Handbook of Research on Cultural and Economic Impacts of the Information Society

P.E. Thomas
Bharathiar University, India

M. Srihari
Bharathiar University, India

Sandeep Kaur
Bharathiar University, India

A volume in the Advances in Human and Social Aspects of Technology (AHSAT) Book Series

Managing Director: Lindsay Johnston
Managing Editor: Austin DeMarco
Director of Intellectual Property & Contracts: Jan Travers
Acquisitions Editor: Kayla Wolfe
Production Editor: Christina Henning
Development Editor: Brandon Carbaugh
Cover Design: Jason Mull

Published in the United States of America by
Information Science Reference (an imprint of IGI Global)
701 E. Chocolate Avenue
Hershey PA, USA 17033
Tel: 717-533-8845
Fax: 717-533-8661
E-mail: cust@igi-global.com
Web site: http://www.igi-global.com

Library of Congress Cataloging-in-Publication Data

Handbook of research on cultural and economic impacts of the information society / P.E. Thomas, M. Srihari, and Sandeep Kaur, editors.
pages cm
Includes bibliographical references and index.
ISBN 978-1-4666-8598-7 (hardcover) -- ISBN 978-1-4666-8599-4 (ebook) 1. Information technology--Economic aspects. 2. Information technology--Social aspects. 3. Information society. I. Thomas, P. E., 1962-
HC79.I55.H3334 2015
303.48'33--dc23

2015012013

This book is published in the IGI Global book series Advances in Human and Social Aspects of Technology (AHSAT) (ISSN: 2328-1316; eISSN: 2328-1324)

British Cataloguing in Publication Data
A Cataloguing in Publication record for this book is available from the British Library.

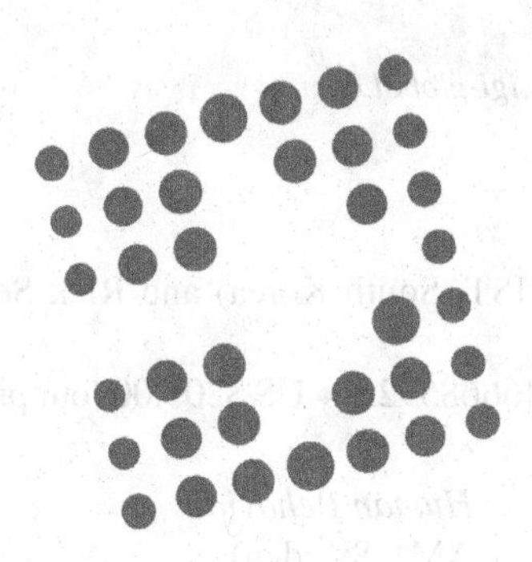

Advances in Human and Social Aspects of Technology (AHSAT) Book Series

Ashish Dwivedi
The University of Hull, UK

ISSN: 2328-1316
EISSN: 2328-1324

Mission

In recent years, the societal impact of technology has been noted as we become increasingly more connected and are presented with more digital tools and devices. With the popularity of digital devices such as cell phones and tablets, it is crucial to consider the implications of our digital dependence and the presence of technology in our everyday lives.

The **Advances in Human and Social Aspects of Technology (AHSAT) Book Series** seeks to explore the ways in which society and human beings have been affected by technology and how the technological revolution has changed the way we conduct our lives as well as our behavior. The AHSAT book series aims to publish the most cutting-edge research on human behavior and interaction with technology and the ways in which the digital age is changing society.

Coverage

- Gender and Technology
- End-User Computing
- Human Development and Technology
- Human-Computer Interaction
- Philosophy of technology
- Technology Adoption
- Digital Identity
- Technology and Social Change
- Human Rights and Digitization
- Cyber Bullying

IGI Global is currently accepting manuscripts for publication within this series. To submit a proposal for a volume in this series, please contact our Acquisition Editors at Acquisitions@igi-global.com or visit: http://www.igi-global.com/publish/.

The Advances in Human and Social Aspects of Technology (AHSAT) Book Series (ISSN 2328-1316) is published by IGI Global, 701 E. Chocolate Avenue, Hershey, PA 17033-1240, USA, www.igi-global.com. This series is composed of titles available for purchase individually; each title is edited to be contextually exclusive from any other title within the series. For pricing and ordering information please visit http://www.igi-global.com/book-series/advances-human-social-aspects-technology/37145. Postmaster: Send all address changes to above address.

Titles in this Series

For a list of additional titles in this series, please visit: www.igi-global.com

Rethinking Machine Ethics in the Age of Ubiquitous Technology
Jeffrey White (Korean Advanced Institute of Science and Technology, KAIST, South Korea) and Rick Searle (IEET, USA)
Information Science Reference • copyright 2015 • 332pp • H/C (ISBN: 9781466685925) • US $205.00 (our price)

Contemporary Approaches to Activity Theory Interdisciplinary Perspectives on Human Behavior
Thomas Hansson (Blekinge Institute of Technology, School of Management (MAM), Sweden)
Information Science Reference • copyright 2015 • 437pp • H/C (ISBN: 9781466666030) • US $195.00 (our price)

Evolving Issues Surrounding Technoethics and Society in the Digital Age
Rocci Luppicini (University of Ottawa, Canada)
Information Science Reference • copyright 2014 • 317pp • H/C (ISBN: 9781466661226) • US $215.00 (our price)

Technological Advancements and the Impact of Actor-Network Theory
Arthur Tatnall (Victoria University, Australia)
Information Science Reference • copyright 2014 • 331pp • H/C (ISBN: 9781466661264) • US $195.00 (our price)

Gender Considerations and Influence in the Digital Media and Gaming Industry
Julie Prescott (University of Bolton, UK) and Julie Elizabeth McGurren (Codemasters, UK)
Information Science Reference • copyright 2014 • 357pp • H/C (ISBN: 9781466661424) • US $195.00 (our price)

Human-Computer Interfaces and Interactivity Emergent Research and Applications
Pedro Isaías (Universidade Aberta (Portuguese Open University), Portugal) and Katherine Blashki (Noroff University College, Norway)
Information Science Reference • copyright 2014 • 348pp • H/C (ISBN: 9781466662285) • US $200.00 (our price)

Political Campaigning in the Information Age
Ashu M. G. Solo (Maverick Technologies America Inc., USA)
Information Science Reference • copyright 2014 • 359pp • H/C (ISBN: 9781466660625) • US $210.00 (our price)

Handbook of Research on Political Activism in the Information Age
Ashu M. G. Solo (Maverick Technologies America Inc., USA)
Information Science Reference • copyright 2014 • 498pp • H/C (ISBN: 9781466660663) • US $275.00 (our price)

www.igi-global.com

701 E. Chocolate Ave., Hershey, PA 17033
Order online at www.igi-global.com or call 717-533-8845 x100
To place a standing order for titles released in this series, contact: cust@igi-global.com
Mon-Fri 8:00 am - 5:00 pm (est) or fax 24 hours a day 717-533-8661

Editorial Advisory Board

List of Reviewers

List of Contributors

Table of Contents

Detailed Table of Contents

Unlike the decisive occupations which facilitated the unambiguous naming of the agricultural and industrial societies, the present one which is tagged with an array of groupings—Post-Industrial, Service, Knowledge, Post-modern, Wired/Networked, Artificial, so on and so forth—can hardly ever be viewed from the perspective of a single occupation. With technology in the forefront working as the driver of information and knowledge, it supports and causes the rampant changes in the provinces of economy, occupation, spatial relations, and culture. And, together they signify the arrival of the 'Information Society'. The obvious shift of a considerable population from the landed labour to industrial labour to knowledge workers marks the transitional phase of the society from agriculture to manufacturing to knowledge society. Hence, this chapter proposes that the dominant phase of a society is not to be visualised as an independent system that is divorced from the other two, but to be understood as an extension of its past.

Typically, designers of ICT based initiatives tend to consider the emerging trends of information and communication technology (ICT) as the starting point for designing an e-initiative rather than first inculcating a clarity on what services are to be delivered by such e-initiatives. 'Technology first' or 'Citizens First' is a conflict all designers have been confronted with, especially in the wake of all technology trends infesting the world now. To resolve this dichotomy, the present study proposes a citizen-centric framework, christened by author as G2C2G framework, which advocates combining technology in equal measures with the respective 'socio-cultural issues' of the local populace.

Innovation capability has increasingly been searched by the ICT sector in cloud computing applications recently. This chapter describes the economic potentials of cloud computing and explores the characteristics of its usage among Hungarian enterprises. Although enterprises are aware of the basic concept of cloud computing, they have concerns about its application mainly due to data security issues and the lack of education. The chance of using cloud computing services is mainly facilitated by the creation of easier application and consultation would positively affect their usage. According to microenterprises and corporations, faster information flow and remote access are the key benefits of cloud usage. In the case of small-sized enterprises, the two main advantages are easier system recoverability and a higher level of mobility in case of a system breakdown. For the medium-sized enterprises, remote access and greater data security were the key benefits of using cloud computing services in 2014.

This chapter analyzes the impact that an open data policy can have on the citizens of India. Especially in a scenario where government accountability and transparency has become the buzzword for good governance and further look at whether the availability of open data can become an agent for socio-economic change in India. What kind of change it can bring to India which has its own complexities when it comes to socio economic issues and whether the steps taken by the government are up to the mark to address these complexities through data sharing. In order to understand the changes which may occur for the good or the bad, the chapter looks at specific examples where the open data platform have been utilized in India and what impact they have had on the Indian society and how the citizens have responded to it.

This chapter analyzes the effect of intangible investment on firm efficiency with an emphasis on its software component. Stochastic production frontier approach is used to simultaneously estimate the production function and the determinants of technical efficiency in the software intensive manufacturing firms in Turkey for the period 2003-2007. Firms are classified based on the technology group. High technology and low technology firms are estimated separately in order to reveal differentials in their firm efficiency. The results show that the effect of software investment on firm efficiency is larger in high technology firms which operate in areas such as chemicals, electricity, and machinery as compared to that of the low technology firms which operate in areas such as textiles, food, paper, and unclassified manufacturing. Further, among the high technology firms, the effect of the software investment is smaller than the effect of research and development personnel expenditure. This result shows that the presence of R&D personnel is more important than the software investment for software intensive manufacturing firms in Turkey.

This chapter which is in line with the global pipelines-local buzz framework addresses the collaboration dynamics of ICT researchers from universities of an emerging economy who are mostly benefiting from national funds and do not have dominating or core roles in international R&D networks. It provides a novel taxonomy to identify the degree of globalisation versus localisation of ICT scientists in Turkey. Based on international and national project portfolios of Turkish ICT researchers who participated in FP6 and other international projects between 2003 and 2006, four groups (gatekeepers, externally oriented researchers, internally oriented researchers, inactive researchers) were formed in terms of their degree of local or global focus. For the period of 2007–2013, the performance of the same population was traced with respect to its international or national project density, publication output, involvement in decision making processes on academic project funding, and contribution to R&D capacity development in the private sector. Findings show that that most of the researchers who are engaged in international collaboration are also locally active and they seem to be the most productive actors within the four groups. The study also implies that having a strong project portfolio at both national and international levels relates to having a work experience abroad after the PhD fulfilment and being at a university with advanced research ecosystem in Turkey. This chapter concludes with key policy recommendations, highlighting the need on moving beyond one-size-fits-all policies which should take in to account the heterogeneity, differentiation on career levels, national priorities and capacity requirements of the research ecosystem.

Educational systems have met information and communication technologies many years ago. Although many years of effort and vast investments, the integration of ICT with educational systems is still weak. Besides many others, lack of interactivity and emotionality in current technologies can be seen as obstacles in front of this integration. We know that learning is associated not only with our cognitive abilities but also with our emotions and affective states. Affective computing is an interdisciplinary branch that is interested in design of systems and devices that can recognize, interpret, process and respond to users' affective states. Affective computing may contribute to interactivity and emotionality of human-computer interaction. Within the scope of this book chapter, related scientific literature was reviewed in order to investigate educational value and potential of affective computing.

interest of police forces in the use of social media to engage groups previously uninvolved in discussion of community policing and for deliberation about priorities of police forces. The chapter concludes that police forces, in general, have been able to exploit the networked characteristics of social media and the potential of user-generated content. Recommendations are provided to achieve more ambitious aims for using social media for policing.

In this chapter, the use of Moodle, an open source Learning Management System (LMS), by the Department of Electronic Media and Mass Communication in Pondicherry University, as a means to supplement classroom teaching has been examined drawing on Actor Network Theory (ANT). This chapter reveals that the use of Moodle gives rise to a new digital culture which is inscribed on the prior cultural template that students, instructors and institutions bring to have a bearing on their teaching and learning activities. However, the rise of such a digital culture is due to the human and material assemblages constituted by how students and instructors inscribe their manifestoes on Moodle and how Moodle inscribes its manifestations on them. Further, the performative potential of Moodle is explained by its networked interaction with other social, human and non-human actors such as the culture of using technology for learning, digital literacy skills, emergent digital divide, access issues among students and teachers, educational and economic background and institutional media ecology among others.

The current state of dialogue within certain South African universities was explored, and if and how dialogue can be used to address the issues of transformation and the lack of social cohesiveness. The role of Information and Communication Technologies (ICTs) in facilitating or inhibiting open conversations was examined. Through qualitative analysis of surveys administered to staff and students at universities, the researchers identified that power disparity, and the slow pace of transformation were prevalent and needed to be addressed. University management generally practice open conversations, and students and staff were willing to participate. Organisational structures were not conducive for open conversations. The ICT infrastructure used had no significant role to play, while Social Network Systems (SNSs) were perceived as enablers of open conversations. This chapter contributes to the existing body of knowledge about change management, and presents open conversations as a means of driving and realising organisational change.

Section 4
Mitigation of End-User Information

Information is crucial for the development of any sector, including agriculture where information needs to be exchanged with farmers and other stakeholders quickly. Thus, efficient linkages for information sharing are essential. ICT innovations enable the shaping and reshaping of communication and interaction. Many of the technology driven information dissemination methods have been initiated by government, private, non-profit making bodies and independent research groups. This chapter explains the integration of ICT within Sri Lankan agriculture communities and how the focus is changing from information dissemination towards facilitating interactions among the stakeholders. The present status of agriculture information dissemination, including the ICT interventions is given. Prevailing issues and limitations in these ICT-based information dissemination approaches initiated by the different entities is explained, giving due recognition to various factors that have contributed to the adoption of ICT initiatives. The chapter ends outlining the possibilities for future focus on ICT activities in an agriculture information society.

In this chapter, the author has discussed India's first rainbow e-governance project encompassing the "ICTs, e-governance, rural development and access to the basic administrative services" aspects in India's hinterland and one of the most backward regions. The paper argues for the "socio economic welfare" stance of the ICTs and the resultants benefits thereof. The present study investigates the socio-economic aspect of community e-governance project named Gyandoot in remote villages of Madhya Pradesh. Out of 18 services offered by Gyandoot, people fully utilized only 3 services (land records, exam results and addressing public grievances) which lead to the considerable fulfillment of target audience's needs (felt needs and expected needs) and improvement in their work efficiency by high scores on convenience, satisfaction, time, cost, reliability and overall benefits factors and a reduction in the time and money for government service delivery. However, Gyandoot could not fare impressively well on spurt in employment and economic activity fronts thus leading to only moderate gains. Only 17% of the Gyandoot's potential could be utilized and 39% was used moderately. Rest 44% could not be utilized at all due to less demand of services. 'Optimism in IT hardware' and 'development of entrepreneurial attitude' were the most noticeable aspects of economic activity generated. The study also posits a few very important questions on the sustainability, interoperability and hierarchical issues relating to the project.

This chapter analyses the social media site Facebook as a communication tool in rural community development. The analysis was focused on the Facebook page of one rural community in Ireland. The research was conducted using a mixed method approach, using Facebook insights, key informant interviews, and questionnaires. The evolution of the Facebook page was documented. The study presents the attitudes towards the Facebook page of users and non-Facebook users. The findings indicate that friends of the community Facebook page believe it plays a vital role in their community forging debate, discussion and higher levels of participation. The non-Facebook users have made the conscious decision not to engage with Facebook, but nonetheless are aware of Facebook and on occasion, kept informed indirectly from sources close to them. Overall the research presented in this chapter illustrates that Facebook can be an effective communication tool in community development even in rural areas.

The concept of automation was first seeded worldwide by Industrial Revolution. Liberalization and privatization has contributed much in the welcome of updated and upgraded technology in India. World Wide Web being the core connector of earth rightly supports Mc Luhan's concept of the 'Global Village'. ICT- Information and Communication Technology is an initiative cum phenomenon that is taken on Public-Private Partnership (PPP) in order to build a bridge between the two sections of the society (technology haves and have nots) so that it is accessible to all. e-Governance, e-Health and e-Commerce are some of its applications. India has witnessed a number of successful E- Projects. Nonetheless, the argument of social exclusion, questions on technology support communication and information dissemination is still on. The article intends to throw light on various aspects keeping in line with the ICT projects in India, the type of ICT usage and a comparison between the already established communication models.

A thorough glance of the ICT and development researches reveal that the qualitative studies reasonably depend on the grounded theory as it is obtained from the phenomenon unlike the study begins with the theory and proves it. Most of the researches concentrated on the adoption of technology, receptiveness of the target audience, organizational structure of the project agencies and of course, the impact of intervention. Fewer researches have been done to gauge the factors affecting the positive or negative impact of the technology. None of the above stated theories were relevant except meta-theoretical perspectives of ICT and society. The authors propose a chapter discusses the contingency factors which affect the positive or negative impact of the rural Information and Communication Technology hubs in India by analyzing the researches which were published after the year 2000. It shall be specifically dealing with the researches which are based on primary data. Thus it could reflect the challenges the Indian rural ICT initiatives face.

Foreword

The all-pervasiveness of information in the present day influences the concept of Information Society. The dilution of its content and meaning has specifically misrepresented the discernment of researchers all around the world to actually define the disorganized information in their interpretative arguments over streamlining the precise significance of the Information Society. In this context, momentous professional deliberation and international cooperation from the academic world has become obligatory to understand the factors influencing development of the Information Society.

The book is intended for the audience researching into human communication aspects in the digital era. The multi-dimensional approach of this book helps frame suitable strategies on consumption of both information and knowledge in the information society or knowledge society. Policy makers, academicians, researchers and government officials will find this book useful in exposing them to various facets in the Information Society.

The chapters in this book make a valuable contribution and are hospitable to the application of Information and Communication Technologies (ICTs) in diverse fields such as health, education, governance, to name a few. The book is targeted to all those who indefatigably work on various research prerogatives to noticeably identify the implication of these ICTs to its potential user.

This anthology has Twenty-Two chapters assembled by the three editors to reflect the contemporary philosophy in the application of ICTs from the ongoing research projects in both developed and developing countries. The editors have focused on the economic and cultural impacts of the Information Society by grouping the chapters into four sections. The first section looks at the components of the information society, its citizen-centricity and meaningfulness in the context of its application and usage. The second section considers various innovative practices of the emerging technologies in the domains previously difficult to reach. The third section addresses the cultural transformation of information by its end user in various ICT based applications. The last section concentrates on the rural development strategies and applications of ICT towards empowering the underprivileged.

I recommend that this be well thought-out as a reference book for the Information Society to facilitate the researchers from both academic and professional entities to develop innovative products for user consumption in the days ahead. It is pertinent to append that the Indian government and the rest in the world have appreciably helped numerous organizations to partake of generating novel expertise in the use of these technologies, hence contributing a rich source to the Information Society. I have no doubt that this edited volume will be yet another resourceful literary addition in understanding the emerging new media and information society paradigms.

Dr. Chinnaswamy Pichandy
Associate Professor and Head Department of Communication PSG College of Arts and Science
Coimbatore – 641014 Tamil Nadu, India

Preface

The world has been witnessing one of the major transformations, the manifestation of Information Society wherein technologies are found facilitating an indispensable societal facet. Martin (1988) states, "the term 'information society' has arisen out of the conventional conviction that information has become a central part of present-day life, both at work and play—so much so, that it has become a symbol of the very age we live in". The new millennium uses the concept of 'Information Society' in the field of social sciences wherein the expression of information in the form of its content has become "diluted". The notion of Information Society has progressively strengthened links with technology in diverse fields such as education, governance, health, agriculture, science, innovation, economy, and culture. Besides, Information has now become an increasingly imperative component in all the spheres of life as societies, at large, in the new millennium are promptly changing around the world. This trend augments organizations with greater use of information to amplify their competence that could benefit their economy besides extending greater public access to goods and services at their own convenience. In this perspective, this book is a valuable approach to study various facets of the promising information culture and economy in both the developed and developing countries.

Ideation for this collected works germinated with the widespread research interest in information and communication technologies (ICTs) around the world that have brought about significant multi-dimensional changes in almost all aspects of life. This also necessitates a better understanding of the users as they are at the heart of user-centered designs of diverse Information and Communication Technology initiatives around the world but are seldom deliberated upon. Also, the use of technology and its practices in a rapidly evolving technological civilization also need to be highlighted. This reflection of thought has motivated the editors to re-examine the Information society theories to form a foundation for both elucidation and organization of innovative technological grounds beyond a mere 'click culture' to a more 'task specified culture' to gain imminence of computer-mediated communication among the so-called digital humans.

Concerning who benefits from this anthology, it is vital to augment the partaking of all, including the vulnerable in the constructive processing of Information to make their right to be heard by implementers and policy-makers of various applications of ICT at dissimilar echelons. The Information Society has a gargantuan prospect to absorb even the most insubstantial people worldwide and make them an integral aspect of their economies through various ICT tools such as e-participation, e-government, e-health, e-education, etc. This resource, from a representation of both developed and developing countries, is an attempt to commence a dialogue on how innovative approaches of ICT could make the digital sphere all-encompassing and participatory taking into account the individual needs for digital inclusion.

Unsurprisingly, a book of this diversity cannot deal with all germane issues in all areas but is an endeavor to provide academicians, researchers, students and working professionals with a strong hypothetical background, placing individual prominence on the potential elucidation of applications of the Information and Communication Technology to the subject concerned. The primary audience of this book symphonizes the research community and students all over the world at all levels – those being introduced to the notion of Information Society, those having a transitional acquaintance with this area in addition to those already conversant about many of the topics incorporated in the same. To congregate the explicit needs of this audience, most chapters of this book have resources that attempt to endow with guidelines for future explorations. The secondary audience for this assemblage is the academicians from diverse fields of expertise such as Agriculture, Health, Education, Governance, E-learning, Research and Development, Mass Media, Information Technology, Environment, Policing, Information Services besides Rural growth and development. The tertiary audience encompasses working professionals and practitioners at the implementation and policy levels of various ICT initiatives such as Internet surveillance, E-governance initiatives and open data regulation agency such as National Informatics Center. Finally, we have also taken into deliberation the needs of readers who have the quest for getting imminence into the realistic implication of the topics covered under the same.

Since the chapters focus on both functional and hypothetical observance in the use of technologies, it becomes imperative to accentuate that this book principally takes the approach of social sciences so that this collection of resources from dissimilar arenas bring about economic and cultural management. This resource will also make available a sound underpinning for researchers and academicians from diverse fields of expertise for more specialized studies on the subject. A comprehensive rationalization of the expansive premise of Information Society to the topics dealt with in this book follows.

The objective of this book is to comprehensively analyze various aspects of ICT applications that aims to be an essential reference source built on the available literature. Researchers around the world argue that the information society is bringing a major thoughtful and wide-ranging revolution in the society. In this book, editors significantly evaluate the stand of the respective authors to illuminate the phenomenon by surveying the works of major information society theorists. This book is an invaluable resource for effortless understanding of the nature of the information society and the technological revolution that made it possible.

This book is a comprehensive amalgamation of various ICT initiatives, its application and implication through an international cooperation with experts at both the global and national levels. This assemblage provides insight into theoretical frameworks, policies and end user perspectives that can notably monitor the expansion of ICT based services to its end user by bringing together contributions from continents such as America (Canada), Europe (Belgium, Ireland, Hungary, United Kingdom), Asia (India, Japan, Bangladesh, Pakistan, Malaysia, Sri Lanka, Turkey) and Africa (Nigeria, South Africa). Collectively, this book provides a description of the key issues influencing the Information Society landscape, both economically and culturally.

The book analyses the recent trends to effectively gauge the ground reality of the consequences of the ICT application in diverse arenas with its content comprising sections commencing from providing an understanding of the components constituting the information society and also examining various ICT applications in areas such as agriculture, education, health, commerce and development. Additionally, the book explores the extensive and significant philosophical debate about the information age in terms of empowerment and democratization that has been fuelled due to several events read as milestones in the road towards the Information Society.

As editors, we have organized the 22 chapters in this volume according to four themes reflected in the sections of the book and outlined below. This book, as a whole, comprises a diverse collection of approaches to cultural and economic underpinnings with Information and Communication Technologies in the Information Society. Section 1 illuminates an understanding of the various concepts in the Information Society. Section 2 represents emerging innovative practices in both the developed and developing nations through Information and Communication technology. Cultural transformation through Information constitutes the Section 3 of this compilation while Section 4 focuses on mitigation of end-user information through various technological applications and initiatives.

Three Chapters are provided in Section 1 that necessitate an **Understanding of the Information Society** with its theoretical underpinnings towards citizen-centricity. Taxonomy of Concepts, Determinants and Implications of the Information Society through an Information Society framework for a 'prosumer' culture helps researchers and academicians to accentuate the user perspective of the Information Society. The following section provides a brief description of specific chapters included in this section:

In his discussion on *The Making of the Information Society: Taxonomy of Concepts, Determinants and Implications*, P.E.Thomas illustrates notable changes in the creation of knowledge and wealth, speedy decision-making, convenience, the feel of a 'psychological neighbourhood' due to the 'shrinking' of the globe, diversity of opportunities and, on the other, the ever-expanding divide between the haves and have-nots, threat of white-collar crimes, invasion of privacy, lack of security, ever-increasing cost of labour and education, and much more in the information era.

Charru Malthotra's manifestation on *Framework for Evolving a Citizen-Centric Information Society* reveals the technology-centricity of ICT initiatives implemented especially in the rural areas of the developing countries, than execution of explicit strategies that deal with citizen-centricity in designing and implementing an Information society at the grassroots.

The corresponding chapter *Consumers as Producers: Information Decomposition Exploiting the Prosumerist Culture* by Sandeep Kaur investigates an information catastrophe that is burgeoning in the electronic era that causes decomposition of information acquired from copious sources online due to type of users, number of users accessing the content, their information skill, and cognitive dispensation of desirable information by quoting a few user generated sites such as the Wikipedia (Online Enclyclopaedia).

Multidimensional approaches to **Emergence of Innovative Practices** comprise Section 2 of this book. The Information Society is radically examined through a pragmatic act of Internet Trolling alongside the importance of Innovation in Sustainable Economic Development; Cloud Computing as an Information Processing method to impact the whole economy in the long term; Open Government Data (OGD) platform that provides access to datasets published by different government entities in open format to facilitate community participation; increasing Productivity through Intangible Investment, Internationalisation of Research and Development (R&D) through international collaboration and practical policy recommendations at micro, meso and macro levels; Affective Computing as an interdisciplinary field standing on the intersection of computer sciences, psychology, and cognitive science and finally, the construction of Sanitary Landfills towards environmental safeguarding. The following section provides a brief description of specific chapters included in this section:

A very radical way to generalize the MacPherson Inquiry of 'institutional racism' to 'institutional sexism' by Jonathan Bishop investigates benevolent sexism in the Information Society as South Wales Police subject women complainants and respondents to harassment and Internet-related crime more favourably than they do men in *Crime recording of Internet Trolling by British Police uncovers Chivalrous*

Attitudes that can be resolved through Transfer of Power: The Thin-Blue Web and hence, recommends the establishment of a professional body to instill professional ethics into the police.

In their contribution *Impact of ICT on Innovation: The Case of Japanese SMEs*, Hiroki Idota, Teruyuki Bunno and Masatsugu Tsuji highlight the importance on the relationship between innovation and ICT use among Small and Medium-sized Enterprises (SMEs), thus postulating two channels from ICT use to innovation, namely direct and indirect, based on factors such as innovation activities, innovation capability, and external linkage.

Through *The Empirical Analysis of Cloud Computing Services among the Hungarian Enterprises*, Peter Sasvari and Zoltan Nagymate examine the Innovation capability and economic potentials of Cloud Computing applications by exploring the characteristics of its usage among Hungarian enterprises based on faster information flow and remote access as its key benefits facilitated by the creation of easier application, the training of employees, and consultation.

D.P. Misra and Alka Mishra attempt to examine the socio-economic planning processes in *Societal and Economical Impact on Citizens Through Innovations Using Open Government Data: Indian Initiative on Open Government Data* that rely on quality data collected, processed and generated by Indian government in its day-to-day functioning by quoting the relevance of non-sensitive data in an open format such as National Data Sharing and Accessibility Policy (NDSAP) to facilitate access to Government of India owned non-sensitive shareable data in machine-readable form through a wide area network all over the country, in a periodically updatable manner.

Using a Stochastic Production Frontier approach in *Intangible Investment and Technical Efficiency: The Case of Software-Intensive Manufacturing Firms in Turkey*, Derya Findik and Aysıt Tansel focus on the link between intangible investments and productivity by analyzing the effect of software investment on firm efficiency for the period 2003-2007 to simultaneously estimate the production function and the determinants of technical efficiency in the software intensive manufacturing firms in Turkey.

Hüseyin Güler and Erkan Erdil elaborate on the involvement of Turkish ICT researchers in Framework Programme 6 (FP6) networks and in other TÜBITAK (Turkish Scientific and Technological Research Council) funded international collaboration projects in *Does Participation in International R&D Networks Enhance Local Dynamism? to* identify the degree of globalisation versus localisation of ICT scientists in Turkey for the period 2007-2013 based on evidence from such chronological data analysis that could highlight the issues such as heterogeneity, career levels, national priorities and capacity requirements of the research ecosystem.

Cenk Akbiyik investigates the role of Affective Computing as a promising area for the integration of ICT with educational systems through his analysis of Affective causes and consequences of the users' behavior in computer based or assisted environments based on 'optimist rhetoric' and 'pessimist rhetoric' in *Understanding Educational Potential and Value of Affective Computing*.

Elmira Shamshiry, Abdul-Mumin, Mazlin Bin Mokhtar, and Ibrahim Komoo expertly review in their contribution *Regional Landfill Site Selection with GIS and Analytical Hierarchy Process Techniques: A Case Study of Langkawi Island, Malaysia: Landfill Site Selection with GIS and AHP in Langkawi, Malaysia* the use of GIS-based Multi-criteria Decision Analysis (MCDA) that examine the essentials of an effective site selection decision making process in Langkawi to meet the environmental legislations and reduce the undesirable effects of the solid waste management in Langkawi.

Section 3 of this compilation describes **Cultural Transformation through Information** in the context of ICT-based economic development; consumer perspective of M-health through mobile phone SMS, a Conceptual Framework describing various uses of Social Media for Policing; a new culture of learning style through 'Moodle'; the role of ICT in facilitating or inhibiting open conversations between students and staff members in higher education institutions; Socioeconomic dimension of Mobile telephony and Electronic Payment System. The following section provides a brief description of specific chapters included in this section:

M-health is an innovative application that potentially deserves support from consumers in terms of its usage. Mahmud AkhterShareef, Vinod Kumar, Uma Kumar and Jashim Uddin Ahmed explore the integration and application of different technological interfaces of Information and Communication Technology in the service delivery system of modern healthcare through the application of mobile phone based message system, Short Message Service (SMS) by identifying customers' perception of SMS as a service delivery channel for Mobile-health or M-health.

Effective use of Social Media in Policing can emerge as a powerful tool to enhance public safety official's ability to disseminate information to the public and access those segments of public that were non-conventional segments of news. Change management by formalizing continuous learning, appropriate support, training and development will be necessary to structure and organize police forces in a more sustainable manner. Amir Manzoor provides an overview of the CCTNS—a revolutionary concept in his contribution *Use of Social Media for Policing* for centralizing the crime-relate information across all levels of law enforcement such as legal frameworks, training of law enforcement officials for Social Media use, and law enforcement collaboration with social network providers by a conceptual framework that describes its various uses.

Information and Communication Technology such as Internet is emerging as an effective tool in the teaching–learning process. In his work *Culture of Use of Moodle in Higher Education: Networked Relations between Technology, Culture and Society*, Shuaib Mohamed Haneef highlights the integration of ICTs in Higher educational institutions by analyzing use of 'Moodle', an open source Learning Management System (LMS), in the Department of Electronic Media and Mass Communication, Pondicherry University, as a means to supplement classroom teaching and the new digital culture it creates against the backdrop of the culture students already have inherited from their previous institutions and social setting.

Kevin Allan Johnston, Bane Nogemane and Salah Kabanda explore the current state of dialogue within certain South African universities in their contribution *The Current State of Dialogue in South African Universities: Change through Open Conversations: The Facilitating Role of ICTs* to address the issues of transformation and the lack of social cohesiveness induced by ICT through qualitative analysis of surveys administered to staff and students at universities.

The chapter *Mobile Phone Revolution and its Dimensional Social and Economic Impacts in Nigeria's Context* by Okanlade Adesokan Lawal-Adebowale highlights the trend of mobile phone development in Nigeria in terms of the telecom sector deregulation policy, emergence of private investors in the sector, available telephone lines and geospatial (rural-urban) distribution of telephony service based on critical observation field events and interviews/consultations with mobile phone subscribers and researchers on mobile phone usage.

Sanghita Roy reveals concern over the alarming, unintended social and economic costs (risks and inconvenience) associated with cash transactions online through interviews and structured questionnaires to analyze the development of new electronic banking and payment products, the introduction of electronic cash, payment mechanisms for the Internet, and new versions of home banking through her work *Overview of Electronic Payment System: A Special Reference to India.*

Five Chapters provided in Section 4 elucidate **Mitigation of End-User Information** in the Information Society through an analysis of ICT interventions in the Agricultural sector; Community E-governance project; Rural community development through Social Media; Rural growth through ICTs and rural Information and Communication Technology hubs in India. The following section provides a brief description of specific chapters included in this section:

Uvasara Dissanayeke and H.V.A. Wickramasuriya, while introducing the latest ICT interventions in the emerging agriculture information society in SriLanka in their contribution *Information Societies to Interactive Societies: ICT Adoptions in the Agriculture Sector in Sri Lanka* discuss ICT-based information dissemination approaches initiated by government, private, non-profit making sectors and independent research groups.

In his work *E-governance for Socio Economic Welfare – A Case Study of Gyanoot Intranet Project in Madhya Pradesh*, Umesh Arya investigates the socio-economic aspect of a community E-governance project 'Gyandoot' in remote villages of Madhya Pradesh.

Using a Mixed Method approach, Padraig Wims analyses the social media 'Facebook' as a communication tool in his chapter *The Potential of Social Media as a Communication Tool in Rural Community Development* for the development of a rural community in the midlands of Ireland to provide an insight into how this community is successfully adopting the social media technology.

Through *ICT- A Magic Wand for Social Change in Rural India* Orance Mahaldar and Kinkini Bhadra explore on the integration of ICT in rural growth by analyzing popularization and propagation of rural ICT policies for the underprivileged beisdes comparing and contrasting the model of ICT with that of several communication models in mass communication such as Shannon & Weaver, Newcomb and Gerbner.

The book closes with a Meta-theoretical Perspective of ICT and society in the chapter *Contingency Factors Impacting the Rural Information and Communication Technology Hubs* by P Govindaraju and M. Maani Mabel who gauge the desirable and undesirable impacts of the rural Information and Communication Technology hubs in India by analyzing published resources evaluating the technology in four views—the utopian view, the dystopian view, the neutral view and the contingency view.

The main source of inspiration for this resource is ascribed to the effortless journey of the editors en route various facets of the Information Society. The aforementioned book chapters indicate the nature and scope of technology-driven Information Society that influence countries around the world. This work is just a beginning and calls for more expert deliberations of various other ICT based challenges. We trust that the readers of this book will find this Handbook of Research on Information Society extremely valuable as it provides thought-provoking theoretical frameworks and observations of finest works by researchers who have contributed to this volume. The combined effort of all the contributing authors has led to the creation of a rich source of knowledge in the issue under investigation and helps make this publication handy for many.

P.E. Thomas
Bharathiar University, India

M. Srihari
Bharathiar University, India

Sandeep Kaur
Bharathiar University, India

Acknowledgment

For almost a year, we have been fortunate to have the company of a team of editorial advisors, contributors and reviewers who have been very forthcoming right from the stage of the ideation of this handbook. On passing down the proposal to them, almost all of them readily responded which truly encouraged us to go ahead with the project.

We anticipated the success of this publication, the moment we received responses from contributors belonging to diverse countries. What pushed us further was their instant support for the minor or major revisions requested for by the reviewers. We are extremely thankful to all the contributors who exercised so much of diligence which actually dispelled the fears we had in the initial stages of this venture. We appreciate and thank all the members of the Editorial Advisory Board who played instrumental roles in providing us the perfect inputs to go ahead with the project. Besides, we wouldn't forget that the real momentum gained came from the hands of the reviewers who played pivotal roles responding immediately to our requests and that too under constrained duration given for the same.

IGI, the publishing house which gave us the support throughout deserves our profuse gratitude. Mr. Brandon Carbough, Mr. Hayley King, Mr. Vince D'Imperio (hope we did not miss out any names) who untiringly synchronized efficiently and kept pushing us every time we neared deadlines. They kept sounding the warning bells which truly acted in our favour, helping us complete the project.

Dr. Chinnaswamy Pichandy, the Head of the Department of Communication at PSG College of Arts & Science, India, who has contributed the foreword to this handbook, deserves a tribute through this venture of ours. At the launch of this handbook Dr. Pichandy will have retired from his academic service which spanned over three decades and a half. Being our teacher and research supervisor, there cannot be a more fitting moment to acknowledge his influence on our lives.

We, the editors, look forward to valuable future ventures with this esteemed publication and thank all for giving us an opportunity to bring out this publication on time.

Section 1
Understanding the Information Society

Chapter 1
The Making of the Information Society:
Taxonomy of Concepts, Determinants, and Implications

P.E. Thomas
Bharathiar University, India

ABSTRACT

Unlike the decisive occupations which facilitated the unambiguous naming of the agricultural and industrial societies, the present one which is tagged with an array of groupings—Post-Industrial, Service, Knowledge, Post-modern, Wired/Networked, Artificial, so on and so forth—can hardly ever be viewed from the perspective of a single occupation. With technology in the forefront working as the driver of information and knowledge, it supports and causes the rampant changes in the provinces of economy, occupation, spatial relations, and culture. And, together they signify the arrival of the 'Information Society'. The obvious shift of a considerable population from the landed labour to industrial labour to knowledge workers marks the transitional phase of the society from agriculture to manufacturing to knowledge society. Hence, this chapter proposes that the dominant phase of a society is not to be visualised as an independent system that is divorced from the other two, but to be understood as an extension of its past.

INTRODUCTION

The explosion of information, spawned by the communication revolution, is today a stark reality and its consequences are profound though the causes are less certain. The direction in which the consequences ply is one of progression in the 'modern' sense. Indications of a progressive society are commonly visible in the form of tangibles like the rising economic status of its people or an encouraging increase in the Gross National Product (GNP). An advancing society reflects not only its economic strength but also a change of people's lifestyle into a more sophisticated one. Economic advancements were precedents in the earlier two societies as well; nevertheless, the pace of change that distinguishes the new society leverages the assumption that it is a fast advancing economy triggered by information. More to the point, when there existed distinct occupations

DOI: 10.4018/978-1-4666-8598-7.ch001

which described the agricultural and industrial societies, the same is not attributed to the present society, for manifold professions continue to take roots on the impulsive imagination of the 'informed' and the 'enterprising'.

The multiplicity of careers that are available today results in an overabundance of classifications—Post-Industrial, Service, Knowledge, Post-modern, Wired/Networked, Artificial, so on and so forth—prefixed to the term 'Society'. These orderings tend to pre-empt the attempts by social scientists to evolving a definitive and unambiguous name for the new society. Since information underscores most activities of this new economic culture, it is not inappropriate to call it the 'Information Society', at least for the sake of expediency.

The three revolutions, the agricultural (1000 BC to the 1800), the industrial (1800 to 1950), and the information (1960 to the present), according to Bell (1976), are discussed as the major stages in technological history and each period is marked by significant changes in the definition of property and work. Earlier, farming underscored the agricultural society, and later on manufacturing, the industrial society, and now, information and knowledge processing has become the backbone of the 'Information Society' (IS). Like-minded scholars like Peter Drucker (2001) explain the characteristics of the new age as a revolution of 'concepts', and that it is the 'information revolution' preceded by the invention of writing in Mesopotamia about 5000 to 6000 years ago, the invention of the written book in China as early as 1300 BC and Gutenberg's invention of the printing press between 1450 and 1455.

THE INFORMATION SOCIETY (IS)

The last century saw a dramatic shift in the fundamentals of the world of information, which in turn, yielded mass concepts of literacy, education, and communication and all of them were spurred by technologies. Technological inventions not only affected dramatic changes in lifestyle, but also intensified interdependence with the exchange of information and, as Low (2000) perceives, technological inventions run parallel to the evolution of the knowledge and information based economy.

The 'IS' paradigm is presented as the realisation of society that brings about a general flourishing state of human intellectual creativity (Mowlana, 1996) instead of affluent material consumption. The superior intellect of the human being stems from the production, process, and distribution of information. In his attempt at characterising the changed work culture, Rogers (1986) identified the US and several West European countries, which became information societies quite early, and whose citizens reflected visible dramatic changes such as fast life, expanded horizons, increased efficiency, and empowerment of a majority of the communities.

The individual in the new era who is also addressed as the 'information man', is perceived to be educated, affluent, and well-travelled (Wresch, 1996). The *nouveau riche* enjoyed expanded leisure, shifts from achievement to enjoyment and from rational work goals to pleasurable play goals. The well-heeled citizen of the 'IS' tends to experience unimaginable number of opportunities made available to him in diverse forms. The one who alone negotiates for himself a comfortable life in the Information Society is the skilled user of the Information Technologies (IT).

A society that embraces the 'doctrine of technological primacy' undergoes changes at a speed proportionate to the form and sophistication of those technologies used. The rapid changes experienced in the global scenario have stemmed from the accelerated growth of international communication whose origin is ascribed to the explosion of technologies, such as TV, satellite, computers, video, fax, Integrated Services Digital Networks (ISDN) and the convergence of computers, television and telephone (Mowlana, 1996). According to Trivedi and Thaker (2001), 'convergence' is perceived as an enabler of the 'Information Society' which drives different technologies towards a common destination. A single channel allows the transmission of information technology, communication technology, and broadcasting services. However, at the base of the new ICTs is telecommunications, the bloodline of the new society, which fuse all other technologies together allowing nations to leapfrog over previous stages of development (Quon, 2001). Things, which were once unimaginable, have been made possible with the advanced technologies.

TECHNOLOGICAL DETERMINISM

Developments in communications technologies are shaping up a second industrial revolution but the forerunners are information, computers, and Internet and not iron and coal. These technologies of the Post-Industrial Society (Bell, 1976) have already begun their impact journey redefining the routine of the people they pass by. The 'technological informational revolution' is propounded as the backbone of all major structural transformations and depicts an 'informational society' which replaces the industrial society as the framework of 'social institutions' (Castells, 1994). When the potential (the amount of information preserved) of the information technology increases, the ability of human beings to process matter and information is enhanced (Low, 1997).

With the emergence of information processing as the basic activity, the new socio-technical paradigm is an information mode of development, conditioning the effectiveness of all processes of production, distribution, consumption, and management (Castells, 1989). The driving force of the new ICTs, discerned to be superior to those in the other societies, acts as a cue for scholars to pronounce that the new Information, Communication and Entertainment (ICE) economy's value is higher than that of the old one.

Theories propounded to define the IS have been doing their rounds without concreteness. Scholars speak out their minds based on their perception of the IS. Mowlana (1996) defines the IS as a mere data society but the other scholars term it as one whose centrality is division of labour and services and a society in which pluralism and secularism exist.

Whether viewed at its surface or in-depth psychological or philosophical levels, the technology is the cause and the way people live, the consequence. A fashionable and popular enthusiasm emerged following the admiration for the new ICT, which in turn sophisticated the domestic and routine lives of people in a dramatic and radical way (Hoffman et al., 2001; Preston, 2001; Maule, 2000; Heeks, 1999).

In his ritual view of communication, Dogra (2002) pointed out that communication via new media also engenders sharing, participation, and possession of common faith. And the shift to a highly technical planetary economy (Kelly, 1988) is sinewy to the idea of McLuhan's 'Global Village' with the 'death of distance' and enables individuals, business firms, and governments to reach around the world faster, farther, and even cheaper than ever before in human history (Lee, 2001; Cairncross, 1997). Admittedly, the ICTs continue to change the way one works, shops, learns and communicates (Brown, 2001). The implication is that there is a need to adopt (Chandler, 2002) technologies to keep pace with changes.

To embrace technology is not just a need alone but also a way of life. The American sociologist and economist ThorsteinVeblen, who lived during 1857-1929 propagated "Technological Determinism," which holds relevance even now, for it emphasises that in a technology-led theory of social change, technology is perceived as a 'prime mover' in history (Chandler, 2001). The technological determinists observe that those technologies such as writing or print or television or the computer changed society at every level. Any surmise that outlines the presence of the new ICTs to be the core of the 'IS' needs no shunning.

TOWARDS DEFINING 'INFORMATION SOCIETY'

That the distinctions among the agricultural, industrial and information ages engendered from the dominant occupations, which prevailed in the respective periods, are not disputed. For, it is a maxim that a society's lifestyle is shaped by those occupations whose benefits attract a majority of the populace.

When the farm hand and the industrial worker identify themselves with the agricultural and industrial ages respectively, the 'Information Age' is not represented by any single occupation. To address one as the 'information worker' is not devoid of ambiguity. The attempts of scholars to categorise the occupations of the 'Information Society' were less than emphatic and varied. Jonscher (as cited in Webster, 2007) identified two sectors—information and production—as dominant occupations of the 'Information Age'. Similarly, Machlup (1984) evolved five broad information groups—education, media of communication, information machines (computer, musical instruments), information services (insurance, law, medicine) and other information activities (R&D, nonprofit activities).

Conversely, Marc Porat (1977) offered a three-fold scheme, classifying 400 occupational types into three categories—production, processing and distribution of information. The first category, comprising the occupational types like scientists, inventors, teachers, etc., produces and sells knowledge, the second category, which gathers and disseminates information comprise managers, secretaries, clerks, etc., and the third, operating information machines and technologies that support the other two categories, consists of occupational types such as computer operators, telephone installers, TV technicians, etc.

The surmise that the 'Information Age' is identified as a result of more people taking to information-based occupations is not contended with. Unlike the 'agricultural' and 'industrial' ages, the 'Information Age' has given way to a numerous variety of white-collar occupations. The 'new age' results in not only diversified occupations, but also spawns a visible growth in many parts of the society. Information Society scholars have been merciless in describing the 'new society' from the point of view of culture. "Pseudo-sophistication" and "artificiality" is the sort of intangibles that have crept up into the society. If this is homogenisation of a global culture, the 'Information Age' could have a setback. Nevertheless, a new facade of the social system has begun to shape up following the increasing use of the ICTs. The socio-economic 'happenings' in the present society are multidimensional, whose causes are even more multiple. There is a sudden explosion of the newfound freedom—social and economic. The rise in literacy is of late, quite visible. The middle-class in the developing nations is capable of accessing its once-dreamed-about lifestyles. Above all, the enterprising are forever on a 'search' realising the potency of the world.

"The information superhighway may be mostly hype today, but it is an understatement about tomorrow. It will exist beyond people's wildest predictions. The digital planet will look and feel like the head of a pin."— Negroponte (as cited in Preston, 2001). Negroponte's observation that the information superhighway is hype continues to hold relevance as the process of initiation into the information revolution has not yet been experienced by a major segment of the world population. It was found that more than 80% of the people in the world have never heard a dial tone, let alone sent an email or downloaded information from the WWW (Black, 1999). The impediment that glares is socio-economic in nature. Most of the Third World Nations and Latin American countries experience obstacles aplenty. Even in India, illiteracy is one of the foremost deterrents for development.

If illiteracy is the concern on the one side, negative economic factors form another one on the other, particularly in the Third World Nations. In his analysis of the rural-urban digital divide Hindman (2000) observed that the era of Information technology was bound to create users and non-users of technologies. In the long run, those who keep the information technologies at a distance or those who do not access them will be ultimately isolated from the forward-looking society. In the digital era, if one were to be classified under the 'non-use' and 'non-access' of information technology categories, it may lead to perceived nonexistence and those who joined the revolution group would be economically forward. Ruet (2002) added that the budget-based development on the traditional public model would be overshadowed by the new economy's valuation of networks. At its base, the Information Society's strength lay in the changes generated in different spheres driven by information, whose spread is the result of technology. Nevertheless, the changes that swept the pre-industrial and post-industrial societies are accredited to the dominant occupations that spearheaded those economies (Rose, 1991). But the social, economic, and cultural changes in the new economy are purported by the 'changes in the role and organisation of information', the key to defining the contemporary society.

CHANGE IS THE KEY

The 'Information Society' experiences explosive changes in many a field, especially education. Both formal and non-formal educations are poised for stupendous growth wherein interactive education, instruction, and distance education will gain mileage from the new technologies (Trivedi & Thaker, 2001). The apparent and inevitable changes now experienced by the society are imminent rather than willed. While imbibing new technologies, social upheavals take place, either spontaneously or force them upon ourselves, for we welcome change at least sub-consciously. Mowlana (1997) propagated four change dimensions—Centralisation of decision-making and control, Homogeneity, Hegemony, and Global system of nation states—that resulted from the ingress of the new ICTs. They point towards a trust-mistrust combination that precipitated in the space between technology and society. While realising the need for existing alongside the advancing technology, man took a fancy to uplifting himself socially by becoming a link in the electronic society and he not only made online courtesy calls but also passed on information to others both, relevant and otherwise.

INFORMATION VS. CHANGE

In his elaborate reviews of the 'Information Society' Frank Webster (1997) observed, "Post Industrialism is widely regarded as an 'Information Society'. The best known characterisation of the 'information society' is Daniel Bell's theory of Post-industrialism." Daniel Bell had projected the pivotal role of information/knowledge as the centrality of the emerging Information society. Bell (as cited in Webster, 1997) contended, "We are entering a new system, a post-industrial society, which, while it has several distinguishing features, is characterised throughout by a heightened presence and significance of information." Daniel Bell also argued that information and knowledge are crucial for Post Information Society, both 'quantitatively and qualitatively.' The "heightened presence" of information as a characteristic of the post-industrial age notwithstanding, one experiences a visible qualitative change, which Bell (1976) called 'theoretical knowledge'. That Bell's theorising pointed towards the increase in information in the social, economic and political fields is neither disputed nor found incorrect, whereas his premise that the 'presence of heightened information' signalling a new kind of society may not be saleable.

Post-Industrial Society stemmed from structural changes in society and not from changes in politics or culture. Bell (1976) asserted that change could seldom originate from any one sector and influence other dimensions of society. He opined that the developed societies were 'radically disjunctive' (Bell, 1980). "That is, there are independent realms—social structure, polity and culture—which have an autonomy one from another such that an occurrence in one realm cannot be presumed to shape another," (Webster, 1997).

The convergence of communications technologies, a cause for structural changes, is likely to have some significant impact on society in terms of change in life-style, viewing pattern, market strategies, employment, formal and non-formal education, etc. The convergence services provide access to information and interactivity leading to a better-informed society. It opens up an opportunity for reaching out to the inaccessible sections of the society (Trivedi & Thakar, 2001). In his interview with Herbert Schiller, Lovink (1997) observed, "Everything you will discover in the areas of television and film will come back in the Net. The patterns are going to be very similar. We are nowhere near to what they like to call an Information Society. This term serves to camouflage the current reality".

All sincere attempts at defining the 'IS' though yielded results, an emphatic bird's-eye view is yet to be achieved. But, the term 'information' largely influences the idea of the new society. From technological angle, that the Internet is second to none in the overwhelming quantum of information available at any given point of time at any single location is a cliché. In his scrutiny of the information industries in Asia, Kyung (2001) pointed out the superiority of the Net in the developed nations. In the US the Internet dominates in terms of contents and traffic of information and the U.S. is more or less the 'hub' of World Wide Web in every respect.

The new media of communications technologies, particularly Internet has a firm footing in the developed nations. Nevertheless, much to the chagrin of the users, these technologies infringe mercilessly upon the privacy of others. Taking cognizance of the danger ahead, the Universal Declaration of Human Rights stepped in. The need to fence the privacy of individuals is as quintessential as the dire need to put the technology to use, for, a society gains impetus when new know-how becomes the means of a more sophisticated life. At the same time, technology alone is insufficient for a society to move into the information mould.

IMPORTANCE OF TECHNOLOGY

The primacy of technologies in creating a society is neither remote nor indiscernible and their dominance is visible quite rampantly in the present. India is not an exception to this condition despite the reality that the advent of the new communications technologies such as Internet and mobile are as recent as the middle nineteen nineties. The growth of the communications industry was not a mere happening but followed a better money inflow into the country in the wake of liberalisation. That the embracing of technology became a reality only when backed up by resources is indisputable and the sidelining of the 'have-nots', an inevitable feature of the IS. Those Americans who revel in the greatest connectivity today are typically high-income households. At the same time, the new ICT can be termed to be the most absorbing for the user. In his study "Uses and Gratifications of the Web Among Students" Ebersole (2000) found that television involves only one's leisure time, whereas the PC/Internet affect work, school and play—personal, family and business relationships. He concedes that the chances of the users of ICT to turn into addicts were rather inevitable or one's attraction for the medium could hamper one's routine.

THE SUPPORT OF ECONOMY

The adoption of a technology gains precedence when the potential user is economically comfortable to own it. Many studies of technology adoption have found that the income of the user was a priority as against education and occupation (Dutton et al, 1989). This leads to the inference that technologies are first tested out by the potential user irrespective of realising their usefulness. Yet, the fact that the new technologies are convenient and reliable as information sources has come to stay. Chung and Rodriguez (as cited in AEJMC, 2012) who explored the patterns of use of information sources such as 'traditional', 'on-line', and 'mixed' among investors, found that on-line investors were more certain about the investing environment. It implies that the credibility of the new technologies as information providers is rated high.

OCCUPATIONAL SUPPORT

The visible changes, which pervade the new society, are in the realm of occupation, especially the notable growth of the information industry. The emergence of the information workers has become a reality with the new-found need for information to manoeuvre the industry successfully. Kuo and Low (2001) pointed out that the long-term growing trend in information-related occupations has been in tandem with and supportive of industrial changes in a developed nation like Singapore. When information becomes the pivot of the post-industrial society, the efficiency of the employee is measured by way of his being a user of the ICT. The Luntz (1997) survey found that as much as 29% of the respondents worked for a "large company", which comprised 51, 47, 30, and 22 percents of the "Super-connected", "Connected", "Semi-connected", and "Not connected" categories respectively. On the contrary, a substantial 27% of the respondents who were "unemployed", "self-employed" (16%), "work for small business" (13%), and "work for medium-sized business" (14%) comprised the other categories. The statistics reveal that the new technologies pave way for the efficient and skilled people who can find placements in large firms. Here, the adverse impact of new technologies is also revealed in the form of the "unemployed". The adoption of technologies results in new ways of performing intellectual tasks and infusing new processes into the daily agenda of individuals and groups. One such is the preference of American government workers to work from home via computer but only a 14% had the opportunity (Temin, 1992).

The new technologies found their footing in India too. The citizenry began to adopt the new technologies at a great pace as (Ruet, 2002) there was a forecast that India's information technology workers would grow from 70,000 a year to 3,50,000 a year by 2008. Taking this cue, the U.S. IT companies decided that along with flying down professionals from India, they could relocate part of the work in India through networking.

VALUE OF 'TIME' AND 'SPACE'

The foremost strength, contraction of space, of the new technologies notwithstanding, the potential user is located in the cities rather than in the suburbs. Hindman's (2000) study reflects that residents in metropolitan cities adopt and use various information technologies than residents of non-metropolitan cities. This is a fact, not only in the case of the West, but also that of the developing nations. The nullifying of the unimaginable distances involves mostly cities due to the dominant presence of users of the new technologies in them. The inference that 'income' was the central reason for technology adoption was also supported by the research finding that the demographics 'occupation' and 'education' equally supported adoption of technologies. Cities, which overwhelm in higher levels of occupational and educational status, would invariably figure among networked places.

CULTURAL HOMOGENEITY

The 'IS' is one in which the general value of life undergoes categorical improvements in the modern sense, wherein the lives of the younger generations are "Much better" than those of their parents (Luntz, 1997). The survey also reveals that the users of the technologies alone do not benefit but also the non-users, thereby the advent of the new communication technologies improves the lifestyle of a society in general.

The positive effects of the ICT are not economic alone, but social too. Technology users are quick to expand their horizons of friends and business partners. In a study of 'dependents' and 'non-dependents' of Internet (Young, 1996), 'Dependents' show a keen interest in creating new on-line relationships by "increasing their immediate circle of friends among a culturally diverse set of world-wide users." They reflect more affinity for on-line relationships as their personal identity could be concealed urging them to build strong bonds. The widening of the social circle, though a positive effect of the new ICT, is often dented by the users' attitude of concealing identities, a peculiarity of the information age.

The technology-driven changes became apparent in the people's lifestyles, in the form of a greatly augmented consumerism with on-line shopping becoming a part of the domestic routine. With satellite technology and the Internet rapidly improving, Internet and cable TV shopping emerge as new types of non-store shopping and is expected to impose a great deal of influence on the traditional store shopping. On the contrary, the online shopper is always wary of the confidentiality online. The groups that express more serious concerns are the same groups that use the Internet more frequently. These concerns could reach great proportions in the future especially when the reported cases of cyber crimes are on the rise.

When sophistication and improved economic value of life as characteristics of the 'IS' are placed on one side of the scale, like in any other form of society, other neutralising concerns might surface on the other. The problem of white collar crimes goes hand-in-hand with pornography, sexual discrimination, and male dominance. Heider and Harp (2000), using textual analysis and a feminist theoretical framework, while examining pornography sites on the WWW, found the Internet to be reifying existing power structures, i.e., male dominance and the exploitation of women. When industrialisation forced replacement of agriculture as an occupation, the repercussions of modernisation of the society did have telling impacts, socially and economically, and continue to do so.

A concrete classification of this new society continuing to be elusive to scholars notwithstanding, the philosophers of the 'IS' have ascertained the determinants that are responsible for its creation. Having acknowledged the deductions of many an author on the 'Information Society', Webster (1997) constricts to five specifics—'Technological', 'Economic', 'Occupational', 'Spatial', and 'Cultural'—that shape and characterize the new civilisation. He posits that the resultant changes in the 'post-industrial society' are visible in many realms particularly the five aspects, the core areas that together mirror the making of the 'Information Society'.

TECHNOLOGICAL

With the presence of technology in the society being realised in the 'post-industrial' era, the overwhelming presence of technology in information storage and dissemination coupled with cheap modes of processing, has begun to redefine the routine and lifestyle of people.

While regarding the new Information and Communications Technologies (ICT) as distinguishing features of a new society, Webster (1997) predicted the formulation of a "techno-economic paradigm" with the rampant spread of the Integrated Services Digital Network (ISDN) at the foundation of the Information Society'. He perceived a 'flexible specialisation' on the work front, as a result of constituting the ICT to spur a new way of administration. All perspectives lead to a point of view that describes the 'Information Society' as one that is technology-driven, as Gates (1995) contends, "I'm optimistic about the impact of the new technology. It will enhance leisure time and enrich culture by expanding the distribution of information. It will give us more control over our lives and allow experiences and products to be custom-tailored to our interests".

The boisterous technological changes that churned the developed societies in the latter half of the 1970s gelled with the emerging 'post-industrial society' as surmised by Bell (as cited in Webster, 1997) in his 'The Coming of Post-Industrial Society'. Castells (1989) also agreed emphatically, "Restructuring could never have been accomplished without the unleashing of the technological and organisational potential of the 'informational'."

According to the Commission of European Communities (Mowlana, 1996), "Telecommunications is the most critical area for influencing the "nerves system" of modern society and it must be viewed as the major component of a conglomerate global sector comprising the management and transportation of information." As rightly positioned, telecommunications, the bloodline of the new Information and Communications Technologies (ICT), creates a social metamorphosis by strengthening the interdependence in society through the mediated form of communication. Preston (2001), while exploring the three-corner relationship involving technology, information, and social change, wrote eloquently about telecommunications that, the explosion of the highly mobile character of telephony and the transition of the personal computer from isolated office automation equipment to a highly flexible form of communication and networking gadget, is noteworthy.

TECHNOLOGY AND SOCIAL CHANGE

The point that there exists an unshaken trust between technological innovations and social changes is not easily contested. The third-wave theorists postulate that the new technologies create many a fundamental change in the social fabric of the advanced societies. It made stronger sense to infer that the developing societies were close on the heels of the advanced ones. Speculations about the winner at the end of the race are meaningless, because only the stronger nations can withstand the inevitable social upheavals that could create dislocations or fractures in the existing system. Toffler (1980) contended that 'a new critical transition' landed the society ushering in 'a third civilisational rupture' creating transformation in the social, economic and political forms.

The theories behind technology-created social change are not new to the new economy but as old as Cohen (as cited in Dogra, 2001) who observed, "the hand mill gives you society with the feudal lord, the steam mill, society with the industrial capitalist." Every society is the result of technological changes. Today, the new media are seen as the crossbreed of communication technologies fetching for itself a social status that runs parallel to the potency of the medium. Yet, the users of the online medium do not see it any different from the older media such as the electronic and print (Lin, 2000). As the purpose of all technologies were to empower the user in some way or other, the ultimate impact of the new technologies was to give end-users greater power to shape their computing systems and to manage their information needs.

The encouraging social and economic changes that trigger the new facade of the society are weighed down by the user's receding trust in the new media. Hoffman et al, (1999) opined that consumers are withdrawn when the electronic network does not safeguard their privacy and security. Conversely, the Indian scenario reflects a more optimistic reaction to using the new media, which helps the society realise for itself the need for easy adaptability to the new technology.

In his analysis of the new media, Paniyil (2001), while mentioning the relief that the ICT brought about for Indian consumers, pointed out that the railway ticketing information is available without the help of touts and examination results, without mobbing in front of notice boards. Indians' easy adaptability to technologies, particularly the Information Technologies (IT), perhaps help in the nation's rating as a topper among 53 nations in terms of IT expertise (Devraj, 2000). At the same time, he placed India at the bottom in terms of telecommunication infrastructure. Though the observation was relevant some years ago, it is otherwise now. The telecommunication technology that runs across the length and breadth of the country is one of futuristic generation. It is rather more pertinent to point out the socio-economic aspects as deterrents that normally plague technology diffusion in India.

While dilating upon the setbacks that impede technology diffusion in India, Shastri (2001) observed that the elite prospered with the private education system, whereas the rural populace (forming more than 60 per cent of the country's population) solely depend upon the public education system, which was faced with a fast-decreasing support from the government resulting in the creation of information haves and have-nots. The distinctions between the two are bound to reflect in intangibles such as upbringing, culture and education. While thinking on similar lines, Trivedi and Thaker (2001) also predicted that the new society would be faced with a new divide—computer literates and illiterates. The computer savvy people would leave behind a large mass of the older (35-50 years) generation in the race for technology adoption.

MEDIA CONVERGENCE

Convergence of different ICT is an intrinsic creation of the Information Society. Though branded as a revolution, Trivedi and Thakar (2001) argued that different perceptions emerged with regard to media convergence. Two schools of thought hold diametrically opposite premises. One thinks that technological convergence leads to media convergence and the other that though convergence is technically possible, divergence of media was bound to continue. When seen from the point of view of countries like India, media convergence could be unaffordable by a major segment of the population. The authors' premise further that the consumers would seek more value for money and simplicity in operation and that if it failed, the reasons were three: cost, complexity and consumer needs.

The issue of affordability is not exclusive to the developing or Third World Nations alone, but also to the developed nations. The former US Asst. Secretary of Commerce, Irving (as cited in Black, 1999) remarked, "Think how powerful the Internet is. Then remind yourself that fewer than 2% of people are actually connected". Lee (2001) also observed that the spread of the Net was rather dramatic and that it had taken only four years for the Internet to reach 50 million users. The amount of traffic carried over the Internet is said to be doubling every 100 days. The power of the medium permeated every nook and corner of the globe but did not touch its entire populace. According to Nua Internet Surveys (as cited in Lee, 2001) the Internet users had skyrocketed since 1998 and it was estimated that some 407 million people were connected to the Internet in 2000, and this reached almost 700 million in 2001. This reflected that the Internet was the fastest growing communication technology in human history. Region-wise, the Internet showed heavy concentration in the North America (40.8%) and Europe (27.8%), claiming 68.6% of the world's Internet users. As of 2014, with a penetration of 40.8% of the world population, the Internet covers nearly 3 billion users (ITU, & UNPD, 2014). It is inferred that among the ICT the Internet is apparently viewed as the foremost technology with one of the fastest growth rates. Though undisputedly, a revolution among technologies, it is improper to expect the medium to find its way into the hands of different economic strata of the society. This expectation never arose when either the television or even the radio made their entry.

ECONOMIC

The trend in the 'new age' is to ascribe an economic value to every piece of information that goes to contribute to the Gross National Produce (GNP). Peter Drucker (2001) deduced that 'knowledge' became the basis of modern economy, shifting from economy of goods to economy of knowledge. Information Society theoreticians argue that the society has evolved into one in which the distinguishing feature is that knowledge and organisation are the prime creators of wealth.

The premise can seldom be refuted, for, the strength of an economic activity is determined by the acceptable use of a piece of information in such a way that it can be converted into 'knowledge' for a congenial output from that activity. The essence of a strong database of information can "homogenise disparate economic activities" (Webster, 1997) and thereby leverage the society economically.

To experience the benefits of a technology by appropriately manoeuvring its potential, means that the objective (to enhance one's life economically) of its user is well-focused. Invariably the educated and the economically forward are likely to be regular participants of the electronic network game. This has the support of Peter Drucker (2001) who opined that the 'next information revolution' would involve all major firms of the present day society. The resultant will be the imperative need to redefine business enterprise as the "CREATION OF VALUE AND WEALTH". He also observed that the computer would be a watershed at the workplace impacting the top management deliberations in business policy, strategy and decisions. It is discerned that all business houses used the ICT not only to expand their business horizons but also to institute value-added services for the customers. This in turn provided the society at large, with an opportunity to enter new realms of consumer activities and trigger the need to address quality in a product and life. The focuses of the Post-Industrial Society are the service sector, which paved way for new opportunities that were non-existent in other societies, and self-employment ventures. Toffler (in Preston, 2001) identified the growth of a new sector that comprises "prosumers", whereby people produce more goods and services, not for sale, or even barter, but for their own use.

The major pitfall that can emerge in the long run would be the economic differences between people with the wherewithal and others without. Patterson and Wilson (2000) referred to the new ICT as 'engines of inequality', that contribute to an ever-widening gap between the rich and the poor, which has now reached 'grotesque' proportions. Irving (in Black, 1999) vouchsafed, "Low-income persons, the less educated are among the groups that lack access to information resources." Contrarily, there are others who contend that ICT has a tremendous equalising potential.

INFORMATION AND ECONOMY

The economic value of the 'IS' is spurred by the informational value developed and information would be the basis of the informational economy, which would cater to all economic needs of the society. Both the economy and the society would grow and develop around the core of production and use of information values (Low, 1997). Information as an economic product will exceed goods, energy and services in importance (Masuda, 1990). The 'intangible' information gains value proportionate to the degree of use it is put to. Those who convert the information into knowledge are slated to ascend higher up and others could be left behind. The power to control information is bound to create income disparities amongst young professionals, which will in turn have a telling impact on the educational system. Similarly, the relatively disadvantaged rural and non-metropolitan economies are likely to suffer from lack of newspapers and contemporary courses in schools and colleges. Hindman (2000) mentioned that if these communities were to be wired residents would read online newspapers and students take up those futuristic courses available in the metropolitan cities. Equipped with telecommunication infrastructure, the 'isolated' societies could evolve themselves into diversified economies and provide jobs for displaced farmers. But in a country like India mere information could be futile. Deb (2001) argued that unless power, water, roads, and other infra-structure improved, reforms might never touch Indians and that a decade of reforms and lowering of import tariff had only ushered in a consumer boom for the strong Indian middle class.

OCCUPATIONAL

Rampant changes in the distribution of occupations are at the core of the most influential theory of the 'Information Society'. Bell's (1976) propagation of the emerging "white collar society', the receding industrial labour, the rising communal consciousness, and the developing of an equality between the sexes, provide a lucid sketch of the Information Society.

The arrival of the 'Information Society' is realised with the domination of the labour market by 'information operatives', which brings together the occupational features and the 'economic measures.' The fundamental premise of the information society's scholars about its evolution points towards the predominance of occupations in the information sector where clerks, teachers, lawyers, and entertainers outnumber coalminers, steel-workers, dockers, and builders. The occupational trends in the 'Information Society' do not signify the fading importance of the agricultural or industrial occupation, rather it emphasises upon the shift in the nature of work, i.e. from hard physical labour to mental deliberations.

In order to define a type of society, it is almost certain that the predominantly prevalent employment is spontaneously used. The most common occupation became a "defining feature" (Bell, 1976) of particular societies. When the agricultural labour pervaded the agricultural society and the factory worker dominated the industrial society, the service specialist surfaced in the post-industrial society. The critical factor in moving from one society to another is that it becomes possible to get "more for less" (Webster, 1997) from work because of the principle of efficiency. In the pre-industrial epoch everyone had to work the land just to eke out a living. However, as it became feasible to feed an entire population without everyone working on the land it was possible to release a portion of the people from farms so that they may do other things while still being assured of an adequate food supply. Accordingly they drifted to the towns and villages to supply factories with labour while buying their food from the excess produced in the country.

To mention that the surpluses in agriculture indirectly led to the proliferation of the other sectors is not incorrect. The 'unthinkable luxuries: e.g., teachers, hospitals, entertainment, and holidays' (Webster, 1997), take roots when the surplus-producing work force of the agricultural sector move to the towns to create industrial wealth, which in turn created new opportunities in 'services'. The process (the automation of industry leading to robotic factories, continuous release of people from industry, and creation of new vistas in services in order to fulfill the new needs) is continuous as the society entered the Information Age. For Bell, (in Webster, 1997) a 'service society' is a post-industrial one. The 'Service sector' transfers employment from one sector to another. The ethos of "more for less" impels automation of first agriculture, and later on industry, thereby getting rid of the farmhand and the industrial working class while simultaneously ensuring increased wealth.

SERVICE SOCIETY

Bell (1976) deduced that the Post-Industrial Society is an Information Society and a service economy reflected the coming of post industrialism. However, Gershuny and Miles (1983) contended that the service occupations, defined as those outputs of which are non-material or ephemeral, are not limited to the service sector. The underscore of the agricultural society is the dependence on raw muscle power (Bell, 1976), the strength of the industrial period was the domination of the machine. Conversely, the pivot of the post-industrial society is based on services—'a game between persons'—where information was the tool. Even history brands as important the presence of the erudite and the skilled for the advancement of any society. The surmise concurs with Perkin's (1990) theory that Britain reflected the resourcefulness of professionals who ruled by the wealth created by the educated and sustained by the exclusion of the unqualified.

In contrast, research and theory has it that the fundamental development of a society became tangible only with the constructive 'inclusion' of the unqualified and the weak. In *The Coming of Post-Industrial Society,* Bell (in Webster 1997) highlighted trends, such as the increased presence of professionals, which have important consequences for politics (Will professionals rule?). Here one could discern not the isolation of realms, but their interdependence as opposed to the view of Bell. In a job-centred society, work represented not only income and sustenance but also self-respect and self-worth. If the 'workers' of capitalist industrialism and informational society are juxtaposed, the distribution of 'social position', 'power', and 'status' would weigh heavier in favour of the latter group. For, the 'information worker' prevails over his counterpart as a 'white-collar worker' (Low, 1997; Rose, 1991).

Popular theories of the information society reflected three types of occupations, 'extractive', 'fabrication', and 'information activities' that pervaded different societies. The dominant group in the post-industrial society is the third in which an overwhelming number of information workers existed. The growing presence of professionals not only meant perennial flow of information but also quality orientation. Here the information worker is the white-collared professional (Bell, 1989). More than the individual, the promotion of the community through valued relationships began to be realised.

The effect of using the IT reflects on the work front and culture or lifestyle, which accompanied work. Private companies, by adopting IT, create professionalism by providing new attire to the roles of information workers. The one new facet of the 'IS' seems to be the importance of education as a "new form of security". In effect, being in possession of a job in the 'IS' is akin to owning a property in another. Because, IT caused the losing of jobs except for those of the skilled. Moreover, the positive effect on the society is that jobs require high levels of creativity for sustenance (Trivedi and Thakar, 2001; Low, 2000).

SPATIAL

The most effective outcome, following the advent of the new ICT is the irreversible "death of distance", resulting in a dramatic effect on time and space. In his thematic analysis of the 'Information

Society' Thomas (2001) observed, "the essence of this society is one of 'wired' where networks play the role of bringing together people and organisations that are separated by continents".

Manufacturing industries, which never looked beyond their own geographical boundaries for transactions, have explosively reached out to unthinkable corners of the world, putting the constraints of space asunder. After scrutinising the possibility of the global strategies of companies made possible by the ICT, Goddard (1992) deducted four elements—1. co-ordination of globally distributed manufacture, 2.computer and communication technologies to enable information processing and distribution, 3.explosive growth of information sector, and 4. integration of national and regional economies—in the transition to an Information Society.

That the New Information and Communications Technologies (ICT) have redefined the geographical space cannot be termed as a vague surmise. The distinct effects of the re-creation of space in the IS are tangible in some forms and intangible in others, besides being both positive and less-than-acceptable intrinsically. What used to be a move towards decentralisation of working is now reverting to a centralised working due to the speed with which governance has become a possibility and that too without too many impediments. With the development of modern science, the universally accepted 'global village' has begun to be realised on the one hand, and the nature of this global space becoming abstract, passive and uniform on the other. The abstract space could be open to exploitation as it is interchangeable with any other space. Radovan (2001), who envisioned the positive aspects of this new 'global culture of the present, predicted a more global human solidarity but cautions that the flattening and shrinking of the space of human experience is liable to have negative effects.

ICT has increased the speed with which economic transactions can be conducted over geographically disparate areas. The reach and extent of speedily activated patterns via computer networks might change the geopolitical influence of states and other organisations, rearrange the time and space of the society and also create a 'symbolic environment' (Mowlana, 1997; Harvey, 1989).

INFORMATION AND SPACE

Although the potential of the new technologies in stringing places on the globe like beads is likely, theyimmobilise people and physically separate them from the society. The primary experience of people when using computers and the Internet is largely immobile and alone, movement is provided on the screen, which may be thought of as a window through which the person looks (Geocities.com, 2002) and as many services will be made available at home on a single device (Trivedi & Thaker, 2001).

At the same time the new ICT networks are propagandist technologies that promote the importance of information transportation around the sphere in order to help in the realisation of economic and social wants while they concurrently reduce the import of places. The flow of information may emerge as the principal aspect of the 'informational society' (Castells, 1994) and the reliance on networks reduces the restrictions of place on contemporary activities (Webster, 1997). The networks ought to have nodal centres through which the information does not merely flow, but where it is collated, analysed and acted upon. While viewing nodal cities like New York, London, and Tokyo as 'highly concentrated command posts of world economy', Sassen (1991) concurred with Castells on branding these cities as 'informational cities', which are spatially dispersed over a wide area and yet interlocked places of economic activity. The rapidity of the expansion of these cities went along proportionately with the equally paced increase in information workers who dealt with the management of the networks, thereby paving way for the 'global control capability'.

The 'global cities' become all the more central functionaries for the world economy as globalisation proliferates. The information producers who form a numerical minority dominate a place in terms of lifestyle. Castells (1989) calls them a "hegemonic social class" that might "not necessarily rule the state but fundamentally shapes civil society".

Though a minuscule minority, the cities that pivot the flow of economic deliberations around the world determine the shaping up of the new society. In Castells' (1994) parlance, this new society is informational and global and makes a vital point that 'informational' refers to more than 'information based' and 'global economy' signifies more than 'a world economy' The 'informational' societies are likely to have an upper hand vis-a-vis those that aren't. The race for a control of the global 'hegemonic social class' could be the near future consequences of the shrinking globe. In a contextual analysis of the changing face of the world, a new form of imperialism is visualised. He observed that the 'global net workers' built overseas hegemony by borrowing from the US its 'comprador' approach for overseas domination, in which local allies (compradors) are assisted to set up new 'independent' countries. These 'comprador' hegemonies administered 'their' spaces in accordance with the needs of their allies in the global centre.

INEQUALITY AND SPACE

The feeling of a shrunken globe due to information technologies notwithstanding, theoreticians do contend that the tedium of distance cannot be eliminated but is but to evolve new types of inequality by making the rural areas more accessible to the dominations of alien corporations. This is quite a truism in the Indian scenario wherein multi-national corporations have made forays into rural India by systematically instituting marketing strategies that deter its lifestyle.

At the same time, contradictions surface from the point of view of other scholars who think that with the neutralising of distance, as a result of networking, jobs will be made available equally to people of both the urban and rural areas. Consequently, the mere knowledge of jobs without adequate skill can make one a misfit, where the rural man continues to be at the receiving end. The inequality, though a bane to society, is inevitable. Nonetheless, the disadvantages posed by geographic isolation would not hinder the "non-metropolitan businesses, which stand much to gain through the adoption of productivity-enhancing technologies" (Gillespie & Robbins, 1989).

Yet, they are also faced with the "rural penalties" of greater distances from markets and a lack of economic diversification (Hudson & Parker, 1990). Barring the inequalities the 'shrinking globe' can create, scholars forecast a major threat, the making of another world. While national boundaries and, in general, space is becoming irrelevant due to the increasing globalisation, scholars conceive of a 'fourth world' that comprises parts of Africa, S. America and Asia that will be excluded as futile to the global network economy. When the strategists advocate the need for uplifting the Third World nations, so as to help even the developed nations enjoy the benefits of the new ICT and the 'shrunken globe', it would be inconsequential if a 'Fourth World' emerged. In effect, the exploitative act of the first two worlds in enhancing their range of possible social networks by controlling the versatility of a medium like the Internet will not only help them reap dividends but also forestall progression of the Third World nations.

CULTURAL

Viewing through the "cultural' microscope Webster (1997) perceived more confusion prevalent in the 'Information Society' and described it as 'wayward' rather than 'organised'. His observation that the "extraordinary increase in information" attributes itself to drastic changes in lifestyle is not an incorrect inference.

The simultaneous access to abundant information from a variety of mass media, ICT, telephone, etc., has redefined social interaction with a sea change. 'Socialising' is preceded by a conscious effort of storage and analysis of global information, which, to a larger extent, controls the lifestyle. If the IS prides itself in evolving a new culture, the chances of 'culture' being considered a determinant of the new society is rather remote. According to the suppositions of scholars, the presence of a unique form of culture determines the emergence of the 'IS'. Contrarily, if the new culture is seen as the consequence of IS, the tools that shape the 'new culture' gain visibility and importance. The machinations of the agricultural and industrial societies are overwhelmingly responsible for the shift in the lifestyle of their peoples.

Today, the change in lifestyle is so abrupt and directionless that the much-valued cultural ethos is threatened leading to both, a shift in lifestyle and a cultural denigration. A state of confusion prevails upon any analyst who tries to define the 'new culture', for a highly complex paradigm has set upon the society. McQuail's (2000) observation that the communication technology has an effect on culture, as communication and culture are intertwined, aligns with the idea that the tools of communication shape the lifestyle of a society. Moreover the "common value system" (Bell, 1976) which was highly regarded throughout a system is now faced with the imminent death.

Irrespective of the nature of changes, Mowlana (1997) agreed that the fundamental form of culture and methods of communication of the industrialised nations are on the decline to give way to a new and different form altogether. The immense opportunities that aid people to form networks, irrespective of distance, open up newer reflections of the society. While examining the potential new marketplace of ideas that exists in cyberspace, Brown (2000) expressed that citizens are provided with universal access opportunities to new media, thereby increasing the diversity of expression and discourse in society.

The high levels of discourse point towards the increasing educational strength of the participants, who eventually become information professionals. As a result of increasing their earning power, the 'IS' professionals are naturally drawn to the luxurious lifestyles offered in large urban centres rather than in the suburbs (Sassen, 1991). The participation of the well-to-do professionals alone is insufficient to promote a collective culture, and ignoring the voice and vision of underserved communities will greatly limit the ability of the Internet to function as a tool that strengthens local communities.

CULTURE AND DEVELOPMENT

If the marginalised are to be supported, they ought to be helped in experiencing the new technologies through applied educational methods. As social scientists have predicted, the non-users of information technologies may find themselves misplaced and incapable of keeping pace with the rest. Hindman (2000) went a step further and reasoned that the perpetuation of status and power in the information society depended on the patterns of use and adoption of the information technologies among the population. Implied, the people who rein in a new lifestyle in the Information Society would be the ones who apply the technologies in the most diverse manner. The benefits of the speed of adoption of technologies might be rocked by certain threats to society, if the speed became uncontrollable and lacks direction.

The profundity of the consequences of the new ICT is proportionate to the uncertainty of their nature and causes (Low, 2000; Mowlana, 1997). The GVU survey (2001) also reflected that users are wary of providing financial information on the Web. To add, the more convenient the technology became, the more the problems to encounter

(Trivedi & Thaker, 2001). Nevertheless, despite the prediction that convergence would influence the life-style of people, experts do opine that for a single device to replace the television, computer, and telephone, it would take some years before it permeates very deep into a social system. For each of the technologies has its intrinsic use and importance.

PLAUSIBLE IMPLICATIONS OF THE INFORMATION SOCIETY

The breakdown of the traditional way of 'discriminating' women socially is becoming a reality. Women are geared to be a part of, and contribute to the new culture in equal vigour as that of men. The prominence of women in the social and political fronts has come to stay with the thinning down of the status of inequality between men and women.

Although the uncomplicated purpose of use of the new technologies is mutual to all to 'cover distance' and achieve 'speed and convenience', users belonging to various age groups think independently of each other when it relates to their own 'spaces'. The prominent presence of the teenagers or youth in their domination of the networking culture cannot be disregarded even though their objective of occupying the virtual spaces is a debatable one.

The youth, in general, reflect a capability for faster adaptability to the changing environment as opposed to the 'cautious' approach of the older age groups. They are, more often than not, prepared to conceptualise a new structuring of the social relations, and interact across indefinite spans of' 'time' and 'space', which Giddens (1990) calls 'disembedding'.

The reality of the environment of the present youngsters is that they were born into a digital world and are strapped to a mobility that is faster than the eye can follow. Although the Information Society' holds plenty of promises for the 'Netizens', their lack of experience of conventions and social life, can alienate them physically from their own surroundings.

The threat of digital divide looms large which results from the increase in the income of one segment which is techno-savvy. In addition to their high educational standing, the users of the Information Technologies can acquire more comforts in life because they are 'information rich'. For those in the 'very low' income bracket, it's extremely tedious to keep pace with the rest and is bound to be relegated to the background, socially and economically.

The deterrent of the Third World nations' progress is lack of adequate governmental support for the educational sector, besides population explosion and poverty. When elementary aspects are neglected, no amount of valiant efforts made in networking the society can result in the genuine form of development, for, the 'ignorant' would always remain dependent on assistance in order to use the new technologies. The sustenance of the government institutions must become a commitment so as to be on a par with the private ones.

As a personal communication technology, the mobile phone which has outpaced the landline is instrumental in the mushrooming of the service industry which is devoid of a 'permanent address'. However, the opportunity for low-investment self-employment seen in the present society is a resultant of the mobile technology.

The new communications technologies have begun to phase out other technologies which were the pivotal forces in office automation. The attempt to create 'paperless office' may see success even in the developing nations, but 'administrative security' never comes with an affordable price tag and even the most advanced nations fear the shelving of hard copies of documents.

With the often slashing of excise duty on personal computers from the government's budget, the markets get buoyed with buyers, due to affordability. India has also gone to the extent of inventing the 'simputer', the common man's computer, to make it affordable for all. The ardent computer user upgrades his system to meet with the equipment of the future, but how would the common man or the illiterate even get to feel the machine when his basic needs are not met and his right to education denied.

Networking has become a reality and is proliferating at an encouraging pace. The aim of achieving efficiency brought in 'decentralisation' of work. But networking has reintroduced the centralised working with a recreated version 'centralised-decentralisation'. The head office keeps a close watch on the working of its branch using the 'wired network' and continues to give directions by the minute.

The perception of the Internet users especially the youth, on the causal factors of the Information Society, run parallel. The future will show an increase in the users' dependence on the medium, making it a part of their lives. Singh's (2001) reservation that all individual media would shed their separate identities and converge on a single platform to provide "more for less" is the premise that cannot be ignored.

The composition of Webster's (1997) 'techno-economic paradigm' is today a realisation that few can rebut. Though the theory of social change engineered by technology is as old as Marxism, the change being felt in totality in the new age was unheard of in the previous societies. The 'third-wave' theorist Toffler (1980) called this change 'a new critical transition which has landed the society in 'a third civilisational rupture'.

The benefits of the new technologies, though numerous, can tend to be weighed down by the burden of the ills they are liable to cause. If the society does not 'stray and instead view the new technologies in the right perspective, the outcome of Preston's (2001) 'three-cornered' relationship involving technology, information, and social change may benefit mankind.

The role of the 'economic' determinant of the 'IS' is a watershed, which can be exploited by the skillful use of the new technologies and a mature analysis of the information disseminated through them. An ingenious handling of the new technologies would help reap better niceties of life. This is seen as a parallel to Drucker's (2001) observation that knowledge has become the basis of the modern economy, which ratifies the theory that "knowledge and organization are the prime creators of wealth."

To comprehend the worth of a piece of information that can be converted to knowledge lies in its intensity to produce a proportionate homogenisation of an economic activity. But, the one major setback that can befall a society, particularly a developing one, is the widening gap of inequality that can forestall any progression with equal strength.

That a major 'occupational' shift has come about in the new society is uncontested, which also confirms the propagations of Bell (1976) that 'white collar society' with a growing number of professionals is emerging and that now it is possible to get 'more for less'(Webster, 1997) the principle of increasing efficiency.

On the other side of the coin, the pull-back could be alarming, when the unskilled and unqualified would neutralise the efficiency of the 'professionals.' In the long run it's imperative that the skilled and the qualified professionals push up the 'weak' in order to stabilise the growth of the society.

The benefits of the 'spatial' aspects of the Information Society are attributable to the new technologies. This characteristic of the society is a long dreamed of phenomenon, helping the world inch closer to McLuhan's "Global Village." Moreover, the making of a new form of 'centralisation' ('centralized-decentralisation') cannot be ignored. Additionally, a networked society could run the danger of making its realities abstract. The swapping of 'abstract' places may take place leading to an insecure feeling of 'invasion of privacy'.

Having gratified their users, the new technologies, when viewed through the 'cultural' microscope, tend to threaten their users' values. The fear is all about an abrupt change that can create a loss of direction, leading to a state of confusion. This could be the 'beginning' of the loss of the local culture. A cultural homogenisation is a proposition that may not sink into the minds of people, especially those of the developing nations. The 'common value system' deduced by Bell (1976), which was regarded for long, could soon cease to exist.

CONCLUSION

In anticipation of the impact of technologies, the observation of one of the pioneers of studies in the province of technology and society deduced that all technologies brought about a social change (Pichandy, 1994), which suits not only the past, but also the future.

Irrespective of being a developed nation, changes accentuated by technologies could demonstrably strengthen and also abruptly pre-empt economic development and healthy progression. The outcome of the nature of developments will engender from the means of channelising the use of technologies. To visualize technological use, strictly on the basis of the realised needs of a society, would be a safe ground to tread on. The co-existence of opposing schools of thought in any given period of time is justified, as changes can be both productive and destructive to any society.

The adversities of the new age, if any, can be borne with equal vigour by neither a developed nor a developing nation like India. The shocks from an onslaught may be absorbed unperturbed by any economically strong nation, but the same might leave the pain unabated for generations in a developing one. The policy-makers of the latter nations need to address the cause of ills, before launching any developmental effort.

No development is sustainable when a major segment of the society is living in wretched conditions as in the Third World nations. The divide between the 'haves' and 'have-nots' will widen further leading to inconsequential effects even on the 'haves'. The government efforts on encouraging privatisation could turn out to be the ill of a developing country. For, there is bound to be a prohibitive hike in the cost of education, further distancing the 'have-nots'. A balanced approach to the policy is most warranted. Similarly, the same goes with the developed nations. Their sustenance will depend on their assistance to the needy nations. To realise the effects of globalisation, sincere attempts to chalk out plans for concerted contributions is the need of the hour.

The new society witnesses the emergence of skilled people, leading to professionalism and a scientific approach to issues. The use of skilled workers could become extremely expensive in the future, forcing the introduction of 'do-it-yourself' kits in the Third World markets. Besides, the notion of 'survival of the fittest' has already found its footing, resulting in downscaling of the work force, and retaining only the skilled. This accepted norm could possibly remove the fangs of the trade union movement in democratic countries, in particular, and eventually cause its extinction. The increasing demand for skilled persons in the new age will create the increase in part-time occupations, wherein those talented would tend to make more money to meet the needs of an 'expensive' future.

One principal outcome of the theories of the contemporary society is the need to use technologies to the hilt. For, the more they are put to use, the better will the economic benefits be. The hierarchies of the workplace are flattened, leading to the easy two-way links between the top management personnel and the floor workers. The traditional hand-me-down businesses in the family are faced with cessation, as the new generations have diverse thinking about novel ventures. The use of English language on the Net are heightened and the diminution of the regional languages is probably not far away. However, to achieve the dream of 'wiring' a developing non-English speaking nation such as India, a multi-lingual approach is crucial.

The strength of occupation in the 'Information Society' is the axiom in this context. The outlook of every kind of job has a changed facade. The change is the transition from the hard labour to the sophisticated mind manager. The information worker has become a reality only due to the machines that are available to help realise his vision. Had there been no industrial society, there wouldn't have been the 'Information Worker'.

The making of the 'Information Society' is discerned to be the extension of the toiling farmer and the industrial labour. It's the transition of one era into another, with changes in its basics. The sophistication and modernity embedded in the 'Information Society' is not actually divorced from the traditions of the yesteryears, but just seemingly discarded. The portrayal of the IS is more or less artificial in nature, which can't dislocate the cultural ethos of any nation. With the dramatic upsurge in the flow of information, its credibility is drowned in distrust, as tens of thousands of individual websites are bursting at the seams, suffocated with 'information'. The increase in cyber and white-collar crimes results in the inevitable rise in the invasion into people's privacy. A much-transparent approach, among peoples and nations, to the use of the new ICTs is undoubtedly commanding and anything opposed to it can brand the 'new society' a myth rather than a reality.

REFERENCES

Bell, D. (1976). *The Coming of Post Industrial Society. New York*. Harmondsworth: Penguin.

Bell, D. (1976). In Webster (1997), Theories of the Information Society. London: Routledge.

Bell, D. (1980). *Sociological Journeys 1960-1980*. London: Heinemann.

Bell, D. (1989). *The Third Technological Revolution and its Possible Socio-Economic Consequences*. Dissent. Spring.

Black, J. (1999). Losing Ground Bit by Bit. *London BBC News Online*. Retrieved from http://news.bbc.co.uk/1/hi/special_report/1999/10/99information_rich_information_poor/472621.stm

Brown, J. (2000). *Realising the Potential, Market place of ideas, Utilizing the First Amendment to Advance Universal Service and Access to the Internet*. Paper presented at 83rd Annual AEJMC Convention, Communication Technology & Policy Division. Phoenix Arizona.

Brown, M. M. (2001). *Democracy and the Information Revolution*. United Nations Development Programme.

Cairncross, F. (1977). *The Death of Distance: How the Communications Revolution will Change Our Lives*. London: Orion Business Books.

Castells, M. (1989). *The Informational City: InformationTechnology, Economic Restructuring and the Urban-Regional Process*. Oxford: Blackwell.

Castells, M. (1994). European Cities, the Informational Society, and the Global Economy. *New Left Review*, *204*(March-April), 18–32.

Chandler, D. (2001). *Technological or Media Determinism.* Retrieved from http://www.aber.ac.uk/media/Documents/tecdet/tdet01.html

Chung, O., & Rodriguez, L. (2012). *Information Source Use and dependencies for Investment Decision-Making.* Communication Technology and Policy 2000 Abstracts.

Cohen, G. A. (2000). In Dogra, (2001). *ICTs for development: A paradox of hope & hype.* Paper presented at International Conference on Community for Development in the Digital Era. University of Madras, Chennai.

Deb, S. (2001, June 25). Hits, Misses and Missing Pride. *Outlook.* Hathway: New Delhi.

Devaraj, R. (2000). *South Asia: Digital Divide Sharpens Rich-Poor Gap.* Retrieved from http://www.ipsnews.net/2000/07/south-asia-digital-divide-sharpens-rich-poor-gap/

Dogra, V. (2002). *ICTs for Developments Paradox of Hope and Hype.* Paper presented at International Conference on Community for Development in the Digital Era. University of Madras, Chennai.

Drucker, P. (2001). *The Next Information Revolution.* Retrieved from http://www.s-jtech.com/Peter%20Drucker%20-%20the%20Next%20Information%20Revolution.pdf

Dutton, W. H., Sweet, P. L., & Rogers, E. M. (1989). Socio-economic status and the early diffusion of personal computing in the United States. *Social Science Computer Review, 7*(3), 259–271. doi:10.1177/089443938900700301

Ebersole, S. (2000). Uses and gratifications of the web among students. Journal of Computer Mediated Communication. University of Southern Colorado, 6(1).

Gates, B. (1995). *The Road Ahead.* London: Viking.

Giddens, A. (1990). *The consequences of modernity.* Cambridge: Polity.

Goddard, J. B. (1992, February 22). *New Technology and the Geography of the UK Information Economy.* London Times. *Times Higher Education Supplement.*

Harvey, J. M. (1989). *Space in the embedding society.* Retrieved from http://www.geocities.com/jp marshall.geo/cybermind/cybertopls.rtf

Heeks, R. (1999). *Information & Communication Technologies, Poverty & Development.* Development Informatics [Working Paper Series No.5]. Manchester, UK: Institute for Development Policy and Management.

Heider, D., & Harp, D. (2000). *New hope or old power: New communication, pornography and the internet.* Retrieved from http://www.AEJMC.orq/convention/abstracts/2000%20/ctp.html

Hindman, D. B. (2000). Infrastructure issues in computer-mediated communication. Retrieved from http://www.AEJMC.org/convention/abstracts/2000/20/ctp.html

Hoffmann, D. L., Novak, T. P., & Peralta, M. A. (1999). Information privacy in market space: Implications for the commercial uses of anonymity on the web. *The Information Society, 15*(2).

Hudson, H. E., & Parker, E. B. (1990). Information Gaps in Rural America: Telecommunications policies for rural development. *Telecommunications Policy, 14*(3), 193–205. doi:10.1016/0308-5961(90)90040-X

Irving, L. (1999) *Losing Ground Bit by Bit.* London BBC News Online. Retrieved from http://news.bbc.co.uk/1/hi/special_report/1999/10/99information_rich_information_poor/472621.stm

ITU, & UNPD. (2014). *Internet Live Stats.* Retrieved from http://www.internetlivestats.com/internet-users/

Jonscher, C. (1999). *In Webster (2007), Theories of the Information Society*. London: Routledge.

Kelly, K. (1988). *New rules for the new economy: Ten ways the networking economy is changing everything*. London: Fourth Estate.

Kuo, E. C. Y., & Low, L. (2001). Information economy and changing occupational structure in Singapore. *The Information Society*, *17*(4).

Lamb, R. (1996). Informational Imperatives and Socially Mediated Relationships. *The Information Society*, *12*(1), 17–38. doi:10.1080/019722496129684

Lee, K. J. (2001). Globalization and infocom industries in Asia: Opportunities and threats. *Media Asia*, 28–29.

Lin, C. A. (2000). *Predicting on-line news activity via motives, innovative traits and news media use*. html

Lovink, G. (1997). *Information inequality: An interview with Herbert Schiller*. Retrieved from http://www.ljudmila.org/nettime/zkp4/20.htm

Low, L. (2000). The Social Impact of New Communication "Technologies. *Media Asia*, *27*(2), 84.

Luntz Research Company. (1997). *The Wired/Merril Lynch Forum Digital Citizen Survey*. Retrieved from http:// hotwired.lycos.com/special/citizen/

Machlup, F. (1984). *Knowledge, its creation, distribution, & economic significance: The economics of information and human capital*. New Jersey: Princeton University Press. doi:10.1515/9781400856022

Masuda, Y. (1990). *Managing in the information society: Releasing synergy Japanese style*. Oxford: Basil Blackwell.

McQuail, D. (2000). *McQuail's Mass Communication Theory*. New York. *Sage (Atlanta, Ga.)*.

Mowlana, H. (1996). *Global communication in transition: The end of diversity?* New Delhi. *Sage (Atlanta, Ga.)*.

Mowlana, H. (1997). *Communication and development--the emerging orders: Global information and world communication*. New Delhi: Sage. doi:10.4135/9781446280034.n10

Negroponte (1995). In Preston (2001), Reshaping communications: Technology information and social change. New Delhi: Sage.

Nua Internet Surveys (n. d.). In Lee (2001), *Globalization and infocom industries in Asia: Opportunities and threats*. Retrieved from [REMOVED HYPERLINK FIELD]http://www.AEJMC.org/convention/abstracts/2Q01conabs/Olmcs.html

Paniyil, M. M. (2001). Media/Information Technology. *Asia Times Online*. Retrieved from http://www.atimes.cpm

Patterson, R., & Wilson, E. (2000). New IT and social equality in Africa: Resetting the research and policy agenda. *The Information Society*, *16*(1).

Perkin, H. (1990). *The rise of professional society: Britain since 1880*. London: Routledge.

Pichandy, C. (1994). *Communication and Social Influence: A study of uses and effects of Home Video (VCR Technology) on the urban and rural audiences* [Unpublished doctoral dissertation]. PSG College of Arts & Science, Coimbatore.

Porat, M. U. (1977). *The information economy: Definition and measurement*. Washington, DC: US Department of Commerce.

Preston, P. (2001). *Reshaping communication: Technology, information & social change*. New Delhi: Sage.

PTI. (2013). *2.97 million professionals employed in IT-ITeS sector in FY13: Government*. Retrieved from http://articles.economictimes.indiatimes.com/2013-05-03/

Quon, A. (2001). Information rich vs information poor: Turning the digital divide into digital dividends. *Media Asia, 28*(3).

Radovan, M. (2001). Information technology and the character of contemporary life. *Information Communication and Society, 4*(2), 230–246. doi:10.1080/13691180110044498

Rogers, E. M. (1986). *Communication technology: The new media in society?* New York: The Free Press.

Rose, M. A. (1991). The post-modern and the post industrial. Cambridge: Cambridge University Press.

Ruet, J. (2002). *IT and development: Clusters as economic policy tools for India.* Retrieved from http://www.joef.ruet@esh-Deihi.com

Sassen, S. (1991). *The Global City: NewYork, London, Tokyo.* Princeton, New Jersey: Princeton University Press.

Shastri, P. (2001, June 25). *Time Travel and Time Warps.* Outlook: New Delhi: Hathway.

Singh, J.P. (2001). *Satellite broadcasting and distributing technology: Retrospect and prospect.* Manthan: DECU-ISRO Publication.

Survey, G. V. U. (2001). *GVU's 5th WWW User Survey.* Retrieved from http://www.cc.gatech.edu/gvu/user_surveys/survey-04-1996/

Temin, T. (1992). *Telecommuting: Many Would, Few Actually Can, NewYork.* McGraw-Hill.

Thomas, P. E. (2001). Information society: A thematic percept of concepts and limits. *Journal of Educational Research and Extension, 38*(3).

Toffler, A. (1980). *The Third Wave.* London: Collins.

Toffler, A. (1980). In P. Preston (2001). Reshaping Communication: Technology, Information & Social Change. New Delhi: Sage.

Trivedi, B., & Thaker, K. (2001). Social dimensions of media convergence in India. *Media Asia, 28*(3).

Webster, F. (1997). *Theories of the Information society.* London: Routledge.

Wresch, W. (1996). *Disconnected: Haves and have-nots in the information age.* New Brunswick: Rutgers University.

Young, K. S. (1996). *Pathological Internet Use: The Emergence of a New Clinical Disorder.* Paper presented at University of Pittsburgh, Bradford.

KEY TERMS AND DEFINITIONS

Centralised-decentralisation: With the decentralising of power came decentralising of work and decision-making. Conversely, the advent of the networking technologies in the workplace tends to diminish the culture of decentralised working since the 'boss' can oversee the employee's work instantly causing sudden interventions.

Convergence: Primarily the term coincides with the combination of different technologies—telephone, computer, broadcasting, and Internet—on a single platform. However, it is pertinent to understand the term from the point of view of multiple activities being performed within a moment using the advances of the new communications technologies.

Cultural: The drastic changes in lifestyles can be experienced with the overwhelming flow of information. The concept of 'cultural shock' may be obliterated from even the conservative societies.

Determinants: If agriculture and manufacturing determined the making of the earlier two societies, a composition of different spheres of activities—technological, economic, occupational, spatial, and cultural—determined the creation of the Information Society.

Economic: Every nature of human activity has a price tag today and hence every piece of information has an economic value.

Information Society: Unlike the predominance of occupations of the agricultural and industrial societies which defined them unambiguously, the Information Society has numerous definitions. However, since information and knowledge is considered to underscore the new age, the term 'Information Society' has a universal applicability.

Occupational: It signifies the transformation from the landed workforce to a sophisticated 'white collar society', the pivot of the Information Society.

Spatial: The advances in communications technologies have resulted in the redefinition of distance and may end up with the creation of 'virtual citizens'.

Technological: The ever-increasing spread of interdependence on technology coupled with mediated form of communication, which replaces interpersonal face-to-face interactions, marks the importance of technology in today's world.

Chapter 2
A Design Framework for Evolving a Citizen-Centric Information Society

Charru Malhotra
Indian Institute of Public Administration, India

ABSTRACT

Typically, designers of ICT based initiatives tend to consider the emerging trends of information and communication technology (ICT) as the starting point for designing an e-initiative rather than first inculcating a clarity on what services are to be delivered by such e-initiatives. 'Technology first' or 'Citizens First' is a conflict all designers have been confronted with, especially in the wake of all technology trends infesting the world now. To resolve this dichotomy, the present study proposes a citizen-centric framework, christened by author as G2C2G framework, which advocates combining technology in equal measures with the respective 'socio-cultural issues' of the local populace.

I. BACKGROUND

In recent times, terms like '*network society*', '*information society* 'and '*knowledge society*' have widely proliferated, due to the value added opportunities offered by Information and Communication Technologies (ICTs) in all domains of life, particularly in the domain of governance. In an attempt to augment the capabilities of its citizens for the information societies of future, several technology-based initiatives (henceforth, referred to as 'e-initiatives') have been designed and implemented across democratic societies such as India. However, despite the best of the intentions and attempts, it has been observed that such e-initiatives are technology-centric and not citizen-centric in nature (Wilson, 2000). Typically, designers of such initiatives tend to adopt a restrictive design approach, focusing a lot on the emerging trends of information and communication technology (ICT)rather than treating the requirements or the contextual background of the citizens as the starting point for their design processes (Pujar; Kamat; Bansode; Kamat & Katigennavar, 2008). As a result, the outcome of such initiatives is not always, what citizens had essentially required and the design approach of such ICT/ e-initiatives is usually a unidirectional

DOI: 10.4018/978-1-4666-8598-7.ch002

approach where citizens remain only passive recipients and not the active constituents of the entire process. (Figure 1)

Literature ruminations (for instance, Malhotra & Chatterjee, 2014) plea that such technology based initiatives must be instead designed using a wider systemic approach that would help to blend technology with economic, social and contextual needs of the citizens. Researchers (for instance, Pujar *et al.*, 2008) further persevere that "*technology cannot thrive unless it is people centered, inclusive, participative, and equitable and improves the quality of life*" (pp. 165). Even design-philosophy advocates that for ensuring citizen satisfaction with products/objects, more design related emphasis may be placed on the needs of the user of the object, than on the object itself (McDonagh-Philp & Lebbon, 2000). Adoption of such a user-focused design approach would ensure sustainability and better utilization of e-initiatives as now "people will act in a way to fulfill their needs regardless of geographic location, nationality, gender, race, religion, political system, and so on….(since it would be)…. a direct manifestation of concept of personal utility" (Hammer & Qahtani, 2009, pp. 138). However, despite the discerning eye of the author, related literature that would clearly specify explicit design strategies for embedding citizen-centricity in e-initiatives could not be sighted. The need therefore, stays on evolving a framework for a more humane 'citizen-centric' design approach that would help to combine 'technology' in equal measures with the respective 'socio-cultural issues' of the local populace in developing countries like India.

Figure 1. Existing Approach to Design of ICT/e- Initiatives

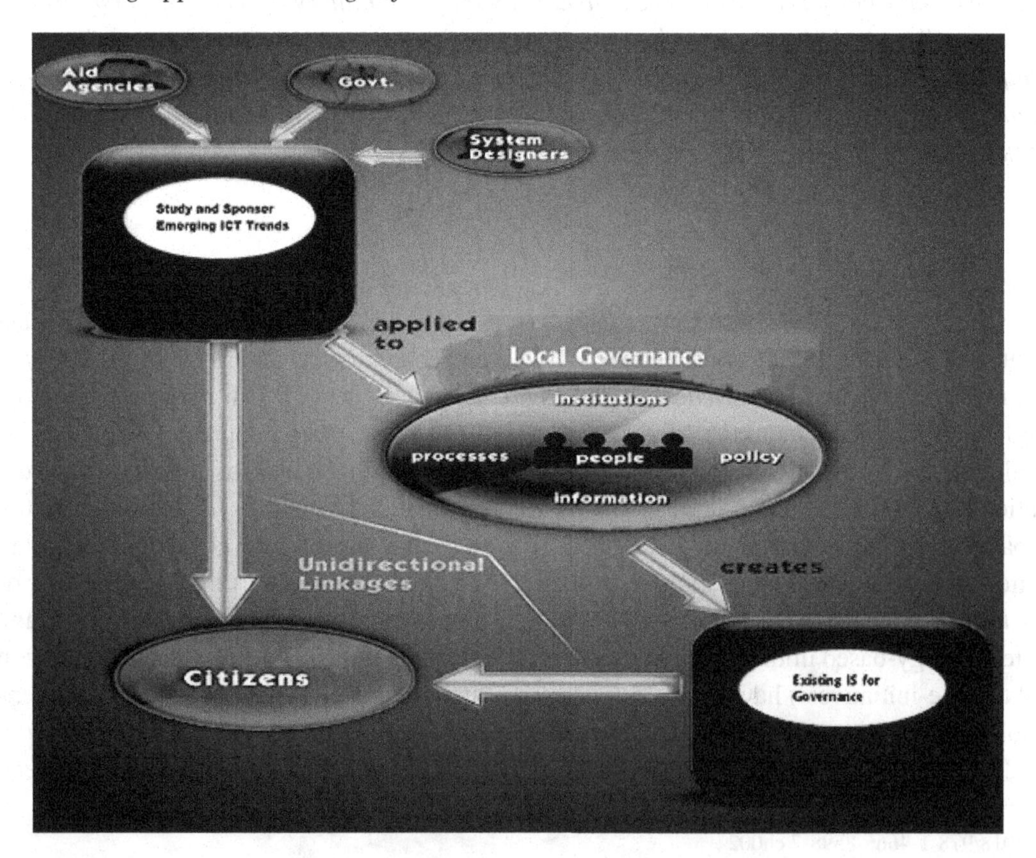

II. REVIEW OF LITERATURE: RELATING INFORMATION TECHNOLOGY, INFORMATION SOCIETY AND E-GOVERNANCE TO ACHIEVE A CITIZEN-CENTRIC E-GOVERNANCE STRATEGIC FRAMEWORK

Information technology (IT), now being popularly referred to as Information and communication technologies (ICT), has largely transformed workflows, livelihood mechanisms, as well as communication options. In fact, information technologies have been widely used as tools for increasing the convenience of provision of government information and services, to facilitate administrative reforms, fuel democratic participations, and even as defense against terrorist threats(Yildiz, 2007).This all-pervading and all-encompassing proliferation of ICT has led to coining of several references such as 'information society' (Bell, 1976), 'network era' (Castells, 2001) and 'knowledge economy' (Heiskanen & Hearn, 2004). Moreover, widespread deployment of ICTs also led to a paradigm shift from 'production and manufacturing' in societies to 'creation and dissemination of information'; thereby, exerting tangible influences everywhere- including on the class structures, on political alignments as well as on social processes established in the societies. Consequently, the erstwhile 'industrial society model' slowly yielded its way to the more contemporary 'information society model' wherein emphasis is not on the creation and distribution of 'material goods' but on management of 'knowledge'. Review of literature indicates that this kind of ecosystem which is primarily based on 'knowledge management' activities, starting from creation, distribution, usage, to integration of information and where these knowledge based activities redefine economic, political and cultural structures, this type of society is to be identified as an 'Information society-IS'. Various researchers have appropriately defined Information Society (IS). For instance, Bell (2007) recognizes IS as, "a society that organizes itself around knowledge in the interest of social control, and the management of innovation and change".

Understandably, IS constantly strives to gain competitive advantage, by exploiting Information technology (IT) in a creative and productive way. A closer look at some other definitions gleaned from review of literature clearly reveal that there is an undeniable, underlying interrelation between IS and IT. For instance, Karvalics (2007) quotes the author Béla Murányi (pp 10), where the latter insists on IS to be very IT-centric viz., "IS is a new type of society in which humanity has the opportunity to lead a new way of life, to have a higher standard of living, accomplish better work and to play a better role in society thanks to the global use of Information and telecommunications technologies". In the same vein, even OECD insists "information society to be a society which makes extensive use of Information and communication technologies and which produces large quantities of Information and communication products and services, and also has a diversified content industry". Indeed, ICT redefine various transactions, processes and institutes in the society such as market-dynamics, institutional setups and governance processes. In particular, Governance has responded to the opportunities offered by the information society by offering their citizens better access to more value-added services with ICTs. Infact, Ngulube (2007) quotes Milner (2002) for having established e-governance in relation with information society. The latter delineates responses by governments to the economic and social demands of an information society as a precursor for Governance to achieve these set of targets for development of the information society and mandates e-governance as an important tool to attain knowledge based economy.

Despite these perceived benefits, some of the researchers (for instance, Malhotra, Chariar & Das, 2013) lament that the design of e-initiatives, particularly for governance has been more techno-centric than citizen-centric. Such researchers assert that the majority of e- initiatives are government-centric; implying that the perceptions and demands of governments stay to be the main focus while deciding the type and nature of information and services to be provided by these initiatives. This perception is usually premised on the trust that governments know exactly what citizens want from e-government (Jaeger & Bertot, 2010), which has repeatedly be proven wrong. As a case in point, websites of some government organizations have focused towards citizens more as a 'customers' than 'consumers' of public services; resulting in creation of government websites more like an online-shop rather than an on-line community that could have encouraged civic engagement of citizens with government and with community (Steyaert, 2000).

To sail over some of these limitations posed by techno-centric and government-centric approaches to design of e-governance initiatives, Malhotra and Chatterjee (2014) mandate that designers/implementers must organize and deliver public information in accordance to the citizens' needs and aspirations and not as per the dictates of technology trends. They assert that this could be done by taking into account five relevant aspects of citizens' reality (referred to as 5Ws in the study) enumerated as "Who", "Where", "What", "Why" and "When". Such a 5W approach may facilitate an integrative understanding of 'citizen satisfaction' with public-sector services.

Several studies (for instance, Bertot & Jaeger, 2006; Chen & Dimitrova, 2006) have investigated factors and their effects on citizen satisfaction with e-government and listed them as e-government use, perceived performance, expectations prior to use, disconfirmed expectations, and procedural justice. More than churning out reams and reams of parameters in a disjointed manner that presumably facilitate or impede the uptake of an e-initiative, it might be far more suitable to develop a comprehensive, well-designed strategic framework that would also save implementers a lot of time, money and disappointments (Rabaiah & Vandijck, 2009).

In consonance with this presumption, several researchers have adopted varied approaches to develop an e-government framework; for instance, Miranda (2000) had conceived the building blocks of e-government framework to be purely technical components (such as ERP, CRM) whereas Wimmer (2002) had perceived her framework as mixture of different views of e-government abstraction layers and progress of public service. Maybe to simplify these two different ends of spectrum, Sharma and Gupta (2003) had based the components of their e-government framework on the maturity levels of e-government implementation. In more recent times, Grant and Chau (2006) had developed their e-government framework to help, assess, categorize, and classify e-government efforts. Irrespective of the parameters/ stages composing an e-government strategic framework, what needs to be emphasized is that a strategic framework is not meant to replace the elaborations of a strategy rather is expected to supplement it.

III. PROPOSED PRINCIPLES FOR IMBUING CITIZEN-CENTRICITY IN DESIGN OF E-INITIATIVES

However, technology characteristics and digital trends would always stay to be a subject of interest for designers of e-initiatives but identification of such e-characteristics and their usability or acceptance by its end-users must not serve as the only guiding standards for design processes. Instead, design efforts for such initiatives must concentrate on citizens needs from the point-of-view of citizens themselves. Such a design approach is referred as 'citizen-centric approach' and is deemed more integrated, citizen-driven and ethnographically sensitive (Malhotra, Chariar & Das, 2011).

It is quite evident that depending on the scope and context of implementation of e-initiatives, several versions and flavors of citizen-centric design approaches are possible.

However, the present study attempts to delineate only one such approach, christened as "G2C2G approach" (Malhotra, Chariar and Das, 2009).

Taking a cue from the basic tenets of democracy, the underlying philosophy governing the proposed approach is that for any e-initiative to be deemed truly citizen-centric, it must fulfill three principles as delineated below:-

1. **'For' the people:** A citizen-centric e-initiative must have 'citizens' as the core reason and 'end' of its design process.
2. **'Of' the people:** A citizen-centric e-initiative must abide by 'fulfillment of needs and aspirations of the citizens' as primary goal of its design process.
3. **'By' the people:** A citizen-centric e-initiative must be participative in nature and simultaneously must accept the local reality of the space inhibited by its citizens as the core reference point of its design process. This principle, therefore, insists that the potentialities and the limitations of citizens' contextual space must be considered as mandatory resource input to the design of such initiatives to ensure that the citizens stay to be the active stakeholders of the entire design process of the proposed e-initiative.

To fulfill these three principles of citizen-centricity, the suggested 'G2C2G approach' avers an e-initiative to be firmly entrenched in the local and indigenous knowledge systems of the region (abbreviated as LINKS, in the study). Malhotra, Chariar and Das (2013) state that such an approach would catalyze local decision-making processes to deliver local solutions to local problems and thus provide better choices to avail regional assets of the local eco-system. The proposed approach, therefore, would help to re-strengthen relationships between the native populace and local governance, leading to a more sustained development in the region (Figure 2).

IV. METHODOLOGY

This paper is a logical derivation of the research study conducted by the author from the years 2006-2009 under the astute mentorship of her research guides. The research had specifically focused on deciphering citizens' concerns with some of the existing e-initiatives that have been currently implemented across various states of India. The e-initiatives that were researched included Rural Access to Services through Internet-RASI (Melur District, Tamil Nadu), Common Service Centres (CSC) (Jhajjar and Gurgoan districts, Haryana), TARA Kendra (Tikkamgarh district, Madhya Pradesh), *Nemmadi* Centres (Raichur district, Karnataka), *Akshaya* Centres (Mallapuram and Ernakulum districts, Kerala), e-*Mitra* (Jaipur district, Rajasthan) and conduct of Citizen Consultation Round (CCR) at Indian Institute of Public Administration, New Delhi.

This field attempt was juxtaposed with review of some of the existing popular technology models *viz.* Innovation Diffusion Theory -IDT (Rogers, 1962), Technology Acceptance Model-TAM (Davis, 1989) and Task Technology Fit-TTF (Goodhue, 1988) models from the contextual perspective of developing countries like India. This point of view of review revealed that to a certain extent Roger's IDT model stays subjective in its approach and that Davis's TAM appears to be quite normative in nature to address contextual diversities of emerging economies. Similarly, Goodhue's TTF model ostensibly adopts a blinkered task-oriented approach without much of explicit reference in its contextual construct. Nevertheless, the latter provided a very good basis for evolving a newer citizen-centric framework and has served as a good take-off point for evolving the hereby proposed G2C2G approach.

Figure 2. Proposed 'LINKS Based G2C2G' Approach

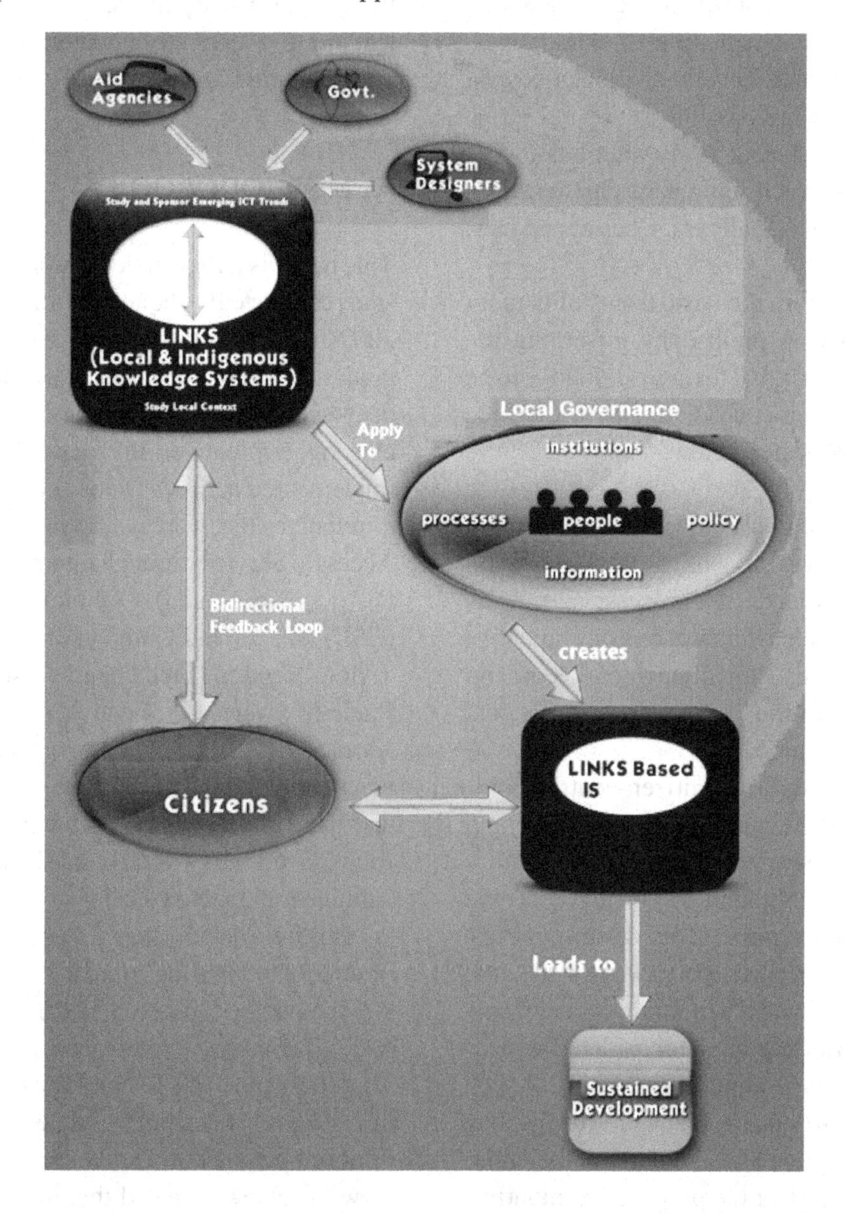

This field experience and in-depth review of literature led to creation of basic set of parameters (constructs and related attributes for each construct) that together constitute a citizen-centric approach for designing e-initiatives.

All these parameters had been meticulously validated using Delphi technique wherein the related expert discussions were undertaken over three web-based rounds, amidst 48 Delphi experts, using predesigned web based questionnaires. These forty-eight Delphi experts had been chosen in a balanced manner ensuring equal and adequate representation of international and national experts drawn from the research, industry, media, academia, government, social sector, and local bodies. Some of the representatives were from organizations included McGill University Canada, Australia Catholic University-ACU Australia, Management Development Institute –MDI Haryana, IIMs, IITs, National Informatics Centre

(NIC), ILFS, and Department of Information Technology from India and so on. Author referred to this Delphi process undertaken in context of e-initiative, as 'Expert Opinion Round-EOR'. EOR had commenced in December-2009 and all its three rounds of review were accomplished by March-2010. Only those constructs and attributes of the proposed G2C2G approach were included in the proposed framework that had elicited affirmative responses with mean values greater than the proposed benchmark of 90% over these three Delphi rounds. Further to this, conclusive remarks of the Delphi experts had also been considered to finalize the attributes for these constructs and related attributes.

Aim and Scope of the Present Study

The present paper could be treated as a logical continuation (sequel) to the related research publications of the author (for instance, Malhotra, Chariar & Das, 2014; Malhotra, Chariar & Das, 2013), emanating from aforementioned research rigor. Herein, the author aims to put forth impartially the citizen-centric framework based on the Delphi-validated G2C2G approach. The study aims to delineate the set of validated and Delphi-approved set of five constructs and attributes constituting the proposed G2C2G approach as well as put forth the background and the justification of inclusion of each of these constructs. However, all other rejected parameters, details of Delphi process and the allied Delphi discussions do not fall within the prerogative of this paper and could be referred elsewhere in the literature (for instance, Malhotra, Chariar & Das, 2014; Malhotra, Chariar & Das, 2013).

V. BUILDING BLOCKS OF THE PROPOSED G2C2G APPROACH

G2C2G approach suggests a holistic framework of constructs and attributes that could be considered by designers and researchers for accomplishing

Table 1. List of Validated Constructs for G2C2G Approach

S. No.	Validated Constructs	Affirmative Ratings by Delphi Experts (Average Value Across Three Delphi Rounds)
6.	Citizen Characteristics (CC)	99.0%
7.	Goal-Task Characteristics (G-TC)	96.0%
8.	Eco-System/ Environment Characteristics (EC)	95.9%
9.	e-Technology Characteristics (e-TC)	95.1%
10.	Regional Characteristics (RC)	91.9%

citizen centricity in their e-design endeavors. The final set of its validated constructs along with the average value of affirmative ratings received the experts, for each of them from over three Delphi rounds, are encapsulated herewith (Table 1):

Constructs and Attributes of the Proposed G2C2G Approach

1. 'Citizen Characteristics': Profiling the Citizens in the Proposed Information Society

Background of the Construct

The first core principle of the proposed citizen- centric philosophy (Section- II) is that a citizen-centric e-initiative must be designed for the people' *i.e.* citizens' must constitute the core reason and 'end' of its design process. Since governance processes are gradually morphing from the conventional, centralized arrangements to more participative and decentralized systems, it becomes particularly relevant for all governance constituents to profile its citizenry. Therefore, it is suggested that the first variable must be the one that would reflect the designers' understanding of detailed caricature of the citizens belonging to the proposed ecosystem of the information society. Such a proposed variable would help the designers to capture basic requisite citizen's details such as her educational background, occupational background and so on. This construct, for ease of reference, has been referred as 'Citizen Characteristics' (abbreviated as CC). 'Citizen Characteristics', had been principally inspired from a construct called 'Individual Characteristics' of TTF model. However, there is a basic difference in the scope between these two constructs. 'Individual Characteristics' of TTF model represents only the end-users of the system whereas 'Citizen Characteristics' construct of the suggested G2C2G approach represents the profile of 'all' the people as citizens (*i.e.* end-users, expected users as well as the present non-users of the e-initiative) and not merely the present or potential 'end-users' of the system. In order to ensure that the output being provided by an e-initiative is completely driven by the end-users as well as potential users, citizens' profile was given prominent consideration while proposing the G2C2G approach.

Definition of Citizen Characteristics

'Citizen Characteristics' could be defined as "*distinctive features of the populace of the proposed IS, that would help to distinguish an individual end-user (or majority of them), their preferences, social orientation and other such attributes*" (Malhotra, Chariar and Das, 2014).

Table 2. Finalized Attributes of Citizen Characteristics (CC)

S. No.	Attributes	Affirmative Ratings by Delphi Experts (Average Value Across Three Delphi Rounds)
7.	Computer self-efficiency	94.4%
8.	Gender profile	91.8%
9.	Educational background	91.1%
10.	Prime occupation	90.2%
11.	Social composition	89.8%
12.	Income slabs	89.6%

Attributes of Citizen Characteristics

'Citizen Characteristics' construct had been validated by the experts to be composed of six attributes which had garnered 90% affirmative response over three Delphi rounds (Table 2).

2. 'Goal-Task Characteristics (G-TC)': Deciding the Prime Aim and Objectives of the E-Initiative Being Designed

Background of the Construct

In accordance to the second proposed principle of the citizen centricity (section –II), the chief motivation of a design processes must be to achieve the overall 'wellbeing and welfare of the citizens', also pronounced clearly in the principles of good governance. In such a scenario, technology obviously would serve merely as the 'means' and not an 'end' in itself and the primary goal (as well as its related objectives) of the e-initiative would be entirely allied to the well-being of the citizens. This insight led to a very important implication of delineating the second construct of 'Goal-Task Characteristics' in the proposed G2C2G approach.

Definition of Goal-Task Characteristics

Goal could be defined as the, "*overarching aim of an e-initiative, which is to eventually attain the goals of governance that could help building an enabling environment conducive for sustainable development* (of the citizens and the society)"(Malhotra, Chariar & Das, 2014). The attainment of these governance goals by any citizen-centric e-initiative could be enabled by automating several definable constituent tasks. Such tasks could, therefore, be defined as "*the actions to be carried out by the governance pro-*

cesses in turning inputs into outputs to achieve welfare of the citizens".

Some of the critical goals of governance (and hence be also could become goals for any citizen-centric e-initiative) could be enumerated as goal of poverty-reduction, goal of non-discriminatory access to government services, ensuring gender-equality and so on. As an example, the tasks for any of these goals, say, the goal of 'non-discriminatory access to government services' could be, 'fulfilment of request for birth and death certificates', 'provision of exact status of citizens' grievances', 'instant feedback about performance of local functionaries' and so on. Therefore, a citizen-centric e-initiative must first establish its aims to achieve the goal of non-discriminatory access to government services and then further endeavour to provide those e-services which fulfil the cited tasks constituting this aim.

Attributes of Goal-Task Characteristics

The attributes of 'Goal-Task Characteristics' have been identified in a manner so that the e-initiative helps in achievement of governance goals by accomplishing the related automated task(s). Following fourteen attributes (Table 3) qualified for being retained in the proposed G2C2G approach after three Delphi rounds.

Table 3. Finalized Attributes of Goal-Task Characteristics (G-TC)

S. No.	Attributes	Affirmative Ratings by Delphi Experts (Average Value Across Three Delphi Rounds)
15.	Time required to accomplish the task	97.0%
16.	Priority of the task	96.8%
17.	Method/technology	94.0%
18.	Using present method/ technology	93.9%
19.	Tasks composing	93.2%
20.	Information generated by the task	92.5%
21.	Cost of the task	92.2%
22.	Time saved for the task using ReGI	90.7%
23.	Feedback	90.5%
24.	Sustainability and revenue task	90.2%
25.	Core task characteristics	90.2%
26.	Importance of task to citizen	89.9%
27.	Participatory rules for citizens	89.8%
28.	Re-engineering specifications	89.6%

3. Eco-System/Environment Characteristics (EC): E-Initiative Must Respond to the Local Practices and Grassroots' Processes

Background of the Construct

The third principle proposed by the author (section-II) states that to be truly participative in its nature, citizen-centric e-initiative must accept the local reality of the space inhibited by its citizens as the core reference point of its design process. This implies that technology specifications must be compatible to the existing values, needs and experiences of the local environment/eco-system. The underlying philosophy of the approach (section-II) also insists a citizen-centric e-initiative to be amenable to its local and indigenous knowledge systems (LINKS). The field experience of the author reveals that LINKS can be best understood by unraveling the eco-system of an area place composed of its prevailing values, demography, existing practices, prior experience, skill-sets, and preferred governance styles of the communities. Even the review of literature affirms that for an e-initiative to be more effective in a local context, an adequate analysis and incorporation of the 'space' defined by such local contextual factors is pertinent (Das, 2005); Padovitz, Loke, & Zaslavsky, 2004). Some philosophers (for instance Agarwal, Angst, & Karahanna, 2006) refer to this local 'space' by representation of 'compatibility' construct of IDT, but a need for inclusion of separate construct, referred to as, 'Eco-System/Environment Characteristics (EC) 'in the proposed approach, had been felt. Author considered that EC could be used to specifically refer to the local and indigenous knowledge systems (LINKS) as well other related attributes of eco system. However, this construct stays to be an enhancement of 'compatibility' variable of IDT (Rogers, 1962).

Definition of Eco-System/Environment Characteristics

Eco-System/Environment Characteristics (EC) could be defined as the "*prevalent knowledge, traditional skills, local resources, community beliefs and norms of the existing* (governance)*systems, with respect to which the proposed e-initiative is being designed*" (Malhotra, Chariar & Das, 2014).

Attributes of Eco-System/Environment Characteristics

In general, since an eco-system refers to all living and non-living things in a particular region or area and their interaction with each other, the attributes of this characteristic refer to the prevalent practices and processes of the grassroots. Following five attributes (Table 4) qualified for being retained in the G2C2G approach after three Delphi rounds.

Table 4. Finalized Attributes of Eco-system/Environment Characteristics (EC)

S. No	Attributes	Affirmative Ratingsby Delphi Experts (Average Value Across Three Delphi Rounds)
6.	Traditional governance solutions	95.7%
7.	Local resources for governance	93.5%
8.	Indigenous means of communication	93.5%
9.	History of traditional governance solutions	90.0%
10.	Health and endemic natural disasters	89.6%

4. E-Technology Characteristics (E-TC): Identifying the Correct Digital Technologies for Designing an E-Initiative

Background of the Construct

For any e-initiative, 'technology 'obviously constitutes an important tool (though not the chief-reason to initiate a design process) to provide services and information to the citizens. The characteristics of the digital technologies that is expected to be used for designing an e-initiative, have been collectively referred as 'e-Technology characteristics (e-TC)'. This construct is broadly representative of the 'Information Systems and Services' of the TTF model (Goodhue, 1988). This construct further considers the 'Perceived Ease of Use' and 'Perceived Usefulness' of TAM (Davis, 1989) as mediating constructs for defining 'e-Technology characteristics'.

Definition of E-Technology Characteristics

Inspired by Malhotra, Chariar and Das (2014), e-Technology characteristics could be defined as '*new and continuously evolving IT-based platform that includes, but not limited to, telecommunication products such as mobile phones, information kiosks, world wide web sites, multimedia, social media or any other interconnected systems, software based applications and support services; designed to facilitate information sharing capabilities which are essential for e-initiatives' implementation*'.

Attributes of E-Technology Characteristics

Eleven attributes qualified for being retained in the G2C2G approach after three Delphi rounds

Table 5. Finalized Attributes of e-Technology Characteristics (e-TC)

S. No.	Finalized Attributes	Affirmative Ratings by Delphi Experts (Average Value Across Three Delphi Rounds)
12.	Availability of local content/ information	98.6%
13.	Use of local language	97.4%
14.	Cost of access	95.9%
15.	Technical support	95.8%
16.	Physical security & H/W security issues	92.0%
17.	Training of stakeholders	91.4%
18.	Social Support	90.4%
19.	Data management attributes	90.4%
20.	Representational vividness of services	89.8%
21.	Design of multiple access mechanisms	89.7%
22.	User–controlled interactive interface	89.6%

(Table 5).While considering these attributes, it is important that one must not lose sight of financial facets too. Even a Delphi expert had pointed out, "I think that before selecting these attributes one must consider the financial resources and the funds being made available in the current plan….for the (considered) areas".

5. Regional Characteristics (RC): Representing the Local Variations in the Proposed Citizen-Centric E-Initiative

Background of the Construct

Another parameter that could substantially affect the design process of an e-initiative is the 'grassroots-reality' that varies from region to region in developing countries. These regional variations could be several such as variations in geographical/demographic indicators, different local infrastructure, dissimilar local governance issues, divergent local resources availability and so on. At the outset, the initially proposed G2C2G approach by the author had failed to account for these regional variations explicitly and considered only four constructs- three of them responding to each of the three proposed principles of citizen-centricity and the fourth one accounting for ICT trends and techniques. However, in the first Delphi round itself several experts directly or implicitly had started insisting that the regional diversity of the local space must be separately reflected. Some such justifications for inclusion of Regional characteristics are justifications cited here with (Table 6).

As a result, a new construct called as 'Regional Characteristics-RC', was put forth to all the experts for approval / rejection. These experts after three rounds of deliberations were of the unanimous view to consider 'Regional Characteristics'; reflected in the average value of 91.9% of affirmative responses (Table 7). Consequently, the construct, R Chad been finally accepted in the proposed G2C2G approach.

Table 6. Some experts' comments averring to incorporate a construct to reflect regional variations whilst designing a citizen-centric e-initiative

"Citizens are the main stakeholders in the process of e-governance (e-initiative). Their characteristics also will vary hugely in a diverse country like India. Say for example, the citizens of Gujarat will be more developed in a socio-economic sense than the citizens of Bihar and their perspectives will also differ".
"*Citizens needs are seasonal in nature (due to the region they inhibit). The needs are different from region to region*".
"*Region selection is important and needs vary from region to region*".

Table 7. Summary of Responses Received for Regional Characteristics (RC)

	Yes	No	Can't Say
EOR-I	96%	2%	2%
EOR-II	87.5%	12.5%	0%
EOR-III	92.1%	7.89%	0%
Mean Values	**91.9%**	7.5%	0.7%
Construct of Regional Characteristics (RC) stands 'Accepted'			

- EOR: Expert Opinion Round/ Delphi Round

Table 8. Finalized Attributes of Regional Characteristics (RC)

S. No	Finalized Attributes	Affirmative Ratings by Delphi Experts
7.	Geographical indicators	93.2%
8.	Infrastructure available	93.2%
9.	Primary language of communication	91.6%
10.	Critical governance needs of the region	90.9%
11.	Citizen groups	90.7%
12.	Social networks/bonding	90.0%

Definition of Regional Characteristics (RC)

Regional Characteristics (RC) can be defined as "*the diverse regional capital and geographical variations of the area in which the e-initiative is to be deployed*" (Malhotra, Chariar & Das, 2014).

Attributes of Regional Characteristics (RC)

Of the set of nine new suggested attributes for Regional Characteristics, six attributes qualified (Table 8) to be retained in the G2C2G approach after three Delphi rounds.

VI. UNIQUENESS AND SIGNIFICANCE OF THE PROPOSED G2C2G APPROACH

All the five constructs and their respective attributes of the proposed G2C2G approach that provides a design framework for designers/ policy visionaries for evolving a citizen-centric information society, are summarized herewith (Figure 3).

The proposed approach attempts to incorporate the diverse influences of the local reality while designing citizen-centric information society, a flexibility that is not fully accounted for in the existing technology models. This has been assured by inclusion of 'Regional Characteristics' and 'Eco-system/environment characteristics' in the proposed approach (Figure 3). This approach also focuses on people as citizens and not merely as the end-users of the technology. The desirable components of citizen-centricity and citizen-inclusiveness have also been inbuilt by taking into consideration 'Citizen Characteristics'. As an outcome of all such suggested constructs, certain pilot communities of practice (COP) should be able to map their own requirements and further serve as a pool of experts to share feedback, create reviews and independently undertake need-assessment exercises to upgrade the existing technology centric e-initiatives to be more citizen-centric in the future.

On a conclusive note, for creating more inclusive and participative information society, a requirement has been perceived in the present study for active involvement of the citizens to liberate the contextual limitations and potentialities of regional spaces while designing e-initiatives as catalysts and empowering tools.

VII. WAY FORWARD

It is an optimistic presumption of the proposed approach that by responding to the local contextual factors and indigenous systems, any e-initiative could closely address the needs and expecta-

Figure 3. The constructs and attributes of the proposed G2C2G Approach
(Source: Malhotra, Chariar and Das, 2014)

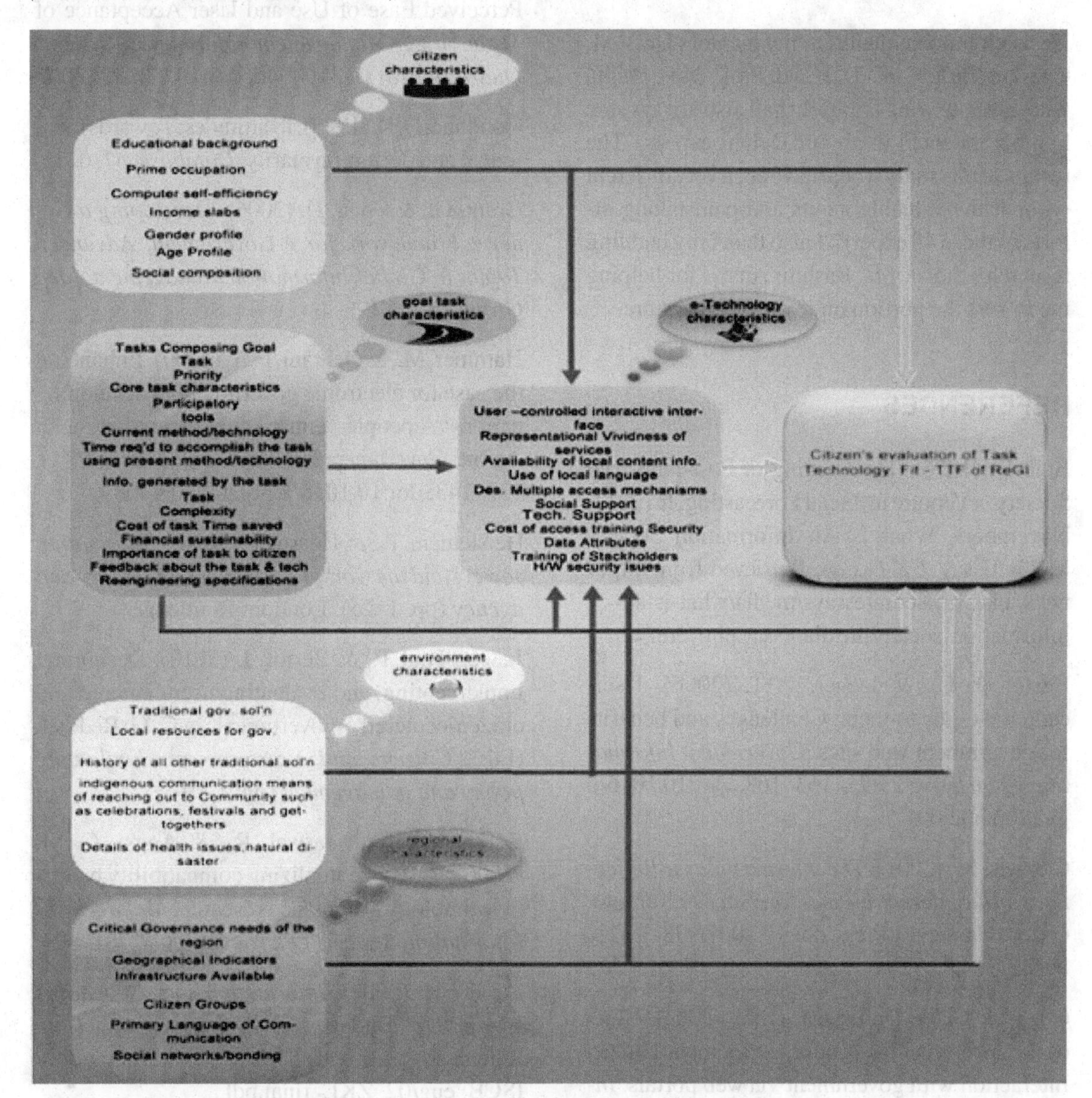

tions of the citizens of diverse and developing economies such as India and hence help to design citizen-centric systems. This might be validated or challenged by future researchers.

Moreover, due to the pre-ordained scope of the present study, priority ranking of the suggested five constructs and their respective attributes could not be undertaken on any criteria. The same could be done using any suitable, systematic method such as Analytic Hierarchy Process (AHP) for the future research.

VIII. ACKNOWLEDGMENT

Heartfelt humble thanks to my mentors Dr. V.M. Chariar, Prof. L.K. Das and Prof. M.P. Gupta who gave me wings to fly. I shall also always stay humbly indebted to all our Delphi experts. The results of this study would have been very different without the valuable inputs and painstaking efforts of these 48 experts. I also thank my budding research scholar, Ms. Rashmi Anand for helping me to sort the portion on review of literature.

REFERENCES

Bell, D. (1976). The Coming of Post-Industrial Society: a Venture in Social Forecasting. In (2013, November), What Is An Information Society Media Essay. *UK Essays*. Retrieved from http://www.ukessays.com/essays/media/what-is-an-information-society-media-essay.php?cref=1

Bertot, J. C., & Jaeger, P. T. (2006). User-centered e-government: Challenges and benefits for government web sites. *Government Information Quarterly*, *23*(2), 163–168. doi:10.1016/j.giq.2006.02.001

Castells, M. (2001). *The internet galaxy: Reflections on the internet, business and society*. Toronto: Oxford University Press. doi:10.1007/978-3-322-89613-1

Chen, Y.-C., & Dimitrova, D. V. (2006). Electronic government and online engagement: Citizen Interaction with government via web portals. *International Journal of Electronic Government Research*, *2*(1), 54–76. doi:10.4018/jegr.2006010104

Das, L. K. (2005). Culture as the Designer. *Design Issues*, *21*(4), 41–53. doi:10.1162/074793605774597523

Davis, F. D. (1989). Perceived Usefulness, Perceived Ease of Use and User Acceptance of Technology. *Management Information Systems Quarterly*, *13*(3), 319–340. doi:10.2307/249008

Goodhue, D. L. (1988). IS attitudes: Towards theoretical and definition clarity. *Database*, *41*, 6–15.

Grant, G., & Chau, D. (2006). *Developing a Generic Framework for e-Government. Advanced Topics in Global Information Management. Idea Group Inc*. IGI.

Hammer, M., & Qahtani, F. A. (2009). Enhancing the case for electronic government in developing nations: A people-centric study focused in Saudi Arabia. *Government Information Quarterly*, *26*(1), 137–143. doi:10.1016/j.giq.2007.08.008

Heiskanen, T., & Hearn, J. (2004). *Information society and the workplace: spaces, boundary and agency* (pp. 1–25). London: Routledge.

Jaeger, Paul T., & Bertot, J. (2010). Designing, implementing, and evaluating user-centered and citizen-centered e-government. In C. G. Reddick (Ed.), *Citizens and e-government: Evaluating policy and management* (pp. 1-19).

Karahanna, E., Agarwal, R., & Angst, C. M. (2006). Re-conceptualizing compatibility beliefs in technology acceptance research. *Management Information Systems Quarterly*, *30*(4), 781–804.

Laszlo, K. (2007). *Information society- what is it exactly?*. Budapest: European Commission. Retrieved from http://www.ittk.hu/netis/doc/ISCB_eng/02_ZKL_final.pdf

Malhotra, C., Chariar, V. M & Das, L. K. (2009 April). User Centered Design Model (G2C2G) for Rural e-Governance Projects. *International Journal of e-Governance*, 1742-7509.

Malhotra, C. Chariar, V. M & Das, L. K. (2011). *Citizen-centricity for e-Governance initiatives in Rural Areas*. Retrieved from http://indiagovernance.gov.in/files/initiatives_in_Rural_Areas.pdf

Malhotra, C. Chariar, V. M & Das, L. K. (2013). Citizen-Centric Approach for Converging Indigenous Knowledge Systems using ICT. In U.M. Munshi & V. Sharma (Eds.), Strategizing Knowledge Management and Environmental Paradigm. New Delhi: Jain Publishing House.

Malhotra, Charru & Chatterjee, T. (2014, August). *ICT4D: Innovating Governance to be more Citizen-Centric using ICT.* Department of Administrative Reforms and Public Grievances, Government of India.

Malhotra, C; Chariar, V.M.& Das, L.K. (2014). A Validated Citizen-Centric Approach using Delphi Technique for Converging Indigenous Knowledge Systems using ICT. *International Journal of e-Government Research (IJEGR), 4.* USA: IGI publications.

Mcdonagh-Philp, D., & Lebbon, C. (2000). The emotional domain in product design. *The Design Journal, 3*(1), 31–43. doi:10.2752/146069200789393562

Milner, E. M. (2002). *Delivering the vision: Where are we going? Delivering the vision: Public services for the information and knowledge economy* (pp. 172–174). London: Routledge.

Miranda, R. (2000). The Building Blocks of a Digital Government Strategy. *Government Finance Officers Association, 16*(5), 9.

Ngulube, P. (2007). The nature and accessibility of e-government in Sub Saharan Africa. *International Review for Information Ethics.* Retrieved from http://www.i-r-i-e.net/about_irie.htm#Publication%20Agreement

Padovitz, A., Loke, S. W., & Zaslavsky, A. (2004). *Towards a Theory of Context Spaces. Proceedings of Workshop on Context Modeling and Reasoning (CoMoRea), at* 2nd IEEE International Conference on Pervasive Computing and Communication *(PerCom'04).* Orlando, Florida. doi:10.1109/PERCOMW.2004.1276902

Pujar, S.M., Kamat, R.K., Bansode, S.Y., Kamat, R.R., & Katigennavar, S.H. (2008). Identifying and exploiting human needs for a people centric evolving knowledge society: A case study of Indian ICT Emergence. *The International Information & Library Review*, 40, 165-170.

Rabaiah. A, & Vandijck. (2009). *A Strategic Framework of e-Government: Generic and Best Practice.* Electronic journal of e-Government, 7(3), 242.

Rogers, E. M. (1962). *Diffusion of Innovation* (1st ed.). New York: Free Press.

Sharma. S., & Gupta, J. (2003). Building Blocks of an E-Government—A Framework. *Journal of Electronic Commerce in Organizations*, 1, 1-15.

Steyaert, J. (2000). Local governments online and the role of the resident: Government shop versus electronic community. *Social Science Computer Review, 18*(1), 3–16. doi:10.1177/089443930001800101

Wilson, M. (2000). *Understanding the International ICT and Development Discourse: Assumptions and Implications* [Unpublished doctoral dissertation]. Development Studies at Oxford University. United Kingdom.

Wimmer, M. (2002). *Towards Knowledge Enhanced E-Government: Integration as Pivotal Challenge.* Johannes Kepler University. Retrieved from http://www.iwv.jku.at/aboutus/wimmer/habilschrift.pdf

Yildiz, M. (2007). E-government research: Reviewing the literature, limitations, and ways forward. *Government Information Quarterly, 24*(3), 646–665. doi:10.1016/j.giq.2007.01.002

KEY TERMS AND DEFINITIONS

Citizen Centricity: The principle of citizen centricity insists that neither the product nor its technology, but the users ('citizens' in case of public service delivery processes) have to be the nuclei of the design strategy. This approach is all about being more responsive and alert to the needs and aspirations of the citizens and stands an anti-thesis to the 'technology-centric approach'. Citizen-centricity, therefore, necessitates more of a socio-cultural approach based on multi-disciplinary perspectives rather than on a mere understanding of tools and trends of technology or economic parameters related to technology implementation. Literature discourse confirms that with adequate citizen-participation, citizen-centricity could be build up more holistically.

Contextual Realities: This term generally refers to the salient influents, such as demographics, cultural norms and so on, which are region specific, and have explicit influence on the usage of e-initiatives by the local citizenry. The author has elsewhere grouped contextual factors in several categories such as Local Administrative Culture, User Profile, User-uncertainty, Physical Infrastructure, security concerns, supporting infrastructure and Socio-Cultural Factors (including Civic mindedness, idiosyncrasies of particular groups, reflecting the group's societal affiliation and position, trust factor, resistance to change and so on).

Delphi Technique: Is a systematic forecasting method employed in situations, instances, experiments where there are inadequate models or historical data available. It involves collecting opinions of varied stakeholders of diversified expertise, over multiple anonymous rounds and after consensus or debate amongst these chosen experts the where collated-judgment is deemed acceptable as a legitimate forecast for the event under consideration.

Design Approach: Design approach refers to preconceiving the process steps and priorities before proceeding with the development of any initiative.

E-Governance Framework: A framework can be conceptual or strategic. A theoretical/conceptual framework of e-governance consists of concepts, together with their definitions, and existing theory/theories that are used for representing a particular case-study of e-governance. It serves as an analytical tool with several parameters to make conceptual distinctions and organize ideas related to various aspects of e-governance initiative. For instance, an e-Engagement Framework of e-Governance would generally illustrate critical elements necessary to ensure smooth and meaningful citizen engagement with decision-making agencies. On the other hand, a Strategic Framework of e-Governance is more at a policy design level for a public organization or could be for a nation as a whole and aims to create a favorable ecosystem for transformation of government related activities by the application of ICT/e-business methods across the public sector for an effective service delivery.

Expert Opinion Round: Also abbreviated as EOR, the author has referred to a specific 'web-based', 'three iterations based', Delphi Technique involving a group of 48 e-governance experts employed in the study to specifically validate the *citizen-centric G2C2G framework* proposed by the author.

G2C2G Approach: The *Government to Citizen to Government* (G2C2G) is a term that has been coined by the author to specifically represent an approach to design e-governance initiatives using principles of citizen-centricity. 'G2 C 2G', like the acronym itself, mandates to keep "*citizens*" at the center of design thinking wherein needs, expectations and potentialities of citizens must be of utmost consideration for a designer of a new e-governance initiative. G2C2G approach also advocates e-governance initiatives to imbue the local cultural wisdom, community knowledge and prevalent traditional practices of the citizens. The proposed G2C2G approach, therefore extends the concept of citizen centricity beyond the mere delineation of needs and expectations of the citizens, by responding to the varied contextual factors of local diversity.

Information Society: Is a new socio-cultural arrangement for a society where there is an extensive use of Information and communication technologies (ICT) for creating better life capabilities and higher standards of living. Such an immense creation, appropriation, and manipulation of information leads to a unique, diversified content industry, and also produces large quantities of information and communication based deliverables and with varied socio-cultural outcomes.

Local and Indigenous Knowledge Systems (LINKS): Refer to a cumulative body of knowledge, expertise, practices and representations that are maintained and developed by the people at the grassroots level. LINKs are an excellent source to provide local solutions to local problems and hence are extremely context specific. Several other studies have also used terms such as Traditional knowledge systems (TKS), indigenous knowledge systems (IKS), people's knowledge systems, ***lok vidya***, vernacular knowledge or local knowledge to connote similar knowledge sets and technical capabilities surrounding specific conditions of communities indigenous to a particular geographical area.

Chapter 3
Consumers as Producers:
Information Decomposition Exploiting the Prosumerist culture

Sandeep Kaur
Bharathiar University, India

ABSTRACT

The present study investigates the decomposition caused by an information catastrophe in the electronic era where an array of information has become extremely easier and cheaper to construct, maneuver and systematize through a qualitative theoretical underpinning from distinguished theoreticians in the field. Quoting a few user generated sites such as the Wikipedia (Online Encyclopedia) that anyone can edit, this chapter highlights critical apprehension over the generation of over-abundant content by unidentified multiple sources over this open sharing model. Recommendations and suggestions on effectual inquiry of published content over user generated sites for scholars around the world to rely on shape the finishing fraction of this chapter.

INTRODUCTION

Communication is equivocal. We are limited by a language where words may mean one thing to one person and quite something else to another. There is no ordained right way to communicate. At least in the absolute sense, it is impossible to share our thoughts with someone else, for they will not be understood in exactly the same way (Wurman, 1989).

Emergence of Information and Communication Technologies (ICTs) have demonstrated manifold ways to revolutionalize the way information is fabricated in this digital era in terms of its production, dispensation in addition to its manipulation, thus, unparalleling the human brain to accommodate the same. This results in a rapid amplification of the information processing skill of an individual to compete with his/her cognitive chattels inquiring the appropriate filtering of the plentiful information to accelerate access to germane content. These technologies have fashioned an information catastrophe that necessitate a measure of control to govern the ecology of information. As Klapp (1986) has fittingly avowed that the quality of information is judged not by its precision and clarity alone, but how it

DOI: 10.4018/978-1-4666-8598-7.ch003

Figure 1.

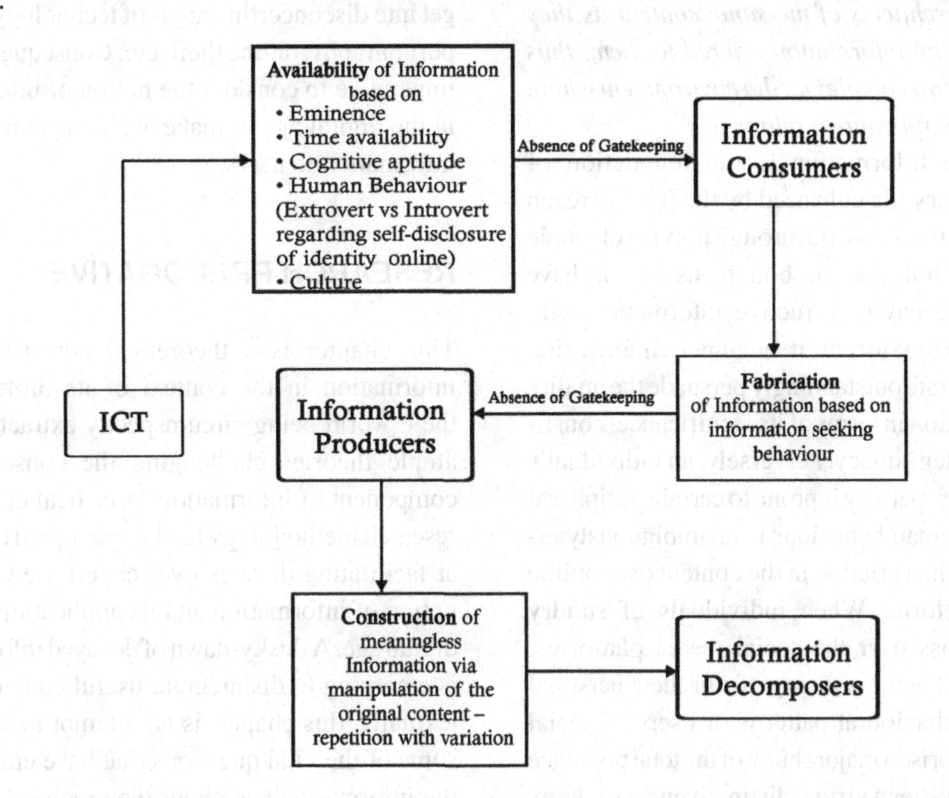

acts upon receivers. Contrarily, these elements may not turn out to be a trouble-free task in the digisphere as communication becomes ineffective when the content generates an absolute loss of its meaning. In the perspective of the escalating accretion of information in the digital epoch, the momentous rationale behind this meaning lag can be associated with the 'facts' that mount up and surpass its subsistence (Klapp, 1982).

'Decomposition' has become branded as an imperative process in the digital ecosystem involving a succession of diverse knowledge workers; one set taking over after the last one has consumed what he/she can, and in doing so, extending the control of information seeking behaviour. Rapid explosion of happenings around the world unparallel one's cognitive ability to process and coalesce rightful information. Klapp (1986) expected that before settling large questions, we go on to new ones, dissatisfied with what we know, no wiser than before. In the meanwhile, information floods on, demanding that something be done (as cited in Walter, 1989, p.6).

Information becomes decomposed when it becomes irrelevant for the consumer. Burgeoning social media and user generated content authorize anyone and everyone to be a fabricator of its content without effectual governance. This decay in the constructive information crops up when multifarious sources are given autonomy to amend a specific section of sector-specific information resulting in the loss of inimitable content personalized for the user needs.

Thus, the information society is on the threshold of becoming an insignificant society if this situation persists. In consequence, decomposition takes the form of a cognitive process in which *an individual's information processing skills corrodes or disintegrates when two or more individuals under similar state of affairs happen to be the architects of the same content as they encounter the information offered to them, thus giving rise to a complex media environment where the meaningful content relapses.*

Though Information is the foundation of contemporary life enhanced by the ICTs to reach every realm of the world through proviso of ample amount of information, bounteous factors have started to decay constructive information with insufficient time to route it sanguinely. Information processing rate outstandingly persuade the quality of information in terms of its significance, constitution and legitimacy. Perversely, an individual's cognitive propensity is prone to certain peripheral aspects. Human behaviour is unambiguously erratic, so is the variation in the content over online media platform. When individuals of sundry milieu amass over the social media platforms, their shared actions diverge from their personal actions. Behavioural patterns of users of social media comprise a major chunk of the total populace that hanker after a virtual distinctiveness of theirs online. Socio-psychological circumstances of individuals mirror his/her individuality in addition to how they perform in online media channel. An individual's capability to engage with the setting contour his/her online conducts as well as articulate himself/herself healthier in writing than speaking. Additionally, each user wishes to create a part of a pack for him/her through either a disclosed or non-disclosed identity. Self-disclosure of the content creator is a concealed schema in the digisphere that calls for vigilance by the experts governing the medium. Culture is yet another factor closely related to how one behaves online. Restrictions of the society on how one should think and act, commanding morals and values, level of socialization, interpersonal skill deficiency, laughable communication specifics, trepidation of being ruining oneself if identity gets unveiled, so on and so forth are a few imperatives concerning online media. Furthermore, noninterventionist outlook makes one build constructive illustration of oneself while non-liberal attitude makes one get into disconcerting areas of technology such as pornography, online theft, etc. Consequently, it is imperative to consider the notion of information in the digital age to make available constructive information to users.

RESEARCH PREROGATIVE

This chapter is a theoretical construction of information in the context of its profusion in the e-world being circumspectly extracted from ample theories challenging the consequential component of information. A critical qualitative research methodology has been adopted that aims at facilitating debates over expert views on the notion of information and its applicability in the digital age. A dusky-dawn of decayed information is emerging to disintegrate useful content. Contextually, this chapter is an attempt to highlight some of the vital questions that have emerged in the information age about the precise definition of information and how it is being embezzled among the digital generation amidst a mirage of content available to them.

NOTION OF INFORMATION

Being regarded as one of the indispensable elements that constitute the world (Floridi, 2003, 2010), the term 'information' has versatile nuances as provided under:

WHAT CAUSES INFORMATION DECOMPOSITION?

Internet has brought in a pandemic syndrome to the society due to impulsive manifestation of Social media platforms, thus, raising an alarm to information-concerned individuals. Apparently, this newly instituted communicable disease is a menace to humanity as the mortality rate of

Table 1.

S.No	Description	Fabrication
1	Information is a difference that makes a difference	Bateson,1972, p.459
2	Information is information, not matter and energy	Wiener,1948, p.132
3	Information has arisen as a concept as fundamental and important as 'being', 'knowledge', 'life', 'intelligence', 'meaning', or 'good and evil', all pivotal concepts with which it is interdependent	Floridi,2001, p.16
4	Information is that part of the process of self-organization that is responsible for generating new features in the system's structure, state or behavior	Hofkirchner,2010, p.62
5	Information is different from meaning. Information is an objective, although abstract, feature of the world in the same way as are physical objects and their properties	Mingers,1995, p.295
6	Information equals data plus meaning	Checkland & Scholes,1990, p.303
7	Information is interpreted data, it is something we get to know, it is knowledge of some sort	Langefors,1993, p.111
8	Information is understood as potential until somebody interprets it	Brier,2004, p.629
9	Information is data that are processed to be useful, providing answers to 'who', 'what', 'where', and 'when' questions	Ackoff,1989, p.5
10	Information is an inward-forming. It is the change in a person from an encounter with data. It is the change in the knowledge, beliefs, values or behavior of that person	Boland,1987, p.363
11	Information-as-expressed-meaning	Basden, 2010,p.18
12	Information is a measurable quantity	Hartley,1928, p.536
13	Information can have attached measure to it	Bar-Hillel & Carnap,1952
14	Information is physical	Landauer,1996
15	Information is transmittable... the fundamental problem of communication is that of reproducing at one point, either exactly or approximately, a message selected at another point	Shannon,1948, p.379
16	The destination of information transmission can be a person or it can be a thing for whom the message is intended	Shannon,1948, p.2
17	Information is an infinite of its characteristics, such as data or knowledge, signal or communication, symbol or meaning ...	Bateson,1972; Boland,1987; Brier,2008; Checkland & Scholes,1990; Hartley,1928; Langefors,1993; Shannon,1948
18	Information is physical, biological, psychical, mechanical, social, digital ...	Bateson,1972; Bates,2006; Brier,1992;2004;2008; Floridi,2010; Maturana & Varela,1980; Mingers,1995;2001
19	Information is been understood as a universal notion	Heidegger,1962
20	Information has been given freedom to be used without consensus in different scholarly domains	Adams,2003; Floridi,2005; Losee,1998; MacKay,1969
21	Information is an ultimately indefinable or intuitive first principle, like energy, whose precise definition always somehow seems to slip through our fingers like a shadow	Gatlin, 1972
22	Like the Iron Age man, Information age Man can recognize and manipulate 'information' but is unable to give a precise definition as to what exactly it is that is being recognized and manipulated	Devlin, 1991
23	Information is generated inside the mind of a person; a subject generated by data stimulus and his/her individual experience	N. Callaos & B. Callaos, 2002
24	Information is a fluid that lacks identity	Lakoff and Johnson 1980
25	Information is processed data which has meaning for the user	Ahituv and Neumann, 1982: 5
26	Information is data that have been organised and communicated.	Broadbent, 1984: 209
27	Information is any physical form of representation, or surrogate, of knowledge, or of a particular thought, used for communication.	Farradane, 1979: 13
28	Information can be described as a commodity or good, but it may be more instructive to think of information as a social and economic lubricant. Information is a resource which conserves other resources: one which facilitates, integrates and enables.	Cronin, 1985b: 129

constructive, significant information is tremendously mounting higher and higher every moment due to a highly competitive environment where each struggles for his/her consideration, thus, generating asymmetrical liaison flanked by an individual and the content generated over the social media.

As quoted by Heraclitus (540-480BC): "There is nothing permanent except change" is fittingly pertinent in a persistently changing world where nothing is assured than transformation. Empirically, one can bring a change in the society through his/her favourable endeavours to revolutionize humanity stirred by the challenges that may occur that cajoles his/her experience with a focus profoundly on an optimistic, constructive upshot. Obstinately, when the transformation is obligated by chance, the individual experience fluctuates with a focus profoundly on a pessimistic, unconstructive upshot with lots of conflict to stand for the same. No matter if the change is instigated by self or the rest, acclimatizing to the situation is an imperative concern. An *information bazaar*, that is sprouting speedily, is parting the social norms that administer the way people guard data about themselves, as there is constantly a relative propensity to amass copious unstructured information held in many different hands obtainable effortlessly upon search. This ubiquitous information authorizes everyone to amend it, in conformity with his own cognitive competence.

In the era of information explosion and technological infiltration, the thoughts of Boland (1987) on information being the inward-forming, that leads to self-discovery and enlightenment, of a person from his engagement with data, is subjected to multiple interpretations that consequentially result in the construction of an incongruous idea. This idea trims down information to routes that take place inside of an individual and reallocate the focus from what was communicated to something that is only a situation-specific result. Benkler (2006) construes a digital uprising in tandem with the emergence of computer networks that has fundamentally transformed the ways in which information, knowledge, and entertainment are created, distributed, accessed, and (re) used.

The so-called 'gatekeepers' accountable for monitoring the content that is packaged and distributed to the audience irrespective of any media has slacken its ties and is almost flagging in its subsistence. Traditional gatekeepers, such as editorial boards, whose task it was to guarantee certain levels of quality in the analog environment, are less important in the online world. As opined by Flanagin and Metzger (2008) and Hargittai (2008a), the co-existence of superfluous mediators such as search engines and information aggregators do not fill the precise role of old gatekeepers, and there are a limited number of standards for quality control and evaluation.

Defiantly, the information society is witnessing a big bang of enormous messages to a knowledge worker resulting in many unprocessed data due to unreceptive consumption by the brain. These observable facts uncouple him of obtaining degraded information. According to Dervin (1983), "all information is subjective (the real) while the objective or external is only the representation of the real". The authors of Belkin (1978) and Luhmann (1990) expressed the 'subjective' orientation towards human communication of the meaning of information while the authors of Brillouin (1962), Landauer (1991), and Stonier (1996) stated the 'objective' orientation towards external physical components of the universe that comprise information.

Aamodt (1993) affirms, "Knowledge is always within a reasoning agent...When we, correspondingly, view information as interpreted data, it only makes sense to talk about data in a book. The information itself has to come from an interpretation process who uses its knowledge in order to understand and thereby 'transform' data into information...Hence, when we in conversation with human being refer to "the information in a book"...we implicitly assume that the interpreter is ourselves or another human being with a similar cultural (and therefore interpretative) background."

Palfrey and Gasser (2008) re-establish a dilapidated rift between the "haves" and "have-nots" through innovative digital tools accessible and used to their full potential. Born into the wired culture, an analogous vision to the intercession of technology in integrating information with a knowledge worker results in him being techno-fluent but completely devoid of "learned behavior" (p. 4). They redefined *Digital Natives (*p.127) as the ability to "build on the shoulders of others," not just to invent with an alarm to not exterminate the obtainable material with the newly fashioned content but to enhance it, stressing strengthening the freedom with the decentralized control of information. They harangue that not everyone has the ability to become familiarized with a completely novel expertise to rummage around for discovering the right information. In the technology-driven era, users confronting copious information are not just passive receivers but also constructors. The pulling out of vital information have to be tailored for users to effectively sift unwarranted information.

Postman (1985), in his work *Amusing Ourselves to Death: Public Discourse in the Age of Show Business* expressed the role of technology in obliterating the modern civilization by fashioning a culture devoid of ethical underpinning. As also, in his thought-provoking book *Technopoly: The Surrender of Culture to Technology* (1993), he conceptualizes the "information glut" (high-speed gargantuan information directed at none in particular), which he defines as cultural "AIDS" (Anti-Information Deficiency Syndrome) leads to the breakdown of a coherent cultural narrative. A few utterances such as "A study has shown . . ." or "Scientists now tell us that . . ." makes one say almost anything without contradiction. Information becomes hazardous and precarious without directives and a pertinent theory to serve its purpose. Technopoly is the social order that considers technology superior to an individual's intellect owing to the outburst of context-free information deficient of a time-honored information filter.

Wurman (1989) articulate concern over the technological stipulation that leads to such a miserable state of affairs, thus creating information anxiety that does not tell us what we want or need to know In his book *Information Anxiety*, Wurman brings out the disparity flanked by data and information to have become more critical as the world moves towards information-dependent economies. It is a product of the ever-widening gap between what we understand and what we think we should understand that results from "too much information as too little information" (as cited in Girard & Allison, 2008) due to the uncertainty around a particular piece of information.

In an exceedingly information concerted social order, Klapp's (1982) notion of 'meaning lag' describes the collective, societal lack of meaning that has resulted from a modern society saturated by information as the amount of data exceeds cognitive capacity of an individual as stated by authors of Hiltz and Turoff (1985), thus building up the feelings of vulnerability (Heylighen, 1999). "The more information is repeated and duplicated, the larger scale of diffusion, the greater the speed of processing, the more opinion leaders and gatekeepers and network, the more filtering of messages, the more kinds of media through which information is passed, the more decoding and encoding, and so on – the more degraded information might be" (Klapp 1986, p.126).

In his book *Inflation of Symbols: Loss of Values in American Culture,* Klapp (1991) comments on the information inflation as the individual pay less attention to it. The information tends to become like noise to human perception (quoted in 1986) and becomes redundant due to its repetitiveness. An individual, thus, becomes cluttered and not integrated. Amount and rate of information are also parameters of noise. A rate too high for the receiver to process efficiently without distraction, stress, increasing errors and other costs can make information poorer. Lack of feedback is yet another noise parameter while the volume of communication increases and adds to the difficulty of finding the fact or the meaning one wants. One grave cause of this occurrence is the media flooding too much information too fast for factual integration making the individual's ability to be selective in finding and retrieving information not subsequently grow in tandem (Hopkins, 1995) as anyone is the creator of any information.

WHAT HAPPENS WHEN USERS CREATE CONTENT OVER THE INTERNET?

The first wave of internet mushroomed as an information-sharing tool where users were mere consumers of content created by web publishers. The second wave of Internet (Web 2.0) has evolved into a participatory information sharing design with user-generated content becoming popular (Cormode & Krishnamurthy, 2008). New media technologies "effectively restore to the audience their capacity to participate" (Cover, 2006, p. 150).

In the views of Wunsch-Vincent and Vickery (2007), publicly accessible content over the Internet that mirror a certain amount of artistic endeavor to be fashioned outside of customary proficient practices characterize the User generated content. The authors of Beer and Burrows (2007), Jenkins (2006), and Mabillot (2007) argued that the resultant of this activity permits a wider distribution of public involvement coupled with their resourceful effort. Perversely, Alexander (2006) finds this situation deteriorating the overall content of a particular piece of information by encouraging everyone to formulate his part of the pack of information online such as blogs, YouTube videos, comments on news articles or blogs, podcasts, so on and so forth with least amount of technical acquaintance. These observable facts can be illustrated by the authors of Cover (2006), Jenkins (2006), Stewart and Pavlou (2002), and Svoen (2007) as a convergence between the contributor of the content and the audience.

Toffler (1980), in his book *The Third Wave* identified the concept of *prosumerism* in line with the convergent scenario of content and audience. He acknowledged Prosumption that was predominant in pre-industrial societies (first wave) to be followed by a "second wave" of marketization that flocked "a wedge into society, thus dawning the concept of producers and consumers (p. 266). In his view, contemporary society is moving away from the anomalous disjointing of production and consumption and towards a "third wave" signaling their reintegration in "the rise of the prosumer" (p. 265).

The creation of prosumerist civilization is leading to an augmented participation of customers in the production process regardless of the fact that there is decentralized assortment for both the publication and promulgation of the generated content. According to the work of Steuer (1991), anyone is permissible to partake in transforming both the form and content of a mediated environment in real time.

Uncooperatively, Ritzer and Jurgenson (2010) dispute over the fact that 'prosumption' is a feature of capitalism for as long as production and consumption have co-existed, and that it is becoming the dominant model in the digital economy and a regular part of everyday life. Prahalad and Ramaswamy (2004) converse this trend as "value co-creation" while Tapscott and Williams (2006) perceive the prosumer as an ingredient of a new "wikinomic" model where businesses put consumers to work. Zwick et al (2008) conclude that prosumption is the granting of freedom to consumers by the companies. Some of the examples include:

1. An Internet forum, or message board, which is an online discussion site where people can hold conversations in the form of posted messages;
2. Wikipedia, where users generate articles and continually edit, update, and comment on them (Konieczny, 2009);

3. Facebook, MySpace, and other social networking websites, where users create profiles composed of videos, photos, and text, interact with one another, and build communities (Boyd, 2006, 2007, 2008);
4. The blogosphere, blogs (Web logs), microblogging (Twitter) and the comments on them produced by those who consume them;
5. YouTube and Flickr, where mostly amateurs upload and download videos and photographs;
6. Linux, a free, collaboratively-built, open-source operating system, and other open-source software applications, like Mozilla Firefox, that are created and maintained by those who use them(Lessig, 2006 & Stewart, 2005);
7. Amazon.com, where consumers do all the work involved in ordering products and write the reviews. Also, the users' buying habits and site navigation are documented to recommend products.

CO-CREATION OF THE GENERATED CONTENT QUESTIONS THE SOURCE CREDIBILITY

Potts et al (2008) discuss the ideation of 'co-creation' through consumer-producer interactions for consumers to use the digital platforms to dynamically fabricate and dispense content over the media as expressed by Deuze and Banks (2009). The term 'produsage' has been instigated by Brun (2008) to define 'the collaborative and continuous building and extending of existing content in pursuit of further improvement.' User-led content 'production' such as Wikipedia is progressions towards extremely decentralized resourcefulness of communities who produce content far from its conventional equivalent. Such scenarios necessitate outsized communities to formulate alteration to the time-honored comprehensive database. Produsage is a shared rendezvous of participant communities wherein content relic are recurrently under development.

Figure 2.

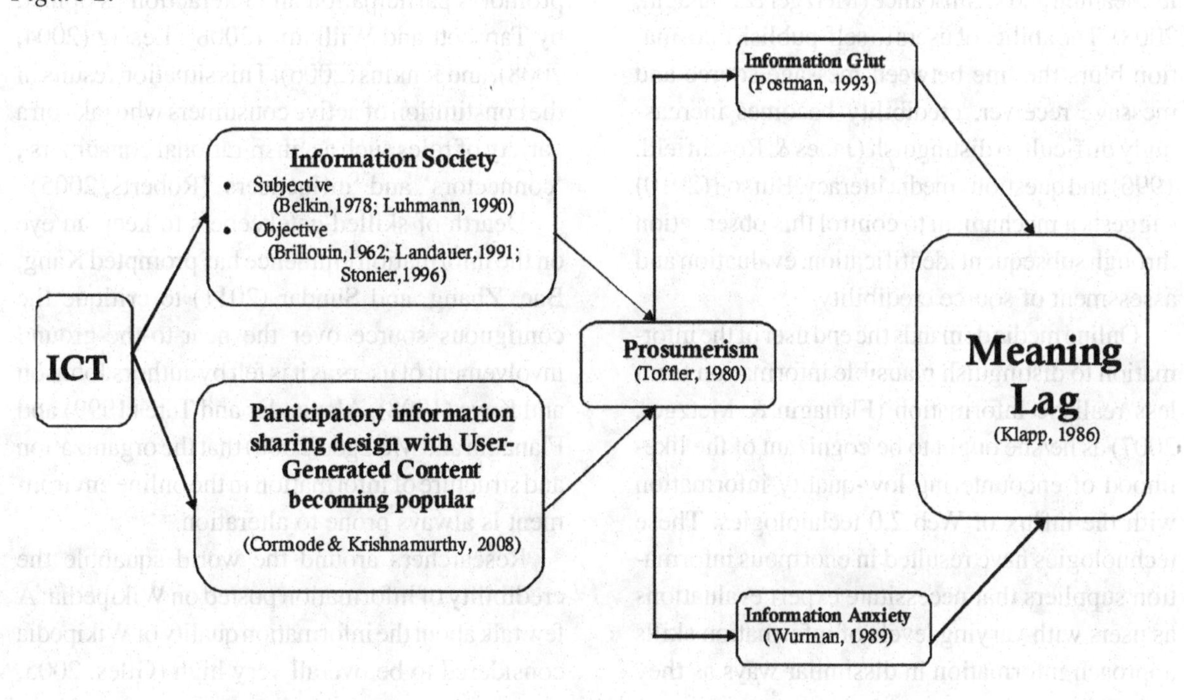

The dawn of social media has brought about an array of information that a user is exposed to in real time. Bontcheva, Gorrell, and Wessels (2013) reveal that two thirds of Twitter users felt that they receive too many posts, and over half of Twitter users felt the need for a tool to sieve out the immaterial posts. Obtaining the pertinent information has become a decisive task for the user owing to inefficiency in locating, organizing and acting upon the accurate information.

Inquiries regarding the one producing content over the social media and the one doing the reparation pose a massive confrontation to the dependability on the information being posted online. Credibility of the content creator optimistically influences the user's potential to be persuaded (Hovland et al., 1953) since social media environment exposes him/her to unidentified sources of information (Lim & Kwon, 2010) that the authors of Sundar and Nass (2001), Kang, Bae, Zhang and Sundar (2011) find travelling through multiple sources before reaching the end-user (). The origin, quality, and veracity of information create an incomparable burden on individuals to unearth apposite information as well as evaluate its meaning and significance (Metzger & Flanagin, 2008). The ability of users to self-publish information blurs the line between message source and message receiver, credibility becomes increasingly difficult to distinguish (Janes & Rosenfield, 1996) and questions media literacy. Burson (2010) suggests a mechanism to control this observation through subsequent identification, evaluation and assessment of source credibility.

Online media demands the end user of the information to distinguish plausible information from less realistic information (Flanagin & Metzger, 2007) as he/she ought to be cognizant of the likelihood of encountering low-quality information with the influx of Web 2.0 technologies. These technologies have resulted in enormous information suppliers that necessitate expert evaluations as users with varying levels of information skills approach information in dissimilar ways as they have an aptitude to identify when information is considered necessary besides to situate, appraise, and employ successfully the needed information (American Library Association Presidential Committee on Information Literacy, 1989).

User Generated Content (UGC) via Web 2.0 assists users to generate content for collective intelligence (Mahmood & Selvadurai, 2006) that does not require IT skills to create and manipulate Internet content. This is corroborated by the works of Isaías et al.(2009) who showed that such enhanced technologies allow anyone to participate in the digital race of content formation and consumption. Social media allows the users to produce the content built on the activity of the users themselves, thus blurring the precincts between users and producers in juxtaposition with the works of authors of Leadbeater (2008), Tapscott and Williams (2008) and Brown (2000). Internet, being a reasonably unrestrained platform for fabrication and publishing, permits everyone to become an architect of content with an ease to produce and edit text, images, and sound. These possibilities have also led to the Web being described as a communication environment that promotes participation and interaction as opined by Tapscott and Williams (2008), Lessig (2004, 2008), and Jenkins (2006). This situation results in the constitution of active consumers who take on a variety of roles such as 'inspirational consumers', 'connectors', and 'influencers' (Roberts, 2005).

Dearth of skilled gatekeepers to keep an eye on the information eminence has prompted Kang, Bae, Zhang, and Sundar (2011) to critique the contiguous source over the near-to-the-ground involvement of users as it is felt by authors Johnson and Kaye (1998), Alexander and Tate (1999) and Flanagin and Metzger (2000) that the organization and structure of information in the online environment is always prone to alteration.

Researchers around the world squabble the credibility of information posted on Wikipedia. A few talk about the information quality of Wikipedia considered to be overall very high (Giles, 2005;

Rajagopalan et al., 2010), while others debate on its open-editing model for umpteen number of articles that confronts users with a hazardous low-quality information (Denning, Horning, Parnas & Weinstein, 2005; Metzger, 2007).

PRODUCTION AFTER CONSUMPTION: CASE OF THE WIKIPEDIA (THE INTERNET ENCYCLOPEDIA)

As of September 2013, Wikipedia has been ranked as the 9th most popular site on the internet for desktop and mobile platforms with 116,835,000 visitors. Of these, about one out of 15,000 contribute five or more edits and of those, a stable 10% contribute more than 100 edits each month. The largest number of these active editors was in March 2007, 4800, and is around 3300 in 2013. As of May 2014, more than 1000 pages are deleted from Wikipedia each day. There are currently 4,536,718 articles in the English Wikipedia of any length, and the combined Wikipedias for all other languages greatly exceed the English Wikipedia in size, giving a combined total of more than 18 billion words in 31 million articles in 287 languages. The English Wikipedia alone has over 2.6 billion words, nearly 60 times as many as the next largest English-language encyclopedia, Encyclopædia Britannica (*Source*: en.wikipedia.org/wiki/Wikipedia:Statistic).

Since its inception in 2001, Wikipedia is being questioned of being a credible source of information due to multiple content creators (Waters, 2007; Dooley, 2010) despite the fact that its accuracy is analogous to a conventional encyclopedia, as highlighted by Giles (2005). The open editing model of Wikipedia exposes users to the risk of encountering counterfeit information (Denning, Horning, Parnas, & Weinstein, 2005). Hence, it calls for credibility appraisal by users themselves under the framework in which information is customized to them. As such, it effectively maintains a virtual memory where qualitative information exists in a concentrated and integrated form (Hayek, 1945; Kankanhalli et al., 2005; Stein & Zwass, 1995).

The present internet trend in India records over 200 million internet users. Though India records 28.16 million unique visitors to Wikipedia as of March 2014, the creator of the content poses a huge challenge despite several attempts to gain insight into the nature of the authors such as WikiScanner mapping the IP-addresses of contributors to organizations across the whole world. This situation gains impetus when users not only launch erroneous information but also probably obliterate formerly written articles.

A decisive feature of the contemporary media environment is the ability of users to be both consumers and providers of information. Online encyclopedias such as Wikipedia permit anyone to incognito contribute content or edit those provided by others, hence questioning the credibility of information. Following this line of research, this chapter focuses on Wikipedia, an archetypal social media platform as an enormous amplification of the information source with its accuracy of the information still under debate.

Users create and exchange user-generated content (Kaplan & Haenlein, 2010) as the variations in the information quality lessens the importance of the credibility of the source when a user becomes more knowledgeable of the content being searched (Eastin, 2001).

Kollock (1999), Kogut and Metiu (2001) and O'Mahony (2003) discuss the emergence of open source production that converts a private commodity (software) into essentially a public good, given that the creation of its content is completely open, quality depends entirely on the types of contributors to Wikipedia. User categorization with distinct characteristics of their contributions to content on Wikipedia as highlighted by Anthony et al. (2007) include *Good Samaritans* (registered users regularly adding and editing information with the quality of their contributions enhanced over time as they become more experienced) and *Zealots (*unregistered users (only identifiable by their IP-addresses) adding or editing information occasionally with the quality of their first contribution often being high but declines over time). Thus, the dynamic role of users to identify and accentuate quality problems could improve Wikipedia.

In a study, Kubiszewski, Noordewier, and Costanza (2011) systematically manipulated the source of information by presenting the same information in the form of a page on Encyclopædia Britannica, Wikipedia, or Encyclopedia of Earth to their participants. Findings revealed that information presented on Encyclopædia Britannica was perceived as having significantly more credibility than on the other two sources.

A similar effect was found by Flanagin and Metzger (2011) while demonstrating that while information presented on Wikipedia was perceived as less credible (regardless of the content), information actually from Wikipedia was perceived as more credible (regardless of the source presented).

The customary updating of information limits the period in which information remains unchanged. As an article evolves due to recurring edits to its contents, the credibility likely improves if user ratings are facilitated to revisions of an article (Korsgaard & Jensen, 2009). However, the authors of Denning, Horning, Parnas, and Weinstein (2005) find its information quality fluctuating heavily between the articles due to its open-editing model.

In his book, *The Sense of Dissonance: Accounts of Worth in Economic Life*, Stark (2009) terms Wikipedia as a *heterarchy*, which is an organization, or a community with multiple worldviews and belief systems and where authority is distributed. An intrinsic attribute of such an organizational structure is a conflict that Stark calls dissonance and "which occurs when diverse, even antagonistic performance principles overlap. However, rather than seeing this conflict as being an impediment to the processes of the organization, Stark sees an organized dissonance as a productive friction which can offer multiple solutions to problems. He warns however, that to be constructive, conflict "must be principled, with the adherents of the contending frameworks offering reasoned justifications." The idea of collaboration and assuming the best in others and their motivations creates a culture where conflict resides in the debates about knowledge and processes rather in the person.

As Stvilia et al. (2008) found in their study on discussions about information quality in Wikipedia, dissonance among users can also have beneficial effects as they seek, "a balance as a social group among those dimensions through the process of negotiation, logical analysis and sense-making of their own and other's actions."In this way, competing views can propel the encyclopedia forward as participants work toward ensuring their viewpoint has the best possible chance of being accepted by the wider community.

While youth are heavy users of Wikipedia for schoolwork and other pursuits (Rainie & Tancer, 2007), children may not be very well equipped to determine the credibility of information they find online due to their relatively limited cognitive and emotional development, lack of life experience, and reduced familiarity with the media apparatus (Metzger & Flanagin, 2008).

User-generated content leverages the potential contributions of a wide variety of users, each of whom may contribute value in some manner to collective endeavors. The essential premise is that, given efficient means of information sharing, collective benefits will emerge from aggregated individual contributions. In this manner, it is argued that networked tools and applications can 'replace the authoritative heft of traditional institutions with the surging wisdom of crowds' (Madden & Fox, 2006).

Wikipedia is perplexed with an unconvinced repute about the quality of its content. Consequently, some people are unremittingly distrusting Wikipedia due to its information not produced or vetted by experts (Metzger et al., 2013). The pervasiveness of exceedingly complex, unidentified, user-generated information bamboozle users in quest of online information. Furthermore, Wikipedia's software platform, MediaWiki, delivers a shared environment, which inspires contributors to iterate persistently on its content in order to perk up its quality. The contributors have a propensity to improve the credibility of an article by challenging a part of the article's content followed by eliciting a debate over it to unearth apposite references, which are later added to the article.

The editorial quality and factual representation of the open nature of Wikipedia has generated much controversy. Stvilia et al. (2005) discuss the Wikipedia's open contribution system that represents an unceremonious peer review to discard superfluous offerings to apparently fabricate its significance. Obstinately, this denunciation considerably diminishes newcomers' contribution rates (Halfaker et al. 2011) in addition to their work in 2009 that showed that editors were more likely to get into conflict when editing the same parts of articles.

Readers sporadically are aware of multiple indistinguishable articles that affirm incongruous specifics over Wikipedia. Articles with few edits and low editorial attention are less likely to be updated (Wilkinson & Huberman, 2007).

CONCERNS OVER THE DECOMPOSED INFORMATION

The technological changes of our era have rendered irrelevant the wisdom of the ages and the sages. The greater the wonders of a technology, the greater will be its negative consequences (Postman, 1998). The volume of information along its length (time-span) and breadth (extensiveness) is becoming devastating. It is not that more information makes us smarter. In his book *The Shallows,* Carr (2010) affirms "What the Net seems to be doing is chipping away my capacity for concentration and contemplation" (p. 6) in harmony with *In Distracted* by Jackson (2009) who disputes that there is so much going on that we are losing our ability for "deep, sustained, perceptive attention" (p. 13). The outcome of this phenomenon is less attention to what is important and more attention to what is not.

Imprecise and ambiguous information can repeatedly lead to considerable harm depending on the intention of the source. Rapid technological bang make available information effortlessly to misinform people. Internet users have an opportunity to contribute and organize information online for individuals and communities (Benkler, 2006).

Content generated over Wikipedia pose challenges to thwart users from falling victim to a myriad of misguided information. Hence, users should employ in their assessments of Internet-based information: accuracy, authority, objectivity, currency, and coverage or scope (Alexander & Tate, 1999; Brandt, 1996; Fritch & Cromwell, 2001; Kapoun, 1998; Meola, 2004; Scholz-Crane, 1998; Smith, 1997). It is found that there is more dissonance over the architects of its content than cohesion due to the disintegration of the information.

High levels of media literacy facilitate users to distinguish whether a message is factual or counterfeit with their ability to access, analyze, evaluate and communicate messages in a variety of forms" and that "a media literate person ...can decode, evaluate, analyze, and produce both print and electronic media" (Aufderheide & Firestone, 1993). As a person's media literacy increases, so does his or her knowledge structures; he or she is then better able to compare information in a media message to the existing knowledge structures in order to draw conclusions about the message (Potter, 2004).

It is not the quantity of information that is disquieting one's realization of what he/she wants from what he/she needs in the name of information but the way the incoming data appears to him/her, hence zeroing the knowledge base and the human intelligence.

REFERENCES

Aamodt, A. (1993). A Case-Based answer to Some Problems of Knowledge-Based Systems. In E. Sandewall & C.G Jansson (Eds.) *Proceedings of the Scandinavian Conference on Artificial Intelligence (pp 168-182). IOS Press.* Retrieved from http://www.idi.ntnu.no/~agnar/publications/scai-93.pdf

Ackoff, R. L. (1989). From data to wisdom. *Journal of Applied Systems Analysis*, *16*, 5.

Adams, F. (2003). The informational turn in philosophy. *Minds and Machines*, *13*(4), 471–501 Retrieved from http://www.uio.no/studier/emner/matnat/ifi/INF5020/h04/undervisningsmateriale/F-ADAMS-informational-turn-in-philosophy.pdf. doi:10.1023/A:1026244616112

Ahituv, N., & Neumann, S. (1982). *Principles of Information Systems for Management*. Dubuque, IA: Wm. C. Brown Publishers.

Alexander, B. (2006). Web 2.0: A new wave of innovation for teaching and learning? *EDUCAUSE Review*, *41*(2), 32–44. Retrieved from https://net.educause.edu/ir/library/pdf/erm0621.pdf

Alexander, J. E., & Tate, M. A. (1999). *Web wisdom: How to evaluate and create Information Quality on the Web*. Mahwah, NJ: Lawrence Erlbaum Associates.

Anderka, M., Stein, B., & Lipka, N. (2012). *Predicting Quality Flaws in User-generated Content: The Case of Wikipedia.* Retrieved from http://www.uni-weimar.de/medien/webis/publications/papers/stein_2012i.pdf

Anthony, D., Smith, S. W., & Williamson, T. (2005). *Explaining Quality in Internet Collective Goods: Zealots and Good Samaritans in the Case of Wikipedia*. Retrieved from http://web.mit.edu/iandeseminar/Papers/Fall2005/anthony.pdf

Anthony, D., Smith, S. W., & Williamson, T. (2007). *The quality of Open Source Production: Zealots and good Samaritans in the case of Wikipedia [Technical Report* TR2007-606]. Dartmouth College, Computer Science. Retrieved from http://www.cs.dartmouth.edu/reports/TR2007-606.pdf

Aufderheide, P., & Firestone, C. M. (1993). *Media Literacy: A Report of the National Leadership Conference on Media Literacy.* Washington, DC: Aspen Institute.

Banks, J. (2009). Co-creative expertise: Auran Games and Fury –A case study. *Media International Australia, 130*, 77-89. Retrieved from http://eprints.qut.edu.au/26176/1/26176.pdf

Banks, J. A., & Deuze, M. (2009). Co-creative labour. *International Journal of Cultural Studies*, *12*(5), 4194–4431 Retrieved from http://eprints.qut.edu.au/31340/2/c31340.pdf doi:10.1177/1367877909337862

Bar-Hillel, Y., & Carnap, R. (1952). *An outline of a theory of Semantic information* [Technical report No. 247]. Cambridge, Massachusetts. Retrieved from http://dspace.mit.edu/bitstream/handle/1721.1/4821/RLE-TR-247-03150899.pdf?sequence=1

Basden, A. (2010). On using spheres of meaning to define and dignify the IS discipline. *International Journal of Information Management*, *30*(1), 13–20. doi:10.1016/j.ijinfomgt.2009.11.006

Bateson, G. (1972). *Steps to an ecology of mind* (p.459). New York: Ballantine Books. Retrieved from http://www.edtechpost.ca/readings/Gregory%20Bateson%20-%20Ecology%20of%20Mind.pdf

Beer, D., & Burrows, R. (2007). Sociology and, of and in Web 2.0: Some initial considerations. *Sociological Research Online*, *12*(5), 17. Retrieved from http://www.socresonline.org.uk/12/5/17.html doi:10.5153/sro.1560

Belkin, N. J. (1978). Information concepts for Information Science. *The Journal of Documentation, 34*(10), 55–85. doi:10.1108/eb026653

Benkler, Y. (2006). *The Wealth of Networks: How Social Production Transforms Markets and Freedom*. New Haven, CT: Yale University Press. Retrieved from http://yalepress.yale.edu/yupbooks/excerpts/benkler_wealth.pdf

Berner, S. (n. d). *Information overload or Information deficiency?* Retrieved from http://www.samberner.com/documents/KM/infoglut.pdf

Boland, R. J. Jr. (1987). The in-formation of information Systems. In R. J. Boland & R. A. Hirscheim (Eds.), *Critical issues in Information Systems Research* (pp. 363–379). New York: John Wiley & Sons.

Boland, R. J., Jr. (1987). In Z.J. Gackowski (Ed.), Informing for Operations: Framework, Models and the First principles (pp. 47). USA: Informing Science Press.

Bontcheva, K., Gorrell, G., & Wessels, B. (2013). *Social Media and Information Overload: Survey Results*. arXiv.

Boyd, D. (2006). Friends, Friendsters, and MySpace Top 8: Writing community into being on social network sites. *First Monday, 11*(12). Retrieved from http://firstmonday.org/article/view/1418/1336 doi:10.5210/fm.v11i12.1418

Boyd, D. (2007). Why youth (heart) social network sites: The role of networked publics in teenage social life. In D. Buckingham (Ed.), *MacArthur Foundation Series on Digital Learning –Youth, Identity, and Digital Media Volume*. Cambridge, MA: MIT Press. Retrieved from http://www.danah.org/papers/WhyYouthHeart.pdf

Boyd, D. (2008). *Taken Out of Context: American Teen Sociality in Networked Publics* [Doctoral Dissertation]. University of California, Berkeley. Retrieved from http://www.danah.org/papers/TakenOutOfContext.pdf

Brandt, D. S. (1996). Evaluating information on the Internet. *Computers in Libraries, 16*(5), 44–46.

Brier, S. (2004). Cybersemiotics and the problems of the information-processing paradigm as a candidate for a unified science of information behind library information science. *Library Trends, 52*(3), 629.

Brillouin, L. (1962). *Science and Information Theory*. New York: Academic Press.

Broadbent, M. (1984). Information management and educational pluralism. *Education for Information, 2*(3), 209–227.

Brown, J. S. (2000). Growing up digital: how the web changes work, education, and the ways people learn. *Change, 32*(2), 10–20. Retrieved from http://www.johnseelybrown.com/Growing_up_digital.pdf doi:10.1080/00091380009601719

Bruns, A. (2008). The Future Is User-Led: The Path towards Widespread Produsage. *Fibreculture Journal, 11*. Retrieved from http://eprints.qut.edu.au/12902/1/12902.pdf

Burson, J. K. (2010). *Measuring media literacy among collegiate journalism students* [Thesis]. Oklahoma State University.

Callaos, N., & Callaos, B. (2002). Toward a systemic notion of information: Practical consequences. *In-forming Science: the International Journal of an Emerging Transdiscipline, 5*(1), 1–11. Retrieved from http://www.inform.nu/Articles/Vol5/v5n1p001-011.pdf

Carr, N. (2010). *The Shallows: What the Internet Is Doing to Our Brains*. New York: W.W. Norton & Company.

Checkland, P., & Scholes, J. (1990). *Soft systems methodology in action* (p. 303). Chichester: John Wiley and Sons.

Chen, H.-T. (n. d). *Understanding Content Consumers and Content Creators in the Web 2.0 Era: A Case Study of YouTube Users*. Retrieved from http://citation.allacademic.com/meta/p_mla_apa_research_citation/2/3/3/7/0/pages233709/p233709-1.php

Comninos, A. (2013). The Role of Social Media and User-generated Content in Post-Conflict Peacebuilding. Retrieved from http://www.tdrp.net/PDFs/TDRP_%20SocialMediaInPostConflictPeaceBuilding.pdf

Cormode, G., & Krishnamurthy, B. (2008). Key differences between Web 1.0 and Web 2.0. *First Monday*, *13*(6), 2. Retrieved from http://firstmonday.org/article/view/2125/1972 doi:10.5210/fm.v13i6.2125

Cover, R. (2006). Audience inter/active: Interactive media, narrative control and reconceiving audience history. *New Media & Society*, *8*(1), 139–158. Retrieved from http://www.academia.edu/655898/Audience_Inter_Active_Interactive_Media_Narrative_Control_and_Reconceiving_Audience_History doi:10.1177/1461444806059922

Cronin, B. (1985). Towards information based economics. *Journal of Information Science*, *12*(3), 129–137. doi:10.1177/016555158601200305

Denning, P., Horning, J., Parnas, D., & Weinstein, L. (2005). Wikipedia risks. *Communications of the ACM*, *48*(12), 152. doi:10.1145/1101779.1101804

Dervin, B. (1983) quoted in Zbigniew J. Gackowski (Ed.) Informing for Operations: Framework, Models and the First principles (2011, p.47). USA: Informing Science Press.

Deuze, M. (2009). Convergence Culture and Media Work. In J. Holt & A. Perren (Eds.), *Media Industries: History, Theory, and Method* (pp. 144–156). Malden, MA: Wiley-Blackwell.

Devlin, K. (1991). *Logic and Information*. Cambridge: Cambridge University Press.

Dooley, P. L. (2010). Wikipedia and the two-faced professoriate. In *Proceedings of the 6th International Symposium on Wikis and Open Collaboration*. New York: ACM. doi:10.1145/1832772.1832803

Druck, G., Miklau, G., & McCallum, A. (n. d.). *Learning to Predict the Quality of Contributions to Wikipedia*. Retrieved from https://people.cs.umass.edu/~mccallum/papers/druck08wikiai.pdf

Eastin, M. S. (2001). Credibility assessments of online health information: The effects of source expertise and knowledge of content. *Journal of Computer-Mediated Communication*, *6*(4). Retrieved from http://www.ascusc.org/jcmc/vol6/issue4/eastin.html

Fallis, D. (n. d.). *A Conceptual Analysis of Disinformation*. Retrieved from http://ischools.org/images/iConferences/fallis_disinfo1.pdf

Farradane, J. (1979). The nature of Information. *Journal of Information Science*, *1*(1), 13–17. doi:10.1177/016555157900100103

Flanagin, A. J., & Metzger, M. J. (2000). Perceptions of Internet information credibility. *Journalism & Mass Communication Quarterly*, *77*(3), 515–540. Retrieved from http://www.jasonmorrison.net/iakm/4006074.pdf doi:10.1177/107769900007700304

Flanagin, A. J., & Metzger, M. J. (2007). The role of site features, user attributes, and information verification behaviors on the perceived credibility of Web-based information. *New Media & Society*, *9*(2), 319–342. doi:10.1177/1461444807075015

Flanagin, A. J., & Metzger, M. J. (2008). (Eds.), Digital media, youth, and credibility (pp. 5-28). Cambridge, MA: The MIT Press. doi:10.1162/dmal.9780262562324.005

Flanagin, A. J., & Metzger, M. J. (2011). From Encyclopædia Britannica to Wikipedia Generational differences in the perceived credibility of online encyclopedia information. *Information Communication and Society*, *14*(3), 355–374. doi:10.1080/1369118X.2010.542823

Floridi, L. (2001). What is the philosophy of information? *Metaphilosophy*, *33*(1/2), 123–145. Retrieved from http://www.philosophyofinformation.net/publications/books/blackwell/chapters/introduction.pdf

Floridi, L. (2003). Two approaches to the philosophy of information. *Minds and Machines*, *13*(4), 459–469. Retrieved from http://www.philosophyofinformation.net/publications/pdf/tattpi.pdf doi:10.1023/A:1026241332041

Floridi, L. (2005). Is Semantic Information Meaningful Data? *Philosophy and Phenomenological Research*, *70*(2), 351–370. Retrieved from http://www.philosophyofinformation.net/publications/pdf/iimd.pdf doi:10.1111/j.1933-1592.2005.tb00531.x

Floridi, L. (2010). *Information: A Very Short Introduction*. Oxford: Oxford University Press. doi:10.1093/actrade/9780199551378.001.0001

Fritch, J. W., & Cromwell, R. L. (2001). Evaluating Internet resources: Identity, affiliation and cognitive authority in a networked world. *Journal of the American Society for Information Science and Technology*, *52*(6), 499–507. Retrieved from https://courses.washington.edu/info320/wi10/readings/fritch.pdf doi:10.1002/asi.1081

Gasser, U. Cortesi, G., Malik, M., & Lee, A. (2012). Youth and Digital Media: From Credibility to Information Quality. Retrieved from http://dmlcentral.net/sites/dmlcentral/files/resource_files/youthanddigitalmediacredibilityreport2.16.12.pdf

Gatlin, L. (1972). *Information Theory and the Living System*. New York: Columbia University Press.

Giles, J. (2005). Internet encyclopaedias go head to head. *Nature*, *438*(7070), 900–901. doi:10.1038/438900a PMID:16355180

Girard, J.P. (n. d.). *Combating Information Anxiety: A Management Responsibility*. Retrieved from http://www.johngirard.net/john/documents/Vadyba%2035-Girard.pdf

Golder, S., Wilkinson, D., & Huberman, B. A. (2007). Rhythms of social interaction: messaging within a massive online network. In C. Steinfeld, B. T. Pentland, M. Ackerman, & N. Contractor (Eds.), *Communities and Technologies 2007: Proceedings of the Third Communities and Technologies Conference* (pp. 41–66). London: Springer-Verlag Limited. Retrieved from http://www.redlog.net/papers/facebook.pdf

Gomez-Rodriguez, M., Gummadi, K. P., & Scholkopf, B. (n. d.). Quantifying Information Overload in Social Media and its Impact on Social Contagions. Retrieved from https://www.mpi-sws.org/~gummadi/papers/icwsm2014-overload.pdf

Halfaker, A., Geiger, R. S., Morgan, J., & Riedl, J. (n. d.). The Rise and Decline of an Open Collaboration System: How Wikipedia's reaction to popularity is causing its decline. Retrieved from http://www-users.cs.umn.edu/~halfak/publications/The_Rise_and_Decline/halfaker13rise-preprint.pdf

Halfaker, A., Kittur, A., & Riedl, J. (2011). Don't bite the newbies: How reverts affect the quantity and quality of Wikipedia work. In *Proceedings of the 7th International Symposium on Wikis and Open Collaboration, WikiSym '11* (pp. 163–172). New York: ACM Press. Retrieved from http://files.grouplens.org/papers/halfaker11bite.personal.pdf

Halfaker, A., Kittur, A., Kraut, R., & Riedl, J. (2009). A jury of your peers: Quality experience and Ownership in Wikipedia. In *Proceedings of the 5th International Symposium on Wikis and Open Collaboration WikiSym '09* (Article No. 15). *New York: ACM Press.* Retrieved from http://kraut.hciresearch.org/sites/kraut.hciresearch.org/files/open/halfaker09-JuryOfYourPeers.pdf

Hartley, R. V. L. (1928). Transmission of Information. *The Bell System Technical Journal, 7*(3), 535–563. Retrieved from http://www.uni-leipzig.de/~biophy09/Biophysik-Vorlesung_2009-2010_DATA/QUELLEN/LIT/A/B/3/Hartley_1928_transmission_of_information.pdf doi:10.1002/j.1538-7305.1928.tb01236.x

Hayek, F. A. (1945). The Use of Knowledge in Society. *The American Economic Review, 35*(4), 519–530. http://www.kysq.org/docs/Hayek_45.pdf Retrieved December 29, 2013

Heidegger, M. (1962). *Being and time* (J. Macquarrie & E. Robinson, Trans). Blackwell: Oxford UK, and Cambridge USA. Retrieved from http://www.naturalthinker.net/trl/texts/Heidegger,Martin/Heidegger,%20Martin%20-%20Being%20and%20Time/Being%20and%20Time.pdf

Heylighen, F. (1999). Change and information overload: Negative effects. In F. Heylighen, C. Joslyn and V. Turchin (Eds.), *Principia Cybernetica Web*. Brussels: Principia Cybernetica. Retrieved January 29, 2014 from http://pespmc1.vub.ac.be/chinneg.html

Hiltz, S. R., & Turoff, M. (1985). Structuring computer mediated communications to avoid information overload. *Communications of the ACM, 28*(7), 680–689http://www.researchgate.net/profile/Starr_Hiltz/publication/220420820_Structuring_Computer-Mediated_Communication_Systems_to_Avoid_Information_Overload/links/0deec51fd15b970b51000000.pdf. RetrievedJanuary272014. doi:10.1145/3894.3895

Hofkirchner, W. (2010). Twenty questions about a unified theory of information: A short exploration into information from a complex systems view. Litchfield Park AZ: Emergent Publications (p.62). Retrieved from http://emergentpublications.com/documents/9780984216475_contents.pdf?AspxAutoDetectCookieSupport=1

Hopkins, R. (1995). Countering information overload: The role of the Librarian. *The Reference Librarian, 23*(49), 305–333. doi:10.1300/J120v23n49_21

Hovland, C. I., Irving, J. L., & Harold, K. H. (1953). *Communication and Persuasion. Psychological Studies of Opinion Change*. New Haven, CO: Yale University Press.

Information Anxiety - Towards Understanding (2012). *Landscape Urbanism Journal 02: Buzz or Noise?* Retrieved from http://scenariojournal.com/lu-information-anxiety/

Information Overload [Ascent White Paper]. Retrieved *from* http://atos.net/content/dam/global/ascent-whitepapers/ascent-whitepaper-information-overload.pdf

Isaías, P., Miranda, P., & Pífano, S. (2009). *Critical Success Factors for Web 2.0–A Reference Framework*. Heidelberg: Springer-Verlag Berlin. doi:10.1007/978-3-642-02774-1_39

Jackson, M. (2009). *Distracted: The Erosion of Attention in the Coming Dark Age*. Amherst: Prometheus books.

Janes, J. W., & Rosenfeld, L. B. (1996). Networked information retrieval and organization: Issues and questions. *Journal of the American Society for Information Science*, *47*(9), 711–715. doi:10.1002/(SICI)1097-4571(199609)47:9<711::AID-ASI7>3.0.CO;2-V

Jenkins, H. (2006). Convergence culture: Where old and new media collide. New York: New York University Press. Retrieved from http://faculty.georgetown.edu/irvinem/theory/Jenkins-ConvergenceCulture-Intro.pdf

Johnson, T. J., & Kaye, B. K. (1998). Cruising is believing? Comparing media and traditional sources on media credibility measures. *Journalism & Mass Communication Quarterly*, *75*(2), 325–340. Retrieved from http://www.aejmc.org/home/wp-content/uploads/2012/09/Journalism-Mass-Communication-Quarterly-1998-JohnsonKay-325-340.pdf doi:10.1177/107769909807500208

Jungwirth, B. (2002). *Information overload: Threat or Opportunity?* Retrieved from http://people.lis.illinois.edu/~chip/pubs/03LIA/13-003.pdf

Kajtazi, M., & Haftor, D. M. (2011). Exploring the Notion of Information: A Proposal for a Multifaced Understanding. Retrieved from http://www.triple-c.at/index.php/tripleC/article/viewFile/280/270

Kang, H., Bae, K., Zhang, S., & Sundar, S. S. (2011). Source cues in online news: Is the proximate source more powerful than distal sources? *Journalism & Mass Communication Quarterly*, *88*, 719–736. Retrieved from http://www.researchgate.net/profile/Shaoke_Zhang/publication/230608544_Source_Cues_in_Online_News_Is_Proximate_Source_more_Powerful_than_Distal_Sources/links/09e41502130a5a870a000000.pdf

Kankanhalli, A., Tan, B. C. Y., & Wei, K. K. (2005). Contributing Knowledge to Electronic Knowledge Repositories: An Empirical Investigation. *Management Information Systems Quarterly*, *29*(1), 113–143.

Kaplan, A. M., & Haenlein, M. (2010). Users of the world, unite! The challenges and opportunities of Social Media. *Business Horizons*, *53*(1), 59–68. doi:10.1016/j.bushor.2009.09.003

Kapoun, J. (1998, July/August). Teaching undergrads WEB evaluation: A guide for library instruction. *C&RL News*, 522-523.

Klapp, O. E. (1982). Meaning Lag in the Information Society. *Journal of Communication*, *32*(2), 56–66. doi:10.1111/j.1460-2466.1982.tb00495.x

Klapp, O. E. (1986). *Overload and Boredom: Essays on the quality of life in the information society*. New York: Greenwood Press.

Klapp, O. E. (1991). *Inflation of Symbols: Loss of Values in American Culture*. New Brunswick, New Jersey: Transaction publishers.

Kogut, B., & Metiu, A. (2001). Open-source software development and distributed innovation. *Oxford Review of Economic Policy*, *17*(2), 248–264. Retrieved from https://www0.gsb.columbia.edu/faculty/bkogut/files/OpensourceSoftware_withMetiu_OREP_2001.pdf doi:10.1093/oxrep/17.2.248

Kollock, P. (1999). The Production of trust in online markets. In E. J. Lawler, M. Macy, S. Thyne, & H. A. Walker (Eds.), Advances in Group Processes, 16, 99-123. Greenwich, CT: JAI Press.

Konieczny, P. (2009). Governance, Organization, and Democracy on the Internet: The Iron Law and the Evolution of Wikipedia. *Sociological Forum*, *24*(1), 162–192. doi:10.1111/j.1573-7861.2008.01090.x

Korsgaard, T. R., & Jensen, C. D. (2009). Reengineering the Wikipedia for Reputation. *Proceedings of the 4th International Workshop on Security and Trust Management (STM 08)*, 71-84.

Kubiszewski, I., Noordewier, T., & Costanza, R. (2011). Perceived Credibility of Internet Encyclopedias. *Computers & Education*, *56*(3), 659–667https://www.uvm.edu/giee/pubpdfs/Kubiszewski_2011_Computers_and_Education.pdf. RetrievedJanuary222014. doi:10.1016/j.compedu.2010.10.008

Lakoff, G., & Johnson, M. (1980). Metaphors We Live By. Chicago: University of Chicago Press. Retrieved from http://shu.bg/tadmin/upload/storage/161.pdf

Landauer, R. (1996). The Physical nature of Information. *Physics Letters. [Part A]*, *217*(4-5), 188–193http://cqi.inf.usi.ch/qic/64_Landauer_The_physical_nature_of_information.pdf. RetrievedJanuary252014. doi:10.1016/0375-9601(96)00453-7

Langefors, B. (1993). Essays on Infology: Summing up and planning for the Future. In B. Dahlbom (Ed.) Gothenburg studies in Information Systems Report 5 (pp.111). Gothenburg: University of Gothenburg Press.

Leadbeater, C. (2008). *We-Think. Mass Innovation, Not Mass Production*. London: Profile Books.

Lessig, L. (2004). *Free Culture: How big media uses technology and the law to lock down culture and control creativity.* London: Penguin Books. Retrieved from http://www.free-culture.cc/freeculture.pdf

Lessig, L. (2006). Code: Version 2.0. New York: Basic Books. Retrieved from http://codev2.cc/download+remix/Lessig-Codev2.pdf

Lessig, L. (2008). *Remix: Making Art and Commerce Thrive in the Hybrid Economy*. London: Bloomsbury. doi:10.5040/9781849662505

Lim, S., & Kwon, N. (2010). Gender differences in information behaviour concerning Wikipedia, an unorthodox information source? *Library & Information Science Research*, *32*(3), 212–220. doi:10.1016/j.lisr.2010.01.003

Losee, R. M. (1998). A discipline independent definition of information. *Journal of the American Society for Information Science*, *48*(3), 254–269. Retrieved from http://www.ils.unc.edu/~losee/book5.pdf doi:10.1002/(SICI)1097-4571(199703)48:3<254::AID-ASI6>3.0.CO;2-W

Lucassen, T. (2013). Trust in Online Information. Retrieved from http://teunlucassen.nl/wp-content/uploads/2013/02/Teun-Lucassen-Trust-in-Online-Information.pdf

Lucassen, T., & Schraagen, J. M. (n. d.). Trust in Wikipedia: How Users Trust Information from an Unknown Source. Retrieved from http://wwwconference.org/proceedings/www2010/wicow/p19.pdf

Luhmann, N. (1990). Meaning as sociology's basic concept. In N. Luhmann (Ed.), *Essays in Self Reference* (pp. 21–79). New York: Columbia University press.

Mabillot, D. (2007). User generated content: Web 2.0 taking the video sector by storm. *Communications & Stratégies*, *65*, 39–49. Retrieved from http://mpra.ub.uni-muenchen.de/4579/1/

MacKay, D. M. (1969). *Information, mechanism and meaning*. Cambridge, MA: MIT Press.

Madden, M., & Fox, S. (2006). Riding the Waves of "Web 2.0": More than a Buzzword, But Still Not Easily Defined. Pew Internet Project. Retrieved from http://www.pewinternet.org/2006/10/05/riding-the-waves-of-web-2-0/

Mahmood, O., & Selvadurai, S. (2006). Modeling "Web of Trust" with Web 2.0. In the *Proceedings of World Academy of Science, Engineering and Technology, 18*.

Maturana, H. R., & Varella, F. J. (1980). R.S. Cohen & M.W. Wartofsky (Eds.), *Autopoiesis and cognition*. Dordrecht Holland: D. Reidel publishing company. Retrieved from http://topologicalmedialab.net/xinwei/classes/readings/Maturana/autopoesis_and_cognition.pdf

Meola, M. (2004). Chucking the checklist: A contextual approach to teaching undergraduates Web evaluation. *Portal: Libraries and the Academy*, *4*(3), 331–344. doi:10.1353/pla.2004.0055

Metzger, M. J. (2007). Making sense of credibility on the Web: Models for evaluating online information and recommendations for future research. *Journal of the American Society for Information Science and Technology*, *58*(13), 2078–2091. doi:10.1002/asi.20672

Metzger, M. J., & Flanagin, A. J. (Eds.). (2008). *Digital Media, Youth, and Credibility*. Cambridge, MA: MIT Press.

Metzger, M. J., Flanagin, A. J., & Medders, R. (2010). Social and heuristic approaches to credibility evaluation online. *Journal of Communication*, *60*(3), 413–439. Retrieved from http://www.pensierocritico.eu/files/Metzger---Social-and-Heuristic-Approaches-to-Credibility-Evaluation-Online.pdf doi:10.1111/j.1460-2466.2010.01488.x

Metzger, M. J., & Pure, R. *Flanagin,A.J., Markov, A., Medders,R. & Hartsell, E.* (2013). The Special Case of Youth and Digital Information Credibility. In M. Folk and S. Apostel (Eds.) *Online Credibility and Digital Ethos: Evaluating Computer-Mediated Communication* (pp. 148-163). *Hershey PA: IGI Global.* Retrieved from http://www.comm.ucsb.edu/faculty/flanagin/CV/Metzgeretal2013%28CredEthos%29.pdf

Mingers, J. (2001). Combining IS research methods: Towards a pluralist methodology. *Information Systems Research*, *12*(3), 240–259. Retrieved from http://gkmc.utah.edu/7910F/papers/ISR%20combining%20IS%20research%20methods.pdf doi:10.1287/isre.12.3.240.9709

Mingers, J. C. (1995). Information and meaning: Foundations for an intersubjective account. *Information Systems Journal*, *5*(4), 295. doi:10.1111/j.1365-2575.1995.tb00100.x

Mueller, B. (2014). Participatory culture on YouTube: A case study of the multichannel network Machinima. Retrieved from http://www.lse.ac.uk/media@lse/research/mediaWorkingPapers/MScDissertationSeries/2013/msc/104-Mueller.pdf

O'Mahony, S. (2003). Guarding the commons: How community managed software projects protect their work. *Research Policy*, *32*(7), 1179–1198. Retrieved from http://flosshub.org/sites/flosshub.org/files/rp-omahony.pdf doi:10.1016/S0048-7333(03)00048-9

Ornebring, H. (2008). The consumer as producer of what?. *Journalism Studies, 9*(5), 771-785. doi:10.1080/14616700802207789

Osman, K. (2013). The role of conflict in determining consensus on quality in Wikipedia article. Retrieved from http://opensym.org/wsos2013/proceedings/p0206-osman.pdf

Palfrey, J., & Gasser, U. (2008). Born Digital: Understanding the first generation of digital natives (Review of the Book). *International Journal of Communication, 4* (2010), 1051–1055. Retrieved from http://ijoc.org/index.php/ijoc/article/viewFile/950/474

Postman, N. (1985). *Amusing Ourselves to Death: Public Discourse in the Age of Show Business.* USA: Penguin Books. Retrieved from https://zaklynsky.files.wordpress.com/2013/09/postman-neil-amusing-ourselves-to-death-public-discourse-in-the-age-of-show-business.pdf

Postman, N. (1993). *Technopoly: The surrender of culture to technology.* New York: Vintage Books. Retrieved from https://mafhom.files.wordpress.com/2013/06/technopoly-neil-postman.pdf

Postman, N. (1998). *Five things we need to know about Technological change.* A Talk delivered in Denver Colorado on March 28. Retrieved from http://web.cs.ucdavis.edu/~rogaway/classes/188/materials/postman.pdf

Potter, W. J. (2004). *Theory of media literacy: A cognitive approach.* Thousand Oaks, California: SAGE Publications, Inc. doi:10.4135/9781483328881

Potts, J., Cunningham, S., Hartley, J., & Ormerod, P. (2008). Social network markets: A new definition of the creative industries. *Journal of Cultural Economics*, *32*(3), 167–185. doi:10.1007/s10824-008-9066-y

Prahalad, C. K., & Ramaswamy, V. (2004). Co-Creation Experiences: The Next Practice in Value Creation. *Journal of Interactive Marketing*, *18*(3), 5–14. Retrieved from http://deepblue.lib.umich.edu/bitstream/handle/2027.42/35225/20015_ftp.pdf doi:10.1002/dir.20015

Presidential Committee on Information Literacy: Final report. (1989). *American Library Association.* Retrieved from http://www.ala.org/acrl/publications/whitepapers/presidential

Quotes of Heraclitus of Ephesus. (540-480BC). Heraclitus of Ephesus. Ancient Greece.

Rainie, L., & Tancer, B. (2007). Wikipedia Users. Pew Internet & American Life Project. Washington, DC. Retrieved from http://www.pewinternet.org/2007/04/24/wikipedia-users/

Rajagopalan, M. S., Khanna, V., Stott, M., Leiter, Y., Showalter, T. N., Dicker, A., & Lawrence, Y. R. (2010). Accuracy of cancer information on the Internet: A comparison of a Wiki with a professionally maintained database. *Journal of Clinical Oncology*, *28*(15), 6058. Retrieved from http://jdc.jefferson.edu/cgi/viewcontent.cgi?article=1008&context=bodinejournal

Ritzer, G., & Jurgenson, N. (2010). Production, Consumption, Prosumption: The Nature of Capitalism in the Age of the Digital 'Prosumer'. *Journal of Consumer Culture*, *10*(1), 13–36. Retrieved from https://sociologiaconsumului.files.wordpress.com/2011/10/overview-production-consumption-prosumption.pdf doi:10.1177/1469540509354673

Roberts, K. (2005). *Lovemarks: The Future Beyond Brands.* New York: Powerhouse.

Samoilenko, A., & Yasseri, T. (2014). The distorted mirror of Wikipedia: A quantitative analysis of Wikipedia coverage of acadèmics. *EPJ Data Science, 3*(1). Retrieved from http://www.epjdatascience.com/content/pdf/epjds20.pdf

Scholz-Crane, A. (1998). Evaluating the future: A preliminary study of the process of how undergraduate students evaluate Web sources. *RSR. Reference Services Review*, *26*(3/4), 53–60. doi:10.1108/00907329810307759

Shannon, C. E. (1948). A Mathematical Theory of Communication. *The Bell System Technical Journal*, *27*(3), 379–423, 623–656. Retrieved from http://worrydream.com/refs/Shannon%20-%20A%20Mathematical%20Theory%20of%20Communication.pdf doi:10.1002/j.1538-7305.1948.tb01338.x

Smith, A. G. (1997). Testing the Surf: Criteria for Evaluating Internet Information Resources. *The Public-Access Computer Systems Review*, *8*(3), 5–23. Retrieved from https://journals.tdl.org/pacsr/index.php/pacsr/article/download/.../5645

Stark, D. (2009). *The sense of dissonance: Accounts of worth in economic life*. Princeton, New Jersey: Princeton University Press.

Stein, E. W., & Zwass, V. (1995). Actualizing Organizational Memory with Information Systems. *Information Systems Research*, *6*(2), 85–117. doi:10.1287/isre.6.2.85

Steuer, J. S. (1991). *Audio-visual space: On the influence of auditory spatial perception in mediated experience* [Unpublished manuscript]. Stanford University, Institute for Communication Research, Stanford, CA.

Stewart, D. (2005). Social status in an open-source community. *American Sociological Review*, *70*(5), 823–842. doi:10.1177/000312240507000505

Stewart, D. W., & Pavlou, P. A. (2002). From Consumer Response to Active Consumer: Measuring the Effectiveness of Interactive Media. *Journal of the Academy of Marketing Science*, *30*(4), 376–396. Retrieved from http://www.uk.sagepub.com/chaston/Chaston%20Web%20readings%20chapters%201-12/Chapter%209%20-%2036%20Stewart%20and%20Pavlou.pdf doi:10.1177/009207002236912

Stonier, T. (1996). Information as a basic property of the universe. *Bio Systems*, *38*(2-3), 135–140. doi:10.1016/0303-2647(96)88368-7 PMID:8734520

Stvilia, B., Twidale, M. B., Smith, L. C., & Gasser, L. (2005). Assessing information quality of a community-based encyclopedia. In F. Naumann, M. Gertz, & S. Mednick (Eds.), *Proceedings of the International Conference on Information Quality–ICIQ 2005* (pp. 442–454). Cambridge, MA: MITIQ. Retrieved from http://mitiq.mit.edu/ICIQ/Documents/IQ%20Conference%202005/Papers/AssessingIQofaCommunity-basedEncy.pdf

Stvilia, B., Twidale, M. B., Smith, L. C., & Gasser, L. (2008). Information quality work organization in Wikipedia. *Journal of the American Society for Information Science and Technology, 59(*6), 983-1001. Retrieved from http://www.researchgate.net/profile/Michael_Twidale2/publication/200772424_Information_quality_work_organization_in_wikipedia/links/00b7d517a7ed9703be000000.pdf

Sundar, S. S., & Nass, C. (2001). Conceptualizing sources in online news. *Journal of Communication*, *51*(1), 52–72. Retrieved from http://www.researchgate.net/profile/Clifford_Nass/publication/2403100_Conceptualizing_Sources_in_Online_News/links/09e4151086146158ba000000.pdf doi:10.1111/j.1460-2466.2001.tb02872.x

Svoen, B. (2007). Consumers, participants, and creators: Young people's diverse use of television and new media. *ACM Computers in Entertainment*, *5*(2), 1–16. doi:10.1145/1279540.1279545

Tapscott, D., & Williams, A. D. (2006). Wikinomics: How Mass Collaboration Changes Everything. New York: Penguin Group. Retrieved from http://labeee.ufsc.br/~luis/egcec/livros/globaliz/Wikinomics.pdf

Tapscott, D., & Williams, A. D. (2008). *Wikinomics: How Mass Collaboration Changes Everything*. London: Atlantic Books.

The notions of information/noise, communication/meaning, author/literature as a self-regulating machine in Italo Calvino's Cybernetics and Ghosts (1967) and Thomas Pynchon The Crying of Lot 49 (1966). (n. d.). Retrieved from http://www.jfki.fu-berlin.de/academics/SummerSchool/Dateien2011/Presentation_Handouts/Handout_-_Iuli_-_September_19_-_Belloni.pdf

Toffler, A. (1980). *Third Wave*. New York: William Morrow and Co.

Tylor, J. (2012). *An examination of how student journalists seek information and evaluate online sources during the newsgathering process* [Published Undergraduate Honors Thesis]. Arizona State University. Retrieved from http://barrettdowntown.asu.edu/wp-content/uploads/2012/05/tylor_An-examination-of-how-student-journalists-seek-information-and-evaluate-online-sources.pdf

Vainikka, E., & Herkman, J. (2013). *Generation of content-producers? The reading and media production practices of young adults.* Retrieved from http://www.participations.org/Volume%20 10/Issue%202/7.pdf

Walter, J. A. (1989). *Overload and Boredom: When the Humanities Turn to Noise.* Paper presented at the Community College Humanities Association Conference (pp. 6). Dayton, Ohio.

Waters, N. L. (2007). Why you can't cite Wikipedia in my class. *Communications of the ACM*, *50*(9), 15–17. doi:10.1145/1284621.1284635

Weissma, S., Ayhan, S., Bradley, J., & Lin, J. (n. d.). *Identifying Duplicate and Contradictory Information in Wikipedia.* Retrieved from http://arxiv.org/pdf/1406.1143.pdf

Wiener, N. (1948). Cybernetics or communication and control in the animal and the machine (pp.132). Cambridge: MIT Press. Retrieved from http://www.allen-riley.com/utopia/cybernetics.pdf

Wunsch-Vincent, S., & Vickery, G. (2007). *Participative Web: User-created content.* A Report prepared for the OECD Committee for Information, Computer and Communications Policy.

Wurman (1989) cited by Girard, J. and Allison, M. (2008). Information Anxiety: Fact, Fable or Fallacy. *The Electronic Journal of Knowledge Management*, *6*(2), 111-124. Retrieved from www.ejkm.com/issue/download.html?idArticle=147

Zwick, D., Bonsu, S. K., & Darmody, A. (2008). Putting Consumers to Work: Co-creation and new marketing governmentality. *Journal of Consumer Culture*, *8*(2), 163–196. Retrieved from http://www.sagepub.com/ellis/SJO%20Readings/Chapter%203%20-%20Zwick,%20Bonsu%20&%20 Darmody.pdf doi:10.1177/1469540508090089

KEY TERMS AND DEFINITIONS

Decomposition: A cognitive process in which an individual's information processing skills corrodes or disintegrates when two or more individuals under similar state of affairs happen to be the architects of the same content as they encounter the information offered to them, thus giving rise to a complex media environment where the meaningful content relapses.

Digital Natives: Segment of the audience who are immersed in a digitally networked environment.

Gatekeepers: People responsible to guarantee the reception of information among the audience based on certain levels of quality.

Information: Values within the outcome of any process.

Information Anxiety: A product reflecting too much information as too little information.

Information Glut: High-speed gargantuan information directed at none in particular.

Information Society: An economical reserve that satisfies the general demand for information facilities and services in public.

Meaning Lag: A point where availability of too much information distorts the exact meaning of the content under debate.

Prosumer: Participation of customers in the production process of content of information.

User Generated Content (UGC): Publicly accessible content over the Internet that mirror a certain amount of artistic endeavor to be fashioned outside of customary proficient practices.

Section 2

Emergence of Innovative Practices

Chapter 4
The Thin-Blue Web:
Police Crime Records of Internet Trolling Show Chivalrous Attitudes That Can Be Resolved through Transfer of Powers

Jonathan Bishop
Centre for Research into Online Communities and E-Learning Systems, UK

ABSTRACT

This chapter using an empirical data-driven approach to investigate crime recording logs of South Wales Police relating to Internet trolling byand towards different sexes. The chapter finds more favourable attitudes towards women as victims in even the most trivial of cases. It finds male victims of trolling are only treated as victims when a form of unwanted face-to-face encounter is needed for action. The chapter shows transferring police powers to local authorities, can cut the cost of community policing by 50% across the board and eliminate sexist attitudes also. The chapter finds that the way social media platforms are exercising 'sysop prerogative' where they have no right to – such as not passing over account information on alleged defamers – puts a huge burden on police resources. Using local authorities, which have many of the same powers as the police and indeed more, can resolve problems without the need to criminalise offenders.

INTRODUCTION

It has been argued that since William Westley's seminal study in the 1950s, descriptions of a "single" police culture have focused on the widely shared attitudes, values, and norms that serve to manage strains created by the nature of police work (Paoline, 2004). As will be explored in this chapter, a police culture of benevolent sexism has crept into the digital age, including with regards to Internet trolling and cyberbullying.

Such attitudes by the police service have a significant effect on the administration of justice and how they are perceived by members of the public as a whole (Porter & Prenzler, 2012). By giving favour or disfavour to one group over another, it

DOI: 10.4018/978-1-4666-8598-7.ch004

means that the police are denying justice to those they do not see as victims but who are, and providing access to criminal remedies for people they see as victims, but who are not. This is no truer than in the recording of and responding to reports of alleged crime (Averdijk & Elffers, 2012), and as this study shows, the reporting of incidents of trolling by men and women in particular.

INTERNET TROLLING AND THE DARK WEB

The act of being provocative or offensive on the Internet is often called Internet trolling or cyber-bullying, which are a huge problems facing the world today (Bishop, 2014c; Buckel, Trapnell, & Paulhus, 2014; Hardaker, 2013). People who abuse others online show no regard for any differences, such as age and sex and will abuse others for occurrences in their life whether happy events or tragic ones (Bishop, 2014a; Bishop, 2014d; Phillips, 2011; Walter, Hourizi, Moncur, & Pitsillides, 2011; Walter, 2014). Internet trolling on websites like Facebook and Twitter are often easy to identify and deal with as they are recorded in a durable form. Others, however, such as those which occur via Skype video calls, where the abuse is not recorded in a durable form, or otherwise accessible via a public-facing website are more problematic, and form part of the 'Dark Web.' The dark web is generally thought of to be the part of the Internet containing websites and file locations that are not indexed by conventional search engines and are therefore hard to find (Stevens, 2009).

Police are now struggling to cope with the number of reports of Internet trolling, and unlocking those dark web networks hiding illegal content. It is often the case that these electronic message faults (EMFts) will be recorded differently depending on the officer and the reporting person in question. Other than through the Data Protection Act 1998 in the UK, it is otherwise unlikely someone will know what information, or misinformation, has been recorded about them by the police, creating a de facto 'dark web' in the police, where what they record about citizens will usually go unchecked (Gürses, Troncoso, & Diaz, 2011). This will be referred throughout this chapter as the 'Thin Blue Web.'

What is apparent from the most prominent of cases brought against trolls since 2011, which have been reported in the media, is that the targets for the authorities have been young men. Namely; Liam Stacey, Reece Messer, Jamie Counsel, Anthony Gristock, and Matthew Woods, among others. One notable exception was Isabella Sorley who was a woman convicted for the trolling of radical feminist Caroline Criado-Perez, known mostly for her misandrist views on wanting less men on banknotes (Bishop, 2014a; Bishop, 2014b; Bishop, 2014d).

REPRESENTATIONS OF WOMEN AS 'TROLLS'

Internet trolls are often depicted in the media as young men (Bishop, 2014c), who go online to target women for misogynistic reasons (Allen, 2014; Faye & Hopgood, 2012). However, research has shown that those likely to display anti-social behaviour on the Internet, such as defriending others – are as often likely to be women as men, sometimes more so (Bishop, 2013c; Bishop, 2013d). Indeed, in the case of discredited feminist, Caroline Criado Perez, who in 2014 was found by the press regulators to have misrepresented domestic violence figures in order to attack men, she should only have expected that people would fight flame with flame, and her sexist remarks against men would not go unchallenged. At the same time another radical feminist, Stella Creasy MP, was targeted, and it was alleged that 63-year-old Brenda Leyland was the person who trolled her, becoming the first recorded death at the hands of neo-feminism. This confirms the finding that those who have the most confrontations online are women – usually with other women (Bishop, 2013d). Indeed, the founding of the group, "Women Against Feminism," shows there are as many divisions between women as there are men (Harrison & Ollis, 2015). Such unequal treatment of men and women by the media and other aspects of society, where the latter is treated more favourably when there are allegations against them, is sexism (Zaikman & Marks, 2014). Where this is done on the perception of women being the 'weaker sex' it is called 'benevolent sexism' (Zaikman & Marks, 2014).

BENEVOLENT SEXISM

Benevolent sexism reflects the tendency to endorse the traditional feminine ideal or to view women in idealised, overly romantic terms or as delicate creatures who require protection (Diekman & Murnen, 2004). Research has indicated that chivalry exists in the police at the stage of arrest for those women who display appropriate gender behaviours and characteristics, whereas female suspects who deviate from stereotypic gender expectations lose the advantage that may be extended to female offenders (Visher, 1983). Observations of police academic training have shown that portraying women as inferior to men is the norm and it is acceptable to those male police officers to refer to those women who get the upper hand on them as "bitches" (Prokos & Padavic, 2002).

BENEVOLENT SEXISM IN THE POLICE FOLLOWING THE MACPHERSON INQUIRY

It has been argued that there is no difference in performance between a police officer who is motivated to take up the role for their eagerness to carry out its duties, whether they are doing it as just a job, or whether they do it because they are not qualified to do any other job (Cordner, 2014). However, it is clear that many police officers take up their roles to be knights in shining armour to women who they see as being vulnerable and in need of their protection. Sexism is far from being eliminated from the police service (Sklansky, 2007). It is thus important to look into institutional discrimination more generally.

The MacPherson Inquiry was a Government inquiry into the way in which the Metropolitan Police dealt with the death of the Black youth Stephen Lawrence in London in the late 1990s (Papadopoulos, Tilki, & Lees, 2004), and can be seen to have applicability here. The report defined the concept of 'institutional racism' as that being a situation where an organisation does not have a concerted effort of being racist, but as a whole, and by not recognising the differing needs of different races that the organisation discriminates against a group. One might therefore argue that a concept of 'institutional sexism' can exist where members of an organisation treat one sex with favour or disfavour in decisions being taken in relation to a person of that given sex in continued opposition to those of the opposite sex (Bartlett & Henderson, 2013). Feminist theorists and activists have argued that at the heart of institutional sexism is the material reality of human reproduction and sexuality, the latter including how a woman is treated and viewed sexually by men and how she views herself (Feagin, 2014). Indeed, when women are portrayed as victims within the family sphere, it is most often seen to be the result of certain traditions that stem from a patriarchal culture (Kealhofer, 2011). The most pervasive form of institutional sexism is patriarchy, a system of social organizations in which men have a disproportionate share of power (Haghighat, 2013), which is known to be a problem with regards to the police service. Indeed in one study where people who had to rate two 'applicants' for police chief (one who had more education and the other who had more experience) participants always chose the man over the woman, but justified their choice as arising from the value they placed on either education or experience (Raymond, 2013).

AN INVESTIGATION INTO THE EXTENT OF BENEVOLENT SEXISM IN THE POLICE AS A MEASURE OF INSTITUTIONAL SEXISM

South Wales Police was the police force chosen as a convenience sample to examine the 'Thin Blue Web,' including because of the locality being in a former coal-fields and industrial area where men were the more dominant economic actors at one point in this environment (Edwards & Chapman, 2000).. Research has shown there are plenty of examples of similar exclusionary attitudes in the literature unrelated to coal-mining areas, which confirm that the problems of sexism, racism and other discriminatory attitudes are not location-specific, but remain as much a general problem for those seeking equality in the South Wales Valleys (Edwards & Chapman, 2000). Whilst other police forces were asked for records, such as Dyfed-Powys Police, they did not have such records needed for the study.

MATERIALS

The study involves using police records of crime reports as embodiments of the 'Thin Blue Web'. Obtained by request of South Wales Police, these records detail a number of incidents of Internet trolling where there are a number of identified individuals involved. The records date from between 2004 and 2014, with numerous incidents of cyber-bullying, which include information on the outcome of complaints to the South Wales Police force about alleged perpetrators and reporting persons.

PARTICIPANTS

The participants in the study were not as in typical studies. An a priori browsing of the police records was conducted to see if there were any obvious cases of trolling and where it was possible issues might arise in relation to the sex of the person – such as online harassment or expression. These people are like 'participants' as it is them that will be considered as individuals rather than analysing the records as a whole in its own right. This allowed for a detailed account of alleged Internet trolling in the records obtained from South Wales Police and testimonies of those involved. The persons investigated by this research are referred to by a pseudonym to protect their identity and the necessary images of them – depicting their visual characteristics displayable to police – have been converted to outlines so they can be considered in an academic sense without unnecessary personal information being conveyed.

METHODOLOGY

Narrative analysis is an umbrella term for an eclectic mix of methods for making sense of, interpreting and representing data that have in common a storied form (B. Smith & Sparkes, 2012). Narrative analysis is increasingly important for examining media discourse, especially news (Su, 2012). Narrative analysis is a structuralism method introduced into literature criticism that tries to find the inner rules of text itself and thus helps to unveil the hidden concepts of structure in the texts (Shen, 2012). In a study like this it would be normal to provide excerpts from the documents, but due to issues of confidentially their contents will be referred to in such a way that the facts cannot be corresponded with the events to which they refer.

RESULTS

The result of the study showed clear differences in how the police handled complaints by men and against men, where the other party was a woman, suggesting a clear bias in favour of women in cases related to Internet trolling and cyber-harassment.

Women Claimants and Respondents

The two claimants discussed in this section come from diverse backgrounds. The first, Person G, is a woman in her 30s, from a mixed race background. The second (Person K) is a much older woman in her from a traditional white background, as is the third claimant (Person T). All have been involved in public life in some way, respectively being a publicly performing musician who received taxpayer funds to enhance her music career, an executive of a publicly funded organization, and finally a political party candidate who manages public funds as part of her day job at a publicly funded institution.

Research has found that in keeping with evidence from both benevolent sexism and the application of racial stereotypes, Afro-Caribbean and other ethnic minority women are perceived as less threatening than those which are men (Plant, Goplen, & Kunstman, 2011). This appeared to be the case in terms of Person G, who was of a mixed race ethic origin. Benevolent sexism toward women often includes the expressed belief that women should be cherished and protected by men (Feather & McKee, 2012). Caucasian females are often the single largest race-gender group portrayed as victims, and such portrayals may change the attitudes of males toward women and male-female relationships (Rich, Woods, Goodman, Emans, & DuRant, 1998). It is therefore clear that men who assume chivalrous roles as police officers will be more likely to be exploited by women who act as victims, especially if they are from a Caucasian background.

Person G was a woman of mixed race origin (i.e. White and Asian). She regularly dyed her hair blonde and wore very feminine makeup. It is known that in cosmetics advertising that women are portrayed as "*victims, subservient, dependent, nurturing, selfless, and sacrificing,*" particularly Asian women (Ali & Shahwar, 2011). It is however well known that Asian women are not entirely the victims they are portrayed to be in media and life in general (Mills, 1999). Person G, who is pictured in Figure 1a, appears with an innocent and vulnerable appeal that might make their case against others a higher priority for chivalrous police officers.

In the media, women tend to be portrayed as passive victims who do not fight back or take other actions to protect or defend themselves (Meyers, 1996). Many women will try to optimise the benefits of both their sex as women and the associated stereotypes. According to (Wryght, 2006) they will want to be viewed as helpless victims, being denied their "rights" by a male dominated world, and as men know such women like jewellery, this can be exploited by them, whilst at the same time appearing "courageous" and "strong" when it suits them in their professional career or public life.

It has been proven that recourse to the 'feminine' by opportunist women seeking more rights than one might consider to be fair and reasonable could be used as a bargaining tool for acceptance within police culture and, even, as a statement of moral superiority (Jackson, 2006). This seems to be true of the police division investigated in this study. Records show that when Person K was accused of the newly created offence of stalking (Section 2A of the Protection from Harassment Act 1997) that the police's response was 'how can one police the Internet?' whereas the officer involved in Person T's case said that the person who was accused of harassment of her should "not treat women that way," and that they "shouldn't get away with something just because it happened on the Internet." Both of the police officers dealing with these cases were men, both working for the same police force.

In terms of Person T she reported a man to the police when he served a legal notice on her following what he believed to be harassment from her. The police, which is the same police division that took action in the case of Person G and Person K, attempted to serve a harassment notice on the man seeking to prevent alleged harassment against him by Person T, which he refused to accept. The document served on him in relation to Person T contained a very biased tone of writing. For instance it said that while the police would not comment on "the truth" of the allegations made against him by Person T, that "if they happened again" then he would be prosecuted. Essentially it claimed that if he did something he knew did not do then they would take action as if he had done the thing that he knew he did not do.

In the records acquired complaints were made against two people from Person D, some of which were public figures and others not so. One of them, was a woman who used an e-dating website called 'OkCupid,' who claimed to be studying at a university in Brussels. It is likely that this person was not whom they said they were because other records show that they asked for money to be sent somewhere in Africa and their English was poor. Even so, there was no investigation by the police, unlike when Persons G, K and T made a complaint. This suggests that this police force were more likely to assess allegations by women, rather than against them. Indeed, as discussed earlier, when a complaint was made against Person K by Person D, alleging she was stalking him on the Internet, there was no formal investigation and the case was quickly closed. However, when Person K made a complaint against Person D, her complaint was investigated and Person D's house attended by police officers.

Male Claimants and Respondents

Person D made a complaint that he was being abused on an Internet website called Pontypridd Town, which was run by another person – Person W – which is a message board based in Pontypridd, with a history of trolling (Bishop, 2013c). Person D complained that he received comments that he was from "cuckoo land," which was by an elected councillor who shall be called Person B. He alleged that he was told by Person W that if he made any further complaints about how he was treated that Person W would visit his home and "break his legs." In investigating the 'Ponty Town' website at www.pontytown.co.uk, the investigating officer noted that there were comments that were "possible civil defamation of character," but that it did not amount to criminal "harassment." It was only when Person B was outside the home of Person D that the police took action – issuing Person B with a police information notice. One can easily compare the difference between how Person D's complaint was handled and those of Person G, K and T. Whilst the remarks made against these three women were not personal in nature – neither of them were threatened or sworn at – their cases resulted in actions being taken for harassment. The only time Person D, a man, got the same treatment was when the person he complained of harassment about was physically proximate. There appears from the data to be a perception in the police that men can "take it like a man," yet somehow women, even if they are public figures, need more protecting in their view.

Person P, who can be seen in Figure 1b, had complaints made against him for harassment. Person P was a local councillor, and was taking part in an undercover investigation into abuses of public trust by other political parties. This included one shop-keeper who was also a local councillor who he alleged would drive into the town centre prior to the pedestrian timeframe coming out – giving her free parking – and would drive out before pedestrianisation ended. He also alleged that another councillor would park in the council car park for free when he was doing shopping, even though his party had a policy that other people using the town centre should pay to do so. When complaints were made against Person P this resulted in the police launching a formal investigation following serving a harassment letter, even seizing Person P's computer and mobile phone. The case even went as far as the Crown Prosecution Service, which brings criminal cases put to them by the police, being asked to take the case. The CPS refused to do so, yet Person P made clear he felt his privacy and home were "invaded."

Figure 1. Person G (left) looks more feminine and Person P (right) more masculine. Person G was treated more favourably by South Wales Police than Person P.

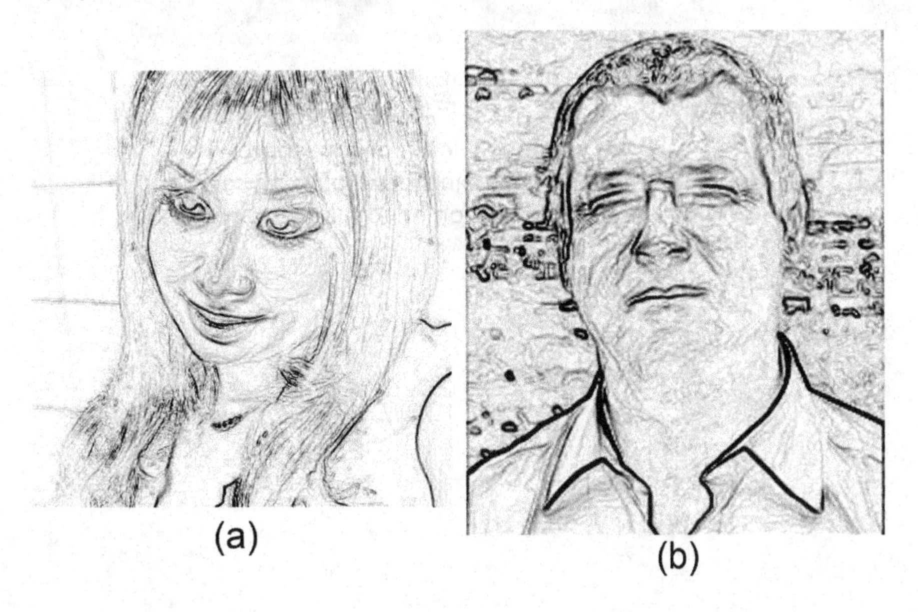

As can be seen from Figure 1, Person P looks much more masculine and rugged than Person G, who was treated more favourably than him. A set of circumstances similar to those of Person P happened with Person D, who is a local journalist. Whilst, as discussed earlier, allegations he made against others did not lead to charges, when less severe allegations were made against him about the content of his journalistic articles, he was charged by the police following being issued with a harassment notice from them. In this instance the CPS were not even consulted when charges were brought – following a woman politician alleging he harassed her, when he posted journalistic articles on a news website alleging that she was claiming to be a disability champion, yet was harassing disabled students. The case went as far as being heard before the local magistrates court, which hears criminal charges, but the Crown Prosecution Service refused to submit the evidence given to them by the police, stating it was not in the public interest to do so.

THE INVOLVEMENT OF SOCIAL MEDIA AND OTHER PLATFORMS

There have been ongoing calls for social media platforms to do more to enforce the statutory rights of citizens, with different platforms having different policies, and often acting in such a way that their policies are in their view above the law. Person G alleged that a video had been posted by Person D, which was not verifiable by the researcher, meaning it was either deleted, she was lying, or the police wrongly recorded her complaint. The abuse of Person D by Person B was verifiable, however, as can be seen from Figure 2. It is also evident to see from Figure 2 that even though Person D had blocked Person B that the latter was still able to post allegedly defamatory posts to others about him, in such a way that it could affect his reputation. It is noted that when a major story within Person D's competence there was no repeat call from the radio station concerned, as there had been on numerous other occasions.

Figure 2. The alleged defamatory statement by Person B to Person D

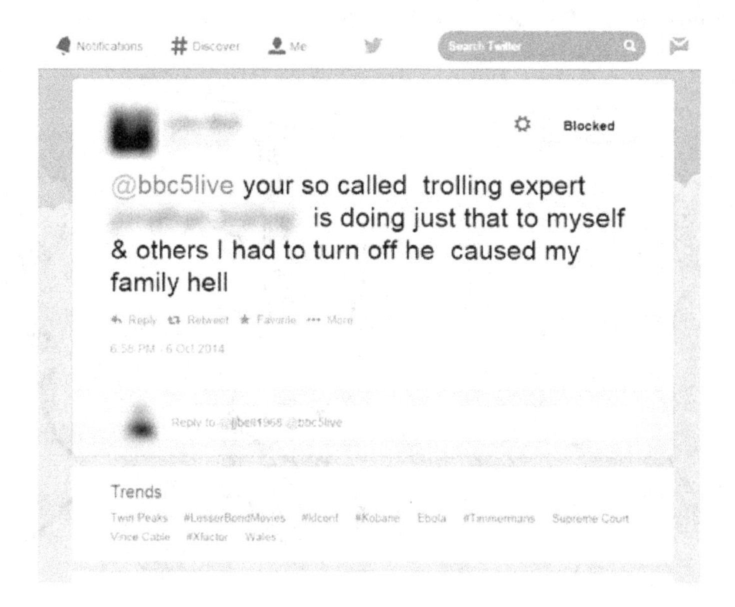

As can be seen from Figure 3 Twitter refused to remove the content alleged to be defamatory saying it was in their rules. Twitter also refused to provide the contact details of Person B to Person D as was his right under Section 5 of the Defamation Act 2013. The policy of Twitter was that those alleging abuse should get in touch with the police, which is totally unrealistic, given that they are expected to prioritise crime, of which Internet trolling may be seen simply as petty name calling.

Figure 3. Twitter's response to the report of the alleged defamatory post

Hello,

Thanks for letting us know about your issue. Here are some tips to help you with your situation:

- Do not respond to the user. We have found that responding to someone who is intentionally attempting to aggravate you or others encourages them to continue their behavior.
- Block the user. You can block the user using the blocking feature described here: https://support.twitter.com/articles/117063
- Learn more about how to deal with abusive users: https://support.twitter.com/articles/15794
- Learn how to flag inappropriate media here: https://support.twitter.com/articles/20069937

We've investigated the account and reported Tweets for abusive behavior, and have found that it's currently not violating the Twitter Rules (https://twitter.com/rules).

The actions of Twitter, as presented in Figure 3, shows that even where statute limits sysop prerogative (i.e. a website owner's right to make independent decisions), in this case, Section 5 of the Defamation Act 2013, which required Twitter to hand over the account information of someone accused of defamation, it does not follow that such a restriction in sysop prerogative will be honoured. It is not right, unlike Twitter expect, for the police authorities to be chasing Internet trolls, and so an alternative means of enforcing the restrictions to sysop prerogative made by legislatures, the courts, and indeed contracts and tortuous obligations, is needed. It therefore should be the case that reform of the police is necessary in order to not reduce the likelihood of benevolent sexism, as discussed earlier, but also to provide more affordable means of dealing with Internet abuse, rather than waste the time of highly paid police constables.

AN AGENDA FOR POLICE REFORM

Reforming the police to make them more fit more purpose has been one that has challenged many a Home Secretary. Rt Hon Michael Howard attempted to make the police focus on the victim of the crime, which failed because it simply allowed for stereotyped forms of victim to be given more attention over victims who are not culturally defined by vulnerability. Rt Hon Jack Straw attempted to focus on introducing simpler to administer penalties to reduce anti-social behaviour, including Anti-social Behaviour Orders and fixed penalty notices, which even though relevant for Internet trolling (Bishop, 2012; Bishop, 2013a; Bishop, 2013b), are rarely used when they could be. Rt Hon David Blunkett updated the sexual offences laws to cover technology-based crimes such as grooming and voyeurism, yet his laws played into the hands of benevolent sexists in the police as definitions of rape focussed on vaginal penetration of women, rather than any forced sexual act (i.e. obtained without informed consent), regardless of whether it was against a man or a woman, boy or girl. Rt Hon Theresa May's highly critical comments of the Police Federation of England and Wales, and tougher penalties for those who unlawfully kill police officers than those murdered in other groups sent out mixed messages. Indeed a predecessor, Shadow Home Secretary David Davis has been highly critical of Section 5 of the Public Order Act 1986, which allows police officials to prosecute anyone who uses foul language in their company. One of the first recorded prosecutions of trolling in Wales was that of Gavin Brent, whom the police had charged after he said to a police officer, "P.S. - D.C. Lloyd, God help your new-born baby." Brent was fined £150 with £364 costs awarded. Had the judgement of DPP v Chambers [2013] 1 W.L.R. 1833 (i.e. the Twitter joke trial) been in existence at the time, and had the case of DPP v Connolly [2008] 1 W.L.R. 276 been applied, it might be reasonable to expect Brent would have been acquitted because it should be expected that a public-facing police officer would be above normal fortitude and that such comments would not cause him apprehension. The fact that the police are bringing charges for offences against the police, when as can be seen from the police records found they have taken little action in the case of the public, then serious reforms need to be made to how the police's powers are distributed and how their officer's conduct is examined.

Reallocation of Police Officials into Local Authorities with Extended Remits for Community Safety and Support

It has long been established that sex discrimination is less in local government than in the private sector (S. P. Smith, 1976). Sex discrimination is grounded in the universal idea that men and women are inherently more capable at particular kinds of work, thereby validating gender roles and sex stereotypes, and sustaining gendered professions that lead to inequality (Sellers, 2014). It is no

Table 1. Positions within South Wales Police and their respective salaries

Level	SFIA Role	Police Position	L Grade	L Salary	U Grade	U Salary
1	Follow	New Constables	0	£19,191.00	7	£36,885.00
2	Assist	Constables	1	£23,493.00	11	£36,885.00
3	Apply	Sergeants	15	£38,145.00	18	£41,451.00
4	Enable	Inspectors	19	£47,256.00	22	£51,258.00
5	Ensure, advise	Chief Inspectors	23	£52,308.00	26	£55,350.00
6	Initiate, influence	Superintendents	32	£62,922.00	36	£74,322.00
7	Set strategy, inspire, mobilise	Chief Superintendents	38	£77,988.00	40	£82,272.00

Data obtained from a FOI request to South Wales Police

wonder, therefore, that this study found that there is sexism in the police, where there are expectations of the police having physical strength, which they assume is not the case of women, whom they perceive as vulnerable. This section shows how the integration of the police into local authorities can have many of the benefits of sex equality that exists within local government.

Integrating the Police into the Local Authority Structure

It has been argued that the creation of public relations units in the police can have either the effect of increasing the connection between law enforcement officials and the public, or provide an easy excuse for those officers seeking to offload their duties to engage with the public (Thibault & Lynch, 1985). Table 1 shows the pay grades and associated salaries as they apply to the various ranks of police constable.

As can be seen from Table 1 and Table 2, the differences in pay between the council workers and police service works is phenomenal. A New Constable who does mainly street patrol duties can earn up to £36,855, which is over twice (2.17) what a Civil Enforcement Officer working for a local authority is paid. Equally a full Police Constable starts their salary at £23,493, which is over £4,000 more (21.62%) than a Streetcare Enforcement Warden doing a similar job, who is paid £19,317. A Police Inspector can earn up to £51,258, which is nearly twice (1.77) that of a Technical Officer, whom does the same management duties of an Inspector. A Chief Inspector can earn up to £55,350, which is £26,428 (52.25%) more than that of a Senior Technical Officer doing a similar job. A Superintendent has a starting salary of £62,922, which is nearly twice (1.96) as much as a Senior Team Leader, who earns £32,072. Finally, a Chief Superintendent who earns up to £82,272, is paid over twice (2.36) that of the equivalent Senior Officer of a local authority, which is £34,894.

Table 2 and Table 3 therefore show that moving the police service into the local authority structure can save the taxpayer around 50% of what is currently being paid. As can be seen from Table 3, among the different levels of autonomy, complexity and seniority are three labels based on the cultural acceptance of police ranks. The term, 'Bobby,' is the name for a police constable who patrols the street, so named after Robert Peel who created them (Victor & Dalzell, 2014). In this case of this new model, a Bobby represents those people who do foot patrols and are the first point of contact with members of the public. The single grade above them is the 'Sarge,' which at present is short for sergeant (Victor & Dalzell, 2014).

Table 2. Positions within Rhondda Cynon Taf CBC and their respective salaries

Level	SFIA Role	Council Position	Grade	Salary
1	Follow	Civil Enforcement Officer	5	£16,998
2	Assist	Streetcare Enforcement Warden	6	£19,317
3	Apply	Technical Officer	8	£28,922
4	Enable	Streetcare Enforcement Officer	9	£26,539
5	Ensure, advise	Senior Technical Officer	10	£28,922
6	Initiate, influence	Senior Team Leader	11	£32,072
7	Set strategy, inspire, mobilise	Senior Officer	12	£34,894

Data obtained from a FOI request to Rhondda Cynon Taf CBC

Whereas under this system bobbies would only be able to detain members of the public who might be suspected of an offence, it would be only a 'Sarge' who could give authority to arrest them should they refuse to co-operate or need to be questioned under caution. After both the Bobby and the Sarge is what is called the 'Super.' In the police as it exists, 'Super' is short for superintendent (Victor & Dalzell, 2014), but in the case of the proposed model it would be sort for supervisor. Use of these terms would ensure the integration of police officials into the local authority structure, and provide re-assurance to the public that the Community Support Officers that replace constables and PCSOs are still the 'Bobbies' that their elected politicians claim to create more of in order to secure their votes.

The roles of 'Inspector' that form part of the current police system would be transferred to the newly created National Crime Agency. These inspectors would need to take examinations to become the equivalent of a FBI agent in the USA and would become part of the proposed 'Territorial Agency,' along with other members of Criminal Investigation Departments and the Territorial Army part of the current Army Reserves. This would create specialists to deal with high level crime with a complexity that council officials could not be expected to deal with, such as homicide and serious sexual assaults. Whilst

Table 3. Proposed integration of policing officials into local authority pay structures and positions

Level	Position	SFIA Role	£ Salary	£ L Saving (%)	£ U Saving (%)
1 (Bobby)	1st Line Community Support Officer	Follow	16,998	2,193.00 (11.4)	19,887.00 (53.9)
2 (Bobby)	2nd Line Community Support Officer	Assist	19,317	4,176.00 (17.8)	17,568.00 (47.6)
3 (Bobby)	3rd Line Community Support Officer	Apply	28,922	9,223.00 (24.2)	12,529.00 (30.2)
4 (Sarge)	Senior Community Support Officer	Enable	26,539	20,717.00 (43.8)	24,719.00 (48.2)
5 (Super)	Senior Technical Officer	Ensure, advise	28,922	23,386.00 (44.7)	26,428.00 (47.7)
6 (Super)	Senior Team Leader	Initiate, influence	32,072	30,850.00 (49.0)	42,250.00 (56.8)
7 (Super)	Senior Officer	Strategy, inspire, mobilise	34,894	43,094.00 (55.3)	47,378.00 (57.6)

Figure 4. An approach to community support based on dualism

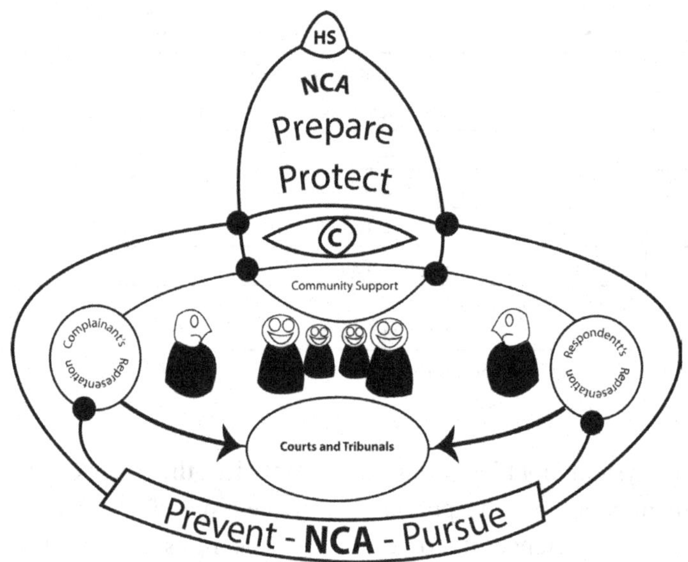

Bobbies might deal with forms of Internet trolling that amount to no more than petty name calling, the more serious forms of Internet trolling that affect national and homeland sexurity – such as extremist language intended to encourage acts of terror – would form part of the National Crime Agency's counter-terrorism arm.

It is important therefore to look in more detail at how this new system of Bobbies, a Sarge and Supers would work. It is argued that these can be understood best through the prisms of the Skills Framework in the Information Age (SFIA+), which provides structured job role descriptions.

Table 4. Proposed job roles for a newly reformed law enforcement personnel structure for 1st and 2nd line CSOs

Position and Details	Duties	Skills Needed
1st Line Community Support Officer (1stCSO) (Level 1: Follow) [Bobby] {Service desk and incident management}	Following agreed procedures, receives requests for support and provides routine advice. Promptly allocates reports which require response from more experienced colleagues, as appropriate. Follows standard procedures, documenting incidents, progress checking.	Has good oral communication skills and takes an analytical approach to problem solving. Completed Secondary Education (to A level, International Baccalaureate or equivalent standard).
2nd Line Community Support Officer (2ndCSO) (Level 2: Assist) [Bobby] {Service desk and incident management}	Following agreed procedures, receives and handles requests for information, and provides routine advice. Following agreed procedures, receives and handles requests for support, provides information to enable problem resolution. Provides an effective interface between public and authorities, including documenting incidents, progress checking.	Experience in a Task requiring customer contact would be advantageous. Has good oral communication skills and takes an analytical approach to problem solving. Completed Secondary Education (to A level, International Baccalaureate or equivalent standard).

Reforming Community Support

It has been put that the creation of community relations units in the police, recently manifested with Partnership and rTogether initiatives, can better achieve effective public relations management and reduction in crime (Thibault & Lynch, 1985). Figure 4 presents a model of how a network of practice for effective law enforcement could exist that brings together different law enforcement agencies to ensure that the rights of the people are upheld. All the personnel identified in Table 3 would be in the part of the diagram marked 'Community Support,' which would be co-ordinated by local authorities initially. As can be seen, these work close with the Police and Crime Commissioner marked 'C,' who would have to give approval for the National Crime Agency to carry out operations. Equally, all agencies would have to cooperate with the solicitors who represent a complainant and a respondent, for whom disputes may be resolved before going to court.

In terms of the first two Bobbies, their roles would resemble those referred to in SFIA as 'Service desk and incident management.' The responsibilities of such persons includes to promptly allocate queries as appropriate and maintain relevant records. Considering the 1st Line Community Support Officer (1stCSO) as presented in Table 4 it can be seen that their role is to follow the lead set my more senior officers in terms of how they complete their duties. It is known that sex equality policies structured around formal elements which address, discrimination in recruitment, promotion and grading, as well as informal elements that address discrimination elements in an organisation (Margetts, 1996). Therefore it would be more possible for a low-skilled 1stCSO to focus on following an effective equality policy than it would for an overqualified police constable.

Table 5 presents the job roles for the officers at Level 3 and Level 4. These are the 3rd Line Community Support Officer (3rdCSO) and the 4th line one (4thCSO) respectively.

Table 5. Proposed job roles for a newly reformed law enforcement personnel structure for 3rd and 4th line CSOs

Position and Details	Duties	Skills Needed
3rd Line Community Support Officer (3rdCSO) (Level 3: Apply) [Bobby] {Service desk and incident management}	Following agreed procedures, provides advice to available options. Responds to requests for support by providing information to enable incident resolution. Provides an effective interface between users and service providers, including external commercial suppliers where applicable. This interface includes documenting incidents, progress checking, and ensuring all diagnostic information is provided for error resolution and incident analysis.	Has achieved proficiency at Level 2 in Service desk and incident management. Has good oral communication skills and takes an analytical approach to problem solving. Probably educated to bachelor degree level or holds a relevant professional qualification.
Senior Community Support Officer (4thCSO) (Level 4: Enable) [Serge] {Stakeholder relationship management}	Engages with stakeholders to seek and record their opinions about products and services supplied. Assesses feedback to help measure effectiveness of stakeholder management, and highlights issues which need to be addresses Works with stakeholders, seeking to develop and enhance relationships. Implements communications strategies, including, for example; handling of complaints; problems and issues; managing resolutions; corrective actions and lessons learned; collection and appropriate dissemination of relevant information appropriately	Probably educated to bachelor degree level or holds a relevant professional qualification. Has knowledge of, a major Service provision Skill and the operational flows of the organisation. Demonstrates up to date knowledge of the organisation's environment, organisational relationships, processes, and reporting. Displays good inter-personal skills, demonstrating the ability to relate to stakeholders in their own language. Has change management experience.

The SFIA framework would suggest a 3rdCSO should be in the 'service desk and incident management' category. This indicates this role involves acquiring a proper understanding of a problem or situation, identifying gaps in the available information required to understand a problem or situation, and also devising means of remedying such gaps. Failures of the police to understand the needs of their communities are nowhere more apparent than with the Israeli National Police. It has been found as a result of this that where the police have an inaccurate understanding of citizen priorities, they may choose to emphasise aggressive crime control at the expense of procedural fairness in their work and claims to legitimacy, which may ultimately weaken their legitimacy in the eyes of the public (Jonathan-Zamir & Harpaz, 2014). This makes it clear, therefore, that the specialisation of a 3rdCSO that focuses on ensuring the proper application of law and procedure would prevent such failings in the Israeli National Police being a problem in Western police forces. Another important part of a 3rdCSO would be communicating effectively in order to establish relationships and maintaining contacts with people from a variety of backgrounds and to be an effective and sensitive communicator in different societies and cultures. It has been argued that police reforms since the 1970s have largely focused on weakening the police subculture and restoring police-community relations (Nhan, 2014). The creation of a 3rdCSO position on this basis, therefore, could increase trust between law enforcement and the public because the role would involve the balancing of community interests more generally with those obligations placed on them by government, such as local councillors.

The role of the 4thCSO, which is the most senior community support officer, equivalent to a sergeant, would fit in the SFIA category of 'stakeholder relationship management.' This means they are responsible for collecting and using feedback from the public and other stakeholders in order to help measure effectiveness of stakeholder management. The 4thCSO would be the only official with the power to arrest and charge, achieving this specification is essential. It is not surprising therefore that such an office holder would be required to be education to degree level in addition to significant experience. The intellectual development that comes from doing a degree would assist in achieving greater accuracy in decision making. In the current policing system, sergeants are in a position of conflict, caught between their responsibility to superior officers and their responsibility for subordinate officers (Engel, 2001). A 4thCSO would thus be concerned more with the administering of justice, looking beyond simply the concerns of the complainant and defence of the respondent, and considering the wider community, as any council official should be expected to do. The number of people arrested with the authority of a 4thCSO should be less than with police constables at present, as the 1stCSOs, 2ndCSOs would only have the power to detain. The judgement of the 4thCSO, therefore, would focus on the bigger picture, such as the opportunity cost of dealing with one crime to the exclusion of another, meaning charging for an offence would be based not on meeting targets, but improving outcomes for community members. Internet trolling offences, therefore, may not be high on the agenda, unless there is actually danger to a person's wellbeing, as was the case when Person B was outside the house of Person D, which was accompanied by Internet trolling. Many online threats are empty threats, as established by DPP v Chambers [2013] 1 W.L.R. 1833, for instance.

A 4thCSO might, according to SFIA, need to help develop and enhance relationships between all stakeholders including the public and to implement a communications strategy. In addition a 4thCSO, in accordance with SFIA, should be responsible for the handling of complaints, problems and issues, as well as managing resolutions, taking corrective actions and learning lessons in addition to ensuring the collection and dissemination of relevant information appropriately.

REFORMING THE ADMINISTRATIVE AND MANAGEMENT STRUCTURE OF THE POLICE AND LOCAL AUTHORITIES

It has been argued that there is little difference between a person being a police chief or owner of a bakery, because all involve the same knowledge, skills and abilities, requiring both to engage in planning of the organisation (Cordner, 2014). However, it has also been argued that there needs to be a clear line of command in a police organisations, where there is often absence of a chief executive officer (Cordner, 2014). These apparently irreconcilable options make even more so the case that integrating the police into a local authority structure, where there is a clearly identifiable chief executive and democratic accountability through elected councillors. Supporting the integration into this structure of superintendents, and where appropriate inspectors, is therefore essential.

As can be seen from Table 6, the role of the Senior Technical Officer, which is the first level of Supervisor (i.e. 1stSuper), would be paired to the SFIA Level 5 role of 'senior level management.' Such a person would therefore ensurs that service delivery meets agreed service levels and negotiate service level requirements and agree service levels. Other parts of this SFIA role include creating and maintaining a catalogue of available services, diagnosing service delivery problems, initiating actions to maintain or improve levels of service and establishing and maintaining operational methods, procedures and facilities in an assigned area of responsibility and reviewing them regularly for effectiveness and efficiency. This therefore requires the use of fact-finding processes in order to generate evidence that identifies community problems and issues that will need to be dealt with (Butler, 1992). The fact that the police already work with local authorities through Partnership and Community Together (PACT) schemes would mean that instead of one or the other passing the buck, it will be the same council official that would be responsible, rather than there being 'opposite numbers' in the council and police respectively.

Table 6. Proposed job roles for a newly reformed law enforcement personnel structure for 1st line Supervisors

Position and Details	Duties	Skills Needed
Senior Technical Officer (1stSuper) (Level 5: Ensure, advise) [Super] {Service Level management}	Liaises with authorities to establish the structure of service level agreements (SLAs). Ensures that operational methods, procedures, and facilities are documented, maintained and reviewed regularly to maintain their effectiveness and efficiency. Negotiates and manages stakeholder expectations and perceptions in order to optimise satisfaction. Regularly reviews Operational Level Agreements, and/or underpinning agreements to ensure that they are in line with SLA targets. Liaises with those responsible for problem management in the diagnosis and resolution of service problems, ensuring that account is taken of agreed levels of service. Initiates action to maintain or improve levels of service, referring issues to higher levels of management as required. Monitors levels of service performance, ensures detailed metrics and records are kept and analysed, provides adequate, accurate and timely reports, to Customers and providers and initiates appropriate action to resolve issues involving other service management processes as necessary. Monitors the effectiveness of all service level management tools and processes in use.	Probably educated to bachelor degree level or holds a relevant professional qualification. Has an extensive understanding of relevant financial principles and procedures including cross charging both internal and external to the organisation. Has the ability to lead teams of staff successfully, when handling complex or high impact problems. Has substantial experience of dealing with the public, specialists and service providers. Is skilled in conducting meetings and team management.

As can be seen from Table 7, the Senior Team Leader, which is the 2nd Supervisor (2ndSuper), takes on a change management role. In the case of the SFIA criteria, this involves them setting the organisation's policy for the management of change in live services and test environments, and ensures that the policy is reflected in practice. In the context of the police, policies go beyond being procedures, rules and regulations, and reflect the purpose and philosophy of the organisation that guide thinking (Cordner, 2014). Such thinking on sex equality is clearly more able to be achieved in a local authority structure where the 'team leader' ethos exists over superintendent position which is more status driven. This includes because it has been argued that the management philosophy and structure of a police organisation, such as whether it is 'top down' or 'bottom up,' will have a significant impact on its effectiveness (Butler, 1992). Indeed, it has been argued that it is no longer expected that superintendents take the role of middle managers, protected within a huge bureaucracy, as they are now required to function as key local political players in negotiating with a range of authorities and reacting quickly to trouble (Stenson, 2013). The local authority structure therefore is more appropriate to achieve this, as it already has strong partnerships lines of communication with various agencies.

As can be seen from Table 8, the role of the Senior Officer (3rdSuper), which replaces chief superintendents, takes on a programme management role. In the case of SFIA this includes setting the organisational strategy governing the direction and conduct of programme management, including application of appropriate methodologies. Such a role in the police focusses more on the technology and systems of the organisation, and how these connect to the attainment of goals and objectives (Cordner, 2014). In the current system, each member of the police service holds the same "office" of constable, but may have a different rank, such as a chief superintendent, who is a constable with the rank of chief superintendent (Baxter, 1996). It therefore makes more sense that their

Table 7. Proposed job roles for a newly reformed law enforcement personnel structure for 2nd line Supervisors

Position and Details	Duties	Skills Needed
Senior Technical Officer (1stSuper) (Level 5: Ensure, advise) [Super] {Service Level management}	Liaises with authorities to establish the structure of service level agreements (SLAs). Ensures that operational methods, procedures, and facilities are documented, maintained and reviewed regularly to maintain their effectiveness and efficiency. Negotiates and manages stakeholder expectations and perceptions in order to optimise satisfaction. Regularly reviews Operational Level Agreements, and/or underpinning agreements to ensure that they are in line with SLA targets. Liaises with those responsible for problem management in the diagnosis and resolution of service problems, ensuring that account is taken of agreed levels of service. Initiates action to maintain or improve levels of service, referring issues to higher levels of management as required. Monitors levels of service performance, ensures detailed metrics and records are kept and analysed, provides adequate, accurate and timely reports, to Customers and providers and initiates appropriate action to resolve issues involving other service management processes as necessary. Monitors the effectiveness of all service level management tools and processes in use.	Probably educated to bachelor degree level or holds a relevant professional qualification. Has an extensive understanding of relevant financial principles and procedures including cross charging both internal and external to the organisation. Has the ability to lead teams of staff successfully, when handling complex or high impact problems. Has substantial experience of dealing with the public, specialists and service providers. Is skilled in conducting meetings and team management.

Table 8. Proposed job roles for a newly reformed law enforcement personnel structure for 2nd line Supervisors

Position and Details	Duties	Skills Needed
Senior Officer (3rdSuper) (Level 7: Set strategy, inspire, mobilise) [Super] {Programme management}	Determines, monitors, and reviews all economics, including costs, projected costs of ownership (including operational costs), staffing requirements, resources, and ensuring that there are appropriate and effective governance arrangements, supported by comprehensive reporting. Ensures the implementation of changes which achieve the objectives that have been set, meets real business needs and measurably improves service and business value. Ensures that the organisation and its staff are managed carefully through the process of change. Ensures that progress is monitored and reviewed throughout this process, and that adjustments are made, as necessary, to achieve the planned results. Manages programme change, through regular reassessment of priorities, resolving resource conflicts, and authorising additions, deletions or modifications. Initiates formal reviews of the programme and its achievements, to assess critically the work carried out and benefits obtained. Evaluates changes to management practices and initiates improvement to organisation practices.	Knows own organisation's policy framework, management structures and reporting procedures for all aspects of the programme's development and operational environment. Has excellent planning, communication and presentation skills, and is expert in project quality management. Is expert in business case development and benefits realisation. Educated to bachelor degree level. May have a postgraduate qualification such as an MSc, MBA, or other business or scientific qualification.

role follows the organisational structure of the local authority, where their powers reflect their duties, which is administrative and strategic as opposed to the day-to-day powers needed by community law enforcers, such as the power to detain, arrest and charge. A 3rdSuper would also take on the SFIA rules of planning, directing and co-ordinating activities to manage and implement complex programmes and to authorise the selection and planning of all related projects and activities. It has been argued that in the case of the police that clear coordination control has been needed at this level (Cordner, 2014), which is something not absent in local authorities. The SFIA framework also says that this role involves the planning, scheduling, monitoring, and reporting of activities related to the programme, ensuring that there are appropriate and effective governance arrangements, supported by comprehensive reporting. This is also common in the equivalent police role, where the holder schedules meetings, whilst also making decisions in-between meetings where required (Cordner, 2014).

REFORMING CRIMINAL AND CIVIL PROCEDURE

Some less serious offences, such as allegations of harassment and other offences by social media could be more effectively managed through alternative dispute resolution (ADR) through legal aid funded solicitors and arbitrators as well as the involvement of 3rd Line Community Support Officers. ADR should perhaps become "ODR" – ordinary dispute resolution – with recourse to the civil and criminal courts for community level crime being named "SDR" – special dispute resolution. It may be that if ODR is unsuccessful that SDR could be used so that where there is a statute of limitation that these should count from when the ODR is commenced, so that legal action is not brought because it is necessary to keep within those limits. At present the only option available to the police not wanting to waste time bringing senseless prosecutions of Internet trolling is to transfer the reported case to the local authority's community safety department so that action such as serving anti-social behaviour orders (ASBOs) can be done, which is an effective method for dealing with Internet trolling (Bishop, 2012; Bishop, 2013a; Bishop, 2013b). As ASBOs do not give someone a criminal record – unless they break it and are subsequently convicted – this may be a possible outcome where an ODR service fails or is not possible, which is an alternative to going straight to the SDR, which often helps no one.

REFORMING LOCAL GOVERNMENT TO ACCOMMODATE THE POLICE

A fault with the current policing system is the representation of rank through the uniform and associated appendages. Such symbolic representations are considered by some to be bordering on fascism (Cullen, 1993; Hall, 1952). Indeed, this may be considered to be the same in all other uniformed professions where the uniform reflects status rather than purpose. For instance the badges worn by military personnel would fit this definition of fascism, whereas the uniforms used by nurses reflect their role. It would therefore be appropriate that all of the CSOs referred to in this paper wear a uniform that identifies them as law enforcement officials, whilst not conferring any rank. Such ranks should instead be reflected through certifications, in the same way other qualifications are, such as in the membership statuses of professional bodies. A law enforcement official should confer authority through how they engage with the public and peers and not any visual representation of rank or other status. Whilst the loss of rank would likely be disliked by the police being transferred to local authorities, being given pieces of paper (i.e. certificates) instead, it would help convey they are working towards crime prevention where the ideal outcome should be that their role becomes redundant.

RECRUITMENT AND SELECTION OF OFFICERS

In order to avoid any discriminatory attitudes, it is necessary to screen officers at the recruitment and selection stage. This can be problematic, as crude examinations can either result in dishonest people acing the exam or people with specific needs failing them unfairly (Cordner, 2014). Indeed, in the context of police recruitment via exams it has been argued that "Generic traits are necessary for effective performance in almost any professional or managerial position and include the ability to communicate orally with sensitivity and a sense of authority to make decisions, to work with many different types of others, and to solve problems under stress and within severe constraints of time and resources" (Thibault & Lynch, 1985). Yet in Australia it has been found that specialised police selection tests such as the Candidate and Officer Personnel Survey (COPS) have been developed, and used, with considerable success (Lough & Ryan, 2010). It is quite clear that in dispensing with inspectors and chief inspectors from community policing and into the National Crime Agency, that prior to the transfer they should be required to sit exams to take on a role that is in essence identical to an FBI agent, which would also be administered to those joining the NCA directly.

FUNDING OF LAW ENFORCEMENT

It was argued in the 1980s that the success of the police management in future would be on the effectiveness of their day-to-day budgeting, as a result of public spending cuts (Thibault & Lynch, 1985), which is no more relevant than today. At present the police in the UK are funded from the precept, which is a type of municipal tax (R. Crawford & Disney, 2012). This is the same with local authorities, but the precept, administered in the form of 'council tax,' based on the property type of the tax payers is unpopular and ineffective. It might therefore be appropriate for a pay-as-you-go model to be introduced where those who use a service are the ones whom pay for it. This could mean that CSOs are funded by premises that should require them, such as public houses. Those court service workers who perform security checks prior to admission, the 'doormen' who are at the doors of clubs and bars, and those who operate security logistics, such as for the banks, among others, could also be replaced with CSOs employed by the local authority. It is argued that having an effective security presence at the door of bar or club offers a practical solution to avoiding drunken or weapon carrying customers entering (Rivera, 2010), but sometimes this results in prejudices leading door staff to exclude people on discriminatory grounds in the same way the police investigated in this study did. It may thus be more effective for such bars to be compelled to hire their door staff from the local council in the form of a CSO. This would mean they are accountable to the public more generally though such elected bodies, meaning the complaints procedures associated with those can be used should they be treated unfavourably.

The funding of the police on this basis bears little resemblance to the day-to-day budgeting in the 1980s (Thibault & Lynch, 1985), and thus it would make more sense for the funding of community law enforcement to be based more on the demand for the particular kind of enforcement. It might be that whilst much of the police component of the precept could simply be transferred to local authorities, that many law enforcement services could be a statutory requirement for some businesses. Business rates from local authorities are currently unfair, because some businesses will pay more than their fair share and others less (Bennett, 1986). The notion of 'polluter pays' is thus one that would be most effectively introduced to fund the police on a demand-led basis. A public house could have a statutory requirement to pay for a 1st Line Community Support Officer (1stCSO) in place of traditional door staff, meaning the effective enforcement of licensing and other laws, such as the requirement to not sell alcohol to someone who is intoxicated, and public order offences respectively. Providing the 1stCSOs are regularly rotated to avoid 'pallyness' then this may be more effective than the use of 'bouncers' directly employed by the establishment.

REFORMING THE SECURITY INDUSTRY AUTHORITY TO REGULATE ALL LAW ENFORCEMENT OFFICERS

Whether one is talking about the police in relation to the MacPherson Inquiry's finding of institutional racism, or this study's findings in relation to institutional sexism, it is clear that there is a lack of professionalism in the police service. Indeed, in 2014 severe criticisms were made of the Police Federation by the Home Secretary, Theresa May. Criticisms have also been levied at the current police complaints system, where complaints against police officers are investigated by that police officer's colleagues. Indeed, in the case of Person D, they made a complaint against the officer from South Wales Police who investigated them, and the complaint was not upheld, even though the Crown Prosecution Service threw out the case against Person D that was put together by that officer.

The Home Office are also looking into reform of the Security Industry Authority to play a greater role in the regulation of security professionals. The SIA is a non-departmental public body that was established in April 2014 and administers the distribution of "personal licences" to all "fit and proper" private security providers (A. Crawford & Lister, 2006; Lister, Hadfield, Hobbs, & Winlow, 2001). It may therefore be seen as an appropriate body for the regulation of all law enforcement personnel, such as the CSOs discussed in this chapter.

According to the SIA some 91,000 private security employees were licensed by it across England and Wales by the end of March 2006 (A. Crawford & Lister, 2006). Expanding to cover council law enforcement staff, including those transferred from the police, then it could ensure that the lack of faith in law enforcement is addressed. As the SIA already has responsibility for regulating those persons using CCTV, it might be that it would be effective at ensuring the stability of the dualist approach to community law enforcement presented in Figure 4, by regulating the members of the National Crime Agency workers as well, especially in relation to inevitable data retention laws, where it is important to make sure such data is not misused. Whilst many are critical of data retention by the government, even though it is done unchecked by the corporations, this could serve to deter crime in the first place, as every solicitor would have the right to request the NCA provide access to records that support the claims of their clients. Organisations currently under the control of the state, like the Police Advisory Board for England and Wales, the Police Discipline Appeals Tribunal and the Police Remuneration Review Body could be transferred to this new independent professional body. Aspects of the Police Federation that are still funded by the state could also form part of it. By the SIA being fully independent of the state, perhaps based on a Royal Charter to allow for professionalisation of the security industry, it would be more able to advise the Home Secretary in these and other areas, without the delinquency one sees in the Police Federation, which is run by the police themselves. Bodies such as the Independent Police Complaints Commission and the Professional Standards Boards of individual police authorities could be split between this body and Police and Crime Commisioners (PCCs). Those complaints relating to the conduct of individual law enforcement officers would be the jurisdiction of the reformed SIA, whereas other complaints, such as about how the police as a whole handled a given report of alleged crime would be dealt with by the directly elected PCCs.

IMPLICATIONS AND FUTURE RESEARCH DIRECTIONS

This chapter has shown clear evidence to support the claim that the police are treating women as trolling victims more often than men, which results in men being treated less favourably than women. A solution has been proposed in this chapter to transfer the powers of the police to local authorities that promote a culture of equality, with a cost saving of 50 percent on wages, and possibly savings through avoiding duplication of other services. Future research will have to consider whether further reform, such as transferring local authority law enforcement powers to Police and Crime Commissioners, would improve the overall strategy for law enforcement. This chapter did not investigate the role of police commanders, and so it might need to be further considered that whether such persons should become 'Deputy Police and Crime Commissioners' directly appointed by and accountable to the elected Commissioner, or be abolished all together. It is thus clear that an agenda of making law enforcement personnel accountable to politicians will ensure pressure is put on them to carry out their duties effectively and without discrimination. It has been strongly put that police are "accountable to the law" and must apply the law but not see themselves as above it (Savage, 1984). This seemed absent in this study in the case of the handling of the complaint against Person D by Person T where although the arresting constable was a liaison officer, and Person T's workplace's policy said they should resolve their complaint, the full weight of the law was launched against Person D. Indeed, the officers that charged Person D did not refer to guidance on Internet trolling set by the CPS (Starmer, 2013), meaning court time was wasted, as the CPS withdrew the case because it did not meet the evidential requirements set out in that guidance. The extent of the 'Thin-Blue Web,' where police reporting of offences go unchecked, may only have been touched on in a minor way by this study, with the problem being far more substantial.

DISCUSSION

This chapter has investigated the existence of 'benevolent sexism' within the South Wales Police area, which as a result of chivalrous attitudes that have manifested in the form of 'institutional sexism.' The MacPherson Inquiry introduced the concept of institutional discrimination, showing how the way an organisation is made of persons with similar attitudes can result in a systematic, even if independent, discriminatory provision towards groups to which that attitude relates. Whilst the MacPherson report looked at the attitudes of the London Metropolitan Police to persons who are of Afro-Caribbean descent or otherwise ethnic minorities, this study has shown that a similar negative attitude exists in South Wales Police to Caucasian men accused of harassment or other offences arising out of social media. Collectively this police force in a former coalfields community, is made up of men who see women in a chivalrous sense, which is that they need protecting from other men. These would-be 'knights in shining armour' treat men accused of harassment less favourably than they do women accused of the same offences. Equally they will treat allegations of trolling against men less seriously than alleged cases of trolling against women. There appears to be an attitude that women need "protecting" whereas men should "just get over it," even where those men are vulnerable adults. Through establishing that there is a clear bias in favour of women complainants and respondents within South Wales Police specifically, policy makers should take action to ensure that law enforcement in relation to Internet trolling is carried out in an objective and unbiased manner for all protected characteristics and not just in support of allegations made by women.

This chapter has suggested the way in which to end benevolent sexism in the police is for their powers to be transferred to local authorities, where equality is stronger and the culture is not based around the rank a worker is at, but their duties and responsibilities. The various ranks of the police would be integrated into the council and whilst the police's precept would be integrated into that of the local authority, there would need to be new measures, such as statutory requirements for public houses to pay the council to provide a community support officer (CSO) to ensure their compliance with the law.

ACKNOWLEDGMENT

The author would like to recognise the support of South Wales Police in accessing the materials used in this study. In particular he would like to thank the responding officers for their co-operation. Particular thanks are due to PC Tim Davies and Sgt John Simmons of Cardiff Bay Police Station, whose involvement in sourcing the data for the study was essential. Thanks are also due to PC Gavin Haines of Pontypridd Police Station who was involved in case study into Twitter in this chapter.

REFERENCES

Ali, S., & Shahwar, D. (2011). Men, women and TV ads: The representation of men and women in the advertisements of pakistani electronic media. *Journal of Media and Communication Studies*, *3*(4), 151–159.

Allen, L. (2014). URL badman (Audio CD ed.). London, GB: Parlophone UK.

Averdijk, M., & Elffers, H. (2012). The discrepancy between survey-based victim accounts and police reports revisited. *International Review of Victimology*, *18*(2), 91–107. doi:10.1177/0269758011432955

Bartlett, A., & Henderson, M. (2013). *Things that liberate: An australian feminist wunderkammer*. Newcastle, GB: Cambridge Scholars Publishing.

Baxter, N. (1996). Constitutionally, can police officers be replaced by soldiers in times of crisis. *The Police Journal*, *69*, 119.

Bennett, R. J. (1986). The impact of Non-Domestic rates on profitability and investment. *Fiscal Studies*, *7*(1), 34–50. doi:10.1111/j.1475-5890.1986.tb00412.x

Bishop, J. (2012). Tackling internet abuse in great britain: Towards a framework for classifying severities of 'flame trolling'. *The 11th International Conference on Security and Management (SAM'12)*. Las Vegas, NV.

Bishop, J. (2013a). The art of trolling law enforcement: A review and model for implementing 'flame trolling' legislation enacted in great britain (1981–2012). *International Review of Law Computers & Technology*, *27*(3), 301–318. doi:10.1080/13600869.2013.796706

Bishop, J. (2013b). The effect of deindividuation of the internet troller on criminal procedure implementation: An interview with a hater. *International Journal of Cyber Criminology*, *7*(1), 28–48.

Bishop, J. (2013c). Increasing capital revenue in social networking communities: Building social and economic relationships through avatars and characters. In J. Bishop (Ed.), *Examining the concepts, issues, and implications of internet trolling* (pp. 44–61). Hershey, PA: IGI Global. doi:10.4018/978-1-4666-2803-8.ch005

Bishop, J. (2013d). The psychology of trolling and lurking: The role of defriending and gamification for increasing participation in online communities using seductive narratives. In J. Bishop (Ed.), *Examining the concepts, issues and implications of internet trolling* (pp. 106–123). Hershey, PA: IGI Global. doi:10.4018/978-1-4666-2803-8.ch009

Bishop, J. (2014a). 'U r bias love:' Using 'bleasure' and 'motif' as forensic linguistic means to annotate twitter and newsblog comments for the purpose of multimedia forensics. *Proceedings of the 11th International Conference on Web Based Communities and Social Media.* Lisbon, PT.

Bishop, J. (2014b). 'YouTube if you want to, the lady's not for blogging': Using 'bleasures' and 'motifs' to support multimedia forensic analyses of harassment by social media. *Oxford Cyber Harassment Research Symposium*. Oxford, GB.

Bishop, J. (2014c). Representations of 'trolls' in mass media communication: A review of media-texts and moral panics relating to 'internet trolling'. *International Journal of Web Based Communities*, *10*(1), 7–24. doi:10.1504/IJWBC.2014.058384

Bishop, J. (2014d). Using the legal concepts of 'forensic linguistics,' 'bleasure' and 'motif' to enhance multimedia forensics. *Proceedings of the 13th International Conference on Security and Management (SAM'14)*. Las Vegas, NV.

Buckel, E. E., Trapnell, P. D., & Paulhus, D. L. (2014). *Trolls just want to have fun. Personality and Individual Differences, Butler, A. J. P. (1992). Police management*. Aldershot, GB: Dartmouth Publishing Company Limited.

Cordner, G. W. (2014). *Police administration* (S. Decker-Lucke, E. S. Boyne, & J. Haynes, Eds.). 8th ed.). Waltham, MA: Anderson Publishing.

Crawford, A., & Lister, S. (2006). Additional security patrols in residential areas: Notes from the marketplace. *Policing and Society*, *16*(02), 164–188. doi:10.1080/10439460600662189

Crawford, R., & Disney, R. (2012). *Reform of ill-health retirement benefits for police in england and wales: The roles of national policy and local finance. (No. w18479)*. Cambridge, MA: National Bureau of Economic Research. doi:10.3386/w18479

Cullen, S. M. (1993). Political violence: The case of the british union of fascists. *Journal of Contemporary History*, *28*(2), 245–267. doi:10.1177/002200949302800203

Diekman, A. B., & Murnen, S. K. (2004). Learning to be little women and little men: The inequitable gender equality of nonsexist children's literature. *Sex Roles*, *50*(5), 373–385. doi:10.1023/B:SERS.0000018892.26527.ea

Edwards, J., & Chapman, C. (2000). Women's political representation in wales: Waving or drowning? *Contemporary Politics*, *6*(4), 367–381. doi:10.1080/713658377

Engel, R. S. (2001). Supervisory styles of patrol sergeants and lieutenants. *Journal of Criminal Justice*, *29*(4), 341–355. doi:10.1016/S0047-2352(01)00091-5

Faye, I., & Hopgood, T. (2012). Thank you hater (MP3 ed.). London, GB: mar.

Feagin, J. R. (2014). *Racist america: Roots, current realities, and future reparations*. London, GB: Routledge.

Feather, N. T., & McKee, I. R. (2012). Values, Right-Wing authoritarianism, social dominance orientation, and ambivalent attitudes toward women. *Journal of Applied Social Psychology*, *42*(10), 2479–2504. doi:10.1111/j.1559-1816.2012.00950.x

Gürses, S., Troncoso, C., & Diaz, C. (2011). Engineering privacy by design. *Computers, Privacy & Data Protection, 14*

Haghighat, E. (2013). Social status and change: The question of access to resources and women's empowerment in the middle east and north africa. *Journal of International Women's Studies*, *14*(1), 273–299.

Hall, J. (1952). Police and law in a democratic society. *Indiana Law Journal (Indianapolis, Ind.)*, *28*(2), 133.

Hardaker, C. (2013). Uh.... not to be nitpicky, but... the past tense of drag is dragged, not drug.": An overview of trolling strategies. *Journal of Language Aggression and Conflict*, *1*(1), 57–85. doi:10.1075/jlac.1.1.04har

Harrison, L., & Ollis, D. (2015). Stepping out of our comfort zones: Pre-service teachers' responses to a critical analysis of gender/power relations in sexuality education. *Sex Education*, *15*(3), 318–331. doi:10.1080/14681811.2015.1023284

Jackson, L. (2006). *Women police: Gender, welfare and surveillance in the twentieth century*. Manchester, GB: Manchester University Press.

Jonathan-Zamir, T., & Harpaz, A. (2014). Police understanding of the foundations of their legitimacy in the eyes of the public the case of commanding officers in the israel national police. *The British Journal of Criminology*, *54*(3), 469–489. doi:10.1093/bjc/azu001

Kealhofer, L. A. (2011). *Cinematic voices of maghrebi migrant women in France*.

Lister, S., Hadfield, P., Hobbs, D., & Winlow, S. (2001). Accounting for bouncers: Occupational licensing as a mechanism for regulation. *Criminology & Criminal Justice*, *1*(4), 363–384. doi:10.1177/1466802501001004001

Lough, J., & Ryan, M. (2010). Research note: Psychological profiling of australian police officers: A three-year examination of post-selection performance. *International Journal of Police Science & Management*, *12*(3), 480–486. doi:10.1350/ijps.2010.12.3.188

Margetts, H. (1996). Public management change and sex equality within the state. *Parliamentary Affairs*, *49*(1), 130–142. doi:10.1093/oxfordjournals.pa.a028663

Meyers, M. (1996). *News coverage of violence against women: Engendering blame*. London, GB: Sage Publications Ltd.

Mills, M. B. (1999). Thai women in the global labor force: Consuing desires, contested selves. *The Journal of Asian Studies*, *59*(01), 217–219.

Nhan, J. (2014). Police culture. In G. Bruinsma & D. Weisburd (Eds.), *The encyclopedia of criminology and criminal justice*. London, GB: Blackwell Publishing Ltd.

Paoline, E. A. III. (2004). Shedding light on police culture: An examination of officers' occupational attitudes. *Police Quarterly*, *7*(2), 205–236. doi:10.1177/1098611103257074

Papadopoulos, I., Tilki, M., & Lees, S. (2004). Promoting cultural competence in healthcare through a research-based intervention in the UK. *Diversity in Health & Social Care*, *1*(2), 107–116.

Phillips, W. (2011). LOLing at tragedy: Facebook trolls, memorial pages and resistance to grief online. *First Monday*, *16*(12). doi:10.5210/fm.v16i12.3168

Plant, E. A., Goplen, J., & Kunstman, J. W. (2011). Selective responses to threat the roles of race and gender in decisions to shoot. *Personality and Social Psychology Bulletin*, *37*(9), 1274–1281. doi:10.1177/0146167211408617 PMID:21566078

Porter, L. E., & Prenzler, T. (2012). Police oversight in the united kingdom: The balance of independence and collaboration. *International Journal of Law, Crime and Justice*, *40*(3), 152–171. doi:10.1016/j.ijlcj.2012.03.001

Prokos, A., & Padavic, I. (2002). 'There oughtta be a law against bitches': Masculinity lessons in police academy training. *Gender, Work and Organization*, *9*(4), 439–459. doi:10.1111/1468-0432.00168

Raymond, J. (2013). Sexist attitudes: Most of us are biased. *Nature*, *495*(7439), 33–34. doi:10.1038/495033a PMID:23467152

Rich, M., Woods, E. R., Goodman, E., Emans, S. J., & DuRant, R. H. (1998). Aggressors or victims: Gender and race in music video violence. *Pediatrics*, *101*(4), 669–674. doi:10.1542/peds.101.4.669 PMID:9521954

Rivera, L. A. (2010). Status distinctions in interaction: Social selection and exclusion at an elite nightclub. *Qualitative Sociology*, *33*(3), 229–255. doi:10.1007/s11133-010-9152-2

Savage, S. P. (1984). Political control or community liaison? *The Political Quarterly*, *55*(1), 48–59. doi:10.1111/j.1467-923X.1984.tb02562.x

Sellers, M. D. (2014). Discrimination and the transgender population: Analysis of the functionality of local government policies that protect gender identity. *Administration & Society*, *46*(1), 70–86. doi:10.1177/0095399712451894

Shen, Y. W. (2012). The narrative express of the concept of structure-pagoda in the fantian temple of shen kuo as example. *Applied Mechanics and Materials*, *209*, 122–125. doi:10.4028/www.scientific.net/AMM.209-211.122

Sklansky, D. A. (2007). Seeing blue: Police reform, occupational culture, and cognitive burn-in. *Sociology of Crime Law and Deviance*, *8*, 19–45.

Smith, B., & Sparkes, A. C. (2012). Narrative analysis in sport and physical culture. *Research in the Sociology of Sport*, *6*, 79–99.

Smith, S. P. (1976). Government wage differentials by sex. *The Journal of Human Resources*, *11*(2), 185–199. doi:10.2307/145452

Starmer, K. (2013). *Guidelines on prosecuting cases involving communications sent via social media*. London, GB: Crown Prosecution Service.

Stenson, K. (2013). Community safety in middle england: The local politics of crime control. In G. Hughes & A. Edwards (Eds.), *Crime control and community: The new politics of public safety* (pp. 109–140). Collumpton: Willan Publishing.

Stevens, T. (2009). Regulating the 'Dark web': How a two-fold approach can tackle peer-to-peer radicalisation. *The RUSI Journal*, *154*(2), 28–33. doi:10.1080/03071840902965687

Su, C. (2012). One earthquake, two tales: Narrative analysis of the tenth anniversary coverage of the 921 earthquake in taiwan. *Media Culture & Society*, *34*(3), 280–295. doi:10.1177/0163443711433664

Thibault, E. A., & Lynch, L. M. (1985). *Proactive police management*. Englewood Cliffs, NJ: Prentice Hall.

Victor, P. T., & Dalzell, T. (Eds.). (2014). *The concise new partridge dictionary of slang and unconventional english*. London, GB: Routledge.

Visher, C. A. (1983). Gender, police arrest decisions, and notions of chivalry. *Criminology*, *21*(1), 5–28. doi:10.1111/j.1745-9125.1983.tb00248.x

Walter, T. (2014). New mourners, old mourners: Online memorial culture as a chapter in the history of mourning. *New Review of Hypermedia and Multimedia,* (ahead-of-print), 1-15.

Walter, T., Hourizi, R., Moncur, W., & Pitsillides, S. (2011). Does the internet change how we die and mourn? an overview and analysis. *Omega*, *64*(4), 275–302. doi:10.2190/OM.64.4.a PMID:22530294

Wryght, I. (2006). *How to date today's modern woman*. Bloomington, IN: AuthorHouse UK Ltd.

Zaikman, Y., & Marks, M. J. (2014). Ambivalent sexism and the sexual double standard. *Sex Roles*, *71*(9-10), 333–344. doi:10.1007/s11199-014-0417-1

KEY TERMS AND DEFINITIONS

Benevolent Sexism: The tendency to endorse the traditional feminine ideal or to view women in idealised, overly romantic terms or as delicate creatures who require protection.

Crown Prosecution Service: The public body in the United Kingdom that decides whether or not a prosecution should be brought.

Harassment: A course of conduct that results in a person feeling harassed, alarmed or distressed, which is not reasonable, or persued in the course.

Institutional Sexism: The result of an organisation made up of persons who share the same attitudes favouring one sex over another in a given situation. Whilst the organisation does not have sexist policies, the attitudes have the equivalent effect.

Narrative Analysis: An umbrella term for an eclectic mix of methods for making sense of, interpreting and representing data that have in common a storied form.

Chapter 5
Impact of ICT on Innovation:
The Case of Japanese SMEs

Hiroki Idota
Kinki University, Japan

Teruyuki Bunno
Kinki University, Japan

Masatsugu Tsuji
University of Hyogo, Japan

ABSTRACT

The innovation process in SMEs (small- and medium-sized enterprises) is complex and in comparison with large firms the causal relationships between promoting factors and innovation have yet not been sufficiently clarified. This chapter attempts to analyze the innovation process using Structural Equation Modeling, in particular focusing on the role of ICT. Seven hypotheses are demonstrated by two models. The results obtained are as follows: (i) top management participation and employee motivation in the innovation process enhance the effect of introducing ICT; (ii) the effect of ICT use raises innovation capability, in particular the ability to connect with external linkages; (iii) ICT use, innovation capability and external linkages enhance innovation activity; and (iv) the effect of ICT use and innovation capability promote innovation directly.

INTRODUCTION

To achieve innovation is essential for sustainable economic development in all economies. In Japan, SMEs (small- and medium-sized enterprises) were looked to as an important economic actor in the Reconstruction Japan Initiative decided by the Cabinet Office in July 2012, in which SMEs were expected to develop into global firms and to create employment opportunities in the region. In reality, on the other hand, SMEs have found themselves facing a severe situation due to the long stagnation. In this environment, only a few SMEs achieved a greater than average rate of profit (The Small and Medium Enterprise Agency, 2009). These SMEs have a number of common features such as strong leadership by top management, quick and flexible decision making, strategies for

DOI: 10.4018/978-1-4666-8598-7.ch005

seeking niche markets, engineering craftsmanship, and effective use of ICT (Information and Communication Technology). Efficiency of the business process is improved by introducing and utilizing ICT. Introducing ICT is considered to be one type of process innovation which includes adopting new production methods and logistics. Moreover, information on customer needs and the market can be promptly obtained by using the Internet and social media, for example. In addition, since communication among employers and top management is activated and intramural knowledge management can be strengthened by ICT, all these lead to innovation (Dodgson, Gann, & Salter, 2006; Lee & Xia, 200; Idota, Bunno, & Tsuji, 2012a).

However, ICT is not the only factor driving innovation, since the innovation process is complex. In this analysis, innovation is categorized into the following four types according to the Oslo Manual (OECD & Eurostat, 2005); (i) product innovation (new products and services); (ii) process innovation (new production methods and new logistic methods); (iii) marketing innovation (changes in design, packaging, and production sites); and (iv) organizational innovation (business practices, workplace environment, and the relationship between the organizations both inside and outside the firm). Since both product and process innovation are created as a result of organizational innovation, and some marketing innovations include product and process innovation, this chapter discusses both kinds of innovation. Regarding the sources of innovation, on the other hand, based on the analysis of many previous studies, the authors' previous studies identified the following three key factors; (i) innovation capability, (ii) external linkages, and (iii) ICT use. The objectives of the paper are (i) to define the content of innovation capability of firms and (ii) to analyze how innovation sources contribute to innovative creation, in particular to examine the causal relationship between the three sources and innovation.

As shown below, although there has been ample research on innovation capability, fewer analyses have been conducted in the context of innovation capability and ICT. Moreover, little research focuses on the *causal* relationship between the above three sources and the final outcome of innovation. These problems have not been successfully clarified yet. Hence, this chapter attempts to analyze the causal relationship by employing Structural Equation Modeling (SEM).

BACKGROUND: PREVIOUS LITERATURE

Definition of Innovation

Schumpeter (1934) defined innovation as a process of "carrying out new combinations" (p. 47). This definition includes the following types of innovations: (i) introduction of a new good; (ii) introduction of a new method of production; (iii) opening of a new market; (iv) acquisition of a new source of supply of raw materials or intermediate goods; and (v) carrying out new organizational forms. The first is termed product innovation, while the others are referred to as process innovations. The Oslo Manual mentioned in the previous section categorized innovation in the similar way.

There are two ways to create product and process innovation; one is called closed innovation, which is achieved by one particular firm, while the other is known as open innovation, which is carried out by collaborating with other firms or organizations. To date, Japanese firms have successfully achieved innovation through "the independence principle," which implies that firms have been accumulating knowledge and knowhow for innovation within a limited number of firms such as their own firm or group firms. Japanese firms constructed industrial groups by connecting related firms vertically or horizontally (Tsuji, 2005). Typical examples of the former are found in the processing and assembly industries, such as automobile, electric appliances, precision machinery, or machine tools, while examples of the latter are groups led by mega-banks. R&D is a typical activity which is conducted by all related firms within the group. The Toyota Motor Corporation, for example, takes the lead in developing new technology by collaborating with its group firms. On the other hand, Chesbrough (2006a) mentioned that in the current environment, closed innovation is not an efficient method, since firms chasing closed innovation cannot catch up with the so-called economies of speed brought about by ICT, such as quicker business decision making or a shorter lifecycle of products. This is one reason why Japanese firms have lost competitiveness in the global market. On the other hand, European or U.S. firms have initiated open innovation by collaborating with other firms and organizations, and have therefore became more active (Chesbrough, 2003; 2006a; 2006b).

Chesbrough (2006a) also asserted that open innovation was the purposive use of inflows and outflows of knowledge to accelerate internal innovation and to expand markets for the external use of innovation (p. 1). Open innovation enhances new innovation by absorbing outside knowledge and combining it with internal innovation resources to create new business models by collaborating with entities outside the firm. In this case, a strategy is required for sharing information and using resources with all firms from suppliers to customers. The use of ICT is, therefore, indispensable for the promotion of open innovation (Gassmann & von Zedtwitz, 2003; Dodgson et al., 2006; Piller & Walcher, 2006; Dittrich & Duysters, 2007; Idota et al., 2012a; Idota, Bunno, & Tsuji, 2010, 2013b, 2014; Idota, Akematsu, Ueki, & Tsuji, 2013a).

Innovation Capability

There are many factors behind the promotion of innovation in an economy, as the endogenous economic growth theory emphasizes, i.e. capital, labor and technology. In reality, it is difficult to raise these factors and promote economic development across the entire economy, but it is more difficult to improve the power of innovation within individual firms. Such power is referred to as innovation capability, which is defined as the ability to continuously transform knowledge and ideas into new products, processes, and systems for the benefit of the firm and its stakeholders (Lawson & Samson, 2001). Innovation capability consists of various factors, which are listed as audit tools, for measuring innovation capability, and related factors are categorized into groups; Mariano & Pilar (2005), for example, categorize these groups of factors as follows: (i) Communication with the external environment; (ii) Level of know-how and experience within the organization; (iii) Diversity and overlap in the knowledge structure; and (iv) Strategic positioning. Causality among these categories is one of this area's major research questions, which aims to identify the causes and results of interactions between the categories (Lawson & Samson, 2001; Perdomo-Ortiza, González-Benito, & Galende, 2009). In order to demonstrate causality, different methodologies such as regression analysis, covariance structure analysis, and structural equation modeling were employed.

Absorptive Capability

In this chapter, these factors are termed internal innovation capability, or internal capability, for short, which is defined as an integrated ability of a firm to create innovation consisting of all resources, which is referred to as core competence, or competitiveness. In more detail, internal capability includes the technological level, such as the number of patents, production facilities, and R&D facilities; human resources, such as the number of engineers with higher degrees or skills, the level of craftsmanship, work ethics; and the organizational nature, such as communication between workers and top management, the speed of decision-making, and leadership by the top management. In what follows, this study also groups these factors into several categories. Traditionally, on the other hand, one part of internal capability was focused on and referred to as "absorptive capability" by Cohen & Levinthal (1990), and Zahra & George (2002) for example. Cohen & Levinthal (1990) defines "absorptive capability" as a firm's ability to reorganize the value of new external knowledge, and assimilate this for commercial benefit (p. 128). They also recognize the innovation process as a learning process consisting of four dimensions; acquisition, assimilation, transformation, and exploitation. Acquisition is the process whereby relevant information is identified from the total amount of information. Assimilation is the ability to process and analyze the information obtained. Transformation is the ability to modify and adopt new knowledge and combine this with knowledge already existing inside the firm. Exploitation is the ability to transform this knowledge into innovation or competitive advantage. Thus the absorptive capability determines the competitive advantage of a firm (Barney, 1991).

Open Innovation

Another source of innovation is to make use of factors outside the firm and utilize them to promote internal capability. New information related to innovation is fundamentally obtained from outside the firm, and the literature mentioned above analyzes this to some extent. Collaboration with entities outside the firm, such as other firms, universities, and local research institutions, for the innovation process came to occupy the center of the research and this was analyzed according to the framework of "open innovation" (Chesbrough, 2003, 2006a, 2006b). The concept of the open innovation process is developed in accordance with the growth of the assembly and processing industries, which handle numerous parts and components, such as in the automotive or electronics industries. New information for innovation is conveyed via the supply chain. In addition, the success of the university-firm collaboration, such as in Silicon Valley or Route 128 in the early 1990s, inspired open innovation. The clustering effect, namely firms finding locations closer to universities, influences open innovation. The open innovation system becomes mandatory for a region or a firm to establish a strategy for innovation. There are two strategies for obtaining information; one is through transactions with other firms, from suppliers and customers (transaction channel), while another is collaboration with research institutions (research channel) (Kagami, Giovannetti, & Tsuji, 2007).

In the context of "absorptive capacity" and "open innovation," external linkage is an important factor which is defined as a network with other firms for the exchange of information related to technologies, consumer needs, the market, etc. and for collaboration with other firms.

ICT Use in the Innovation Process

ICT use is also essential for innovation. ICT, such as ERP (Enterprise Resource Planning) packages, groupware, CAD/CAM, B2B E-commerce, B2C E-commerce, EDI (Electronic Data Interchange), SCM (Supply Chain Management) and Social media, has been regarded as a tool that improves the productivity of firms and enhances innovation activities.

ICT becomes important as a platform to promote capability creation. Many previous studies mentioned ICT was viewed as effective tools for innovation (e.g. Gretton, Gali, & Parham, et al., 2004; Tsuji 2005; Dodgson et al., 2006; Lee & Xia, 2006; Tsuji & Miyahara, 2010, 2011; Spiezia, 2011; Idota et al., 2010, 2012a, 2013a, 2013b, 2014; Idota, Bunno, & Tsuji, 2011 2012b; Idota, Ogawa, Bunno, & Tsuji, 2012c). For example, Gretton et al. (2004) mentioned ICT provided an indispensable platform for innovation. And Spiezia (2011) used the four categories of innovations in the Oslo manual and used firm data of 11 OECD countries. He highlighted that ICT acted as an enabler of innovation, particularly for product and marketing innovation, in both manufacturing and service industries. Dodgson et al. (2006) clarified the following two points from the case study of the Procter and Gamble Co.: (i) ICT supports communications for open innovation in the community or between communities; and (ii) ICT such as data mining, simulation, design of prototype and a virtual system are useful for supporting open innovation.

Thus, ICT contributes to firms by: (i) improving the efficiency of management and communication inside the firm; (ii) enabling networking and collaboration among business entities and organizations by reducing the time required for communication and overcoming geographical constrains; and (iii) creating new markets for business, such as e-commerce. As a result, ICT has become one of the essential bases for promoting innovation activities (Dodgson et al., 2006; Lee & Xia, 2006; Idota et al., 2010, 2011, 2012a, 2012b, 2012c, 2013a, 2013b, 2014).

It is reported that even the simple use of social media such as SNSs (Social Networking Services), Twitter, and blogs among employees promotes innovation (Idota et al., 2011). In addition to ICT use inside the firm, ICT is also used for supporting collaboration with entities outside the firm. In particular, cooperation with other firms, universities, and local research institutions has been an important factor for innovation (Chesbrough, 2003, 2006a, 2006b). In the open innovation process, a strategy for sharing information and resources with other firms, from suppliers to customers, for example, is required. The use of ICT is therefore indispensable for the promotion of open innovation, since ICT can connect firms and expedite the sharing of information related to innovation).

Based on the above discussions, ICT has the following two functions: (i) ICT promotes the efficiency of firms by sharing information among employees and employers, and activates communication, which leads to the enhancement of knowledge management activities for innovation inside the firm; and (ii) ICT enables firms to share, exchange, and communicate with external agents, connecting them more tightly with other firms or universities, consultants, or research institutes. Thus firms can absorb technology, know-how, and information from outside. Taking these two ICT functions into consideration, ICT influences the promotion of innovation through the following two channels: (i) enhancement of internal innovation capability; and (ii) support for internal capabilities leading to innovation.

Thus these three key factors, innovation capability, external linkage and ICT use promote innovation activity. As a result, firms are able to achieve greater innovation in a more efficient way.

MAIN FOCUS OF THE CHAPTER

Causality between ICT Use and Innovation

Most analyses of innovation are based mainly on two methods, regression analysis and factor analysis. Although there are various related methods, the underling basic theory is almost the same. The former is used to verify statistical relationships between observed variables, but it can deal only with issues that are observable variables, which raises the problem of endogeneity. As a result, the obtained relationships are "seemingly related," but this does not signify casuality. Factor analysis, on the other hand, can deal with endogenous variables, but cannot explain causality. This chapter employs SEM, which is able to overcome the problems of both regression and factor analysis.

Although papers on innovation employing SEM have appeared, there are few analyses that use SEM to examine the relationship between ICT and innovation. For example, Chen (2012) demonstrated the relationship between IT-enabled resources and R&D capability. This chapter has various points in common with this paper.

Model and Hypotheses

This chapter attempts to analyze how ICT use contributes to innovation. Based on the authors' previous papers and papers listed in the previous literature, three variables, innovation capability, external linkages, and ICT use are cited as the most important sources of innovation. Innovation capability inside the firm contains factors such as technological level, managerial organization, human resources, and so on. Factor analysis is used to identify the representative variables which coincide with the above factors.

Data

This chapter is based on a mail survey conducted in February 2012 with respect to 3, 959 innovative Japanese SMEs in the manufacturing, service, information processing service and construction industries[1].

The number of valid responses was 647 (16.3%). Questions in the survey consist of the number of innovations achieved for the most recent five years, business resources, management behavior, the effect of ICT, and so on.

The aim of the analysis is to verify whether the seven hypotheses indicated below are verified or not by using SEM (Structural equation modeling). SEM is a statistical method that can examine causal relationships between plural constructs through the use of models.

SEM is said to be a mixture of factor analysis and regression analysis; the former constructs latent variables from observed variables by using factor analysis, while the latter examines the causal relationships between latent variables by regression analysis. Thus, SEM analysis can be used even for cases in which the variables are endogenous and the usual Least Squares cannot be applied. The idea of SEM was initially proposed as CSA (Covariance structural analysis) by Bock (1960) and developed by Bock & Bargmann (1966) in order to solve issues related to multivariate analysis. Later Bagozzi (1980) and Bollenn (1989) termed this SEM.

The merits of SEM are summarized as follows: Regression analysis, which enables the causal relationships between variables to be verified, can handle only the observed variables, that is, endogenous variables, which are referred to as "latent variables" in SEM. Factor analysis can construct latent variables, which exist as common characteristics behind observed variables, but it cannot analyze their causal relationships. SEM makes it possible to solve the issues related to factor and regression analysis, and integrate these two methods. In other words, SEM introduces latent variables which are not observable, and by fixing the causal relationship between latent and observed variables, statistically examines social as well as natural phenomena.

Table 1 indicates basic statistics. Data not used in the analysis are excluded from the table. "Presence of product innovation" and "Presence of process innovation" are dummies. The other questions were answered according to the Likert five-point scale.

Confirmatory Factor Analysis

To conduct SEM, it is necessary to obtain latent variables. To specify these variables, confirmatory factor analysis is conducted by the maximum likelihood method (Varimax Rotation). The results are shown in Tables 2 to 4. Table 2 indicates latent variables related to human factors, and as a result, two factors are extracted as a result of factor analysis, "Top management" and "Employee." Since the first factor consists of employee pride and understanding, atmosphere in the office and so on, it is termed "Orientation of employee motivation." As for the second factor, Top Management presenting their ideas, leadership of the top management and top management participation in projects are extracted, and this is therefore referred to as "Orientation of top management participation."

Table 1. Basic statistics

		N	Min	Max	Avg.	Std. Dev.
Innovation	Presence of product innovation	468	0	1	.71	.453
	Presence of process innovation	468	0	1	.52	.500
Top Management Participation	Top managers voluntarily show their ideas and decide on new business.	468	1	5	3.71	1.005
	Top managers take the leading role in new business.	468	1	5	3.88	.972
Employee Motivation	The employees understand the target of the firm.	468	1	5	3.96	.725
	The employees are proud of their firm.	468	1	5	3.83	.696
	The employees understand the strong points of the firm.	468	2	5	3.91	.692
	The atmosphere in the firm allows easy consultation with colleagues.	468	1	5	3.77	.782
	The employees understand the situations in which in-house products are used.	468	1	5	3.92	.829
	Employees help others with their work even if it is unrelated to their own work.	468	1	5	3.63	.806
Innovation Capability	Capability to create new products and services	468	1	5	3.39	1.027
	Capability to solve customers' problems	468	1	5	3.85	.804
	Original core technology and R&D capability	468	1	5	3.57	.912
External Linkages	Positively offers other companies its own technology	468	1	5	2.81	1.098
	Receives technical proposals from other companies	468	1	5	2.81	1.074
	Understands the strong points of the partner, and is collaborating in the fields of each other's strong points	468	1	5	3.41	1.061
Innovation Activity	Ideas for new products and services are often created within the firm.	468	1	5	3.18	1.125
	Basic research and R&D are coordinated.	468	1	5	2.75	1.099
	R&D is directly connected to new products and services	468	1	5	2.91	1.146
	Analysis is performed on products and services of the company as well as those of competitors	468	1	5	2.94	1.062
Effect of ICT	Useful as PR for goods	468	1	5	3.13	1.243
	Improvement in speed of managerial judgments and business development	468	1	5	3.43	1.084
	Shortening of product lead time	468	1	5	2.86	1.098
	Increase in the number of new products and services in development	468	1	5	2.72	1.049
	Ease of awareness of customer needs	468	1	5	3.19	1.059

Source: Authors

Table 2. Factor analysis of top management and employee

	Top Management and Employee	
	Employee Motivation	Top Management Participation
The employees understand the target of the firm.	**.669**	.037
The employees are proud of their firm.	**.742**	-.002
The employees understand the strong points of the firm.	**.733**	.028
The atmosphere in the firm allows easy consultation with colleagues.	**.623**	-.013
The employees understand the situations in which in-house products are used.	**.536**	.034
Employees help others with their work even if it is unrelated to their own work.	**.637**	-.086
Top managers voluntarily show their ideas and decide on new business.	-.010	**.827**
Top managers take the leading role in new business.	.009	**.908**
Factor Correlation Matrix		
1	1.000	.087
2	.087	1.000
Cronbach's α	.816	.858

Source: Authors

The result regarding the innovation basis of the firm is summarized in Table 3, three factors being extracted as a result of factor analysis. Since the first factor consists of "Capability to create new products and services," "Capability to solve customers' problems" and "Original core technology and R&D capability," these are singled out as one variable termed "innovation capability." As for the second factor, "Positively offers other companies its own technology," "Receives technical proposals from other companies" and "Understands the strong points of the partner, and is collaborating in the fields of each other's strong points" were extracted, and the relating variable referred to as "External linkages." In the same manner, for the third factor, "Ideas for new products and services are often created within the firm," "Basic research and R&D are coordinated" and "Data on products and services of the company and competitors are analyzed" were extracted, and this accordingly named "Innovation activity" [2].

One factor was extracted as a result of factor analysis regarding the effect of ICT (Table 4). Since the factor consists of "Useful as PR for goods," "Improvement in speed of managerial judgments and business development," "Shortening of product lead time," "Increase in the number of new products and services in development," and "Ease of awareness of customers' needs," the variable was termed "Effect of ICT."

The list of latent and observable variables used in the analysis is indicated in Table 5.

Hypotheses

In this chapter, two models of the causal relationship between the three sources and innovation are presented and verification of seven hypotheses is attempted. The difference in the two models lies in examining the causal relationships among the three key sources and innovation. Namely, one model postulates that ICT use promotes in-

Table 3. Factor analysis of innovation capability and activity

	Innovation Capability and Activity		
	Innovation Capability	**External Linkages**	**Innovation Activity**
Capability to create new products and services	**0.801**	-0.03	0.069
Capability to solve customers' problems	**0.679**	0.079	-0.129
Original core technology and R&D capability	**0.629**	-0.045	0.127
Positively offers other companies its own technology	0.073	**0.678**	-0.049
Receives technical proposals from other companies	-0.076	**0.641**	-0.028
Understands the strong points of the partner, and is collaborating in the fields of each other's strong points	0.03	**0.528**	0.103
Ideas for new products and services are often created within the firm.	-0.078	-0.017	**0.936**
Basic research and R&D are coordinated.	-0.011	-0.01	**0.878**
R&D is directly connected to new products and services	0.211	-0.061	**0.514**
Products and services of the company as well as those of competitors are analyzed	0.026	**0.277**	**0.445**
Factor Correlation Matrix			
1	0.612	0.446	1
2	1	0.21	0.612
3	0.21	1	0.446
Cronbach's α	0.757	0.690	0.822

Source: Authors

novation capability and attracts external linkages, while the other model hypothesizes the reverse relationship, that is, external linkages promote ICT use. This chapter analyzes the suitability of the two models using SEM. In order to make the discussion clear, the causal relationships among key variables, that is, the three sources are categorized into four groups, and hypotheses are presented for each group.

Human Factors

The hypotheses in the first group are related to human factors, which are represented by top management participation and employee motivation in this chapter. Top management takes the leadership in business management in general, and this includes positive activities to promote innovation capability, to collaborate with external linkages, and to introduce ICT. In addition to top management, employees are engaged in actual activities to achieve the objectives, and thus their motivation and business ethics are also essential.

Table 4. Factor analysis of the effect of ICT

	Effect of ICT
Useful as PR for goods	**.878**
Improvement in speed of managerial decision-making and business development	**.872**
Shortening of product lead time	**.685**
Increase in the number of new products and services in development	**.681**
Ease of awareness of customer needs	**.566**
Cronbach's α	.852

Source: Authors

Table 5. Variables for Structural Equation Modeling

	Latent Variables	Observable Variables
	Innovation	Presence of product innovation
		Presence of process innovation
Human Factors	Top Management Participation	Top managers voluntarily show their ideas and decide on new business.
		Top managers take the leading role in new business.
	Employee Motivation	The employees understand the target of the firm.
		The employees are proud of their firm.
		The employees understand the strong points of the firm.
		The atmosphere in the firm allows easy consultation with colleagues.
		The employees understand the situations in which in-house products are used.
		Employees help each other with their work even if it is unrelated to their own work.
Innovation Basis	Innovation Capability	Capability to create new products and services
		Capability to solve customers' problems
		Original core technology and R&D capability
	External Linkages	Positively offers other companies its own technology
		Receives technical proposals from other companies
		Understands the strong points of the partner, and is collaborating in the fields of each other's strong points
		Analysis is performed on products and services of the company as well as those of competitors
	Innovation Activity	Ideas for new products and services are often created within the firm.
		Basic research and R&D are coordinated.
		R&D is directly connected to new products and services
ICT Use	Effect of ICT	Useful as PR for goods
		Improvement in speed of managerial judgments and business development
		Shortening of product lead time
		Increase in the number of new products and services in development
		Ease of awareness of customer needs

Source: Authors

Therefore, causal relationships between these two human factors and the three sources are presented as follows:

H1: Top management participation and employee motivation promote ICT use.

H2: Top management participation and employee motivation improve innovation capability.

H3: Top management participation and employee motivation promote external linkages.

There is no need to mention the rationale for these hypotheses. Regarding H1, Damaskopoulos & Evgeniou (2003) and Cragg & Zinatelli (1995), for example, emphasize the importance of top management participation in the adoption of ICT, while Caroli & van Reenen (2001) emphasize worker motivation for ICT adoption. As for H2, Tidd, Bessant, & Pavitt, (2001) lists top management participation and employee motivation as important factors in constructing an innovative organization by claiming that the former must have a shared vision, leadership and a strong will to innovation.

Causality among the Three Sources

The following two hypotheses are related to the causal relationship among the three sources of innovation, which is the main research question of this chapter:

H4.1: ICT use promotes innovation capability and external linkages.
H4.2: Innovation capability and external linkages promote ICT use.

The hypotheses examine whether ICT use is the cause or the result of innovation capability and external linkages. Differing results arise from these hypotheses. Namely, Chen (2012) showed that IT-enabled resources have impacts on R&D capability, whereas Park, Fujimoto, & Hong, (2012) showed that ICT causes innovation via organizational capability. Hollenstein (2004), Carlsoon (2004), and Beccheti, Londono Bedoya, & Paganetto (2003) showed that ICT use enhances only product innovation.

Resources and Innovation Activity

This hypothesis is related to how the sources affect innovation activity, which is a variable constructed by the following questions.

H5: Innovation capability, external linkages and ICT use promote innovation activity.

Of previous studies, Chen (2012) shows that ICT promotes innovation capability and then capability enhances financial performance via his "strategic objectives." This chapter also intends to show the same process, but here "strategic objectives" is the same as the concept of "innovation activity" described in this chapter.

Sources and Innovation

This hypothesizes the final causality between the sources and innovation.

H6: Innovation activity promotes innovation.
H7: Innovation capability, external linkages and ICT use directly promote innovation.

In order to examine the above hypotheses, this chapter presents the two models depicted in the following Figures 1 and 2. The hypotheses are summarized in Tables 6 and 7. The difference between the two models lies in whether the "Effect of ICT use" is the cause or the result of "Innovation capability" and "External linkages."

RESULTS OF THE ANALYSIS

Selection of the Model

Tables 8 and 9 indicate the fit of the two SEM models. Both GFI (Goodness of Fit Index) and AGFI (Adjusted Goodness of Fit Index), which indicate criteria for the explanatory power of the model, give a value between 0 and 1. If GFI>=AGFI and both indices have a value of 0.9 or more, the model can be judged as proper. CFI (Comparative Fit Index) evaluates the model in terms of goodness-of-fit, which indicates how much the model is improved in comparison with an independent model estimated under the assumption that there is no correlation among the observed variables. CFI takes a value from 0 to 1, and the model is judged as being a good fit if the CFI value is 0.9 or more. Moreover, RMSEA (Root Mean Square Error of Approximation) is an index that expresses divergence between the estimated and actual distribution of the model expressed in terms of the amount of degree of freedom. The model can be judged as being a good fit if the value is 0.05 or less. The values of those indices in both models are very similar

Figure 1. Model 1: "Effect of ICT" is a cause of "Innovation capability" and "External linkages"
Source: Authors

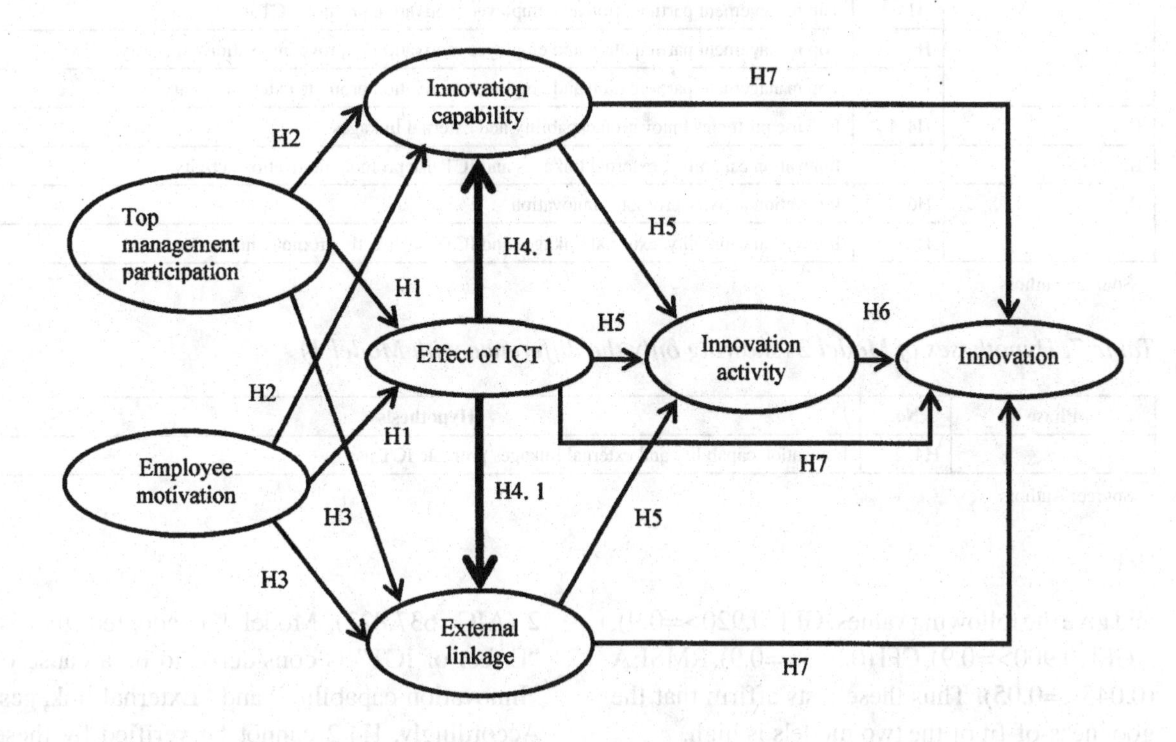

Figure 2. Model 2: "Effect of ICT" is a result of "Innovation capability" and "External linkages"
Source: Authors

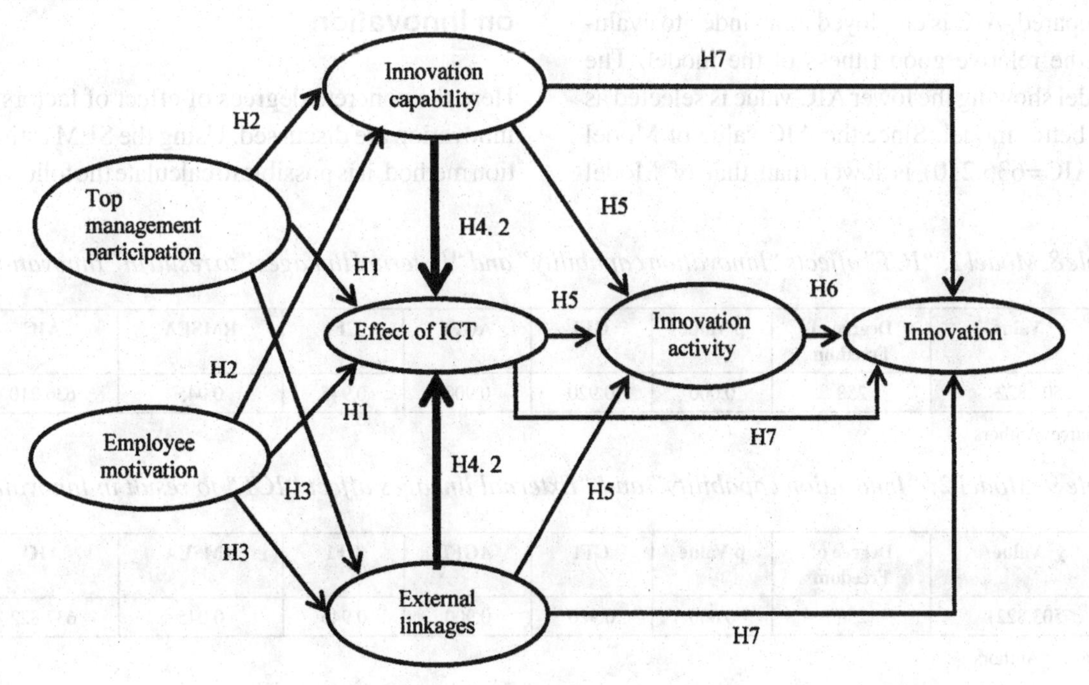

Table 6. Hypotheses of Model 1

Phase	No.	Hypothesis
I	H1	Top management participation and employee motivation promote ICT use.
	H2	Top management participation and employee motivation improve innovation capability.
	H3	Top management participation and employee motivation promote external linkages.
II	H4. 1	ICT use promotes innovation capability and external linkages.
III	H5	Innovation capability, external linkages and ICT use promote innovation activity.
IV	H6	Innovation activity promotes innovation.
	H7	Innovation capability, external linkages and ICT use directly promote innovation.

Source: Authors

Table 7. Hypotheses of Model 2 (showing only the difference with Model 1)

Phase	No.	Hypothesis
II	H4. 2	Innovation capability and external linkages promote ICT use.

Source: Authors

and give the following values: GFI (0.920>=0.9), AGFI (0.900>=0.9), CFI (0.945>=0.9), RMSEA (0.045<=0.05). Thus these tests affirm that the goodness-of-fit of the two models is high.

Next, which model is to be selected is determined according to the Akaike Information Criterion (AIC). When two or more models are compared, AIC is employed as an index to evaluate the relative good fitness of the model. The model showing the lower AIC value is selected as the better model. Since the AIC value of Model 1 (AIC=636.210) is lower than that of Model 2 (AIC=637.822), Model 1 is adopted, that is, "Effect of ICT" is considered to be a cause of "Innovation capability" and "External linkages. Accordingly, H4.2 cannot be verified by these two models.

Direct and Indirect Effects on Innovation

Here the concrete degrees of effect of factors on innovation are discussed. Using the SEM estimation method, it is possible to calculate the following

Table 8. Model 1: "ICT" affects "Innovation capability" and "External linkages" to result in "Innovation"

χ^2 Value	Degree of Freedom	p Value	GFI	AGFI	CFI	RMSEA	AIC
503.822	258	0.000	0.920	0.900	0.945	0.045	636.210

Source: Authors

Table 9. Model 2: "Innovation capability" and "External linkages affect "ICT" to result in Innovation

χ^2 Value	Degree of Freedom	p Value	GFI	AGFI	CFI	RMSEA	AIC
503.822	258	0.000	0.920	0.900	0.945	0.045	637.822

Source: Authors

three effects separately: (i) the standardized total effects (Table 10); (ii) direct effects (Table 11); and (iii) indirect effects (Table 12). First, Table 10 shows effects termed the standardized total effects, implying that the direct effects and the indirect effects are added together. Table 11 shows the standardized direct effects, which indicates the effect of one variable on another variable. Table 12 indicates the standardized indirect effects, which implies the effect of one variable on another via related variable(s).

In order to see the effect more clearly, let us take the example of innovation capability and examine its effect on innovation. Table 10 shows that the standardized total effect on innovation amounts to 0.345. This effect is decomposed into the direct and indirect effects. Table 11 shows the direct effect on innovation, which amounts to 0.171, while the indirect effect on innovation shown in Table 12 amounts to 0.173. As a result, the total effect amounts to 0.345. Innovation capability thus promotes innovation both directly and indirectly, but the indirect effect is larger than the direct effect.

Next, let us discuss the effect of ICT on innovation. The standardized total effects amount to 0.384 (Table 10), which is the largest among all the factors listed in the table. This value can be decomposed into direct and indirect effects. The former is 0.185 (Table 11), while the indirect effect via innovation activity is 0.199 (Table 12). It should be noted that the indirect effect is larger than the direct effect.

In sum, it is also shown that the factor which provides the largest effect on innovation is the effect of ICT use. The values of all effects are summarized in Figure 3.

Verification of Hypotheses

As mentioned above, Model 1 is selected, and the discussion below is based on Model 1. Table 13 summarizes the estimation results related to H1-H7. Let us examine the hypotheses one by one.

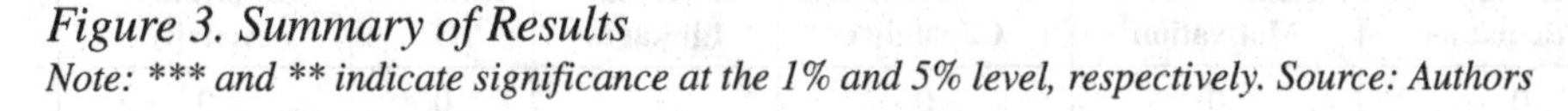
Figure 3. Summary of Results
*Note: *** and ** indicate significance at the 1% and 5% level, respectively. Source: Authors*

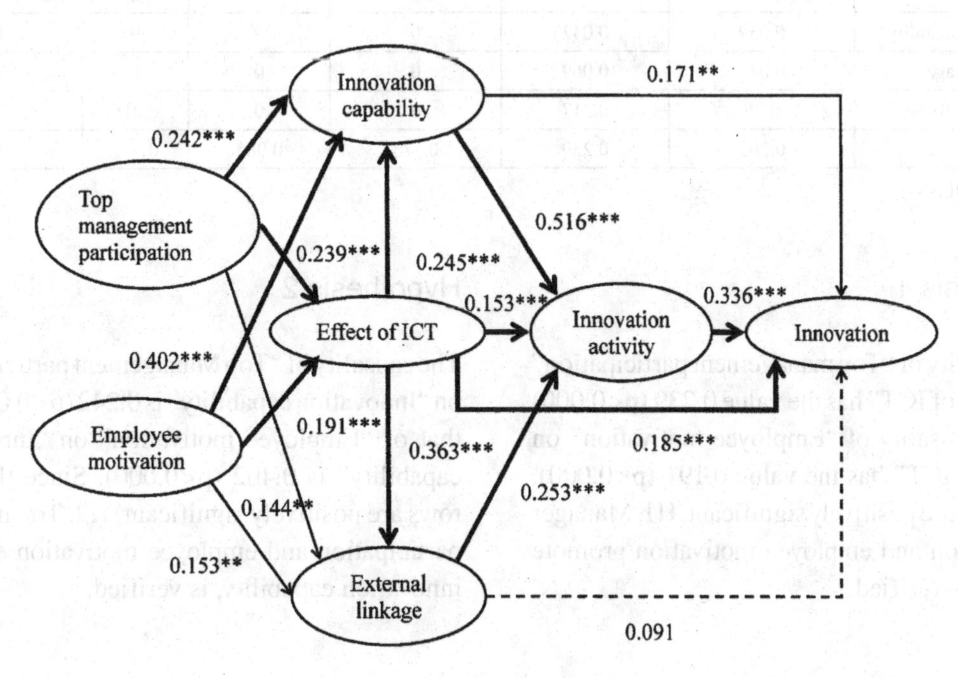

Table 10. Standardized total effects

From/ To	Top Management Participation	Employee Motivation	Innovation Capability	External Linkages	Effect of ICT	Innovation Activity
Effect of ICT	0.239	0.191	0	0	0	0
Innovation capability	0.301	0.449	0	0	0.245	0
External linkages	0.231	0.223	0	0	0.363	0
Innovation activity	0.25	0.317	0.516	0.253	0.37	0
Innovation	0.201	0.239	0.345	0.176	0.384	0.336

Source: Authors

Table 11. Standardized direct effects

From/ To	Top Management Participation	Employee Motivation	Innovation Capability	External Linkages	Effect of ICT	Innovation Activity
Effect of ICT	0.239	0.191	0	0	0	0
Innovation capability	0.242	0.402	0	0	0.245	0
External linkages	0.144	0.153	0	0	0.363	0
Innovation activity	0	0	0.516	0.253	0.153	0
Innovation	0	0	0.171	0.091	0.185	0.336

Source: Authors

Table 12. Standardized indirect effects

From/ To	Top Management Participation	Employee Motivation	Innovation Capability	External Linkages	Effect of ICT	Innovation Activity
Effect of ICT	0	0	0	0	0	0
Innovation capability	0.059	0.047	0	0	0	0
External linkage	0.087	0.069	0	0	0	0
Innovation activity	0.25	0.317	0	0	0.218	0
Innovation	0.201	0.239	0.173	0.085	0.199	0

Source: Authors

Hypothesis 1

The causality of "Top management participation" on "Effect of ICT" has the value 0.239 ($p<0.000$) and the causality of "Employee motivation" on "Effect of ICT" has the value 0.191 ($p<0.000$). Since both are positively significant, H1, Manager participation and employee motivation promote ICT use, is verified.

Hypothesis 2

The causality of "Top Management participation" on "Innovation capability" is 0.242 ($p<0.000$) and that of "Employee motivation" on "Innovation capability" is 0.402 ($p<0.000$). Since these arrows are positively significant, H2, Top manager participation and employee motivation enhance innovation capability, is verified.

Hypothesis 3

The effect of "Top Management participation" on "External linkages" is 0.144 (p<0.016) and that of "Employee motivation" on "External linkages" is 0.153 (p<0.012). Since both are positively significant, H3, Top management's participation and employees' motivation promote external linkages, is verified.

Hypothesis 4

The "Effect of ICT" on "Innovation capability" is 0.245 (p<0.000) and that of "Effect of ICT" on "External linkages" is 0.363 (p<0.000). Since these are positively significant, H4. 1, the Effect of ICT use promotes innovation capability and external linkages, is verified. It should be noted that, since Model 2 is not adopted, H4.2 cannot be examined by these models.

Hypothesis 5

The "Effect of ICT" on "Innovation activity" is 0.516 (p<0.000), that of "Innovation capability on "Innovation activity" is 0.253 (p<0.000), and that of "External linkages" on "Innovation activity" is 0.153 (p<0.000). Since all show positively significant values, H5, Innovation capability, external linkages and effect of ICT use promote innovation activity, is verified.

Hypothesis 6

The effect of "Innovation activity" on "Innovation" is 0.336 (p<0.000), which is positively significant. H6, Innovation activity promotes innovation, is therefore verified.

Hypothesis 7

The "Effect of ICT" on "Innovation" is 0.171 (p<0.044) and that of "Innovation capability" on "Innovation" is 0.185 (p<0.008), which show positively significant values. However, the causality of "External linkages" on "innovation" was not found to be significant. Therefore, H7, Innovation capability, external linkages, and ICT use directly promote innovation, is only partly verified.

DISCUSSION

This study demonstrates the causal relationships among three sources of innovation and that between the three sources and innovation itself. The main findings of this chapter may be summarized as follows.

Rigorous Examination

Regarding the relationship between the effect of ICT use and sources of innovation such as innovation capability and external linkages, two models were constructed and analyzed using SEM to determine their validity. Two opposing relationships can be considered between ICT use and innovation capability. Namely, ICT enhances innovation capability, or firms with higher innovation capability can easily introduce ICT and promote efficiency. It is necessary to analyze the two models for, and verify, true causality. In doing so, this chapter has constructed two models with opposing causality, and has showed that ICT use affects innovation capability and external linkages. Chen (2012) shows that IT-enabled resources have an impact on R&D capability, but do not examine the reverse relationship. It might be the case that the reverse relationship is also viable.

Intermediate Parameter

Many studies, such as Perdomo-Ortiza et al. (2009), Menguc & Auh (2010), Yam, Lo, Tang, & Lau, (2011), Kmieciak, Michna, & Meczynska (2012) and so on, attempt to clarify the direct relationship between capability and managerial performance. However, firms with high capability

Table 13. Result of Structural Equation Modeling (Model 1)

	From	To	Standardized Coefficient	SE	*t* Value	*p* Value
H1	Top Management Participation	Effect of ICT	0.239	0.043	4.374	0.000***
H1	Employee Motivation	Effect of ICT	0.191	0.087	3.498	0.000***
H2	Top Management Participation	Innovation Capability	0.242	0.049	4.507	0.000***
H2	Employee Motivation	Innovation Capability	0.402	0.11	6.833	0.000***
H3	Top Management Participation	External Linkages	0.144	0.042	2.408	0.016**
H3	Employee Motivation	External Linkages	0.153	0.088	2.51	0.012**
H4. 1	Effect of ICT	Innovation Capability	0.245	0.062	4.584	0.000***
H4. 1	Effect of ICT	External Linkages	0.363	0.061	5.38	0.000***
H5	Innovation Capability	Innovation Activity	0.516	0.053	8.32	0.000***
H5	External Linkages	Innovation Activity	0.253	0.068	4.08	0.000***
H5	Effect of ICT	Innovation Activity	0.153	0.053	2.836	0.005***
H6	Innovation Activity	Innovation	0.336	0.044	3.534	0.000***
H7	Innovation Capability	Innovation	0.171	0.033	2.015	0.044**
H7	External Linkages	Innovation	0.091	0.04	1.141	0.254
H7	Effect of ICT	Innovation	0.185	0.032	2.66	0.008***

Note: *** and ** indicate significance at the 1% and 5% level, respectively.
Source: Authors

may not necessarily achieve a high performance automatically. In contrast, it is natural to consider that in such firms, high capability promotes business behavior, and as a result firms elevate their performance. This chapter adds a variable termed innovation activity, which is an intermediate variable between capability and innovation. Chen (2012) adds "Strategic objective" between capability and performance, and Bergh & Lim (2008) adds "Sell-off" and "Spin-off."

Implications of the Results

The results of the analysis above lead to the following implications.

1. For effective use of ICT, Top management participation (0.239) is more important than Employee motivation (0.191). This implies that top management has to take the initiative in promoting ICT use rather than leaving it to employees.

Most SMEs lack of leadership of top management, low ICT investment, absence of ICT experts or advisor, lack of knowledge regarding ICT use, and so on (Yap, Soh, & Raman, 1992; Cragg & Zinatelli, 1995; Thong & Yap, 1995; Doukidis, Lybereas, & Galliers, 1996; Delone, 1988; Igbaria, Zinatelli, & Cavaye, 1998; Levy & Powell, 2000; Caldeira & Ward, 2002; Tsuji 2005; Ruiz-Mercader, Merono-Cerdan, & Sabater-Sanchez, 2006; Kauremaa, Karkkainen, & Ala-Risku, 2009). Top management should play the most important role to promote ICT use among SMEs (Delone, 1988; Martin, 1989; Yap et al., 1992; Thong & Yap, 1995; Igbaria et al., 1998; Calderia & Ward, 2002).

2. Innovation capability requires Employee motivation (0.402) more than Top management participation (0.242). This implies that employees have a greater role to play in the promotion of innovation capability than management in Japanese innovative SMEs.

Japanese firms are famous for "*Kaizen* (improvement activity)" at the production site or job shop. Quality management (quality control) is a typical example. Voluntary participation of improvement which is employee's motivation is important for innovation capability (Idota et al., 2012b).

3. For external linkages, Top management participation (0.144) and Employee motivation (0.153) are required, but their importance is almost the same.
4. The effect of ICT is influenced more by External linkages (0.363) than Innovation capability (0.245), implying that ICT is more effective for obtaining information and collaborating with external organizations.

This results mention that the use of ICT for sharing information and knowledge with external organizations is indispensable for the promotion of innovation (Gassmann & von Zedtwitz, 2003; Dodgson et al., 2006; Piller & Walcher, 2006; Dittrich & Duysters, 2007; Idota et al., 2010; 2012c).

5. Innovation activity is affected by Innovation capability (0.516), followed by External linkages (0.253), and Effect of ICT (0.153).

It follows from the above discussions that Innovation capability is the most important factor for promoting Innovation activity, but that External linkages and Effect of ICT are also useful.

FUTURE RESEARCH DIRECTIONS

Although this study demonstrates a new dimension regarding the role of ICT use in the innovation process, it also has some limitations. The following are indications of directions for future study:

1. The paths from innovation capability, effect of ICT, external linkages, and innovation activity to innovation were examined. The reverse paths, however, may also exist, such that achieved innovation in turn strengthens these factors. The causal relationship between innovation and the factors is not necessarily one way. Both directions of causality must be considered in the analysis.
2. In the innovation process, external factors such as business environments might influence innovation, but these have not been considered in this analysis.
3. Innovation activity was analyzed as an intermediate parameter in this analysis. Other intermediate parameters, such as the amount of R&D investment, could also be examined.
4. This analysis focused on innovative SMEs, but to obtain more general conclusions large firms should also be included in the analysis.

Future analyses should address these problems.

CONCLUSION

In this chapter, the relationship between ICT use and innovation in Japanese SMEs was analyzed by SEM. As a result of the analyses, the model "ICT affects innovation capability and external linkages" was selected according to AIC. That is, innovation capability and external linkages are activated by ICT use, and thus innovation is promoted. On the other hand, the model "ICT use is improved by innovation capability and external linkages, and then innovation is promoted," was found not to be suitable.

Limitations of the Study

A limitation of the study was that the data used referred only to Japanese SMEs, though the mechanism by which ICT use promoted innovation was clarified in this chapter. However, all other coefficients are positively significant according to the adopted model, except the hypothesis that external linkages promote innovation directly. The result indicates the following; (i) top management participation and employee motivation promote the effect of ICT use, innovation capability and external linkages; (ii) the effect of ICT use raises innovation capability and external linkages; (iii) the effect of ICT use, innovation capability and external linkages activate innovation activity and promote innovation as a result; and (iv) the effect of ICT use and innovation capability promote innovation directly. The effect of ICT use is the largest variable contributing to innovation. From this, it is verified that ICT use is indispensable for innovation in Japanese SMEs.

It should be noted, however, that ICT itself does not create innovation, but rather ICT further promotes the effects of top management as well as employees who participate positively in creating new business. Similarly ICT promotes the roles of innovation capability and absorptive ability in the same way. Human and organizational factors are important in the utilization of ICT for creating innovation.

Toward the General Theory of ICT Capability

Finally, let us consider the further use of ICT for innovation in the age of rapid transformation. Market environments are shifting faster and more drastically than expected, and in order to cope with the dynamism of the market, firms are required to develop agility to catch up with changes (Goldman, Preiss, & Nagel, 1995). That is, firms have to supply new goods and services meeting consumers' desires or restructure their business processes to correspond with the new environments. In so doing, it is important to make use of or combine new ICT applications such as SNS, cloud computing, or standardized package software such as ERP. This could be achieved by enhancing *ICT capability*, which is defined by Bharadwaj as "the ability to mobilize and deploy IT-based resources in combination with other resources and capabilities" (Bharadwaj, 2000). IT-based resources consist of the following three factors; (i) IT infrastructure, which is composed of information technology, technological platforms and databases, (ii) human IT resources such as employee skills, training, experience, insight, and relationships between employees; and (iii) intangible IT-enabled resources such as know-how, organizational culture, reputation, and environmental adaptability (Bharadwaj, 2000). The factor with the most variability is not the individual engineering of IT-based resources, but the capability to incorporate various systems and resources, such as human and organizational resources, with ICT to create a synergistic effect. Innovative firms literally have to "own" their ICT capability. In this sense, ICT will become more and more indispensable for innovation, whatever shape the future economy will take.

ACKNOWLEDGMENT

This chapter is partly supported by JSPS grants titled "Research on Organization IQ and the Strengthening that Contributes to Creation of Innovation" (c-23530307) and "Business Innovation Strategy by Social Media" (Grant number c-24530435) and the Ministry of Education, Culture, Sports, Science and Technology, Japan (MEXT) Program for Strategic Research Bases at Private Universities (2012-16) project "Organizational Information Ethics" S1291006. Financial supports are gratefully acknowledged.

REFERENCES

Bagozzi, R. P. (1980). *Causal Models in Marketing*. New York, NY: Wiley.

Barney, J. (1991). Firm resources and sustained competitive advantage. *Journal of Management*, *17*(1), 99–120. doi:10.1177/014920639101700108

Beccheti, L., Londono Bedoya, D. A., & Paganetto, L. (2003). ICT Investment, Productivity and Efficiency: Evidence at Firm Level using a Stochastic Frontier Approach. *Journal of Productivity Analysis*, *20*(2), 143–167. doi:10.1023/A:1025128121853

Bergh, D. D., & Lim, E. N. (2008). Learning how to restructure: Absorptive capacity and improvisational views of restructuring actions and performance. *Strategic Management Journal*, *29*(6), 593–616. doi:10.1002/smj.676

Bharadwaj, A. S. (2000). A Resource-Based Perspective on Information Technology Capability and Firm Performance: An Empirical Investigation. *Management Information Systems Quarterly*, *24*(1), 169–196. doi:10.2307/3250983

Bock, R. D. (1960). Components of Variance Analysis as a Structural and Discriminal Analysis for Psychological Tests. *British Journal of Statistical Psychology*, *13*(2), 151–163. doi:10.1111/j.2044-8317.1960.tb00052.x

Bock, R. D., & Bargmann, R. E. (1966). Analysis of Covariance Structures. *Psychometrika*, *31*(4), 507–533. doi:10.1007/BF02289521 PMID:5232439

Bollenn, K. A. (1989). *Structural Equations with latent Variables*. New York, NY: Wiley. doi:10.1002/9781118619179

Caldeira, M. M., & Ward, J. M. (2002). Understanding the successful adoption and use of IS/IT in SMEs: An explanation from Portuguese manufacturing industries. *Information Systems Journal*, *12*(2), 121–152. doi:10.1046/j.1365-2575.2002.00119.x

Carlsoon, B. (2004). The Digital Economy: What is New and What is Not? *Structural Change and Economic Dynamics*, *15*(3), 245–264. doi:10.1016/j.strueco.2004.02.001

Caroli, E., & van Reenen, J. (2001). Skill-biased organizational change? Evidence from a panel of British and French establishments. *The Quarterly Journal of Economics*, *116*(4), 1449–1492. doi:10.1162/003355301753265624

Chen, J. (2012). The synergistic effects of IT-enabled resources on organizational capabilities and firm performance. *Information & Management*, *49*(3-4), 142–150. doi:10.1016/j.im.2012.01.005

Chesbrough, H. W. (2003). *Open innovation: The new imperative for creating and profiting from technology*. Boston, MA: Harvard Business School Press.

Chesbrough, H. W. (2006a). Open innovation: A new paradigm for understanding industrial innovation. In H. W.Chesbrough, W. Vanhaverbeke, & J. West (Eds.), Open Innovation: Researching a New Paradigm (pp. 1-12). Oxford, UK: Oxford University Press.

Chesbrough, H. W. (2006b). *Open business model: How to thrive in the new innovation landscape*. Boston, MA: Harvard Business School Press.

Cohen, W. M., & Levinthal, D. A. (1990). Absorptive capacity: A new perspective on learning and innovation. *Administrative Science Quarterly*, *35*(1), 128–152. doi:10.2307/2393553

Cragg, P. B., & Zinatelli, N. (1995). The evolution of information systems in small firms. *Information & Management*, *29*(1), 1–8. doi:10.1016/0378-7206(95)00012-L

Damaskopoulos, P., & Evgeniou, T. (2003). Adoption of new economy practices by SMEs in Eastern Europe. *European Management Journal*, *21*(2), 133–145. doi:10.1016/S0263-2373(03)00009-4

Delone, W. (1988). Determinants of success for computer usage in small business. *Management Information Systems Quarterly*, *12*(1), 51–61. doi:10.2307/248803

Dittrich, K., & Duysters, D. (2007). Networking as a means to strategy change: The case of open innovation in mobile telephony. *Journal of Product Innovation Management*, *24*(6), 510–521. doi:10.1111/j.1540-5885.2007.00268.x

Dodgson, M., Gann, D., & Salter, A. (2006). The role of technology in the shift towards open innovation: The case of Procter & Gamble. *R & D Management*, *36*(3), 333–346. doi:10.1111/j.1467-9310.2006.00429.x

Doukidis, G. I., Lybereas, P., & Galliers, R. D. (1996). Information systems planning in small business: A stages of growth analysis. *Journal of Systems and Software*, *33*(2), 189–201. doi:10.1016/0164-1212(95)00183-2

Gassmann, O., & von Zedtwitz, M. (2003). Trends and determinants of managing virtual R&D team. *R & D Management*, *33*(3), 243–262. doi:10.1111/1467-9310.00296

Goldman, S. L., Preiss, K., & Nagel, R. N. (1995). *Agile Competitors and Virtual Organizations: Strategies for Enriching the Customer*. New York, NY: Van Nostrand Reinhold.

Gretton, P., Gali, J., & Parham, D. (2004). The effects of ICTs and complementary innovation on Australian productivity growth. In OECD (Ed.), *The economic impact of ICT: Measurement, evidence and implications* (pp. 105–130). Paris, FR: OECD Publishing.

Hollenstein, H. (2004). Determinants of the Adoption of Information and Communication Technologies. *Structural Change and Economic Dynamics*, *15*(3), 315–342. doi:10.1016/j.strueco.2004.01.003

Idota, H., Akematsu, Y., Ueki, Y., & Tsuji, M. (2013a). Empirical Analysis on Innovative Capability and ICT Use in Firms of Four ASEAN Economies. *Proceedings of 2013 AAA ITS Regional Conference* (pp. 1-30). Perth, Australia.

Idota, H., Bunno, T., & Tsuji, M. (2010). Open innovation success factors by ICT use in Japanese firms. *Proceedings of the 21th European regional ITS Conference* (pp. 1-23). Copenhagen, Denmark.

Idota, H., Bunno, T., & Tsuji, M. (2011). Empirical Analysis of Internal Social Media and Product Innovation: Focusing on SNS and Social Capital. *Proceedings of the 22nd European regional ITS Conference* (pp. 1-20). Budapest Hungary.

Idota, H., Bunno, T., & Tsuji, M. (2012a). Open innovation strategy of Japanese SMEs: From viewpoint of ICT use and innovative technology. *Proceedings of the 23th European regional ITS Conference* (pp. 1-14). Vienna, Austria.

Idota, H., Bunno, T., & Tsuji, M. (2012b). Empirical Study on ICT Use and Business Strategy for Innovation among Japanese SMEs. *Proceedings of the 19th ITS Biennial Conference* (pp. 1-17). Bangkok, Thailand.

Idota, H., Bunno, T., & Tsuji, M. (2013b). Covariance Structure Analysis of Innovation and ICT Use among Japanese innovative SMEs. *Proceedings of the 24th European Regional ITS Conference* (pp. 1-22). Florence, Italy.

Idota, H., Bunno, T., & Tsuji, M. (2014). An Empirical Analysis of Innovation Success Factors Due to ICT Use in Japanese Firms. In T., Tsiakis, T., Kargidis, & P. Katsaros (Eds.), Approaches and Processes for Managing the Economics of Information Systems, (pp. 324-347). Hershey, PA: IGI. doi:10.4018/978-1-4666-4983-5.ch020

Idota, H., Ogawa, M., Bunno, T., & Tsuji, M. (2012c). An empirical analysis of organizational innovation generated by ICT in Japanese SMEs. In S., Allegrezza, & A., Dubrocard (Eds.), Internet econometrics (pp. 259-287). Hampshire, UK: Macmillan. doi:10.1057/9780230364226.0020

Igbaria, M., Zinatelli, N., & Cavaye, A. L. M. (1998). Analysis of information technology success in small firms in New Zealand. *International Journal of Information Management*, *18*(2), 103–119. doi:10.1016/S0268-4012(97)00053-4

Kagami, M., Giovannetti, E., & Tsuji, M. (Eds.). (2007). *Industrial Agglomeration: Facts and Lessons for Developing Countries*. Cheltenham, U.K.: Edward Elgar.

Kauremaa, J., Kärkkäinen, M., & Ala-Risku, T. (2009). Customer initiated interorganizational information systems: The operational impacts and obstacles for small and medium sized suppliers. *International Journal of Production Economics*, *119*(2), 228–239. doi:10.1016/j.ijpe.2009.02.007

Kmieciak, R., Michna, A., & Meczynska, A. (2012). Innovativeness, empowerment and IT capability: Evidence from SMEs. *Industrial Management & Data Systems*, *112*(5), 707–728. doi:10.1108/02635571211232280

Lawson, B., & Samson, D. (2001). Developing innovation capability in organisations: A dynamic capabilities approach. *International Journal of Innovation Management*, *5*(3), 377–400. doi:10.1142/S1363919601000427

Lee, G., & Xia, W. (2006). Organizational size and IT innovation adoption: A meta-analysis. *Information & Management*, *43*(8), 979–985. doi:10.1016/j.im.2006.09.003

Levy, M., & Powell, P. (2000). Information systems strategy for small and medium sized enterprises: An organizational perspective. *The Journal of Strategic Information Systems*, *9*(1), 63–84. doi:10.1016/S0963-8687(00)00028-7

Mariano, N., & Pilar, Q. (2005). Absorptive capacity, technological opportunity, knowledge spillovers, and innovative effort. *Technovation*, *25*(10), 1141–1157. doi:10.1016/j.technovation.2004.05.001

Martin, C. J. (1989). Information management in the smaller business: The role of the top manager. *International Journal of Information Management*, *9*(3), 187–197. doi:10.1016/0268-4012(89)90006-6

Menguc, B., & Auh, S. (2010). Development and Return on Execution of Product Innovation Capabilities: The Role of Organizational Structure. *Industrial Marketing Management*, *39*(5), 820–831. doi:10.1016/j.indmarman.2009.08.004

OECD, & Eurostat (2005). *Oslo Manual: Guidelines for collecting and interpreting innovation data* (3rd ed.). Paris, FR: OECD Publishing.

Park, Y., Fujimoto, T., & Hong, P. (2012). Product architecture, organizational capabilities and IT integration for competitive advantage. *International Journal of Information Management*, *32*(5), 479–488. doi:10.1016/j.ijinfomgt.2011.12.002

Perdomo-Ortiza, J., González-Benito, J., & Galende, J. (2009). The intervening effect of business innovation capability on the relationship between Total Quality Management and technological innovation. *International Journal of Production Research*, *47*(18), 5087–5107. doi:10.1080/00207540802070934

Piller, F. T., & Walcher, D. (2006). Toolkits for idea competitions: A novel method to integrate users in new product development. *R & D Management*, *36*(3), 307–318. doi:10.1111/j.1467-9310.2006.00432.x

Ruiz-Mercader, J., Meroño-Cerdan, A. L., & Sabater-Sánchez, R. (2006). Information technology and learning: Their relationship and impact on organizational performance in small businesses. *International Journal of Information Management*, *26*(1), 16–29. doi:10.1016/j.ijinfomgt.2005.10.003

Schumpeter, J. A. (1934). *The theory of economic development*. Oxford, UK: Oxford University Press.

Spiezia, V. (2011). Are ICT users more innovation? An analysis of ICT-enabled innovation in OECD firms. *OECD Journal: Economic Studies*, *2011*, 99–119. doi:10.1787/19952856

Thong, J. Y. L., & Yap, C. S. (1995). CEO characteristics, organizational characteristics and information technology adoption in small businesses. *Omega*, *23*(4), 429–442. doi:10.1016/0305-0483(95)00017-I

Tidd, J., Bessant, J., & Pavitt, K. (2001). *Managing Innovation - Integrating Technological, Market and organizational Change* (2nd ed.). Chichester, U.K.: Wiley.

Tsuji, M. (2005). Information technology use in Japan. In M., Kuwayama, Y., Ueki, & M., Tsuji (Eds.). Information technology for development of Small and Medium-sized Exporters in Latin America and East Asia (pp. 345-373). Santiago de Chili, Chili: ECLAC/United Nations.

Tsuji, M., & Miyahara, S. (2010). A Comparative Analysis of Organizational Innovation in Japanese SMEs Generated by Information Communication Technology. In A., Kuchiki, & M. Tsuji (Eds.). From Agglomeration to Innovation: Upgrading Industrial Clusters in Emerging Economies (pp. 231-269). Basingstoke: Palgrave Macmillan.

Tsuji, M., & Miyahara, S. (2011). Agglomeration and Local Innovation Networks in Japanese SMEs: Analysis of the Information Linkage. In A., Kuchiki & M., Tsuji, (Eds.). Industrial Clusters, Upgrading and Innovation in East Asia (pp. 253-294). Cheltenham, U.K.: Edward Elgar.

Small and Medium Enterprises in Japan-Finding Vitality through Innovation and Human Resources [White Paper]. (2009). The Small and Medium Enterprise Agency. Tokyo, JPN: Ministry of Economy, Trade and Industry (METI). Retrieved from http://www.chusho.meti.go.jp/pamflet/hakusyo/h21/h21_1/2009hakusho_eng.pdf

Yam, R. C. M., Lo, W., Tang, E. P. Y., & Lau, A. K. W. (2011). Analysis of sources of innovation, technological innovation capabilities, and performance: An empirical study of Hong Kong manufacturing industries. *Research Policy*, *40*(3), 391–402. doi:10.1016/j.respol.2010.10.013

Yap, C. S., Soh, C., & Raman, K. (1992). Information systems success factors in small business. *Omega*, *20*(5-6), 597–609. doi:10.1016/0305-0483(92)90005-R

Zahra, H., & George, G. (2002). Absorptive Capacity: A Review, Reconceptualization, and Extension. *Academy of Management Review*, *27*(2), 185–203. doi:10.5465/AMR.2002.6587995

ADDITIONAL READING

Antonioli, D., Mazzanti, M., & Pini, P. (2010). Productivity, innovation strategies and industrial relations in SMEs. Empirical evidence for a local production system in northern Italy. *International Review of Applied Economics*, *24*(4), 453–482. doi:10.1080/02692171.2010.483790

Barney, J. B., & Clark, D. N. (2007). *Resource-based theory*. Oxford, NY: Oxford University Press.

Bartel, A., Ichniowski, C., & Shaw, K. (2007). How does information technology affect productivity? Plant-level comparisons of product innovation, process improvement, and work skills. *The Quarterly Journal of Economics*, *122*(4), 1721–1758. doi:10.1162/qjec.2007.122.4.1721

Brynjolfsson, E., & Hitt, L. (2000). Beyond computation: Information technology, organizational transformation and business performance. *The Journal of Economic Perspectives*, *14*(4), 23–48. doi:10.1257/jep.14.4.23

Brynjolfsson, E., & Kahin, B. (2000). *Understanding the digital economy: Data, tools, and research*. Cambridge, MA: MIT Press.

Brynjolfsson, E., & Saunders, A. (2009). *Wired for innovation: How information technology is reshaping the economy*. Cambridge, MA: MIT Press.

Burgelman, R., Christensen, C., & Wheelwright, S. (2008). *Strategic management of technology and innovation* (5th ed.). New York, NY: McGraw-Hill/Irwin.

Bygstad, B., & Lanestedt, G. (2009). ICT based service innovation: A challenge for project management. *International Journal of Project Management*, *27*(3), 234–242. doi:10.1016/j.ijproman.2007.12.002

Chesbrough, H. W. (2011). *Open services innovation: Rethinking your business to grow and compete in a new era*. San Francisco, CA: Jossey-Bass; doi:10.1007/978-88-470-1980-5

Corso, M., Martini, A., Paolucci, E., & Pellegrini, L. (2001). Information and communication technologies in product innovation within SMEs: The role of product complexity. *Enterprise and Innovation Management Studies*, *2*(1), 35–48. doi:10.1080/14632440110056319

Davenport, T. H. (1993). *Process innovation*. Boston, MA: Harvard Business School Press.

Davenport, T. H., & Prusak, L. (2000). *Working Knowledge: How Organizations Manage What They Know*. Boston, MA: Harvard Business School Press.

Dibrell, C., Davis, P. S., & Craig, J. (2008). Fueling innovation through information technology in SMEs. *Journal of Small Business Management*, *46*(2), 203–218. doi:10.1111/j.1540-627X.2008.00240.x

Gago, D., & Rubalcaba, L. (2007). Innovation and ICT in service firms: Towards a multidimensional approach for impact assessment. *Journal of Evolutionary Economics*, *17*(1), 25–44. doi:10.1007/s00191-006-0030-8

Hamel, G., & Prahalad, C. K. (1994). *Competing for the future*. Boston, MA: Harvard Business School Press.

Hammer, M., & Champy, J. (1993). *Reengineering the corporation: A manifesto for business revolution*. New York, NY: HarperCollins.

Helfat, C. E., Finkelstein, S., Mitchell, W., Peteraf, M., Singh, H., Teece, D., & Winter, S. G. (2007). *Dynamic capabilities: Understanding strategic change in organizations*. Malden, MA: Blackwell.

Johannssen, J. A., Olaisen, A. J., & Olsen, B. (1999). Strategic use of information technology for increased innovation and performance. *Information Management & Computer Security*, *7*(1), 5–22. doi:10.1108/09685229910255133

Keen, P. G. W. (1997). *The process edge: How firms thrive by getting the right process right*. Boston, MA: Harvard Business School Press.

Keen, P. G. W., & McDonald, M. (2000). *The e-process edge: Creating customer value and business wealth in the Internet era*. Berkeley, CA: McGraw-Hill.

Mandelson, H., & Ziegler, J. (1999). *Survival of the smartest*. New York, NY: Willy.

Melville, N., & Ramirez, R. (2008). Information technology innovation diffusion: An information requirements paradigm. *Information Systems Journal*, *18*(3), 247–273. doi:10.1111/j.1365-2575.2007.00260.x

Miyazaki, S., Idota, H., & Miyoshi, H. (2012). Corporate productivity and the stages of ICT development. *Information Technology Management*, *13*(1), 17–26. doi:10.1007/s10799-011-0108-3

Nambisan, S., Agrarwal, R., & Tanniru, M. (1999). Organizational mechanisms for enhancing user innovation in information technology. *Management Information Systems Quarterly*, *23*(3), 365–395. doi:10.2307/249468

Nonaka, I., & Takeuchi, H. (1995). *The knowledge creating company*. Oxford, NY: Oxford University Press.

Parker, M. M., Benson, R. J., & Trainor, H. E. (1998). *Information economics: Linking business performance to information technology*. Englewood Cliffs, NJ: Prentice Hall.

Peansupap, V., & Walker, D. H. T. (2006). Innovation diffusion at the implementation stage of a construction project: A case study of information communication technology. *Construction Management and Economics*, *24*(3), 321–332. doi:10.1080/01446190500435317

Pijpers, G. G. M., & Montfort, K. (2005). An investigation of factors that influence senior executives to accept innovations in information technology. *International. Journal of Management*, *22*(4), 542–555.

Sambamuthy, V., Bharadwaj, A., & Gorover, V. (2003). Shaping agility through digital options: Reconceptualizing the role of information technology in contemporary firms. *Management Information Systems Quarterly*, *27*(2), 237–263.

Teece, D. J. (2009). *Dynamic capabilities & strategic management organizing for innovation and growth*. Oxford, NY: Oxford University Press.

Teece, D. J., Pisano, G., & Shuen, A. (1997). Dynamic Capabilities and Strategic Management. *Strategic Management Journal*, *18*(7), 509–533. doi:10.1002/(SICI)1097-0266(199708)18:7<509::AID-SMJ882>3.0.CO;2-Z

Tidd, J., & Bessant, J. (2009). *Managing innovation: Integrating technological, market and organizational change* (4th ed.). London, UK: Willy.

Utterback, J. M. (1994). *Mastering the dynamics of innovation: How companies can seize opportunities in the face of technological change*. Boston, MA: Harvard Business School Press.

Wang, P. (2009). Popular concepts beyond organizations: Exploring new dimensions of information technology innovations. *Journal of the Association for Information Systems*, *10*(1), 1–30. doi:10.5465/AMBPP.2007.26529396

Wang, P., & Ramiller, N. C. (2009). Community learning in information technology innovation. *Management Information Systems Quarterly*, *33*(4), 709–734.

KEY TERMS AND DEFINITIONS

Employee Motivation: Voluntary behavior of employees toward their work, particularly innovation, which characterizes the competitiveness of firms.

External Linkages: External organizations such as customers, suppliers, universities or research organizations, for example, providing information on technologies, consumer needs or the market, or engaging in joint R&D with other firms.

Innovation: To create new products and services and to promote productivity by renovating management. This mainly consists of product and process innovation.

Innovation Activities: Activities for innovation which include not only R&D but also data analysis on customers' needs, the market, and rival firms.

Innovation Capability: Organizational capability related to the creation of new products and services, which is the basis for innovation of firms.

SMEs (Small- and Medium-Sized Enterprises): Japanese SMEs are defined by Article 2 of the Small and Medium- sized Enterprise Basic Act as firms in manufacturing industries with 300 employees or less, or with capital of JPY 300 million (USD 3 million) or less, firms in other industries with 100 employees or less, or with capital of JPY 100 million (USD 1 million) or less, firms in the wholesale industry with 50 employees or less or with capital of JPY 50 million (USD 500 thousand) or less and firms in the retail industry with 100 employees or less or with capital of JPY 50 million (USD 500 thousand) or less.

Top Management Participation: Leadership of top management engaging in innovation activity including R&D, establishing project teams, and so on.

ENDNOTES

1. The questionnaire survey targeted unlisted innovative SMEs which have the following characteristics: (i) the number of employees exceeds 20; (ii) the amount of sales was in the range JPY one million to 9.9 billion in FY2011; (iii) the latest growth rate of sales exceeds 20%; and (iv) the SME has achieved continuous surplus in profit in the most recent three terms.
2. Cronbach's α is 0.676, which is rather low. In the case of Explanatory Factor Analysis (EFA), it is acceptable if the value of Cronbach's α is larger than 0.6 (Bagozzi, 1994), although it is generally required to be larger than 0.7.

Chapter 6
The Empirical Analysis of Cloud Computing Services among the Hungarian Enterprises

Peter Sasvari
University of Miskolc, Hungary

Zoltán Nagymate
University of Miskolc, Hungary

ABSTRACT

Innovation capability has increasingly been searched by the ICT sector in cloud computing applications recently. This chapter describes the economic potentials of cloud computing and explores the characteristics of its usage among Hungarian enterprises. Although enterprises are aware of the basic concept of cloud computing, they have concerns about its application mainly due to data security issues and the lack of education. The chance of using cloud computing services is mainly facilitated by the creation of easier application and consultation would positively affect their usage. According to microenterprises and corporations, faster information flow and remote access are the key benefits of cloud usage. In the case of small-sized enterprises, the two main advantages are easier system recoverability and a higher level of mobility in case of a system breakdown. For the medium-sized enterprises, remote access and greater data security were the key benefits of using cloud computing services in 2014.

1. INTRODUCTION

The increasingly fierce economic competition requires companies to respond to the environmental changes as quickly as possible. Keeping pace with the speed of the technological development is difficult but the identification of revolutionary innovations and their adaptation within a short period of time might be a turning point in the life of an organization. The development level of information technology (IT) at an enterprise also indicates its ability to innovate because in lack of proper equipments innovation is impossible (Sasvari, 2012).

IT tools provide support for an enterprise in several areas. With their help, inter alia, production processes can be optimized, communication can be facilitated, information flow becomes faster and

DOI: 10.4018/978-1-4666-8598-7.ch006

data processing becomes more efficient. However, the operation of an IT department involves challenges as well. Establishing the IT-infrastructure is on the one hand a capital-intensive task, not to mention the additional maintenance and development costs. On the other hand, system operation requires a high level of expertise, which is reflected both at management and employee levels (Shaw, 2011).

If the organization's information technology is not cost-effective and its operation is not in proper hands, it doesn't support the implementation of targets. *Cloud computing* offers solution for the two mentioned basic as well as many other problems.

The newest stage in the evolution of IT is the emergence of cloud, which has fundamentally changed the industry. The English definition of "cloud computing" means a service. Its essence is that the customer obtains IT tools via Internet connection, so their IT department or at least a part of it can be outsourced.

The appearance of the model has a complex impact on the whole economy in the long term. This concept is not only present at a company-level but also in the everyday life of people. The range of services involves not only the simple e-mail sending but also the data storage and the operation of web-based management functions in the company. There were many professional studies dealing with the questions that served as a basis when the secondary research was carried out.

We focused on the enterprise as a customer and a recipient of cloud-based services. The aim of our research was to find out what the impact of the partial or full changeover to the new technology was in the case of Hungarian organizations in their everyday life and competitiveness. The basic questions of the research were the following:

- To what extent is the concept of cloud computing known among the Hungarian enterprises?
- What are the characteristics of using this technology in Hungarian organizations?
- What are the critical decision factors?
- Is the use of cloud computing services effective?

2. DEFINITION AND CLASSIFICATION OF CLOUD COMPUTING

In the background of cloud computing development is the idea, according to which information processing method is much more efficient when it is accessible via network and it is processed through centrally aligned computer and storage systems.

The term "cloud" is derived from how the Internet is presented on network diagrams, with which the unknown or irrelevant parts of the system are marked.

In the practice the most widely accepted definition was developed by the U.S. National Institute of Standards and Technology (NIST). This definition is also used in the European Union's publications which reads as follows:

"Cloud technology is a model that enables anywhere a convenient and on-demand access to shared set of customized IT resources (networks, servers, storage, applications, services), while it requires minimal administrative activities and service intervention."

The clouds can be classified in many ways. The cloud models can be differentiated on the basis of how many tenants have the resources used by the customer, by whom the background infrastructure is operated, where the tools are located (Bőgel, 2009). According to Mell and Grance (2011), four types of clouds can be differentiated:

- Private cloud,
- Community cloud,
- Public cloud,
- Hybrid cloud.

Private cloud is a computing infrastructure reserved for only one organization. We differentiate two types: they are established inside or outside the company's plant. The private cloud can be owned and operated by the given organization, the service provider, a third party or by one of their any other combinations. This solution has the advantage that the resource is not shared with other tenants which means that a higher performance can be provided. It can be adapted to the individual interests of the company and combined with any organizational level. The key is that the exclusive usage provides a greater security. As a drawback, high acquisition costs have to be mentioned since in this case the investment is done by the user of the infrastructure. In addition, the question of long-term commitment can be mentioned. The company cannot terminate the installed units in a flexible and cost effective way (Molnár et al., 2012).

Community cloud operates also like the private cloud in a closed system. However, not only a single company but a group of them has access to the infrastructure. Organizations are linked together by a common interest, such as efficiency considerations, compliance with government regulations, and reduction of security risks. A community cloud can be owned and operated by one or more partners or a third party. It can also be installed inside or outside the company. Its main advantage is to share the investment costs because the purchase of hardware and software tools is made jointly. In terms of data storage, a closed group of tenants is associated with less risk that is why mutual trust between the parties is a very important condition. The model is a kind of transition between private and public clouds in terms of costs and security. It has the disadvantage that the fulfillment of individual interests can only be reached by the organization when making compromises. In addition, the existing systems must be harmonized with each other, which often involve the replacement of tools.

Unlike in the past, the infrastructure of public cloud can be accessed by anyone. The resources are owned, managed and operated by the service provider on their own premises. In practice, the term refers in many cases to traditional cloud computing. Thus the experts researching the trends of cloud computing take only public clouds into account, which can be misleading. This model offers the cheapest solution of all because there is no need to purchase expensive equipment. The commitment for the service is short-term or temporary. Access to the system is much more flexible than private clouds. The disadvantage is that the user has less influence on the operation because the cloud is managed exclusively by the service provider. The security risks are high; the isolation of users is a key issue. There might be difficulties with the accessibility and availability time. The support or assistance can be due to the large number of customers impersonal.

Hybrid cloud is defined as the combination of the above-mentioned variants. In this case a high level of personalization is applied. The company may carry out certain functions via public cloud and others via private cloud. A barrier may be the creation of integrity belonging to different systems and the lack of knowledge utilization. In many cases it is difficult to differentiate in which system the application is running.

The second main classification method is based on the method of service. The three basic methods are as follows:

- Infrastructure as a Service – (IaaS)
- Platform as a Service – (PaaS)
- Softvare as a Service – (SaaS)

The infrastructure as a service is the most elementary level. In this case the service provides hardware devices that are fundamental computing resources for a company. The hardware is accessible for the user through a virtual interface, which means that the user installs and runs the necessary operating system and applications on his own. Customers are responsible for the installed software, they keep them under control. The running and supervision of the basic infrastructure belong to the responsibility of the service provider. In this method the enterprise has a major task, including resource management and updating, and is also responsible for the implementation of security services exceeding the basic infrastructure.

In the case of platform as a service the customer rents not only the hardware devices but also the operating system. Indeed, the customer is provided with a full programming toolkit and a complex environment for development by the service provider. The user installs on his own the applications he has created or acquired for the system that can be controlled in this way however he also bears the responsibility. The provider is responsible for managing the infrastructure. The fulfillment of security measures is equally divided between the parties.

Software as a service is at the highest level of the hierarchy. In this model the customer has access to the applications running on the provider's infrastructure. The user needs only one so- called client to use the software. The client can be a device (e.g., laptop, smartphone and tablet) or a program (e.g. web browser). The operation of the infrastructure as well as the implementation of security activities are under the responsibility of the service provider. In addition, he installs, configures and updates the applications.

3. ADVANTAGES FROM THE USE OF CLOUD COMPUTING

Certain types of cloud computing have their own special advantages which mainly depend on the aim of usage. However, some of them are generally valid for all types of cloud.

Here are the most important ones (Buest et al, 2013):

- **Cost reduction** (low level of capital investment or no capital investment at all; less IT employees are required to maintain the system; higher fixed costs can be converted into low variable and operation costs; reducing the system-related administrative tasks) (Szucsne, 2012)
- **Data security and data protection** (More efficient data management and control; Better order of data; Better data security; Easier recoverability in case of system failure),
- **Remote access** (Faster information flow, more efficient employee collaboration; remote access to information systems; easier access to hardware and software tools for the company; flexible service)
- **Fast installation** (High-level mobility)

More complex advantages:

- Change of working method and organizational culture.
- Improvement of competitiveness.

Cost reduction appears in many fields. There is no need for investment because the hardware devices are granted by the service provider. High capital costs can be turned into lower operational costs and with their help even less capital-intensive enterprises can access to the necessary infrastructure. The need for human resource in computing falls significantly, which also means savings (Mozsik, 2010).

The changeover of traditional IT into cloud-based computing is usually executed due to cost restraints. The examination of the cost reduction level is not a simple task because it has several elements. There are evident and less visible factors as well. Revealing the latter, in a particular case, significantly facilitates to choose between traditional and cloud-based information technology (Nanterme et al., 2013).

It is evident that in contrast with the traditional IT system the investment into hardware devices, buying software or having a large number of employees at the IT department are not required when using the service. However, when making efficiency calculations, few companies remember the opportunity costs. A study examining the cost effectiveness of the cloud classifies the financial factors in the following way (Kepes, 2012):

- Lowering the opportunity cost of running technology;
- Allowing for a shift from capital expenditure to operating expenditure;
- Lowering the total cost of ownership (TCO) of technology;
- Giving organizations the ability to add business value by renewed focus on core activities.

The examination of the factors cannot be fully separated because they interact with each other. Opportunity cost is closely related to the more effective concentration on value adding IT processes. The reduction of capital cost affects the examination of the total „costs" of ownership.

Opportunity cost is one of the basic terms in the economic studies. Though its understanding varies from accounting and economic point of view, its essence is in both cases the same. The basis is what other activities we have given up therefore to what extent we have lost the yield with the realization of a given activity. The last part of the sentence implies that it is not about costs but about profit category.

The term can be described in the conception of managerial economic sciences as follows: (Samuelson et al., 1987, pp. 667): „The opportunity cost of a given decision consists of things that are given up when a certain decision is made instead of an alternative decision."

In terms of IT, opportunity cost appears mainly due to the unequal usage of resources. 80% of the IT department's total costs contain maintenance costs (Kepes 2012), which means only one fifth of the resources are spent on value adding processes. The applications are running smoothly only in this way. The main part of the time is spent on updating the operating systems, recovery activities of servers and data centers. In an ideal case the proportions would be reciprocal. While IT specialists invest their energy into secondary tasks, the company loses yields. Opportunity cost can be reduced significantly when cloud-based services are available for the organization. Depending on the service method, the handling of hardware devices, updating the operating systems, renewal of application licenses are in the responsibility of the service provider so the time investment into supporting functions can be shortened to the minimum (Harris, 2013).

From a financial point of view, one of the most important characteristics of the cloud is that it can turn high capital costs into low operational and maintenance costs. The establishment of a traditional data center within the company is often goes hand in hand with unacceptable investment costs that is why it needs to be determined carefully (Fajszi et al., 2010).

As it is shown in Figure 1, the equipment (electronic-, holding-, cooling devices all together 26%), construction costs (18%), the necessary energy (20%), maintenance (15%) and the reservation of place itself (15%) are factors weighted relatively equal. In the case of a rental only a part of it is charged to the company.

The costs of the shown data center for the whole life of operation mount up to around 120 thousand dollars (APC, 2003). Considering the introduction of cloud, the simple comparison of the value with the service fee may lead to incorrect decisions. Frequently, the continuous daily continuous use of external infrastructure is compared to the daily running of a traditional system. The result might be disadvantageous for the cloud, though an essential point is missing in the calculation, i.e. exploring the relationship between capital and operating costs (Golden, 2009).

The investment into servers and other devices means the long-term commitment of the company. The costs of unused capacity must be paid and the capital goods lock up the money of the

Figure 1. General cost structure of establishing a data centre

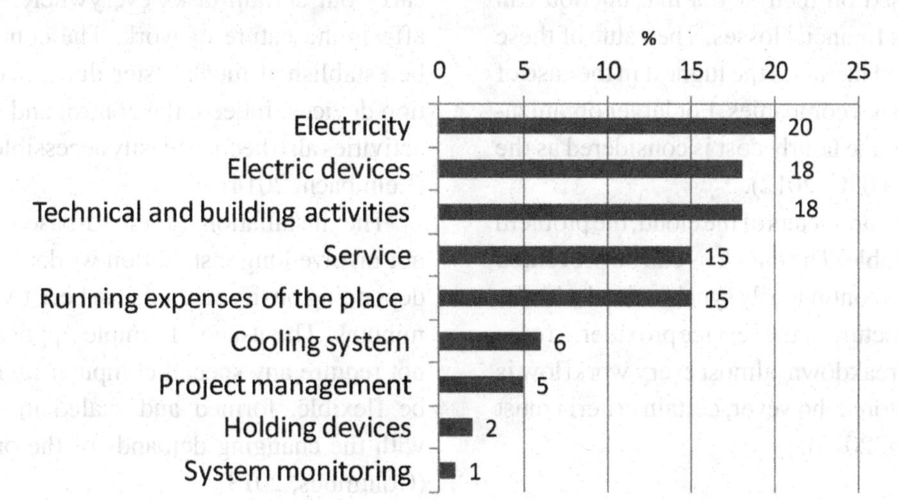

organization. In the case of the cloud, since the infrastructure is rented, the payment is done in the proportion of usage. The price of this flexibility is the availability fee that is why the conventional system seems to be cheaper. The added value of the cloud is its scalability and flexibility when necessary. The framework of capital investment is limited at most companies because the management is not interested in the lockup. With the help of the service the liquidity becomes sustainable in the future, which is expressively an important task while running the company because the need for resources often occurs unexpectedly.

Data security means the easier recoverability after a possible system crash. With the data synchronization the risk of information loss can be reduced. The backups also have cost implications because the potential maintenance, recovery works set back the production, which leads to loss of revenue (Safranka, 2013).

The increase of data protection effectiveness means the reduction of risks related to system crashes. The factor is closely related to the former point because the recovery also causes costs. Its average value based on a study dealing with the topic (Aberdeen Group, 2012) increases from year to year parallel to the emergence of automation activities. The damages related to the system interruption of data centers are summarized in Table 1.

It shows that all size categories are significantly affected by the yearly average cost. The end sum is formed due to the different components. The average duration and number of downtime at micro and small-sized enterprises are relatively high. In

Table 1. Yearly average cost of data center downtime by size category

	Micro-, Small-Sized Enterprise	Medium-Sized Enterprise	Corporation
Avg. number of downtime	1.7 pcs/year	3.5 pcs/year	3.0 pcs/year
Avg. duration of downtime	2.2. hour/pcs	3.4 hour/pcs	0.8 hour/pcs
Avg. hourly cost of downtime	6,900 $/hour	74,000 $/hour	1,130,000 $/hour
Yearly avg. impact	25,806 $/year	880,600 $/year	2,712,000 $/year

this way, based on their size a malfunction can cause serious financial losses. The value of these two mentioned factors is the highest in the case of in medium-sized companies. For larger organizations, the average hourly cost is considered as the critical point (IDC, 2012).

Due to the parameters of the cloud, the problem becomes evitable. The data loss can be prevented if the system is continuously synchronized with the local infrastructure of the service provider. In case of a system breakdown, almost every workflow is able to be restored; however, certain criteria must be kept (Baig, 2013):

- Cloud computing is only effective if the data stored on the provider's infrastructure can be managed without downloading,
- The files are normally saved in encrypted and zipped way in external storage places that cannot be modified in this way,
- The only solution is when the business data is stored virtually and in real format, so that they directly become readable or editable with the applications associated with the service.

In addition to its use a backup, the cloud has other added values in data handling. Software as a service is a technology that the firm does not need to update annually so the necessity of planning the maintenance is ended. The problems of effectiveness associated with the data duplications can also be excluded. The latter concept demands additional tasks from the company, which significantly reduces the efficiency. Due to the redundant copies, sooner or later the company will need more storage space, not to mention the problems with file management and transparency. The same copy of a document stored in the cloud is available to all employees who use them.

Remote access allows the geographically free accessibility to database and applications. Its precondition is the existence of Internet connection. Due to the mobility, employees are able to carry out certain tasks everywhere, which also affects the nature of work. The connection can be established much faster due to communication devices. Indeed, the control and monitoring activities also become easily accessible for people (Leimbach, 2014).

The installation of cloud-based tools does not involve long installation works. The service, depending on the method, can be activated within minutes. The usage of simple applications does not require any special computer literacy. It can be flexible, formed and scaled in accordance with the changing demands of the organization (Columbus, 2013).

There are applications that have an extremely high rate of cloud-based usage. E-mail is one of the most commonly used services. Today, it is almost always associated with spam or virus filtering, which is a kind of value-added business. The storage space rental and data synchronization are identified with cloud computing by most of the people. The business value is given by the device and place independent remote access to information. The basic infrastructure with an integrated application makes it possible not only to download your data but also to edit them in the cloud. Document management and software supporting employee cooperation are also typical. It is especially considered a business model, a solution for handling customer relationships (Lepenye, 2010).

In the past easily programmable and transparent processes were characteristic to working activities. The performance and time consumption could be easily separated from each other. But complexity has appeared also in this field, partly due to the mobile devices and cloud services. It is perspective dependent whether the opinion about these changes is positive or negative. With the help of e-mail, the contact does not cause a problem anymore and social networks allow the cooperation of colleagues independent from the working time. In this way the tracking of the workflow and the performance evaluation is a challenge for the company.

Certain parts of the cloud help the organization to get advantages. They have a major impact on the business (D'Arcy, 2011):

- With the help of cloud computing, the resource can be assigned to the task almost promptly which means the knowledge in the given situation. The contact with the employees, customers, suppliers helps the company to valuable information and ideas, not to mention the continuous feedback. The task to be executed can be divided into parts in a more easier way, their solution can be outsourced and tracked.
- The spread of cloud, i.e. remote work causes problems in the measurement of productivity. The working time of the employees becomes "continuous" so performance-based benefits can be realized. Effectiveness depends on the employees; the chance to take forward the company's innovation will be in their hands. They decide on the devices, applications used by them and the IT department acts upon their demands.

The improvement of competitiveness can be identified as the quick and cost-effective adaptation of business processes to the changing circumstances. The effectiveness is mainly shown in the below capabilities (Ernst & Young's, 2010):

- Faster yield increase.
- Long-term cost reduction.
- Effective risk management.
- Ability to concentrate on value-adding processes.
- Preservation of company reputation, etc.

The cloud is used by the IT manager of the company not only to improve the adaptability of the IT department but also to gain complete business advantages. The cloud computing helps to eliminate the risks accompanied with uncertainty. Its main instrument is the flexible capacity and the often mentioned scalability. The usage of private and public cloud services enables the distribution of sudden load on the resources. To the effectiveness belongs naturally cost reduction as well. The minimum capital requirement is a critical factor. Due to the outsourcing of IT, less employees are needed to support the necessary processes with which significant cost saving can also be reached. Transparent service tariffs enable planning with further reduction of the possible uncertainty. The advantage of a standardized application is that the devices belonging to them and their price are in their value for money comparable for the organization.

The cloud-based technology contributes to the quick recognition of trend changes, market introduction of new products and services, reallocation of resources in order to meet the demands (European Commission –MEMO/12/713, 2012).

4. AIM, METHODOLOGY OF THE RESEARCH, AND SAMPLE SIZE

The aim of the research was to explore the characteristics of cloud-based service usage among companies located in Hungary. For the assessment of cloud computer usage we conducted a questionnaire survey. The research was based on four main pillars:

1. Awareness of the definition cloud computing among companies,
2. Characteristics of using the technology,
3. Exploring the critical decision factors,
4. Efficiency of the application.

During the examination, we formulated the following hypotheses:

1. The awareness of the term cloud computing varies in the size categories.

2. Less than one third of Hungarian companies use cloud-based services.
3. Data security is the main drawback of using the application in Hungarian companies.
4. Cost effectiveness is the main positive factor and advantage of the service in each size category.

The questionnaire was filled in by 97 enterprises altogether. The filled-in questionnaires taken from the analyzed business sector are part of an exploratory research. This research is designed to have an insight into the knowledge on the concept of cloud computing in Hungary and explore the position of various business organizations. Little prior knowledge has been gained on this issue since no researcher has studied it in Hungary so far.

From the research's point of view, the grouping fields of activity and size category are relevant.

By taking a look at the activities, the sample is heterogeneous. The answers were sent from almost every sector. 19% of people giving answers are operating in the wholesale and repairing of motor vehicle. They are followed by the sectors agriculture and professional, scientific, technical activities both with 10%. It is worth mentioning the sectors hospitality service and public administration with their 8% (see Figure 2).

In terms of size category, 34% of the answers result from questionnaires filled in by small-sized enterprises. They are followed by microenterprises with 27%. The corporations are represented in a high number, 22% of the sample resulted from this category. The proportion of medium-sized enterprises was 17% in the sample.

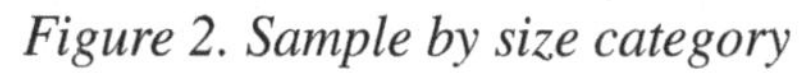

Figure 2. Sample by size category

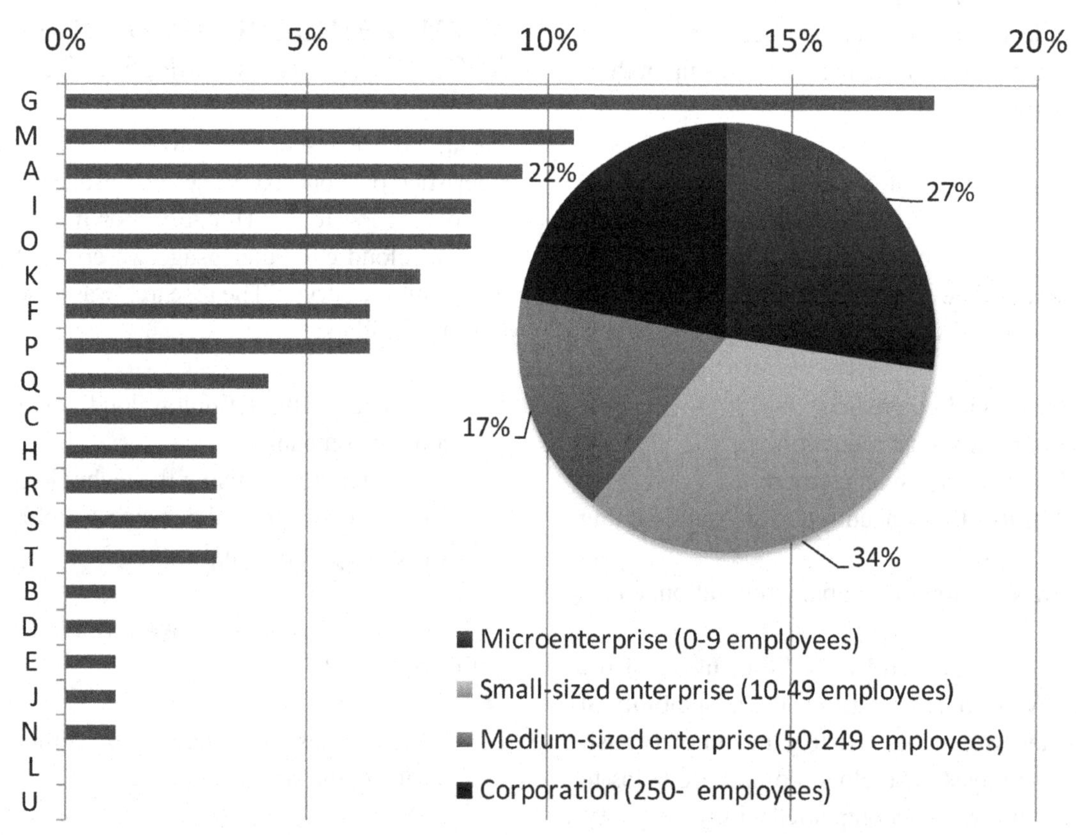

5. THE INFORMATION DEVELOPMENT LEVEL OF HUNGARY

In terms of area and population, Hungary belongs to the group of smaller countries and, on the basis of GDP per capita, it can be classified among the less developed countries in the European Union.

After its political system change in 1990, a sharp fall in GDP occurred but the country's GDP experienced a moderate growth once again in 1994. The Hungarian economy became more open and there was a significant increase in the number of foreign-owned companies and the proportion of FDI. One of the effects of the transition to the market economy was that in a ten-year period the number of registered companies increased tenfold.

The role of the service sector plays an increasingly powerful role in Hungary. Based on the GDP distribution, services are at 64%, industry is at 31%, and agriculture represents only 5% of the GDP. For the development of the Hungarian economy, the role of multinational companies is absolutely important in the fields of manufactured goods, machinery manufacturing, automobile manufacturing and electronics. Some of these businesses export more than half of the goods they produce.

After Hungary's accession to the European Union in 2004, the economy gained significant resources, such as capital transfers, which contributed to the growth and modernization of capital as a production factor. Hungary is still lagging behind most of the member states of the EU as it is underdeveloped compared to the countries leading the list. In 2008, the arrival of an unexpectedly severe economic crisis caused by changes in the world financial markets shook Hungary as well. The crisis called the financing of public debt into question, budget cuts and austerity measures did not help, and, as a result, the financial management of the country was forced to resort to a loan package provided by the IMF and the EU to maintain financial stability.

The main problems of the Hungarian economy include unemployment and decline in earnings, which decrease consumption and investment in the long run, resulting in a reduction of state budget revenues. The national debt currently amounts to 100 billion US dollars and its financing forces the country into a spiraling debt trap.

Different international indices and surveys show that in terms of ICT usage and application, Hungary is associated with the bottom of the table among the EU member states. The country's ranking is much lower than its economic development level would indicate. Compared to the average of the EU member states, the penetration of broadband and Internet usage are lower, and even at a regional level, e-shopping, online commerce, e-payment and e-invoicing are significantly lower.

In Hungary, about 100,000 people work directly in the ICT sector and nearly another 100,000 in other sectors using ICT solutions. More than 14,000 businesses deal with the development of information and communication technology, tools and software. Sound and television services are available for 100% of the population, 97% of the settlements have fixed line broadband connection, mobile broadband is available across 500 cities, nearly 55% of the population have retail PCs, and the penetration of corporate PCs is virtually 100%. More than four million people regularly use the Internet, there are 11 million mobile phones, 1.7 million fixed broadband, one million mobile Internet subscriptions in Hungary, and 99% of the households have a television set. The very rapid spread of mobile Internet access service increased bandwidth requirements for servicing the cellular base stations many times. For meeting increased demand, high-capacity optical networks are needed. The spread of new technologies and services resulted in increased competition. Electronic communications service providers in the television market, while cable TV providers compete for the Internet, phone and mobile Internet services market. Furthermore, the penetration of wireless and mobile services became more important.

Compared to the EU, the structure of Hungary's domestic IT market still contains a significant shift towards hardware, and it can be characterized by the lack of appropriate software, although the share of IT services is closer to European levels (Racskó, 2012). Forty percent of the IT expenditures are made with corporations, 26% with medium-sized companies, and 17% with small-sized enterprises. The remaining 16% of IT-related expenses go to micro-enterprises and households. All in all, companies employing more than 100 workers take a 70% share in IT expenditure so the segment of small-sized businesses remains fairly modest.

The electronics industry is and certainly will be the world's most dynamic industry in the coming decade. The Hungarian electronics industry has already played an important role in rural development. Most of the production facilities have been established outside Budapest. The electronics industry is global by its very nature; it holds great potential for the country.

The most important goal of economic development is to strengthen the competitiveness of domestic enterprises. A number of factors contribute to the fact that IT and ICT development will materialize only through a slow process in Hungary.

Hungary's fiscal, economic and administrative legal systems are still not conducive to the rapid development of e-business, the business culture of SMEs and corporate innovation culture are less developed, business plans are often short-sighted.

6. AWARENESS OF THE TERM CLOUD COMPUTING

At very first we examined to what extent the definition of cloud computing is clear for the Hungarian enterprises is. This aspect is important because of the followings (Csobán, 2014):

- On the one hand it establishes the exploration of the usage characteristics. With its help we can filter if the organization doesn't apply the technology because they have not heard about it or because of other drawbacks.
- On the other hand if a given decision maker thinks he is aware of the term but his answers refer to the opposite the root of a newer problem can be detected. Namely, the incomplete knowledge, and the expectations resulting from inefficient usage lead to false expectations.

1. Have you ever heard about the concept of cloud computing?
2. Have you ever heard about any of the listed concepts?
   a. Types of cloud: private, public, community, hybrid cloud;
   b. Types of installation: Infrastructure as a service (IaaS); platform as a service (PaaS) and software as a service (SaaS)

The results demonstrated in Table 2 are as follows:

- 89% of those people who are fully aware of the concept of cloud computing heard about the **private cloud**. It confirms our statement, so there is no conflict in the answers. 91% of people who are just beginning to learn the concept of cloud have also heard about the private cloud. It is observable in each size category that at bigger enterprises the concept of cloud is in a bigger proportion known (at a corporation it also reaches the 100%).
- The awareness of the concept **public cloud** is the lowest among the microenterprises (more than 70%) but it can also be stated that people perfectly knowing the concept of cloud are also aware of the concept of public cloud. Here such as both at corporations and medium-sized enterprises the concept is known. Who are beginning to

Table 2. The knowledge of the concept and types of cloud computing among Hungarian enterprises in 2014

	Micro-Enterprise	Small-Sized Enterprise	Medium-Sized Enterprise	Corporation	Avg
People Who Are Perfectly Aware of the Concept of Cloud		**Types of Cloud**			
Private cloud	86%	89%	83%	100%	89%
Public cloud	71%	89%	100%	100%	89%
Community cloud	57%	89%	100%	100%	85%
Hybrid cloud	43%	67%	80%	60%	62%
		Types of Installation			
IaaS	57%	89%	100%	80%	81%
PaaS	57%	78%	83%	80%	74%
SaaS	86%	100%	100%	80%	93%
People Beginning to Learn the Concept of Cloud at the Moment		**Types of Cloud**			
Private cloud	86%	93%	83%	100%	91%
Public cloud	90%	88%	67%	63%	80%
Community cloud	100%	68%	83%	63%	77%
Hybrid cloud	50%	44%	50%	38%	45%
		Types of Installation			
IaaS	70%	74%	50%	63%	67%
PaaS	80%	68%	67%	63%	70%
SaaS	80%	84%	83%	100%	86%

learn about the concept of cloud at the moment, their awareness rate reaches 60%.

- In terms of **community cloud,** a similar knowledge can be seen as in the case of public cloud. 85% of people being perfectly aware of the concept of cloud have also heard about this cloud type.
- In case of **hybrid cloud** there are differences. 48% of people who have stated that they perfectly know the cloud in their own statement haven't heard about the hybrid cloud. Only 45% of people who are beginning to learn about the concept of cloud know the hybrid cloud, so this is the lowest rate in comparison to the other types.

The examination was also done in regard to the other models with the following results:

- In the case of **infrastructure as a service,** 81% of organizations that are aware of the concept of cloud have heard about the IaaS. 67% of enterprises that have newly begun to learn about cloud computing have heard about the infrastructure as a service.
- In the case of PaaS -**platform as a service**-, the situation is similar to the former ones. 26% of the respondents who stated that they know the cloud computing haven't heard about the platform as a service. 70% of people who are beginning to learn about the technology have heard about the concept of PaaS, which means they are at the beginning of the learning period.
- In the case of **software as a service,** 93% of those who completely know the concept system of cloud have heard about the

SaaS model. This is a very high rate. 86% of people who are now getting to know the concept of cloud computing are aware of the SaaS which is also a positive aspect. The result means that the enterprises that are operating based on this model know the applications well.

It makes a much more differentiated picture about the situation if we examine the received answers grouped by their size category (see Figure 3).

38% of medium-sized enterprises are perfectly aware of the concept of cloud, while in terms of the other size categories it can be stated that at only about a quarter of the companies little differences are shown. The most visible is that among small-sized enterprises the rate of those who are now beginning to learn about the concept is the highest and reaches nearly the 60%. About small-sized enterprises it can be said that the lowest rate was assessed among those who have never heard about the concept of cloud in any form. This option was chosen by 13% of the respondents. In the case of corporations this is the highest rate, reaching a rate of 38%.

7. SURVEY ON THE USAGE OF CLOUD COMPUTING

Our research was aimed at exploring how the IT systems of Hungarian enterprises adapt to the new IT trends. We compared the data about the application of traditional and cloud-based infrastructure and pointed out the most widespread installation and service types as well as the kind of tasks they most widely applied.

As it is shown in Figure 4, the Hungarian enterprises use in the rate of 70% traditional, in 30% cloud-based technologies for their data storage.

The examination of the operation types shows that 26% of the companies are operating with partly cloud-based information technology. At the forefront stays the private cloud with 14%. The public cloud and community cloud slightly lag behind it. The former was chosen by 9%, the latter was marked by 6% of the sample participants. The hybrid solution is applied by surprisingly few companies, by 2% of them altogether. A high difference between the planned usages cannot be seen because in three cases it hardly exceeds the 10%. The hybrid cloud is the only one that reaches merely the half of it.

Figure 3. Awareness of the concept of cloud by size category at Hungarian enterprises in 2014

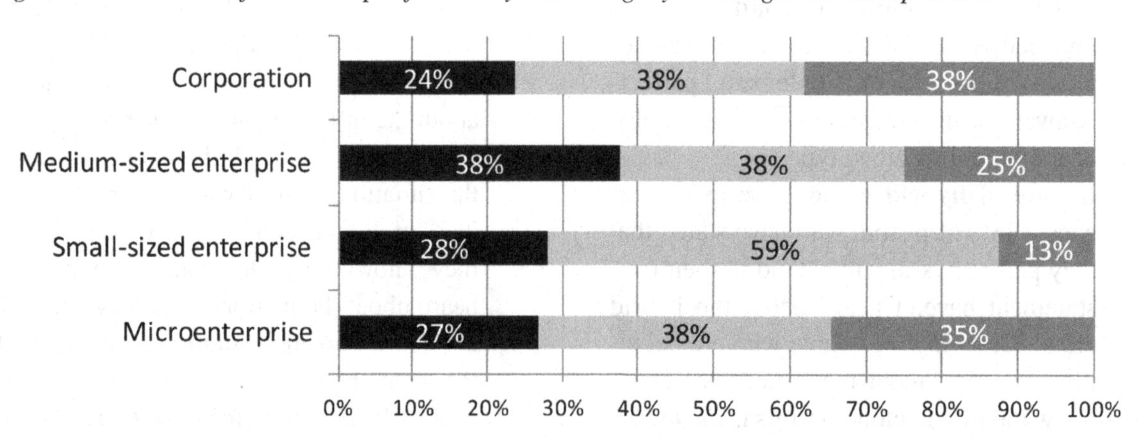

Figure 4. The structure of the average computer infrastructure at Hungarian enterprises in 2014

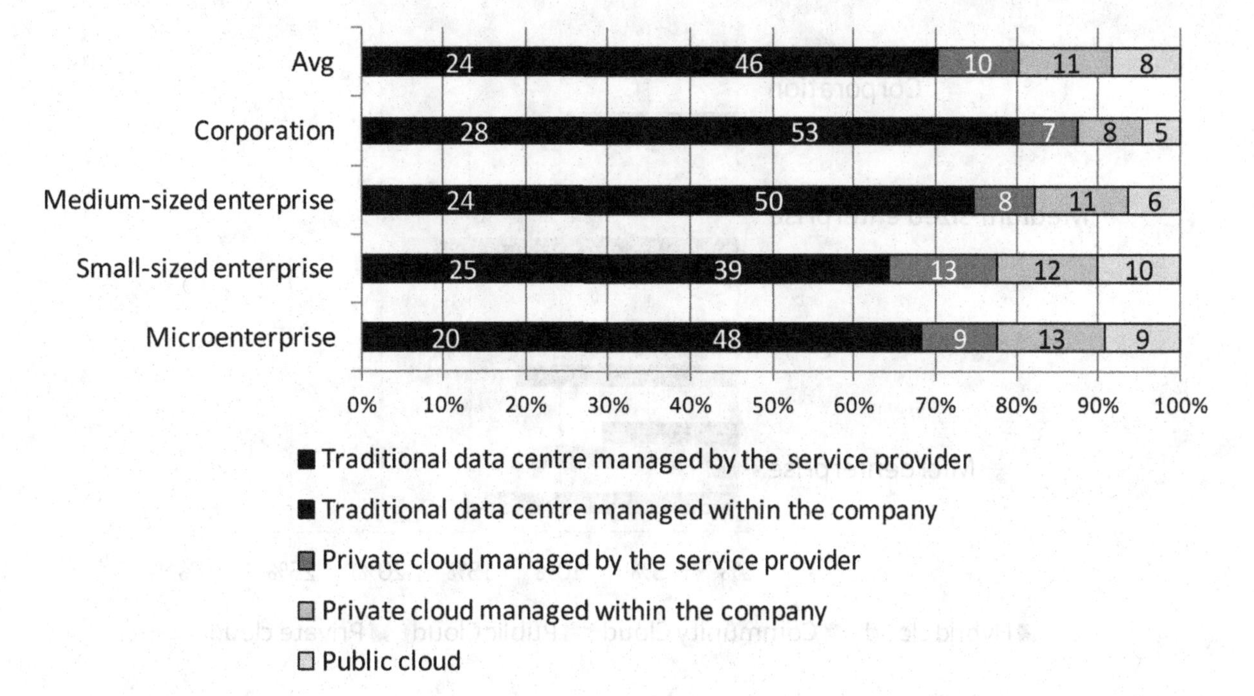

Studying the usage of installation types, considerable discrepancies are visible by the size categories. The microenterprises are the only ones where all the four models are applied. The biggest ratio is given by the private cloud. The public cloud was marked by a very little number of respondents, by only 34%. In the case of small-sized enterprises, the usage of private and public cloud is equal. In terms of technology usage, the medium-sized enterprises are the foregoers. In their case the public cloud is the most widespread installation method. The cloud, more exactly the private type of it is used by only 9% of the corporations (see Figure 5).

Based on the data according to the planned usage, the current usage structure is going to change significantly (see Figure 6). 14% of the microenterprises plan the introduction of the community cloud in Hungary. This means that the model will be used by one quarter of the enterprises belonging to the size category so it overtakes the private cloud. The usage of the latter is planned by 25% of the small-sized enterprises; moreover the hybrid technology will have its place too. The situation of the medium-sized enterprises is the same, nearly 20% of them count with the usage of private cloud in the future. The corporations mainly prefer the introduction of public cloud, whereas the hybrid cloud is not even planned.

Regarding the service models it can be seen that the overall results are true also by the size categories, which means that the SaaS is the leading model everywhere (shown in Figure 7). It is applied by more than 40% of the microenterprises. The situation is the same with the small-sized enterprises. In case of the latter nearly the quarter of the respondents uses also the infrastructure and platform as a service. From the aspect of usage 56% of the medium-sized enterprises marked the SaaS, nearly one third the PaaS and IaaS. The corporations use the platform as a service the least that slightly reaches the 10%.

Examining the planned data, some significant differences can be observed. Both the micro-, and small-sized enterprises are planning the usage of all three types in the future but the two other groups

Figure 5. The usage of the operation types by size category at Hungarian enterprises in 2014

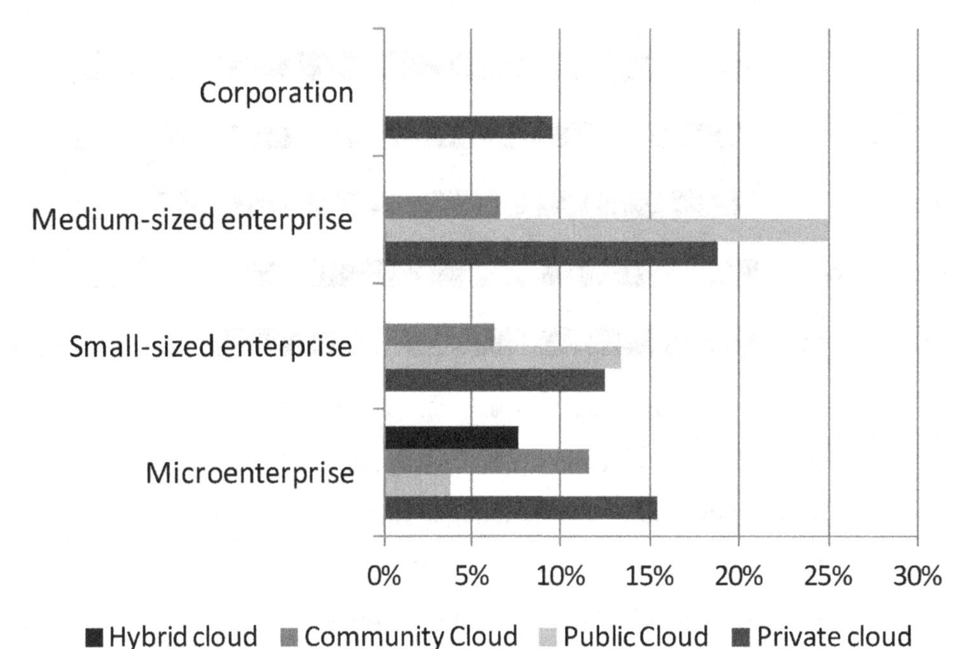

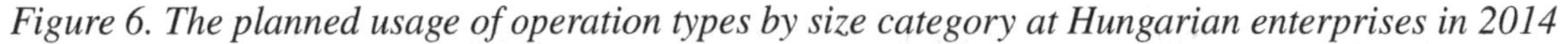

Figure 6. The planned usage of operation types by size category at Hungarian enterprises in 2014

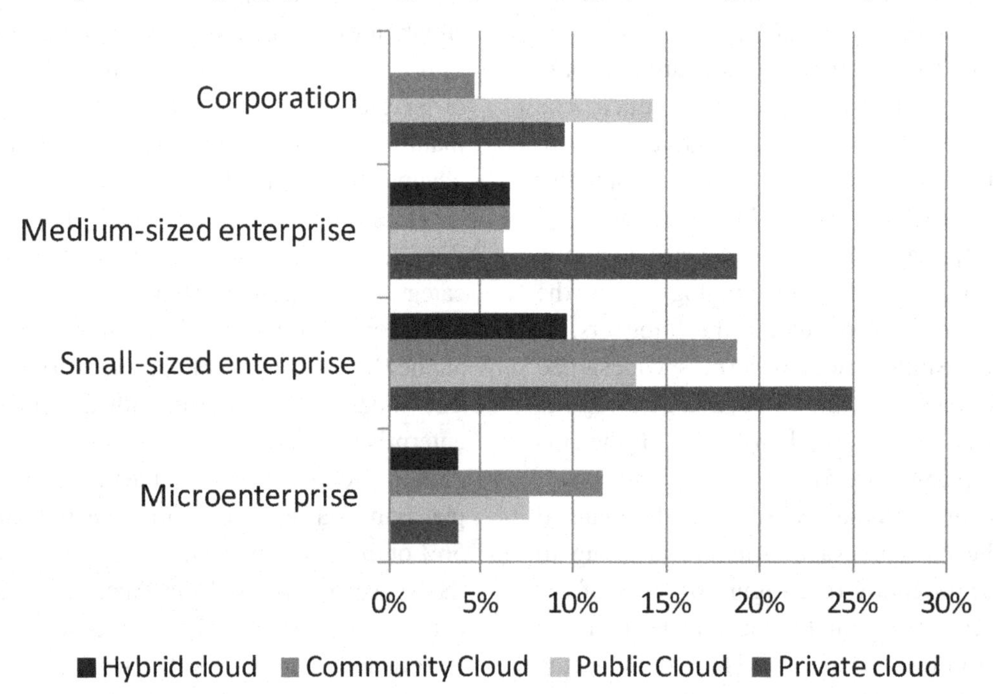

Figure 7. The usage of service models by size category at Hungarian companies in 2014

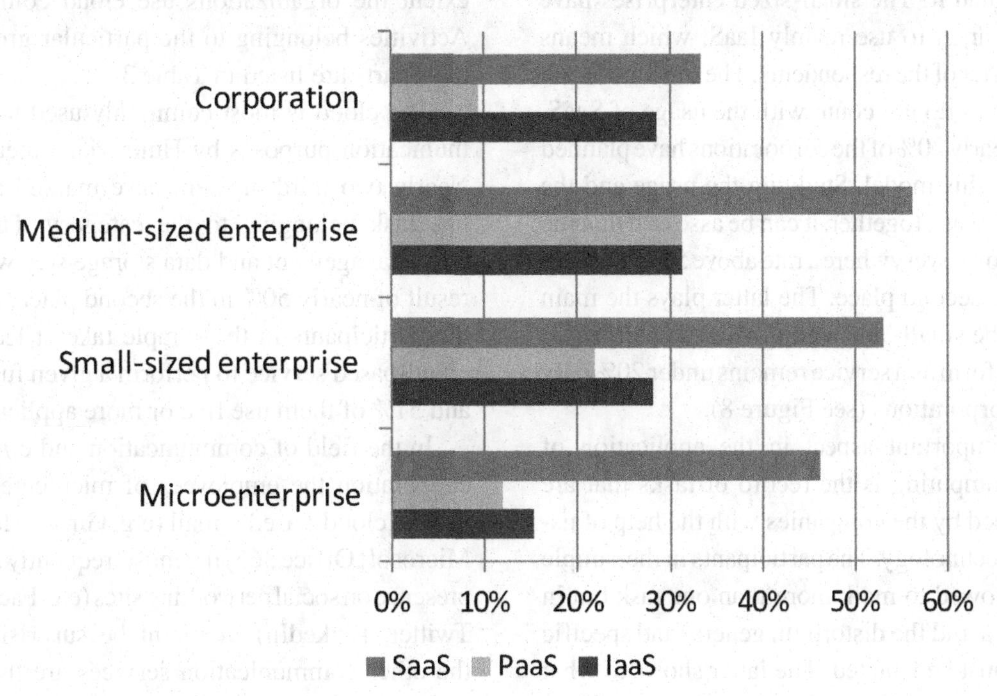

Figure 8. The planned usage of service models by size category at Hungarian enterprises in 2014

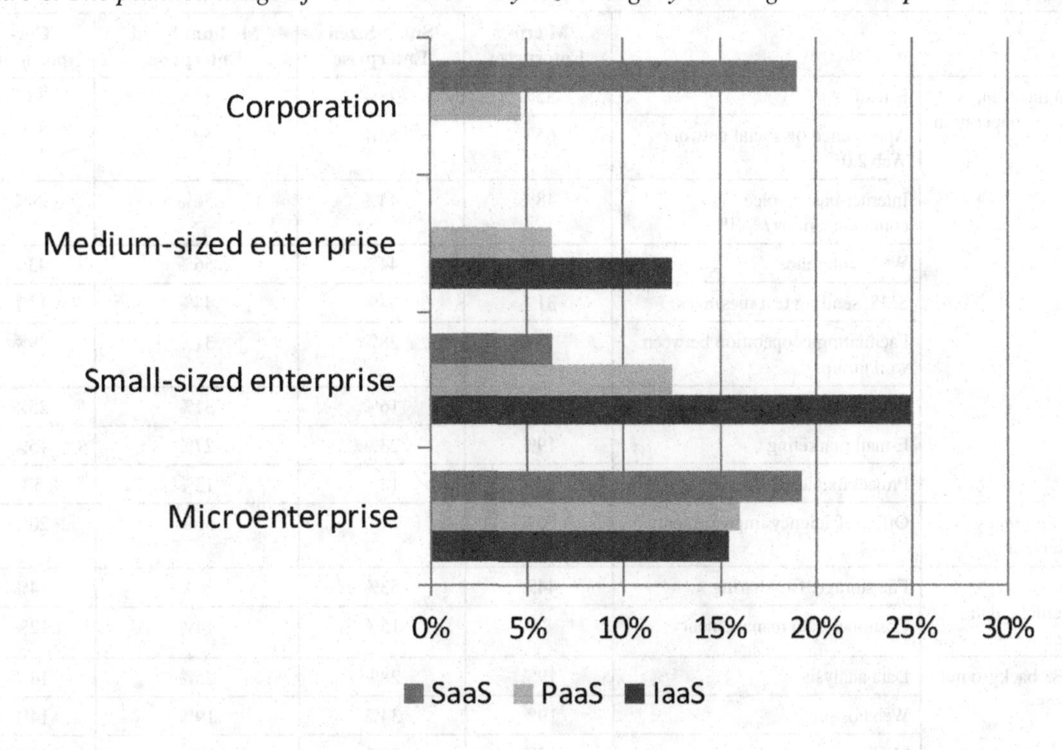

do not plan it. The small-sized enterprises have set the target to use mainly IaaS, which means one quarter of the respondents. The medium-sized enterprises do not count with the usage of SaaS, while nearly 20% of the corporations have planned to apply this model. Studying the usage and the planned usage together, it can be assessed that the SaaS shows everywhere a rate above 50%, the IaaS is on the second place. The latter plays the main role at the small- and medium-sized enterprises. The platform as a service remains under 20% only at the corporations (see Figure 8).

An important aspect in the application of cloud computing is the record of tasks that are performed by the companies with the help of using the technology. The participants in the sample were allowed to mark more than one task but in order to avoid the distortion, general and specific fields must be isolated. The latter shows to what extent the organizations use cloud computing. Activities belonging to the particular groups as their parts are listed in Table 3.

The cloud is most commonly used for communication purposes by Hungarian enterprises. Nearly two third of them have marked at least one task belonging to the category. The data base management and data storage stay with the result of nearly 50% in the second place. 85% of the participants in the sample take at least one cloud-based service to perform a given function, and 51% of them use five or more applications.

In the field of communication and employee cooperation the employees of microenterprises use the cloud-based e-mail (e.g. Gmail, Hotmail, Microsoft Office 365) the most frequently and the presence on social networking sites (e.g. Facebook, Twitter, LinkedIn). It might be surprising but the other communication services are the most

Table 3. Classification of cloud-based executed tasks and their frequency rate in percentage at Hungarian enterprises in 2014

		Micro-Enterprise	Small-Sized Enterprise	Medium-Sized Enterprise	Corporation
Communication, employee cooperation	E-mail	85%	78%	81%	33%
	Appearance on social networks, Web 2.0	65%	53%	50%	30%
	Internet-based voice communications / VoIP	48%	44%	56%	29%
	Web conference	24%	44%	56%	43%
	SMS, sending text messages	31%	34%	44%	19%
	Facilitating cooperation between workgroups	15%	28%	31%	29%
	Education, training	19%	16%	31%	25%
	E-mail marketing	19%	23%	27%	15%
	Project management	8%	13%	13%	5%
Office efficiency improvement	Office efficiency improvement	50%	71%	56%	20%
Data base management, data storage	File storage, file sharing	44%	53%	36%	14%
	Costumer data management	8%	15%	14%	12%
Business background processes	Data analysis	19%	28%	25%	14%
	Web hosting	19%	34%	19%	14%
	Media monitoring	12%	29%	19%	19%

frequently used by medium-sized enterprises. Here, in this size category more than the half of the enterprises use the web conference (e.g. Skype, Citrix Go To, Meeting, ReadyTalk) and the internet-based communication (e.g. Skype, Cisco, CloudVoIP). Moreover, one third of Hungarian enterprises use this modern technology for working (e.g. Basecamp, Huddle) and for teaching and training activities (e.g. Citrix Go To Webinar, ReadyTalk).

The cloud-based office work (e.g. Google Docs, Microsoft Office 365) is the most frequently used at small-sized enterprises, exceeding the 70%. The small-sized enterprises are also the best in cloud-based file storage, file sharing (e.g OneDrive, Dropbox, Microsoft Office 365) and customer database management (e.g. Microsoft Dynamics CRM, Salesforce).

The Hungarian small-sized enterprises stand out in the Hungarian business background processes. One third of the enterprises makes data analysis (e.g. Stasoft, STATISTICA software family, Crystal Reports), webhosting (e.g. Google Sites, Microsoft Office 365) and media monitoring (e.g. Google Alerts, Wildfire) with a sort of cloud-based application.

Although our research is not representative, it reveals a lot about the awareness and the attitude of using the cloud at Hungarian enterprises. A considerable part of the respondents struggle with conceptual confusions in the subject. Regarding the operation types, the participants of the sample are, with the exception of the hybrid cloud, quite well-informed. The application of the latter one is connected to many advantages that the organizations cannot utilize in this way.

In the case of the service types, a bigger spread is shown among those who are aware of the concepts and who are not. In general terms, the concept of cloud is known by the respondents but they are less aware of its individual types. The lack of real awareness is in case of SaaS the most observable. 73% of those who stated, they have not met the cloud, have heard about the software as a service. It is partly logical that the user level sees only the application but not the technology behind. But since it is about enterprises, in our opinion the awareness must be broadened, and it is necessary to get a better insight into the background processes.

By size category, the rate of those who are beginning to learn the concept is the highest among the small-sized enterprises. From this we draw the conclusion that the cloud will play an important role at these companies in the future.

The usage shows differences in the classification of service and operation types. The former was selected by 54%, while the latter by only 26% of the respondents. We would like to point out its connection with the awareness, which means that the SaaS is used by the organizations in the highest rate, while the hybrid cloud as an installation type is just slightly applied. Examining the size categories, only 4% of microenterprises use the public cloud. This rate reaches 25% altogether in the case of medium-sized enterprises. The corporations only use the private cloud, which means only 9% of them. Among the services, the software is outstanding in each category, at medium-sized enterprises the application usage reaches the rate of 56%.

In the fulfillment of tasks the general cloud services such as e-mail, software for improving the office efficiency or the presence on community sites were not considered as part of our research in order to avoid distortions. The results show that the application of software supporting the communication and cooperation has the greatest weights. The data storage and data management are also important. The former was emphasized by 65%, the latter by 50% of the respondents.

8. OBSTACLES IN THE USAGE OF CLOUD COMPUTING AND THE SUPPORTING FACTORS AT HUNGARIAN ENTERPRISES

In the selection of the obstacles, the respondents had certainly the possibility to choose several aspects that they considered important in their opinion (see Table 4). The reasons of data security were the most commonly named as a main problem; exactly 77% of the respondents have chosen this. To this category belong the possibility of data loss and the distrust against the service and its provider. Slightly behind them stays the second most frequent obstacle, the lack of staff qualifications. The latter is meant as the lack of competency at employee and management level. In the case of the two third of the organizations, the main contributing factors are computer independent reasons. These are elements that cannot be influenced, for instance the unstable network of Internet or electricity, and their unreliability. At the end, cost stays as an interfering component, with almost 60%. Not only the service fee but also the relocation costs of the existing applications are part of this group.

Considerable differences can be seen while examining the question by size categories. In the case of microenterprises, the most important obstacles are the two factors below:

Table 4. Obstacles in the usage of cloud computing at Hungarian enterprises in 2014

Ranking	Name	Micro-Enterprise		Small-Sized Enterprise		Medium-Sized Enterprise		Corporation	
		Value	Ranking	Value	Ranking	Value	Ranking	Value	Ranking
1	Distrust against the service and its provider	3,32	5	3,35	5	3,60	2	3,95	1
2	Data security issues	3,50	2	3,35	4	3,27	9	3,67	5
3	Problems with the strength, stability and reliability of internet	3,48	3	3,13	9	3,47	4	3,70	3
4	The senior management does not understand and does not support cloud-based computing	3,15	8	3,55	1	3,27	8	3,52	6
5	Lack of staff qualifications	3,42	4	3,39	3	3,33	7	3,33	10
6	Possibility of data loss	3,73	1	3,13	8	3,13	11	3,38	9
7	No access to the Internet	3,31	6	2,94	10	3,60	3	3,81	2
8	The relocation of existing equipment is too expensive	2,96	10	3,42	2	3,36	6	3,67	4
9	The relocation of existing equipment is too difficult	3,04	9	3,26	6	3,64	1	3,19	11
10	Unstable electrical network	3,27	7	2,84	11	3,43	5	3,48	8
11	High price of cloud computing	2,80	11	3,26	7	3,13	10	3,50	7
12	Expensive Internet access	2,46	12	2,45	12	2,47	12	2,90	12

Table 5. Supporting factors of using the cloud computing at Hungarian enterprises in 2014

Ranking	Name	Micro-Enterprise		Small-Sized Enterprise		Medium-Sized Enterprise		Corporation	
		Value	Ranking	Value	Ranking	Value	Ranking	Value	Ranking
1	Decreasing security risks related to cloud-based services	3,58	1	3,88	1	3,86	3	3,76	2
2	Facilitating the integration of the existing systems with cloud-based systems	3,38	6	3,68	3	4,00	1	3,81	1
3	Decrease in the price of cloud-based services	3,58	2	3,72	2	3,50	5	3,57	4
4	Providing consulting assistance with cloud-based services	3,46	5	3,45	5	3,71	4	3,76	3
5	Providing training for the employees on cloud-based services	3,50	4	3,48	4	3,93	2	3,48	5
6	Easier customization of cloud-based services	3,54	3	3,19	6	3,29	6	3,43	6

- Possibility and risk of data loss;
- Question of data security.

Surprisingly, the high price of Internet connection and cloud-based services means the least problem in this size category.

In the case of small-sized enterprises, the qualification of the senior management is considered as the most retentive aspect as well as the relocation costs of the existing applications means a serious problem.

In the case of the Hungarian medium-sized enterprises, the problems related to the technical and human resource side of existing applications and the existing distrust against cloud-based services also mean a huge obstacle.

This distrust is also characteristic to Hungarian corporations, which is also connected to the problems of Internet signal strength, stability and reliability.

In the way of the spread of cloud computing mainly stay -depending on the size category- the risks of data security, the lack of qualifications, cost aspects and other factors that are independent from the technology.

Supporting factors for the spread of the application are considered as the driving forces and the solutions. Supporting factors mean such changes that positively influence the adaptation and accelerate the speed of spread. Based on the answers, the usage would be mainly supported if the service provider facilitated *the integration of the existing systems* with cloud-based systems and the easier customization of cloud-based services. The latter is mainly typical of microenterprises.

The Hungarian enterprises see the strongest supporting function in the reduction of security risks of cloud-based services independent from the size category.

68% of the participants in the survey stated that there was a need for consulting assistance, training and coaching. Exactly 60% is the rate of those who pointed out cost reductions. In the case of lowering the security risks of data storage and data relocation, only 60% of the companies would consider using the cloud (see Table 5).

Among the supporting factors of the Hungarian micro- and small-sized enterprises in the sample, the decrease of security risks and the price reduction of cloud-based services are regarded as the most important ones. In case of medium-sized enterprises the emphasis is placed on the integration of existing systems and the importance of trainings. The integration, to that also the question of data security is connected, is also important at the corporations.

Independent from the size category, the easier customization of cloud-based services is considered as the least important (except for the microenterprises).

9. ADVANTAGES OF USING CLOUD COMPUTING AT HUNGARIAN ENTERPRISES

The majority of Hungarian enterprises are of the opinion that the cloud technology help and may help the faster information flow and the better cooperation of employees between and within the companies (shown in Table 6). Moreover the use of cloud may help in the faster learning of the foregoer software applications, in the easier acquisition of software, as well as in the flexible and scalable usage. Among the advantages are also the better data handling and the question of the

Table 6. Advantages in the usage of cloud computing at Hungarian enterprises in 2014

Ranking	Name	Micro-Enterprise		Small-Sized Enterprise		Medium-Sized Enterprise		Corporation	
		Value	Ranking	Value	Ranking	Value	Ranking	Value	Ranking
1	Faster information flow, more efficient employee collaboration	3,88	1	3,88	3	4,07	3	4,10	1
2	High-level mobility	3,85	3	4,00	2	3,69	8	4,10	2
3	Remote access to information systems	3,85	2	3,75	4	4,13	1	4,05	4
4	Easier recoverability in case of system failure	3,72	5	4,03	1	3,75	7	3,95	7
5	Flexible service	3,68	6	3,58	6	3,80	6	4,05	5
6	Better order of data	3,58	8	3,47	8	4,07	2	3,71	11
7	More efficient data management and control	3,73	4	3,25	12	4,06	4	3,81	9
8	Reducing administrative tasks related to the system	3,62	7	3,44	9	3,93	5	3,75	10
9	Better data security	3,42	11	3,66	5	3,13	12	4,10	3
10	Less IT employees are necessary to maintain the system	3,42	9	3,56	7	3,44	10	4,00	6
11	Easier access to hardware and software tools for the company	3,42	10	3,44	10	3,56	9	3,86	8
12	Low level of capital investment or no capital investment at all	3,00	13	3,38	11	3,38	11	3,52	13
13	Higher fixed costs can be converted to low variable and operation costs	3,04	12	3,22	13	3,13	13	3,68	12

better data security. The latter has to be meant as the better recoverability. This is followed by the mobility and the remote access at the Hungarian enterprises in 2014. Among Hungarian companies, the capital investment and the possibility of cost reduction are regarded as less important.

Independent from the size category, the Hungarian enterprises emphasize the following advantages:

- Faster information flow, more efficient employee cooperation;
- High level of mobility;
- Remote access to information systems;
- Easier recoverability in case of system crash; and
- Flexible service.

In the opinion of microenterprises, faster information flow and remote access are the most important advantages. Surprisingly, the least importance is given to the lower costs and lower capital investments. It is interesting, that for the small-sized enterprises the easier recoverability of a system crash and the high level of mobility are the most important advantages. It may be rather surprising that the more effective data control and ensuring of monitoring are listed among the smaller advantages. In the case of the Hungarian medium-sized enterprises, the biggest advantages of the cloud computing were the remote access and the higher data security in 2014. Though, the corporations -analogical to the microenterprises- see the biggest advantage in faster information flow.

From the answers it can also be seen that the respondents are rarely dissatisfied with the applied cloud services. The percentage of those who are dissatisfied with it has not reached 5% in any of the size categories. The number of those who could not answer inter alia because it is too early to tell their opinion about the effect is very high.

Examining the size categories, significant differences can be experienced in the assessment if the results were reached. The rates are the lowest in the case of the microenterprises. The characteristics of the effectiveness of cloud have reached only 50% of the expected rate. However in the case of small- and medium-sized enterprises outstanding rates can be experienced. In the former case every criteria -flexibility, effectiveness and cost reduction- were evaluated above 80%, whereas in the latter case, only the fulfillment of the requirements in terms of costs were worst (see Table 7). The corporations gave sub average points and the particular factors met the requirements almost at the same rate.

The identification of the decision-making criteria helped to get to know the reasons of usage or the avoidance of the cloud usage. Among the risks, the question of data security appears the most commonly that frustrate the usage of cloud computing in 76% of the cases. The lack of qualifications is nearly equally weighted. We think, in practice. the globally appearing preconceptions against security are deeply rooted in the case of Hungarian companies, too. The control and handling of data is not given with please into the hands of an external partner. Here is this phenomenon

Table 7. Fulfillment rate of the requirements by company size categories in Hungary in 2014

	Micro-Enterprise	Small-Sized Enterprise	Medium-Sized Enterprise	Corporation
Flexibility	67%	87%	73%	64%
Effectiveness	50%	83%	73%	64%
Cost reduction	56%	83%	55%	55%

connected with the problem of qualification. The potential in the cloud, certainly together with its disadvantages has to be familiarized with the organizations. The most important is that the decision maker should be able to weigh situation dependent. In certain cases, the interests at a company level make some less important disadvantages of the technology negligible.

The companies participating in the research have mentioned in several cases interfering aspects that are independent from the cloud computing such as the stability, reliability or availability of the Internet connection. These points mean a huge problem because it is not possible to influence them by the service provider. Their importance is determining mainly for the microenterprises.

The introduction of the obstacles makes a larger insight into the situation. The respondents put the training and consulting assistance in the first two places, where a subsequential change would considerably raise the possibility to use the cloud. We must underline, that the motivating aspects have their effect not one by one but together. That is why we have the opinion if the service providers take this fact into account their measures become much more complex and they satisfy the customer needs more effective.

Examining the advantages of using the cloud, we came to the conclusion that the administrative aspects dominate by more than 90% in decision making. The respondents rate the faster accessibility to the foregoer applications and the flexible and scalable infrastructure as the main positive aspects. It is surprising that the existence of these functions dominate over the cost effectiveness, mobility, as well as the cooperation. By size category, our main realization is that the medium-sized enterprises and the corporations use all the advantages in a more efficient way than the smaller ones.

The results experienced during the usage reached or overtook the expectations in terms of flexibility, effectiveness and cost reduction. However, many organizations apply the cloud in such an early stadium that they could not report on this. During the research it became clear that the enterprises regarded the role of quality changes as more important against cost reduction.

10. EXPECTED ORGANIZATIONAL CHANGES

The main tasks of numerous organizations in the business sector are collecting, processing information and decision-making. The hierarchical structures characteristic of our time have formed in a way that could be framed into the structure of information and decision-making of a former period. As we climb the organizational hierarchy from the bottom upwards, the level of the amount of information together with its processing becomes higher and higher. In parallel to this, the level of decision-making also gets higher, requiring greater responsibility. Lower-level organizations often have the task to generate information for the upper level in a desired structure. The creation of information systems (e.g. integrated business information systems, data warehouses) and later the IT departments of companies both followed this structure during their formation over time.

The penetration of cloud computing in the business sector, is very much likely to transform this traditional structure and the communication part of a company's culture since, if an organizational unit such as a department can freely choose between an internal and external IT service provider, it might opt for an occasionally higher-quality, more flexible and, above all, cheaper external service. Thus the building of an organizational structure becomes possible in which the individual units are not dependent on internal IT services, and the relationship between the organizational units is mostly built on the exchange of information rather than on a strict organizational structure. This phenomenon of cloud-based organizations has been called *'wirearchy'* in the literature which means that organizational units are not linked by hierarchy but by various information channels. In order to achieve this, first the levels of trust and confidence need to be created which eventually allows the conversion of traditional structures.

This projection is underpinned by the Gartner 2014 forecast, according to which the effect of the economic crisis has forced companies to cut their IT costs and this can be clearly realized by shifting some parts of their IT functions to cloud services.

ENISA (European Union Agency for Network and Information Security) examined the cloud-based applications in 23 European countries. According to the ENISA Report 2013 (Helmbrecht, 2014), the United Kingdom, Spain and Italy are included in the group of the earliest users of the technology. The report found significant differences between the investigated countries, and therefore made a proposal to formulate a national cloud strategy, explore the specific barriers of application, disseminate best practices and develop a common set of standards based on them.

CONCLUSION

This chapter aimed at introducing the economical possibilities in the cloud computing and revealing the characteristics of their usage among the Hungarian enterprises.

The most important advantages of using the technology are cost effectiveness, data protection, remote access and quick installation. As an obstacle of its introduction, reliability, commitment to the service provider, loss of control, and accidental system breakdowns in terms of availability are generally mentioned in the literature. While exploring the positive and negative factors accentuated by the Hungarian companies, it turned out that it was really about critical factors but their weighting is different in certain cases.

The characteristics of the Hungarian cloud usage were the followings:

- The Hungarian enterprises are clear about the basic concept of cloud but they often do not link its different types to it;
- Classified by operation types, the usage reaches 26%, while the service method is 54%. Most of the companies use the cloud in order to perform tasks related to communications and cooperation. Exactly 66% of the respondents gave this answer.
- Opposite to the application is mainly the data security, 77% of the respondents have marked this choice. The lack of qualification is also a significant problem, nearly equal to the former one;
- The chance to use the cloud would be mainly supported by the creation of an easier application, beside this, the training and consulting assistance provided for the employees would also positively influence the adaptation;
- The administrative characteristics of the technology mean the main advantage for the Hungarian enterprises. Less system control, scalability, and the accessibility to the flexible capacities are ranked before the cost factors;
- The requirements of cloud-based services have reached or overtaken the expectations at most of the companies. Its parts are better flexibility, increased effectiveness and cost reduction.

After processing this issue, our main conclusion was that due to its modernity the Hungarian companies had a lot of reservations against the technology. The Hungarian enterprises can close up in this matter only if:

- *More widely orientation of people who are willing to use the cloud:* beyond the learning of global tendencies, it is reasonable to use the Hungarian information sources because the information revealing the local relations is more relevant for decision-making.

- *Careful decision-making*: when making decisions several criteria must be considered, not only the main drawbacks or advantages. It is important that the company should be able to weigh and should feel the weight of the certain criteria dependent on the situation. The aim of usage, the service provider, the type of data stored on external storage places, the capacity and security specifications of the used infrastructure, etc. must be known. We also would like to point out that the degree of the independency relationship must be considered in every case so the tasks are only allowed to be relocated in any extent to the service that the possible disturbances do not appear in the given company, or at least not to a critical extent.
- *Creating real expectations:* it must be known that the cloud has got an availability fee as well. Standard functions do not adapt perfectly to any of the companies and the possibility of scalability is also finite. So if the customer collects information they do not have to confront with surprises, and the advantages of cloud computing do not remain hidden. They positively contribute to the effective application of the information technology.

It is highly probable that the spread of cloud-based computing solutions among the Hungarian enterprises – in view of cost reduction opportunities and other benefits - will accelerate in the near future (Racskó, 2014).

Its natural prerequisite is to reduce the currently existing risks of data security, privacy, business and management. Given the benefits of cloud computing, the European Union, in the role of a regulator and certifier, is actively seeking to reduce the risks and overcome some diffusion barriers. Despite the efforts of the European Commission, it is still not possible to speak about a common European cloud computing framework, furthermore there are important differences between the strategies of member countries.

However, the development will certainly enforce a more intense standardization process and a few years' experience in the application will show the advantages and disadvantages of various corporate uses, and cloud computing is expected to become a utility-like service on this basis.

ACKNOWLEDGMENT

This research was partially carried out in the framework of the Center of Excellence of Mechatronics and Logistics at the University of Miskolc.

REFERENCES

Four Steps to Setting the Right Budget for Downtime Prevention. (2012, April). *Aberdeen Group*. Retrieved from http://www.stratus.com/~/media/Stratus/Files/Library/AnalystReports/Aberdeen-4-Steps-Budget-Downtime.pdf

Baig, A. (2013). Data protection designed for the cloud era. *GigaOM research.*

Bőgel, G. (2009). *Az informatikai felhők gazdaságtana, (The Economics of IT clouds)* (pp. 673–688). Közgazdasági Szemle.

Buest, R., & Miller, P., (2013). *The state of Europe's homegrown cloud market*, GigaOM research

Columbus, L. (2013). *Gartner Predicts Infrastructure Services Will Accelerate Cloud Computing Growth.* Retrieved from http://www.forbes.com/sites/louiscolumbus/2013/02/19/gartner-predicts-infrastructure-services-will-accelerate-cloud-computing-growth/

Csobán, J. (2014). *A felhőalapú számítástechnika elterjedésének empirikus vizsgálata a magyar vállalatok körében, (The empirical study of the spread of cloud-based computer technology among the Hungarian enterprises)*. Szakdolgozat, Miskolci Egyetem.

D'Arcy, P. (2011). *7 trends driving the evolving workforce - are you ready for change?* Retrieved from http://en.community.dell.com/dell-blogs/direct2dell/b/direct2dell/archive/2011/10/18/7-trends-driving-the-evolving-workforce-are-you-ready-for-change.aspx

Determining Total Cost of Ownership for Data Center and Network Room Infrastructure, White Paper #6. (2003). *American Power Conversion*. Retrieved from http://www.linuxlabs.com/PDF/Data%20Center%20Cost%20of%20Ownership.pdf

Ernst & Young's. (2010). *Cloud computing issues and impacts*, Global Technology Industry Discussion Series. Retrieved from http://www.ey.com/Publication/vwLUAssets/Cloud-computing_issues_and_impacts/$FILE/Cloud_computing_issues_and_impacts.pdf

European Commission - MEMO. 12/713 (2012). *A számítási felhőben rejlő potenciál felszabadítása Európában - mi is jelent ez pontosan és milyen módon érint bennünket? (Unleashing the Potential of Cloud Computing in Europe - What is it and what does it mean for us?)*, Retrieved from http://europa.eu/rapid/press-release_MEMO-12-713_hu.htm

Fajszi, B., Cser, L., & Fehér, T. (2010). *Üzleti haszon az adatok mélyén, Az adatbányászat mindennapjai, (Business gains in the depth of data, The daily routine of data mining)*. Alinea Kiadó- IQSYS.

Gartner (2013). Predicts 2014: *Government CIOs Are Key to Moving the Digital Enterprise Forward*. Retrieved from http://www.gartner.com/document/2625824

Golden, B. (2009). *Capex vs. Opex: Most People Miss the Point About Cloud Economics*, Retrieved from http://www.cio.com/article/484429/Capex_vs._Opex_Most_People_Miss_the_Point_About_Cloud_Economics

Harris, T. (2013). *Cloud Computing - An Overview, School of Software*, Sun Yat-sen University Retrieved from http://south.cattelecom.com/rtso/Technologies/CloudComputing/Cloud-Computing-Overview.pdf

Helmbrecht, U. (2014). *ENISA Annual Report 2013, European Union Agency for Network and Information Security*. Luxembourg: Publications Office of the European Union.

IDC (2012). *Quantitative Estimates of the demand for cloud Computing in Europe and the likely barriers to take-up*

Kepes, B. (2012). *Cloudonomics, The Economics of Cloud Computing*, Retrieved from http://www.cloudstratagem.com.au/Cloudonomics-The_Economics_of_Cloud_ Computing.pdf

Leimbach, T. (2014). *Potential and impacts of cloud computing services and social network websites*. Brussels: European Union.

Lepenye, T. (2010). *Felhős ég az IT felett - Bevezetés a számítási felhők világába*, (*A cloudy sky over information technology – An introduction into the world of cloud computing*) Retrieved from http://lepenyet.wordpress.com/2010/04/23/felhos-eg-az-it-felett-%E2%80%93-bevezetes-a-szamitasi-felhok-vilagaba/

Mell, P., & Grance, T. (2011). *The NIST Definition of Cloud Computing*. Retrieved from http://csrc.nist.gov/publications/nistpubs/800-145/SP800-145.pdf

Molnár, B., Szabó, Gy., Benczúr, A., & Tarcsi, Á. (2012). *Felhő számítástechnika a közigazgatásban, (Cloud computing in public administration)*. Információs Rendszerek Tanszék

Mozsik, T. (2010): *5 tipp a számítási felhők felhasználásához, (5 tips of using cloud computing)* Retrieved from http://bitport.hu/vezinfo/5-tipp-a-szamitasi-felho-vallalati-felhasznalasahoz

Nanterme, P., & Cole, M. (2013). *Accenture Technology Vision 2013*, Every Business Is a Digital Business, Retrieved from http://www.accenture.com/SiteCollectionDocuments/PDF/Accenture-Technology-Vision-2013.pdf

Racskó, P. (2012). *A számítási felhő az Európai Unió egén, (Computerized clouds in the sky over the European Union)* (pp. 1–16). Vezetéstudomány.

Racskó, P. (2014). A felhőalapú számítástechnika az elektronikus közigazgatásban, (Cloud computing in the field of electronic public administration) (pp. 191-209). Budapest: E-közszolgálatfejlesztés, Nemzeti Közszolgálati Egyetem.

Safranka, M. (2013). *A felhő definíciója, System Center Mindenkinek, (The definition of cloud computing – System Centre for everyone)* Retrieved from http://blogs.technet.com/b/scm/archive/2013/02/08/a-felh-defin-237-ci-243-ja.aspx

Samuelson, P., & Nordhaus, W. (1987). Közgazdaságtan I-II. (Economics Vol. 1-2.) (pp. 667). Budapest: Közgazdasági és Jogi Könyvkiadó,.

Sasvari, P. (2012). Adaptable Techniques for Making IT-Related Investment Decisions. *International Journal of Advanced Research in Computer Science and Software Engineering*, *2*, 2.

Shaw, N. (2011). *The Cloud Broker Business Paradigm*, Retrieved from http://blogs.perficient.com/businessintelligence/2011/08/15/the-cloud-broker-business-paradigm/

Szucsne, M. K. (2012). A Comprehensive Review of Scientific Literature on Methods for Determining Discount Rates in Corporate Practices. *Theory Methodology Practice: Club of Economics in Miskolc*, *8*(02), 81–87.

ADDITIONAL READING

Biró. Sz., Bujna A., Cser, L., Fajszi, B., Fehér, T., Hosszu, M., Járási, I., Masanja, Á., Máté, A., Móra, K., Szél, M., & Zimmer, M. (2012). Business value in an ocean of data (pp. 302). Budapest: Alinea.

Carr, N. (2004). *Does IT Matter?* Boston: Harvard Business School Press.

Carr, N. (2008). *The Big Switch*. New York: W. W. Norton & Co.

Curko, K., Bach, M. P., & Radonic, G. (2007). *Business Intelligence and Business Process Management in Banking Operations*, Information Technology Interfaces, 2007. ITI 2007. Proceedings of 29th International Conference on Information Technology Interfaces doi:10.1109/ITI.2007.4283744

Cusumano, M. (2008). The Changing Software Business: From Products to Services and Other New Business Models. *The MIT Center for Digital Business*, research paper no. 236.

Davenport, T., & Harris, J. (2007). *Competing on Analytics*. Boston: Harvard Business School Press.

Doctorow, C. (2008). Welcome to the Petacentre. *Nature*, *455*(4), 16–21. doi:10.1038/455016a PMID:18769411

Krauth, P. (2008). *Közműszerű IT-szolgáltatás, (IT as a public utility service) Megjelent: Dömölki Bálint (szerk.): Égen-földön informatika*. Budapest: Typotex Kiadó.

Pastuszak, Z. (2010). Use of the e-business reception model to compare the level of advanced e-business solutions reception in service and manufacturing companies, *International Journal of Management and Enterprise Development*, 8(1), 1-21.

Rogers, E. (2003). *Diffusion of Innovations*. New York: Free Press.

Suha, P., & Martinek, P. (2011). *Auto scaling solutions in enterprise cloud computing*. In: Proceedings of the XXV. microCAD International Scientific Conference (pp. 91-96). Miskolc, Magyarország, 2011.03.31-2011.04.01.

KEY TERMS AND DEFINITIONS

Broad Network Access: Capabilities are available over the network and accessed through standard mechanisms that promote use by heterogeneous thin or thick client platforms (e.g., mobile phones, tablets, laptops, and workstations).

Cloud Computing: It is a model for enabling ubiquitous, convenient, on-demand network access to a shared pool of configurable computing resources (e.g., networks, servers, storage, applications, and services) that can be rapidly provisioned and released with minimal management effort or service provider interaction. This cloud model is composed of five essential characteristics, three service models, and four deployment models.

Community Cloud: The cloud infrastructure is provisioned for exclusive use by a specific community of consumers from organizations that have shared concerns (e.g., mission, security requirements, policy, and compliance considerations). It may be owned, managed, and operated by one or more of the organizations in the community, a third party, or some combination of them, and it may exist on or off premises.

Data Protection: An umbrella term for various procedures that ensure information is secure and available only to authorized users.

Data Security: Protection against illegal or wrongful intrusion. In the IT world, intrusion concerns mostly deal with gaining access to user and company data.

Gross Domestic Product (GDP): It is the market value of all officially recognized final goods and services produced within a country in a year, or over a given period of time. GDP per capita is often used as an indicator of a country's material standard of living.

Hybrid Cloud: The cloud infrastructure is a composition of two or more distinct cloud infrastructures (private, community, or public) that remain unique entities, but are bound together by standardized or proprietary technology that enables data and application portability (e.g., cloud bursting for load balancing between clouds).

Information Technology: Processing information by computer, which encompasses "information management" and "computer science." IT is also the latest moniker for the industry as a whole, and the term became popular in the 1990s. It actually took 40 years before the industry settled on what to call itself. First it was "electronic data processing" (EDP), followed by "management information systems" (MIS) and "information systems" (IS) and finally "information technology" (IT).

Infrastructure as a Service (IaaS): The capability provided to the consumer is to provision processing, storage, networks, and other fundamental computing resources where the consumer is able to deploy and run arbitrary software, which can include operating systems and applications. The consumer does not manage or control the underlying cloud infrastructure but has control over operating systems, storage, and deployed applications; and possibly limited control of select networking components (e.g., host firewalls).

Measured Service: Cloud systems automatically control and optimize resource use by leveraging a metering capability at some level of abstraction appropriate to the type of service (e.g., storage, processing, bandwidth, and active user accounts). Resource usage can be monitored, controlled, and reported, providing transparency for both the provider and consumer of the utilized service.

On-Demand Self-Service: A consumer can unilaterally provision computing capabilities, such as server time and network storage, as needed automatically without requiring human interaction with each service provider.

Opportunity Cost: It is a key concept in economics. Opportunity costs are not restricted to monetary or financial costs: the real cost of output forgone, lost time, pleasure or any other benefit that provides utility should also be considered opportunity costs.

Platform as a Service (PaaS): The capability provided to the consumer is to deploy onto the cloud infrastructure consumer-created or acquired applications created using programming languages, libraries, services, and tools supported by the provider. The consumer does not manage or control the underlying cloud infrastructure including network, servers, operating systems, or storage, but has control over the deployed applications and possibly configuration settings for the application-hosting environment.

Private Cloud: The cloud infrastructure is provisioned for exclusive use by a single organization comprising multiple consumers (e.g., business units). It may be owned, managed, and operated by the organization, a third party, or some combination of them, and it may exist on or off premises.

Public Cloud: The cloud infrastructure is provisioned for open use by the general public. It may be owned, managed, and operated by a business, academic, or government organization, or some combination of them. It exists on the premises of the cloud provider.

Rapid Elasticity: Capabilities can be elastically provisioned and released, in some cases automatically, to scale rapidly outward and inward commensurate with demand. To the consumer, the capabilities available for provisioning often appear to be unlimited and can be appropriated in any quantity at any time.

Remote Access: The ability to log in to a computer or network within an organization from an external location. Remote access is typically accomplished via a connection to the Internet or by dialing directly via an analog modem. See virtual private network, remote control software and RAS.

Resource Pooling: The provider's computing resources are pooled to serve multiple consumers using a multi-tenant model, with different physical and virtual resources dynamically assigned and reassigned according to consumer demand. There is a sense of location independence in that the customer generally has no control or knowledge over the exact location of the provided resources but may be able to specify location at a higher level of abstraction (e.g., country, state, or datacenter). Examples of resources include storage, processing, memory, and network bandwidth.

Software as a Service (SaaS): The capability provided to the consumer is to use the provider's applications running on a cloud infrastructure. The applications are accessible from various client devices through either a thin client interface, such as a web browser (e.g., web-based email), or a program interface. The consumer does not manage or control the underlying cloud infrastructure including network, servers, operating systems, storage, or even individual application capabilities, with the possible exception of limited user-specific application configuration settings.

Chapter 7
Societal and Economical Impact on Citizens through Innovations Using Open Government Data:
Indian Initiative on Open Government Data

D. P. Misra
National Informatics Centre, India

Alka Mishra
National Informatics Centre, India

ABSTRACT

This chapter analyzes the impact that an open data policy can have on the citizens of India. Especially in a scenario where government accountability and transparency has become the buzzword for good governance and further look at whether the availability of open data can become an agent for socio-economic change in India. What kind of change it can bring to India which has its own complexities when it comes to socio economic issues and whether the steps taken by the government are up to the mark to address these complexities through data sharing. In order to understand the changes which may occur for the good or the bad, the chapter looks at specific examples where the open data platform have been utilized in India and what impact they have had on the Indian society and how the citizens have responded to it.

BACKGROUND

A piece of content or data is open if anyone is free to use, reuse, and redistribute it - subject only, at most, to the requirement to attribute and share-alike. (Opendefinition.org)

For a country as diverse as India, the process of governance is a complex one which involves a lot of deliberations with the various stakeholders within and outside the government. Given the significant social and economic issues which the government has to deal with in India, it has become more and more imperative that the government's decision making process has to be an informed one to ensure the success of its schemes and initiatives. These schemes and initiatives which are targeted towards the citizens also requires an inbuilt process to ensure accountability and transparency to ensure that these schemes are actually

DOI: 10.4018/978-1-4666-8598-7.ch007

benefitting the needy. Therefore, for an informed decision making and accountable review of the government policies the essential ingredient is the availability of data.

Evidence-based planning of socio-economic development processes rely on quality data. Governments across the globe and particularly in India collect process and generate a large amount of data in its day-to-day functioning, which are lying in silos and are difficult to put in effective use. Asset and value potentials of data are widely recognized at all levels. Data collected or generated through public investments, when made publicly available and maintained over time, their potential value could be more fully realized. It helps building a comprehensive statistical picture of the country and allows maximum use/reuse of data, which has the tremendous potential to benefit the citizens socially and economically through data-driven innovation. However, most of such data, which are non-sensitive in nature, remains inaccessible to citizens buried deep down in the government records and files.

Governments become more transparent by proactively publishing timely, relevant, and comprehensive information and data on the Internet. This is done so that it can be easily accessed, analyzed, reused, and combined with other data by anyone for any purposes free of charge and without any restrictions. Open data provides the foundation to enable citizens to better understand how their government works, how their tax money is spent, and how decisions and laws are made. Better understanding through increased access to information can be beneficial to governments, citizens, and society as a whole, as it: (Department of Economic and Social Affairs, Division for Public Administration & Development Management, United Nations, 2013)

- Helps citizens to hold their government and administration accountable, which can reduce corruption and mismanagement.
- Helps citizens to better understand why and how decisions are made, which can help restore trust and can lead to better acceptance of policy decisions once enacted.
- Supports and empowers citizens to make informed decisions and engage with the government, thus enabling citizens to have a more-active voice in society.
- Supports decision-makers in government and public administration to make better and fact-based policy decisions and thus to increase government efficiency and effectiveness.
- Supports governments, citizens, academia, and the private sector to work together and collaboratively find new answers to solve societal problems.

The need of the hour is to facilitate sharing and utilization of the large amount of data generated and residing among the entities of the Government of India at all the tiers be it at the central, state, district or even Panchayat level. This is possible if the data is available in open formats and free from licenses to encourage its innovative use, reuse and redistribution. In this backdrop; the National Data Sharing and Accessibility Policy (NDSAP) was formulated with the objective of facilitating access to Government of India owned non-sensitive shareable data in machine readable form through a wide area network all over the country, in a periodically updatable manner.

National Data Sharing and Accessibility Policy (NDSAP), gazette notified on 17th March 2012, envisages proactive dissemination of Government owned data through the Open Government Data (OGD) Platform India - http://data.gov.in. In compliance to the NDSAP, the OGD Platform provides an enabling provision and platform for proactive and open access to the data generated through public funds available with various ministries/departments/organizations of Government of India. The need of the hour is to unlock significant social and economic value for the use/reuse and redistribution of Open Government Data. With the release of thousands of datasets pertaining to different sectors such as census, energy, health, commerce, postal, agriculture, transport etc. on the Platform, various communities ranging from developers, start-ups, industries, and academia to researchers, etc. have started engaging with the Open Government Data for data-driven innovation and service delivery. In the coming years there is a decisive impact envisaged in the socio economic impact on the society

According to the preamble of NDSAP, there has been an increasing demand by the community that data collected with the deployment of public funds should be made more readily available to all, for enabling rational debate, better decision making for progressive research and analysis and use in meeting civil society needs.

NDSAP aims at the promotion of a technology-based culture of open data management and community engagement there on for development of a societal and economical eco-system. As per NDSAP, Data sharing and accessibility are based on the principles – Openness, Flexibility, Transparency, Legal Conformity, Protection of Intellectual Property, Formal Responsibility, Professionalism Standards, Interoperability, Quality, Security, Efficiency, Accountability, Sustainability and PrivacyIt envisages a state-of-the-art data warehouse and data archive with online visualization capabilities, which includes provision of multi-dimensional and subject oriented views of the datasets to give better graphical.

INTRODUCTION

Open Government Data (OGD) Platform India (http://data.gov.in), developed completely using Open Source Stack and has been set up to provide access to datasets published by different government entities in open format. It facilitates community participation for further development of the product with Visualizations, APIs, Alerts, Notifications etc. It has an easy to use and user friendly interface with dynamic/pull down menus, search based reports, secured web access, bulletin board, based on Dublin Core metadata standards defining core as well as extensible metadata and parametric & dynamic reports in exportable format. The platform reflects how innovative use of information technology has led to a paradigm shift in accommodating huge data potential of the country.

The Platform has a rich mechanism for citizen engagement, which could help Ministries/ Departments/ Organizations prioritize the release of Government Datasets by asking for datasets/ apps which are not available on the platform. Besides, enabling citizens to express their need for specific datasets or apps, it also allows them to rate the quality of datasets, seek clarification or information from nodal officers of participating government entities.

In this Internet age and digitally connected population, Social Media plays pivotal role in dissemination of information and awareness. People can share the information about datasets published on the portal through their social network accounts. People can also share their experiences, stimulate new ideas and demonstrate the power of putting open data to work through social networking sites. The platform has social media connectors be it through Facebook or Twitter.

The Platform also acts as a knowledge-sharing platform through online communities. Citizens with specific interests are encouraged to contribute blogs and join online forums around various datasets of their domain of interest such as agriculture, education, health, etc. This would further encourage the data-driven innovation around the specific domain.

Platform demonstrated its potential to the App Developers' Community through various contests such as '12th Plan Hackathon', 'In Pursuit of an Idea' 'CMA Hackathon', etc. Out of which '#OpenDataApps Challenge 'was launched in association with National Association of Software and Services Companies (NASSCOM) a trade association of Indian Information Technology and Business Process Outsourcing industry and 'Code for Honor 2014' was launched with M/S Microsoft to target industries for developing mobile Apps for societal good even on commercial models.

Several innovative and useful prototypes as well as full-fledged Apps have been developed across platforms and devices ranging from Mobile/Tablet, SMS to Voice-based ones, using Open Government Data and Open Source Technologies and Tools, which helped the government to empower its citizens with information and services. Therefore, we see the advent of innovation building in India using government data through various types of Apps, mash-ups, info-graphics, visualizations by slicing and dicing data and even service delivery. In the process, it is envisaged to impact our economy as it is had been in other developed countries as well. Looking forward, the immediate plan in data collection is involving a number of dynamic data generating projects including online services as well as government's stand on commercial use of Apps.

- First, target Ministries/Departments to persuade them to release as many datasets as possible on proactive/auto consumption basis from the e-Government Service Applications particularly from Mission Mode Projects (MMPs) of the country.
- Second, take relevant action viz. releasing APIs/Tools/Services in line with the feedbacks/ suggestions received from citizens on datasets they are looking for.
- Third, OGD Platform to offer an integrated repository of data portal which will not only hold data for various central ministries/departments but would also encompass data generated by various State Governments and UTs over a period of time.
- Fourth, in view of the feedbacks and queries received from various communities, clear cut guidelines should be issued on commercial use of these Apps developed using OGD. Many of the apps developed have a huge potential.

BIG PICTURE ON OPEN DATA

Big bang for Open Data in a single platform will spur a frenzy of activities. Pollution numbers will affect property prices. Restaurant reviews will mention official sanitation ratings. Data from tollbooths could be used to determine prices for nearby hoardings. Combining data from multiple sources will yield fresh insights. The revolution across the industries fueled by open data is starting to do for the modern world what the industrial revolution did for the past century. The Economist says "Open Data a new Goldmine" ("new goldmine | The Economist," 2013) –

Economically, it can play pivotal role in breaking down information gaps across industries which would help companies share benchmarks and spread best practices that raise productivity. The OGD analytics can also help industries know consumer preferences to improve products and services. In addition to helping the industry, it also allows a much more informed decision making process as open data would enable NGOs and Think Tanks also to contribute their value to the government's decisions where economics is

Figure 1. A screen shot of "The Economist"

involved. Publicly available resources contributed by the Government and a growing number of businesses and citizens have reached the critical mass necessary to trigger a step-change in business attitudes towards open data. Businesses in all industries can now find relevant open data and use it to improve their products and services. New businesses, like Duedil, i3 Education Services, Parkopedia and Spotlight on spend, are emerging whose commercial models are predicated on the insight they deliver from open data. (Deloitte Analytics Paper, 2012)

According to Open Data Handbook, a project of Open Knowledge Foundation, several studies have estimated the economic value of open data at several hundreds of billions of Euros annually added to the GDP of EU alone. New products and companies are re-using open data. The Danish husetsweb.dk (http://www.husetsweb.dk/) helps you to find ways of improving the energy efficiency of your home, including financial planning and finding builders who can do the work. It is based on re-using cadastral information and information about government subsidies, as well as the local trade register. Google Translate uses the enormous volume of EU documents that appear in all European languages to train the translation algorithms, thus improving its quality of service. (see Figure 2)

The Open Government Data has the potential to create social value as well. There are numerous instances of the ways in which open data is creating social value. According to Open Data Handbook, Open Government Data can also help you to make better decisions in your own life or enable you to be more active in society. A woman in Denmark built findtoilet.dk (http://www.findtoilet.dk/), which showed all the Danish public toilets, so that people she knew with bladder problems can now trust themselves to go out more again. In the Netherlands a service, vervuilingsalarm.nl (http://www.vervuilingsalarm.nl/), is available which warns you with a message if the air-quality in your vicinity is going to reach a self-defined threshold tomorrow. In New York you can easily find out where you can walk your dog, as well as find other people who use the same parks. Services like 'mapumental' (https://mapumental.com/) in the UK and 'mapnificent(https://mapumental.com/)' in Germany allow you to find places to live, taking into account the duration of your commute to work, housing prices and how beautiful an area is. All these examples use open government data. (WARSAW Institute of Economic Study & Centre for European Stratergy, 2014)

According the first UK-wide market assessment of public sector information produced by Deloitte between October 2012 and March 2013, the value of public sector information to consumers, businesses and the public sector in 2011/12 was approximately £1.8 billion (2011 prices). This is a mid-point estimate, with the sensitivity analyses giving a range between £1.2billion and £2.2 billion.

While an aggregate figure on the social value of public sector information is difficult to reach without more information on the way data is used and how it then permeates society, on the basis of conservative assumptions, it is estimated this figure could be in excess of £5 billion for 2011-12 (2011 prices). This estimate is likely to increase as public sector information is used more widely and in more impactful ways. Adding this social value estimate to the calculated value of public sector information to consumers, businesses and the public sector, gives an aggregate estimate of between £6.2 billion and £7.2 billion in 2011-12 (2011 prices). Future uses of public sector information that have the potential to generate much more value include greater combining of public and private sector information, exploiting the benefits of linked data, embedding geospatial and location data across more and more products and services and more informed policymaking based on better utilized public sector information (Department for Business Innovations & Skills, Delloite, 2013)

Figure 2. The representative graphic on contribution of Data Driven Solutions to EU GDP

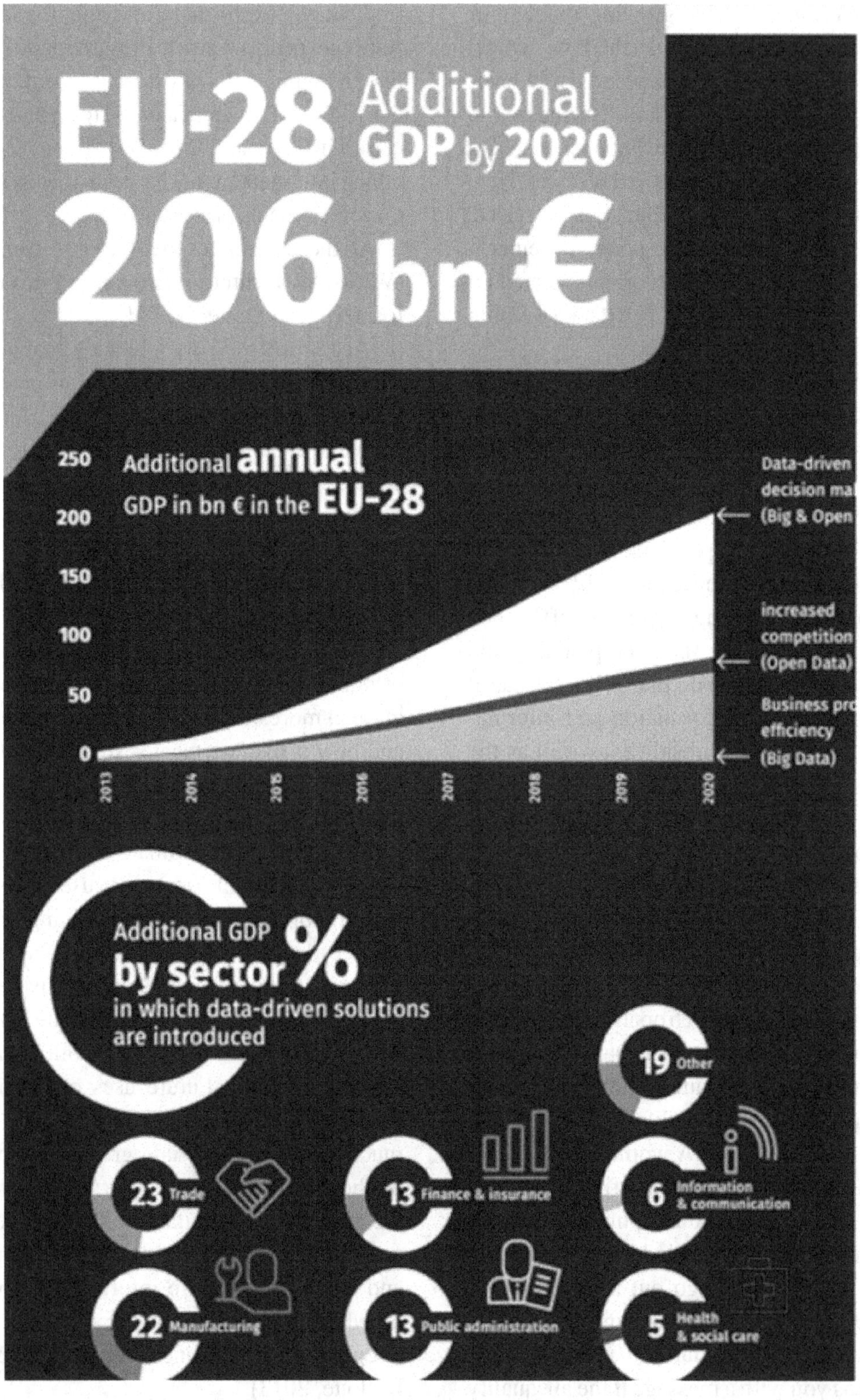

POTENTIAL ECONOMIC AND SOCIAL IMPACT

New Business Opportunities for Firms and Companies

The Open Government Data has the potential to create business opportunities. It has the potential to raise productivity, to improve products and services and most importantly to pave way for the data-driven innovation with new products and services. Moreover, it stimulates creation of new firms and companies.

Seattle-based company called Porch.com, which uses city work permits, licenses and other residential construction information to create a searchable database, is one of the examples. The company raised $6.25 million from angel investors in October 2012 and expects to hire nearly 80 more workers by the end of 2014, as it continues to expand the online service nationally. (Loten Angus, 2014)

US-based health care technology company, iTriage(https://www.itriagehealth.com/) is another example. It offers a portfolio of location-aware mobile apps, which provides consumers instant access to information about healthcare providers and facilities in their neighborhood. The apps mash up health data, public-domain records about insurance products and public directories of healthcare providers to disseminate this information.

Several countries, including USA, Spain and Finland, have witnessed tangible impact of Open Data on the volume of business activity in their geographies. In USA, it has listed 500 companies working on Open Data related innovations and businesses whereas in Spain, a study estimates that there are over 150 companies focused solely on the informediary (the term is a composite of information and intermediary) sector ("Open Data 500 Companies," n.d.) . There are many such success stories……..

Innovation in Business

Broader and more rapid access to scientific papers and research data will make it easier for researchers to focus on research and analysis rather than on data collection whereas businesses to build on the findings of public-funded research. This will help boost a country or region's innovation capacity across all fields. Taking the example of the European Union, it will give that region a better return on its €87 billion (USD $106 billion) annual investment in R&D. (Open Government Partnership, 2012)

Leading businesses, such as Google and Asos, are adopting new business models, which are based on free access to their data as it has the potential to generate a good return on investment. It gives impetus to increased engagement with consumers and developers. Their success will lead to creation of new commercial ventures, which will generate new sources of revenue and herald new opportunities for innovation.

According to a Deloitte Analytic paper on Open Data, in late 2011, Duedil, an open data start-up, was valued at around £20 million by investors keen to acquire the company. In 2010, Factual, a US-based start-up and aggregator of publicly available data received a first tranche of investment funding of $25 million. (Deloitte Analytics Paper, 2012)

Creating New Products and Services

Small and medium companies with products and services based on Open Data, such as Global Positioning Systems, financial services and software applications, also generate new businesses and jobs. The Weather Channel, an American television network and Garmin, a firm that develops consumer, aviation and marine technologies (with market cap of over $7 billion at end of January 2013) were built using raw government data. Furthermore, businesses can generate high returns through the development of new products and services based on high value data domains. For instance, Bright Scope, a California financial information startup, used government data to help the consumers understand fees associated with their retirement savings accounts. Similarly, data domains such as Economic, Geospatial and Environmental have higher commercial impact. For instance, Open Data from the US National Weather Service supports a private weather industry worth over $1.5 billion per year. (Capgemini Consulting, n.d.)

Also, innovative solutions can be developed through a mix of public sector and proprietary information such as data as-a-service. For instance, CloudMade (http://cloudmade.com/), an applications development company, leverages OpenStreetMap data from the transport domain and supplements it with various datasets from alternative sources in order to create comprehensive location data. Revenue is generated by supplying this information at a price to developers and application publishers of geo-enabled products.

Some Country-Specific Examples (Open Government Partnership, 2012)

- **Australia:** A study of the aggregate economic impacts of spatial data on the national economy conducted by the Australian government suggested that open spatial data and high precision positioning systems can increase productivity by billions of Australian dollars across a range of industry sectors. For instance spatial information industry revenue in 2006-07 could have added cumulative gain of AUD 6.43-12.57 billion (USD $6.7-13 billion), equivalent to 0.6-1.2% of GDP.
- **Denmark:** A study (in Danish) on Quantifying the value of open government data showed that banking, insurance and energy indicated that better access to public sector information could be of significant value, with the energy industry estimating that in conjunction with the construction industry the potential national market for energy improvements drawing on various government data sources is €0.54-2.7 billion (USD $0.55-3.3 billion).
- **European Commission:** A recent European Commission Communication on Open Data predicts that overall economic gains from opening up public data could amount to €40 billion (USD $48.7 billion) a year in the EU.
- **Ireland:** A study by TASC has shown that charging for data does not lead to cost recovery, that the country's FOI law is not "expensive" as such and that the estimated value of the business potential of reusing public data is between €83-399 million (USD $101-486 million) per annum.
- **Kenya:** Kenya became Africa's first country to digitize its information as part of a wide-scale open data initiative. The initiative is yielding a secondary economy with a range of apps that are being created to help people access, manage and comment on government information.
- **Spain:** a government-commissioned study found in-country business volume directly associated with open data released by national government was €550-650 million (USD $669-791 million) and between 5,000 and 5,500 employees were directly assigned to activities related to re-using information.
- **US:** Opening its weather data led to gross receipts by commercial weather industry of USD $400-700 million a year with 400 firms employing 4,000 people. By comparison, Europe had a similar sized economy but with largely closed weather data and had only 30 firms with 300 employees and receipts of USD $30m-50m a year.

Innovative Apps Developed across the Globe using Open Data

- **Brazil:** The interactive mapping platform InfoAmazonia (http://infoamazonia.org/#!/map=49) provides a crowd sourced map of news and reports on environmental threats facing the Amazon rainforest.
- **USA:** Procure.io (http://www.knight-foundation.org/grants/20102539/): The Oakland and Atlanta-based technologists behind this project will produce a streamlined procurement system for making government contract offerings more accessible, using a simple interface in which government officials can submit requests for proposal to a publicly accessible and easily indexed database. By simplifying the contracting process, Procure.io stands to broaden the pool of applicants and thereby encourage lower bids.
- Outline.com(http://outline.com/): This Cambridge, MA-based "policy simulation" startup will let users input their age, income and other general details on a website and then use sophisticated economic models to output a positive or negative dollar amount that represents their expected net income change from a proposed policy. Outline will also provide a transparent version-control system to catalog changes in the policies and platforms for communities and government officials to comment.
- Oyez(http://www.oyez.org/): Founded in 1997 at IIT Chicago-Kent College of Law, Oyez has overseen successful digitization and annotation initiatives for U.S. Supreme Court documents and now the organizers hope to apply the same model to state supreme courts. The effort will collect, catalog, standardize, annotate and release to the public the records of the supreme courts of the five largest states (CA, FL, IL, NY and TX). The organization will also work to annotate the records with metadata and plain-English summaries, in partnership with local "academic or other public-spirited institutions."
- GitMachines (http://www.gitmachines.com/): The Washington, DC-based team will provide free, cloud-based virtual machines that are compliant with NIST and GSA software standards and come pre-configured with commonly used open government tools such as the Apache Tomcat web server and data workflow management tool Drake. By offering these servers from a central, virtual depot, Git Machines will also reduce costs associated with ad hoc server-side IT staffing.
- Civic Insight (http://civicinsight.com/): Building off their work on BlightStatus, an urban blight data visualization tool for New Orleans, the San Francisco-based Civic Insight will expand the scope of their dynamic mapping solution, working with other cities on applications related to economic development and public health.
- Plan in a Box (http://blog.openplans.org/2013/04/plan-in-a-box/): A Philadelphia- and New York-based team will build a simple web publishing platform designed for municipal planning activities. Aimed at geographically-constrained projects in small and medium-sized cities, Plan in a Box will offer a centralized news and feedback repository, with mobile device and social network integration.
- **World Bank:** It has put financial data for more than 200 countries onto individual pages, pulling data from seven different sources to one attractive and user-friendly interface. World Bank in India had done a short survey recently for around 100 companies in India who are interested to continue and scale up their business based on Open Data in India. Following are the graphs representing existence of companies and working on various sectors of the economy. (see Figure 3 & 4)

Figure 3. The representative graphic of Companies & Sectors they are working is showcased in Figure 3.

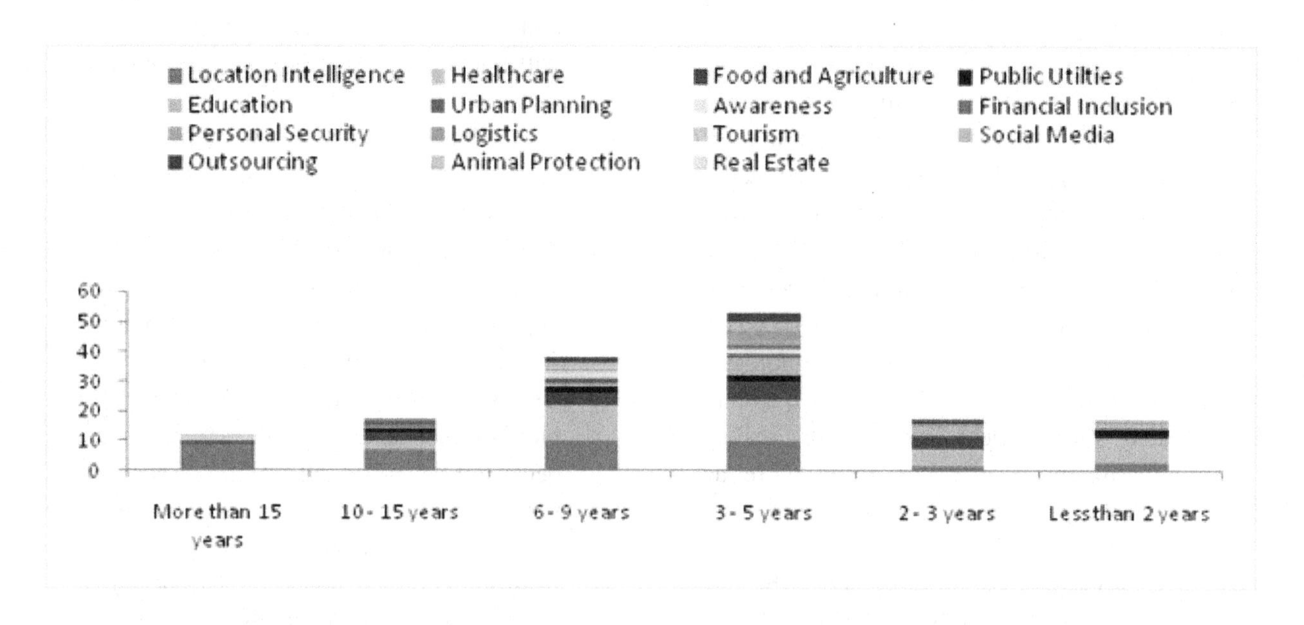

Figure 4. The representative graphic of Financing Needs by Companies & Sectors they are working is showcased in Figure 4.

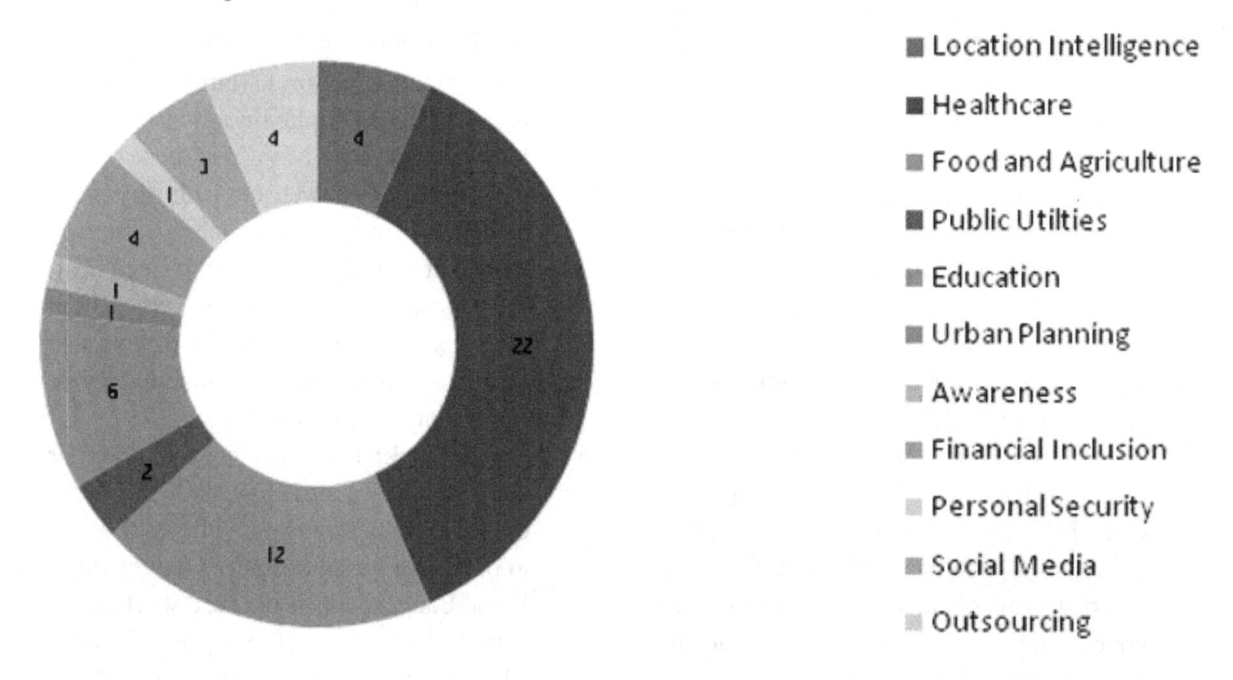

- **King County Elections** (http://www.kingcounty.gov/elections.aspx): Its pushed elections data out to citizens on a mobile app for the first time ever, serving over 200,000 voters on its Nov. 6 election night.
- **Edmonton, Alberta** (http://www.socrata.com/blog/the-way-we-live-edmonton/): introduced its Citizen Dashboard, making government performance data, such as on-time bus arrivals and number of potholes filled, more easily available to citizens.
- **European Commission** announced the winners of the European Prize for Innovation in Public Administration 2013. Helsinki Region Infoshare (HRI) (http://www.hri.fi/en/) is a regional Open Data initiative, where the cities of the Helsinki Metropolitan Area make accessible their data to all. Aporta is an initiative of the Spanish Government for promoting the Re-Use of Public Sector Information and fostering an open data culture.

WHAT IS OPEN GOVERNMENT DATA AND CITIZEN ENGAGEMENT

The term Open Government Data (OGD) came into prominence in recent past. The two main elements of open government data can be defined as follows:

- Government data is any data and information produced or generated by any government or public sector body
- Data is said to be 'open', no matter the source, only if it can be accessed, reused and redistributed by anyone, for any purposes, including commercial reuse, free of charge and without any restrictions – subject only, at most, to the requirement to attribute and share alike. While the full definition gives precise details as to what this means but to summarize the most important are:
    - **Availability and Access:** the data must be available as a whole at no more than a reasonable reproduction cost, preferably by downloading over the Internet. The data must also be available in a convenient and modifiable form.
    - **Reuse and Redistribution:** the data must be provided under terms that permit reuse and redistribution including the intermixing with other datasets.
    - **Universal Participation:** everyone must be able to use, reuse and redistribute - there should be no discrimination against fields of endeavor or against persons or groups. For example, non-commercial restrictions that would prevent commercial use, or restrictions of use for certain purposes (e.g. only in education), are not allowed ("Open Definition, n.d.) .

While opening or using open government data it may be a good idea to understand the technical and legal openness of government data on one hand and its usefulness in service delivery or transparency, accountability and citizen engagement on the other hand.

The evolution of the Internet, mobile and social networking technologies as well as other advances in information and communication technologies (ICT) have enabled the transformation of governance and contributed to a shift in the balance of power between citizens and the government. There is a growing demand by citizens for information held by government so they can actively participate in government affairs. At the same time, governments and Public Sector Bodies are increasingly experimenting with citizen engagement and new consultative processes by utilizing new communication channels provided by ICTs, especially social media.

Citizen engagement is often seen as the interaction between governments and citizens in order to share information and involving them in policy processes, including public service delivery, and more specifically in defining the issues that affect them, identifying possible solutions, and developing priorities for action, often jointly with the government bodies. E-participation has developed in pace with technological and political developments from public information over public consultation towards engagement and collaboration. These have come from simple websites, blogs and FAQs to the use of social media networks (e.g. Twitter and Flickr and Facebook. etc.) on to more sophisticated and interactive systems such as e-voting or modern ICT to facilitate decision-making processes. The various forms cater to different needs by disseminating public service information, giving and receiving feedback. E-participation has the potential to make citizen engagement cheaper, easier, faster, and more transparent. Citizen engagement should occur at all stages of policy development and be an iterative process. Key benefits include (Department of Economic and Social Affairs, Division for Public Administration & Development Management, United Nations, 2013):

- Increasing citizens' sense of responsibility and understanding of complex issues.
- Understanding of each other's priorities and values and thereby sharing ownership between government bodies and citizens for policies and decisions, thereby increasing their legitimacy.
- Developing more informed and more consensual policy choices.
- Increased trust and sense of cooperation between citizens and Public Sector Bodies.
- Possibilities for government bodies to tap into the creativity and technical know-how of citizens.

MOMENTUM STARTED GAINING IN INDIA

After gazette notification of National Data Sharing and Accessibility Policy (NDSAP) on 17th March 2012; proactive dissemination of Government owned data through the Open Government Data (OGD) Platform India (http://data.gov.in) has started picking up. This is the first-ever Open Data initiative in India, which aims at providing an enabling provision and platform for proactive and open access to the data generated through public funds available with various ministries/departments/ organizations of Government of India.

Open Government and More Efficient Governance

The Open Data Initiative of India paves the way for more efficient governance by facilitating easy access to plethora of Government owned datasets to public.

- **Transparency:** The data collected by Government gives the statistical picture of the country. It paves way for strengthening transparency in the governance as it is important that citizens know what Government is doing. The Open Government datasets can be used as one of the effective ways to monitor policies, services and other steps being taken by the Government for welfare of the people. Moreover, it has the potential of being an important step in delivering the promises of the Right to Information Act more efficiently and effectively in near future, and ultimately a step towards greater transparency and accountability in governance. (Ministry of Law & Justice, Government of India, 2005)

- **Avoiding Duplication and Cost Saving:** Sharing and accessibility help avoiding duplication in collection, generation of data, as separate bodies wouldn't have to collect the same data. It will lead to significant cost savings in data collection as it is now being collected through different sources.
- **Maximized Integration:** Datasets can be combined to provide it with more useful and meaningful context. And adoption of common standards for the collection and transfer of data may make integration of individual datasets feasible.
- **Ownership Information:** Users are able to identify owners of the principal datasets. This will bring accountability and transparency. In the long run the secondary owners may discontinue collecting data.
- **Better Decision-Making:** Ready access to valuable data may enable more informed and better decision-making. For example: If quality datasets are available, it would be easy to make efficient decisions regarding protection of the environment, development planning, managing assets, improving living conditions, disaster management, etc.

Social Inclusion in Governance

Citizen Engagement/Public Participation in governance and Community Collaboration for data-driven innovation is one of the key objectives of the Open Government Data Initiative of India. It envisages collaboration and cooperation between government entities and public for more accountability and efficiency in governance.

Data Portal India (https//:data.gov.in) has a strong component of citizen engagement. It provides a platform to the public to share ideas on new/required datasets as well as endorse the suggestions given by others. Hence, apart from enabling the public to seek required datasets, it also helps ministries/departments/organizations to prioritize the release of datasets. Moreover, users can rate the published datasets on three aspects i.e. Quality, Accessibility and Usability, which helps Government entities serve people better. The users can also directly connect with the Nodal Officers of the ministries/departments/organizations seeking more information or clarification on any dataset.

Community Collaboration (http://data.gov.in/community/agriculture-community): OGD India also provides a platform for interaction and knowledge sharing. People can connect, interact and share their views with like-minded people through online communities on the portal. The online communities open up the avenues for data-driven innovation through creative collaboration on Open Government Datasets and brainstorming in discussion forums. People are also encouraged to share their stories, experiences and knowledge on anything related to Open Data through blogging on the Data Portal India.

Maximizing use of public resources: Easy access to government owned data enhances values of the public resource. It enables more extensive use of data for the benefit of the community.

Currently, more than 11,000 resources (datasets/apps) have been made available on the OGD Platform. The need of the hour is data-driven innovation to make use of these thousands of datasets, available on the OGD Platform, in a more meaningful manner and relevant for people. So far, several initiatives have been taken to explore avenues to connect with the community ranging from data journalist, academia researchers to developers in order to encourage active engagement with the datasets.

12th Plan Hackathon

Planning Commission and National Innovation Council organized a two-day Hackathon for exploring the 12th Five Year Plan Document and its relevant data during 6th-7th April, 2013 on the OGD Platform. Students and professionals from all walks of life across the country came up with short films, web/mobile applications and data visualizations to articulate insightful content of the 12th Plan Document.

The sectors shortlisted for the Hackathon were Macroeconomic Framework, Health, Urban Development, Education and Skill Development, Energy, Agriculture and Rural Development and Environment.

The event was held simultaneously at 10 prestigious Universities/Institutes i.e. University of Jammu, IIT Delhi, Delhi University, Aligarh Muslim University, IIT Kanpur, IIT Kharagpur, TISS Mumbai, IIIT Hyderabad, IISc Bangalore, IIT Madras and IIM Shillong. Many participants also joined the event online.

For the event, the OGD Platform facilitated online registration, which occurred in two phases: the first from 22nd – 25th March' 13 and the second from 28th March – 2nd April' 13. The portal also featured a special section "12th Plan Hackathon" (http://data.gov.in/hackathon) to keep the users always updated.

More than 1900 participants across the country registered for the 32-hour Hackathon and Total 217 submissions were made. Among 10 locations, IISc Bangalore witnessed the highest submissions i.e. 42. Online Applications (virtual participation) had 37 submissions, followed by 32 in Aligarh Muslim University; 25 in IIT Delhi, 18 in IIT Madras; 15 in TISS Mumbai, 14 IIT Hyderabad; 12 in IIT Kanpur, 9 in Delhi University; 8 in IIT Kharagpur and 5 submissions in University of Jammu. (Sonam Sandhya, 2013)

The following are the two of the apps and info-graphic developed during the Hackathon:

Help My City – 1st Prize in 12th Five Year Plan Hackathon at Indian Institute of Technology (IIT), Delhi; Category: Applications

The main focus of the project is to bridge the gap between the Government and the Citizens by providing an integrated platform where common people can not only raise their problems but also can give suggestions, ask questions and bring some innovative solutions for different sectors as they experience in their daily lives to the government.

Figure 5. The representative graphic of the Help My City

Maternal & Child Care –1st Prize in 12th Five Year Plan Hackathon at IIT Delhi; Category: Info-Graphic

The info-graphic throws light on why and how the 12th Year Plan proposes to improve healthcare conditions (preventive and curable) especially relating to maternal health and child care.

In Pursuit of an Idea

National Informatics Centre (NIC) in association with the Institute of Informatics and Communication (IIC), University of Delhi initiated a unique

Figure 6. The Infographic on Maternal & Child Care

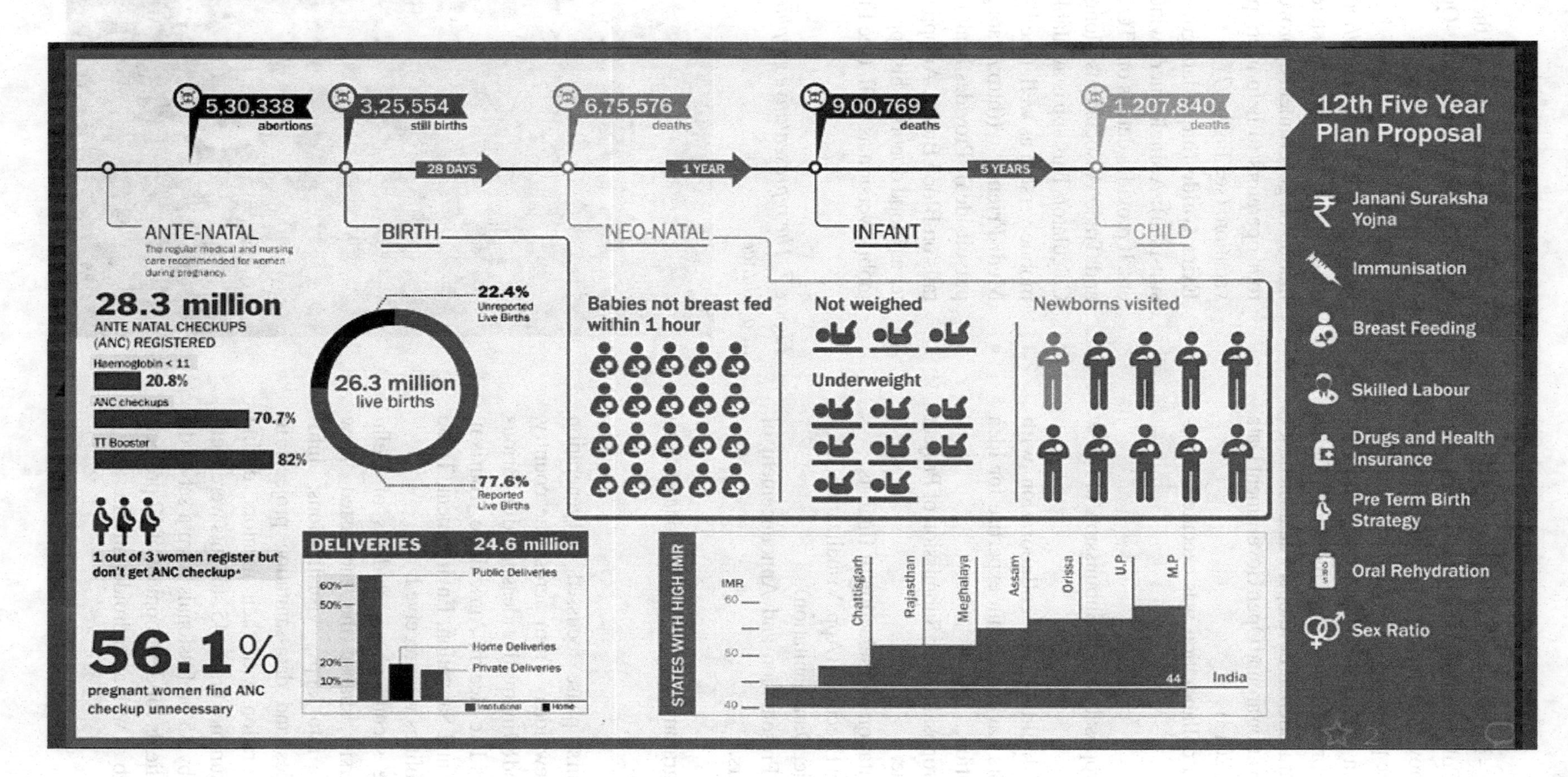

programme – In Pursuit of an Idea with the theme "Creative Collaboration on Open Government Data for Innovation" on 24th May, 2013. The objective of the program was to encourage creative collaboration among the students of Delhi University and professionals from the varied fields ranging from academia, developers, data scientists, etc. for innovation around Open Government Data (Misra D P, 2013)

The Idea collaboration was executed in following steps:

1. Pre proposal round: Submission of 'New Ideas'.
2. Team building and collaboration with mentors having domain expertise for Idea Execution.
3. Full proposal round: Submission of Project Outline.
4. Presentation and selection of finalists.
5. Project Execution (App, Visualization, Infographic, Data Sanitation).
6. Final Presentation and Announcement of winners.

The programme took place in two phases from May to July.

- The first phase focussed on generation of 'New Ideas' from across the country. Around 80 innovative ideas based on various sectors like Health, Agriculture, Tourism, Water and Sanitation, Environment, Trade and Politics were received.
- In the second phase, students of Delhi University shaped the shortlisted 'New Ideas' into apps, visualizations, infographics and data-sanitation projects in collaboration with their mentors, during their summer break. 45 students were mentored by 35 professionals from a set of diverse fields for development of 17 projects on web as well as android platform.

The following are some of the useful apps prototypes developed using the Open Government Datasets:

- **India at a Glance** (http://india.gov.in/india-glance)**:** Provides the state-wise information on government approved hotels and tour operators to help users plan for their vacation. (see Figure 7)
- **Exim Guide** (http://data.gov.in/event/pursuit-idea)**:** A single query window for traders. It provides details on ITC & IEC codes and Trade Associations along with Tariff Calculator. This app is available in Android mobile version as well. (see Figure 8)
- **Medi-Friend** ((http://data.gov.in/event/pursuit-idea)**:** Provides health tips and details on Blood Banks. An app to find/register as blood donors. This app is available in mobile version as well. (see Figure 9)

Figure 7. The representative graphic of the India at a Glance

Figure 8. The representative graphic of the Exim Guide

Figure 9. The representative graphic of the Medi-Friend

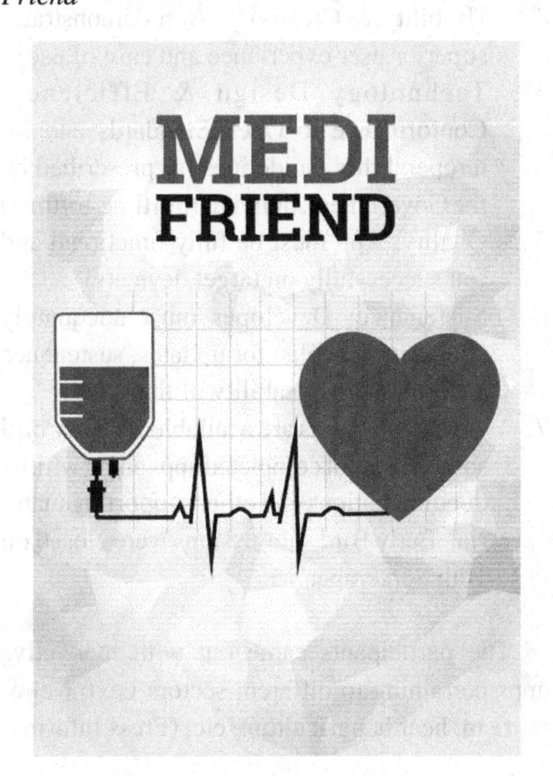

- **My Water My Condition** (http://data.gov.in/event/pursuit-idea)**:** Provides state-wise information on Cause of Water Contamination, Impact and Remedies for purification. (see Figure 10)
- **Alerts for Piped Water Supply** (http://data.gov.in/event/pursuit-idea)**:** Provides state-wise, district-wise and block/taluk-wise information on piped water supply. Total population in number habitations covered can be drilled down on the Map of India. (see Figure 11)

These developed projects are available at http://data.gov.in/event/pursuit-idea and http://iic.ac.in/projects/. The source codes along with documentation are in public domain. Source codes are available at https://github.com/DataPortalIndia/Ideadu.

Figure 10. The representative graphic of the My Water My Condition

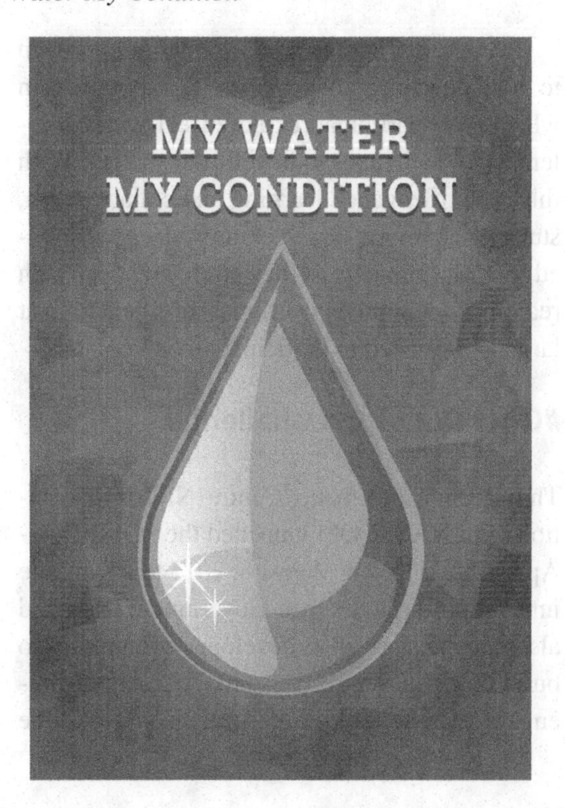

Figure 11. The representative graphic of the Alerts for Piped Water

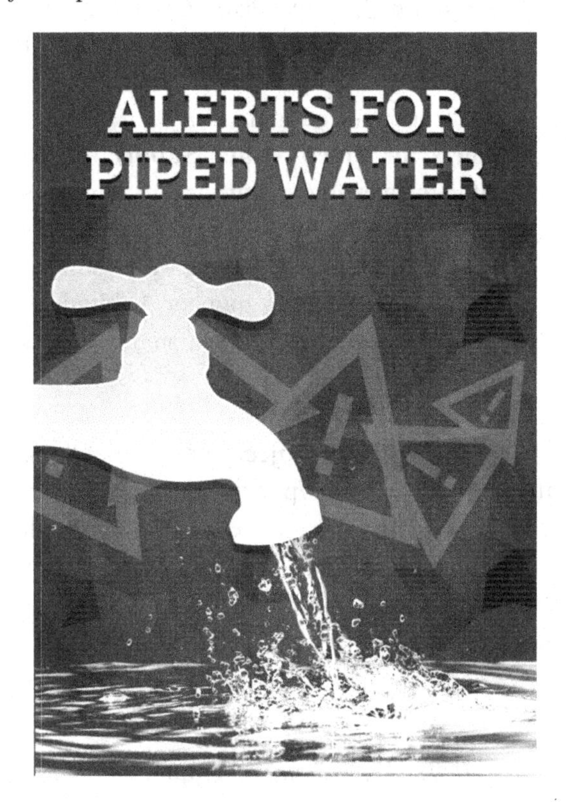

In Pursuit of an 'Idea' was a dynamic approach to both teaching and creative collaboration in which every participant explored real-world problems and challenges to benefit the society. With this type of engaged learning and collaboration, students get motivated to obtain a deeper knowledge of the subjects as they study and deal with real time data of the government, while public at large is inspirited to participate in governance.

#OpenDataApps Challenge

The National Informatics Centre (NIC) in association with NASSCOM launched the #OpenDataApps Challenge on August 8, 2013 to encourage innovation through Open Government Data and also engage start-up & developer community to build an open data ecosystem. A series of pre-engagement sessions were organized at Adobe India, Microsoft India, International Institute of Information Technology - Bengaluru & Wipro for active participation of start-ups and developers in the Challenge (http://storify.com/DataPortalIndia).

The entrepreneurs, developers from industry and community were invited to create unique and useful Apps across platforms and devices ranging from Mobile/Tablet, text-based SMS to voice-based applications using Open Government Data.

A total of 231 proposals on various ideas for a solution were submitted and finally 99 completed applications were submitted for assessment for across the country for the #OpenDataApps Challenge. All apps were reviewed and rated on the basis of parameters listed below:

1. Data Sources: The primary source of the datasets must be on the Open Government Data Platform, India (data.gov.in)
2. Concept Note: How the solution will improve delivery of government services, promote government transparency, accountability and public participation
3. Usability & Creativity: App demonstrates superior user experience and ease of use
4. Technology Design & Efficiency: Conformance to Open Standards and interoperability Guidelines (as prescribed by the Government. of India from time-to-time)
5. Quality: App must be fully-functional and run successfully on target device(s)
6. Sustenance: Developer must adequately demonstrate a plan for updates, sustenance and continuing usability of the app
7. +5 Bonus Points are available for early bird submissions of completed apps along with its documentations and other supporting material. Early Bird submissions were closed on 10th September'13.

The participants came out with innovative apps pertaining to different sectors i.e. travel & tourism, health, agriculture, etc. (Press Information Bureau (PIB), Government of India, 2013). Some of the Apps Developed for #OpenDataApps Challenge are:

GoTourist Mobile App (http://www.tekmindz.com/news-highlights-open-data)developed by TekMindz, IT consulting & technology Services Company with headquarters in India, serving clients across Asia/Pacific, Middle East, North America and Africa, was one of the winners of the award for #OpenDataApps Challenge for Innovation in Governance. The app is a gateway to information related to government-approved hotels, restaurants, resorts and travel agents. (see Figure 12).

Features of the App

- Notifications: Apart from the features using the open dataset, it can also send real time notifications and news to tourists.
- Feedback Mechanism: There is a feedback mechanism to give a view of the quality of service being offered.
- Guides: There are short audio files and video animations which will work as guide to explain about the history of the place being visited. This, again, is Government-approved data.
- Trip Planner: A tourist can place his query and get the list of all places that he can visit. It will give an effective way in sequence manner of what places to visit, travel approach such as taxi stand and the cost of taxi also.
- Decision Support System: Based on the feedbacks received and analytics in place a basic decision support system is provided.
- Transport Systems All Airlines, Railways can promote the tourism by using the QR Code and NFC features of the app.
- Information Access through NFC: NFC tags will be placed on tourists places and as tourists pass by certain points they will be provided with information.

Figure 12. The representative graphic of the GoTourist

- Tourist Book: Tourists frequently visiting various places can place their experiences, photos and memories in it for lifetime.

The app has the potential to economically benefit the Government with robust tourism industry as it would give impetus to tourism by increased footfalls. The list of other is available on the OGD Platform at http://data.gov.in/featured-community-apps-all.

Market Watch (http://mocioun.com/marketwatch/) app provides the wholesale price information of commodities as per the datasets powered by the OGD Platform (http://data.gov.in) for public use. It provides live price updates of commodities from various markets (mandis) across India. (see Figure 13)

Figure 13. The representative graphic of the Market Watch

Figure 14. The representative graphic of the Earth Core

Features of the App

- Check Price: By selecting the combination of commodity and market, user will get the maximum, model and minimum price of commodities from various markets across India.
- Watch List: In order to keep a constant watch and easy access, user can add few particular combinations of a commodity and market to watch list, which will be refreshed if there is any update.
- Product Reports: Using product report option, users can generate the price report of a particular commodity from various markets across India.
- Market Reports: Using market report option, user can generate the price report of all commodities available at a particular market in India.
- Around Me: User can see the nearest markets around his/her location on Google map and can generate the market report with a single click on the location.
- Market Watch is available in iPhone android and Windows Phone.

Earth Core (see Figure 14) App enables user to detect and utilize the mineral ores hidden deep below the Earth's crust to provide rich returns to the Indian economy and strengthen it. It provides the location and miscellaneous information of various ores and minerals. The user can also visualize the quantity and values for the minerals and metals that have been imported and exported in last few years. The App also contains the information regarding the quantity and quality about the production of mineral during last few years.(Bharadwaj, 2014)

CMA Hackathon

The Commissionerate of Municipal Administration (CMA), Tamil Nadu organised the first Hackathon with the theme "Code for Urban Governance" at Anna University, Chennai from 14th-15th December, 2013. The objective was to encourage innovation in Urban Governance through development of mobile and web applications. The CMA published up-to-date datasets from the municipalities of Tamil Nadu on Data Portal India - http://data.gov.in/ in open formats for the Hackathon. All apps were reviewed and rated on the basis of parameters listed below: (see Figure 15)

1. Basic Idea: How the solution will improve delivery of government services, promote government transparency, accountability and public participation and spur citizen engagement. The ideas presented should be using the high level themes to improving the service delivery for urban governance
2. Usability and Creativity: Application demonstrates superior user experience and ease of use. Its uniqueness and innovativeness, use of Tamil Language and leverage the latest advances in information technologies including mobile platforms and responsive design.
3. Technology Design and Efficiency: Conformance to Open Standards and interoperability Guidelines (as prescribed by the Government of India. Innovative use of technology elements to solve the problem statement
4. Quality: Application must be fully-functional and run successfully on target device(s) or a completely done prototype and wireframe with part working application for the said idea.

The participants came out with innovative apps pertaining to different sectors i.e. travel & tourism, health, agriculture, etc.

Figure 15. The representative graphic of the Earth Core

1. **TrashIt** is an Android app to enable crowd sourced garbage reporting. In order to motivate users to participate, we introduce a gamification element to this.
2. **KYC – Know Your City** is an integrated feedback, information & grievance redressal website for CMA officials and public to connect effectively for a better tomorrow.
3. **State Health Analyzer** is to analyze the performance of each ward on the parameters - Health, Road, Sanitation Assign weightage to each area, high performing wards will be highlighted in map and drill down charts on the parameters will be available.(EFY Times, 2013)

Code for Honor 2014

Code for Honor is Microsoft's award for solution excellence. In collaboration with NIC, Microsoft included the "Best Solution for Social Good using Open Government Data" award as an exclusive category within the contest that encourages creation of apps for Social Good using datasets available on OGD Platform India - http://data.gov.in. The contest was launched on 19th December, 2013. All apps were reviewed and rated on the basis of parameters listed below:

1. The contest was open to Technology startups, ISV companies, Non-Governmental Organizations, Civil Society Organizations and Not-For-Profit organizations registered in India and that are less than 8 years old with fewer than 200 employees
2. Round 1: Novelty of the Solution, Economic viability, Feasibility of implementation
3. Round 2: Solution Architecture, System Design, Optimal use of relevant technologies (including devices, if applicable), Quality of Implementation, Solutions with emphasis on Accessibility
4. Round 3: Quality of working prototype of the Solution, Optimal use of relevant technologies (including devices, if applicable), Economic viability, Feasibility of implementation
5. Final and Round 4: Quality of working Solution, Impactful use of devices and services, Innovative use of technology, Relevance in consumer/commercial scenarios, Feasibility of Go-To-Market plan

The participants developed innovative apps pertaining to sectors like agriculture and travel.

1. **Let's Carpool** (Point 2 Point Solutions, Mumbai) a solution for eco-friendly users, which suggests carpool options based on a user's travel trends and offers incentive options to promote carpooling. This app was one of the finalists.
2. **Rainbow** (Greeno Tech Solutions, Chennai) information exchange platform for farmers to make informed decisions through the entire life cycle of a crop. This app was one of the finalists.
3. **MandiTrades** (Appface Technologies Pvt Ltd, Bangalore) a solution that aims to achieve direct selling of products between farmers and consumers. This app was declared winner of the contest.*(see Figure 16)*

Features and Uses of the App

- Commodity Prices – Farm Produce Information is provided directly from the "Government of India" Data Servers hosted on http://www.data.gov.in
- Farmer Produce Information – This can be done directly from the field by the farmer and the data is immediately available in the Smart Phone App on a Map

Figure 16. The representative graphic of the Mandi Trades

Figure 17. The representative graphic of the Great Indian Toilet Tracker

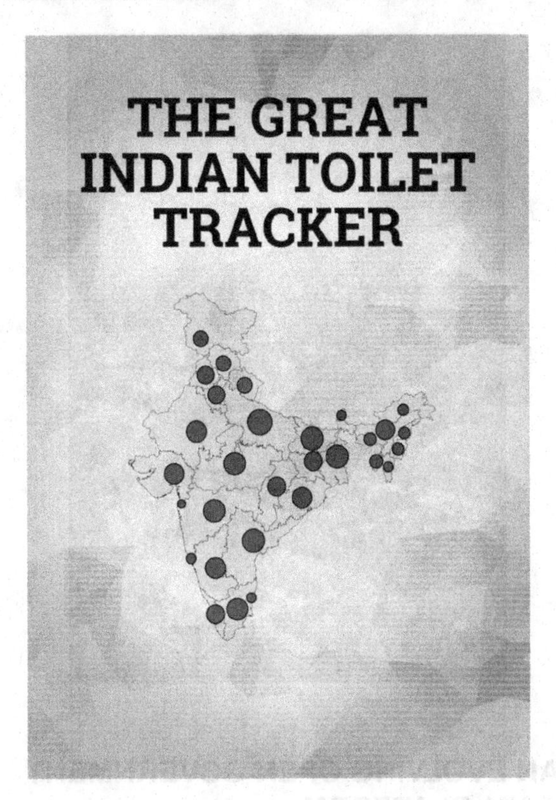

- Auto Geo-Tagging of Farmer Location – This helps in traceability of the produce to the place in the earth where it was grown
- Map based View of Available Farm Products – Anyone (Home user, Organized Retailer, Transporter, Whole Sale Buyer) can view the details and connect directly with farmer with a phone

Collaborate with Us

NIC also took a "Collaborate with Us" initiative to encourage citizen engagement with Open Government Data. The Public at large were invited to build innovative apps, visualizations, info-graphics etc around the datasets available on OGD Platform. Community developed apps are featured in the Featured Apps section of the portal. The following apps have been contributed by the community on the OGD Platform:

The Great Indian Toilet Tracker: Rural Sanitation Scheme - Progress and Performance

We can find out how the rural sanitation scheme is doing because of the data that is published on the Ministry of the Drinking Water and Sanitation website. This project aims to create simple tools that will demystify the large datasets and compare it to other relevant datasets.(http://data.gov.in/community-application/great-indian-toilet-tracker)

Know Your Representative: (see Figure 18) With this application users can know the attendance of their representatives in Parliament for both the houses i.e. Rajya Sabha members and Lok Sabha members(http://data.gov.in/community-application/know-your-representative).

Figure 18. The representative graphic of the Know Your Representative

AN EVOLVING OPEN GOVERNMENT DATA PLATFORM

The first version of the platform, namely 'Data Portal India' was opened to public use in October 2012.(see Figure 19) Following the overwhelming response to a survey conducted to enhance the features and functionalities of Portal and feedbacks from government entities and public at large, the revamped portal rechristened as Open Government Data (OGD) Platform India to provide better user experience to both the data providers and data consumers. To maximize benefits of the Open Government Data, it is a constant endeavor of the NDSAP Programme Management Unit, NIC to update and upgrade the Open OGD Platform on a continuous basis. Its key features include:

- A single point web access for various resources of government viz. Statistics, Datasets, APIs, Web Services, Tools, Visualizations and Apps.
- Based on Dublin Core metadata standards having Core & Extensions architecture ensures scalability on metadata
- It has a configurable multilevel pre-defined workflow system to be used by Govt. Depts. to contribute, approve and publish datasets
- It has configurable and scalable modules viz. Data Management System, Content Management System, Visitor Relationship Management System, Communities, Visualization, Dataset Conversion Tool, APIs to consume datasets, etc.
- Machine-readable datasets help innovators, researchers, developers, academia to ideate and develop apps & mesh-ups for any innovative way of information/service delivery
- It has a built-in open source visualization engine to create and view visualizations with sanitized datasets.
- Enabled for active citizen engagement through rating, suggest, discuss, collaborate, forums, blogs, etc.
- Better User Experience & efficient discoverability of resources
- Additional options to search & filter resources by Frequency, Sectors, Coverage etc.
- Usage trend in Tag Cloud
- Organized cataloguing of similar resources (Datasets/Apps) like time series datasets of Consumer Price Indexes (CPIs) comes under a catalog. Multiple Resources (Datasets/Apps) under a catalog.
- Catalog and Resources revisions with timestamp
- New Enhanced Visualization Platform
- Enhanced User Experience through the Visualization Gallery
- Separate instance for its Demo Site with role based credentials to have a first-hand feel of the workflow
- Responsive Web Layout design

Figure 19. The representative graphic of the OGD Platform

- Option to enable SMS and Email Alerts
- Dedicated Event Section for Contests and showcasing community contributed Apps
- Application Programming Interfaces (APIs) to query within datasets
  - Integrated API for the Developers
  - Public can request for API
  - Detailed API page for individual Data Source.
  - Data can be requested on different parameters given with examples in Data API on Resources Page.

Product Innovation

- Quick Response Code enabled – Datasets published on the Data Portal India is QR enabled and hence can be read by an imaging device, such as a camera, and formatted algorithmically to be appropriately interpreted.

- Metadata – Datasets are published along with standard metadata based on International Dublin Core. It uses controlled vocabularies on government sectors, jurisdictions, dataset types, access mode etc. Besides facilitating easy access to datasets, it would be extremely useful in the future for federation / integration of data catalogs for the whole country as such as OGD is also being offered as a service i.e. SaaS model to the other states of India.
- Tool for Intra-operability of Data formats – Utility has been developed to convert the source datasets to different formats like XML, JSON, JSONP etc. which are of great use to developer community for further development of Apps.
- Metrics – Dashboard has been developed to give a bird's view of the Ministry wise number of datasets/apps published, which could be further drilled down to organization wise details. The Visitors Statistics are also available at the dashboard as well as the status of feedback received.
- Custom Widgets to Consume Sector Specific Catalogs – A widget is provided to choose their sector specific datasets for consumption either through a object of custom banner or XML format or JSON format.

Major Issues

- Understanding on Open Government Data and its potential benefits within government is low. Though many datasets are already available on the portals of ministries/departments/ organizations but are not in open format. Hence it is a challenge to spread awareness and motivate Government entities to proactively participate in this initiative by publishing datasets in open format.
- Quality, Consistency and Relevancy are some of the important aspects to harness the power of Open Government Data. Dataset identification and sanitization has been a concern because of the lack of domain knowledge amongst users.
- Availability of Open Government Datasets alone doesn't make any difference until citizens take advantages of those. Hence, encouraging various communities ranging from Data Enthusiasts, Developers and Researchers to Data Journalists, Civil Societies, etc. to engage with available datasets is a challenge, which is requires a lot of persuasion, engagement sessions through workshops and conducting of data meets across the country.
- Open Government Data Platform India is also offered as a service (SaaS) model on following:
    - Modular Components – Content Management System, Dataset Management System, Visitors Relationship Management, Community
    - Functionality – Feedback, Rating, Social Media Connectors, Embed Feature, Widgets
    - Catalog – Dataset or Apps
    - Dashboard – Analytics, Metrics, Visitor Stats.
    - Dynamic Visualization Engine

Data Quality

- Data Compositeness/Completeness – Check for the constituent elements within the dataset. The dataset should be well explained in terms of the variable present therein the dataset through a descriptive metadata. The metadata should well describe the units, definitions, frequency, data source and notes to special mention in the dataset.

- How to comprehend – Look at the details with regards to the above mentioned aspects. In case, all is present then try interpreting the data as a layman and ensure that the dataset is well supplemented by the metadata. Otherwise understand these details from the data generator unless it is comprehended to the fullest.
- Data Consistency – Check for the consistency in the timestamps across the variable values and data values are aligned across systems. There should be no gaps between the timestamp and validity time frame of data is clearly mentioned as well as the series should be continuous in nature. Check for the consistency in the data values with the earlier datasets and any discrepancy therein present should be relooked and confirmed with the respective source data.
- How to comprehend – There are automated algorithms to check for consistency in time stamp. Create graphs to find the movement of the values of the variables across the time period. In case, there exists any previously published dataset we cross check with it to ensure there are no gaps in both the datasets.
- Data Coverage – Check for the completeness in the dataset with the source in terms of granularity. Dataset should be made available at the lowest possible levels to allow users correctly describe the phenomena being measured. And data confirms to industry standards.
- How to comprehend – Check for the granularity of the datasets on the source website apart from talking to the contributor.

While, above factors brings a degree of relevance for the users, they are achieved through the most integral part of the framework which is "Data Cleansing". The normal standardization process includes:

- Assigning string, date, character and numbers to the required fields
- Abbreviations and acronyms to be replaced by full forms.
- No special characters and blank spaces in the matrix.
- No special character in column header.
- Column header should be self explanatory
- Similar font size with no formulas and merged columns.
- Dataset should be de-normalized without any merged column
- No formula of calculated column should appear in dataset like Total or Average of available column or rows
- Footer note should be in column rather putting it in the bottom with merged columns
- Above all it must be in machine readable format viz. CSV, XML, JSON, ODS, XLS etc.

Best Practices

As per NDSAP, data sharing and accessibility are based on the following principles

Openness, Flexibility, Transparency, Legal Conformity, Protection of Intellectual Property, Formal responsibility, Professionalism Standards, Interoperability, Quality, Security, Efficiency, Accountability, Sustainability and Privacy.

Sunlight Foundation, a nonprofit, nonpartisan organization that uses cutting-edge technology and ideas to make government transparent and accountable, has identified ten principles to evaluate the openness and accessibility of Government owned data (Sunlight Foundation, 2010).

1. Completeness: Released dataset should clearly reflect "what is recorded about a particular subject". Metadata, explaining the raw data, should also be included along with formulas and explanations on calculation of

data. This will enable users to have nights into the scope of the information, which will help in understanding the data better.

2. Primacy: Datasets released by the Government must include the original information, details on how the data was collected and original source documents recording the data collection. This will enable users to verify the information.
3. Timelines: Timely release of datasets is one of the important factors to maximize the utility of information people can obtain. If possible, information collected by the Government should be released as soon as it is collected.
4. Ease of Physical and Electronic Access: People should be able to easily locate and download content. A simple interface for users to access information stored in a database at once and the facility to make specific calls for data through an Application Programming Interface (API) make data readily accessible.
5. Machine readability: Data should be stored in widely used file formats that are suitable for machine processing.
6. Non-discrimination: This refers to who can access data and how they must do so. However, barriers such as registration or membership requirements, and authorized applications to access data, are applicable.
7. Use of Commonly Owned Standards: Commonly owned or open standard implies who owns the format in which data is stored. Freely available formats can be accessed without the need for a software license. This would increase the number of potential users.
8. Licensing: Government owned data should be labeled as public resource, hence, should be available without restrictions.
9. Permanence: Government datasets should be maintained over time. It should be available on-line with appropriate version tracking and archiving.
10. Usage Costs: Imposing fees for access to Government datasets can discourage potential users. It may also hinder transformative uses of data.

Five Star Open Data:

Tim Berners-Lee, the inventor of the Web and Linked Data initiator, suggested a 5 star deployment scheme for Open Data, explaining costs and benefits that come along with it. Cost and benefits of these open data levels.(Tim Berners-Lee, n.d.):

★ Data accessible on the Web under an open license (such as PDDL, ODC-by or CC0). However, the data is locked-up in a document. Other than writing a custom scraper, it's hard to get the data out of the document

★★ Available as machine-readable structured data on web (e.g. excel instead of image scan of a table). However, the data is still locked-up in a document. To get the data out of the document you depend on proprietary software.

★★★ as (2) plus non-proprietary format (e.g. CSV in-stead of excel)

★★★★ All the above features. Besides, use of open standards from W3C (RDF and SPARQL) to identify things, so that people can point at your stuff using an URI

★★★★★ Data in the Web linked to other data.

CONCLUSION

This is just the beginning. The Open Government Data initiative is in its infancy days in India and there are miles to go.... However, there is a potential to unlock significant social and economic value from the use/re-use of Open Government Data. Various communities ranging from developers, start-ups to researchers, etc. have started to actively engage with the Open Government Data for both societal and economic benefits. There are many milestones to reach and landmarks to create in order to harness the benefits of the Open Government Data. This initiative is on the progressive road and in near future envisages tapping the benefits of Open Government Data more efficiently with enhanced people participation.

REFERENCES

A new goldmine. (2013, May 18). *The Economist*. Retrieved from http://www.economist.com/news/business/21578084-making-official-data-public-could-spur-lots-innovation-new-goldmine

Auer, S. R., Bizer, C., Kobilarov, G., Lehmann, J., Cyganiak, R., & Ives, Z. (2007). Lecture Notes in Computer Science: Vol. 4825. *DBpedia: A Nucleus for a Web of Open Data* (p. 722). The Semantic Web; doi:10.1007/978-3-540-76298-0_52

Bharadwaj, S. N. (2014, February 4). Open Data Apps are All the Rage in India-Enterprise Efficiency. Retrieved from http://www.enterpriseefficiency.com/author.asp?section_id=2405&doc_id=272552

Capgemini Consulting. (n.d.). Page 7 - The Open Data Economy, Unlocking Economic Value By Opening Government & Public Data. Retrieved from http://ebooks.capgemini-consulting.com/The-Open-Data-Economy/files/assets/basic-html/page7.html

Code For Honor - Awards 2014 (2014). *Open Government Data (OGD) Platform India*. Retrieved from https://data.gov.in/event/code-honor-awards-2014

Defining Open in Open Data, Open Content and Open Knowledge. (n. d.). *Open Definition*. Retrieved from http://opendefinition.org/od/index.html

Open Data Driving growth, ingenuity and innovation. (2012). *Deloitte Analytics Paper*. Retrieved from https://www.deloitte.com/assets/Dcom-UnitedKingdom/Local%20Assets/Documents/Market%20insights/Deloitte%20Analytics/uk-insights-deloitte-analytics-open-data-june-2012.pdf

Market Assessment of Public Sector Information. (2013). Department for Business Innovations & Skills. Retrieved from https://www.gov.uk/government/uploads/system/uploads/attachment_data/file/198905/bis-13-743-market-assessment-of-public-sector-information.pdf

Department of Economic and Social Affairs. Division for Public Administration & Development Management, United Nations, (2013). Guidelines on Open Government Data for Citizen Engagement. Retrieved from http://workspace.unpan.org/sites/Internet/Documents/Guidenlines%20on%20OGDCE%20May17%202013.pdf

Gazette of India. (2012). National Data Sharing & Accessibility Policy (NDSAP). Retrieved from http://data.gov.in/sites/default/files/NDSAP.pdf

Hackathon, C. M. A. (2013). Code of Urban Governance. India: Government of Tamil Nadu; Retrieved from cma.tn.gov.in/cma/en-in/Pages/Hackathon.aspx

Loten Angus. (2014, January 8). Open Data a Boon for Entrepreneurs - WSJ. Retrieved from http://online.wsj.com/news/articles/SB10001424052702304887104579307000606208592

Ministry of Law & Justice, Government of India. (2005). Right to Information Act. Retrieved from http://rti.gov.in/rti-act.pdf

Misra, D. P. (2013, May 25). The Launch of in Pursuit of an Idea - Creative Collaboration on Open Government Data for Innovation-Informatics. Retrieved from http://informatics.nic.in/news/newsdetail/newsID/450

Open Data 500 Open Government Partnership. Companies. (n. d.). Retrieved from http://www.opendata500.com/list/

Open data and economic growth: which link, if any? (2012, July 21). Retrieved from http://www.opengovpartnership.org/blog/blog-editor/2012/07/20/open-data-and-economic-growth-which-link-if-any

Open Knowledge Foundation. (2012, November 14). Open Data Handbook Documentation. Retrieved from http://opendatahandbook.org/pdf/OpenDataHandbook.pdf

OpenDataApps Challenge. (n. d.). *Open Government Data (OGD) Platform India.* Retrieved from https://data.gov.in/event/opendataapps-challenge

Planning Commission, Government of India. (2013). 12th Five Year Plan Hackathon. Retrieved from http://planningcommission.gov.in/hackathon/

Shri Kapil Sibal inaugurates Conference on 'Open Data Apps for Innovation in Governance. (2013, August 8). *Press Information Bureau (PIB), Government of India.* Retrieved from http://www.pib.nic.in/newsite/erelease.aspx?relid=97925

Sandhya, S. (2013, April 9). Planning Commission's hackathon gets over 1,000 participants. *The Times of India.* Retrieved from http://timesofindia.indiatimes.com/tech/tech-news/internet/Planning-Commissions-hackathon-gets-over-1000-participants/articleshow/19460398.cms?referral=PM]

Ten Principles for Opening up Government Information. (2010, August 11). Sunlight Foundation. Retrieved from http://sunlightfoundation.com/policy/documents/ten-open-data-principles/

The Launch of in Pursuit of an Idea - Creative Collaboration on Open Government Data for Innovation. (n. d.). Retrieved from http://informatics.nic.in/news/newsdetail/newsID/450

The White House, Memorandum on Transparency and Open Government. (2009). Retrieved from www.whitehouse.gov/the_press_office/Transparency_and_Open_Government/

Tim Berners-Lee. (n. d.). 5 star Open Data. Retrieved from http://5stardata.info/

Commissionerate Of Municipal Administration (CMA) And ThoughtWorks Conduct Hackathon Dedicated To Improving Governance In The City. (2013, December 20). *E. F. Y. Times.* Retrieved from http://efytimes.com/e1/124753/Commissionerate-Of-Municipal-Administration-CMA-And-ThoughtWorks-Conduct-Hackathon-Dedicated-To-Improving-Governance-In-The-City

Big & Open Data in Europe: A growth engine or a missed opportunity. (2014). WARSAW Institute of Economic Study & Centre for European Strategy. Retrieved from http://www.microsoft.com/global/eu/RenderingAssets/pdf/2014%20Jan%2028%20EMEA%20Big%20and%20Open%20Data%20Report%20-%20Final%20Report.pdf

ADDITIONAL READING

Big & Open Data in Europe. (n. d.). A growth engine or a missed opportunity. *WARSAW Institute of Economic Study & Centre for European Strategy.*

Open Data Driving growth, ingenuity and innovation. (2012). Deloitte Analytics Paper.

Market Assessment of Public Sector Information. (2013, May). Department for Business Innovations & Skills Delloite:

Guidelines on Open Government Data for Citizen Engagement. (2013Department of Economic and Social Affairs. *Division for Public Administration & Development Management, United Nations.* New York:

Dinand, T. (2013). Capgemini Consulting The Open Data Economy, Unlocking Economic Value By Opening Government & Public Data.

Memorandum on Transparency and Open Government. (2009). *The White House*.

National Data Sharing and Accessibility Policy. (n. d.). *The Gazette of India.*

Open Data Handbook Documentation (2012, November 14). Open Knowledge Foundation.

Ten Principles for Opening up Government Information. (2010, August 11). Sunlight Foundation.

KEY TERMS AND DEFINITIONS

Application Programming Interfaces (APIs): Allows users particularly developers to retrieve data programmatically.

CSV: A comma-separated values (CSV) (also sometimes called character-separated values, because the separator character does not have to be a comma) file stores tabular data (numbers and text) in plain-text form.

Dublin Core metadata standards: The Dublin Core Metadata Initiative (DCMI) began in 1995 with an invitational workshop in Dublin, Ohio that brought together librarians, digital library researchers, content providers, and text-markup experts to improve discovery standards for information resources. The original Dublin Core emerged as a small set of descriptors that quickly drew global interest from a wide variety of information providers in the arts, sciences, education, business, and government sectors.

Hackathon: A hackathon (also known as a hack day, hackfest or codefest) is an event in which computer programmers and others involved in software development, including graphic designers, interface designers and project managers, collaborate intensively on software projects.

Informediary: The term is a composite of information and intermediary. As the name suggests, infomediaries specialize in information management, collecting and storing customer information and controlling the flow of commerce on the Web. Yahoo! is one of the most popular and powerful infomediaries in the world.

Interoperability: Interoperability is the ability of different information technology systems and software applications to communicate, exchange data, and use the information that has been exchanged.

JSON: JavaScript Object Notation, is an open standard format that uses human-readable text to transmit data objects consisting of attribute–value pairs. It is used primarily to transmit data between a server and web application, as an alternative to XML.

JSONP: JSONP or 'JSON with padding' is a communication technique used in JavaScript programs running in web browsers to request data from a server in a different domain, something prohibited by typical web browsers because of the same-origin policy. JSONP takes advantage of the fact that browsers do not enforce the same-origin policy on <script> tags.

Mandi: Mandi, in Hindi refers to a trading hub or a market, generally for agricultural produce.

Mission Mode Project (MMP): A mission mode project (MMP) is an individual project within the National e-Governance Plan (NeGP) that focuses on one aspect of electronic governance, such as banking, land records or commercial taxes etc.

National Data Sharing and Accessibility Policy (NDSAP): National Data Sharing and Accessibility Policy (NDSAP), gazette notified on 17th March 2012, envisages proactive dissemination of Government owned data through the Open Government Data (OGD) Platform India - http://data.gov.in.

ODS: An operational data store (or "ODS") is a database designed to integrate data from multiple sources for additional operations on the data. Unlike a master data store the data is not passed back to operational systems. It may be passed for further operations and to the data warehouse for reporting.

Open Data: Open data is data that can be freely used, reused and redistributed by anyone.

Open Government Data (OGD) Platform India: Single point access to Government catalogues and resources (datasets/apps).

Panchayat: Village Council in India.

Parametric: Relating to or expressed in terms of a parameter or parameters. Parametric statistics is a branch of statistics which assumes that the data has come from a type of probability distribution and makes inferences about the parameters of the distribution.

SaaS Model: Software as a service is a software licensing and delivery model in which software is licensed on a subscription basis and is centrally hosted. It is sometimes referred to as "on-demand software". SaaS is typically accessed by users using a thin client via a web browser. SaaS has become a common delivery model for many business applications.

XML: Extensible Markup Language (XML) is a markup language that defines a set of rules for encoding documents in a format that is both human-readable and machine-readable. The design goals of XML emphasize simplicity, generality and usability across the Internet.

Chapter 8
Intangible Investment and Technical Efficiency:
The Case of Software-Intensive Manufacturing Firms in Turkey

Derya Fındık
Yıldırım Beyazıt University, Turkey

Aysit Tansel
Middle East Technical University, Turkey

ABSTRACT

This chapter analyzes the effect of intangible investment on firm efficiency with an emphasis on its software component. Stochastic production frontier approach is used to simultaneously estimate the production function and the determinants of technical efficiency in the software intensive manufacturing firms in Turkey for the period 2003-2007. Firms are classified based on the technology group. High technology and low technology firms are estimated separately in order to reveal differentials in their firm efficiency. The results show that the effect of software investment on firm efficiency is larger in high technology firms which operate in areas such as chemicals, electricity, and machinery as compared to that of the low technology firms which operate in areas such as textiles, food, paper, and unclassified manufacturing. Further, among the high technology firms, the effect of the software investment is smaller than the effect of research and development personnel expenditure. This result shows that the presence of R&D personnel is more important than the software investment for software intensive manufacturing firms in Turkey.

INTRODUCTION

In recent years, the share of investment in intangible assets of the firms in manufacturing industries increased in most of the EU countries while the share of investment in tangible capital has decreased (Corrado, Haskel, Jona-Lasinio, & Iommi, 2013). Intangible investment is defined as "the claims on future benefits that do not have a physical or financial embodiment"(Lev,2000). Many authors proposed different ways of classifying the intangible assets (van Ark & Piatkowski,

DOI: 10.4018/978-1-4666-8598-7.ch008

2004; Young, 1998; Vosselman, 1998; MERITUM, 2002; Oliner, Sichel & Stiroh, 2008; Hulten & Hao, 2008; Cummins, 2005). A more recent classification is proposed by Corrado, Hulten & Sichel (2009). According to him, there are three main components of intangibles. These are computerized information, scientific and creative property, and economic competencies. The computer software and computerized databases are in the first group. The second group includes science and engineering R&D, mineral exploration, copyrights and license costs, and other activities for product development such as design and research. The third group emphasizes the "soft" part of the intangible assets, such as brand equity, firm specific human capital, and organizational structure.

Studies that focus on the link between intangible investments and productivity found that intangible investments increase the productivity (Oliner et al. 2008; Corrado et al. 2009, Bosworth &Triplett, 2000; van Ark, Hao, Corrado & Hulten, 2009; Park & Ginarte, 1997). However, there is little evidence on the effect of intangible investments on firm efficiency (Becchetti, Bedoya & Paganetto, 2003). In this chapter, we analyze the effects of software investment and R&D personnel expenditure which are components of intangible investment on firm efficiency in Turkey. We consider the software intensive manufacturing firms in Turkey for the period 2003-2007. We observed two main trends. First, the number of firms making software investment decreased during the period investigated. Second, firms which already make software investment became more software-intensive. The main question asked is the increase in the intensity of software investment results in efficiency gains for the Turkish manufacturing firms. We also included R&D personel expenditure as another component of intangible investment in this chapter.

This chapter is organized as follows: Background section provides the review of literature on intangible investment of the firms. Model section explains the specifications of the production function and the technical efficiency. In this chapter, we also provide an extant review of literature on determinants of technical efficiency. The other section is devoted to data and methodology. We, then discuss empirical results. The last section introduces concluding remarks.

BACKGROUND

The 1970s marks the beginning of a period referred to as post-Fordist Era. This period is characterized with a transition from manufacturing based economy to services based economy. This change has resulted in a shift from tangible assets such as physical, financial, and human to the intangible ones in the production process (Shapiro & Varian, 2013). The history of the concept of intangible investment dates back to Machlup (1962). He conceived the knowledge as an intangible asset and emphasized the difficulties in isolating the effects of intangible investment on the knowledge producing industries. Therefore, the much of the concern with the intangible asset is related to their identification and the measurement.

Intangible investment refers to investment in human capital such as education and socialization activities (Webster, 1999). Adams & Oleksak (2010) consider the intangible assets such as the personal networks, reputation, or innovation capability and refer to them as "invisible assets". More recently, the definition of intangible assets is broadened to include software and databases, research and development activities, intellectual property rights, human capital, and organizational structure.

Empirical studies that use intangible investment as a production factor increased since the 2000s. Jalava & Pohjola (2008) found the positive effect of intangible investment on Finnish economy by using non-financial business sector data and emphasized the increasing role of the quality of the investment rather than the quantity in the economic growth. The positive effect of intangible investment on economic growth is also observed in cross country studies. Van ark et al.(2009) used the computerized information, innovative property, and economic competencies to proxy the intangibles and found that the combined effect of these variables accounts for a quarter of labour productivity growth in the US and several countries in the EU. Park & Ginarte(1997) analyzed another component of the intangibles, namely intellectual property rights (IPRs). They found that IPRs directly affect inputs such as research and development expenditure and physical capital.

Other components of intangible investments received considerable attention in the literature. The software investment as productive asset was not considered often (Basu & Fernald, 2007). In recent years, this component became capitalized as an expenditure in order to observe its contribution to GDP. According to Borgo, Goodridge, Haskel & Pesole (2013) asset training, design, and software have the largest shares in knowledge spending especially in the services sector in UK, while R&D has only a small share. Further, Becchetti et al. (2003) found that software investment has a complementary effect on skilled labour and increases both labour productivity and the firm efficiency. When ICT is considered as a general purpose factor, ICT investment could also facilitate firm efficiency. Castiglione & Infante (2014) have observed that positive effect of ICT on technical efficiency of Italian firms manufacturing firms during the period 1995-2006. The effect of ICT on technical efficiency is much stronger for the firms that make changes in their organizational structure, that invest in research and development and that are open to international markets. In a similar vein, Dimelis & Papaioannou (2014) examined the diffusion of ICT in manufacturing and services sectors in EU for the period 1995-2005. In their study, ICT variable is decomposed into three factors such as computing equipment, communications' equipment, and software. They found that software and communications equipment have a strong negative effect on technical efficiency and this effect remain robust after controlling the degree of market regulation. Further, Berghall (2014) have found that new ICT technologies improve the performance of Finnish industries that lag behind the frontier. When industry and time effects are controlled for, ICT has a significant effect on technical efficiency during the period 1986-2003 in Finnish industry.

MODEL

We use stochastic production frontier approach to simultaneously estimate the production function and the determinants of technical efficiency. The stochastic frontier model with panel data specification is given by

$$y_{it} = \alpha + \sum \beta_x x_{kit} + \varepsilon_{it} \quad (1)$$

$$\varepsilon_{it} = V_{it} - U_{it} \quad (2)$$

$$t = 1,...,T \; i = 1,2,...,N$$

$$U_{it} \geq 0 \quad (3)$$

where y_{it} and x_{kit} are the output and the vector of inputs of firm i at time t. β is the vector of unknown parameters, V_{it} and U_{it} are independent, unobservable random variables. Accordingly, V_{it} indicates statistical noise which is normally distributed with mean zero and variance σ_v^2 and the σ_u^2. U_{it} is the non-negative random variable associated with technical inefficiency and it is allowed to vary over time. U_{it} can be described as:

$$U_{it} = \{\exp[-n(t-T)]\} U_{it} \quad (4)$$

where n_{it} is an unknown parameter to be estimated and U_{it} are independent and identically distributed non-negative random variables.

Production Function

In this study, four types of variables are used to estimate production function which is in translog form. These are capital, labor, raw material, and energy. Table 1 displays the variable definitions.

$$\ln Y_{it} = \beta_0 + \beta_1 t + \beta_2 t^2 \beta_3 \ln(K_{it}) + \beta_4 \ln(L_{it}) + \beta_5 \ln(RM_{it}) + \beta_6 \ln(E_{it}) + \beta_7 \ln(K_{it})^2 + \beta_8 \ln(E_{it})^2 + \beta_9 \ln(L_{it})^2 + \beta_{10} \ln(RM_{it})^2 + \beta_{11} \ln(K_{it})\ln(L_{it}) + \beta_{12} \ln(K_{it})\ln(RM_{it}) + \beta_{13} \ln(K_{it})\ln(E_{it}) + \beta_{14} \ln(L_{it})\ln(RM_{it}) + \beta_{15} \ln(L_{it})\ln(E_{it}) + \beta_{16} \ln(RM_{it})\ln(E_{it}) + \beta_{17} \ln(K_{it})t + \beta_{18} \ln(E_{it})t + \beta_{19} \ln(RM_{it})t + \beta_{20} \ln(L_{it})t + v_{it} - u_{it}$$

$$t = 1,...,T \; i = 1,...,N \; E_{it} \quad (5)$$

where Y_{it} is the real output firm i in year t, K_{it} is the capital stock measured by depreciation allowances in year t, is the electricity and fuel purchased by firm i in year t, RM_{it} is the total value of intermediate goods used in the production of inputs by firm i in year t. Time variable indicates technological change. v_{it} indicates random errors that are independently and identically distributed with $N(0, \sigma_v^2)$ and u_{it} represents technical inefficiency term following normal distribution with mean μ_{it} and variance σ_u^2.

Capital stock variable is created based on the Perpetual Inventory Method (PIM). In the Equation (6) below, K_t represents the capitak stock at time t. K_{t-1} indicates initial capital stock, *d* shows the depreciation rate and I_t is the investment. Initial capital stock is calculated assuming that there exists permanent growth at the sum of the industrial rate of growth and the rate of depreciation.

Table 1. Variable definitions

Output (Q)	Output which is measured as manufacturing sales-changes in finished good inventories
Capital Stock (K)	Depreciation Allowances
Labor (L)	Average Number of Employees
Raw Material (RM)	Total value of intermediate goods
Electricity and Fuel (E)	Electricity and fuel purchased
Time (T)	Time (t,1,...5)
Industry Dummies	Food (Nace 15-16),textile (Nace 17-18), leather (Nace19),wood (Nace20),paper (Nace21-22),chemicals (Nace25),plastics (Nace25),nonmetals (Nace 26), metals(Nace 27-28),machinery(29), electricity(Nace30-33),transportation equipment(Nace 34-35), and unclassified manufacturing(Nace 36-37)
R&D Personnel	Dummy variable which takes the value of 1 if the firm invests in R&D personnel expenditure
Regional Agglomeration	Share of the firm's revenues to the total revenue of the region
Software Investment	Share of software investment to total intangible investment
Trade Openess	Share of total product and services exports to total revenues
Outsourcing revenue	The share of total outsourcing expenditure to total expenditure
Outsourcing expenditure	The share of total outsourcing revenues to total revenues
Subsidy	Dummy variable which takes the value of 1 if the firm receives subsidy and 0 otherwise
Suncontracting	The share of subcontracting expenditure to total expenditure
Time Effects	Dummies for each year from 2004 to 2007. 2003 is a reference year(d_2004, d_2005, d_2006, d_2007)

$$K_t = (1-d)K_{t-1} + I_t \quad (6)$$

Nominal values of capital stocks are deflated by the corresponding sectoral producer price indices at four digit. All variables in the production function are in the logarithmic form.

Technical Efficiency Function

Technical efficiency is defined as the distance of a firm from an efficient frontier (Battese & Coelli, 1992). The efficiency of a firm consists of two components: technical efficiency and allocative efficiency (Farrel, 1957). Technical efficiency indicates the ability of a firm to obtain maximum output from a given set of inputs. A more specific definition belongs to Koopmans (1951). Accordingly, a producer can be considered as technically efficient if the increase in the output is achieved by the reduction in at least one other output or increase in at least one input.

In this study, the inefficiency model is formed by including a list of explanatory variables that are classified as firm specific variables in order to explain the firm efficiency denoted by μ_{it}.

$$\mu_{it} = \delta_0 + \delta_1 Tradeopenness + \delta_2 Outsourcing / Subcontracting + \delta_3 RegionalAgglomeration + \delta_4 R\&DPersonnel + \delta_5 SoftwareInvestment + \delta_6 TimeEffects + \delta_7 SectorDummies \quad (7)$$

In Equation (7), δ_0 is the constant term which represents differences in production that cannot be explained by firm specific variables. Trade openness is measured as the share of total products and services exports to total revenues. Outsourcing is measured at two levels. The first one is outsourcing expenditure which is defined as the share of outsourcing expenditure to total expenditure. The second one is the outsourcing revenue which is measured by the share of outsourcing revenues to total revenues. We added outsourcing revenue, subcontracting expenditure and government subsidy in the estimation of low technology firms[1]. Subcontracting expenditure is measured by the share of subcontracting expenditure to total expenditure. Subsidy is a dummy variable that takes the value of 1 if firm received subsidy between 2003-2007. Regional agglomeration is measured as the share of the firm's revenues to the total revenue of the region. Research and development (R&D) personnel is measured by dummy variable which takes the value of 1 if the firm invests in R&D personnel expenditure and 0 otherwise. This variable is selected due to the importance of qualified personnel for firms making software investment. Software investment is measured as the share of software investment in total intangible investment. Year and sector dummies are also included in the study in order to control for heterogeneity.

EMPIRICAL LITERATURE ON DETERMINANTS OF TECHNICAL EFFICIENCY

There is an extensive literature on the determinants of technical efficiency (see, Table 2). In this study, we focus on a part of those variables such as trade openness, outsourcing, government subsidy, regional agglomeration, R&D personnel, and software investment. Adding year effect is considered to be relevant because the time period in this study corresponds to the period of privatization in Turkish telecommunication sector. Following sections deal with the determinants of technical efficiency of Turkish software intensive manufacturing firms.

Table 2. A list of Literature on the determinants of firm Efficiency and Expected Signs

Variables	Expected Sign	Motivation	Literature
Trade Openness	+	Small firms with managerial abilities	Aw & Batra (1998)
		Access to foreign market	Sun et al. (1999)
		Learning through exporting	Delgado et al. (2002)
		Greater capacity of utilization International market competition Specialization in production	Piesse &Thirtle (2000); Gumbau-Albert & Maudos(2002); Hossain & Karunaratne (2004)
	-	When combined with non-production labor its effect on the firm efficiency turns out to be negative	Grether(1999)
Outsourcing	+	Allocation of resources to the activities that provide comparative advantage	Heshmati(2003); Taymaz & Saatçi(1997)
Regional Agglomeration	+	Agglomeration effect	Driffield & Munday(2001);Taymaz & Saatçi (1997)
	-	Efficiency benefits could decrease after some point that cities reach a certain population	Mitra(1999)
		As the communication costs decline and the quality of interaction with the partners outside the region increases, the positive effect of geographical proximity could dissappear	Curran & Blackburn (1994)
R&D Personnel Expenditure	+	Absorptive capacity	Cohen & Levinthal (1989)
		Spillover effects from R&D in developed countries to developing ones	Coe et al. (1995); Huang & Liu (1994)
ICT	+	Higher growing firms exploit the adoption integrated technologies more than lower growing firms	Brasini & Freo(2012)
		Investment in ICT is not the only way of achieving higher economic growth. ICT generates complementary effects on the variables as human capital and structural change in the different sectors	Castiglione (2012)
		Higher economic growth depends on technological progress	Dimelis & Papaioannou.(2010)
	n.s.	Lack of significant effect of the internet use for sales in firm's efficiency	Romero & Rodriguez(2010)
Software Investment	+	Software investment increases the scale of firm operations	Becchetti et al. (2003)
Subcontracting Expenditure	+	Network effect	Aoki(1989);Lazonick(1990);Burki & Terrel(1998);Taymaz & Saatci(1997)
Subsidy	-	Renk seeking behaviour	Martin et al.(1983)
	n.s.	Subsidies go to R&D performers	González et al. (2005)
Time effect	+	Privatization of the state monopoly	Jha & Majumdar (1999);Ross et al. (1996);Bortolotti et al (2002), Lam & Shiu (2010)

Trade Openness

One of the determinants of technical efficiency is trade openness which indicates the exporting activities of the firm. Production efficiency of firms that compete in international market could be high because competition forces firms to allocate resources more efficiently, to exploit scale economies, and to improve their technology (Balassa, 1978; Feder, 1983; Ram, 1985; Bodman, 1996).

The positive effect of export on firm efficiency is found by Aw & Batra,1998; Sun, Hone & Doucouliago,1999; Piesse & Thirtle, 2000; Gumbau-Albert & Maudos,2002; Delgado, Farinas & Ruano, 2002, Hossain & Karunaratne,2004. Negative effect is found by (Grether, 1999) or no relation is observed by (Alvarez & Crespi, 2003). Trade openness of the economy explains regional and industrial variation in terms of efficiency in the case of China (Sun et al., 1999). Economic reforms in China after 1980 targeted coastal regions, therefore, the economy in those regions became much exposed to foreign trade that results in efficiency gains. For the Canadian manufacturing sector, both import penetration and export share increased in the period of 1973-1992. Those years were also marked by the reduction in protection under the North American Free Trade Agreement (NAFTA). This generated two main effects on Canadian manufacturing firms. The first was to lose tariff protection on some goods. The second was to gain tariff-free access to international product markets. The ultimate effect of openness to international competition decreased inefficiency of Canadian manufacturing firms (Bodman, 1996). In Taiwan, exporting activities had positive effect on the productivity of the small and localized firms which did not invest in a specific technology (Aw & Batra, 1998). This result indicates that there are some unobservable factors such as managerial ability of the small firms that provide efficiency gains.

The effect of the export share on technical efficiency of the firm, on the other hand, increases at a decreasing rate and reaches a maximum point in Bangladesh (Hossain & Karunaratne, 2004). When the export share is interacted with non-production labor, the positive effect of export share becomes negative (Grether, 1999). The reason for negative effect of exports on efficiency could be explained by technological disparities between domestic firms and foreign counterparts.

Outsourcing

Outsourcing is taken as another determinant of technical efficiency which indicates all subcontracting relations between firms including hiring temporary labor. Transaction cost approach elaborates the outsourcing activities in terms of cost reduction functionality (Williamson, 1973). Firms can either outsource production activities or business related services. Therefore, they can allocate the resources to the activities which provide comparative advantage. As a result, firm can attract more highly skilled staff through investment in its core competences.

Some part of the literature concerns with the effect of outsourcing on profitability and productivity because outsourcing could produce significant differences in the quality of final products and sales even if there is no change in the efficiency[2] (Görzig & Stephan, 2002; Lacity & Wilcocks, 1998; Gianelle & Tattara, 2009). In addition, the long term and short term effect of outsourcing could be different from each other. Windrum, Reinstaller and Bull (2009) argued that in the long term, productivity of outsourcing firms decreases.

The effect of outsourcing on firm efficiency is studied by Heshmati, 2003; Taymaz & Saatçi, 1997. They found the positive effect of outsourcing on firm efficiency. In fact, the effect of outsourcing depends on the content of the outsourced activity.

If non-productive activities are outsourced, the effect of outsourcing on efficiency could be positive since outsourcing decrease the costs of production. In addition, firm became much focused on the core fields which results in increase in quality of the products. However, if there is a mismatch between outsourcing firm and the external supplier in terms of organization of the work, problems could emerge based on the quality concerns.

Government Subsidy

Firms in the developing countries mostly struggle with financial difficulties to sustain themselves. Public subsidy programmes are developed to support those firms. In recent years, this mechanism has become conditional on implementing innovative activities such as producing a new product or a process.

The relation between subsidy and the firm efficiency could be negative. This implies that subsidized firms are less efficient than their non-subsidized counterparts (Martin, John & Page, 1983). Accordingly, government regulation which targets to reduce input and output prices, encourages rent–seeking behaviour among entrepreneurs. In some cases, subsidies go to firms that already conduct R&D activities[3], therefore, the positive effect of subsidy on decision to innovate is not clearcut (González, Jaumandreu & Pazo, 2005). In this study, the term subsidy is only included in the estimation of low technology manufacturing firms since a considerable number of firms in this group are subsidized by the government.

Subcontracting

Subcontracting and outsourcing activities can be considered similar to each other. Both of them reflects the provision of services by the external vendors. As for the case of subcontracting, firm may have the required facilities to operate the activities but it prefers to subcontract them. For the case of outsourcing, firm does not have in house production capability of the activity and it depends on the external supplier (Van Mieghem, 1999).

Several studies analyzed the effect of subcontracting on the firm efficiency. The positive effect of subcontracting on technical efficiency is conditional on the emergence of network effects as a result of subcontracting activity (Aoki, 1989; Lazonick, 1990; Burki & Terrel, 1998; Taymaz & Saatci, 1997).

Regional Agglomeration

Firms making software investment are included in this study. Although it could be ambigious to classify them as "software firms", allocating resources into the software component of the information and communication technologies (ICT) is an indication of innovativeness (Bessen & Hunt, 2007). Therefore, the effect of location could be analyzed in this frame. Geographical proximity could facilitate technological improvement, competitiveness, market linkages and collaboration among firms through such mechanisms as trust (Romijn & Albaladejo, 2002).Tacit knowledge[4] is facilitated by the trust between firms in the same location. This situation eases the knowledge transfers from one organization to another. The close interaction among firms clustered in a specific geography reduces the risk and uncertainty towards adopting a new technology decreases.

Taking those considerations into account, expected effect of regional agglomeration on efficiency is positive (Driffield & Munday, 2001; Taymaz & Saatçi,1997). On the other hand, efficiency benefits could decrease after some point that cities reach a certain population (Mitra, 1999). As the communication costs decline and the quality of interaction with the partners outside the region increases, the positive effect of geographical proximity could dissappear (Curran & Blackburn, 1994).

R&D Personnel

In the efficiency literature, the effect of research and development (R&D) activities are analyzed by using various proxies such as R&D capital intensity (Kumbhakar, Ortega-Argiles, Potters, Vivarelli, & Voigt, 2012) R&D capital stock (Wang, 2007), or R&D expenditure (Perelman, 1995).

Regardless of how it is measured, R&D activities are intangible assets carrying the notion of creative property. Therefore, the presence of R&D personnel which reflects the absorptive capacity of the firm (Cohen & Levinthal, 1989) is crucial especially for firms operating in the capital intensive industries such as electiricity, machinery, and chemicals. Based on this, the positive effect is expected for this variable (Dilling-Hansen, Madsen, & Smith, 2003; Griliches, 1998; Coe, Helpman, & Hoffmaister, 1995; Tassey,1997; Huang & Liu,1994). There could be long term and short term effect of R&D activities. Dilling-Hansen et al. (2003) emphasized that when the R&D activities of the firms are based on basic research, its effect on firm performance emerges in the long run.

Software Investment

The effect of intangible investment on productivity has been studied only recently. Most of the evidence belongs to developed countries (Corrado et al. 2013). To consider the effect of ICT on productivity, the positive effect of computer networks is found (Atrostic & Nguyen, 2005). As for the comparison between US and Japan in terms of the effect of computer networks, Japan lags behind the US. One possible reason is that complementary activities such as innovation or process change is lower in Japan (Atrostic, Motohashi, & Nguyen, 2008). In addition, complementarity could exist among the ICT components such as the relation between information networks and business networks (Motohashi, 2007).

The effect of intangibles on economic growth or productivity in developing countries was not investigated due to lack of data. In this study, we analyze the effect software component of intangible investment on Turkish manufacturing firms for the years between 2003-2007 by using information on software investment. In those years, there has been an increase in the software investment intensity while there is no increase in the number of firms that make that investment.

The motivation for using this variable is to investigate whether investing in software component of ICT generates differential effect on the efficiency among software-intensive firms. There are several studies on the effect of ICT (see, Table 3). Empirical evidence establishes a positive link between ICT and technical efficiency (Brasini & Freo, 2012; Castiglione, 2012; Castiglione & Infante, 2014; Dimelis & Papaioannou, 2010; Berghall, 2014; Bechetti et al., 2003; Lee & Barua, 1999; Romero & Rodriguez, 2010; Repkine, 2008; Bertschek, Fryges, & Kaiser, 2006; Criscuolo & Waldron, 2003; Rincon, Robinson, & Vecchi, 2005). Milana and Zeli (2002) and Repkine (2009) have found no significant effect of ICT on firm efficiency. Accordingly, ICT may not change the technology frontier for countries having a high level of telecommunication investment.

Time Effects

Reforms in the telecommunication sector on a global scale were started in 1980s. Those reforms include the directions such as commercialization of the telecom services, involvement of private firms in the telecommunications sector, diversification in the service supply, competition enhancing, and the elimination of government from the ownership status (Wellenius & Stern, 1994). The United States and the United Kingdom are the two countries that initiated the liberalization process in the telecommunications sector. British Telecom was privatized by the act of Telecommunications in 1984 and the Office of Telecommunications (Oftel), which

Table 3. Empirical Studies on the Effect of ICT on Efficiency

Authors	Title of the Paper	Targeted Population	Result	ICT Component
Castiglione(2012)	Technical efficiency and ICT investment in Italian manufacturing firms	3452 Italian manufacturing firms over the period 1995 to 2003	• Positive and significant effect of ICT investment on technical efficiency. • Group, size, and geographical position have positive influence on technical efficiency. • Older firms are more efficient than younger firms	ICT investment takes the value of 1 if firm makes ICT investment
Becchetti et al. (2003)	ICT investment, productivity, and efficiency evidence at firm level using a stochastic frontier approach	4400 Italian SME's over the period 1995 to 1997	• Software investment increases the scale of firm operations • Telecommunication investment creates flexible production network which products and processes are more fequently adapted to satisfy consumers' taste for variety	This indicator is used as a decomposed form; hardware, software, and telecommunication investment
Romero & Rodriguez(2010)	E-commerce and efficiency at the firm level	Spanish manufacturing firms over the 2000 to 2005	Positive influence of e-buying on efficiency while e-selling has no effect	Binary variable if firms makes e-buying or e-selling
Shao & Lin(2001)	Measuring the value of information technology in technical efficiency with stochastic frontier productions	US firms over the the period 1988 to1992	Positive effect of IT on efficiency	Hardware investment and information systems staff expenditure
Dimelis & Papanniou (2010)	The role of ICT in reducing inefficiencies. A Stochastic Production Frontier Study across OECD countries	17 OECD countries countries over the period 1990 to 2005	• A significant ICT impact in the reduction of cross country inefficiencies. • European countries are less efficiency and have not yet converged to the efficiency levels of the most developed OECD countries.	ICT investment as a share of GDP
Mouelhi(2009)	Impact of adoption of information and communication technologies on firm efficiency in the Tunisian manufacturing firms	Tunisian manufacturing firms	Positive effect of ICT capital on efficiency is observed after controlling for human capital related firm characteristics	ICT index composed of communication ratio, hardware acquisitions ratio, and software acquisitions ratio
De Vries & Koetter (2011)	ICT adoption and heterogeneity in production technologies: Evidence for Chilean Retailers	Chilean Retail Firms	Positive effect of ICT on determining production technologies	ICT index varying from 0 to 7. Index is generated by using internet, intranet, extranet, and webpage onership

was publicly funded and independent agency, was established as a regulator of the sector. In the same year, under the state antimonopoly ruling, AT&T, the largest American telecommunications company, was broken up into 7 regional companies. For both countries, the main motivation was to encourage competition in the sector. The UK Government chose the duopoly policy because the presence of lots of competitors in the sector might result in failure of the sector (Gabel & Pollard, 1995). Therefore, Mercury Communications obtained license as a first competitor for the British Telecom.

In the following years, privatization in the telecommunications sector spread throughout the developing countries. The first move in the liberalization of telephony services in Turkey dates back to 1994 when the Telsim and Turkcell operators made an agreement with Telecom based on the revenue sharing and few years later, in 1998, they obtained the licenses. By the end of 2003, the monopoly rights of the Turkish Telecom have abolished which started the privatization process in the telecommunication sector. In the following years, competition has become higher in mobile sector relative to fixed telephony or broadband (Atiyas, 2011). We introduce year dummies for this period in order to investigate the effect of privatization on efficiency in software-intensive firms for the years between 2003-2007.

Some writers consider that the creation of the competitive environment with the privatization of the state monopoly enhances productive efficiency (Jha & Majumdar, 1999; Ross, Beath, & Goodhue, 1996; Bortolotti, D'Souza, Fantini, & Megginson, 2002, Lam & Shiu, 2010). From the economic development perspective, the main issue is based on whether privatization generates inequity while it increases efficiency. Birdshall and Nellis (2003) state that it is possible to increase efficiency without decreasing equity. For countries that experienced inefficiency and inequality in the distribution of the services, conditions of failure in privatization were introduced in pre-privatization period such as mismanagement of the privatization or low technical infrastructure.

DATA AND METHODOLOGY

In this study, five waves of the Structural Business Statistics of Turkey administered by Turkish Statisical Institute (TURKSTAT) are used in order to analyze the effect of software investment on firm efficiency. It includes the data from the year 2003 to 2007. The dataset has detailed information on sales, revenues, and costs for each firm. First, 2003-2006 dataset was shared by TURKSTAT then 2007 wave was introduced as a single dataset. Two datasets are merged with the help of the key dataset including the common id numbers for the two waves, 2007 and 2003-2006 dataset. After deleting the duplicated observations, 17131 observations remained for each year[5]. Only manufacturing firms are included in this study, since measuring productivity in services sector is quite different from that of production sectors. There are 45900 manufacturing firms in the dataset.

In this study, capital stock is proxied by depreciation allowances. Some observations of this variable have zero values which indicates that those firms do not have any production activities. Therefore, firms with no information on capital stock in any of the years are removed from the sample. The same procedure is applied to the employment variable. Since firms employing less than 20 workers are sampled, observations for micro firms are deleted. Moreover, manufacturing industry revenues which are used to construct output variable is cleaned of the zero observations. In this study, firms that do not invest in software are excluded. A number of observations are also removed following the construction of the variables. For instance observations which exceed 1 for the variable export share are cleaned of the sample. Therefore the final sample includes 8450 observations.

We use OECD (1997) classification to group firms in terms of their technological sophistication. Accordingly, firms operating in electronics, machinery, and chemicals are high technology firms, while textiles, food, paper are low technology sectors. The distinction between high technology and low technology firms are based on the R&D intensity. High technology sectors are more R&D intensive while low technology industries are conceived as low R&D performers[6].

In this study, there are 2212 observations for the high technology firms. The number of observations for low technology sectors are 4160. We aim to compare the effect of production function variables and the effect of determinants of technical efficiency. For this purpose, we discuss the estimation results for high technology and low technology separately.

As for the methodology, stochastic frontier model with time varying efficiency is used in this study. The advantage of using panel data in stochastic frontier production is that inefficiency term and input levels do not have to be independent as cross section models (Schmidt & Sickles, 1984). In addition, there is no need for distribution assumption for the inefficiency effect. We assume the translog functional form since it does not impose any prior restrictions on the production function unlike Cobb Douglas. The appropriateness of translog form is tested by introducing Cobb Douglas for each estimation.

EMPIRICAL RESULTS

Table 4 reports the empirical results of the stochastic frontier and the determinants of technical efficiency in high technology manufacturing firms for the period 2003-2007. High technology manufacturing sectors are named as "capital intensive sectors". Table 5 shows the empirical results of the stochastic frontier and the determinants of technical efficiency in low technology manufacturing firms for the period 2003-2007. All models used in this study have a panel characteristic. The advantage of using panel data in stochastic frontier production is that inefficiency terms and input levels do not have to be independent as in cross section models (Schmidt & Sickles, 1984). In addition, there is no need for distributional assumption for the inefficiency effect. We assume the translog functional form for the technology since it does not impose any prior restrictions on the production function, unlike Cobb Douglas. In addition, for each model, the appropriateness of the translog form is tested by introducing Cobb Douglas.

Each table is composed of two parts. The first part shows the frontier function variables, which are output, capital stock, labor, raw material, and electricity and fuel. Taking the heterogeneity issue into account, sector dummies are introduced in the production function. The second part shows the inefficiency frontier function variables which are trade openness, outsourcing, regional agglomeration, R&D personel, and software investment. All these explanatory variables display sufficient variation regarding their distribution. This model is time variant production frontier with year dummies that are introduced in both production function and technical efficiency. All variables are in logarithmic form.

Starting with the variables in the frontier function, we expect a positive effect of capital stock on output in high technology manufacturing firms. Therefore, increase in capital intensity indicates the efficient use of machinery which results in overall increase in the firm efficiency. The output increases with capital stock at 14 percent. The positive sign of capital stock squared indicates that the effect of capital stock increases at an increasing rate. As for the low technology manufacturing firms, the effect of capital stock on output is positive and significant but lower than that of high technology sectors. The positive and significant sign of the squared term shows that it increases at an increasing rate.

When the capital stock interacts with labor, raw material, electricity and fuel, the coefficient gives negative, negative, and positive effect, respectively for the high technology manufacturing firms. Interaction with labour is negative and insignificant whereas interaction with raw material is negative and significant. Therefore, the existence of raw material results in a decrease in the effect of capital stock on output. The interaction effect with electricity and fuel, on the contrary, is positive, implying that these two inputs are complementary. As for the low technology manufacturing firms, the interaction with labor, raw material, electricity and fuel gives positive, negative, and

Table 4. Stochastic Production Frontier Estimation Results for High Technology Firms

	Coefficients	t-Statistics
A. Frontier Functions		
Constant	0.10	5.19
K	0.14	17.09
L	0.02	2.13
RM	0.59	72.43
E	0.05	5.86
T	0.04	5.98
*K*K*	0.02	5.73
*K*L*	-0.01	-2.07
*K*RM*	-0.08	-11.89
*K*E*	0.04	6.14
*K*T*	-0.01	-2.29
*L*L*	0.00	0.47
*L*RM*	0.01	1.46
*L*E*	0.00	-0.49
*L*T*	0.00	-0.56
*RM*RM*	0.09	27.70
*RM*E*	-0.05	-8.29
*RM*T*	0.03	6.14
*E*E*	0.01	3.01
*E*T*	-0.01	-2.00
*T*T*	0.03	5.80
Chemicals	0.19	7.37
Electricity	0.05	2.27
Machinery	0.03	1.29
B. Inefficiency Effects Model		
Constant	-0.88	-1.98
Trade Openness	-1.11	-5.84
Outsourcing	-3.66	-7.37
Regional Agglomeration	-2.13	-7.30
R&D personnel	-0.44	-4.40
Software investment	-0.12	-5.60
Year 2004	-1.15	-7.85
Year 2005	-1.54	-8.08
Year 2006	-2.31	-12.71
Year 2007	-0.83	-7.36

continued

Table 4. Continued

	Coefficients	t-Statistics
Variance Parameters, Loglikelihood, and Mean Efficiency		
$\sigma^2 = \sigma_2^u + \sigma_2^v$ $\gamma = \sigma_2^u / (\sigma_2^u + \sigma_2^v)$	0.75 0.94	9.34 116.99
Loglikelihood	-357.52	
Mean Efficiency	0.83	
Number of Observations	2212	

Transportation is the base sector

positive effect, respectively. Among these, only interaction of capital with the raw material gives significant result. This indicates the same result with the high technology manufacturing firms. However, the coefficient of the interaction term is lower for low technology manufacturing firms.

The effect of labor is also positive and significant with a small coefficient for high technology manufacturing firms. In addition, the labor squared gives zero and insignificant result. Interaction terms with other inputs do not give significant results. In contrast to high technology sectors, labour has a negative effect on output. The positive sign of the squared term of this variable indicates that the effect of labor decreases at an increasing rate.

When the labour variable is interacted with the raw material, electricity and fuel separately, the coefficients are positive for the high technology manufacturing firms. However, those coefficients are not significant. Similar results are obtained for the low technology manufacturing firms.

The coefficient of raw material has the highest share in comparison to other production inputs for the high technology manufacturing firms. The effect of its square term gives positive and significant result indicating that the use of raw material in the production generates increasing effect on output. Examining the interaction of raw material with the other input variables, the interaction with electricity and fuel has a negative and significant effect on output. So, the presence of raw material results in a decrease in the effect of electricity and fuel

Table 5. Stochastic Production Frontier Estimation Results for Low Technology Firms

	Coefficients	t-Statistics
A. Frontier Functions		
Constant	-0.01	-0.30
K	0.08	13.80
L	-0.01	-1.67
RM	0.66	98.28
E	0.03	4.51
T	0.03	4.84
*K*K*	0.01	5.20
*K*L*	0.01	1.62
*K*RM*	-0.04	-8.21
*K*E*	0.00	0.65
*K*T*	0.00	-0.20
*L*L*	0.00	1.21
*L*RM*	0.00	0.71
*L*E*	0.00	0.60
*L*T*	0.00	0.35
*RM*RM*	0.10	35.80
*RM*E*	-0.04	-6.97
*RM*T*	0.02	4.68
*E*E*	0.02	4.88
*E*T*	-0.01	-2.80
*T*T*	0.03	5.08
Food	-0.01	-0.37
Textiles	0.14	4.65
Paper	0.17	5.32
Unclassified manufacturing	0.02	0.62
B. Inefficiency Effects Model		
Constant	0.39	2.62
Export share	-5.63	-13.13
Outsourcing expenditure	-0.21	-3.38
Outsourcing income	0.00	0.00
Subsidy	0.03	0.75
Regional Agglomeration	-0.07	-1.00
R&D personnel expenditure	-0.23	-5.75
Software investment	-0.08	-4.00
Subcontracting expenditure	-0.52	-5.77
Year 2004	-0.21	-3.50
Year 2005	-0.36	-4.50

continued

Table 5. Continued

	Coefficients	t-Statistics
Year 2006	-0.97	-6.06
Year 2007	-0.23	-3.29
Variance Parameters,Loglikelihood, and Mean Efficiency		
$\gamma = \sigma_2^u / (\sigma_2^u + \sigma_2^v)$ $\sigma^2 = \sigma_2^u + \sigma_2^v$	0.28 0.78	7.00 19.50
Loglikelihood	-1111.6	
Mean efficiency	0.82	
Number of observations	4160	

expenditure. As for the low technology manufacturing firms, the effect of raw material is positive and significant and higher than that for high technology manufacturing firms. Its square is also positive and significant indicating that the effect of raw material on output increases at an increasing rate. The interaction with electricity and fuels negative and significant. This implies the same result with the high technology manufacturing firms.

The sign of electricity and fuel is positive and significant. The positive sign of the squared term of this variable indicates that its effect on output increases at an increasing rate. As for the low technology manufacturing firms, the sign of the electricity and fuel gives positive and significant result and the positive sign of the squared term indicates that it increases at an increasing rate.

The positive and significant effect of the time variable indicates that the mean technical progress is 4 percent per year in high technology industry. When the time interacts with capital stock, labor, raw material, electricity and fuel, the coefficient gives negative, zero, positive, and negative effect, respectively. Among these, only the interaction of time with raw material gives significant result, indicating that technical change is raw material saving. As for the low technology manufacturing firms, the effect of time on output is positive and significant as in the case of high technology sectors. However, the sign of the squared term indicates that its effect decreases at an increasing rate.

Considering the variables in the inefficiency frontier function, we have trade openness, outsourcing, regional agglomeration, R&D personnel, software investment, and year dummies. The effect of trade openness is negative and significant, therefore, exporting activities increase the technical efficiency of the firm. However, its effect is lower than that of low technology sectors. This result indicates that export activities play a much more crucial role in explaining technical efficiency for low technology firms. In 1996, quota restrictions on exporting textile products to EU are abolished with the Customs Union Agreement in Turkey. Export share of the country increased during the period investigated. This result is in line with the cases of China (Sun et al., 1999); Hungary (Piesse & Thirtle, 2000), Spain (Gumbau-Albert & Maudos, 2002), and Chile (Tybout, De Melo, & Corbo, 1991).

We next consider the effect of outsourcing expenditure on technical efficiency. It has the highest share in the technical efficiency estimation with a negative sign. As for the low technology manufacturing firms, the effect of outsourcing expenditure on efficiency is positive and significant. Its effect is higher than that for the high technology sectors which indicates that outsourcing activities are more important in explaining the technical efficiency in low technology sectors. This result is in line with Heshmati (2003) and Taymaz and Saatci (1997). The positive effect of outsourcing on efficiency could be based on allocation of activities that provide comparative advantage.

The relation between regional agglomeration and technical efficiency is positive. It has the highest coefficiency following the outsourcing expenditure. It is higher than that of low technology firms. This result emphasizes the importance of location in explaining the technical efficiency in high technology sectors (Driffield & Munday, 2001; Taymaz & Saatçi, 1997).

The presence of R&D personnel is also an important determinant of technical efficiency in high technology sectors, implying that R&D intensive firms are more efficient (Cohen &Levinthal, 1989; Coe et al.1995; Huang & Liu,1994). This finding is in line with R&D supporting policy in high technology sectors in Turkey. As for the low technology manufacturing firms, the coefficient of R&D has negative and significant effect on technical inefficiency. On the other hand, its effect is smaller than that of the high technology industry.

The effect of software investment is positive and significant. However, the coefficient is the smallest in comparison to the other variables. This indicates that software investment is still not the main factor in explaining technical efficiency since software investment is quite a new factor of investment. As for the low technology manufacturing firms, software investment has also positive and significant effect on technical efficiency for low technology manufacturing firms.

Time effects are also introduced in the estimation. All of them are positively related to technical efficiency. This result is in line with the assumption that links positive association with the privatization and technical efficiency (Jha & Majumdar, 1999; Ross et al., 1996; Bortolotti et al. 2002; Lam & Shiu, 2010).

For the low technnology manufacturing firms, we included some additional factors such as subsidy, outsourcing revenue, and subcontracting expenditure in the technical inefficiency function. Interestingly subsidy does not appear to be significant for low technology sectors although the considerable number of firms in the low technology sectors are subsidized in Turkey.

It is crucial to make a distinction between outsourcing reveue and outsourcing expenditure. For the first one, outsourcing is the main activitiy of the firm that generates a large part of the turnover while for the second, firm may outsource part of its activities to the external suppliers. We included outsourcing revenue in the efficiency estimation of the low technology manfacturing firms since outsourcing revenue accounts for considerable amount of the firm turnover for that group of firms. Nevertheless they do not have the same degree of impact with outsourcing expenditure. This indicates that firms that do outsource their activities to other firms are more efficient than for firms in which outsourcing is the main activity.

Table 6 displays the test results for the models. The first null hypothesis is based on the presence of Cobb-Douglas functional form, therefore, all squared and interaction terms are excluded from the model. These tests are applied for each technology group. The likelihood ratiosof test statistics are calculated by the formula as

$$-2\{\log[likelihood(H_0)] - \log[likelihood(H_1)]\} \quad (8)$$

If the value exceeds the 5% critical value, H_0 is rejected. For this study, it implies that Cobb Douglas is not the appropriate functional form. The second null hypothesis is based on the absence of inefficiency in the model. If the paramater gamma is zero, the variance of the inefficiency effects is zero. This indicates that the model is

Table 6. Test results

Null Hypothesis	Loglikelihood Value	Test Statistic	Decision
Cobb Douglas Production			
All β's are equal to zero			
High Technology Sectors	-691,03	666,06	Ho Reject
Low Technology Sectors	-1738,4	1253.6	Ho Reject
No Inefficiency			
$H_0 : \gamma = \delta_0 = ...\delta_{n=0}$			
High Technology Sectors	-632	548	Ho Reject
Low Technology Sectors	- 1456	688.8	Ho Reject
Non Stochastic Inefficiency			
$H_0 : \gamma = 0$			
High Technology Sectors	-632	533,2	Ho Reject
Low Technology Sectors	-1456	314	Ho Reject
No Inefficiency Effects			
$H_0 : \delta_1 = ...\delta_n = 0$			
High Technology Sectors	-365,4	14,8	Ho Reject
Low Technology Sectors	-1299	375	Ho Reject
Time Invariant Inefficiency			
$H_0 : \delta_3 = \delta_4 = \delta_5 = \delta_6 = 0$			
High Technology Sectors	-363.8	32.4	Ho Reject
Low Technology Sectors	-1154.01	86	Ho Reject

reduced to traditional response function that include determinants of efficiency into the production function. The test statistics reject this null hypothesis. For high technology industry, a key parameter γ is 0.94. For the low technology industry, this variable is 0.78. This implies that much of the variation in the composite error term is due to the inefficiency component. The third null hypothesis is that firms in the high technology sectors and low technology sectors are fully efficient. When the only gamma is set to zero, it specifies that the inefficiency effects are not stochastic. However, this assumption is rejected in this study.

The forth null hypothesis is that there is no inefficiency effect. When only inefficiency effects are set to zero, it specifies that the inefficiency effects are not a linear function of the inefficiency parameters. This hypothesis is also rejected which indicates that the joint effects of these inefficiencies of production are significant, although individual effects of one or more variables may not be significant.

The fifth null hypothesis is that inefficiency effect is time invariant. As reported in the Table 3 and 4, year dummies give negative and significant results for the technical inefficiency. This implies that the null hypothesis is rejected.

CONCLUSION

The adoption and the use of Information and Communication Technologies (ICTs) are indications of technological progress and important keys for the development of knowledge-based economy and its future sustainability. The existence of ICT infrastructure provides business opportunities and helps firms build up business networks between suppliers, buyers and customers. A large number of business tasks are succeeded through the internet by means of personal computers and external network facilities which, in turn, decrease the transaction costs. Moreover, use of ICTs provides an efficient channel for advertising, marketing and direct distribution of goods and services. ICTs play a dual role in the business world. It is both a technology stock of the firms and a channel for technology transfer from one firm to another (Hsieh & Lin 1998).

ICT have three main components. These are telecommunication investment, hardware investment and software investment. Unlike hardware and telecommunication investment, measuring the software investment is difficult since it is generally supplied with the hardware component. In recent years, a considerable effort has been directed to isolate the effect of software investment as a part of intangible investment on firm efficiency. In Turkey, there has been an increase in the software investment of Turkish manufacturing firms during the period 2003-2007. In this study, we analyzed whether the increase in software investment resulted in efficiency gains for software-intensive manufacturing firms in Turkey by using time varying stochastic frontier approach. The main motivation was to increase output by increasing efficiency with given amounts of resources. Therefore, the term efficiency can be simply defined as the success in producing as large as possible with the given input. Our results show that software investment is crucial both for the high technology and the low technology manufacturing firms. However, its effect is much higher in the high technology sectors such as electricity, chemicals, and machinery as compared to the low technology sectors such as clothing, textiles, food, paper, and unclassified manufacturing.

Despite its positive and significant effect on the firm efficiency, software investment does not generate an effect as large as the research and development personnel which is another component of intangible investment. Software intensive firms mostly rely on the skilled workforce which is competent in research and development activities. This result shows that the presence of R&D personnel has a crucial role for productive efficiency of the manufacturing firms in Turkey.

REFERENCES

Adams, M., & Oleksak, M. (2010). *Intangible Capital: Putting knowledge to work in the 21st century organization*. Santa Barbara: ABC-CLIO.

Alvarez, R., & Crespi, G. (2003). Determinants of technical efficiency in small firms. *Small Business Economics*, *20*(3), 233–244. doi:10.1023/A:1022804419183

Aoki, M. (1989). *Information, incentives and bargaining in the Japanese economy: A microtheory of the Japanese Economy*. New York: Cambridge University Press.

Atiyas, I. (2011). Regulation and competition in the Turkish telecommunications industry. In *The Political Economy of Regulation in Turkey*. New York: Springer. doi:10.1007/978-1-4419-7750-2_8

Atrostic, B. K., Motohashi, K., & Nguyen, S. V. (2008). Computer Network Use and Firms' Productivity Performance: The United States vs. Japan (US Census Bureau Center for Economic Studies Paper No. CES-WP-08-30). Retrieved from http://papers.ssrn.com/sol3/papers.cfm?abstract_id=1269425

Atrostic, B. K., & Nguyen, S. V. (2005). IT and productivity in US manufacturing: Do computer networks matter? *Economic Inquiry*, *43*(3), 493–506. doi:10.1093/ei/cbi033

Aw, B. Y., & Batra, G. (1998). Technology, exports and firm efficiency in Taiwanese manufacturing. *Economics of Innovation and New Technology*, *7*(2), 93–113. doi:10.1080/10438599800000030

Balassa, B. (1978). Exports and economic growth: Further evidence. *Journal of Development Economics*, *5*(2), 181–189. doi:10.1016/0304-3878(78)90006-8

Basu, S., & Fernald, J. (2007). Information and communications technology as a general-purpose technology: Evidence from US industry data. *German Economic Review*, *8*(2), 146–173. doi:10.1111/j.1468-0475.2007.00402.x

Battese, G. E., & Coelli, T. J. (1992). *Frontier production functions, technical efficiency and panel data: with application to paddy farmers in India*. Netherlands: Springer.

Becchetti, L., Bedoya, D. A. I., & Paganetto, L. (2003). ICT investment, productivity and efficiency: Evidence at firm level using a stochastic frontier approach. *Journal of Productivity Analysis*, *20*(2), 143–167. doi:10.1023/A:1025128121853

Berghall, E. (2014). Has Finland advanced from an investment to an innovation-driven stage? *LTA*, *1*(14), 11–32.

Bertschek, I., Fryges, H., & Kaiser, U. (2006). B2B or Not to Be: Does B2B e-commerce increase labour productivity? *International Journal of the Economics of Business*, *13*(3), 387–405. doi:10.1080/13571510600961395

Bessen, J., & Hunt, R. M. (2007). An empirical look at software patents. *Journal of Economics & Management Strategy*, *16*(1), 157–189. doi:10.1111/j.1530-9134.2007.00136.x

Birdshall, N., & Nellis, J. (2003). Winners and losers: Assessing the distributional impact of privatization. *World Development*, *31*(10), 1617–1633. doi:10.1016/S0305-750X(03)00141-4

Bodman, P. M. (1996). On export-led growth in Australia and Canada: Cointegration, causality, and structural stability. *Australian Economic Papers*, *35*(67), 282–299. doi:10.1111/j.1467-8454.1996.tb00051.x

Borgo, M. D., Goodridge, P., Haskel, J., & Pesole, A. (2013). Productivity and growth in UK Industries: An intangible investment approach. *Oxford Bulletin of Economics and Statistics*, *75*(6), 806–834. doi:10.1111/j.1468-0084.2012.00718.x

Bortolotti, B., D'Souza, J., Fantini, M., & Megginson, W. L. (2002). Privatization and the sources of performance improvement in the global telecommunications industry. *Telecommunications Policy*, *26*(5), 243–268. doi:10.1016/S0308-5961(02)00013-7

Bosworth, B. P., & Triplett, J. E. (2000). *What's new about the new economy? IT, economic growth and productivity*. Washington, DC: Brookings Institution, Mimeo.

Brasini, S., & Freo, M. (2012). The impact of information and communication technologies: An insight at micro-level on one Italian region. *Economics of Innovation and New Technology*, *21*(2), 107–123. doi:10.1080/10438599.2011.558175

Burki, A. A., & Terrell, D. (1998). Measuring production efficiency of small firms in Pakistan. *World Development*, *26*(1), 155–169. doi:10.1016/S0305-750X(97)00122-8

Castiglione, C. (2012). Technical efficiency and ICT investment in Italian manufacturing firms. *Applied Economics*, *44*(14), 1749–1763. doi:10.1080/00036846.2011.554374

Castiglione, C., & Infante, D. (2014). ICTs and time-span in technical efficiency gains. A stochastic frontier approach over a panel of Italian manufacturing firms. *Economic Modelling*, *41*, 55–65. doi:10.1016/j.econmod.2014.04.021

Coe, D. T., Helpman, E., & Hoffmaister, A. W. (1995). North-South R&D spillovers. *The Economic Journal*, *107*(440), 134–149. doi:10.1111/1468-0297.00146

Cohen, W. M., & Levin, R. C. (1989). Empirical studies of innovation and market structure. Handbook of Industrial Organization, 2, 1059-1107.

Corrado, C., Haskel, J., Jona-Lasinio, C., & Iommi, M. (2013). Innovation and intangible investment in Europe, Japan, and the United States. *Oxford Review of Economic Policy*, *29*(2), 261–286. doi:10.1093/oxrep/grt017

Corrado, C., Hulten, C., & Sichel, D. (2009). Intangible capital and US economic growth. *Review of Income and Wealth*, *55*(3), 661–685. doi:10.1111/j.1475-4991.2009.00343.x

Criscuolo, C., & Waldron, K. (2003). E-commerce and productivity. *Economic Trends*, *60*, 52–57.

Cummins, J. G. (2005). A new approach to the valuation of intangible capital. In C. Corrado, J. Haltiwanger, & D. Sichel (Eds.), *Measuring capital in the new economy* (pp. 47–72). USA: University of Chicago Press. doi:10.7208/chicago/9780226116174.003.0003

Curran, J., & Blackburn, R. (1994). *Small firms and local economic networks: the death of the local economy?* London, UK: Paul Chapman.

De Vries, G. J., & Koetter, M. (2011). ICT Adoption and heterogeneity in production technologies: Evidence for Chilean retailers. *Oxford Bulletin of Economics and Statistics*, *73*(4), 539–555. doi:10.1111/j.1468-0084.2010.00622.x

Delgado, M. A., Farinas, J. C., & Ruano, S. (2002). Firm productivity and export markets: A non-parametric approach. *Journal of International Economics*, *57*(2), 397–422. doi:10.1016/S0022-1996(01)00154-4

Dilling-Hansen, M., Madsen, E. S., & Smith, V. (2003). Efficiency, R&D and ownership–some empirical evidence. *International Journal of Production Economics*, *83*(1), 85–94. doi:10.1016/S0925-5273(02)00302-X

Dimelis, S. P., & Papaioannou, S. K. (2010). Technical efficiency and the role of information technology: a stochastic production frontier study across OECD countries. In S. Allegrezza & A. Dubrocard (Eds.), *Internet Econometrics* (pp. 43–62). UK: Palgrave McMillan.

Dimelis, S. P., & Papaioannou, S. K. (2014). Human capital effects on technical inefficiency: A stochastic frontier analysis across industries of the Greek economy. *International Review of Applied Economics*, *28*(6), 797–812. doi:10.1080/02692171.2014.907246

Driffield, N., & Munday, M. (2001). Foreign manufacturing, regional agglomeration and technical efficiency in UK industries: A stochastic production frontier approach. *Regional Studies*, *35*(5), 391–399. doi:10.1080/713693833

Farrell, M. J. (1957). The measurement of productive efficiency. *Journal of the Royal Statistical Society. Series A (General)*, *120*(3), 253–290. doi:10.2307/2343100

Feder, G. (1983). On exports and economic growth. *Journal of Development Economics*, *12*(1), 59–73. doi:10.1016/0304-3878(83)90031-7

Gabel, D., & Pollard, W. (1995). *Privatization, deregulation, and competition: learning from the cases of telecommunications in New Zealand and the United Kingdom*. Retrieved from http://citeseerx.ist.psu.edu/viewdoc/download?doi=10.1.1.230.4447&rep=rep1&type=pdf

Gianelle, C., & Tattara, G. (2009). Manufacturing abroad while making profits at home: a study on Veneto footwear and clothing global value chains. In M. Morroni (Ed.), *Corporate Governance, Organization and Design and Inter-Firm Relations: Theoretical advances and Empirical Evidence* (pp. 206–213). UK: Edward Elgar. doi:10.4337/9781848446120.00019

González, X., Jaumandreu, J., & Pazó, C. (2005). Barriers to innovation and subsidy effectiveness. *The Rand Journal of Economics*, *36*(4), 930–950.

Görzig, B., & Andreas, S. (2002). Outsourcing and firm level performance (DIW Berlin (Discussion Paper No. 309). Retrieved from http://www.econstor.eu/bitstream/10419/18045/1/dp309.pdf

Grether, J. M. (1999). Determinants of technological diffusion in mexican manufacturing: A plant-level analysis. *World Development*, *27*(7), 1287–1298. doi:10.1016/S0305-750X(99)00054-6

Griliches, Z. (1998). Issues in assessing the contribution of research and development to productivity growth. In Z. Griliches (Ed.), *R&D and Productivity: The Econometric Evidence* (pp. 17–45). USA: University of Chicago Press. doi:10.7208/chicago/9780226308906.001.0001

Guidelines for Managing and Reporting on Intangibles. (2002). *MERITUM Project.* Retrieved from www.pnbukh.com/files/pdf_filer/pdf_filer/MERITUM_Guidelines.pdf

Gumbau-Albert, M., & Maudos, J. (2002). The determinants of efficiency: The case of the Spanish industry. *Applied Economics*, *34*(15), 1941–1948. doi:10.1080/00036840210127213

Haskel, J., Jona-Lasinio, C., & Iommi, M. (2012). Intangible capital and growth in advanced economies: Measurement methods and comparative results (IZA Discussion Paper No.6733). Retrieved from ftp://ftp.mpls.frb.fed.us/pub/research/mcgrattan/sr472/data/MacroData/Intangibles/Corrado12.pdf

Heshmati, A. (2003). Productivity growth, efficiency and outsourcing in manufacturing and service industries. *Journal of Economic Surveys*, *17*(1), 79–112. doi:10.1111/1467-6419.00189

Hossain, M., & Dias Karunaratne, N. (2004). Exports and economic growth in Bangladesh: Has manufacturing exports become a new engine of export-led growth? *The International Trade Journal*, *18*(4), 303–334. doi:10.1080/08853900490518190

Hsieh, C., & Lin, B. (1998). Internet commerce for small businesses. *Industrial Management & Data Systems*, *98*(3), 113–190. doi:10.1108/02635579810213116

Huang, C. J., & Liu, J. T. (1994). Estimation of a non-neutral stochastic frontier production function. *Journal of Productivity Analysis*, *5*(2), 171–180. doi:10.1007/BF01073853

Hulten, C. R., & Hao, X. (2008). What is a Company Really Worth? Intangible Capital and the" Market to Book Value" Puzzle (NBER Working Paper No. w14548). Retrieved May 14, 2015 from http://infolab.stanford.edu/pub/gio/CS99I/nber_w14548.pdf

Jalava, J., & Pohjola, M. (2008). The roles of electricity and ICT in economic growth: Case Finland. *Explorations in Economic History*, *45*(3), 270–287. doi:10.1016/j.eeh.2007.11.001

Jha, R., & Majumdar, S. K. (1999). A matter of connections: OECD telecommunications sector productivity and the role of cellular technology diffusion. *Information Economics and Policy*, *11*(3), 243–269. doi:10.1016/S0167-6245(99)00017-7

Koopmans, T. C. (1951). Analysis of production as an efficient combination of activities. *Activity Analysis of Production and Allocation*, *13*, 33–37.

Kumbhakar, S. C., & Lovell, K. (2000). *Stochastic frontier analysis*. UK: Cambridge University Press. doi:10.1017/CBO9781139174411

Kumbhakar, S. C., Ortega-Argilés, R., Potters, L., Vivarelli, M., & Voigt, P. (2012). Corporate R&D and firm efficiency: Evidence from Europe's top R&D investors. *Journal of Productivity Analysis*, *37*(2), 125–140. doi:10.1007/s11123-011-0223-5

Lacity, M. C., & Willcocks, L. P. (1998). An empirical investigation of information technology sourcing practices: Lessons from experience. *Management Information Systems Quarterly*, 22(3), 363–408. doi:10.2307/249670

Lam, P. L., & Shiu, A. (2010). Economic growth, telecommunications development and productivity growth of the telecommunications sector: Evidence around the world. *Telecommunications Policy*, *34*(4), 185–199. doi:10.1016/j.telpol.2009.12.001

Lazonick, W. (1990). *Competitive advantage on the shop floor*. USA: Harvard University Press.

Lee, B., & Barua, A. (1999). An integrated assessment of productivity and efficiency impacts of information technology investments: Old data, new analysis and evidence. *Journal of Productivity Analysis*, *12*(1), 21–43. doi:10.1023/A:1007898906629

Lev, B. (2000). *Intangibles: management, measurement, and reporting*. Washington, DC: Brookings Institution Press.

Machlup, F. (1962). *The production and distribution of knowledge in the United States* (Vol. 278). USA: Princeton University Press.

Martin, J. P., & John, M. Jr. (1983). The impact of subsidies on X-Efficiency in LDC industry: Theory and an empirical test. *The Review of Economics and Statistics*, *65*(4), 608–617. doi:10.2307/1935929

Milana, C., & Zeli, A. (2002). The contribution of ICT to production efficiency in Italy: firm-level evidence using data envelopment analysis and econometric estimations (No. 2002/13). Paris: OECD Publishing. Retrieved from http://www.oecd-ilibrary.org/docserver/download/5lgsjhvj7m5d.pdf?expires=1431686341&id=id&accname=guest&checksum=235816053C0ABA10933BC3CB14BE1F82

Mitra, A. (1999). Agglomeration economies as manifested in technical efficiency at the firm level. *Journal of Urban Economics*, *45*(3), 490–500. doi:10.1006/juec.1998.2100

Motohashi, K. (2007). Firm-level analysis of information network use and productivity in Japan. *Journal of the Japanese and International Economies*, *21*(1), 121–137. doi:10.1016/j.jjie.2005.08.001

Mouelhi, R. B. A. (2009). Impact of the adoption of information and communication technologies on firm efficiency in the Tunisian manufacturing sector. *Economic Modelling*, *26*(5), 961–967. doi:10.1016/j.econmod.2009.03.001

Information Infrastructures: their impact and regulatory requirements. (1997). OECD. Retrieved from http://www.oecd.org/sti/broadband/2095181.pdf

ISIC REV.3 Technology intensity definition, classification of manufacturing industries into categories based on R&D intensities. (2011). OECD. Retrieved from http://www.oecd.org/sti/ind/48350231.pdf

Oliner, S. D., Sichel, D. E., & Stiroh, K. J. (2008). Explaining a productive decade. *Journal of Policy Modeling*, *30*(4), 633–673. doi:10.1016/j.jpolmod.2008.04.007

Park, W. G., & Ginarte, J. C. (1997). Intellectual property rights and economic growth. *Contemporary Economic Policy*, *15*(3), 51–61. doi:10.1111/j.1465-7287.1997.tb00477.x

Perelman, S. (1995). R&D, technological progress and efficiency change in industrial activities. *Review of Income and Wealth*, *41*(3), 349–366. doi:10.1111/j.1475-4991.1995.tb00124.x

Piesse, J., & Thirtle, C. (2000). A stochastic frontier approach to firm level efficiency, technological change, and productivity during the early transition in Hungary. *Journal of Comparative Economics*, *28*(3), 473–501. doi:10.1006/jcec.2000.1672

Polanyi, M., & Sen, A. (1967). *The tacit dimension*. New York: Doubleday.

Ram, R. (1985). Exports and economic growth: Some additional evidence. *Economic Development and Cultural Change*, *33*(2), 415–425. doi:10.1086/451468

Repkine, A. (2008). ICT Penetration and Aggregate Production Efficiency: Empirical Evidence for a Cross-Section of Fifty Countries. *Journal of Applied Economic Sciences*, *3*(2), 137–144.

Repkine, A. (2009). Telecommunications Capital Intensity and Aggregate Production Efficiency: a Meta-Frontier Analysis (MPRA Working Paper No. 13059). Retrieved from http://mpra.ub.uni-muenchen.de/13059/1/MPRA_paper_13059.pdf

Rincon, A., Robinson, C., & Vecchi, M. (2005). The productivity impact of e-commerce in the UK: 2001 evidence from microdata (NIESR Working Paper No. 257). Retrieved from http://www.researchgate.net/profile/Michela_Vecchi/publication/5200599_The_Productivity_impact_of_E-Commerce_in_the_UK_2001_Evidence_from_microdata/links/09e4150a4a6e814ae1000000.pdf

Romero, Q. C., & Rodríguez, R. D. (2010). E-commerce and efficiency at the firm level. *International Journal of Production Economics*, *126*(2), 299–305. doi:10.1016/j.ijpe.2010.04.004

Romijn, H., & Albaladejo, M. (2002). Determinants of innovation capability in small electronics and software firms in southeast England. *Research Policy*, *31*(7), 1053–1067. doi:10.1016/S0048-7333(01)00176-7

Ross, J. W., Beath, C. M., & Goodhue, D. L. (1996). Develop long-term competitiveness through IT assets. *Sloan Management Review*, *38*(1), 31–42.

Schmidt, P., & Sickles, R. C. (1984). Production frontiers and panel data. *Journal of Business & Economic Statistics*, *2*(4), 367–374.

Shao, B. B., & Lin, W. T. (2001). Measuring the value of information technology in technical efficiency with stochastic production frontiers. *Information and Software Technology*, *43*(7), 447–456. doi:10.1016/S0950-5849(01)00150-1

Shapiro, C., & Varian, H. R. (2013). *Information rules: a strategic guide to the network economy*. USA: Harvard Business Press.

Sun, H., Hone, P., & Doucouliago, H. (1999). Economic openness and technical efficiency: A case study of Chinese manufacturing industries. *Economics of Transition*, *7*(3), 615–636. doi:10.1111/1468-0351.00028

Tassey, G. (1997). *The economics of R&D policy*. USA: Greenwood Publishing Group.

Taymaz, E., & Saatci, G. (1997). Technical change and efficiency in Turkish manufacturing industries. *Journal of Productivity Analysis*, *8*(4), 461–475. doi:10.1023/A:1007796311574

Taymaz, E., Voyvoda, E., & Yılmaz, K. (2008). Türkiye Đmalat Sanayiinde Yapısal Dönüşüm, Üretkenlik ve Teknolojik Değişme Dinamikleri (ERC Working Paper No. 08/04) (Structural Transformation of Turkey Manufacturing Industry, Productivity and Technological Change Dynamics). Retrieved from http://www.erc.metu.edu.tr/menu/series08/0804.pdf

Torii, A., & Caves, R. E. (1992). Technical efficiency in Japanese and US manufacturing industries. In R. Caves (Ed.), *Industrial Efficiency in Six Nations* (pp. 423–457). Cambridge: MIT Press.

Tybout, J., De Melo, J., & Corbo, V. (1991). The effects of trade reforms on scale and technical efficiency: New evidence from Chile. *Journal of International Economics*, *31*(3), 231–250. doi:10.1016/0022-1996(91)90037-7

Van Ark, B., Hao, J. X., Corrado, C., & Hulten, C. (2009). Measuring intangible capital and its contribution to economic growth in Europe. *EIB papers, 14*(1), 62-93.

Van Ark, B., & Piatkowski, M. (2004). Productivity, innovation and ICT in Old and New Europe. *International Economics and Economic Policy*, *1*(2-3), 215–246. doi:10.1007/s10368-004-0012-y

Van Mieghem, J. A. (1999). Coordinating investment, production, and subcontracting. *Management Science*, *45*(7), 954–971. doi:10.1287/mnsc.45.7.954

Vosselman, W. (1998). Initial guidelines for the collection and comparison of data on intangible investment. OECD. Retrieved from http://www1.oecd.org/dsti/sti/industry/indcomp/prod/intang.htm

Wang, E. C. (2007). R&D efficiency and economic performance: A cross-country analysis using the stochastic frontier approach. *Journal of Policy Modeling*, *29*(2), 345–360. doi:10.1016/j.jpolmod.2006.12.005

Webster, E. (1999). *The economics of intangible investment*. UK: Edward Elgar Publishing Limited.

Wellenius, B., & Stern, P. A. (1994). *Implementing reforms in the telecommunications sector: Lessons from experience*. Washington, D.C.: World Bank Publications. doi:10.1596/0-8213-2606-6

Williamson, O. E. (1973). Markets and hierarchies: Some elementary considerations. *The American Economic Review*, *63*(2), 316–325.

Windrum, P., Reinstaller, A., & Bull, C. (2009). The outsourcing productivity paradox: Total outsourcing, organisational innovation, and long run productivity growth. *Journal of Evolutionary Economics*, *19*(2), 197–229. doi:10.1007/s00191-008-0122-8

Young, A. (1998). Towards an interim statistical framework: selecting the core components of intangible investment. *OECD*. Retrieved from http://www1.oecd.org/dsti/sti/industry/indcomp/prod/intang.htm

KEY TERMS AND DEFINITIONS

Intangible Investment: This term indicates all products or services that cannot be measured directly (e.g. knowledge, R&D, software,... etc.).

R&D: Research and development activities.

Software-Intensive Firms: Firms that invest heavily in software products or services.

Stochastic Frontier Analysis: A parametrical method of measuring technical efficiency.

Tangible Capital: This term includes all types of physical capital such as buildings and machinery.

Technical Efficiency: It is measured as a distance of a firm from efficient production frontier.

Translog Production Function: A flexible functional form that does not impose any prior restrictions on production function.

ENDNOTES

1. The share of high technology firms receiving government subsidy and being involved in subcontracting relations is quite low. Those variables are not included in the efficiency estimation of high technology firms.
2. Changes in productivity occurs due to the differences in production technology, differences in the efficiency of production process, and differences in the production environment(Kumbhakar & Lovell,2000). Hence, efficiency is only one of the components meaning that productivity can increase or decrease even there is no change in the efficiency.
3. R&D activities are used as a proxy for innovation.
4. Tacit knowledge cannot be transmitted through communication in a direct way, rather it is built up by direct experience Polanyi &Sen (1967). In a trust relation, firms learn from each other without awareness. Therefore, it refers to the process of assimilating ourselves things from outside.
5. We constructed balanced panel dataset in order to trace the firms making software investment each year between 2003-2007.
6. The classification based on the R&D intensity has some deficits. To illustrate, high technology firms can produce goods in the range from low technology to high technology. The idea behind creating such an index was to determine a common trajectory for OECD countries (OECD, 2011).

Chapter 9
Does Participation in International R&D Networks Enhance Local Dynamism?

Hüseyin Güler
Bahçeşehir University, Turkey

Erkan Erdil
Middle East Technical University, Turkey

ABSTRACT

This chapter which is in line with the global pipelines-local buzz framework addresses the collaboration dynamics of ICT researchers from universities of an emerging economy who are mostly benefiting from national funds and do not have dominating or core roles in international R&D networks. It provides a novel taxonomy to identify the degree of globalisation versus localisation of ICT scientists in Turkey. Based on international and national project portfolios of Turkish ICT researchers who participated in FP6 and other international projects between 2003 and 2006, four groups (gatekeepers, externally oriented researchers, internally oriented researchers, inactive researchers) were formed in terms of their degree of local or global focus. For the period of 2007–2013, the performance of the same population was traced with respect to its international or national project density, publication output, involvement in decision making processes on academic project funding, and contribution to R&D capacity development in the private sector. Findings show that that most of the researchers who are engaged in international collaboration are also locally active and they seem to be the most productive actors within the four groups. The study also implies that having a strong project portfolio at both national and international levels relates to having a work experience abroad after the PhD fulfilment and being at a university with advanced research ecosystem in Turkey. This chapter concludes with key policy recommendations, highlighting the need on moving beyond one-size-fits-all policies which should take in to account the heterogeneity, differentiation on career levels, national priorities and capacity requirements of the research ecosystem.

DOI: 10.4018/978-1-4666-8598-7.ch009

INTRODUCTION

The particular combination of local buzz and global pipelines generates a dynamic of knowledge creation within a research ecosystem (Bathelt, 2007). In line with the global pipelines-local buzz framework this study looks from the perspective of universities at emerging economies which are participating in international R&D networks formed to conduct frontier research in advanced technology fields. It gives clues about research dynamics of emerging economy universities that are mostly benefiting from national funds and do not have dominating or core roles in international R&D networks. Barnard, Cowan & Müller (2012) analyses global pipelines-local buzz at researcher level on scientific publications, this paper in addition to that adds project based analysis to the literature while also other types of contributions to the local system are also has been taken into account. This type of analysis can be considered as a unique approach, because in fields like biotechnology, pharmaceutical and information and communication technology (ICT) collaboration networks are at the core of new knowledge generation where they are dominated mostly by the advanced country organization, that's why most studies are about dynamics of developed countries. Considering the lack of studies about research dynamics of emerging economy universities, it is also aimed to contribute to the debate about the internationalization of R&D by putting emphasis on the local impact of international collaboration and derive practical policy recommendations at micro, meso and macro levels.

With this paper we attempt to highlight the significance of local buzz created by Turkish researchers belonging to EU-funded ICT R&D and other TÜBİTAK funded international collaboration projects. In other words, this paper is about global pipelines' effects on local buzz. The paper documents the role of globally and locally engaged researchers in the innovation system of an emerging economy.

From evolutionary perspective of innovation, research collaboration and external knowledge flows are seen as important catalyzers for acquiring new capabilities for innovative organizations which cannot rely only on internal knowledge base (Castellani, Zanfei, & Muendler, 2006). The theoretical framework followed in this study is based on contemporary studies on innovation from the perspective of evolutionary economics, the core–periphery model of economic development and recent literature on research networks and sociology and organization of science in emerging economies. Following, Krugman's core–periphery model of economic geography, this study is grounded on local deployment of knowledge gathered from international R&D networks and based on the findings it tries to provide actionable policy recommendations for the countries at the periphery in order to enhance synergies between local buzz and global pipelines.

Network literature implicitly treats the researchers who are involved in different collaboration actions as gateways between different projects. Such researchers may also transmit knowledge gathered from international platforms to the local level, which can enhance the local buzz. On the other hand, rather than contributing to local knowledge spillovers, these gateways may serve to transfer local tacit knowledge into international forums, which may have limited or no positive effects on the local competitiveness level. As a third option, rather than acting as gateways bridging the local and the global, they may have limited local connections while preferring to interact mostly with global players and transmitting all of their gains from international collaboration projects to other foreign partners.

In the light of these statements, the paper is organized around the following research questions: Within the framework of Turkish participation in EU FP6 IST projects and other international collaboration projects does participation in international R&D networks create local buzz in Turkey? How can the profiles of participant Turkish ICT researchers be framed in terms of their significance in focus on local buzz and global pipelines? How the differences or similarities in the degree of global/local base be explained at a researcher level? How leading Turkish universities are constructing the mix of international versus local focus? What kind of policy implications can be framed in terms of the findings of the study?

To answer these questions, both qualitative and quantitative methods are applied within the time frame of 2003–2012, focusing on global and local buzz generated by Turkish ICT researchers that take part in EU-funded R&D projects and other international projects funded by TUBITAK. Different than EU level studies on ICT research such as Malerba, Vonortas, Breschi & Cassi (2006), this study brings together the national and international portfolios and matches them to set the degrees of localization versus globalization at researcher level. Therefore, project portfolios of ICT researchers are divided and analyzed within two time intervals. First period is between 2003 and 2006 which encompasses the timeframe of FP6. Similarly, second period covers the period after finalization of FP6 till July 2013.

In order to obtain insights regarding the paths followed after participating into international collaboration, descriptive analysis linking different data sets are performed prior to generation of a taxonomy to map the density of global versus local focus of researchers. Similar to Graf (2011) the taxonomy is formed based on four groups while arguing that different groups have different research outputs in a certain period of time. This argument is tested on the basis of key indicators like international or national project density, publication output, involvement in national governance bodies, and contribution to R&D capacity development in private sector for the period 2007-2013. Using the two-sample t-test differences or similarities among the groups is analysed.

After justification of the four groups for positioning the global and local based project portfolios of researchers, the study focuses to find statistically significant answers on why such grouping is there. This part holistically covers the period between 2003 and 2013 without dividing into two time intervals and traces the backgrounds of researchers while questioning the similarities and differences in PhD education, publication outputs before 2003, research ecosystem of the university and work experience after PhD fulfillment.

The last parts of the study are constructed with findings of in-depth interviews and focus groups which assist for setting policy recommendations to exploit the synergy between global pipelines and local buzz for the benefit of a national innovation ecosystem.

BRIDGING NETWORKS LITERATURE WITH LOCAL BUZZ-GLOBAL PIPELINES PHENOMENON

Network studies have gained popularity in the academic world. The number of papers about the networks formed under EU Framework Programs has risen, as well. Breschi & Cusmano (2004), Barber, Paier & Scherngell, (2009), Roediger-Schulga & Dachs (2006), Cabo (1999), Roediger-Schulga & Barber (2006) and Ortega & Aguillo (2010) are some examples of such studies. Derived from the small world phenomenon (high clustering and short average relational distances), most studies assume perfect knowledge flow among the partners of a network, which is not the case in reality. Moreover, studies focused on EU programs are conducted at the supranational level and leave unaddressed issues related to fluidity of knowledge flows between the local actors of the innovation system - the firms, universities and research institutions and the people at national level. EU level studies are extensively focused on the core of networks while little effort is made to understand the impact of EU networks on periphery.

Contemporary studies on European networks generally focus on a partnership structure as a whole rather than investigating the future performance of different nodes in research networks. In contrary to well-known approaches, looking from the perspective of less-connected nodes of a network could lead to alternative findings which may challenge the contemporary understanding. Such kind of focus may provide an opportunity to expose the nonlinearity of knowledge flows from international collaboration and also local deployment dynamics of collaborative research at international level.

The way of handling globalization versus localization or flattening versus spikiness is affected mainly by the political sphere. Such controversial approaches to economic geography and spatial economic are clarified by Christopherson, Garretsen & Martin (2008) as follows:

More 'globalized' world brings different views as to what globalizations means and whether it is a trend for good or ill. Those on the neoliberal right are typically pro-globalization, arguing that it has opened up markets across the globe, that it is a force for spreading opportunity and wealth across nations and that the intensification of competition it engenders stimulates innovation and productivity. Those on the political left tend to be anti-globalization, arguing it is a process dominated by global corporations that have become more powerful than nation states, that it increases inequality within advanced economies and undermines the ability of the world's poorer countries to improve social welfare or protect their natural environment (Christopherson, Garretsen & Martin, 2008, p. 1).

Castells (2011) states that globalization forces changes in our understanding of spatial concepts, assuming that anything can be located anywhere and thus moved somewhere with ease. Similarly, there are many studies that state that "innovation takes place in international networks reaching far beyond their region's boundaries" (Benneworth & Dassen, 2010).

Dominance of approaches favoring the international dimension of innovation creates a challenge for local policy-makers. On the other hand, the role of the local ecosystem as an important knowledge base to enhance local firms' capabilities of gaining advantageous positions in the global market has been widely recognized under concepts such as regional innovation systems, industrial clusters, localized learning and innovative milieus (Freeman, 1995; Cooke, Gomez, Uranga, & Etxebarria, 1997; Porter, 2000; Malmberg & Maskell, 2006).

Besides the black and white sides of this debate, there are empirical analyses that exhibit trends towards both increasing globalization and localization (Trippl, Tödtling, & Lengauer, 2009). Similarly, the necessity for both strong local and global interactions is highlighted in a study of a high-tech aerospace cluster in Taiwan (Eriksson, 2006). Tödtling & Trippl (2007) find that the Austrian biotechnology sector needs local-level and global-level exchanges simultaneously.

In this paper it is argued that the dichotomy of "local buzz and global pipelines" (Bathelt, Malmberg & Maskell, 2004) should be replaced with a more balanced approach blending both in the basket of knowledge creation. The local buzz–global pipelines approach argues that local interaction or 'buzz' and interaction through trans-local 'pipelines' create a dynamic process of learning, knowledge production and innovation that is central to understanding a cluster's success (Bathelt, 2007).

Further investigation is required about the outcomes of international collaboration on local research capacity upgrading. The literature highlights that strengthening the local research capacity of developing countries relies on knowledge networks that are connected both locally and globally (Lall, 2001; Marin & Bell, 2006; Narula & Duning, 2000; Barnard, Cowan & Müller, 2012). Starting from 2003, thanks to the gained access for participation in European networks and increased support of TUBITAK for international collaboration projects, many researchers were engaged more extensively in global research activities, but the outcomes of the initiatives remains to be analyzed. Going beyond the boundaries of the project networks involved it is required to study how researchers manages global versus local trade-off and potential heterogeneities at research level in creating scientific outputş. These concepts can be handled within the context of the local buzz–global pipelines framework, which emphasizes both the need for enhanced local networks and strong extra-local or global linkages while paving the way to balance them all (Maskell, Bathelt, & Malmberg, 2006). The approach argues that local interaction or 'buzz' and interaction through trans-local 'pipelines' create a dynamic process of learning, knowledge production and innovation that is central to understand a cluster's success (Bathelt, 2007).

In order to unlock the gains from international research collaboration and their relation to future outputs of researchers, there is a need to reveal the dynamics of researchers and main drivers to have a strong project portfolio at both national and international level. Such study cannot be built on quantitative analysis only and it requires in-depth analysis as well. In order to develop recommendations for future policies, in-depth interviews and focus group meetings are essential to assist to exploit the open issues to create synergy between global pipelines and local buzz for the benefit of a national innovation ecosystem

METHODOLOGY OF RESEARCH

This paper uses a mixed methodology combining qualitative and quantitative approaches. The quantitative method makes possible to analyze the similarities and differences in their research outputs for selected groups of researchers; while qualitative part which is complementary to quantitative study provides insights into managing the mix of researchers from different categories and also how Turkish research ecosystem influences or may influence the outcome of researchers by applying new polices.

The objective of this research is to understand the collaboration dynamics of Turkish ICT researchers engaged in international researchers and to see whether they create local dynamism at individual level. Moreover, the study put special interest to Turkish university participation to FP6, in other words on participants originally funded by the European Commission between 2003 and 2006.

The paper is based on data of 79 Turkish ICT researchers who were engaged in at least one international project based collaboration activity in a timeline between 2003 and 2006. These individual researchers constitute the target population of the study. A target population is the complete collection of researchers we want to learn something about and also we should note that the choice of target population affects the statistics that result from data (Lohr, 2009). The unit of analysis in this study is the project portfolio of a Turkish ICT researcher. If a project is funded by FP6 Information Society Technologies sub-theme or Electrical, Electronics and Informatics Research Support Group of TUBITAK it is considered that this is an ICT project. In line with this private sector participants from Turkey were disregarded from our framework since they are funded at firm level. However, the funded projects of researchers from private sectors under Electrical, Electronics and Informatics Research Support Group of TUBITAK was not eliminated since they are funded at researcher level and firms in such projects acts as hosting institution rather than a performing body.

It is also crucial to define what we understand from international collaboration. It should be noted that here we mean project based collaboration which exceeds the national boundaries and funded by an authority. In this study the international project based actions are defined as being a partner in a funded European FP6 project or international collaboration projects funded by TUBITAK which started between 2003 and 2006.

Towards Defining Heterogeneous Groups of ICT Researchers

Methodically, in line with the global pipelines-local buzz literature (Bathelt, Malmberg & Maskell 2004; Maskell, Bathelt & Malmberg, 2006; Gertler & Levitte, 2005; Moodysson, 2008; Trippl, Tödtling, & Lengauer, 2009, Grabher & Ibert, 2013) it is expected that the agents which constitute the population show heterogeneous features where some researchers have extensive international actions, while some are locally focused and others are balanced in terms of taking part in global and local collaboration projects. This is also in parallel with the literature on social networks where the agents holding a brokering position between two groups of actors are defined as gatekeepers (Gould & Fernandez, 1989; Graf & Krüger, 2011, Graf, 2011, Foster, Borgatti & Jones, 2011). Therefore, we framed a taxonomy based on data of Turkish researchers participating into at least one international ICT project funded by academic funding department of TUBITAK or European Commission between 2003 and 2006. Based on Graf (2011) we divide the researchers into two main groups where some of them are internal oriented while others are external oriented actors. Therefore we can argue that some agents will perform below the average in terms of number of international projects while they have more project involvement in national level or vice versa.

Based on the literature (Graf, 2011; Dubois, Copus & Hedström, 2012; Akçomak, Akdeve & Fındık, 2013), we can create a simple typology to categorize actors in four sub-groups in terms of their intensity in local and international collaboration where we can expect differentiation in scientific outputs or performance (in a given time interval) among different categories.

Following the works of Akçomak, Akdeve & Fındık, (2013) and Graf (2011) obtaining two dimensional degrees from the matching and weighted sums allows mapping the researchers' positioning. The two dimensional data can be plot on a two-dimensional Cartesian system where the data are divided into quadrants based on the mean of the variables, in our case which are the degrees of international and local engagements respectively. Using Graf (2011)'s typology where actors (i.e. Researchers in our case) are categorised in terms of their intensity of internal and external relations (Figure 1).

Figure 1. Taxonomy of ICT researchers in Turkey in terms of degrees of external relations and internal relations (Adapted from Graf, 2011)

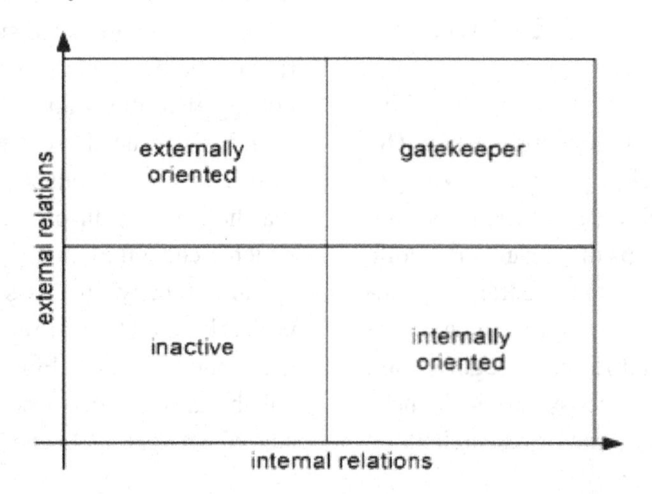

Table 1. Descriptive Statistics on International Project Portfolios

Int. Project Portfolio	Group	Frequency	Median	Mean	Std. Dev.	Min.	Max.
Gatekeeper	I	18	212,5	265,3	161,6	150	775
Externally oriented	II	13	150	189,4	65,3	150	300
Internally oriented	IV	17	125	99,3	31,7	62,5	125
Inactive	III	31	62,5	84,7	30,4	62,5	125
Total		79	125	146,2	111,0	62,5	775

Table 2. Descriptive Statistics on Local (National) Project Portfolios

Local Project Portfolio	Group	Frequency	Median	Mean	Std. Dev.	Min.	Max.
Gatekeeper	I	18	100	106,4	58,9	50	300
Externally oriented	II	13	0	0	0	0	0
Internally oriented	IV	17	100	98,8	39,8	50	200
Inactive	III	31	0	0	0	0	0
Total		79	0	45,5	60,6	0	300

Descriptive statistics related to the distribution of intensity of internal and external relations are provided in Table 1 and 2 respectively.

According to the applied sampling design which based on separating the population into four categories, where Group I is called gatekeepers, Group II externally oriented researchers, Group III inactive researchers and Group IV as internally oriented researchers. Below the features of each category are explained briefly:

- **Gatekeepers:** While they are engaged in international collaboration above the mean value, they simultaneously lead at least one nation-wide project.
- **Externally Oriented Researchers:** They are totally internationally focused for the period between 2003 and 2006. Although they have only international projects, their weights are mostly less-than-gatekeepers who used to manage national and international projects.
- **Inactive Researchers:** Bulk of researchers is fitting in this group. They are mostly contributors to funded projects, rather than being investigators of the projects. Their weights lay below the mean values of both axes.
- **Internally Oriented Researchers:** They are engaged in international projects but they are mostly inward looking researchers in the years 2003 and 2006.

Quantitative Analysis

It is argued that scientific outputs of these groups are not same in a given period. We test this argument on the basis of key indicators for the period 2007-2013. Scientific outputs of the researchers were traced for the period 2007-2013 with respect to each group's international project portfolio, international project portfolio, publication output, involvement in national governance bodies and contribution to R&D capacity development in private sector.

Differences or similarities among the groups are detected through two-sample t-test. Multiple t-tests are performed to compare the means of these four groups separately, and to understand which groups are different at all. There are three different ways to construct the hypothesis for comparing the means of two independent samples through traditional hypothesis testing. These are one tailed t-test (right-tailed and left-tailed) and two-tailed t-test. Two-tailed t-test considers the extreme effect in both directions whereas one-tailed t-test considers it for only one direction. Here, two-tailed t-test is preferred instead of one-tailed t-test not to miss the effect in the untested direction and see the total extreme effect in both directions. Therefore, the null hypothesis is tested where means of two groups are equal versus the alternative one assuming they are different as given below:

$$H_0 : \mu_1 \quad \mu_2$$

$$H_1 : \mu_1 \, / \, \mu_2$$

There are also two different options for the use of t-test. One of them is used when the variances of the populations are not equal, and the other one is used when they are equal. The formulas are given below for both options respectively.

$$\frac{\left(\bar{X}_1 \ \bar{X}_2\right)\left(\mu_1 \ \mu_2\right)}{\sqrt{\frac{s_1^2}{n_1} \,|\, \frac{s_2^2}{n_2}}},$$

$$degrees\ of\ freedom : smaller\ of\ n_1 1\ or\ n_2 1$$

$$\frac{\left(\bar{X}_1 \ \bar{X}_2\right)\left(\mu_1 \ \mu_2\right)}{\sqrt{\frac{\left(\Re_1 \ 1\right)s_1^2 \,|\, \left(\Re_2 \ 1\right)s_2^2}{n_1 \,|\, n_2 \ 2}}\sqrt{\frac{1}{\Re_1} \,|\, \frac{1}{n_2}}},$$

$$degrees\ of\ freedom : n_1 \,|\, n_2 \ 2$$

If the positive critical t-value for the defined significance level is smaller than the positive t value calculated in above formulas or if the negative critical t-value for the defined significance level is greater than the negative t value calculated in above formulas, then one can claim that there is enough evidence to reject the null hypothesis $\left(H_0\right)$.

To determine which formula is appropriate for using t-test, f-test should be performed to check whether the variances are equal or not. In f-test, the null hypothesis is the equality of the variances of two populations, and the formula is the ratio of two variances with $n_1 - 1$ and $n_2 - 1$ degrees of freedom for the numerator and the denominator respectively. The results of f-tests and t-tests are plotted in Table 3.

Involvement in National Governance Bodies

Here we test whether internationally engaged researchers are contributing to national decision making and monitoring processes regarding academic research projects for the period between 2007 and 2013. We do reject null hypothesis for the following comparisons: gatekeepers and internally oriented researchers, externally oriented researchers and internally oriented researchers, externally oriented researchers and inactive researchers. Therefore we use two different formulas to perform T-test. After F-test, T-test is performed and we find that concerning the involvement in decision making processes of TUBITAK, gatekeepers and internally focused researchers are not different at 0.05 significance level. Also, the performance of externally oriented and inactive researchers is not different at 0.05 significance level as well.

These findings imply that, involvement of gatekeepers and internally focused researchers in the assessment processes of TUBITAK are more common than the other two groups. Those who are not active at the local level, in other words, those who are only active in the international dimension did not pay much attention for being evaluator or reviewer for TUBTAK funded academic projects.

Table 3. Summary of F-tests and T-tests

		f-Test for Variance Comparison			t-Test for Mean Comparison				
		Externally Oriented	Internally Oriented	Inactive	Externally Oriented	Internally Oriented	Inactive	Mean	STDEV
Involvement in National Governance Bodies	Gatekeepers	0.046	0.6	0	0	0.38	0	8.2	5.4
	Externally Oriented		0.12	0.64		0	0.71	1.5	3
	Internally Oriented			0.1			0	6.6	4.7
	Inactive							1.2	4.7
Contribution to R&D Capacity Development in Private Sector	Gatekeepers	0.02	0.09	0.1	0.01	0.75	0	23.2	19.3
	Externally Oriented		0	0.19		0.11	0.76	7.6	9.6
	Internally Oriented			0		0.07		20.5	29.4
	Inactive							6.3	13.8
Density of National Projects	Gatekeepers	0.2	0.64	0	0.09	0.55	0.01	84.6	86.7
	Externally Oriented		0.4	0.18		0.22	0.28	35	60.3
	Internally Oriented			0.01			0.02	67.6	76.9
	Inactive							17.1	44.7
Density of International Projects	Gatekeepers	0.96	0.3	0	0.81	0.32	0.01	52.8	65.1
	Externally Oriented		0.31	0		0.51	0.06	47.1	65.4
	Internally Oriented			0.08			0.09	33.1	50
	Inactive							8.9	34.5
Publication Output	Gatekeepers	0.00	0.00	0.00	0.07	0.09	0.02	43.4	49
	Externally Oriented		0.3	0.12		0.85	0.26	18.5	17.4
	Internally Oriented			0.69			0.12	19.6	13.1
	Inactive							12.5	12.4

In other words, it can be said that researchers only engaged internationally do not present dynamism to participate in national research governance mechanisms. They look more isolated.

Researchers active in both local and global level show extremely high interest to take part in the national governance systems. Wherever possible, the researchers in this kind of want to be active. They bring suggestions, but also share their problems. But no matter what they do not offend against the system.

Contribution to R&D Capacity Development in Private Sector

Another indicator we test in tracking the performance of four groups is researchers' contribution to R&D capacity development programs. Here, in a similar way, we analyze the similarities and differences of four groups regarding their data on contributing the capacity enhancement of Turkish private sector. Initially, F-test is performed which is followed by T-test for each pairs of groups.

The findings say that gatekeepers and internally oriented researchers; externally oriented and inactive researchers; externally oriented and internally oriented researchers are not different at 0.1 significance level. The researchers who are only active globally, surprisingly, tend to contribute on deployment of R&D in private sector (previous analysis stated that those same group of researchers were that much effective in governance mechanism of academic programs at the 5% significance level). This trend is not as strong as gatekeepers or internally oriented researchers, but this group is not indifferent to contribute to R&D processes in the industry. It seems wiser to encourage these people to contribute on private sector R&D rather than the governance processes for the management of academic R&D funding mechanisms in Turkey.

Density of National Projects

To find the density of national projects of a researcher, the track record (2007-2013) of each researcher in national academic research programs is matched with its relevant groups. Then, a weighted sum corresponding to a degree of local dynamism is calculated for each researcher.

Based on the results we can say that there is enough evidence to reject the null hypothesis for the means of gatekeepers and externally oriented researchers at 0,10 significance level; and also for gatekeepers and inactive researchers, internally oriented researchers and inactive researchers At 0,05 significance level.

We have enough evidence to claim that gatekeepers and internally oriented researchers perform better on a project basis at national level. Those who are active in both global and local are going ahead in this category as well. Externally oriented researchers and inactive researcher in this category are not having significant visibility in national projects between 2007 and 2013.

Density of International Projects

Following the similar steps done for comparing the densities of national projects, here at initial stage raw data of international project performance covering the period between 2007 and 2013 of the population is weighted based on a project type and accomplished roles in the projects. After getting the weighted scores, F-tests and T-test are performed to compare the means of four groups with respect to their international project performance.

International project performance analysis reveals a striking result. Surprisingly, researchers who were active only at local basis between 2003 and 2006, increased their international project performance between 2007 and 2013. We cannot reject the null hypothesis for the mean comparisons three cases: Gatekeepers and Externally Oriented researchers, Gatekeepers and Internally Oriented Researchers, Externally Oriented Researchers and Internally Oriented Researchers. Naturally, gatekeepers and externally oriented researchers is leading this category again. As a result, both global and local in the title continues to be the leading researchers in carrying out the project. As a result, gatekeeper researchers are continues to be a pioneer under that heading as well.

Publication Output

In this section four groups are compared with respect to their publication outputs between 2007-2013.

Mean comparisons of publication data presents an interesting situation. Researchers interacting both globally and locally are publishing more than other three groups. This led us to argue that the high number of interactions, can link to access more information. The other three groups do not differ significantly in scientific publishing performance. The findings state that statistically Externally Oriented, Internally Oriented, and Inactive Researchers are not different at 5% significance level.

Factors Related with Strong Project Portfolio at Global and Local Levels

After we have justified that four groups show differences in global and local connectedness, the study focuses on finding out statistically significant answers on why such grouping is there. At this stage, the review was performed on backgrounds of the researchers that make the population of the study. In another words this section of the paper is aiming to explore individual and organizational level factors influencing to have a strong project portfolio at both national and international levels.

This part holistically covers the period between 2003 and 2013 without dividing into two time intervals and traces the backgrounds of researchers while questioning the similarities and differences in PhD education, publication outputs before 2003, holding a position at one of best performing Turkish universities and overseas work experience after PhD fulfilment.

The first one is about whether holding a PhD degree from a university which is listed among top 400 universities at Times Higher Education World University Ranking makes difference in the project performance of ICT researchers. The second one includes bibliometric data authored by ICT scientists from our population which are published before 2003, in other words it covers the publication outputs which are published prior to period of our study. The third one is related to holding a position at one of best performing Turkish universities. It is supposed that being a member of an advanced research ecosystem will enhance the project outputs of the ICT researchers. And the fourth one is about the overseas work experience of the researchers after the fulfilment of PhD. These analyses are focused on investing the project portfolio of researchers with each factor mentioned above. Therefore, again multiple t-tests are performed to compare the means of the four groups (gatekeepers, externally oriented

Table 4. F-tests and T-tests for Factors Related with Strong Project Portfolio

		f-Test for Variance Comparison			t-Test for Mean Comparison				
		Externally Oriented	Internally Oriented	Inactive	Externally Oriented	Internally Oriented	Inactive	Mean	STDEV
PhD Education	Gatekeepers	0.9	0.6	0.16	0.94	0.15	0.03	71	24.8
	Externally Oriented		0.58	0.37		0.2	0.11	70.2	25.2
	Internally Oriented			0.05			0	83.2	21.6
	Inactive							48.1	35.1
Publications Before 2003	Gatekeepers	0.86	0.99	0.16	0.68	0.52	0.06	19.1	18.1
	Externally Oriented		0.86	0.29		0.87	0.19	16	16.8
	Internally Oriented			0.17			0.26	14.7	18.1
	Inactive							8	12.2
Position at Best Turkish Uni.	Gatekeepers	0.12	0.63	0.1	0.09	0.74	0	0.9	0.3
	Externally Oriented		0.24	0.76		0.16	0.19	0.6	0.5
	Internally Oriented			0.24			0	0.8	0.4
	Inactive							0.4	0.5
Overseas Work Experience	Gatekeepers	0.92	0.92	0.45	0.16	0.198	0.02	0.6	0.5
	Externally Oriented		0.98	0.62		0.72	0.72	0.3	0.5
	Internally Oriented			0.51			0.34	0.4	0.5
	Inactive							0.2	0.4

researchers, internally oriented researchers, inactive researchers) for each of the four factors in order to check whether there is relationship between researcher's current standing and his/her mentioned background information. The results are listed in Table 4.

Quality of PhD Education

Here, it is examined whether there is a significant relationship between quality of the PhD degree of a researcher and his project performance. The level of the quality of the university from where a researcher got his PhD degree is obtained by combining the values of two indexes namely the Times Higher Education World University Ranking and academic parts of the Entrepreneurial and Innovative University Index in Turkey.

One time, in order to have a considerable project portfolio at both national and international levels, it is envisaged that quality of the university where the doctoral degree is received should above the average. The findings show that the researcher profiles in first three groups do not differ in terms the quality of the university where the PhD education is fulfilled. While the means for gatekeepers, externally oriented researchers and internally oriented researchers are close to each other, the education background of inactive researchers is not as good as the other three groups.

It is found that in the first three groups' doctoral education roots of the researchers show similarities. However it is not possible to reveal the sources of differences in their performance quantitatively. We need to make qualitative interviews in order find evidences for such differences. 79% of the researchers from the first three groups completed their PhDs in Turkey or abroad in a university which is listed in the Times Higher Education World University Ranking. Therefore the doctoral education cannot be stated as a distinguishing feature for researchers among four groups.

Publications Before 2003

The publication analysis has been conducted for the years prior to the period of 2003-2013. Therefore similar study was performed to see whether there is a relationship between construction of the four groups with respect to the project performance of researchers and prior publication performance of the same researchers. After conducting the F-tests and T-tests for six possible pairs of groups, we found that past publication performance does not seem to relate the project performance where the results are not statistically significant. It means that there are other reasons behind the differences in the ten years project performing capacity of the ICT researchers.

Holding a Position at One of Best Performing Turkish Universities

According to the findings of our descriptive analysis 69% of the international projects in ICT are executed by six universities which are METU, Bilkent University, Bosphorus University, ITU, Koç University and Sabancı University. Therefore we test whether holding a position in one these six universities makes statistically significant difference in the project portfolios of the four groups. We set "Holding a Position at One of Best Performing six Universities" as a dummy variable.

Here we find that means of gatekeepers and internally oriented researchers are not different at 0.05 significance level. Similarly the means of externally oriented and inactive researchers not different at 0.05 significance level as well. Similarities in the means of gatekeepers and internally oriented researchers show that they are working at similar universities. So the two groups are consisting of the researchers of the most successful six universities. Despite the fact that those two groups are doing research at similar universities, differences in their performance needs to be examined more deeply.

Interestingly, the group conducting only international activities resemblances to those who are less active researchers. This finding reinforces our view that the aptitudes of externally engaged researchers need to be investigated in detail.

Overseas Work Experience

Overseas work experience is referring amount of working time abroad which spent for post-doctoral education in academic institutions or professional experience in private sector. Looking of the overseas working experience of the population, a striking result comes out: 58% of gatekeepers have more than 2.5 years international work experience. Thanks to the contribution of overseas work experiences of these individuals it is estimated that they are able to sustain their international connections.

In the meantime, global work experiences of those involved only in international research projects is below than our initial expectations. In fact, researchers who work at the only local level put effort in developing additional international links. Looking at this point, it can be said that locally engaged researchers are progressing better that externally oriented researchers in terms of rate of extending international linkages.

Findings from Quantitative Analysis

We found that significant portion of researchers engaged strongly in international co-operation is active at the local as well. Even they provide a significant contribution to their research environment within the case of involvement in governance mechanisms from academic research programs and contribution to R&D capacity development in the private sector.

A small fraction of researchers are visible only in externally oriented actions. It seems that they are lacking a focus on the national basis. Researchers active only on a national basis in the period 2003-2006, showed a progress at international level. The quantitative findings state after a while such researchers wanted to interact externally with the global players.

So, why such grouping is happening? The most meaningful results we found that it is related with overseas work experience and the ecosystem conditions of the university in Turkey where they work. A suitable research climate established by a University is a notable argument for better project performance at both levels. It is also expected that such universities probably are following strategies and they have certain principles for choosing the most suitable academic profiles.

The basic question which constitutes the starting point of the study was how much ICT researchers engaged in international collaboration are active at national basis. Quite frankly, it was expected that a lot of these people were not concerned significantly about national issues. It can be said that most of the quantitative results are in contrary to initial expectations.

The most active makers of international collaboration for the period of 2003-2006, were also the researchers who led the national basis with respect to their national project portfolio. Coupled with engagements in strengthening the public and private sector research capacity as well, this situation continued in the period 2007-2013. Taking into account these findings in can be said that gatekeepers are the most valuable and efficient mass of researchers in ICT sector in Turkey.

Looking at the 10-year performance of those who are engaged only global collaboration (in the period 2003-2006), they are staying relatively behind the gatekeepers and internally oriented researchers and the number of researchers in this group is disappearing slightly.

The results show that researchers are active mostly on a national basis in the period 2003-2006, have taken steps to improve their international co-operation activities in 2007-2013. This finding corresponds to the national vision to strengthen international ties and to make Turkey a part of European Research Area and being open to rest of the world. It is argued that enhancements of international links should be triggered with additional steps in following years, because the descriptive analysis clearly pictured that most of the Turkish universities are lacking project based ties with their counterparts abroad.

Initially it was expected that some universities might have originally been more isolated than others, because of infrastructure, collaboration records of its researchers and lack of roots favoring the collaborative research culture. The findings are relevant with initial thoughts, where the research capacity of a university is statistically significant to make better project performance. However, differences in outputs of researchers with similar backgrounds who are holding a position in a same university is an open area for further questioning in in-depth interviews. The only valuable quantitative finding at an individual level is about the relationship between project performance and post-doctoral research or professional work experience abroad. Those who have over 2.5 years abroad other than PhD study are more appetite than others in terms of project development. Moreover, in the case of six universities the institutional research ecosystem can also contribute to find relevant expressions about the factors influencing the project performance. However we should also note that the international collaboration level of other universities is very low.

Qualitative Analysis

This research is about the further collaboration dynamics and research related performance of ICT researchers engaged in international collaboration. Data limitations prohibit benefiting fully from quantitative methods, so qualitative methods are complementary to understand the processes about local versus international collaboration, and also the determinants lying behind the heterogeneous performance of researchers with similar backgrounds. Moreover, prior research deploying quantitative methods provided evidences on individual level which needs to investigate deeply on institutional level. Hence, in that part, a case study method has been implemented. According to Yin (1994) a case study is an empirical research that investigates a contemporary phenomenon within its real-life context. It provides the collection of detailed and multi-dimensional data about a small number of cases answer specific questions (Eisenhardt, 1989). Yin (1994) also states that evidence of multiple case studies is more convincing and therefore the study will be regarded as more robust.

In quantitative part we have justified that project performance of ICT researchers are heterogeneous, and so we have classified them into four groups in terms of combinations of local versus international projects. It is also shown that researchers engaged intensively in both levels are concentrated in few numbers of universities. Based on descriptive statistics it seen that six universities (METU, ITU, Koç, Sabancı, Bilkent and Bosphorus University) in Turkey have conducted 69% of all funded ICT projects which have international dimension. Initially it seems that they are clustered, but their intensity of project portfolios is heterogeneous at national and international levels. Hence, although they are presented as successful cases we have a mixture of universities, some are dedicated more for international collaboration; some are still locally oriented but somehow they are generating the biggest portion of the ICT project capacity of higher education in Turkey. Moreover, we need to understand why researchers with similar performance differ with respect to their project portfolio, so we need to capture the issues and attitudes relating with such kind of variations among researchers. Taking into account the open issues of coming from quantitative part, the qualitative study is based on semi-structured interviews focused on 6 university-level case studies. The main themes covered during the interviews are listed below:

- Policy for recruiting researchers.

- Motivations to conduct a research project.
- Trade-off concerning publishing versus conducting projects.
- Trade-off concerning national versus international collaboration.
- Performance based evaluation system.
- Reasons differences in performance of researchers with similar backgrounds.

Prior to each interview we have reviewed the quantitative findings about that university which provided ground for more detailed questions. For example in the case METU, we have questioned additionally the declining performance in international ICT collaboration, while in the case of Koç University we have tried to unlock policies behind the more intensive focus on international collaboration.

At an interview stage first we have tried to reach vice-rectors responsible for research policy, if not we shift to other related administrators responsible for the coordination of research at a university level or senior people knowing the dynamics of ICT departments at that university. Luckily we have interviewed with four vice rectors, one contact point for handling relations with the governmental institutions, and one senior researcher who has deep understanding about history and dynamics at ICT departments of his university. The interviews were realized on the phone, at initial stage we have provided information about the findings from the quantitative part mentioning about the standing of their university.

In other words interviews were performed on a guided conversations basis; at the beginning we have provided the overall picture of study and its scope, and then continued with more detailed questions to get insights from the university representatives about institutional level policies, principles and strategies. We have tried to extend the conversations on a mutually agreed basis, because the probability of getting more useful information increases.

The length of interviews changed from 50 minutes to 2 hours. In order to get more insights none of the interviews were digitally recorded; but each valuable detail was noted simultaneously to the notebook. After each interview we carefully re-read transcribed text and shared through e-mails with advisor of the study to allow timely recommendations regarding the follow up steps. Sharing the details about each interview provided an opportunity to revise and update the general findings from the in-depth analysis. During the coding phase grounded theory building approach is followed (Glaser & Strauss, 2009; Eisenhardt, 1989). We primarily followed Eisenhardt (1989), who said: "The inductive case method suits

Figure 2. Conceptual model of grounded theory (Source: Whetten, 2000)

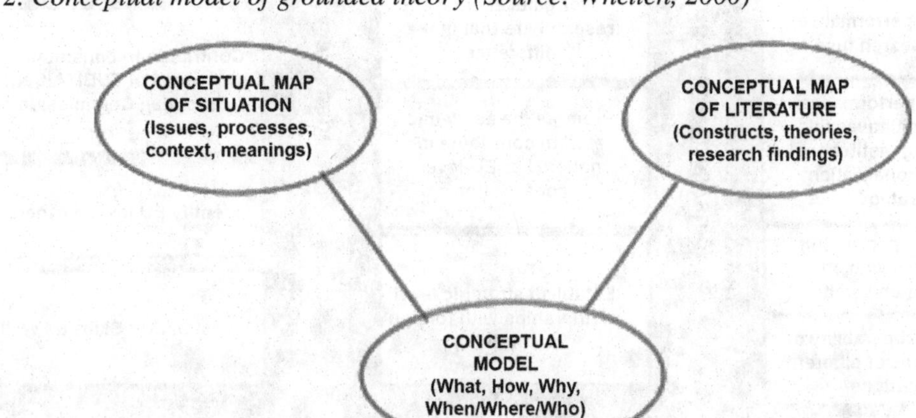

research that poses 'how' or 'why' questions, involves complex causal links, and seeks to generate novel theory that is empirically testable". In that phase Uzzi (1996) was deeply analyzed. During the interpretation of findings, Whetten (2000) was followed as well (Figure 3).

Linking the conceptual issues with empirical findings was a kind of bridging activity covering the literature on European R&D networks, research policies for higher education, STI indicators, local buzz-global pipelines, etc.

Findings from Qualitative Analysis

Based on the interviews findings from qualitative analysis were categorized into six levels (Table 5) aiming to present and discuss findings of the qualitative research from a policy making perspective.

POLICY RECOMMENDATIONS

This paper has proposed and empirically examined the taxonomy of local buzz and global pipelines in the context of ICT research in an emerging economy. In this part, a multi-level framework will be incorporated with the emphasis on individual skills and practices at institutional and national bases. Here, we review the main findings of the research and discuss policy options at three levels (micro, meso and macro levels).

The aim of designing policy recommendations is to increase the number of ICT gatekeepers in higher education sector and to improve the added value of ICT ecosystem. Some implications derived from the study can be summarised as follows:

Figure 3. Policy recommendations at three levels (macro, meso, micro)

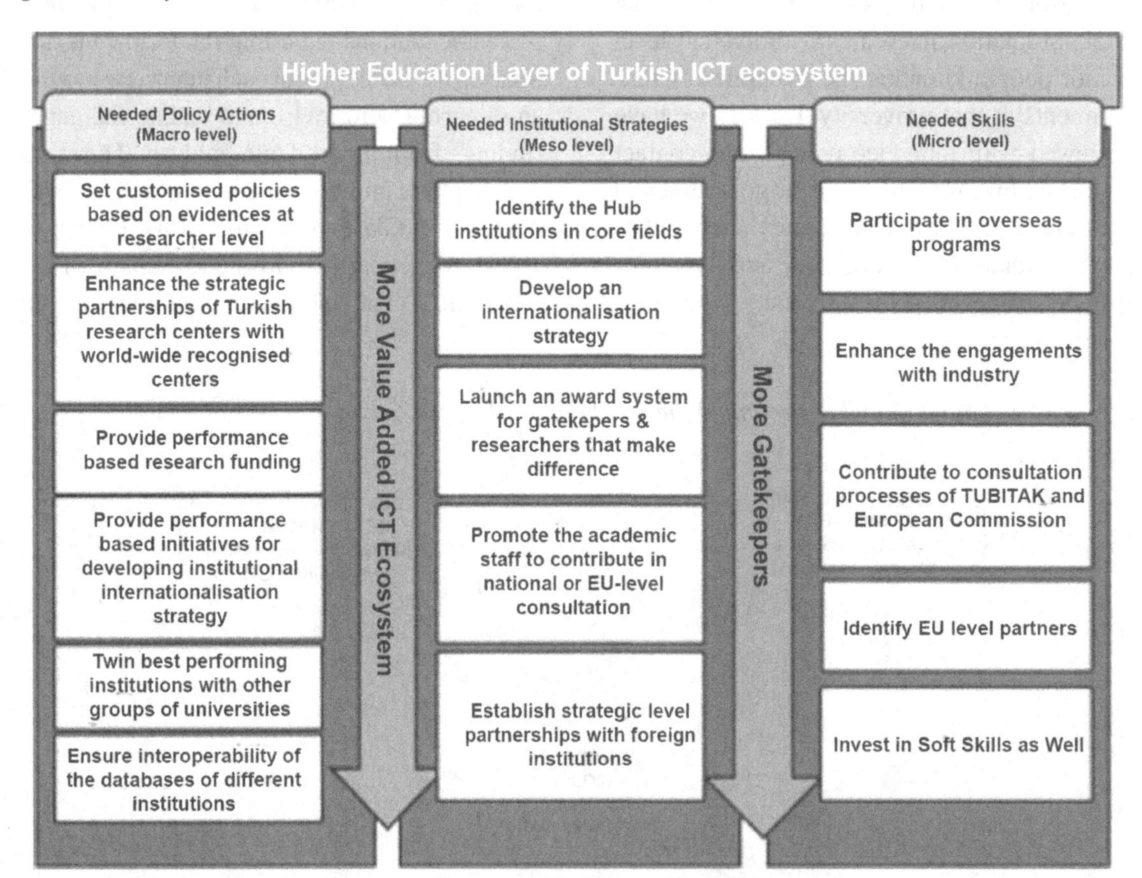

Table 5. Findings of the qualitative study

	Recruitment Policy	Motivations for Research	Publishing vs Projects	National vs International Engagements	Performance Based Evaluation	Explanations for Differences in Research Outputs
Bilkent University	Strict rules for selecting researchers (i.e. publications in high-impact journals, reference letters) Marie Curie seen as useful tool to attract talents	Evaluation committee for seeking the research components Softening the rules because of entrepreneurship index Access to EU level infrastructures Awareness raising campaign leaded by the Rector Projects offers carrots like best graduates and incentive bonus	Optimal trade-off between publishing and research projects Special care for potential star scientists Technology and product oriented projects seen as strategic	Recently adopting strategies for shifting their focus to national projects because of pragmatic reasons (less bureaucratic burdens, ease to get funding, new mechanisms for big projects) Initial steps to set strategic initiatives with private sector (e.g AVEA)	Merit based performance system Salaries are flexible depends on scientific outputs A young Asst.Prof could receive more salary than a senior Prof.	It should be elaborated case by case -having a big team triggers the needs for projects in order to sustain -Focusing in one and only one specific topic (i.e 3DTV)
Bosphorus University	Rather than a policy they have principles coming from the historical roots of the university (do not recruit graduates w/ external experience, need for consensus for recruiting a certain researcher, sustaining the independence of the university)	Competition triggers the motivations for having funded projects Matching fund for pre-project phases	Primary focus for publishing papers BAP fund is enough for satisfying publishing requirements for academic tenure No favors for project makers	Projects are seen as engagement activities Indifferent among national vs international No priority to lead 1007 projects with societal objectives International projects preferred to 1007 projects A lack of institutional coordination for managing project portfolios	No need for performance based system, because not possible to change the salary	Personal factors and different career paths have an impact on research outputs: -entrepreneurial spirit -being engaged with networks (i.e international or industry linkages)
	Recruitment Policy	Motivations for research	Publishing vs Projects	National vs International Engagements	Performance Based Evaluation	Explanations for differences in research outputs
Sabancı University	Strict rules for selecting researchers ---competence level checking -consulting to prominent researchers -thematic area -Individual and independent research capability -non-academic working experience	Individual research funding based on performance -soft money -no punishment, just for motivation Stick and carrot approach for Assoc. Professors (3 or 5 assessments) Assessments create competition among researchers for funding opportunities	Dominant policy favoring publication Emerging policy on big projects (especially for defense sector)	No differentiation, but most successful in national projects No clear strategy for promoting international projects expect project money provided for time allocated in an international collaboration project. Overheads of FP projects are seen as attractive tool (Complaints about the national approach for not covering the overhead spending)	Well defined merit based performance system If performance is not satisfactory termination of the contract	Soft skills and personal factors have an impact on research outputs Moreover there are disgruntled researchers who are sceptical about the national system.

continued on following page

Table 5. Continued

	Recruitment Policy	Motivations for Research	Publishing vs Projects	National vs International Engagements	Performance Based Evaluation	Explanations for Differences in Research Outputs
Koç University	Policy to select right people while providing the appropriate ecosystem for research Strict rules for selecting researchers -being graduated from best universities -publications during the PhD study at journals w/ low acceptance rate -post-doc experience	No direct reward or punishment mechanisms It is important to select the best people and provide appropriate ground to play Start-up fund provided for the 1st year	Primary focus for publications at best journals However playing an important role in world class project also contribute to the tenure	Focus on world-class international projects Policy for collaborating with best research universities Engagement with industry is also important (1003 and 1007 programs provides good ground for collaboration with private sector)	Well defined merit based performance system If performance is not satisfactory termination of the contract	Two reasons: -Soft skills and personal factors (i.e. being a demanding researcher) -research discipline (some topics in ICT are theory-oriented while others are practice-oriented)
	Recruitment Policy	Motivations for research	Publishing vs Projects	National vs International Engagements	Performance Based Evaluation	Explanations for differences in research outputs
METU	Rather than an explicit policy they have principles coming from the historical roots of the university -dense network with graduates - job market paper presentation - a sense of belonging to METU and corporate culture	Competition triggers the motivations for having funded projects No clear strategy, but "research in the air" environment Guiding senior academics to engage with techno park companies Performance based department budgets for creating and sustaining linkages	Primary focus for publishing papers because of the tenure procedure (High impact publications triggers projects) But recently shifting to a differentiated policy assessing equal weights to academic research, teaching, entrepreneurship and engagement with society	Recently adopting strategies for shifting their focus to international projects and especially to Horizon 2020. The diminishing international collaboration reflected to drastic increase in national funds, a lack of institutional approaches to leverage multipliers and not having an international engagement strategy	Incentives for best performing researchers and departments rather than a tough performance system Publications, patents, theses, design of new courses, money generated from contract research are part of the incentive system.	Systemic reasons - lack of a strategic approaches to trigger internal collaboration (it is expected that central coordination will decrease such differences)
ITU	Rather than an explicit policy they have principles coming from the historical roots of the university (preferring researchers with PhD from abroad, being a preferred university because of its brand value and advantages of being in Istanbul)	No clear strategy for the promotion of research projects. Recently catalyzing the TTO offices to promote conducting research projects.	Indifferent between publications and projects An emerging priority issues is about patenting activities (they think that patents attributed to ITU researchers are very small)	Indifferent between national and international projects; no matter whether it is international or national it is important to bring funded projects. More successful in national projects Government does not follow balanced approaches between int. and national mechanisms (Too many national mechanisms)	No need for performance based system, because not possible to change the salary	Soft skills and personal factors (connections boost the international projects) Research experience in foreign countries (PhD fulfilled at a EU university increases the changes to find consortia to be funded by the EC)

1. The project-performing intensities of ICT researchers are heterogeneous. The empirical investigation suggests that there are significant differences in recent national and international project portfolios of Turkish ICT researchers that were involved in international collaboration between 2003 and 2006. Generally, the observed differences suggest the need for differentiated policies for different clusters concerning their degree of local and global focus. Thus, a holistic perspective which takes into account the variety of profiles should be adopted instead of one-size-fits-all policies.
2. Officials and policy-makers should be aware of such clusters of researchers that are just active in one dimension (who are active internally or externally only). More studies must be conducted focusing on different segments of the population. Several methods should be found to activate the potential of those performing under their potential.
3. Despite the growing funding for international collaboration in Turkey, the number universities engaged in ICT is still low.
4. Low level of collaboration under European Framework Programs should be addressed by internationalization strategies developed by universities that can be supported by public authorities on a performance basis.
5. The number of gatekeepers should be increased. Hence, policies that encourage international collaboration will contribute to the knowledge stock of the country since it is shown that gatekeepers create positive outcomes at the local base as well. Such policies should not limit the project involvement of gatekeepers at the national level. The need to remove quotas prohibiting managing more than two ARDEB-funded projects simultaneously is commonly mentioned by vice-rectors due to the fact there are qualified researchers who can manage more than two projects at the same time.
6. As shown in this study, only six Turkish universities are active in international ICT collaboration. The number of internationally active universities can be increased by twinning those universities with at least another six having the potential to be engaged in international activities.
7. In the previous ten years, the government invested heavily in research centers and central research laboratories. However, the international level of performance of those centers is negligible. Special policies to activate the potential of research centers are needed.
8. The number of project-based support mechanisms has been increased recently. There are several available tools that allow researchers to submit proposals and apply for grants. It is assumed that such a variety of tools increases the knowledge that is circulated. However, the governance mechanisms from which policy-makers can acquire valuable information are not sufficient. More mechanisms must be developed to get feedback from project investigators.

Based on the experiences shared during the in-depth interviews, several recommendations have emerged. These recommendations can be considered at the individual (micro), institutional (meso), and system (macro) levels, which are presented in Figure 3.

Macro-Level Policy Recommendations

Macro-level recommendations cover the nationwide policy issues regarding the ICT research in Turkey:

Set Customised Policies Based on Evidences at the Researcher Level

Often governments launch mechanisms to enhance project-performing culture or innovation capacity as a whole, where their objectives are very broad. Such mechanisms do not specify the needs of heterogeneous groups as stated in this study. Different approaches and policies should be developed for different researcher profiles, besides the more traditional one-size-fits-all policies. Such new types of policies must be based on evidence from data-mining studies at the researcher level. Instead of replacing all the current policy, a new kind of mixture of policies should find breadth in the policy-making sphere. Evidence-based policies rely on extensive data processing, such that there is a clear need to strengthen the infrastructure for storing and handling databases. It is believed that placing evidence-based approaches at the heart of policy-making will provide ground for ex ante impact analysis and then ease the measuring of the outcomes of the mechanisms.

Enhance the Strategic Partnerships with World-Wide Recognised Centres

Thirty-six per cent of ICT researchers of our population have been affiliated to a research center funded by Ministry of Development. It is expected that researchers working in these centers have the potential to establish more international linkages. Infrastructure and human power come together in these centers, and so possibility that these groups will be engaged in larger-scale projects is higher than in the other parts of the ICT ecosystem. The case of Boğaziçi University clearly indicates that infrastructure support for a research center provided an enabling environment, which boosted the number of international projects (for a 214% increase in number of international projects between 2007 and 2013). Based on their experience, a representative of Boğaziçi University states that "research centers should be triggered more to take a key and central role in the innovation system". In that sense, the South Korean and Singapore experiences are interesting because they set initiatives to draw the divisions of internationally leading research centers such as Max-Planck, Pasteur, and Fraunhofer to their countries.

For example, according to the National Research Foundation of Singapore (2013) under the Campus for Research Excellence and Technological Enterprise (CREATE) program, 10 research centers that are established in collaboration with leading universities in the world are supported in performing advanced research in specific fields. Centers that are supported under The CREATE Program have a budget that is available for human resources and research infrastructure. The first CREATE center was formed by an alliance with MIT followed by other leading universities to come to Singapore in the following timeframe. While the research that is performed by the CREATE centers does not directly aim for commercialization, this result can be attained with the assistance of the technology transfer offices. The patent rights that are obtained by the local (Singapore) universities and the foreign universities are realized on a 50%–50% basis. In the second phase of the CREATE program, it is expected that financial contribution from the private sector will be sought.

Such program can be launched in Turkey to support strategic level partnerships of national research centers funded by the Ministry of Development.

Provide Performance-Based Research Funding

It was particularly highlighted by the representatives of state universities that the current central system is prohibiting them from performing better in terms of research outputs, or, in other words one of the reasons for low levels of international performance is the burden regarding not being able to recruit staff to increase the visibility of the university at the EU level. Therefore, they want to be more autonomous in managing financial resources.

European Platform Higher Education Modernisation (2010) states that more autonomy should be linked to monitoring processes and fulfilment of research targets of universities. For example, New Zealand is assessing the research performance of tertiary education organisations and then funding them on the basis of Performance-Based Research Fund (The Tertiary Education Commission, 2015)

Similarly, in Turkish higher education system, more autonomy may not be granted unless the universities reach their targets set by the public authorities. Deploying wise practices may speed up the smooth transition into a performance-based system. Below, three semi-level proposals are made which could be put into practice via the Ministry of Finance, Ministry of Development, and TÜBİTAK:

- Conducting a competency assessment for all types of research institutions, starting from research centres settled at universities, funded by the Ministry of Development, and providing funding with respect to their competency level.
- Paying overhead based on different percentages with respect to the project portfolios of state and foundation universities
- Removing quotas for high-performance researchers in national research programs.

Provide Performance-Based Initiatives for the Preparation of Institutional Internationalization Strategies at Universities

In-depth interviews show that none of the universities have international engagement or internationalization strategies. They do not have clear targets regarding obtaining funds from programs like Horizon 2020; which means that they lack a strategy for international collaboration. Moreover, derived from the overall findings of the six interviews, disappointment regarding international collaboration is related to insufficient institutional structuring (i.e. separate branches at the universities for the coordination of research, burdens to recruit competent experts with non-academic backgrounds).

The efficiency of the governmental funding for international collaboration can become more inclusive if it is reflected strategically at the meso-level. The statistics show that 22 universities in Turkey constitute 91% of all international collaboration in ICT, while 69% of international collaboration is performed by only 6 universities. Therefore, in order to activate the international focus of Turkish universities, the government, on a performance basis, may provide support for developing international strategies.

Twinning the Best-Performing Institutions with Lagging Universities

As mentioned before, international collaboration in ICT is centered in six universities. In an environment where so many funds are available, other universities also need to enter the competition. Therefore, balanced trade-offs should be created between leading and laggard universities. Present findings state that universities like Kocaeli, Yıldız Teknik, Dokuz Eylül, Hacettepe, Fırat, Anadolu, TOBB ETÜ, İzmir Yüksek Teknoloji, Yeditepe, Gebze Yüksek Teknoloji, Ege, Süleyman Demirel, Işık, Erciyes, Pamukkale, and Özyeğin have the capacity to become engaged more intensively in international collaboration.

It is important to twin the best-performing universities primarily with those that have a capacity to conduct international collaboration. Such an effort would be most probably helpful in increasing the funds received from upcoming Horizon 2020 programs. If such twinning becomes successful, it will be coupled with pairs consisting of a university and a private sector company. It can be stated that not only do the inter-linkages between the private sector and successful universities in FP6 IST facilitate the participation of private sector actors in EU projects, but they also enable the management and maintenance of previously connected networks with the aid of the experience of the university actors. It can be argued that the most visible Turkish universities in the EU ICT ecosystem can play a pivotal role in transforming the Turkish private sector, and particularly SMEs, in the context of the Horizon 2020 programme. Therefore, enhancement of partnerships between successful Turkish universities like METU, Bilkent, Sabancı, and Koç and private sector institutions that perform research activities could be an alternative to trigger involvement in funded EU projects.

Ensure Interoperability of the Databases and Data Quality of Different Institutions

In this study, I have tried to match different sources. This was done mostly manually because there are no possible ways yet to combine researchers' data from different sources. Because of the present state of databases, we cannot always do exactly what we want. For example, it was not possible to properly match ICT researchers' name with their patent data on a chronological basis. Moreover, it was not possible to include the consultancy services provided by the population in public funded private sector R&D projects. Similarly, we could not benefit from bibliometrics on international collaboration dynamics of the population because of time limitations. In order to make better evidence-based policies, playing with and manipulating data ensuring the interoperability of the databases and data quality of different institutions is crucial. Therefore, comprehensive effort should be made toward developing sustainable systems to match different data sources and ensuring the availability of data for national and international collaboration dynamics.

Meso-Level Policy Recommendations

At the meso-level, five main recommendations for Turkish universities are listed:

Identify the Hub Institutions in Core Research Fields

One of the findings of the in-depth interviews is that the most successful universities do not have a clear view about what are the best possible EU-level partners with which to collaborate. Framework Program projects are heavily dominated by a small number of hub institutions including Fraunhofer, CNRS, the Ecole Polytechnique Federale de Lausanne, Philips, Nokia, Siemens, and France Telecom (Wagner et al., 2004; Malerba, Vonortas, Breschi & Cassi, 2006). These organizations serve to orchestrate research and facilitate the exchange of knowledge among peripheral groups. Hubs dominate both the connectivity between the research organizations from different participant countries, either member states or associated countries, and that between different technology areas and research disciplines (Johnston, Pestel, Mladenic, Grobelnik, & Stefan, 2003).Therefore, universities should make more effort to identify the best possible partners among central organizations that serve as "hubs" in FPs. There are useful sources like www.ist-world.org which provides information regarding the hubs in ICT at the EU level. After obtaining the initial reports, it is believed that universities can identify potential partner at EU level.

Develop an Internationalisation Strategy

It can be stated that accompanying actions were not effective enough to trigger Turkey's participation in FP7. For example, the TÜBİTAK EU Framework Coordination Office took part in seven FP6 projects (HAGRID, IST-MENTOR+,

IDEALIST34, Idealist7fp, IST World, EPIST, and CEEC IST NET) that aimed to help to increase, directly or indirectly, the participation of the country in FP6 IST. While the overall funding from FP7 increased 215% in comparison to FP6, ICT funding increased just 22%. This situation can be attributed to lack of institutional policies for international collaboration in ICT and also to trade-off between internationalization versus local consultancy options stressed by METU, İTÜ, and Boğaziçi University representatives. The current trade-off accommodates the risk of lock-in and lack of ability to update the knowledge stock if over-embeddedness becomes a reality in the Turkish ICT ecosystem. Therefore, comprehensive internationalization strategies at the institutional level are needed. This is a complementary recommendation to the macro-scale views presented in a previous section. Internationalization of the institutions should be seen as a capacity-building effort, to build more effective and sustainable impact at the national and international scales. As mentioned before, none of the six top institutions have an internationalization strategy, and just METU has preparations to build a special strategy for the upcoming Horizon 2020 program. Setting clear objectives and scanning the research potential at the university level can help to align target-oriented actions and will serve to enhance research outputs of the university. Such kinds of planning for the near future will also map clearly the upcoming openings, avoid missed opportunities, and set the ground to fill the gaps in the knowledge stock of recent dynamics in ICT research.

Launch an Award System for Gatekeepers and Researchers that Make a Difference

The METU case provides a useful feedback regarding rewarding the well-performing scientists and departments. The METU representative stated that "regardless of the money they receive as bonus, the awarding mechanism has a pushing role". He mentioned that "Your quartile of performance is shared with the others, so you push yourself to be better". Awards systems should be coupled with sharing best practices because it is a good way to improve research performance of lagging researchers by replicating successes throughout the university. At that point, the award mechanism of the University Economic Development Association (2015) could be a benchmark for universities willing to establish such types of incentives. The association has several categories of awards including:

- Talent Development
- Innovation and Entrepreneurship
- Community-Connected Campus
- Collaboration and Leadership
- Research and Analysis
- Talent Development
- Innovation and Entrepreneurship
- Community-Connected Campus
- Collaboration and Leadership
- Research and Analysis

Especially for the state universities, such mechanisms can be treated as performance tracking systems at individual and departmental levels.

Encourage Academic Staff to Contribute in National or EU-Level Consultation Mechanisms

The number of project-based support mechanisms has been increased recently. There are several available tools that allow researchers to submit proposals and apply for grants. It is assumed that such a variety of tools increases the knowledge that is circulated. TÜBİTAK and other institutes are trying to establish governance mechanisms for designing future policies. Recently the number of such mechanisms has started to grow rapidly. For example, from the beginning of 2013, TÜBİTAK conducted 23 consultations in several fields. Most of the researchers perceive them as fatiguing duties or works that do not add any value. It should be noted that most of new calls in the TÜBİTAK funding system are based on the outputs of the consultation processes, which are open for all research. Such types of new governance structures provide a window to influence future research priorities. Therefore, it is believed that if university management encourages researchers to take part in such discussions, it will enable more inclusive governance among universities and central organizations.

Establish Strategic Level Partnerships with Foreign Institutions

This in-depth study showed that most of the collaboration actions of universities are ad-hoc based or initiated at the researcher level. The only exception is the strategic partnership between Sabancı University and MIT. On the other hand, international collaboration has become integral to higher education in the 21st century, and perhaps nowhere is this more apparent than in the recent proliferation of international partnerships among colleges and universities (Sutton, Obst, Louime, Jones & Jones, 2011). It is often advantageous to formalize collaborative links with foreign partners at the institutional level by recognizing that they can turn into partnerships under Framework Program or other funding mechanisms.

During the interviews, the İTÜ representative highlighted the importance of EU-level connections mostly coming from researchers doing PhDs in EU countries. This situation implies the need for joint PhD program with EU institutions. A recent Joint Doctoral Scholarship Program in Turkey offered institutional level incentives. Within the scope of the new program, Turkish students will be eligible to get scholarship for conducting joint doctoral training/research for up to 24 months in universities abroad in the fields of natural sciences, engineering and technology, medical sciences, agricultural sciences, social sciences, and the humanities if institutional protocols are signed between Turkish and foreign universities.

Micro-Level Policy Recommendations

Micro-level recommendations are listed under seven items:

Participate in Overseas Programs

Findings of the quantitative study proved that having over 2.5 years of work experience abroad contributes to having a more comprehensive project portfolio at the researcher level. Post-doc studies especially open doors to further research careers, change career directions, pursue a passion for a particular subject, enter a profession that needs a specific qualification, gain a clear insight into industry, or create invaluable contacts (Higher Education Academy, 2015). Another advantage of postgraduate study is that it allows the researcher to continue his/her career while adding additional skills and knowledge. During the interviews, the İTÜ representative stated, "Researchers who performed studies in EU countries enter more easily into EU networks", which implies a networking effect and cognitive proximity with the EU agenda. Additionally, the Koç University representative stated that: "Broadening the spectrum of research is important. In addition to the main field of activity, additional areas of specialization provide ability to manage EU-level projects with different people from several areas". He added that if they found such researchers, they would recruit them without looking at their research areas. Therefore, researchers should look for ways to broaden their research areas. Considering the general research environment in emerging economies, it seems that the most pragmatic way to do so is to conduct a post-doc study abroad.

Enhance the Engagement with Industry

Many researchers lack an understanding of the relevance of their studies at the industry level. It is believed that within the economic conditions of a country like Turkey it is important to uncover industry-related opportunities for collaboration. The qualitative part of this research clearly shows that gatekeepers engage closely with industry, as well. Sabancı University's representative highlighted the significance of strategic initiatives, especially with the private sector's R&D centres. Similarly, guiding senior researchers to set up links with the techno park firms is a key action at METU. Our analysis also stressed that most collaborative arrangements are on an ad-hoc basis or initiated at the researcher level. Moreover, in one-to-one discussions with the area experts, it was stated that in some specific cases hub organisations choose partners from the periphery who own or have the ability to reach local knowledge. Therefore, for researchers in ICT, it seems crucial to establish and maintain close relations with industry, which may provide future opportunities and open new doors.

Contribute to Consultation Processes of TÜBİTAK and European Commission

Wide consultation processes with partners across the higher education and research sectors is a trendy topic among policy-makers of OECD countries and was clearly highlighted in the OECD Innovation Strategy report (OECD, 2010). Consultative governance mechanisms are promoted in Turkey, as well. The sector-oriented standpoint adopted within the National Science, Technology, and Innovation Strategy 2011-2016 has been promoted by two result-driven and targeted call-based funding programmes designed by TÜBİTAK recently. Accordingly, temporary governance mechanisms have been established by TÜBİTAK in priority areas, which allows an environment for a bottom-up and entrepreneurial discovery of the technology needs of each sector. These governance mechanisms comprised high-level representatives from academia, the private sector, and the public sector. In the high-level prioritisation meetings of these actors, a consultative and consensus-building process takes place to designate R&D priorities in each sector. Calls are opened in each sector through the ongoing TÜBİTAK funding mechanisms in technology needs and/or topics that have been previously identified and prioritised at such high-level prioritisation meetings. Adopting roles in these processes provides access to novel policy tools and data sources, as well as occasion to be recognised by the public authorities.

Identify EU-Level Partners

Based on the findings published in the ICT Technology Audit Study for Turkey (METU, 2011) it can be stated that the low levels of participation by Turkish organizations in official and non-official EU networks is the most crucial, since much of the participation in submitted projects resulted in unsatisfactory performance[1]. It should be noted that 67% of gatekeepers and 60% of the researchers in the three groups excluding inactive researchers received their PhDs from US institutions, which makes it somewhat harder for them to be visible at EU levels at initial stages. This requires further effort in engagement and networking at the EU level and proactive approaches to get EU funding.

Invest in Soft Skills

During the interviews, the Bilkent University representative stated that "the number of researchers who can lead big international projects does not exceed the fingers of one hand", stressing the importance of soft skills.

Listed as hard-working attitude, public speaking skills, managing personal relationships, ability to work independently, ability to work in teams, creative skills and ability to formulate new problems and ideas, and ability to accept and learn from criticism (DavideChicco, 2012). In other words, soft skills are crucial in in academic career such as teaching, presenting, and the writing of funding applications. The combination of skills a researcher requires for the future are listed as deep, narrow, and discipline-focused skills and broad soft or life skills (Allen Consulting Group, 2010). In international project work it is also essential to spend time developing personal relationships with project partners as well as to have ability to read the unspoken and unwritten language of cultural norms of other countries (Grinstead, 2013).

CONCLUSION AND FURTHER RESEARCH

Concluding Remarks

This chapter examines whether ICT researchers engaged in international collaboration have significant local activity at the national level. To conduct tests on their local focus, first we categorized the profiles of ICT researchers in terms of their degree of globalization versus localization, and so their global and local project portfolios were mapped against each other for two periods of time. Global and local performance of the population was traced with respect to five indicators, which are international and national project densities, publication output, involvement in decision making processes on academic project funding, and contribution to R&D capacity development in the private sector. We see that the results are situational. There is a group of researchers who are extremely successful at both levels, which means that they create local buzz. On the other hand, there are two additional groups that have only a one-dimensional focus for a given time interval, either local or global. The last group consists of more or less inactive researchers who did not show significant scientific performance above the average for either of the two dimensions.

Following the setting up of the framework for mapping international and national dynamics of an ICT researcher in Turkey, we have also found that better performance at both levels has a relationship with overseas work experience after PhD fulfilment and the research landscape provided by the university with which the researcher is now affiliated. Such types of limited findings implied that further analysis should be conducted to unlock the dynamics of ICT research in Turkey. Based on that, objective in-depth interviews were conducted with high-level representatives of the six most successful universities in ICT in Turkey. In-depth interviews clearly highlighted the needs for differentiated policy tools in terms of the different researchers' profiles, as well as internationalization strategies at the university level. Both actions seem crucial, because the Turkish ICT landscape is not connected internationally except these six universities. Moreover, other policy recommendations were dedicated in a special chapter organized in three dimensions: macro, meso, and micro.

Further Research

This study presents the Turkish case and offers taxonomy for assessing local–global collaboration dynamics at the researcher level. It would be fruitful to test the taxonomy in BRICS and EU12 countries and also to build a ground for performing country level comparisons.

Similar grounds can be deployed for different sectors in Turkish innovation ecosystems. For example studies in other priority areas listed in the National Science, Technology, and Innovation Strategy 2011-2016, is suggested can be conducted as well.

Further examination about origins and determinants explaining the differences in research portfolios of researchers with similar backgrounds could contribute to development of more evidence-based policies.

In line with the argument stated above, further analysis to explore the impact of local–global links bridged by the best-performing researchers will be helpful for further testing of evidence-based policies.

Noting that most of the Turkish ICT researchers in this study's population have received their PhD degrees from US universities, it would be interesting to perform a similar study to explore dynamics of US–Turkey collaboration linkages.

REFERENCES

Akçomak, S., Akdeve, E., & Fındık, D. (2013). *How do ICT firms in Turkey manage innovation? Diversity in expertise versus diversity in markets (No. 1301)*. STPS-Science and Technology Policy Studies Center, Middle East Technical University. Retrieved from http://stps.metu.edu.tr/sites/stps.metu.edu.tr/files/1301.pdf

Employer Demand for Researchers in Australia, Report to the Department of Innovation, Industry, Science and Research. (2010). *Allen Consulting Group*. Retrieved from http://www.industry.gov.au/research/ResearchWorkforceIssues/Documents/EmployerDemandforResearchersinAustraliareport.pdf

Barber, M. J., Paier, M., & Scherngell, T. (2009). *Analyzing and modeling European R&D collaborations: Challenges and opportunities from a large social network. Analysis of Complex Networks: From Biology to Linguistics*. Chicago: Willey-Blackwell

Barnard, H., Cowan, R., & Müller, M. (2012). Global excellence at the expense of local diffusion, or a bridge between two worlds? Research in science and technology in the developing world. *Research Policy*, *41*(4), 756–769. doi:10.1016/j.respol.2011.12.002

Bathelt, H. (2007). BuzzandPipeline Dynamics: Towards a Knowledge Based Multiplier Model of Clusters. *Geography Compass*, *1*(6), 1282–1298. doi:10.1111/j.1749-8198.2007.00070.x

Bathelt, H., Malmberg, A., & Maskell, P. (2004). Clusters and knowledge: Local buzz, global pipelines and the process of knowledge creation. *Progress in Human Geography*, *28*(1), 31–56. doi:10.1191/0309132504ph469oa

Benneworth, P., & Dassen, A. (2010). *Strengthening Global-Local Connectivity in Regional Innovation Strategies–A Theoretical and Policy Reflection*. CHEPS. Twente, Netherlands.

Breschi, S., & Cusmano, L. (2004). Unveiling the texture of a European Research Area: Emergence of oligarchic networks under EU Framework Programmes. *International Journal of Technology Management*, *27*(8), 747–772. doi:10.1504/IJTM.2004.004992

Cabo, P. G. (1999). Industrial participation and knowledge transfer in joint R&D projects. *International Journal of Technology Management*, *18*(3), 188–206. doi:10.1504/IJTM.1999.002766

Castellani, D., Zanfei, A., & Muendler, M. A. (2006). *Multinational firms, innovation and productivity*. Cheltenham: Edward Elgar. doi:10.4337/9781847201591

Castells, M. (2011). *The rise of the network society: The information age: Economy, society, and culture* (Vol. 1). West Sussex: John Wiley & Sons.

Christopherson, S., Garretsen, H., & Martin, R. (2008). The world is not flat: Putting globalization in its place. *Cambridge Journal of Regions. Economy and Society*, *1*(3), 343–349.

Cooke, P., Gomez Uranga, M., & Etxebarria, G. (1997). Regional innovation systems: Institutional and organisational dimensions. *Research Policy*, *26*(4), 475–491. doi:10.1016/S0048-7333(97)00025-5

DavideChicco. (2012, May 29) Which soft skills for research career? [Web log comment]. Retrieved from http://academia.stackexchange.com/questions/1799/which-soft-skills-for-research-career (2015, May 16).

Dubois, A., Copus, A., & Hedström, M. (2012). Local embeddedness and global links in rural areas: Euclidean and Relational Space in Business Networks (pp. 103-121). In C. Hedberg & R.M. do Carmo (Eds.), Translocal Ruralism. Springer Netherlands. doi:10.1007/978-94-007-2315-3_7

Eisenhardt, K. M. (1989). Building theories from case study research. *Academy of Management Review*, *14*(4), 532–550.

Eriksson, S. (2006). Cluster creation and innovation within an emerging Taiwanese high-tech sector. *International journal of technology transfer and commercialisation, 5(3),* 208-236.

Funding Higher Education: A View across Europe. (2010). *European Platform Higher Education Modernisation*. Retrieved from http://www.utwente.nl/bms/cheps/publications/Publications%202010/MODERN_Funding_Report.pdf

Foster, P., Borgatti, S. P., & Jones, C. (2011). Gatekeeper search and selection strategies: Relational and network governance in a cultural market. *Poetics*, *39*(4), 247–265. doi:10.1016/j.poetic.2011.05.004

Freeman, C. (1995). The 'National System of Innovation in historical perspective. *Cambridge Journal of Economics*, *19*(1), 5–24.

Gertler, M. S., & Levitte, Y. M. (2005). Local nodes in global networks: The geography of knowledge flows in biotechnology innovation. *Industry and Innovation*, *12*(4), 487–507. doi:10.1080/13662710500361981

Glaser, B. G., & Strauss, A. L. (2009). *The discovery of grounded theory: Strategies for qualitative research*. New Jersey: Transaction Books.

Gould, R. V., & Fernandez, R. M. (1989). Structures of mediation: A formal approach to brokerage in transaction networks. *Sociological Methodology*, *19*, 89–126. doi:10.2307/270949

Grabher, G., & Ibert, O. (2013). Distance as asset? *Journal of Economic Geography*, lbt014.

Graf, H. (2011). Gatekeepers in regional networks of innovators. *Cambridge Journal of Economics*, *35*(1), 173–198. doi:10.1093/cje/beq001

Graf, H., & Krüger, J. J. (2011). The performance of gatekeepers in innovator networks. *Industry and Innovation*, *18*(1), 69–88. doi:10.1080/13662716.2010.528932

Grinstead, J. (2013, August 22). The Soft Skills of International Project Management. Retrieved from http://www.nasa.gov/offices/oce/appel/ask/issues/49/49s_soft_skills_ipm.html

Postgraduate Taught Experience Survey (PTES). (2015, May 16). *Higher Education Academy*. Retrieved from https://www.heacademy.ac.uk/consultancy-services/surveys/ptes

Johnston, P., Pestel, R., Mladenic, D., Grobelnik, M., & Stefan, J. (2003). *European Research Co-Operation as a Self-Organising Complex Network: Implications for Creation of a European Research Area*. Brussels: DG Information Society.

Lall, S. (2001). *Competitiveness, Technology and Skills. Williston*. Edward Elgar Publishing. doi:10.4337/9781781950555

Lohr, S. (2009). *Sampling: design and analysis*. Boston: Cengage Learning.

Louime, C., Jones, J. V., & Jones, T.-A. (2015). Developing Research-Based Partnerships: Florida A&M University's US-Brazil Cross-Cultural Initiative. In S. B. Sutton & D. Obst (Eds.), Developing Strategic International Partnerships: Models for Initiating and Sustaining Innovative Institutional Linkages. New York: Institute of International Education and the AIFS Foundation; Retrieved from http://www.tec.govt.nz/Funding/Fund-finder/Performance-Based-Research-Fund-PBRF-/

Malerba, F., Vonortas, N., Breschi, S., & Cassi, L. (2006). *Evaluation of progress towards a European Research Area for information society technologies. Report to European Commission*. Brusells: DG Information Society and Media.

Malmberg, A., & Maskell, P. (2006). Localized learning revisited. *Growth and Change*, *37*(1), 1–18. doi:10.1111/j.1468-2257.2006.00302.x

Marin, A., & Bell, M. (2006). Technology spillovers from Foreign Direct Investment (FDI): The active role of MNC subsidiaries in Argentina in the 1990s. *The Journal of Development Studies*, *42*(4), 678–697. doi:10.1080/00220380600682298

Maskell, P., Bathelt, H., & Malmberg, A. (2006). Building global knowledge pipelines: The role of temporary clusters. *European Planning Studies*, *14*(8), 997–1013. doi:10.1080/09654310600852332

ICT Technology Audit Study for Turkey. (2011). *Middle East Technical University*. Retrieved from http://stps.metu.edu.tr/sites/stps.metu.edu.tr/files/task9.pdf

Moodysson, J. (2008). Principles and practices of knowledge creation: On the organization of "buzz" and "pipelines" in life science communities. *Economic Geography*, *84*(4), 449–469. doi:10.1111/j.1944-8287.2008.00004.x

Narula, R., & Dunning, J. H. (2000). Industrial development, globalization and multinational enterprises: New realities for developing countries. *Oxford Development Studies*, *28*(2), 141–167. doi:10.1080/713688313

Campus for Research Excellence and Technological Enterprise (CREATE). (2015, May 16). National Research Foundation. Retrieved from http://www.nrf.gov.sg/about-nrf/programmes/create

OECD. (2010). *Ministerial report on the OECD Innovation Strategy*. Retrieved from http://www.oecd.org/sti/45326349.pdf (2015, May 16).

Ortega, J. L., & Aguillo, I. F. (2010). Shaping the European research collaboration in the 6th Framework Programme health thematic area through network analysis. *Scientometrics*, *85*(1), 377–386. doi:10.1007/s11192-010-0218-4

Porter, M. E. (2000). Location, competition, and economic development: Local clusters in a global economy. *Economic Development Quarterly*, *14*(1), 15–34. doi:10.1177/089124240001400105

Roediger-Schluga, T., & Barber, M. J. (2006). *The structure of R&D collaboration networks in the European Framework Programmes* (p. 36). UNU-MERIT.

Roediger-Schluga, T., & Dachs, B. (2006). *Does technology affect network structure?-A quantitative analysis of collaborative research projects in two specific EU programmes (No. 041)*. United Nations University.

Sutton, S. B., Obst, D., Louime, C., Jones, J. V., & Jones, T. A. (2011).*Developing strategic international partnerships: Models for initiating and sustaining innovative institutional linkages*.

Todtling, F., & Trippl, M. (2007). Knowledge links in high-technology industries: Markets, Networks or Milieu? The case of the Vienna biotechnology cluster. *International Journal of Entrepreneurship and Innovation Management*, *7*(2), 345–365. doi:10.1504/IJEIM.2007.012888

Trippl, M., Tödtling, F., & Lengauer, L. (2009). Knowledge sourcing beyond buzz and pipelines: Evidence from the Vienna software sector. *Economic Geography*, *85*(4), 443–462. doi:10.1111/j.1944-8287.2009.01047.x

Best Practice Sharing. (2015, May 16). University Economic Development Association. Retrived from http://universityeda.org/value-to-members/best-practice-sharing/

Uzzi, B. (1996). The sources and consequences of embeddedness for the economic performance of organizations: The network effect. *American Sociological Review*, *61*(4), 674–698. doi:10.2307/2096399

Wagner, C. S. (2005). Six case studies of international collaboration in science. *Scientometrics*, *62*(1), 3–26. doi:10.1007/s11192-005-0001-0

Wagner, C. S., Cave, J., Leydesdorff, L., Allee, V., Graafland, I., Perez, R., & Botterman, M. (2004). *ERAnets Evaluation of Networks of Collaboration Between Participants in IST Research and Their Evolution to Collaborations in The European Research Area (ERA). Inception Report*. Brussels: DG Information Society and Media.

Whetten D.A. (2000). *Developing "Good" Theory through Articulation and Examination*. Brigham Young University.

Yin, R. K. (1994) Case study research Design and Methods (2nd ed.). Thousand Oaks: Sage publication.

KEY TERMS AND DEFINITIONS

EU Framework Programs: These programs are designed by European Union as funding programs to support and foster research in the European Research Area (ERA). The first framework program starts in 1984 and the final funding scheme called Horizon 2020 covers the period 2014-2020.

Information Society Technologies (IST): It is one of seven sectors of the European Union's Fifth Framework Program for Research and Technological Development for 1998-2002. It also continued under the Sixth Framework program. The IST program features four key actions, each focused on technologies, issues and objectives of strategic importance to Europe. The objective is to ensure that all European citizens and companies benefit from the opportunities of the emerging Information Society.

International R&D Networks: Organizations need to interact at different levels. They need enhanced local networks and strong extra-local or global linkages, while paving the way to balance those. Through interactions in international networks, they explore and, then, exploit the new knowledge for facilitating their R&D activities.

Knowledge Flows: From evolutionary perspective of innovation, research collaboration and external knowledge flows are seen as important catalyzers for acquiring new capabilities for innovative organizations which cannot rely only on internal knowledge base.

Local Buzz–Global Pipelines: The local buzz–global pipelines approach argues that local interaction or 'buzz' and interaction through trans-local 'pipelines' create a dynamic process of learning, knowledge production and innovation that is central to understanding a cluster's success

National Innovation System: The national innovation systems approach stresses that the flows of technology and information among people, enterprises and institutions are key to the innovative process. Innovation and technology development are the result of a complex set of relationships among actors in the system, which includes enterprises, universities and government research institutes.

Chapter 10
Understanding Educational Potential and Value of Affective Computing

Cenk Akbiyik
Erciyes University, Turkey

ABSTRACT

Educational systems have met information and communication technologies many years ago. Although many years of effort and vast investments, the integration of ICT with educational systems is still weak. Besides many others, lack of interactivity and emotionality in current technologies can be seen as obstacles in front of this integration. We know that learning is associated not only with our cognitive abilities but also with our emotions and affective states. Affective computing is an interdisciplinary branch that is interested in design of systems and devices that can recognize, interpret, process and respond to users' affective states. Affective computing may contribute to interactivity and emotionality of human-computer interaction. Within the scope of this book chapter, related scientific literature was reviewed in order to investigate educational value and potential of affective computing.

AFFECTIVE COMPUTING

If we want computers to be genuinely intelligent and to interact naturally with us, we must give computers the ability to recognize, understand, and even to have and express emotions. - Rosalind W. Picard, 1997

Affective computing is an emerging computing paradigm (Kwon & Hong, 2013, p. 93). In 1995, Rosalind. W. Picard wrote a technical report, more a thought paper, where she presented the very initial ideas on affective computing. Depending on Picard's work we can define affective computing as a branch that deals with design of systems and devices that can recognize, interpret, process and respond to users' affective states. As seen in the definition, responding to users' affective states is the critical issue in affective computing.

Affective computing is a powerful and deeply important topic, full of extremely difficult technical, scientific, philosophical, and ethical challenges (Picard, 2010, p. 16). It has contributed to various fields in at least four ways (Kaliouby, Picard, & Cohen, 2006, p. 230):

DOI: 10.4018/978-1-4666-8598-7.ch010

1. Designing novel sensors and machine learning algorithms that analyze multimodal channels of affective information.
2. Creating new techniques to infer a person's affective or cognitive state.
3. Developing machines that respond affectively and adaptively to a person's state.
4. Inventing personal technologies for improving awareness of affective states and its selective communication to others.

Affective computing is an interdisciplinary field standing on the intersection of computer sciences, psychology, and cognitive science. That's why it has been attracting various scientists and specialists such as computer scientists, educators, psychologists, and cognitive scientists.

Basically affective computing aims to use power of affect to enhance human-human communication and human-computer interaction. There is an enthusiasm among scientists, researchers, and system developers that affective computing has been enabling or will enable users to interact with computers in a more efficient, more humane and friendlier manner.

AIM AND METHOD

The current study is a literature search aiming to investigate educational value and potential of affective computing. Throughout the chapter, affective computing was studied from the viewpoint of learning and instruction. Several scientific articles and dissertations on affective computing and affective states were reviewed to seek answers to these questions:

- What is affective computing?
- What are applications of affective computing?
- How important are affective states for learning?
- What are instructional constructs related with affective computing?
- What are ethical issues regarding design and use of affective computing systems?

AFFECTIVE STATES

Affective states and therefore emotions are critical components of an affective computing system. In related literature, these two are generally used interchangeably. Although, they are two closely related constructs, they have their own meanings.

Minsky (2004; cited in Axelrod & Hone, 2006, p. 160) defines emotions as complex neurophysiological systems with visceral, behavioural and reflective levels operating on biological, neurological and psychological systems. These systems help us organise and regulate other systems such as cognition, memory and problem-solving. In other words, emotions are subjective experiences. They result in physical and psychological changes that influence thought and behaviour. These changes are adaptive responses of an organism in order to cope with the environment. Research showed that patients who have lost the ability to experience emotions due to brain damage function try to maximize the performance of their task by analysing all the benefits and drawbacks of each possible choice. This process causes them to fall into an infinite diatribe that does not eventually bring them to a final decision (Tennov 1994; cited in Bianchi-Berthouze & Kleinsmith, 2003, p. 259).

Affect, on the other hand, is an encompassing term, used to describe the topics of emotion, feelings, and moods together, even though it is commonly used interchangeably with emotion (Fox, 2008, p. 16). Affective states are considered psycho-physiological constructs and are split up into three main categories: valence, arousal, and motivational intensity (Harmon-Jones, Gable, & Price, 2013, p. 303). Where valence is the positive-to-negative evaluation of the subjectively experienced state, arousal is extent of reaction to stimuli and motivational intensity is the strength of urge to move toward or away from a stimulus.

CLASSIFICATION OF EMOTIONS

From the viewpoint of affective computing studies, classification of affective states and emotions are important. Hence, many experimental studies and artificial intelligence systems requires a classification of emotions.

A number of classification systems of emotions have been proposed. Among them perhaps the simplest one is categorizing emotions according to their valence as positive and negative. Although this bipolar categorization may provide the required simplicity to some research studies, interaction among environment and human affective states seem far more complex and a bipolar categorization may not always be the right path to follow.

One widely accepted classification of emotions rely on Ekman's (1972) influential work. Ekman's research findings led him to classify six emotions as basic: anger, disgust, fear, happiness, sadness and surprise. Ekman also found that the six basic emotions are not culturally determined; instead they appear to be universally recognized.

Another classification belongs to Plutchik where he developed the "wheel of emotions", suggesting eight primary emotions grouped on a positive or negative basis: joy versus sadness, anger versus fear, trust versus distrust and surprise versus anticipation (Plutchik, 2011).

The circumplex model of emotion was first developed by Russell (1980). This model suggests that emotions are distributed in a two-dimensional circular space, containing arousal and valence dimensions. Arousal represents the vertical axis and valence represents the horizontal axis, while the centre of the circle represents a neutral valence and a medium level of arousal.

Though it is not a classification system, a technique called the multidimensional scaling may be used to locate emotions on two dimensions. Through the use of multidimensional scaling, a visual depiction of emotional distance between experiences can be made (Schacter, 2011).

APPLICATIONS OF AFFECTIVE COMPUTING

Based on the studies conducted, we can state that affective computing studies are still in their childhood. Many of them are R&D studies which are mostly isolated from social context, aiming to develop and test affective technologies. But computer systems sensitive to human affective states have a huge variety of, at least potential, applications. Many technological imprints such as communication devices, wearable devices, virtual environments, smart house technologies, speech recognition systems, stress monitoring systems, intelligent agents and affective decision making systems fallout the area of impact of affective computing. In fact many software systems would significantly improve performance if they could adapt to the emotional state of the user, for example if intelligent tutoring systems, ATMs, or ticketing machines could recognize when users were confused, frustrated or angry they could provide help which would improve the service quality (Akbiyik, 2010, p. 195).

If we focus on educational use of affective computing, we see that affective technologies such as affective tutorials, pedagogical agents and artificial intelligence systems have been developed to promote learning. Basically these applications aim to promote learning by arranging learning content and by enriching human-computer interaction. Such systems have the ability to arrange the learning content considering learners' affective states, such as emotions, to increase attention time and motivation and to maximize learning performance.

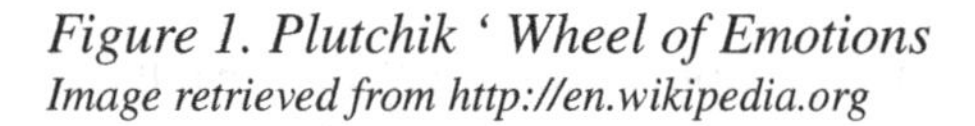

Figure 1. Plutchik ' Wheel of Emotions
Image retrieved from http://en.wikipedia.org

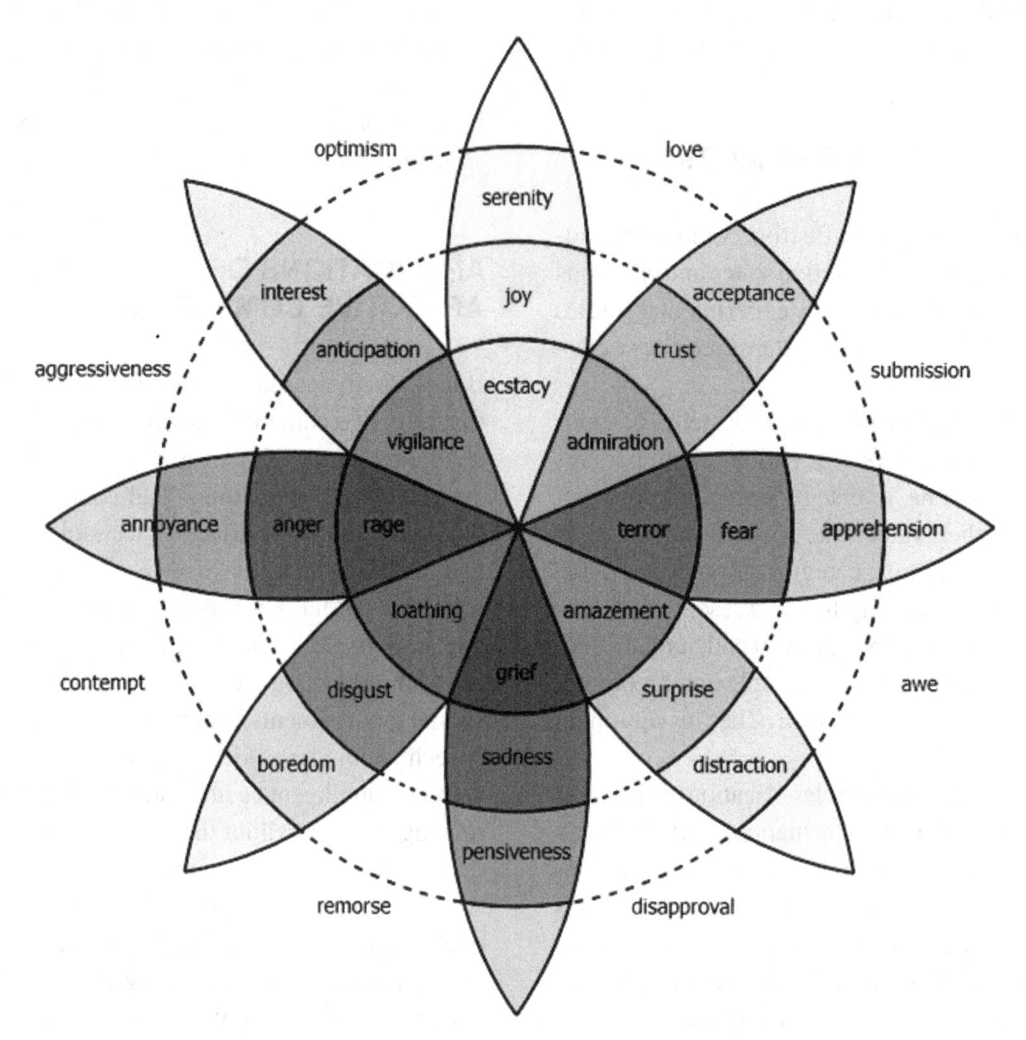

Figure 2. Multidimensional Scaling of Emotions

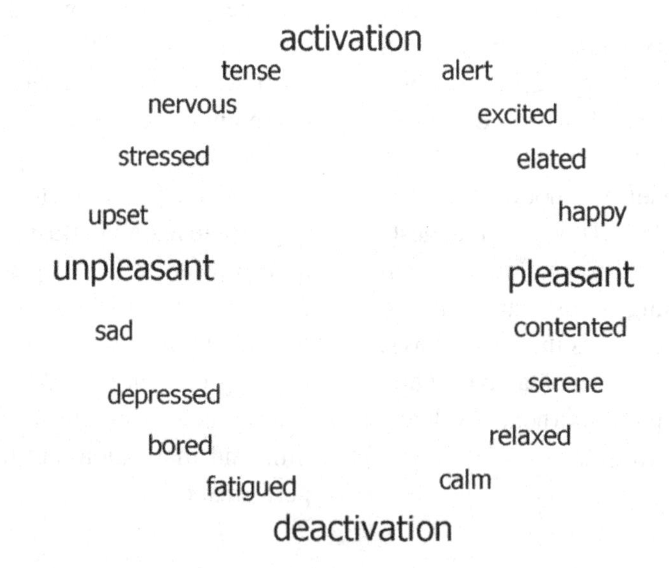

Affective social networks and affective communication systems are other educational applications of affective computing. According to Bandura (1997), a great deal of psychological modelling occurs when learners observe behaviours of their everyday associates. Learners come to understand phenomena through negotiating meanings with people in the environment, and they achieve goals through interacting, both explicitly and implicitly, with the instructor, peers, materials, and atmosphere embedded in the context (Kim & Baylor, 2006, p. 576). Affective computing systems may provide an emotional touch to convert present social networks and communication tools to affective systems to increase interactivity and facilitate communication.

Affective computing has many possible applications in health sector. For instance Chittaro and Sioni (2014) has proved affective computing may be influential on relaxation training. One other example to such applications is on stress management. Villani and Riva (2012) developed a stress management protocol and tested it in a controlled study comparing three interactive experiences (virtual reality, video, and audio). Results of the study showed the efficacy of all three interactive experiences in inducing positive emotions and integrating different approaches to manage stress.

Bio-feedback is another promising application area of affective computing. A bio-feedback interface means that the affective data that are gathered through an affective computing system and are fed back through the stimulators of instant affection technologies, and consequently enable a self-regulation of the user, since they control the interaction intentionally in order to master the interface (Zics, 2011, p. 74). Many industries from gaming to automotive may find correct applications of biofeedback technology in order to improve their products.

Development of social robots which express emotions is another attracting application field of affective computing. Social robots shoe behaviours similar to humans: they interact and communicate with humans by following a set of social rules, e.g., by using modalities of communication also used in human-human interaction (Cid, Moreno, Bustos, & Nunez, 2014, p. 7712). With social robots, more humanly interactions, increased empathy and acceptance levels are desired.

Affective systems may have interesting present and future applications in many other sectors. In criminal science for example, brain waves of a suspect may be used to reveal whether he hides any information. Another interesting application is about parental guidance and has been realized by Eyben et al. (2013) where they developed an affective computing application to automatically detect violent scenes in movies.

Although some people may find them dysfunctional, affective computing has also amusing and creative applications. One of the applications is on fashion. Merging fashion with affective computing technologies is termed "affectiveware" and it aims to create clothing that is personalised by the emotions of an individual. This kind of affective clothing is able to represent and stimulate emotional responses by changing colours (Goulev, Stead, Mamdani, & Evans, 2004). Another amusing application of affective computing has been realized by Shahid et al. (2013) where they developed and tested a multimodal affective interface called "the affective mirror" which tries to make users happy by showing a distorted representation of their face.

AFFECTIVE STATES AND LEARNING

It is generally accepted that affective states have effects on cognitive tasks in some way. Affective states can order as well as disorder thinking and learning. Research indicate that positive affect does foster intrinsic motivation, and enjoyment and performance of enjoyable tasks (Isen & Reeve, 2005, p. 297) and conversely, negative emotional states, such as anger and sadness, have been shown to have a negative impact on learning and motivation (Goleman, 1995; cited in Moridis & Economides, 2008, p. 315).

However, dealing with affect-cognition relation in a positive-negative manner may be an over simplification. Different emotions can influence cognitive mechanisms in different ways (Pekrun, Goetz, & Titz, 2002). Affect-cognition relations seem to be much more complicated where we have to consider kind of cognitive task as well as emotions, and their valance and arousal. For example it is well known that learning or remembering something in a state of anxiety, anger, or depression can be difficult for any individual (Goleman, 1995; cited in Moridis & Economides, 2008, p. 316). However, negative affect initially focuses the mind, leading to better concentration (Schwarz and Bless, 1991; cited in Moridis & Economides, 2008, p. 316). Likewise, positive affect widens the thought processes, making it easier to be distracted. But when the problem involves focusing, positive affect may interfere with the subject's concentration (Bower, 1992; cited in Moridis & Economides, 2008, p. 316)

Akbiyik (2010, p. 198) proposes to use power of emotions in computer based or assisted learning environments. He suggests certain features of computer technologies such as simulations, videos and music to produce an emotionally sound learning environment. But in order to be able to incorporate power of affective states to instruction, developers need instructional strategies. FEASP and Kort-Reilly-Picard dynamic model of emotions are examples to these instructional frameworks. The FEASP model has been offered by Hermann Astleitner (Astleitner, 2000). FEASP signifies the five most important dimensions of instructional related emotions: Fear, Envy, Anger, Sympathy, and Pleasure. The FEASP approach refers to 20 instructional strategies aiming to decrease negative feelings (fear, envy, and anger) and to increase positive feelings (sympathy and pleasure) during instruction. These strategies are both applicable in traditional and computer assisted learning environments. For example the model offers to intensify relationships, install sensitive interactions, establish cooperative learning activities and implement peer helping programs in order to increase sympathy.

On the other hand, the Kort-Reilly-Picard dynamic model of emotions for SMET (Science, Math, Engineering, Technology) considers learning as an emotional process with four main repeated stages. According to this model, during learning the student repeatedly passes from curiosity to disappointment, frustration, and acceptance (Kort, Reilly, & Picard, 2001). The learning process is separated by two axes, vertical and horizontal, labelled learning and affect,

Figure 3. The Kort-Reilly-Picard Dynamic Model of Emotions

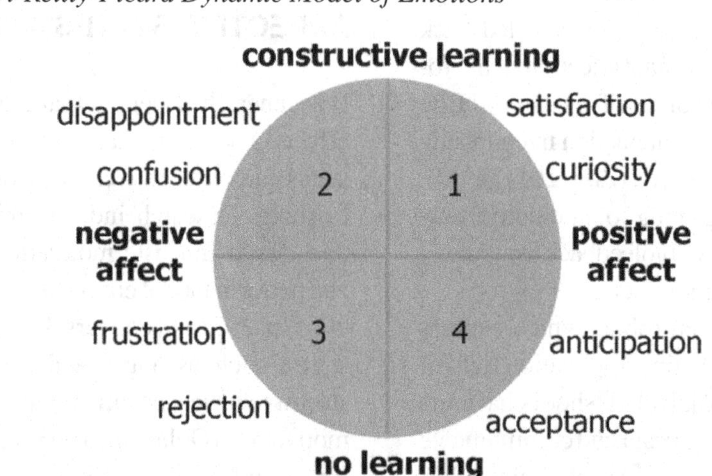

respectively. The affect axis ranges from positive affect on the right to negative affect on the left. The learning axis ranges from "constructive learning", where new information is being integrated into schemas, to "no learning", where misconceptions are identified and isolated from schemas.

AFFECT RECOGNITION

Affect recognition is a critical and vital component of affective computing systems. These systems require recognizing user's affective states in order to be able to respond them. Affective computing systems use a variety of affect recognition technologies. These include analysis of facial images, posture, voice and biological signals. Biological signals contain heartbeat, state of tension, skin temperature, skin conductivity, blood pressure and brain waves. But affective computing systems do not only rely on affect recognition to evaluate affective states. Self reporting techniques are also used in these systems.

Considering the complexity of affective states, one recognition technology may not be enough to capture and interpret all affective states. For example while there is evidence for the existence of a number of universally recognised facial expressions for emotion happiness, surprise, fear, sadness, anger and disgust (Ekman, 1972) there are also a number of psycho-physiological correlates of emotion most of which cannot easily be detected by observation (Hone, 2006, p. 228). Besides, empirical studies revealed that certain emotion states such as neutral and surprise are more clearly recognized from the visual-facial modality rather than the audio-lingual one. But other emotion states, such as anger and disgust are more clearly recognized from the audio-lingual modality (Virvou et al. 2012, p. 25). Moreover, while galvanic skin response technology may be useful to detect individual's stress level, heart rate data may be used to recognize a positive or negative affective state. Electromyography may be used to detect if the user is tense while respiratory measures may be used to interpret an emotional arouse. That's why some researchers prefer to use a group of these recognition technologies together to get better results in affect sensing. For instance, Shen, Callaghan, and Shen (2008) has reported accuracy rate of emotion recognition rises from 68.6% to 86.5% when data from brainwave signals were added to the analyses.

Existing approaches to identifying affective states may be summarized as bio-physiological measures, self reporting and observation techniques:

- Bio-physiological measures: Approaches to measuring affect as an internal state tend to concentrate on bio-physiological observations, using data such as heart rate, galvanic skin response (GSR) and cardiac inter-beat interval. However the level of arousal shown by these measures does not map exactly to the subjective experiences of participants, and does not always give clear indication of valence, or exact emotional expression. Functional magnetic resonance imaging (fMRI) is now providing fascinating data on brain activity during emotional processing, but fMRI is currently restricted to laboratory settings, which may not accurately reflect real life situations (Axelrod & Hone, 2006: 161). Bio-physiological measures are more difficult to conceal or manipulate than facial expressions and vocal utterances, they are a more reliable representation of inner feelings (Shen, Wang, & Shen, 2009, p. 178).
- Self Report: When affect is conceptualised in terms of subjective experience, measures can be obtained by asking someone about their feelings via direct probes, questionnaires or narrative means, either during interaction or retrospectively. However, these very questions may disrupt the normal flow of affect, while semantic and perceptual

differences between individuals mean that such measures may be imprecise (Axelrod and Hone, 2006, p. 161). An example to self reporting technique was developed by Broekens and Brinkman (2009) where users use an interface to provide affective feedback in terms of valence, arousal and dominance.

- Observation: The recognition of emotional expressions from observation has the potential to be particularly useful within the context of HCI, because it is non-intrusive and should therefore not disrupt ongoing interaction. In addition, although emotional expressions may not always match internal affective state, they still typically convey useful information (Axelrod and Hone, 2006, p. 161). A number of studies have been conducted regarding affect detection by observation techniques. For example in their study Pedrotti et al. (2014) have recorded pupil diameter and some other measures during a driving task and have shown that affective computing systems can use pupil diameter data for successful stress detection.

Clearly, sensors are critical technologies to affect recognition. Researchers have developed portable sensors to recognize affective states. Examples include tiny video camcorders to record facial expression, head gesture and posture changes, microphones to record vocal inflection changes, skin-surface sensing of muscle tension, heart-rate variability, skin conductivity, blood-glucose levels (Kalioub, Picard, & Baron Cohen, 2006, p. 233). Some of these devices may also function as integrated devices in other mobile devices. On the other hand, affective wearables are increasingly getting more attention. Affective wearables are wearable devices, such as a glove or a ring, that measure biological signals. The wearer can take it off, or turn it off. For example Lanata, Valenza, and Scilingo (2012) has developed a electrodermal glove which based on a fabric glove, with integrated textile electrodes placed at the fingertips, able to acquire and process the electrodermal response (EDR) to discriminate affective states. Researchers has reported promising results in the field of affective computing.

AFFECTIVE AGENTS

One main application lane of affective computing systems is on affective agents. Affective agents are animated characters integrated in applications to promote interaction. Affective agents have the ability to simulate a social interaction. In some cases they even provide information and encouragement. Moreover, these agents may even respond to users with apparent empathy.

But why are affective agents important for affective computing systems? Because these agents are a way for machines to interact with us in a humanly manner. As Rosalind W. Picard explains (Picard, 2003, p. 58):

What motivates much of affective computing—how can we enable computers to better serve people's needs—adapting to you vs. treating you like some fictional idealized user, and recognizing that humans are powerfully influenced by emotion, even when they are not showing any emotion?

Reeves and Nass (1996 ; cited in Kim & Baylor, 2006, p. 570) concluded from more than 10 years of studies, people may apply the same social rules and expectations to computers as they do to humans in the real world. In human-computer interaction, people often experience and interpret interactions with a computer as interactions with other people. The social agency theory suggests that social cues like face and voice of an agent motivate this interpretation. Studies conducted on affective agents yield promising results. For example in an experimental study Moridis (2012) found that an agent performing parallel empathy displaying emotional expressions relevant to the emotional state of the student may cause this emotion to persist. Moreover, the agent performing parallel and then reactive empathy appeared to be effective in altering an emotional state of fear to a neutral one. Accordingly, this study has shown that empathetic feedback expressed through an agent can change the affective state of the learner.

Affective agents are also considerably important for learning systems. The benefit of peer interaction has widely been accepted by educators. Intellectual development is achieved when learners are involved in learning activities in which they interact with others (Vygotsyky et al, 1978). In particular, pedagogical agents can be designed to simulate social interaction that may facilitate learners to engage in learning task (Kim & Baylor, 2006, p. 569). And indeed pedagogical agents seem to simulate a type of social interaction (Kim and Baylor, 2006, p. 576) making learning more meaningful at computer based environments. Based on the given research, we can say that an "emotional-learning agent" is supposed to (Moridis & Economides, 2008, p. 329):

1. Recognize the running emotional condition of the student;
2. Recognize when to intervene in order to influence the student's emotional state;
3. Produce the most optimal emotional state for learning.

Baylor and Ryu (2003; cited in Krämer & Bente, 2010, p. 72) also suggest that human-likeness creates a strong motivating effect. A supporting study comes from Louwerse, Graesser, Lu, and Mitchel (2005) where in their experimental study they found that learners preferred natural agents with natural voices, as predicted by the social-cue hypothesis. Likewise, the term "believability" is often used to describe expectations concerning virtual agents. Increasing believability may affect users' satisfaction and agents' evaluation (Demeure, 2011, p. 432). But studies also revealed that integrating affective agents to increase learning performance is not a straightforward path. Beale and Creed (2009, p. 775) reports that results of related studies are often inconclusive and contradictory.

Understanding how we experience agency in HCI is a problem of considerable practical significance, given the widespread use of interactive Technologies that either explicitly or implicitly rely on social cues and response (McEneaney, 2013, p. 811). Though several studies have highlighted the potential for simulated emotion to both enhance and hinder interactions with agents, many others in the education and learning domain generally found that use of emotion had little positive impact on the interactions. It is likely that simply integrating a human like character is not enough. Many other variables such as age, personal traits and learning styles of the learner as well as learning content and agents' characteristics such as voice, appearance, non verbal abilities and feedback style should be taken into account.

EDUCATIONAL VALUE AND POTENTIAL OF AFFECTIVE COMPUTING

Affective computing seems to be a promising area from the viewpoint of educational technology. Educational technology is a complex, integrated process involving people, procedures, ideas, devices, and organization for analyzing problems and devising, implementing, evaluating, and managing solutions to those problems, involved in all aspects of human learning (AECT, 1977, p. 2). That is to say educational technology is an interdisciplinary branch. It involves in using scientific knowledge for solution of educational problems. Educational applications of information and communication technologies are among interest of educational technologists.

Unfortunately, affective computing and learner emotions have not become a serious research interest among educational technologists. One of the reasons of this lack of interest may be that instructional designers have been too busy with cognitive and motivational objectives. Another reason may be the research difficulties in front of researches because conducting research on emotions in education presents a number of potential challenges (Akbiyik, 2010, p. 192).

The educational value and potential of affective computing can be reviewed under 5 intertwined constructs which are motivation, suggestion, valance, arousal, and feedback.

Motivation

Motivation is among the most important variables affecting learning outcomes. Motivation is the key factor that starts and continues human action. Low motivated learners tend to quit learning tasks or drop classes. Human motivation is complex and it is related many factors such as expectations, beliefs, past experiences, curiosity, and emotions. There are various theories and models trying to explain human emotion. Behaviourism is among them. Behaviourists tend to explain human learning as a consequence of external factors such as conditioning and punishment (Sen, 2006, p. 12). Human motivation in behaviourist sense is about joy and satisfaction of learning experiences. Thus, if an individual has positive learning experiences his or her motivation increases.

Affective computing can be used to increase one's learning motivation in behaviourist sense by enabling him or her to enjoy the learning task. This can be achieved by pedagogical agents where they may be employed to make the learner feel pleased by visual and auditory cues.

The ARCS model is an instructional model that puts motivation in the very centre of instruction. ARCS is an acronym and stands for attention, relevance, confidence, and satisfaction. The ARCS model is a method for improving the motivational appeal of instructional materials (Keller, 1987, p. 2). Affective computing may be successfully applied to achieve principles of ARCS model. For example an affective system may recognize boredom of learner and gain his or her attention by exposing learner to a discrepant event or using humour. Moreover, pedagogical agents may give messages about future usefulness of the learning task to maintain relevance. Confidence is an important element of ARCS model. Learner confidence may be raised in a number of ways. The system may give hints and clues to help encourage learner or decrease difficulty level of the tasks when it senses a disappointment. People tend to be satisfied when they accomplish challenging tasks. An affective system may calculate the appropriate level of challenge to maintain learner satisfaction. Agents may also be used to praise learner for positive outcomes.

Suggestion

Suggestions are messages. They are proposals offered for acceptance or rejection. They may come from environment or from the individual himself. In the golden era of mass communication we can confidently state that every day we are under a bombardment of media messages. Media constantly sends us messages on what to buy, where to go, how to live, etc. In fact these messages are suggestions offered us to accept them.

Lozanov (1978), developer of Accelerated Learning model, claims that reserved learning capacities of individuals could be released by suggestion. Suggestions may be direct or indirect. A direct suggestion is explicit while an indirect one contains implicit messages. Indirect messages aim to influence human emotions and cognition by employing many factors such as values, beliefs, culture, and expectations.

Both direct and indirect suggestions may be employed in affective learning systems. In case of a learner needs to be praised or encouraged affective system may supply what he or she needs.

Indirect verbal suggestions may be provided using stories or videos. Such a suggestive system may also provide a degree of guidance to the learner to show him the path he or she should follow.

Valance

Valence is related with how much positive or negative do we perceive an affective state. Because they are seen to foster learning, generally positive affective states are desired at learning environments. This viewpoint is partially true. Although positive emotions such as joy or pleasure widen cognition and help us to think better, they also make distraction easier. On the other hand, negative emotions such as anxiety help us to narrow our mind and focus. This mechanism does not allow oversimplification. It is related both with the kind of emotion and the type of learning task. That's why valance should be carefully taken into account in an affective learning system. An affective system which can recognize learner's affective state and decides type of learning task may serve to learn more efficiently. Further, such a system may try to put the learner into the correct affective state by changing his or her emotions. Different kinds of music, visuals, design elements, and agents can be employed to achieve this goal. For example, a fun video may be shown to the learner to cheer him up. Or on the contrary, an agent may give information about complexity of the learning topic to help learner to focus.

Arousal

Regarding affective learning systems, arousal in another variable that should be taken into account. High levels of arousal may inhibit learning. This is valid for both positive and negative emotions. For instance high levels of anxiety may inhibit learner from thinking and focusing. But research show that a low level of anxiety, such as test anxiety, is desirable to motivate learner and force the learner to complete learning task. An affective system should detect arousal level, decide and bring learner's arousal level to a feasible level for learning. Direct or indirect messages, relaxing exercises, relaxing music, sounds from nature may be used to decrease arousal.

Feedback

Feedback is an important construct found within many theories of learning (Mory, 1992, p. 5). It promotes learning by supplying information about learners' performances and conditions. Feedback in behaviourist sense is reinforcement for correct answers (Mory, 1992, p. 6). This kind of feedback has been widely used in computer based instruction. "Correct" or "try again" kind of feedback is seen quite often in programmed learning materials.

Clues are also a kind of feedback. Clues are short messages which help learner to overcome learning problems. Teachers frequently use clues during instruction. "Try another way, remember the principles you have just read, look from a different angle, you are on the right path, keep going" are examples of these clues. They may have significant positive effects on learning performance. An affective learning system may use power of clues to enhance learning. But giving the right clue at the right time is not simple for a computer system. Such a system surely needs sophisticated artificial intelligence capabilities.

Ethical Issues

Regardless of good intentions, the design of a technology may be overturned to undesirable paths. As Reynolds and Picard (2005) state, there are a number of important ethical considerations that arise with the computer's increasing ability to recognize emotions. The most important one out of these ethical issues is on privacy of affective states. Emotions, perhaps more so than thoughts, are ultimately personal and private. They provide information about the most intimate motivational factors and reactions. Any attempts to detect, recognize, not to mention manipulate, a user's emotions thus constitutes the ultimate breach of ethics and will never be acceptable to computer users (Picard, 2003, p. 61). Another ethical consideration is whether exposing affective state information creates opportunities for others to manipulate one's behaviour and thoughts using this information (Kalioub, Picard, & Baron Cohen, 2006, p. 242). Moreover, it should be noted that certain categories of physiological data may also be used to detect medical conditions (e.g., cardiac arrhythmias, hypertension, and epilepsy) of which the individual may be unaware. The introduction of physiological computing should not provide a covert means of monitoring individuals for routine health problems without consent (Fairclough, 2009, p. 141).

In order to overcome these ethical issues some strict measures should be taken. Users of an affective computing system should know exactly what data is being collected, why it has been collected, where it has been stored, and who has access to this data. Storing affective data on secure servers, preventing access except of the user, and breaking the link between users' identification and data on their affective states may be other precautions to prevent misuse of these systems.

CONCLUSION

Affective computing is a promising multidisciplinary area. Although it is far away from maturity, it is attracting many scientists, researchers and developers from various disciplines. The pioneering studies are promising. I think that it has a strong potential to provide the desired interactivity to human-computer interaction and computer based or assisted learning environments.

REFERENCES

Akbiyik, C. (2010). Can affective computing lead to more effective use of ICT in Education? *Revista de Educacion*, *352*, 179–202.

Astleitner, H. (2000). Designing emotionally sound instruction: The FEASP-approach. *Instructional Science*, *28*(3), 169–198. doi:10.1023/A:1003893915778

Axelrod, L., & Hone, K. S. (2006). Affectemes and all affects: A novel approach to coding user emotional expression during interactive experiences. *Behaviour & Information Technology*, *25*(2), 159–173. doi:10.1080/01449290500331164

Bandura, A. (1997). *Self-efficacy: The exercise of control*. New York: W. H. Freeman.

Beale, R., & Creed, C. (2009). Affective interaction: How emotional agents affect users. *International Journal of Human-Computer Studies*, *67*(9), 755–776. doi:10.1016/j.ijhcs.2009.05.001

Bianchi-Berthouze, N., & Kleinsmith, A. (2003). A categorical approach to affective gesture recognition. *Connection Science*, *15*(4), 259–269. doi:10.1080/09540090310001658793

Broekens, J., & Brinkman, P. (2009). Affect button: A method for reliable and valid affective self report. *International Journal of Human-Computer Studies*, *71*(6), 641–667. doi:10.1016/j.ijhcs.2013.02.003

Chittaro, L., & Sioni, R. (2014). Affective computing vs. affective placebo: Study of a biofeedback controlled game for relaxation training. *International Journal of Human-Computer Studies*, *72*(8-9), 663–673. doi:10.1016/j.ijhcs.2014.01.007

Cid, F., Moreno, J., Bustos, P., & Nunez, P. (2014). Muecas: A multi-sensor robotic head for affective human robot interaction and imitation. *Sensors (Basel, Switzerland)*, *14*(5), 7711–7737. doi:10.3390/s140507711 PMID:24787636

Demeure, V., Niewiadomski, R., & Pelachaud, C. (2011). How is believability of a virtual agent related to warmth, competence, personification, and embodiment? *Presence (Cambridge, Mass.)*, *20*(5), 431–448. doi:10.1162/PRES_a_00065

Ekman, P. (1972). *Universal and cultural differences in facial expressions of emotion*. Lincoln: University of Nebraska Press.

Eyben, F., Weninger, F., Lehment, N., Schuller, B., & Rigoll, G. (2013). Affective video retrieval: violence detection in Hollywood movies by large-scale segmental feature extraction. *PLoS ONE*, *8*(12), 1–9. doi:10.1371/journal.pone.0078506 PMID:24391704

Fairclough, S. H. (2009). Fundamentals of physiological computing. *Interacting with Computers*, *21*(1-2), 133–145. doi:10.1016/j.intcom.2008.10.011

Fox, E. (2008). *Emotion Science: An integration of cognitive and neuroscientific approaches*. Palgrave: MacMillan.

Goulev, P., Stead, L., Mamdani, E., & Evans, C. (2004). Computer aided emotional fashion. *Computers & Graphics*, *28*(5), 657–666. doi:10.1016/j.cag.2004.06.005

Harmon-Jones, E., Gable, P. A., & Price, T. F. (2013). Does negative affect always narrow and positive affect always broaden the mind? Considering the influence of motivational intensity on cognitive scope. *Current Directions in Psychological Science*, *22*(4), 301–307. doi:10.1177/0963721413481353

Hone, K. (2006). Empathic agents to reduce user frustration: The effects of varying agent characteristics. *Interacting with Computers*, *18*(2), 227–245. doi:10.1016/j.intcom.2005.05.003

Isen, A. M., & Reeve, J. (2005). The influence of positive affect on intrinsic and extrinsic motivation: Facilitating enjoyment of play, responsible work behavior, and self-control. *Motivation and Emotion*, *29*(4), 297–325. doi:10.1007/s11031-006-9019-8

Kaliouby, R., Picard, R. W., & Cohen, S. B. (2006). Affective computing and autism (1093, 228–248). New York: Annals New York Academy of Sciences.

Keller, J. M. (1987). Development and use of the ARCS model of instructional design. *Journal of Instructional Development*, *10*(3), 2–10. doi:10.1007/BF02905780

Kim, Y., & Baylor, A. L. (2006). A social-cognitive framework for pedagogical agents as learning companions. *ETR & D*, *54*(6), 569–596. doi:10.1007/s11423-006-0637-3

Koda, T., & Maes, P. (1996). *Agents with faces: The effect of personification.* Paper presented at the 5th IEEE International Workshop on Robot and Human Communication. Tsukuba, Japan. doi:10.1109/ROMAN.1996.568812

Kort, B., Reilly, R., & Picard, R. (2001). *An affective model of interplay between emotions and learning: reengineering educational pedagogy—building a learning companion*. *Proceedings of the IEEE International Conference on Advanced Learning Technology: Issues, Achievements and Challenges*. Madison, USA. doi:10.1109/ICALT.2001.943850

Kwon, H. J., & Hong, K. S. (2013). A method to predict human emotion using sentimental similarity. *International Journal of Bio-Science and Bio-Technology*, *5*(3), 93–101.

Lanata, A., Valenza, G., & Scilingo, E. P. (2012). A novel EDA glove based on textile-integrated electrodes for affective computing. *Medical & Biological Engineering & Computing*, *50*(11), 1163–1172. doi:10.1007/s11517-012-0921-9 PMID:22711069

Louwerse, M. M., Graesser, A. C., Lu, S., & Mitchel, H. M. (2005). Social cues in animated conversational agents. *Applied Cognitive Psychology*, *19*(6), 693–704. doi:10.1002/acp.1117

Lozanov, G. (1978). *Suggestology and Suggestopedia: Theory and practice*. Paris: UNESCO. Retrieved online at: http://unesdoc.unesco.org/images/0003/000300/030087eb.pdf

McEneaney, J. E. (2013). Agency effects in human–computer interaction. *International Journal of Human-Computer Interaction*, *29*(12), 798–813. doi:10.1080/10447318.2013.777826

Moridis, C. N., & Economides, A. A. (2008). Toward computer-aided affective learning systems: A literature review. *Journal of Educational Computing Research*, *39*(4), 313–337. doi:10.2190/EC.39.4.a

Moridis, C. N., & Economides, A. A. (2012). Affective learning: Empathetic agents with emotional facial and tone of voice expressions. *IEEE Transactions on Affective Computing*, *3*(3), 260–272. doi:10.1109/T-AFFC.2012.6

Mory, E. H. (1992). The use of informational feedback in instruction: Implications for future research. *Educational Technology Research and Development*, *4*(3), 5–20. doi:10.1007/BF02296839

Pedrotti, M., Mirzaei, M. A., Tedesco, A., Chardonnet, J.-R., Mérienne, F., Benedetto, S., & Baccino, T. (2014). Automatic stress classification with pupil diameter analysis. *International Journal of Human-Computer Interaction*, *30*(3), 220–236. doi:10.1080/10447318.2013.848320

Pekrun, R., Goetz, T., Titz, W., & Perry, R. P. (2002). Academic emotions in students' self-regulated learning and achievement: A program of qualitative and quantitative research. *Educational Psychologist*, *37*(2), 91–105. doi:10.1207/S15326985EP3702_4

Picard, R. W. (1995). *Affective computing (*Technical Report No. 321*)*. Cambridge: M.I.T Media Laboratory Perceptual Computing Section.

Picard, R. W. (1997). *Affective computing*. Cambridge: MIT Press. doi:10.1037/e526112012-054

Picard, R. W. (2003). Affective computing: Challenges. *International Journal of Human-Computer Studies*, *59*(1-2), 55–64. doi:10.1016/S1071-5819(03)00052-1

Picard, R. W. (2010). Affective computing: From laughter to IEEE. *IEEE Transactions on Affective Computing*, *1*(1), 11–17. doi:10.1109/T-AFFC.2010.10

Pulutchik, R. (2011). The nature of emotions. *American Scientist*, *89*(4), 344–350. doi:10.1511/2001.4.344

Reynolds, C., & Picard, R. W. (2005). *Evaluation of affective computing systems from a dimensional metaethical position*. Paper presented at the First Augmented Cognition Conference, Las Vegas, Nevada.

Russell, J. (1980). A Circumplex model of affect. *Journal of Personality and Social Psychology*, *39*(6), 1161–1178. doi:10.1037/h0077714

Schacter, D. L. (2011). *Psychology*. New York: Worth Publishers.

Sen, M. (2006). *Effects of English lessons, based on multiple intelligences theory, on students' motivation, self efficacy, self-esteem and multiple intelligences*. [Masters Dissertation]. Ankara University Institute of Social Sciences, Ankara Turkey. Retrieved from www.yok.gov.tr(191346)

Shahid, S., Krahmer, E., Neerincx, M., & Swerts, M. (2013). Positive affective interactions: The role of repeated exposure and copresence. *IEEE Transactions on Affective Computing*, *4*(2), 226–237. doi:10.1109/T-AFFC.2012.39

Shen, L., Wang, M., & Shen, R. (2009). Affective e-learning: Using "emotional" data to improve learning in pervasive learning environment. *Journal of Educational Technology & Society*, *12*(2), 176–189.

The definition of educational technology. (1977AECT. Washington, D.C.: Association for Educational Communications and Technology.

Villani, D., & Riva, G. (2012). Does interactive media enhance the management of stress? suggestions from a controlled study. *Cyberpsychology, Behavior, and Social Networking*, *15*(1), 24–30. doi:10.1089/cyber.2011.0141 PMID:22032797

Virvou, M., Tsihrintzis, G. A., Alepis, E., Stathopoulou, O., & Kabassi, K. (2012). Emotion recognition: Empirical studies towards the combination of audio-lingual and visual-facial modalities through multi-attribute decision making. *International Journal of Artificial Intelligence Tools*, *21*(2), 1–28. doi:10.1142/S0218213012400015

Vygotsky, L. S., Cole, M., John-Steiner, V., Scribner, S., & Souberman, E. (1978). *Mind in society*. Cambridge: Harvard University Press.

Zics, B. (2011). Engineering experiences in biofeedback interfaces: Interaction as a cognitive feedback loop. *Journal of Visual Art Practice*, *10*(1), 71–82. doi:10.1386/jvap.10.1.71_1

KEY TERMS AND DEFINITIONS

Affective Computing: An interdisciplinary branch that deals with design of systems and devices that can recognize, interpret, process and respond to users' affective states.

Affective State: An encompassing term, used to describe the topics of emotion, feelings, and moods together.

Emotions: Complex neurophysiological systems with visceral, behavioural and reflective levels operating on biological, neurological and psychological systems.

Human-Computer Interaction: A discipline concerned with the study, design, construction and implementation of human-centric computer systems.

Instructional Design: The process of creating instructional experiences.

Instructional Technology: Application of scientific knowledge at solution of instructional problems.

Learning Environment: Environment in which learning occurs.

Chapter 11

Regional Landfill Site Selection with GIS and Analytical Hierarchy Process Techniques:

A Case Study of Langkawi Island, Malaysia

Elmira Shamshiry
University Kebangsaan, Malaysia & Research Management Center (RMC), University Malaysia Terengganu (UMT), Malaysia

Abdul Mumin Abdulai
University Kebangsaan, Malaysia

Mazlin Bin Mokhtar
University Kebangsaan, Malaysia

Ibrahim Komoo
Universiti Malaysia Terengganu (UMT), Malaysia

ABSTRACT

Increasing population and urbanization pose a huge challenge for municipal authorities to select suitable landfill site to dispose the increasing quantities of solid waste. Wrong landfill siting can result in social, environmental and economic cost. Therefore, suitable approaches are required to select landfill sites because that can enhance sound waste disposal practice in the fast-growing urban areas. The Geographic Information System based Multi-criteria Decision Analysis has been used in this chapter to examine the essentials of an effective site selection. GIS-based MCDA is an intelligent system that transforms spatial data into valuable information which can be used to make critical decisions. The analytical hierarchy process is utilized to assist the prioritization process. In Langkawi, disposal of municipal solid waste into open sites could lead to different adverse impacts on public health and the physical environment. This paper represents simple but effective method to assist landfill site selection efforts in the Langkawi.

1. INTRODUCTION

Municipal solid waste (MSW) is seen as fundamental issue to city management and policy makers. Financial, social, political and environmental concerns are major considerations that complicate the decision making procedures (Baban & Flannagan, 1998). Among the different techniques employed to treat municipal solid waste solid wastes, landfills are the last destination (Gbanie et

DOI: 10.4018/978-1-4666-8598-7.ch011

al., 2013). Although not much attention has been paid to landfills, they form integral components of the waste management chain and require much more attention in order to reduce their environmental impacts (Mahini & Gholamalifard, 2006; Rahman et al., 2008). Landfill is not as expensive and complicated as other kinds of waste treatment (e.g., incinerator). Nevertheless, landfill siting is a complex, intricate, and tedious process that needs thorough assessment using various kinds of criteria (Chang et al., 2008). Site selection seems to be also a significant and essential issue in waste management in the fast-growing urban and tourist areas, particularly in the developing nations.

Due to the complexity of waste management systems, the selection of the suitable solid waste landfill site needs a careful consideration of the different and alternative assessment criteria (Gbanie et al., 2013). Selecting appropriate sanitary landfill places is a significant decision which requires an enhanced land assessment procedure in order to determine the optimum disposal locations (Tınmaz & Demir, 2006). Such locations must meet the legal conditions of the government, and also must reduce economic, health, environmental and social expenses (Siddiqui, et al., 1996). Sanitary landfill can constitute one of the basic approaches of municipal solid waste disposal. Interestingly, optimized siting decisions have obtained notable significance for ensuring minimum harm and destruction to the different environmental sub-components, and also could decrease the stigma related to the residents living in the vicinity, thereby increasing the overall sustainability with regard to the life cycle of a landfill (Sumathi et al., 2008).

There is abundant evidence in the literature to show that identifying an appropriate site for municipal landfill has never been an easy procedure, as it requires careful environmental, social, technical and economic considerations. Generally, problems related to organization and planning in waste management that occur usually due to legal and financial limitations further complicate landfill site selection process in the majority of the developing nations. Inadequate information poses a challenge in the site selection process because of the rules and principles governing the use of data in the Municipalities (Daneshvar et al., 2005; Mokhtar et al., 2008).

Geographic Information System (GIS) is a digital database management system that manages huge volumes of spatially distributed data from different resources. GIS seems to be suitable for site-selection research since it can store, analyze, retrieve, and represent information based on user-defined details (Shamshiry et al., 2011). GIS is a useful instrument that can be used to bolster the management of natural resources (Luis E. Marín, et al., 2012).

GIS has the benefit of storing, analyzing and retrieving a remarkable amount of information from different resources and showing the results with much ease and accuracy (Al-Hanbali et al., 2011; Mokhtar et al., 2008; Siddiqui et al., 1996; Sumiani et al., 2009). Spatial planning issues demanding complex and diverse data can be determined through the use of multi-criteria assessment methods (Nas et al., 2008). The benefit in using the GIS-based methods for site selection is that while GIS can handle a huge amount of spatial data, Multi-criteria Decision Analysis (MCDA) can blend expert opinions with factual information that is more appropriate for optimal landfill siting. Such method assesses different criteria, all potential outcomes and conflicting goals arising from the analysis (Al-Hanbali et al., 2011). Such methods use GIS to perform a primary screening of the study area in order to determine the appropriate regions. In the last decade, MCDA was highly employed by various scholars for landfill site selection in different approaches. A GIS-based MCDA transforms and integrates spatial data into a decision. It includes the use of geographical data, the decision maker's priorities and the management of data and priorities to achieve uni-dimensional values of alternatives (Sumathi et al., 2008).

Since the 1950s, along with the proliferation of GIS technology, multiple criteria decision making methods (MCDM) have been developed as a main device to help decision makers analyze and solve various criteria decision issues. Examples of studies that used GIS to determine possible waste disposal sites include: Muttiah et al., (1996); Charnpratheep et al., (1997); Kao & Lin (1996); Kao et al., (1997); Lin & Kao (1998); Sarah & Susan (2000); Leao et al., (2001); and Sumathi et al., (2008). MCDM techniques have been enhanced to help decision makers in ranking a recognized set of alternatives for an issue or making a choice among this set while paying attention to the conflicting principles. The alternatives are compared with each other, and to determine their relationship with each criterion. Likewise, some approaches need comparison of the criteria to achieve the relative significance of each criterion. Thus, MCDM approach uses this method to appoint ranks to the alternatives. Siddiqui et al., (1996) combined geographic information system (GIS) and AHP process to study appropriate solid waste site selection process in the fast urbanizing areas due to technological advances, globalization and population growth. Siddiqui has found that the utilization of GIS and analytical hierarchy process (AHP) can enhance the efficiency of choosing suitable landfill sites for the disposal of solid wastes (Sumathi et al., 2008).

GIS mixes the spatial data with quantitative and qualitative data that are able to support a huge range of spatial queries (Montserrat et al., 2008). The possible benefit of a GIS-based method for landfill siting emerges from the idea that it not only decreases the cost and time of site selection, but also represents a digital data bank for long-term controlling of the site. GIS can also have a main function in keeping data to facilitate gathering operations, customer service, the planning of routes for waste transportation to transfer stations, and from transfer stations to landfills, the analysis of optimal locations for transfer stations, and the long-term control of landfills (Sumathi et al., 2008). The benefits of utilizing GIS for waste disposal as well as landfill site selection have been shown in many different studies (Montserrat et al., 2008).

AHP is a systematic decision making process which was first expanded by Saaty (1980) (Bhushan & Rai, 2004). This method represents a tool of decomposing the issue into a hierarchy of sub-issues that can be more easily understood and subjectively assessed. The subjective assessments are changed into numerical values ranked on a numerical scale (Bhushan & Rai, 2004, Şener et al., 2010).

Two major reasons for the increasing solid waste growth in Langkawi Malaysia include the rapid transformation of lifestyles and increasing population of residents as well as tourists visiting the Island. In Langkawi, the disposal of some of the MSW into open sites could lead to different adverse impacts on public health and the physical environment. Thus, constructing sanitary landfills to meet the environmental legislations and reducing the undesirable effects of the current practices is the major preference for MSW management in Langkawi. Such problem is getting more significant when we understand that Langkawi has many internationally renowned and interesting Islands for visitors. Thus, the chapter represents simple but effective method to assist landfill site selection efforts in the Langkawi Island. To achieve this objective, this study has explored the standard specifications for landfill sitting using the case of Langkawi.

2. BACKGROUND

The methods and the criteria used in the landfill site selection process have been examined in this section. Also, brief information about the study area has been presented.

Table 1. Number of tourists, in Langkawi 2003-2009

Years	2003 *	2004*	2005*	2006**	2007**	2008**	2009**
Tourists	1,981,946	2,179,629	1,835,287	2,981,646	3,426,426	2,879,270	1,044,163
Increase population%	1.22	1.45	0.97	2.88	14.92	15.97	5.79

Source:* Shafeea Leman et al. (2007), **Langkawi Tourist Information Center (Jan 2010)

Table 2. Population growth rates in Langkawi Island (1980-2009)

Years	1980*	1991*	2000*	2001**	2003***	2004***	2005*	2008*	2009*
Population	28,340	42,938	69,597	73,091	82,552	85,336	88,125	96,726	97000
Increase in population%	3.09	4.68	6.09	6.4	7.23	7.47	7.71	8.46	8.49

Source: * MHLG (2009), ** National census (2010), *** Shafeea Leman et al. (2007)

2.1. The Study Area

As a primary Geopark in Malaysia and Southeast Asia, Langkawi Geopark consists of 99 Islands located in the Kedah State, Malaysia. The idea of a Geopark was initiated by Langkawi Development Authority (LADA), and the Kedah State Government, which is basically due to their motivation and desire for the consistent progress of Langkawi as the main source of geological heritage and a tourism hub in the Asian subregion. This has been shown in the activities of the planning authorities like the Majlis Daerah Langkawi and Majlis Perbandaran Langkawi Bandaraya Pelancongan (MPLBP) (Shafeea Leman et al., 2008).

An economy that is based largely on cultivation of paddy and rubber and fisheries is quickly being overtaken by a tourism-based economy, which is due to the ecological beauty of the island coupled with public sector support.

The landfill in Langkawi is placed at Kampung Belanga Pecah, Jalan Air Hangat, Kuah. It has a total area of 20 hectares, with 12 working staff and 3 machines. The disposal method adopted usually is land filling. This landfill is about 10-years old. In 2000, the average daily load was 80 tons. While the latest statistics is not available, the daily load of waste moved to this landfill has been projected to increase considerably. This can affect the ability of the Island to attract tourists.

The benefits envisioned in making Langkawi a Geopark and tourism hub make it essential to follow the appropriate standards for siting landfill in the Island.

Number of tourists in Langkawi Island is shown in Table 1. Population growth rate is shown in Table 2 and average amount of weekly waste produce between 2004-2009 is shown in Figure 1.

2.2. The Method

Before performing the spatial analysis, the factor criteria should be determined based on the local principles, international practices, and then outlined according to the assessment of the physical as well as socio-economic problems. Factor criteria are employed to assess the remaining fields for landfill according to their suitability. First of all, GIS data were gathered for study area from various resources. Maps with the scale 1:20,000 were digitized and converted (Fig. 3 A-L). All of the analysis, digitization, and conversion of the maps were carried out through GIS software; Arc GIS Desktop 9.2. The AHP weights were counted by Microsoft Excel.

Figure 1. Statistical analysis diagram of average weekly waste produce at MSW Langkawi Island, (2004-2009)

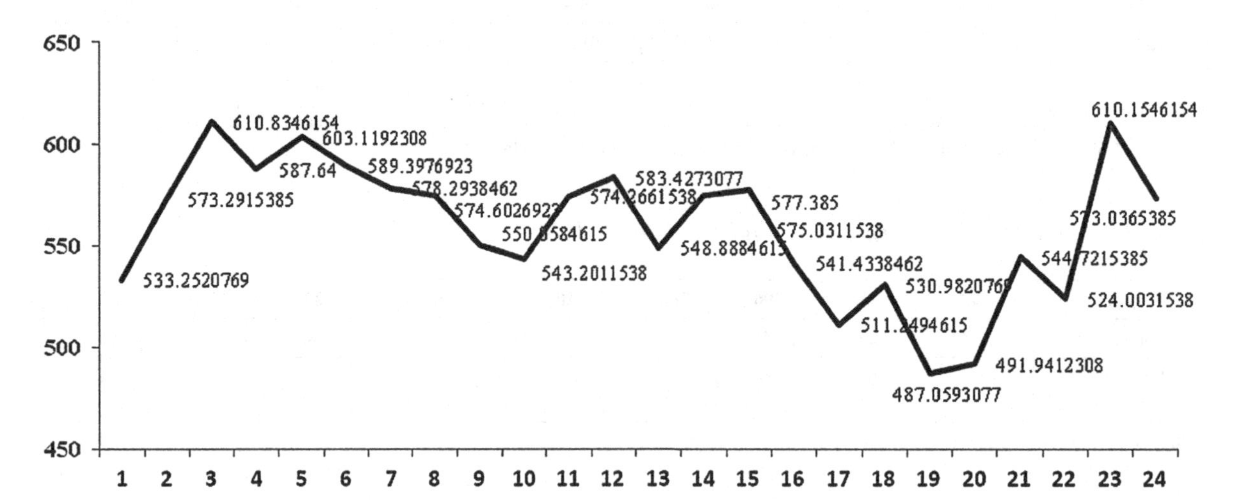

The GIS-aided landfill siting examined here mixes the spatial analysis devices provided by GIS, which are based on particular assessment criteria. The methodology includes the following steps:

1. To develop a digital GIS database including all spatial information.
2. To determine the assessment criteria/sub criteria and formation of the hierarchical structure of the multiple criteria issue.

To prepare feature definition images for the extract analysis, we need to perform spatial analytical operations. All the relevant criterion maps pertaining to landfill were made for the extraction procedure (Siti Zubaidah et al., 2013). Multi-criteria decision analysis provides the chance to incorporate the various criteria into the site selection assessment. This approach thus aids decision makers to select the suitable option. The use of GIS as decision supporting system helps decision makers in each site selection. AHP approach accelerates decision making via breaking an intricate decision issue into an easier one. Also, decision elements are compared through the utilization of pair-wise comparison for weight identification, which helps in decreasing the complexity of the decision process.

2.2.1. *Criteria Description and Application*

The following factors were examined in the landfill site selection procedure in this chapter.

There were two main groups of determinant criteria. The first group included physical factors. The second group consisted of socio-economic factors. Seven criteria were indentified in two major groups for site selection procedure for the study area. Each criterion is described as follows:

The selected potential site maps consider more analysis. At this level, factor criteria were employed to further assess these sites based on their suitability for indicating the most ideal site for locating landfill. Thus, seven factor criteria were determined and each one was classified based on its suitability (Wan Hussin et al., 2010). In this analysis, the first step is to apply the constraint criteria to make a map of the excluded fields; see Figures 2 through 13.

Figure 2. The map layer for the geomorphology criteria. Different color in the legend of photo clarified characteristics of per map.

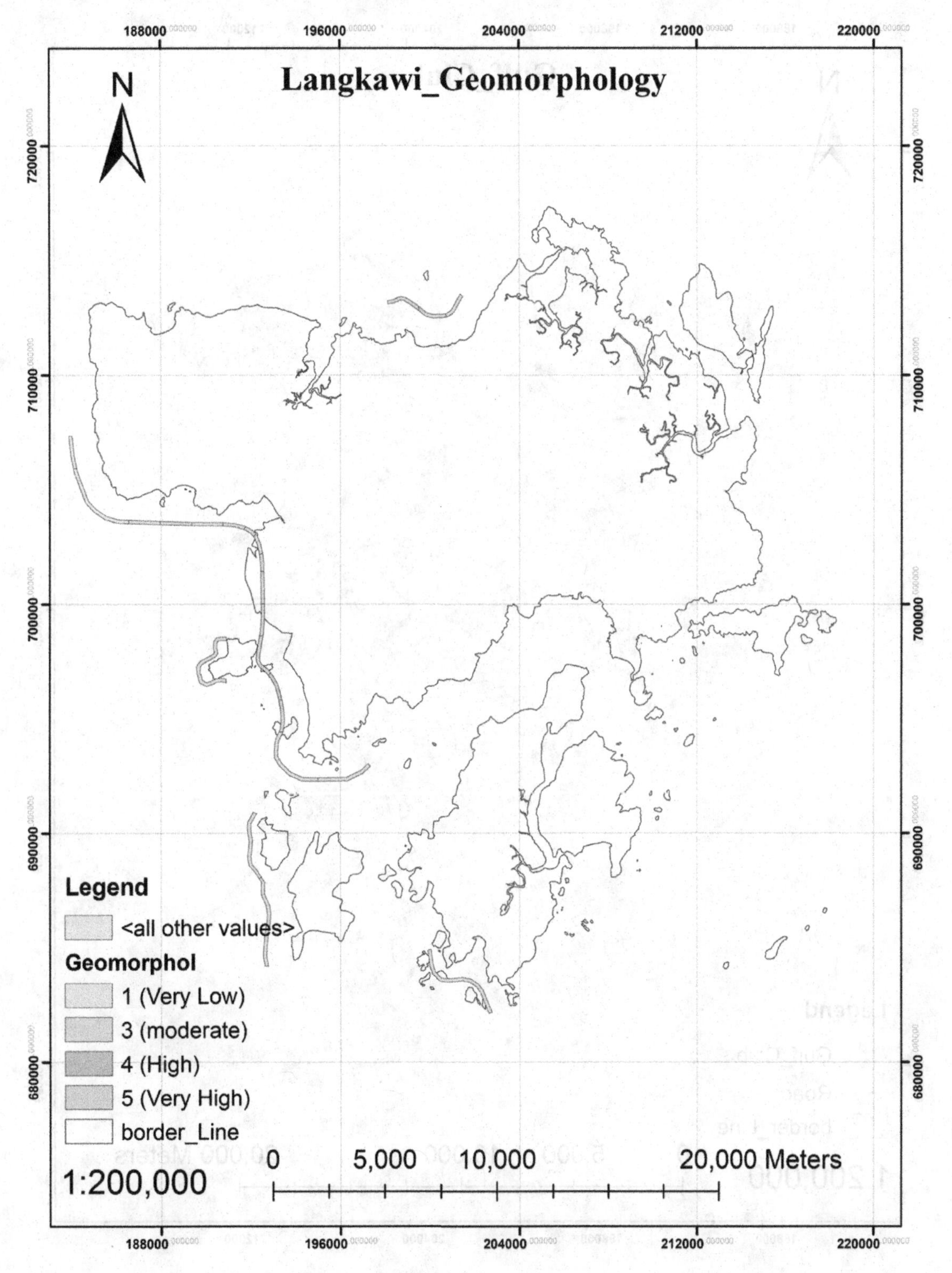

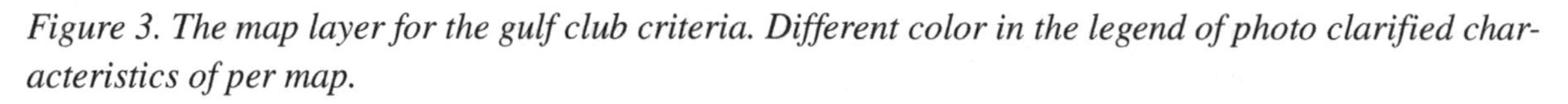

Figure 3. The map layer for the gulf club criteria. Different color in the legend of photo clarified characteristics of per map.

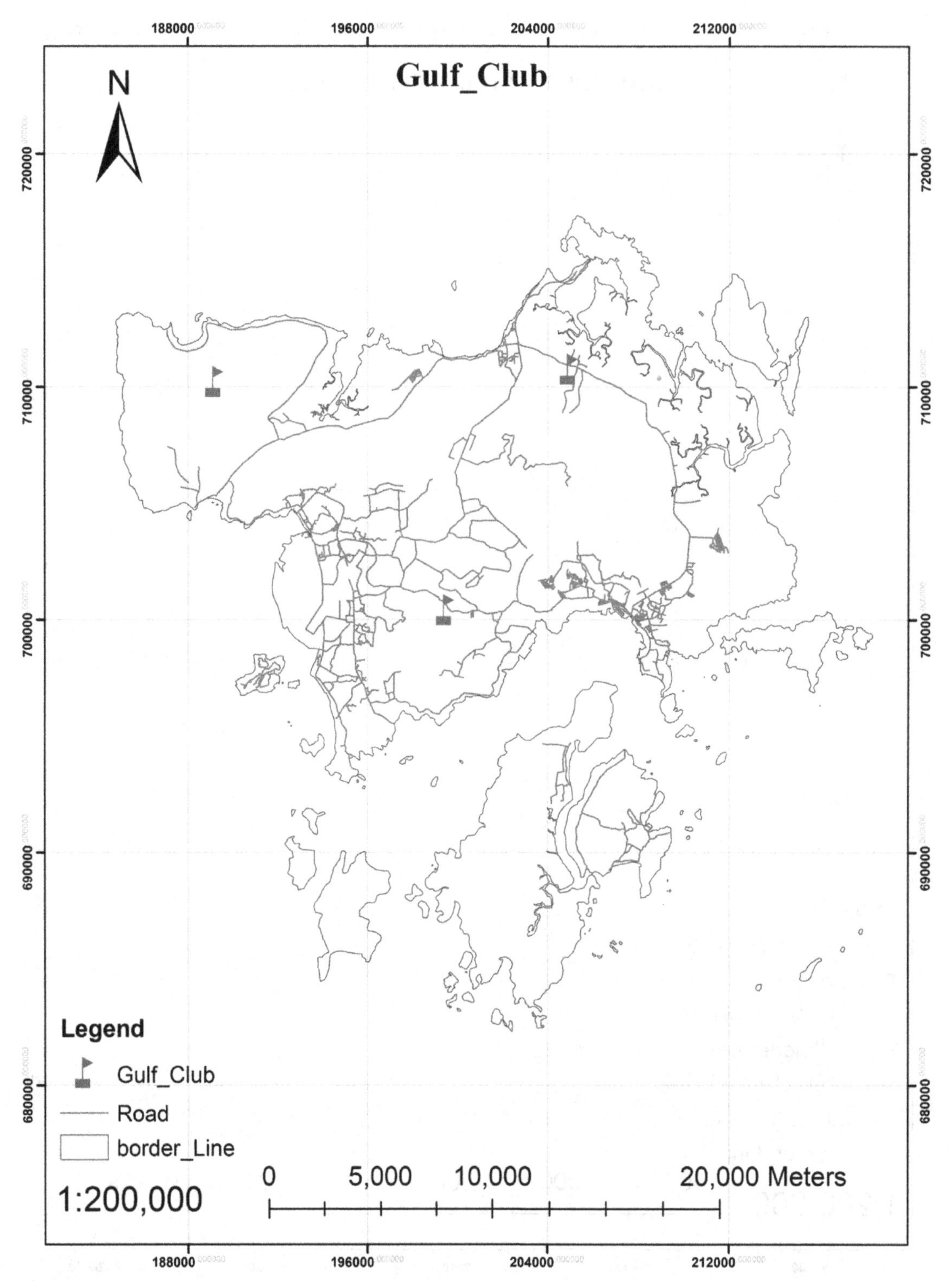

Figure 4. The map layer for the land use criteria. Different color in the legend of photo clarified characteristics of per map.

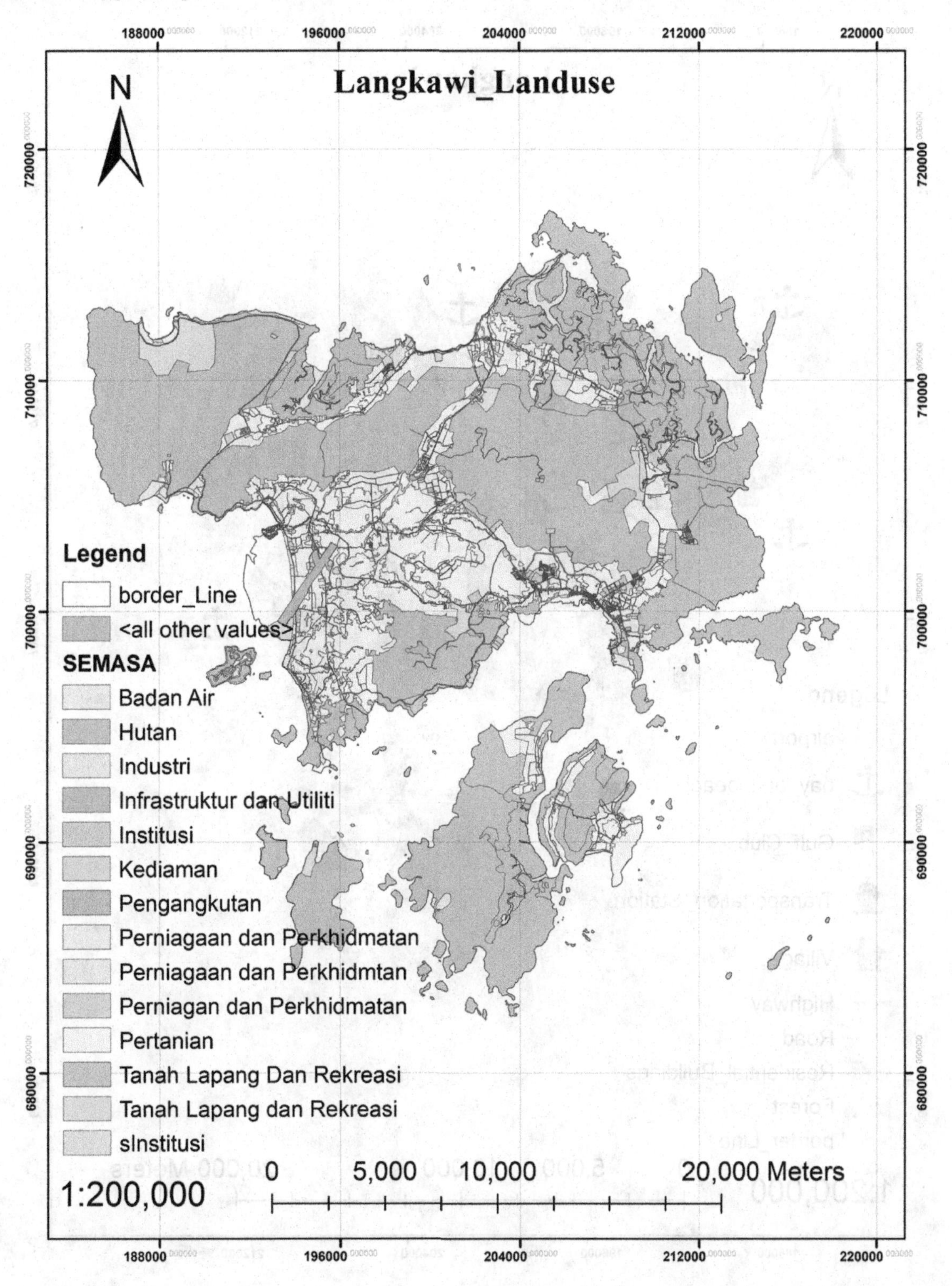

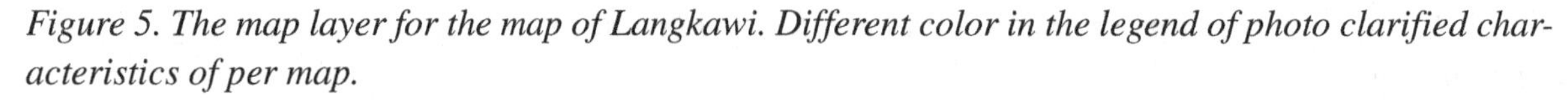

Figure 5. The map layer for the map of Langkawi. Different color in the legend of photo clarified characteristics of per map.

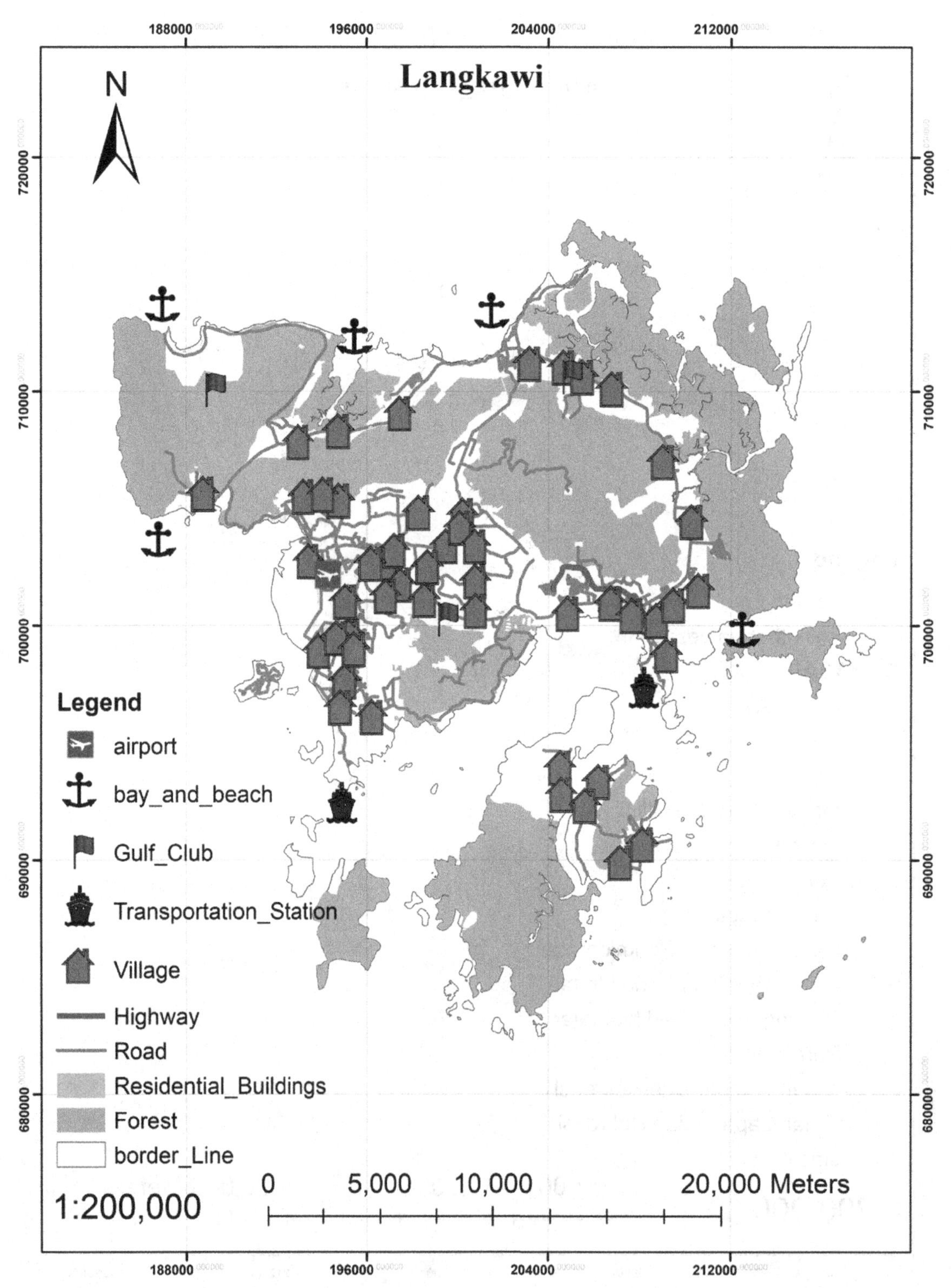

Figure 6. The map layer for the parcel. Different color in the legend of photo clarified characteristics of per map.

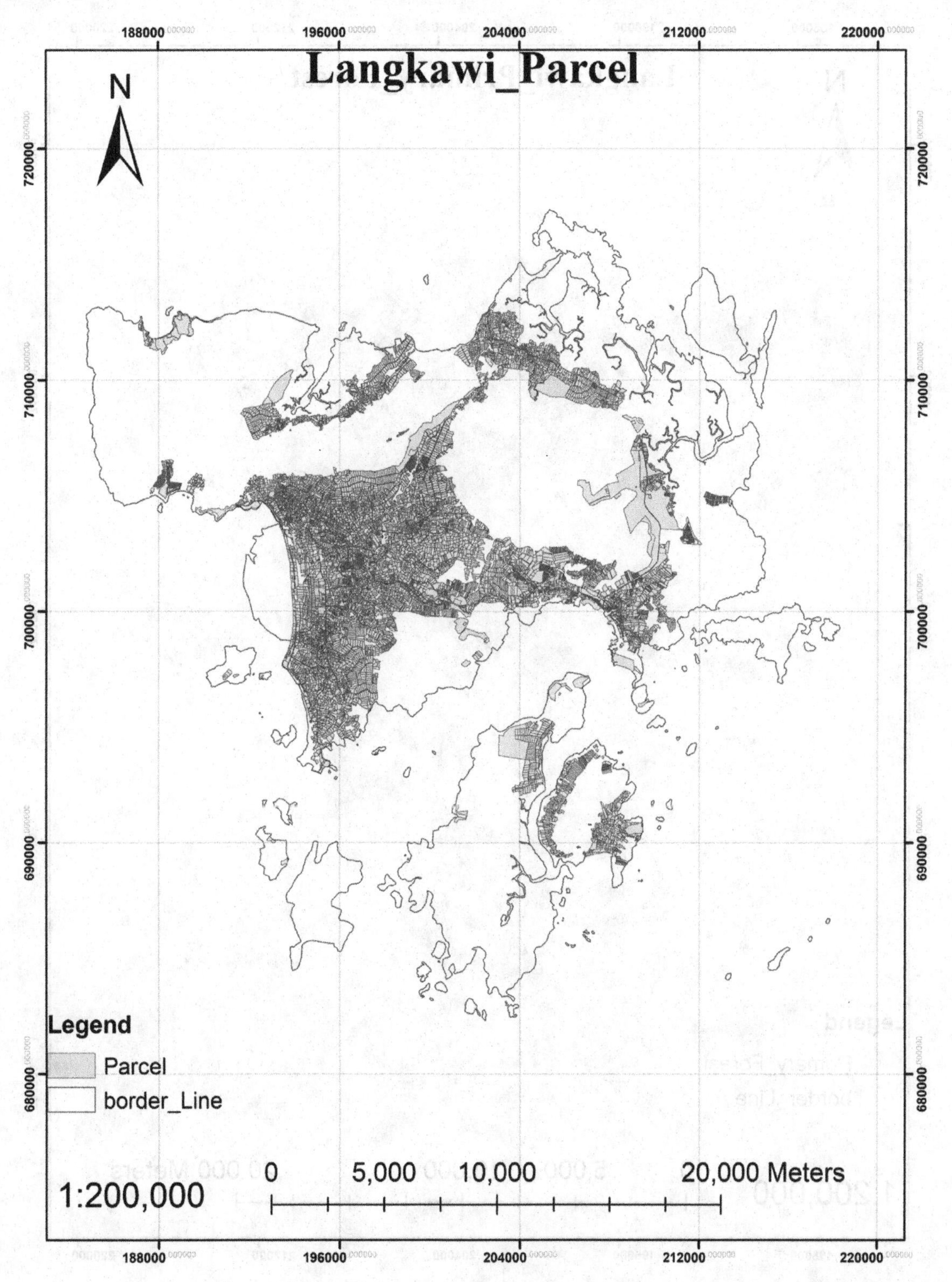

Figure 7. The map layer for the primary forest criteria. Different color in the legend of photo clarified characteristics of per map.

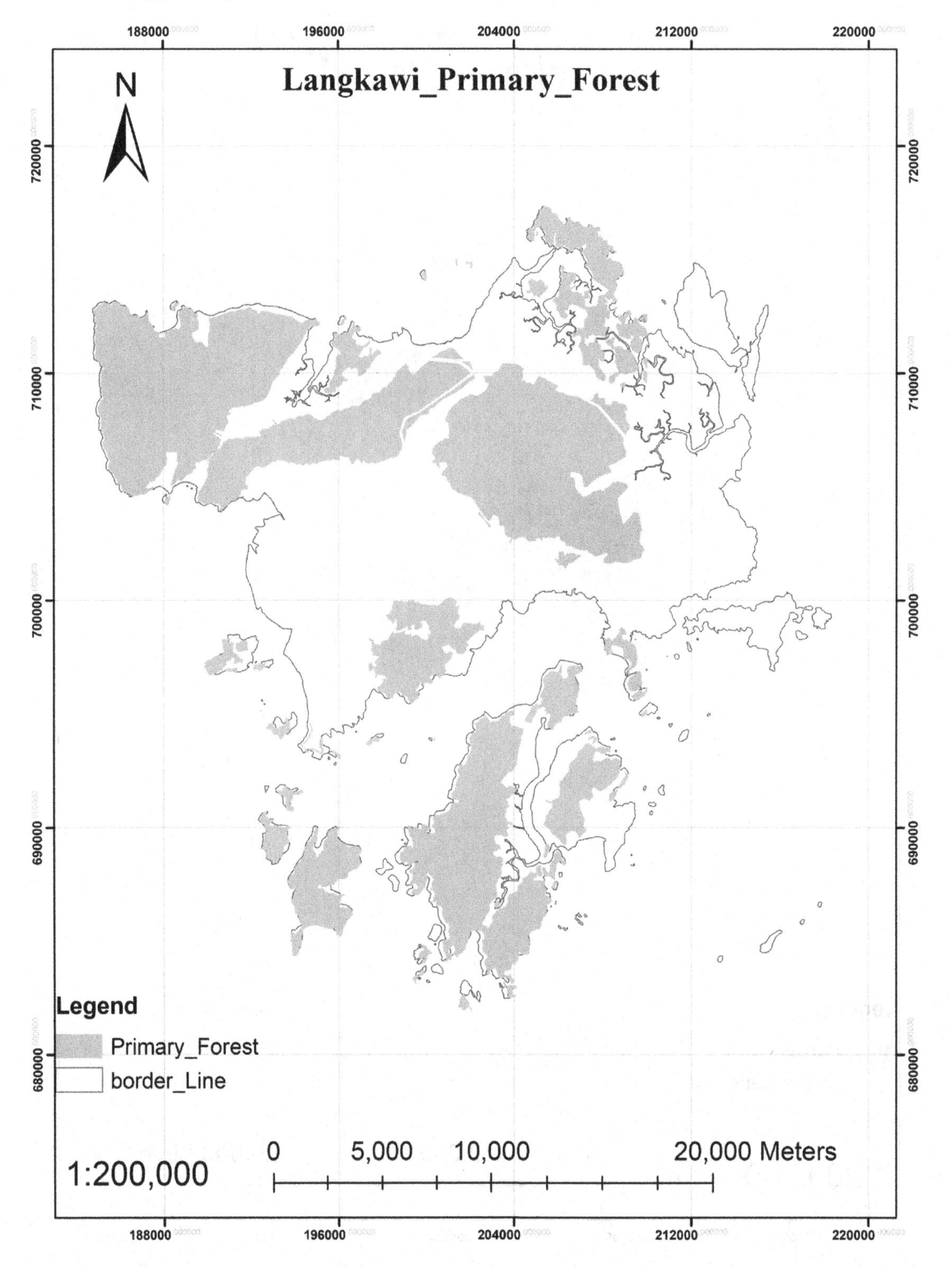

Figure 8. The map layer for the aspect. Different color in the legend of photo clarified characteristics of per map.

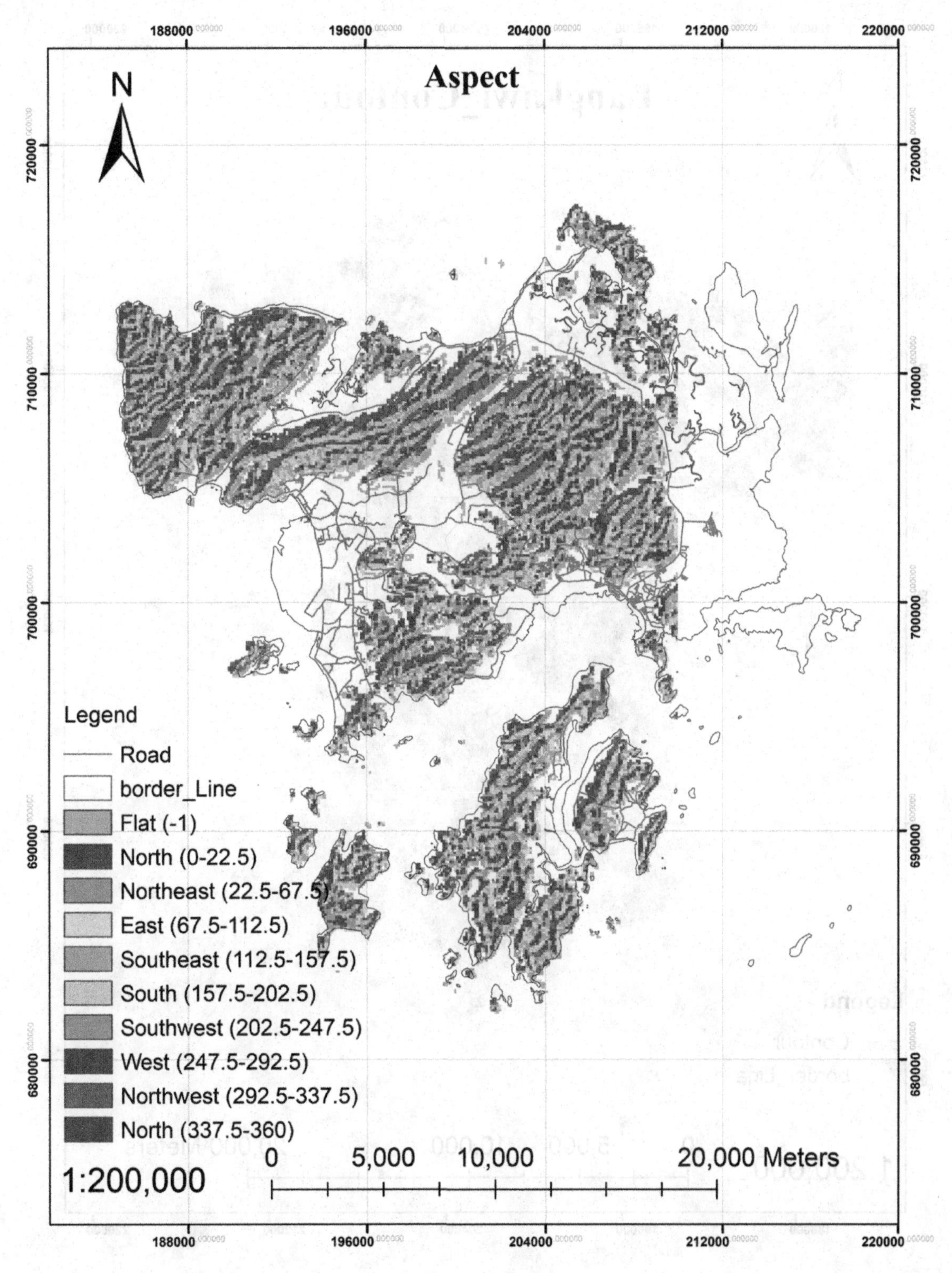

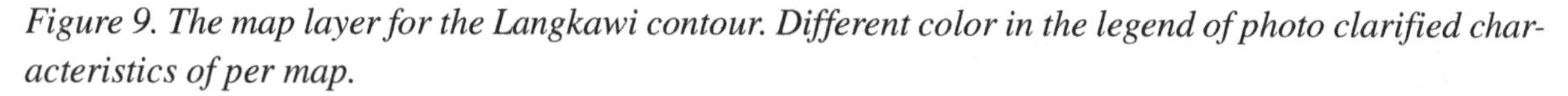

Figure 9. The map layer for the Langkawi contour. Different color in the legend of photo clarified characteristics of per map.

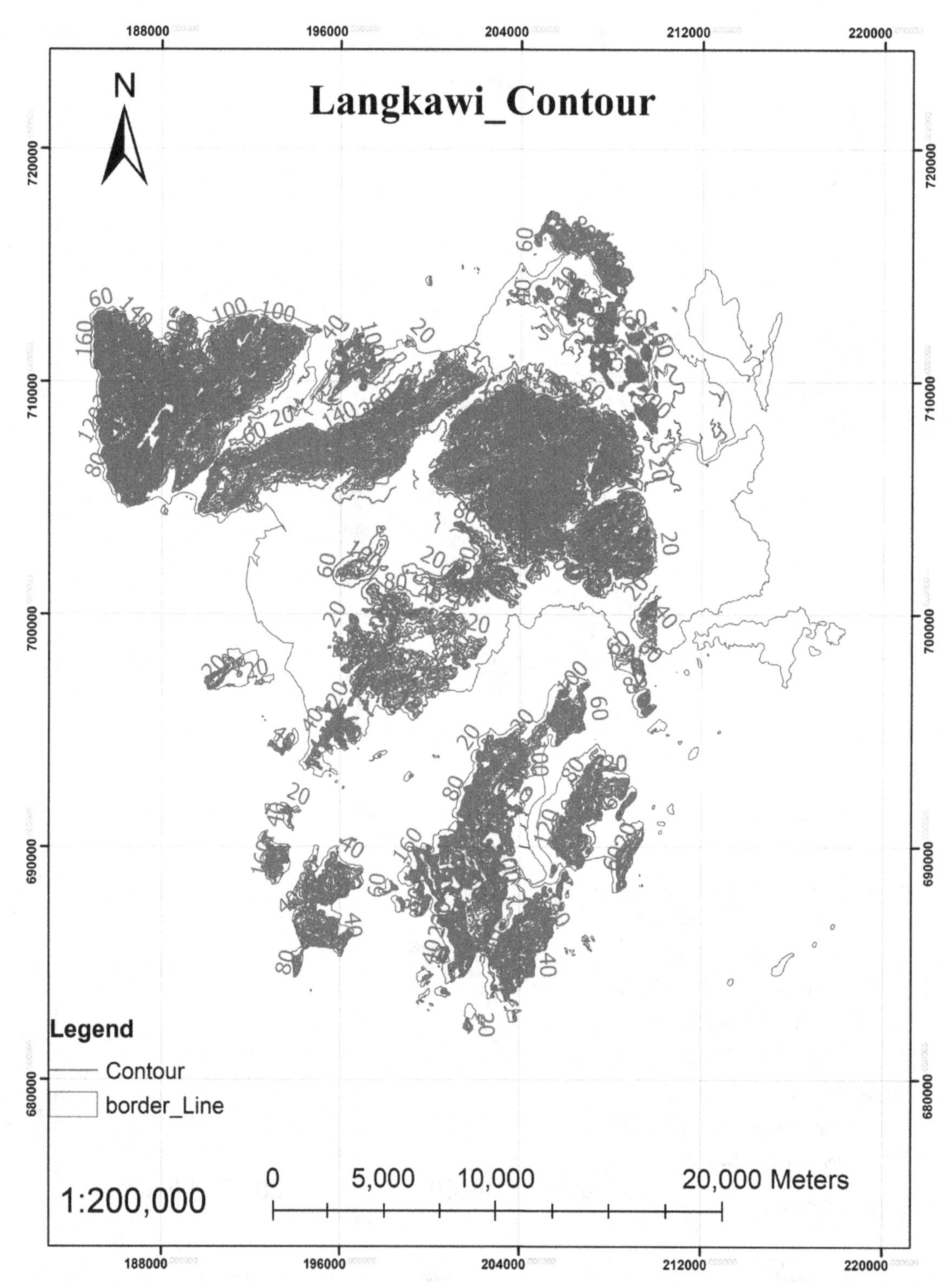

Figure 10. The map layer for the roads criteria. Different color in the legend of photo clarified characteristics of per map.

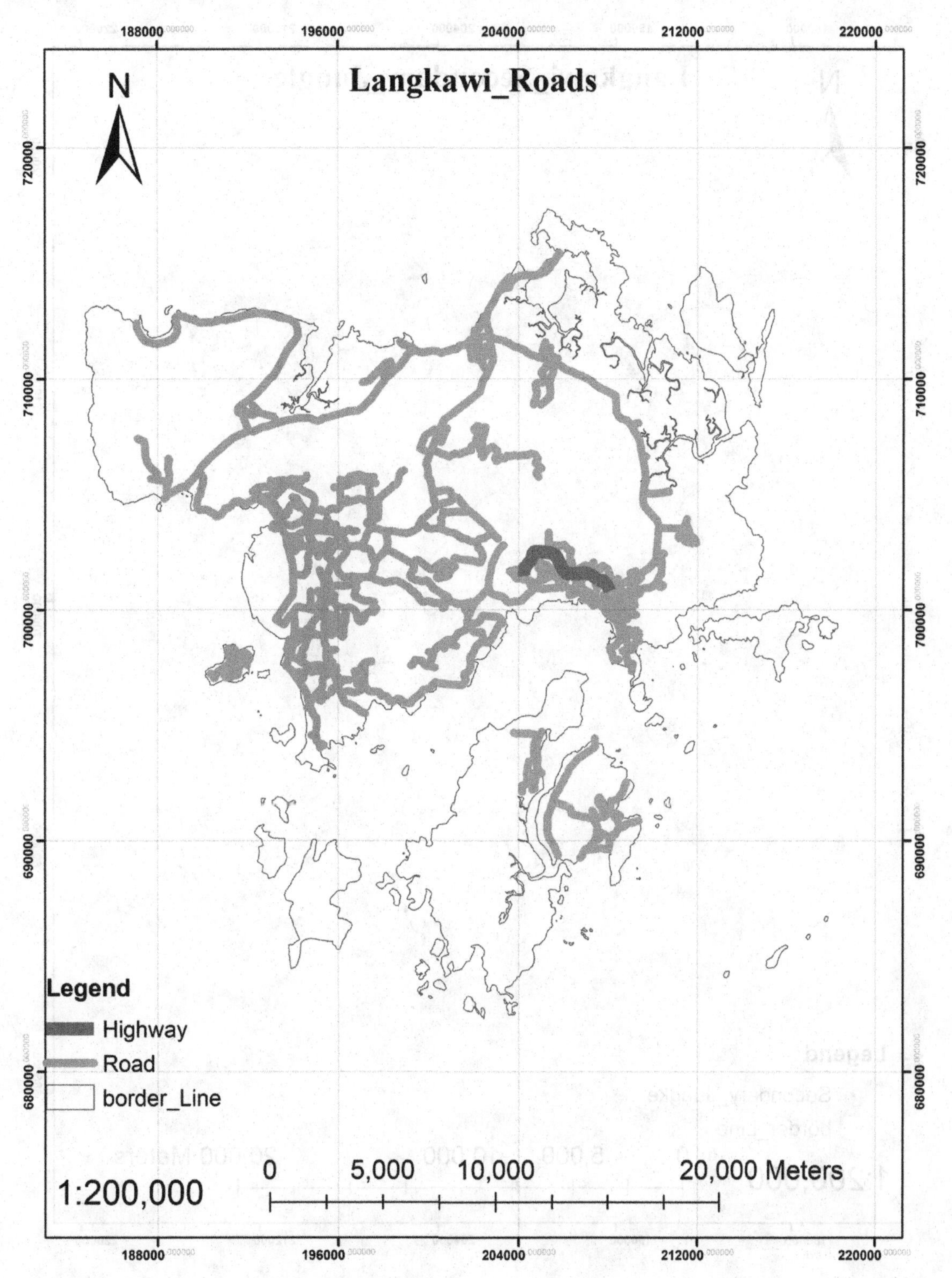

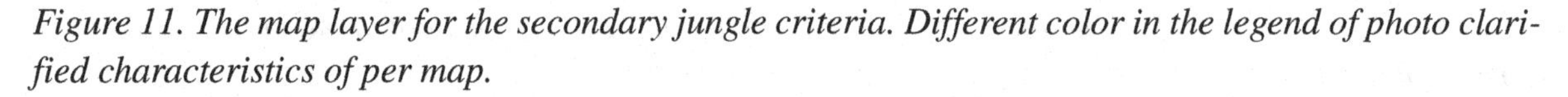

Figure 11. The map layer for the secondary jungle criteria. Different color in the legend of photo clarified characteristics of per map.

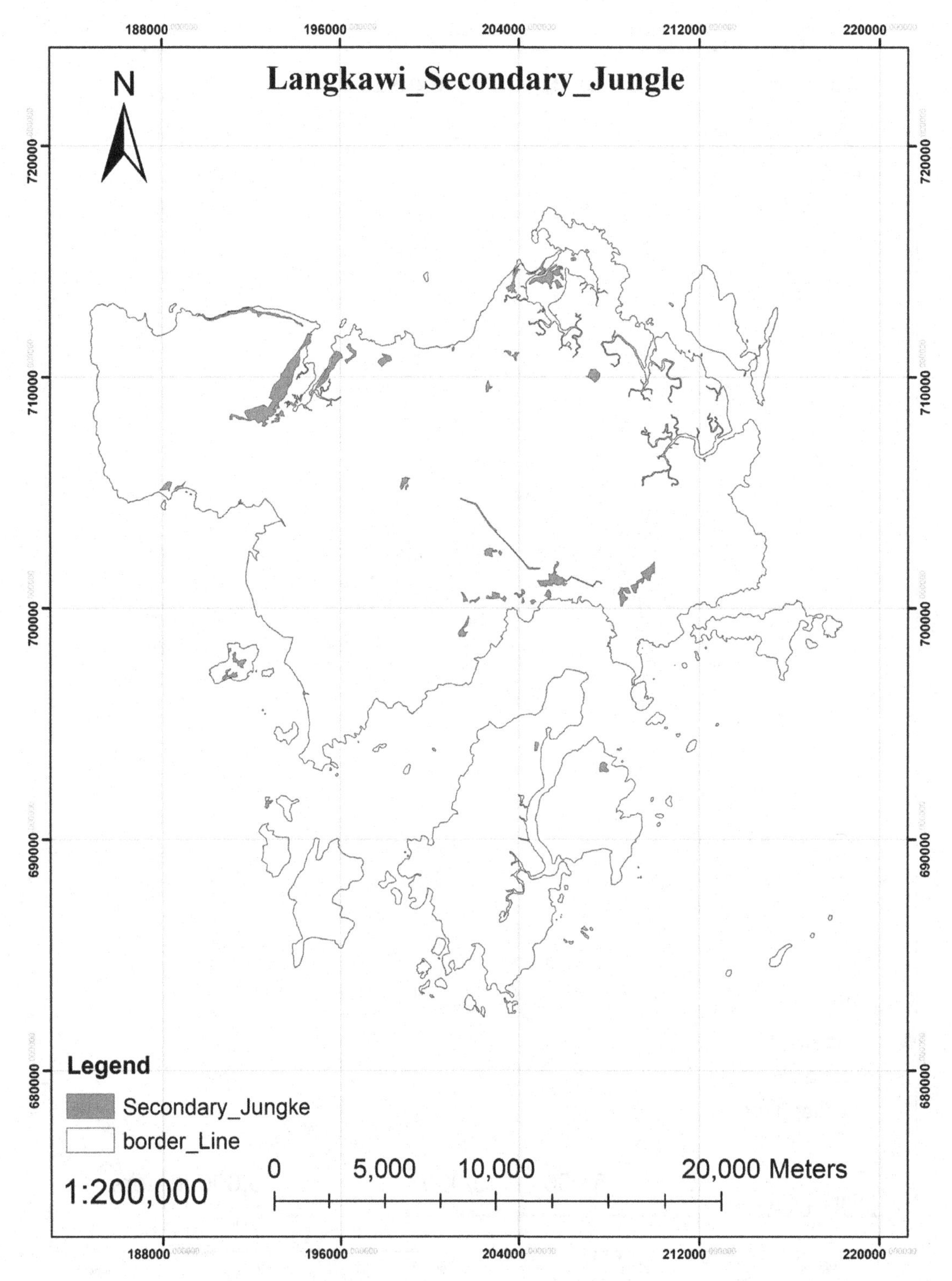

Figure 12. The map layer for the slope criteria. Different color in the legend of photo clarified characteristics of per map.

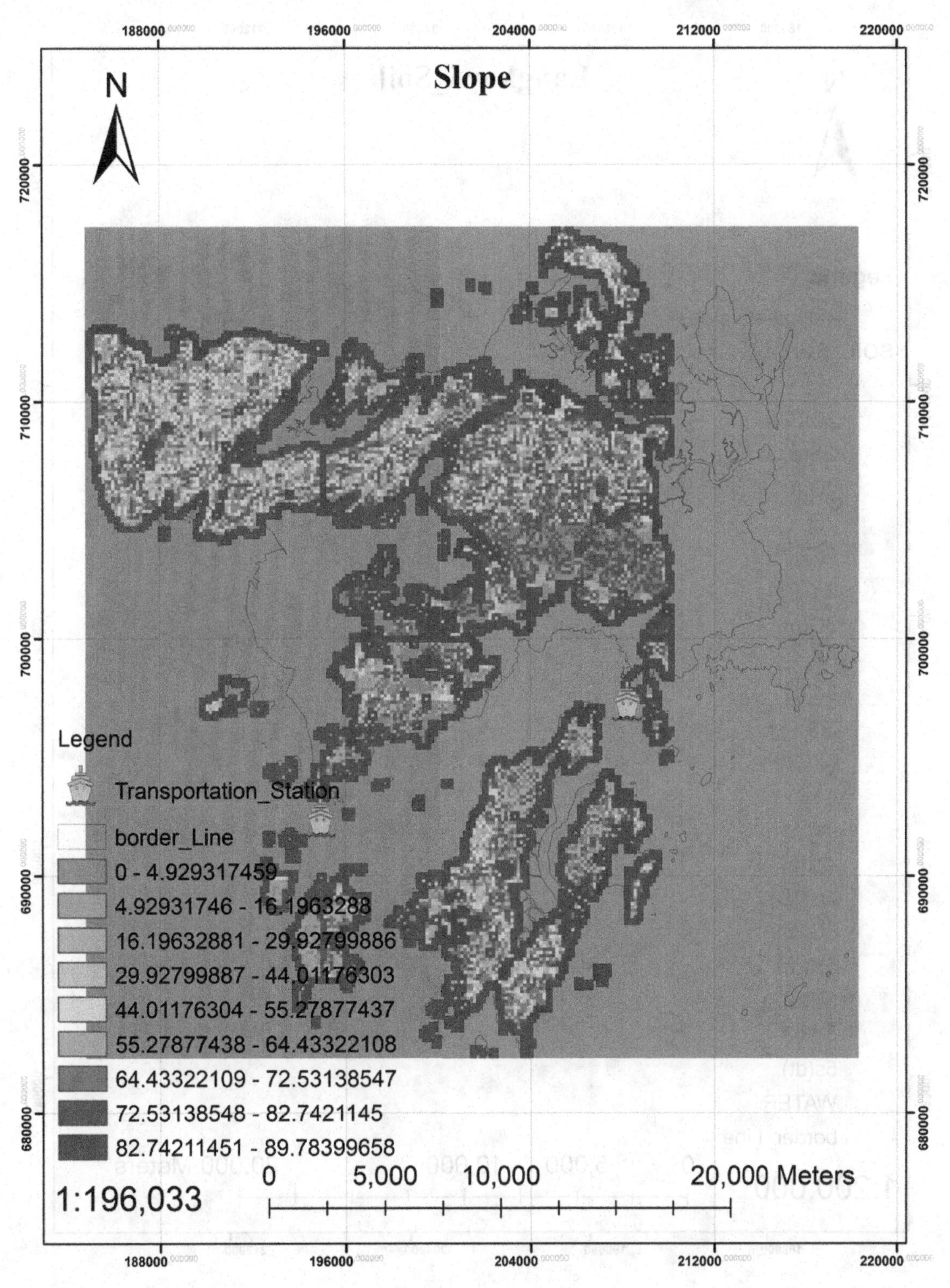

Figure 13. The map layer for the soil criteria. Different color in the legend of photo clarified characteristics of per map.

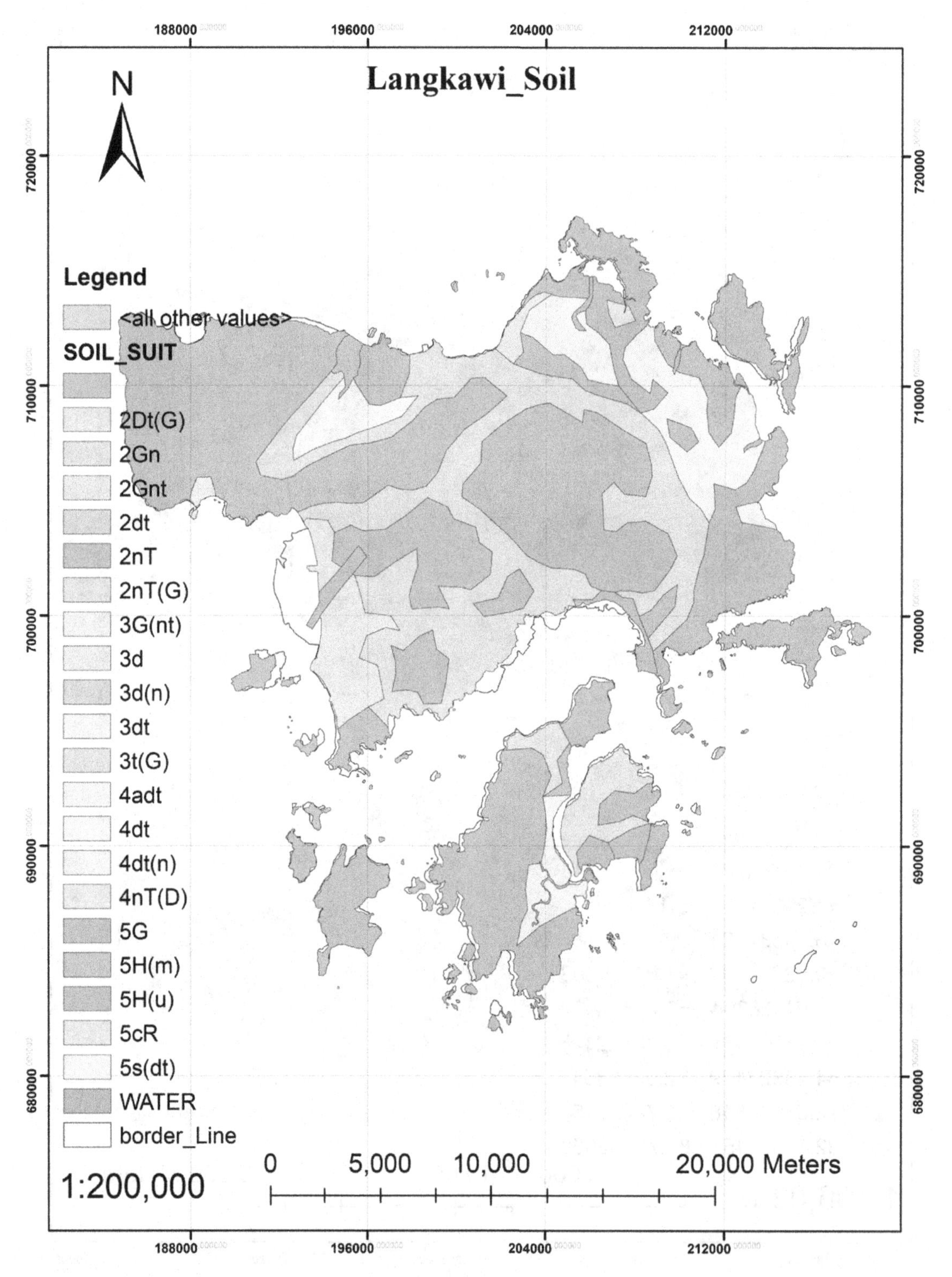

2.2.2. Physical Criteria

The physical criteria examined include water, forest, slope, and aspect.

- **Water:** This criterion seems to be significant from both the economic and environmental view-points because of the need for an effective drainage system with probably high costs (Gemitzi et al., 2007, Afzali et al., 2011). Totally, waste disposal regions should not be sited near to lakes, rivers, ponds or swamps.
- **Forest:** Indeed, forest is a physical criterion. Mangrove forest in Kilim River (Geopark branch) is included in this category. This criterion is significant since it leads to degradation to, and pollution of sensitive ecosystems.
- **Slope:** Land morphology is another significant factor in siting of landfill. Land morphology is assessed by slope gradation determined in percentages or degrees (Kontos et al., 2005). Steep slopes are not appropriate for landfill establishment in which the construction expenses of excavation are exorbitant in higher slopes (Gemitzi et al., 2007). Furthermore, the appropriate slope of land surface is significant in preventing the flowing of leachate (Khorasani & Nejadkorki, 2000; Afzali et al., 2011). The best slope to locate landfill is below 10 degrees for minimizing erosion and water runoff. Slope is the measure of the rate of change of elevation at a surface location and normally represented by percentage or degree (Chang, 2010).
- **Aspect:** Aspect is known as the measure of the direction of slope. It starts with 0° at the north, and then in a clockwise direction goes to an end at 360° again at the north. It is usually categorized into four main directions including; north, east, south, and west or into eight main directions such as north, northeast, east, southeast, south, southwest, west, and northwest.

2.2.3. *Socio-Economic Criteria*

The socio-economic criteria examined in this section include road, built up areas, land use, and terminal and transportation station and airport.

- **Road:** Building roads for access to the landfill, particularly in long distances, involves high preliminary cost. Thus, the selected site is suggested to be as close as to the freeways and main roads (Abdoli, 1993). If landfill is located too far from the road, expenses for solid waste collection and transportation will are go up. Also, it cannot be located too close because of aesthetic aspects. This criterion is considered as the distance from main roads, minor roads, etc in the city (Akbari et al., 2008).
- **Built up areas:** Landfill should be placed far away from populated areas and down town. Otherwise, it can affect aesthetic values of the surrounding region (Chang et al., 2008). With regard to providing adequate landfill capacity for the city's long term requirements, landfill site should not be constrained by the development plans of the city (Abdoli, 1993).
- **Land use:** Land use is not on the foundation of particular directions and may change based on the study area (Kontos et al., 2005). Economically, it is suggested to select bare lands that have the capacity to be used after landfill site completion or can be sold (Abdoli, 1993).
- **Terminal and Transportation Station and Airport:** Landfill sites can attract birds and some animals. This problem can affect the operation of airplanes. Thus, it is necessary to consider appropriate distance of landfill site from airports and other transportation stations (Daneshvar, 2004).

Table 3. Example of scale for comparisons

Intensity of Importance	Description
1	Equal importance
3	Moderate importance of one factor over another
5	Strong or essential importance
7	Very strong importance
9	Extreme importance
2,4,6,8	Intermediate values Reciprocals Values for inverse comparison

(Source: Saaty 1980)

There is a limitation in this research related to soil and groundwater criteria that are not found raw data to make digital map.

Next, the weights for each of the identified physical as well as socio-economic criteria were evaluated by using AHP as one of the MCDM approaches, and Microsoft Excel to carry out overlay analysis through GIS for site selection. Multi-criteria evaluation (MCE) is a tool that enables individuals to make decisions appropriately. The AHP is a mathematic technique used for different criteria decision making. The AHP was developed by Saaty in 1977. It is used for investigating complex decisions involving different criteria. Pairwise comparison, applied within the area of the AHP technique, represents a comparison of criteria used in decision analysis and identifies values for each of these criteria. In AHP, a matrix is produced as consequence of pairwise comparisons and criteria weights are achieved as a consequence of these evaluations (Saaty, 1997).

A matrix is made in this method in which a value is given to every criterion based on its significance compared to all other criteria, and the weight of its comparative significance is computed for each criterion. Overall, the method compares every likely pair of criteria through an appreciation scale usually from 1 to 9 as a relative matrix, to characterize equal rank to extreme significance; see table 3 that describes importance intensity (Saaty, 1980, 1996).

In addition, it seems to be possible to identify the consistency ratio (CR) of decisions in pairwise comparison. CR shows the random probability of values that are gained in a pairwise comparison matrix (Ahmad, HA et al., 2013; Saaty 1997).

In the AHP the pairwise comparisons in a judgment matrix are considered to be adequately consistent if the corresponding consistency ratio (CR) is less than 10% (Saaty, 1980). Thus, when the $CR \leq 0.10$, the degree of consistency is acceptable.

Where λmax is the eigen value of the pairwise comparison matrix, subsequently, the CI assessment is estimated with applying this method:

$$CI = (\lambda \max - n) \,/\, (n - 1) \tag{1}$$

After that the consistency ratio (CR) is obtained by dividing the CI value by the Random Consistency index (RCI) as given in the Table 4 with different numbers of n. If the CR rate is greater than 0.10, then it is necessary to re-examine the problem and re-check the pairwise judgments. At last, to assure the consistency of the pairwise comparison matrix, the consistency judgment must be checked for the appropriate value of n by CR, that is, *CR = CI/RI.*

Table 4. Mean values of random consistency index

n	1	2	3	4	5	6	7	8	9
RCI	0	0	0.58	0.90	1.12	1.24	1.32	1.41	1.45

(Source: Saaty and Kernas 1985)

Table 5. Judgments matrix on the influences of physical criteria

Criteria	Water	Forest	Slope	Priority Vector
Water	1	2	8	0.593
Forest	½	1	6	0.341
Slope	1/8	1/6	1	0.066

Table 6. Judgments matrix on the influences of socio-economic criteria

Criteria	Built Up Areas	Terminal and Transportation Station	Airport	Roads	Priority Vector
Built up areas	1	5	3	7	0.553
Terminal and Transportation Station	1/5	1	1/3	5	0.131
Airport	1/3	3	1	6	0.271
Roads	1/7	1/5	1/6	1	0.045

When a normalized pairwise comparison matrix is found, it is necessary to: (i) Compute the sum of each column; and (ii) Divide each entry in the matrix by its column sum; (iii) Take average across rows to obtain the relative weights. For controlling the consistency of the estimated weight values, the consistency ratio (CR) is estimated as follows: First, assess the eigenvector and the maximum eigenvalue for each matrix. Second then, estimate an approximation to the consistency index.

2.2.4. Overlaying and Identifying Suitable Sites

Weighted Overlay is a technique for applying a common measurement scale of values to diverse and dissimilar inputs to create an integrated analysis (ESRI ArcGis 9.2 Spatial Analysis) (Hala & Mohamed, 2012).

To identify suitable sites, various weights were assigned to all the parameters. When the weight is larger, the criterion in the overall utility becomes more significant. The weights were enhanced by providing a range of pair wise comparisons of the relative significance of factors to the suitability of pixels for the activity being assessed. The process through which the weights were generated pursues the logic enhanced by Saaty (1980) under the Analytical Hierarchy Process (AHP). Pair wise comparison of 9-point continuous scale gives the rates of the weight. Such pair wise comparisons were analyzed to generate weights that sum to 1. The results of combination map layer demonstrated in Figures 14 to 19 and the suitable final place are shown in Figures 20 and 21.

3. RESULTS AND DISCUSSION

Weights were estimated for all of the criteria via AHP and the results are shown in Tables 5, 6, 7 and 8. Seven criteria were utilized in the computation procedure, and were divided into two major groups. The following is the judgment matrix for the case of comparing the importance of the four decision criteria.

Table 7. Decision matrix and solution when the original AHP is used for physical criteria

Physical Criteria	Weight
Water	0.593
Forest	0.341
Slope	0.066

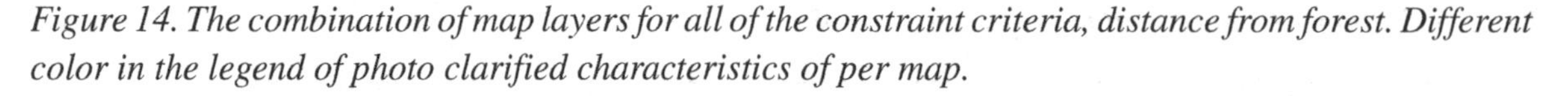

Figure 14. The combination of map layers for all of the constraint criteria, distance from forest. Different color in the legend of photo clarified characteristics of per map.

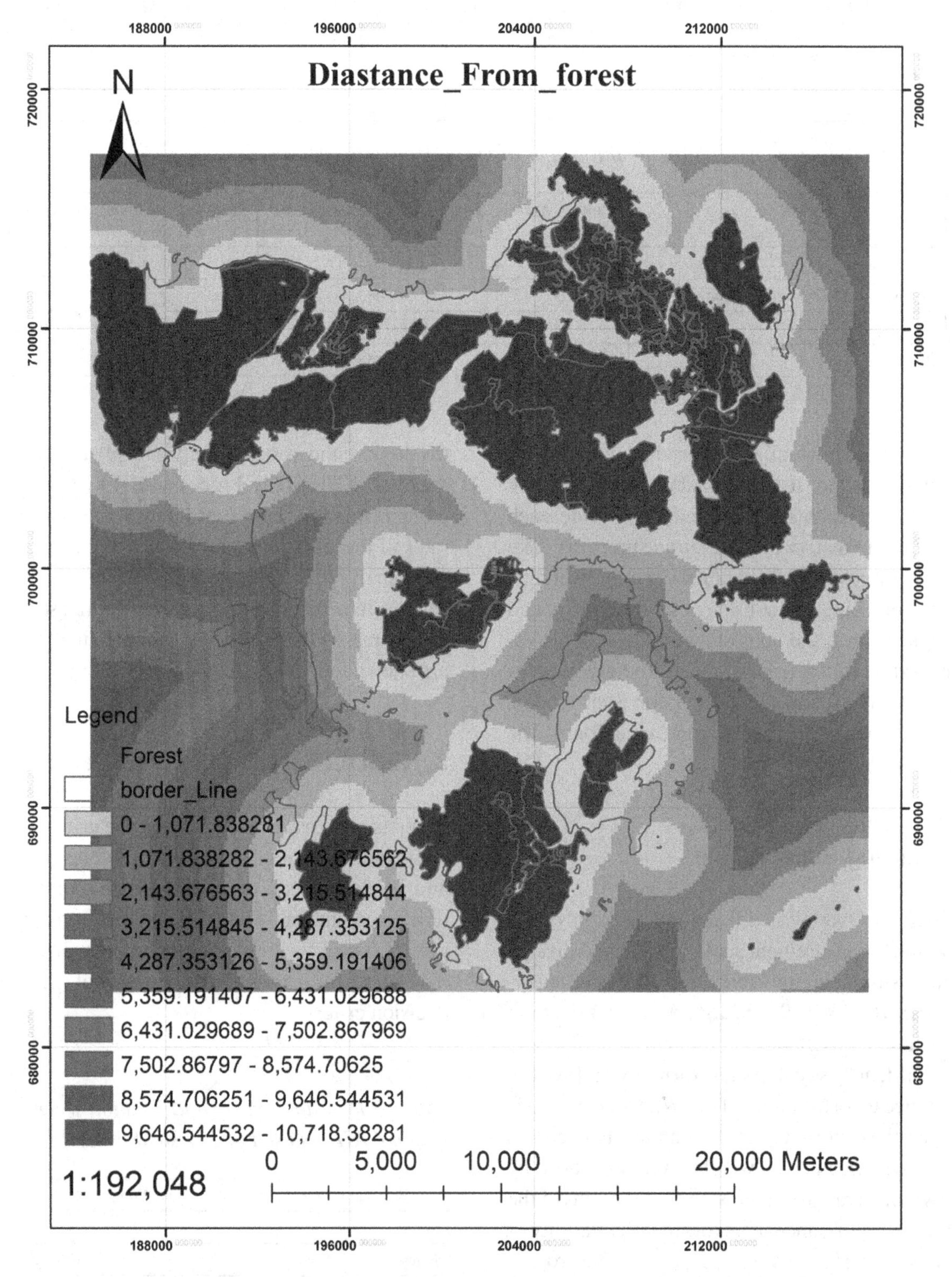

Figure 15. The combination of map layers for all of the constraint criteria, distance from residential. Different color in the legend of photo clarified characteristics of per map.

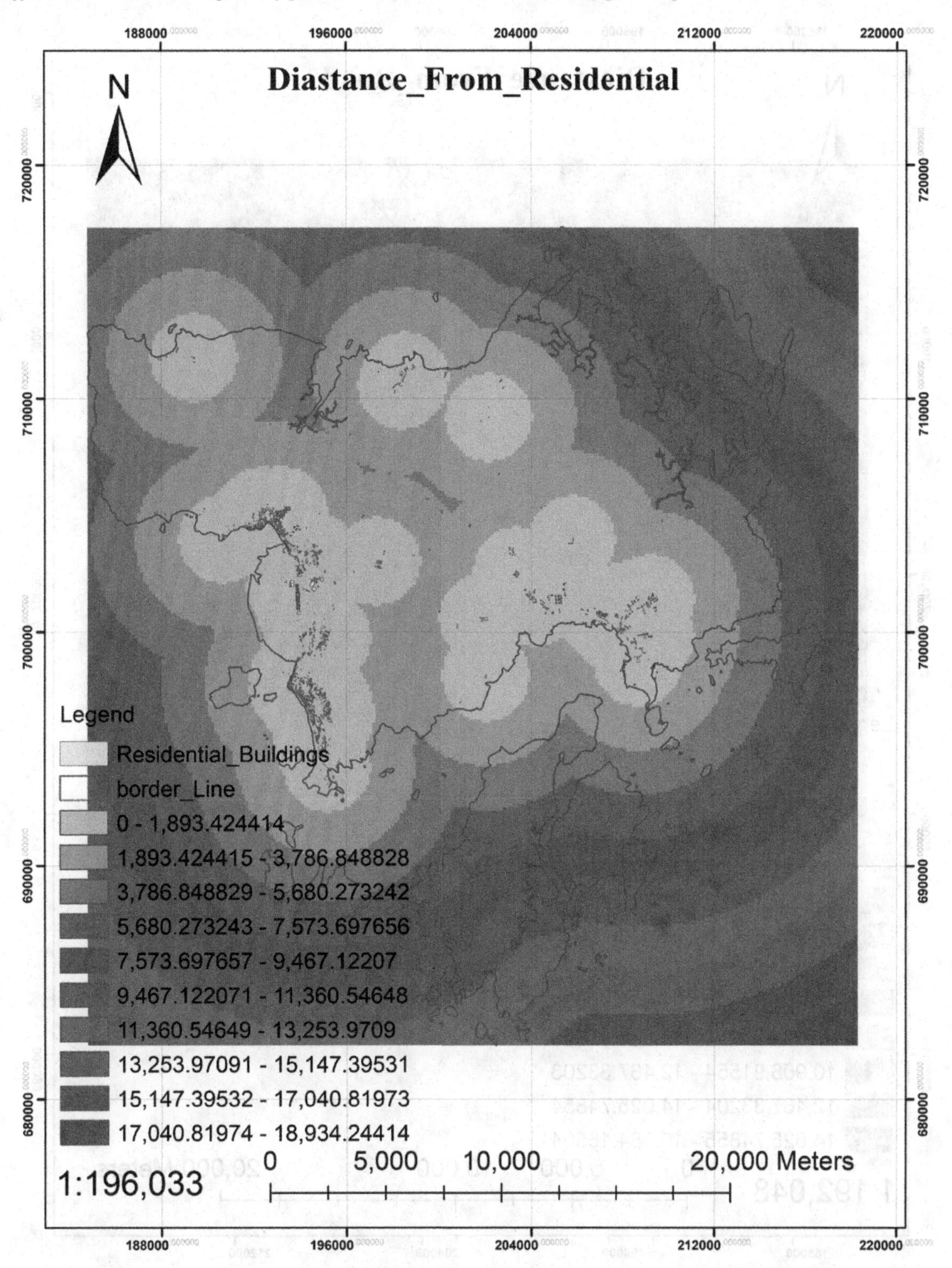

Figure 16. The combination of map layers for all of the constraint criteria, distance from road. Different color in the legend of photo clarified characteristics of per map.

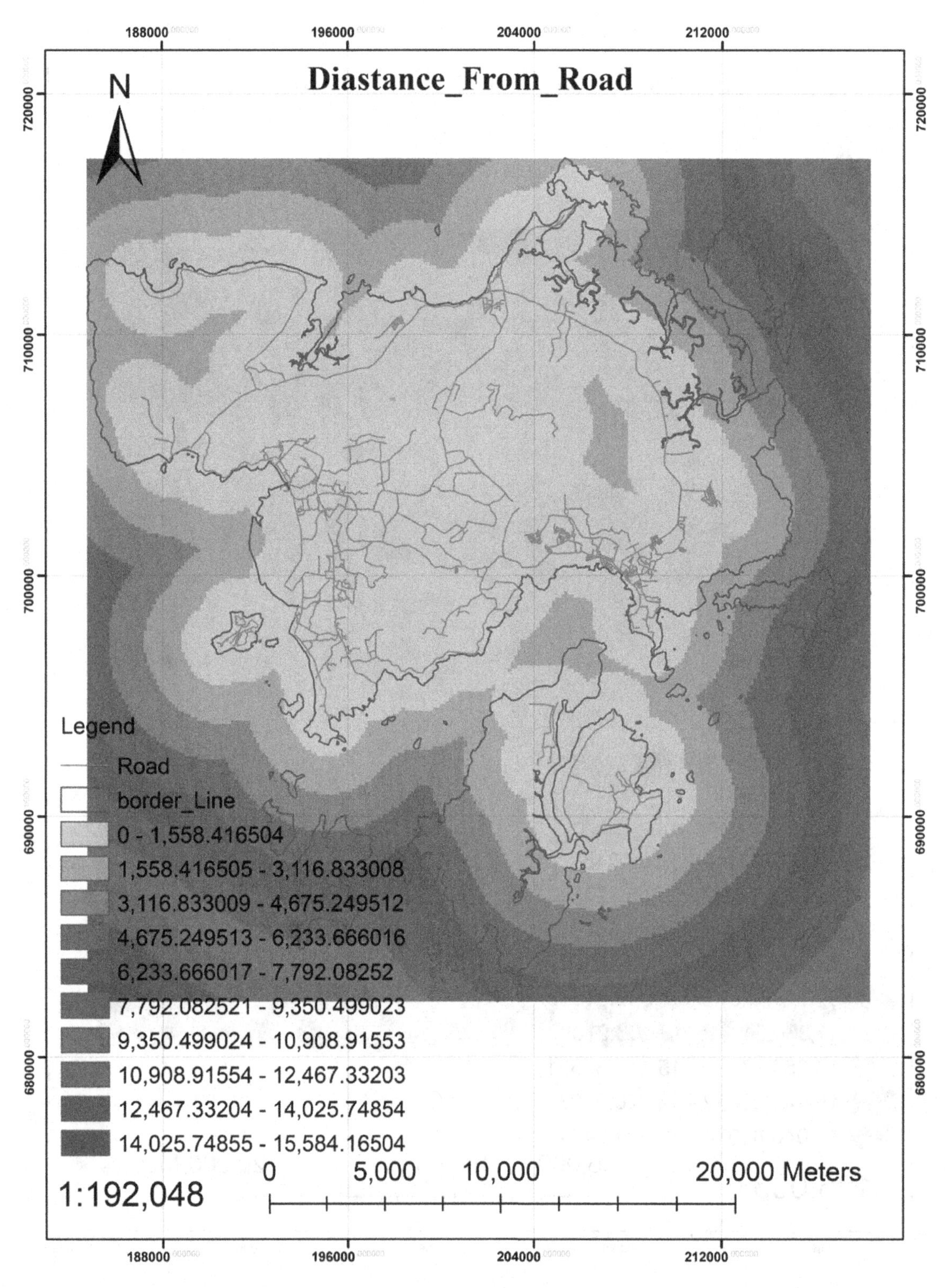

Figure 17. The combination of map layers for all of the constraint criteria, distance from terminal and transportation. Different color in the legend of photo clarified characteristics of per map.

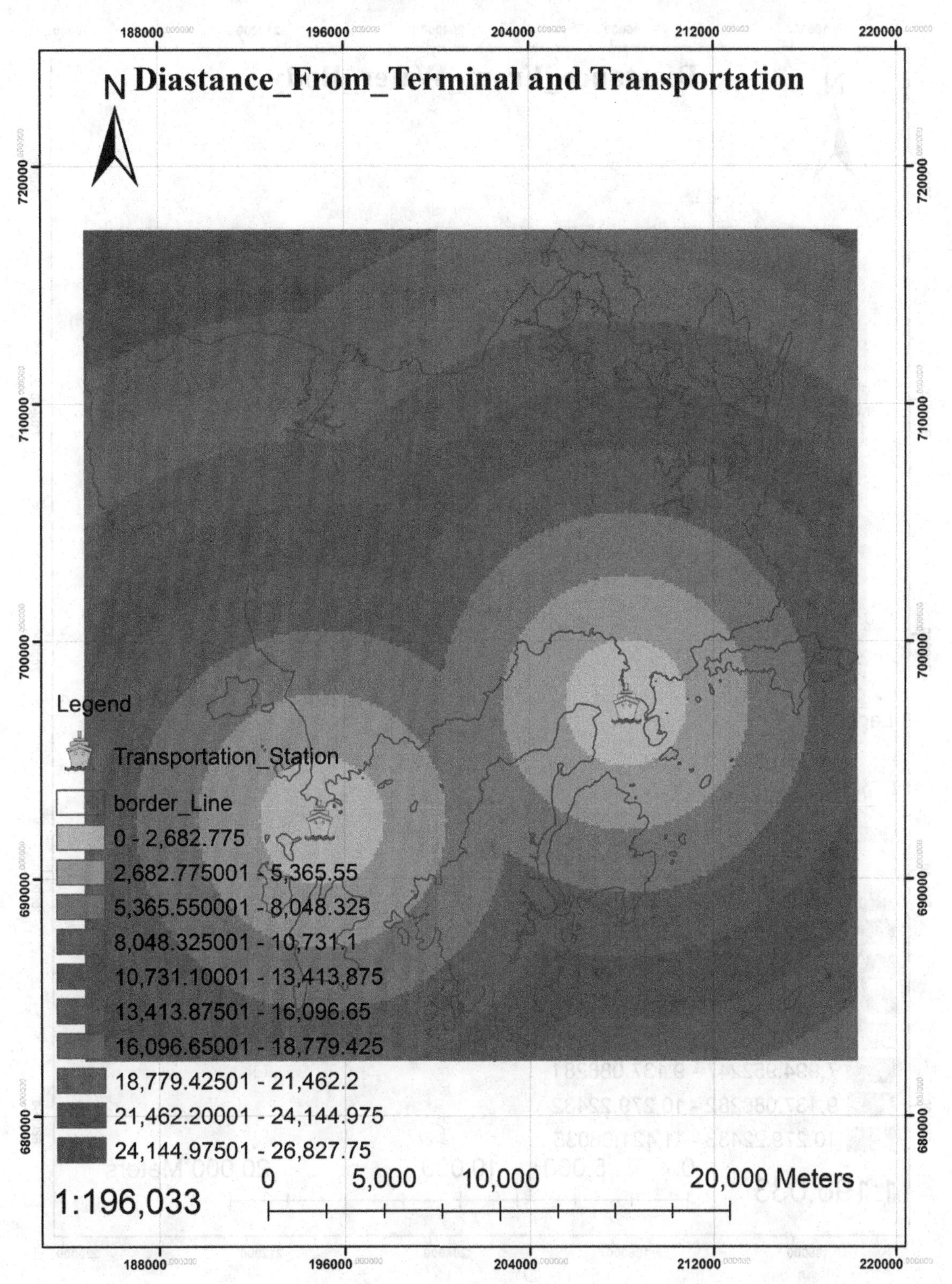

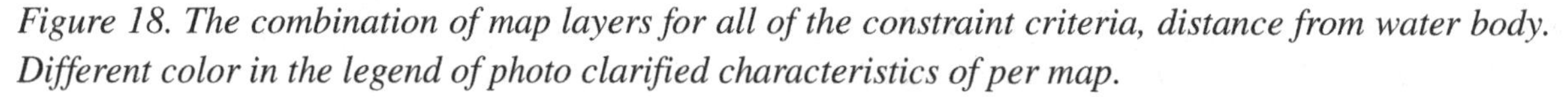

Figure 18. The combination of map layers for all of the constraint criteria, distance from water body. Different color in the legend of photo clarified characteristics of per map.

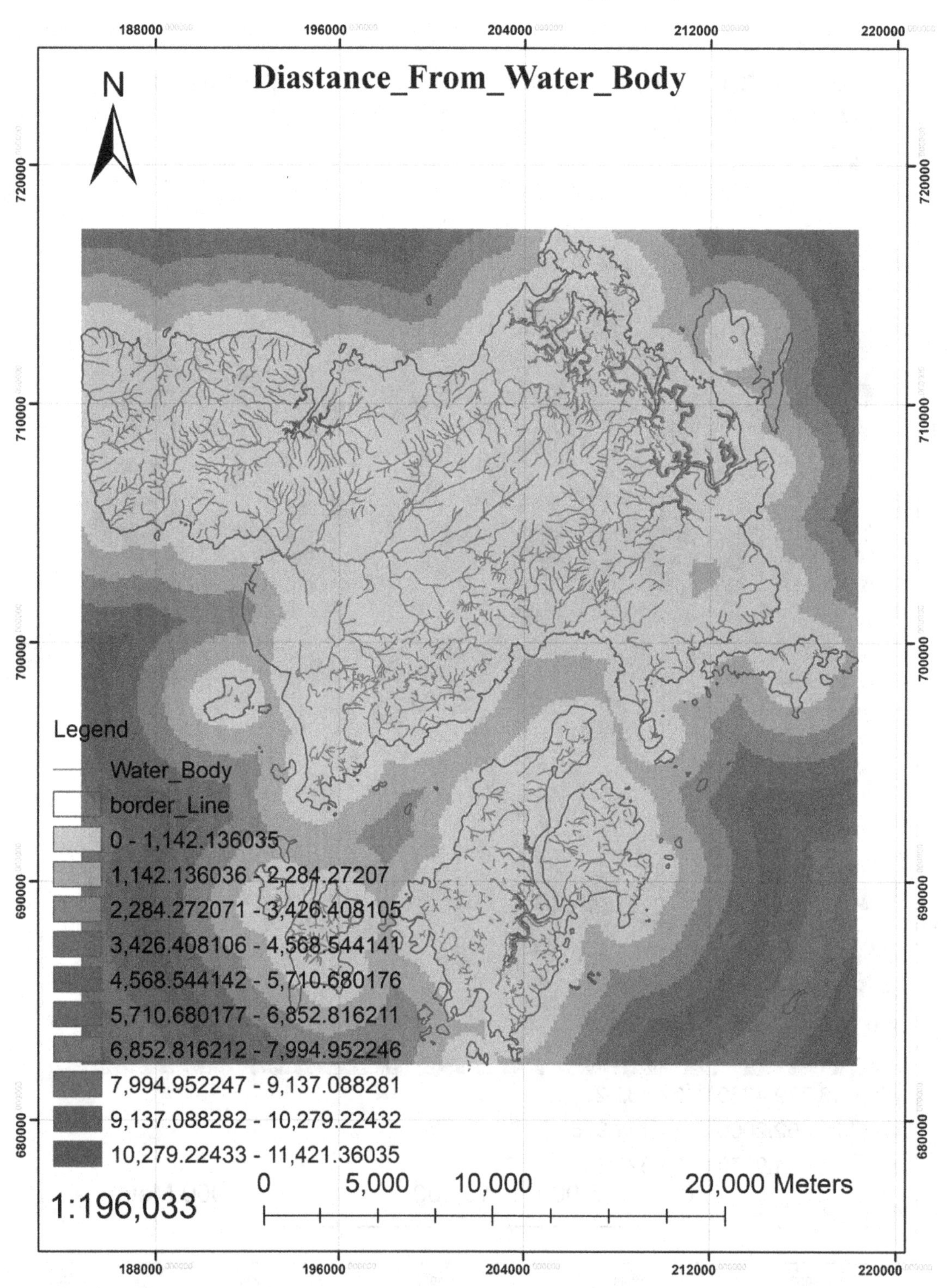

Figure 19. The combination of map layers for all of the constraint criteria, distance from airport. Different color in the legend of photo clarified characteristics of per map.

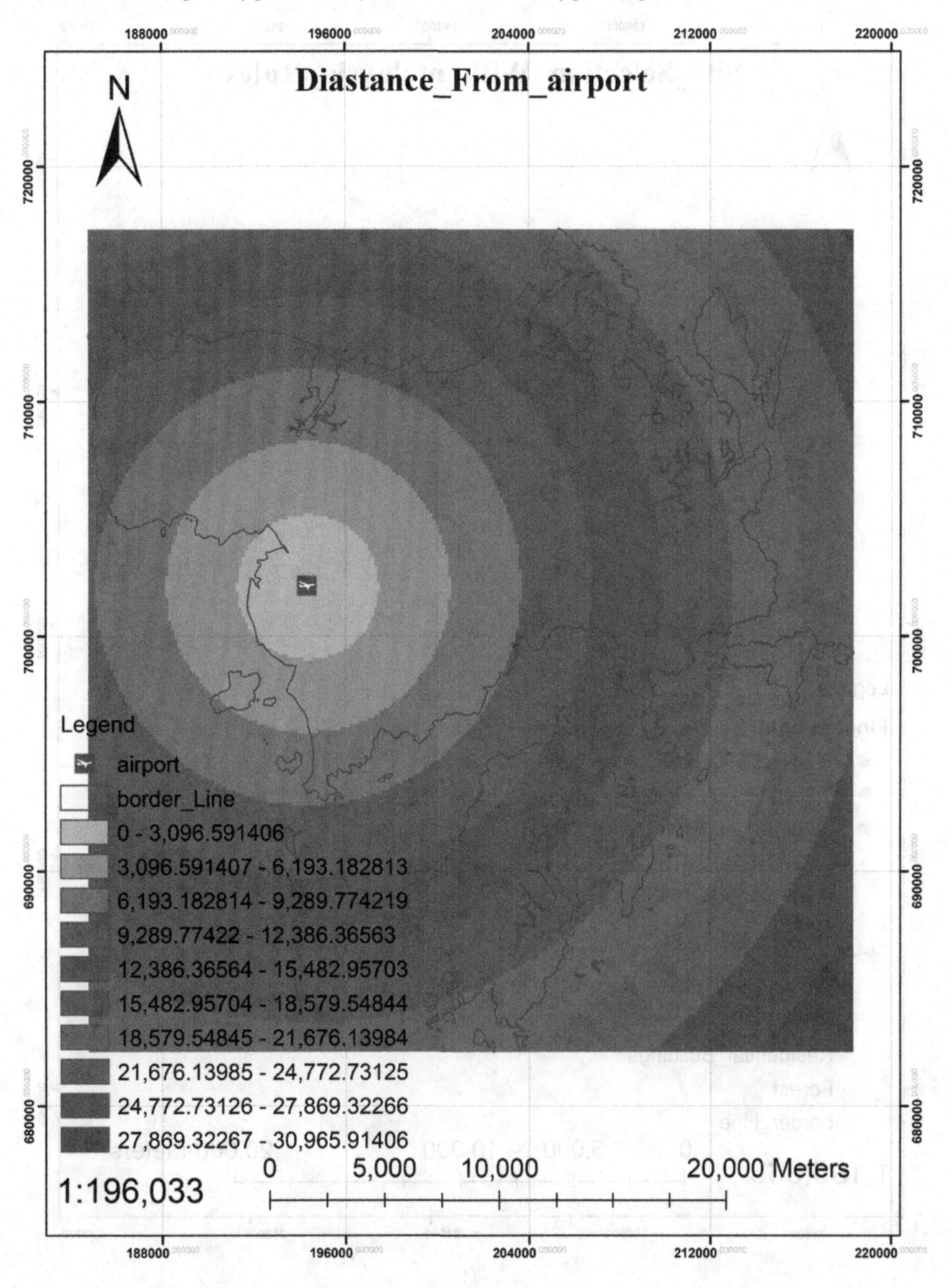

Figure 20. Final overlay maps for landfill site selection of Langkawi Island based on Malaysia rules. Different color in the legend of photo clarified characteristics of per map.

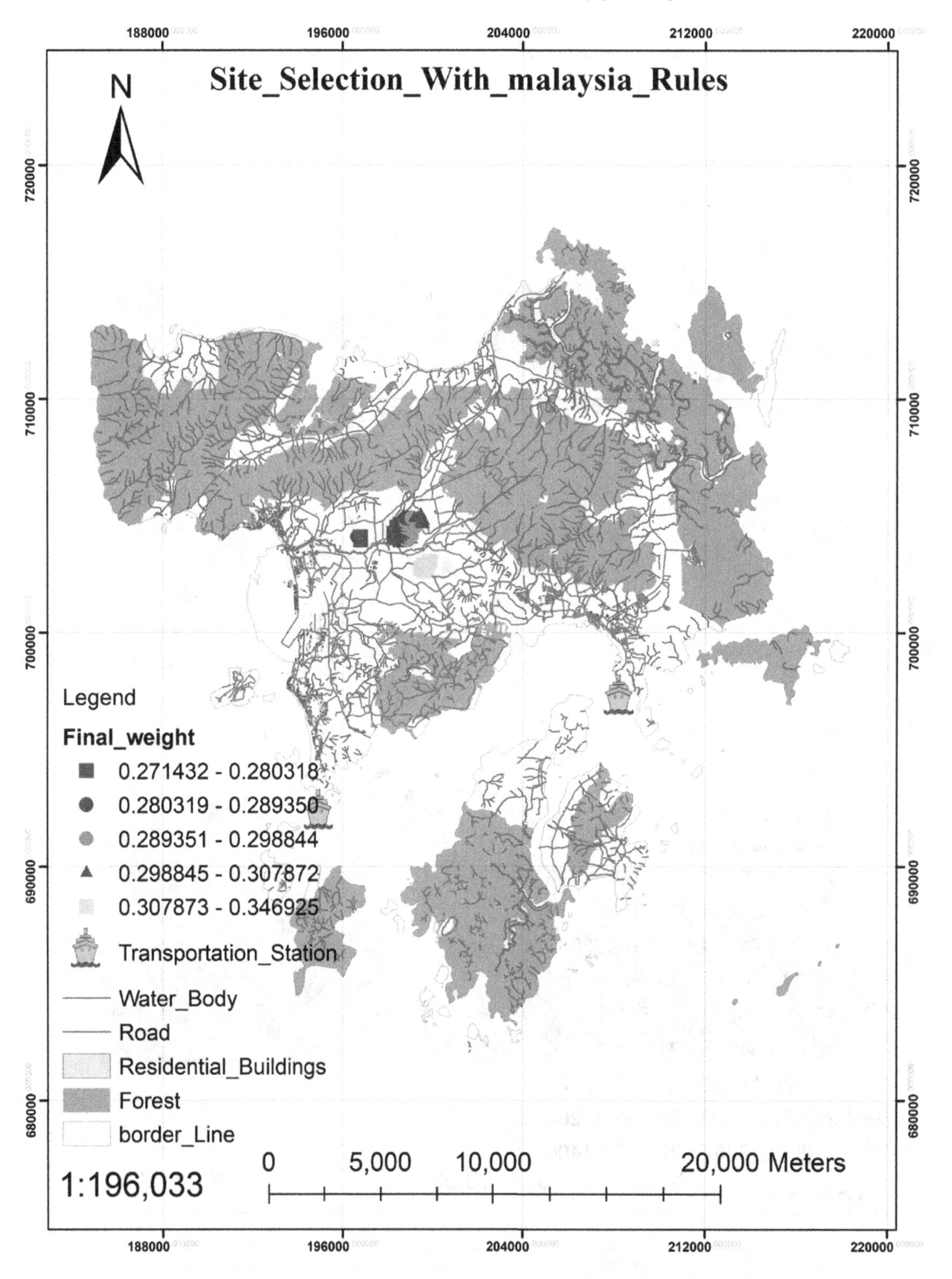

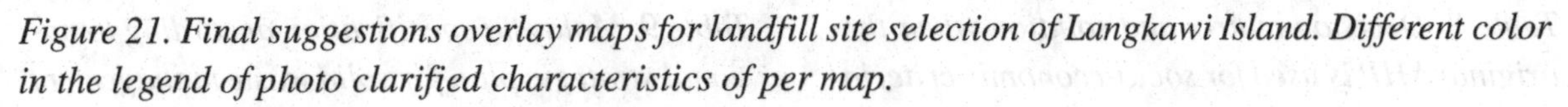

Figure 21. Final suggestions overlay maps for landfill site selection of Langkawi Island. Different color in the legend of photo clarified characteristics of per map.

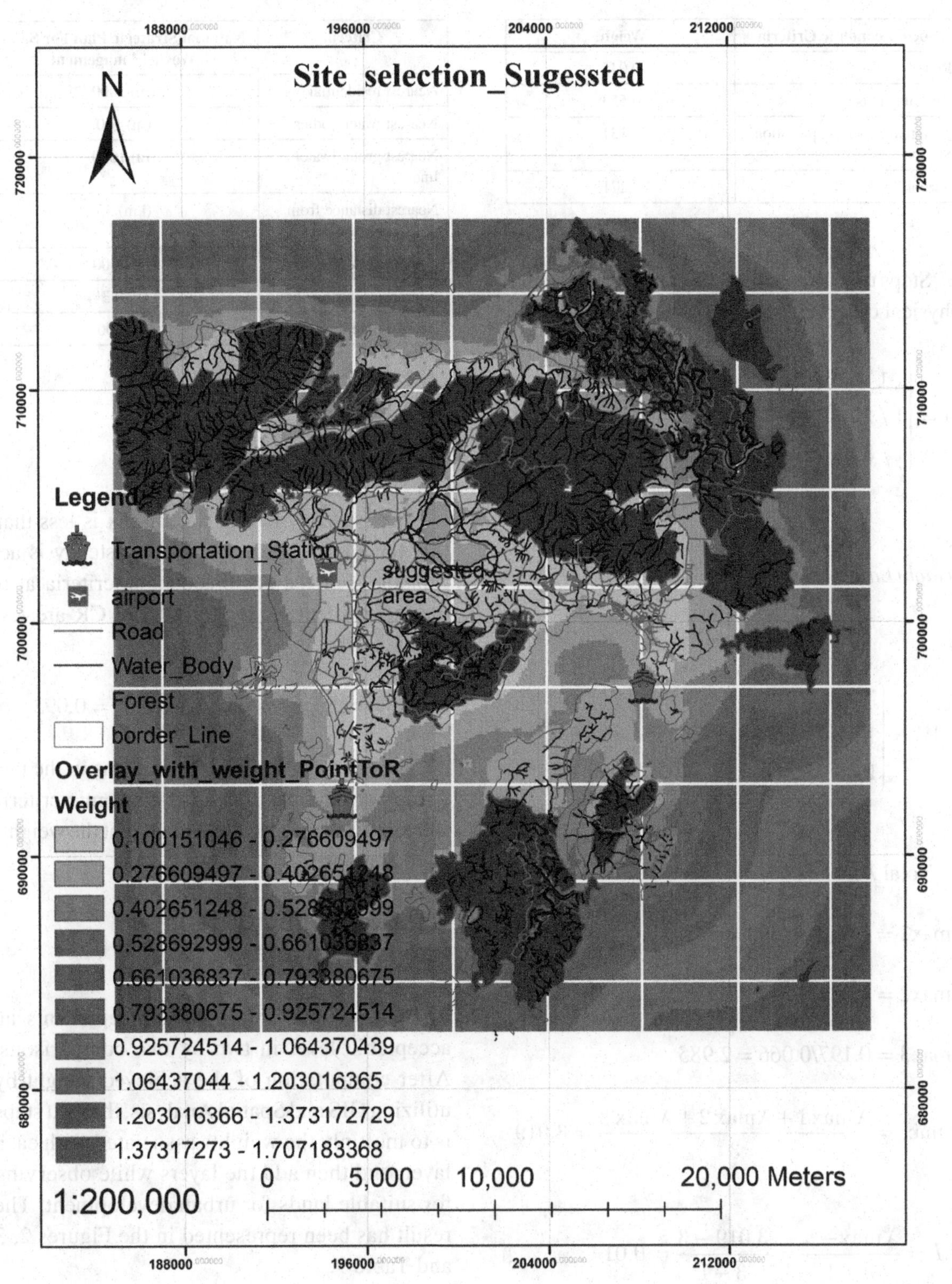

Table 8. Decision matrix and solution when the original AHP is used for socio-economic criteria

Socio Economic Criteria	Weight
Roads	0.045
Built up areas	0.553
Terminal and Transportation Station	0.131
Airport	0.271

Steps used to calculate the consistency rate for physical criteria is shown as follows:

$$A = \begin{pmatrix} 1 & 2 & 8 \\ 1/2 & 1 & 6 \\ 1/8 & 1/6 & 1 \end{pmatrix}$$

$$weightLayers = \begin{pmatrix} 0.593 \\ 0.341 \\ 0.066 \end{pmatrix}$$

$$A.W = \begin{pmatrix} 1 & 2 & 8 \\ 1/2 & 1 & 6 \\ 1/8 & 1/6 & 1 \end{pmatrix} \times \begin{pmatrix} 0.593 \\ 0.341 \\ 0.066 \end{pmatrix} = \begin{pmatrix} 1.803 \\ 1.034 \\ 0.197 \end{pmatrix}$$

Total λ max is:

$\lambda max1 = 1.0803/0.593 = 3.040$,

$\lambda max2 = 1.034/0.341 = 3.032$,

$\lambda max3 = 0.197/0.066 = 2.985$

$$\lambda \max = \frac{\lambda \max 1 + \lambda \max 2 + \lambda \max 3}{3} = 3.019$$

$$I.I = \frac{\lambda \max - n}{n-1} = \frac{3.019 - 3}{3-1} = 0.01$$

Table 9. Malaysia specification according to national strategic plan for solid waste management

Criteria	National Strategic Plan For Solid Waste Management
Nearest residential	(m) 1000
Nearest water bodies	(m) 100
Nearest groundwater line	(m) 1000
Nearest distance from transfer station	(km) 25
Nearest protected forest	(m) 3000
Nearest airport location	(km) 3
Nearest road line	(m) 500

$$I.R. = \frac{I.I.}{I.I.R3 \times 3} = 0.017 \leq 0.1$$

Inconsistency rate in this matrix is less than 0.1; therefore, the degree of consistency is acceptable. For the socio-economic criteria also, the inconsistency rates for CI and CR are less than 0.1. That is,

$\lambda max = 4.252$, $CI = 0.084$, and $CR = 0.093$

The CR values of all comparisons in the two groups of physical and socio-economic criteria were lower than 0.10. This shows that the weights were appropriate.

3.1. Converting Criteria into Map Layers

In such situation, this relation represents an acceptable level in two by two comparisons. After computation of the achieved weight by utilizing GIS and Spatial Analysis, the next steps is to multiply the weights associated with each layer, and then add the layers while observing for suitable lands for urban development. The result has been represented in the Figures 2, 3 and Table 9.

Figure 2 shows the map layers for criteria of geomorphology, gulf club, land use, parcel, primary forest, aspect, Langkawi contour, roads, secondary jungle, slope and soil.

As Hala and Mohamed (2012) stated weights emphasize the relative importance of one criterion to another and are often determined by research specialists, stakeholders, or interest groups and/or decision-makers. In general, in the procedure of multi-criteria evaluation using a Weighted Linear Combination it is necessary that the weights are normalized. In this research between Water, Forest, Slope criteria shows in Table 5 and between criteria built up areas, terminal and transportation station, airport, roads shows in Table 6. The Figure 3 clarifies for this discussion. Figure 3 shows the combination map layer for all of the constraint criteria after buffering, restriction and distance from forest, residential area, road, terminal and transportations, water body and airport.

The final site of landfill result in Figure 4 is quite reasonable for Langkawi area based on protection Geopark.

Using a mixture of GIS and multi criteria assessment methods to determine the selection of a suitable landfill site, the result indicated that the physical as well as socio-economic criteria are significant. The extension of some appropriate areas is very important for landfill site. Applying GIS as well as multi-criteria decision analysis is therefore significant in the site selection process. This is because GIS has been found to be much more useful and flexible in its application. The result of factor maps overlay is multiplied by the result of limitation maps overlay.

In accordance with Figure 4, the appropriate land area suitable for land fill siting is less than 10%. This means that many places of the study area were not appropriate to site land fill.

In other words, less than 10% of the study area was preserved from more landfill sitting explorations due to the restrictions of land use in the Geopark and airport areas. Among them, Geopark and Kilim River, the beach, golf club, residential area and forest mangrove were eliminated as areas for potential sites, and the emergence of slope has a small function in the elimination process.

The regions with rivers and the level of surface water and road network play an important role in the elimination process. Indeed, due to the high physical structure as well as operation costs of landfill, the ideal is that the landfill site should provide the long-term needs of the city in the year 2025. By considering population, solid waste generation rate, the amount of cover matter and compact solid waste density in the landfill site, there is the high need of more land area.

Thus, the benefits of utilizing GIS and AHP technologies for the identification of appropriate solid waste dumping site will reduce the environmental danger and human health issues.

3.2. Solutions and Recommendations

The selection of suitable landfill sites is of great significance that can enhance managing effectively the rapidly increasing solid waste in Langkawi Island. However, the landfill in Langkawi has been sited close to the Geopark, which is also near to the Kilim River. Therefore, it is very important to identify new landfill site in the Island. Moreover, the result has shown that GIS is an effective tool to determine the optimal siting of landfills. Landfill site selection should, therefore, consider environmental and socio-economic factors, particularly in the case study area due to its status as a Geopark. If this technique is used by a company and/or the public sector in landfill siting procedure, it can improve decision making with regard to suitable site selection in Langkawi Island. This research found that GIS-assisted and the AHP have the capacity to enhance the efforts of policy makers and solid waste management practitioners who are directly engaged in the process of selecting appropriate sites for municipal landfills. The use of GIS can increase their knowledge of the physical terrain and the analytical process.

3.3. Future Research Directions

Solid waste has constituted a huge challenge to sustainable development goals, including environmental and personal health. Effective solid waste management is, therefore, essential if Langkawi Island is to continue as a viable tourism hub in Malaysia as well as in the Southeast Asian subregion. This makes the use of GIS and AHP in landfill site selection very crucial. In that regard, future research should target how to improve the efficiency of these important techniques in solid waste management process, particularly in selecting the most appropriate and cost-effective landfill sites. Innovative ways to fund this important technology should also form part of future research directions in solid waste management in Langkawi Island.

4. CONCLUSION

The increasing rate of MSW in Langkawi Island is one of the biggest issues that the authorities are grappling with. To mitigate the effects on the environment of the Geopark and public health will require effective decision making process in Langkawi. This was the motivation for the present study. The method used in this study was a land screening approach that enhanced site selection as well as environmental impact evaluation of the landfill. Based on the findings of this study, it would be valuable to combine GIS and AHP and the user could assign various weights to the two parts (physical and social-economic criteria). Such a system is very effective to bridge the gap between decision makers and analysts during discussion of the different visions and priorities.

The crossed different apparition maps allow the stakeholders to determine the landfill suitability index of each vision for every site of the area. Thus, they can choose the best site according to their own facilities. Also, the use of GIS can significantly help landfill site selection. GIS is used for potential site location in order to evaluate compliance with the conventional standards and site specifications. It is an important instrument that allows the user to examine the suitability of sites versus the national guidelines. If one works in an area or region where there are national or municipal guidelines, such criteria can be built into the model.

Thus, constructing sanitary landfills to meet the environmental legislations and reducing the undesirable effects of the current practices is the major preference for MSW management in Langkawi. Such a problem is getting more significant when we understand that Langkawi has many internationally known and interesting places for visitors. Thus, this paper represents simple but effective method to assist landfill site selection efforts in the Langkawi Island. To achieve this objective, the standard specifications for landfill sitting have been examined in this paper using the case of Langkawi.

ACKNOWLEDGMENT

I wish to acknowledge the Institute for Environment and Development (LESTARI), UKM, Malaysia, and Research Management Center (RMC), University Terengganu Malaysia (UMT) for providing resources and collaborative efforts. I am very grateful to all of the experts who had contributed to our survey.

REFERENCES

Abdoli, M.A., (1993). Municipal solid waste management system and its control methods. *Metropolitan recycling organization publication*, 142-154.

Afzali, A., Samani, J. M. V., & Rashid, M. (2011). Municipal landfill site selection for Isfahan City by use of fuzzy logic and analytic hierarchy process. *Iranian Journal of Environmental Health Sciences & Engineering*, *8*(3), 273–284.

Ahmad, H. A., Zainura, Z. N., Rafiu, O. Y., Fadhil, M. M. D. D., & Ariffin, M. A. H. (2013). Assessing environmental impacts of municipal solid waste of Johor by analytical hierarchy process. *Resources, Conservation and Recycling*, *73*, 188–196. doi:10.1016/j.resconrec.2013.01.003

Akbari, V., Rajabi, M. A., Chavoshi, S. H., & Shams, R. (2008). Landfill site selection by combining GIS and fuzzy multi-criteria decision analysis, case study: Bandar Abbas, Iran. *World Applied Sciences*, *3*(1), 39–47.

Al-Hanbali, A., Alsaaideh, B., & Kondoh, A. (2011). Using GIS-Based weighted linear combination analysis and remote sensing techniques to select optimum solid waste disposal sites within Mafraq City, Jordan. *Journal of Geographic Information System*, 3, 267-278. Retrieved from http://www.SciRP.org/journal/jgis doi:10.4236/jgis.2011.34023

Baban, S. J., & Flannagan, J. (1998). Developing and implementing GIS-assisted constraints criteria for planning landfill sites in the UK. *Planning Practice and Research*, *13*(2), 139–151. doi:10.1080/02697459816157

Bhushan, N., & Rai, K. (2004). *Strategic Decision Making: Applying the Analytic Hierarchy Process* (p. 172). New York: Springer-Verlag.

Chang, K. T. (2010). *Introduction to Geographic Information System* (5th ed.). Mc Graw-Hill.

Chang, N. B., Parvathinathan, G., & Breeden, J. B. (2008). Combining GIS with fuzzy multicriteria decision-making for landfill siting in a fast-growing urban region. *Journal of Environmental Management*, *87*(1), 139–153. doi:10.1016/j.jenvman.2007.01.011 PMID:17363133

Chang, N. B., Parvathinathan, G., & Breeden, J. B. (2008). Combining GIS with fuzzy multicriteria decision-making for landfill siting in a fast-growing urban region. *Journal of Environmental Management*, *87*(1), 139–153. doi:10.1016/j.jenvman.2007.01.011 PMID:17363133

Charnpratheep, K., Zhou, Q., & Garner, B. (1997). Preliminary landfill site screening using fuzzy geographical information systems. *Waste Management & Research*, *15*(2), 197–215. doi:10.1177/0734242X9701500207

Daneshvar, R., (2004). Customizing Arcmap Interface to Generate a User- Friendly Landfill Site Selection GIS Tool. Department of Civil Engineering. University of Ottawa Canada, 7-13.

Daneshvar, R., Fernandes, L., Warith, M., & Daneshfar, B. (2005). Customizing arcmap interface to generate a user- friendly landfill site selection GIS tool. *Journal of Solid Waste Technology Management*, *31*(1), 1–12.

Gbanie, S. P., Tengbe, P. B., Momoh, J. S., Medo, J., & Tamba Simbay, K. V. (2013). Modelling landfill location using geographic information systems (gis) and multi-criteria decision analysis (MCDA): Case study Bo, Southern Sierra Leone. *Applied Geography (Sevenoaks, England)*, *36*, 3–12. doi:10.1016/j.apgeog.2012.06.013

Gemitzi, A., Tsihrintzis, V. A., Voudrias, E., Petalas, C., & Stravodimos, G. (2007). Combining geographic information system, multicriteria evaluation techniques and fuzzy logic in siting MSW landfills. *Environ Geol*, *51*(5), 797–811. doi:10.1007/s00254-006-0359-1

Hala, A. E., & Mohamed, N. H. (2012). Mapping potential landfill sites for North Sinai cities using spatial multicriteria evaluation. *The Egyptian Journal of Remote Sensing and Space Sciences*, *15*, 125–133. doi:10.1016/j.ejrs.2012.09.002

Kao, J. J., Lin, H., & Chen, W. (1997). Network geographic information system for landfill siting. *Waste Management & Research*, *15*(3), 239–253. doi:10.1177/0734242X9701500303

Kao, J. J., & Lin, H. Y. (1996). Multifactor spatial analysis for landfill siting. *Journal of Environmental Engineering*, *122*(10), 902–908. doi:10.1061/(ASCE)0733-9372(1996)122:10(902)

Khorasani, N., & Nejadkorki, F. (2000). Site selection for urban waste in arid lands by the application of GIS: A case study for the city of Kerman, Central Iran. [in Persian]. *BIABAN*, *5*(1), 59–66.

Kontos, T. D., Komilis, D. P., & Halvadakis, C. P. (2005). Sitting MSW landfills with a spatial multiple criteria analysis methodology. *Waste Management (New York, N.Y.)*, *25*(8), 818–832. doi:10.1016/j.wasman.2005.04.002 PMID:15946837

Leao, S., Bishop, I., & Evans, D. (2001). Assessing the demand of solid waste disposal in urban region by urban dynamics modeling in a GIS environment. *Resources, Conservation and Recycling*, *33*(4), 289–313. doi:10.1016/S0921-3449(01)00090-8

Lin, H., & Kao, J. (1998). Enhanced spatial model for landfill siting analysis. *Journal of Environmental Engineering*, *125*(9), 845–851. doi:10.1061/(ASCE)0733-9372(1999)125:9(845)

Luis, E. M., Vicente, T., Andrea, B., José, A., Reyna, O. P., & Hernández-Espriú, A. et al. (2012). Identifying suitable sanitary landfill locations in the state of Morelos, México, using a Geographic Information System. *Physics and Chemistry of the Earth*, *2*(9), 37–39.

Mahini, S. A., & Gholamalifard, M. (2006). SitingMSWlandfills with a weighted linear combination (WLC) methodology in a GIS environment. *International Journal of Environmental Science and Technology*, *3*(4), 435–445. doi:10.1007/BF03325953

Ministry of Housing & Local Government Malaysia (MHLG), (2009). *National strategic plan for solid waste management*.

Mokhtar, A. M. D., & Wan, Z. W. J. Rev. M.M. O., & Wan M.A.W.H., (2008). How Gis Can Be A Useful Tool To Deal With Landfill Site Selection. *Proceedings International Symposium on Geoinformatics for Spatial Infrastructure Development in Earth and Allied Sciences, Hanoi, Vietnam, 4-6 December 2008, ISBN 978- 4-901668-37-8, pp 377-382.*

Montserrat, Z., & Emilio, M. (2008). Evaluation of a municipal landfill site in Southern Spain with GIS-aided methodology. *Journal of Hazardous Materials*, *160*(2-3), 473–481. doi:10.1016/j.jhazmat.2008.03.023 PMID:18423853

Muttiah, R. S., Engel, B. A., & Jones, D. D. (1996). Waste disposal site selection using GIS-based simulated annealing. *Computers & Geosciences*, *22*(9), 1013–1017. doi:10.1016/S0098-3004(96)00039-8

Nas, B., Cay, T., Iscan, F., & Berktay, A. (2008a). Selection of MSW landfill site for Konya, Turkey using GIS and multi-criteria evaluation. *Environmental Monitoring and Assessment*, *160*(1–4), 491–500. PMID:19169836

Rahman, M. M., Sultana, K. R., & Hoque, M. A. (2008). Suitable sites for urban solid waste disposal using GIS approach in Khulna city, Bangladesh. *Proceedings of Pakistan Academy of Sciences*, *45*(1), 11–22.

Saaty, T. (1980). *The Analytic Hierarchy Process*. New York, USA: McGraw-Hill.

Saaty, T. L. (1977). A scaling method for priorities in hierarchical structures. *Journal of Mathematical Psychology*, *15*(3), 234–281. doi:10.1016/0022-2496(77)90033-5

Saaty, T. L. (1996). *Decision making with dependence and feedback: The analytic network process*. Pittsburgh: RWS Publications.

Saaty, T. L., & Kearns, K. P. (1985). Analytical planning: the organization of systems. A. Wheaton & Co. Ltd. GB ISBN 0-08-032599-8.

Sarah, W., & Susan, J. E. (2000). Environmental risk perception and well being: Effects of the landfill siting process in two Southern Ontario Communities. *Social Science & Medicine*, *50*(7–8), 1139–1154. PMID:10714933

Şener, Ş., Şener, E., Nas, B., & Karagüzel, R. (2010). Combining AHP with GIS for landfill site selection: A case study in the Lake Beyşehir catchment area (Konya, Turkey). *Waste Management (New York, N.Y.)*, *30*(11), 2037–2046. doi:10.1016/j.wasman.2010.05.024 PMID:20594819

Shafeea Leman, M., Abdul Ghani, K., Komoo, I., & Ahmad, N. (Eds.). (2007). *Langkawi Geopark*. Bangi: Lestari, Ukm and Lada publication.

Shafeea Leman M., Komoo I., Roslan Mohamed K., Aziz Ali C., Unjah T., Othman K. & Yasin M. H.M., (2008). Geology and geoheritage conservation within langkawi geopark, Malaysia. *Articles and Publications*.

Shamshiry, E., Nadi, B., Mokhtar, B. M., Komoo, I., & Saadiah, H. H. (2011). Urban solid waste management based on geoinformatics technology. *Journal of Public Health and Epidemiology*, *3*(2), 54–60.

Siddiqui, M. Z., Everett, J. W., & Vieux, B. E. (1996). Landfill siting using geographic information system: A demonstration. *Journal of Environmental Engineering*, *122*(6), 515–523. doi:10.1061/(ASCE)0733-9372(1996)122:6(515)

Siti Zubaidah, A., Mohd Sanusi, S. A., & Mohd Suffian, Y. (2013). Spatial comparison of new landfill sites using criteria derived from different guidelines. *International Surveying Research Journal*, *3*(2), 29–40.

Sumathi, V. R., Natesan, U., & Sarkar, C. (2008). GIS-based approach for optimized sitting of municipal solid waste landfill. *Waste Management Journal*, *28*(11), 2146–2160. doi:10.1016/j.wasman.2007.09.032 PMID:18060759

Sumiani, Y., Onn, C. C., Mohd Din, M. A., & Wan Jaafar, W. Z. (2009). Environmental planning strategies for optimum solid waste landfill siting. *Sains Malaysiana*, *38*(4), 457–462.

Tınmaz, E., & Demir, I. (2006). Research on solid waste management system: To improve existing situation in Corlu Town of Turkey. *Waste Management (New York, N.Y.)*, *26*(3), 307–314. doi:10.1016/j.wasman.2005.06.005 PMID:16112565

Wan Hussin, W. M. A., Shahid, K., Mohd Din, M. A., & Wan Jaafar, W. Z. (2010). Modeling landfill suitability based on multi-criteria decision making method. *Interdisciplinary Themes Journal*, *2*(1), 20–30.

KEY TERMS AND DEFINITIONS

Analytical Hierarchy Process (AHP): AHP is a mathematic technique used for different criteria of decision making, especially for investigating complex decisions.

Aspect: Aspect refers to the measure of the direction of slope. It starts with 0° at the north, and then in a clockwise direction goes to 360° again at the north.

Geographic Information System (GIS): Geographic Information System (GIS) is a digital database management system that manages huge volumes of geographical or spatial data from different resources.

Land Site: It is the land area where something is located or selected for its future location. For instance, the land areas where landfill for solid waste disposal, hospital, school, etc, are located.

Landfill: It is a site or place for the disposal of waste materials by using either incineration or by burial.

Langkawi Island: Langkawi Island is located in the Andaman Sea, which is approximately 30 km from the mainland coast of North-western Malaysia. Langkawi hosts the first global Geopark in Southeast Asia. Administratively, Langkawi Island is a District in the Kedah State. Its economy is largely driven by tourism due to its historic geophysical environment.

Multi-Criteria Decision Analysis: MCDA is GIS-assisted method that helps decision makers to analyze and solve various criteria decision issues by using a combination of geographical data and the decision maker's priorities.

Section 3

Cultural Transformation through Information

Chapter 12
Effect of Mobile Phone SMS on M-Health:
An Analysis of Consumer Perceptions

Mahmud Akhter Shareef
North South University, Bangladesh

Jashim Uddin Ahmed
North South University, Bangladesh

Vinod Kumar
Carleton University, Canada

Uma Kumar
Carleton University, Canada

ABSTRACT

This chapter is engaged in identifying consumer perceptions regarding short message service (SMS) of the mobile phone as an alternative service delivery channel for Mobile-health (M-health) and studying the cultural impact of this change. In this connection, the Unified Theory of Acceptance and Use of Technology (UTAUT) model was used as the theoretical base to perceive consumer perceptions about M-health. The authors have performed an empirical study of diabetic patients in Bangladesh and Canada. Path analysis was conducted on the results of both samples. Analysis results confirmed that the UTAUT model fits quite nicely in predicting consumer perceptions of M-health-driven mobile technology. It also acknowledged that differences in cultural traits have an impact on consumer behavior.

INTRODUCTION

Globalization, economic development, regular monitoring of the human development index, health consciousness, and soaring life expectancy are factors that voluntarily and forcibly push and diffuse the healthcare service system worldwide. Many consumers are now extremely concerned about better service quality of the healthcare system as they are not satisfied with the present health service delivery system. In this context, health service providers, including physicians, are very interested in exploring the integration and application of different technological interfaces of information and communication technology in the service delivery system of modern healthcare. One of many possible opportunities to be applied in the service delivery of healthcare, which many practitioners are recently exploring, is the application of a mobile phone-based message system, such as short message service (SMS), as the newest addition to the service delivery system of better

DOI: 10.4018/978-1-4666-8598-7.ch012

quality healthcare. In this present effort to reveal the effectiveness of modern technology on the healthcare system, the current study is engaged in identifying customer perceptions of SMS as a service delivery channel for modern healthcare, which we termed here as Mobile-health or M-health.

Mobile-health or M-health can be defined as providing right healthcare service at right time continuously to any remote patients without hampering their regular lifestyle. In this service system patients' physical presence in hospitals, clinics, and/or doctors chambers is not required. They will be communicated through ICT-driven wireless systems, software, and health monitoring devices. Several wireless communication systems can be used for medical professionals' interaction with patients like, any kind of smartphones, body sensors containing accelerometers, pedometers, electrocardiograms, pulse oximeters, blood-glucose meters, weight scales, etc. Other required technologies may include SMS, multimedia messaging service (MMS); remote communicators and location tracking technology like radio frequency identification (RFID); GPS etc.; data processing tools like personal data assistant (PDA), pocket PC, palm and laptop as well as wireless network like the WiFi Internet network. Through sensor, the patient's health conditions will be monitored, recorded, and analyzed. And then through connected smartphone, essential information will be continuously transferred to medical professionals from a remote place. Medical professionals will receive any data, related to patients' health condition, through their laptop, tablet PC, PDA, or other wireless-based Internet communication. This communication will be a continuous regular pattern; however, if urgent advice is required due to any deteriorating health conditions of the patients, two-way communication will be established through SMS from physicians.

M-health researcher Kahn et al. (2010) illustrated: "Innovative applications of mobile technology to existing healthcare delivery and monitoring systems offer great promise for improving the quality of life." Since the beginning of modern information and communications technology (ICT), wireless communication, electronic health recording, and monitoring devices predominate in a major driving role of the technological and social beliefs of consumer decision-making processes and their complex buying behavior. This is composed of the cognitive, affective, and conative, or behavioral, components of attitude, which play a significantly comprehensive role in accepting an ICT-driven healthcare system. Theorizing this integrated health and technological adoption behavior for consumer complex buying behavior has the potential to help us discover better future designs of a culture and market economy governed by ICT for an innovative and revolutionary M-health system.

Consumers generally are not engaged in buying or pursuing M-health as a regular product. Its purchase frequency, oriented with only a small number of patients, is insignificant to general consumers. In the M-health service system, self-service technology is predominant and this needs extensive self-explanatory skills. From the perspective of a health-concerned matter, M-health-related issues potentially deserve a higher consideration from consumers in the light of usage (Yu et al., 2006). Therefore, the systematic adoption of M-health necessitates a complex buying behavior, and consumers must integrate several different ideas to justify their decision to receive M-health services.

The worldwide proliferation of mobile phone SMS as the service delivery channel contains several issues, challenges, barriers, and limitations. Many researchers (He et al., 2007; Moynihan et al., 2010; Muk, 2007; Srisawatsakul & Papasratorn, 2013; Zhang & Mao, 2008; Zhang & Li, 2012) have asserted from extensive empirical studies that service delivery to the intended segments of customers through messaging on a mobile phone SMS will be successful if it can capture the ubiquitous opportunities of wireless devices such as providing time, location, and customer-context-based messages of service. The findings of the studies suggested that service delivery through mobile phone SMS could be accepted among consumers if it can maintain continuous connectivity with reliability. The authors also affirmed that for the most effective SMS interactivity, authenticity of information and delivery of the correct content to the right customer is important. It is especially important in M-health, as the content of healthcare is extremely important and privacy is a prevalent factor in this context. As a result, consumers will perceive service delivery through SMS of their mobile phone as an effective service delivery channel if it can deliver trustworthy, personalized information, at any time and in any location. To reveal the effectiveness of M-health service delivery through mobile phone SMS, understanding customer perceptions about adopting this new trend of service delivery channel is potentially important; however, researchers have not comprehensively examined the possibility of adding this service delivery channel in M-health.

Consumer behavior about any ICT-related adoption cannot be generalized, as cultural traits have a significant impact on consumer attitudes toward ICT. This argument is justified by many researchers who conducted research on the impact of the cultural differences in consumer attitudes (Jamieson, 2012; McDonald & Dahlberg, 2010). Irani et al. (2007) claimed that ICT adoption behavior is highly controlled by socio-psychological traits which signify the impact of culture. With reference to the study of Goodman and Green (1992), where ICT adoption behavior for Middle Eastern countries was explored, Ein-Dor et al. (1993) acknowledged that any attempt to theorize consumer behaviors cannot be generalized without comparing the cultural differences among consumers of different nations. Other researchers, like Kettinger et al. (1995) and Winsted (1997), investigated consumer behavior for ICT in the USA and some Asian countries and finally concluded that a trend could be generalized considering the effect of impulsive cultural differences. Tajfel's social identity theory (1972) identified that behavioral and social differences among cultures have potential implications for modeling consumer behaviors. The theory of planned behavior (Ajzen, 1991) suggested that there were different beliefs concerning an attitudinal, subjective norm and behavioral control in predicting behavioral intention and actual behavior. Several researchers, such as Straub et al. (1994), while verifying the technology adoption model (TAM) (Davis, 1989) among consumers of three different countries (Japan, Switzerland, and the United States), postulated that those beliefs predicting actual behavior might not be similar among consumers of different countries having observable dissimilarities in cultural traits. Donthu and Yoo (1998) analyzed the cultural influences on service perception among the consumers of four countries – Canada, India, UK, and USA – and noted significant differences in perceiving service quality among consumers who had different cultural traits.

This current study is engaged in identifying consumer perceptions regarding the SMS of mobile phones as an alternative service delivery channel for M-health and studying the cultural impact of this type of service delivery.

Theoretical Model

Before reacting to any system, consumers first expose themselves to the new system and attempt to decide if it is acceptable or not. If they find the new system to be favorable in terms of their intention, they try to create their motive for the system as acceptable, i.e., to perceive it positively. Perception can be defined as the process by which individuals receive information, organize it, and then interpret their sensory impressions in order to impart significant meaning to the system. This project has two significant issues: one is M-health and the other one is the SMS of mobile phones as the service delivery channel.

About SMS-based connectivity, many researchers have identified that SMS provides additional values, such as perceived usefulness to recipients, which is deemed as a significant driving factor for positive perception about the system (Carroll et al., 2007; Cheng et al., 2009). They revealed that consumer perceptions of usefulness, enjoyment, and cost effectiveness are important factors for them to create a positive perception about any system if it is delivered through mobile phone-based SMS as an alternative service delivery system. Researchers (Turel et al., 2007; Zhang & Mao, 2008) also identified that users have a positive attitude toward wireless information like SMS (Trappey & Woodside, 2005) and thus willingness to be exposed (Zhang & Mao, 2008; Zhang & Li, 2012), because it can provide process, socialization, and content motivations. The findings of several studies (Qureshi et al., 2012; Srisawatsakul & Papasratorn, 2013) of the effect of SMS on consumer perceptions indicated that since SMS-based service delivery has many interactive; personalized; and time, place, and context-based benefits, customers have appreciated SMS.

To examine and conceptualize consumer perceptions about M-health where service is being delivered through mobile phone-based SMS, the authors used the Unified Theory of Acceptance and Use of Technology (UTAUT) (Venkatesh et al., 2003) model. According to the UTAUT model, performance expectancy, effort expectancy, social influence, and facilitating conditions are the four potential constructs to explain user perception and acceptance behavior.

Performance expectancy (PE): Venkatesh et al. (2003) developed this construct from the integrated paradigms of different behavioral theories based on system usefulness, and defined it as "the degree to which an individual believes that using the system will help him or her to attain gains in job performance" (Venkatesh et al., 2003). We propose based on UTAUT, that,

H_1: Performance expectancy (PE) has a positive influence on customer perceptions of SMS (PER) as a service delivery channel for M-health.

Effort expectancy (EE): This formative construct of the UTAUT model captures integrated notions of ease of use and is defined as "the degree of ease associated with the use of the system." The effect of this construct has been proposed as,

H_2: Effort expectancy (EE) has a positive influence on customer perceptions of SMS (**PER**) as a service delivery channel for M-health.

Social influence (SI): SI has captured the overall influence of society on creating consumer perceptions; it is defined as "the degree to which an individual perceives that important others believe he or she should use the new system." We have proposed this construct in this theoretical development process as,

H_3: Social influence (SI) has a positive influence on customer perceptions of SMS (**PER**) as a service delivery channel for M-health.

Facilitating conditions (FC): For M-health, SMS-based service delivery can facilitate the system as an alternative service delivery channel. It is defined as "the degree to which an individual believes that an organizational and technical infrastructure exists to support use of the system."

H_4: Facilitating conditions (FC) has a positive influence on customer perceptions of SMS (PER) as a service delivery channel for M-health.

Research Methodology

For M-health, we designed a hybrid model of an ICT-driven health service delivery system for diabetic patients. The system is illustrated as follows:

Diabetic patients would wear a hospital-provided sensor system as a wristband and this sensor system would be connected to the patients' smartphone. Through analytical software added to the smartphone, the patient would be directly connected with and continuously monitored by health professionals of any hospital. Health professionals would periodically monitor patient health-related data, which is transmitted directly and continuously to their personal laptop or any hand-held computing system. Whenever the medical professionals find that any diabetic-related parameters have dropped to the danger limit they alert the patient by sending SMS to the patients' smartphone for regular instructions and tips. This remote health service delivery system through SMS is considered here as M-health.

To capture consumer perceptions and explore the effect of culture on the perception process of SMS as a service delivery channel for M-health, the study was conducted in Bangladesh and Canada among diabetic patients. All other measuring items were extracted directly from the UTAUT model and then revised to align the measuring items with the notion of M-health and SMS as the service delivery channel. The scale items of the four constructs were measured by a five-point Likert scale ranging from 1 (strongly disagree) to 5 (strongly agree). Diabetic patients of these two countries who are now taking diabetic monitoring services almost every week from direct presence in any healthcare service provider facility were presented with the proposed hybrid model of M-health. They were asked to respond to the questionnaire based on their perceptions of seeking that alternative healthcare service through SMS operated by mobile phone from any remote locations.

The same procedure was used to collect data from patients in Canada and Bangladesh. For Bangladesh, the survey was conducted in Dhaka City among registered diabetic patients in the Bangladesh Institute of Research and Rehabilitation in Diabetes, Endocrine and Metabolic Disorders (BIRDEM). The total number of respondents was 127. The same questionnaire was distributed in Ottawa, Canada, at two different centers in the diabetes management community program. 115 responses were collected from Ottawa.

Results and Discussions

Since the measuring items are extracted directly from the UTAUT model, we did not conduct any factor analysis; rather we directly conducted path analysis following structural equation modeling (SEM). However, before that we verified the reliability of the constructs through Cronbach's alpha for the two samples. Since the coefficient alpha for all the constructs varied from 0.801 to 0.923, the constructs' reliability (Nunnally & Bernstein, 1994) was approved.

The path diagram displays factor loadings for the independent variables. After several iterations with inclusion of several error covariants among the determinants of perception, the authors accepted the final model for the Bangladeshi and Canadian sample as shown in Figures 1 (Consumers' Perception of M-health through SMS, Path coefficients, Bangladesh) and 2 (Consumers' Perception of M-health through SMS, Path coefficients, Canada) respectively.

The standardized path coefficients, Chi-Square statistic, degree of freedom (df), p-value, and RMSEA are also shown in Figures 1 and 2, which are the final cause and effect relationship between the independent constructs and perception of M-health conducted through SMS for Bangladesh and Canada. The $\chi 2$ statistic of 6.85 and 5.36 for Bangladesh ((df = 4, p-value 0.224976) and Canada respectively (df = 4, p-value 0.111239) indicates that the null hypothesis of the model is a good fit for the data, or at least cannot be rejected. The root mean square error of approximation (RMSEA) (0.045 and 0.061 for Bangladesh and Canada respectively) is quite reasonable as goodness of fitness (Kline, 2005, pp.133-144). Other fit measures such as CFI, IFI, RFI, GFI, AGFI, NFI, and NNFI are verified (all range from 0.97 to 0.99), which indicate that the model fit compares reasonably with the literature (Segars et al., 1993; Chau, 1997.

Figure 1. Consumers' Perception of M-health through SMS (Path coefficients) (Bangladesh)

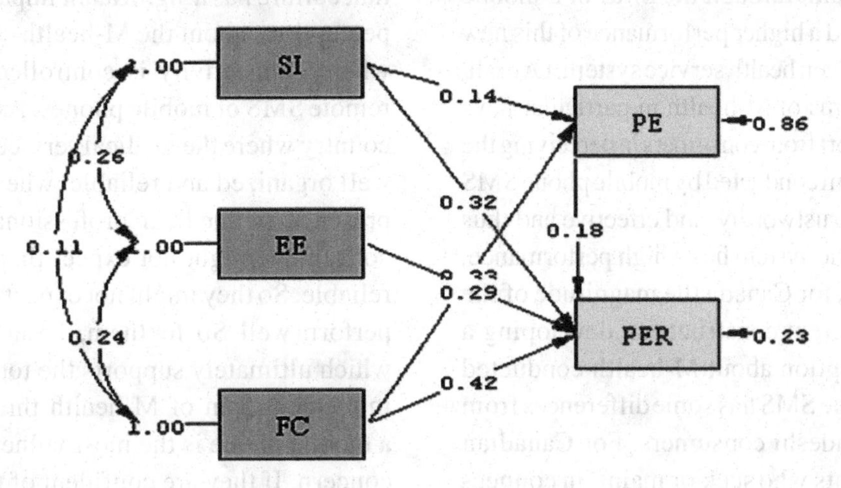

The results show that the UTAUT model could perfectly predict consumer perceptions for M-health, which is primarily operated through mobile phone-based SMS. All the independent variables are found significant at 0.05 level. For Bangladeshi consumers, FC is the most important attribute (path coefficient 0.42) to impart a positive perception about M-health service operated through SMS. SI is the second most (path coefficient 0.32) important construct to create a positive impression for M-health. Load coefficients for EE and PE are 0.29 and 0.18 respectively. Other than these regular relations captured by the UTAUT model, two new relations emerged from the LISREL analysis for the proper fit of the model as per sample. Other than the predicted relations of FC and SI to perception, these two constructs also influence PE. It indicates that if the supporting environment and condition is well organized and consumers feel the normative effect

Figure 2. Consumers' Perception of M-health through SMS (Path coefficients) (Canada)

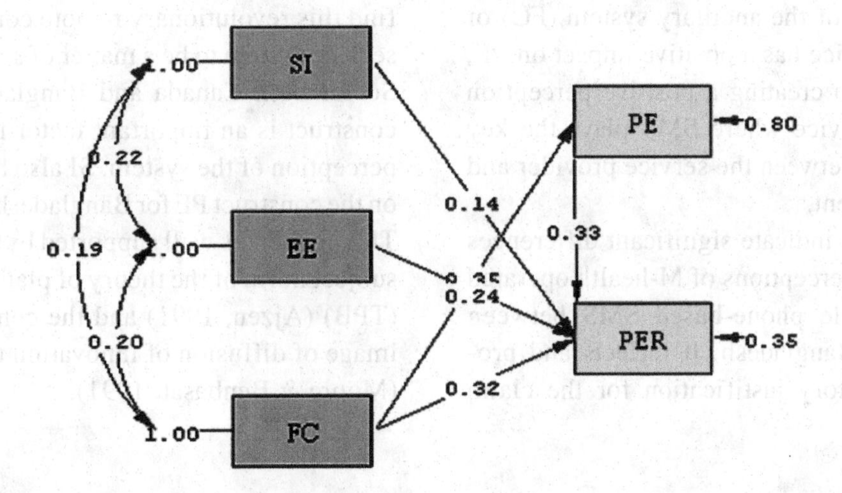

of using M-health through the SMS of a mobile phone, they find a higher performance of this new technology-driven health service system. Overall, ancillary systems of M-health in particular have immense support from consumers in perceiving the M-health system conducted by mobile phone SMS to be reliable, trustworthy, and effective and thus they find that the system has a high performance.

In contrast, for Canada the magnitude of the effects of different constructs on developing a positive perception about M-health conducted by mobile phone SMS has some differences from that of Bangladeshi consumers. For Canadian diabetic patients who seek or maintain connectivity with M-health service through the SMS of mobile phones, the expected performance (PE) of this particular remote control service is the most important reason (path coefficient 0.33) to create a positive perception about this service. Overall, ancillary support (FC) is the second most vulnerable issue (path coefficient 0.32) for them to develop positive perception. Two other constructs, ease of system use (EE) and the normative influence of society (SI), are also important predictors for pursuing a positive perception about the system. The load coefficients for EE and SI are 0.24 and 0.14 respectively. Again, for Canadians the integrative effect of the ancillary system (FC) of M-health service has a positive impact on PE, which leads to creating a positive perception about this service where SMS plays the key connectivity between the service provider and service recipient.

The results indicate significant differences of consumer perceptions of M-health operated through mobile phone-based SMS between Canada and Bangladesh. It reflects and provides exploratory justification for the claim that culture has a significant impact on forming perceptions about the M-health service system where connectivity is controlled through the remote SMS of mobile phones. As a developing country where the medical service system is not well organized and reliable, when the physical presence of medical professionals is absent, consumers might not expect this system to be reliable. So they might not expect this system to perform well. So, for them, the ancillary system which ultimately supports the total design and implementation of M-health through SMS of a mobile phone is the most vulnerable issue of concern. If they are confident of the FC of this system, they develop a positive perception of the system. For Bangladeshi users the normative influence of the society has an impact on the perception of the M-health system as a high performance system. In a developing country, this finding can be justified for a new technology-driven system as an alternative to traditional brick and mortar healthcare services. When diabetic patients use a wrist band directly connected with doctors through a smartphone and receive continuous feedback through SMS from doctors, so that they do not need to go to a medical center and can continue their daily life without hampering their regular jobs, they find this revolutionary remote control medical service system to be a matter of social prestige. So for both Canada and Bangladesh, this SI construct is an important factor for a positive perception of the system. SI also has an impact on the construct PE for Bangladeshi consumers. This concept is well supported by the construct subject norm of the theory of planned behavior (TPB) (Ajzen, 1991) and the construct of the image of diffusion of innovation theory (DOI) (Moore & Benbasat, 1991).

Theoretical and Managerial Implications

This exploratory study has potential contribution in the advancement of revolutionary health service delivery system through modern ICT. Both the academics and practitioners can be benefited from the findings of this study. UTAUT model is suggested to assume consumers behavior for ICT. Although, M-health is a very new and exploratory research issue, this study revealed that this model can also be used to conceptualize consumers behavioral intention for seeking M-health through mobile phone SMS. This theoretical identification can provide deep insight for the researchers, practitioners, and policy makers to advance this new kind of health service delivery system for all patients living in remote areas. Practitioners and policy makers can be assured that creating reference group and pushing this new trend of service through them can be an effective idea to positively motivate general consumers. Like all ICT related consumers behavior, M-health adoption is also highly dependent on how easy it is to use. For reliability, this apparently virtual service system must be authentically supported by required policies and arrangements.

It is identified that patients' perception about M-health delivered through mobile phone SMS is notably different for Canadian and Bangladeshi consumers. From cultural perspective, social influence (SI) is an important issue to pursue behavioral intention (Ajzen, 1991). For Bangladeshi patients, in seeking M-health through mobile phone SMS, they are highly motivated by reference group and social norms, where as for Canadian patients, although significant, surrounding social influence has the least impact on consumers perception about M-health delivered through mobile phone SMS. It reflects the impact of culture on consumers' behavior. Several researchers (Ein-Dor et al., 1993; Espinoza, 1999; Pavlou & Chai, 2002; Shareef et al., 2011) who conducted research on consumers' behavior for ICT adoption acknowledged that culture has significant impact on consumers' behavior.

CONCLUSION AND FUTURE RESEARCH DIRECTION

Beginning in the last century, the substantial advancement and revolutionary accomplishments of the healthcare service system helped consumers to create enormous expectations in identifying and accepting new healthcare services (Kahn et al. 2010). As an essential, precious, and emergency product, consumers demand healthcare services to be flexible, accessible, available, and compatible with a maximum price-value trade-off. They also prefer to streamline their high expectations for cost-effectiveness, quality, efficiency, life-pattern-congruency from health professionals (Wu et al. 2007). However, and not specifically for ICT, consumers desire a competent service compatible to a modern-day life pattern. It needs to be dynamic, flexible, and an easy-going medical service which would at the same time pressure all the stakeholders in a healthcare service system to incorporate and integrate the core characteristics of a wireless communication system in the selection of delivery of healthcare services to the patients.

The research had two objectives. As the first goal, the authors attempted to identify the causes which can induce consumers to have positive perceptions about M-health driven by the SMS of mobile phone. In this connection, the UTAUT model was used as the theoretical base to perceive consumer perceptions about M-health. The authors have conducted an empirical study among diabetic patients in Bangladesh and Canada. Path analysis has been conducted for both samples. The results confirmed that PE, FC, SI, and EE are the significant constructs for capturing consumer perceptions about M-health conducted by the SMS of mobile phones. Therefore, the UTAUT model fits quite nicely in predicting consumer perceptions for M-health-driven mobile technology. Nevertheless, the degree of convergence and magnitude of effect of different constructs in learning consumer perceptions for M-health are potentially different for Bangladeshi and Canadian consumers. This identification reflects the cultural effects on the consumer perception process for an ICT-driven, M-health system that is predominantly controlled from remote places.

Several researchers (Espinoza, 1999; Irani et al., 2007; Posey et al., 2010; Shareef et al, 2014), in exploring the impact of culture on consumer behavior for ICT-driven service, acknowledged this finding. Pavlou and Chai (2002) addressed consumer adoption behavior for Chinese and USA consumers, and, in the light of Hofstede's (2001) cultural dimensions, revealed that any attempt to formulate a standardized ICT-related consumer behavior model is impractical. The authors asserted that culture, indeed, has potential implications for consumer attitudes and behavioral norms. Tajfel (1972), in a social identity theory, strongly asserted that social identity, which is potentially governed by cultural traits, has a substantial impact on paradigms of consumer behavior. Technological, behavioral, and social beliefs of the system's functional, organizational, and professional benefits will render it congruent with a life pattern comprising an attitude toward using it. However, this research has been conducted in only two countries. To justify the cultural impact on perception process of consumers, future researchers can conduct similar research in several countries having significant differences in cultural traits.

REFERENCES

Ajzen, I. (1991). The Theory of Planned Behavior. *Organizational Behavior and Human Decision Processes*, *50*(2), 179–211. doi:10.1016/0749-5978(91)90020-T

Carroll, A., Barnes, S. J., Scornavacca, E., & Fletcher, K. (2007). Consumer perceptions and attitudes towards SMS advertising: Recent evidence from New Zealand. *International Journal of Advertising*, *26*(1), 79–98.

Chau, P. Y. K. (1997). Reexamining a Model for Evaluating Information Center Success: Using a Structural Equation Modeling Approach. *Decision Sciences*, *28*(2), 309–334. doi:10.1111/j.1540-5915.1997.tb01313.x

Cheng, J. M. S., Blankson, C., Wang, E. S. T., & Chen, L. S. L. (2009). Consumer attitudes and interactive digital advertising. *International Journal of Advertising*, *28*(3), 501–525. doi:10.2501/S0265048709200710

Davis, F. D. (1989). Perceived Usefulness, Perceived Ease of Use and User Acceptance of Information Technology. *Management Information Systems Quarterly*, *13*(3), 319–340. doi:10.2307/249008

Donthu, N., & Yoo, B. (1998). Cultural Influences on Service Quality Expectations. *Journal of Service Research*, *1*(2), 178–186. doi:10.1177/109467059800100207

Ein-Dor, P., Segev, E., & Orgad, M. (1993). The Effect of National Culture on IS: Implications for International Information Systems. *Journal of Global Information Management*, *1*(1), 33–44. doi:10.4018/jgim.1993010103

Espinoza, M. M. (1999). Assessing the cross-cultural applicability of a service quality measure A comparative study between Quebec and Peru. *International Journal of Service Industry Management*, *10*(5), 449–468. doi:10.1108/09564239910288987

Goodman, S. E., & Green, J. D. (1992). Computing in the middle east. *Communications of the ACM*, *35*(8), 21–25. doi:10.1145/135226.135236

He, D. H., & Lu, Y. B., (2007). *Consumers Perceptions and Acceptances towards Mobile Advertising: An Empirical Study in China*. IEEE.

Hofstede, G. (2001). *Culture's Consequences* (2nd ed.). Thousand Oaks: Sage.

Irani, Z., Love, P. E. D., & Montazemi, A. (2007). e-Government: Past, present and future. *European Journal of Information Systems*, *16*(2), 103–105. doi:10.1057/palgrave.ejis.3000678

Jamieson, K. (2012, October 15-17). *SMS Advertising: A Cross-national Study on Acceptance and Response. Proceeding of the 13th West Lake International Conference on Small and Medium Business, (WLICSMB 2011)*. Hangzhou, China.

Kahn, J. G., Yang, J. S., & Kahn, J. S. (2010). 'Mobile' Health Needs and Opportunities in Developing Countries. *Health Affairs*, *29*(2), 252–258. doi:10.1377/hlthaff.2009.0965 PMID:20348069

Kettinger, W. J., Lee, C. C., & Lee, S. (1995). Global measures of information service quality: A cross-national study. *Decision Sciences*, *26*(5), 569–588. doi:10.1111/j.1540-5915.1995.tb01441.x

Kline, R. B. (2005). *Principles and Practice of Structural Equation Modeling*. NY: The Guilford Press.

McDonald, J., & Dahlberg, J. (2010, March 8-10). US Consumer Attitudes Toward And Acceptance Of SMS Mobile Text Advertising, *Proceeding of the 4th International Technology, Education and Development Conference (INTED)*. Valencia, Spain.

Moore, G., & Benbasat, I. (1991). Development of an Instrument to Measure the Perceptions of Adopting an Information Technology Innovation. *Information Systems Research*, *2*(3), 173–191. doi:10.1287/isre.2.3.192

Moynihan, B., Kabadayi, S., & Kaiser, M. (2010). Consumer acceptance of SMS advertising: A study of American and Turkish consumers. *International Journal of Mobile Communications*, *8*(4), 392–410. doi:10.1504/IJMC.2010.033833

Muk, A. (2007). Consumers' intentions to opt in to SMS advertising - A cross-national study of young Americans and Koreans. *International Journal of Advertising*, *26*(2), 177–198.

Nunnally, J. C., & Bernstein, I. H. (1994). Psychometric Theory. New York: McGraw-Hill.

Pavlou, P. A., & Chai, L. (2002). What Drives Electronic Commerce across Cultures? A Cross-Cultural Empirical Investigation of the Theory of Planned Behavior. *Journal of Electronic Commerce Research*, *3*(4), 240–253.

Posey, C., Lowry, P. B., Roberts, T. L., & Ellis, T. S. (2010). Proposing the online community self-disclosure model: The case of working professionals in France and the U.K. who use online communities. *European Journal of Information Systems*, *19*(2), 181–195. doi:10.1057/ejis.2010.15

Qureshi, I. M., Batool, I., & Shamim, A. (2012). Consumer Perception In Response To E-Marketing Stimuli: The Impact of Brand Salience, *Actual. Problems of Economics*, *2*(4), 137–143.

Segars, A., & Grover, V. (1993). Re-examining Perceived Ease of Use and Usefulness: A Confirmatory Factor Analysis. *Management Information Systems Quarterly*, *17*(4), 517–527. doi:10.2307/249590

Shareef, M. A., Kumar, U., Kumar, V., & Dwivedi, Y. K. (2011). E-government Adoption Model (GAM): Differing Service Maturity Levels. *Government Information Quarterly*, *28*(1), 17–35. doi:10.1016/j.giq.2010.05.006

Shareef, M. A., Kumar, V., Dwivedi, Y. K., & Kumar, U. (2014). Global Service Quality of Electronic-Commerce. [IJICBM]. *International Journal of Indian Culture and Business Management*, *8*(1), 1–34. doi:10.1504/IJICBM.2014.057947

Srisawatsakul, C., & Papasratorn, B. (2013). Factors Affecting Consumer Acceptance Mobile Broadband Services with Add-on Advertising: Thailand Case Study. *Wireless Personal Communications*, *69*(3), 1055–1065. doi:10.1007/s11277-013-1065-4

Straub, D. W. (1994). The Effect of Culture on IT Diffusion: E-Mail and FAX in Japan and the U.S. *Information Systems Research*, *5*(I), 23–47. doi:10.1287/isre.5.1.23

Tajfel, H. (1972). La Categorisation Sociale (Social categorization). In S. Moscovici (Ed.), *Introduction a La Psychologie Sociale, 1* (pp. 272–302). Paris: Larousse.

Trappey, R. J., & Woodside, A. G. (2005). Consumer responses to interactive advertising campaigns coupling short-message-service direct marketing and TV commercials. *Journal of Advertising Research*, *45*(4), 382–401.

Turel, O., Serenko, A., & Bontis, N. (2007). User acceptance of wireless short messaging

Turel, O., Serenko, A., & Bontis, N.services. (2007, January). Deconstructing perceived value. *Information & Management*, *44*(1), 63–73. doi:10.1016/j.im.2006.10.005

Venkatesh, V., Morris, M. G., Davis, G. B., & Davis, F. D. (2003). User Acceptance of Information Technology: Toward a Unified View. *Management Information Systems Quarterly*, *27*(3), 425–578.

Winsted, K. F. (1997). The service experience in two cultures: A behavioral perspective. *Journal ofRetailing*, *73*(3), 337–360. doi:10.1016/S0022-4359(97)90022-1

Wu, J.-H., Wanga, S.-C., & Lin, L.-M. (2007). Mobile computing acceptance factors in the healthcare industry: A structural equation model. *International Journal of Medical Informatics*, *76*(1), 66–77. doi:10.1016/j.ijmedinf.2006.06.006 PMID:16901749

Yu, P., Wu, M. X., Yu, H., & Xiao, G. C. (2006, June 21-23). The Challenges for the Adoption of M-Health. *IEEE International Conference on Service Operations and Logistics and Informatics (SOLI 2006)* (pp. 181-186). Shanghai, China. doi:10.1109/SOLI.2006.329059

Zhang, J., & Mao, E. (2008). Understanding the acceptance of mobile SMS advertising among young Chinese consumers. *Psychology and Marketing*, *25*(8), 787–805. doi:10.1002/mar.20239

Zhang, R. J., & Li, X. Y. (2012). Research on Consumers' Attitudes and Acceptance Intentions toward Mobile Marketing. In L. Hua (Ed.), *2012 International Conference on Management Science & Engineering* (pp. 727-732). doi:10.1109/ICMSE.2012.6414259

ADDITIONAL READING

Archer, N. (2007). Mobile eHealth: Making the Case. In I. Kushchu (Ed.), Mobile Government: AN Emerging Direction in E-government (pp. 155-170). Hershey, PA: IGI Publishing.

Assael, H. (1995). *Consumer Behavior and Marketing Action* (5th ed.). Cincinnati, Ohio: ITP, South-Western College Publishing.

Bloch, P. H., & Marsha, L. R. (1983). A Theoretical Model for the Study of Product Importance Perceptions. *Journal ofMarketing*, *47*(3), 69–81. doi:10.2307/1251198

Cadogan, J. (2010). Comparative, cross-cultural, and cross-national research: A comment on good and bad practice. *International Marketing Review*, *27*(6), 601–605. doi:10.1108/02651331011088245

Kotz, D., Avancha, S., & Baxi, A. (2009). A Privacy Framework for Mobile Health and Home-Care Systems. SPIMACS'09. Chicago, Illinois, USA.

Kumar, V., Kumar, U., Shareef, M. A., Chowdhury, A. H., & Sharan, V. (2013). Developing Citizen-centric Service: Adoption Behavior for Mobile Health. *Proceedings of the Administrative Sciences Association of Canada Conference*. Calgary, Alberta, Canada.

Mallat, N. (2007). Exploring consumer adoption of mobile payments – A qualitative study. *The Journal of Strategic Information Systems*, *16*(4), 413–432. doi:10.1016/j.jsis.2007.08.001

Mattila, A. S. (1999). The role of culture in the service evaluation process. *Journal of Service Research*, *1*(3), 250–261. doi:10.1177/109467059913006

McSweeney, B. (2013). Fashion Founded on Flaw - The Ecological Mono-Deterministic Fallacy of Hofstede, GLOBE, and Followers. *International Marketing Review*, *30*(5), 483–504. doi:10.1108/IMR-04-2013-0082

Meingast, M., Roosta, T., & Sastry, S. (2006). Security and privacy issues with health care information technology, *Proceedings of the 28th IEEE EMBS Annual International Conference*, August, DOI doi:10.1109/IEMBS.2006.260060

Michael, R. T., & Becker, G. S. (1973). On the New Theory of Consumer Behavior. *The Swedish Journal of Economics*, *75*(4), 378–396. doi:10.2307/3439147

Miyazaki, A. D., & Fernandez, A. (2001). Consumer Perceptions of Privacy and Security Risks for Online Shopping. *The Journal of Consumer Affairs*, *35*(1), 27–44. doi:10.1111/j.1745-6606.2001.tb00101.x

Nelson, K. G., & Clark, T. D. Jr. (1994). Cross-Cultural Issues in Information Systems Research: A Research Program. *Journal of Global Information Management*, 2(4), 19–29. doi:10.4018/jgim.1994100102

Neslin, S., & Shankar, V. (2009). Key Issues in Multichannel Customer Management: Current Knowledge and Future Directions. *Journal of Interactive Marketing*, *23*(1), 70–81. doi:10.1016/j.intmar.2008.10.005

Payan, J., Svensson, G., & Hair, J. (2010). A "cross-cultural RELQUAL-scale" in supplier distributor relationships of Sweden and the USA. *International Marketing Review*, *27*(5), 541–561. doi:10.1108/02651331011076581

Robertson, T. S. (1974). A Critical Examination of Adoption Process Models of Consumer Behavior. In J. N. Sheth (Ed.), *Models of Buyer Behavior*.

Shareef, M. A., Archer, N., & Dwivedi, Y. K. (To be published in 2015). An Empirical Investigation of Electronic Government Service Quality: From the Demand Side Stakeholder Perspective. Total Quality Management & Business Excellence.

Shareef, M. A. & Dwivedi, Y. K. (To be published in 2015). A Bird Eye View of Existing Research on Consumer Behavior in the Context of SMS Based Marketing, The Marketing Review, 15(1),

Shareef, M. A., Kumar, V., Dwivedi, Y. K., & Kumar, U. (2014). *Citizen Attitudes toward Service Delivery through Mobile-Government (mGov): Driving Factors and Cultural Impacts, Information Systems Frontiers*.

Shareef, M. A., Kumar, V., & Kumar, U. (Forthcoming). Predicting Mobile Health Adoption Behavior: A Demand Side perspective. *Journal of Customer Behavior.*

Shareef, M. A., Kumar, V., Kumar, U., & Dwivedi, Y. K. (2014). Factors affecting citizen adoption of transactional electronic government. *Journal of Enterprise Information Management*, *27*(4), 385–401. doi:10.1108/JEIM-12-2012-0084

Shareef, M. A., Kumar, V., Kumar, U., & Dwivedi, Y. K. (To be published in 2015). Consumer online purchase behaviour: perception versus expectation. International Journal Indian Culture and Business Management.

Sun, G., D'Alessandro, S., Johnson, L. W., & Winzar, H. (2014). Do we measure what we expect to measure? Some issues in the measurement of culture in consumer research. *International Marketing Review*, *31*(4), 1–38. doi:10.1108/IMR-03-2012-0055

Swoboda, B., Pennemann, K., & Taube, M. (2012). The Effects of Perceived Brand Globalness and Perceived Brand Localness in China: Empirical Evidence on Western, Asian, and Domestic Retailers. *Journal of International Marketing*, *20*(4), 25–77. doi:10.1509/jim.12.0105

Taylor, S., & Todd, P. (1995). Decomposition and crossover effects in the theory of planned behavior: A study of consumer adoption intentions. *International Journal of Research in Marketing*, *12*(2), 137–155. doi:10.1016/0167-8116(94)00019-K

Vallerand, R. J. (1997). In M. Zanna (Ed.), *Toward a Hierarchical Model of Intrinsic and Extrinsic Motivation* (Vol. 29, pp. 271–360). Advances in Experimental Social Psychology New York: Academic Press. doi:10.1016/S0065-2601(08)60019-2

Venkatesh, V., Davis, F. D., & Morris, M. G. (2007). Dead or Alive? The Development, Trajectory and Future of Technology Adoption Research. *Journal of the AIS*, *8*(4), 268–286.

Venkatesh, V., Thong, J. Y. L., & Xu, X. (2012). Consumer Acceptance and Use of Information Technology: Extending the Unified Theory of Acceptance and Use of Technology. *Management Information Systems Quarterly*, *36*(1), 157–178.

Wu, I.-L., Li, J.-Y., & Fu, C.-Y. (2011). The adoption of mobile healthcare by hospital's professionals: An integrative perspective. *Decision Support Systems*, *51*(3), 587–596. doi:10.1016/j.dss.2011.03.003

KEY TERMS AND DEFINITIONS

Consumer: In this article, actually, patients are terms as consumers. Generally consumers can be defined as anyone who use any products or services.

Culture: Culture, in this article, is defined as overall traits of any society or nations which can distinctly identify their characteristics to develop a unique identity.

Mobile-Health or M-Health: Can be defined as providing right healthcare service at right time continuously to any remote patients without hampering their regular lifestyle. In this service system patients' physical presence in hospitals, clinics, and/or doctors chambers is not required. They will be communicated through ICT-driven wireless systems, software, and health monitoring devices.

Perception: It is a process by which individuals organize and interpret their sensory impressions in order to give meaning to their environment or any objects.

Short Message Service: Any message delivered through mobile phone is termed as "short message service" (SMS).

UTAUT Model: The full name of UTAUT Model is Unified Theory of Acceptance and Use of Technology (UTAUT) (Venkatesh et al., 2003) model. According to the UTAUT model, performance expectancy, effort expectancy, social influence, and facilitating conditions are the four potential constructs to explain user perception and acceptance behavior.

Chapter 13
Use of Social Media for Policing

Amir Manzoor
Bahria University, Pakistan

ABSTRACT

An overwhelming amount of information (and misinformation) is available on today's social media sites (e.g., Twitter, Facebook, Flickr, YouTube). Law enforcement agencies actively seek to leverage these resources to improve services and communication with public. Various factors have forced law enforcement agencies to have an active voice on social media. This chapter examines the growing interest of police forces in the use of social media to engage groups previously uninvolved in discussion of community policing and for deliberation about priorities of police forces. The chapter concludes that police forces, in general, have been able to exploit the networked characteristics of social media and the potential of user-generated content. Recommendations are provided to achieve more ambitious aims for using social media for policing.

1. INTRODUCTION

Social media is a complex concept that generally refers to a broad range of non-traditional forms of electronic communication including blogs and micro blogs, discussion forums, media sharing websites, social networks, social news, social bookmarking, and Wikis (Varano & Sarasin, 2014). One common feature of all these is that they are all consumers of content. In contrast to traditional media (such as TV), a user of social media can be both a consumer and a producer of user-generated content and timely news.

One definition of social media is that "it is a group of Internet-based applications that build on the ideological and technological foundations of Web 2.0, and that allow the creation and exchange of User Generated Content (Kaplan & Haenlein, 2010). Kaplan and Haenlein (2010) divided social media into six types (see Table 1).

Another very significant feature of social media is rich user interaction that makes social media most successful (Wang, Tang, Gao, & Liu, 2010). Different governments agencies especially police have been using social media for many years now (Walters, 2014; Wagner, 2014). Some early examples of social media use for policing include the 2011 fires at City of Los Angeles that caused extensive damage to vehicles and property worth more than $350,000 (CNN, 2012). Pushed to their limits, public safety officials used social media as a bi-directional communication tool to both collect

DOI: 10.4018/978-1-4666-8598-7.ch013

Table 1. Social Media Types

Type of Social Media	Description	Example
Collaborative Projects	Allow for the joint and simultaneous creation of content by end-users.	Wikipedia
Blogs and Micro-Blogs	Websites that provide date stamped content entries in reverse chronological order	Twitter
Content Communities	Sites that provide their users a platform to share media content	YouTube
Social Networking Sites	Sites that provides their users ability to connect by creating profiles, sending emails and instant messages to other users	Facebook
Virtual Game Worlds	Platforms that represent a 3-D environment whereby users can create and appear in the form of personalized avatars and interact with each other.	World of Warcraft
Virtual Social Worlds	Sites similar to virtual game worlds. One difference is that there exist no restrictions on the possible number of interactions that users can have with other.	Second Life Application

and communicate real time information from the public about a rash of fires. In this situation, social media played a critical role in a quick resolution to this crisis by greatly enhancing public safety official's ability to disseminate information to the public and accessing those segments of public that were non-conventional segments of news (Sutton, Palen, & Shklovski, 2008).

In London terrorist attack in 2005, eyewitnesses used blogs to tell their experience i.e. first-hand reports of the incident. In the Iranian presidential election of 2009, witnesses tweeted during the bloody clash that took place between protesters and government forces. This suggests that people do turn to social media in case of disaster/emergency (LeVeque, 2011; Burns & Eltham, 2009).

During the last decade, social media has brought significant changes in the way we communicate and share information. Nearly 1.11 billion people across the globe, or 16% of the world's population, were estimated to have accessed Facebook by March 2013(Facebook, 2013). The social media has impacted social landscape, from basic interpersonal communications to playing a central role in toppling of tyrannical governments during Arab Spring of 2011 (Howard & Hussain 2011).

Such breadth and depth of social media impact has caught attention of law enforcement agencies around the globe. Law enforcement agencies, in a bid to expand the scope of their communication strategies, have started to adopt social media strategies. It was estimated that by October 2013, 92% of 600 US law enforcement agencies reported using some form of social media (International Association of Chiefs of Police, 2013).

Despite such potential advantages of social media capacity, some law enforcement agencies across the globe still reluctant to accept this new form of communication (Maynard, 2013). It is clear that at least some of this apprehension is due to basic lack of familiarity and expertise (Varano & Sarasin, 2014). Another factor could be that social media are rich, but overwhelming sources of information which required time and resources for proper analysis (Kavanaugh et al., 2012).

This chapter aims to explore the state-of-the-art of social media use for policing to discover its various uses, enablers of its user, usage trends, and issues to come up with specific guidelines/recommendations for future use of social media by law enforcement agencies.

2. BACKGROUND

2.1. Explosion of Social Media Use

In recent years, there has also been a considerable expansion in the levels of use of social media. According to (Pew Internet, 2013), some 73% of online adults used a social networking site of some kind. Facebook was the dominant social networking platform in the number of users, but a striking number of users were diversifying onto other platforms. Some 42% of online adults used multiple social networking sites. According to (eMarketer, 2013), nearly one in four people worldwide expected to use social networks in 2013. The number of social network users around the world was expected to rise from 1.47 billion in 2012 to 1.73 billion in 2013, an 18% increase. By 2017, the global social network audience was expected to reach a total of 2.55 billion. According to (Smith, 2011), "stay connected" to family and friends was the most cited reason for use of social media. The magnitude and speed of this growth defies comprehension. As a result, many corporations now invest time and money into creating, purchasing, and promoting social networking sites. According to Boyd and Ellison (2007), the rise of social networking sites suggested a shift in the organization of online communities with social networking sites getting organized around people and structured around personal networks. Therefore, social media is an extremely active and evolving domain that now accounts for a significant proportion of Internet traffic. As a result, a new breed of crimes has emerged that uses social media (Heatherly, Kantarcioglu, & Thuraisingham, 2013).

2.2. Crimes Linked to Social Media

The National White Collar Crime Center identified following typical crimes that used social media (National White Collar Crime Center, 2013).

2.2.1. Burglary via Social Networking

This crime involved the perpetrator perusing users' profiles and looking for potential victims in the vicinity who will not be home. Myspace and Facebook users' posts by users are used to find victims who will not be home for a specific period. This information gives potential thieves a good time window to burgle the property. Facebook and Twitter's new "my location" feature allows readers to see where they were and how long ago it was when they posted their update. That makes it much easier for criminals to attack. According to (Stadd, 2013), more than 75% of burglars reportedly use Twitter, Facebook and Foursquare to target potential properties.

2.2.2. Phishing and Social Engineering

Phishing, the most widespread Internet and email fraud today, is a crime in which perpetrators send out many emails with the hopes of getting response in return. Social engineering refers to gaining access to information by exploiting human psychology rather than using traditional hacking techniques (Goodchild, 2012). A classic example of this starts when a friend on your network sends you a message and asks for a quick loan to get car repairs so he/she can get home for work on Monday. At the end, you find that your friend never needed car repairs and that the person you transferred money to was a fraud artist. The risks of data breaches that can result from these attacks are incredibly high – there were over 552 million identities exposed in data breaches during 2013 (Deschatres, 2014). In 2012, there were nearly 33,000 phishing attacks globally each month, which totaled a loss of $687 million. In 2013, the number of phishing attacks reached 37.3 million, an increase of 87%.

2.2.3. Malware

Social networking offers opportunities for virus and malware users. Users clicking on links, opening attachments, and responding to messages on networks can become victims without knowing it, resulting in adware, viruses, and malware being loaded onto their machines. The number of malware increased from 22.25 million in 2012 to 28.4 million in 2013, an increase of 27.6%. In 2013, According to a 2013 global survey conducted by B2B International and Kaspersky Lab (Kaspersky, 2013) malware attacks meant financial losses for about 36% of users – with many people forced to pay to restore damaged devices to working order. 27% respondents suffered at least one malware attack in 2013.

2.3. Setting the Stage for Social Media for Policing

For law enforcement agencies around the globe, social media has developed into an issue that they need to understand and harness. Policing is in many ways a technology driven profession that has historically embraced technology and integrated it into policing in highly visible and instrumental ways (Alderson, 1979). The increasing number of crimes linked with social media and the significant losses incurred have provided a strong basis for police use of social media.

Social media represents one of the next biggest waves of technological advancement in law enforcement (Kavanaugh et al., 2012). Many police departments around the world have been quick to adopt the use of social media to communicate with the public. According to International Association of Chiefs of Police2013 Social Media Survey (International Association of Chiefs of Police, 2013), 95.9% of 500 US agencies used social media in some capacity. The most frequently used social media platforms were Facebook (92.1%), Twitter (64.8%), and YouTube (42.9%). These strategies, in many ways, lie at heart of more innovative policing strategies such as community-policing or problem-oriented policing, both of which hold police-citizen communication/ interaction as a core philosophy. The most common use of social media was for criminal investigations at 86.1%. 57.1% of agencies not currently using social media were considering its adoption while 69.4% of agencies had a social media policy and an additional 14.3% were in the process of constructing a policy. 80.4% of agencies reported that social media had helped solve crimes in their jurisdiction while 73.1% of agencies stated that social media had improved police-community relations in their jurisdiction. Use of social media is a great opportunity for bi-directional communication with the public in general and youngsters in particular. For youngsters, social media is the preferred way to stay connected with family and friends, a primary source of information about the world around them, and for emotional support (Ellison et al. 2007; Greenhow & Robelia 2009). There is a growing sense that exploitation of social media will soon become a necessity given the rapid emergence of new forms of communication and expansion in their dominance of the social landscape and discourse.

2.4. Factors Underlying the Adoption of Social Media for Policing

The trend of using social media for policing is being driven by the idea that police should increase communication with the public. The concept of community policing is centered on community and police department as allies that play a direct role and actively participate in shaping organizational processes and priorities of the police department. (Friedmann, 1992) In community policing, community is a customer with needs are worthy of consideration and police have a responsibility for sharing information with the public. This information sharing is both a service to the public and an image control mechanism for police to create positive public presences.

However, community policing is one of the many reasons behind social media use for policing. Another factor is resource constraints. The shrinking resources have overwhelmed police departments across the globe and forced them to develop innovative ways to reduce workload without compromising public safety or community relations (Stadd, 2013). Alternate crime reporting strategies, such as 311 systems and phone-based police reports, have been developed in parallel to the traditional 911 system. These alternative systems, largely, have been effective alternatives of the traditional reporting systems (Mazerolle et al., 2003). The explosion of Internet, has also given rise to a new set of relatively inexpensive online crime reporting systems. It was anticipated that these systems would play an important role in future given the growing online presence of police departments (Cisneros, 2009).

In Europe, we see many more issues that are tenacious. These issues are driving police for establishing their online presence on social media (Composite Project, 2012). First, irrespective of whether a particular police department has presence on social media or not, there were active discussions on social media about police matters. Second, there was a proliferation of bogus social media accounts and channels, both in small and big cities, that were used specifically to provide police- related information. In Berlin, Germany an unofficial Facebook page with police news listed more than 15,000 fans. In the Dutch region Haaglanden, an unofficial Twitter feed by a self- proclaimed police fan listed 2,500 followers (BBC News, 2012). This situation calls for an ever growing space for rumors and speculations in social media until police establishes a credible presence online. Third, normal citizens were using social media to perform actions traditionally performed by police only. One such action was search warrants for missing people. In many cases, the relatives and friends of the missing person started using social media at their own and provided non-trustworthy information. For normal citizens, such situations became difficult because they had no means to differentiate between trustworthy and non-trustworthy information. Fourth, police increasingly faced the problem of traditional media communication not reaching the relevant people. For many police affairs, bi-directional communication with younger and better-educated people is relevant and important. However, a large majority of these people didn't use traditional media for communication and instead relied solely on social media to get news. These segments of population were important because they were the highest users of social media sites of police (Ruddell & Jones, 2013). Therefore, active social media presence of police was crucial to communicate with their target audience. Fifth, social media increasingly impacted everyday life and people used social media to organize events (such as parties), make announcements (such as suicide attempts), and report child abuse. This increasingly complex situation calls for a police force with competence in social media and able for an effective bi-directional communication with citizens. Social media has shown to be an effective and relevant tool in crisis management. Social media helps people to self-organize, to get and share important, current and local information. The UK riots in the summer of 2011 is a clear example that during times of crises police forces highly benefit from established connections and trained practices on social media(Denef, Bayerl, & Kaptein, 2013; Tonkin, Pfeiffer, & Tourte, 2012; Scholes-Fogg, 2013).

Another pressing issue is increased use of social media by criminals (Rizzo, 2013). According to Pelgrin (2013), there were three reasons why criminals used social media to find their targets. First, a very large number of users, who were sharing a lot of information, provided an enormous repository of potential victims and data. Second, increased amount of information posted on these sites provided an ever increasing dossier of information available to do many crimes such as password cracking and identity theft. Third, social media acted as prime medium for malware distribution. According to 2013 Symantec Internet Security Threat Report, 43% of attacks that used social networking websites were related to malware. The technologies used on social networking sites can not only invite user participation but also make these sites easier to infect the user's system with malware that can shut down the system or install keystroke loggers that can steal user's credentials. More recently we are seeing many examples of how criminals use social media to track police and recruit their members. According to Buttler (2013), criminals used information gathered from social media to engineer relationships with police for the purpose of securing access to law enforcement information. One example as to how criminals are using social media is the Mexican cartels (Purvis, 2011).Today's organized crime syndicates use Facebook page and IP address as the new weapons to fight law enforcement agencies in their new battleground i.e. Cyberspace. These cartels use social media and blogs to significantly shorten the process of intelligence gathering for their criminal activities, for target selection in human trafficking operations, and gleaning information to help them determine an individual's value, visibility, and vulnerability. These cartels are also using social media to instill fear in others and deter journalists and private citizens to voice against their criminal activities. They are using geo-location technology to find computers that have been used to post dialogue that negatively affects their illicit businesses. In a documented case, a Mexican blogger threatened to expose members of a cartel. In response, the cartel threatened to kill 10 people for every person whose details will be leaked. As a result, the blogger backed down and didn't reveal the information he had (Barker, 2013).

3. THE USE OF SOCIAL MEDIA IN POLICING

Utilizing social media has several benefits and can be extremely invaluable in a contemporary policing environment. Police departments vary greatly in the extent to which they have adopted social media. Below is an overview of how social media has been integrated into policing (Lons, 2010; Stevens, 2010).

3.1 Social Media for Recruitment

Police recruitment in the twenty-first century is faced with various challenges such as budget-related attrition, retiring baby-boom generation, and generational trends that cause move of qualified candidates to other professions (Wilson & Castaneda, 2011). Social media offers law enforcement an opportunity to become a competitive employer by providing an ability to attract, engage, and inform potential applicants. Law enforcement agencies can use social media as an inexpensive way to connect with both passive and active job seekers, and to answer any questions about a future career in law enforcement (International Association of Chiefs of Police. 2011). The law enforcement agencies can also post recruitment and other career-related videoson their YouTube channel, while already having presence on Facebook, Twitter, Flickr, Pinterest, and Blogger.com (Gazaway, 2011; Mustian & Wallace, 2014; Knell, 2013). Another tool is recruitment blogs. Blogs give agencies a method to communicate more regularly and more personally than a conventional department website offers. Facebook posts allow applicants to have specific conversations that can be viewed by other applicants.

In China, a verified account of the Chengdu public security bureau on SinaWeibo, the Chinese equivalent of Twitter, published a series of movie poster-like photos Wednesday in an effort to attract talents to join the police force (People Daily, China, 2014). In Canada, police departments in many cities such as Vancouver, Regina, Edmonton, and Calgary actively used their Facebook pages for recruitment. In 2012, Toronto Police department initiated 'Youth in Policing Initiative (YIPI), to promote youth participation in and exposure to the work environment through diverse, educational, and productive work assignments (Toronto Police, 2012a). In New Zealand, the most popular police Facebook and Twitter accounts were the NZ Police Recruitment page which had more than 18,500 "likes" and the @BetterWorkStory account which had more than 4500 followers (3news, 2013). In United States, police departments of various cities such as Boston, New York, Los Angeles, and Oakland actively used their Facebook pages and YouTube channels to recruit new officers (KGO, 2014). In UK, police force of several cities, such as London, Manchester, and Essex were actively engaged in using social media to get new recruits (Lee, 2103). The Victoria Police Department in Australia initiated a 'Twitter Recruit' campaign in which Victoria Police recruits shared the experience of being at the Police Academy with the world (in particular, potential recruits) via Twitter (Commissioner for Law Enforcement Data Security, 2012).

3.2 Social Media for Passive Intelligence and Investigations

Social media has tremendous potential for investigation purposes (Zeng, Chen, Lusch, & Li, 2010). Social media is transforming the way in which law enforcement agencies conduct investigations. Investigations performed by the police can benefit greatly from information that is available on social media. Information about offenders and crimes found online has shown to be valuable for police operations. US Law enforcement agencies used social media for investigative purposes when seeking evidence or information about missing or wanted persons, gang participation, as well as Internet crimes such as cyberstalking or cyberbullying. Information found online helped supplement other evidence already gathered by the police (National Law Enforcement Policy Center, 2010).

In Australia, the State Intelligence Division (SID) monitored social media for passive intelligence gathering. The SID was trialing cybercrime analysis software that operated on publicly available information, providing an analysis of friendship networks. Information from social network sites was largely used to corroborate other intelligence. Where relevant, a 'screen capture' or a copy of text was placed on a file (Commissioner for Law Enforcement Data Security, 2012). A special E-crime squad was established by Victoria Police where crime analysts accessed publicly available material on social media to gather intelligence about persons of interest.

In Europe, many police departments found that, in many cases, Internet and social media helped to find information that otherwise would have required a much greater investigative effort or would not have been available at all (Composite Project, 2012).Performing such investigations in social media extends existing policing practice. Police and prosecutors in USA used information found on social media sites to gather and enhance the evidence against an individual (National Law Enforcement Policy Center, 2010). Take example of Melvin Colon, the suspected New York gang member. He posted public photos on Facebook that showed him flashing gang signs. However, in private posts he mentioned references to past violent crimes and threats against others. One of Colon's Facebook friends agreed to give police access to Colon's "private" information. The court ruled that Colon lost all claims to privacy when he shared those details with friends (CNN, 2012).In some cases, people turned themselves in, possibly out of fear or embarrassment. In other cases, people who recognized the pictures and videos contacted the police department with information.

Social media empowers the community to get involved in the crime fighting process (International Association of Chiefs of Police, 2012). This leads to enhanced relationships with community members. In United States, according to a July 2012 survey of 1,221 federal, state, and local law enforcement agencies that used social media in some way, four out of five agencies said they use social media for investigations (Public Intelligence, 2013).

3.3 Social Media for Active Intelligence and Covert Operations

Police departments also make active use of social media for covert operations. These covert operations were carried out by trained intelligence professionals. However, certain security risks were identified in use of social media for covert operations. In a research by (Stilgherrianon, 2011) it was found that everybody in police department aged 26 years or younger had uploaded their photo onto the internet and 85 percent were using at least one of the major social networking sites. Some 47 percent were using them daily, and another 24 percent weekly. Australian governments had introduced laws to protect the privacy of individuals and there are also legal protections for those who need to conceal their identities as part of their job. However, Australin police uncovered evidence of at least one organized crime group having photographs taken at police graduation parades. With the ease with which these images could be spread and stored, potentially forever, that posed an unforeseen threat (Bowden, 2011).

3.4 Social Media for Internal Intelligence

Police departments also used social media sites to investigate cases of Police members behaving inappropriately online. Many police departments had issued guidelines for proper use of social media use by their member. In some case, police didn't actively seek information from social media sites and the cases of improper behavior were reported by third parties (Commissioner for Law Enforcement Data Security, 2012). Police departments normally formulated a profile of a target member under investigation using social media and other tools. They then developed and applied integrity tests on suspected members. Police departments used stand-alone computers to access social media sites and acquire information. As a result, these computers could not be traced back to the Police network.

3.5 Social Media for Enforcement

This is an infrequent use of social media for policing. Where a Magistrate is satisfied that it is not reasonably practicable to serve a copy of an Intervention Order, the Magistrate ordered the document to be served in another manner such as via Facebook, or other social media sites if deemed appropriate (Commissioner for Law Enforcement Data Security, 2012). Documents served via a social media site were strictly from an official Police Social Media profile, and the full details of the police officer serving the document ere provided. The police also required to establish that the online location it was serving the document to was actually the respondent's page/site.

3.6 Social Media for Community Policing

Law enforcement agencies have begun to use social media tools to enhance community policing initiatives. For example, police departments across the globe are using social media for posting crime prevention tips, crime reporting, posting crime maps and other data, and disseminating alerts to the community (National Law Enforcement Policy Center, 2010; Sherman, 2011). Police agencies are also using social media platforms to reach out to their community members in order to foster better relationships and connections. However, the challenge for the police will be to find a way to embrace the spirit of the new social media in such a way that the content that is developed is convincing and feels authentic to users (Copitch & Fox, 2010).

In Netherlands and the United Kingdom, police departments either have social media officers, responsible for social media communication with local communities, or adopted social media as standard tool for community police officer. Local police officers communicate with the community on social media networks on their own behalf. They are free to publicly post their own message and only follow higher-level guidelines. They talk about their current operations, their contact details, and post safety remarks about local safety issues. This communication is independent of the press officers of their force. Police headquarters usually monitor what their local officers are posting on social media. Some police headquarters also have access to their officers' accounts and can independently change messages posted by the local officers. The purpose of this monitoring is to share knowledge and best practice among each other and to be aware of current policing matters in other areas. In Netherlands, the website 'www.politie20.nl' specifically deals with police intelligence and social media for police work. In addition, this website provides reports of meetings that are being organized with citizens in local communities to define the best use of social media for police work (Webster, 2013). Other than considering social media as a tool to support traditional community policing, social media networks are also considered as another type of community that requires police presence. This type of activity is sometimes described as "virtual community policing" that takes place on the social media networks such as Facebook. The police actively seek contact to people online to answer questions and file crimes (European Crime Prevention Network, 2009). In Helsinki, Finland, police had three officers working full time for virtual community policing. In Limburg Zuid, Netherlands, police had a special virtual character that identified himself as a police officer and operated a virtual office in the social network habbo hotel. This website was used by young children mostly who used avatars to walk around and talk to each other. This service was popular and the children talked to the officer about issues within and beyond the virtual world (European Crime Prevention Network, 2009).

Still the use of social media for community policing is not a common practice even in Europe because it doesn't fit with the current practice and hierarchic work structure in which police organizations usually operate in many countries. Another factor could be the perceived risks of using social media (National Executive Institute Associates, 2013). Whether such approach is feasible and would be adopted by police forces in other countries, is yet unknown.

3.7 Social Media as Information Outlet

The most straightforward communication use of social media by police is to publish police-related information using accounts that are setup by police and that citizens can subscribe to.The use of a particular social networking site by police depends on the local popularity of different social networks. The most popular social networks used by police are Facebook and Twitter (Varano & Sarasin, 2014).In a wide selection of networks available, selection of these two sites allows police to minimize the maintenance efforts while reaching the largest number of people. In addition, police departments have been using YouTube channels to publish videos and Flickr for publishing photos. Such communication using social media and other outlets is usually performed by the communications department of police force. This communications serves as an additional outlet of information that previously was prepared for press statements to be release by police. Police forces across Europe, such as in Belgium, the

Netherlands and the United Kingdom, are publishing this type of information for many years. Police forces in Finland, Iceland, and Ireland performed similar activities (Bennett, 2012). The Austrian Criminal Intelligence Service and city police of Zurich, Switzerland had also established presence on social media (Drandreagalli, 2011). To kick-off this effort initially, the police forces initiated a 24-hour 'tweet-a-thons' campaign in which police used Twitter messages to communicate with community (The Burlingame Voice, 2103). The purpose of the campaign was to show the public the broadness of police operations and to build special attention from the media in order to further increase the number of followers. A large scale publishing of information becomes especially relevant in times of large scale crises when citizens need to be informed in time and look for a credible source of information and advice. In 2011, riots erupted in different cities of the United Kingdom and in Vancouver, Canada. Police forces in both cases used Twitter to publish information on their operations and to provide information updates to citizens. This information received great interest by the public and all police forces saw significant rise in their follower numbers (CBC News, 2011).In both cases, public welcomed this new type of police service while police monitored the discussion of the general social media audience to issue trusted statements for fighting rumors. Social media allows police to push large amount of information to public with relatively little effort and resources required. Another advantage of social media is that even non-users of social media can get the updates through their friends because social media encourages sharing information across people and networks. Use of social media also allows police to become more independent from the press with an open and real-time communication with general public. As witnessed in the riots of UK and Vancouver, Canada, this new type of communication can become especially relevant in crises situations. Victoria Police Department in Australia developed a Facebook page in 2004 primarily to release information and to reach beyond regular viewers of the Victoria Police News Page. The majority of posts were news articles that were automatically posted onto the Facebook page using the RSS feed of the Victoria Police News Page. Victoria Police used the RSS Graffiti application, a free service that allowed users to periodically update one or multiple social network pages with any information feeds of their choosing (Commissioner for Law Enforcement Data Security, 2012).

3.8 Social Media to Leverage the Collective Wisdom

In United Kingdom or the Netherlands, various police departments routinely publish search warrants on social media for daily operations. For police, crowd sourcing is the main tool used to identify suspects in cases that receive a lot of public attention. One example is UK riots in 2011. The police used Twitter and photo-sharing site Flickr to extensively support investigations and to seek information on offenders (Procter, Crump, Karstedt, Voss, & Cantijoch, 2013; Vis, 2013). Social media appears to be a useful tool to seek investigation help from public. At the same time the public responses through social media constitutes a very large amount of data. Distilling this data can provide critical criminal information that may not be gathered with traditional means. However, it is not an easy task.

3.9 Social Media to Interact with the Public

Social media provides police ability of two-way, interactive communication with citizens. This communication with public using social media allows police to respond to queries from citizens in a way that it becomes shared knowledge and is accessible for others, too. Most police forces use social media to push communication in a similar fashion they used press announcements.

However, in long term, this interaction with public using social media is more interactive and on individual basis. This interactive communication is a consequence of design of social media sites. For example, any user of Twitter can send a message to another Twitter user. The user is then notified of the message and can choose to reply. In contrast to electronic mail, this conversation is public that other users can also choose to read too. In a similar fashion, Facebook allows users to see comments posted by other users or simply express their appreciation using 'Like' button. In a social media world, police forces need to make many choices regarding the kind and tone of message, how to respond to feedback received, and how to deal with the messages that don't follow police guidelines. The answer to these questions may sometime simply require following existing police regulation but in many cases the answer is not that clear. It is specially challenging given that using social media police is engaged in an open dialogue and police officers need more reliance on their skills and judgment rather than the guidelines. For police social media is an opportunity to engage in dialogue with an average citizen that they might, typically, have had less contact with. Such open dialog also provides a tool to resolve conflicts and provide direct feedback to police work. For citizens, social media is an opportunity to interact with police and know more about work they probably know very little about i.e. policing. In 2011, a 24 hour 'tweet-a-thon' campaign started by Zurich city police posted on Twitter and Facebook most of the police activities on that day. In UK, the Birmingham police started the day-long "tweet-a-thon" on 18th November, 2011 (BBC News, 2011). Birmingham Police already had about 8,000 Twitter followers and attracted 2,000 more over the course of the day. Police in the city tweeted regularly under the handle @brumpolice, with news of incidents in the city and safety and security advice. People showed great interest in in the interaction with the police and generally were supportive. In USA, Halton police received a good tip in an unsolved homicide during their "tweet-a-thon" on July 02, 2014(O'Reilly, 2014). In 2012, Victoria Police in Australia undertook a trial of Eyewatch, an online community engagement tool targeted at the regional level that uses the Facebook platform. Police found both positive and negative aspects of using Eyewatch with potential to be effective particularly in 'ethnically homogenous, low crime neighborhoods with high levels of baseline confidence in police (Commissioner for Law Enforcement Data Security, 2012). Victoria Police also used its Twitter page as a tool to increase the reach of media releases from the Victoria Police News Webpage. Victoria Police uses(d) YouTube as a storage facility for publicly released video – ranging from news stories and CCTV footage, to public relations videos. Users were not allowed to post comments but they could share the videos on other social media sites. Instagram is a social media platform where members share images along with a caption. While still in its infancy, Instagram was viewed by Victoria Police as another tool for community engagement. Victoria police ran two PSA blogs using Google's Blogger site to publish localized blogs designed to engage and inform their communities. The Victoria Police Wikipedia page began in October 2004 and developed to contain in-depth information about Victoria Police's historical background, ranking system and equipment used.

3.10 Social Media to Show the Human Side of Policing

When using social media for policing, the tone of the message is very important. Usually, police forces opt for a formal and impersonal tone. However, the experience of police forces with social media suggests that the tone of the message on social media should be different. The way of delivering message often has more impact on the audience than the actual words used. This is also true in the messages sent via social media. Consistency in voice is the key. A consistent message, delivered in a reliable that remains the same throughout, regardless of authorship, makes the communication more professional. A stoic and unemotional tone should be relaxed when appropriate by choosing to show some personality and even humor at times. Just like in-person interactions, online social interactions are a chance for police departments to show their human side. Agencies have long recognized that communities who get to know their officers usually like them, as well. The current trend of online communities and friendships, getting to know a police department virtually can have the same effect (Burns & Perron, 2014). A tone that projects professionalism, competence, and confidence is fundamental. To go the extra mile and win over the public, police department needs to remain approachable and human on their social media channels. People often share or retweet those messages that show compassion, empathy, and humor. This approach also leads to a broader audience/follower base and increased exposure to the police department's humanity. Using a nontraditional voice or tone, police can reach segments of their communities previously unreachable by traditional communication channels. In a similar fashion, a message from the police department in support of a local football team can generate social media inroads with followers of the team. However, the non-traditional tone may not be suitable in every jurisdiction. Police departments need to get advice from their social media specialists or public affairs team, to determine the most appropriate voice and tone for their department. Posting of content not directly connected with current police operations has received warm positive feedback by citizens. For instance, the Greater Manchester Police (GMP) promoted the anniversary of their police museum. They posted links to images showing historic police cars and GMP officers of the past. Citizens then who were interacting with the police welcome the human side of policing (Denef, Bayerl, & Kaptein, 2013).In a letter to the editor of Jamaica Observer, a citizen shared the story of police officers who participated in a game with the youngsters in a poor neighborhood. This interaction of police with the citizens changed their views about police and their view of the police became one of a positive and endearing image (Jamaica Observer, 2012).This closer connection with public provides police an increased perceived support from and trust of the community. An open dialogue with public provides police widen their topics of discussion with the public and touch a larger number of topics that related to citizens' and police officers' everyday lives.

3.11 Social Media to Support Police IT Infrastructure

It is normal to observe an extraordinary pressure on police IT systems for communication with the public when there is a large-scale crisis or investigation of a case that receive special attention from the public. The people seeking information in these cases may belong to geographic boundaries well beyond the jurisdiction of the police department since local news can be virally distributed through social media. Usually, the IT infrastructures of police departments cannot handle these peaks in demand for information. One successful way of dealing with these peaks in demand for information is to use various social media sites to better balance peak loads in their IT infrastructures. However, there is a caveat in using this approach. Social media can virally spread the news in minutes transforming it from local news to global news. The resulting peaks in loads on police IT infrastructure can significantly impact the police ability to communicate. For the famous UK murder case of Joanna Yeates during Christmas 2010 who first went missing and later was found dead, the Police had to deal with high peaks in demand (Morris, 2011). In that case, the public's interest overwhelmed police website making it inaccessible during peak times. The police therefore chose to use a set of social media networks to publish important information. You-

Tube served as the network to distribute CCTV footage and asking the public for information. Also the police actively used Twitter and Facebook to communicate. Using this set of social media platform allowed the police to be the central voice and remain communicating even in cases when their own website was unreachable. This issue is, however, not only relevant for smaller forces who suddenly see high interest from a national or global community. During the 2011 riots in London, the Metropolitan police (MET), for instance used Flickr to publish images of suspects. With announcements on Twitter, the photos were extremely popular. Within 12 hours of the posting of photos there had been more than 4 million views. For this, even the police reached the limits of Flickr and had to distribute the images so that they would show up. The MET's website traffic increased dramatically during and just after the riots. Hosting images on a separate server through Flickr helped ensure their site was not overloaded and could run at optimal levels, thus ensuring the public could still gain policing information and advice (Webster, 2013). As these examples show, and while these cases are surely exceptional, the freely available global infrastructures of social media networks allow police forces to handle the peaks in demand and make them communicative even in exceptional cases.

3.12 Social Media for Background Investigations

Social media is also used to screen potential police officers for any disqualifying information. In fact, many law enforcement agencies require applicants sign waivers that allow investigators to have access to their accounts on various social media. Some agencies even require candidates to provide private passwords, Internet pseudonyms, text messages, and email logs as part of the expanding cybervetting process for law enforcement jobs (Rose et al., 2010).According to a report on law enforcement social media use, more than a third of 728 law enforcement agencies checked applicants' social media sites during background checks (Johnson, 2010).Many law enforcement agencies aggressively warn to delete any social media accounts they have maintained sooner than later. The prevailing theory is that departments who fail to properly screen/monitor potential and current employees are open to negative media attention. In a survey by IACP of 800 law enforcement agencies, a third mentioned their agency had experienced negative media attention from social media use by on-duty or off-duty employees (International Association of Chiefs of Police 2011, p. 11).

3.13 Social Media for Efficient Policing

Currently, police forces across the globe are confronted with the task of performing their work with reduced financial resources, due to budget cuts following the economic downturn. By using social media, police forces have been able to increase the efficiency of their communication and develop a closer connection with the general public despite shrinking budgets. Often, when adopting a new technology or putting additional effort in using it, police forces need to account for the effectiveness and benefits of these activities, given that they are publicly funded(Composite Project, 2012). The Icelandic police operated in one of the toughest economic conditions with heavy budget constraints and heavy lay-offs. They specifically used social media to engage with the general public and were able to sustain the perceived level of trust. The free availability of the networks and the high adoption rate of social media in Iceland helped their strategy. In the similar fashion, Greater Manchester Police (GMP) in the United Kingdom performed their social media communication with public without any additional budget and was successful to achieve effective in public communication. In Germany, the police use of social media required extra efforts but police were able to handle it without additional personnel.

Clearly, use of social media has become a tool for police to deal with budget cuts. However, the use of this tool in future require a long-term evaluation, cost-benefit analysis, and require resources and additional training. The integration of social media into daily policing routines is a question for future research.

It is also worth mentioning the explosion in mobile apps some of which may link to social media. These include the UK Metropolitan Police app (used to find your nearest police station/street level crime map/emerging information/Twitter), US local sheriffs' apps (used to provide police information in real time), and Brooklyn Quality of Life app (used to report crime).

4. ENABLERS OF SOCIAL MEDIA USE FOR POLICING

Effective use of social media for policing requires many enablers such as information systems for crime and criminal tracking systems, appropriate legal frameworks, training of law enforcement personnel, and collaboration with social network providers.

4.1. Information Systems for Crime and Criminal Tracking

Without doubt, policing is an information-intensive business. The data stored within police information systems help determine to what a police department pays attention. The arrangement of this data helps determine the types of analysis that can be performed and the uses to which they can be put. The way information flows around police department determines the level of attention attached to different matters at different levels and determines who makes which decisions. The content and form of information released to the public help making police department accountable and meet people expectations. Properly managed, information systems can serve as a powerful tool for police executives. These systems can cut labor costs, improve resource allocation, increase efficiency, and effectiveness of existing operations, help redefine the work, emphasize new values, and facilitate the development of new partnerships. Poorly managed information systems can frustrate managerial purposes, enshrine old values, emphasize outdated and inappropriate performance measures, give power to the wrong people, perpetuate old ways of doing business, create false or misleading public expectations, destroy partnerships, and impose crippling restrictions on new styles of operation-apart from their propensity to consume millions and millions of tax dollars (Sparrow, 1993).

There exist various information systems for crime and criminal tracking and networking both at national and international level. The software, called the Domain Awareness System, was New York City's attempt to build a truly one-stop shop for crime and counterterrorism data that's accessible in real time to New York Police Department officers and other law enforcement personnel (Williams, 2012; Wasserman, 2011). Interpol and Europol are promoting international cooperation and fast and secure information exchange and analysis to fight crime globally. Interpol's i-24/7 system enables police officials from 190 participating countries to search and cross-check a wide range of global databases from any location. In 2011, 1 billion searches were conducted, 10,000 notices issued and 7,958 arrests made. Interpol and Europol have established a secure communications line directly linking the two organizations, and endorsed operational action plans of cooperation in key areas. Europol has supported more than 13,500 cross-border cases in 2011 through intense use of intelligence, an increase of more than 17 percent compared with 2010 (Europol, n.d.). The Information System for Direzione Nazionale Antimafia (SIDNA) at the Italian National Anti-Mafia Department, part of the Ministry of Justice, is used for investigation activities by more than 700 different users, including detectives, administrative staff, judges, and police across Italy. All stakeholders were able to access the same details on crime cases and research, enabling cross-pollination of information for nationwide investigations. The computerized system ECRIS was established in April 2012 to achieve an efficient exchange of information on criminal convictions between EU countries (European Commission, n.d.). eJusticeNY is a browser-based application designed to give users from qualified agencies a single point of access to computerized information within and beyond New York State. eJusticeNY embodied the concept of coordinated and integrated criminal justice information systems for New York State. The system's security and ease of use allowed qualified users to obtain current status information for a defendant at any key decision point in the processing of a criminal case (New York State Division of Criminal Justice Service, n.d.).Germany had implemented centralized databases at a federal level, such as the police information system INPOL at Federal Criminal Police Office (BKA). All Germany's regions used this centralized search database to access crime-related data for many years. The intent of the centralized system was to allow the regional areas to better communicate with each other using a more standardized data exchange structure (Bundeskriminalamt, 2012).

The Crime and Criminal Tracking Network & Systems (CCTNS) is revolutionary initiative of Indian government to centralize the policing system in India. In India, there had been many computerization initiatives in the past that included initiatives by both federal and state governments of India. In 1990, federal government of India initiated Crime and Criminals Information System (CCIS), Initiative to create crime-and criminals-related database, and 7 Integrated Investigation Forms (IIF) (Times of India, 2014a,b). In 2004, Common Integrated Police Application –CIPA and Application for police station operations and investigation process were initiated. Various state governments also started initiatives such as Andhra Pradesh (e-COPS), Gujarat (HD-IITS), Karnataka (Police-IT), Tamil Nadu (CAARUS), and West Bengal (TTS).Adoption and success of these applications has varied for several reasons. First was limited utility at the police station, which was the primary data generation point. These applications were generally considered data sinks with lots of input and little output. These applications also lacked adequate local language support. Secondly, these were standalone systems that did not share data with other police stations and other police formations. Thirdly, these applications were not adequately user-friendly and poorly handled at police stations.

CCTNS was an effort to bring paradigm shift in crime control and tracking in India by moving from standalone and centrally managed CIPA (Common Integrated Police Application) to all India connected, service-oriented and distributed management based system (TNN, 2014). CCTNs is not just a checklist of product & service deliverables. It is an integrated service delivery model. The government of India started CCTNS project with the goal of enhancing outcomes in crime investigation and criminals tracking and increasing efficiency and effectiveness of Police departments across India (Shekhar, 2014; Sharma, 2014; PTLB, 2011). The key objectives of CCTNS were to provide enhanced tools for investigation, crime prevention, and law & order and to increase operational efficiency. The CCTNS is a common data repository for sharing crime and criminal data of state and central level. It improves service delivery to the Citizen/Stakeholders/within department and provides access to the citizens for availing police services.

4.2. Legal Frameworks

Existing legal frameworks need to be transposed to social media. It is necessary because these frameworks, when developed, either ignored or did not expect that one day social networking will become so important. The real problems is that which activity should be considered as illegal while using social media. In the words of John Cooper QC, a leading barristers of UK, stalking, threats to kill, sending obscene material and harassment were "age old" offences and the fact that they were being committed on Twitter did not make any difference. While revenge porn, where people upload sexually explicit content of ex-partners without their permission, was already against the law to "send any form of obscene picture". He further added that social media was a "positive, inspiring arena" which was self-policing to a "high degree", but like society in general there were those who spoiled it for the rest ...but that did not mean new laws were needed to deal with it (BBC News, 2014). Existing legal frameworks need to come up with clear explanation of what constitutes anti-social behavior on social media.

Take US example of the case of Caroline Criado-Perez, the writer and feminist campaigner (O'Flinn, 2014). In July 2013, Criado-Perez received threats via Twitter to rape and kill her. Two of the offenders, Isabella Sorley and John Nimmo pleaded guilty to sending by means of a public electronic communications network messages which were menacing in character. That was an offense according to Section 127(1)(A) of the Communications Act 2003 (TCA). The Communications Act 2003 pre-dated Twitter's creation. The prosecution of this case under a pre-dated legislation demonstrated the difficulty in controlling the increasing challenge of online abuse. Currently, threats made via Twitter can be prosecuted under the US Malicious Communication Act 1989 (MCA) and the TCA. Under the MCA, sending any form of electronic communication that conveys a threat, false or misleading information, or indecent or grossly offensive content is an offense. Under the TCA, sending a message via public electronic communications network, that is grossly offensive, indecent, obscene or of menacing character, is an offense. Public electronic communications network covers internet communications generally, including those sent via Twitter. Both MCA and TCA coul be used to prosecute the case involving Twitter. The main issue was anonymity that the internet could provide which caused significant issues with investigation and prosecution. Tracing individuals consumes limited police resources and requires cooperation from ISPs and social media networks themselves.

In Germany, police developed a legal framework for social media investigations that was also used as a training material for police officers. The framework established the relation between police operations and regulations of commercial social media platform operators.

In UK, the home office planned to introduce a new law allowing police and security services to extend their monitoring of the public's email and social media communications (The Guardian, 2012). The new system was expected to allow security officials to scrutinize who is talking to whom and exactly when the conversations are taking place, but not the content of messages. Civil liberties campaigners strongly criticized the plan because of the risk it could breach the privacy of law-abiding Britons. Internet service providers also voiced concern at the law, questioning the cost and practicalities of installing systems fulfill the requirements of the new law. They were also worried that their customers would not tolerate the compilation of personal communications information.

Social media sites, including Twitter, are facing pressure to pro-actively tackle abuse head on. New laws that would require social media sites to reveal the identities of trolls are being considered. A significant problem facing social media sites is the issue of online abusers simply creating new anonymous accounts when existing accounts are suspended. In the case of Caroline Criado-Perez, one offender, Nimmo sent his tweets via six separate accounts. Until such time as new legislation is adopted, prosecutors will have to continue to rely upon the co-operation of social media site operators, and the increasingly dated legislation (such as MCA and TCA) and media benevolence.

4.3. Police Training

There is a strong need that law enforcement administrators establish appropriate controls over the use of social media. It is necessary so that police departments can benefits from its use while reducing incidents of misuse of social media by police officers. This would require setting criteria for social media use and training police personnel on these policies. In doing so, police forces can fully realize the true potential of social media as a law enforcement tool. Police forces need further training of their officers to perform investigations on social media. Simple social media investigations in open sources are about to become standard. Demand for social media capabilities cannot be handled by IT departments of police alone. For police forces around the globe, developing social media capabilities and more specialized skills appears to be one of the major challenges for the years ahead.

According to Stuart (2013), training officers on social media guidance can be done in two steps. The first should address general computer, Internet, and social media security and privacy issues, while the second should look at the practical application of social media policy as related to officers. Many police departments, such as Toronto Police Department has established specific guidelines for their officers use of social media (Toronto Police, 2012b). The training curriculum should be frequently updated and repeated to keep up with evolving technology and ensure the information remains fresh in officers' minds. Once educated, officers can take the initiative to properly protect themselves and their departments. Compliance can occur when officers understand the problem and buy into the solution.

4.4. Collaboration with Social Network Providers

The investigation of closed sources, such as private messages exchanged on social networks, IP addresses of users' computers, users' email addresses, and phone number require close collaboration of law enforcement agencies and social network platform operators. In Europe and North America, this collaboration is not complicated as it follows national laws and orders from prosecution authorities. However, the situation gets complicated when data is required from operators outside the national boundaries of Europe and North America. In that case, police forces are required to follow official procedures for international police support and it can take long before the requested data can be made available, if at all. While few operators, such as Facebook, collaborates with police forces in international operations not all operators are expected to do so. Upon request by the law enforcement agencies, Facebook offers to freeze the users' data. This data is shared with law enforcement agency once the official international police support request has been provided.

5. PRACTICAL/MANAGERIAL IMPLICATIONS AND SUGGESTIONS

The discussion of this chapter provides several managerial implications for use of social media for policing. The future police departments would require an integrated approach for engagements with the citizens in order to have more informed and flexible interactions with the citizens. Police officers would need location-independent access to real-time information that provides them with a single complete picture of events they are dealing with or about to be confronted by. Following are the significant implications and suggestions to help police transform and able to meeting the future challenges related to social media use in policing (Accenture, 2012; Accenture, 2013; Rutter, 2014;Donlon-Cotton, 2012).

Citizens Engagement

Police forces need to embrace a range of contact channels that provide citizen engagement online, social as well as face to face. These channels should provide new ways of interaction, underpinned by trust, that provides personalized interactions in cost effective manner. Self-servicing portals can be used crime reporting, search warrants, crime maps, basic police and licensing enquiries. Reporting non-emergency crimes through an online portal could dramatically reduce costs and officers' time (Australian Institute of Police Management, 2012). Emerging technologies, such as mobile apps, can be used to engage with citizens, aid investigations, and glean intelligence information. These self-service portals can be latest police tool to help keep the public informed while reducing pressure on police resources. Check My Crime web portal is an initiative by Western Australia Police. The portal provides victims of stealing and damage related crimes with opportunities to access 'self-service' functions over the internet. Users can also generate and print an up-to-date abridged record of the report to provide to their insurance company, and retain for their own records. This saves time and money for both the victims and police (Western Australia Police, 2013).

Empowerment of Law Enforcement Officers

Police officers need to be empowered with real-time access to information. To achieve fiscal and efficiency gains, this information must be presented in an intuitive and interactive way. Police officers can use integrated technologies to provide quick response and reduce investigation time. Mobile technologies bring immediate and accurate intelligence to further empower officers. Interactive information sharing at crime scene enables officers to perform real-time analysis and investigation. Officers can use mobile devices to check photographic, voice or fingerprint biometric details of suspects and most importantly confirm the suspect's identity with the victims and witnesses.

Houston, the largest city in the state of Texas, is home to more than 2.1 million people. Houston police department comprised 5,200 sworn officers and 1,300 civilian employees. To help officers on the street more effectively fight crime and preserve public safety, the department set up a real-time crime center (RTCC)as part of its Law Enforcement Analytics (LEA) solution. The RTCC was designed to make critical information – derived from crime, jail booking, probation, and other databases – immediately available to officers responding to calls. Vital information about addresses, vehicles, or named persons were available instantaneously to officers before or as they arrive on the scene. The department also deployed a management dashboard for tracking crime statistics and trends (Information Builders, 2013).

Optimization of Law Enforcement Work

To address future demands, police forces need to create agile departments with optimized infrastructure to cut costs and with speed and efficiency gains. By collaboration with other public/private organizations, police force can focus on its core activities. A re-visit of resource planning and demand management can help police best use their assets and re-allocation of its work force to areas where it is most needed. Predictive modeling techniques allow police to link resources to demand and real time action by police force. The Richmond, Virginia, USA police department used data mining and predictive analytics for a variety of law enforcement and intelligence applications, including tactical crime analysis, risk and threat assessment, behavioral analysis of violent crime, and proactive deployment strategies (The Police Chief Magazine, 2013).New technologies allow police to better manage information demand of citizens by using social media sites as an alternative outlet of information. A scrutiny of existing structures may help police identify the need of specialized skills or shift of focus on new priorities. Resource assessment/adjustment can provide a police service with a manpower equipped with a diverse skill set that is more effective in proactive fight with crime. Police needs an integrated information management approach with automation of work processes and optimized departmental resources to create more efficient, location-independent police force. Non-core activities, such as administrative functions, can be outsources to cut costs and put more focus on core policing activities.

Use of Analytics in Law Enforcement

Police force can use analytics for risk management by identifying criminal networks and predicting crime based on real-time information. Geographic profiling, combined with criminal analytics is anticipated to be a very significant police tool in future. Geographic profiling is an investigative methodology that predicts the serial offender's most likely location including home, work, social venues, and travel routes. It uses the locations of a connected series of crimes to produce a map showing the areas in which the offender most likely lives and works. Although it is generally applied in serial murder, rape, arson, robbery, and bombing cases, geographic profiling also can be used in single crimes that involve multiple scenes or other significant geographic characteristics. According to the National Institute of Justice, at least 13 percent of the police departments in the USA were using geographic profiling to solve crimes, and more importantly, to prevent them (Brendle, 2002). Predictive analytics can help police to identify and prevent persistent reoffenders quickly (Kamensky, 2013; Moskvitch, 2012; Kelly, 2012; Aponte, 2014; Byrne & Marx, 2011). In USA, predictive analytics technology working its way into law-enforcement stations around the country. Using predictive analytics software, for example, police can create a map of a city showing precisely where cars may be stolen, houses robbed, people mugged etc. The software calculates its forecasts based on times and locations of previous crimes, combined with sociological information about criminal behavior and patterns (Kelly, 2014). There have been a number of predictive crime mapping pilot projects in UK and they are considered "the next generation of intelligence-led policing" (BBC News, 2012; Steve, 2013). The interoperability of systems and crime databases, combined with improved data standards and management is essential for successful proactive crime fighting. There exist many firms that specialize in social media analytics. One such example of use of these companies is Boston bombing case where the Boston Police Department sough help of an analytics company Buzzient to help catch the people behind the case (O'Leary, 2013).

Enhanced Collaboration of Law Enforcement Agencies

An effective collaboration of various law enforcement agencies around the globe is necessary to support different aspects of policing and to create a more agile and responsive police service. Such collaboration is also necessary to fight today's borderless crime. Local governments and public sector organizations could work closely with police to deal with matters under their jurisdiction such as lost property or issuing passports. Working closely with other justice organizations can help speed up investigations and convictions. Working closely with other public sector organizations can help police monitor criminal activity and develop a more responsive service.

Proactive Change Management

Future police leaders must equip themselves with effective change management skills as they will be at the forefront of managing change and making it happen. They must have IT and business to structure sustainable change management. They must be able to foster a climate of change acceptance and readiness in their respective department. Future police service would need to adopt structured change management approach to maintain internal and external ownership and accountability in order for stakeholders to accept new processes and technology. Future police officers would need right tools of change management with a clear understanding of the value of change. Introduction of the culture of continuous learning and improvement and making change management an ongoing effort can help officers get the best out of the change efforts (Police Executive Research Forum, 2013).

6. FUTURE RESEARCH DIRECTIONS

Present research into social media use for policing has been directed towards exploring the ways in which social media can be used by law enforcement agencies. Emerging work has focused on the sociological relevance of social media policing (Trottier, 2012), success and failure of social media use for policing (Crump, 2011), and attitudes about surveillance strategies on social media (Trottier & Schneider, 2012), and use of social media by police to engage with community (Ho, Yu, & Lai, 2014).There are, however, other issues that are of particularly importance in evaluating the institutional possibilities of adopting social media for policing.

First, research is required to investigate the ethnographic studies of police social media behaviors. This is important keeping in view the two cases of riots in London and Vancouver. In the case of London riots, it was found that the one very significant reason police lost control of riots was that the issue of race impaired their ability to do the job(Green, 2011).

Second, research is required to investigate the social media users to understand the effect of police interventions. The research might attempt to understand how enthusiastic are followers of police sites, and how impactful are police interventions.

Third, an investigation of structural approaches to police networks is needed. The research might attempt to understand the entities involved, how do they change over time, and their working. One particular emphasis can be placed on their working under times of stress, such as a major incident or a controversial issue.

Third, research is required to investigate the ethical and privacy issues involved in using social media for policing. Emphasis may be placed on issues of legitimacy, transparency and regulation. With increasing use of social media by criminals is forcing law enforcement agencies to have an active presence on social media. Law enforcement agencies continue to request more access to user's social media. There is a need dig deep into this issue to unearth various ethical and privacy issues of police use of social media.

Fourth, an investigation of the impact of social media on police organizations would be helpful as we mixed results of social media use in law enforcement agencies around the globe. It is important to understand the factors that improve the probability of success of social media use for policing. A particular emphasis can be placed on the context and background in which the social media is used for law enforcement. For example how the culture of a society impacts the key success factors of social media for policing.

7. CONCLUSION

During the last decade, we have seen significant changes in the way we communicate and share information. With its great depth and breadth of information, social media has provided new opportunities for law enforcement agencies to enhance their service and engage with the public. Another significant feature of social media is its rich user interaction that makes social media most successful.

In recent years, there has also been a considerable expansion in the levels of use of social media. Social media is an extremely active and evolving domain that now accounts for a significant proportion of Internet traffic. The popularity of social media has also brought new types of crimes associated with its use such as burglary via social networking, phishing and social engineering, and malware.

For law enforcement agencies around the globe, social media has developed into an issue that they need to understand and harness. Policing is in many ways a technology driven profession that has historically embraced technology and integrated it into policing in highly visible and instrumental ways. Social media represents one of the next biggest waves of technological advancement in law enforcement. Many police departments around the world have been quick to adopt the use of social media to communicate with the public. Despite such potential advantages of social media capacity, some law enforcement agencies across the globe still reluctant to accept this new form of communication. It is clear that at least some of this apprehension is due to basic lack of familiarity and expertise. Another factor could be that social media are rich, but overwhelming sources of information which require time and resources for proper analysis.

We have witnessed recently an increasing number of crimes related to social media and the significant damages suffered by the users. This factor has provided a strong basis for police to use social media actively. There exist several factors that give rise to police use of social media. Community policing is one significant factor. There are also many other factors. Irrespective of whether a particular police department has presence on social media or not, there are active discussions on social media about matters. There is a proliferation of bogus social media accounts and channels, both in small and big cities, that are used specifically to provide police- related information. Normal citizens are using social media to perform actions traditionally performed by police only. In this case an active police voice on social media becomes necessary to assist public distinguish between trustworthy and non-trustworthy information. People are increasingly used social media to organize events and make announcements (such as suicide attempts), and report child abuse. This increasingly complex situation calls for a police force with competence in social media and able for an effective bi-directional communication with citizens. Another pressing issue is increased use of social media by criminals who are using social media for a variety of criminal activities including recruiting the new members of their criminal organizations.

Police departments vary greatly in the extent to which they have adopted social media. Some of the common uses of social media in policing include police recruitment, passive intelligence and police investigation, community policing, spreading information, leveraging the wisdom of crowd, interaction with the public, to show human side of policing, to provide support for police IT infrastructure, to perform background investigations, active intelligence and covert operations, and internal intelligence, enforcement.

Effective use of social media for policing requires many enablers such as information systems for crime and criminal tracking systems, appropriate legal frameworks, training of law enforcement personnel, and collaboration with social network providers. Policing is an information-intensive business. These information systems provide several benefits to the police departments including better engagement with citizens and global information exchange for better crime control. There exist various information systems for crime and criminal tracking and networking both at national and international level such as Domain Awareness System of New York Police Department, Interpol's i-24/7 system, System for Direzione Nazionale Antimafia (SIDNA) at the Italian National Anti-Mafia Department, and the European computerized system ECRIS. The Crime and Criminal Tracking

Network & Systems (CCTNS) is revolutionary initiative of Indian government to centralize the policing system in India. CCTNS is an effort to bring paradigm shift in crime control & tracking in India by moving from standalone & centrally managed CIPA (Common Integrated Police Application) to all India connected, service-oriented and distributed management based system. Existing legal frameworks need to be transposed to social media. The main issue is anonymity that the internet can provide which causes significant issues with investigation and prosecution. Tracing individuals consumes limited police resources and requires cooperation from ISPs and social media networks themselves. New laws that would require social media sites to reveal the identities of trolls are being considered. There is a strong need that law enforcement administrators establish appropriate controls over the use of social media. For police forces around the globe, developing social media capabilities and more specialized skills appears to be one of the major challenges for the years ahead. The investigation of closed sources, such as private messages exchanged on social networks, IP addresses of users' computers, users' email addresses, and phone number require close collaboration of law enforcement agencies and social network platform operators. The future police departments would require an integrated approach for engagements with the citizens in order to have more informed and flexible interactions with the citizens. Some recommendations to help police transform to enable them for meeting the future challenges include citizen engagement, empowerment of law enforcement officers, optimization of law enforcement work, use of analytics in law enforcement, enhanced collaboration of law enforcement agencies, proactive change management and proactive change management.

The discussion of this chapter provides several managerial implications for use of social media for policing. The future police departments would require an integrated approach for engagements with the citizens in order to have more informed and flexible interactions with the citizens. Police officers would need location-independent access to real-time information that provides them with a single complete picture of events they are dealing with or about to be confronted by. To address future demands, police forces need to create agile departments with optimized infrastructure to cut costs and with speed and efficiency gains. Police force can use analytics for risk management by identifying criminal networks and predicting crime based on real-time information. An effective collaboration of various law enforcement agencies around the globe is necessary to support different aspects of policing and to create a more agile and responsive police service. Such collaboration is also necessary to fight today's borderless crime. Future police leaders must equip themselves with effective change management skills as they will be at the forefront of managing change and making it happen. They must have IT and business to structure sustainable change management.

This chapter contributes to the understanding of social media use in policing, particularly how social media connects the police departments, and the citizens for an effective engagement for better crime control. The chapter also indicates that the policy makers should be aware of the opportunity to use social media in policing and their policies and strategies should be formulated accordingly. Furthermore, effective use of social media require various enablers, most important of which is the transformation of existing legal frameworks to support use of social media in policing. Furthermore, the collaboration among social media networks provides and law enforcement agencies are significant for effective use of social media for policing. This raises a significant challenge that warrants an increased global cooperation among governments and law enforcement agencies. This, in turn, also supports the idea that use of social media in policing is not a local but rather an international phenomenon.

REFERENCES

3. *news*. (2013, June 21). Police reap benefits of social media. Retrieved from http://www.3news.co.nz/Police-reap-benefits-of-social-media/tabid/423/articleID/302718/Default.aspx

ABC7 News. (2014, June 25). Oakland Police Department turns to social media to find new recruits. Retrieved from http://abc7news.com/technology/oakland-police-uses-social-media-to-recruit/140708/

Accenture. (2012, January 11). Tap the Power of Social Media to Drive Better Policing Outcomes. Retrieved from http://www.accenture.com/us-en/Pages/insight-tap-power-social-media-drive-better-policing-outcomes.aspx

Accenture. (2013, June). Preparing Police Services for the future. Retrieved from http://www.accenture.com/us-en/landing-pages/Documents/13-1583/download/preparing-police-services-for-the-future.pdf

Alderson, J. (1979). *Policing freedom*. Macdonald and Evans Plymouth.

Aponte, V. (2014, January 31). Police use social media to inform public about crime hot spots. *ValleyCentral.com*. Retrieved from http://www.valleycentral.com/news/story.aspx?id=1001273

Australian Institute of Police Management. (2012, June). *Preparing police services for the future: Six steps toward transformation. Australian Institute of Police Management*. Retrieved from http://www.aipm.gov.au/know-it-now/police/preparing-police-services-for-the-future-six-steps-toward-transformation/

Bargent, J. (2013, April). Mexico Crime Tracking Social Media Page Disappears. *InSight Crime | Organized Crime in the Americas*. Retrieved from http://www.insightcrime.org/news-briefs/mexican-crime-tracking-social-media-pages-disappear

Barker, B. (2013, March).Social Media and Criminal Organizations. *Security Management*. Retrieved from http://www.securitymanagement.com/article/social-media-and-criminal-organizations-0010271

BBC News. (2011, November 18). Thousands in force "tweet-a-thon." Retrieved from http://www.bbc.co.uk/news/uk-england-birmingham-15790457

BBC News. (2012, December 7). Social media "benefits police." Retrieved from http://www.bbc.co.uk/news/technology-20641190

BBC News. (2014, July 2). Plea for no new social-media laws. Retrieved from http://www.bbc.com/news/uk-politics-28104937

Bennett, J. (2012, December 11). Study Shows That Social Media Benefits Police. *Social Media Today*. Retrieved from http://www.socialmediatoday.com/content/study-shows-social-media-benefits-police

Boyd, D. M., & Ellison, N. B. (2007). Social network sites: Definition, history, and scholarship. *Journal of Computer-Mediated Communication*, *13*(1), 210–230. doi:10.1111/j.1083-6101.2007.00393.x

Brendle, A. (2002, November 20). Police Use GIS in D.C. Area Sniper Case and More. *National Geographic*. Retrieved from http://news.nationalgeographic.com/news/2002/11/1120_021120_GIScrime.html

British Columbia - CBC News. (2011, June 15). Riots erupt in Vancouver after Canucks loss. Retrieved from http://www.cbc.ca/news/canada/british-columbia/riots-erupt-in-vancouver-after-canucks-loss-1.993707

Bundeskriminalamt (2012). *BKA Electronic Search and Information Systems*. Retrieved from http://www.bka.de/nn_194550/EN/SubjectsAZ/ElectronicSystems/electronicSearchAndInformationSystems__node.html?__nnn=true

Burns, A., & Eltham, B. (2009). Twitter free Iran: An evaluation of Twitter's role in public diplomacy and information operations in Iran's 2009 election crisis.

Burns, D., & Perron, Z. (2014). Considerations for Social Media Management and Strategy. *The Police Chief*, (81): 31–32.

Buttler, M. (2013, July 7). Criminals use social media to track police. *Herald Sun*. Retrieved from http://www.heraldsun.com.au/news/law-order/criminalss-use-social-media-to-track-police/story-fni0fee2-1226675624831

Byrne, J., & Marx, G. (2011). Technological Innovations in Crime Prevention and Policing. A Review of the Research on Implementation and Impact. *Journal of Police Studies*, *3*(20), 17–40.

Cisneros, T. (2009, April 1) Santa Ana launches online crime-reporting tool. http://www.ocregister.com/news/reports-168503-police-online.html

CNN. (2012). Official: Los Angeles arson suspect under investigation in Germany. Retrieved from http://articles.cnn.com/2012-01-04/us/us_california-arson_1_los-angeles-arson-fireshollywood-apartment?_s=PM:US

Commissioner for Law Enforcement Data Security. (2012). *Social Media and Law Enforcement*. Retrieved from http://www.cleds.vic.gov.au/content.asp?a=CLEDSBridgingPage&Media_ID=98370

Composite Project. (2012, December 7). *COMPOSITE deliverable - Best Practice in Police Social Media Adaptation*. Retrieved from http://www.composite-project.eu/tl_files/fM_k0005/download/COMPOSITE-social-media-best-practice.pdf

Copitch, G., & Fox, C. (2010). Using social media as a means of improving public confidence. *Safer Communities*, *9*(2), 42–48. doi:10.5042/sc.2010.0226

Crump, J. (2011). What Are the Police Doing on Twitter? Social Media, the Police and the Public. *Policy & Internet*, *3*(4), 1–27. doi:10.2202/1944-2866.1130

Denef, S., Bayerl, P. S., & Kaptein, N. A. (2013). Social Media and the Police: Tweeting Practices of British Police Forces During the August 2011 Riots. In *Proceedings of the SIGCHI Conference on Human Factors in Computing Systems* (pp. 3471–3480). New York, NY, USA: ACM. doi:10.1145/2470654.2466477

Deschatres, S. (2014, July 8). Social Engineering: Attacking the Weakest Link in the Security Chain. Retrieved from http://www.symantec.com/connect/blogs/social-engineering-attacking-weakest-link-security-chain

Donlon-Cotton, C. (2012, January). Implementing Social Networking into Law Enforcement Ops: Community Relations. *Hendon Publishing*. Retrieved from http://www.hendonpub.com/resources/article_archive/results/details?id=1185

drandreagalli. (2011, November 27). Organized Crime in Central Europe. *Economic crime intelligence*. Retrieved from http://economiccrimeintelligence.wordpress.com/2011/11/27/organized-crime-in-central-europe/

Ellison, N. B., Steinfield, C., & Lampe, C. (2007). The benefits of Facebook "friends:" social capital and college students' use of online social network sites. *Journal of Computer-Mediated Communication*, *12*(4), 1143–1168. doi:10.1111/j.1083-6101.2007.00367.x

eMarketer. (2013). Social Networking Reaches Nearly One in Four around the World. Retrieved from http://www.emarketer.com/Article/Social-Networking-Reaches-Nearly-One-Four-Around-World/1009976

European Commission. (n. d.). ECRIS (European Criminal Records Information System) - Justice. Retrieved from http://ec.europa.eu/justice/criminal/european-e-justice/ecris/index_en.htm

European Crime Prevention Network. (2009, December 30). Good practice documents - Virtual Community Policing. Retrieved from http://www.eucpn.org/goodpractice/showdoc.asp?docid=247

Europol. (n. d.). About Europol. Retrieved from https://www.europol.europa.eu/content/page/about-europol-17

Facebook. (2012). Timeline statistics. Retrieved from http://www.facebook.com/press/info.php?statistics

Friedmann, R. R. (1992). Community policing: Comparative perspectives and prospects.

Gazaway, C. (2011) KSP turning to social media for recruits. http://www.wave3.com/story/15176887/kspturning-to-social-media-for-recruits

Goodchild, J. (2012, December 20). Social Engineering: The Basics. *CSO Online*. Retrieved from http://www.csoonline.com/article/2124681/security-awareness/social-engineering-the-basics.html

Green, D. (2011, August 8). London riots: why did the police lose control? *Telegraph*. Retrieved from http://www.telegraph.co.uk/news/uknews/crime/8689004/London-riots-why-did-the-police-lose-control.html

Greenhow, C., & Robelia, B. (2009). Old communication, new literacies: Social network sites as social learning resources. *Journal of Computer-Mediated Communication*, *14*(4), 1130–1161. doi:10.1111/j.1083-6101.2009.01484.x

Heatherly, R., Kantarcioglu, M., & Thuraisingham, B. (2013). Preventing private information inference attacks on social networks. *Knowledge and Data Engineering. IEEE Transactions on*, *25*(8), 1849–1862.

Ho, K. K. W., Yu, C. C., & Lai, M. C. L. (2014). Engaging and Developing the Community Through Social Media: A Pragmatic Analysis in Policing Context in Hong Kong. In L. G. Anthopoulos & C. G. Reddick (Eds.), Government e-Strategic Planning and Management (pp. 263–285). Springer New York; Retrieved from http://link.springer.com/chapter/10.1007/978-1-4614-8462-2_14 doi:10.1007/978-1-4614-8462-2_14

Howard, P. N., & Hussain, M. M. (2011). The role of digital media. *Journal of Democracy*, *22*(3), 35–48. doi:10.1353/jod.2011.0041

Information Builders. (2013, June). Houston Police Department Creates Real-Time Crime Center. Retrieved from http://www.informationbuilders.com/applications/houston

International Association of Chiefs of Police. (2013). *92% of U.S. law enforcement agencies use social media*. Retrieved from http://www.iacpsocialmedia.org/Portals/1/documents/2013SurveyResults.pdf

International Association of Chiefs of Police. (n. d.). Houston, Texas, Police Department – Blogging for recruitment and beyond. Retrieved from http://www.iacpsocialmedia.org/Resources/CaseStudy.aspx?termid=9&cmsid=4734

International ICT Policies and Strategies. (2011, September 2). International ICT Policies and Strategies: CCTNS Project of India to Be Launched Shortly. Retrieved from http://ictps.blogspot.com/2011/09/cctns-project-of-india-to-be-launched.html

Johnson, K. (2010, December 11). Police recruits screened for digital dirt on Facebook, etc. *USA TODAY*. Retrieved from http://usatoday30.usatoday.com/tech/news/2010-11-12-1Afacebookcops12_ST_N.htm

Kamensky, J. M. (2013, November 5). Fighting Crime in a New Era of Predictive Policing.*Governing| The State and Localities*. Retrieved from http://www.governing.com/blogs/bfc/col-crime-fighting-predictive-policing-data-tools.html

Kaplan, A. M., & Haenlein, M. (2010). Users of the world, unite! The challenges and opportunities of social media. *Business Horizons*, *53*(1), 59–68. doi:10.1016/j.bushor.2009.09.003

Kaspersky Lab. (2013, September 17). Taking a malware hit – more than one in three attacks costs users money. Retrieved from http://www.kaspersky.com/about/news/press/2013/Taking_a_malware_hit_more_than_one_in_three_attacks_costs_users_money

Kavanaugh, A. L., Fox, E. A., Sheetz, S. D., Yang, S., Li, L. T., Shoemaker, D. J., & Xie, L. et al. (2012). Social media use by government: From the routine to the critical. *Government Information Quarterly*, *29*(4), 480–491. doi:10.1016/j.giq.2012.06.002

Kelly, H. (2012, August 30). Police embrace social media as crime-fighting tool. *CNN*. Retrieved from http://www.cnn.com/2012/08/30/tech/social-media/fighting-crime-social-media/index.html

Kelly, H. (2014, May 26). Police embracing tech that predicts crimes. *CNN*. Retrieved from http://www.cnn.com/2012/07/09/tech/innovation/police-tech/index.html

Knell, N. (2013, January 3). Pinterest Helps Police Catch Criminals. *Governing The State and Localities*. Retrieved from http://www.governing.com/news/local/gt-pinterest-helps-police-catch-criminals.html

Lee, C. (2103, August 27). New Media Knowledge - Social media's role in recruitment unveiled. *New Media Knowledge*. Retrieved from http://www.nmk.co.uk/article/2013/8/27/social-media%E2%80%99s-role-in-recruitment-unveiled

Leishman, F., Loveday, B., & Savage, S. P. (2000). *Core issues in policing*. Pearson Education.

LeVeque, T. (2011) Introducing social media to an emergency operations center. Retrieved from http://lawscommunications.com/category/tom-le-veque

Lon, C. (2010, March).6 Ways Law Enforcement Uses Social Media to Fight Crime. *Mashable*. Retrieved from http://mashable.com/2010/03/17/law-enforcement-social-media/

Maynard, M. (2013, October 31). Public agencies still don't do social media very well. *Governing- The State and Localities*. Retrieved from http://www.governing.com/news/headlines/Public-Agencies-Still-Dont-Do-Social-Media-Very-Well.html

Mazerolle, L., Rogan, D., Frank, J., Famega, C., & Eck, J. E. (2003). *Managing citizen calls to the police: an assessment of non-emergency call systems*. Washington, DC: United States Department of Justice.

Morris, S. (2011, October 28). Joanna Yeates murder: the full truth may never be known. *The Guardian*. Retrieved from http://www.theguardian.com/uk/2011/oct/28/joanna-yeates-case-vincent-tabak

Moskvitch, K. (2012, October 29). Can you predict crime with tech? *BBC News*. Retrieved from http://www.bbc.co.uk/news/technology-20068722

Mustian, J., & Wallace, B. (2014, July 2). Police using social media to track down criminals. *The New Orleans Advocate*. Retrieved from http://www.theneworleansadvocate.com/news/9576282-171/gotcha-police-using-social-media

National Executive Institute Associates. (2013, July). Social media: a valuable tool with risks. Retrieved from http://www.neiassociates.org/storage/FBINEIA-2013-SocMediaTool.pdf

National Law Enforcement Policy Center. (2010). *Social media: concepts and issues paper*. Alexandria: International Association of Chiefs of Police.

National White Collar Crime Center. (2013, June). Criminal Use of Social Media. Retrieved from http://www.nw3c.org/docs/whitepapers/criminal-use-of-social-media.pdf

New York State Division of Criminal Justice Service. (n. d.). *What is eJusticeNY? - NY DCJS. NYS Division of Criminal Justice Services*. Retrieved from http://www.criminaljustice.ny.gov/ojis/ejusticeinfo.htm

O'Flinn, J. (2014, January 14). Twitter trolls: the existing legal framework. *The Lawyer*. Retrieved from http://www.thelawyer.com/analysis/opinion/twitter-trolls-the-existing-legal-framework/3014808.article

O'Leary, A. (2013, April 18). One on One: Tim Jones of Buzzient, Hunting Chatter on Explosives. *Bits Blog*. Retrieved from http://bits.blogs.nytimes.com/2013/04/18/buzzient-boston-marathon-investigation/

O'Reilly, N. (2014, July 2). Halton police get homicide tip in tweet-a-thon. *The Spec*. Retrieved from http://www.thespec.com/news-story/4610107-halton-police-get-homicide-tip-in-tweet-o-thon/

Observer, J. (2012, May 11). Showing the human side of the police. *Jamaica Observer*. Retrieved from http://www.jamaicaobserver.com/letters/Showing-the-human-side-of-the-police_11430692

Pelgrin, W. (2013, June 5). 3 reasons why criminals exploit social networks (and tips to avoid getting scammed). *CSO Online*. Retrieved from http://www.csoonline.com/article/2133563/social-engineering/3-reasons-why-criminals-exploit-social-networks--and-tips-to-avoid-getting-scamme.html

People's Daily Online. (2014, July 4). Chengdu police use social media to boost recruitment. Retrieved from http://english.peopledaily.com.cn/n/2014/0704/c98649-8750616.html

Pew Research Center's Internet & American Life Project. (2013, December 30). Social Media Update 2013. Retrieved from http://www.pewinternet.org/2013/12/30/social-media-update-2013/

Police Executive Research Forum . (2013, July). Social Media and Police Leadership: Lessons. *Boston*.

Procter, R., Crump, J., Karstedt, S., Voss, A., & Cantijoch, M. (2013). Reading the riots: What were the police doing on Twitter? *Policing and Society*, *23*(4), 413–436. doi:10.1080/10439463.2013.780223

Public Intelligence. (2013, October 13). Social Media and Tactical Considerations for Law Enforcement. Retrieved from http://publicintelligence.net/cops-social-media/

Purvis, C. (2011, June 17). A Look at Mexican Drug Cartel Membership Trends. *Security Management*. Retrieved from http://www.securitymanagement.com/news/a-look-mexican-drug-cartel-membership-trends-008644

Purvis, C. (2012, January 20). Researcher Reports a Surge in Social Media Use By Subversive Groups. *Security Management*. Retrieved from http://www.securitymanagement.com/news/researcher-reports-a-surge-social-media-use-subversive-groups-009428

Rizzo, T. (2013, October 15). Most Gang Members Use Social Media, Study Finds. *Government Technology Solutions for State and Local Government*. Retrieved from http://www.govtech.com/public-safety/Most-Gang-Members-Use-Social-Media-Study-Finds.html

Rose, A., Timm, H., Pogson, C., Gonzalez, J., Appel, E., & Kolb, N. (2010). *Developing a cyber-vetting strategy for law enforcement*. Alexandria: International Association of Chiefs of Police.

Ruddell, R., & Jones, N. (2013). Social media and policing: Matching the message to the audience. *Safer Communities*, *12*(2), 64–70. doi:10.1108/17578041311315030

Rutter, T. (2014, January 27). How police can join the digital revolution – roundup. *The Guardian*. Retrieved from http://www.theguardian.com/public-leaders-network/2014/jan/27/police-digital-revolution-roundup

Scholes-Fogg, T. (2013, December 12). Police and Social Media, a report for the Independent Police Commission of England and Wales. *ConnectedCOPS.net*. Retrieved from http://connectedcops.net/2012/12/13/police-social-media-report-independent-police-commission-england-wales/

Sharma, N. K. (2014, June 30). Criminal tracking system in a limbo. *Times of India*. Retrieved from http://timesofindia.indiatimes.com/city/jaipur/Criminal-tracking-system-in-a-limbo/articleshow/37484919.cms

Shekhar, R. (2014, July 16). Delhi cops teach how to fight cyber crime. *Times of India*. Retrieved from http://timesofindia.indiatimes.com/india/Delhi-cops-teach-how-to-fight-cyber-crime/articleshow/37875118.cms

Sherman, A. (2011, August 31). How Law Enforcement Agencies Are Using Social Media to Better Serve the Public. *Mashable*. Retrieved from http://mashable.com/2011/08/31/law-enforcement-social-media-use/

Smith, A. (2011). *Why Americans use social media*. Washington, DC: Pew Research Center.

Sparrow, M. K. (1993). *Information Systems and the Development of Policing*. US Department of Justice, Office of Justice Programs, National Institute of Justice.

Stadd, A. (2013, June 24). How Burglars Are Using Social Media [INFOGRAPHIC] - AllTwitter. *Mediabistro*. Retrieved from http://www.mediabistro.com/alltwitter/burglars-social-media_b45302

Steve, A. (2013, July). Cambridge Police Launch Map Database Showing Crime Stats.*Boston Magazine*. Retrieved from

Stevens, L. (2010). Social media in policing: nine steps for success. *Police Chief Magazine, 77*.

Stilgherrianon. (2011, August 25). Has Facebook killed the undercover cop? *CSO Online*. Retrieved from http://www.cso.com.au/article/398581/has_facebook_killed_undercover_cop_/

Stuart, R. D. (2013, February). Social Media: Establishing Criteria for Law Enforcement Use. *Federal Bureau of Investigation*. Retrieved from http://www.fbi.gov/stats-services/publications/law-enforcement-bulletin/2013/february/social-media-establishing-criteria-for-law-enforcement-use

Sutton, J., Palen, L., & Shklovski, I. (2008). Backchannels on the front lines: Emergent uses of social media in the 2007 southern California wildfires. *Proceedings of the 5th International ISCRAM Conference* (pp. 624–632). Washington, DC.

The Burlingame Voice. (2103, October 31). Tweet BPD. Retrieved from http://www.burlingame-voice.com/2013/10/

The Guardian. (2012, April 1). Government plans increased email and social network surveillance. Retrieved from http://www.theguardian.com/world/2012/apr/01/government-email-social-network-surveillance

The Police Chief Magazine. (2003). Connecting the Dots: Data Mining and Predictive Analytics in Law Enforcement and Intelligence Analysis, *70*(10). Retrieved from http://www.policechiefmagazine.org/magazine/index.cfm?fuseaction=display_arch&article_id=121&issue_id=102003

The Times of India. (2014b, July 19). Crime and Criminal Tracking Network System project in Allahabad district likely to be completed by December. Retrieved from http://timesofindia.indiatimes.com/city/allahabad/Crime-and-Criminal-Tracking-Network-System-project-in-Allahabad-district-likely-to-be-completed-by-December/articleshow/38667452.cms

The Times of India. (2014c, July 4). Police station to go online. Retrieved from http://timesofindia.indiatimes.com/city/kanpur/Police-station-to-go-online/articleshow/37766775.cms

The Times of India Crime tracking system to connect south Goa police stations. (2014a, July 18).. Retrieved from http://timesofindia.indiatimes.com/city/goa/Crime-tracking-system-to-connect-south-Goa-police-stations/articleshow/38575478.cms

Tonkin, E., Pfeiffer, H. D., & Tourte, G. (2012). Twitter, information sharing and the London riots? *Bulletin of the American Society for Information Science and Technology*, *38*(2), 49–57. doi:10.1002/bult.2012.1720380212

Toronto Police. (2012a). Toronto Police Service: To Serve and Protect. Retrieved from http://www.torontopolice.on.ca/yipi/

Toronto Police. (2012b). Toronto Police Service Social Engagement Guidelines. Retrieved from www.torontopolice.on.ca/publications/files/social_media_guidelines.pdf

Trottier, D., & Schneider, C. (2012). The 2011 Vancouver riot and the role of Facebook in crowd-sourced policing. *BC Studies*, *175*, 57–72.

Varano, S. P., & Sarasin, R. (2014). Use of Social Media in Policing. In G. Bruinsma & D. Weisburd (Eds.), Encyclopedia of Criminology and Criminal Justice (pp. 5410–5423). Springer New York; Retrieved from http://link.springer.com/referenceworkentry/10.1007/978-1-4614-5690-2_387 doi:10.1007/978-1-4614-5690-2_387

Vis, F. (2013). Twitter as a Reporting Tool for Breaking News. *Digital Journalism*, *1*(1), 27–47. doi:10.1080/21670811.2012.741316

Wagner, K. (2014, March 17). Police Turn to Social Media to Fight Crime, Dispel Rumors. *Mashable*. Retrieved from http://mashable.com/2014/03/16/police-departments-social-media/

Walters, J. (2014, July). Governments Struggling to Get Social Media Right. Retrieved from http://www.governing.com/topics/mgmt/gov-government-social-media.html

Wang, X., Tang, L., Gao, H., & Liu, H. (2010). Discovering Overlapping Groups in Social Media. In *2010 IEEE 10th International Conference on Data Mining (ICDM)* (pp. 569–578). doi:10.1109/ICDM.2010.48

Wasserman, T. (2011, August 10). NYPD Creates Unit To Track Criminals Via Social Media. *Mashable*. Retrieved from http://mashable.com/2011/08/10/nypd-unit-social-media/

Webster, R. (2013, February 11). Social media for community policing. Retrieved from http://www.russellwebster.com/social-media-for-community-policing/

Western Australia Police. (2013). Check my crime now available. Retrieved from http://www.police.wa.gov.au/Aboutus/News/Checkmycrimenowavailable/tabid/2013/Default.aspx

Williams, M. (2012, August 9). New York City Unveils Crime-Tracking Data Software. *Governing| The State and Localities*. Retrieved from http://www.governing.com/topics/technology/gt-nyc-unveils-crime-tracking-data-software.html

Wilson, J. M., & Castaneda, L. W. (2011). Most wanted: Law enforcement agencies pursue elusive, qualified recruits. *RAND Rev*, *35*(1), 25–29.

Zeng, D., Chen, H., Lusch, R., & Li, S.-H. (2010). Social media analytics and intelligence. *IEEE Intelligent Systems*, *25*(6), 13–16. doi:10.1109/MIS.2010.151

KEY TERMS AND DEFINITIONS

Community Policing: Community policing is a philosophy that blend traditional and non-traditional aspects of law enforcement to promote partnerships and problem-solving in order address conditions that give rise to public safety issues.

Internal Intelligence: Internal intelligence refers to the activities conducted within the country that threatens internal security.

Malware: Malware is short form of Malicious Software and refers to the software specifically designed to damage computer systems.

Passive Intelligence: Passive intelligence refers to evaluating available information for law enforcement purposes.

Phishing: Phishing is a type of e-mail fraud in which a perpetrator attempts to acquire sensitive information (such as bank financial pin) for malicious reasons.

Social Media: Social media is a collection of online communication channels that allow people to create and share information, ideas, and images with others.

Viral: It refers to popular Online content that quickly spreads through social media networks.

Chapter 14
Culture of Use of Moodle in Higher Education:
Networked Relations between Technology, Culture and Learners

M. Shuaib Mohamed Haneef
Pondicherry University, India

ABSTRACT

In this chapter, the use of Moodle, an open source Learning Management System (LMS), by the Department of Electronic Media and Mass Communication in Pondicherry University, as a means to supplement classroom teaching has been examined drawing on Actor Network Theory (ANT). This chapter reveals that the use of Moodle gives rise to a new digital culture which is inscribed on the prior cultural template that students, instructors and institutions bring to have a bearing on their teaching and learning activities. However, the rise of such a digital culture is due to the human and material assemblages constituted by how students and instructors inscribe their manifestoes on Moodle and how Moodle inscribes its manifestations on them. Further, the performative potential of Moodle is explained by its networked interaction with other social, human and non-human actors such as the culture of using technology for learning, digital literacy skills, emergent digital divide, access issues among students and teachers, educational and economic background and institutional media ecology among others.

INTRODUCTION

Higher education is the lynch pin of intellectual capital and hence it has an essential role to play in the evolution and development of an information society. Technological innovation in the contemporary era points to the emergence of 'informationalism' era wherein knowledge production is predicated on collaborative, interactive and networked technologies (Castells, 1996). Universities and colleges are required to incorporate internet technologies into teaching and learning. While adoption of technologies and infrastructure do not indicate a widespread embracing of e-learning practices, government norms prescribing understanding of technology-mediated learning as one of the eligibility criteria for teaching posts in higher institutions have brought about substantial

DOI: 10.4018/978-1-4666-8598-7.ch014

changes in the pedagogic practices. The survival of educational institutions will be determined by the technology capital or resources and infrastructure they would invest in for augmenting teaching and learning (Mlitwa, 2005).

This is apart from the internet cultures adults grow up in. With the introduction of computer into education and its use in social life, reading as a performative activity has found new meanings in the digital environment. Reading text as an enterprise depends on the materiality of the medium. The material affordances of the digital medium require users to possess literacy or competency to not only read and construe content but also know how to engage with the remediated content (Bolter, 2000).

While emphasis is laid on technology, the social and cultural contexts in which technology is placed cannot be excluded or studied in isolation. Since the digital technology's invasion, assumptions about its application in education and society have been either to invest in the precepts of technological determinism or the oppositional social determinism. Technological determinism essayed the position of medium as an omnipotent influencer having unassailable impact on events in society and on people. On the other hand, social determinism posited that technology is shaped by society.

However, both approaches seek to advance their claims discounting their mutual influence. There is a systemic failure to understand the need for interleaving technology and society. The discourse of technology (Foucault, 1988) expounds on how self is shaped and honed by technology and the interaction between the self and society whereby governmentality of technology over the self and the self over technology is mediated through symbiotic relations built between the humans and non-humans. Extending this concept, what one would find in web 2.0 is an empowered reader whose agential potential to interact and influence a communicative and cognitive ecology is sustainable and tenable.

In the specific domain of education and ICTs, research on learning is dependent on human and non-human actants. "Purposeful action and intentionality may not be properties of objects, but they are not properties of humans either. They are the properties of institutions, of apparatuses, of what Foucault called dispositifs" (Latour 1999, p.192). According to Latour, the ability of a human to 'act' is made possible through a distributed system of human and non-human actants that are both tangible and intangible. The inscription of human actions on infrastructure and the imposition of programmed actions of technologies on humans interweave and mesh together producing fibrous, rhizomatic and fluid networks.

Use of digital artifacts in learning is an intersection of infrastructure, institutions and their policy, preparedness of teachers to adopt technology-mediated instruction, users and their varied cultural background, power structure in operating a technology such as LMS, use of open sources and peer-peer learning. The type of institution, its policy, and perception of using technology for imparting instruction and the culture of teachers and students in using technology or willing to shift the pedagogy from traditional to technology-mediated practice are essential parameters of e-learning adoption (Holt & Challis, 2007; Weaver Spatt & Sid Nair, 2008).

Culture of an institution primarily concerns with the culture of learners and instructors. Culture is both an individual product when considered as knowledge acquired by a person; it is also a collective entity that generates groups of differential capabilities and practices (Savard, Bourdieu & Paquette, 2008). In the context of learning and technology, culture is predicated on their exposure to digital technologies, the user experience in having used the Internet (or any other digital technology) for learning as well as teaching, having understood the participatory spaces technologies afford and having engaged in participatory activities in a decentralised network for top-bottom and peer-peer learning. The culture also indicates the need for infusing pedagogy (learning and sharing, instead of learning and teaching) with technological inputs and relocating one's identity, personality and self from the past traditions of learning to the computer-mediated online learning.

Understanding culture lays out the learning styles, local beliefs and local experiences of learners. The technology use by learners indicates that user practice does not take place in a vacuum. Exploring the culture of use of Moodle, an open source LMS, I examine the performative aspects of technology and the relationship between the learners, their culture and infrastructural or media ecology. I seek to gain insights into the following questions:

a. How does the relationship between user, technology and culture play out in the use of Moodle for higher education?
b. Does the Moodle facilitate a new culture of learning style and how does the divide (cultural and digital), which is a heterogeneous concept, re-centre its position towards realising a homogenous goal of learners pursuing the same goal (of learning by using Moodle)

BACKGROUND

This paper focuses on how technology is employed in the academia by teachers and students for imparting education using Moodle. Technology amplifies the learning experiences of students (Tinio, 2002) and it also enhances education (Muianga, 2004).

Literature available on technology and learning has been produced using situated paradigms, social constructivism and activity theory. Activity theory focuses on the users' perspectives and their needs (Rajkumar, 2005) by examining the subject, the object or the goal of the learning activity, technology as an artefact and division of labour. Subjects (humans) are mediated by culture, tools, rules and contexts (Rajkumar, 2005; Miettinen, 1997).

Later, new approaches such as considering technology as value-laden and that (inter)actions are not only controlled by human beings but are also seen as having the potential to influence and shape social perceptions and identities emerged. Feenberg (2003) calls this perspective of looking at technology as capable of shaping society and getting shaped by the society as the critical perspective of technology. In other words, to understand the use of technology, it is essential to focus on both human activities and non-human artefacts as both human and non-human actants influence each other. This is amply explained by actor-network theory.

Actor-Network theory from Science and Technology Studies (STS) emphasizes the embedding of knowledge in a network of social process, conceptual systems and technological artefacts (Latour, 1992; Callon, 1991). Actor-Network theory puts emphasis on the agency of non-human actants in the heterogenous assemblages of human-material interaction. The theory postulates that human actions and non-human influences form networks to redistribute and reformulate action. ANT demonstrates that any object, despite appearing to be a totalised and self-contained entity, is actually a production of a rhizome of entities connected through space and time by networks. This challenges the networked assemblages of knowledge production which seemingly posit less fluid forms of production of knowledge and discourses. As rhizomes, knowledge production in educational setting is emergent and is characterized by fluidity or *fluid space* (Law & Mol, 2001).

Knowledge Production in Learning Management System

Knowledge production within an LMS functionality is an activity that is mediated by humans through their interactions with tools, infrastructure, rules, contexts and policies of educational institutions.

Evident in the subject-tools interactions or human and non-human actors is the interface and usability of LMSs such as Moodle or proprietary tools that include BlackBoard. Bjoko (2006) conducted a usability study using eye-tracking method to evaluate the user-friendliness of a newly improved website of the American Society of Ontology against its older version. His study points to users using technology to achieve their ends or satisfy their goals. Interfaces facilitate interactions between human and non-human actors making online learning effective. However, there is a danger in subscribing to instrumentalist notions of seeing technologies as neutral tools that are used only to achieve user end goals (Kellner, 1998).

Mlitwa (2007) develops a model to represent LMS functionality of user interaction with tools, hardware and content through the optic of Activity Theory. "It is the usability of the LMS applications and the entire learning environment that mediates and transforms the object (learning) through the activity of learning – into the final outcome: enhanced learning and learning experiences" (Mlitwa, p. 60). Actor Network Theory (ANT) offers an alternative value-laden perspective of technology removed from an essentialist notion in which it claims that the social and contextual aspects embedded within technology shape its use. ANT eliminates any a priori assumptions between the technical and the social (Callon, 1986) and both continually negotiate to have a mutual influence in network process (Tuomi, 2001). Each actor is connected to the other parts of the network. The socio-technical network is an assemblage created by people who construct and contribute to e-learning courses through collaborative actions (Lamb & Davidson, 2002).

The *after* actor-network theory is a breakaway from the traditional ANT perspective wherein it dispenses with the network modality and embraces *spatial formations*. In so doing, the cardinal feature of ANT is to negate ontological and sociological binaries of nature/society; agency/structure; human/material to stress the interconnected and networked entities that comprise a system.

The presence of or an assemblage of actors distributed across a network are entities of technique, resource, bureaucracy or information (Latour, 1987). In the same vein, SØrensen (2009) explains the performative potential of technologies, in that patterns of socio-technical relations are formed by technologies and humans. In educational practices, the participative role of both humans and technologies in formulating what and how the actors do and contribute to the social process of learning. The resultant outcome is due to a chain of relations enacted in and through activities thereby forming a network of actors. An actor can literally be anything as long as it is a source of action (Latour, 1999). For instance, the socio-economic background of students can affect their uptake of educational content mediated through technologies.

The influence on the network will be reflected in various levels including (any actor at any level) bureaucratic, technical or otherwise and that learning is a *distributed action* (Latour, 1999). Every actor, be it a technical object or scientific network, is deployed within the complex ecologies of the networks which support their existence and enable their ability to perform the tasks usually understood to be causally located in a discrete space.

This paper uses actor-network theory and media ecology to assess the presence of technology infrastructure in Pondicherry university and how learning is influenced by Moodle, the competency and digital literacy of faculty and students to use it, the dove-tailing of content and pedagogy into the technological framework and its impact on learning as well as other social and cultural environments such as the shift from a paper-based and book reading culture to electronic mode of writing assignment and online exams. In higher education, ICT predominantly implies deploying the Web for teaching and learning practices (Czerniewicz, et al., 2005; Muianga, 2004).

In this study, the use of Moodle or a technology is located in the network of various actors that include digital literacy skills, the prior experience of students in using the Internet for information and other purposes, infrastructure and internet access facilities in the university and outside, inclination to use Moodle by teachers for imparting knowledge, digital divide among students and the divide between students and teachers as well the one within the teaching community. Thus, use of technology is not a phenomenon of *universality;* it is an act of *mobility* (Latour, 1987) where learning through technology is influenced by various actors that are social and cultural too.

Actors in E-Learning Process

The socio-economic background of students and their ethnicity determine how students adjust to and embrace innovative pedagogies and teaching methods introduced by higher education institutions (Wong & Tatnall 2009). In one of the studies, Wong (2010) indicates that students with low levels of academic ability and no prior exposure to internet infrastructure prefer face-to-face interaction with their lecturer and tutor to online learning methods.

There are many actors that are both human and non-human in a university setting. University policy, infrastructure, computer labs and wi-fi among others constitute non-human actors (Tummons, 2009; Wong & Tatnall, 2010). As Law (1987) states the administrator and the subject coordinator are the 'Heterogeneous Engineer'. The subject coordinator or the instructor crafts lesson plans for both offline and online class room content delivery. Students are also human actors and technological infrastructure accounts for non-human actors (Wong & Tatnall, 2010).

The adoption of technologies by students and teachers is illustrated by the translation of events starting from problematisation through Interessement, Enrolment, and Mobilisation. In problematisation, actors, teachers and instructors involved, advocate the use of technologies for teaching and learning. While subject coordinators contribute to popularizing the use of technologies in educational institutions, the policies of the institution such as providing wi-fi facilities and generating e-learning content, as non-human actors, can impact or problematise the e-learning endeavour undertaken.

Interessement is about making e-learning content interesting to comprehend, providing easy-to-use interface so that students do not disillusioned with technologies (Wong & Tatnall, 2010). The subject coordinator or the one who pioneers this effort in an educational institution has to work collaboratively with other instructors in order to make online teaching and learning very effective and interesting.

Enrolment is not only about registering for a course but also establishes how online courses are designed and how they attract students to join and do their classes. Enrolment, in that sense, involves student motivation and the courses designed should strive to keep the motivation level of students at an optimum level. For instance, online courses cannot afford to draw students at the cost of encouraging students to absent from face-to-face sessions. de Lange, Suwardy, and Mavondo (2003) identified that "the challenge for educators is to develop strategies that ensure any novelty effect does not wear off with an end result of technology impeding learning." Mobilisation brings together all teachers who are convinced by the potential of the technologies to be used as supplementary learning tools in addition to face-to-face training.

Further, media ecology is an intricately intertwined feature of the user's emergent attitude towards and use of technology. The Internet, extending its meaning beyond a medium, reshapes the structure of society and culture by furthering the communication process and altering the interaction patterns. Combined with actor-network theory, media ecology is used to inquire into the university media ecosystems in terms of computer, internet and wi-fi facilities and their contribution to technology-mediated learning.

METHOD

Data were collected through focus group discussions held with a group of five students and three instructors in the Department of Electronic Media and Mass Communication. The discussion was recorded and later transcribed for analysis.

Focus Group

Focus group allows participants to share and respond to comments. It is 'a carefully planned discussion designed to obtain perceptions on a defined area of interest in a permissive, non-threatening environment' (Krueger 1994, p.6). Focus group discussion adds new ideas, thoughts, gives rise to new hypotheses, reflections (Hydén & Bülow, 2003).

Focus group discussions help in unearthing and eliciting information that are deeply entrenched in individual memory (Kamberelis & Dimitriadis, 2008). They are also invaluable in facilitating 'the exploration of collective memories and shared stocks of knowledge' (p. 396). The data collected through focus group discussions are immense compared to interviewing and observation methods thereby resulting in discerning insights into social, political, cultural and economic nuances of the phenomenon under study.

Focus group discussions are facilitated and moderated in informal ways to allow participants in the discussion to express freely their thoughts, angst and reflections across temporal and spatial dimensions on a specific set of topics or issues of the everyday life. The more informal a focus group discussion can get, the more comfortable participants will feel in sharing their experiences.

The hallmark of focus groups is the explicit use of the group interaction to produce data and insights that could be less accessible without the interaction found in a group (Morgan, 1988, p.12)

In this study, five students were identified for focus group discussion from a class exposed to Moodle-based learning for subjects that include Photography, Media Research Methods and Radio Production. The students, comprising three girls and two boys, were drawn using convenient and purposive sampling techniques. Three students were selected based on the references provided by their faculty in the Department of Electronic Media, Pondicherry University, and the other two students were selected from the same class by the researcher using convenient sampling. Selecting students from the same class presuppose that they share same characteristics besides becoming relevant to the study. The questions floated to facilitate participants reflect on their use of internet, Moodle for learning, their inclination to appropriate technologies, digital literacy of learners and instructors and prior experience of using technology for teaching and learning brought out varied opinions with different points of view. The reflective process encouraged participants to bring out the heuristic knowledge which helped the researcher to cull out commonalities and differences. The focus group discussion lasted close to 55 minutes. The discussion in the audio format was later transcribed as a textual record and was analysed for emergent themes on how participants used Moodle, interacted with technologies, socio-cultural factors that impeded and facilitated their use of Moodle for learning.

The discussion was recorded after obtaining informed consent from the participants. The recorded discussion was transcribed and coded to gain insights into the interface between users and Moodle founded on actor-network theory. The themes emerged posit the differential use of internet by students with prior experience and those who come from impoverished socio-economic background.

As part of the study, three teachers from the same department, who used Moodle to supplement their face-to-face classroom teaching, were interviewed separately and their views on using technology for teaching, their perception of Moodle and its affordances, and how students co-opt Moodle into their learning practices were elicited. Their views were also recorded and coded.

In the first phase of data analysis, the study employed microanalysis of the transcribed data gleaned from the focus group discussion and interviews with instructors separately. Through this technique, the data were broken into detailed and meaningful segments and categories. The identified codes were labelled and concepts and categories were developed. Some of the identified categories include cultural shift wrought by internet practices in reading and writing assignments, Moodle and digital literacy, institutional ecology, user interface design and performative communication through Moodle among others.

ANALYSIS AND DISCUSSION

The use of Moodle has changed the reading and writing practices of the respondents. This has some resonances with the changing literacy that is predicated on engagement with text mediated through digital technologies and the Internet. One of the key features of digital literacy is the materiality of the medium in which the text is embedded. As opposed to the text in print literature characterised by definite markers such as finite origin and closure and reading text from a material such as paper, the hypertext by virtue of its unmooring of text from spatial dimensions makes materiality a malleable and fluid concept vesting the power with the reader and his/her subjectivity to exploit the potential of the medium.

Much of the difficulty in appropriating technologies was faced by students who had poor functional literacy by way of their social and economic background which perilously ties to technological access and use. This combined with their non-English speaking characteristic affected their academic performance, at least in the beginning, to adapt to using Moodle as a resource for learning. A wide assemblage of factors was at play in determining the culture of use of Moodle among students from downtrodden place. Although the department imposed, not as a rule but as a habit and as an initiative to embrace technology, their initial reluctance and retardation was inscribed by their prior experience. For them to be able to reinscribe their attuning to using Moodle, they depended on media ecologies of the institution which played a favourbale role to use Moodle. That includes physical setting such as labs, computer access and wi-fi facility. Uninterrupted exposure to technologies facilitated them to adopt and adapt Moodle for learning. Such translations occurred in stages from wi-fi facility to having their own laptops to accessing computers in labs. The spatial formations of the network of factors involved in producing course content, accessing it, participating in forums and submitting assignments constitute the diffuse nodal points without any centrality.

Reading and Writing through Moodle: A Cultural Shift

Moving away from the culture of submitting assignments on paper, the shift to the electronic mode has met with some concern. Respondents suffer from time pressure with the deadline closing on a particular date and time. Despite the fact that Moodle helps to reorganise the working practice of students by disciplining them, the closing time set by teachers to submit the assignment online is seen as disfavour.

Respondents claim that for paucity of time little reading is undertaken and that they open Moodle an hour before to submit their work. There is an element of rigidity in the flexible learning system. The LMS per se does not afford rigidity but the user actions and performances contribute to it underlying the fact that materiality of the medium is contingent on the user actions. The rigidity in the form of deadline is contingent on students' attitude towards assignment. In the old cultural practice of handwritten assignments and learning activities, students would start on them in advance while use of Moodle seems to suggest that students have learnt to strike a balance between the fear for submitting assignments in Moodle and the ease with which they can acquire information on the Web.

According to them, the use of Moodle has opened up a new possibility of reading content but it has killed ingenuity connected to writing. Respondents clearly distinguish their writing in networking sites from the academic writing as two different works of art. Writing is viewed as a serious academic activity involving the cognitive faculty to think through and articulate one's views. As opposed to writing in networking sites, respondents engage in writing in Moodle by copying and pasting content from the Internet to submit their assignments online, let alone a few exceptions.

R: If we are writing on paper, we will be sincere
R: Moodle has spoilt the writing skill or any attempt to write has been severely affected.

One of the respondents, with a higher level of competency in using the Internet, said that she finds Moodle facilitating her writing skills. It is evident that students with varied exposure and Internet skills are likely to experience dissimilar perceived usefulness of Moodle illustrating that its adoption and use are strongly grounded in the user experience (culturally embedded) and Moodle, i.e. user, his/her subjectivity, and the technology – a mesh of human and non-human actors. Simultaneously, students with varied exposure and Internet skills experience dissimilar perceived usefulness of technology illustrating that adoption of technology and its use is strongly grounded in the social-technical framework.

Students confess that they copy and paste while a faculty respondent says that the university has purchased *turnitin* software and that it is possible to check plagiarism. However, use of another technology is found to be burdensome on the part of faculty – so they haven't started using *turnitin*. It is not about using *turnitin* which is important but inculcating in students the need for zero-level plagiarism and devising a pedagogy that will not allow learners to copy and paste. In other words, a compendium of entities that involve deployment of technology and cultural values are the basis for augmenting the performance of learning/teaching through Moodle.

What can be inferred is that the presence of software does not reduce the incidence of plagiarism. The culture of checking for authenticity of content and appropriate references has led to increased habit of lifting content from the Internet within academic circles. The performance of students is attributed to the performance of instructors and it needs a paradigm/fundamental shift in understanding the notion of 'assignment and other student activities'. What can be inferred from the discussion is that the culture of copying and pasting has become a nuanced form of using the Internet for learning.

The non-human actors are interconnected with the social aspects of literacy constituting the socio-technical network. The non-human actors - *turnitin* software and Moodle - have the 'agency' to influence the reading and writing practices of students and teachers.

Respondents claim that the reading habit has declined and is limited to perusing materials posted in the Moodle by teachers in the form of Power Point presentations, PDF files and external hyperlinks. However, all instructors are not providing a rich fund of information apart from PPTs and sometimes a few PDFs. The text, video, audio, hyperlinks refer to the 'participation' space (Brown & Alder, 2008).

R: One teacher is an exception. He gives us many links and websites to go through.

This further illustrates that the human agents – instructors and students – who participate in the teaching and learning process are one of the primary nodes of the network of various factors affecting the use of Moodle for learning and academic achievement.

In the absence of external hyperlinks, the reading material such as PPTs does not elucidate concepts and this further proscribes wide in-depth reading. There is a cultural shift from reading books to reading PPTs in Moodle. Respondents said that they used Google to search for content whenever they had to submit assignments. Reading extended beyond the materials uploaded in Moodle only during the time of working on out-of-class assignments. One respondent differs when she says:

R: There is very limited information on Moodle. I go to Google to search for more information. I use both Google and Moodle for information.

It is to be evaluated whether the decline of reading for learning as claimed by the respondents is exacerbated by the technology or transferred from the traditional system to the technology-mediated learning process. Changing to a new cultural practice that involves a shift in digital literacy and the institutional obligation to use *Moodle* further brought about a new change in terms of reading which has adversely affected the habit of visiting libraries.

Technology and Learning Behaviour

Stress and Technology

It cannot be elided that students add their own meanings to material practices which are interwoven with cultural and spatial forms (see Latour 2005). The co-existence of media artifacts and spatial settings define how Moodle is co-opted into the learning system by students who experience a shift from traditional pedagogy to techno-pedagogic practices. According to students, the use of Moodle is surcharged with anxiety or stress in terms of workload and pressure to carry out responsibilities as students. However, the stress or the non-trivial effort needed to use Moodle is relatively less as one does not read content and sift through information before submitting it. However, it would be incorrect to attribute stress to use of Moodle. Instead, it is born out of productive meanings that users add to the already inscribed significations in the LMS.

Although Moodle was initiated as a tool to supplement traditional learning and teaching pedagogies, students do not shown enthusiasm to straddle both traditional and technological systems/cultural artefacts. Moodle represents dematerialization of learning methods, resulting in the abandoning of traditional materialistic cultural artefacts such as books or the performative actions of reading books in libraries. From the responses, it could be gauged that drudgery and efforts are associated with materialistic forms of traditional media than with dematerialized digital artefacts. Moodle not requiring students to refer books does not establish a mere causal relationship but produces meanings derived from networks of relations between Moodle and their previous encounter with materialistic artefacts in traditional libraries with spatial settings different from digital libraries. In addition, Moodle can also be leveraged to steer students to read books online. The ease of use of Moodle, in terms of it not exerting students to read or it becoming an easy choice for learning compared to books, only points out fault lines to be taken care of in pedagogies.

R: While writing on paper, we experience stress and also fear of submitting it (assignment). Also, we work more going to the library and search for information by reading books. In Moodle, we do not search for extra information other than what we find in it.

According to a respondent, with the introduction of Moodle, the stress experienced in class rooms is also low.

R: When a teacher is teaching, we sit relaxed because it is going to be there in PPT in Moodle. In traditional classroom, we used to take notes seriously and the attention span will be more. But now, our mindset is that we have a backup in Moodle and it doesn't matter even if we don't pay attention to the class.

Feedback as an Interactive Feature

The feedback was immediate in real class as opposed to the virtual environment learning. The social presence of the teacher and his/her remarks on what a student does and says may stay longer than the feedback received from the instructors in the Moodle.

R: Every day and in every class, we get response from teachers.

It is evident from the above response that technology can change the learning practice of students. The feedback being asynchronous, respondents feel that they do not await the feedback. Another reason they attribute to not considering the feedback with concern is that it is shared but not discussed in the social presence of everyone.

R: We are not scared. We are submitting our assignment. Whatever feedback comes, we are okay with it.

This scenario brings to explain the gap between the home-grown culture of students engaging in discussion in real setting that they bring from their previous experience and the host culture of virtual sharing and discussion they are initiated into in the university now. The gaps are multidimensional and they refer to gaps of access to technologies, gaps of digital literacy (students' knowledge and experience in using websites) and gaps of social and economic factors all of which are intricately intertwined.

USER INTERFACE AS NON-HUMAN ACTANT

User-interface design of Moodle constitutes the performative potential of technologies (SØrensen (2009). Faculty members and students explained that they are not familiar with the user interface of the LMS which could be another factor that dissuades them from exploiting its varied features.

Faculty: The user interface of Moodle is rugged and it is not as user-friendly as one would expect it to be.

Faculty: I am still learning. I am not clear how we can effectively use it. It depends on the person who is using it and his logical thinking.

One of the faculty respondents despite his knowledge of Moodle and using it to deliver course work to students could not leverage on it or optimize his use of the LMS. Apart from one's knowledge of how the LMS functions, the teacher says, one needs to know how to logically connect the curriculum and what is to be delivered online. This also hints at the futility of describing Moodle in its essentialist forms based on their characteristics. The spatial formations that Moodle produces are not limited to its materialist conceptions but are networked with its performative potential that subsumes how its characteristics contribute to effective learning. In the process, the LMS gives rise to a new pedagogic discourse in the educational setting. In other words, the relational spaces of technology, users, institutional policies and availability of internet facility among others constitute the performance of the assembled entities.

The media use of Moodle by the user depends on both technological and material features. For instance, user interface of Moodle, which is both technological and material, is perhaps experienced and evaluated from their use of Facebook. The features are embedded in a raw framework in Moodle as it is an open source software and allows users to customize the look and feel of pages. A respondent with experience in web designing says:

R: It is not organised and user-friendly. For few subjects, assignment links were not displayed. I didn't know where the links are.

Another respondent who pursued Visual Communication as his undergraduate degree said that user-friendliness is not a fixed and predefined feature but can be grasped with usage. This refers to the participatory culture of users in redefining the digital space and comprehending its dimensions. It also elucidates the nexus between human and non-human actors (users and user interface) that mutually influence the learners and the software.

R: It (Moodle) is easy to adapt. When I started using Facebook, I didn't know anything. I signed the application and went through it. I got new experiences. Initially there will be some struggle and it can be overcome. We learn as we use.

The response above highlights how users invest digital material objects with their greater meaning by overcoming the imposed inscriptions of technology such as Facebook. Initially, they attempt to navigate through the technological affordances and later they participate in modifying media forms and contents signaling a cultural shift towards 'participatory culture' (Jenkins, 2006). Relatively, Moodle is easy to use. However, the respondent's experience with Facebook does not necessarily indicate that the social networking site was difficult to use but his use of Facebook as an actant would have made his encounter with Moodle less arduous.

MOODLE, DIGITAL LITERACY AND DIGITAL DIVIDE

The arguments surrounding the user-interface design indicate that students from rural places and other backward towns got themselves exposed to technologies much later than those from urban cities began. In this context, the shift from traditional to a progressive technology-inclusive culture is more radical for the students from rural background.

The availability of the infrastructure in institutions and schools create a viable and desirable environment for students to maximise their Internet use in turn resulting in better understanding of the interface. Prior experience obtained through institutional norms further helps in co-opting such exposure into the host culture engendered by the Pondicherry University to embrace Moodle. This highlights the concept of media ecology that underlies a conflation of environments consisting of techniques, technologies, symbols, information systems and machines.

In addition, the gap between the home-grown culture of students, where their Internet usage is presumably limited, and the host culture of learning online through Moodle in the university lays out, quite starkly, the paradoxes of literacy. The gaps are multidimensional and they refer to gaps of access to technologies, gaps of digital literacy (students' knowledge and experience in using websites) and gaps of social and economic factors all of which are intricately intertwined.

At another level, access to laptops guarantees access to Moodle institutionalising digital divide. For those who do not possess laptops, the dependency on computer labs and browsing centres is inevitable to complete assignments. The economic background of many results in delayed submission of works assigned to them. The economic factor is also an actant that determines the use of Moodle.

Another divide erupts from the incompatibility between teacher's expectations and students' performance within the department. There is a small danger of assuming that all students are equally capable of embracing the technology effectively. On the other hand, students contend that a workshop or a small training should be given before they start using Moodle. The gap between the teachers' expectations laced with their techno idealism and students' failure to cooperate, caused primarily due to lack of knowledge to use the LMS, leaves a black hole to be filled.

TEACHERS, STUDENTS AND THEIR USE OF MOODLE

Faculty members attempt to layer traditional teaching with their competency in virtual learning. Two faculty members of the four have a different historicity of using the Internet. As one of them claims, to use a computer with very low configuration and a black and white monitor in an era when radio was the fastest medium of communication offered him thrills and challenges.

Faculty: We have to write our own commands. It was participatory and a creative challenge. I was thrilled to type it even though it took us 2 hours to type one page then. Television was not available then and the presence of computer in the bio-technology department (MK University, Madurai) was empowering. That experience is unmatched even today.

The prior experience of the two respondents does not have any bearing on their current use of the Internet but their exposure to the Internet generated fresh enthusiasm. One of them worked in an Open University and brings his competency to bear upon the Moodle experience in this university. Crediting Pondicherry University for providing the infrastructure including the server to run the Moodle initiative, the respondent feels that students are interested in exposing themselves to any new technology.

The Moodle initiative is currently in limbo following new policy decisions to shift the server to the department. The process appears to be long-winding and the use of technology is dependent on human actors and institutional ecology.

INSTITUTIONAL ECOLOGY

The wi-fi enabled campus of the university makes the use of Moodle for teaching and learning among Electronic Media students possible. With an informal training, the experiment was launched and subsequently it heralded a shift in teaching pedagogy from being teacher-centric to learner-centric. The Moodle technology has affordances to facilitate participation and thereby debunks one-way transmission of knowledge. Although, the server infrastructure in Pondicherry University is not robust, Moodle privileges both instructors and learners to use 10 MB and 2MB space respectively. This inheres in the participatory mechanism of the technology facilitating learners to interact and upload content thereby making Moodle learner-centric as well. After embracing Moodle, its technological inscriptions impose demands on instructors to change their pedagogy. The networked assemblage of human-material relations among Moodle, wi-fi infrastructure, instructors, content and learners works in mutual relationships contributing to each other in equal measures to realize effective learning.

It is perceived that there is a strong correlation existing between the discipline and other faculty members, as their profession in the discipline would demand, are well-versed in computer software and these experiences came as an actant influencing their use of Moodle for teaching.

The media ecology of Pondicherry University comprises the exclusive infrastructure and lab facilities afforded by it. Implicit in this argument is the divide between the digital natives and digital immigrants and divide within digital immigrants and within digital natives (the use of the Internet is variable across teachers and students and creates a divide). Media ecology as a non-human actant reiterates its confluence of user performance, the infrastructure in the university and how these ecologies are sustained and strengthened further by the use of students and teachers.

Implicit in this argument is the divide between the digital natives and digital immigrants and divide within digital immigrants (the use of the Internet is variable and creates a divide).

Faculty: *Had the university extended this facility to all, the experience would have been better.*

He, however, felt that Pondicherry University was better off as the infrastructure was good and he received immediate compliance from the university whereas his previous experience in a state university reveals that he did not have access to printers. As an empowered digital user (citizen), he does not want to depend on the university for procedural actions.

Faculty: *If you are interested in innovation, let's not depend on the VC or the university. It is my own and I am doing it for my students and for my own interest. If the server facility is denied, we will work at another level.*

The faculty respondent's words demonstrate his competency and skills in addition to his passion for using technology and consequently attempting to help students realise its benefits. The human actants are predominant here influencing the intersecting with the non-human actants. His specific reference to server facility stems from a recent obstacle he and his colleagues face in using the LMS which has to be shifted from its present location in the administration building to the department – another example of how the centre-periphery paradigm is reconfigured by de-centred operation of the Moodle. The respondent also expresses confidence to upgrade Moodle to its 2.0 version and carry forward the success and progress the department has achieved in the last one year.

Faculty: Luckily, we have sustained it (Moodle) for one year. We will move it to the department now. Moodle 2.0 should have been introduced now. I have great confidence and faith in similar lines.

MOODLE AS IMMUTABLE MOBILE

Faculty: Everything has changed. Anyone can audit and monitor all my materials, questions and other activities (I assign to students). My care and attention has improved and this has made me more perfect to prepare.

Indicating a shift in methodology, one of the faculty members emphasises on transparency. This could be a newly cultivated habit that has emerged after his use of technology for education. Besides, he validates and re-works on new materials every year. The content uploaded is stored in the LMS and is accessible to students of all years for reference. Thus, according to him, technology is not a short cut to teaching but an innovative mechanism that facilitates collaborative learning. In other words, it is a knowledge bank or a database or a small library that feeds content to students as and when required. It is not the technology that has perfected him to perform better and he does not subscribe to technological determinism. Instead, he exercises caution while using Moodle as he treats it as an open and public space that reflects his identity as a teacher.

The need to inscribe his role as a teacher is informed both by technology and social values inherent in the profession, a socio-technical framework. Further, the archives of lesson materials on specific courses taught by the faculty become immutable mobile as the digital assets allow coalition building around learning among students. On the other hand, the Moodle space functions as an immutable mobile for the teacher as what he is as a teacher and his performative roles are enunciated by the map – lessons and course materials in Moodle. Further, information is passed between agents such as students and other scholars as well as transferred to different spatio-temporal fluidities by which the teacher uses the material to reinscribe, reconstruct, recirculate and remediate the content for the next semester and across different batches of students.

Actor-network theory suggests that some relevant actors such as the archiving of lessons every year in Moodle are themselves constructed by artefacts. In the process, artefacts and humans mutually shape each other. From this perspective, the Actor-network theory promotes the faculty member as a collector and an archivist. These uses of Moodle by him and users on their part assemble to recreate a typical metaphoric bookshelf. Moodle is a library translated into an archive consisting of "links". Moodle, therefore, is a 'personified and embodied reflection of the World Wide Web'.

CONCLUSION

Understanding the various actors playing a key role in adding meanings to the working of Moodle as well as appropriating it into everyday life in the university point to how Moodle use in the digital environment is challenged, renewed and renegotiated. The way students and instructors organize their use of Moodle, technologies and artefacts, co-exist in networks in a human-material assemblage. The digital technology, including Wi-fi, and human actants mutually shape each other in the context of institutional policies and infrastructure provided to facilitate the use of Moodle. As Latour (1987) explains, no single object such as Moodle or wi-fi facility is self-contained but they are explained by their networked interaction with other social and non-human actors involving the culture of using technology for learning, digital literacy skills, emergent digital divide and access issues among students and teachers. In the same vein, social actors such as students and teachers cannot be defined in the secluded socio-cultural contexts but need to be intertwined with the technological framework. In all, the use of Moodle in Pondicherry University is a richly variegated phenomenon due to varying digital literacy, prior cultural experience of using Internet for learning, and due to gaps in access, educational background, economic background and institutional media ecology.

This paper contextualises the use of LMS (Moodle) for learning in a centralised monolithic infrastructural regime that explains that the spaces facilitating peer-peer learning were not used and encouraged. Chat facility was utilised to facilitate interaction except by one faculty and the lack of interest to participate in interaction remains a major concern. In one of the online exams conducted by a faculty, the incidence of copying and pasting content from the Internet was high and the students reported that they were ill-prepared for the new examination system. The drawbacks help in understanding the relationship between the culture, technology and human beings besides helping in demystifying the pre-defined assumptions of the relationship.

The culture of use of Moodle among students of Electronic Media and Mass Communication is a microcosmic enterprise in Pondicherry University. For one, intrusion of technology is seen as a threat to traditional teaching methods. There is also a fear of breaking or reconfiguring the existing tradition – the move is perhaps considered to be anti-essentialist. Extrapolating this weak and fragile proposition, it is possible to see that the role of technology has not been understood thoroughly and especially that computer-mediated learning will be a strong supplement to classroom learning. These are undesirable impediments while the nation and the MHRD are generating discourses on teaching, learning and technology, through various initiatives such as NME-ICT and presently through plans to develop MOOC (Massive Online Open) courses.

REFERENCES

Bjoko, A. (2006). Using eye tracking to compare web page designs: A case study. *Journal of Usability Studies*, *3*(1), 112–120. Retrieved from http://uxpajournal.org/using-eye-tracking-to-compare-web-page-designs-a-case-study/

Bolter, J. D., & Grusin, R. (2000). *Remediation: Understanding new media*. Massachusetts: MIT Press.

Brown, J., & Alder, R. (2008). Minds on fire: Open education, the long tail and learning 2.0. *EDUCAUSE Review*, *43*(1), 16–32.

Callon, M. (1986). Some elements of a sociology of translation: domestication of the scallops and the fishermen. In J. Law (Ed.), *A sociology of monsters: Essays on power, technology and domination* (pp. 196–229). London: Routledge.

Callon, M. (1991). Techno-economic networks and irreversibility. In J. Law (Ed.), *A sociology of monsters: Essays on power, technology and domination* (pp. 132–165). London: Routledge.

Castells, M. (1996). *The rise of the network society: The information age, economy, society and culture*. Oxford, MA: Blackwell Publishers.

Czerniewicz, L., Ravjee, N., & Mlitwa, N. (2005). Information and communication technologies (ICTs) and South African higher education: Mapping the landscape.

de Lange, P., Suwardy, T., & Mavondo, F. (2003). Integrating a virtual learning environment into an introductory accounting course: Determinants of student motivation. *Accounting Education*, *12*(1), 1–14. doi:10.1080/0963928032000064567

Feenberg, A. (2005). Critical theory of technology: An overview. *Tailoring Biotechnologies, 1* (1), 47-64. Retrieved from https://www.sfu.ca/~andrewf/books/critbio.pdf

Foucault, M. (1988). Technologies of the self: A seminar with Michel Foucault. In L. H. Martin, H. Gutman, & P. H. Hutton (Eds.), *Technologies of the self* (pp. 16–49). Amherst: University of Massachusetts Press.

Holt, D., & Challis, D. (2007). From policy to practice: One university's experience of implementing strategic change through wholly online teaching and learning. *Australasian Journal of Educational Technology*, *23*(1), 110–131.

Hydén, L., & Bülow, P. (2003). Who's talking: Drawing conclusions from focus groups – some methodological considerations. *International Journal of Social Research Methodology*, *6*(4), 305–321. doi:10.1080/13645570210124865

Jenkins, H. (2006). *Fans, bloggers and gamers: Exploring participatory culture*. New York: New York University Press.

Kamberelis, G., & Dimitriadis, G. (2008). Focus groups: Strategic articulations of pedagogy, politics, and inquiry. In N. K. Denzin & Y. S. Lincoln (Eds.), *Collecting and interpreting qualitative materials* (p. 396). New Delhi: Sage.

Kellner, D. (1998). Multiple literacies and critical pedagogy in a multicultural society. *Educational Theory*, *48*(1), 103–122. doi:10.1111/j.1741-5446.1998.00103.x

Krueger, R. A. (1994). *Focus groups: A practical guide for applied research*. Thousand Oaks, California: Sage.

Lamb, R., & Davidson, E. (2002, March 7-10). Social scientists: Managing identity in socio-technical networks. Paper presented at the Hawai'i International Conference on System Sciences. Big Island, Hawaii. doi:10.1109/HICSS.2002.994034

Latour, B. (2005). *Reassembling the social. An introduction to actor network theory*. New York: Oxford University Press.

Latour, B. (1987). *How to follow scientists and engineers through society*. Milton Keynes: Open University Press.

Latour, B. (1992). The sociology of a few mundane artefacts. In W. Bijker & J. Law (Eds.), *Shaping technology/building society studies in sociotechnical change*. Cambridge, MA: MIT Press.

Latour, B. (1999). *Pandora's hope: Essays on the reality of science studies*. Cambridge: Harvard University Press.

Law, J., & Mol, A. (2001). Situating technoscience: An inquiry into spatialities. *Environment and Planning. D, Society & Space*, *19*(5), 609–621. doi:10.1068/d243t

Miettinen, R. (1997, July). The concept of activity in the analysis of heterogeneous networks in innovation processes. Proceedings of the CSTT Workshop, Actor Network and After. University of Helsinki. Retrieved from http://communication.ucsd.edu/MCA/Paper/Reijo/Reijo.html

Mlitwa, N. (2005). Higher education and ICT in the information society: A case of UWC. 2nd Annual Conference of the Community Informatics Research Network (CIRN). 24-26 August, 2005, Cape Peninsula University of Technology (CPUT), South Africa.

Mlitwa, N. (2007). Technology for teaching and learning in higher education contexts: Activity theory and actor network theory analytical perspectives. *International Journal of Education and Development using Information and Communication Technology*, *3*(4), 54-70.

Morgan, D. L. (1988). *Focus groups as qualitative research*. Newbury Park, CA: Sage.

Muianga, X. (2004). Blended online and face-to-face learning – a pilot project in the faculty of education at the Eduardo Mondlane University, Mozambique. Emerge2004 Online Conference. South Africa: University of Cape Town; Retrieved from http://emerge2004.net/connect/site/UploadWSC/emerge2004/file19/emerge2004paperfinal.pdf

Rajkumar, S. (2005). *Activity theory*. Retrieved from www.slis.indiana.edu/faculty/yrogers/act_theory

Savard, I., Bourdeau, J., & Paquette, G. (2008). Cultural variables in the building of pedagogical scenarios. In E. Blanchard & D. Allard (Eds.), *Culturally aware tutoring systems* (pp. 83–94). Montreal, Canada: University of Montreal.

SØrensen. E. (2009). The materiality of learning. Cambridge, MA: Cambridge University Press.

Tinio, V. L. (2002). ICTs in Education. In e-Primers for the Information Economy, Society and Polity. Retrieved from http://www.eprimers.org/ict/index.asp

Tummons, J. (2009). Higher education in further education in England: An actor-network ethnography. *International Journal of Actor-Network Theory and Technological Innovation*, *1*(3), 55–69. doi:10.4018/jantti.2009070104

Toumi, I. (2001). Internet, innovation, and open source: Actors in the network. *First Monday*, *6*(1). Retrieved from http://firstmonday.org/issues/issue6_1/tuomi/index.html

Weaver, D., & Nair. (2008). Academic and student use of a learning management system: Implications for quality. *Australasian Journal of Educational Technology*, *24*(1), 30–41.

Wong, L., & Tatnall, A. (2009). The need to balance the blend: Online versus face-to-face teaching in an introductory accounting subject. [IISIT]. *Journal of Issues in Informing Science and Information Technology*, *6*(1), 309–322. Retrieved from http://iisit.org/Vol6/IISITv6p309-322Wong611.pdf

Wong, L. (2010). The e-learning experience - Its impact on student engagement and learning outcomes. Proceedings of *Business & Economics Society International Conference*. Bahamas.

Wong, L., & Tatnall, A. (2010). Factors determining the balance between online and face-to-face teaching: An analysis using actor-network theory. *Interdisciplinary Journal of Information, Knowledge, and Management*, *5*(1), 167-176. Retrieved from http://www.ijikm.org/Volume5/IJIKMv5p167-176Wong450.pdf

KEY TERMS AND DEFINITIONS

Immutable Mobility: Immutable mobile is a term coined by Latour (1986) and he used it to describe things that are easy to reproduce and transport without changing their inherent characteristics. Latour explains this term by drawing on the printing press. The printing press, for the first time, allowed ideas to move out of local and temporary places and spaces and spread across the world unlike the primal way of information dissemination that circulated within small territories. Besides, the printing press reproduced messages without distortion unlike face-to-face communication in which the message gets modified from person to person. We encounter immutable mobiles in internet technologies when the objects have the properties of being mobile (technologies and textual mobilities) but also immutable.

Dematerialized Digital Artefacts: Digitality of information and artefacts is the spinoff of the internet era. With digitalization, the authenticity and centrality of information is destabilized. A book is a material artifact and the material form of the book not only stands for the cultural meanings contained in it but also for the attendant material authority. Digital artefacts are stripped of such canonical laws as everyone participates in the creation of digital texts. In that sense, digitalization has led to increasing dematerialization of texts and information artefacts. Materiality of a digital artifact is an emergent property and is not inherent in the information or the device that contains it (*See Writing Machines by Katherine Hayles*). Materiality is therefore not a technological feature but what the user/reader does with both technology and information contained therein. Further, the meanings of information are derived from the users' interaction with both medium and content. The meaning making practices are therefore material and performative.

Technological Affordances: This term is used to refer to new technologies and what tasks users can possibly perform with technologies at their disposal. The term *technological affordance* was coined by Ian Hutchby as a reaction against social constructivism. He used it to describe the material constraints of a technology and their specific applications. For example, we perceive staircase in terms of what it facilitates – climbing floors – which constitutes its affordance(s). Similarly, Google Plus or Kindle has its own affordances; Kindle is used for reading books and cannot be used the way we use an iPad. Thus, affordances are linked to material-constraints of technologies in question.

Media Ecology: The inspiration for media ecology comes from Marshall McLuhan although it was introduced by Neil Postman in 1968. It is being used an optic to understand media environment that we live in today. According to Neil Postman, media ecology refers to the media environment human beings encounter. He explains that media ecology deals with the interaction between the technology and human beings as the interaction defines the culture and the existence of human kind in a media-saturated environment. Further, media ecology examines how media is affected by culture, language, technology in line with Latour's actor network theory. In the course of our interaction with media, it structures how and what we see, perceive and conduct ourselves. For instance, a research that explores how text messaging or Skype affects intimacy and love draws on media ecology.

Participatory Culture: Participatory culture is a broad-based term that subsumes a wide array of activities that users perform in the digital age. Henry Jenkins has contributed a lot to the popularity as well as for the uptake of participatory culture as a theoretical framework. Some of the activities users perform frequently such as Do IT Yourself mashing up of music to create identities, crowd sourcing, blogging, fan cultures, community organizing exemplify participatory cultures. Jenkins defines participatory culture as one which allows free expression of artistic talent and civic engagement sharing one's creations with others. In the process, everyone becomes a produser (producer and user). Users also establish social connection with others by sharing their creations. Participatory cultures are productive, creative and collaborative. For more, read *The Participatory Culture Handbook* edited by Aaron Delwiche and Jennifer Jacobs Handerson and also *Confronting the Challenges of Participatory Culture: Media Education for the 21st Century* by Henry Jenkins.

Performative Potential of Digital Technologies: Drawing on Judith Butler's performativity, Science and Technology Studies posits that the materiality of things as well as the man-machine interactions is produced in social performances. Science and Technology Studies (STS) offers a different ontology of performativity, which is neither overly discursive (as Butler argues) nor does it overemphasise materiality at the cost of discursive constructions. This outlook therefore commingles both human and non-human entities in socio-technical frameworks such as online learning environments that put together offline and online contexts besides bringing together learners and technologies. The non-human actant represents material conditions while human entities account for social action with utterances. Technological failures apart, human entities can also be held responsible for the failure or success of a performative action that a technology ought to be facilitating in combination with the social action to be performed by the learner or the teacher. The performative potential of online exams of several entrance tests held for higher education or for admission to higher institutions posit the necessity of social-technical agencies wrought by both students who take exams and institutions that conduct them, teachers who prepare the exam, technicians who control the system and facilitate the smooth conduct of online exams. The failure of the performative potential of the technologies in this context is due to the assembly of socio-technical agencies, that is human and non-human entities.

Collaborative Learning: Collaborative learning is an instruction method in which learners participate in small groups working towards achieving a common goal. The small groups work at various levels based on their performance and knowledge levels. The groups of learners supplement one another in their learning activity besides learning on their own. Such a shared learning practice gives learners an opportunity to participate in discussions.

Chapter 15
The Current State of Dialogue in South African Universities:
Change through Open Conversations and the Facilitating Role of ICTs

Kevin Allan Johnston
University of Cape Town, South Africa

Bane Nogemane
Standard Bank, South Africa

Salah Kabanda
University of Cape Town, South Africa

ABSTRACT

The current state of dialogue within certain South African universities was explored, and if and how dialogue can be used to address the issues of transformation and the lack of social cohesiveness. The role of Information and Communication Technologies (ICTs) in facilitating or inhibiting open conversations was examined. Through qualitative analysis of surveys administered to staff and students at universities, the researchers identified that power disparity, and the slow pace of transformation were prevalent and needed to be addressed. University management generally practice open conversations, and students and staff were willing to participate. Organisational structures were not conducive for open conversations. The ICT infrastructure used had no significant role to play, while Social Network Systems (SNSs) were perceived as enablers of open conversations. This chapter contributes to the existing body of knowledge about change management, and presents open conversations as a means of driving and realising organisational change.

DOI: 10.4018/978-1-4666-8598-7.ch015

SUMMARY

This chapter explored the current state of dialogue within certain South African universities, and if and how dialogue can be used to address the issues of transformation and the lack of social cohesiveness. South Africa has a history of segregation, antipathy and violence between racial groups. South African universities are currently receiving greater diversity among their students and staff in terms of racial, socioeconomic background, and gender. It is a moral and civic responsibility of universities to undergo transformation and redress socio-economic historical imbalances. However, transformation has been marred by the lack of institutional dialogue, and lack of openness. The role of ICTs in facilitating or inhibiting open conversations was examined.

The researchers identified that power disparity, and the slow pace of transformation were prevalent and needed to be addressed. University management generally practice open conversations, and students and staff were willing to participate. Organisational structures were not conducive for open conversations. The ICT infrastructure used had no significant role to play, while Social Network Systems (SNSs) were perceived as enablers of open conversations. The chapter contributes to the existing body of knowledge about change management, and presents open conversations as a means of driving and realising organisational change.

INTRODUCTION

South Africa is 'a society torn by a long history of antipathy and violence between groups' (Dixon et al 2010, 402). In the early nineties, racial segregation was officially disbanded to allow equal participation of Black people in public and economic life (Durrheim & Dixon, 2010). However, to undo centuries of segregation requires effort from all stakeholders involved, for example the government, people, and higher institutions of learning. Compared to previous years of segregation and unfair discrimination, South African higher institutions are currently receiving greater diversity among their students and staff in terms of racial, socioeconomic background, and gender. This diversification if not carefully monitored, has the potential of creating and fostering historical discrimination and inequality within higher learning institutions in South Africa. It is therefore a moral and civic responsibility of higher learning institutions to undergo transformation and redress socio-economic historical imbalances that are as a result of the apartheid government (Ramdass, 2009). However, transformation has been marred by the lack of institutional dialogue, lack of openness and inactivity of institutional forums (Lewins, 2010; Soudien et al., 2008). These inhibitors call for the need for communication – a dialogue process for people to engage on issues of transformation. Information and communication technologies (ICTs) have been associated with bridging communication gaps between people, and could therefore potentially be a tool for facilitating institutional dialogue, enhancing institutional forum activities and openness within higher education institutions. Bull and Brown (2012) posit ICTs as an ideal medium for this participation to occur, as ICTs can cut geographical and organisational boundaries, allowing more people to get involved. Traditionally conversations happen face to face or in meetings, but with the advent of technology, conversations can take place via ICT mediums such as email. As open conversations are inclusive in their nature and seek to encourage the participation of all individuals, ICTs have been put forward as the ideal means of facilitating such conversations (Bull & Brown, 2012; Byrne & Sahay, 2007; Yang & Li, 2012). If properly implemented and contextualized, ICTs can increase communication operational efficiency, quality, and transparency (Zimmermann & Finger, 2005).

The purpose of this chapter was to explore the current state of dialogue of university students and staff members over issues related to transformation (or lack thereof) within South African institutions of higher education. Particular emphasis was placed on the role of Information and Communication Technology (ICT) in facilitating or inhibiting open conversations at universities in South Africa.

The chapter is organised as follows: Section 1 provides the theoretical framework on which this chapter is based. Section 2 outlines the research methodology. The findings and the discussion of findings are presented in section 3, and then the chapter concludes.

1. RELATED WORK

The state of dialogue in South African universities refers to the level, extent and degree of participation to which university stakeholders and structures engage with one another through dialogue in order to overcome the issues of transformation and lack of social cohesion (Soudien et al., 2008). The reported state of dialogue in South African universities in 2008 was depicted by the following quote; "there seemed to be little or no internal dialogue between institutional constituents on issues of transformation. Of particular concern is the fact that institutional forums (IFs), which should be facilitating such dialogue, appear to have largely become inactive" (Soudien et al., 2008, p. 13). All South African universities have been legislated by Government to create Institutional Forums (IFs) (stakeholder forums) (Harper, Olivier, Thobakgale & Tshwete, 2002). The IF serves as an advisory body to the university councils, the highest decision making body. The Higher Education Act of 1997 (Section 31,2) specifies that there should be representatives from management, council, senate, academics, other staff, and students (Harper et al., 2002).

The importance of change in South African universities is that of creating an inclusive space with increased and broadened access for all (Akoojee & Nkomo, 2007; NCHE, 1997) . Organisations need to change so as to adapt and compete in hypercompetitive business environments (Biedenbach & Söderholm, 2008; Luftman, Zadeh, Derksen, Santana, Rigoni, & Huang, 2013). Organisational change in the context of this chapter refers to altering the beliefs, attitudes, and behaviours of university stakeholders in order to redress past inequalities and overcome discrimination of all forms in South African universities (NCHE, 1997). Much of the work in organizational change has been reported in literature (Beer & Eisenstat, 2011; Kerber and Buono 2007; Korte and Chermack 2007; Weick and Quinn 1999). Soudien et al. (2008) identified four content issues that required change: power disparity, transformation, discrimination and employment equity as shown in Figure 1. Soudien et al. (2008) indicated that in higher education, power disparity was exhibited by senior students who had considerable authority and power over their juniors and expected 'blind obedience' from them. Staff members questioned the power departments had in the appointments process as they felt that the final decision is at the hands of the Heads of School. In some universities, male authority and power was justified as traditional culture.

Soudien et al. (2008) suggested that all institutions had comprehensive policies in place to deal with transformation; however there was a disjunction between policy development and implementation. There were differing views on the progress and pace of transformation. Soudien et al. (2008) further indicated that discrimination was still prevalent, with racial discrimination constituting the main problem. Homophobia and discrimination based on gender and disability were pertinent in most universities. Given the changes in social and economic structure of South Africa post-apartheid, class discrimination was becoming more significant. Finally, Soudien et al. (2008)

Figure 1. Motivators for change: Aspects of transformation Soudien et al. (2008)

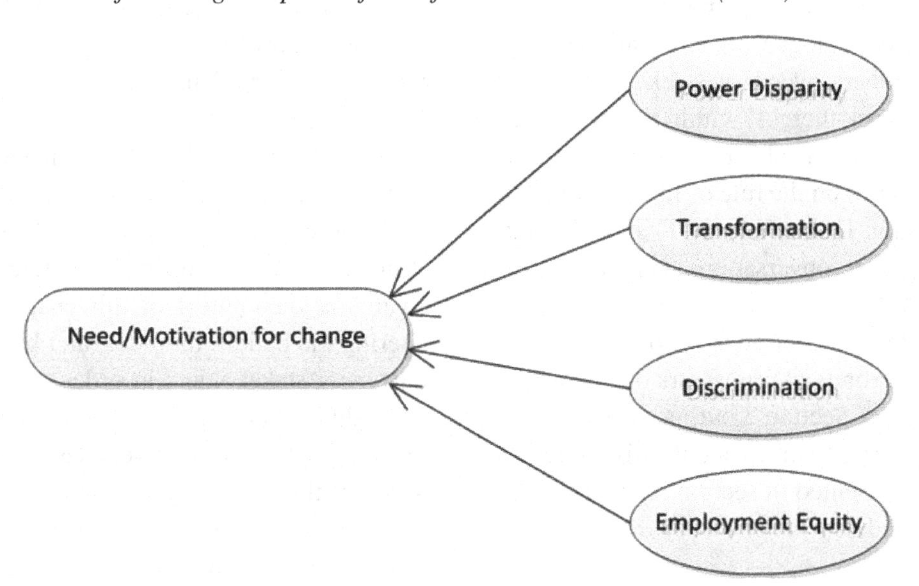

indicated a lack of understanding of the importance of employment equity. The key opinion held by university stakeholders on employment equity was that it's planning had 'become a compliance exercise with no focused discussions, leadership and direction on confronting the manner in which employment equity, particularly with regard to black South Africans is compromised by the traditional hierarchy of higher education institutions' (Soudien et al. 2008, p. 40). Soudien et al. (2008) attributed these challenges to the lack of internal dialogue between university stakeholders and the inactivity of institutional forums designated to openly discussing transformation issues through open conversations. As a starting point to making the change envisioned by transformation policies more realisable, Soudien et al. (2008) recommended remedying the current inactive state of dialogue in South African universities by encouraging participation and engagement through strengthening institutional forums and promoting open conversations. This led to the research question (RQ1) what is the current state of the factors that motivate the need for institutional change in South African universities? In attempting to answer this research question, this chapter seeks to bridge the gap in organisational change theory identified by Hempel and Martinsons (2009). The gap being the under-examined change content aspect of organisational change (Armenakis, 1999; Hempel & Martinsons, 2009).

A dialogue is a conversation between university stakeholders regarding issues related to transformation and social cohesion. Conversations in their nature can be either open or closed. An open conversation is more than just simple telling-listening situations, it entails interactive situations in which any person can freely ask open-ended questions without fear, where individuals are energized and inspired; where individuals listen attentively and learn from one another (Denning, 2010). Closed or private conversations are interactions that take place between only a few select individuals and are characterized by the reluctance and fear to openly discuss the same issues in a public forum, eventually leading to a culture of silence (Stacey, 2003).

Effective communication and cross-organisational dialogue between change stakeholders has been suggested as one of the factors in implementing and managing change successfully (Beer & Eisenstat, 2011; Sahadath, 2011). There are however dissenting views in organisational change literature, based on which level of the organisation the conversation on change needs to originate from. An authoritarian view suggests that change should be enacted by top management in order to be successful and sustainable (Beer & Eisenstat, 2011; Klein, 1996). Within this view, a line hierarchy is the most effective sanctioned channel for driving and managing change. Cameron and Caza (2004), Boyd and Bright (2007) however, called for the need to understand the processes, characteristics, and behaviours of exceptional or positively deviant organisations. The use of inclusive open conversations as a means of driving change is an example of this positive deviance which fosters dialog in the organisation through which individuals can reveal, analyse and share ideas, thus opening their minds to new possibilities (Korte and Chermack 2007).

Regardless of the view, the success of the change or failure thereof is influenced by management support, organisational structure and the culture (Armenakis, 1999; Fernandez & Rainey, 2006; Sahadath, 2011). Managers should be in support of change and transformation, they should not impede the dialogue process on transformation, but should strive to create an organisational structure and an overall environment that does not make it difficult to share views with people at different levels of the institution, hereby avoiding the patriarchy approach and a culture of silence (Soudien et al. 2008). These are possible if people are willing to engage and participate in the change process (Chermack et al., 2007; Intaganok et al., 2008; Kykyri, Puutio, & Wahlstrom, 2010). To achieve a deep organisational capacity for change, willingness to engage and assume responsibility for the change is required from the part of the recipients, implementers and leaders of the change (Kerber & Buono, 2007). This led to the research question (RQ2) what are the personal and organisational factors that shape and influence open conversations? In answering this question this research seeks to add to body of Positive Organisational Scholarship (POS) knowledge and also make recommendations on how or if open conversations are a viable means of driving managing organisational change. Cameron and Caza (2004), Boyd and Bright (2007) defined POS as the focus on understanding the processes, characteristics, and behaviours of exceptional or "positively deviant" organisations.

Information and communication technologies (ICTs) bracket a large number of technologies from hardware to software. For the purpose of this research, ICTs will entail, hardware devices and software applications primarily used for communication and that are easily accessible to university students and staff (e.g. Desktops, Mobile phones, Email, SMS, etc.) (Kennedy, Krause, Judd, Churchward, & Gray, 2008).

Traditionally conversations happen face to face, or in meetings but with the advent of technology, conversations can take place via ICT mediums such as email, chat rooms, SMSs (Bull & Brown, 2012; Byrne & Sahay, 2007; Yang & Li, 2012). Participatory design literature suggests the need for participation of marginalised people across different levels of an organisation in to develop and sustain positive change (Byrne & Sahay, 2007). Bull and Brown (2012) posit that ICTs can cut geographical and organisational boundaries allowing more people to get involved. Social networking sites (SNSs) have been touted as the ideal platforms for rich social engagement and conversation (Schinasi & Schultz, 2012). The power SNSs have to enable and facilitate change-driving conversations in the political sphere can see through the Arab spring. The Arab spring being the wave of protests in the Arab world in 2010 that forced from power the long-standing regimes of Egypt, Libya, Tunisia, and Yemen, where social networks such as twitter were used extensively to discuss and organize the protests (Khondker, 2011). The need to establish the effectiveness of ICTs in encouraging participation led to the research question (RQ3) what role does Information and Communication Technologies play in facilitating open conversations? The question in its answer seeks to answer the call to look at how and if ICTs can be used in the change process.

Figure 2. Research Framework for exploring the role ICTs play in open conversation

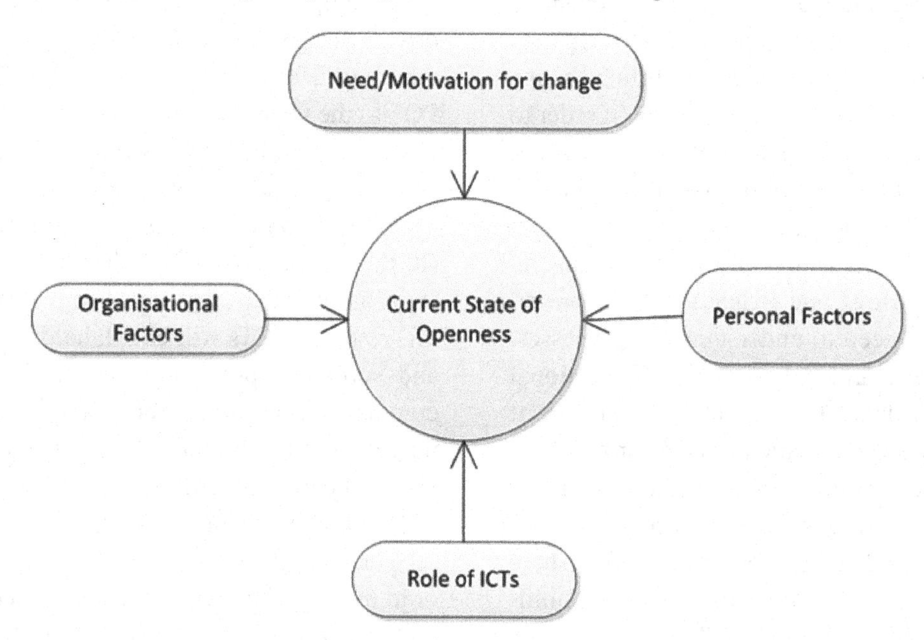

Figure 2 shows the research framework this chapter used to explore the role ICTs play in open conversation. To fulfil the research purpose of exploring and presenting a cross-sectional view of the current state of dialogue in South African universities; the state of the motivators that led to the impetus for change in 2008 will be assessed (RQ1), the organisational and personal factors that influence Open Conversations taking place in South African universities will be investigated (RQ2), And the perceived role of ICTs in facilitating Open Conversations will be investigated (RQ3).

2. RESEARCH METHODOLOGY

The research was quantitative in nature and conducted in an exploratory manner. Data were collected from two higher learning institutions situated in the Western Cape of South Africa. Access to the Universities was obtained through the National Education Health and Allied Workers Union (NEHAWU) that has branches in all 23 higher learning institutions in the country. NEHAWU was also ideal as it was the only union whose membership allowed for students, academic staff and non-academic staff. The survey was sent to NEHAWU shop stewards who then passed it on to their members, this sampling technique is known as chain sampling or snowballing, and ensures information-rich cases (Agerfalk & Fitzgerald, 2008).

The self-administered questionnaire was distributed via email to students and staff members over a 2-week period. As suggested by Presser et al., (2004) for this type of research, a majority of the questions were closed-ended, using five-point Likert scales or required yes or no answers. There were a few open-ended questions that sought to gauge participant's unguided insights/views. Keeping in line with (Soudien et al., 2008), the questions sought to understand people's views and opinions on issues relating to transformation, discrimination and social cohesion within higher education institutions. Prior to distribution, the questionnaire was pre-tested on two professors and five postgraduate students. This was done in order to improve instrument validity and to ensure maximum and valid responses to the survey.

Table 1. Change motivation questions

	Q9: Do you think there is inequality in the distribution of power in your University?	Q17: Do you think people at your University are discriminated against?	Q20: Are you happy with the pace of Transformation at your University?	Q22: Do you think employment equity (EE) is well implemented at your University?
Yes	47	33	30	35
	68.1%	47.8%	43.5%	50.7%
No	16	36	38	31
	23.2%	52.2%	55.0%	44.9%
Unsure	6	0	1	3
	8.70%	0.0%	1.5%	4.4%
Total	**69**	**69**	**69**	**69**
	100.0%	**100.0%**	**100.00%**	**100.00%**

The completed questionnaires were captured into an Excel spread sheet. Once all the questionnaires had been captured, a check was carried out to eliminate any invalid questions. The elimination of invalid questions was primarily based on whether respondents answered key questions in the questionnaire. After being cleaned and freed of errors, the data was analysed via a statistical computer program, SPSS. The Statistical Package for Social Sciences (SPSS) was a useful tool for analysing questionnaires due to its flexibility and ease of use.

3. FINDINGS AND DISCUSSION

In total 72 students and staff members, respondent to the survey, 3 surveys were incomplete and invalid and were not used, which brought the total number of respondents to 69. Ninety percent of staff and student respondents were from two Universities (UCT and CPUT), with 81% being staff members.

3.1 RQ1. Current State of the Factors That Motivate the Need for Institutional Change in South African Universities

The results of the influencing factors represented in Table 1, highlight the key findings for the motivation for change of the investigation.

On the question of power disparity, 68.1% of respondents thought that there is inequality in the distribution of power, 23.2% thought there wasn't any disparity in power and 8.7% were unsure. The finding that the majority of the respondents thought that there is unequal power distribution is similar to that of Soudien et al. (2008) where senior students expected 'blind obedience' from their juniors, along other forms of noted disparity in power. This similarity could be because of other factors such racial discrimination taking precedence and are paid more attention to and thus the power disparities at universities still persist.

On the issue of discrimination within universities; 47.8% of the respondents believed that people were discriminated against. On the contrary, 52.2% of the respondents believed there was no discrimination happening in their universities. Soudien et al. (2008) stated that the volume of complaints regarding discrimination was too significant to ignore. As per findings of this research where 52.2% of the respondents believed there was no discrimination, no conclusive comparison can be made as Soudien et al. (2008) did not quantify the volume of complaints.

When asked about the pace of transformation, 43.5% of the respondents were happy with the pace of transformation, 55% were not happy, and 1.5% respondents were unsure. The second part of the question on transformation was whether the respondents thought the pace of transformation should be increased or decreased. The majority (87%) of the respondents felt that the pace of transformation should be increased, while 10% thought the pace should decrease, and 3% were unsure of whether it should decrease or increase. The near-even split between respondents who were happy with the pace of transformation and those who weren't, shows that there are still differing views on the progress of transformation as found by Soudien et al. (2008). The persistence of these differing views, points to the pervasiveness of the transformation process. There was an unexpected consensus on the increasing pace of transformation, which was found to be 87%. The implications of this finding could mean that university stakeholders are becoming more accepting of the transformation process albeit not completely happy about it.

When asked about how well employment equity was implemented, 50.7% thought that employment equity was well implemented, while 44.9% thought it wasn't, and 4.4% of the respondents were unsure. The even split of 50.7% to 44.9% marks a difference from the findings made by Soudien et al. (2008). Soudien et al. (2008) found that key opinion held was that employment equity was not well implemented planning lacked. This difference could be attributed to improved understanding of the importance of employment equity in the last four years.

Based on the findings of this chapter, the respondents' views on whether employment equity was well implemented or not, were evenly split. The split however still marked an improvement from the state employment equity was in four years ago. There was a similar split in opinions on whether there was discrimination or not. There was a consensus on power disparity being still a key issue that needed to be overcome. There was also a consensus on the need for the pace of transformation to increase.

3.2 RQ2. Personal and Organisational Factors That Shape and Influence Open Conversations

The motivation for institutional change in South African universities is driven by the need to address the issues of; power disparity, transformation, discrimination, and employment equity. The majority of respondents (68%) were of the opinion that there is inequality in the distribution of power. The lack of equity in higher education has always been debated (Amsler 2013; Bowman 2010, Hey & Morley 2011), and this is a concern especially in South Africa where higher education institutions are becoming increasingly diverse in terms of students and staff racial groupings. The possible reason could be the belief from 62% of the respondents that the organisational structures and culture did not facilitate open conversations. This lack of open conversations resulted in a substantial number of people (48%) feeling discriminated against, and the majority (55%) not being happy with the pace of transformation despite having a significant number of respondents (67%) believing that management supported or practiced open conversations. These findings are similar to those of Soudien et al. (2008), who stated that the volume of complaints regarding discrimination was too significant to ignore, and organisation structures of universities are disengaging. Although the number of respondents who felt discriminated against was 48%, this could be a distorted reality because personal experiences of discrimination may distort perceptions of group discrimination by creating a false consensus effect (Dixon et al 2010). The perception that transformation change was slow called for improvements from the majority (87%) of respondents. Respondents also called for a thorough implementation of the employment equity act to ensure equality.

A significant number of respondents (75%) showed willingness to participate in open conversations. Their willingness was attributed to the possibilities that open conversations could be an avenue for sharing new ideas and gaining new perspectives on issues of transformation as a respondent indicated,

It is a forum to air what needs to be said and where preconceived judgements and stereotypes can be broken. If open conversations are not done, it leaves room for assumptions which lead to beliefs that may harm the society at large. It helps to clarify grey areas in a subject matter.

A second respondent agreed stating that open conversations

... will always lead to enrichment of knowledge, as it enhances the positive dialogue amongst students. It gives checks and balances to the authorities, thereby improving the academic environment.

The remaining (25%) were unwilling to participate in open conversations; they were of the opinion that it was not useful and a waste of time.

Although the majority of respondents were willing to participate in open conversations, the findings showed low levels of awareness regarding open meetings. For example, the majority (74%) of respondents were aware of any open meetings taking place, while 13% of the respondents were aware of 6 to 20 open meetings taking place, and 13% of the respondents were aware of 21 or more open meetings taking place, Furthermore, attendance at these meetings was low, with 90% of respondents attending between 0 to 5 open meetings with the purpose of '*finding out what is going on on Campus. Sometimes when you are on campus you are in a bubble. If you do things out your norm then you get informed*'. Eight percent of respondents attended 6 to 20 open meetings, and only 3% of the respondents had attended 21 or more open meetings. Closed meetings were also attended, with 59% of respondents having attended between 0 to 5 closed meetings, while 28% of the respondents had 6 to 20 closed meetings (conversations), and 13% had taken part in 21 or more closed meetings. The topic discussed most frequently in both meetings was academic fees (see Figure 3). Admissions were the second most discussed topic in closed meetings, while transformation was the second most discussed topic in the open meetings. The topic discussed the least in both meetings was employment equity. The reason behind the findings is most likely the demographics of the respondents being composed of more students than staff. Transformation and admissions issues are discussed more in open meetings than in closed meetings, while the frequency with which accommodation was discussed is the same in both meetings. The findings show that the willingness therefore exists, but there is lack of awareness of meetings that would facilitate the transformation process. Organisational members need to encouraged to participate in meetings where positive interracial contacts with other people is possible – a process that could lead to positive outcomes of transformation and a sense of eliminating the perception of living in a society characterized by racial discrimination and socio-economic injustice (Dixon et al, 2010). Since such meetings can act as one of the most influential interventions for prejudice reduction (Tadmor et al 2012), participants need to be encouraged to attend and be informed that the power to implement change is in their hands, as the people who seek to benefit from such transformational change (Durrheim & Dixon 2010). Therefore there is a need for strong leadership to strengthen institutional forums that facilitate open dialogue that will enable transformation.

3.3 RQ3. Role of ICTs in facilitating Open Conversations

The majority of respondents had access to software (68%) and hardware (59%) outside university. The fact that some of the respondent's did not have access to software and hardware outside university, could be a potential problem that might reflect

Figure 3. Topics discussed at Open Meetings vs. topics discussed in closed conversations

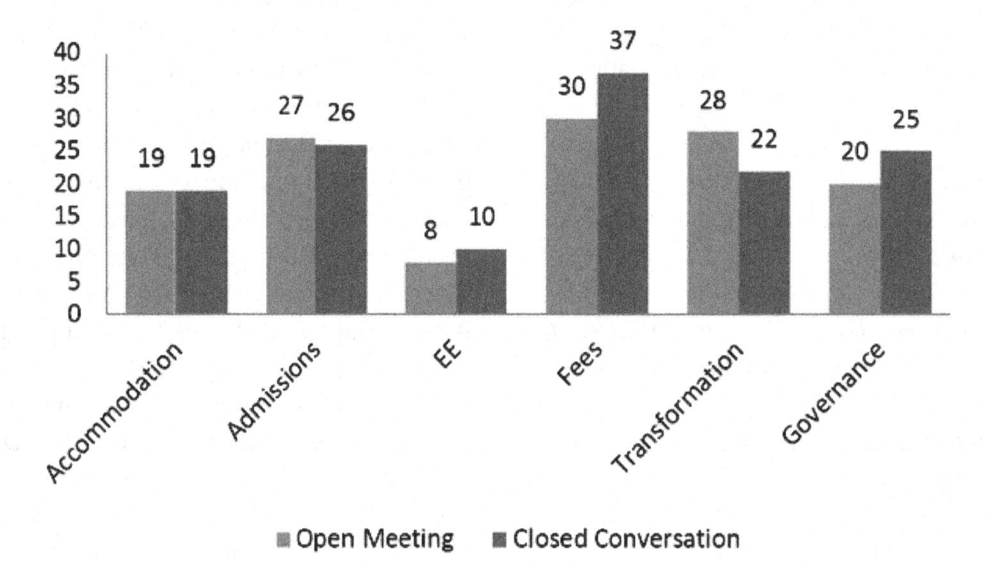

and even enlarge existing social inequalities, just as the lack of Internet access creates existing social inequalities (Mesch & Talmud, 2011). The primary software application used for conversations was Email (61%), followed by SMS which was used by 18% of the respondents (Figure 4). Conferencing was the least used software medium with the blogs and other media coming higher than conferencing in terms of use. The majority (63%) of respondents rated themselves as being skilled with the software used for conversations. Desktops are the most used hardware devices (42%), followed by laptops and mobile phones with 25% usage each. Tablets being relatively new and expensive their usage was expectedly low at 7%. A significant number of respondent's (94%) found the ICT devices easy to use.

Few (33%) respondents indicated that it was not difficult to share views with the whole organisation. This is a very low response given the need to promote and create means of supporting transformation through dialogues. Twenty-nine

Figure 4. Software applications and devices used for conversations at University

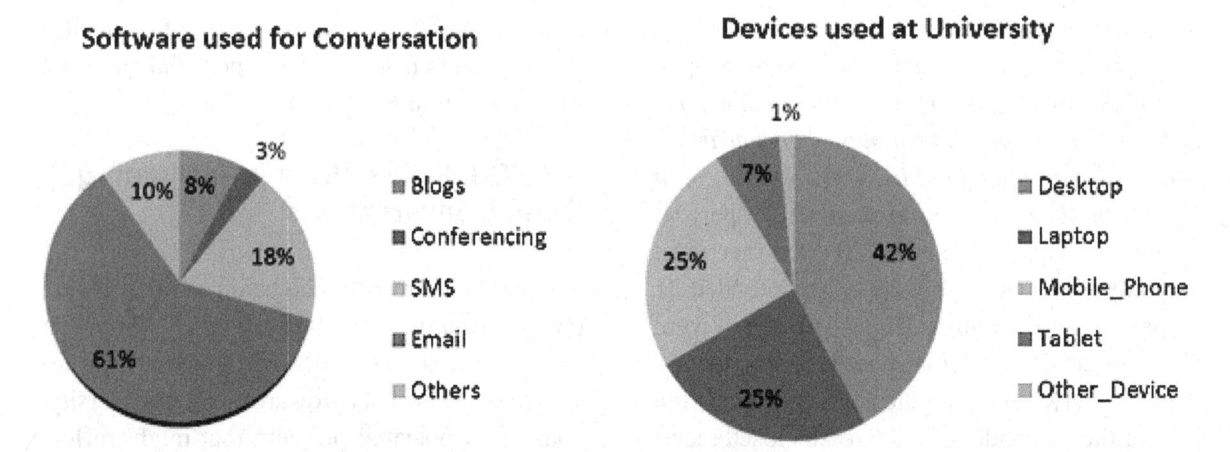

percent of respondents found it difficult to share their views, and the remaining 38% were unsure on the easiness of sharing views with the whole organisation. Part of the reason could be attributed to the organisation's ICT infrastructure being perceived as not being supportive of sharing views and experiences with the whole organisation. For example, 49% were of the opinion that their universities ICT infrastructure does not support open conversations. Despite these findings, a significant number (93%) of respondents conceived that social network systems (SNSs) such as Facebook were a possible means of facilitating open conversations at their respective universities and therefore an agent of social change. This is backed up by research which states that SNSs provide novel ways of communication between people, and can strengthen conversations and relationships (Johnston, Kawalsky, Lalla & Tanner, 2013). SNSs were perceived to be a tool that could create awareness about meetings taking place on campus and ultimately create a path towards transformation. Currently however, SNS were not used for such purposes because of a '*lack of a dialogue culture between ourselves. We tend to dialogue with others outside the circle of work*'. With SNSs, participants are able to not only participate in dialogues related with work (professional relationships); but also may help participants to know each other better as persons, that is in addition to professional relationships (Zhao and Rosson 2009).

CONCLUSION

The purpose of this chapter was to explore the current state of dialogue within South African universities. The findings indicate that higher institutions are still faced with challenges necessary for transformation. Specifically, there is unequal power distribution at higher institutions which results in the presence of racial discrimination. There was an average perception on the increasing pace of transformation, an indication that stakeholders of higher institutions of learning are becoming more accepting of the transformation process. However, this pace was also seen as being too slow given the changing institutional climate. For example, transformation challenges such as employment equity were not thoroughly implemented. Partly because of the lack of strong management support for such initiatives, especially efforts aiming at establishing open conversations; and also the lack of an organisational structures that are conducive for open conversations. This is in spite of the willingness of institutional stakeholders (staff and students) to take part in open conversations. The willingness therefore exists but there is lack of awareness of meetings that would facilitate the transformation process. Therefore there is a need for strong leadership to strengthen institutional forums that facilitate open dialogue that will enable transformation. ICT has been used as a tool to enhance open conversations. Its role however is not seen as pivotal to the facilitation of transformation through open conversations. Through this chapter, social networks sites are perceived as an avenue that can enable and facilitate open conversations at universities.

REFERENCES

Akoojee, S., & Nkomo, M. (2007). Access and quality in South African higher education: The twin challenges of transformation. *South African Journal of Higher Education*, *21*(3), 385–399.

Amsler, S. (2013). The politics of privatisation: insights from the Central Asian university. In Educators, Professionalism and Politics: Global Transitions, National Spaces and Professional Projects. NY and London: Routledge, 2012.

Armenakis, A. A. (1999). Organizational Change: A Review of Theory and Research in the 1990s. *Journal of Management*, *25*(3), 293–315. doi:10.1177/014920639902500303

Beer, M., & Eisenstat, R. A. (2011). How to have an honest conversation about your business strategy. *Harvard Business Review*, *82*(2), 82–89. PMID:14971272

Biedenbach, T., & Söderholm, A. (2008). The challenge of organizing change in hypercompetitive industries: A literature review. *Journal of Change Management*, *8*(2), 123–145. doi:10.1080/14697010801953967

Bowman, N. A. (2010). College Diversity Experiences and Cognitive Development: A Meta-Analysis. *Review of Educational Research*, *80*(1), 4–33. doi:10.3102/0034654309352495

Boyd, N. M., & Bright, D. S. (2007). Appreciative Inquiry as a Mode Action Research for Community Psychology. *Journal of Community Psychology*, *35*(8), 1019–1036. doi:10.1002/jcop.20208

Bull, M., & Brown, T. (2012). Alternative workplace strategies Change communication : The impact on satisfaction with alternative workplace strategies. *Facilities*, *30*(3), 135–151. doi:10.1108/02632771211202842

Byrne, E., & Sahay, S. (2007). Participatory Design for Social Development: A South African Case Study on Community-Based Health Information Systems. *Information Technology for Development*, *13*(1), 71–94. doi:10.1002/itdj.20052

Cameron, K. S., & Caza, A. (2004). Contributions to the Discipline of Positive Organizational Scholarship. *The American Behavioral Scientist*, *47*(6), 731–739. doi:10.1177/0002764203260207

Chermack, T. J., van der Merwe, L., & Lynham, S. A. (2007). Exploring the relationship between scenario planning and perceptions of strategic conversation quality. *Technological Forecasting and Social Change*, *74*(3), 379–390. doi:10.1016/j.techfore.2006.03.004

Denning, S. (2010). *The leader's guide to radical management: Re-inventing the workplace for the 21st century*. San Francisco: Jossey-Bass.

Dixon, J., Durrheim, K., Tredoux, C., Tropp, L., Clack, B., & Eaton, L. (2010). A paradox of integration? Interracial contact, prejudice reduction, and perceptions of racial discrimination. *The Journal of Social Issues*, *66*(2), 401–416. doi:10.1111/j.1540-4560.2010.01652.x

Durrheim, K., & Dixon, J. (2010). Racial contact and change in South Africa. *The Journal of Social Issues*, *66*(2), 273–288. doi:10.1111/j.1540-4560.2010.01645.x

Fernandez, S., & Rainey, H. G. (2006). Managing successful organizational change in the public sector. *Public Administration Review*, *66*(2), 168–176. doi:10.1111/j.1540-6210.2006.00570.x

Harper, A., Olivier, N., Thobakgale, S., & Tshwete, Z. (2002). *Institutional Forums*. Sunnyside, South Africa: Centre for Higher Education Transformation.

Hempel, P. S., & Martinsons, M. G. (2009). Developing international organizational change theory using cases from China. *Human Relations*, *62*(4), 459–499. doi:10.1177/0018726708101980

Hey, V., & Morley, L. (2011). Imagining the university of the future: Eyes wide open? Expanding the imaginary through critical and feminist ruminations in and on the university, Contemporary Social Science. *Journal of the Academy of Social Sciences*, *6*(2), 165–174.

Intaganok, P., Waterworth, P., Andsavachulamanee, T., Grasaresom, G., & Homkome, U. (2008). Attitudes of staff to information and communication technologies. *The Electronic Journal on Information Systems in Developing Countries*, *33*(3), 1–14.

Johnston, K. A., Kawalsky, D., Lalla, N., & Tanner, M. (2013). Social Capital: The Benefits of Facebook "Friends". *Behaviour & Information Technology*, *32*(1), 24–36. doi:10.1080/0144929X.2010.550063

Kennedy, G., Krause, K.-L., Judd, T., Churchward, A., & Gray, K. (2008). First Year Students' Experiences with Technology: Are they really Digital Natives. *Australasian Journal of Educational Technology*, *24*(1), 108–122.

Kerber, K. W., & Buono, A. F. (2007). Enhancing Change Capacity. Client-Consultant Collaboration. *SYMPHONYA Emerging Issues in Management*, *n*(1), 81-96.

Khondker, H. H. (2011). Role of the New Media in the Arab Spring Role of the New Media in the Arab Spring. *Globalizations*, *8*(5), 37–41. doi:10.1080/14747731.2011.621287

Klein, S. M. (1996). A management communication strategy for change. *Journal of Organizational Change Management*, *9*(2), 32–46. doi:10.1108/09534819610113720

Korte, R. F., & Chermack, T. J. (2007). Changing organizational culture with scenario planning. *Futures*, *39*(6), 645–656. doi:10.1016/j.futures.2006.11.001

Kykyri, V., Puutio, R., & Wahlstrom, J. (2010). Inviting Participation in Organisational Change through Ownership Talk. *The Journal of Applied Behavioral Science*, *46*(1), 92–118. doi:10.1177/0021886309357441

Lewins, K. (2010). The Trauma of Transformation: A Closer Look at the Soudien Report. *South African Review of Sociology*, *41*(1), 127–136. doi:10.1080/21528581003676077

Luftman, J., Zadeh, H. S., Derksen, B., Santana, M., Rigoni, E. H., & Huang, Z. D. (2013). Key information technology and management issues 2012–2013: An international study. *Journal of Information Technology*, *28*(4), 354–366. doi:10.1057/jit.2013.22

Mesch, G. S., & Talmud, I. (2011). Ethnic differences in internet access: The role of occupation and exposure. *Information Communication and Society*, *14*(4), 445–471. doi:10.1080/1369118X.2011.562218

NCHE. (1997). Education White Paper 3- A Programme for Higher Education Transformation. Retrieved from http://www.info.gov.za/view/DownloadFileAction?id=70435

Presser, S., Couper, M. P., Lessler, J. T., Martin, E., Rothgeb, J. M., Bureau, U. S. C., & Singer, E. (2004). Methods for Testing and Evaluating Survey Questions. *Public Opinion Quarterly*, *68*(1), 109–130. doi:10.1093/poq/nfh008

Ramdass, K. (2009). The challenges facing education in South Africa. Proceedings of *Educational and Development Conference* (pp. 111 – 130). Thailand. Tomorrow People Organisation.

Sahadath, K. C. (2011). Leading Change One Conversation at a Time. *ACMP Global Conference* (pp. 1 – 10). Orlando, Florida.

Schinasi, K., & Schultz, I. (2012). Paying Attention to Society and Culture. In B. V. Ark (Ed.), The Linked World: Executive Editor Bart van Ark (pp. 118 – 134).

Soudien, C. W., Michaels, S., Mthembi-Mahanyele, M., Nkomo, G., Nyanda, N., Nyoka, S., et al. (2008). *Report of the ministerial committee on transformation and social cohesion and the elimination of discrimination in public higher education institutions*. Department of Education, Republic of South Africa. Retrieved from http://www.vut.ac.za/new/index.php/docman/doc_view/90-ministerialreportontransformationandsocialcohesion?tmpl=component&format=raw

Stacey, R. (2003). Learning as an activity of interdependent people. *The Learning Organization*, *10*(6), 325–331. doi:10.1108/09696470310497159

Tadmor, C. T., Hong, Y. Y., Chao, M. M., Wiruchnipawan, F., & Wang, W. (2012). Multicultural experiences reduce intergroup bias through epistemic unfreezing. *Journal of Personality and Social Psychology*, *103*(5), 750–772. doi:10.1037/a0029719 PMID:22905769

Weick, K. E., & Quinn, R. E. (1999). Organizational Change and Development. *Annual Review of Psychology*, *50*(1), 361–386. doi:10.1146/annurev.psych.50.1.361 PMID:15012461

Yang, S., & Li, J. (2012). The Use of ICT Products and "White- Collarization" of White-Collar Workers: An Everyday-Life Perspective. In P. Law (Ed.), *New Connectivities in China* (pp. 159–169). Springer Netherlands. doi:10.1007/978-94-007-3910-9_13

Zhao, D., & Rosson, M. B. (2009, May). How and why people Twitter: the role that micro-blogging plays in informal communication at work. In *Proceedings of the ACM 2009 international conference on supporting group work* (pp. 243 - 252). ACM. doi:10.1145/1531674.1531710

Zimmermann, P., & Finger, M. (2005). Information- and Communication Technology (ICT) and Local Power Relationships : An Impact Assessment. *The Electronic. Journal of E-Government*, *3*(4), 231–240.

KEY TERMS AND DEFINITIONS

Dialogue: A conversation between university stakeholders regarding issues related to transformation and social cohesion.

Facilitating Role: A role which makes a process or path possible or easier.

ICT: Information and Communications Technology (ICT), includes computer hardware, software, and networking technology.

Open Conversations: Entail interactive situations in which any person can freely ask open-ended questions without fear, where individuals are energized and inspired; where individuals listen attentively and learn from one another.

Organisational Change: Refers to altering the beliefs, attitudes, and behaviours of university stakeholders in order to redress past inequalities and overcome discrimination of all forms in South African universities.

South African Universities: South African Universities were restructured after the fall of Apartheid to widen access and reset the priorities of the old apartheid-based system.

Transformation: The processes to redress socio-economic historical imbalances that are as a result of the apartheid government in South Africa.

Chapter 16
Mobile Phone Revolution and its Dimensional Social and Economic Impacts in Nigeria's Context

Okanlade Adesokan Lawal-Adebowale
Federal University of Agriculture, Nigeria

ABSTRACT

The emergence of mobile phone telecommunication in the last thirteen years in Nigeria has greatly revolutionized the dynamics of information exchange and usage by group of individuals in the country. Unlike the past years before 2001 whereby physical contacts and/or letter writing were the major means of interaction between individuals that are farther apart on geospatial dimension, spatial interaction is now the order of the day as a result of institutionalisation of the mobile telephony services in the country. By virtue of the telecom sector deregulation in 2001 and competition for dominance by the four major mobile phone network providers in the country, namely Airtel, MTN, Globacom and Etisalat, as much as 162, 719, 517 lines were actively connected in the country with a teledensity of 94.4 as at July 2014. Based on this, exploitation of the communication tools by Nigerian has effected a transformed social and economic condition of the country in terms of attraction of investors into the telecom sector, generation of income for the Nigerian Government, creation of employment opportunities, ease of business and financial transactions as economic impacts. The social impacts of the mobile phone revolution in the country include facilitation of prompt interactive linkages and exchange of information, entertainment and social networking. Other forms of impacts include its influence on educational and health services in the country. Despite the transformation impact of the mobile phone revolution in the country, exploitation of the communication tool for social vices by unscrupulous individuals was too obvious to be underplayed. The negative impacts arising from nefarious acts-mediated mobile phone usage include loss of hard earned income by unsuspecting individuals to swindlers, road accidents as a result of usage of phone while on the wheel and provision of deceptive information by one person to the other while on phone. This notwithstanding, the telecom sector has proven to be of great value to most Nigerian's as it enabled them to readily interact with one another, facilitate business and financial transactions thereby enhancing their social and economic wellbeing.

DOI: 10.4018/978-1-4666-8598-7.ch016

INTRODUCTION

The need to forge effective and interactive communication between two or more individuals, especially over space, engendered the need for development and integration of electronic communication tool(s) in human communication interface. Consequently, the turn of the 21st century witnessed the upsurge of telephony and internet-based communication tools in human's social and economic interaction on a global scale. This is reflected in the growth of connected telephony lines, either as fixed or mobile lines, from about1.4billion in 1999 to nearly 7billion lines in 2014 (Isiguzo, 2010; ITU, 2014). Such increment is brought about by the advancement of the information-driven technology from the traditional fixed line communication tools, such as wired telephones, fax and telex, and even postal services, to a more robust mobile communication tools, such as mobile phones and internet-based information communication applications such as electronic mail (e-mail) and social media (Facebook, Whatsapp, 2go, LinkedIn, Twitter, etc.). Given the convergence of these information-driven tools in a simple and single device as smart phones, the telephony device has not only serves as tool of communication, but of facilitation of socioeconomic development and transformation of human society. The dexterity with which the mobile communication device functions and its dynamic of applications to meet and satisfy various human needs engendered the information-driven technology as a tool for accelerated development of national and global economies (Isiguzo, 2010). In the same vein, the World Bank (2006) and the World Economic Forum (2005 – 2006) emphasise that economic development of a nation largely depends on overall development of the country's telecommunication sector. This is based on the fact that sectors with the integration of information and communication technology (ICT) in their operational functions are more productive and profitable than those not making use of the communication driven-technology.

In view of the growing trend of ICT development, particularly the telephony component, and the successful outcome of its integration in all spheres of human's life informed the need for the Nigerian government to revolutionise the countries telecommunication sector between 1990 and 2000 through Government enacted privatisation policy of the telecommunication sector. The privatisation action, under the affairs of the Nigerian Communication Commission (NCC) brought about the emergence of private investors in the telecommunication sector and eventual widespread availability of mobile telephony services in the country (Lawal-Adebowale, 2010). The observed widespread of mobile phone in the country is facilitated by nationwide penetration of the mobile telephony network services put in place by the telecom investors, namely MTN Nigeria, Airtel, Globacom and Etisalat, in the country. Supporting these service providers are the fixed/wireless and CDMA (Code Division Multiple Access) network providers among which are Multilinks, Starcomms and Visafone. With the dexterity of mobile communications, the network services providers did not limit their services to voice communication, which of course was the initial primary function, but have had it advanced to internet service provision, video calls, graphics text messages and mobile television thus creating the platform for dynamic usage of the telephony applications and services in the country.

In view of this, field observation shows that mobile phones and its integrated applications had been extensively utilised in various ways and for different purposes. As indicated by Isiguzo (2010), mobile phones had been extensively applied by Nigerians in their daily and essential social and economic endeavours, among which are information communication, entertainment, shopping, education, banking and medicare. With mobile phone applications creating enabling environment for interaction and bringing a wide variety of services to most Nigerians, Pyramid Research

(2010) indicated that mobile communication services have had greater impact on the citizenry. In view of this, and with nearly one and a half decade of mobile telephony service delivery and usage in Nigeria (2001 – 2014), it becomes essential to evaluate the extent and dimension impacts of mobile phone usage in the country.

Methodological Approach

Development of this paper was based on collection of telecom-based documentations, both in print and virtual, from Government and private-based telecommunication agencies for extensive critical analysis of the documented data and information on the impact of mobile phone service delivery and usage in Nigeria. The Government agencies include NCC, National Information Technology Development Agency (NITDA), National Bureau of statistics (NBS), and the private bodies include Pyramid Research, Mobility Nigeria, BuddeCom. In addition to this, was conscious monitoring of the trends of the impact of mobile phone applications on Nigerians in the context of accessibility, affordability, connectivity, social interactions, entertainment and economic impact – in terms of employment, income generation and facilitation of business transaction, for empirical presentation in this research output. Furthermore, field observation of telecom-based events and reports in the media and interactive discussion with mobile phone users, vendors and marketers were harnessed for logical presentation of thought in the write up.

This methodological approach, inferred from combination of qualitative and secondary analysis research approach (Levin and Fox, 2000; Babbie, 2005), was found appropriate as it afforded the research work to depend on secondary data from relevant agencies and personal observation and monitoring of field events for analysis and empirical presentation of thought. In view of this, the research report is presented in the order of historical trend of telecommunication development in Nigeria, telecom sector deregulation and policy implications in Nigeria, mobile phone revolution in Nigeria, mobile phone usage in Nigeria, trend of mobile phone growth in Nigeria and the global perspective, and the social and economic impact of mobile phone usage in Nigeria.

Historical Trend of Telecommunication Development in Nigeria

The history of telecommunication development in Nigeria dated back to 1886 with the laying of first telegraphic submarine cable by a British firm – Cable and Wireless Limited, through which London was connected with Lagos, under the British imperial administration (Ndukwe, 2003a; Nigeriafirst, 2003). Usage of telephony communication however began in 1893 following the provision and connection of government offices in Lagos with telephone lines, though purposely for effecting administrative communication and functions (National Policy on Telecommunications – NTP, 2000). Notwithstanding the streamline purpose of telecommunication by the imperial government, the installed cable connections paved way for a number of regions and cities to be connected for electronic communication in the country (Longe & Longe, n.d.; Ajayi, Salawu & Raji, n.d.). This provision continued till the country's independent in 1960. By then, Nigeria had less than 100, 000 telephone lines in place for a population of about 40million inhabitants (Ige, n.d.) thereby making telephony accessibility and usage limited to government officials and other technocrats in the country.

Thereof the independence, the operation, and management of telephony services was solely under the administration of the Federal Government Nigeria (FGN), and an attempt to ensure the provision of functional, accessible and affordable telephony services for use by Nigerians in general led to the establishment of the Departments of Posts and Telecommunications (P&T) under the

Ministry of Communication in 1960 (Mawoli, 2009). By 1962, the FGN, in conjunction with the British firm launched the Nigerian External Telecommunications (NET) Limited (Ndukwe, 2003a). While the P&T assumed responsibility for provision and management of internal telecommunication services, NET took responsibility for the operation and administration of the external telecommunication services (Usoro, 2007; Mawoli, 2009). With these two departments of communication in place, the country was able to install a number of microwave radio transmission systems by which cities such as Lagos, Ibadan, Benin, Enugu and Port Harcourt were connected within the first decade of independent. Despite the observed city to city connectivity, the communication outfit could only provide about 18,724 functional telephony lines, against the expected 60,000 lines for use of an estimated population of about 40 million, with a resultant teledensity of 0.5 or 0.5 telephone lines per 1000 people (NTP, 2000; Lawal-Adebowale, 2010). An attempt to improve the telecommunication services in the country led to the reformation of the P&T and the NET communication Departments thereby leading to emergence of the Nigerian Telecommunication Limited (NITEL) in 1985 as the new telecommunication outfit in the country.

A decade and an a half (between 1985 and 2001) of NITEL's operation in the country could not in any way salvage the problem of telephony accessibility and usage by the general populace as it could only provide about 400, 000 lines for about 120 million Nigerians with a resultant teledensity of 0.49 (Federal Ministry of Information and National Orientation – FMINO, n.d.). The available lines, as it were under the imperial government, were mainly concentrated in the urban areas and in the hands few individuals, most of whom were top government officials, captains of industries and affluent members of the society. With this category of users and attraction of operating subsidies of over N30million between 1975 and 1999, the FMINO (n.d.) describes Nigeria as the country with most expensive telephone network and one of the lowest telephone density rates in the world. With this situation, telephony accessibility and usage was highly expensive and extremely difficult for common man or average income earners in the country to acquire; and those who could then afford the telephony service may have to wait for months, or years in some cases, before they could obtain telephone line(s). In addition, the quality of service was very poor – as telephone lines may remain dead for weeks and/or months with no timely remedy from any quarters. At the same time subscribers were made to pay bills of telephone service they never used or never used to satisfaction as a result of poor operational telephony services in the country by NITEL (Alabi, 1996; FMINO, n.d.; Lawal-Adebowle, 2010). As indicated by Ndukwe (2003b); Mawoli, (2009), NITEL had no remarkable improvement in its performance between 1987 and 1992 as consumers' demands were largely unmet.

Consequently, prompt information exchange between two or more individuals had no place in the then Nigeria as the general populace had to rely on postal service for postage of written letters as means of communication within and outside the country. With postage letters taking days or months for information to reach the intended receiver and for feedback to get to the written communication initiator, it implies that information flow in the then Nigeria was not just foot dragging or disparagingly slow, but time-wise expensive and less supportive of human social and economic development. This situation equally put the nation's economy at bay with little or no prowess for entrepreneurship and investment drives, and information management for livelihood development of Nigerians. According to Ndukwe (2003a), private investment in the telecom sector was mere US$50million up till 1999 and one telephone lines to 250 Nigerians. Against this backdrop was the need for further reformation and deregulation of the communication sector by the Nigerian Government and other development stakeholders in the country.

Telecom Sector Deregulation and Policy Implications in Nigeria

Based on the poor performance of NITEL and the need to facilitate transformational development of the telecom sector for nationwide availability of functional, accessible and affordable telephony services in Nigeria the FGN found it necessary to revamp the telecommunication sector, most especially the telephony communication subsector. The reform thus began with partial liberalization of the telecommunication sector in 1992, with the National Communication Commission (NCC) put in place to facilitate the reform. According to NPT (2000); NCC (2014), the commission, which was established in November 1992 and began operational functions in July 1993, serves as independent national regulatory authority for the telecommunications industry in Nigeria with the mandate of bringing about an efficient, reliable, affordable, universally accessible and cost effective telecommunications system in the country.

To achieve its set mandate, NCC, as indicated by NTP (2000); Ndukwe, (2003c; 2005), functions to liberalize the market for private sector participation and investment in the country's telecom sector through the following functions:

- Licensing of telecommunications operators;
- Assignment and registration of frequency to duly licensed operators;
- Administration of national numbering plan
- Facilitating private sector participation and investment in the telecommunications sector of the Nigerian economy;
- Promoting and enforcing a fair competitive environment for all operators, as outlined in this policy;
- Defining standards for economic regulation of dominant operators, including tariff regulation as outlined in this policy.
- Establishing mechanisms for promoting universal access to telecommunications services in Nigeria, as outlined in this policy;
- Establishing and enforcing technical operational standards and practices for all operators including the imposition of penalties for violations.
- Ensuring that the public interest is protected.

To create a leveling ground for all investors in the Nigerian telecom NCC conducted bids for licensing in a public, transparent and unbiased manner in the form of:

- Public tender invitation,
- Competitive bidding,
- Open application,
- Unregulated entry.

In addition, all criteria for application, award, and denial of license requests are clearly disclosed to all parties and published for the enlightenment of Nigerians. In view of this were the emergence and successful licensing of five digital mobile operators, namely Electronic Communication Network (ECONET) wireless, Mobile Telecommunication Network (MTN) Nigeria, Mobile Telecommunication (M-Tel), Globacom and Etisalat between 2001 and 2003.

Mobile Phone Revolution in Nigeria

Prior to the emergence of GSM in the country in 2001, cellular phone service had been in place in the mid 1980 (Ndukwe, 2001) and became operated as Mobile Telecommunication Service in 1992 under the joint venture of NITEL and Digital Telecommunications of Atlanta. As the sole Mobile Telecommunication Service provider in the country NITEL was able to provide about 55,000 cellular lines by 1994, thereby putting the nation's telephony penetration at a low rate of 8 direct exchange line per thousand people. Although, NITEL's capacity network increased from 450,516 lines in 1991, through 600,000 lines in 1992, to 1 million lines in 1995, the telecom outfit could not meet the public's demand for mobile telecommunications in the country (Longe & Longe, n.d.). As at 2000, there were about 20,000 connected cellular lines, representing an average annual growth rate of 1,250 subscribers per annum

Partial deregulation of the telecom sector and privatisation of NITEL in 1992 led to emergence of the Code Division Multiple Access (CDMA) telephone in the country in November 1997 (Ojo, 2011). The CDMA operators thus began competitive provision of telephony services either as fixed wired access and/or fixed wireless access, which are respectively known as landline and mobile telephony services, in the country. This development thus puts Nigeria's telephony penetration on the rise. With increased number of available fixed wired and wireless service providers from 9 in 1999 to 24 in 2005, the number of the telephony subscribers surged from 23, 144 to 568,925 between these years. As a matter of fact, the fixed wired access holds 95% of the telephony penetration in the country by the year 2000. (Ndukwe, 2006). Alongside the CDMA telephony services was the ground-breaking emergence of Global Communication for Mobile System (GSM) in the country in 2001 under the auspices of ECONET wireless (which later became V Mobile Nigeria, Celtel, Zain and now Airtel) and MTN Nigeria. Each of these service providers paid a bid price of US$285million to the Nigerian Government (FMINO, n.d.) and thus officially began operation of mobile communication services in the country in August 2001.

Thereof the launch of GSM, mobile phone diffusion took a gradual step to spread from a few cities of Lagos, Port Harcourt and Abuja, where the communication network were first launched and concentrated, to becoming widespread in all 36 states of the federation; and from initial concentration in urban areas to a number of rural communities in the country. As much as the advent of the mobile phone service operation in the country was a welcome development, the initial cost of acquisition and operation of the telephony service was on a high side and as such was less affordable to most Nigerians by then. For instance, as at 1999, the CDMA telephone lines cost as much as N100, 000 (about USD$833 at the rate of N120 to a dollar); a starter pack of the GSM mobile line costs as much N60, 000 (about USD$500) at inception in late 2001 (Ndukwe, 2006; Usoro, 2007) and N20,000 (USD$167) in early 2003 (NCC, 2007a). Similarly, the least handset, though not necessarily marketed by the mobile phone network service providers, goes for about N25, 000 (about US$208). Given the economic situation of most Nigerians these prices were beyond the reach of average income earners and as such mobile phone usage became restricted to a few high income earners who could afford the lines (CDMA and GSM) and the handset at such high prices.

In addition to this was the issue of air time expiration period whereby subscribers were expected to exhaust their phone credit within a specified time period that is reflective of the amount of air time credit loaded at a time. For instance, the least credit voucher by Airtel service provider (then known as ECONET) which was five hundred N500 (US$4.2 at N120 to a dollar) had to be exhausted within 5days while that of MTN which was N1500 (US$12.5 at N120 to a dollar) was expected to be consumed within 15days. Going by the tariff charge of N50 (US$0.42 at N120 to a dollar) per minute, it implies that a subscriber *must* make at least a minute call per day and failure to do so results in barring a concerned subscriber from making use of the remaining call credit after the expiration of the air time period. For the barred subscriber(s) to be able to use the barred call credit such one would have to load additional credit voucher.

Apart from the high cost of mobile phone usage by subscribers was the issue of geospatial coverage of the telephony network as the service provision was initially limited to major cities such Lagos, Port Harcourt and Abuja in the country. The obvious reason for this was the peculiarities of these states/cities in the Nigerian economic and political climate. While Lagos State was the commercial nerve of the country, Abuja constitutes the administrative centre and Port Harcourt as the resource base for foreign exchange earnings. By implication, spatial communication via the telephones was limited, not just to a few ones who could afford the services at a high cost, but also to the urban areas in the country. This situation continued till August 2003 when the terms of agreement for two years of operation mainly by Airtel and MTN expired and the window for other private investors in the telecom sector became opened. The expiration period thus paved way for the incoming of other two mobile phone service providers, namely M-Tel and Globacom, who were both regarded as national carriers, in 2003. By November 1st 2008, the fifth service provider – Etisalat, came on board for provision telephony services in the country.

Ever since then, competition among the main functional mobile phone service providers, namely Airtel, MTN, Globacom and Etisalat, for market dominance had not only brought about a continued downward prices of mobile phone kits and call tariffs, but engendered a geospatial spread of the telephony network services across the country. Unlike the initial concentration of the telephony services in major cities of Lagos, Abuja and Port Harcourt, other major towns and communities have become connected in the country (Ndukwe, 2009); and by virtue of radial coverage of the installed telephone masts across the major towns, a large number of rural communities have become connected for mobile phone usage. Field survey by Lawal-Adebowale (2008) however showed that most of the connected rural communities were those that fell alongside the major roads connecting states and major towns, with the remotely located ones remaining unconnected. The non-connection of certain communities in Nigeria with mobile phone network was corroborated by MTN Nigeria indications that about 40million rural dwellers remained unconnected with any communication network (Vanguard, 2010; TheNigeriaDaily.com, 2011).

Given the value of mobile communication, and as recognized by the members of the rural areas, a number of the communities had make-shift masts (Figure 1) erected for reception of telephony signals. By this intuition, usage of mobile communication in the areas rather became 'fixed mobile phone' than actually being mobile phone on the ground that the mobile handset had to be wire-connected with make-shift mast for signal reception and communication (Figure 2). This suggests that much has to be done in order to ensure rural inclusion in the wider spectrum of mobile phone revolution in the country.

Consideration of statistics on telephony connectivity in Nigeria by NCC showed an exponential growth in the number of telephone lines from an average of 10,000 lines per annum between 1960 and end of 2000, to an average growth rate of 1 million lines per annum in the in the first two years of GSM operation in the country. As of September 2003, Nigeria had attained over 3 million lines, (2.3 million of which were digital mobile lines), with a teledensity of 2.6 per 100 inhabitants (Ndukwe, 2003). A run through of the annual telephony (mobile phone, CDMA and fixed wired/wireless) subscriber data on NCC database showed a monumental increase of connectivity from 866, 782 lines in 2001 to 172, 625, 725 lines in January 2014 – with mobile phone connectivity accounting for 30.7% (266, 461 lines) and 94.3% (162, 719, 517 lines) between the 2001 and January 2014; thereby putting the nation's teledensity at 91.4.

Mobile Phone Usage in Nigeria: Basis for Accessibility and Affordability

Against the high cost of telephony acquisition and usage in Nigeria under NITEL and at the onset of the telecom sector deregulation comes the cheap rate at which telephone lines could be acquired and used by anyone in the country today. The cheapness of telephony services was due to

Figure 1. Makeshift mast for reception of mobile telephony signals in one of the surveyed rural communities in Ogun State, Nigeria (picture by author).

market liberalisation of the telecom sector and competitive spirit for market dominance among the four mobile phone service providers. For instance, emergence of M-Tel and Globalcom in 2003 broke the Airtel-MTN strong market alliance on high cost of telephone lines and call tariffs. Against the N14, 000 and N12, 000 cost prices of Airtel and MTN telephony lines respectively, and a tariff charge of N50 per minute of calls by both service providers as at July 2003, were sales

Figure 2. Fixed/wired mobile handset for making and receiving calls at a fixed location (picture by author)

of M-Tel line at N9, 000 and tariff charge of N21 per minute. This development swiftly gave ground for other intending subscribers and even some of those already connected on Airtel and MTN lines to take up the M-Tel line. This advancement by M-Tel thus posed a threat to the patronage of Airtel and MTN services in the country. An attempt to check mate this new development, both Airtel and MTN refused interconnectivity with M-Tel thereby restricting M-Tel subscribers to M-Tel lines as it was not possible for them to link any other person on both Airtel and MTN lines. On this ground, some subscribers had to be on both M-Tel and Airtel/MTN lines for convenient links with other subscribers. This situation became a serious issue that the National Assembly- the legislative arm of the Nigeria Government and NCC had to wade in, directing that all operators of telephony services in the country *must* interconnect with one another.

While issue of interconnectivity was being addressed, Globacom – the forth mobile communication service provider and an indigenous national carrier emerged on the telecommunication scene with a tariff charge of per second billing. With this routing development on the telephony communication scene, both Airtel and MTN had to take up the option of per second billing with a drastic reduction in cost of starter pack acquisition in order to retain their subscribers. By late 2003 cost of mobile line starter pack had reduced to N2, 500 and by early 2004 it had become N500. Now a starter park, which cost N100, is near free as every new line comes with pre-loaded voucher of N100. Based on this, acquisition and patronage of mobile phone services had continued with an upward trend of subscribers. As indicated by Ndukwe (2006); Mojekwe (2012), demand for mobile lines took a steady increase from 2001 till date against the downward trend of demand for the CDMA and fixed wired/wireless phones. For instance, the CDMA which had active subscriptions of 6.18 million in January 2011 went down drastically to 4.78 million by November 2011. The same goes for the Fixed Wired/Wireless telephone lines, which had 1.03 million users in January 2011 and declined to 753,383 by November of the same period. Out of the 127.2 million connected telephone lines in 2011 in the country, GSM operators had 89.9 million subscribers; the CDMA operators had 4.78 million subscriptions while the Fixed Wired/Wireless operators had 753,383 users. This scenario and the prospect of higher demand for mobile phone services could have informed Etisalat's entry into the nearly saturated mobile telephony service in the country by November 1st 2008 as the fifth mobile service provider. Etisalat equally came on board with per second billing of phone calls.

In addition to downward cost of telephony line acquisition and per second call billings as bases for increased usage was availability of lower denominations of credit voucher and long term duration of fixed expiration period. Against the initial minimum credit voucher of N500 on Airtel network and N1500 on MTN network were introduction of smaller denominations in the range of N50; N100; N200 and N400 by the service providers. On another note was the introduction of lower tariff charge of 20kobo per minute within a network lines and between 25 and 30k per minute between lines of the different telephony networks. To further encourage subscribers continued and sustained patronage of their chosen network, various low-cost or cost effective tariffs were introduced by the network providers. Instance of such lower tariff packages were family and friends, zone calling, extra call credit in relation to every recharge by subscribers etc. In addition to these were weekends, non-peak and free night calls. Alongside this was the extended duration of air time expiration from 5days by Airtel and 15days by MTN to 90 days by all the four telephony service providers in the country. Text messaging tariffs also reduced from N15 per page within network and from N30 per page between networks to N4 per page across all network. These provisions thus stimulate regular and good use of mobile phones among Nigerians.

Outside the provisions of the network service providers was the mobile phone market with various brands of handsets or cell phones. Unlike the early season of mobile phone revolution in the country whereby the least phone sold for as much as N25,000; and with much of the then available phones having limited functions for voice calling and text messaging, expanded mobile phone markets, had brought about reduction in prices of cell phones. As a matter of fact, a functional phone with features such as radio, camera and torch light, in addition to the normal voice call and text messaging functions, cost as little as N2000 in today's Nigeria. Based on this, an intending mobile phone user could readily acquire the communication device at will. In addition to this is the emergence and introduction of advanced mobile phones with varying features and applications in the Nigerian telephone markets. Such phones include iPhone, Android, Blackberry, and of recent, IPAD or personal assistance, with capacity for installation of various phone apps. The common apps characterising such phones include call related apps such as voice call, video call; chat features such as Palmchat, Whatsaap, Blackberry Messenger (BBM); graphics communication apps such as Bluetooth, Flash share; Quickoffice characterised by quick word, quick sheet, quick point, quick PDF (Portable Document File). Other features include Assistant for information management, Geographic Positioning System (GPS), internet features for online connectivity and Google Maps for geographic mapping, and play store for assessing and harnessing any Apps of value for personal use.

Trend of Mobile Phone Growth and Penetration in Nigeria

Ever since the revolution of mobile phone in the Nigeria, the trend of usage by Nigerians, both in terms of connectivity and types of phone usage, has ever been on the increase. In terms of connectivity, a Wikipedia-based global statistics of mobile phone usage across 68 countries of the world shows that Nigeria ranked 7th with the total numbers of 167,371,945 subscribers and 18th in terms of teledensity of 92.14 as at February 2014 (Table 1). An updated mobile usage in Nigeria as at July 2014 however puts the number of mobile phone subscribers at 179,588,986, with a teledensity of 94.42 (NCC, 2014). Based on this, it suggests Nigeria not only constitutes the foremost mobile usage nation in Africa, but the trend of usage is ever on the increase on monthly basis (Table 2). The continuous growth of mobile phone subscription in Nigeria goes in line with International Telecommunication Union – ITU (2014) submission that mobile phone subscription rate has ever been on the increase in the developing countries; and this will continue with a penetration rate (3.1%) that doubles that of the developed countries (1.5%). Out of the expected 7billion worldwide mobile-cellular subscriptions, with a penetration rate of 96% by the end of 2014, the developing countries would account for more than three-quarter or 78% of the growth rate with the penetration rate of 90% by the end of 2014. And among the developing countries, Africa, of which Nigeria is one, would account for 69% penetration rate thereby making the continent, though alongside the Asian-Pacific, the strongest region of mobile phone growth in the world. And given the mobile phone subscription rate in Nigeria, the country is considered the fastest growing mobile phone market in the world and is believed to have overtaken South Africa to be the largest mobile phone market in Africa (Mobility Nigeria, 2014a; BuddeComm, 2014).

On account of smartphone usage statistics, Africa accounted for 2% of the estimated 1billion units of the phone in use globally as at 2102 (Mobility Nigeria, 2013). With about 4million units of smartphones usage in Nigeria as at April 2013, the country was third to South Africa, with 11million, and Egypt with 7million units (Mobility Nigeria, 2013). A further report in the same year by Punch (2013), however showed that Nigeria,

Table 1. List of countries by number of mobile phones in use

Rank	Country or Regions	Number of Mobile Phones	Connections/100 Citizens	Data Evaluation Date
	World	6,800,000,000	97	2013
01	China	1,227,360,000	90.9	December 2013
02	India	924,318,927	74.16	31 August 2014
03	United States	327,577,529	103.1	April 2014
04	Brazil	276,200,000	136.2	July 2014
05	Russia	256,116,000	155.5	July 2013
06	Indonesia	236,800,000	99.68	September 2013
07	Nigeria	167,371,945	94.5	Feb 2014
08	Pakistan	140,000,000	77	July 2014
09	Japan	121,246,700	95.1	June 2013
10	Bangladesh	116,508,000	69.5	August 2014
11	Germany	107,000,000	130.1	2013
12	Philippines	106,987,098	113.8	October 2013
13	Iran	96,165,000	130	February 2013
14	Mexico	92,900,000	82.7	Dec. 2011
15	Italy	88,580,000	147.4	Dec. 2013
16	United Kingdom	75,750,000	122.9	Dec. 2013
17	Vietnam	72,300,000	79	October 2013
18	France	72,180,000	114.2	Dec. 2013
19	Egypt	92,640,000	112.81	August 2013
20	Thailand	69,000,000	105	2013
21	Turkey	68,000,000	89.9	2013
22	Ukraine	57,505,555	126.0	Dec. 2013
23	South Korea	56,004,887	111.5	2014
24	Spain	55,740,000	118.0	Feb. 2013
25	Argentina	56,725,200	141.34	2013
26	Poland	47,153,200	123.48	2013
27	Colombia	49,066,359	104.4	2013
28	South Africa	59,474,500	117.6	2013
29	Algeria	33,000,000	94.2	2013
30	Taiwan	28,610,000	123.33	September 2013
31	Kenya	28,080,000	71.3	2013
32	Venezuela	27,400,000	98.0	2013
33	Peru	33,000,000	110.0	Oct. 2013
34	Romania	22,800,000	108.5	Not stated
35	Canada	26,543,780	74.1	2012
36	Morocco	36,550,000	113.6	Q1 2013
37	Netherlands	20,000,000	121.1	Nov. 2013
38	Australia	30,200,000	133.0	December 2013
39	Saudi Arabia	46,000,000	169.5	Jun 2013
40	Malaysia	30,379,000	143.8	Apr 2014

Source: http://en.wikipedia.org/wiki/List_of_countries_by_number_of_mobile_phones_in_use (October 20, 2014)

Table 2. Monthly telephony subscriber data (January – July, 2014)

	Operator	July	June	May	April	March	February	January
Connected lines	Mobile (GSM)	175,425,162	165,716,078	173,697,287	172,913,989	168,595,831	167,371,538	162,719,517
	Mobile (CDMA)	3, 802,931	3,974,106	4,081,300	4,076,933	4,083,672	7,620,525	7,667,314
	Fixed wired/ wireless	360,893	342,696	340,831	328,388	327,524	2,238,458	2,238,894
	Total	179,588,986	170,032,880	178,119,418	177,329,661	173,007,027	177,230,928	172,625,725
Active lines	Mobile (GSM)	129,978,598	130,536,850	128,896,631	126,958,904	124,884,842	126,246,648	125,173,177
	Mobile (CDMA)	2,021,214	2,061,458	2,107,389	2,256,612	2,039,391	2,398,581	2,421,970
	Fixed wired/ Wireless	187,028	182,395	178,038	172,876	172,963	357,612	365,433
	Total	132,186,840	132,780,703	131,182,058	129,391,392	127,097,196	129,002,841	127,960,580
Teledensity*		94.42	94.84	93.70	92.42	90.78	92.14	91.40

Source: Nigerian Communication Commission data base (2014)

* Teledensity was based on population of 140million and active lines in Nigeria

with about 25% of its mobile phone subscribers on the use of smartphone, became second to South Africa, with 33% of the country's mobile phone subscribers on the use of smartphones (Table 3).

Table 3. List of countries with smartphone usage in Africa

Rank	Countries	Proportion of Smartphone Users (%)	Proportion of Basic Feature Phone Users(%)
1	South Africa	33	48
2	**Nigeria**	**25**	**59**
3	Egypt	22	71
4	Ghana	18	64
5	Cameroon	17	74
6	Kenya	13	50*
7	Senegal	11	81
8	Cote d'Ivore	10	78
9	Uganda	10	75
10	Tanzania	6	77

Source: Adapted from published TNS statistics on smartphone usage in January 8, 2013 online Punch news paper

* Actual figure not provided but indicated figure was interpolated from indications that South Africa and Kenya had lesser basic phone usage than Nigeria

The high rate of smartphone penetration in South Africa, as indicated by the Technology Marketing Corporation – TMC.Net (2014), was underscored by the country's mobile phone subscribers' drive for use of WhatsApp – an instant messaging apps that characterises the smartphone features. Notwithstanding the leading position of South Africa, the trend of smartphone usage in Nigeria has continued to be on the increase with about 10million units of the phones now in use in the country (Mobility Nigeria, 2014). And in view of the projection that about 30million units of smartphone is expected to be sold in Nigeria between now and 2015 (Punch, 2013), it suggests that the country is on the verge of becoming the largest potential market for smartphone usage in Africa.

Impact of Mobile Phone Usage in Nigeria: The Social and Economic Dimension

The herald of mobile phone in Nigeria in 2001 and its aftermath revolution is known to have engendered social and economic transformation in various dimensions in the country. Key indicators of such socio-economic development, as highlighted by NCC (2007), include provision of telecommunications infrastructure, development of Small and Medium Scale Enterprises, ICT and Rural development, development of policy framework, human capacity development, Technology development etc. Alongside this development was intuitive exploitation of the mobile phone device beyond the primary usage for information communication between two or more individuals to usage for facilitation of interactive linkages, entertainment, educational activities, efficient and improved productivity, service provisions, innovativeness, creativity and new possibilities, and better quality of life by Nigerians (Ndukwe, 2001). The dimensional impacts of such mobile phone exploitation and usage in the country are thus x-rayed as follows:

The Economic Impact of Mobile Phone Revolution in Nigeria

- **Economic Investment:** The soundness of a nation is largely judged by the strength of its economy, using indicators such as the Gross Domestic Product (GDP), per capita income, industrial development, enhanced purchasing power and employment opportunities. Based on the observed positive relationship between mobile phone revolution and economic growth in Nigeria (Ndukwe, n.d.), the advent of mobile communication network in Nigeria has strengthened the nation's economic base, judging by the worth of attracted investment in the country and its contribution the national GDP. According to Ndukwe (2003d), the mobile communication network attracted as much as USD$2.55 billion worth of investment as at June 2003 – a phenomenal 5000% increment over the attracted USD$50 million investment worth in 1999. Based on this, investment worth in the country's telecom sector ranked second only to the oil industry; contributing a steady growth to the nation's GDP, from 1.77% in 2007 to 8.5% as at April 2014 (Ndkwe, n.d.; NCC, 2014). As indicated by Ndukwe (n.d.), a 1% increase in mobile telecommunication demands in Nigeria generates about 0.14% growth in the nation's economy (Ndukwe, n.d.). Consequently, the telecommunication technology is known to present copious opportunities for the creation of unprecedented wealth for Nigeria as a nation.

The telecom sector also serves as income generating venture to the Nigerian government in form of tax. According to Bottomline (2006), MTN paid about N9.8 million as tax to the Federal Government of Nigeria 2005 while the company workers tax deduction amounted to about N1.1 billion. In the same vein, the mobile phone company remitted about N34.8 billion to the government in the form of license fees, duties, taxes, and other statutory payments. In 2007, about N150 billion was paid to the Federal Government of Nigeria by MTN since it began operations in the country in 2000 (Bottomline, 2007). Also, the Federal Government has earned over 242 billion naira from spectrum licensing fees (NCC, 2008). As a result of increase in the number of mobile phone subscribers and to mitigate the issue of connectivity congestion for improved service delivery, the network providers, as indicated by BuddeCom (2014), are investing billions of dollars on additional base stations and optic fibre transmission.

- **Employment Opportunities:** The telecom investment drives created employment opportunities in the country. For instance, about 15,000 persons had direct employment on the pay role of the GSM operators, either as engineers, administrative, technical and non-technical staff (Ndukwe, 2009). For instance, Globacom had about 2,500 employees on its pay role as at 2007 (Bottonline, 2007). In the same vein, an estimated 400,000 Nigerians are indirectly employed by the GSM operators and this takes the form of contracts to construction firms, research companies and media consultants or advertising practitioners (Ndukwe, 2003; 2009). Others are groups of individuals categorized as wholesale dealers, and sub-dealers in sales of credit vouchers, and the retailers who sell to the end (phone) users.

On another note are inestimable number of individuals who had inadvertently become self-employed and/or employer of labor based on exploration and exploitation of the mobile revolution in the country. In this regard are dealers in the sales of various brands of phones and phone accessories in major markets across the country. While the major dealers in the phone business are self-employed on one hand, they constitute employer of labor on the other hand as such ones employ quite a number of individuals as sales representatives or sales point attendants. In the same are several individuals that have become self-employed on account of rendering phone-based services such as retail sales of credit voucher, sales of phone accessories such as batteries, earpiece, memory cards, phone jackets and cases, and phone chargers. Other services rendered by such self-employed individuals include repairs of faulty phones and running of phone kiosk or 'umbrella-stand' as call centers (Figure 3). Paradoxically, the epileptic electricity supply in the country turned out be a ground for creation of telephony-based employment for some individuals who harnessed this opportunity to run alternative power supply which entails the use of generator to recharge dead or flattened phone batteries at a fee. An interview of one of such service providers by a reporter on a Small and Medium Enterprise (SME) sub-section of the national news on the Nigerian Television Authority in 2007 indicated that an average of N2000 is made per day as proceed from the phone battery recharging service.

Figure 3. A self-employed call centre operator in one of the surveyed communities on impacts of mobile phone usage in Nigeria (photo by author)

Another value of mobile phone in the employment process was application of the communication tool as means of contact by both prospective employees and the potential employing organisation(s). Although, applicants may be requested to indicate either or both their life electronic mail (e-mail) addresses and functional mobile phone numbers as means of contact in their résumé or curriculum vitae, observation showed that it is faster and more convenient to contact the applicants by means of their indicated mobile phone numbers. This cannot be unconnected with the fact that text messaging in form of short text messages (SMS) does not require special applications, either for sending or retrieving messages, unlike the e-mail that is Internet-based and requires phones with special applications for usage. Experiences in this regard thus showed that applicants for employment are largely contacted by means of their mobile lines either for the purpose of invitation for interview(s) or informing and inviting them to pick up their appointments. Applicants without functional mobile lines are automatically screened out of the employment process as it becomes difficult to get in touch with such one, even where they are found suitable for being shortlisted for interview or appointment. Based on this, every prospective applicant ensures that s/he has functional and life mobile phone number(s) for ease of contact with or by the prospective employer(s).

- **Institutionalisation of Linkages for Business Transaction:** Given the value of mobile phones for facilitation of spatial interaction, the communication device has been greatly harnessed by entrepreneur for business transactions in various ways. For instance, advertisers of products and services either in print or electronic media always include phone numbers in the advertorial message for possible use by prospective customers for linkage with the advertisers or manufactures of the advertised product(s). In the same vein are phone number inscriptions by small scale entrepreneurs at the door posts or entrances of their business premises or workshop; and in some cases on walls and sign posts on the streets as a way to facilitate linkages with them for patronage of their businesses. A field observation in this regard shows that practitioners such as plumbers, painters, carpenters, interior decors and window and pane fitters write phone numbers on the walls of on-going building constructions for attraction of the property owners' for patronage of their services. An interaction with some of such practitioners with a view to ascertaining the outcome of such inscription of phone numbers at their target areas showed positive results in terms of favorable response and eventual linkage with them by the prospective customers through the wall-inscribed telephone numbers.
- **Financial Transaction:** The banking and other financial sectors have developed phoned-based services by which customers can easily transact businesses without having to visit or be at the banks. For instance, bank customers could readily check their account balance or receive alerts on every cash deposit or withdrawal made at any point in time. This application is of great value to paid-employed workers whose salaries are paid into their respective bank account. Such workers are alerted via the mobile phone the moment their accounts are credited with their paid salaries; and whenever withdrawal is made from the accounts the concerned customers are alerted and informed of such withdrawal with indications of the precise amount of money withdrawn and time of withdrawal. By this, the customers could readily monitor their account. In the same vein, the use of the alert mode by the commercial banks serves as a protection the bank customers' account in

that such customers readily become aware of any financial impropriety that might be committed against them by fraudsters who might sometimes hacked into someone else's account using the Automated Teller Machine (ATM) card.

On another note is the application of mobile phone for effecting cash transfer from a person's account to another, either within a particular bank or between banks; and as soon as the accounts are rightly debited and credited by the transacting banks the concerned customers are alerted of the effected transactions via an internet-generated text messages, providing the customers details of the effected transaction for their information and records. In view of the recently enacted cashless policy by the Central Bank of Nigeria (CBN) whereby individuals cannot withdraw cash in excess of N500,000 at once and N3,000,000 by cooperate bodies (CBN, n.d.), most of the commercial banks in the country had embarked on electronic banking (e-banking) or mobile money (mMoney). In this wise, financial transaction could be effected by bank customers – be it individual or corporate organisations – using electronic device such as the mobile phone. To enhance the mobile phone-based financial transaction, the commercial banks had developed mobile phone Apps which could be downloaded onto the phone by means of the Play Store Apps, and used for financial transaction of choice right from the comfort of one's home or office. In view of this, bank customers thus use the mobile phone to effect financial transactions such as confirmation or cancellation of posted cheques, transfer money to those who not operate bank account, transfer money from one's account to that of another person, payment of utility bills, booking and reservation of tickets for both local and international travels and purchase of air time for one's phone or any other person. With this provisions, the mobile banking Apps allows for convenient banking at one's finger tips.

- **Location and Creation of Markets for Goods and Services:** The need for business transaction, particularly in an efficient and profitable manner by individuals necessitated the need for deployment of mobile phone for creation and location of markets for their goods and services. For instance, entrepreneurs or producers of goods and services readily exploit the mobile phone to ascertain the market situation in terms of the current market price, availability and rate of demand for the goods and services they might intend to bring to the market at a particular time or period. By this, the entrepreneurs are saved the torrent of market glut and as such are able to sell at better price at any other time. In the same vein was the use of mobile phone to link established customers and other intending buyers either by directly calling or text messaging such ones to inform them about availability of demanded products or when it will be available, and the selling price. By this, the entrepreneurs become certain of the available markets for their goods and services.

On another note was the use of the mobile phone-internet interface to create or participate in an online marketing where some Nigerian sales outlets such as Kaymus, Jumia and Konga display varying brands of products which range from household goods to equipment, electronic gadgets, wears, phones, laptops/computers and automobiles for the attention of interested buyers in the country. In addition to the online sales outlets is the online-based market tagged OLX. This constitutes a market platform whereby an intending seller of a particular household goods or automobile could have such goods, which could be brand new or fairly used, displayed with a price tag for attention of the prospective buyers. On this platform, individual buyers could use the mobile phone-based Internet App to access available products for sales or use it to upload goods or products one intend to market, doing so in the comfort of one's abode. Once a buyer showed interest in a particular product, the marketer is contacted for transaction through the online address and once payment is effected, the buyer either have the goods or products delivered at his/her door step or make arrangement to pick it up at the sales point.

With this mobile phone-enabled provision, it becomes possible for phone and online users to have access to arrays of products, as it were in shopping malls, from which they make purchases with convenience. The platform is as well used as an open market in a similar manner to trade fair, where goods and products could be displayed for the attention and patronage of the prospective buyers. Unlike the trade fair which runs for a short period of time, the online market remains to time indefinite thereby given both the marketers and buyers the leverage of continuous and timeless interaction for business transaction.

The exploit of mobile phone-based market application is equally of great value to rural farmers and other agro-product marketers in Nigeria as it enabled such ones to create and locate markets for their agro-products thereby bypassing the middle men who are known for taking advantage of the farmers by buying from them at a give-away price either at the farm gate or in the open market as result of perishability of the agro-produce and market glut arising from jam packing of the open market with same agro-produce at the same time by the farmers. By exploit of the mobile phones the farmers are saved from creating market glut and given off their produce at a giveaway price as they use the phone to seek advance information from, or make arrangement with fellow or group of farmers on the type and quantum of agro-produce to be brought to the market either in a particular market day or period. By this mobile phone-driven arrangement the farmers are able to attract better market prices for their products and as such make better gains with the realisation that agriculture is a profitable venture.

The Social Impact of the Mobile Phone Revolution

- **Facilitation of Information Exchange:** The primary purpose of mobile usage for information communication and exchange is intensively and extensively manifested in the social context of human interactions and communication in Nigeria. With over 177million subscribers on mobile lines in the country as at April 2014 (NCC, 2014), and coupled with the leverage of network coverage across cities, towns and rural communities, family members, relatives, friends and business associates readily interact and/or communicate with one another via the mobile phones, irrespective of global distances between them. That is, calls could be put through by anyone to friends, relatives and associates who might be residing within or outside the country. A vivid experience in this regard was Ndukwe (2003c) indication that

... my mother lives in my village in Oraifite, Anambra State and the only way to contact her is by mobile phone. Knowing that she can call me at any time and that I can reach her bringsme a peace of mind that is invaluable

Mobile phone-mediated communication was not only integrated for communication between two or more individuals at distant locations but between those within vicinity. Instance in this regard was the use of mobile phone for communication between couples, and other family members within the same building or apartments, between neighbors and between colleagues in offices, which could be for seeking the whereabouts of one another, exchange pleasantries, seeking information for immediate use etc. By this regular contact bonds of love and friendships are thus strengthened and sustained between individuals in the country. As culled from *USA Today* by Awake (2009), as much as 70% of couples now use the mobile phone to communicate with each other while apart during the day – a scenario that was never possible before the advent and widespread of the mobile phone. As indicated by this information source, *'not too long ago, family members would go their various ways in the morning and not speak to one another again until evening.'* But now, reverse is the case as family members readily get in touch with one another at any point in time. In this regard, the same Awake indicates that about 64% of the couples contact each other to coordinate schedules and 42% of parents contact or communicate with their children while away from them during the day. By this telephony exploit, the line of communication is ever opened between couples and family members.

- **Facilitation of Contacts between Known and Unknown Individuals:** Another point of mobile phone impacts was the use of the communication device to predetermine the possibility of meeting an individual at any specified location and time. This is often done by making advance phone calls or text messages to one another indicating where to meet at a particular time. By this mobile phone mediated contact, one is saved of making fruitless journeys, financial and time wastages that would have been expended on such journeys. A similar scenario was possibility of meeting an individual one had never seen or met for once. Provision of mobile phone numbers of the two prospective contacts, particularly by a third party who is linking up the two, is all that is needed for the two to meet each other as may be arranged by two of them over the phone. With the given phone numbers, calls are made and information exchanged with regards to where and when to meet, and when eventually within the vicinity of the pre-arranged locations, description of worn clothes or taken vehicles by either of them is provided via the phone for actual sighting and meeting of each other. This possibility saved the concerned individuals the rigor of having to ask several other individuals or having to walk round the streets, as it used to be before the advent of mobile phone revolution in the country, for location of the prospective contact one might be meeting for the first time.
- **Voucher-Turned-Money Transfer:** The emergence of mobile phone had been intensively exploited by Nigerians for a tool of 'money' transfer. This is based on the fact that credit voucher, which ordinarily are meant to be loaded as call credit on phones, is considered and treated as money by Nigerians. In essence, the credit voucher is alternatively used as legal tender by individuals in the country. Based on this, credit voucher of a certain amount of money is readily transferred by a person to an intending recipient(s)/beneficiaries who on receipt of the credit voucher convert it to equivalent cash on sales. Although, this system of money transfer is mostly undertaken by group of individuals who do not operate bank account, it is a safe and faster way of transferring money to one's relations or beneficiaries who is far away from home. And in as much as this practice was common, the attendant disadvantage was the relative difficulty of getting a buyer for the received credit voucher on time; and where such is eventually found, it is mostly sold or bought at a price lesser than the actual worth of the sent credit voucher. This is based on the fact the credit voucher is readily available for intending users to get at any point in time from the widely available and strategically located phone kiosks. And where it becomes difficult for a person hoping to convert credit voucher to cash, such one often resort to the phone kiosk operators to buy over the credit voucher,

though at a lesser price than the actual face value or worth of the credit voucher. As a matter of fact the phone-kiosks operators constitute the readymade buyer of such voucher for cash conversion.

- **Monitoring of Fellow Human's Movement:** An important aspect of human. life is regular movement from one place to the other and as such, one may need to move within the locality or travel on a distant journey for various reasons or purposes. As a way to ascertain the safety of friends and relatives on journeys at any point in time, phone calls are often put through by the relations back at home to the person on journey at a regular interval. As expressed by some individuals interacted with on this matter, majority of them acknowledge the social value of mobile phone in this regard as it enable them to monitor their family members, friends and relatives on journeys either away from or when returning home. By this, it becomes possible to know where the travelling ones are at any point in time and what the situation or condition such one was while on the journey. This monitoring continues till the travelling ones arrived at their destinations. The same principle applies for monitoring of family members' movement within the locality. For instance, the mobile phone makes it possible for parents to monitor the movement of their children when sent on errant or while away to school or elsewhere and also use it to ascertain the situation with them when left all alone at home. In the same vein, couples and other family members equally integrate the mobile phones for monitoring the movement and/or wellbeing of one another, thereby maintaining regular contacts any point in time or throughout the day. This negates the normal practice of having to meet and see one another only at end of the day when all would have returned home from their various endeavours of the day to which all normally departed for in the early hours of the day. This practice thus brings about a sigh of relief to everyone involved in the mobile phone-mediated contacts as all in the contact chain are certain of the safety and welfare of one another.

On a similar note, employers make use of the mobile phone to monitor and coordinate their employees at any point in time irrespective the distance between them. For instance, employers relay information with regards to transactions and specific action to be taken by the employees on business function at a particular time. On another note, the mobile phone is used by certain employers, most especially the sole proprietors, to ascertain whether or not their staffs are at the duty post as expected. This is achieved either by having a phone, which is not expected to be taken about, for use of the business centre to which the employer calls anytime he/she hopes to communicate with the staffs during the business hour. In some cases, the call may be to the personal phone of his/her employee; but to be sure that such employee is actually at the duty post or at the business centre, the proprietor often speak with two or more of the staffs in sequence on the same phone. By this arrangement, the proprietor becomes rest assured of his/her employees' presence or absence from duty post and/or what is generally going on in the centre in his/her absence. In the same vein, staff on business trip is monitored by the employer by means of the mobile phone to ascertain the outcome of the business trip and to properly guide the employee appropriately on effected transaction on his/her behalf.

Notwithstanding the advantage of the mobile phone-mediated contact practice in the social and economic life of humans, field observation showed that the practice sometimes creates emotional anxieties on the part of the person who is putting a call through for a contact but could not have such contact established with the intended person. Such contact failure is often induced by network failure or sometimes by user-induced contact failure arising from such ones' failure to pick up the phone on several calls, or possibly because the phone is in silent mode or it is completely switched off due to flattened battery. Based on this, the person who puts the calls through become unnecessarily worried, wondering what could be happening or could have happened to the prospective contact within that period of contact or connection failure.

- **Facilitation of Emergency Contacts/ Security Alert:** Due to unforeseen occurrence that characterises human's endeavours, the need for emergency calls, which is as well referred to as 'Save Our Soul' (SOS) calls or text messages, for stimulation of quick response(s) from help a desk or helping hands becomes necessary. Experiences in this regard include the use of mobile phone for eliciting the responses of one's neighbours for help in case of being in a distress or distressing situation either at home or elsewhere. This has equally been applied in the case of road or traffic accidents whereby Road Marshals or health workers are quickly contacted for their attention and action to be taken on behalf of the accident victims and control of the consequent traffic build ups. In the same vein, families and relatives of the accident victims are readily contacted via the phone for their quick response to the needs of their family members involved in an accident.

In the same vein, the electronic broadcast, particularly radio, and mobile phone link is exploited by security outfits to provide security tips to the public. The issue of security information is a regular feature on both Rock City and Ogun State Broadcasting Cooperation (OGBC) radio broadcast whereby security personnel provide the public useful security-based information by means of phone call into an ongoing life programme. With this provision, the public is sensitized of the need to be security conscious and how such security could be ensured. Commonly provided security tips centers on theft and burglary prevention, guard against kidnapping and child molestation, prevention of fire outbreak and other environmental risks. Alongside this is integration of the mobile phone for securing the safety of one's environment usually by putting calls through to the neighbors, other members of the community and even to the police or security agents for the purpose of alerting them on lurking dangers or threats to lives and properties in the neighborhood or to stimulate their responses for action to quell any emerging security threats in the neighborhood. To further aid effective policing or any other security services in the country, specially coded security numbers are developed for security outfits such as the Nigerian Police and Federal Road Safety Commission for easy dialing and linkage with the security outfits by the public. Although, there is no absolute security anywhere, deployment of the mobile communication device had impacted on security of lives and properties, at least against the attacks of hoodlums, in the neighborhood.

- **Traffic Information Impact:** With heavy vehicular movement across the country, the resultant effect is usually long lines of traffic build ups. In view of this is the need to inform road users of the traffic situation on the high ways by traffic marshals. This is often achieved through a mobile phone-radio link whereby an assigned traffic officers calls into the life radio programme at a specified time to give report of traffic situation on the high ways for the benefit of motorists and other road users. Based on this, road users are informed about the high ways traffic build ups and as well provided information on alternative roads with light traffic to which the motorists might need to take to avoid the built up traffics. In the same vein, this platform is used to sensitise and forewarn road users on the dangers of misuse of the roads arising from such traffic related activities as over speeding, making or receiving phone calls while on the wheel and other unnecessary distraction that may result in accidents or car crash. With this background, the mobile phone had become a tool for enhancing the safety of road users and smooth vehicular movement.

Given the connectivity and inter-linkage potentials of the mobile phones, the communication tool bas been exploited by the vehicle licensing and insurance units to assure motorists of actual and authentic documentation of their vehicle particulars by sending short text messages via the mobile phones to the vehicle owners, informing them of such documentations. An example of such authentication message by Ogun State Vehicle registration unit as retrieved from inbox message of a vehicle owner reads "Dear Oladehinde T. O., your vehicle registration/permit details for LSD 756 CN was successful. You will get a reminder a month to expiry of the document. Expiry date is May 21 2016. Thank you". In addition to this a message by the Mutual Care Insurance to the same vehicle owner reads Dear Sir/Ma, MUTUAL has received your premium of NGN5,000 for policy: PRM/24/4/07751/15-26396ID. Transaction date: 21/05/2015. Thank you. This was authenticated by the National Insurance Industry Database (NIID) with a follow up message that read "your insurance policy no PRM/24/4/07751/15-26396ID for license plate no: LSD 756 CN is genuine". By this exploit, the antics of licensing touts and the usual issuance of fake vehicle particle particulars to unsuspecting vehicle owners at are thus automatically eliminated. In addition to this is a phone message alert to the vehicle owner in about a month to expiration of validity of the vehicle license. A vivid example in this regard is message from the Ogun State Vehicle Registration Unit to a vehicle owner which reads "Dear Mr. Bowaleade, O. A., please be reminded that that your vehicle registration with plate number KRD 338 BF will expire on 09 Jun 2015. Thank you. With this the vehicle owner is sensitised to work toward renewal of the vehicle particulars on or before the indicated expiry date.

- **Social Networking Impact of the Mobile Phone:** Although Internet Service Providers (ISP) were licensed to provide internet services for use by Nigerians at affordable rates, accessibility to the service is largely through the privately-run cyber cafés, whereby intending users visit the cafés for internet use at a fee of N100 or N150 per hour. With the mobile phone network-powered internet services, quite a number of individuals now readily accessed the internet via their mobile handsets at any point in time and location. Iterative discussion with some mobile phone users, particularly the school (secondary school and tertiary institution) age youths, on the use of phone-based internet revealed that most of them used the application for social networking via the Facebook, Twitter, 2go Whatsapp and pinging. In addition to this was the use of the phoned-internet for exchange of electronic messages, monitoring of current events in and outside the country as may be posted by news agencies, Wikileaks, media broadcasting organisations and by individuals or groups. By this, mobile phone users are able create and maintain social interaction with friends, families and relations and as well become updated with current events on a global scale.

On another note was application of the multiple or group caller services provided by the telephony network service providers, as a tool of social networking. This is similar to electronic conferencing (e-conference) whereby a group of callers are connected via the phone for social and/or economic interactions. Although the group caller service is restricted to a particular telephony line, i.e all in the group must be on the same network, as no interconnectivity is possible for this provision, the provision provided group of individuals to simultaneously interact with one another thereby using the platform to promptly address issues of concern by the group members.

- **Feedback Integration in Electronic Media Broadcast:** Electronic media – radio and television (TV) – broadcast is traditionally known to be devoid of feedback or immediate reaction from the listeners and/or viewers. With the emergence and exploitation of the mobile phones in media broadcast it becomes possible for listeners and/or viewers of radio and TV programs to effect feedback or immediate reaction in relation to subject matter of discourse on air. This possibility however takes place on provision of certain phone number(s) or short text message code to which listeners or viewers of a phone-in programme on radio or TV might call or send message(s). By this arrangement listeners or viewers of broadcast programme were thus able to contribute to issues of discourse either by asking questions to seek further clarifications on subject of discussion or by providing additional information or insight on the subject matter. Based on this, it becomes possible for concerned individuals to share their views, experiences, and establish their positions on national burning issues.

This application is daily feature in electronic media broadcast, particularly radio. For instance, Rock City FM radio feature a current affair related programme tagged "Day Break Show" between the hours of 8am and 10:30am, Monday to Friday, whereby current political, social, economic and environmental issues are discussed by a resources person and thereafter a phone line is thrown open for listeners to participate either by making calls or send messages via the provided phone number. Ogun State Broadcasting Cooperation (OGBC) runs a similar programme tagged *Morning Flight* and takes place between Monday and Friday. A similar programme tagged *Sunday Morning* takes place every Sunday, between 8:30 and 10am, whereby burning issues on social, economic, environmental, security, health and political status of the country are given in-depth discussion by resource persons after which the public are allowed to contribute to the issue of discussion by calling or sending messages into the programme by means mobile phone.

With the revolution of radio/television broadcast and mobile phone link, the electronic media functions not just to inform, educate and entertain the public but afford them the opportunity to participate in issues of discussion and to air their views or express their disposition to an ongoing issue in the country. In addition to this, the electronic media and mobile phone links serves as a platform for the public to give reports of on-going events or happenings in their environment by calling into a radio or television programmes that are meant for that purpose. By this, attention of concerned authorities is called to issues that might be raised by the callers. For instance, residence in Ogun State used the radio-mobile phone-link to call the attention of the State Government to the needs and issues of serious concern to them. Such issues include cases of dilapidated roads, traffic congestion, need for water and power supply, health issues, and economic matters. And where some of these issues are attended to by the authorities concerned, some members of the benefiting communities do use the same radio-phone platform to express appreciation for the kind gesture.

- **Entertainment Impact of the Mobile Phone:** With the development of phone-based applications or Apps, as obvious in smart phones, the mobile phone is greatly deployed for entertainment purposes by young and old in Nigeria. Field observation in this regard shows that the camera component of the mobile phone is highly deployed for taking pictures of persons and images of interest for documentation and sharing. Pictures sharing between two or more persons are made possible by the *Bluetooth* and *Flash Share* features of the phones, and Multimedia Message Services (MMS) rendered by the mobile phone network providers. While the Bluetooth and Flash Share are used for transferring pictures within a close range, whereby the sender and receiver must be beside each other, the MMS supports long distance picture transfer in the same manner as the text message. In addition to this is the use of the video feature of the mobile phone for recording events of choice or interest and for playback of such recorded events for viewing. The quantum of recorded video bites however depends on storage capacity of the phones and/or the installed memory card in the phone.

Music, often regarded as soul of life, constitutes a common application of mobile phones by individual users, particularly the in-school youths, in Nigeria. Based on this, series of musical albums are generally saves on the phones and playback for listening and entertainment by users. In view of the musical download on the phones, hardly do Nigerians make use of default ringing tones of the phones but largely use music of choice as customized ringing tones. In addition, such ringing tone may be made general or customised with a particular number for immediate recognition of the caller even before taking a look at the phone.

In addition to the video and camera components of the mobile phones were the television and FM (Frequency Modulation) radio features that enables phone users to either watch television-based or listen to radio-based programmes such as news, music, dramas, sports and current affairs. Based on the mobile phone Apps, individual phone users are readily informed and updated on the occurring events, be it social, economic, political or environmental issue, in the country. The phone radio App however functions not only as broadcast media, but equally as a recording device. By this, aired radio programme could be recorded and documented for later use. Field observation in this regard shows that a number of individuals used the device to record short announcement, say when giving out numbers to the public, which is later played back for better understanding.

The inbuilt or downloaded games of various types in the phones equally serve as means of entertainment for the phone users. Such games cut across Sudoku or puzzles, snakes, mini game planet, soccer/football, numeral café etc. Interaction with mobile phone users on the use of phone games reveals that the game feature creates the platform for relaxation and recreation; and in some cases, serves a useful educational purpose and for intellectual development.

Impact of Mobile Phone Revolution on Media Practice in Nigeria

The media practice which entails electronic broadcast and prints is a professional practice by which the public is informed, entertained and educated on local and international events or occurrences. To gather essential information of value to the public the Nigerian journalists heavily depended on the use of midget or portable analogue recording device and pen and paper for recording and jotting of information on field events. But with the advent of mobile phone and its revolution in Nigeria, journalists in the country now exploit the camara, voice and video recording features of the phones, which are in digital forms, for recording of interviews or field events with more convenience. By this, media reporters had their news and event coverage done in an effective and efficient manner. In the same vein, the Quickoffice App component of the iPhones or Personal Assistance is exploited as word processor for letterings of information that is later used for news writing either in print or broadcast media.

On another note, the internet component of the mobile phones enables individuals to access news and other information of interest from the webpage of both the print and broadcast media in and outside Nigeria. For instance, all the daily newspapers, and radio and television stations in the country are readily assessed online by any interested individual for news, entertainment or information. In addition to having the opportunity to view and listen to life radio and television broadcast online via the mobile phone is the prospect of accessing podcast of the same news and entertainment documented online by the electronic media houses. By this, any missed radio and television programmes could thus be accessed online as podcast at any other convenient time by interested individuals. Such podcast could be accessed through the streamline web address, facebook, twitter or instagram, as may be indicated by the media houses. In addition to this is development of radio and television Apps by the electronic media houses in the country for ready download from the PLAYSTORE tool onto mobile phones and use for receiving information or viewing events by interest individuals.

Further exploitation of the mobile phones for journalistic practice has brought about increased number of freelance practitioners with such ones recording field events either in video or photographic format for onward transmission, through the internet or Multimedia Message (MMS) phases of the mobile phone network, to the media house(s) to which such freelance practitioner is listed. The essence of acceptability of the video and/or photographic format from the freelance practitioners by the media houses is based on the credence it gives to the sent information to the media houses. In addition to this is acceptability of the video and photographic formats from any individual from general public. This practice is much common with the Channels Television – a privately owned television station based in Lagos State, southwest Nigeria, which generally calls on the public to upload useful and informative video and photographic scene on its television data base for relay to the public either in the course of news casting or presentation of related issue on the screen. In the same vein, it is common with most radio stations in the Nigeria to allow the public reportage of events and occurrences in their areas life on via the mobile phone.

The dynamics with which the mobile phone functions has equally transform the media practice from the traditional one-way communication to two-way communication by effecting linkages between the electronic media broadcast presenters and the listeners or viewers. In essence, the essential feedback or interactive mechanism that lacking in mass communication methods is now graciously integrated in the media broadcast by integration of mobile phone usage such that television viewers and radio listeners readily call or phone-in into the broadcast programme to seek for clarifications or contributes to issues of discussion. In the same vein, inclusion of mobile phone number or electronic mail addresses, such as e-mail, facebook and twitter, in the prints – newspapers, magazines, journals and bulletins, creates opportunity for readers to interact with the writers through the provided number and addresses. As indicated by Lawal-Adebowale and Adebayo (2006), mobile phone-media broadcast integration though enables the farmers to effect *immediate interaction* with extension practitioners through phone calls or text messaging such interaction becomes possible only in the face of life media broadcast. There is however no *immediate feedback* or interaction in the case of the print media since it takes time for printed information to reach a particular reader.

It therefore equally takes time for feedback and interaction to be effected by means of the mobile phone between the writers of printed information and the readers.

Educational Impact of Mobile Phone Revolution

Mobile phone was observed to be of value in execution of educational activities by students in Nigeria as such ones heavily deploy the internet, video, audio and camera components of the phones for information sourcing, data generation and documentation. By virtue of the internet component of the phones, students are able to source needed and relevant information on subject matter of concern to complement taught lessons for better understanding or execution of given academic assignments. In addition to this was the use of the documentation App of the smart phones for storage of written document, particularly as a backup, which could then be retrieved in case of loss of the main file.

The camera components is as well deployed for taking pictures of specimens or models of educational materials for later use in writing term papers, dissertations and theses, as the case may be. Similarly, the video and voice recorder components of the mobile phones are deployed for educational purposes, such a recording of interviews, delivered lectures and other field events that are eventually used to buttress point of discussion either in written form or oral presentations. The calculator App of the mobile phones serves as useful tool for working out mathematics and related mathematical tasks. By this application, workings of mathematical tasks by the students are enhanced.

Impact of Mobile Phone Revolution on Health Issues

Health is wealth and as such every individual tends to take good care of his health status by consulting doctors and taking genuine drugs as may be medically prescribed. In this wise, mobile phone users often use the tool to contact their hospitals or doctors for medical attention. In the same sense, the communication is tool is used to book appointments with specific doctors or to call the doctor in the case of emergency. Access to genuine drugs is however greatly impeded by pervasive fake and adulterated drugs in the country which often results in health complications, and death in some cases, on administration of such drugs. To overcome this situation were inscription of special numbers on cases or packs of drugs by pharmaceutical companies such that intending user of a particular drug could confirm the genuineness or fakeness of the drug by dialing the inscribed numbers or text message the number to a 5-digit codes by means of the mobile phone; and where the drug is actually a genuine one, an immediate response is generated from the concerned pharmaceutical company's electronic information base to affirm or dispute the genuineness of the purchased drug. The response is communicated in form of text message to the one making the enquiry via the mobile phone. An example of genuineness of a drug confirmation was the case of COMBIART – a malaria drug by Strides ACOLAB LIMITED, an Indian Pharmaceutical Company with sales representative in Nigeria. On the case of the drug was the inscription of alpha-digit code 'CBB4X2UJ' to be text messaged by intending user of the drug to 38351. Alongside this is the inclusion of a free toll number – 08089261133, to which a call be made. On text messaging the alpha-digit code to the given number, a response message which read *"OK Authentic product. Questions? Call 08089261133 NAFDAC. Powered by PharmaSecure"* was received by the sender. By this message, genuineness of the malaria drug was affirmed and was then taken with convenience. But where the message indicated No or not authentic, or where there was no response to the sent confirmation message the drug is then affirmed to be a fake one and as such would be readily discarded for safety of one's health.

By integration of the mobile telephony services in the pharmaceutical healthcare delivery it becomes possible for intending user of a particular drug to be sure of the genuineness of the purchased drugs; saved as much people that care to confirm the genuineness of purchased drug(s) the danger of health complications and untimely death, and ultimately guaranty effective treatment or control of the ailment under medical consideration. In addition, mobile telephony integration in the pharmaceutical healthcare services enables the pharmaceutical companies to jealously safeguard the genuineness and effective marketing of their drugs, tactically forced the imitation of their drugs out of the market as a result of little or no patronage by intending users, and as well make it possible for producers of the genuine drugs to make better sales and/or turn over.

On another note was the use of mobile phones to sensitise the public on health issues by the Ministry of health and other health agencies in Nigeria. An experience in this regard was sensitisation of the public on the outbreak of Ebola disease and the preventive measures to be taken by individuals by means of text messages. A received message from the Ministry of health on the need to report cases of Ebola infected persons to the appropriate authority or agency in the country thus read as *"Govt action against Ebola: Identifying & monitoring exposed persons, air/seaports & land borders. Report cases to 08037879701, 08037154575. ebolainfo@health.gov.ng"*. A similar health message on Ebola disease was the symptoms to look out for in any suspected case of the disease and the symptoms include fever, head ache, chest and abdominal pain, coughing with blood, red eye, diarrhea, . Alongside this was preventive message such as avoidance of contact with infected person, animals like bat, monkey and gorilla, regular hand washing with sanitizers. With this mode of health information communication, most Nigerian had become sensitised to the virulence of Ebola disease and are taken actions on the preventive measures to ensure safety of their health. In addition, individuals had taken it upon themselves to have the information on Ebola disease communicated to friends and relatives either by phone call or text message so as to ensure that their loved ones are aware and well informed about the deadly disease.

Other health care tips service are equally provided by the mobile phone network providers in the country, though at a fee of N50 per health tips message. Such health tips, which are often generated from the network providers' health information or data base, are delivered in form of message to the intending user(s) of the health information on request. Available health tips for use include management and prevention stress, Human Immuno Virus/Acquired Immune Deficiency Syndrome (HIV/AIDS), cholera, diarrhea, typhoid and malaria. Based on this, users of health messages are able to mange related health issue that might be affecting them.

Social Vices Impacts of the Mobile Phone Revolution

- **Swindling:** In as much as the mobile phone revolution in Nigeria is of great value to social and economic development of the country, deployment of the communication tool for heinous activities by unscrupulous individuals cannot be overlooked. Among the terrible acts committed with the use of mobile phone was duping of unsuspecting individuals by tricksters. The commonly employed tactics by the dupers was to present themselves as a known person to their prey and persuasively ask such ones to send certain sums of money to meet a pressing need. An instance in this regard as related by a mobile phone user on reception of false message that reads 'you have a package from your relative abroad and I need certain amount of money to parcel the package to you and as such, you need to send the sum of N3000 by means of credit voucher to be converted to cash on sales for the package to be parcel to you'. Another instance is presentation of falsehood such as 'certain relative of yours was involved in a traffic accident and receiving medical attention, and to care for the medical bill, kindly send certain amount of money by means of credit voucher to be converted to cash for such need'. In view of this, several innocent individuals had been duped of their hard earned income by the tricksters.

- **Deceptive Impression:** Among several other uses of mobile phones was the use of the communication device as a tool of deception in terms of given distorted information, especially about where an individual may be at a particular time. An instance in this regard is the given impression by a caller that he/she is far away somewhere when actually within vicinity. Established reasons for such deceptions include the need to either avoid the caller or keep the caller waiting at a spot until the receiver is able to arrive the spot for physical interaction with the caller. A Voxpop on this matter on a television broadcast shows an individual who affirmed that he sometimes use the mobile phone to give deceptive impression with regards to where he might be at a particular time for the purpose of fulfilling certain task. Citing an instance of such expression of deceptive impression, he claimed to have given a customer an impression that he was 5kilometers away from office when actually was 35kilometers away with the underlying reason that he cannot afford to let the particular customer leave without meeting him in the shortest time for business transaction. On another note are individuals who because of the need to have themselves excused or do not want to welcome the visit of a particular person might give such one a deceptive impression of being out of town when actually in town or at home.

Although, this example of deceptive impression is without an evil intent, in some cases is the use of the mobile phone for facilitation of evil intent by unscrupulous individuals. A vivid example in this regard was presentation of self as a known or friendly person by unscrupulous individuals to unsuspecting person(s) with view to swindle such ones or lure them into uncanny deeds. For instance, a Postgraduate young lady named Cynthia Nkogosu was lured via the mobile phone-mediated social media chat and pinging, all the way from Nassarawa State in the North Central region of Nigeria to a hotel in Lagos – a Southwest State in Nigeria, by a social media-met friend who eventually raped, robbed and killed her.

- **Traffic Accidents:** A common trend of traffic accident in Nigeria is the mobile phone-induced accident arising from the use of the handset while on the wheel. Against this background was the occurrence of motor accidents that often result in loss of properties and lives. According to the Nigerian Federal Road Safety Commission (FRSC), a larger proportion of road accidents in the country were due to mobile phone-induced concentration losses by drivers on wheel. Due to the ever increasing rate of phone-induced traffic accidents, a ban on the use of mobile phone while on the wheel was enacted by the FRSC with a view to stemming of such road accidents in the country. A feature by Awake (2009) on this issue reveals that motorists who talk on either handheld or hands-free devices are as impaired as drunk drivers. It however indicates that approximately 40% of such drivers are mostly within the age range of 16 and 17. In essence, a phone call or a simple text messaging or reading while on the wheel is lethal and often lead to crash, not only Nigeria but on the global scale.

In the same vein was the use of phones by pedestrians while walking on high ways and inner roads; using it either for making or receiving calls; pinging and playing games. A more disastrous act of mobile phone usage was blocking the ears with earpieces while listening to music such that it becomes difficult for such phone users to hear the sounds of moving and horning vehicles. The resultant effect of such losses of concentration while walking the roads is traffic accident which are either critically maiming or fatal.

- **Examination Malpractice:** In as much as mobile phone serves useful educational purpose when put to good use, it is staggering to observe the deployment of the communication device for examination malpractice among Nigerian in-school youths. A personal observation and observations of several individuals who had served as invigilators on various national and school examinations conducted in the country showed that mobile phones are intensively used by students to facilitate cheating during examinations in various ways. For instance, the short text message component of the mobile phones is highly deployed for communication of answers to multiple choice examinations between students in the examination halls; and in some cases between student(s) who is/are writing the examination and someone else outside the examination halls. This is more common during national examinations such as the Unified Tertiary Matriculation Examination (UTME) conducted by Joint Admission and Matriculation Board, Senior Secondary Certificate Examination (SSCE) by National Examination Council (NECO), and West African Senior Secondary Certificate Examination (WASSCE) by the West African Examination Council (WAEC). It is on this account that these examination bodies are the option of Computer-Based Test (CBT) as way to control examination malpractices among the students.

In same vein was the use of mobile phone for effecting examination malpractices by matriculated students or students of tertiary institutions either by recording lesson notes in audio format, documenting it on safe files or short text codes/ messages which are then secretly retrieved for copying during examinations. The audio files are often retrieved by means of the earpiece or headset thereby limiting the play sound to a user of the phone. Another dimension to mobile phone-induced examination malpractice was going online to source information in relation to a subject matter of concern from the web pages for retrieval and copying during an examination. Based on these experiences mobile phones are out rightly prohibited in any examination in the country.

- **Learning Distraction:** Alongside the use of mobile phone as a tool of examination malpractice was its distractive influence on learning concentration among the students. This becomes apparent as students focused on the use of mobile phone, either for playing games or browsing the net for whatever reason known to them, rather than paying the deserved attention to ongoing educational instruction in the classroom. Awake (2009) considers the practice of working on a computer while watching television and talking on the phone, or toggling between say, electronic mail (e-mail) and other programmes as multitasking. In the same vein, lecture attendance alongside the use of phones either for browsing, making calls, reading text messages, playing games or watching films becomes multitasking and as such, it becomes impossible to gain a depth of knowledge of any of the tasks, especially the academic learning.

That is, in no way could someone follow a number of things at the same time hoped to have indepth knowledge of all. Hence, mobile phone usage during lecture hours by students results in superficial learning and poor retention of taught of lessons.

In addition to distractive learning influence of the mobile phone as induced by students multitasking with the communication tool was the regular and noisy ringing of the phones and the frequent exit of students to receive such calls. Observation and interactive discussion with both students and lecturers on this issue reveals this occurrence as a serious problem and hindrance to effective teaching and learning in academic environment. To stem the tide of mobile-phone-induced distraction among students, lecturers often urged them to switch off their phones during lecture hours and disobedient to such instruction attracts seizure of the students' phones and other necessary sanctions against the erring students.

- **Inducement of Immorality:** While mobile phones serve as element of entertainment in terms of usage for playback of video and audio files of recorded or downloaded films and music, and for playing games, application of the communication device to the extreme of entertainment has resulted in debasing or induced immorality among the phone users. Specific immorality-mediated phone include pornographic viewing whereby nude pictures or videos are downloaded for viewing. In the same vein was the use of the camera and/or video component of the phones for taking and recording self nudity or that of immoral partners. This may in turn be forwarded to other immoral fellows in of 'sexting' – the practice of sending lewd images of either self or that of someone else to another person. In this wise, taking of nude pictures or construction of sexuality messages are readily communicated in for of text message between immoral partners or posted on the web for attractions of other unsuspecting individuals into immoral entertainment. With this practice on the mobile phone platform, Awake (2009) describe the internet-based phones as a "shopping mall" for sexual predators and others with bad motives. But due to socio-cultural dissonance or unacceptability of such immoral practices, the phone-induced immoral act is often done secretly by the phone users.

CONCLUSION

A conscious observation, interviews and discussion with mobile phones users, and critical review of literature on mobile telephony development and usage in Nigeria showed that the country has witnessed a tremendous growth and transformation in the telecom sector. With four mobile network service providers in the country and competition for market dominance among them, the cost of mobile phone acquisition and operation had greatly decline such that functional lines subscribe to by phone users surged from more or less 18,724 lines between 1960 and 2000 to an outstanding 172,625,725 lines between 2001 – when the mobile communication services commenced in the country As at April 2014, the nation's teledensity was 91.4, indicating a fast growing mobile communication in the country – and 2014. Exploitation of the mobile communication tool for social and economic purposes has thus transformed the socioeconomic status of the country in terms of attraction of investors into the telecom sector, generation of income for the Nigerian Government, creation of employment opportunities, ease of business and financial transaction as economic impacts. The social impacts of the mobile phone revolution in the country include facilitation of prompt interactive linkages and exchange of information, entertainment and social networking. Other forms of impacts include its influence on educational and health services in the country. Despite the transformation impact of the mobile phone revolution in the country, exploitation of the communication tool for social vices by unscrupulous individuals was too obvious to be underplayed. The negative impacts arising from mobile phone-mediated nefarious acts include losses of hard earned income to swindlers by unsuspecting individuals, road accidents as result of usage of phone while on the wheel and provision of deceptive information by one person to the other during phone calls. This notwithstanding, the telecom sector has in general be of great value to most Nigerian and has enabled them to readily interact with one another, facilitate business and financial transactions thereby having their social and economic well being transformed.

REFERENCES

Ajayi, O., Salawu, R. I., & Raji, T. I. (n. d.). A century of telecommunications development in Nigeria –what next? Retrieved from http://www.vii.org/papers/nigeria.htm

Alabi, G. A. (1996). Telecommunications in Nigeria. University of Pennsylvania, African Studies Centre. Retrieved from www.africa.upenn.edu/ECA/aisi_inftl

Technology: Blessing or curse. (2009, November). *Awake!* New York: Watch Tower and Tract Society. (pp. 1 – 9).

Babbie, E. (2005). *The basics of social research*. Australia: Wadsworth.

Nigeria mobile market: Insight statistics and forecast. (2014). *BudeComm*. Retrieved from http://www.budde.com.au/Research/Nigeria-Mobile-Market-Insights-Statistics-and-Forecasts.html

Cash-less Nigeria. (n. d.). Central Bank of Nigeria. Retrieved November 22, 2014 from http://www.cenbank.org/cashless/

The Olusegun Obasanjo reforms: Telecommunication sector. (n. d.). Federal Ministry of Information and National Orientation – FMNIO.

Gallup (2010). Mobile phone access varies widely in sub-Saharan Africa: Average phone owner is more likely to be male, educated, and urban. Retrieved from http://www.gallup.com/poll/149519/mobile-phone-access-varies-widely-sub-saharan-africa.aspx

Ige, O. (n. d.). Evolution of the telecommunications industry. Retrieved from http://www.ncc.gov.ng/archive/Archive%20of%20Speeches/telecomevolution-olawale_ige170402.pdfSlide presentation 49pp

ICT: Facts and figures. (2014). International Telecommunication Union. Retrieved from https://www.itu.int/en/ITU D/Statistics/Documents/facts/ICTFactsFigures2014-e.pdf

Isiguzo, K. (2010). Foreword. In *The impact of mobile services in Nigeria: How mobile technologies are transforming economic and social activities*. Pyramid Research.

Lawal-Adebowale, O. A. (2010). Telecom sector policy deregulation and mobile phone diffusion in Nigeria – an assessment of impact on adoption and usage. P*roceedings of the 3rd Annual Conference of African Society for Information and Communication Technology* (pp. 177 – 185).

Lawal-Adebowale, O. A. (2008). Fixed Wireless telephony system: A help line for bridging rural digital divide and transformation of rural communities in southwest Nigeria. Proceedings of the 16th Annual Conferee of the Nigerian Rural Sociological Association (pp. 241 – 245).

Lawal-Adebowale, O. A., & Adebayo, K. (2006). *Information and Communication Technologies: Pathways for Effecting Feedback in Mass Method of Extension Message Delivery. In proceedings of Agricultural Extension Society of Nigeria* (pp. 183–189). AESON.

Levin, J., & Fox, J. A. (2000). *Elementary statistics in social research* (8th ed.). Needham Heights, MA: Allyn & Bacon.

Longe, O. M., & Longe, O. D. (n. d.). An overview of the development in the telecommunication industry of Nigeria. Retrieved from http://www.ircabfoundation.org/ journals/st/an%20overview%20of%20the%20development%20in%20the%20telecommunication%20industr%20of%20nigeria.pdf

Mawoli, M. A. (2009). Liberalisation of the Nigerian telecommunication sector: A critical review. *Journal of Research in National Development, 7* (2), not paged. Retrieved from http://www.transcampus.org/JORINDV7Dec2009/journalV7NO2Dec2009.html

Mobility Nigeria. (2014a). Mobipedia Nigeria: Facts and figures. Retrieved from http://mobility.ng/quick-facts/

Mobility Nigeria. (2014b). 2014 Stats: Is Nigeria becoming a smartphone market? Retrieved from http://mobility.ng/2014-is-nigeria-becoming-a-smartphone-market/

Mobility Nigeria. (2013). Nigerian smartphone market figures for 2012. Retrieved from http://mobility.ng/nigerian-smartphone-market-figures-for-2012/

National Communication Commission. (2014). Subscriber data base. Retrieved from http://www.ncc.gov.ng/index.php?Option=com_content&view=article&id=1390:vanguard-23rd-april-2014-telecom-activities-may-keep-nigerias-rebased-gdp-green&catid=86:cat-Mediapr-headlines

National Communication Commission - NPT. (2000). National Policy on Communication. Ministry of Communication. Retrieved from http://www.ncc.gov.ng

Ndukwe, E. C. A. (n. d.).Telecommunications as a vehicle for socio-economic development. Slide presentation. 12pp. Retrieved from http://www.ncc.gov.ng/archive/speeches_presentations/EVC's%20Presentation/2009/socio.pdf

Ndukwe, E. C. A. (2003a). Telecommunication in national development. A Slide Presentation, 45pp. Retrieved from http://ncc.gov.ng/archive/speeches_presentations/EVC's%20Presentation/The%20Role%20of%20Telecommunications%20in%20National%20Devep.pdf

Ndukwe, E. C. A. (2003b). An overview of evolution of the telecommunication industry in Nigeria and challenges ahead (1999-2003). Retrieved from http://www.ncc.gov.nig/ speeches-presentation/EVC's%20Presentation/overview%20of %20Telecom%20.

Ndukwe, E. C. A. (2003c). The role of telecommunications in national development. Proceedings of the 19th Omolayole Annual Management Lecture, held at the Chartered Institute of Bankers' Auditorium Victoria Island, Lagos. Retrieved from http://ncc.gov.ng/archive/speeches_presentations/EVC's%20Presentation/The%20Role%20of%20Telecommunications%20in%20National%20Devep.pdf

Ndukwe, E. C. A. (2003d). Telecommunication regulation: Nigerian challenges & direction. Proceedings of Telecommunications workshop NICON. Hilton, Abuja.

Ndukwe, E. C. A. (2005). Telecom liberalization in Nigeria: Opening up the market and sector reform. Proceedings of SATCOM. Retrieved from http://ncc.gov.ng/archive/speeches_presentations/EVC's%20Presentation/Telecoms%20Liberalisation%20in%20Nigeria.pdf

Ndukwe, E. C. A. (2006). Country experience in telecom market reforms [Slideshow]. Retrieved from http://ncc.gov.ng/archive/EVCSpeches/2009_NITDEL_Lecture.pdf

Ndukwe, E. C. A. (2009). Telecom in the service of the modern society.

Telecom Development Lecture (n. d.). NITDEL. Retrieved from http://ncc.gov.ng/archive/EVC-Speches/2009_NITDEL_Lecture.pdf

Ndukwe, E. C. A. (2004). The imperative of accelerating the deployment of Information and communications technologies (ICTs) for social and economic development. Proceedings of the 11th Herbert Macaulay Memorial Lecture. Retrieved from http://www.ncc.gov.ng/archive/speeches_presentations/EVC's%20Presentation/11th%20Herbert%20Maculay%20Memorial%20-%20220704.pdf

Ndukwe, E. C. A. (2004). Communications technology in the 21st century. Proceedings of annual general meeting of the Nigerian Society of Engineers, Enugu Branch, Enugu.

Nigeriafirst (2003), *Telecommunication in Nigeria.* Retrieved from http://www.nigeriafirst.org/Tcom

The impact of mobile services in Nigeria: How mobile technologies are transforming economic and social activities. (2010). Pyramid Research. Retrieved from www.pyramidresearch.com

25% Nigerian mobile phone subscribers use smartphones. (2013, January 8). *Punch.* Retrieved from http://www.punchng.com/business/technology/25-of-nigerian-mobile-subscribers-use-smartphones-tns

Why South Africa is Africa's top destination for smartphone debuts. (2014). *Technology Marketing Corporation.* Retrieved from http://www.tmcnet.com/usubmit/-why-south-africa-africas-top-destination-smartphone-debuts-/2014/10/19/8074353.htm

Usoro, P. (2007). Telecommunications Law and Practice in Nigeria [Slideshow]. Proceedings of the Nigerian Bar Association Bar Week.

Ojo, J. (2011). Appraisal of a decade of GSM revolution in Nigeria. Public Affairs Analyst. Retrieved from http://jideojong.blogpost.com/

Rural telephony: Huge investments, low impact. (2011). *TheNigerianDaily.com.* Retrieved from http://www.thenigeriandaily.com/

Vanguard (2010). Rural Telephony: MTN covers 350 uncovered villages with smart technology. Retrieved from http://www.thevanguardnr.com

Chapter 17
Overview of Electronic Payment System:
A Special Reference to India

Sanghita Roy
West Bengal University of Technology, India

ABSTRACT

The emergence of e-commerce has created new financial needs that in many cases cannot be effectively fulfilled by the traditional payment systems. The advent of the Electronic commerce has prompted the invention of several payment tools to facilitate the completion of business transactions over the Internet. There are different methods to pay electronically. Recognizing this, virtually all interested parties are exploring various types of electronic payment system and issues surrounding electronic payment system and digital currency. Broadly electronic payment systems can be classified into four categories: Online Credit Card Payment System, Online Electronic Cash System, Electronic Cheque System and Smart Cards based Electronic Payment System. Each payment system has its advantages and disadvantages for the customers and merchants. These payment systems have numbers of requirements: e.g. security, acceptability, convenience, cost, anonymity, control, and traceability. Therefore, instead of focusing on the technological specifications of various electronic payment systems, the researcher has distinguished electronic payment systems based on what is being transmitted over the network; and analyzed the difference of each electronic payment system by evaluating their requirements, characteristics and assessed the applicability of each system. To sustain in the competition more banks are following e-commerce and especially using e-payment mechanism. Though Indian economy is basically cash driven, still India is not far behind in adopting E-payment services in retail and banking sector.

INTRODUCTION

Financial system is the backbone of every economy. In order to handle staggering number of monetary transactions every economy requires a reliable financial system. By financial system it means banks and non-bank financial institutions which provide various types of financial services to the customers. In the payment system fund transfer service and financial clearing are the

DOI: 10.4018/978-1-4666-8598-7.ch017

two most important services than other services. Payment system improves financial intelligibility, stimulating business growth and helps in banking sector reform. Attitude of people towards a new payment system has been changing for the last two decades largely due to the following reasons:

1. **Increased either Volume or Value of Transaction:** As people are becoming more conscious regarding their financial matter, numbers as well as value of the transactions are increasing. This phenomenon is attributed to the rapid growth in financial market activity around the world and the payment generated by such activity.
2. **Technological Enhancement:** From last two decades there is an incredible technological improvement in banking and financial sector. It is due to the advancement of Information and Communication Technology and massive growth of Internet. As a result, financial institutions and consumers both have the ability and the resource to move funds much faster through the system, at a lower cost.
3. **Effect of Globalization:** With the effect of globalization more and more businesses have started to overcome geographical boundaries. As a result more financial transactions are flowing across the countries. The company that has the capability to streamline its payment mechanism is able to trim costs and thus achieve competitive advantage. This can be possible only in cross-nation payment.

Globalization and financial revolution have changed specially the developing countries in many aspects.[1] Opportunity of trade and investments have increased, consumers taste and preferences have changed, demands for foreign products and services have increased. Technological advancements make the world more and more borderless. Advancements in communication and information technology bundled with Internet have produced unprecedented opportunities in the global economy, where Internet connects digitally all countries and regions. Electronic money, which is an electronic replacement for cash, is a product of such digital convergence. It is storable, transferable and perhaps unforgettable. The purpose of this chapter is to provide a comprehensive idea of Electronic money and Electronic Payment System and its acceptance in India.

Since the late 1970's and early 1980's, a variety of schemes have been proposed to allow payment over the computer network. The idea of paying for goods and services electronically is not a new one. Aristotle (384 – 322 B.C.) said that – everything must be assessed by money; for this enables men always to exchange their services and so makes society possible.

The arrival of Internet has changed the whole world. It brings the whole universe into our palm. The growth of Electronic Commerce has been possible only due to the availability of World Wide Web (WWW) technology. Initially the focus of Electronic Commerce was to sell goods like computer peripherals and software, books, music CDs etc. to consumers. Around 1999, industries shifted their focus on the trade that the companies can do with each other. They tried to build online electronic market place using the benefits of Electronic Commerce. With this Business-to-Business (B2B) Electronic Commerce it becomes possible to bring together businesses such as car manufacturer with its ancillary suppliers or computer manufacturers with its dealers. B2B E-Commerce has larger potential than Business-to-Consumer (B2C), as per estimation B2B had reached $226 billion worldwide in 2000 and $2.7 trillion on 2004.

In both B2B and B2C sector, firstly, Internet was used as a means of searching of products and services, payment being carried out off-line by some conventional payment method i.e. cash or check.

In early 90's, when the first edition of Electronic Payment System was released, a huge variety of various payment methods were available in the market which were developed either by academic researchers or commercial interests. Some of these got success and most of them failed to get acceptance from mass. Early market leaders such as First Virtual Inc., Cyber Cash Inc. and Digicash launched payment systems that achieved some quite extensive deployment but failed to generate an economic return. At the same time, many new companies started up, offering new methods of payment for B2B and B2C sector. In case of B2B payment it requires large amount of money transfer and bank plays the role of mediator for large value transfer.

In the primitive age by payment meant direct exchange of goods and services for other goods and services. This system is known as '*double coincidence of wants*'. This means, for example, if a person wants to exchange food for a cow he must first find another such type of person who is both hungry and also has a cow. Over the centuries this system has been replaced by various forms of money.

The earliest money was called *commodity money*, where physical commodities (such as corn, salt, cotton) whose values were known and were used to make payment. After Industrial revolution in the 1800s gold and silver coins were used as commodity money as they were portable and divisible. The next step in the progression of money was the use of tokens such as paper notes. This is referred to as adopting a commodity standard.

In a stable economy, it becomes unnecessary to have commodity backing for notes that are issued. This is referred to as *fiat money* since the tokens only have value by virtue of the fact that the Government declares it to be so, and it is widely accepted.

LITERATURE REVIEW

Sumanjeet Singh (2009) has classified Electronic Payment System into four categories – online credit card payment system, online Electronic cash system, Electronic check system and Smart card based Electronic Payment System. Several advantages and disadvantages of various payment system in view of customers and merchants are discussed. Instead of focusing on technological specification, primary thrust was given on what is being transmitted over the network and analyze the difference of each Electronic Payment System by evaluating their requirements, characteristics and assess the applicability of each system.

From the study it is clear that despite the existence of variety of E-payment options, credit cards are the most dominant payment system. Second option is debit card. Like many other study, the present study reveals the prospect of smart card based Electronic Payment System and predicts that in future smart card will eventually replace other Electronic Payment System options. On the other hand, due to limited user-base, e-cash has not gained much popularity. There are a number of factors which affect the usage of Electronic Payment System. Among all these user base is most important. Apart from this, other factors are consumer preferences, ease of use, cost, industry agreement, authorization, security, authentication, accessibility, reliability and public policy.

Aastha Gupta and Munish Gupta (2013) in the paper tried to examine and analyze the stage-wise development of Indian Payment System from the ancient age to present time. The article focused on only payment settlement system and it is based on secondary data sources. The developments in Information and Communication Technology (ICT) resulted in numerous innovations in the payment system of India. There are variety of electronic clearing options but they are limited than demand of bank customers in India. Due to lack of ICT, connectivity and other infrastructure problems – all these facilities are not provided at sufficient level to the rural India.

Raganish Dass and Sujoy Pal from IIM, Ahmedabad tried to explore the factors affecting the adoption of Mobile Financial Services (MFS) among rural under banked. From the study it was revealed that the demand for banking and financial services along with the hardship faced by the population in availing such services through the existing channels of delivery, were prime drivers for adoption of MFS among the rural under-banked. On the other hand, lack of trust and low technology readiness were found to be the prime bottlenecks in adoption of such services. Perceived financial cost is also a matter of concern among the rural people. Such laggings can be removed through increased awareness and usage among peers.

Aaron L. Philips (1998) explained migration of corporate payments from check to electronic format. The Treasury Management Association (TMA) in USA conducted a survey in early 1998 to identify the barriers, benefits and incentives for converting corporate paper check payments to electronic forms (ACH and EDI). The result revealed that federal and state mandates (e.g. tax payments) to be the most common incentives for organizations to adopt electronic payments. The major disadvantages was lack of vendor (trading – partner) capability to receive Electronic Payment accompanied by remittance information, lack of systems integration and cost of additional technology. The most important benefits are lower costs, certainty of payment date and improved cash-flow projections.

In Iran the research was carried out to evaluate the specifications of Electronic Payment System. Four types of specifications are considered, such as – technical, legal, security and socio-economic. At the end of the study it is found that socio-economical factors like factors of economical development, per capita income level, unemployment rate, multiple rate of foreign exchange, cost of internet etc. plays a major role in acceptance of Electronic Payment System in Iranian bank users.

Khalili et. al.(2012) tried to evaluate Electronic Payment System in Iran and the result showed that debit card is the most preferred Electronic Payment System, followed by Credit Card and Electronic check.

Khiaonarong(2000) examined the creation of modern Electronic Payment System in Thailand and concluded that this creation has helped to facilitate the turnover of fund in the economy.

Nigerian payment system has been predominantly cash based. In 1st January, 2009 Electronic Payment System was introduced in order to prevent corruptions and delay in Government payment. To know the feedback of Electronic payment implementation a study was carried out among 200 respondents in 2010. Majority of the respondents agreed that the new payment system is better than the old system of cash and check in spite of its minor drawbacks which can be overcome in near future.

In 2012 a study was done in Lagos, Nigeria to examine payment pattern adopted by Nigerian consumers and motivational factors for using debit card. The result of the analysis shows that in spite of various difficulties cash and check continue to remain a dominant form of payment in Nigerian economy. Convenience of use and time saving benefits are the factors behind the popularity of use of debit cards. Nigerians basically use a combination of various payment instruments based on their convenience, specially ATM/debit card or debit card/check.

Credit card is a small plastic card which was first launched in Indian market in 1960 by Diner's club card. Between foreign and Indian banks, foreign banks have a dominant share due to various reason. Credit cards have changed the way people look at money. Previously only the rich people in selected cities could use it. Today, it is a way of life for the middle class too, even in smaller location across the country. The utility of cards varies from person to person depending on their profile. Majority people are only aware of cash withdrawal facilities of credit card. But most of them are not aware of all the detail benefits of credit card like – interest free credit period, money lending facility etc.

All around the globe, credit card ownership and usage have increased substantially in last few years. Research showed that debt associated with credit card usage has been on the rise in recent decades. (Wickramasinghe & Gurugamage, 2009) In a paper Godfrey Themba showed that credit card ownership and its usage in Botswana are relatively high and very much influenced by consumers demographics i.e. income, age, education, gender and marital status as well as attitude towards debt. In case of attitude towards debt age and gender are significantly related where the youths and females are more likely than other demographic groups to have negative attitude towards debt.

Talwar(1999) examined IT revolution in banking sector which has not only provided services to the customers but has also reduced the operational cost. Wenninger (2000) examined the impact of Electronic Commerce in banking sector. E-commerce created new form of competition among banks and banks adopted E-payment techniques as a survival strategy. Monoharan (2007) highlighted the Electronic Payment System in India and its impact on Indian banking sector. In a paper Singh et. al. (2012) studies the impact of E-banking on payment and clearing system and identifies the important factors for the customers to choose electronic banking as a mode of payment

A survey on Greek bank's customers was done whose target was to demonstrate revised Technology Acceptance Model (TAM) to measure users' attitude towards adoption of online electronic payment services which will offer increased security on payment via Internet. There are a number of factors which affect adoption of payment instruments such as switching barriers between alternatives, attractiveness of alternatives and switching cost. Initial findings prove a positive relation between ease of use and actual usage of the new service.

Till date, a large section of our society prefer transactions that involve physical contact of people, cash and checks. That's why, security, trust and convenience are among the major contending factors that affect adoption of Electronic Payment System in Nigeria. E-payment initiative began in Nigeria in 2009 and this service is available mostly in capital city and some bigger cities nationwide. Factors which hinders progress of E-payment services in Nigeria are – lack of trust, poor infrastructure, slow development of information and communication technology and also banking sector.

Gholami et. al. (2010) defined Electronic Payment System as the use of pre-loaded debit and credit cards on Internet and other electronic devices to perform daily transactions which include paying for goods and services, money transfer and bill payment at any time of the day. By Electronic Payment System we mean use of credit card, Magnetic Ink Character Reader (MICR) check, Automated Teller Machine (ATM), E-cash, Electronic Fund Transfer (EFT) etc. that are used to facilitate the customer's decision to pay for a product or services. (Vassiliou, 2004)

Ayo (2006) tried to investigate the Electronic Payment System in Nigeria using Ability, Motivation and Opportunity (AMO) model. From the study it was found that only a good number of Nigerian companies have some sorts of online exposure. Ayo also mentioned that motivation and opportunities for E-business is low mainly due to lack of E-payment infrastructure and access to ICT facilities. In his next study Ayo used extended TAM which showed that perceived ease of use and perceived usefulness were not only antecedents of E-payment and banking acceptance in Nigeria, these factors also mattered in promoting continued usage of such innovations among businesses and the Nigerian populace.

With an intention to expand use of Electronic Payment System in Nigerian small firms, it is found that top management support, organizational readiness and IS vendor support are essential. While perceived usefulness is found to be an important factor, perceived ease of use does not have any meaningful influence on small firms' intention to expand Electronic Payment System use. Variables of Government support and financial resource support did not positively influence the intention to expand Electronic Payment System use in Nigerian small firms.

in a study the author has tried to examine the association between retail bank customers' ATM usage patterns and their perceptions of ATM attributes by identifying those variables which distinguish users and non-users. By assessing ATM usage patterns and perceptual variables, the study concludes that a strategy of stressing the most important perceived attribute of relative advantage is crucial to the success of the current efforts by bank marketers aimed at increasing ATM usage.

In a paper Chang-tseh Hsich reviewed some intriguing features of some major online payment instruments, such as – E-cash, Smart Card, Electronic wallet. Their potential problems and some practical strategies to reduce the possible frauds associated with the use of those instruments on the NET was discussed. However, most of the payment instruments have not gained acceptance by either merchants or customers or both for reasons ranging from cost to security concerns. The most commonly used tool is credit card, through certain degree of risks are involved in it. In this situation support of banking industry is essential. Banks must play more proactive roles in setting up the standards for using those instruments and to coordinate the transaction payment operations among all parties involved.

For real-time online credit card processing, a merchant needs to install a third party proprietary software in the merchant Electronic Commerce server. Mohammad and Emmanul (2003) discussed about various issues that need to be resolved before integrating a third party payment solution to a merchant E-commerce system. Critical factors such as cost, complexity and security associated with the implementation and maintenance of such systems are also discussed. Such a result can be extremely valuable to small businesses that are venturing into E-commerce.

David Wright has done a comparative evaluation between credit card payment system, e-check system and digital cash system. It also evaluates their advantages and disadvantages to the customer, merchant, service provider and financial institutions. In order to protect the system from the risk of hacking, cryptographic technique is suggested which will provide security. The paper concludes with a description of a new system, which is designed to relieve that concern by allowing payments over the telephone network for purchases made over the Internet.

Reddy (2012) classified Electronic Payment System into four general types – Online Credit Card Payment System, Electronic Check System, Electronic Cash System and Smart Card Based Electronic Payment System. From his study, it was found that despite the existence of variety of Electronic Payment options, Credit Cards are the most dominant payment system, followed by Debit card. Interestingly this fact is supported by a recent study of the leading research firm Nielsen. With respect to online purchase India has third biggest credit card users followed by Turkey and Ireland. Amongst various credit cards, more than half or about 53% Indian prefer Visa card. India has a good market for Electronic Commerce and Smart Card based Electronic Payment System has the potential to replace all the other E-payment options. There are a number of factors which affect the usage of Electronic Payment System. Among all these user base is most important. Success of Electronic Payment depends on several options, like consumer preferences, Ease of use, cost, industry agreement, authorization, security, authentication, accessibility and reliability and public policy.

Despite the growth of Internet In 2001 Chiravari and Nazareth tried to realize the challenge experienced between business and consumers in electronic Commerce world. They found that trust as a major concern for consumers to buy online. In a paper trust and its antecedents, usefulness and ease of use are identified and Technology Acceptance Model (TAM) is used to present an alternative framework of the consumer's usage of Internet for Electronic Commerce.

Nigerian economy is basically paper-based with an objective to introduce modern banking techniques Central Bank of Nigeria (CBN) started cashless system of payment. Their objective was to reduce robbery, high cost of processing cash, revenue leakages, inefficient treasury management etc. The study indicated that Electronic Payment System has a great influence on Nigerian economy. It leads to significant decrease in deposit mobilization and credit extension by Nigerian deposit money banks. Bulks of Nigerian economy are run by SME and micro traders. It is expected that the policy of cashless economy in Nigeria will influence specifically the low income group, who are currently deeply rooted in using cash and see it as a convenient and easy way of receiving and making payments.

Apart from several benefits of Electronic Payment System James J. McAndrews (1999) discussed about various types of risks associated with Electronic Payment System. Operational risk, fraud and legal risk pose new challenges to payment system risk control. System operators should learn the lessons from the previous failures in similar system. Electronic Payment System providers should have well understood procedures to resolve problems and detecting counterfeiting or other fraud. Contracts assigning liabilities between technology companies and financial companies should be explicit to reduce legal uncertainty. He suggested that consumers should be informed of the system procedures to resolve operational problems, detection of frauds or use of counterfeits. All these efforts will help to reduce uncertainties that might otherwise prevent wide spread acceptance of this new system.

Malaysian Researchers tried to understand how user trust can enhance the acceptance of Electronic Commerce. The key research model is reviewed using Technology Acceptance Model proposed by Davis for E-Commerce trust from different perspectives and integrate them into a single model. This study focuses on factors that are perceived to affect user trust from a psychological, cultural and even interface design point of view. In the field of electronic Commerce and trust building, the use of TAM, infused with the trust element is perceived to be adequate and efficient to assess users' trust levels and acceptance of a presence-based virtual shopping environment.

Delali Kumaga(2010) in his thesis attempted to investigate challenges of implementing Electronic Payment System in Ghana. In addition, it also attempts to assess the degree of usage of e-zwich, debit and credit card. E-zwich is a national domestic smart card whose purpose is to reduce large amount of cash held outside the banking system. Despite the attempt taken by Government to automate the payment system, it is estimated that only 20% of the population have bank accounts and 90% of the cash issued by the Bank of Ghana is still held by the non-bank public. Basically people are not aware of the benefits of Electronic Payment and are therefore slow to adopt it. Finally the study revealed that e-zwich payment system has the potential to reduce the number of unbanked in Ghana. However, more education of the public especially the rural people and banks are necessary to realize its full potential. The challenges faced by the Government in implementing Electronic Payment System in Ghana is categorized into four main group i.e. security, infrastructure, legal and regulatory issues and socio-cultural issues. Electronic Payment in Ghana during the past few years have undergone significant progress, but still it is paper-based. Only few restaurants and shops have established Point Of Sale machines to perform transaction through debit card. Still 80% population in Ghana is unbanked. Mass campaign, advertisement and training on Electronic Payment is necessary so that it attracts Ghanaian population and they start using E-payment products.

REQUIREMENTS OF AN ELECTRONIC PAYMENT SYSTEM

Before discussing Electronic payment system in depth, we start our discussion on conventional payment systems i.e. payment by cash. Nowadays cash transaction is the most popular and simplified form of money transfer. But as the amounts get larger, security becomes an issue and people avail the services of various financial Institutions such as bank, Post Office etc. Cash can be easily transferred from one individual to another or from one account to another. In paper form, it is quite portable and larger amounts can be carried in a pocket or in briefcase – where no transaction charges are levied.

But on contrary cash is not free. High value printing costs are involved in it. Risks are involved in carrying cash. There is a chance of theft or robbery. Once the cash has been produced, it must then be transferred to banks or companies under very high security. Vaults must be built to store it and high insurance premium is charged to cover losses due to theft. There is a risk of counterfeit notes. Nevertheless, cash is the most commonly used form of payment. In our country still 80% transactions are cash based. One of the reason behind the popularity of cash payment is the development of automated Teller Machine (ATM) which allow consumers to access money in cash form much easily.

WHAT IS E-MONEY AND HOW DOES IT WORK?

Traditionally, people or businesses use tokens or objects as a symbol of money. Tokens represents a standard monetary value. By token we mean quarters or dollars in US, rupees in India. With the advent of Internet, market place is expanding virtually and society is becoming more and more paperless. E-Money is sometimes viewed as electronic transfer of funds from one party to another where the transfer may be debit or credit. Electronic-money or Electronic cash or digital cash is basically a combination of stream of 0 and 1 which is stored on an electronic storage device. E-Money cannot be restricted within geographic boundaries. It can be carried on a number of devices viz. magnetic swipe card, smart card, computer memory, mobile phone or Personal Digital Assistant (PDA). Electronic money may be useful when making payment over the Internet, where credit cards are uneconomical or whether the individuals making the payments do not own credit cards.

BASIC OF ELECTRONIC PAYMENT SYSTEM

In Electronic Payment System transaction of goods and services take place using Internet network. The main objectives of Electronic Payment System

Figure 1. Electronic payment scheme

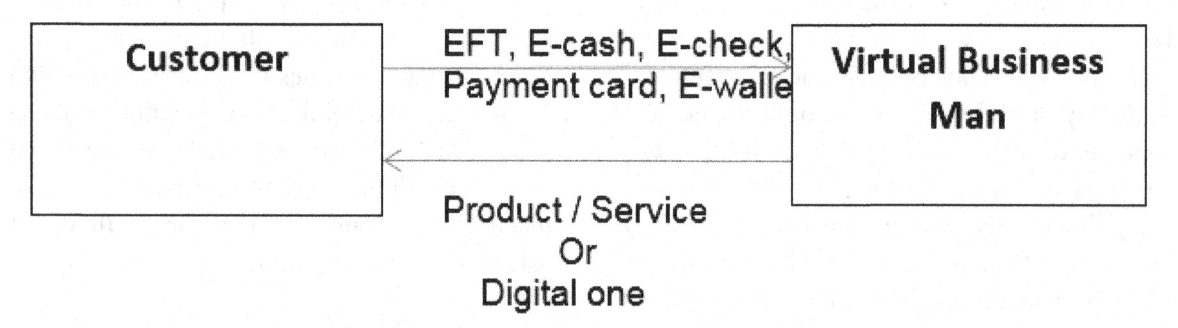

are to increase efficiency, improve security, and enhance customer convenience.

For online transactions online buyers may use one of the following EPSs to pay for products/ services:

- **Electronic Funds Transfer (EFT)**: EFT involves electronic transfer of money by financial institutions.
- **Payment Cards**: It contains stored financial value that can be transferred from the customer's computer to the businessman's computer.
- **Credit Cards**: These are the most popular method used in EPSs and are used by charging against the customer credit.
- **Smart Cards**: It includes stored financial value and other important personal and financial information used for online payments.
- **Electronic Money (e-Money/e-Cash)**: This is standard money converted into an electronic format to pay for online purchases.
- **Online Payment**: This can be used for monthly payment for Internet, phone bills, etc.
- **Electronic Wallets (e-Wallets)**: These are similar to smart cards as they include stored financial value for online payments. Basically, function of e-wallet is overlapping. E-***wallets*** can be classified as ***payment cards*** when they are used to store credit card information or as ***e-money*** when they store electronic currency.
- **Electronic Gifts**: Here electronic currency or gift certificates are sent from one individual to another. Using this the receiver can purchase through online stores provided they accept this type of currency.

It is very much essential to standardize the various payment mechanism. Transaction through Internet must be secure and valid. Security issues is crucial to the acceptance of online payment standards: consumers and merchants must believe that their information is kept unaltered and remains secure during transmission. SET and SSL are two standards that protect the integrity of online transactions.

FEATURES OF ELECTRONIC PAYMENT SYSTEM

Evaluation of Electronic Payment System (EPS) is quite difficult and it is done based on few parameters[2]. These are:

1. **Identifiability** – If the system is able to keep record of all the transactions as a sequence of separate transaction then the system is considered as identifiable.
2. **Scalability** – A scalable system should be able to accommodate varying transaction sizes that may differ greatly in volume of traffic.
3. **Consistency** – A system is considered consistent if it is able to capture comparable information for comparable transactions. The information captured by the system depends upon the type of transaction.
4. **Interoperability** – Different countries have different forms of currencies and values. The system is considered interoperable if the owner of one form of money is able to convert it into another form.
5. **Transaction Cost** – An Electronic Payment System is sure to cost something to the user. So long as the cost of an electronic transaction is comparable to current physical money standards, we may not have anything to complain about. Although few banks and businesses charge their customers a fee when customers use notational forms of money.
6. **Security** – The whole Electronic payment services lies on browser based Internet protocol that are relatively open, the infrastructure

supporting electronic commerce must be resistant to attacks in an environment where eavesdropping and modification of messages is easy.

   a. **Authentication** is needed to make sure that persons in a transaction are who they claim to be.
   b. **Message Integrity** is needed to ensure that information has not been altered since the data was signed.
   c. **Double-Spending Prevention** is needed to prevent copied coins being spent repeatedly. This parameter is applicable only to token-based systems.

7. **Privacy-** Information must not be revealed to unauthorized people. This is achieved by using encryption technology. Only with the appropriate key the information can be easily decrypted and understood. In the privacy aspect of electronic payment systems we can distinguish three principles:
   a. **Payment Confidentiality**: payment details including payer, payee, account numbers, amounts, date and time must not be known to electronic observers who are monitoring the network traffic.
   b. **Payment Anonymity**: only a payer's pseudonym is known to the payee.
   c. **Payer Untraceability**: payment system cannot trace payments back to the payer.
8. **Online Verification:** Electronic payment systems that need the help of a distant computer throughout the transaction are said to be *online* systems. They have to be more secure to prevent problems of double spending and dishonest transactions. Paper money or gold coins can be traded for years without being deposited in a bank, but this is because they cannot be counterfeited. But digital notes are easy to copy. The cryptographic algorithms can catch counterfeiters, but only when the money is processed through a bank.

TYPES OF ELECTRONIC PAYMENT SYSTEMS

With the rapid growth of Electronic commerce, different Electronic payment systems have appeared in last decade. The grouping can be made on the basis of what information is being transferred online. According to Anderson (1998) E-payment system can be broadly divided into four general types –

1. Online Credit card or Debit card based payment system
2. Electronic check system
3. Electronic cash system
4. Smart card based E-payment system

There is one more transaction type which has not been included in the group i.e. *Electronic Fund Transfer*. Electronic Fund Transfer is one of the pioneer of paperless transaction. EFT is used for transferring money from one bank account directly to another without any paper money changing hands. The advantages of EFT contain the following:

- Simplified accounting
- Improved efficiency
- Reduced administrative costs
- Improved security

1. **Online Credit Card or Debit Card Based Payment System** – This is the most popular online payment tool, especially in the retail sector. Throughout the world most of the consumers and merchants have widely accepted it (Loudon and Traver, 2002) [3]. The most attractive features of credit card payments are: privacy, integrity, compatibility, good transaction efficiency, acceptability, convergence, mobility and low financial risk [3]. But payment system has raised several

problems before consumers and merchants, which include lack of authentication, repudiation of charges and credit card or debit card fraud.

Nowadays, there are two types of credit cards available in the market:

(i) Credit card issued by Credit Card companies like Visa, MasterCard
(ii) Credit card issued by various banks like ICICI, HSBC, SBI etc.

Customer's income level, credit history, and total wealth are the factors for issuing credit card. Credit cards are suitable for medium range of purchases. Often businesses offer incentives to attract customers to open an account and get one of these cards. But they are unsuitable to use for very small or very large payments. It is not cost-justified to use a credit card for small payments. Also, due to security issues, these cards have a limit and cannot be used for excessively large transactions.

Debit Cards

The difference between credit cards and debit cards is that in debit card there is no limit of purchase. The purchased amount will be automatically deducted from your account after the transaction is over. In credit card the amount is repaid during billing time.

2. **Electronic Check Payment System** – An e-check uses the same legal and business protocols associated with traditional paper checks. It is a new payment instrument that combines high-security, speed, convenience, and processing efficiencies for online transactions. An e-check can be used by large and small organizations, even where other electronic payment solutions are too risky or not appropriate.

The function of E-check method is almost same as paper check. An account holder will issue an e-check which will contain name of bank or financial Institution, person's account number, name of payee and amount. Like ordinary check E-check holds a MICR number. Electronic check system has many advantages - (1) during auction they do not require consumers to reveal account information to other individuals (2) they do not require consumers to continually send sensitive financial information over the web (3) it is less expensive than credit cards and (4) much faster than paper based traditional cheque. But, this system of payment also has several disadvantages-such as-relatively higher fixed costs and limited use in virtual world. So, this type of transaction is not so popular among retail users. It is generally useful in government sector and for B2B operations where anonymity is not required and amount of transactions is generally large enough to cover fixed processing cost.

3. **Electronic Cash Payment System** – E-cash is a digital form of cash that have limited convertibility into other forms of value and require intermediaries to convert. E-cash transaction takes place directly and immediately to the participating merchants and vending machines. E-cash usually operates on a smart ard, which includes an embedded microprocessor chip. The microprocessor chip stores cash value and the security features that make electronic transactions secure. Mondex, a subsidiary of MasterCard (Mondex Canada Association) is a good example of e-cash. This payment system offers numerous advantages like authority, privacy, good acceptability, low transactions cost, convenience and good anonymity. But, this system of payment also has many limitations like poor mobility, poor transaction efficiency and high financial risk, as people are solely responsible for the lost or stolen.

4. **Smart Card Based Electronic Payment System** – Smart cards are like credit cards with built-in memory chips or in some cases, microprocessor embedded in them so as to serve as storage devices which hold larger amount of encrypted information than credit cards with in-built transaction processing capability. Some smart cards have provisions to allow users to enter a Personal Identification Number or PIN code. It provides greater level of security than credit cards. Smart cards based electronic payment systems do not need to maintain a large real time database. Currently, the two smart cards based electronic payment system- Mondex and Visa card.

Apart from this, cash is stored in encrypted form onto the chip. In order to pay via smart card it is necessary to introduce the card into a hardware terminal. The device requires a special key from the issuing bank to start a money transfer in either direction. Smart cards can be disposable or rechargeable. A popular example of a disposable smart card is the one issued by telephone companies. After using the pre-specified amount, the card can be discarded.

Some of the advantages of smart cards include the following:

- Stored many types of information
- Not easily duplicated
- Not occupy much space
- Portable
- Low cost to issuers and users
- Included high security

The disadvantages of smart cards are the lack of universal standards for their design and utilization.

OVERVIEW OF CREDIT CARD PROCESSING

Credit cards are payment cards which works on "Pay Later" method of payment. The cards are issued by banks against a special purpose with some

Figure 2. Entities in conventional Credit Card Processing System

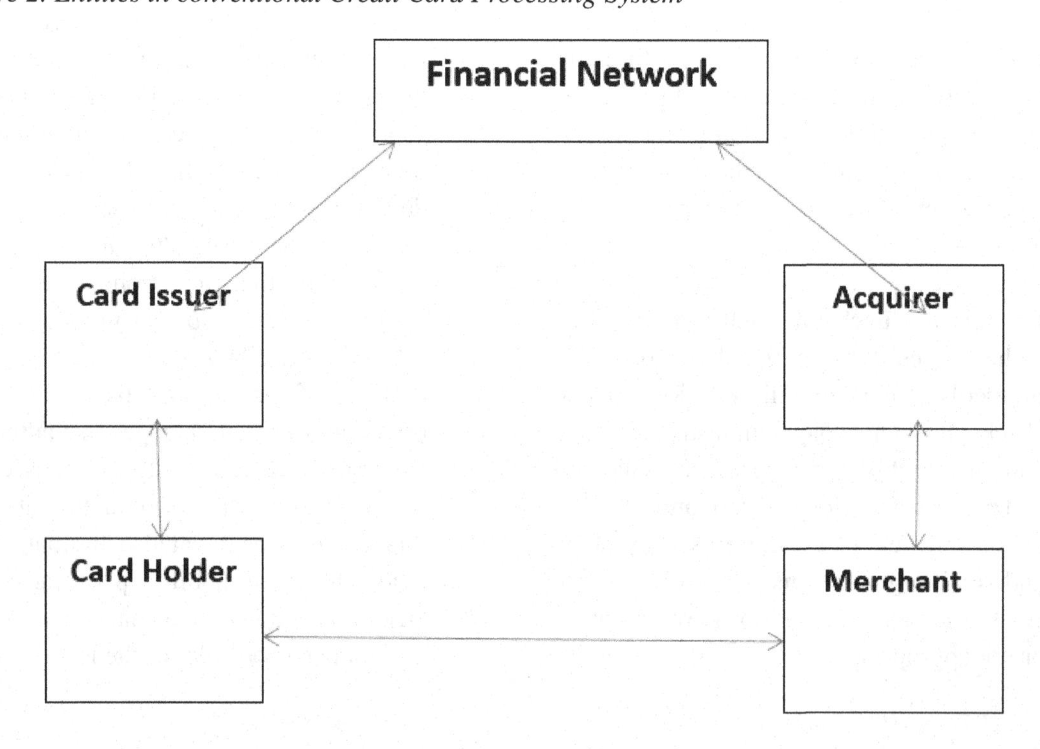

form of installment based repayment scheme [4]. Credit card was first introduced in 1958 by Diner's club. Today, there are two major organizations which capture 80% of the credit card market, they are Visa International and Mastercard.

There are four parties involved in credit card transaction. The issuing bank issues credit card to the buyer and maintains account of the buyer. Bank decides the limit of purchase using the credit card and decides the percentage of interest on the unpaid portion of the bill. The cardholder or the buyer performs a transaction. The merchant is the seller of goods or services. Merchant maintains an account with a bank or a financial institution known as the acquirer. When a Credit card transaction is performed acquiring institutions contracts with merchants and charges a certain percentage of fees for the transaction. Some of the well-known acquirers are Paymentech and Wells Fargo. Acquiring institutions sometimes outsource merchant services to third party processing systems like FDC (First Data Corporation), or Global Payment Systems (GPS). Acquiring institutions provide merchants services by using the existing financial network either directly or through third party processing system. Credit card payment takes place in two phase. The first phase is Authorization and the second phase is capture / settlement.

Authorization

Through Internet browser the consumer sends CC data to the merchant. Now Authorization starts, the merchant first verifies the cardholder's identification and credit limit. Then sends the credit card information like the card number, expiration date, and amount to the acquirer. The acquirer will forward the card details to the issuing bank via the existing financial network. The bank will either approve or decline the request or referral response where there is lack of information. If the transaction is approved, then the merchant can deliver the goods purchased to the buyer. A transaction can be declined for various reasons like unavailable credit, bad credit history, wrong address, etc.

Capture / Settlement

Here, the actual transfer of funds from the cardholder's account to the merchant's account takes place. As per the regulations imposed for Internet, a merchant cannot charge the buyer's credit card until the goods have actually been delivered. The transaction details of the card will be captured and the sale amount will be credited to the merchant's deposit account through the acquiring financial institution and posted to the cardholder's credit card account.

OVERVIEW OF ELECTRONIC CHECK PROCESSING

Electronic Check Processing is similar to the traditional check processing which is designed to debit consumers' checking accounts for payment of goods and/or services. ECP is mainly used in Corporations to centralize, disburse or collect funds from their branches, franchises, agents, or from other corporations. Electronic check contains digital signature of the payer and it provides mechanism to verify the funds on-line in real time. The digital signature is generated based on some public key based identity scheme. Variations of an electronic check can provide the functionalities of traveler's check or a certified check. If the currency field is changed, then and electronic check can be used as a traveler's check. If the check contains the signature of the payer's bank, then it becomes a certified check.

ECP can be achieved in any of two ways for processing:

- By using the Automated Clearing House (ACH) network when the customer's bank is a member of a financial institution, or

Figure 3. Hierarchy of Net Check servers

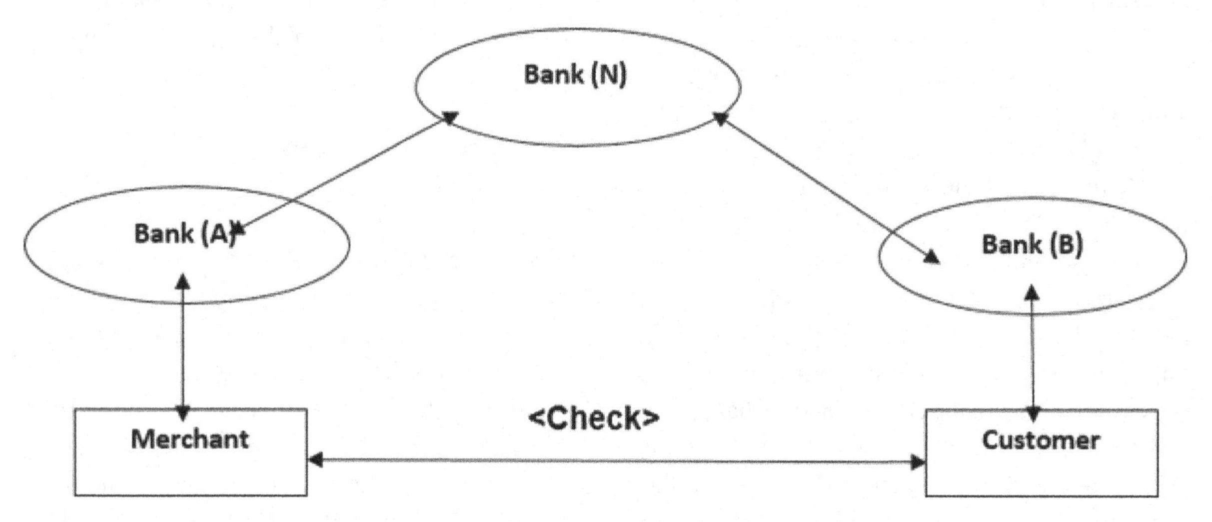

- By generating a facsimile draft
- At the direction of the merchant or
- When the customer's bank is not a participant of the ACH network

There are 3 steps that occur when the check is forwarded by the merchant's bank to the financial network.

1. **Validation** – This is the first step. This process includes format and data edit checks, bank routing number checks and comparison to the data stored in the database.
2. **Verification** permits merchants to compare each transaction to an external negative file to locate accounts, which have a history of bad checks outstanding or are closed for cause.
3. **Prenotification** permits merchants to validate account information prior to submitting an ACH transaction for deposit.

If the check fails any of the above reason, then it will be rejected to the consumer. ECP can also handles failures as returns.

OVERVIEW OF ELECTRONIC CASH PROCESSING

Electronic Cash Payment System is similar to conventional cash payment where anonymity and security is maintained. There are two ways in which Electronic Cash Payment Systems can be implemented: using Smart Card Technology or using an electronic mint.

FUNCTION OF ELECTRONIC CASH SYSTEM

Entities in an E-cash system are merchant, consumer and E-cash bank or Mint. Consumers and merchants open an account with the E-cash Bank. E-cash provides front-end software called E-cash cyber-wallet that resides on the consumer's computer. CyberWallet stores and manages consumer's coins, and keeps record of all transactions. Consumer first withdraws coins from E-cash bank to their wallet software on the local disk. In order to provide anonymity the withdrawal protocol prevents a bank from being able to see the serial numbers of the issuing coins.

Figure 4. Entities and their functions within the E-cash system

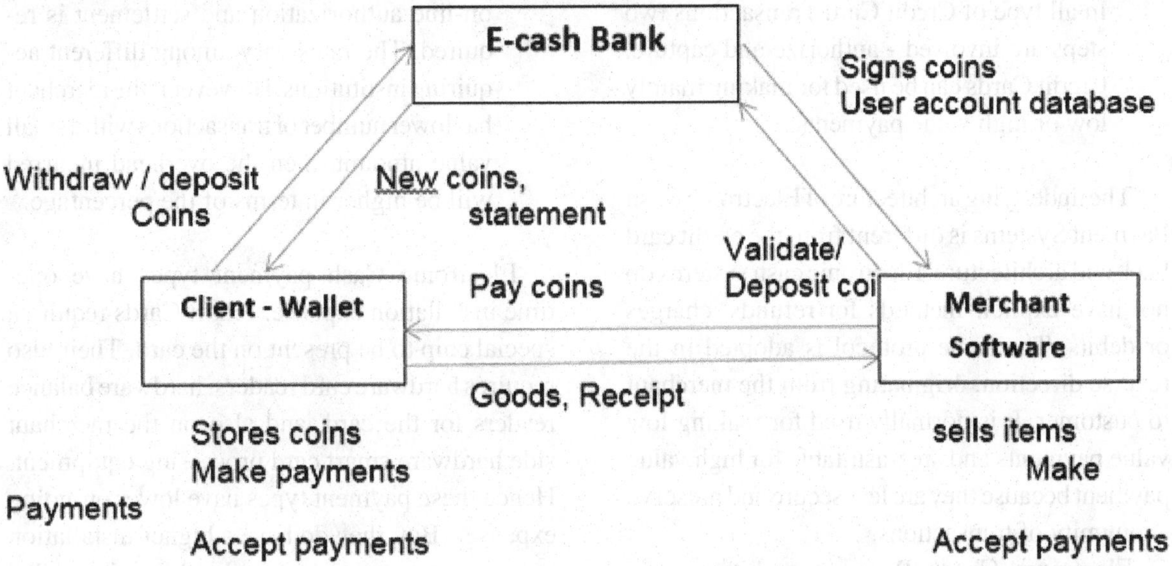

E-cash Bank
Signs coins
User account database
Withdraw / deposit
Coins
New coins,
statement
Validate/
Deposit coi
Client - Wallet
Pay coins
Merchant
Software
Goods, Receipt
Stores coins
Make payments
Payments
Accept payments
sells items
Make
Accept payments

Each coin has a serial number that is generated randomly by the customer's wallet software. The serial number is masked and sent to the bank so that the bank cannot log the serial numbers of the coins with a particular customer. The bank checks the consumer's account to determine whether the consumer has the amount desired to be stamped on the coins. If the consumer has the desired amount, the bank signs the coin blindfolded and assigns a denomination to it. Consumer's account is deducted by the denomination. Coins are sent back to the wallet. Wallet decrypts the coins and makes it ready for use.

When the customer chooses to purchase an item on the web, the customer sends the request to the merchant. The merchant responds by sending a payment request to the client. The payment request contains the currency to be used, amount, timestamp, merchant bank ID, merchant account ID and a short description. This request is not encrypted which makes it unsecured. If the consumer decides to pay, coins valuing the requested amount are gathered from the wallet and the exact amount is sent to the merchant. The wallet is capable of withdrawing new coins from the E-cash. Bank if more denomination is needed to make a payment. The merchant forwards the coins to the E-cash Bank. The Mint verifies that the consumer has not already spent the coins. If the consumer has not yet spent the coins, the coins will be deposited in the merchant's account. The merchant then sends the goods and a receipt to the customer. Refunds and payout services are also handled in the same way but this time payment is originating at the merchant and ending at the customer. E-cash Bank is not capable of processing coins from other banks. Similarly E-cash coins cannot be processed at other bank. This is a severe limitation in propagating electronic cash payment.

COMPARISON OF DIFFERENT PAYMENT METHODS

The payment system can be analyzed and compared based on several factors.

1. **Architecture** - Credit Card Systems are designed to handle complex payment needs like refunds, charges and returns where separate

protocol is followed in each of the cases. In all type of Credit Card Transactions two steps are involved - authorize and capture. Credit Cards can be used for making mainly low or high value payments.

The underlying architecture of Electronic Cash Payment Systems is different from the credit card back end architecture. Electronic cash systems do not have explicit methods for refunds, charges or debits. The same protocol is adopted in the reverse direction, originating from the merchant to customer. It is normally used for making low value payments and are unsuitable for high value payment because they are less secure and preserve anonymity of transactions.

Electronic Check Payment architecture is similar to the existing Credit Card architecture. But unlike Credit Card no on-line authorization is required. Checks are batched and set to the clearinghouse periodically.

Electronic Checks are designed to handle returns from the payee's bank. They however do not have the concept of refund. Checks are processes sequentially from the payer to the payee's bank in one step involving anywhere from a few hours to a day. Electronic Checks are used to make low to medium value payments.

2. **Security** - For the purpose of secure payment transaction Credit Card Payment Methods adopts SET protocol, whereas Electronic Check and Electronic Cash payment methods do not have such a standard protocol for securing the transactions. Credit Cards also have AVS and CVV2 for verification and authorization. This adds security to credit card processing. Electronic Checks use digitize signatures and transmit checks within a digital envelope. Electronic Cash systems have electronic cash banks (Cash servers) that digitally sign the coins to be issued to a customer.

3. **Cost** - Every time in Credit Card Transactions on-line authorization and settlement is required. The rates vary among different acquiring institutions. However if the merchant has lower number of transactions with a small value amount, then the overhead incurred will be higher in terms of the percentage.

Electronic Cash payment types have one-time installation expense. Smart Cards require a special chip to be present on the card. Their also requires hardware card readers, hardware balance readers for the card, and also on the merchant side hardware smart card processing equipment. Hence these payment types have lower on-going expenses. But, they do have a higher installation expense since some special hardware is needed to process them.

Electronic Checks have the lowest cost. The transaction fees charged by ACH to process electronic checks is lower than that of credit cards. The process of digitally signing a check and masking it inside a digital envelope involves purchase of special software to do that. But it is a one-time expense and is not incurred with time unlike credit cards expense. It has also been reported that the number of fraudulent transactions is lower with electronic checks resulting in lower expenses.

4. **Flexibility** - Credit Card Systems have the ability to accommodate new types of cards and to handle ever-changing protocols. The SET protocol used by Credit Card Processing is very open-ended making it more flexible. However the electronic cash systems (like Mondex and Ecash) are based on proprietary protocols and proprietary architectures. This makes it difficult to adapt these products for any changes. Another major drawback of being proprietary is that of integrating these products with other applications like Billing Software. Ecash system is not able to process coins from other banks. Similarly other banks

are not capable of processing Ecash coins. Hence there is no open-end architecture for Ecash payment systems. Electronic Check Payment Systems are being standardized by FSTC. FSTC's check payment processing is yet to be incorporated into commercial products and accepted as a standard.

5. **Performance** - Credit Card Processing System requires on-line authorizations. There should not be any delay due to slow transmissions across the network. With the increased popularity of credit card transaction it is important that we work towards eliminating the delays associated with on-line authorizations needed for each transaction. Electronic Cash and Electronic Check have all the necessary data available on the hosting server. Hence these systems need not contact financial institutions on-line.
6. **Ease of Use** - Credit Card payment can be done without the need of sophisticated software at the consumer site. Most of the user have the basic know-how of using a credit card. Minimal or no training is needed for customers to make payments using credit cards. Electronic Check payment system needs installation of software and sometimes special hardware at the customer site to be able to create and process electronic checks.

Electronic checkbooks are also maintained at the customer site. People need to be trained to use the special technology for issuing electronic checks.

Electronic cash payment system has a special software called electronic purse that needs to be installed at the customer site. The purse will store coins, maintain the balance and communicate with the electronic cash banks. People need to be trained to use electronic purse.

SECURE ELECTRONIC PAYMENT SYSTEM INFRASTRUCTURE

In order to ensure the integrity and security of each electronic payment transaction following measures and technologies are directly used: *Authentication, public key cryptography, digital signatures, certificate, certificate authorities, SSL, S-HTTP and secure electronic transmission (SET).*

1. **Authentication:** This is the process of verifying the authenticity of a person and a transaction. There are many tools available to confirm the authenticity of a user. For instance, passwords and ID numbers are used to allow a user to log onto a particular site.
2. **Public Key Cryptography:** In Public key cryptography one public and one private is used to encrypt and decrypt data respectively. Cryptography is the process of protecting the integrity and accuracy of information by encrypting data into an unreadable format, called cipher text. Only those who possess a private key can decrypt the message into plain text. Though the private key is not publicly known.
3. **Digital Signature:** A digital signature includes any type of electronic message encrypted with a private key that is able to identify the origin of the message. The followings are some functions of digital signature.
   a. **The Authentication Function:** Generally, digital signature adds a string of characters to an electronic message that serves to identify the sender or the originator of a message.
   b. **The Seal Function:** Checking is performed against any alteration of the text of the message after the digital signature was appended.

c. **The Integrity Function:** This function is of great interest in cases where legal documents are created using such digital signatures.

4. **Certificate:** A certificate provides a mechanism for establishing confidence in the relationship between a public key and the entity that owns the corresponding private key.
5. **Certificate Authorities:** Certificate authorities are similar to a notary public, a commonly trusted third party. In the e-commerce world, certificate authorities are the corresponding of passport offices in the government that concern digital certificates and validate the holder's identity and authority.
6. **Secure Sockets Layer (SSL):** Secure Sockets Layer transmits private documents via the Internet. SSL uses a cryptographic system that uses two keys to encrypt data - a public key known to everyone and a private or secret key known only to the recipient of the message. It operates between the transport and the application layers in the network stack and uses both public and private key cryptography. SSL provides a relatively secure method to encrypt data that are transmitted over a public network such as the Internet, also offers security for all Web transactions, including file transfer protocol (FTP), HTTP, and Telnet-based transactions. The protocol is vulnerable to attacks on the SSL server authentication. Despite its vulnerabilities, when properly implemented, SSL can be a powerful tool for securing Web-sensitive data.

Advantages of SSL

Some of the advantages of SSL contain the following:

- *Authentication:* Permits Web-enabled browsers and servers to authenticate each other.
- *Access Limit:* Permits controlled access to servers, directories, files, and services.
- *Data Protection:* Guarantees that exchanged data cannot be corrupted without detection.
- *Information Share:* Permits information to be shared by browsers and servers while remaining out of reach to third parties.

Disadvantages of SSL

Some of the disadvantages of SSL contain the following:

- *Simple Encryption:* This might increase the chances of being hacked by computer criminals.
- *Stolen Certificate/Key:* One important drawback of SSL is that certificates and keys that originate from a computer can be stolen over a network or by other electronic means.
- *Point-to-Point Transactions:* SSL handles only point-to-point interaction. Credit card transactions involve at least three parties: the consumer, the merchant, and the card issuer. This limits its all-purpose applications.
- *Customer's risk:* Customers run the risk that a merchant may expose their credit card numbers on its server; in turn, this increases the chances of credit card frauds.
- *Merchant's risk:* Merchants run the risk that a consumer's card number is false or that the credit card won't be approved.
- *Additional overhead:* The overhead of encryption and decryption means that secure HTTP (SHTTP) is slower than HTTP.

1. **Secure Hypertext Transfer Protocol (S-HTTP):** Another protocol for transmitting data securely over the World

Wide Web is Secure HTTP (S-HTTP). Whereas SSL creates a secure connection between a client and a server, over which any amount of data can be sent securely, SHTTP is designed to transmit individual messages securely.

2. **Secure Electronic Transmission (SET):** The Secure Electronic Transmission protocol imitates the current structure of the credit card processing system. This can generate a large number of data packets. The SET protocol offers packets of data for all these transactions, and each transaction is signed with a digital signature.

This makes SET the largest consumer of certificates, and it makes banks by default one of the major distributors of certificates. The privacy of messages in the SET payment environment is accomplished through encryption of the payment information using a combination of public key and private key algorithms. The most important property of SET is that the credit card number is not open to the seller.

Advantages of SET

Some of the advantages of SET contain the following:

- *Information security:* Neither anyone listening in nor a merchant can use the information passed during a transaction for fraud.
- *Credit card security:* There is no chance for anybody to steal a credit card.
- *Flexibility in shopping:* If a person has a phone he/she can shop.

Disadvantages of SET: Some of the disadvantages of SET include its *complexity* and *high cost for implementation.*

E-PAYMENT SYSTEM IN INDIA

In the post liberalization era all Indian banks have adopted technology enabled banking services to remain competitive and to provide best services to their customers. Irrespective of their ownership status (private sector or public sector) almost all of them have given maximum importance to technology development and deployment. The journey on IT was started in 1989, based on Rangarajan Committee Recommendation followed by Saraf Committee Recommendation in 1993 and Vasudevan Committee Recommendation in 1998. V. Leeladhar (2006), Deputy Governor, RBI has described technology as a key driver in banking Induatry. Banks which have not made enough investments in technology are at peril as they will soon find their customer base eroding and the banks which have invested in technology have gained great mileage through improved competitive advantage and are potentially poised to attract increased market share. Technology adoption has also improved the quality of risk management systems in banks.

Banking sector is considered to be the backbone of Indian economy. Due to economic reforms and the various E-Banking techniques followed by the banks during the last two decade strengthened their financial position. However, Indian payment system is basically cash driven. The unintended social and economic costs (risks and inconvenience) associated with cash transactions are alarming. It is for some of these reasons that a forward looking economy should seriously think of embracing the modern e-payment system. Active users of Electronic Payment system use it because it is convenient, easy to use, saves time and meets their transaction needs (Adesina and Ayo, 2010). E-Payment helps banks to increase speed, shorten processing periods, improve the flexibility of business transactions and reduce costs associated with having personnel serve customers physically.

According to the report of RBI, in India during the last two decade the performance of all electronic mode of payment have shown better growth than the physical cash or check-based system. RBI has already taken initiative to efficiently utilize the e-payment system and also to take steps to mitigate the associated risks and losses for both consumers and financial institutions. Still e-payment system has not become mainstream mode of transaction activities in India.

The first technology enabled banking service is ATM which came in India by HSBC bank in 1987. Internet banking was first introduced in 1996 by ICICI bank. Several definitions of Electronic payment exists in literature. Gholami et. al. (2010) with Andam(2003) stated Electronic payment system is "the use of debit and credit cards on the Internet or other electronic devices to perform daily transactions which include paying for goods and services, transfer of money and bill payments at any time of the day". Encyclopaedia Britannica (2010) refers E-payment systems as automated processes of exchanging monetary value among parties in business or personal transactions and transmitting this value over the information and communication technology (ICT) networks to the respective account. The common e-Payment channels include the payment cards (debit or credit), online web portals, automated teller machines (ATM), Real Time Gross Settlement (RTGS) system, Electronic Fund Transfer (EFT), National Electronic Fund Transfer (NEFT), Electronic Clearing Service (ECS) (Nnaka, 2009).

Electronic payment systems have become increasingly popular in India. In fiscal year 2012, growth of electronic payments is 26.8% to 1.21 billion transactions from 0.96 billion transactions in fiscal year 2011, while the amount of check clearance slid from 1.39 billion units to 1.34 billion units over the same period. In terms of total transaction value, 98% of all electronic payments consist of large value payments through Real Time Gross Settlement (RTGS) systems and the remaining 2% comes from retail electronic payments, including credit cards, debit cards, electronic clearing services (ECS) credit and debit payments, and electronic funds transfers (EFTs). Although large value payment systems have mostly shifted to electronic payment mode, retail payment remains rather paper-centric, and the growth of different retail electronic payment systems varies. The total number of transactions of retail payments only increased five times, from 229 million units during fiscal year 2006 to 1.15 billion units during fiscal year 2012. Of all transaction volume handled by the retail electronic payment systems in fiscal year 2012, 55.8% was conducted through credit cards and debit cards. ECS credit payments, ECS debit payments, and EFTs accounted for of 10.5%, 14.2%, and 19.5%, respectively.

Debit cards transactions have seen more vibrant growth than credit cards in the past few years, even though they entered the market 10-years later than credit cards. As of June 2012, the transaction volume of debit cards grew by 38.29% year-on-year, while credit card payments grew by 21.95% during the same period. The transaction volume of credit card payments shrunk from 2009 to early 2010, however, whereas year-on-year growth rates of debit cards stood first, averaging 33.9%, in part due to the 2008 financial crisis. During the same period, the growth of ECS credit (a facility for companies to pay salary, pension, dividends, interest, and other regular incomes) decreased by 5.06% year-on-year, while ECS debit (a similar facility for paying regular bills, such as utilities or school/college fees) saw an 8.61% growth during the same period. At the same time, the EFT system – which facilitates the transfer of funds electronically by giving mandate to the bank branch or through internet banking – has seen rising popularity over time. Although it only covered 1% to 2% of the retail electronic payment systems in 2005, it now accounts for approximately 20%-25% of all retail electronic systems.

REVIEW OF INDIAN FINANCIAL SYSTEM

As mentioned in the mission statement of Reserve Bank of India's publication on Payment Systems in India (2009-12) – payment system of a country should be "safe, secure, sound, efficient, accessible and authorize". Payment systems are the most essential standard of the economic system of a country. GDP of a country depends on the development of payment system. So there is a continuous effort in finding innovative ways of making payments which are hassle free.

An electronic means of payment are both safe and efficient BPSS (Board for Regulation of *Payment* and Settlement Systems) is continuously trying to change the mindset of people from paper to electronic. An efficient payment system forms the backbone of economic well-being of a nation. [1]

As of March 2014, in India, there are 21 nationalized and public-sector banks, SBI and 8 SBI group of bank, 80 regional rural banks, 19 private sector banks, 32 foreign banks are operating in India along with 29 foreign banks are doing business in India. Computerization of banking were started from 1985. Now, 97% of public sector banks, cent percent of private and foreign banks are computerized. All those banks offer lots of Information and Communication Technology based banking services to bank customers and are using modern technology to internal business operations. After financial reform in 1991, various foreign and private sector banks entered into Indian banking industry with their high-tech banking services. In order to compete in the competition RBI, Institute for Banking Research and Development of Technology has continuously trying to enhance the system by required facilities to banking and financial institutes in India.

ANCIENT PAYMENT SYSTEM IN INDIA

Indian payment instruments and mechanism have a very long history. Early Indian used coins, they were either punched marked or cast in gold, silver or copper as a payment instrument.

In ancient India, loan deed forms called *rnapatra* or *rnalekhya* were in use. These contained details such as the name of the debtor and the creditor, the amount of loan, the rate of interest, the condition of repayment and the time of repayment. The deed was witnessed by a person of respectable means and endorsed by the loan-deed writer. Execution of loan deeds continued during the Buddhist period, when they were called *inapanna.*

In the Mauryan period, there was use of *adesha*, which was an order on a banker desiring to pay the money to a third person, which is very much similar to nowadays bill of exchange. During the Buddhist period, there was considerable use of these instruments.

In Mughal period loan deeds were called *dastawez* and were of two types: *dastawez-e-indultalab* which was payable on demand and *dastawez-e-miadi* which was payable after a stipulated time.

In the Mughal period, few great foreign travellers came in India. From their writings, it may be noted that Indian bankers issued bills of exchange on foreign countries, mainly for financing sea-borne trade. These bills were widely accepted and were traded at high discounts, as the discounts included the insurance premium covering the risk representing safe arrival of goods.

Another instrument in use during the Muslim period was the Pay order. Pay orders were issued from the Royal Treasury on one of the District or Provincial treasuries. They were called *Barattes* and were very much similar to present day drafts or cheques.

In twelfth century one of the most important financial instrument were evolved that is Hundi, it has been continued till today. Hundis were used

- As remittance instruments (to transfer funds from one place to another)
- As credit instruments (to borrow money)
- For trade transactions (as bills of exchange)

Hundis were of various kinds and each type had certain distinguishing features.

1. **Darshani Hundi:** It was a demand bill of exchange, payable on presentation according to the usage and custom of the place.
2. **Muddati Hundi:** It was a type of bill and is payable after stipulated time or on a given date or on a determinable future date or on the happening of a certain stipulated event.

The states of India ruled by kings or nawabs had their own distinct coins. An example of this was the Arcot Rupee coin struck by the Nawab of Arcot in the Madras Presidency. By 1740, the Europeans had secured the privileges of coining this rupee, and the coins came to be known as English, French and Dutch arcots. During the British period, in 1835 East India Company introduced company's rupee to bring uniformity of currency system. In 18th century, Bank of Hindoostan first implemented paper currency, then after issued by General Bank in Bengal and Behar, the Bengal Bank and three Presidency Banks. Each Presidency Bank had the right to issue notes within certain limits. The Bank of Bengal notes generally circulated within the environs of Calcutta and were mainly used for effecting large transactions. The largest proportion of the Bank of Bengal notes consisted of notes of Rs.100 and upwards. The notes sometimes bore a small premium, so great was the public confidence in the bank. The Paper Currency Act of 1861 conferred upon the Government of India the monopoly of Note Issue bringing to an end note issues of private and Presidency Banks.

The private banks and the Presidency Banks introduced other payment instruments in the Indian money market. Cheques were introduced by the Bank of Hindoostan, the first joint stock bank established in 1770.

Post Bills were introduced by the British in 1827. These were Inland Promissory notes issued by the bank on a distant place, the holder of which would be paid on acceptance after a specified number of days (seven days' sight or thirty days' sight) and were similar to muddati hundis. These bills had a much smaller currency than bank notes, mainly because the government refused to authorise their receipt in payment of public dues. They were mainly used by European businessmen for purposes of internal remittances.

In 1833, cash credit accounts were added to the Bank of Bengal's array of credit instruments. The bank used to grant loans against the security of Company's paper, bullion, plate, jewels or goods of non-perishable nature or goods not liable to great alteration in their value up to a limit of 1 lakh sicca rupees. Buying and selling bills of exchange became one of the items of business to be conducted by the Bank of Bengal from 1839.

In 1881, the Negotiable Instruments Act (NI Act) was enacted, formalising the usage and characteristics of instruments like the cheque, the bill of exchange and promissory note. The NI Act provided a legal framework for non-cash paper payment instruments in India. With the steady growth in volumes of trade and commerce and the growing confidence of the public in the usage of cheques etc., transactions through the use of these payment instruments grew at a rapid pace. Bank employees had to frequently walk to other banks, collect cheques and drafts, and present them to drawee banks and collect cash over the counter. There was danger of loss in transit of the instruments. Besides, such methods could only serve for limited volumes of instruments. With the development of the banking system and higher turnover in the volume of cheques, the need for an organised cheque clearing process emerged amongst the banks. Clearing associations were formed by the banks in the Presidency towns and the final settlement between member banks was effected by means of cheques drawn upon the Presidency Banks. With the setting up of the Imperial Bank in 1921, settlement was done through cheques drawn on that bank.

The Calcutta Clearing Banks' Association, which was the largest bankers' association at that time, adopted clearing house rules in 1938. The association had twenty-five large banks as its members and eight sub-members. There were two ordinary clearings on each business day, except on Saturday when there was one clearing. However, the association did not cover many banks functioning in Calcutta. The cheques, drafts etc. of such non-clearing banks were collected by the clearing banks only on payment of charges. This affected their business prospects adversely, as the public was not likely to maintain accounts with banks whose cheques suffered a serious handicap of market acceptability. To overcome this problem, these banks formed themselves into a group called the Metropolitan Banking Association with fifty members, which conducted the Metropolitan Clearing House, in 1939. This association arrived at an understanding with the Calcutta Clearing House in 1940. In addition, two other clearings were conducted in Calcutta - the Pioneer clearing and the Walks Clearing.

The Bombay Clearing House was the only association to conduct clearings in Bombay. It had no parallel systems/institutions comparable to the Metropolitan Clearing House of Calcutta. The uniform procedures and charges for collection of non-clearing banks' cheques, drafts, dividend warrants etc. were adopted by the Bombay Clearing House in 1941-42. After the setting up of Reserve Bank of India under the RBI Act 1935, the Clearing Houses in the Presidency towns were taken over by Reserve Bank of India.

MODERN PAYMENT SYSTEM IN INDIA

The Reserve Bank of India is doing its best to encourage alternative methods of payments which will bring security and efficiency to the payments system and make the whole process easier for banks. Though Indian payment systems have always been dominated by paper-based transactions, but after the emergence of Electronic Commerce it becomes essential to upgrade the traditional payment systems. Ever since the introduction of e-payments, the banking sector has witnessed growth like never before. According to a survey by Celent, the ratio of e-payments to paper based transactions has considerably increased between 2004 and 2008. This has happened as a result of advances in technology and increasing consumer awareness of the ease and efficiency of internet and mobile transactions.

From early 1990's banks and financial institutions gradually started using computers for their daily activities. Since 1991, RBI had started 'BANKNET' which is a network among the banks. Another is 'INFINET' which is a satellite based wide area network where VSAT (Very Small Aperture Terminal) technology is used. It was set up in June 1999. In Indian Banking System ATM (Automated Teller Machine) plays a crucial role. ATM can be used for payment of utility bills, fund transfer between accounts, deposit of checks and cash into accounts, balance enquiry and several other banking transactions. Apart from ATM, RBI has already introduced MICR technology, ECS, EFT, NEFT, Card based clearing and RTGS etc. RBI has made it compulsory for banks to route high value transactions through Real Time Gross Settlement (RTGS). Also NEFT (National Electronic Funds Transfer) and NECS (National Electronic Clearing Services) has encouraged individuals and businesses to switch to electronic methods of payment.

In India payments are of two types - firstly, large-scale payments and small-scale payments and secondly, paper-based payment and electronic payment. Most of the large-scale payments are corporates or government payments which are settled by RBI. Small-scale payments are mainly retail payments concerning individuals which are generally paper-based. Most large-value payments are handled electronically. However, even the retail payments are showing a tendency of shifting to the e-payment mode, mainly because of consumer awareness and regulations by the RBI.

Nowadays more than 75% of all transactions are done electronically, including both large-value and retail payments. Out of this 75%, 98% come from the RTGS (large-value payments) whereas a meager 2% come from retail payments. This means consumers have not yet accepted this card based transaction as a regular means of paying their bills and still prefer conventional methods. Retail payments if made via electronic modes are done by ECS (debit and credit), EFT and card payments.

ROLE OF RBI IN ENCOURAGING ELECTRONIC PAYMENT SYSTEM

1. Being the apex financial and regulatory institution in India, it is compulsory for RBI to upgrade the payment system and in view of this aim, RBI has already taken several initiatives to strengthen Electronic Payment System in India and encourage people to adopt it.
2. The Payment and Settlement Systems Act, 2007 enables RBI to regulate, supervise and lay down policies involving payment and settlement space in India". Apart from some basic instruction to banks RBI has actively encouraged all banks and consumers to embrace Electronic Payment System.
3. RBI has given permission to NBFC (Non Banking Financial Companies) to issue co-branded credit cards in order to form partnerships with commercial banks.
4. In order to meet credit needs of farmers NABARD launched Kisan Credit Card Scheme. By using this plastic card farmers can be free from paper money hassles.
5. National Payments Corporation of India (NPCI) jointly with Indian Banks Association (IBA) has already been started "Rupay", a domestic card scheme. Initially functioning as an NPO, Rupay will focus on potential customers from rural and semi-urban areas of India. It is expected that Rupay will have a much wider coverage than Visa, MasterCard or American Express Cards.
6. Though, RBI has taken active initiative to effectively spread Electronic Payment culture, but due to certain socio cultural reason growth of Electronic Payment is hindered. Despite the Electronic Payment infrastructure, 63% of all payments are still made in cash. A small percentage of urban - metropolitan population pay their bills electronically. Almost in some cases the transaction is done partially online and partially offline. The main reason for this apathy switch to Electronic Payment System comes from lack of awareness of the customer despite various efforts by the Government.

A FIELD STUDY REPORT ON ACCEPTANCE OF ELECTRONIC PAYMENT SYSTEM BY THE CUSTOMERS IN EASTERN INDIA

The study was based on primary data. The tools constructed for the collection of data were Interview Schedule using structured questionnaires. Data for this study were collected by means of a survey conducted mainly in metro city Kolkata, West Bengal and its surrounding suburb areas from August to October 2013. The structured survey questionnaires were in English and those were distributed randomly select 650 participants. Participants were mainly from Education sector.

Others were from Banking, Government services, IT professionals, students, retired persons or even housewives. The respondents were asked beforehand whether they had knowledge about online banking and Electronic Payment services. Only those who answered in affirmative were given the questionnaire to complete. The questionnaire was designed to collect demographic informations like age, gender, occupation, educational qualification etc. 235 responses were received and after checking the validity of the questions 167 respondents were fit for carrying out descriptive analysis. Data thus collected were posted in a master table to facilitate further processing. Statistical analysis of the data were done through SPSS 16 software in computer. In the analysis 5 point Likert scale was used. Scores were allotted for the usage such as totally agree -1, agree-2, neutral-3, disagree-4 and totally disagree-5. The questions were initially tested with a focus group of 30 respondents mainly professionals from Education sector in West Bengal.

The response rate is 36.15 percent (235). Among these, 167 (71.06 percent) of the responses are usable as most items are adequately responded. A total of 70.06% are male respondents. A majority of the respondents (45.78%) is in the range of 26 to 40 years of age. Next falls the age group of 18 to 25 years, they are keen to adopt the latest technology. People with age of above 40 or above 60 years basically prefer conventional method (8.0 percent) i.e. cash and check. Most of them are aware of latest technology but as they are not tech-savvy they are afraid of doing so.

In consideration with marital status 48.73 percent respondents are married while 47.46% respondents are single. As both the percentage are all most same, marital status is not a significant factor in Electronic-payment adoption. The survey shows that users of E-payment system are mostly highly educated people- master degree holder (38.32 percent) and next the graduate people (28.143%). More than three-quarters (66.46%) of the respondents perform online transactions and have previous experience in surfing internet. Only minority 26.34 percent is techno-phobic and might simply be reluctant to change. During survey most of the participants came from education sector. So majority users 56.88 percent are from this sector, 20.58% respondents are in IT & Telecom, 17.38% in Govt. service, 23.7% people are involved in business and only 14.22% are house-wives. Tremendous responses came from students, almost 80% of them are users of electronic payment system. Majority have a moderate income level, which is below Rs. 50,000 (40.96%), though while doing this survey 34.93% people had not disclosed about their income.

Survey report shows that E-payment system is accepted only by the urban people (82.03%), while rural and sub-urban people hardly know about it. Majority of them are rare users of ATM card only. From this survey one thing is clear that people still have faith on public bank (74.25%) and State Bank of India tops this list. SBI have 35.92% online users, followed by United Bank of India- 10.17 percent online users. All the private bank users are urban people. Majority of them are customers of HDFC bank (9.58% online users), followed by Axis bank (5.98% online users), ICICI bank (4.19% online users) respectively. Those who are users of online all of them primarily perform ATM transaction. Next comes use of Debit card, credit card and rest. According to the survey report VISA has largest customer base than Master.

CONCLUSION

There are a wide variety of payment systems available today. However there arises a need to provide a single universal payment system that provides the advantages of all the existing payment systems. It is clear that Credit Card Payments have adopted SET as a standard for payment transactions. However, no protocol is currently available for electronic check payment.

Financial Service Technology Consortium (FSTC) is working towards bringing in a standard for electronic checks. Electronic Cash products like E-cash that do not make use of banking infrastructure are finding it difficult to push into the market. However smart card systems like Mondex are not popular in the market because of not being backed up by major banking institutions. Electronic Payment Industry has an extensive potential for growth considering the growth of Internet. We should take advantage of this and make the best use of available technology for the betterment of mankind.

If the usage of electronic money continue to increase, it has the potential to significantly reduce the use of paper currencies in the near future and perhaps lead us to a new kind of banking and monetary system. Can Electronic Payment System become a substitute for present conventional system? It is still too early to say. However, a number of issues need to be addressed and resolved before E-payment system enjoys the universality of currently used system.

REFERENCES

Adeoti, O.O., Osotimehin, K.O., & Olajide, O.T. (2012). Consumer Payment Pattern and Motivational Factors using Debit Card in Nigeria. *International Business Management*, 6(3), 352-355

Alhudaithy, A.I. and Kitchen, P.J., (2009). Rethinking models of technology adoption for Internet banking: The role of website features. *Journal of Financial Services Marketing*, 14(1), 56–69.

Anik, A.A. & Pathan, A.K. (2002). A framework for managing cost effective and easy electronic payment system in the developing countries.

Arkalgud, S. (2000). Electronic Payment Systems [Unpublished student report]. San Jose State University.

Asaolu, O. T., Ayoola, J. T., & Yemi, E., (May 2011). Electronic payment system in Nigeria: implementation, constraints and solutions. *Journal of Management and Society*. 1(2).16-21

Ayo, C. K., Adewoye, J. O., & Oni, A. A. (2010). The State of e-banking Implementation in Nigeria: A Post-Consolidation Review. *Journal of Emerging Trends in Economics and Management Science*, *1*(1), 37–45.

Crede, A. (1998) Electronic payment System, Electronic money and the Internet: The United Kingdom Experience to Date. University of Sussex. Retrieved from www.susx.ac.uk/spru

Geetha, K., & Malarvizhi, V. (2012). Assessment of a Modified Technology Acceptance Model among E-Banking Customers in Coimbatore City. *International Journal of Innovation, Management and Technology.*, *3*(2).

Hamidinava, F., & Madhoushi, M. (2010, December). Evaluating the features of electronic payment systems in Iranian bank users' view. *International Review of Business Research Papers,* 6(6), 78–94

Khalili Amozad, H., Ebrahimi Babak, S., & Nalchigar, S. (2012, May). Evaluation of e-payment systems in Iran using analytic hierarchy process. *African Journal of Business Management*, 6(19), 5950-5956. http://www.academicjournals.org/AJBM

Lee, H. H., Fiore, A. M., & Kim, J. (2006). The role of the technology acceptance model in explaining effects of image interactivity technology on consumer responses. *International Journal of Retail & Distribution Management*, *34*(8), 621–644. doi:10.1108/09590550610675949

Li, H. Y., & Huang, J. (2009). Applying Theory of Perceived Risk and Technology Acceptance Model in the Online Shopping Channel. *International Journal of Bank Marketing*, *2*(2).

Manoharan, B. (2007). Indian e-Payment System and Its Performance. *Professional Banker, 7*(3), 61–69.

Mantel, B. (2000). Why Don't Customers Use e-Banking Products: Towards a Theory of Obstacles, Incentives and Opportunities [FRB Chicago Working Paper No. EPS-2000-1].

Nargundkar, R. (2002). *Marketing Research*. New Delhi: Tata McGraw-Hill.

Pikkarainen, K., Pikkarainen, T., & Karjaluoto, H., & Pahnila, S. (2006). The measurement of end-user computing satisfaction of online banking services: empirical evidence from Finland. *International Journal of Bank Marketing*, 24(3), 158-172. Retrieved from www.emeraldinsight.com

Poon W.-C. (2008). User's adoption of e-banking services: The Malaysian perspective. *Journal of Business and Industrial Marketing, 23*(1), 59–69.

Ravi, V., Mahil, C., & Sagar, N.V. (2007). Profiling of internet banking users in India using intelligent techniques. *Journal of Service Research, 6*(2).

Ramana, R.N.R.V. (2002, December). A study on value network theoretical model to examine the e-banking services. *Indian Journal of Research*, 1(12).

Ramani, D. (2007). The E-Payment System. *E-Business, 7*(5), 35–41.

Sanzogni, L., Sandhu, K., & Ghaith, A. W. (2010). Factors influencing the adoption and usage of online services in Saudi Arabia. Retrieved from http://www.ejisdc.org

Sekaran, U., & Bougie, R. (2010). Theoretical framework In theoretical framework and hypothesis development. In *Research Methods for Business: A Skill Building Approach* (p. 80). United Kingdom: Wiley.

Singh, M., & Kaushal, R. (2012). Factor Analysis Approach to Customers' Assessment of Electronic Payment and Clearing System in Indian Banking Sector. *The IUP Journal of Information Technology, 11(3), 64-75.*

So, W. C. M., Wong, T. N. D., & Sculli, D. (2005). Factors affecting intentions to purchase via the internet. *Journal of Industrial Management & Data Systems, 105*(9), 1225–1244. doi:10.1108/02635570510633275

Sudhagar, S. (2012). A Study on Perception and Awareness on Credit Cards among Bank Customers in Krishnagiri District. *Journal of Business and Management,* 2(3), 14-23. (IOSRJBM) ISSN: 2278-487X

Talwar, S. P. (1999). IT and Banking Sector. *RBI Bulletin, 53*(8), 985–992.

The eCommerce B2B Report. (2001, February). *Emarketer.* Retrieved from http://www.emarketer.com

Johar, M.G.M., & Awalluddin, J.A.A.(2011). The role of technology acceptance model in explaining effect on e-commerce application system. *International Journal of Managing Information Technology, 3*(3).

Themba, G., & Tumedi, B. C. (2012). Credit Card Ownership and Usage Behaviour in Botswana. *International Journal of Business Administration, 3*(6). doi:10.5430/ijba.v3n6p60

Wenninger, J. (2000). Emerging Role of Banks in e-Commerce. Current Issues in Economics and Finance. 6(3)

KEY TERMS AND DEFINITIONS

Architecture: The complex or carefully designed structure of something.

Credit Card: A small plastic card issued by a bank, building society, etc., allowing the holder to purchase goods or services on credit.

Debit Card: A payment card that deducts money directly from a consumer's checking account to pay for a purchase.

E-Cash: Electronic financial transactions conducted in cyberspace via computer networks.

E-Check: A form of payment made via the internet that is designed to perform the same function as a conventional paper check. Because the check is in an electronic format, it can be processed in fewer steps and has more security features than a standard paper check.

E-Commerce: E-commerce, short for electronic commerce, is trading in products or services using computer networks, such as the Internet.

Electronic Payment System: A means of making payments over an electronic network such as the Internet.

Online Fraud: A crime in which the perpetrator develops a scheme using one or more elements of the Internet to deprive a person of property or any interest, estate, or right by a false representation of a matter of fact, whether by providing misleading information or by concealment of information.

Section 4
Mitigation of End-User Information

Chapter 18
Information Societies to Interactive Societies:
ICT Adoptions in the Agriculture Sector in Sri Lanka

Uvasara Dissanayeke
University of Peradeniya, Sri Lanka

H.V.A. Wickramasuriya
University of Peradeniya, Sri Lanka

ABSTRACT

Information is crucial for the development of any sector, including agriculture where information needs to be exchanged with farmers and other stakeholders quickly. Thus, efficient linkages for information sharing are essential. ICT innovations enable the shaping and reshaping of communication and interaction. Many of the technology driven information dissemination methods have been initiated by government, private, non-profit making bodies and independent research groups. This chapter explains the integration of ICT within Sri Lankan agriculture communities and how the focus is changing from information dissemination towards facilitating interactions among the stakeholders. The present status of agriculture information dissemination, including the ICT interventions is given. Prevailing issues and limitations in these ICT-based information dissemination approaches initiated by the different entities is explained, giving due recognition to various factors that have contributed to the adoption of ICT initiatives. The chapter ends outlining the possibilities for future focus on ICT activities in an agriculture information society.

AGRICULTURE INFORMATION SOCIETY

Agriculture plays an important role in the Sri Lankan economy. Agriculture provides a direct source of income for around 31% of the population (Central Bank of Sri Lanka, 2013b). The rural population in Sri Lanka is around 85% (World Bank, 2014), and agriculture is both a direct and indirect source of living for about 65% of

DOI: 10.4018/978-1-4666-8598-7.ch018

the population who live in these rural areas. The contribution of agriculture to the country's gross domestic production is about 10.8% (Central Bank of Sri Lanka, 2013a).

Right information delivered at the right time is vital for successful farming. Farmers need information regarding crop growth, pest and disease problems, and marketing. A study conducted by De Silva and Ratnadiwakara (2008) reports that information search cost accounts for 11% of the total cost, and nearly 70% of the transaction cost. Information search costs arises from the need to obtain information related to decisions such as the crops to plant, agronomic practices, pest and disease identification and management, harvesting, storage and post-harvest practices. Information systems which provide the required information are described in Table 1. Transaction costs are incurred in transactions related to the purchase of inputs such as seed, fertilizer, and pesticides, and also in the sale of produce. Additional transaction costs are seen when farmers deal with external agents indirectly through Farmer Organizations. In such instances transaction costs arise between farmers and the Farmer Organizations, and also between the Farmer Organizations and the external agencies such as input suppliers or buyers. Appropriate information systems can reduce the transaction costs incurred in such situations.

At present most of the information obtained, and transactions conducted are through traditional mechanisms. Generally in Sri Lanka farmers have been obtaining information through the farm visits of, or the office visits to, extension agents. Thus, if the time spent by the farmers for this activity is taken also into account appropriately the information cost is bound to increase. Furthermore, it is noted that this cost analysis is from the perspective of the farmer. When the time and other associated cost, such as the transport cost, of the extension agent is also taken into account the actual cost of such information would vastly increase. Hence mechanisms which obviate the need for such meetings could reduce the associated information costs. ICT mechanisms are very well positioned for this, thus being able to reduce this information costs. It is not argued that ICT mechanisms are appropriate for all situations. Rather, that it would be appropriate in many situations. The reasons for such an assertion are as follows. Unlike in mass communication, or even group communication methods adopted in agricultural extension, the information provided through ICT mechanisms could be tailored to the particular requirements of the specific farmer, as in the traditional individual extension methods. For example, the requirements for a particular crop, or variety, could be provided. The needed information could be obtained irrespective of the location of the farmer. Transport and time costs too would be almost eliminated. Interactivity, which is not generally used or possible through many other information providing channels, could also be used. For example, Smartphones could be used to take photographs of field problems such as pests or diseases which are sent for possible identification, after which requests for further information, or recommendations for the management of such problems, or the links to the appropriate information which is already available could be sent back to the farmer. The added advantage of this mechanism lies in the fact that if the first level of personnel handling such requests are unable to provide the information that they can channel it to increasingly higher levels of experts, according to the nature of the question, and then respond to the information seeker. Access to such higher levels of expertise would not normally be possible for most information seekers. Even in instances where such access may be possible, the time taken for access to personnel and awaiting their response could possibly lead to a situation where the response is of lesser value due to the associated delays. For example, measures against a pest or disease attack should be taken as quickly as possible. Even a delay of a few days could lead to substantial losses. A further advantage lies in the fact that the proficiency of the limited experts could be more widely utilized to service a larger group of people. Thus, the expertise of officers based in central stations could be utilized from almost any area of the country.

There are many traditional sources of agricultural information as seen in Table 1. Technical advice was traditionally provided by extension agents, including subject matter specialists, attached to various government departments and institutions. For example, the Department of Agriculture had a vast network of field level extension agents who catered to the needs of farmers in the food crop sector. However, it is noted that this coverage has been greatly diminished due to the transfer of the field level extension agents to another department. Technical advice on crops such as tea, rubber and coconut, as well as information on subsidy schemes are provided by different agencies related to these crops. Whilst these agencies use mass media too, the 1920 Agri-Advisory Service is a telephone based service introduced by the Dept. of Agriculture. However, as seen in Table 1, apart from these sources there are numerous other information providers too. Though information suppliers like input suppliers are likely to be biased, farmers obtain information from them due to the relative convenience. Whilst physical markets also provide marketing information, its range and accuracy is certainly limited. Accordingly, most of the traditional information sources could be vastly improved as seen by the steps already taken, as given in this chapter, and also by initiatives that could be taken in the future.

Information Needs of the Farmers

As mentioned previously, farmers need information throughout the cultivation process until they harvest and sell the products. De Silva and Ratnadiwakara (2008) proposed a six stage value chain for agriculture information starting from the decision on which crop to cultivate until selling the harvest. During the first stage the farmers have to decide on several aspects such as which crop to cultivate, the extent of land to be allocated for

Table 1. Agriculture information sources which cater for farmers information needs

Sources of Information	Information Needs
Input suppliers (Agro chemical merchants)	• Seeds and planting materials • Agro chemicals: fertilizers, pesticides, herbicides • Agriculture equipment, machinery
Markets /buyers	• Market prices • Places
Extension agents	• Technical advice • Training opportunities, demonstrations, plant Clinic • Government subsidy schemes, loans
Subject matter experts and researchers	• Solutions for farm management practices • Latest innovations
Mass media	• Weather information • Market prices
Farmer organization	• Cultivation plans • Water availability
1920 Agri advisory service	• Technical information related to farming • Purchasing inputs • Marketing

Sources (Dissanayeke & Wanigasundera, 2014; Wijerathna, 2011; Dissanayake, Wijekoon, Madana, & Wickramasinghe, 2009)

a particular crop, when to start cultivation, and making arrangements for working capital. Selecting a suitable crop would be depending on many factors such as climatic conditions, season of the year, availability of seed and other raw materials including labour and, fertilizer.

The second stage is where they purchase or use their own seeds saved from previous cultivations. Land preparation and planting is regarded as the third stage in which plant beds are prepared and subsequently planting seeds. During this stage the farmers have to decide on labour; whether to hire or use family labour, and use of machinery in land preparation.

Growing is the fourth stage in the agriculture value chain, where farmers are faced with issues such as managing pest attacks, diseases, irrigation, fertilizer, weeding. During this stage, the farmers look for fertilizer and subsidy programmes. In the next stage farmers engage in harvesting, sorting and packing. During this period they have to find labour for harvesting, storing spaces. They would also look up to information on post-harvest management and value addition too. Selling represents the last stage of the value chain in which farmers have to make decisions on market prices, places to sell the produce and transport arrangements. Accordingly a farmer has to take numerous decisions regarding the cultivation of crops. Thus, a farmer is basically a manager who has to make numerous decisions from selection of crop to ultimate sale of produce. Thus, decisions support systems, which go beyond just the provision of generalized technical information, are needed for commercial farmers. A pilot product for such a decision support systems for the vegetable sector has been developed by one of the co-authors with the collaboration of many other technical personnel. It provides information to help decide what vegetable to grow, seed requirements, cultivation practices, input requirements including labour for specific growing areas, pest and disease control measures, harvesting and post-harvesting practices. The costs and returns of all these practices, as well as the cash flows and the overall income and expenditure are provided to facilitate farmers to take decisions.

In certain areas of the country farmers make collective decisions at the Farmer Organization level with respect to field and irrigation channel maintenance activities, as well as cultivation aspects such as cultivation dates and crops. Collective decisions are especially important when dealing with external agencies as in agreements related to Forward Sales Contracts, where Farmer Organizations could agree to provide a crop to a particular purchaser at agreed upon prices. In such instance access to market information to negotiate prices would help in reducing associated transaction costs. Furthermore, such systems should facilitate communication between the Farmer Organizations, or network/s of Farmer organizations, and the produce buyers. As Farmer Organizations make collective purchases of inputs, such as fertilizer, these information systems should enable the aforementioned communication abilities with potential suppliers of agricultural inputs too.

As indicated the need for information in agriculture is very wide. This need is further expanded as it includes a very large number of entities requiring widely differing types of information. In terms of sectors it needs to cater to the sectors such as crop, animal husbandry, and fisheries. Within a sector such as the crop sector it needs to cater to differing segments such as the food crop sector, the plantation sector, the protected agriculture sector, the floriculture sector, and the food processing sector. Within each segment it needs to provide information on crop and variety selection, cultivation practices, pest and disease management, harvesting and post-harvest practices as well as marketing information. Due to this diversity it is essential that an overall strategy to provide agricultural information take cognizance of this fact. Accordingly, multiple initiatives, rather than just a few, are needed by different players to provide the information requirements in agriculture. Institutions, which have developed strong ICT capabilities and initiatives, such as the Department of Agriculture, could be supported to provide advice and training to other agriculture organizations to develop their own information services. Such a mechanism should provide for new initiatives from the different organizations, to enable adaptation and innovation to develop and deliver products most suited for their clientele.

Arising from the diversity of requirements noted above, another perspective is possible in terms of Agricultural Information Systems. Roling (1988) in his work on Agricultural Knowledge Systems identified many sub-systems such as the research, dissemination (or extension), user (or farmer), training, input supply/ marketing, policy, and NGO sub-systems. This view broadens the scope of agricultural information systems, indicating user needs beyond that of the farmer. An overall information strategy for the agricultural sector certainly needs to take account of all these needs. Clearly priority areas of importance, and possibility, need to be the initial initiatives. However, an overall strategy should not get bogged down only with the initial initiatives, and their maintenance, but also forge ahead to meet the other information requirements too.

Traditional Systems of Agriculture Extension

Traditionally, the scientific research and new knowledge related to agricultural practices were delivered to farmers through a process of farmer education, aiming to increase produce and productivity of agriculture. Provision of such information can lead to improved yields (Rosegrant & Cline, 2003). This process of disseminating agriculture information is known as *agricultural extension* whilst a village bound extension agents typically play the main role in bridging the gap between research and practice. A variety of teaching methods, such as individual methods e.g farm visits, group methods e.g. demonstrations, and mass methods e.g. television and radio programmes are used to educate the beneficiaries.

In a given agriculture education system, learning could take place along four paradigms; technology transfer, advisory work, human resource development, and facilitation and empowerment (National Agricultural and Forestry Extension Service [NAFES], 2005). Technology transfer involves a top-down approach to deliver specific recommendations related to cultivation practices the farmers need to adopt, while advisory services help farmers in clarifying problems, by responding to their queries with technical prescriptions. Facilitation for empowerment involves facilitating experiential learning and farmer to farmer exchanges. Farmers are encouraged to make their own choices, by interacting with each other.

However, it is seen that the traditional methods of information dissemination have become less successful and less cost effective due to various reasons. The average number of farm families to be served by a single extension officer has exceeded 4000, which is an extremely hard target to achieve. The withdrawing of grass root extension workers from extension activities and overburdening of extension workers with duties other than provision of extension services are two of the other constraints that affected the agriculture extension system in Sri Lanka. Decentralization of the extension services to provincial government has weakened the extension service seriously affecting the research –extension linkage, and the efficiency of the national agriculture extension system. Weak knowledge management systems especially in the areas of information sharing, dissemination of information, and agricultural extension is being regarded as one of the major challenges ahead of agriculture research and extension today.

Given the fact that many farmers are literate, and the growth of ICTs in the recent years, integration of ICT is seen as one of the promising solutions, which can be used to provide up-to date information to the agriculture sector. The efforts to harness ICTs in reaching agricultural communities were evident during last decade, when looking at the investments made by the agriculture organizations, including major projects such as the cyber extension project, which will be discussed later in this chapter. A number of agriculture based organizations have started websites and have started offering web based services.

Access to ICTs

Compared to other low income countries Sri Lanka performs exceptionally well in its affordable ICT services, as it has remarkably lower mobile broad band prices (International Telecommunication Union [ITU], 2012). The ICT development index (IDI) ranks Sri Lanka in 105th position in year 2011, out of 155 countries. The same index places Sri Lanka at 50th position in terms of ICT prices. Table 2 shows the sub-indices used to

Table 2. IDI sub indices and rank of Sri Lanka (Source ITU, 2012)

Index	Sub-Indices	Rank 2011	
ICT access/ readiness infrastructure	fixed-telephony mobile telephony international Internet bandwidth households with computers households with Internet	103rd	3.3
ICT intensity/ Usage	Internet users fixed (wired)-broadband mobile broadband	112th	0.67
ICT capability or skills	adult literacy gross secondary enrolment gross tertiary enrolment	98th	6.45

calculate the IDI, and the rank of Sri Lanka based on the sub indices. Sri Lanka provides one of the lowest mobile –cellular prices thus being ranked in the 14th position in the mobile–cellular price category of the IDI. Mobile subscriptions per 100 people is as high as 99.2 at the end of year 2013 (TRCSL, 2013). It is noted that this value does not indicate the percentage of subscribers as it is fairly a common practice in Sri Lanka to have multiple subscriptions, probably due to the fairly low cost, and in some cases, free availability of such mobile subscriptions.

Internet

Sri Lanka has a well developed broadband infrastructure; however the penetration is relatively low. Fixed line penetration is 2.35%, while mobile broadband subscriptions are around 5.9% (Telecommunications Regulatory Commission of Sri Lanka [TRCSL], 2013). At present there is a well developed broadband market, with different fixed and mobile operators providing broadband services through different technologies. There is a potential to increase the broadband use in the future. Both the TRCSL and the Information and Communication Technology Agency of Sri Lanka (ICTA) have made broadband access a policy focus. Examples of recent ICT development projects include the setting up of over 500 rural tele-centers, a subsidy scheme to build and operate a fiber backbone in rural areas, and the development of e-government applications (ITU, 2014).

Literacy

The adult literacy rate in Sri Lanka is around 91% (Central Bank of Sri Lanka, 2013b) which indicates that the majority of the population, including the farmers, can read and write. High literacy levels give a definite advantage in using various ICT resources, and it is an important factor to be considered in planning for information and communication interactions.

ICT INTERVENTIONS

There are many ICT based interventions to serve the agriculture society in its various stages of the production process. Some projects stand out due to its coverage of population, publicity and investments: Among these are, the government initiated a cyber extension project, agri-advisory service, and other collaborated projects on SMS based market price dissemination systems. Websites are the most commonly adopted web technology by most of these organizations, which is similar to the observations reported by Rhoades and Aue (2010) who studied the use of social media in agriculture information dissemination. Use of social network sites like Facebook or micro blogging sites such as Twitter is not commonly seen at the organizational level. Interactive Voice Response (IVR) methods are still at research level and are successfully tried out with smaller communities. This section discusses some of the important ICT interventions that attempted to use ICTs in reaching various levels and categories of the farming community.

Cyber Extension Project

The DOA initiated a cyber extension project way back in 2004 as an "appropriate information exchange mechanism which seems affordable and convenient for rural farmers in satisfying their information needs" (Wijekoon, Emitiyagoda, Rizwan, Rathnayaka, & Rajapaksha, 2014). This was established in two phases; as a wireless extension strategy at first and as a real cyber extension mechanism with internet and telecommunication facilities as the second phase. It was felt necessary and important that farmers were provided with necessary information needed in the various stages of the farm decision making process and the extension system was facing criticisms that it was not being able to satisfy the information demands from the farmers. The Department of Agriculture was thus looking for alternative methods powered by the latest ICTs and their solutions is to introduce computer based learning to the farmer community.

Forty five agrarian service centers, out of the 550 centers, were selected to establish cyber extension units (CEU). A cyber unit was provided with a computer, digital camera, internet facility, telephone, printer and a scanner, similar to a rural information center with the aim of supporting the agriculture community in the area. Thus, a set of Interactive Multimedia CDs (IMMCDs) were designed as an offline cyber extension strategy to provide crop related information to the farmer community. Typically a CD contained information on various aspects of the growth of a particular crop including cultivation and management aspects of crops such as chili, big onion etc. There are also a few CDs which present information on more general topics such as 'integrated pest management', home gardening, and micro irrigation, which discuss important management practices that are common for a group of crops. The learning contents in the CDs were developed with the assistance of Research Officers who verified the technical information. These IMMCDs included video clips, audio narrations, graphics, images and text based illustrations.

The extension agent is to act as the officer in charge of the cyber unit while farmers can use the CDs when they visit the extension agents' office and learn the technical information provided in the CDs. The extension officer may also use the CDs in farmer training classes to design training aids. A list of IMMCDs that have been produced by the Department of Agriculture and is available in the sales outlets is presented in Table 3. These CDs are available mostly in Sinhala, some in Tamil, and a few in English.

Lack of awareness of the cyber mechanism was seen as one of the major problems according to (Wijekoon et al., 2014). Later the DOA had taken steps to popularize the CEUs among farmers. However there are other problems such as poor computer skills by the farmers to use CDs on their own (Dissanayeke, Wickramasuriya, & Wijekoon, 2009). Certain farmer groups are seen more confident in using CDs to obtain information. These are the well-educated and mostly part time farmers who have a main source of income other than agriculture. Some of them even had computer facilities in the home and they made copies of these CDs for later reference. However the majority of the famers had to mainly depend on the cyber extension unit to use these CDs, while they need the extension agent's assistance to select the relevant pieces of information. This interferes with the schedule of the extension agent because he is pre-occupied with other major responsibilities, rather than only managing the CEU. Considering this difficulty, the DOA is

Table 3. List of CDs available in the cyber extension units (Source Department of Agricutlure Sri Lanka [DOA], 2010)

Title of the CD	Languages [S] –Sinhalese, [T]- Tamil, [E] – English
Anthurium	[S], [E]
Banana cultivation	[S]
Bean cultivation	[S]
Betel	[S]
Big onion cultivation	[S] [T]
Brinjal cultivation	[S] [T]
Chili	[S]
Coconut (I, II)	[S]
Compost making	[S]
Cucurbitaceae plants	[S]
Forages	[S]
Gerbera cultivation	[S]
Home gardening	[S]
Integrated pest management	[S]
Jack	[S]
Leafy vegetables	[S]
Maize cultivation	[S]
Micro irrigation	[S]
Mushroom (I, II)	[S]
Orange /Citrus	[S]
Orchid	[S]
Paddy	[S] [T]
Papaya cultivation	[S] [T]
Potato cultivation	[S]
Protected agriculture	[S]
Pulses	[S]
Rambutan cultivation	[S]
Red onion cultivation	[S] [T]
Royal botanical garden	[E]
Soil conservation	[S]
Tibbatu	[S]
Tomato cultivation	[S] [T]
Underutilized fruit crops	[S]
Upcountry vegetables	[S]
Vegetable insect pests	[E] [S]

planning to appoint a separate officer to manage the CEU and help with farmers to find the necessary information.

The IMM CDs have an interactive user interface where the users have some control in selecting what information to be viewed and when. This can be considered as a positive development because farmers, being adult learners, need to have some control over what they want to view. However the best uses of these could not be harnessed by many farmers mainly due to the poor computer skills and less access to computer facilities.

A substantial amount of resources has been expended to develop good ICT material such as the IMM CDs for the food crop sector in Sri Lanka as mentioned above. However, as with any other information source, it is important to continuously update such material. While updating may not be as glamorous and rewarding as the initial development of a product, it is very important to ensure that the information seekers are provided with current information. Apart from the greater fulfillment of the information needs leading to greater customer satisfaction, it will also enhance the trust and credibility of these sources of information. This is especially so when such material becomes available online. To facilitate such updating and appropriate technical system, key responsible persons whose work will be appropriately recognized, adequate support staff and financial allocations are important.

Another important consideration of the cyber extension project is to link farmers with the other major agriculture stakeholders such as, wholesale traders, researchers and policy makers. It is considered necessary and important to regulate the information flow between stakeholders i.e. researchers and farmers, farmers and policy makers, farmers and traders. It is expected that this would enable farmers to make email queries to researchers seeking technical assistance to solve field problems. However this objective is achieved to a lesser extent so far due to limitations such as low computer literacy of farmers, Extension officers are overburdened with responsibilities other than managing the cyber unit and assisting farmers to send emails will add to their already heavy workload.

Marketing Information Systems

According to Dharmaratne (2013), Sri Lanka had commenced an Agriculture Market Information System (AMIS) as early as 1980s. Market data had been collected, analysed and finally disseminated to interested parties. The main purpose of the system was to measure food security and provide price signals to agriculture marketing stakeholders including the small farmers, traders and policy makers. AMIS had been initiated as two bulletins; a weekly publication that included information on wholesale and retail market prices of nine food items, including price comparisons with the previous week, producer price, statistical indicators such as range and average price. The bulletin was made available for policy makers, general public, and media agencies. The second publication was a monthly information system, which provided key indicators of prices, production, crop situation and food stocks.

Some of the major problems with the initial years of implementing AMIS were poor understanding of the purpose of data and information collection, underutilization of data and information, ineffective communication and presentation, lack of internationally comparable and compatible methodologies for data and information handling and limited capacity of national programs. Farmers were also unable to use the system as the information provided by the system was limited to a few crop types. These were hardly enough to make right decisions. In addition the small farmers and traders were not skilled enough to interpret some of the data presented in the bulletin. It is also noted that these earlier systems did not meet the actual needs of farmers for real time information. Whilst this information is certainly useful for academic studies and policy decision makers, its utility to farmers is limited. However, present data collection, analysis, and dissemination possibilities have enabled the rapid collection and provision of user required specific information almost in real time. Thus, the use of present day Agricultural Marketing Systems by farmers too is bound to increase. However other stakeholders such as policy makers, scientists, and academics are also able to use the system in a useful way.

Agriculture Advisory Service

A call centre solution known as Agriculture Advisory Service is implemented by the DOA as a supplementary service to the present extension system in the country. This is foreseen as a quick mechanism of disseminating agriculture information to strengthen the linkages between research, extension, training, and farmers. This type of a system helps to facilitate a demand driven extension service, as the farmer initiates the communication process.

The extension officers, working in the call center, assist farmers in solving their various problems such as agriculture related technical matters, inputs and marketing problems. The service, which is available in the local languages, receives nearly 100 to 250 calls from the agriculture community every day and is regarded as one of the most wide spread ICT related agriculture activites in Sri Lanka (Dissanayake et al., 2009; DOA, 2010; Wijerathna, 2011). A study conducted by Dissanayake et al. (2009) reports that the farmer community is satisfied with the information provided, while the field extension staff regards the service as an effective solution which eases their work at the field level.

Mobile Based Information Services

Mobile based information dissemination methods recieved wide attention in the recent years mainly due to the availability of mobile phones among people in Sri Lanka, including the farmers. A recent study shows that about 73% of the rural farmers have access to a mobile phone while some extended farm families had access to more than one mobile phone at a time (Dissanayeke & Wanigasundera, 2014) making it a common household item. When compared with the use of computers with internet facilities, the mobile phone was found to be the most common ICT facility among the farmers. Wide usage and accessibility to mobile phones has given opportunities to see how to use mobile based information systems in reaching the farming community. Short message service (SMS) based systems to send market prices, toll free call line facilities to inquire about agriculture based queries, and interactive voice response systems have been experimented with, and later some used by government, private sector, non-government based organizations as well as by independent research groups. Some of the important mobile based initiations are discussed later in this chapter.

Use of mobile SMSs to deliver important pieces of information has become popular worldwide due to the simplicity, effectiveness and low cost (Dhaliwal & Joshi, 2010; Fafchamps & Minten, 2012). Information related to commodity prices, market opportunities, crop advisory, and weather information are the main types of information that are sent to farmers using SMSs in the above studies. Many farmers preferred to have these informative SMSs as it is an inexpensive way to get access to important information. Given this fact that the present access and use of mobile devices is very high, and also that it could be expected to grow even further, this should be seriously considered as a tool that would have even more importance in the future. Initiatives should not be limited to basic cell phones but should cover applications for Smartphone too. While the majority of the present farming population may not own Smartphone yet, their prices will undoubtedly come down making them more affordable. Further, given the large number of migrant workers who have gone overseas from rural areas, the want for communicating with them will propel more people to purchase Smartphone even as prices come down as well. Thus ownership per se of Smartphone in the rural areas is bound to increase. Even if people may not have their own Smartphone, they are bound to have access to them through other rural people who own them. If the information is valuable enough farmers will probably be willing to pay enterprising people who could look up the information on behalf of the farmers for a small reasonable charge. Owners of communication centres that are spread all over the country could be one group that might show interest in such an enterprise.

Mobile SMS Based Price Information Dissemination Services

"Govi Gnana Seva"

The Govi Gnana Seva (GGS) project started as an independent price collection and dissemination service to help farmers get the best possible prices for their produce. This is one of the pioneer projects to initiate sending vegetable market prices to farmers in Sri Lanka (De Silva, 2008). The project operated from the Dambulla Dedicated Economic Center from where vegetable spot prices are collected and then sent by SMSs to the farmers who are registered with the system. Traditionally low farm-gate prices, especially for perishable crops such as vegetables, have been reported even when consumer prices for the same products are relatively much higher. Whilst the low bargaining power of individual small scale farmers is one factor, another factor is their lack of knowledge regarding the prevailing wholesale prices in major agricultural markets closer to the urban areas. Hence, the attempts to fill the information gap between farmers and markets became significantly important.

Later the GGS project started a partnership with a leading mobile company and continued to offer the service on a Tradenet platform (Dialog Axiata PLC, 2009). They have also expanded the service to collect price information from 2 other dedicated economic centers. The system can match the buyers with possible sellers and send alerts to both parties with their respective contact details (de Soyza, 2014). The buyer and seller can negotiate and proceed with the transactions. Buyers and sellers can upload posts to the Tradenet using web, WAP, call centre and IVR, SMS and USSD access technologies using English language or the two local languages.

Interactive Voice Response (IVR) Systems

IVR System for Mushroom Farmers

The Ruhunu University together with a private mobile service provider developed an Interactive Voice Response (IVR) system to educate small-scale mushroom farmers. This is implemented as a technology dissemination programme under the Life Long Learning for Farmers (L3F) employing ICT for one of its components. The IVR system embedded pre-recorded messages of two minutes duration for six months to guide listeners on how to establish, and manage a mushroom shed. Business planning and financial management lessons are also included (Wijeratne & Silva, 2013). About 5000 farmers have taken part in the programme. Farmers are able to obtain needed information quickly and accurately using ICTs. The study reports that the majority have accessed the knowledge system, which can be considered as a positive development. They have listened to the voice mail during their free time. Poor feedback from farmers is seen as one of the limitations by the researchers. The L3F have recently started a similar programme in collaboration with the Open University of Sri Lanka (OUSL) and the same mobile service provider to offer financial management lessons to rural women using IVR systems.

Agricultural Price Information Index

In the recent years a government based agricultural research institutions have started offering daily whole sale vegetable price information, collected from eight markets Island wide with the assistance of a private mobile service provider, one of the leading mobile service providers in the country (Hector Kobbekaduwa Agrarian Research and Training Institute [HARTI], 2014; Mobitel Pvt Ltd, 2014). The service is made available in the two local languages using an Interactive Voice Response System (IVR) to the customers of the same mobile service provider. The callers have to bear the cost for using the IVR system.

Decision Support Systems

Social Life Network

Social Life Network (SLN) is an attempt in developing a holistic mobile based system to aid farmer information needs, throughout the farming life cycle (De Silva, Goonetillake, & Wikramanayake, 2012). The SLN will address issues such as ‘how to strengthen the linkages among various agriculture stakeholders using mobile based systems’, and ‘how to capitalize on the latest mobile technologies such as inbuilt sensors and processing capabilities’. As implied in its name, this system intends to create a network of the users, who would generate real time information, through their participation in the SLN, which will eventually be accessible for the same user community in return. It is assumed that such systems would eventually help the stakeholders to make informed decisions by opening up opportunities for predictive models to strengthen the decision making process. Mobile interfaces of the SLN have been continuously tested with the stakeholders, using action research approaches, to assure user-friendly and usable designs

Websites

The Internet and websites play a major role in today's information culture. A website can be used to post important information that could make the farming community instantaneously aware of relevant information (Reddy & Ankaiah, 2005). Websites can further act as an important medium to ensure the dissemination and sharing of essential agriculture information that fits the agriculture community's interests and needs. A content analysis study, which evaluated 27 agriculture related websites in Malaysia, concludes three important categories of information that should be there in agriculture websites namely technical information with regard to crops, fisheries, and livestock, training opportunities offered by the institutions, and the financial aspects related to capital, loan facilities and interest rates (Ramli, Hassan, Samah, Sham, & Ali, 2013).

A number of agriculture related organizations in Sri Lanka have marked their web presence (Table 4) providing useful information for the visitors. In fact reports do indicate a high impact on the agriculture sector, next to the telecommunications sector (Jayathilake, Jayaweera, & Waidyasekera, 2010). The types of information and services available through these websites include; technical information related to crop and livestock, marketing information, online services, training opportunities, organizational structure and administrative divisions, vision and mission, news briefs, and contact information.

Almost all the websites are available in English, while the majority has accommodated Sinhalese language as well. Only a few websites have the complete Tamil translations, while this facility is under construction on many sites. For systems where the target group is the farmers, in most instances the content material will have to be in both local languages which are Sinhala and Tamil. As the availability of the same content in both languages is not seen on all sites, this needs to be done. Hence efforts for automatic translation from one language to another needs to be enhanced. Such a facility, together with verification by experts, should be used to enhance the efficiency and reliability of having the content in both languages. To the extent possible, English versions are to be made available to meet requirements of multi-lingual companies and NGOs, as well as other users such as students.

The Department of Agriculture (DOA) website has been recognized both locally and internationally for its pioneer work in using ICTs for agriculture information dissemination in Sri Lanka. According to the website statistics, the number of hits exceeded 3 million as of 2014 whilst thousands of online users visit the website every day. This website has been recognized as the best website among the government websites over several years and provides an example for the other websites which followed. Thus we discuss some of the important features in the DOA website, which is of prime importance to understand the agriculture information culture in the country.

Technical Information Dissemination

Most of the websites presented in Table 4 have made efforts to share technical information related to cultivation aspects in their websites. Online learning resources, including pdf versions of printed publications, and video documentaries are most commonly used to achieve this objective.

The DOA website publishes technical information related to important crop varieties that are grown in the country under the crop recommendation section. These crops belong to the food crop sector including rice, vegetables, fruits, grains, tubers, oilseed crops and condiments. Specific information related to the nutritious value of the produce, recommended varieties, suitable climatic conditions, and crop management practices such as propagation, pest and diseases, fertilizer application, post-harvest handling, and value addition are presented in English and one other local language (Sinhalese). This technical information is pre-

Table 4. Websites of some of the main (government) agricultural organizations

Organization	Some of the Important Features
Department of Agriculture (DOA) http://www.agridept.gov.lk	• Technical information dissemination – Video documentaries, online learning resources, publications • Market information • Training opportunities • Languages–Sinhalese, Tamil, English
Institute of Post Harvest Technology (IPHT) http://www.ipht.lk	• Technical information dissemination • Training opportunities • Languages: Sinhalese and English languages only
Department of Export Agriculture (DEA) http://www.exportagridept.gov.lk	• Subsidy schemes • Farm gate prices of export agriculture crops • Technical information dissemination related to crop management practices • Video documentary • Training opportunities • Languages
Tea Research Institute (TRI) http://tri.lk	• Technical information dissemination – list of publications and advisory circulars • Languages: Sinhalese and English languages only
Rubber Research Institute (RRI) http://www.rubberdev.gov.lk	• Technical information dissemination – online learning resources • Price information • Download applications for various services offered by the institution • News updates • Statistics • Languages – English, Sinhalese, Tamil
Rubber Development Department of Sri Lanka (RDD) http://www.rubberdev.gov.lk	• Services- subsidies, extension services • Download applications • Statistics • Price information
Coconut Research Institute (CRI) http://cri.gov.lk	• Technical information dissemination using, online learning resources, publications, and video documentaries • Online forms to make inquiries • News updates • Languages: English, Sinhalese, Tamil
Coconut Cultivation Board (CCB) http://www.coconut.gov.lk	• Technical information dissemination using online learning resources. • Subsidy programmes, credit facilities and loans facilities • Download loan applications • Crop input prices • News and event information • Languages: English, Sinhalese, Tamil
Coconut Development Authority (CDA) http://www.cda.lk	• Information on key products • Online directory to find exporters and traders • Publications • Statistics • Languages: English, Sinhalese, Tamil
Department of Animal Production and Health (DAPH)	• Online application portal to apply for import and export permits • Publications • Livestock statistics
Hector Kobbekaduwa Agrarian Research and Training Institute (HARTI) http://www.harti.gov.lk	• Display market information • Publications • Facilities available • News and events

sented in the format of online learning resources, using interactive menus to locate learning contents. Text based illustrations were the most commonly used medium, while graphics and photographs are also used appropriately to illustrate facts. Similar efforts have been made by several other organizations to disseminate technical information.

It is a positive trend to observe that many of these organizations have shared their printed publications on the website as a portable document format (pdf) files, giving an opportunity for online users to download them easily without any cost. These publications otherwise have to be purchased from selected sales outlets. Sales outlets sometimes face problems when certain publications are sold out, and when the farmers who are coming for the particular publication has to wait for the next print. Some other organizations have displayed the list of publications in the webpage with the respective prices, directing farmers to the sales centers where a copy can be obtained. Publications include books, leaflets, agriculture magazines, advisory circulars, and other agro-technology based reports that are originally designed to be in the printed format.

Video is a very powerful source to provide information, compared to other mediums as it can combine several media at the same time. It is seen that only a very few agricultural organizations other than the DOA is utilizing online videos to reach agriculture audiences. This situation is similar to the observations made elsewhere (Goodwin & Rhoades, 2009; Rhoades & Aue, 2010). The Department of Agriculture has a repository of video documentaries produced for national television that is made available for the online users. The DOA has its own video production unit at the Audio Visual Center where these documentaries have been produced. Thus a rich collection of more than 300 video documentaries are now available in the DOA website. The Department of Export Agriculture and the Coconut Research Institute are two other organizations that have made good use of online videos in agriculture related technical information dissemination. Both these organizations have shared these videos on YouTube, which is an important step in reaching non-agriculture audiences and especially young farmers. In fact it is important to get more agriculture related videos on such common platforms to reach a majority of the community.

Agriculture Information Management Systems

The Agriculture Information Management System (AgMIS) is developed by the DOA to share information related to food crops such as cultivation extents, production or yield forecast, and contact details of the farmers and officers involved. This is an interactive system which is developed to minimize marketing problems, while it is also expected that it would provide a comprehensive database for policy makers to help in planning and decision making (Food and Agriculture Organization of the United Nations [FAO], 2014). Latest news updates related to the food crop sector is displayed in the website for the frequent visitors in English and the two local languages. Only a few organizations are seen supporting online databases to manage information on buyers and sellers. The Coconut Development Authority maintains an online directory to provide information on manufacturers and importers for interested parties. Users can search a manufacturer based on the district, product and product type using an interactive menu in this website which help stakeholders to access important information easily.

Agricultural Price Information

Use of websites to display market information is seen as one of the recent developments. As seen in Table 4, several organizations have started publishing market prices of the relevant crops as well as related products on their websites so that online users can glance through these prices before making important decisions. Some organizations are using multiple methods such as publishing on the website using interactive menus, mobile IVR based systems, and publishing as PDF documents. For instance the Hector Kobbekaduwa Agrarian Research Training Institute started publishing the daily and weekly food prices on their website for easy access. This is an interesting difference from the earlier system they had, which was available on printed format only. Wholesale, retail and farm gate prices of more than 100 commodities can be obtained through the web site in the two local languages and also in English. Interactive menu items help the users to locate and view a specific category of product easily, and this saves time as otherwise time has to be spent on browsing a long list of items. The same information available in the website is accessible using a mobile based IVR system too, as discussed under mobile based systems.

Farm gate prices for all the export agriculture crops, collected weekly by the Economic Research Unit of the Department of Export Agriculture, are displayed on their website. A mobile version of the website is also available, making it easier for the export agricultural crops stakeholders to view information using a Smartphone. Information for the past few years have been saved on the website that helps users to compare prices in different years and different seasons of the year, thus making it easier in taking important decisions such as selling the produce. The Rubber Development Department is yet another organization that uses their website to publish price information. The latest information is published on the home page itself, making it much easier for the users to have a quick glance over the prices. Detailed information related to a specific year or month or a date can be obtained easily using the interactive menus.

Agriculture Related Services

A comprehensive list of services offered by a particular organization is available on many of the web sites. These services include training opportunities, credit and loan facilities, subsidy programmes, provision of export /import permission, agriculture inputs, certifications and some analytical services such as soil testing. In most of these cases, the website is simply being used to create an awareness in the public of the types of services, posting a brief description of the services. A few organizations such as CCD and RRI have moved a step forward by enabling the download of a copy of an application form through the website. DAPH has an online application portal, which can be used to submit applications and track the progress of the application to obtain import and export permits, which is an interesting development.

Extension and training opportunities were displayed on most of the websites mainly to make the public aware about these programmes. Furthermore, information related to credit facilities and subsidy schemes are also seen, along with facilities to download application forms from the website, as in the case of the Coconut Cultivation Board.

Information and Communication Technology Agency (ICTA) of Sri Lanka

Most of the websites and the features discussed in the section above are funded by the ICTA, which is the single apex body, owned by the government, involved in ICT policy and direction in the country. Its work includes improving technological capacity of the country, such as building ICT infrastructure, and the ICT readiness of its people, through education and human resources development. ICTA has provided financial support to a number of agriculture based organizations to establish interactive information services that are directly related to agriculture information dissemination. A complete list of these organizations and types of services financially supported are presented in Table 5.

ICTA has also supported disseminating agricultural best practices through e-Learning by funding two important projects namely Wikigoviya by

Table 5. Interactive information services funded by ICTA (source Information and Communication Technology Agency [ICTA], 2013)

Organization	E-Service Offered by the Website
Rubber Development Department of Sri Lanka (RDD)	Provide Rubber Prices
Department of Animal Production and Health (DAPH)	• Online Application Submission portal • DAPH Application Manager
Department of Export Agriculture (DEA)	Market Information
Department of Agriculture (DOA)	• Farmer Database • Classifieds - Advertising platform for farmers to sell their products • Agriculturists – to get contact information of agriculture specialists and their publications
Hector Kobbekaduwa Agrarian Research and Training Institute (HARTI)	• Weekly food prices • Daily food prices
Tea Small Holdings Development Authority (TSHDA)	Subsidy Information
Sri Lanka Tea Board	• Tea Price • Tea Directory

the Department of Agriculture, and Navagoviya by a private organization. Wikigovia consists of an e-learning system, agri-forum to discuss agricultural issues of importance, and an agriculture Wikipedia that can be edited by users ("Wikigoviya," 2014). The Navagoviya website is an initiation from a leading private sector company to develop and deploy e -earning and digital content to build awareness of new techniques and technologies in the agricultural sector. Most of these websites are published in English and two other local languages.

Rural resource centers, with internet facilities have been established to disseminate information at the village level. These centers are referred to as "*Nenasala* Centers" and currently there are 667 such centers. *Nenasala* centers provide a range of services including high speed internet access, e-mail, telephone, computer training classes and other ICT related services. The content essential to the rural community is available to all users in the Sinhala and Tamil languages. *Nenasalas* also caters to the diverse needs of the village community including agriculture, fisheries, and trade, which make it an important landmark in agriculture and related information culture in Sri Lanka.

ICTA has also funded a SMS enabled platform to exchange dairy product information among a small community of farmers. The system helped farmers to access a database to obtain necessary information, connect with the extension officer, the veterinarian, and other service providers. In addition a network of computers with touch screens were set up in public places for the easy access by farmers who does not have mobile phones (Mubarak, 2009).

PROBLEMS AND LIMITATIONS

ICT adoption is seen to be moderate among the farmer community, and a large part of this success can be attributed to the growth of the telecommunication sector in the recent years. The latest ICT based inventions in the agriculture sector can be seen as more of an effort to harness the best uses of ICTs in the agriculture information dissemination process. In this context, it is more likely to expect the emergence of information dissemination systems that are more of a technology driven nature than that of user driven nature, which could be a major drawback. In the future it is more important to see how to develop systems that would cater to actual information needs of the farmer community, by getting their involvement in the design process.

On the other hand we can see reasons such as cost of technology, lack of ICT proficiency, and inability to cater for the actual user needs slowing down the adoption and use of ICTs in agriculture. According to Jayathilake et al. (2010) the cost of technology can be seen as the main drawback that limit ICT adoption among farmer. Farmers' reluctance to invest on ICT based services could be due to a low awareness of the benefits of such services, less trust on the return of the investment, and high initial cost. This especially affects small farmers who practice subsistence agriculture, who see spending on ICTs as a waste of money, and who do not see the benefits of investing on them. During the inception of ICT projects, we can see more farmers using the systems when the services are offered free of charge, and there is no financial cost to the farmer. Latterly the farmer has to bear at least a very small part of the cost such as the cost of the telephone call, which was toll free at the inception.

Lack of ICT proficiency is seen as another important reason that affects the use of ICT in agriculture. For instance the unfamiliarity with mobile based technologies may lead to poor adoption of mobile SMS based price information systems. The majority of the farmers would be more conversant with the voice based services, while only a few are comfortable with SMS due to various reasons such as lack of technical know-how, and language proficiency (Wijerathna, 2011). Poor language proficiency is mainly due to the inability in using the English alphabet in sending and receiving text messages, rather than their literacy levels. Sri Lanka enjoys fairly high literacy rates due to the free education system thus there is a high potential to impart technology based education. As most of the mobile phones used in the country have English language in-built, it is necessary to come up with solutions to have phones with local language facilities and information systems. Interestingly the young and progressive farmers are seen mostly using these ICT based systems, and generally, low income, elderly farmers lag behind being unable to use the SMS facility.

Little or no emphasis has been given on linking farmers with the other important stakeholders such as extension agents, researchers, subject matter experts, traders, and input suppliers. Even though the present ICTs can be successfully used in strengthening the existing networks, and can be used to facilitate interaction among stakeholders very little attention is paid in this regard. This does not encourage interaction between the various stakeholders and the farmer is generally unaware of who else will be there in the network. This might be one of the reasons for the poor adoption of such technologies. The other possible reasons may be lack of awareness, negative attitude of some individuals at senior management levels, and administration problems, as with the case of cyber extension project (DOA, 2010)

It is seen that most of the attention is presently devoted to developing websites however the power of other web technologies such as social media, video sharing, and micro blogging has not yet being recognized. Rhoades and Aue (2010) noted similar observations with a group of agriculture journalists from the United States. Accordingly, most participants have seen the benefits of such tools, but some are still doubtful to adopt them because of the fear of time and resources needed.

FUTURE FOCUS

The landscape of agriculture information systems is changing. Commercialization, intensification and a greater involvement of the private sector is seen. Furthermore an expansion of the food processing sector is also seen. Thus, the need for agriculture related information has changed and grown in terms of the end users as well as the need for specialized information as in the case of protected agriculture. With the drastic reduction of the field extension workers in the 1980's, the agricultural extension role of the Department of Agriculture too has changed. The private sector and the NGO sector have undertaken the provision of agricultural extension, or information, services. However, these are but limited initiatives. The varying ICT initiatives already undertaken have tried to address this gap between the need for enhanced information and the reduction in the traditional extension services provided. There certainly is the need for more initiatives, some, if not many, of which should be from the ICT sector.

An apex body, such as a joint one between the Council for Agricultural Research Policy (CARP) and the Information and Communication Technology Agency (ICTA) which are the main respective government bodes at the national level, together with representation from the private agricultural companies, the plantation companies, and representatives of the farming communities should be formed. Such a body should map out the overall policy and strategy for agricultural related ICT initiatives. Seed funding should be provided for initiatives. Funding could be under different categories serving different purposes. It could also be under different scopes to include small short term projects, as well as more complex and longer term projects. Joint proposals by a technical agricultural agency and ICT competent personnel should be encouraged. The technical agency should prove its commitment and capability to maintain such a system once developed. The rationale for the above are elaborated upon below.

Whilst efforts of individual agencies and personnel do contribute to the availability of agricultural information, those would be dependent on their priorities, capabilities, and interests. When uncoordinated, such efforts may be duplicated, not completed due to the lack of competence or funds, and not adequately maintained over time. Furthermore, important areas may not be addressed. Hence, the coordination of information systems in the agricultural sector is important. The strategy for such coordination should be done by a representative body. Thus for Sri Lanka, representatives keen and committed to this initiative, from the following organizations could be considered for such a body. The Sri Lanka Council for Agricultural Research Policy (CARP) is the main body for agricultural related activities, whilst the Information and Technology Agency (ICTA) is the main organization involved in public funded ICT initiatives and thus, is in a good position to play a key role. Representation from the Ministry of Agriculture would be required to align initiatives to related policy, and also to influence the formulation of such policy. The Department of Agriculture, whilst being the main organization for the food crop sector, is also the organization that has been innovative and done the largest amount of work in agricultural ICT sector, as indicated before, and thus should continue to play a leading role in this sector. It would also be important to obtain representation from other agriculture related Departments, and the plantation crop sector as well, as they generate the technology and information for such sectors as well as providing the agricultural extension services. Another sector to be included would be representation from the Universities, with Faculties of Agriculture, as they represent another important source of knowledge and research in agriculture. Whilst the organizations identified above are mainly the information providers, it would be important to include the actual users of such information too to make such initiatives more demand driven. Hence the importance of key farmer representatives who are in a position to understand the possibilities and requirements from anticipated information systems. These could be from different categories identified to be important. The consideration of the needs of larger entities such as the Regional Plantation Companies, which are responsible for the management of the private plantation estates, as well as the requirements of the small-holders in these sectors too need to be ensured through appropriate participation. Similarly the requirements of the private sector agricultural organizations that are playing an increasing role, especially in catering to the more commercialized agricultural ventures need to be ensured. The requirement of NGOs for reliable agricultural information is also high since many have agricultural components in their projects, and hence their needs also should be considered. A committee comprising all those identified might be too large. However, their representation and input would certainly add value to future efforts. Hence, one way to balance these competing requirements of wider representation and a leaner committee could be to have a committee with permanent representation from the relatively more important organizations, and rotating membership of the other segments. Wide representation of this nature would enable clearer identification of key ICT initiatives that need to be focused on, coverage of a wider area in terms of both technical areas and information requirements, and better maintenance and future enhancements to the products. This forum would also enable the determination of possible lead-roles, such as the Department of Agriculture providing leadership and support to other organizations in their areas of ICT development. It could also determine those with multiplier effects, such as a base ICT system that is developed for the technical content only to be included by the different agencies. Since many agricultural organizations could lack personnel competent to develop full information systems, systems such as these would enable those organizations, normally unable to do so, to provide information to their clients through these 'pre-written shells' of ICT systems.

The role of a committee, such as the one proposed above, should be mainly to determine overall policy, priorities, strategy, and funding mechanisms. Deliberations of such a committee should be infrequent, but well planned and prepared for, and of high intensity, whereby substantial objectives are accomplished. If implementation is to be handed over to such a committee, apart from the need for frequent meetings of the main personnel, it would also need additional support staff and other resources. Thus, a more feasible alternative for implementation of the coordination of initiatives would be the handling of such activities by an existing national level organization, such as the ICTA in Sri Lanka. Such an agency could call for proposals according to the guidelines determined by the main committee, and coordinate the selection of projects, fund disbursement, and the progress monitoring and evaluation of agricultural ICT projects, which would be then and addition to the nature of activities already undertaken by them. An agency such as this could be involved in ensuring the maintenance and thus the longer term sustainability and continued utility of these ICT initiatives.

Clearly, a mechanism to propel activities towards desired goals, as determined by a representative committee as outlined above, would be to provide funding for the determined areas. Given the fact that most ICT information system initiatives are of relatively lower cost in comparison to infrastructure projects or organizational expansion, and also the relative availability of funds as countries strive to become more knowledge based economies and allocate funds accordingly, the availability of funds for these purposes is probably not a constraint. Funds could be provided mainly for the development of products. This funding should cover the period beyond the testing and prototype stages to actual initial use by the end users. This funding would act as an incentive for innovative ideas and possibilities. It would also enable those agencies lacking the needed ICT personnel for product development to hire them for the period needed. Whilst the major portion of the available funding could be for new initiatives, it would also be prudent to allocate funds for enhancement of previous products. In any field, and especially in ICT products, continuous improvements are almost essential. Hence, whilst the agency undertaking the initiative should be able to fund and undertake normal maintenance of the product, periodic major revisions could be supported as in its initial development.

The allocation of available funds should be pre-determined based on the needs and priorities identified for ICT activities in agriculture. For example allocations could be done proportionate to both the relative importance and need of different sectors such as the crop, animal husbandry, fisheries, and food processing sectors. Even though important, the funding for an area could be curtailed if suitable ICT applications already exist for that area. Within a sector, such as the crop sector, a similar pre-determination of the allocation of funds could be done for the food crop and plantation sectors. This process could be continued to a reasonable level to ensure that adequate coverage is provided. Such pre-determination of allocations should allow for reasonable margins of cross over, whereby provisions for certain areas are increased above the pre-determined allocation, and another/others reduced correspondingly. This would minimize the acceptance of a weak proposal purely because of it falling within a given area of allocation, and also increase the acceptability of a good proposal which might not have been funded due to other better proposals being allocated the available funds for that particular area.

In the allocation of funding for different areas it would be beneficial to strategically allocate funds based on short term, and probably smaller and simpler systems, as well as more long term, and probably larger information systems. Whilst many ideas for the short term could be projects with a relatively limited scope the longer term projects could be more complex and of greater scope. A mix of both would be needed. Smaller applications could be completed quicker and show results fast, thus giving a quick return on investment, as well as being a motivating factor for further work by the basically non-ICT personnel who probably would be a major group desiring to develop such systems. The areas considered could either be technical areas of importance, or areas of information systems which are complex systems akin to Enterprise Resource Planning systems of other sectors. Thus, the need for more complex systems to cater for more integrated information requirements should not be overlooked. Especially in such instances the involvement of ICT professionals should be ensured.

In general the strength of a technical agency would be its personnel, knowledge base and research output in the crops or areas related to the agency. In terms of ICT initiatives a weakness in many of these agencies, especially the smaller ones, would be the lack of personnel competent enough to develop and continuously maintain information systems. Hence, it would be beneficial to promote collaboration between personnel in these organizations and ICT competent technical organizations or personnel. This could be accomplished through the specific indication of such a requirement for funding purposes. The evaluation of proposals could be based on the agricultural competence and accomplishments, as well as the ICT competence and accomplishments of the personnel involved.

In an era of knowledge explosion, updating data to minimize obsolete information is essential. Furthermore, maintenance of an information system by rectifying bugs, or errors in the system, and also minor modifications and upgrading of the system has to be done. Thus, to enhance the continued utility, and thus the use, of the information systems developed, the capacity and commitment of an organization desiring to develop a new system, to maintain such a system in the future should be determined. Possibilities for an external agency, or agencies, to provide such backup if needed should be determined. A network of practitioners could also be promoted to help both in the initial development, as well as this latter aspect of maintenance.

Facilitation of the Interaction among Agriculture Stakeholders

Use of ICT based information exchange systems is most commonly seen among young and progressive farmers. Thus, future ICT based agricultural information systems need to be able to cater to their information needs, by identifying these farmers as special target communities. While doing so it is vital to move toward more interactive systems and building communities of stakeholders those who would interact and learn from each other's. Facilitation of interactions is important for two reasons. Firstly, farmers are likely to learn more from their colleagues than the extension agent or other authorities, as the problems they experience in the field are similar to the other farmers. They are much more likely to follow the footsteps of a successful farmer from the same community as the results are proven readily. Farmers, in general, are knowledgeable on whom to go for advice, while they relate to their own community and colleagues first when they have a problem. Secondly, the farmers would like to discuss and share what they found as a useful piece of information with their colleagues. The farmers prefer to see the opinion of the others in the community before adopting agricultural practices even when the information is passed down by the extension agent or any other important source. Thus it is necessary to create ICT based systems that can be used to facilitate interaction and information sharing among the agricultural communities. Participation of agricultural extension officers and other subject matter experts in such systems is crucial for successful functioning of such systems. These officers can initiate interactions, aware farmers on latest technologies and practices, and various other opportunities available for their training and development. Using the traditional system of extension to give away such information would be more time consuming when compared to an ICT based system.

When implementing such ICT based mechanisms, we need to pay attention to three important aspects; use of existing technologies when and where applicable in order to minimize the cost, go for participatory methods in developing and implementing ICT based agriculture information systems, and providing training for target communities.

Ideally we can develop applications and software to facilitate farmer collaboration using ICTs. However this could take a long time, and may involve substantial costs for development and maintenance of such systems. One alternative is to choose from the existing web based technologies, namely social networking, blogging, sending and receiving SMSs and IVR services, that are freely available with minimum or no maintenance cost. Some of these technologies have been tested out with smaller communities and has given promising results. Being in the category of a middle income country, it would be useful for Sri Lanka to explore existing and emerging technologies and modify them based on the specific requirements of the target groups.

Adoption of such ICT based information systems by the agriculture community depends on a number of aspects. One important question is 'how a given farmer community choose a suitable web based technology for collaboration?' This could be made possible in a number of ways. Ideally the community could make use of web technology, including social media, which the members are already familiar with. There are farmers and other stakeholders, those who already use web based technologies for interactions. Especially, the young farmers today are well aware of social networks and they can be encouraged to use such networks to link with other farmers. Another option would be an outside facilitator, such as the extension agent or any other authoritative person, introducing farmers to networking using social media. With a little help from the government or another organization in training these officers, they can easily initiate these networks at village level.

Use of participatory and interactive project designs when implementing ICT interventions with agricultural communities would improve the chances of sustainable impacts on target communities (Donovan, 2011). Accordingly future projects can adopt design research approaches, while ensuring stakeholder participation throughout the design process. This would lead to higher participation, easy adoption and sustainability, as farmers would get a sense of ownership for the outcome.

In many instances the average farmers may not have the necessary skills and attitudes to use a given ICTs although they are willing to do so. Thus, it is important to provide necessary training for them. The farmers who are conversant in using such technology could be identified and they could be assigned to help the other farmers.

There are informal leaders and followers in the community. We need to identify these groups and help them identify suitable ICT based communication systems to facilitate collaboration. It is important to identify the existing means of communication (such as face-to-face gatherings) that can be enhanced, or replaced, with modern ICTs, to strengthen the networks that are already present in the community. This would give recognition to each stakeholder in the system and users would be more comfortable in interacting with people who are already known to them.

CONCLUSION

Information and communication technologies have revolutionized the traditional systems of information exchange mechanisms, while opening up number of gateways to integrate ICTs in the development process. The agricultural information society has been significantly affected by these latest ICTs. A number of interventions made to harness best use of ICTs in agriculture information dissemination. Computer based learning methods, mobile based information dissemination systems and websites are the most common.

The major challenges ahead of the agriculture information society are less emphasis on networking stakeholders, duplication of work due to poor coordination, cost for developing and maintenance of ICT based systems, lack of ICT proficiency among farmers, and inability to cater to the actual user needs by the existing systems The possibility of using existing web based technologies, which are freely available, have not been adequately explored.

Addressing the above limitations is going to be very challenging. However, some of them can be addressed by ensuring proper coordination among the organizations, developing suitable ICT based agriculture information systems by following participatory research approaches, choosing from the existing web based technologies such as social media and modify them to suit local situations, and provide support for target communities by providing necessary training.

REFERENCES

Central Bank of Sri Lanka. (2013a). *Annual Report 2013*. Colombo: Si Lanka. Central Bank of Sri Lanka.

Central Bank of Sri Lanka. (2013b). *Sri Lanka Socio-Economic Data 2013* (Vol. XXXVI). Colombo, Sri Lanka: Central Bank of Sri Lanka.

De Silva, H. (2008). *Using ICTs to create efficient agricultural markets: A future vision for Sri Lanka* [PDF document]. Retrieved from http://www.lirneasia.net/wp-content/uploads/2008/03/de-silva_transaction-costs-in-sri-lanka-the-future.pdf

De Silva, H., & Ratnadiwakara, D. (2008). Using ICT to reduce transaction costs in agriculture through better communication : A case-study from Sri Lanka. Retrieved from http://www.lirneasia.net

De Silva, L. N. C., Goonetillake, J. S., & Wikramanayake, G. N. (2012). A holistic mobile based information system to enhance farming activities in Sri Lanka. In *Engineering and Applied Science (EAS 2012), IASTED Conferences, Vol 785* (pp. 91–99). ACTA Press. doi:10.2316/P.2012.785-092

de Soyza, M. (2014). Dialog Tradenet. *Digital Knowledge Center*. Retrieved from http://digitalknowledgecentre.in

ICT for Agriculture in Sri Lanka. (2010). Department of Agriculture Sri Lanka (DOA). Retrieved from http://www.afaci.org

Dhaliwal, R. K., & Joshi, V. (2010). Mobile Phones - Boon to Rural Social System. [LICEJ]. *Literacy Information and Computer Education Journal*, *1*(4), 261–265.

Dharmaratne, T. A. (2013). Agricultural market information system in Sri Lanka: Costs, transmission, reliability, volatility and adequacy to the policy needs. Proceedings of the International Conference on Agricultural Statistics VI. Rio de Janeiro, Brazil. Retrieved from http://www.fao.org

Dialog Axiata, P. L. C. (2009). Dialog Tradenet and GGS partnership set to revolutionise agri market access. Retrieved from http://www.dialog.lk

Dissanayake, D. M. L. B., Wijekoon, R. R. A., Madana, P., & Wickramasinghe, Y. W. (2009). Awareness and effectiveness of the toll free agricultural advisory service of the department of agriculture. *Abstract of Final Year Research Symposium 2009, Volume 03*. Faculty of Agriculture Rajarata University of Sri lanka. Retrieved from http://repository.rjt.ac.lk/7013/1685

Dissanayeke, U., & Wanigasundera, W. A. D. P. (2014). Mobile based information communication interactions among major agriculture stakeholders: Sri Lankan Experience. *Electronic Journal of Information Systems in Developing Countries*, *60*, 1–12.

Dissanayeke, U. I., Wickramasuriya, H. V. A., & Wijekoon, R. (2009). Evaluation of Computer Based Learning Materials in Agricultural Information Dissemination in Sri Lanka. *Tropical Agricultural Research*, *21*(1), 73–79.

Donovan, K. (2011). Anywhere, anytime - mobile devices and their impact on agriculture and rural development. Proceedings of the ICT in Agriculture: Connecting Smallholders to Knowledge, Networks, and Institutions (pp. 49–70). Washington. Retrieved from http://www.ictinagriculture.org

Fafchamps, M., & Minten, B. (2012). Impact of SMS-based agricultural information on Indian farmers. *The World Bank Economic Review*, *26*(3), 383–414. doi:10.1093/wber/lhr056

Food and Agriculture Organization of the United Nations (FAO). (2014). *Agriculture Management Information System. Department of Agriculture, Government of Sri Lanka (DOASL)*. Retrieved from http://www.agmis.lk/

Goodwin, J., & Rhoades, E. (2009). Agricultural Legislation: The Presence of California Proposition 2 [YouTube video]. Proceedings of the *Annual National Agricultural Education Research Conference*. Louisville, Ky.

Hector Kobbekaduwa Agrarian Research and Training Institute (HARTI). (2014). Mobitel agri price information index. Retrieved from http://www.harti.gov.lk

Information and Communication Technology Agency of Sri Lanka (ICTA). (2013). List of Interactive Information Services. Retrieved from http://www.icta.lk

Measuring the Information Society CH 1211. (2012). (p. 213). International Telecommunication Union. Geneva, Switzerland. Retrieved from http://www.itu.int

Statistical market overview: Sri Lanka. (2014). International Telecommunication Union (ITU). Retrieved from http://www.itu.int

Jayathilake, H. A. C. K., Jayaweera, B. P. A., & Waidyasekera, E. C. S. (2010). ICT adoption and its' implications for agriculture in Sri Lanka. *Journal of Food & Agriculture*, *1*(2), 54–63. doi:10.4038/jfa.v1i2.1799

Agri Price Information Index. (2014). Mobitel Pvt Ltd. Retrieved from http://www.mobitel.lk

Mubarak, C. (2009). e-Sri Lanka: What is in it for agriculture. Proceedings of *Joint National Conference on Information Technology in Agriculture* (pp. 7–10). Colombo, Si Lanka. University of Moratuwa, Sri Lanka and University of Ruhuna, Sri Lanka.

National Agricultural and Forestry Extension Service (NAFES). (2005). Consolidating Extension in the Lao PDR (p. 77). Retrieved from http://www.laolink.org

Ramli, N. S., Hassan, S., Samah, B. A., Sham, M., & Ali, S. (2013). Comparison of crop, fisheries and livestock information displayed on agriculture websites. *Journal of Basic and Applied Scientific Research*, *3*(6), 760–765.

Reddy, P., & Ankaiah, R. (2005). A framework of information technology-based agriculture information dissemination system to improve crop productivity. *Current Science*, *88*, 1905–1913.

Rhoades, E., & Aue, K. (2010). Social agriculture: Adoption of social media by agricultural editors and broadcasters. Proceedings of *107th Annu. Mtg. Of Southern Association of Agricultural Scientists* (pp. 1–20). Orlando, Florida.

Roling, N. (1988). *Extension Science: Information Systems in Agricultural Development* (p. 233). UK: Cambridge University Press.

Rosegrant, M. W., & Cline, S. A. (2003). Global food security: Challenges and policies. *Science*, *302*(5652), 1917–1919. doi:10.1126/science.1092958 PMID:14671289

Telecommunications Regulatory Commission of Sri Lanka (TRCSL). (2013). *Statistical Report -2013*. Retrieved from http://www.trc.gov.lk

Wijekoon, R., Emitiyagoda, S., Rizwan, M. F. M., Rathnayaka, R. M. M. S., & Rajapaksha, H. G. A. (2014). Cyber extension : An information and communication technology initiative for agriculture and rural development in Sri Lanka. *Food and Agriculture Organization. Document for Technical Consultant*. Retrieved from http://www.fao.org

Wijerathna, S. (2011). Mobile telephony for agricultural development of Sri Lanka (p. 45). Retrieved from http://papers.ssrn.com/sol3/papers.cfm?abstract_id=1976180

Wijeratne, M., & Silva, N. D. (2013). Mobile phone intervention for Sri Lankan mushroom producers. Proceedings of *27th Annual Conference of Asian Association of Open Universities*. Pakistan: Allama Iqbal Open University, Pakistan.

Wikigoviya. (2014). Retrieved from http://www.goviya.lk/index.php/en

Urban population Data. (2014). World Bank. Retrieved from http://data.worldbank.org

Chapter 19
E-Governance for Socio Economic Welfare:
A Case Study of Gyandoot Intranet Project in Madhya Pradesh, India

Umesh Kumar Arya
Guru Jambheshwar University of Science and Technology, India

ABSTRACT

In this chapter, the author has discussed India's first rainbow e-governance project encompassing the "ICTs, e-governance, rural development and access to the basic administrative services" aspects in India's hinterland and one of the most backward regions. The paper argues for the "socio economic welfare" stance of the ICTs and the resultants benefits thereof. The present study investigates the socio-economic aspect of community e-governance project named Gyandoot in remote villages of Madhya Pradesh. Out of 18 services offered by Gyandoot, people fully utilized only 3 services (land records, exam results and addressing public grievances) which lead to the considerable fulfillment of target audience's needs (felt needs and expected needs) and improvement in their work efficiency by high scores on convenience, satisfaction, time, cost, reliability and overall benefits factors and a reduction in the time and money for government service delivery. However, Gyandoot could not fare impressively well on spurt in employment and economic activity fronts thus leading to only moderate gains. Only 17% of the Gyandoot's potential could be utilized and 39% was used moderately. Rest 44% could not be utilized at all due to less demand of services. 'Optimism in IT hardware' and 'development of entrepreneurial attitude' were the most noticeable aspects of economic activity generated. The study also posits a few very important questions on the sustainability, interoperability and hierarchical issues relating to the project.

INTRODUCTION

E-governance is defined as the application of electronic means in (1) the interaction between government and citizens and government and businesses, as well as (2)in internal government operations to simplify and improve democratic, government and business aspects of governance (International Institute of Communication and Development, 2001).This word has gained tre-

DOI: 10.4018/978-1-4666-8598-7.ch019

mendous popularity in today's information age. Dharampur Sub-District Infrastructure planning for development (1977) is an early example of attempts to use computer applications for cost optimization and decision-making. The Karwar Rural Development Information System (1984) was yet another initiative formulated with a focus on reducing delay and curbing corruption through a monitoring programme based on computer applications (Kaul, M. et al.).However, the modern age e-governance started near millennium (2000) in India when idea of technology driven governance joined the chorus of numerous other issues for the betterment of citizenry. Role of technology powers competitiveness and leads to the creation of brand institutions and the use of right technology could bring in the right non-linear elements in all sectors, including water, power, education and healthcare (Kalam, 2004). The government realized the importance of ICT as a tool of national development and appointed a task force on IT and software development. The task force submitted its report in 1998, envisioned India as IT superpower by 2008, and suggested 108 recommendations. The government implemented most of them and it virtually sowed the seeds of e-governance in India. Much weightage was given to IT considering its tremendous impact on the society. Internet policy 1998 was a result of these recommendations which led to privatization of internet services in India. According to Heeks (1999), ICTs mean 'Electronic means of capturing, processing, storing and communicating information', usually in digital form. The possibilities with technology are unimaginable (Thomas,2005). It is believed that ICTs lead to Informatization. This is the process through which the new communication technologies are used as a means for furthering development as a nation becomes more and more an information society (Rogers, 2000; Singhal & Rogers, 2001).

Why E-Governance?

It is a vexed question whether technology can provide the solution to the daily ordeal faced by citizens in executing transactions with the government. It is a million dollar question whether e-governance is really the answer to end the citizens' sufferings. Citizen is the epicenter of e-governance (Presiss & Steven, 1996). Abraham Lincoln once said that public sentiment is everything. With public sentiment, nothing can fail and without it, nothing can succeed (*ibid*). As marketing starts with customer's needs and ends with customer's satisfaction, similarly, governance starts with citizens' needs and ends with citizens' welfare leading to their satisfaction. Citizen is the epicenter of e-governance (Presiss & Steven, 1996). Mahatma Gandhi once said, "A customer is the most important visitor in our premises. He is not dependent on us, we are dependent on him. He is not an interruption in our work, he is the purpose of it. He is not an outsider to our business, he is part of it. We are not doing him a favour by serving him but he is doing us a favour by giving us an opportunity to do so." According to a TNS mode market research survey, in order to pay a bill, a consumer travels an average distance of 10.5km, spends over 64 minutes and incurs an average expenditure of Rs 12 over and above the actual bill amount (Ramalingam, 2006). Another study conducted by Internet and Mobile Association of India, IMAI (2006) found that an average household in top 10 Indian cities pay 42 bills online in a year in finance, telecom and utilities companies. They save 24 hours a year citing convenience (54%), time saving (35%) and fancy (5%) as reasons. The government departments till date are as faceless and working mysteriously as they were invented and handed over to us by the Britishers. (Singla quoted by Mahapatra, Raghunath, 2004). The originators have abandoned this system in their own country while moving towards more accountability (*ibid*).

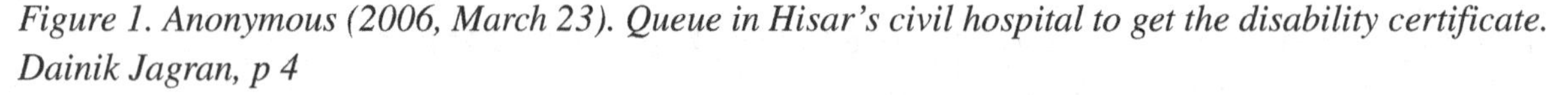
Figure 1. Anonymous (2006, March 23). Queue in Hisar's civil hospital to get the disability certificate. Dainik Jagran, p 4

Some writers have stressed the two main functions of government.

- Obligatory
- Optional

Obligatory functions relate to the preservation of state like right to life, security, employment, freedom of speech and expression whereas optional functions, not being essentials, bring a better system of governance and better living conditions of society. E-governance comes under optional function of government but due to the multiple dynamics attached to this concept, it is fast resulting into an obligatory function of government.

The endless queues and numerous rounds to the government offices seem to be the ordeal for a citizen. They have to spend their precious time, money, energy and that too at the cost of other important assignments so much that old man died

Figure 2. Anonymous (2004, February 12). An unending queue. Dainik Bhaskar, p 3

Figure 3. Times Photo (2005, September 14). Files destroyed in the irrigation department in Mumbai Floods. Hindustan Times, p 6

at the counter of house tax in Delhi when he was standing in the line under the scorching sun waiting to fill up his house tax at the Municipal Corporation of Delhi's office (Bhaskar News, 2004).

Corruption has become a part of Indian culture (Nayar, 2004). It has been seen that the departments with maximum public interaction like police, income tax, land and revenue matters etc. score high on corruption ladder. The originators have abandoned this system in their own country while moving towards more accountability (*ibid*).

The 8th goal of UN millennium development goals (2004) to be achieved by the member states by 2015 is "Develop a global partnership for development (In cooperation with the private sector, make available the *benefits of new technologies—especially information and communications technologies*). The words information, communication and technology are axial to the discourse on information society and have even formed a subfield of their own (Arya, 2010) Benefits of technologies are all pervasive but they often go unnoticed or do not get proper attention perhaps because they are "too simple but highly effective". The Hindi mega movie "Nayak" released in 2003 featuring Anil Kapoor is such a fascinating example. The Hero becomes the Chief Minister for a single day of the Maharashtra state ridden by corruption, lawlessness, nepotism, anarchy etc which he is determined to end. The Hero has a single day's time to improve the affairs. He checks out the status of their complaints on phone from the concerned government departments. In all the cases, he sends a suspension letter to the guilty typed on the spot directly through the fax machine thereby obviating the tardy and cumbersome task of departmental enquiry, witnesses etc. This shows that even simple electronic instruments like telephone, fax and television, which are oldest ICTs available since decades, can be put to novel use with astounding success. This potential increases as we move higher on the interactivity ladder of the state of the art modern gadgets. ESIA (Eliminate, Simplify, Integrate and Automate) framework by Singla (2004) is worth considering. The physical public interaction must be minimized and eventually eliminated, processing of files simplified, various interdepartmental functions integrated and finally automated. Since networks are immune to corruption, delays and unnecessary objections on the files. It has been seen that the departments with maximum public interaction earn the bad name of "insensitive" and corrupt public needs. Here e-governance can come to their rescue. Networks or the computer-mediated communication treat every user with equal respect and are immune to the nepotism, favoritism and external influence. Here ICTs can come to the rescue of common man.

About Gyandoot

On January 1, 2000 in Dhar district of central Indian state of Madhya Pradesh, a unique low cost and self-sustainable e-governance project named Gyandoot (Messenger of Knowledge) was launched with 21 telecenters (soochnalayas) situated in different gram panchayats of 5 blocks of the district. The telecenters were connected through dial up access to the central server placed at the office of Zila Panchayat at District Collectorate. Gradually, Gyandoot spread to all 13 blocks. The manager of the telecenter was chosen from the local community and trained by the Gyandoot Samiti. The soochak doesn't get any salary or stipend. Instead, s/he is charged 10% of income as commission to Gyandoot Samiti. Later on, the concept was extended to allow private telecenters with a license fee of Rs 5000/- in order to increase the reach and public participation. As a result, the number of telecenters increased to 31. The number of telecenters increased to 38 in 2002 but only 25 telecenters were operational at the time of survey in June 2006. The project got extensive media publicity and it bagged the prestigious Stockholm Challenger Award in June 2000 in the section of "Public service and Democracy" out of 109 entries from around the world.

Literature Review

Singhal and Roger (1990) reported that in an evaluation survey of the 74 telephones in Kittur village of Karnataka in 1986, the benefits found were - savings in time and money, higher prices for agricultural products, increased sales of farm products, quicker medical attentions, increased social interaction with friends and relatives, better law and order situation and faster information and news flows. *"Information Needs Assessment for Rural Communities, An Indian Case Study"* (CRISP Group, 2003) concludes that government entitlements, education, agriculture, fisheries, health, weather reports and bus time tables are the popular areas of information access among the rural communities. It found 9 categories of needs which include basic needs (livelihood, drinking water etc.), government information (BPL list, land records etc.), self employment (traditional skills, enterprises etc.), access to justice (addressing grievances, rights etc.), daily information (daily news, market prices etc.), environmental awareness (pollution, disaster management), classifieds and entertainment (employment news and matrimonial), announcements (health camps, SHG meetings etc.), Area profile (fact sheet, niche & opportunities). Khataokar and Chaturvedi (2004) in their research titled *"Future Perspectives of E-Governance in Madhya Pradesh: Initiatives towards G2C and G2B"* describe how each of the employees and the businessmen can partner with the government in its development initiatives found that there is significant positive correlation between efficiency and implementation of e-governance in G2B and G2C area. *"e-Suvidha: A Citizen Service at the Community Information Center in Northeast"* by Das, Rey and Prasath (2004) talks about e-governance package designed for CICs in 487 blocks of 8 states to automate the citizen centric services of submitting forms and monitor the progress online. They found that despite diversity in formats and procedures of government services, it is possible to develop generic software flexible to customizing according to local needs and highlighting the use of local language support. A similar study by *Kumari* (2004) titled *"Impact of E-Seva in Andhra Pradesh: A Study"* indicates that 70% of the customers using online payment of bills facility expressed satisfaction at "one stop shop" service, 25% are highly satisfied for all the services. E-seva is utilized by all the citizens irrespective of the difference in age, educational background and employment status. Educated class had a higher level of satisfaction. The study also highlights the significant role played by the informal sources of information like friends, relatives and other reference groups. A Study titled *"What Works: Tarahaat's Portal*

For Rural India" by *Lawlor, Sandel and Peterson* (2001) revealed its social impact in terms of more avenues of computer education for girls and women, increased self-confidence among rural children leading to entrepreneurial efforts and better crop price due to readily available mandi rates. *Saukaryam* (meaning facility) Project by Jaju (2004) in *"Saukaryam: A Case Study of Municipal E-Governance"* details the public private partnership project by Vishakhapatnam Municipal Corporation to deliver citizen services online. Jaju analysed that people were enthused by the ease of delivery of services, lack of harassment, elimination of corrupt practices, jump in revenue collection, the establishment of bulletin boards for discussions, prompt addressing of grievances. This is what he calls "Digital Unite".

Lobo and Balakrishnan (2002) in "Report Card on Service of Bhoomi Kiosks: An assessment of Benefits by Users of the Computerized Land Records System in Karnataka" found the benefits of the ease in use of the Bhoomi kiosks, reduced complexity of procedures, error free documents to more users, fast rectification of errors, reasonable cost of service (Rs 15), zero hidden costs, improved staff behaviour etc *Bhatnagar* (2000) in his research on CARD (Computer Aided Registration of Deeds) in *"Land/Property Registration in Andhra Pradesh"* found that earlier 11 step procedure of land's purchase/sale transaction was replaced by 10 minutes user friendly experience. Land registration completes in few hours unlike 7-15 days earlier. *Kukreja* and *Grover* (2004) in *"Innovative Approach in Deed Registration"- PRISM (Property Registration Information System Module"* in Punjab mention that it resulted in reduction in cycle time, elimination of frauds, convenience to citizens, increased transparency and efficiency etc. *Jafri, Dongre, Tripathi, Aggrawal and Shrivastava* (2002) stated that Gyandoot has provided the rural youth with an opportunity for self-employment and helped to enhance their entrepreneurial skills. *Vijayaditya* (2002) reported that the Warana project has been successful in generating employment opportunities for the local population in Maharashtra. Another study conducted by IMAI (2006) found that an average household in top 10 Indian cities pay 42 bills online in a year in finance, telecom and utilities companies. They save 24 hours a year citing convenience (54%), time saving (35%) and fancy (5%) as reasons.

Need and Significance of the Study

- **The study** - The present study would explore the effectiveness of community ICT project in fulfillment of target audience's needs, work efficiency and enhancement of employment opportunities of the target audience. Hence it would be of great importance and help to the development agencies, research organizations, sociologists etc. owing to its multidisciplinary orientation.
- **Limitations** - The study's findings do not claim to be relevant to other e-governance projects outside Dhar district. The research doesn't claim to extrapolate the findings in every social setup in India. The scope of finding out the fulfillment of the RQ is restricted to the adoption of the definition standardized by the experts. The findings are relevant only for the duration of the time spent in the field by the researcher. A rural society is polarized according to caste, color, creed, income, education, gender etc. hence it might have affected the quality of answers in the interview schedule method.
- **Theoretical Framework** - This study will follow two frameworks. The work of Whyte (1999) argues that the following dimensions should be covered in evaluating a telecentre:
    - The services offered
    - The finances
    - The usage of the services

- The users of the services
- What benefit the users of the services perceive.

Loader, Hague and Eagle (2000) provide a framework for "Community Informatics". In their opinion, the key element of CI is the ability to build community capacity through connection to electronic tools.

Objectives

RQ1. To find out the potentiality of IT in fulfillment of target audience needs.

RQ2. To find out the potentiality of IT in enhancement of work efficiency.

RQ3. To find out the potentiality of IT in enhancement of employment opportunities and economic activity.

- **Research design** - The study adopted "case study" methodology to fulfill the RQs. Case study consists of a detailed investigation often with data collected over a period of time of phenomenon within their context (Heartly, 2004). The aim is to provide an analysis of the context and processes which illuminate the theoretical issues being studied (ibid). Interview schedule method was employed to measure the empowerment pre and post Gyandoot scenario for "better, "good" and "same" options.
- **Sample selection** - A Pilot study was done during a pre survey visit of the study area by the researcher which found that most citizens in rural areas were agriculturists having few bighas of land and limited disposable income, less educated, Hindi speaking, information deficient, intermediary driven and less assertive. This indicated towards homogeneity of the sample. A sample of 50 citizen respondents was chosen. Firstly, random sampling method was adopted in selecting four blocks out of ten where the soochnalayas (telecenters) were situated. The blocks selected were Nalchha, Tirla, Dhar central and Sardarpur. Thirteen operating telecenters were listed operating under these blocks out of the total 28 telecenters running in the entire district. Secondly, under quota sampling method, 4 respondents were allotted to each telecenter (except Dehri sarai, where only 2 respondents were interviewed) and the citizen respondents were interviewed. Incidentally, more than 50% of the total 28 operational telecenters in 10 blocks are present in these four randomly selected blocks.
- **Tools and techniques** - Interview schedule, non-participatory observation and informal discussion with the soochaks and project staff for pre and post Gyandoot scenario.
- **Data analysis** - The responses gathered were analyzed using percentage analysis since data is in descriptive form and the quantitative technique was adopted in order to arrive at the objective.
- **Operationalising variables** – The following definitions were standardized by the experts.
- **ICTs** – According to Heeks (1999) ICTs mean „Electronic means of capturing, processing, storing and communicating information", usually in digital form.
- **E-governance** - is defined as the application of electronic means in (1) the interaction between government and citizens and government and businesses, as well as (2)in internal government operations to simplify and improve democratic, government and business aspects of governance (International Institute of Communication and Development, 2001).
- **Soochak** – The owner or operator of the telecenter.

- **Soochanalya** – The telecenter where ICT services are accessed.
- **Need** - The definition of the need adopted for the study is "the gap between current and desired (or required) results or the gap in results between "what is" and "what should be".
- **Employment** - The study has defined employment as the situation in which people have work.
- **Economic activity** - The economic activity is defined as the industry, jobs, earning a living and producing wealth.
- **Work efficiency** - The operational definition adopted for this objective is "skillfulness in avoiding wasted time and effort.

The operational definition adopted for this sub objective is skillfulness in avoiding wasted time and effort. DOI[1] (Digital Opportunity Initiative, 2004) report observed that IT enables people and enterprises to capture economic opportunities by increasing process efficiency, promoting participation in expanded economic networks, and creating opportunities for employment. UN global survey[2] (2004) on e-governance states that ICTs cut across all sectors to bring greater efficiency and opportunities to people. The Central Board of Secondary Education (CBSE) started the telecounselling of second phase through IVRS (Interactive Voice Response System)[3] conducted by 39 principals and trained counselors thus saving the hassle of traveling and queues. Citizens have immensely benefited from the online delivery of exam results, railway and airline tickets, registration of public grievances and participation in the online polls through SMS and mobile phones.

EMPLOYMENT OPPORTUNITIES AND ECONOMIC ACTIVITY

The study has defined employment as the situation in which people have work whereas the economic activity is defined as the industry, jobs, earning a living and producing wealth. DOI's final report states that ICT can contribute to income generation and poverty reduction. It enables people and enterprises to capture economic opportunities by increasing process efficiency, promoting participation in expanded economic networks, and creating opportunities for employment (*ibid*). The MP state task force on IT observes the following -

"Depending on the share in the national output that the state aims for, the employment opportunities would range from approx. 4 lacs to 1 million by the year 2008 engaged in the IT related activities. An estimated sixty percent of the jobs could come from services, of which some one-third would be low skilled data entry jobs and the balance from the growth of internet related services such as information kiosks in urban and rural areas. Software development could give employment to another 20%, trade and commerce could contribute 10%, and the rest of the employment opportunities would be contributed by training-related jobs and jobs relating to communications and hard ware maintenance".

Gurstein (1999)[4] explored factors that can limit the success of community informatics projects. He found that a key feature of failure is the inability to link the projects with local economic activity, and an absence of strong leadership to unite community efforts. ICTs represent a vast grid of virtual opportunities tunneling through a new configuration power, agency and structure of meaning capable of revolutionizing real-life settings (Luke, 1998). Similarly, in order to generate economic activity in the villages Indian Railways Catering and Tourism Corporation decided to write to all district magistrates in order to know the PC connections with broadband internet connections in villages so that the rural people could be provided the licenses and codes to offer railway reservation to the customers from just a click of computer.[5]

Hypothesis – Following hypotheses were coined after extensive review of literature.

H1 - IT has the considerable potential for fulfilling the target audience's needs.

H2 - IT has the considerable potential for improving the target audience's work efficiency.

H3 - IT doesn't have the potential of enhancement of employment opportunities and economic activity.

Findings and Discussions

RQ1: Fulfillment of the needs

This RQ was divided into two elements – felt needs and expected needs of the target audience. A comprehensive need assessment survey for the felt needs was done by the administration in 1999 before launching Gyandoot. The outcome of this survey formed the basis of Gyandoot services. The needs' profile is liable to change over a time period of 6 years. The expected needs are those which have emerged after the inception of project and they are not yet on Gyandoot's services menu but have lot of potential of fulfilment.

Felt Needs

The following charts explain the effectiveness of Gyandoot from citizens' point of view in providing the felt needs of people in getting government services on the parameters of convenience, satisfaction, cost (travel, stay, bribe, wage, labour lost etc), days in getting the work done, benefits (big, medium, same and worse), preference (traditional or IT enabled) and bribe paid (earlier and now). Some services were not availed by the respondents at all. These include, income certificate, below poverty line list, rural Hindi mail (mainly used by soochaks), rural matrimonials, village newspaper, advisory module, vermin compost khad booking. Most frequently used services were land records, exam results and public grievances redressal (sent through rural Hindi e-mail).

Satisfaction

As shown in Figure 4, Khasra or Land records (97%), government. forms (100%), exam results (96%), e-education (computer courses) and domicile certificates (100% each) did draw maximum satisfaction from all respondents. The reason being the direct relation with the routine life of populace. This is followed by respondents of government. information regarding notices and announcements (88%), employment news and caste certificate (80%), and public grievances (67%). It is clear that there is a positive relationship between the widely used services and satisfaction level. All respondents (mainly farmers) were totally dissatisfied with mandi rates information. Obsolete information was cited as the main reason as Gyandoot team feeds previous day's market rates which could be quite different from the prevailing rates. The researcher found that the area had good coverage of mobile signals and respondents told that they used to contact the agents in the mandi for the latest prevailing rates for their farm produce. Ironically, this service lost its sheen to the mobile revolution whereas it used to be most sought after service by people initially in 2000 when mobile phone was a luxury and very expensive.

Convenience

As it is clear in *Figure 5*, on the parameter of convenience relating to availing land records (khasra), government. forms, exam results, e-education, domicile certificates and caste certificates, 100% respondents cited convenience for these services. Government. information was convenient for 88% respondents and for grievances, it was 78%. E-news (employment news) provided convenience to 77% respondents. Mandi rates information was not at all convenient to get as reported by 100% respondents.

Figure 4. Satisfaction

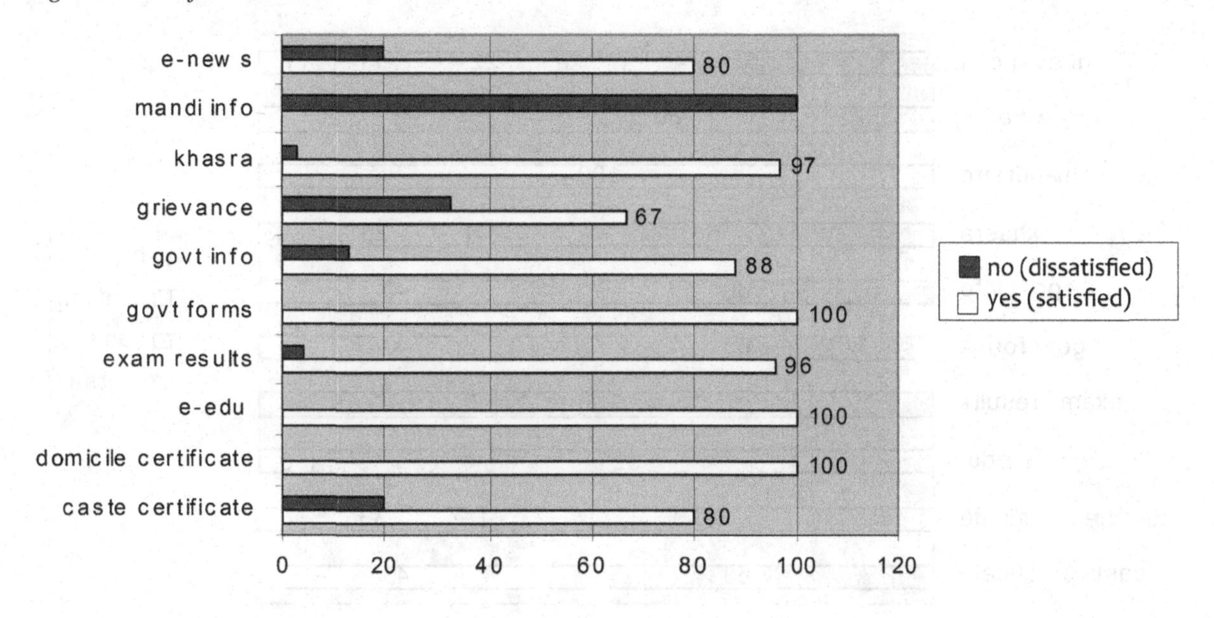

Figure 5. Convenience

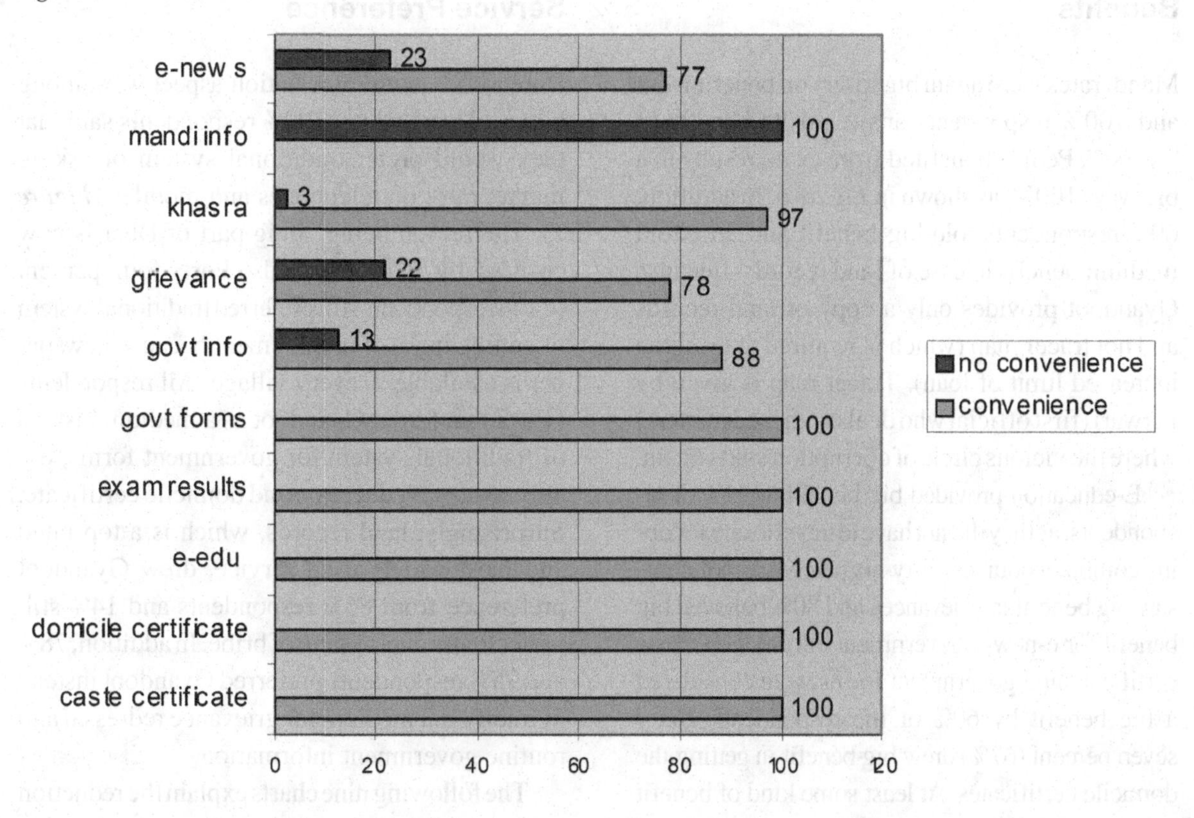

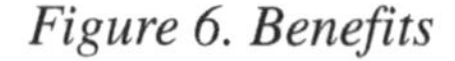

Figure 6. Benefits

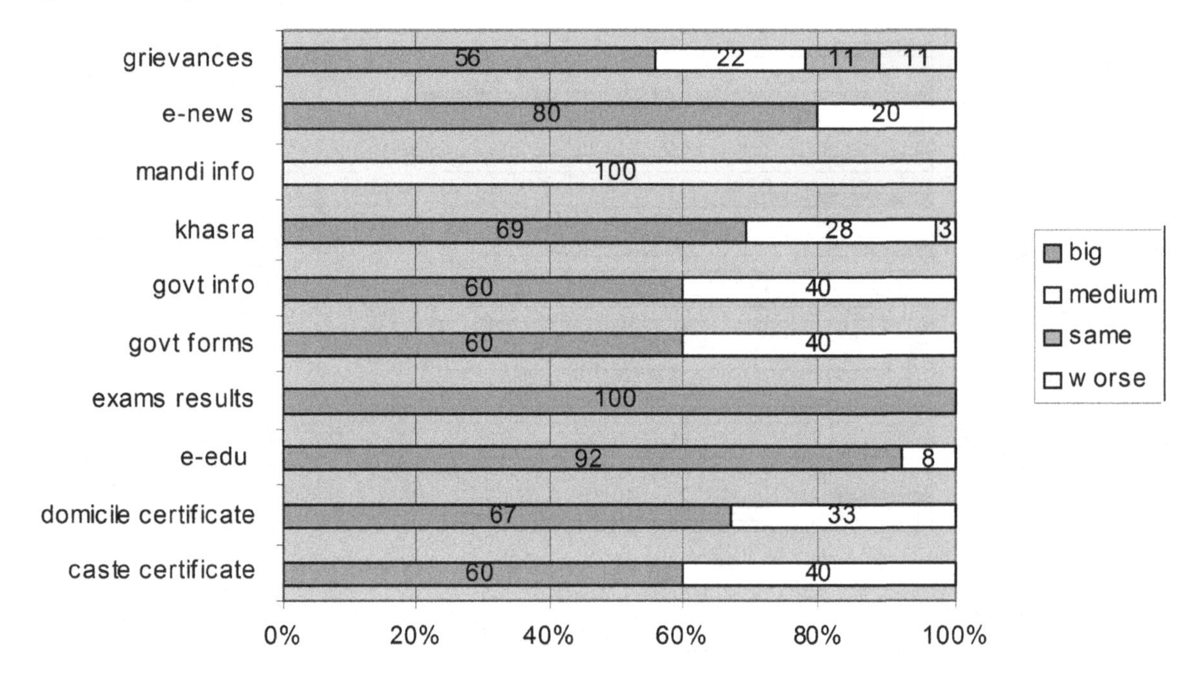

Benefits

Mandi rates were again big losers on benefit front and 100% respondents answered its benefit as "worse". People benefited from exam results in a big way (100%) as shown in *Figure 6*. In addition, 69% respondents told big benefit and 28% told medium benefit in case of land records. Because Gyandoot provides only a copy of land records and not tracer map (which is required to avail the increased limit of loan). Tracer map is given by Patwari (first official who deals with land matters) where the vicious circle of corruption starts again.

E-education provided big benefit to 92% of respondents, as they did not have to travel to city for doing computer courses. Fifty-six percent respondents saw big benefit in grievances and 80% believed big benefit for e-news. Government information, caste certificate and government forms were considered a big benefit by 60% of the respondents. Sixty seven percent (67%) drew big benefit in getting the domicile certificates. At least some kind of benefit (medium) was cited by almost all respondents for all the services whereas answers like "same" or "worse" were less except mandi rates.

Service Preference

Here also, mandi information aspect was among biggest losers where 100% respondents said that they would prefer traditional system of asking market rates on telephones and mobiles (*Figure 7*). The reason being, a big part of Dhar is now covered by mobile signals. Forty-four percent (44%) respondents still preferred traditional system of getting news of employment because newspaper is available in every village. All respondents (100%) preferred Gyandoot as a medium instead of traditional system for government forms, exams results, e-education and domicile certificate. Surprisingly, land records, which is a top rated and most widely used service, drew Gyandoot preference from 86% respondents and 14% still prefer traditional system of bribe. In addition, 78% and 75% respondents preferred Gyandoot instead of traditional medium for grievance redressal and routine government information.

The following nine charts explain the reduction in cost and time for availing different services pre and post-Gyandoot periods.

Figure 7. Service Preference

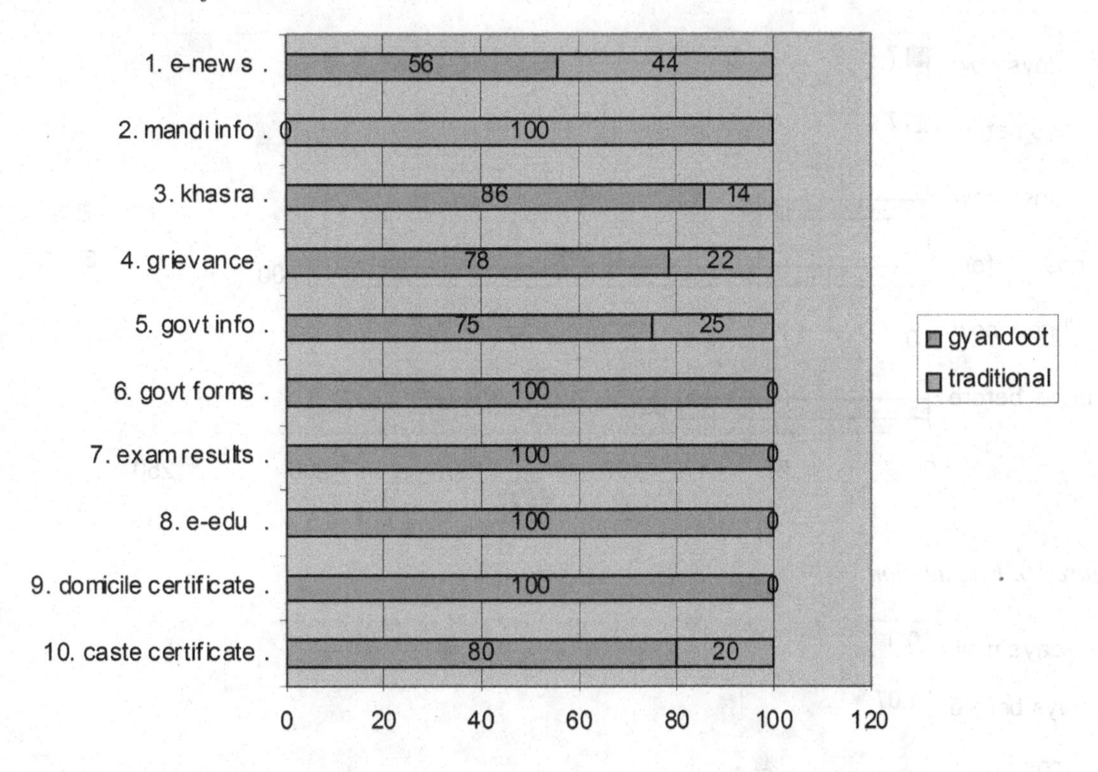

Figure 8. Cost, bribe, and days for caste certificate

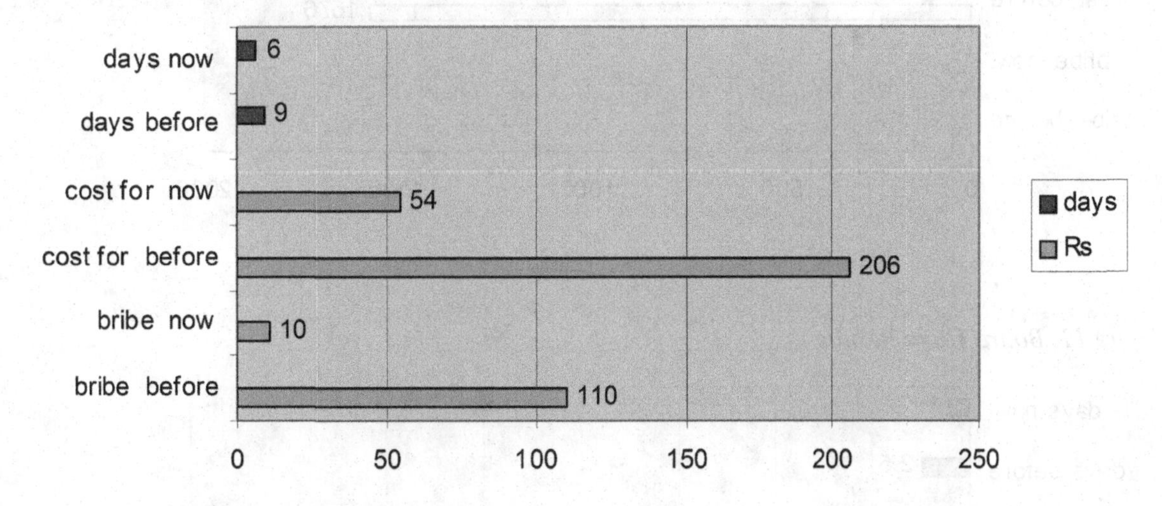

The Figure 8 clearly indicates the reduction of 3 days time, saving of 152 rupees and reduction of 100 rupees in bribe for getting caste certificate through Gyandoot. These amounts to considerable savings in rural settings.

The Figure 9 indicates no reduction in time, but cost reduction was by 150 rupees and reduction of 83 rupees in bribe for getting domicile certificate through Gyandoot.

Figure 9. Domicile Certificate

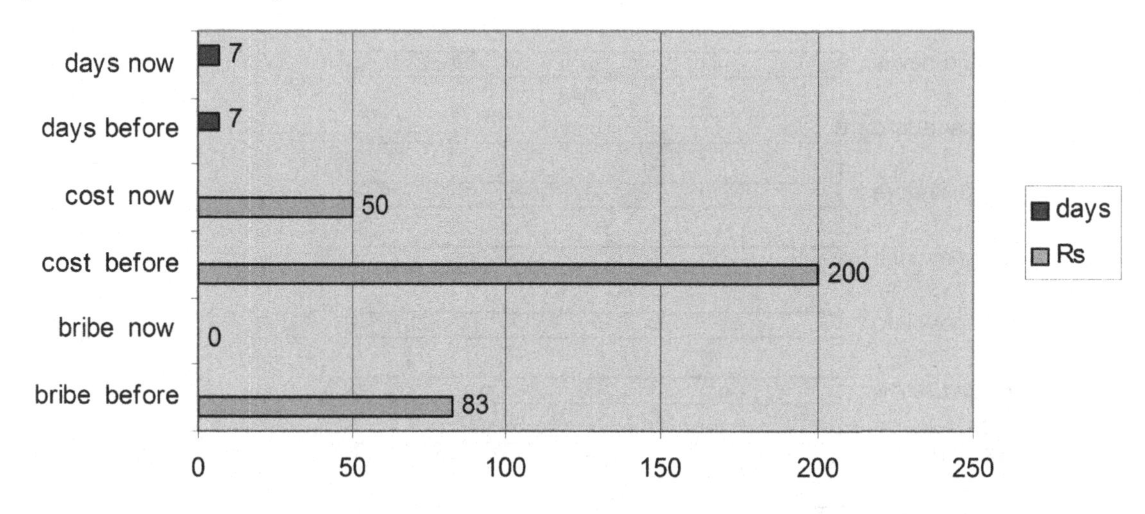

Figure 10. E-education

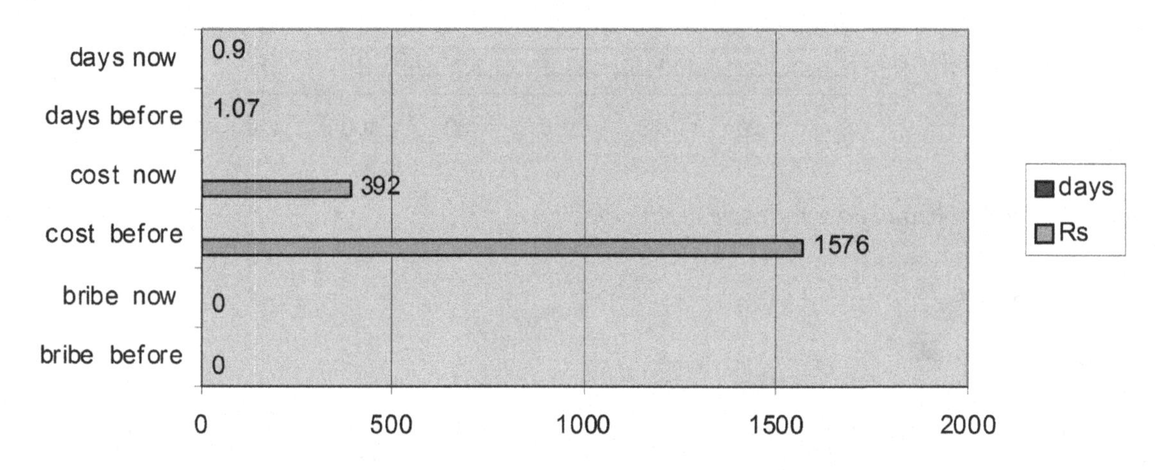

Figure 11. Board Exam Results

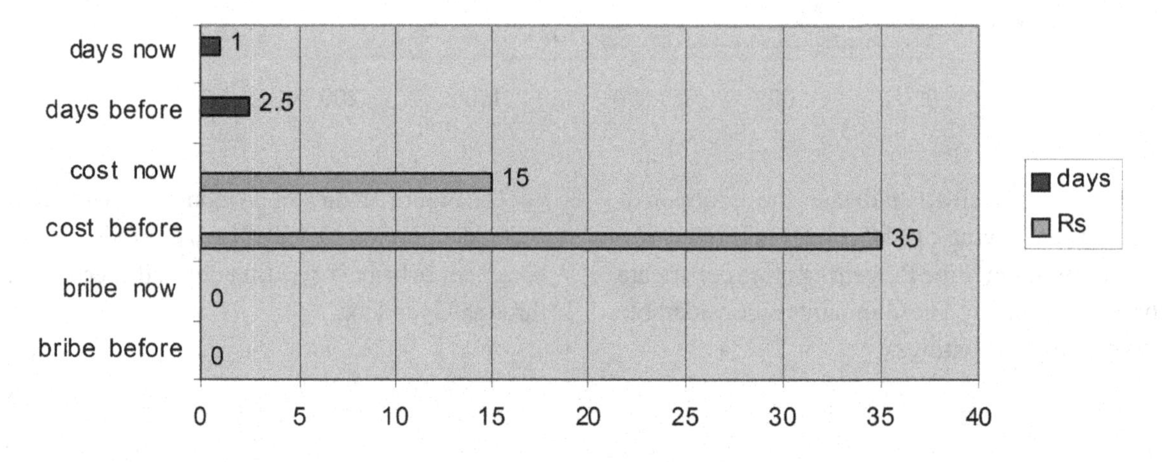

Figure 12. Forms for Government Services

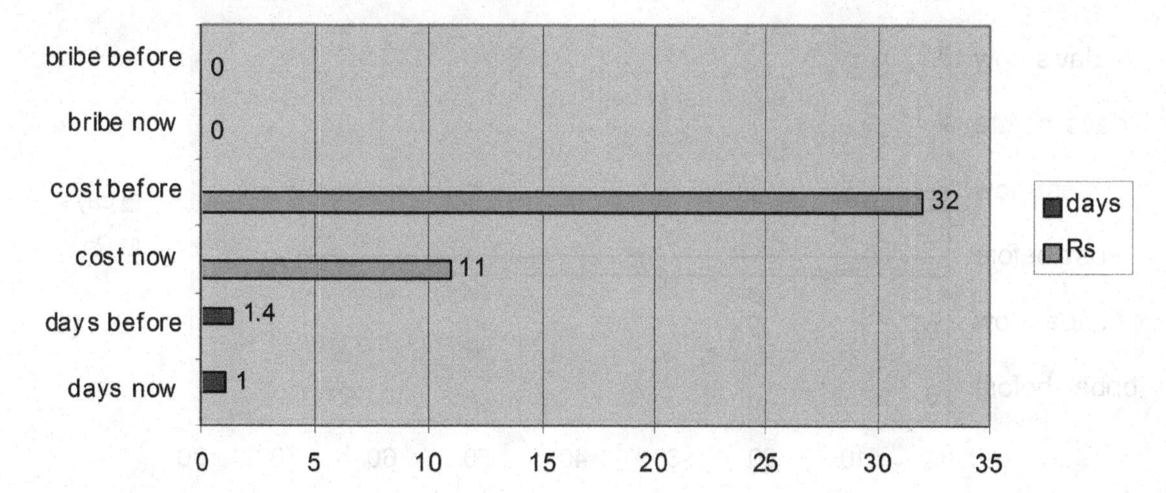

E-Education

There is a reduction of one day's time, a saving of whopping 1184 rupees. However, no bribe was paid to do computer courses pre and post-Gyandoot (Figure 10). The students had to visit the city daily earlier to pursue computer courses, which was made available in the villages itself post-Gyandoot.

It is clear that there was reduction of 1.5 days time, saving of 20 rupees. No bribe was paid earlier also to know the exam results (Figure 11).

There was reduction of roughly half-day's time, saving of 21 rupees for getting forms for different government services e.g. ration card, arms license etc. (Figure 12). No bribe was paid earlier also to get these forms. In addition, people get help and counseling from soochaks in filling their forms.

Grievance & complaints redressal days were reduced by 6.5 days whereas 18 rupees were saved on an average. (Figure 13). No bribe was paid pre and post-Gyandoot for this service. Perhaps, the respondents sent complaints regarding public facilities and officials where no speed money was required. However, for some special complaints, money was still paid to add wings to files.

Figure 13. Grievances

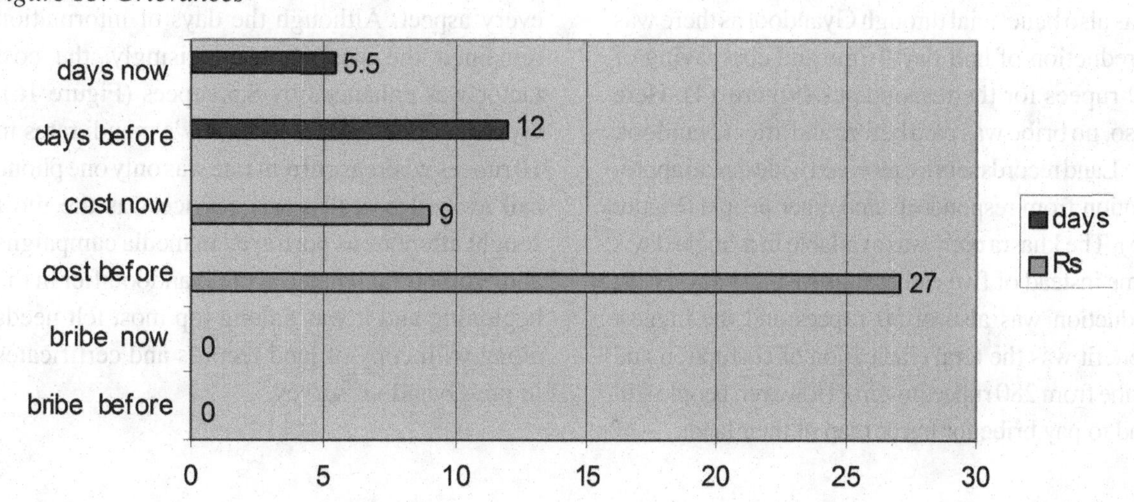

Figure 14. Government Information

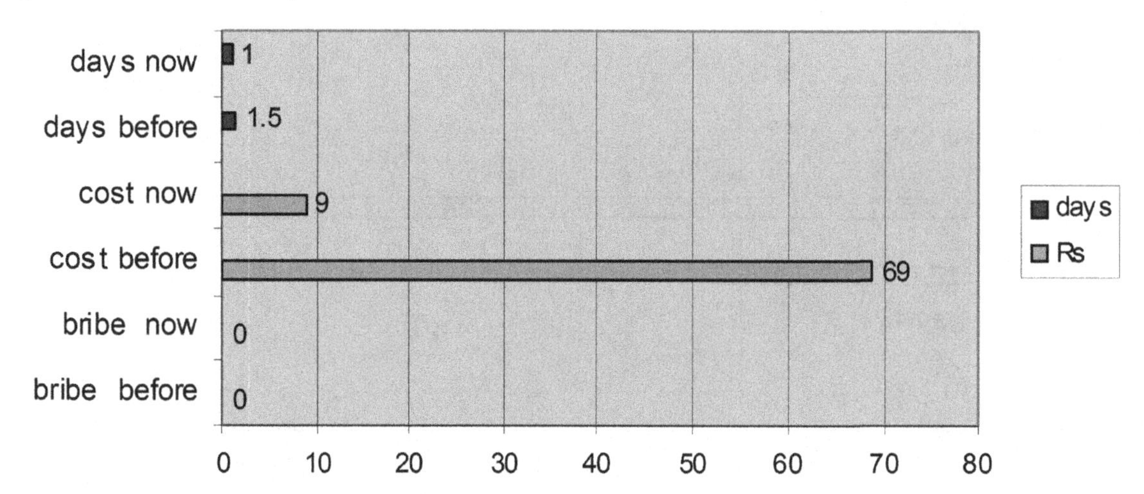

Figure 15. Land Records

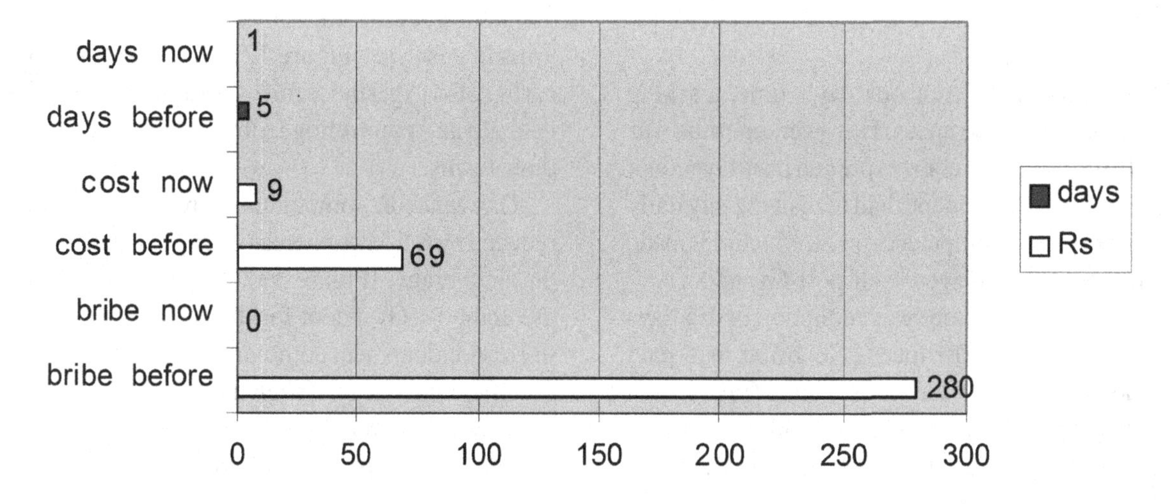

Routine information from government agencies was also beneficial through Gyandoot as there was a reduction of half days' time and cost saving of 60 rupees for the respondents (Figure 14). Here also, no bribe was paid before and after Gyandoot.

Land records service received widespread appreciation from respondents and other people (Figure 15). The khasra copy was available in a single day's time instead of five earlier thus saving 4 days. Cost reduction was also of 60 rupees and the biggest benefit was the total eradication of corruption and bribe from 280 rupees to zero. However, people still had to pay bribe for tracer map of their land.

Mandi information proved to be a laggard in every aspect. Although the days of information remained the same but surprisingly, the cost factor was enhanced by 8.5 rupees (Figure 16). Gyandoot delivers previous day's mandi rates in 10 rupees whereas current rate was only one phone call away. Ironically, this service was the most sought after one as portrayed in media campaigns and promotional material of Gyandootafter in the beginning and it was among top most felt needs along with copy of land records and certificates in pre-Gyandoot survey.

Figure 16. Mandi Information

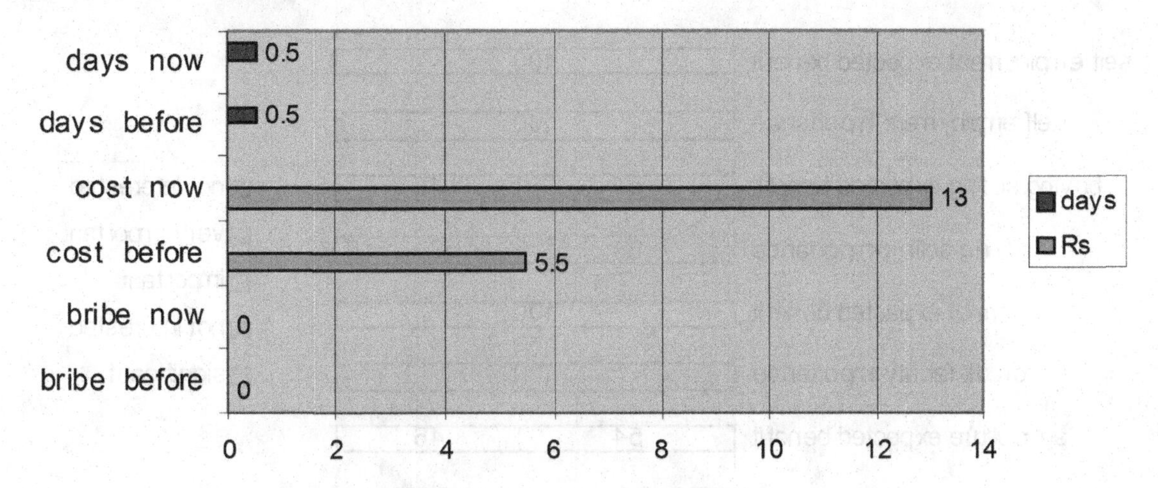

Figure 17. Employment News

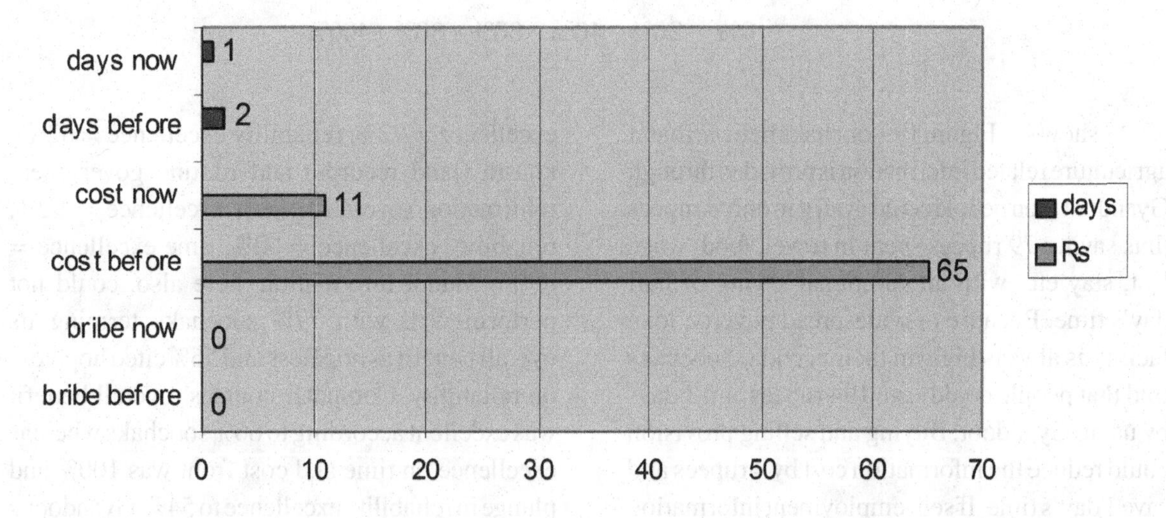

Employment news' days were reduced by one and cost came down to 11 rupees from 65 rupees (Figure 17). Bribe was not paid in pre and post-Gyandoot periods for this service.

Expected needs – Soocaks being the convergence point for availing the services, felt the pulse of people with whom they share their personal problems and seek solutions hence only soochaks were administered the questionnaires for fulfilling this objective. The expected needs were framed by the researcher after consulting the available literature on e-governance projects in India. Next two charts consist of the soochaks' perception of expected needs, their benefits, days, cost and importance.

Questions regarding needs of health information, entertainment, investment, shopping, telemedicine etc. were given "not interested" answer. Self employment'a and credit facility's benefits and importance was rated as excellent by 100% soohaks (Figure 18). This finding is on expected lines due to the 10.8% unemployment rate in India.[6] Buying and selling alongwith agriculture need was also deemed to be of great importance by 46% soochaks with 46% believing its benefit as significant. Agriculture is the hazardous occupation to health worldwide(Srinivas, 2006). In MP alone, the value of human lives lost to fatal accidents plus the cost of non fatal injuries, has been estimated at almost $30 million (ibid).

Figure 18. Expected Needs, Benefit, Days, Cost, and Importance

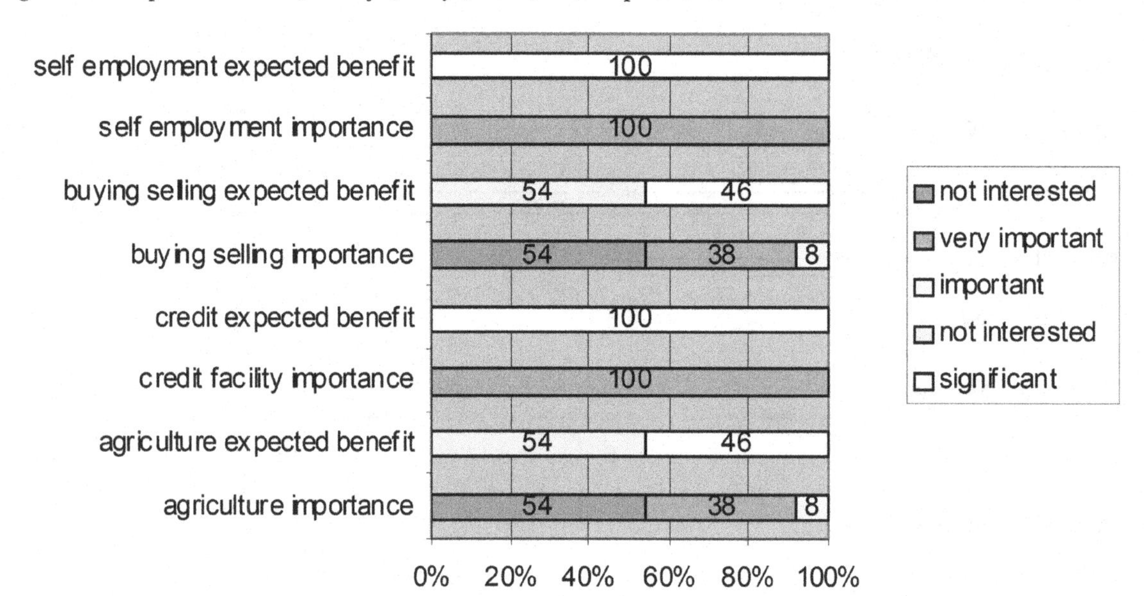

As shown in Figure 19, soochaks believe that if agriculture related information is provided through Gyandoot then people could avail it in only 4 rupees thus saving 79 rupees spent in travel, food, wage lost, stay etc. with an additional saving of half day's time. Because of widespread poverty, loan facility is always high on their agenda. Soochaks told that people could save 194 rupees and 3 days by using Gyandoot. Buying and selling provision could reduce the information cost by 4 rupees and save 1 day's time. If self-employment information is given through Gyandoot then 17 rupees and 5 rupees would be saved vis a vis present traditional system. Null hypothesis is rejected and first hypothesis H_1 is accepted here.

This following chart consists of soochaks' perception of services on the parameters of time, cost reliability and overall benefit.

RQ 2. Work efficiency –Time, cost, reliability and overall benefits were taken as criteria to measure the efficiency.

Figure 20 shows that reliability, time, cost, and overall benefit were rated as excellent for board exam results, below poverty line list (BPL), government forms, rural Hindi mail (overall benefit excellence = 92%, reliability excellence = 62%), khasra (land records) and routine government information (overall benefit excellence = 92%, reliability excellence = 92%, time excellence = 89%). Mandi information, here also, could not perform well with 77% soochaks terming its overall benefit as hopeless and 56% cited hopeless on reliability. Computer courses' overall benefit was excellent according to 60% soochaks whereas excellence on time and cost front was 100% and plunge in reliability excellence to 54%. Gyandoot's excellent track record in public grievance redressal can be mainly attributed to the rural Hindi mail service which enabled people to send complaints to administration through soochaks.

Employment news was rated as average by 69% soochaks whereas 54% termed its reliability as excellent and for time and cost, it was 69% and 77% respectively. Grievance redressal's overall benefit was excellent according to 54% soochaks with reliability as average = 54% and time as average = 62%. However, costwise its excellence was 100% because people directly lodged their complaints from telecenters @ 10/- per complaint. Overall benefit for different certificates was rated

Figure 19. Expected Needs' Cost and Days

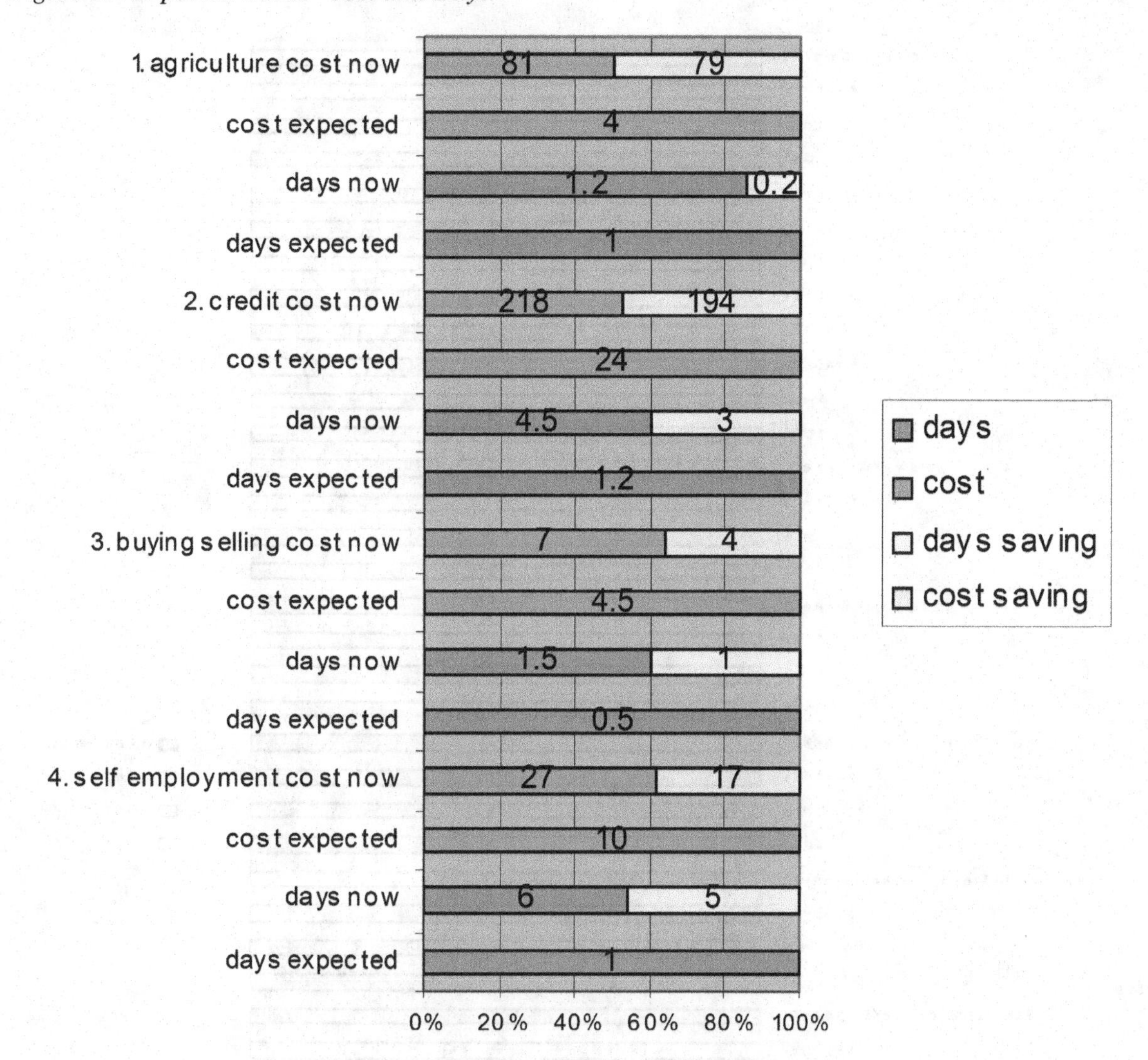

as average by 69% soochaks with a cost excellence by 85% soochaks. These findings relate to the work of Singhal Arvind, Roger Evernett, (1990), Khataokar, Chaturvedi (2004), Jaju Sanjay (2004), Lobo and Balakrishnan (2002) and Kukreja and Grover (2004).

RQ3. Employment Opportunities and Economic Activity

The next two charts provide citizens' and soochaks' responses on the questions of employment, entrepreneurship, total number of people benefited in pre and post-Gyandoot periods.

Optimism in ITES (Information Technology Enabled Services) turned out to be significant one as felt by 88% respondents and 94% said that ITES's scope has increased from Gyandoot. Respondents could recall that 89 people were benefited form ITES (*Figure 21*). This shows the tremendous opportunity of ITES in rural areas. Only 32% respondents told that entrepreneurship has increased post-Gyandoot, 52% termed it as moderate and many people started their own small communication services shops providing computer services, STD/PCO, mobile recharge cards, fax, photocopy etc. and 61% benefited from Gyandoot's entrepreneurship. As the chart shows, it has increased after the advent of Gyandoot.

Figure 20. Perception on Time, Cost, Reliability, and Overall Benefit

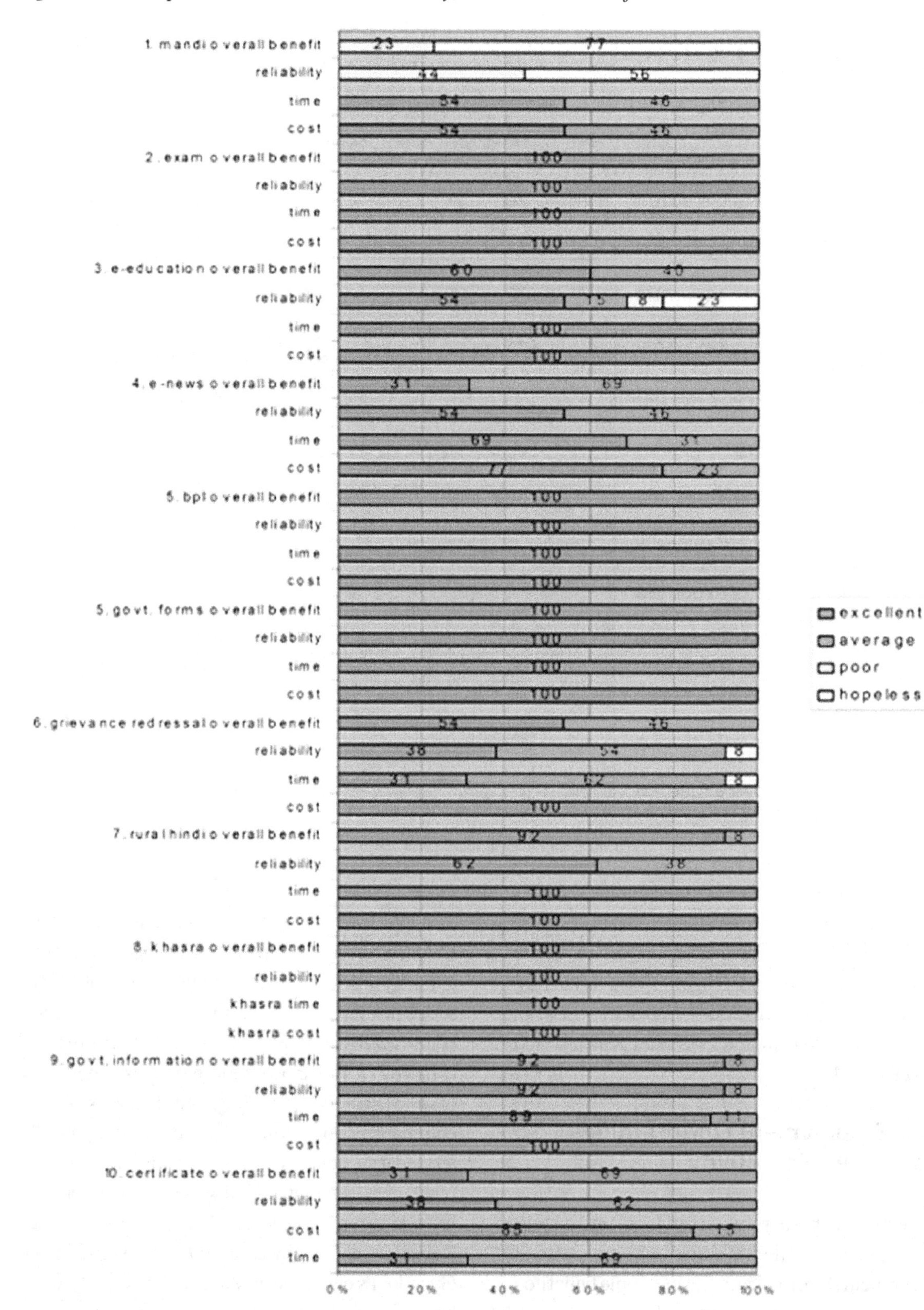

Figure 21. Employment Scenario

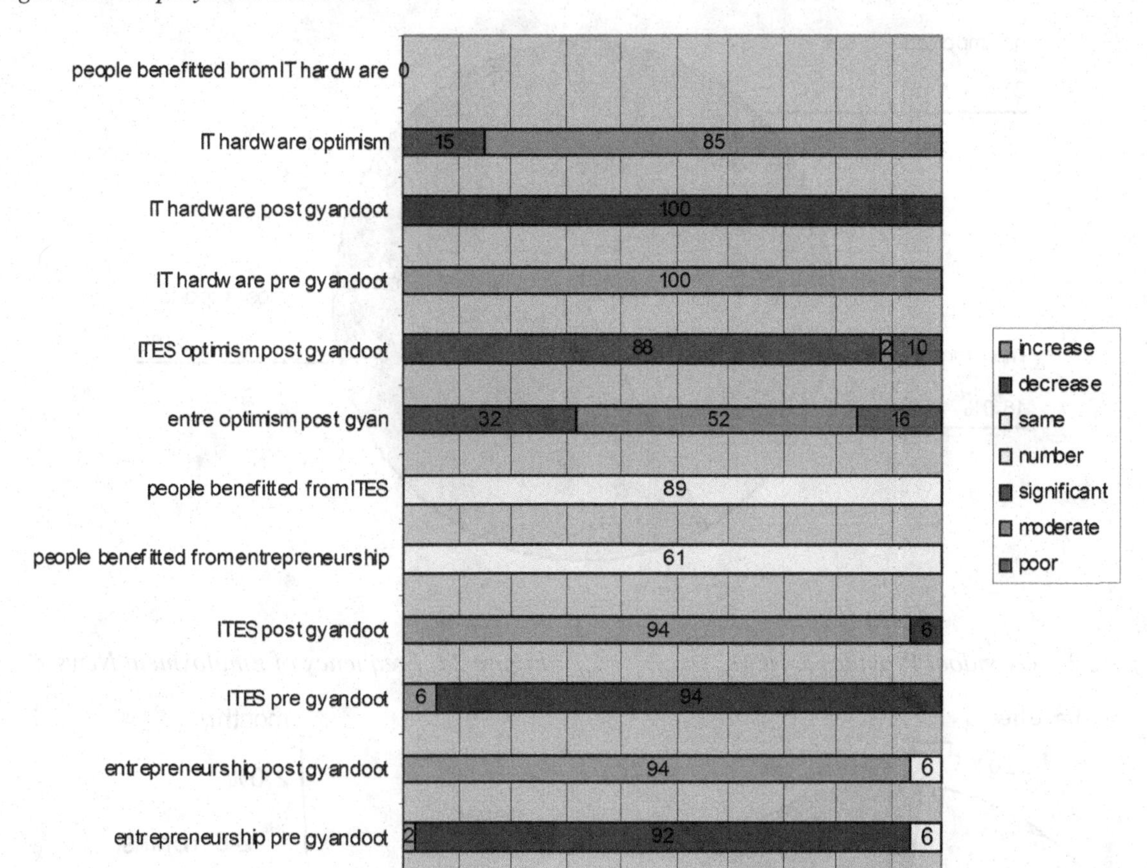

Optimism in hardware field proved to be a dampener as 85% termed it as poor and rest 15% as moderate. All respondents (100%) told that scope of IT hardware has increased post-Gyandoot. Respondents could not recall the total number of people benefited from IT hardware related activities.

Following eight pi-charts describe some more employment related aspects of Gyandoot.

Employment was rated as most important by 58% respondents whereas it was important for 18% respondents, 24% said that employment was not important for them (Figure 22). Hence, it can be assumed that career aspiration of one-fourth respondents was very low.

Thirty-four (34%) respondents did not know that Gyandoot provides news related to employment, 64% answered "yes" for this question (Figure 23). Despite five years of glorious existence, 1/3rd of respondents did not know this very important service of Gyandoot.

Biggest number of respondents (37%) told that they regularly need news related to employment. It points out the grave need of employment for the target audience (Figure 24). However, 8% respondents told that they do not need employment information at all.

Whether Gyandoot provided employment to the people was answered as "yes" by 22% of the respondents and 13% told that they could recall the number of people who got employment through Gyandoot (Figure 25). Almost half (56%) of respondents said that they have not heard about anybody getting employment through Gyandoot.

Figure 22. Importance of Employment

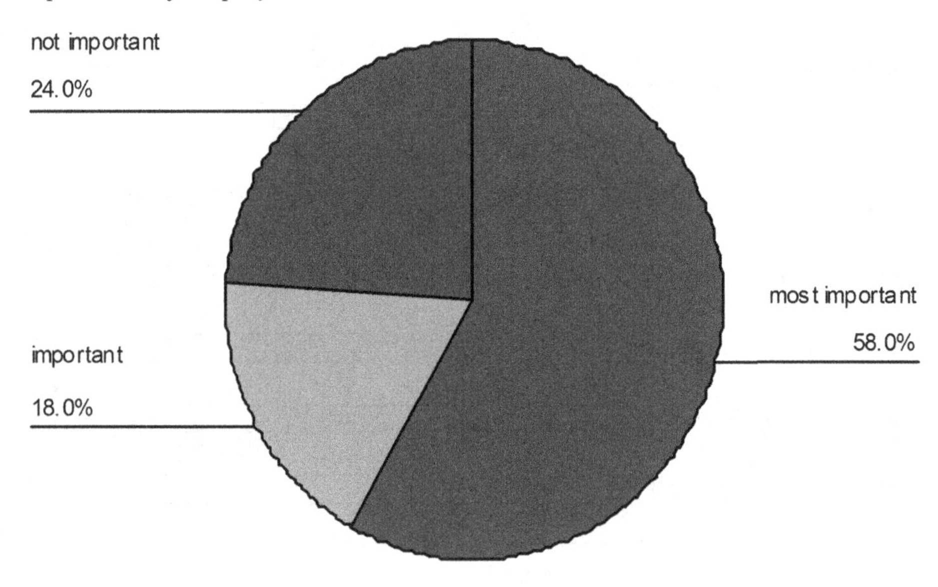

Figure 23. Gyandoot Provides E-News

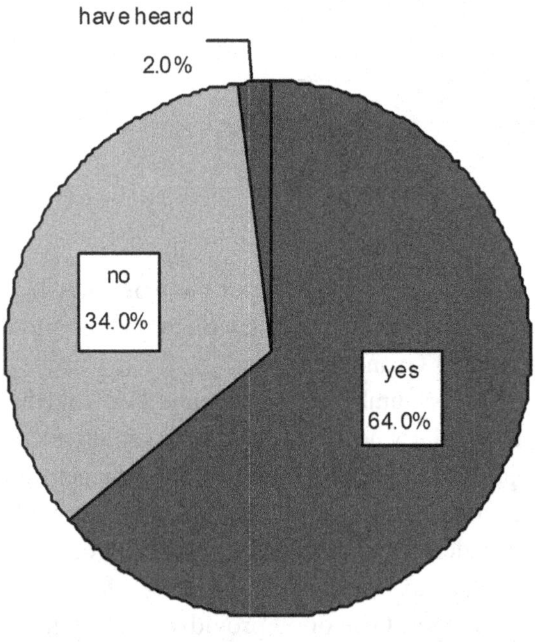

have heard
2.0%
no
34.0%
yes
64.0%

Figure 24. Frequency of Employment News

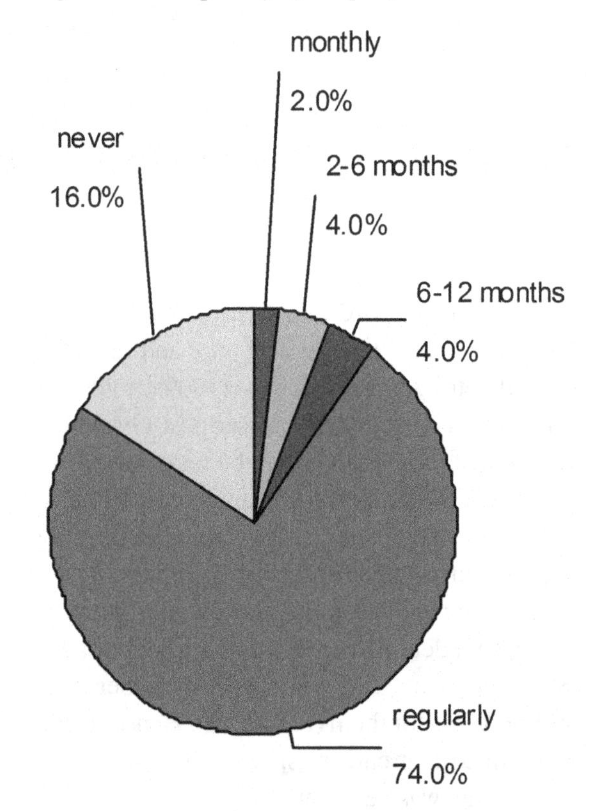

Figure 25. Heard of Getting Employment through Gyandoot?

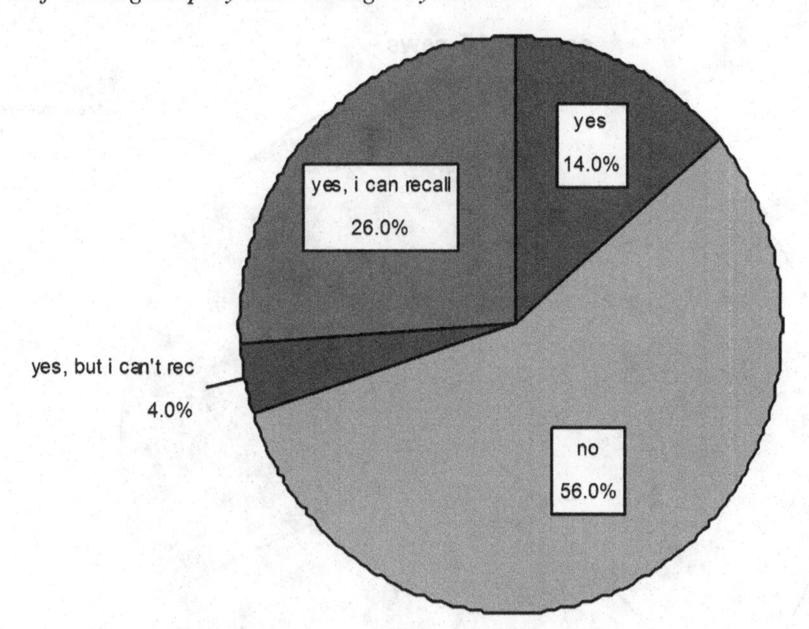

On the question of main source of employment news, 15 out of 50 respondents cited newspaper as a source of information and 19 said that they get information from their relatives and friends (Figure 26). Only 16 respondents answered in favour of Gyandoot as the main source of information.

The strength of informal channels of communication in a community can be gauged from the fact that highest number (28) of respondents still prefers traditional interpersonal system for getting e-news than Gyandoot, which was the preference of 22 (44%) respondents (Figure 27).

Regarding people's belief in the information provided by Gyandoot, 58% said that they would believe it subject to the soochak's endorsement, only 42% respondents, who comprised mainly educated youth, said that they would believe themselves and will not need soochak's endorsement (Figure 28). It is clear that intermediation in information delivery systems is here to stay, no matter what kind of direct communication channels are provided to the target audience. The above findings are not in concurrence with Jafri, Dongre, Tripathi, Aggrawal and Shrivastava (2002), world's bank report on Gyandoot and Vijayaditya (2002). The researcher found that impact on employment was not so high vis a vis Gyandoot's five years of existence.The null hypothesis $H_3$is neither accepted nor rejected fully here. Hence it can be inferred that IT has a moderate potential or generating the employment opportunities and economic activities.

CONCLUSION

As pointed by some other studies, Gyandoot because of it newness and innovative mechanism of service delivery was quite successful in fulfilling in many of its objectives. However this success is marked by the acute polarisation in IT's usage. Out of the total 18 services of Gyandoot, only 3 (17%) were used to the maximum (land records, exam results and public grievances redressal). Eight (39%) services were not used at all (Mandi rates, income certificate, below poverty line list, rural Hindi mail (mainly used by soochaks), rural matrimonials, village newspaper, advisory module, vermin compost khad booking) . Rest 7 services (domicile certificate, government information,

Figure 26. Source of Employment News

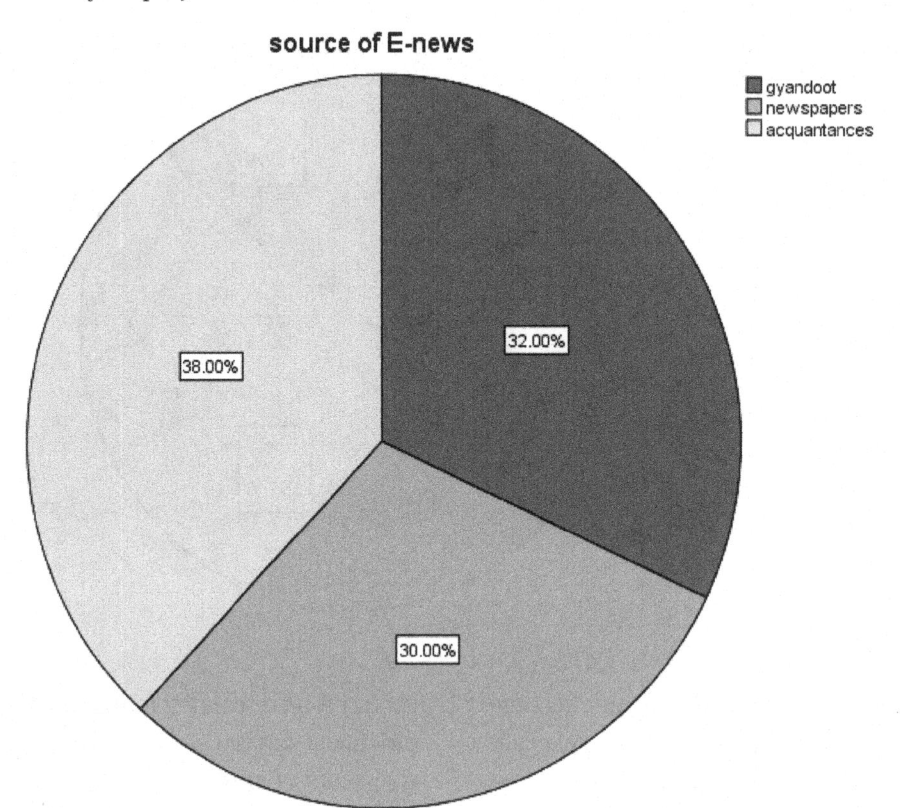

Figure 27. Preferred Sources of Employment News

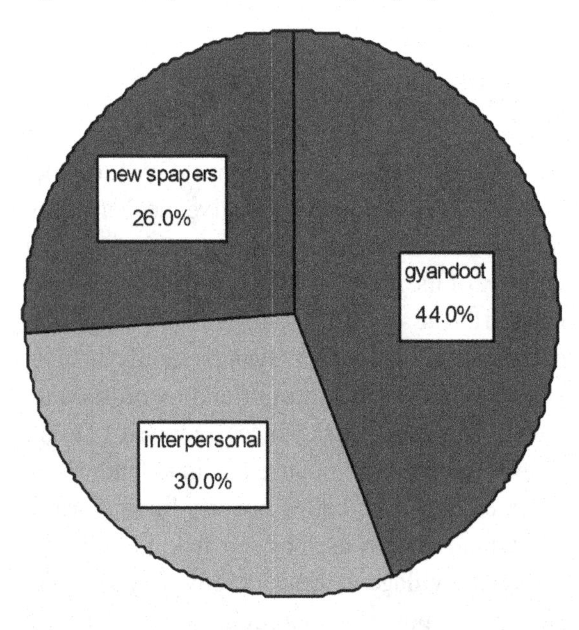

caste certificate, government forms, employment news, rural market, e-education) were used moderately. Hence it can be easily deduced that only 17% of the Gyandoot's potential could be utilized and 39% was used moderately. Rest 44% could not be utilized at all owing to the misplaced needs, lack of appeal in the services or the trust. Majority of the respondents were above poverty line, having 10th to 12th education. They were self-employed having Rs 25000 annual income, average land 13 bighas, Hindi speaking and writing enabled, soochaks dependent for Gyandoot services but they possess at least one phone in every 1.4 kms from their homes. The soochaks had good hardware. Ninety four percent (94%) respondents said that IT did not help them reduce indebtedness whereas 46% said that it helped in a better way in promoting a desire among them to migrate to cities, 24% believed that it did not

Figure 28. Belief in Employment News through Gyandooot

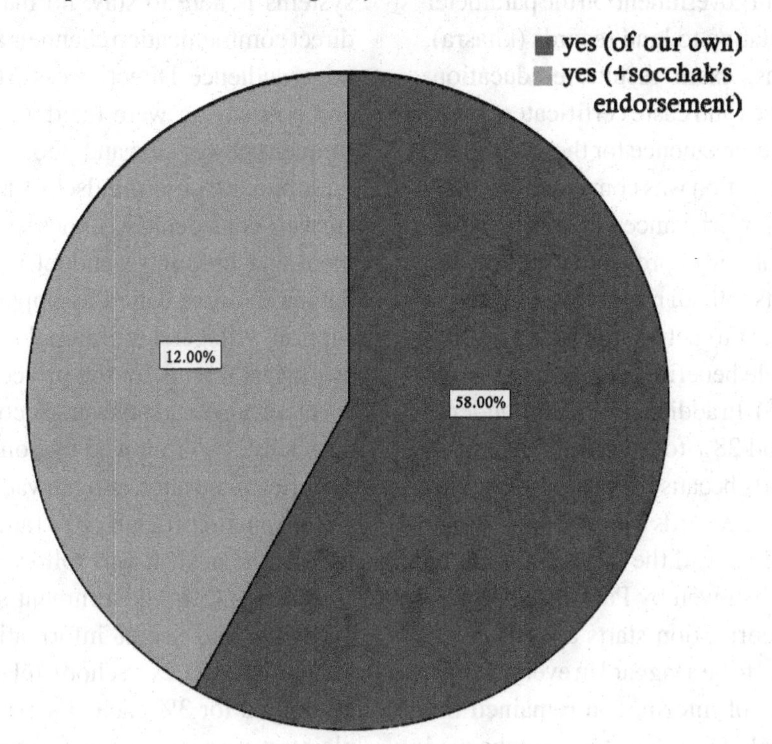

help them in doing so. Total 76% respondents felt that Gyandoot provided better help in formation of desire to earn money from computer related jobs.

Besides, 94% and 96% felt that Gyandoot provided great help to avail the services at reduced cost and saving money respectively. Almost all respondents (98%) believed that Gyandoot failed to help them in securing better price of crop and cattle, 90% said it did not help them in getting loan facility. Enhancement of awareness regarding surrounding was rated as a big help as answered by 94% of respondents. Overall, 84% felt that they got a lot of help in realizing their right of information, 60% answered good help in refusing bribe to government Most of the respondents (92%) gave credit to IT for development of a desire to learn and gather more skills for upliftment and 86% said that Gyandoot's help was significant in their ability to learn computers. The respondents felt increased faith in the importance of computers, science and education 88%, 90% and 92% respectively. Thus, IT can be used to spread and reinforce the technological awareness. Interestingly, 56%, 56% and 66%respondents told that Gyandoot has helped them in a big way in enhancing communal harmony, brotherhood and trust respectively. Ninety four (94%) believed that Gyandoot changed their way of thinking on some particular issues. This finding is supportive of the media effects of IT. Gyandoot provided benefit to all strata of society irrespective of caste, income, status, literacy etc. as told by 94% people. A very heartening finding was that 74% respondents believed that Gyandoot has been successful in removing the malady of female illiteracy and more people were considering education for girl child in the computer age. All respondents (100%) cited no influence of Gyandoot on the cultural practices and rituals like manner of worship, child birth ritual, folk songs and dances. People's belief in government increased as 88% respondents answered in affirmative and they admitted that Gyandoot has tremendously increased their faith in government On the parameter of convenience relating to land records (khasra), government forms, exam results, e-education, domicile certificates and caste certificates, 100% respondents cited convenience for these services. Government information was convenient for 88% respondents and for grievances, it was 78%. E-news (employment news) provided convenience to 77% respondents. Mandi rates information was not at all convenient to get as reported by 100% respondents. People benefited from exam results in a big way (100%). In addition, 69% respondents told big benefit and 28% told medium benefit in case of land records because Gyandoot provides only a copy of land records and not tracer map (which is required to avail the increased limit of loan). Tracer map is given by Patwari where the vicious circle of corruption starts again. Mandi information proved to be a laggard in every aspect. Although the days of information remained the same but surprisingly, the cost factor was enhanced by 8.5 rupees. Gyandoot delivers previous day's mandi rates in 10 rupees whereas current rates were only one phone call away. Self-employment and credit facility needs were rated very important and its benefits could be significant as told by 100% soochaks. Buying and selling along with agriculture need was also deemed to be of great importance by 46% soochaks with 46% believing its benefit as significant. Reliability, time, cost and overall benefit were rated as excellent for board exam results, below poverty line list (BPL), government forms and rural Hindi mail. Optimism in ITES (Information Technology Enabled Services) turned out to be significant one as felt by 88% respondents and 94% said that ITES's scope has increased from Gyandoot. Regarding people's belief in the information provided by Gyandoot, 58% said that they would believe it subject to the soochak's endorsement, only 42% respondents, who comprised mainly educated youth, said that they would believe on their own and will not need soochak's endorsement. It is clear that intermediation in information delivery systems is here to stay, no matter what kind of direct communication channels are provided to the target audience. Direct access to the administration and cost saving were rated as biggest strengths, frequent power cuts and poor connectivity along with bureaucratic mindset of the administration etc were considered weaknesses, scope of employment and linking Gyandoot with other national databases were hailed as opportunities and corruption, villagers' traditional mindset were rated as biggest threats for the project.

Questions and answers accounted for biggest number (31%) followed by complaints of public facilities like water, aanganwadi, certificates etc. Complaints of officials (10%) and financial matters (9%) came next. It was followed by land related complaints (5%), government schemes, medical problems and secret information passing each having 4% shares. School related and "others" accounted for 3% each. As expected, 33% complaints were regarding government officials, 22% each for panchayat secretary and other panchayat members, 8% each for sarpanch, soochak, rest 6% regarding excesses and atrocities on weaker sections of the society. It shows that people are mostly dissatisfied with the government officials. There lies the potential of e-governance. 'Sawali Ram se puchhiye' (ask question from experts) subcategory was most popular with 38% questions; the administration got 25% share; agriculture related questions were 19%; questions & suggestions regarding employment were 14% on various problems and issues. The "secret information passing" category included complaints against encroachment of land complaints (46%) against neighbours, sarpanch, panchayat officials and relatives, against tree felling (23%), child marriages (15%) and others (15%). This category provided chance to whistleblowers or aware citizens to pass on the information without being identified. In this way, the administration was able to stop three child marriages. Gyandoot received maximum number (46%) of complaints during its first year (2000) of operation. It dropped to 36% in 2001 and miser-

Figure 29. Characteristic Model of E-Governance

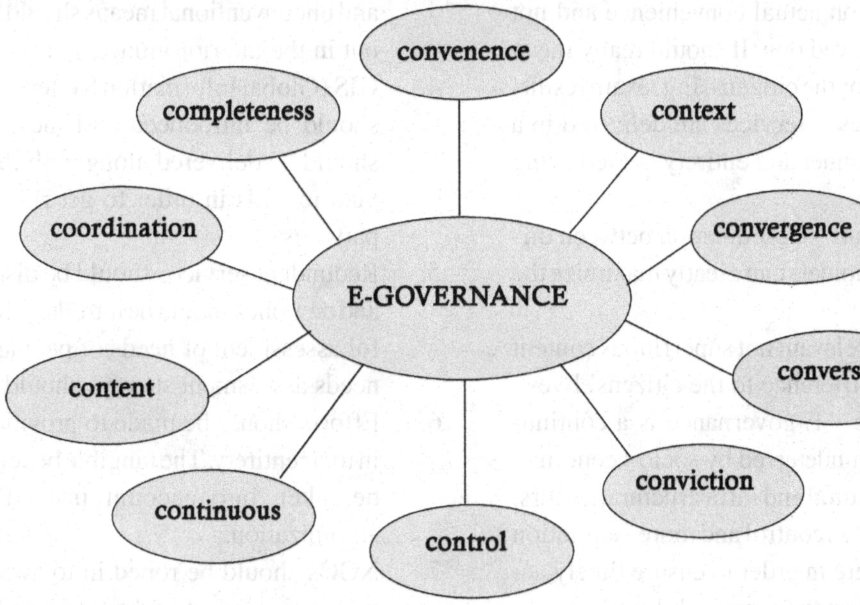

ably low (0.3%) in 2002. However, the volume again picked up to 6% in 2003 and 2004. Gyandoot received 2.1% complaints in 2005. Eighty percent of the complaints received were replied. Around one-fourth i.e. 23.2% complaints were answered the very next day and 8.8% complaints were answered after 6 days. Forty-seven percent (47%) complaints received "done" answer. All the complaints of mid-day meal scheme in schools were found wrong. It shows the magnitude to which technology was misused. Teachers were appointed in 75% of complaints against lack of teachers in schools. Out of total 17 land related complaints, 50% encroachment cases were solved and the researcher did not find record of rest 50%. In addition, 38% land complaints and 14% land dispute complaints were solved. One child marriage was stopped and another one was referred to concerned official. It was quite relieving to know that 270 complaints (80%) were replied and requisite action was taken. The project staff started the delivery of all services with zest initially but consequently it had to focus on its 'core' which resulted into the discontinuation of some services by its disuse (vermin compost khad booking etc.) and misuse (lodging false complaints of the neighbours to the administration to settle the personal scores). However, IT scored high on needs and work efficiency parameters for the selected services. The findings concur to the Amara's aw which postulates that we tend to overestimate the effect of a new technology in the short term and underestimate its effect in the long term (Johnson, 2007). This impressive record could not match the pace with 'employment opportunities and economic activity' variables and the silver line was the 'development of an entrepreneurial attitude' among people. In order to further probe this area and standardize the conceptual framework, more such studies are recommended in this filed.

RECOMMENDATIONS

The researcher would like to suggest 10 Cs characteristics model for successful implementation of e-governance projects:

1. **Convenience**– E-governance project lays stress more on actual convenience and not on the perceived one. It should really mean something for the citizens. E.g. exam results
2. **Completeness**- Services are delivered in a complete manner and entirety not requiring ifs and buts.
3. **Coordination** – Coordination between different stakeholders can greatly maximize the benefits.
4. **Content** – Relevant not superfluous content makes the difference to the citizens' lives.
5. **Continuous** – E-governance is a continuous process undeterred by socio-economic, political, cultural and infrastructural factors.
6. **Control** – Less control and more facilitation has to be there in order to ensure timely action and fixing the responsibility.
7. **Conviction** – E-governance must portray and develop strongly held belief in its effectiveness.
8. **Convergence** – It has to be an amalgamation of different technologies, not computer alone, to achieve the goal.
9. **Converse** – E-governance must generate dialogue and debate among citizens, media circles, polity, policy-makers and academia.
10. **Context** – E-governance services must fit in the local circumstances peculiar to a particular area.

The following recommendations may be considered by the agencies concerned:

1. Investment should first be made in electricity, roads and communication networks in the rural areas. If the basic infrastructure is in place, other things like e-governance and e- participation will follow automatically.
2. Public grievance module should be developed into a full-fledged entity and a separate department should be formed to entertain the complaints. Facility of lodging complaints must be provided through a toll free number.
3. Extensive media campaign with conventional and unconventional means should be carried out in the interior villages.
4. GIS (Global Information System) technique should be introduced and the tracer map should be delivered along with the copy of land records in order to get rid of corrupt patwaris.
5. Redundant services should be discontinued and new ones should be introduced after careful assessment of needs of people. Regular needs assessment surveys should be done.
6. Efforts should be made to provide services in their entirety. The tangible benefits should be taken into account instead of mere automization.
7. NGOs should be roped in to aware people with the need of technology and to serve as vertical and horizontal channel of communication and feedback.
8. Services of Gyandoot should be outsourced and third party involvement with district administration should be encouraged. Highly sensitive e-governance projects like Transport Authority of Delhi have been outsourced with impeccable security.
9. Since the area has good mobile coverage, shifting from dial-up system of telephones to mobile technology would be advisable for connecting to Gyandoot servers.
10. Mobile Gyandoot stations should be set up on vehicles, which can traverse the length and breadth of the area and provide the required services through laptops and mobile phones. The government must emphasize the penetration of telecommunication network in the interior areas.
11. Government should continue to fund or subsidize the rural computerization in order to make the people reach a threshold level of technology usage.
12. Stress should be put on the actual usage and benefits rather than fad and fancies associated with computers.

13. Women should be provided incentives in the form of awards, scholarships, prizes, etc. to learn technology.
14. Frequent seminars, workshops, road shows and community meetings should be held regularly in order to develop and sustain the people's belief in e-governance and information technology.
15. Process re-engineering should take place in the departments and number of channels should be reduced by making suitable amendments in the rules and regulations.
16. A MIS should be developed, maintained and updated relating to the project for prompt retrieval of information and fast decision-making.

OBSERVATIONS OF THE RESEARCHER

1. Some members of Gyandoot team tried to do their best in order to provide good service to soochaks.
2. Team members rarely acknowledge the shortcomings of the project; they prefer to talk about positive aspects instead.
3. Connectivity and electricity appeared to be the main problem in Gyandoot implementation.
4. Villagers rely on Gyandoot for other non-Gyandoot services also e.g. advice, discussion, etc.
5. Silent telecommunication revolution is sweeping the region with telecom signals (mobile) available in most of the villages and every village having STD/PCO facility in multiples.
6. There is loss of business for soochaks due to lack of electricity. Still they have adopted some creative methods to overcome this problem. E.g. they collect whole day's work and process the same at one go when the light comes.
7. Kundli, computer software courses, photocopy, internet, typing, etc. have been widely employed by the soochaks.
8. Gyandoot has resulted into "spin off effect" with many people setting up their own computer centers and allied services.
9. Seasonal services like exam results are popular rather than the routine services as some of them have never been used on some centers since inception.
10. Kiosks' strength lies in single window shop for many services.
11. Soochnalayas cannot survive in absence of non-Gyandoot services.
12. In spite of all shortcomings and non-fulfillment of hopes, people are hopeful that at least some kind of benefit is available instead of nothing.
13. People see telecenters with great hopes. In most of the cases, the soochaks being community leaders counsel and advise people who respect them as an extension of the administration.
14. One MLA used Gyandoot to seek information on village roads and its photocopy so that he can present it to the Chief Minister for seeking grant.
15. Any kind and every kind of complaint had been sent through Gyandoot.
16. The administration was so upbeat during the initial period of commencement of Gyandoot that concerned authorities were asked to send their reply on the telephone to the district collector who in turn used to instruct his staff to inform the result of complaint to the soochak on phone. However, the situation took a U-turn in the later years.
17. The complaints and grievance module is fast losing its relevance due to the advent of www.mpsamadhan.org (official website of MP government for statewide complaints).
18. District administration can ensure grievance redressal within 7 days only for the 22 services prescribed for it as these directly

come under the collector whereas other complaints which require in-depth investigations, litigation tangles, multiple hierarchy of departments, searching of papers etc., take considerable time (sometimes upto 3 months). The Gyandoot team stopped grievance redressal service for few months after having been fed up with frivolous complaints, which wasted manpower and resources.

19. Gyandoot team kept no proper record of complaints, although quick action was ensured for each complaint. The telecenters, who are doing good business, are of the firm opinion that they will not be able to survive if they do not provide non-Gyandoot services.
20. It is a big fallacy that villagers themselves can work on computers and access what they want. Factually, even the most literate person asks soochak to do their work, as villagers feel hesitated and incapable. Besides; they do not own the equipment. Moreover, the soochaks do not allow the people to touch the expensive instruments.
21. Students use Gyandoot for results or doing computer courses and no E-clubs exist in reality as mentioned in the websites.
22. Educated people and outspoken respondents seem to have a high aspiration level for Gyandoot. As a result, most of them are grossly dissatisfied with Gyandoot. They call it a 'total failure' and brand it as a scheme for awards. However, they still recognize that it has given people at least some kind of benefit.
23. Some telecenters, while sensing the opportunity started offering services like electricity bill collection, telephone bill collection, etc. thus reinventing the wheel and reflecting potential of interactive e-governance.
24. Soochaks felt increase in their status among people due to extension of administration perception of the people.
25. Block headquarters telecenters are more profitable due to more work plus some additional facilities like inverter provided by the authorities. Block telecenters earn roughly Rs 4000/- per month from non-Gyandoot services and Gyandoot services contribute only Rs 1000/- approximately.
26. Soochaks were providing non-Gyandoot services like color photos, printing jobs, visiting cards, photocopy, computer courses like Photoshop, tally, Corel draw, DTP, MS-office. Almost all of them have provided employment to at least one person who manages the telecenters in their absence. These persons are mostly students who have done computer courses from Gyandoot.
27. All soochaks were of unanimous opinion that it is simply not viable to run the telecenter without the support from non-Gyandoot services.

REFERENCES

Arya, U. (2010). Public relations facet of information and communication technologies: A cross sectional analysis of public grievances variables. *Governance & Public Policy*, *5*(4), 7–30.

Average Indian household pays 42 bills online a year: study. (2006, April 14). *Business Line*, 135, 9.

Backus, M. (2001). *E-Governance and developing countries-Introduction and examples* [IICD Research Report No. 3]. Retrieved from http://www.ftpiicd.org/files/research/reports/report3.doc

Bhaskar News. (2004, September 22). Man dies on the municipal committee counter in Delhi. *Dainik Bhaskar*.

Bhatnagar, S. (2000). Land/Property registration in Andhra Pradesh. *WorldBank*. Retrieved from www1.worldbank.org/publicsector/egov/cardcs.htm

Bhatnagar, S. (1990). E governance and social exclusion: Experiences from the fields.

Cassell, C., & Symon, G. (2004). *Essential guide to qualitative methods in organizational research.* New Delhi: Sage Publications. Retrieved from http://preview.tinyurl.com/4s84c84

Gupta, M. P. (Ed.), *Promise of E-Governance: Operational Challenges*. New Delhi: Tata McGraw-Hill Publishing Company Limited.

Heeks, R. (1999). Information and communication technologies, poverty and development. Retrieved from http://www.man.ac.uk/idpm/diwpf5.htm

Information Needs Assessment for Rural Communities: An Indian Case Study (2003). Retrieved from http://ruralinformatics.nic.in/files/4_12_0_229.pdf

Jafri, A., Dongre, A., Tripathi, V.N., Aggrawal, A., Shrivastava, S. (2002, April). Information and communication technologies and governance: The Gyandoot experiment in Dhar district of Madhya Pradesh, India. *Overseas Development Institute*.

Johnson, L. (2007). The maverick: Dispatches from an unrepentant capitalist. Hampshire, UK: Harriman House Limited. Retrieved from http://tinyurl.com/amara-law

Kalam, A. P. J. (2005, May 16). Technologies for societal transformation. *The Hindu*.

Kukreja, S., & Grover, M. (2004). Quoted In M.P. Gupta (Ed.), Promise of E-Governance: Operational Challenges. New Delhi: Tata McGraw-Hill Publishing Company Limited.

Lawlor, A., Sandel, V., & Peterson, C. (2001). What works: Tarahaat's portal for rural India. Retrieved from www.digitaldividend.org/pdf/tarahaat.pdf

Lobo, A., & Balakrishnan, S. (2002). Report card on service of Bhoomi kiosks: An assessment of benefits by users of the computerized land records system in Karnataka. Retrieved from http://www.nisg.org/egovgateway/kb_docs/casestudy/Bhoomi%20evaluation%20Nov%202002.pdf

Luke, A. (1998) quoted in Sreekumar, T.T. (2004). E governance and social exclusion: Experiences from the fields. Retrieved from www.11iacc.org/download/add/WS11.2/TTS%20Paper.pdf

Millennium Development Goals, 149. (2004). Millennium Development Goals. Retrieved from http://www.un.org/millenniumgoals/

Nayar, M. (2004, October 22). Aiming to get a true picture of corruption. *The Hindu*.

Peter, B. (2001). Telecentres and universal capability: A study of the telecentre programme of the Universal Service Agency in South Africa, 1996 - 2000 [Unpublished doctoral dissertation]. Aalborg University, Denmark.

Ramalingam, A. (2006, January 22). Now, no long queues to pay your bills. *The Times of India*.

Roger, E., & Shukla, P. (2001). The role of telecenters in development communication and the digital divide. *The Journal of Development Communication*, *12*, 26–30. Retrieved from http://wsispapers.choike.org/role_telecenters-development.pdf

Singhal, A., & Roger, E. (1990). *India's information and communication revolution*. New Delhi: Sage Publications.

Srinivas, N. (2006, August 17). Not so simple life, farming can take a toll on health. *The Hindu*.

Thomas, K. T. (2005). Beware! cops may soon go mobile. *Business Line*, *105*, 1.

Vijayaditya, N. (2002). *A wired village: The warana experiment* (S. Bhatnagar & R. Schware, Eds.). New Delhi: Sage Publications.

Whyte, A. (1999). *Understanding the role of community telecenters in development - A proposed approach to evaluation in telecenter evaluation – A global perspective*. Ottawa: Retrieved from https://rgomez.ischool.uw.edu/sites/rgomez.ischool.uw.edu/files/documents/99%20TC%20evaluation,%20global%20perspective.pdf

KEY TERMS AND DEFINITIONS

Bureaucracy: A well laid down structure (mostly known for slow work, discrimination and corrupt work practices) of the government to carry out the administrative functions of the state.

Economic Activity: Any process, service or the facility which helps to generate the value in terms of money, immediate or potential one.

Efficiency: A measure of increase in the work output in less time.

Empowerment: A subjective term though, it has different meanings for different people. Most commonly, it involves the strengthening of the skills, knowledge base, earning potential etc. in pre and post phase of any project or scheme.

Intranet: A local network of computers which may or may not be connected to the internet. It is basically a secure medium unlike internet.

Local Needs: The needs of the local population which may vary from group of villages from another group of villages.

Telecenter: An ICT kiosk in the village where the villagers can access the basic administrative services from the district administration.

ENDNOTES

1 Digital Opportunity Initiative (2004). Digital Opportunity Initiative. Retrieved April 1, 2004, from www.opt init.org/framework/onepage/onepage.htm

2 UN Global Survey (2004). UN Global Survey. Retrieved May 27, 2005, from http://www.unpan.org/egovernment2.asp

3 Staff Reporter(2005, May 20). CBSE tele-counselling from May 23. *The Hindu*. Retrieved from http://www.thehindu.com/2005/05/20/stories/2005052001431300.htm

4 Gurstein (1999) quoted by Benjamin Peter, "Telecentres and Universal Capability: A study of the Telecenter Programme of the Universal Service Agency in South Africa, 1996 – 2000 " (Ph. D. diss., Aalborg University, 2001), 54

5 Kumar,R. (2005, September 25). Be e-ticket vendor if you have broadband and PC.*Dainik Jagran*, 4

6 The World Fact Book. (2005). The World fact book. Retrieved September 15, 2005, from https://www.cia.gov/library/publications/the-world-factbook/rankorder/2129rank.html

Chapter 20
The Potential of Social Media as a Communication Tool in Rural Community Development

Pádraig Wims
University College Dublin, Ireland

ABSTRACT

This chapter analyses the social media site Facebook as a communication tool in rural community development. The analysis was focused on the Facebook page of one rural community in Ireland. The research was conducted using a mixed method approach, using Facebook insights, key informant interviews, and questionnaires. The evolution of the Facebook page was documented. The study presents the attitudes towards the Facebook page of users and non-Facebook users. The findings indicate that friends of the community Facebook page believe it plays a vital role in their community forging debate, discussion and higher levels of participation. The non-Facebook users have made the conscious decision not to engage with Facebook, but nonetheless are aware of Facebook and on occasion, kept informed indirectly from sources close to them. Overall the research presented in this chapter illustrates that Facebook can be an effective communication tool in community development even in rural areas.

INTRODUCTION

The aim of the chapter is to analyse the social media site Facebook as a communication tool in rural community development. Using a case study approach, the analysis is primarily focused on the Facebook page of one rural community in the midlands of Ireland and the complex interplay between those who use the page and those who do not engage with the technology. The aim of this approach is to provide an insight into how one rural community is successfully adopting social media which may in turn help other rural communities develop a similar service.

When we think of communication, most people probably think of talking, texting, email or maybe even silent physical forms of communication such as smiling or hugging. However, how we communicate has fundamentally changed. The informality of social communication has brought about a new playing field. It is not just about the traditional media of newspapers, TV and radio,

DOI: 10.4018/978-1-4666-8598-7.ch020

but also the Internet, both mobile and interactive. Rural communities are also changing and adapting to the modern world of communication. The old art of communicating with friends over a casual meeting on the street is being challenged by the ever increasing presence of Facebook. Local news, reports of burglaries, places to visit and calls to action are all daily occurrences on Facebook, replacing the community bulletins of old. Facebook is revolutionising how people communicate and community groups and organisations are embracing the new technology.

Social media and networks are essentially Internet sites where people interact freely, sharing and discussing information about each other and their lives, using a mix of personal words, pictures, videos and audio. At these web sites, individuals and groups create and exchange content and engage in person-to-person conversations. They appear in many forms including blogs, forums and message boards, social networks and wikis. There are lots of well-known sites such as Facebook, LinkedIn, Myspace, Twitter, YouTube, Flickr and WordPress. Three of the most popular in Ireland are Facebook (62% of adults have Facebook accounts), Twitter (30%) and LinkedIn (26%) (Ipsos MRBI, 2014).

The efficiency of calling around to somebody's house for face to face meetings in an urban setting is very different from the reality in dispersed rural areas. Allowing a community to engage people in the same physical space, even though they may be geographically and remotely apart is a major benefit to any rural community organisation. A well designed Facebook page can help to alleviate some of these disadvantages. The implementation of Facebook can help to innovate and reduce response time in times of key decision making, providing the tools to easily search out relevant information from similar experiences elsewhere, relevant to a particular group or area. On the surface, it would appear that Facebook has all of the credentials to deliver a connected community in rural areas. Facebook is now an accepted means of communication. It is changing the way many people relate to one another and share information. But can Facebook be used as effectively as a communication tool in rural community development?

Successful rural community development is the process of helping a community to strengthen itself and develop towards its full potential. Communication is a key component of any sustainable development. Engaging people for community development purpose is important but members of communities can only be engaged when communication is effective. Good community communication leads to successful collaborative efforts and transformation of a community which in time helps to bring about social change among the marginalized and vulnerable groups within the community. Successful communication will help move people to a collective and community focused model of participation, appreciation and equity. More and more communities have realized the potential that Facebook has to offer in bridging the community gaps in rural Ireland. Using one such community, Abbeyleix in County Laois, Ireland this study investigates their community Facebook page to help analyse if Facebook can indeed be an effective communication tool in community development.

The central research question for this chapter is: can Facebook be used as a communication tool in rural community development?

A rapidly growing body of research has accompanied the meteoric rise of Facebook as social scientists assess the impact of the social network on social life. However, while researching this chapter it was clear that very little has been written about utilising Facebook in rural communities. Hence, the purpose of this chapter is to present research to provide an overall view about the use of Facebook in rural community development. This will be done through a study of one rural area and its community Facebook page. It aims to demonstrate how the community of Abbeyleix are using Facebook to increase transparency and e-participation, opening real community dialog on what has become their community virtual notice board.

With more than a billion active accounts worldwide, it can be easy to forget that not everyone is on Facebook. After all effective communication is about spreading the message to as many people as possible and a percentage of people still prefer to keep in touch by traditional communications methods. Indeed, some prefer to not have a Facebook account at all. The research will look at this objectively and establish the reasons why these people do not engage with social media. For these reasons, Facebook in rural communities presents a rich environment for research and raises a set of complex and intriguing questions which need to be explored.

The following research questions are addressed in this chapter:

- Is a community Facebook page an effective means of communications for rural communities?
- What are the primary benefits for a rural community in having a community Facebook page and is there an established model that can be rolled out as a working model for other communities?
- Why are some people choosing not to engage with a community Facebook page?
- Can the Abbeyleix community Facebook page be used a working model for other rural communities?

As the research topic has been set, the study will draw on both the interdisciplinary expertise of the Abbeyleix Facebook page users, page management and non-Facebook users providing an all inclusive perspective on the subject matter. From the outset, the research was planned and constructed relating to different research philosophies and research approaches. The study area for the research is Abbeyleix in Co Laois and their use of the social network site Facebook. Three separate types of stakeholders participated in this research. They included:

- The friends of the Abbeyleix community Facebook page who interact with the page on a regular basis.
- The people of Abbeyleix.
- The creator, manager and administrator of the Abbeyleix community Facebook page which is being used as a case study in this chapter.

The research was conducted using a mixed method approach, whereby both qualitative and quantitative approaches were used. This project took an interpretive perspective as it was mostly concerned with gaining an insight into the mechanics of Facebook in a rural setting. Therefore this was an interactive study with the research methods and the findings of the study developing on an ongoing basis throughout the project as information became available or was needed.

A socio-economic profile of the catchment area of Abbeyleix further informed the project and demonstrated the local context within which The Abbeyleix Facebook page has developed. Secondary sources of information used, included but were not limited to various books, academic journals, Central Statistics Office (CSO) statistics, government agency reports and other publications relevant to the study. Existing documents specific to Facebook such as online articles, company information and newspaper/magazine articles also provided secondary data useful for this research. Primary research for this study involved a combination of both quantitative and qualitative research methods which are described in more detail below.

The quantitative method used was a survey with data gathered through two questionnaires as follows: The Facebook User survey questionnaire was compiled and administered through the web- based software, Survey Monkey, and delivered and promoted through the Abbeyleix Facebook page. This allowed for the best use of time resources in a cost effective manner providing the best possible coverage of the study population. The survey was launched on 20th March 2014 through the Abbeyleix Facebook page with a closing date of 26th March. At all times anonymity was guaranteed as only the researcher had access to individual questionnaires returned online. A cover letter introducing the topic and completion requirements was included at the front of each survey. Of the total 2021 friends of the Facebook page, 33 surveys were completed and submitted. While the total number of returns was disappointing, the final respondents gave a good demographic spread.

The second survey questionnaire was targeted at non Facebook users in order to bring balance to the research. The questionnaire which contained 17 questions was developed in Microsoft Word and used the on-board features of radio buttons and tick boxes to help speed up the completion process for the respondent. The survey was delivered either face to face or via email to a targeted group of 17 individuals who choose not to engage with Facebook. By using both an in-person and online questionnaires, the aim was not to exclude those who may not have regular access to Internet or Facebook, and to get a wide spectrum of respondents. One week was given for the respondents to complete the survey.

In this research both convenience sampling, the process of selecting those cases that are easiest to obtain for samples and snowball sampling, where an element of referrals from initial subjects was relied upon to generate additional subjects (Sarantakos, 2005) were used.

BACKGROUND

This section reviews relevant literature to provide a context for this research and to synthesise the findings of previous research that is relevant to this subject.

This research is positioned in Ireland, a small, trade-dependent economy in the extreme West of the European Union. Ireland is a predominantly rural country; according to most recent census of population conducted in 2011 (CSO, 2011) the proportion of the Irish population living in rural areas is 37.8%. This is high by international standards for developed economies, for instance the comparable value for the OECD (average of 28 countries) is 34% (Brezzi, Piacentini, Rosina & Sanchez-Serra, 2012). Because of its rural characteristics Ireland represents an appropriate case study country to examine the potential of social media as a communication tool in rural community development.

Ireland experienced rapid economic expansion from 1995 to 2007, when annual GDP growth averaged 6%, but economic activity dropped sharply since 2008 when Ireland entered into a deep recession with the onset of the world financial crisis and a severe slowdown in property and construction markets. As a result of this recession, there are now many villages without a shop, many post offices are closed and many more under threat. Many police stations are closed, patrol cars are scarce and ambulance services are curtailed. The availability of doctors at night-time is restricted and many small towns have lost their banks. All this does not augur well for the future, nor does it encourage young people to live in rural areas, and those who do find it difficult to own a home or find employment. This has resulted in significant emigration from rural Ireland. In Abbeyleix, for example, the unemployment rate is at 24.1% compared with a national average of 19.0%. This has resulted in 3.5% moving to live elsewhere in the county, 3.0% living elsewhere in Ireland, while 0.6% live outside the State, all of whom were resident twelve months before the census on April 10, 2011 (CSO, 2011). This indicates that people are moving to find work or better living standards. This brings added pressure on the maintenance of key local services (both public and private) as well as continued investment in the key social and infrastructure development that is required to enable rural areas and communities to reach their full potential. In more remote, less accessible rural communities, additional problems appear to centre around the lack of connectivity (transport, energy and broadband), lack of timely, affordable access to key services such as specialist healthcare or to well-paid employment and demographic imbalance (Walsh, 2010). Walsh further adds that at local level the strong sense of rural as a place and as a distinct identify has in the past, been an inhibiter to communities working together. This fear must be overcome as communities and community organisations need to collaborate and network with one another to raise the issue of rural poverty and exclusion. It is now considered that this situation may be ameliorated through developments in Information and Communication Technology (ICT).

ICT can empower rural communities and give them "a voice" that permits them to contribute to the development process. With new ICTs, rural communities can acquire the capacity to improve their living conditions and become motivated through training and dialogue with others to a level where they make decisions for their own development (Balit, 1998). Giving rural people a voice means giving them a seat at the table to express their views and opinions and become part of the decision making process. To this end, the world has become a much smaller place where every day people connect and share with one another, adapting cultures and customs, dissolving borders, and uniting disparate cultures (Solis, 2010). In the era of social media, interpersonal networks are much larger than they have ever been, and there are more ways to communicate with people in them. In the past individuals, families and communities had a set of contacts, all of whom generally knew how to reach each other, either via phone, e-mail, or post. Today, thanks in large part to social networks there are many different levels of communication, each with a specific purpose and etiquette (Gordhamer, 2010).

As people become more comfortable using the internet, they are increasingly likely to use Social Network Sites (SNS) such as Facebook. It is the second-most visited site, after Google. Unlike just about any other website or technology business, Facebook is profoundly, centrally about people. It is a new form of communication, just as was instant messaging, email, the telephone and the telegraph (Kirkpatrick, 2010). Facebook connects people to one another in ways that enable them to do entirely new and novel things.

Wilson, Gosling and Graham (2012) reported that a rapidly growing body of research has accompanied the meteoric rise of Facebook as social scientists assess its impact on social life. However, research on Facebook emanates from a wide variety of disciplines with countless academic articles, journal articles, grey literature and blogs discussing social media with results being published in a broad range of journals and conference proceedings. This makes it difficult to keep track of various findings and because Facebook is a relatively recent phenomenon, uncertainty still exists about the most effective ways to do Facebook research (Wilson et al, 2012). Facebook's mission is to help make the world more open and connected and indeed it is changing how many people interact online. Mark Zuckerberg once said "... history tells us that systems are most fairly governed when there is an open and transparent dialogue between the people who make decisions and those who are affected by them" (Kirkpatrick, 2010).

There is a knowledge gap in how social media in the Internet age can be used as an effective community development tool. It is based on these gaps that this research was conducted. Gilbert, Karahalios and Sandvig (2008) note the lack of data in how rural communities use modern technology, such as social networking sites. As people continue to emigrate, keeping in contact with family and their wider community will be even more important than before.

Community Development in Rural Ireland

The relationship between social ties and community participation is complementary in nature -the more connected people are to their community, the more likely it is that they will participate in voluntary activities that work toward local benefit (Ryan, Kerry, Agnitsch, Zhao and Mullick, 2005). People are also more likely to feel attached to their communities if they interact with local ties (Wilkinson, 1991; Bell, 1998). For example, "people who report frequent conversations and meetings with friends and acquaintances" are more likely to become involved in voluntary or community activities than those who have limited social interactions (Wilson and Musick, 1997). This sense of shared identity can increase the rate of volunteering at the local level (Wilson, 2000). In his study of rural places, Wilkinson (1991) describes this social phenomenon as the "community field," or "a process of interrelated actions through which residents express their common interest in the local society."

The term community, in the 21st century, has evolved from its original roots; from a sense of a physical place, to a sense of place that is geographically unlimited (Lee, Kim, Lee and Kim, 2012). Communities in the 21st century know no geographic bounds and play a larger role in people's lives than ever before. A community can be any type of social interaction, and today that can take place on a blog or social network, or in person (Yong-Yeol, Han, Kwak, Moon and Jeong, 2007). Because of this evolution of community, the terms community and social network are often used interchangeably.

The focus on how social capital is built and reinforced recently expanded to include the influences of the Internet and other Information and Communication Technologies (ICTs). This research typically focuses on how Internet use can increase or at the very least, supplement social capital. For example, some have shown that ICTs can make it easier for people to participate in community voluntary organisations through providing a conduit for information about local happenings (Wellman, Haase, Witte & Hampton, 2001). Other research in rural areas has shown that Internet users are more likely to be involved in community events, organizations, and to take leadership roles in local undertakings than non-Internet users (Stern & Dillman, 2006).

Gilbert et al. (2008) concluded that rural communities are famous for using technology in novel ways. It is widely accepted that the Internet confers benefits on its users in a variety of ways, ranging from simple information acquisition and purchasing goods and services, to interacting with a range of individuals and groups in the wider processes of governance. Rural citizens stand to gain more than most, since the use of the Internet reduces, if not removes, geographical barriers to such interaction (Warren, 2007). At the simplest level, the benefits of the internet and broadband are easier access, faster data transfer and more accurate relay of complex digital information, but its real value is in its emergent properties (Rennie and Mason, 2005). To that extent, the shrinking of the 'digital divide' and particularly the increased availability of broadband in the countryside is crucial to the development of social capital in rural communities.

Because of the disparity in access to broadband, some rural communities in Ireland have fewer chances to take advantage of the types of social, political, and economic opportunities at the local level that comprise the common working definition of social capital. Mossberger, Tolbert and McNeal (2008) argue that while the Internet may have the potential to mitigate some 30 years of decline in civic engagement, there still exists a difference between people who use broadband technology and those who do not. For instance, being able to email large groups of individuals about local happenings and events, as well as searching out civic and political information quickly and easily, could potentially help to mobilise people, especially among the younger generations.

An issue for consideration is that the Internet can help overcome several limitations to community participation that have been documented in the past. For example, working mothers, housebound individuals, and people who lack transportation can utilise the Internet to become involved in their community in their own time, rather than having to attend meetings (Sproull and Kiesler, 2005). This type of participation can also have benefits for the volunteers themselves, as it can open doors to social networks that may have been previously untapped or underdeveloped (Norris, 2002).

Given that rural communities are behind other types of places in terms of the availability and use of high-speed broadband technology, they may experience disadvantages in two ways. At the individual level, people in rural areas may not be as well able to take advantage of tools and opportunities available on the Internet that would improve their daily lives through accessing their finances or seeking out medical information (Stern, Adams, and Boase, 2011). At the community level, the Internet provides an important medium for communication and information exchange regarding community groups and activities. Without this tool, community members may be less likely to be recruited, find information about these activities, or communicate with others regarding these types of participation. Again, this may also have particular implications for rural areas, as their vitality, development, and growth are often dependent on citizen participation in community-building efforts (Aigner, Flora, Tirmizi & Wilcox, 1999).

In the recent past, there has been concern about the "digital divide," or the disparity between those with access to the Internet and those without. Internet technology diffused faster to urban and suburban areas than to rural places (Horrigan, 2006; Townsend, 2001). As a result, researchers and policymakers were concerned about the effects of the lack of Internet access within rural communities (Donnermeyer and Hollifield, 2003).

Acknowledging these facts, the Irish Government's Broadband plan, "Delivering a Connected Society" in 2012, concludes that "targeted State intervention could achieve positive economic returns, positive socio-economic benefits and a positive benefit-cost ratio. The collective aim is to deliver the full benefits of a digitally enabled society, an aim which can only be achieved where the essential underlying infrastructure is available to everyone in the country". (Department of Communications, Energy and Natural Resources, 2012).

Access to Facebook or social media in general cannot be effected without internet connections. While Ireland still tends to lag behind the EU average in relation to broadband accessibility, this situation is improving slowly. In March 2014, The Commission for Communications Regulation (ComReg) released its Quarterly Report on the Irish Telecommunications market for the period October to December 2013. It found that average fixed broadband speeds continue to increase with approximately 53.4% of all fixed broadband subscriptions equal to or greater than 10Mbps, up from 31.5% in Q4 2012. Some 35.2% of all fixed broadband subscriptions were equal or greater than 30Mbps, up from 20.4% in Q4 2012. The estimated fixed broadband household penetration rate was 60.6% in Q4 2013 (Comreg, 2014).

Comreg added that at the end of December 2013 the mobile penetration rate was 122.2%. The number of smartphone/tablet users increased by 1.9% from Q3 2013 and up by 9.2% compared to Q4 2012. This information is important as it indicates a trend towards people accessing online content on their mobile devices. However, Preston, Cawley and Metykova (2007) note that providing access to broadband is only one piece of the puzzle; rural communities need to be shown how beneficial broadband access is to their area. If broadband is universally important from the small rural communities to the government, then more people should have access.

Evolution of the Internet and Social Media

The Internet as we now know it began in the 1960s as a way for government researchers to share information. The World Wide Web (commonly known as the web) is not synonymous with the internet but is the most prominent part of the internet. Web 1.0 as it is now known was an early stage of the evolution of the World Wide Web. Users could only view webpages but could not contribute to the content of the webpages. According to Cormode and Krishnamurthy (2008) "content creators were few in Web 1.0, with the vast majority of users simply acting as consumers of content". Web 1.0 was the first generation of the web which according to Tim Berners-Lee, the man credited with inventing the internet, could be considered the read-only web and also as a system of cognition (Berners-Lee, 1999). Web 1.0 began as an information place for businesses to broadcast their information to people. The early web provided limited user interactions or content contributions and only allowed users to search for information and read it.

Web 2.0, in comparison to Web 1.0, is much better oriented for social, political, and business users and provides better appliances and services to such those groups of users (Cormode and Krishnamurthy, 2008). Eijkman defined Web 2.0 as a trend of Internet services that promote "users to collaboratively create, share and recreate knowledge from multiple sources, leverage collective intelligence and organized action" (Eijkman, 2008). The fundamental advantage of Web 2.0 is that it allows users to contribute to the web as much as they consume the web itself. By September, 2005, the term Web 2.0 had taken hold and been cited 9.5 million times in Google. The essential difference between Web 1.0 and Web 2.0 is that content creators were few in Web 1.0 with the vast majority of users simply acting as consumers of content. In contrast, any participant can be a content creator in Web 2.0 and numerous technological aids have been created to maximize the potential for content creation.

Web 2.0 has had two main consequences of importance to global marketers. First, it has given rise to what has been termed 'social media' or Social Network Sites (SNS) and second, it has allowed the phenomenon that has been termed 'creative consumers' to flourish. It is important to distinguish between the media and the consumers. The media (e.g., YouTube, Facebook, and Twitter) are essentially vehicles for carrying content. This content in the form of words, text, pictures, and videos is generated by millions of consumers around the world, and from a marketer's perspective can indeed be inspired to create value (Muniz and Schau, 2011). At the outset there is the need to distinguish between the concepts of Web 2.0 and social networks. Web 2.0 is both a platform on which innovative technologies have been built and a space where users are treated as first class objects. The platform consists of various new technologies on which a variety of popular social networks, such as Facebook, Myspace, etc. have been built (Cormode and Krishnamurthy, 2008).

Brogan (2010) explains that Social Media are the product of Internet-based applications that build on the technological foundations of Web 2.0. Typically, social media are highly accessible (easy to get to) and scalable (can be used to reach large numbers). These social media support the democratisation of knowledge and information, and transform individuals from mere content consumers into content producers. Kaplan and Haenlein (2010) describe social media as "a group of Internet-based applications that build on the ideological and technological foundations of Web 2.0, and that allow the creation and exchange of user-generated content." As Hanna, Rohm, and Crittenden (2011) argued, the real power of the social media ecosystem is that "we are all connected."

According to Mason and Rennie (2007) the web has always supported some forms of social interaction e.g. computer conferencing, email and listservs. The recent proliferation in the use of social networking sites (SNS) has resulted in new research examining the role that SNSs play in identity construction. SNSs are defined as internet-based services that give individuals three major capabilities: first, the ability to construct a public or semi-public profile; second, the ability to identify a list of other users with whom a connection is shared and third, the ability to view and track individual connections as well as those made by others within the system (Boyd and Ellison, 2007). Kaplan and Haenlein (2010, p. 63) define a social networking site as applications that enable users to connect by creating personal information profiles and inviting friends and colleagues to have access to those profiles and sending e-mails and instant messages between each other.

What makes social network sites unique is not that they allow individuals to meet strangers, but rather that they enable users to articulate and make visible their social networks. This can result in connections between individuals that would not otherwise be made, but that is often not the goal, and these meetings are frequently between "latent ties" who share some offline connection (Haythornthwaite, 2005). On many of the large SNSs, participants are not necessarily "networking" or looking to meet new people; instead, they are primarily communicating with people who are already a part of their extended social network.

Although exceptions exist, the available research suggests that most SNSs primarily support pre-existing social relations. Lampe, Ellison and Steinfield (2007) suggest that Facebook is used to maintain existing offline relationships or solidify offline connections, as opposed to meeting new people. These relationships may be weak ties, but typically there is some common offline element among individuals who befriend one another, such as a shared class at school. Research in this vein has investigated how online interactions interface with offline ones. For instance, Lampe, Ellison, and Steinfield (2006, pp. 167 - 170) found that Facebook users engage in "searching" for people with whom they have an offline connection more than they "browse" for complete strangers to meet. Likewise, research found that 91% of U.S. teens who use SNSs do so to connect with friends (Lenhart and Madden, 2007).

This is a key point of the research presented in this chapter. Rural Irish communities are made up of local networks of people who overlap between different groups and organisations relaying and sharing the latest community news. Likewise the Facebook community is made up of networks of people who overlap between different groups and organisations through their pages relaying and sharing news. The vital difference is the speed at which the message can be spread using Facebook over a much wider audience.

Facebook is by far the largest online social network. It was founded in February 2004 by Mark Zuckerberg and fellow Harvard students Eduardo Saverin, Andrew McCollum, Dustin Moskovitz and Chris Hughes. Facebook was originally designed for college students and within 24 hours, 1,200 Harvard students had signed up. After one month, over half of the undergraduate population had a Facebook profile. The network was promptly extended to other Boston universities and eventually to all US universities. US high schools could sign up from September 2005, then it began to spread worldwide, reaching UK universities the following month.

During September 2006 the network was extended beyond educational institutions to anyone with a registered email address. The site remains free to join, and makes a profit through advertising revenue. The site's features have continued to develop. Users can now give gifts to friends, post free classified advertisements and even develop their own applications popular.

With the growth in popularity of smart phones, the Facebook mobile application makes it easy to connect on the go. An estimated 945 million active users use Facebook mobile products. In fact, over fifty percent of Facebook users regularly access the site from a mobile device (Facebook, 2014). As Facebook gained popularity internationally, other social networking sites that had been developed were swept aside and lost momentum, some even closing down. Orkut was an example of the latter; this was a social networking site that was developed by Google in 2004, the same year as Facebook was established. It gained popularity especially in India and Brazil, but closed down in September 2014.

Facebook continues to grow at astonishing rates. In 2008 Facebook had 100 million users and as at December 2013 had 1.3 billion monthly active users worldwide. It is estimated that there were in excess of 1 billion mobile monthly active users as of March 2014 (Facebook, 2014). People use Facebook to keep up with friends, upload photos, share links and videos, and learn more about the people they meet. Like other SNSs, Facebook enables users to create visible profiles. At a minimum, profiles require a user's name, gender, date of birth, and e-mail address. Information posted beyond these basic fields is at the discretion of the user. Users can add basic facts about themselves, such as home town, add contact information, personal interests, job information and a descriptive photograph (Boyd and Hargittai, 2010). With regard to the uptake of Facebook in Ireland the social media monitoring site Social Bakers (2014) recently advised that 2.25 million Irish people use Facebook. As expected, Dublin, the capital city, has the highest penetration of Facebook users of any county with 3 in 4 having a Facebook profile. Outside of Dublin the number of users drops significantly.

The "Facebook Penetration" for each country is measured and published by Miniwatts Marketing Group (2013); the term "Facebook Penetration" is define as the ratio of Facebook users in relation to the estimated total population in each world region. According to this source, the Facebook penetration for Ireland as a country is 45.2%, compared with 38.0% for all European Union Member States and 49.9% for North America (the highest penetration). Thus the Facebook penetration rate for Ireland compares favourably with other developed countries.

In recent years Facebook has become increasingly popular in Ireland with community clubs, groups and organisations as a communications tool. According to Social Bakers (2014) this is because it is free to setup and maintain, it is easy to use and widely available all over the world and it allows users to generate content. Facebook makes up 63 per cent of Irish social-media activity, twice as much as all other social-media sites combined. The figure puts Irish Facebook activity higher than that in the UK (55%) and significantly higher than that in the US (47%) (Facebook, 2014).

Research from University College Cork in 2013 reported that Irish emigrants maintain strong connections with home via social networks, texts, Skype, email and telephone calls. Over 70 per cent of emigrants use Skype and telephone calls to regularly maintain contact with family and friends in Ireland. Over 90 per cent of emigrants use Facebook and other social network sites to keep updated with home (Glynn, Kelly and MacEinri, 2013).

But is Facebook helping to build social capital? Social capital broadly refers to the resources accumulated through the relationships among people (Coleman, 1988). Social capital is a term with a variety of definitions in multiple fields (Adler and Kwon, 2002), conceived of as both a cause and an effect (Resnick, 2001). Bourdieu and Wacquant (1992 p. 14) define social capital as "the sum of the resources, actual or virtual, that accrue to an individual or a group by virtue of possessing a durable network of relationships of mutual acquaintance and recognition". The resources from these relationships can differ in form and function based on the relationships themselves.

If social capital declines, a community experiences increased unrest, reduced participation in civic activities, and distrust among community members. Greater social capital increases commitment to a community and the ability to mobilise collective actions. In general, social capital is seen as a positive effect of interaction among participants in a social network (Helliwell and Putnam,

2004). For individuals, social capital allows a person to draw on resources from other members of the networks to which he or she belongs. These resources can take the form of useful information, personal relationships, or the capacity to organize groups (Paxton, 1999).

The Internet has been linked both to increases and decreases in social capital. Nie (2001), for example, argued that Internet use detracts from face-to-face time with others, which might diminish an individual's social capital. However, this perspective has received strong criticism (Bargh and McKenna, 2004). Some researchers have claimed that online interactions may supplement or replace in-person interactions, mitigating any loss from time spent online (Wellman et al, 2001). Indeed, studies of geographical communities supported by online networks have concluded that computer-mediated interactions have had positive effects on community interaction, involvement, and social capital (Hampton and Wellman, 2003).

Recently, researchers have emphasized the importance of internet-based linkages for the formation of weak ties, which serve as the foundation of bridging social capital. Because online relationships may be supported by technologies like distribution lists, photo directories, and search capabilities (Resnick, 2001), it is possible that new forms of social capital and relationship building will occur in online social network sites. Bridging social capital might be augmented by such sites, which support loose social ties, allowing users to create and maintain larger, diffuse networks of relationships from which they could potentially draw resources. It is claimed (see for instance Donath and Boyd, 2004; Resnick, 2001 and Wellman et al., 2001) that SNSs could increase the weak ties one could form and maintain, because the technology is well-suited to maintaining these ties cheaply and easily. If a message is powerful enough it can spread to a vast sea of connected individuals, regardless of who originated it (Kirkpatrick, 2010 p. 296). It is clear that the Internet facilitates new connections, in that it provides people with an alternative way to connect with others who share their interests or relational goals (Ellison, Heino and Gibbs, 2006). Increasing online interactions do not necessarily remove people from their real communities, but may indeed be used to support relationships and keep people in contact, even when life changes.

This literature reviewed above has given a context to this research, examined community development, Government intervention, evolution of the internet and social networking, explained the Facebook phenomenon and explained the relationship between the online and off line communities as the author seeks to thread the subject matter together. The review suggests that given the continued emergence and integration of technology in everyday life, it is important to understand how and where it is being used. As the Internet has evolved over the past 30 years, so has its role in everyday life. The Internet is an expected service in today's world, much like electricity. It tells us that Facebook shows a strong "offline to online trend," meaning that online contacts are typically known before being added to the friends list (Bonneau, Muniz, Anderson, & Stajano, 2009). This suggests that an individual's offline social environment has a strong influence on decisions as to whether to actively participate on Facebook. Kujath (2011), for example, reported that Facebook and other social networks serve as an extension of face to face communication, although some individuals seemed to be relying more on communication via social networks than on "offline" interactions. This is seen as extremely important amongst users who live away from their communities in the search for work. It is tools like Facebook that can help bring communities and people closer together regardless of physical location, for the benefit of society as a whole.

DEVELOPMENT OF ABBEYLEIX COMMUNITY FACEBOOK PAGE

Abbeyleix is a small town situated in County Laois, in the midlands of Ireland. County Laois has a total population of 80,458 people (CSO, 2011). Abbeyleix is a fine example of an 18th century town, situated on the N8 approximately 14km south of the county town of Portlaoise on the old Dublin to Cork road. It is one of only 24 officially designated heritage towns of Ireland. County Laois has several small towns and a scattering of isolated villages. Abbeyleix is one of the larger urban centres outside Portlaoise and has a rich architectural heritage and boasts a significant number of fine Victorian buildings. This architectural style is quite distinct and gives Abbeyleix a very individual character. The opening of a new motorway (M7/M8 toll route) in 2010 has diverted a huge proportion of traffic away from the town. Whilst the reduction in the volume of traffic was welcomed in the wider community it has posed a threat to the business community and consequently the vibrancy of the community as a whole. A number of businesses have closed in recent years due to the down turn in the economy. This has increased pressure on public services such as the longstanding threat to close the local community nursing home and the withdrawal of the daily public bus service. The closures and withdrawals have led to an increase in unemployment, forcing people to emigrate away from the area in search of work. In the 2011 census of population, 751 persons aged 15 years and over were in the labour force and of these, 75.9 per cent (570 persons) were at work. The unemployment rate for the area was 24.1 per cent compared with a national average rate of 19.0 per cent.

Abbeyleix is traditionally characterised by having a very strong social capital with very active residents' associations, community and sports groups operating in the community. All of these groups and organisations have the effect of creating loose social networks overlapping in the same geographical area.

In terms of population, Abbeyleix had a population of 1,827 in April 2011 (CSO, 2011).

Of the 686 private households in Abbeyleix in April 2011, some 454 had some form of internet connection, as detailed in Table 1. This figure does not include access to broadband via smartphone.

According to the All-Ireland Research Observatory (AIRO, 2012) between 40-50% of households in Abbeyleix had a broadband connection.

Table 1. PC ownership and Internet access in Abbeyleix

Households with a Personal Computer		
	No	%
Yes	463	67.5
No	206	30.0
Not stated	17	2.5
Total	686	100
Households with Internet Access		
Broadband	400	58.3
Other	54	7.9
No	212	30.9
Not stated	20	0.3
Total	686	100

Source: CSO (2011)

The Abbeyleix Community Facebook Page

The Abbeyleix Facebook page was established in February 2010 by a local man who was interested in local community development and who had a deep understanding and insight into the everyday running of a community Facebook page. The aim in setting up the Facebook page was to bring together the community, keep them informed of local events and promote the area on a wider stage to encourage tourism. To date the Facebook page is run purely on a voluntary basis, has been in operation for over four years and is deemed to be a successful working model of a community Facebook page as a case study for this research.

It was felt that an Abbeyleix community page could be created for the role of intermediary for other people to post their updates, messages and events on the page making it a 'go to' site for the latest news and views about the town. According to Quinn (2014), who was page creator and administrator, these were the main reasons behind setting up the Abbeyleix community Facebook page.

Constructing the Abbeyleix Facebook page was relatively quick and easy. All that is required to set up a community Facebook page is a username and valid e-mail address; this allows the creator to have access and administration responsibilities. Once created the administrator becomes the content generator/manager for the page. It is then just a matter of detailing (profile) what the page is about. The Abbeyleix Facebook page is acting as a 'Virtual Community Noticeboard' alongside other forms of communication medium such as local newspapers, parish newsletters and local radio stations. The administrator has full control over the page allowing access to new members (friends) or additional moderators (screen and add content) to help with the maintenance and generation of new user content.

The page creator and administrator, drawing on the experience of having a personal presence on Facebook and seeing how Facebook was becoming more and more popular, felt the time was ripe for Abbeyleix to have its own community based page. Prior to this local information was shared via the conventional means of word of mouth, local papers and parish newsletter. These had drawbacks as information was often misinterpreted, misunderstood or out of date by the time it was received. Important decisions often went unnoticed which resulted in plans being put in place without the consent of the community. From its origins the aims of the community page were simple:-

- To keep the community informed;
- To promote 'Unity in the Community' wherever possible; and
- To promote the area on the wider Facebook stage to encourage visitors and tourists to the area.

In the initial stages, the page creator and administrator spent approximately 7-10 hours per week updating and commenting on all social aspects of the town, including social events, fundraisers, public bulletins and community notices. This led to a quick uptake on new friends joining the page. A decision was made early in the life of the page to grow organically and not to go joining (liking) other pages in an attempt to try to boost page numbers (friends). The number of friends grew virally as people with an association to the Abbeyleix area became aware of the page's existence through their friends on Facebook. Currently the maintenance of the site takes approximately 4 hours per week.

By August 2010, less than 6 months after its creation the page had 600 friends rising to its present total of 2122, or 116% of the town population. Presently the page is adding between five and ten new friends each week and these cover a wide geographical spread. The gender split reveals that the number of female friends is almost twice that of male friends in contrast to all Facebook trends. Analysis of the demographic breakdown reveals that most of the male and female users fall in the middle age range, as in Ireland the middle age groups tend to use Facebook more actively as shown in Table 2. This has resulted in the page becoming one of the primary reference sources for both locals and visitors to the area. These numbers may seem unusual as social networking is often associated with the younger age groups, but according to the Pew Research Centre (Duggan and Brenner, 2012), the average age of people who use Facebook falls within the 18 to 29 year-old range.

Table 2. Audience reach on the Abbeyleix Page

Country	Fans of Abbeyleix Facebook Page	City	Fans of Abbeyleix Facebook Page	Language	Fans of Abbeyleix Facebook Page
Ireland	1714	Abbeyleix	531	English (USA)	1100
United kingdom	183	Dublin	278	English (UK)	979
United States of America	96	Portlaoise	193	Spanish	5
Australia	40	Durrow	63	French	5
Canada	16	Kilkenny	56	Italian	5

Source: Facebook (2014)

The audience this Facebook page reaches is quite impressive (Table 2), as it spans across 38 different countries, ranging from Ireland and the United Kingdom to Australia, Canada, Italy, Ghana, Czech Republic, Indonesia and Bangladesh. Not surprisingly, the largest number of followers is from Ireland with the United Kingdom coming in second. More specifically to a community page, followers can be found all around Ireland, with most are located in Abbeyleix, followed by Dublin and the neighbouring towns of Portlaoise and Durrow. The page creator and administrator reported that many of the friends located outside of Abbeyleix and Ireland are former residents of Abbeyleix or have a direct connection to the town through family. They therefore use the Facebook page to keep in touch with their town or ancestral home.

An additional source of traffic has been the local website. When the local development group, Abbeyleix Business and Community Development Forum launched their website (www.abbeyleix.ie), links were forged between the two sites to promote one another. Information and features are shared by the sites constantly, allowing cross referencing and visiting traffic to flow in both directions.

The Abbeyleix page has positioned itself as a community page to be used by the community as an alternative means to deliver local news directly to people's pockets (mobile) or home (PC). This 'virtual notice board' has been acting as a conduit or central location successfully now for nearly 4 years. The page creator and administrator acts as moderator for the page and uses discretion to remove inappropriate or offensive material. The page creator and administrator continued that "Recent innovations in social media and smart phone technology have made a huge difference to this local community, facilitating neighbourhood co-operation and a marked increase in social action" (Quinn, 2014). Some recent examples of this include:-

2011 and 2012 Hospital Marches

When the HSE threatened to close the local community services hospital, the page played a vital part in raising awareness, through constant updates, circulation of posters and public meeting times and dates. Over 5,000 people marched through the town in protest in October 2011, gaining national media coverage. The campaign is still ongoing and the page is highly active in channelling key details to the public, when required.

2011 Abbeyfest

Now in its third year, Abbeyfest has become a vital part of the Arts and Music calendar in the Midlands showcasing an array of talent catering for all ages. The Abbeyleix page again played an integral part in widening the potential audience, showing support for the festival's own Facebook and webpage.

2011 Christmas Market and Craft Fair:

Like Abbeyfest, the Abbeyleix Christmas Market and Craft Fair is now in its third year. The event is held in early December every year and has proved to be a significant success attracting over 1,000 people each year with local choirs, stalls and artisan foods being the main attractions.

2012 Christmas Tree Campaign

When friends of the page were asked should the town re-introduce a Christmas tree in the Market Square of Abbeyleix in 2012, over 120 people replied with a resounding yes. This led to a tree being erected by local volunteers each year since then.

2013 St Patricks Day Parade

Re-introduced after a 30 year absence, the parade was attended by an estimated crowd of over 1,500 people in 2014. Advertisement and updates on the event through the page played a large part in the success of the Parade. This was publicly acknowledged by the organising committee.

2013+ Other Initiatives:

Too numerous to mention, but every event that is brought to the attention of the Abbeyleix Facebook page is supported and promoted on the page include bringing the cannonball run to town in 2013, showing ongoing support for Abbeyleix Tidy Towns and the promotion of local businesses, events and news on a daily basis.

Page Insights

Facebook provides access to its Insights service which allows page administrators to monitor the users of the page under the headings Likes, Reach, Visits, Posts and People. This data can provide useful information. Insights provides continuous measurements on the Page's performance and anonymized demographic data about a page audience to see how people are discovering and responding to posts and updates. It provides ongoing feedback on who likes the Page and who likes, comments, and shares posts to help improve targeting (Facebook, 2014). In addition, Facebook provides Page administrators with aggregated anonymous insights about people's activity on their Page. The *People Reached* section in the *People* tab of a Page Insights provides the following information about the people the Page is reaching:

- **Gender and Age:** The percentage of people who saw any content about the page for each age and gender bracket. This is based on the data people enter in their personal timelines.
- **Countries:** The number of people who saw any content about the Page, broken down by country. This is based on an IP address.
- **Cities:** The number of people who saw any content about the Page, broken down by city. This is based on an IP address.
- **Language:** The number of people who saw any content about the Page, broken down by language. This is based on a default language setting.

Facebook's Insights have proven to be a valuable source of information for the Abbeyleix page. The latest update shows the best types of posts for Pages, better engagement data and when fans are online.

"Days" indicates on average, how many of the page fans are actively seeing any posts on Facebook in an hour for each day of the week. These include posts from friends, Pages, apps etc.

"Times" shows, on average, how many of the page fans see posts in an hour.

Administrators can also hover over each day of the week and Facebook will overlay a graph on the "Times" to give information about that specific day. This information is beneficial when trying to engage as many of the page's friends as possible, allowing targeted posts and updates. The peak times on the Abbeyleix Facebook were found to be Saturday evenings from 6pm to 10pm.

In order to get people to check the page regularly and remind them of its existence a number of initiatives were devised, such as:-

1. Weekly Profile Photo – Friends are asked to submit a photo depicting the area, which is used as the cover (masthead) picture for the coming week or ten days. This proved to be very popular and also showcases the area to potential visitors.
2. Use of Funny Video/Pictures: Trending videos linked from YouTube or other Facebook sites are posted to stimulate reaction during quieter periods on the page.
3. Events listings: Organisation and clubs can avail of this facility to post their events in the events guide at the top of the page.

As the page has continued to evolve there are plans to introduce a number of new updates, such as:-

- Competitions;
- Daily Deals from local businesses as an incentive for people to carry out business in the town; and
- Additional contributors.

Based on additional feedback taken from the insights facility, the page has learned that friends of the page tend to be more engaged with the visual aspect of video links or photos. This indicates that people are more inclined to like or discuss visual content uploaded to the page rather than text-based content.

This section has documented the evolution of the Abbeyleix Facebook page as a real community page reaching out not just to the community but worldwide. Because of the ease of sharing information and the popularity of Facebook, followers have interacted with the page, which in turn allows their Facebook friends to see what pages they have interacted with. This causes a chain (viral) reaction allowing for information to easily be shared with an infinite amount of people over a very short timeframe. Since the creation of the page, the focus and posts have remained consistent helping to create a virtual community notice board for the community.

Survey Findings: Analysis of Users and Non-Users of Abbeyleix Facebook Page

This section presents both quantitative and qualitative primary data gathered during this research to determine if Facebook can be used as a community development tool. This data will give an insight into the service user experience with The Abbeyleix Facebook page as well as the perspective of those involved in the operation of the service. Running parallel to this will be research findings from respondents who do not engage with Facebook. The non-Facebook user survey investigates why some people do not engage with Facebook and looks for the trends among non-users.

On 20th March 2014, an online questionnaire was fielded to the Abbeyleix Facebook page requesting people to participate in a short survey. All 2022 (as of 20/03/14) of the Abbeyleix Facebook users were sent a public invitation from the page administrator, with a short description of the study and a link to the survey. Two reminder updates were subsequently posted on the page. The survey was hosted on Survey Monkey, an online survey hosting site. The survey contained 29 questions and was split into 3 parts. The survey was left open for one week resulting in a 33 people responding to the questionnaire. The thrust of the questionnaire was to gauge people's interaction with the Abbeyleix Facebook page and to catalogue the benefits. While it is acknowledged that the response to the survey was considerably lower than expected considering the total number of friends of the page, the total of 33 respondents was comparable to other means of carrying out similar surveys in a community environment.

Of the 33 respondents 67% were female and 33% were male. This corresponds well with the demographic breakdown of the Abbeyleix Facebook page where the split is 65% female and 35% male. The age profiles of respondents to the research surveys together with those of Abbeyleix Facebook users and all Irish Facebook users are presented in Table 3.

The data in Table 3 illustrate that although the respondents were selected randomly, there was a spread across all of the age categories. However, a slightly higher proportion of respondents were in the 45-64 year age category than the overall Abbeyleix Facebook users.

During March 2014, a survey was also targeted at residents of Abbeyleix who did not use Facebook. These respondents were identified randomly by word of mouth. Questionnaires were either hand delivered face to face or emailed to recipients. Fifteen questionnaires were completed and returned. The questionnaire contained 17 questions and the thrust of the questions was to establish why some people in Abbeyleix were not engaging with Facebook. In the non-user Facebook survey the author sought to understand the ways in which people who decided not to become users of Facebook differed from those who were users.

Of the fifteen respondents 67% were male and 33% were female. This is the reverse of the Facebook user survey and demographic breakdown of the Abbeyleix Facebook page. When the demographics of this sample is compared with the population of Abbeyleix, this sample appears to be representative with one exception. Females (which in Abbeyleix is 51 per cent), were slightly under represented and males were over represented in the sample. The respondents were selected randomly with a spread across all of the age categories, as presented in Table 3.

Abbeyleix Facebook Use - The main research question set for this chapter was to determine if the Abbeyleix Facebook page can be an effective means of communication for the local community. Based on the findings presented in this section, the answer to this question can be answered in the affirmative. According to CSO (2011) Abbeyleix has a total population of 1,827. The Abbeyleix Facebook page insight tools shows that 540 fans of the page are based in Abbeyleix. Over 61% rated the page as being either excellent or very good. Over 96% of Facebook users when surveyed, said they would miss the page if it were to cease operation.

Some 73% of the non-Facebook users surveyed said there is someone in their household with access to Facebook. This indicates that people are exposed to Facebook by both direct and indirect means. While non-Facebook users may not want

Table 3. Age profiles of survey respondents, all Abbeyleix Facebook page friends and all Irish Facebook users

Age Category (Years)	Survey Respondents (Facebook Users) N=33 (%)	Survey Respondents (Non-Facebook Users) N=15 (%)	Abbeyleix Facebook Page Friends N=2022 (%)	Irish Facebook Users (%)
Under 25	9	13	23	34
25-44	45	67	51	48
45-64	39	13	21	15
65+	6	7	5	3

to engage with social networking sites, nonetheless over 80% stated that the local community benefits from an informative Facebook page.

Analysis of engagement on the Abbeyleix Facebook page illustrated that female friends (74%) of the page engaged with the page nearly three times more than their male (25%) counterparts over the previous 28 days. This is related to the fact that more men than women are friends of the page. The most active age profile on the page are women aged between 35 – 44 years (23%), followed by 45-54 (18%) respectively. Males between 35-44 years (8%) are the most active category amongst the men.

The busiest time on the page is between 6pm and midnight, peaking around 9pm. Respondents were asked if they considered the Abbeyleix Facebook page to be an effective means of communication in the community. The majority, over 96%, gave a positive response. When asked about the amount of time they spend on the Abbeyleix page over 30% reported that they spent between 6 – 10 hours per week, 27% between 1 to 5 hours per week, followed by those who claimed to live on it coming in at just under 24% and 18% between 11 to 20 hours. When asked which devices were used most often to connect to the internet it emerged that over 42% of respondents used a PC/ Laptop, 36% used smartphones and the remaining 22% used tablets.

Respondents were asked if they were engaging with Facebook more or less with than they were 12 months previously. A resounding 94% of the respondents said that they were using Facebook more with only 6% saying less.

Respondents were also asked to give one advantage and one disadvantage to Abbeyleix in having a community Facebook page. The main advantages stated included "It keeps people up to date on local events" and "It provides updates of what is going on in Abbeyleix" or as one person put it "Crucial information hub for new residents"

The main disadvantages included: "Not everyone, particularly older people, uses Facebook" and "It's addictive".

Some 15% of respondents reported that they visited the Abbeyleix Community Facebook page numerous times daily, 21% once a day, and a further 15% visited every other day or a couple of times a week. Twelve percent of the respondents visited the page once a week to keep abreast of local news.

When asked, 89% of the respondents reported that the Abbeyleix page helps to promote a higher level of participation and community dialogue amongst friends of the page. The respondents were asked about their membership of other forms of online accounts. The top three online accounts held by the Facebook users were email (87%), Skype (59%) and Twitter (53%). This suggests that users of the Facebook page are computer literate and not afraid to acquire alternative accounts to keep connected with family and friends in the digital era. When asked which methods they use most to keep in contact with family and friends it emerged that Facebook came out on top at 46%, nearly as popular as all of the other methods combined. Text messaging was second at 19% with phone third at 11%. Further study of these results would appear to indicate a trend away from conventional methods of communication towards newer methods of direct contact by Facebook users at least.

When questioned directly, 38% of respondents stated that Facebook is a most effective means of communication when used with local newspapers, 15% with parish newsletters and 11% when used with text messaging.

Over 61% of the respondents stated that the Facebook page was either excellent or very good. In addition over 92% stated that the page has provided them with information that they might not otherwise have had access to and 84% reported that they attended an event that they saw advertised on the community page. Most noteworthy is that nearly 85% claimed they would respond positively to a 'Call to Action' if posted on the page.

Table 4. Percentage of respondents ranking these content items most important (N=33)

	1st Preference %	2nd Preference %	3rd Preference %	Total Ranking These Items among Their Top Three Preferences %	Overall Position in Ranking (Combining Top Three Preferences)
Death notices	7	18	18	43	4
Local news	50	18	7	75	1
Friday fun	4	4	11	19	6
Breaking news	11	14	25	50	3
Sports news	4	4	4	12	8
Community news	7	28	18	53	2
Gigs	4	4	0	8	9
Local photographs	4	7	14	25	5
Events & festivals	11	4	4	19	6

In order to determine what type of post engages friends of the page most the respondents were asked which type of status update (Posts) on the page engaged them most. Nearly three quarters (72%) indicated that a picture post was the most engaging, followed by a text update (25%) and a video link at just over 3%.

One of the aims of the research was to decide if the Abbeyleix page could be used as a model for other communities who were considering joining Facebook. When asked if other rural communities would benefit from such a page over 89% replied in the affirmative. Asked what should be added to such a page to further meet the needs of a community it emerged that good, reliable, local information or insider knowledge, such as contact details and opening hours for local services and tradesmen, appeared to be the common trend.

When asked to rank in order of preference the features of the page 50% ranked local news as their priority, followed by breaking news and events and festivals. The results are summarised in Table 4.

A reccuring theme throughout the answers was the need to keep the information updated and fresh. While the question was an open question the message coming through from the replies showed that sharing of information and keeping people in touch was of key importance.

Non-Facebook Users - The findings from the non-Facebook user survey are now presented. Some 87% of non-Facebook users confirmed they had access to the internet. This eliminates the hypothesis that lack of Facebook engagement may be explained by absence of internet access. Of those with internet access, over 39% accessed the internet via a PC/Laptop, 38% with smartphones and the remaining 23% with tablet devices.

While those surveyed did not engage with Facebook, the study set out to determine if there was a trend in usage of other online media types. The most popular application used by this cohort was email (at 29%), followed by WhatsApp (20%) and Skype (14%). This indicates a trend of communication on a more one to one basis, as both email, WhatsApp and Skype are direct forms of communication between sender and receiver. All of these applications require an email address and password as a minimum requirement, when joining. For this reason these respondents cannot be labelled as technology laggards, just more likely to have shunned joining Facebook for one reason or another.

Respondents were asked which methods (excluding Facebook) they used to keep in contact with family and friends. Contact via phone was the most popular at 47%, followed by text at 40% and face-to-face at 13%.

When asked to explain how they stay informed about local events and news in their community, ten out of the fifteen respondents (67%) mentioned that they received their community news from the local newspaper. Friends was the next most popular answer with one person using the age old communication channel in rural Ireland, replying "My Mother knows all the gossip".

While this category does not engage with Facebook, 100% of them declared that they were aware of the social networking site. Some 87% added that they did not feel they were missing anything by not being on the site. Only 13% had previously engaged with Facebook in the past.

Privacy issues, lack of time and lack of interest were all cited as reasons for not having a Facebook account. One person added: "I am not interested in broadcasting my business on the internet where it can be viewed by people that I am not actually "friends" with".

Asked if they intended to open a Facebook account in the next 12 months, the majority at 87% replied that they did not intend to do so. Even though they liked the idea of an informative community Facebook page 93% indicated that this would not entice them to join Facebook. This group believed that relevant, up to date information is the key ingredient to the success of such a page. Other than having suggestions on what the page should contain this group indicated a real reluctance to ever engage with Facebook. This confirms that the majority of those polled have made a conscious decision not to join Facebook. Interestingly, 73% of respondents have someone in their household with access to Facebook which may go some way to explaing their awareness of the site. It also means that while some people are not on Facebook they may be receiving information second-hand via a Facebook user in their home.

Benefits of the Community Facebook Page to the Community

The experience presented in this chapter illustrate that Facebook is an excellent opportunity for a community to connect with families and share information rapidly. If a community is consistent in keeping the information updated and accurate, people will come to rely on the Facebook Page as a reputable resource to find information about the area. There are many different types of information that a community could choose to share on its Facebook Page. A Facebook Page is a great place to post noteworthy happenings around the community via a status update that posts on the Page's wall. This is an easy way to keep people informed as to what's going on locally and it only takes moments to do.

It is important to frame the discussion with a warning about protecting people on the page. Before launching a Facebook Page, a community must ensure they've thought through the types of content they're going to share with the world. Before sharing any information about any friend of the page (including pictures, videos, first names, work samples, etc.) the page administrator must ensure they have obtained consent from the rightful owner and clearly acknowledge all copyright. Additionally, community pages should respect people's privacy. Not everyone is on Facebook to share their personal details with the world. Likewise clear warnings must be posted periodically warning about the use of explicit mater or offensive content not being tolerated.

Facebook allows a community to lower the barriers to participation for its members. By effectively using Facebook, a community can make it easier for people to get involved and share their opinions on a variety of fronts. While some communities may fear this increased participation, others will embrace it as it not only increases involvement, but can also lead to a healthy discourse about what's happening in the community.

Additionally, as the numbers of page friends continue to increase people and associated groups are generating increased amounts of content. By posting their comments, news and view along with video links and pictures the page will constantly refresh and stay up to date. This is a criticism often aimed at conventional websites as the content rapidly becomes out dated. Recruiting additional administrators will share the work load of maintaining and monitoring the site and allow cover during holiday periods or busy times during local events. More importantly it will provide a couple of different perspectives on the community as the page enters the next stage of development.

DISCUSSION AND CONCLUSION

This chapter has analysed the social media site Facebook as a communication tool for rural community development. The analysis was primarily focused on the Facebook page of one rural community, that of Abbeyleix in Ireland, with the aim of providing an insight into how this community is successfully adopting the social media technology. The research was conducted using a mixed method approach, whereby both qualitative and quantitative approaches were used.

It is clear from this research that local communities engaging with pages such as the Abbeyleix community Facebook page become more informed, responsive, innovative, and most importantly feel involved in community decisions. However, it is evident that other forms of media such as local newspapers and parish newsletters will continue to play a vital role in spreading the message, especially for older generations.

If the community feels informed and can have their say it makes a great difference to the dynamics within that community. To do this a community must have an open line of communication or open forum to enter debates, discuss topics and network with other like-minded people. The Abbeyleix Facebook page has proved to be an invaluable tool for their community. Based on the survey results and the Facebook insight data, it is clear that people are engaging with the page. This 'virtual notice board' has been acting as a conduit or central location for all of the people and groups of the area relaying information, news and more. For the last four years the page has helped rally the residents to band together to support various causes and events, ranging from Christmas Markets, St Patrick's Day parades, protesting at the hospital closure or promoting businesses in town. It has brought closeness to the community, whether they live locally or overseas. The town and by wider association the world has become a much smaller place where every day people connect and share with one another.

Unlike just about any other website or technology business, Facebook is profoundly, centrally about people. Facebook connects people to one another in an entirely new way. The 96% of respondents who answered positively in the research are evidence that Facebook is very effective. In the case of Abbeyleix, this is a means of communication that is being used to deliver messages or call to action in real time without incurring a cost to over 2100 people. While some elements within the community may be suspicious of the new technology it is clear that there is now widespread acceptance of the technology which promotes a higher level of participation and dialogue within the community.

While non-users may have privacy concerns the research findings indicate that the advantages of Facebook far outweigh the disadvantages. Crucial information for residents and keeping people up to date on local issues are all key components of what a community Facebook page is about. The more connected people are to their community, the more likely it is that they will participate in voluntary activities that work toward local benefit (Ryan et al., 2005). But its real value is in its emergent properties (Rennie and Mason, 2005). To that extent, the shrinking of the 'digital divide' and particularly the increased availability of broadband in the countryside is crucial to the development of social capital in rural communities.

The results of this research have shown that ordinary members of the community are now technologically advanced. They are members of a large number of social network sites, accessing the internet on a range of devices and spending long periods of time online. The Facebook survey found that the respondents regularly and frequently visited the Abbeyleix Community Facebook page and the majority said the page was either excellent or very good. All the responses were very positive showing a clear knowledge and positive attitude to the page. Even the non-Facebook users' survey illustrates that 100% of the respondents were aware of the Facebook page and 80% of them felt their community was benefiting from the page.

The findings of this research indicate that the Abbeyleix Facebook page is an ideal template for other communities considering developing their own Facebook pages.

REFERENCES

Adler, P., & Kwon, S. (2002). Social capital: Prospects for a new concept. *Academy of Management Review*, *27*(1), 17–40.

Aigner, S. M., Flora, C. B., Tirmizi, S. N., & Wilcox, C. (1999). Dynamics to Sustain Community Development in Persistently Poor Rural Areas. *Community Development Journal: An International Forum*, *34*(1), 13–27. doi:10.1093/cdj/34.1.13

AIRO. (2012). The Atlas of the Island of Ireland - Mapping Social and Economic Change, All Ireland Research Observatory. Retrieved from http://www.airo.ie

Balit, S. (1998). Listening to farmers: communication for participation and change in Latin America. In Training for agriculture and rural development: 1997-98, 29-40. Rome Italy: FAO.

Bargh, J., & McKenna, K. (2004). The Internet and social life. *Annual Review of Psychology*, *55*(1), 573–590. doi:10.1146/annurev.psych.55.090902.141922 PMID:14744227

Bell, M. (1998). The Dialogue of Solidarities, or Why the Lion Spared Androcles. *Sociological Focus*, *31*(2), 181–199. doi:10.1080/00380237.1998.10571100

Berners Lee, T. (1999). *Weaving the Web: The Original Design and Ultimate Destiny of the World Wide Web, Orion Business Books* (1st ed.). Collins.

Bonneau, J., Muniz, J., Anderson, R., & Stajano, F. (2009). Eight Friends are Enough: Social Graph Approximation via Public Listings. *Proceedings of the Second ACM Workshop on Social Network Systems*. doi:10.1145/1578002.1578005

Bourdieu, P., & Wacquant, L. (1992). *An Invitation to Reflexive Sociology*. Chicago: University of Chicago Press.

Boyd, D. M., & Ellison, N. B. (2007). Social Network Sites: Definition, History and Scholarship. *Journal of Computer-Mediated Communication*, *13*(1), 210–230. doi:10.1111/j.1083-6101.2007.00393.x

Boyd, D. M., & Hargittai, E. (2010). Facebook Privacy Settings: Who cares? First Monday peer reviewed journal of the web, *13*(6). Retrieved from http://firstmonday.org/article/view/3086/2589

Brezzi, M., Piacentini, M., Rosina, K., & Sanchez-Serra, D. (2012). Redefining urban areas in OECD countries. In *Redefining "Urban": A New Way to Measure Metropolitan Areas*. OECD. doi.10.1787/9789264174108-en

Brogan, C. (2010). *Social media 101* (1st ed.). Hoboken, N.J.: Wiley. doi:10.1002/9781118256138

Coleman, J. S. (1988). Social capital in the creation of human capital. *American Journal of Sociology*, *94*(s1Supplement), S95–S120. doi:10.1086/228943

Comreg -. (2014). *Quarterly Key Data Report - Data as of Q4 2013 Document No: 14/19*. Dublin: The Irish Communications Regulator.

Cormode, G., & Krishnamurthy, B. (2008). Key differences between Web 1.0 and Web 2.0. First Monday peer reviewed journal of the web, *13*(6). Retrieved from http://firstmonday.org/article/view/2125/1972

CSO. (2011). Census of Population 2011, Preliminary Results *(PDF download)* Central Statistics Office. Retrieved from www.cso.ie

Department of Communications. Energy and Natural Resources (DCENR) (2012). Delivering a Connected Society, A National Broadband Plan for Ireland. Retrieved from http://www.dcenr.gov.ie/Communications/Communications+Development/Next+Generation+Broadband/

Donath, J., & Boyd, D. (2004). Public displays of connection. *BT Technology Journal*, *22*(4), 71–82. doi:10.1023/B:BTTJ.0000047585.06264.cc

Donnermeyer, J., & Hollifield, C. (2003). Digital Divide Evidence in Four Rural Towns. *IT & Society*, *1*(4), 107–117.

Duggan, M., & Brenner, J. (2012). *The Demographics of Social Media Users – 2012*. Retrieved.

from http://www.pewinternet.org/2013/02/14/the-demographics-of-social-media-users-2012/

Eijkman, H. (2008). Web2.0 as a non-foundational network-centric learning space Campus-Wide. *Information Systems*, *25*(2), 93–104.

Ellison, N., Heino, R., & Gibbs, J. (2006). Managing impressions online: Self-presentation processes in the online dating environment. *Journal of Computer-Mediated Communication*, *11*(2), 415–441. doi:10.1111/j.1083-6101.2006.00020.x

Facebook statistics. (2014, June 30). Facebook. Retrieved from http://www.xmarks.com/site/www.facebook.com/press/info.php%3Fstatistics

Gilbert, E., Karahalios, K., & Sandvig, C. (2008). *The Network in the Garden: An Empirical Analysis of Social Media in Rural Life*. University of Illinois at Urbana-Champaign.

Glynn, I., Kelly, T., & MacÉinrí, P. (2013). *Irish Emigration in an Age of Austerity. Project funded by The Irish Research Council Hosting Institutions: Department of Geography and the Institute for the Social Sciences in the 21st Century*. University College Cork.

Gordhamer, S. (2010). 5 Levels of Effective Communication in the Social Media Age. *Mashable*. Retrieved from http://mashable.com/2010/02/08/communication-social-media/

Hampton, K., & Wellman, B. (2003). Neighboring in Netville: How the Internet supports community and social capital in a wired suburb. *City & Community*, *2*(4), 277–311. doi:10.1046/j.1535-6841.2003.00057.x

Hanna, R., Rohm, A., & Crittenden, V. L. (2011). We're all connected: The power of the social media ecosystem. Northeastern University, Boston, MA.

Haythornthwaite, C. (2005). Social networks and Internet connectivity effects. *Information Communication and Society*, *8*(2), 125–147. doi:10.1080/13691180500146185

Helliwell, J. F., & Putnam, R. D. (2004). The social context of well-being. *Philosophical Transactions of the Royal Society*, *359*(1449), 1435–1446. doi:10.1098/rstb.2004.1522 PMID:15347534

Horrigan, J. (2006). Home Broadband Adoption 2006. *Pew Internet & American Life Project*. Retrieved from http://www.pewinternet.org/files/old-media/Files/Reports/2006/PIP_Broadband_trends2006.pdf.pdf

Ipsos, M. R. B. I. (2014). Social Networking Quarterly. Retrieved from http://www.ipsosmrbi.com/social-networking-may-2014.html

Kaplan, M. A., & Haenlein, M. (2010). Users of the World unite! The challenges and opportunities of Social Media Original Reseach Article. *Business Horizons*, *53*(1), 59–68. doi:10.1016/j.bushor.2009.09.003

Kirkpatrick, D. (2010). *The Facebook Effect: The Inside Story of the Company That Is Connecting the World*. Simon & Schuster.

Kujath, C. L. (2011). Facebook and Myspace: Complement or substitute for face-to-face Interaction? *Cyberpsychology, Behavior, and Social Networking*, *14*(1-2), 75–78. doi:10.1089/cyber.2009.0311 PMID:21329446

Lampe, C., Ellison, N., & Steinfield, C. (2006). A Face(book) in the crowd: Social searching vs. social browsing. [New York: ACM Press.]. *Proceedings of CSCW-2006*, 167–170.

Lampe, C., Ellison, N., & Steinfield, C. (2007). A familiar Face(book): Profile elements as signals in an online social network. *Proceedings of the SIGCHI Conference on Human Factors in Computing Systems* (435–444). New York: ACM Press. doi:10.1145/1240624.1240695

Lee, J. W. Y., Kim, B., Lee, T. L., & Kim, M. S. (2012). Uncovering the Use of Facebook During the Exchange Program. *China Media Research*, *8*(4), 62–76.

Lenhart, A., & Madden, M. (2007). Teens, Privacy and Online Social Networks: How teens manage their online identities and personal information in the age of Myspace. *Pew Internet and American Life Project Report*. Retrieved from http://www.pewinternet.org/files/old-media/Files/Reports/2007/PIP_Teens_Privacy_SNS_Report_Final.pdf.pdf

Mason, R., & Rennie, F. (2007). Using Web 2.0 for learning in the community. *The Internet and Higher Education*, *10*(3), 196–203. doi:10.1016/j.iheduc.2007.06.003

Facebook Penetration Growth. (2013). Miniwatts Marketing Group. Retrieved from http://www.internetworldstats.com/facebook.htm

Mossberger, K., Tolbert, C., & McNeal, R. (2008). *Digital Citizenship: The Internet, Society, and Participation*. Cambridge, MA: The MIT Press.

Muniz, A. M. Jr, & Schau, H. J. (2011). How to inspire value-laden collaborative consumer-generated content. *Business Horizons*, *54*(3), 209–217. doi:10.1016/j.bushor.2011.01.002

Nie, N. H. (2001). Sociability, interpersonal relations, and the Internet: Reconciling conflicting findings. *The American Behavioral Scientist*, *45*(3), 420–435. doi:10.1177/00027640121957277

Norris, P. (2002). The Bridging and Bonding Role of Online Communities. *The Harvard International Journal of Press/Politics*, *7*(3), 3–13. doi:10.1177/1081180X0200700301

Paxton, P. (1999). Is social capital declining in the United States? A multiple indicator assessment. *American Journal of Sociology*, *105*(1), 88–127. doi:10.1086/210268

Preston, P., Cawley, A., & Metykova, M. (2007). Broadband and Rural Areas in the EU: Recent Research and Implications. *Telecommunications Policy*, *31*(6-7), 389–400. doi:10.1016/j.telpol.2007.04.003

Quinn, R. (2014). An analysis of Facebook as a Communication Tool in Community Development [Student Research Paper]. University College Dublin.

Rennie, F., & Mason, R. (2005). Bits or Baubles: The opportunities for broadband to add value to education and learning. *Scottish Affairs*, *53*(1), 31–47. doi:10.3366/scot.2005.0055

Resnick, P. (2001). Beyond bowling together: Sociotechnical capital. In J. Carroll (Ed.), HCI in the New Millennium (247–272). Boston, MA: Addison-Wesley.

Ryan, V., Kerry, D., Agnitsch, A., Zhao, L., & Mullick, R. (2005). Making Sense of Voluntary Participation: A Theoretical Synthesis. *Rural Sociology*, *70*(3), 287–313. doi:10.1526/0036011054831198

Sarantakos, S. (2005). *Social research* (3rd ed.). Basingstoke: Palgrave Macmillan.

Solis, B. (2010). Facebook Connects 500 Million People: Defines a New Era of Digital Society. Retrieved from http://www.briansolis.com/2010/07/facebook-connects-500-million-people-defining-a-new-era-of-digital-society/

Ireland Facebook Statistics. (2014). Social Bakers. Retrieved from http://www.socialbakers.com/facebook-statistics/ireland

Sproull, L., & Kiesler, S. (2005). Public Volunteer Work on the Internet. In W. Dutton, B. Kahin, R. O'Callaghan, & A. Wyckoff (Eds.), *Transforming Enterprise*. Cambridge, MA: The MIT Press.

Stern, M., & Dillman, D. (2006). Community Participation, Social Ties, and Use of the Internet. *City & Community*, *5*(4), 409–424. doi:10.1111/j.1540-6040.2006.00191.x

Stern, M. J., Adams, A. E., & Boase, J. (2011). Rural Community Participation, Social Networks, and Broadband Use: Examples from Localized and National Survey Data. *Agricultural and Resource Economics Review*, *40*(2), 158–171.

Townsend, A. (2001). The Internet and the Rise of the New Network Cities, 1969–1999. *Environment and Planning. B, Planning & Design*, *28*(1), 39–58. doi:10.1068/b2688

Walsh, K. (2010, October 21). *New Ideas, New Directions*. Proceedings of the Pobal All-Island Conference. Boyne Valley Hotel, Drogheda. KW Research & Associates Ltd.

Warren, M. (2007). The digital vicious cycle: Links between social disadvantage and digital exclusion in rural areas. *Telecommunications Policy*, *31*(6–7), 374–388. doi:10.1016/j.telpol.2007.04.001

Wellman, B., Haase, A. Q., Witte, J., & Hampton, K. (2001). Does the Internet increase, decrease, or supplement social capital? Social networks, participation, and community commitment. *The American Behavioral Scientist*, *45*(3), 436–456. doi:10.1177/00027640121957286

Wilkinson, K. (1991). *The Community in Rural America*. New York: Greenwood Press.

Wilson, J., & Musick, M. (1997). Who Cares? Toward an Integrated Theory of Volunteer Work. *American Sociological Review*, *62*(5), 694–713. doi:10.2307/2657355

Wilson, J. (2000). Volunteering. *Annual Review of Sociology*, *26*(1), 215–240. doi:10.1146/annurev.soc.26.1.215

Wilson, R. E., Gosling, S. D., & Graham, L. G. T. (2012). A Review of Facebook Research in the Social Sciences.

Yong-Yeol, A., Han, S., Kwak, H., Moon, S., & Jeong, H. (2007). Analysis of topological characteristics of huge online social networking services. *Proceedings of the 16th international conference on World Wide Web* (pp. 835-844). New York, NY, USA

KEY TERMS AND DEFINITIONS

Broadband: Broadband constitutes any form of high-speed Internet access.

Civic Engagement: Civic engagement is the process whereby the local community are facilitated to become involved in making decisions about the issues that affect them. It is the local community coming together to be a collective source of change.

Community Facebook Page: A social media application which communities may use as a virtual community notice board. A community Facebook page can be a resource for community members and can benefit a community by keeping everybody informed of local events which are of concern and making it easier for community members to engage and support local activities, organisations and businesses.

Digital Divide: The term Digital divide refers to the gap between those who have access to information and communication technology (ICT) and the skills to use ICT and those who do not have the access or skills to use these technologies within a geographic area, society or community. In the context of this chapter, it refers to differences between rural and urban communities.

Rural Community Development: The process of helping rural communities to strengthen themselves and develop towards their full potential. Good communication contributes to successful collaborative efforts and transformation of communities which in time help to bring about social change among marginalised or vulnerable groups.

Social Media: Social media refer to the diverse range of web-based highly interactive tools that allow users to create, share, exchange and comment among themselves in virtual communities and networks.

Web 1.0: Web 1.0 was the first generation of the world wide web, also referred to as the read-only web. Web 1.0 began as an information place for businesses to broadcast their information and only allowed users to search for information and read it.

Web 2.0: Web 2.0 allows users to contribute content to the web. The essential difference between Web 1.0 and Web 2.0 is that content creators were few in Web 1.0. In contrast, any participant can be a content creator in Web 2.0. This has given rise to 'Social media'.

Chapter 21
ICT: A Magic Wand for Social Change in Rural India

Orance Mahaldar
Ghent University, Belgium

Kinkini Bhadra
Jadavpur University, India

ABSTRACT

The concept of automation was first seeded worldwide by Industrial Revolution. Liberalization and privatization has contributed much in the welcome of updated and upgraded technology in India. World Wide Web being the core connector of earth rightly supports Mc Luhan's concept of the 'Global Village'. ICT- Information and Communication Technology is an initiative cum phenomenon that is taken on Public-Private Partnership (PPP) in order to build a bridge between the two sections of the society (technology haves and have nots) so that it is accessible to all. e-Governance, e-Health and e-Commerce are some of its applications. India has witnessed a number of successful E- Projects. Nonetheless, the argument of social exclusion, questions on technology support communication and information dissemination is still on. The article intends to throw light on various aspects keeping in line with the ICT projects in India, the type of ICT usage and a comparison between the already established communication models.

INTRODUCTION

The seeds of Industrial Revolution and technological innovation have grown up to spread its roots much strongly in the 21st Century in the form of telecommunication, computation and World Wide Web. Landing in the technology driven era where automation is the central concept; distances are shortened and spaces are virtually killed while paving a way to a more transformed and transparent world. Communication technology has made it possible to propagate information in a much faster and easier way. This has enabled to build a society enriched with information – "Information Society".

Information society is one of the key terms that describe the modern world we live in today. It is said to be an outcome of the industrial and post-industrial society (Sarrocco, n.d.), where the creation, distribution, use and integration of information is recognized as an active political, cultural and economic activity in order to enhance

DOI: 10.4018/978-1-4666-8598-7.ch021

participation and promote social inclusion (DESA, 2009). But information dissemination alone is not the magic solution of problems like hunger or poverty. In fact 'Right information at the right time' is the key to solution (Chhavi, 2008). Be it the cost of seeds and other raw materials required by farmers or the recent health care planning by the government, that plans to provide free health check up for expecting mothers; information stand alone is not important, but dissemination of it at the right time such that the end users can utilize the information and benefit themselves from the same is vital. Rural population in India are undereducated in terms of the policies, plans and programmes taken to aid them of facilities and amenities required for sustainable development and better living.

Information society concerns the use of information for societal upliftment, social control, management of innovation in order to ensure a better quality of living, break the boundaries of community and ensure better and organized work, that also finds application in solving rural problems of poverty, inequality, illiteracy and environmental degradation (Rahman, 2008). Therefore, information deals with human intellect. In a nutshell, information society combines human intelligence and technical innovation together to give rise to the concept of 'technology-support development' where the 'way to use' a technology is focused at. It can be put in two ways- One, technology providers make use of the right technology at the right place (also referred to as 'context' by some experts), i.e. at the planning and execution level. Two, the end users make use of the technology for their own benefits (with reference to e-literacy). For example, installation of kiosks and computers in rural areas are not enough until it is the right technology for the purpose targeted and the target mass is capable of using them for own benefits.

A quick sneak peak in the history of social & technical development unearths the fact of the matter of the long going debate of technology supporting development. The first seed of development paradigm, as highly known today among the academicians, is the modernization theory or the dominant paradigm of development. This era was marked by technological innovation, capitalistic capability and experimentation to pave the way towards an economic boost. Advocates of the theory- Wilber Schramm (1964), Everett M. Rogers (1969) and Lerner (1958) greatly believed in technology bringing development (Fig- 1). Some of the primary features of the industrial society could be categorized as power production, increase of per capita production, high mass consumption, human liberalization and maximization of profit. However the negative peripheries include strikes, labour movement, urbanization and unemployment (Masuda, 1980).

Figure 1. The above model describes the course of development according to modernization theory.

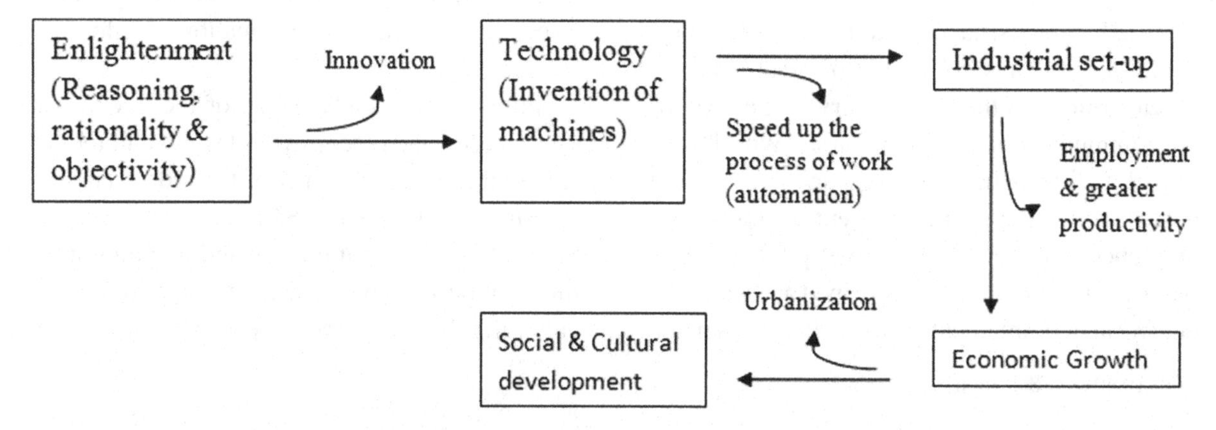

The process of innovation in the West eventually penetrated in the developing nation like India, where application of technological innovation can be rightly segregated in two forms:

- **Setting up of Industries:** For better & speedy productivity leading to economic development and growth of
- **Mass Communication Technologies:** For reaching the mass people and encouraging the implementation of the Right to Information Act.

Setting up of industries provided employment and improved the quality of living; while mass communication technologies made it possible to diffuse information into every layer of the society. Another important goal which is achieved with the development of mass media technology in India is less dependency on foreign sources of news or biased news[1].

ICT in Indian Context

The journey of technology as a catalyst to social change was started in India by proper, systematic and equal dissemination of news and information. Later it was relayed forward with the help of several experiments done with Television and Radio. Both the government owned mediums were used successfully in educating a brief segment of people living in remote villages on an experimental basis (*SITE* & *KHEDA* projects, 1975). The economic liberalization in India opened the door to several Multinational Companies (MNCs) and 100% FDI in selected sectors boosted the journey of technology in India. Internet being one of the greatest inventions and innovations of the modern society, standing in 2014, Information and Communication Technology (ICT) has taken over most of the charge as more and more private companies as well as the government sector takes aid of ICT at domestic level in the form of e-Governance, e-commerce and e-health to bring up the information revolution close to the people of rural and remote areas (Thomas, 2009).

Even in the present scenario, 70% of India depends on agricultural source of income. Thereby, agriculture plays a vital role in India's economy in terms of poverty mitigation and employment generation, and contributes up to a quarter of national income (Siriginidi, 2009). Rural poverty is a complex phenomenon. The idea of several factors made responsible for rural poverty, like economic, social and environmental (Reimer, 1997; Bosworth & Atterton, 2012), make 'rural poverty' more complex as a concept and problem. (Giles, Bosworth & Willett, 2013). ICT is a fuel to global economy (Siriginidi, 2009; Chhavi, 2008). But its share in the recent past saw a steep declination from 56.5% in 1951 to 24.3% in 2002. The agricultural workforce too saw the retardation from 76% in 1961 to 60% in 2000 and with the continuous growth of the population of 15.5 million and existing government polices is would be very difficult to develop rural areas successfully. Therefore, new plans and programmes should be developed in order to keep pace with the recent changes, install 'innovations of information technologies' (ICTs) with active participation from development organizations (Siriginidi, 2009). ICT is the new hope that can eradicate problems of rural poverty, inequality and environmental degradation (Bhatnagar, 2000).

In a country like India where 3/4th of the population still depends on agrarian source of income, introduction of innovations of technology and digitalization has created a digital divide between the technology haves and have-nots as most of the people are either uninformed and technology illiterate or they do not have the purchasing power to avail the same. Also, in the developing scenario, it is greatly important for a country like India to penetrate information at every level in order to minimize communication lag and foster transparency in each of the three tiers of the government.

Another important thing that also became necessary to develop is the logical reasoning and power to differentiate between the right and the wrong. ICT serves the bridge between them and tries to teach the rural mass how to drive the technology for their own benefit. This is one of the features of information society where it advocates the concept of technology being driven by human intellect and for their own benefit and not the other way round.

ICT avoids dependency on technology and favours development support communication. Rural poverty with reference to India is a complex phenomenon and a dominant approach to solve it can only cut down the ambition. (Bhatnagar, 2000). Development Support Communication- the word and concept was coined and ideated by one of the communication scientist Robert Erskine Childers (1976). It was re-postulated and recognized that development communication is an offshoot of dominant paradigm where economic development forms the main route to development. But later it was found that, in Indian scenario, sustainable growth and development was important over/ at par with economic development as most of the rural India is deprived of the modern facilities and stay in poor conditions of live (Melkote & Steeves, 2001).

But ICT alone cannot solve all rural problems. It requires infrastructure to establish distribution channels. Also, it is important to reduce costs of reaching to the people (Siriginidi, 2009). Hence, The rural ICT applications mostly tries to offer the services of governmental bodies like district administration, cooperative union and the state and central bodies to the citizens at their door step. Steps have also been taken to smoother the procedure by implementation of several Government- Citizen (GC) e-Governance pilot projects. Some of the numerous factors of ICT for which it is being highly recommended today may be summarized as:

Figure 2. DSC Model vs DC Model

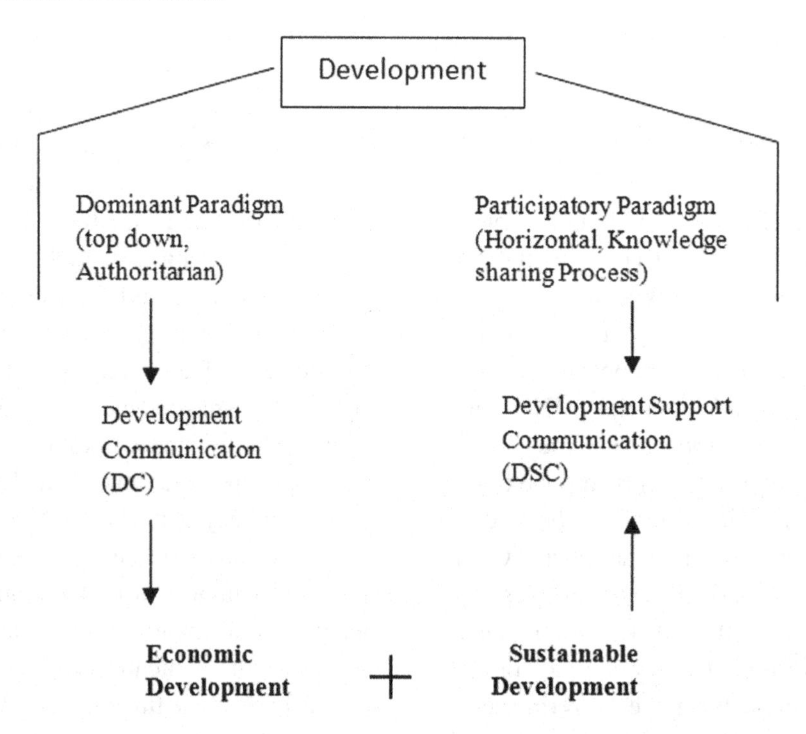

1. It supports participatory method of communication which is highly preferred as a developmental model in rural India.
2. It is cost-effective, user friendly and efficient.
3. It is a people inclusive medium and involves knowledge sharing process.
4. It intends to promote the transparency between public and the government.
5. It acts to build an information society by active learning process and development of human intellect.
6. It helps to build true democracy by encouraging mass participation.
7. It helps enhancement of revenue for the government and the service provider.
8. It supports Right to Information Act and the universal right to freedom of Speech and Expression.

Information and Communication Technology (ICT) in India has spread its tentacles through Reliance Infocom's roll out of low-cost mobile cellular phones, numerous civil society based initiatives aimed at establishing affordable access to information and knowledge and Village Public Telephones (VPTs) to its enabling the computerization of land records such as the *Bhoomi* project in Karnataka. Some other similar projects include that of *APSWAN* (Andhra Pradesh), *Sustainable Access in Rural India* (*SARI* in Tamil Nadu), *Akshaya* Project (Kerala), *SETU* (Maharashtra), *Gyan Ganga* (Gujarat) and *WBSWAN*- a government-to-citizen portal (West Bengal), *LOKMITRA* Project (Himachal Pradesh) to name a few. ICT has also spread wings in the health sector with projecs like '*Solidarity and action against the HIV infection in India*' or *SAATHII* (2000), *Sisu Samrakshak* or *SSK* (2000) and *Apollo Telemedicine* (2000). India accounts for 60% of the ICTs projects in Asia tracked by The World Resources Institute (Thomas, 2009).

The present article would discuss about the success of the ICT in India keeping account of its type of usage which is of primary importance in this matter. The chapter would highly discuss the ways and features that made it greatly penetrating by doing a thorough case-study based on the past and ongoing E-projects in India. Since the success of ICT is recognized today, thereby analyzing, comparing and contrasting the model of ICT with that of several communication models in mass communication like- Shannon & Weaver, Newcomb and Gerbner will give a different angle to observe it. The chapter would also include in itself the problems and hindrances (both from social and individual perspective) faced by ICT in its acceptance among the masses (if any).

BACKGROUND

To move on with the article it is important to define ICT for better understanding. A proper and apposite definition will help conceptualize the whole term in terms of application and improved academic understanding.

Information and Communication Technology *aka* ICT also referred to as IT or Information Technology previously, is the most modern and upgraded technology used in order to foster better communication and information dissemination for the joint purpose of education, health and rural empowerment in a developing society especially in the rural sector. ICT is a technology that deals with information gathering and dissemination to storing and presenting of data in the desired format (Ifueko, Omoigui, Okauru, 2011; Accra, 2012). ICT comprises of elements of processes which link different entities and locations leading to compression of space, coordination in time, and globalization (Castells, 2000; Sahay et al., 2003, Hayes & Westrup, 2012, Niall & Chris, 2012). It may also be noted that ICT, in other terms may also be referred to as computer or computer technology and network while including television and radio also (Chandler, Daniel; Munday, Rod, Iaugust 2012; Accra, 2012). ICT is a broader concept that comprises of three main things- services, applications and technologies. ICT serves by providing sole or a combination of telecom services such as telephony, mobile telephony, fax and computer services like internet, e-mail, file transfers, etc. The applications of ICT cover video conferencing, teleworking, e-commerce, e-health, distance learning, management information systems (MIS), stocktaking, etc. Technologies used by ICT in providing the services range from old technologies such as radio and TV to new ones such as cellular mobile communications (Siriginidi, 2009).

ICT therefore has three key terms: *Technology, Information* and *Communication*. All the three terms in ICT are highly interlinked with each other and are also interdependent aiming for a certain fixed role. For example: Technologies like television and radio started to be used as a part of developmental project since its early advent with projects like *SITE* (1975) and *KHEDA* (1975) for television and various other projects related to health and agriculture through radio were broadcasted. Counting on the results of these experiments it was concluded that these technologies had effect on the target people and that it could, with well structured and planned programmes, may serve a social purpose and help eradicate rural problems and issues. It was then predicted that radio and television had high capability to create change in the society and can penetrate at the grassroots level. Since then development programmes were structured keeping in mind the acceptability in the rural sections of the society and were also designed skillfully and tactfully. In recent days, internet has formed a World Wide Web which unifies every individual and also exposes to innumerable ideas and information. After The United Nations has already declared access to the internet as another basic human right, The Govt. of India's National Telecom Policy too envision the implementation of 'Right to Broadband' scenario by the year 2020 (Ganapathy, 2014). Also, in the recent endeavour to improve ICT services according to NeGP 2006 (National e-Governance Plan), Government of India (GI) has aimed to transform all the Government activities from manual to computerized system (Sanyal et al, 2014).

Information can be interpreted as a message or better said, the content of any message, which is usually encoded by the speaker and then processed through a well recognized channel to reach the receiver in its understandable form. The channel may be of various types that includes verbal, telephonic and written forms. Information encoding is an important part and should be done carefully in case of rural program designing. The message should be in favour of the target audience and therefore must be understandable for them. One of the significant hindrances in the way of rural communication is the language. Since, computers talk in universal language English; therefore it does not favour rural understanding. In order to enable rural understanding, soon options to convert into language were allowed by Microsoft and started practicing. This created a revolution on its own as the language barrier was overcome. Information is a supporting hand to carry forward basic human right which includes right to information and freedom of expression (Chhavi, 2008). Therefore, uniform information dissemination is the key to democracy and information empowerment is essential for successful democracy (Siriginidi, 2009). Social exclusion is much deep a problem. It marks the exclusion of people from a range of benefits, access and services which mark the basic human rights in the modern society from exchanging (Commission of the European Communities 1993; Magno, 2014).

But for successful and effective *communication* there are two more important things: targeted decoding of the message or proper and correct understanding of the meaning along with the positive feedback mechanism. Medium has a close relationship with message interpretation or 'Medium is the message' (McLuhan, 1964) and are therefore symbiotic in nature. Marshall McLuhan's concept of medium was broad and he put together that it was the medium, which 'shaped and controlled the scale and form of human association and action'. Therefore it might be concluded that medium of communication should be chosen very carefully as it is very much specific for a defined purpose and rural communication is that defined area.

ICT plays a major role in nation's politics, economy, social and cultural development (Siriginidi, 2009; Chhavi, 2008). It is not just limited to rural development alone. ICT has changed our lives from the way we do business, shopping, and do banking to access information, get entertained and communicate with people (Chhavi, 2008). Role of ICT in both established medium like radio, TV, video, computer disc, etc. and emerging medium like internet, wireless and broadband as a powerful tool is responsible for speedy scaling up and inter-linkage of development interventions and its outcomes (Siriginidi, 2009). ICT has an integrated relation with human rights also, i.e. it supports the freedom of expression and right to information according to Article 19 of the Universal Declaration of Human Rights. (Siriginidi, 2009; Chhavi, 2008)

However, the unification of specific technology for the transmission of specific information will lead to effective communication in rural areas which may act as the weapon for social change in India. ICT in the 21st century is one such magic wand for social change (Fig- 3).

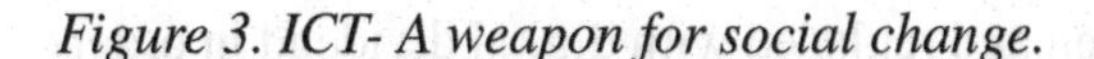

Figure 3. ICT- A weapon for social change.

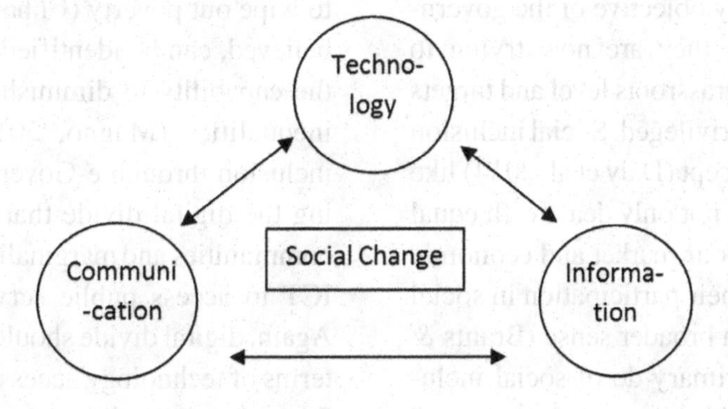

ICT or Information and Communication Technology is a special extension of IT or Information Technology which deals with the skills of bridging the communication gap between the urban and rural area through effective and structured plans and programs. The World Wide Web with high speed internet plans is now installed even in the remotest villages of Gujarat and Andhra Pradesh in India. ICT negates social exclusion and supports social inclusion, participation and democracy by bringing transparency of information in each tier of the administration. ICT helps upgrade the rural mass to match the urban tech savvy society and also to make them e-Literate. ICT helps them to be 'future ready' in the globalised world.

Eradicating the Digital Divide

Digitalization is inherent with the concept of *social exclusion*. Technology has its own advantages that embed our daily life including the way of living, but not all the citizens get close to its friendly assistance on equal share. This unequal distribution of Information and Communication technology disapproves equal participation in social, economic and cultural forum. This can be briefly called as social exclusion. The problem is not to be measured just in economic terms, but it also includes unequal rights in education, health, housing, and access to services (Commission of the European Communities 1993; Magno, 2014). Therefore, we see that social exclusion has a multi disciplinary approach. (Daly et al. 2014).

The concept of social exclusion gained notice only in the 1990s. It is related to the lack of engagement in governance processes. (Magno, 2014). Segment suffering from social exclusion experience intricacy in claiming a range of citizen rights, which also includes access to adequate health care and education. This can be attributed to their weak social integration and incapacity to participate in public decision-making (Shortall, 2008; Magno, 2014). In social exclusion, poverty must be seen as the refusal of basic capabilities and not just the lack of income (Sen, 1999). Exclusion in the information age can be identified in two ways- (i) When a person is not connected to the digital network. (ii) When a person is unable to participate in the debates and discussion related to politics and public discourse (Magno, 2014); while another side of exclusion in the information age can emanate from existing social and cultural circumstances along with institutional and political factors (Zheng & Walsham, 2008; Magno, 2014). Therefore, it can be said that social exclusion is caused by irregular employment, gender, ethnicity, disability or ill health, and lack of opportunities for participation, along with low income.

The concept of social inclusion can therefore be seen in terms of underprivileged people acquiring rights, access, and benefits from improved education, health, governance services, and digital connectivity (Magno, 2014). Social inclusion is the primary objective of the government organizations as they are now trying to implement ICT at the grassroots level and targets to empower the underprivileged. Social inclusion is a double layered concept (Daly et al. 2014) like social exclusion which not only deals with equal participation in the labour market and economic life but also includes their participation in social and cultural issues in a broader sense (Brants & Frissen, 2003). The primary do of social inclusion is to create equitable access to Internet and other technologies. It is also very important to focus on another factor which is 'context', i.e. the framework required by the technologies to alleviate key problems of development in rural areas (Bhatnagar, 2014). Social inclusion is required and preferred for it gives the person the capability to think and make his own decisions. In a developing and democratic country like India, it becomes very necessary for every citizen to take part in economic as well as political activities for national benefit. Without being able to keep updated with the technological changes of the modern world, 70% of the total population (who reside in the rural structure) would be vulnerable to economic and social crisis.

Digital divide is another offshoot of social exclusion that again can be related to a dichotomous concept and has multiple levels (Brants & Frissen, 2003). Digital divide is directly proportional to the inability to use or access of technology (Archmann & Guiffart, 2014). However there is another argument which highlights the fact that digital divide or digital exclusion may be a voluntary choice of an individual also (Bhalla & Lapeyre, 1997), whereby exclusion may reflect un-intention to participate, negligence towards technological use, social and cultural taboos that reject interaction with the upgraded world, patterns of interests or a contractual relationship between actors or 'distortions' to the system, such as discrimination, market failures and unenforced rights. Therefore, the much argued digital divide needs to be diminished and replaced with digital dividend in order to wipe out poverty (Chhavi, 2008). ICT, as it is believed, can be identified as the tool which has the capability to diminish spatial and temporal inequalities (Magno, 2014). Fostering social inclusion through e-Governance requires bridging the digital divide that prevent slow income communities and marginalized groups from using ICT to access public services (Magno, 2014). Again, digital divide should not be seen simply in terms of technology access. It is a wider concept. Several social, political, institutional, and cultural conditions should be considered in understanding why particular communities are deprived in gaining access, developing content and using ICT (Warschauer, 2003). The digital divide is a long time concern of the government and internet being recognized as essential for economic competitiveness, government services, citizen participation and engagement, social inclusion and learning; is gaining priorities in government policies (Daly et al. 2014). There are international evidences that authenticate the negative effect of digital divide in exacerbating inequality by failing to equip its audience with the needed skills and other personal characteristics required to pave way to the knowledge society. Therefore, it implies that the divide can reduce the life chances of the disadvantaged, reducing learning opportunities and chances for career advancement and adversely impacting on access to government information and services (Selwyn, 2002; Daly et al. 2014). But on the other hand, there is also a group of policy makers who believe that the diffusion of internet can alone lessen the digital divide (Daly et al. 2014). Therefore, a paradigm shift is required in the sense that understanding and recognizing the problems of the poor and then enacting the best technology innovation for the purpose would be the correct way to solve any part of the problem instead of vice versa (Mc Namar, 2003; Bhatnagar, 2014).

In order to fulfil the target which is to eradicate the poverty, requirement of third person involvement becomes highly necessary in the form of Opinion Leaders (Lazarsfled, Berelson & Gaudet, 1944; Katz & Lazarsfled, 1955). They together postulated the Two-step Flow of Information, where it was predicted that the rural mass do not readily accept the norms of the urban society and thereby rejects the ideas coming from the same. With the help of opinion leaders it was much easier to reach and get connected to the rural mass. Opinion leaders are generally the most influential people in a village like headmaster, village doctor, *sarpanch*, etc. If ICT is one such taboo, then it can be well introduced with the help of opinion leaders via NGOs and Integrated Rural Development plans by the public sector. This is also one of the way by which participation of the rural mass can be encouraged and made successfully acceptable. In the recent ICT initiatives, the role of opinion leaders has been kept in mind to get high rated success in the developmental programs.

The role of ICT in rural development do not just relate to the ease in daily life with e-Literacy, but it also deals with other phenomenal factors like awareness to social, political, environment and health threats, ability to take own decision, develop critical thinking and opinion formation and thus resulting into equal participation, attitude and personality formation, building self confidence by involving into discussion forums and taking part in dialogic communication. ICT in this way enables smooth functioning of the administration by enabling horizontal knowledge sharing process and vertical flow of information.

Digitalization comes with yet another concept called *convergence*. The technology used in ICT fairly involves internet as the primary tool. Most of the ICT devices are for multipurpose usage like mobile phones, laptops, tabs, computers and cable television networks offering phone services, internet television and mergers between media and telecommunication firms (Singh & Raja, 2010). These devices find an integrated approach for communication by enabling speedy access to all types of information in the local or native language. ICT convergence plays a promising positive role in the fields of education, health, medicine, finance and government (Huang, Guo, Xie, & Wu, 2012). ICT convergence in health sector and medical industry can help people from the less developed areas gain access to superior health care resources worldwide. With ICT one can take the aid from medical expert sitting miles away through HD video equipments and medical apparatus that may pass on vital datas from medical devices at a lightning fast speed. In case of education sector ICT convergence can take to the world's biggest library for information as well as provide distance learning facilities from the world's top most universities. Similarly, ICT convergence finds its applications in other sectors related to finance and economy too.

ICT, another form of digitalization, aims to form e-democracy as a part of its successful implementation and usage marked by political engagement and open discussion among educated mass to help create a space of convergence in which all the citizens are enabled to recognize themselves as co-working for a common deed (Molinari, McPherson & Singh, 2014). E- Democracy is the new horizon… the outcome of specially designed plans and programmes where the scattered mass gets accumulated, each with motivation and an opinion that constructs a true democracy. It is the individual level motivation that can lead to collective movement of the population for future establishment of a better public administration and knowledge society. E-democracy is free from constraints of conflict, orthodox ideas and leads to innovation and better future. E- Democracy, as the authoritative source like OECD says in an often quoted 2004 publication, can be achieved in terms of e-participation, whose objectives are as follows (Macintosh, 2004):

- Reaching out and engaging a broader audience of active participants;
- Support participation through a range of technologies to cater for the diverse technical and communicative skills of citizens;
- Provide relevant information in a format that is both more accessible and more understandable to the target audience to enable more informed contributions.
- Engage with a wider audience to enable deeper contributions and support deliberative debate.

E-Governance: It is the concept shaped through the policy of e-Government which essentially targets the use of information technologies (typically the internet) to foster the delivery of government information and services, re-structure administrative procedures, and enhance citizen participation (Mahizhnan, 2014). The term governance is also a 'goal oriented process which denotes the outcomes of interaction of government, public services and citizens throughout the political process' (Das, 2010). It is also recognized as a set of 'technology mediated process' that are changing the ways of public service delivery and also the interaction between the citizen and the government (Kate, 2002). Thereby the right technological use will result in bringing social upliftment and skill development (Figure 4).

ICT: THE MAGIC WAND FOR SOCIAL CHANGE IN RURAL INDIA

Information and Communication Technology in the 21st Century has created a sensation by showcasing its vast use in various fields like health, finance, administration, politics, education and several others. Not just in name, but also in deed did ICT become one of the important bridges to level down the gap between the rural and urban areas. With proper planning and strategies along with the merge of the private and the public partnerships, ICT flourished in Indian rural sector within a short span of time. Villagers started accepting soon the technology as their friend in their daily life as it helped them in greater productivity and yield of crops through e-krishi and other similar agriculture programs.

Through effective changing of government policies and increasing public- private partnerships, a lot of improvements are carried out in effective e-Governance programs (Jamaluddin, 2013). Application of ICT can be done in diverse platform; from accelerating information dissemination, improve efficiency of public services and increase the transparency and accountability of government administration to reduce corruption and facilitate citizen participation in local governance. But full potential of ICT in terms of its

Figure 4. Information dynamics in social uplift (Rahman, 2008)

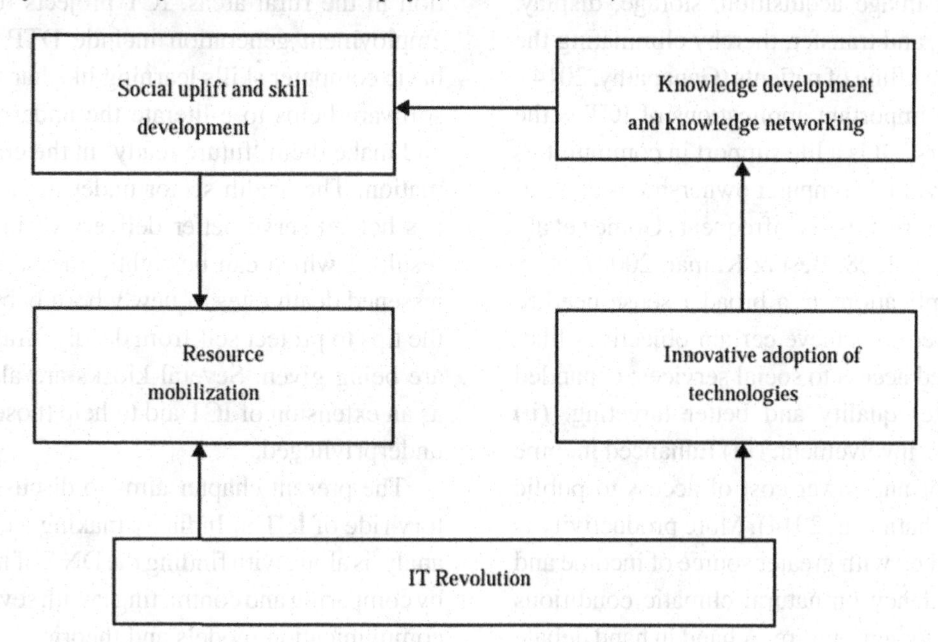

application and usage as a catalyst for development is yet to be reached (Bhatnagar, 2014). ICT costing was cumbersome. But the rapid smooth technological advancement is making it more affordable to reach a place where the high cost will no more be the biggest barrier in bridging the digital divide. Government as a part of successful ICT implementation has correctly used the same for proper execution of internal efficiency and improved delivery of services (Bhatnagar & Singh, 2010; Bhatnagar, 2014). Some of the most successful ICT projects in India owe their credits to several partnerships. For example, the incredible success of e-Choupal is one such example where experts from their respective fields came in to make it a successful mission. In e-Choupal, ICT agents provide the infrastructure (lab or warehouses), government provided information like weather forecasts and commodity prices from government mandis, while experts from Universities were reached for their valuable advice all throughout the implementation process (Bhatnagar, 2014).

India is the first address, when it comes to experimentation with ICT for sustainable development (Bhatnagar, 2014). Internet plays a vital role in agribusiness leading to new market places and also as an information resource (Jamaluddin, 2013). e-Commerce has found its way successfully to agriculture. Both the B2B and B2C categories of transactions have used Internet in Agriculture, Remote service, and Maintenance referred to as agribusiness –to–agribusiness (A2A) and agribusiness-to-grower (A2G).Therefore, the participation is directly linked with the adoption o internet mutually by both the ends- buyers and sellers (Jamaluddin, 2013). m- Governance hold a major division in the National e-Governance Plan which establish the exceptional growth and development in ICT (Ganapathy, 2014). With the motto of providing high quality and affordable healthcare to people irrespective of their financial, technological and geographical reach, Apollo started with Apollo Telemedicine whereby patients health are investigated, monitored and treated via image acquisition, storage, display, processing, and transfer, thereby eliminating the physical travelling of patients (Ganapathy, 2014). One of the important applications of ICT is the "Telecenters". It is a life support in communities where individual computer ownership is uncommon and internet use is infrequent (Gomez et al., 1999; Heeks, 2008; Best & Kumar, 2008).

ICT applications in a broader sense need to be developed to achieve certain objectives like- (i) Improved access to social services; expanded reach, better quality and better targeting. (ii) Community involvement. (iii) Enhanced income for the poor and lower cost of access to public services (Bhatnagar, 2014). More productivity is directly linked with greater source of income and less dependency on natural climatic conditions favourable for agriculture. A hand in hand debate which follows at parallel argues the dependency of technology vs dependency on natural climate? The dependency on natural climatic conditions for yield of crops often curtailed their profit with huge loss. Thereby acceptance of technological aid seemed to be a better option. Services like weather report, land conditions, use of fertilizers and very importantly the actual rates in the market helped the farmers. Apart from this ICT use in the field of education and health is beyond parallel. As discussed earlier, rural population is very orthodox in nature and they tend to reject any foreign ideas and imagination readily. In order to gain trust and acceptance, messages and programmes were designed just in the way best acceptable. For example, most of the girl children are not allowed to move out of home for education purpose. ICT, with distance learning programmes made it possible to get higher education sitting from home itself. Even the whole library is digitalized today in order to make it accessible from any nook and corner of the world. The prime key area of ICT that makes it this much accessible is the affordability. Government of India has taken great initiatives in rural development projects by installing devices that would impart high speed internet connection in the rural areas. ICT projects relating to employment generation include DTP learning, basic computer skills learning like hardware and software helps to e-literate the underprivileged and make them 'future ready' in the era of automation. The health sector under the aid of ICT has helped serve better delivery of infants, the result of which can be rightly measured by the lessened death rates of newly born babies. Also, the tips to protect self from deadly viral diseases are being given. Several kiosks are also set up as an extension of ICT aid to help those who are underprivileged.

The present chapter aims to discuss the victory ride of ICT in India by making a case study analysis along with finding the DNA of its success by comparing and contrasting it with several other communication models and theories.

Case Study

The chapter aims to see the success of ICT in India for which some of the important projects are being discussed and analyzed here. This analysis of the several important projects will help infer the effective penetration of ICT in rural India and the overview will highly serve to get to an anawer of one of the objectives. The primary projects discussed in here are The *Akshaya* Project (Kerala), *E-Gram* (Gujarat), *Gyan Ganga* (Gujarat) and *WBSWAN* (West Bengal).

The Akshaya Project

This is one of the biggest ICT projects that India has ever witnessed. Introduced in Malappuram district of Kerala, this initiative soon spread its web to the other parts of the state. The high success project was the first of its kind which extended the 'district-wide e-literacy' in the state. The project included the largest Internet Protocol (IP) based wireless networks in the world to make Malappuram India's first E-literate district. In Phase I of the project 100% e-literacy was achieved in 8 districts of the state. The project has conducted one of the largest awareness missions for the need of computer literacy and has reached over 3.6 million people to fulfil its mission of generating e-literacy awareness. Multiple computer access centres has been set up throughout the state, primarily funded and run by the state government, leading to a colossal wireless communication infrastructure which has opened up multiple opportunities and wide range of services. Prof. Kenneth Keniston, Founder and Director of MIT India Programme commented on the project and added his valuable views on it:

There are many good projects sponsored by State Governments and NGOs which are admirable; but nowhere has the kind of vision and strategy been as demonstrable as in Akshaya. Neither do I think any other state has the wherewithal for accomplishing these because without literacy, without commitment on the part of the people concerned, without a certain level of social justice, these things would be very difficult to achieve.

The services that are conducted by the project include (i) e-Pay: Electronic paying system helps the online payment of monthly bills such as electricity, land phone, drinking water, university fees etc. sitting in the comfort of home. (ii) e-Krishi: It primarily aimed to help and provide online agricultural information to rural people, particularly farmers. Through this program the farmers were made literate of the several modern techniques that can be up brought for better growth and productivity of crops. It also helped to provide the price and values of seeds and other trading requirements in order to help them overcome fraud situations. (iii) e-Vidya: Vidya means knowledge and e- Vidya dealt with electronic advanced education courses on Information Technology (IT) for e-literates and others. (iv) e-Ticketing: It helped to pre book online train, flight and bus ticket reservations over internet. (v) Village Kiosks were set up aiming for transparent collectorate program to facilitate citizen- government interface and minimize the gaps in communication by access to information.

"ICT accessibility for anyone and everyone" was the primary concern for the project which was carried out with much success. ICT accessibility for all sections of people had led to better lifestyles, information accessibility and transparency in governance and welfare programmes funded by the state government. The project has resulted in considerable socio-economic growth for the state. The project, as of now, is being conducted in other districts as well like Thiruvanathapuram, Kollam, Alappuzha, Kottayam, Kannur and Idukki to name a few.

However the CAG audit report on Kerala's Akshaya contradicts some points by saying that billions of money would be wasted if bureaucracy does not learn quickly from its failures as it challenges the success of the project by saying that the target of giving 50,000 jobs by means of this project in three years (2003- 2006) was not fulfilled as the employment generated was just 6,818 in eight years (Upadhyaya, 2010).

Gyan Ganga

Like Akshaya Project in Kerala, Gyan Ganga too is one of the ICT initiatives taken by the government of Gujarat with the sole objective of providing wireless internet connectivity to all 18,000 villages. The project was initiated by the Department of science and technology on behalf of the Government of Gujarat (GOG) and has signed MOU with M/s n- Logue communications Pvt. Ltd. It can therefore be identified as one of the Public-Private-Partnership (PPP) aiming common goals of providing internet connectivity through wireless technology called CorDect in order to provide employment to village entrepreneurs and building of knowledge societies at the grassroots level. The ICT facilities provided by *Gyan Ganga* includes online registration of various applications, online public grievance forum, information on Government programmes, online application forms, update Government information, etc.

Gyan Ganga undertook quite a few progressive steps to achieve considerable economic growth by reducing farming costs, increasing crop yield, enabling effective post harvest management, reducing risks, providing expertise in animal husbandry and watershed management and enabling better credit options and facilities to the rural mass.

Some of the services offered by *Gyan Ganga* include- Computer education, Blue book, Green book, Red book, Online testing tutorial, Online Photoshop tutorial, Health, E-mail and web browsing, e- Governance and Bio data maker. The *Gyan Ganga* project enabled top class services in a single click, provided solutions with an Agriculture expert, veterinary services, e-Government services, Distance health care or e-health, Distance learning or e-learning, Remote Eye Care, e- Agriculture and many more with the help of internet.

E-Gram

The primary objective of this mission is to enable the gram panchayats to adopt a computerized official system. The initiation of this project was a huge step to develop the rural areas particularly for official purposes such as instant processing of birth and death registration, issuance of certificates such as caste, income and electricity. The success of existing ICT services in the state had led the state government to take up this project to expand ICT services in the rural areas. The state government had planned to cover 1400 villages in the initial phase of the project. The *E-gram* project enables the villagers to have access to relevant and full information through e-mails and government websites. The *E-gram* remains one of the most successful projects undertaken by the government of Gujarat.

Some of the services carried on by *E-gram* include: (i) Birth and death registration along with issuance of respective certificates via computerised and easily handled system. (ii) Property Assessment was easily accessible and reproducible. (iii) Tax Collection, availability of printed bills and details of taxes. (iv) Accounts of gram panchayats were made easily accessible and available. (vi) Issuance of various certificates such as caste certificate, income certificate, farmer certificate, availability of easy verification and easily maintained records. *E-Gram* is initiated by a software system specially developed by the Government of Gujarat. The technologies used for incorporating IT in e-Governance include Back end - MS-Office 2000, MS-Access 2000, SQL Server 2000, Front end – Visual Basic, ASP, ODBC, Operating System- Windows 2000, Networking -GSWAN dial up connectivity. Computer system, Dot matrix Printer, Modem, Telephone and Inverter were among the hardware that as a part of the project was provided along with *E-Gram* panchayat as the only software (Kokil, n.d.).

West Bengal State Wide Area Network (WBSWAN)

Based on Internet Protocol (IP), *WBSWAN* is a modern networking system for computerized connectivity within the administration run by the West Bengal state government. It enables the government to function more productively and effectively by supporting both horizontal and vertical flow of information and communication in order to carry out its initiatives better. *WBSWAN* is a network system for data, voice and video communication that runs throughout the state of West Bengal. This network helps the government to carry out administrative programmes through a computerized system. The project is officially run by West Bengal Electronics Industry Development Corporation Limited or Webel Technology Limited. IIT (Kharagpur) is the formally appointed 'External Network Consultant' for the project. WBSWAN network offers connectivity of Data, Voice & Video Communication facilities from State Switching Centre at Kolkata up to all District Headquarters on 2 Mbps (E-1 link) leased line of BSNL. According to the guidelines of DIT, GOI, twenty horizontal offices are to be linked with

WBSWAN backbone at the District, sub- division level and five horizontal at the block level. Each District Headquarter has video conferencing facility along with Multi- conferencing facility through Multipoint Conferencing Unit (MCU).

The primary objective of this networking system is to provide connectivity among all the government departments as well as to improve government-citizen and government-industry ties. It also supports projects such as government Application Service Provider (ASP).

An Inference from the Case Study

From the above four case studies, it could therefore be outlined that ICT is highly preferred as a tool for social change in the government sector and that it can bring transparency between the administration and the public. It is for this reason that both the private companies and public wings are now collaborating together for the betterment of the rural societies. Some of the facts and figures coming out of the case studies can be inferred as:

- Government bodies are putting their step forward for ICT Implementation at various levels with the aim of equal dissemination of information.
- Rural population is now more e-literate and has access to high speed internet connectivity to make their daily life easier.
- More job options have opened up in the form of business entrepreneurs and DTP learning.
- ICT is securing transparency at several levels of the government administration and therefore supporting the Right to Information Act 2005.
- ICT initiates having a public forum which encourages debates and discussion in a pluralistic society.
- ICT is able to bridge the gap between the rich and the rural section of the society, between the technology haves and have-nots.
- ICT favours social inclusion by more easy access to technology at affordability.
- It is also very necessary to use ICT in the most effective way or there are chances of it to be misused and loss or drainage of money may occour.
- Successful Public-Private coordination for social purpose.

COMPARISON WITH DIFFERENT MODELS OF COMMUNICATION

The core area involving ICT is 'technology' as the medium for communication. In ICT a message is passed on via technologies like telephone, fax, computer, e-mail etc. Which means a message from the source (here the policy makers) is first encoded in the machine language (binary language or others) and is transmitted via signal (internet). The encoded message then reaches the receiver who decodes the message and perceives the meaning and gives his/her feedback. The same notion can be traced in one of the founding communication models 'Shannon and Weaver Model', 1949.

Shannon and Weaver Model too talks about an Information source, who is also the decision maker and designs the message accordingly, the message is transmitted via a transmitter in the form of signal and then received by the receiver who decodes it and gives a feedback. Some of the converging areas in both the cases may be listed as below:

1. **Source as the primary decision maker:** Shannon and Weaver says that 'source' designs the message and is the primary 'decision maker' who selects over which message and how much information is to be passed on. In case of ICT, the source or the decision maker is The State i.e. the government plans and programs meant for rural upliftment.

2. **Identification of noise:** Since the message passes through a machine (technology) and has to undergo several conversion procedures in order to be 'transmission ready', therefore, high chances of intervention are there. These interventions are recognized by Shannon and Weaver as 'noise'. In case of ICT, 'noise' may occur with slow internet connectivity. Lower the noise, better the communication. For this reason, government has installed high speed internet connection in rural areas. Noise in this model also gets a different dimension of barrier. In such a case ICT has a language barrier which is also overcome by recent options of translations provided by technology.
3. **Identification of 3-tier problems in communication:** Shannon and Weaver identified three levels of problem. Level A dealt with technical problems, Level B with semantic problems and Level C with effectiveness problems…one complex than the other. In ICT too, the same problems are identified and care has been taken on all the three factors to minimize the problem.

Drawbacks

1. Linear Model of communication: While ICT approaches for two way communication with transparency and interaction, Shannon and Weaver does not recognize the same, instead the model identifies communication as a linear movement of information from left to right.
2. No place for feedback mechanism: Shannon and Weaver Model do not talk about feedback, but is very concerned about the 'effect' of the information on the receiver. In ICT also, the effect of message on the receiver is given priority and so the message is designed in the way understandable and absorbed by the audience.

Keeping in mind the use of ICT in rural development it may also be compared to two-step-flow theory: the theory developed by Elihu Katz and Paul Lazarsfeld in 1944 and later in 1955, states the importance of a middleman in the process of communication. The middleman is termed here as Opinion Leader. He, the opinion leader is a member of the same group of people who are targeted. The function of opinion leader is to build a bridge between the outer world and his group. Since, he is a person of primary importance in the group; his opinions are readily acceptable to the rural mass.

It is here, where ICT's success can be identified. ICT deals with installation of technologies at fixed places in the village. Selected volunteers are given the duties of providing training session to a group of people and then they are asked to relay the learnt lessons. In this way, ICT do not directly communicate with the rural mass, but it goes via opinion leaders.

Two-step-flow theory has certain advantageous factors identified as under:

- High level of penetration in the rural mass
- Enactment of regular interaction
- Enactment of horizontal communication
- Systematic involvement
- Less risk of failure
- Integrated approach

Since ICT works at multilevel, therefore it can rightly be compared with Newcomb's Model (Das, 2010). Also, it must be noted that Newcomb's model aims for a social equilibrium as his proposition was based on consistency or balance theory (Andal, 2010). His approach is much broader than just transmission of message; but deals with the interpretative process involved between individuals or groups or institutions during the process of communication.

Newcomb's model, 1953, briefly states that there is high interdependency between the members taking part in a communication. Newcomb argues by saying that if A and B are communi-

Figure 5. ICT in Two-step flow theory

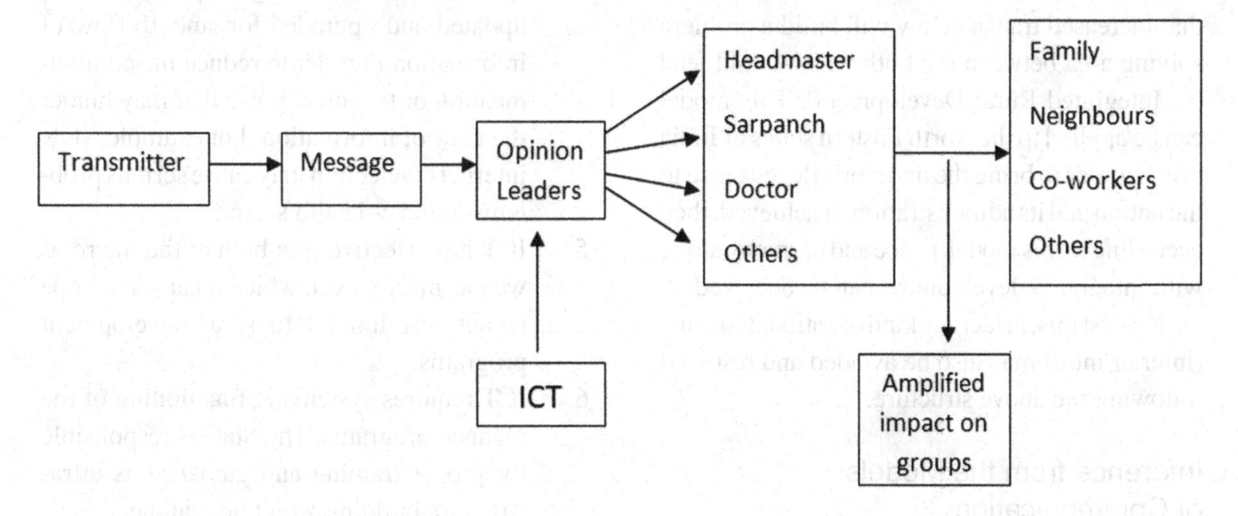

cators and X is a part of their system, then ABX altogether are interdependent. All the three must have equal attitudes towards each other in order to maintain equilibrium. Change of any one of the member would break the structure.

In case of ICT, the interaction between the rural mass and the government plays a crucial in fostering rural development. Since, the target approached is 'integrated development' of the rural sector by increasing the quality of living, sanitation, health and economy, through proper flow of information (via e-Governance) between the target people and the government; we can say that rural development is dependent on the relation between public (rural mass) and government. Other way round, we may also say that, both the public (rural mass) and government must have the same approach or goal, in this case 'the rural development' in order to achieve it.

From Figure 6, it can be stated that through transparency between the government and the rural mass, there can be a healthy relationship at-

Figure 6. ICT in Newcomb's Model

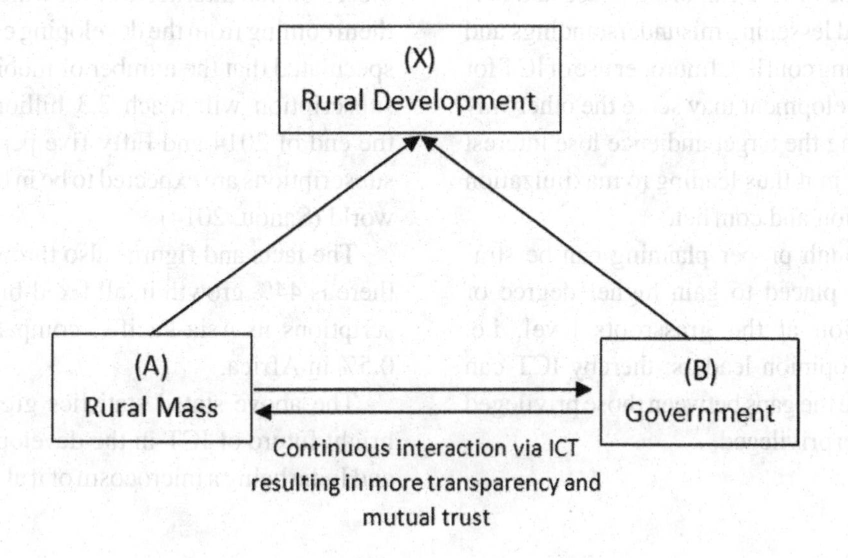

tained between the both. It can also be speculated that increased transparency will build a problem solving area between the both which could lead to 'Integrated Rural Development'. This model can be applied to the North Eastern states of India also in order to bring the underprivileged close to the nation and its administration. If achieved, then according to this model, peace and harmony along with integrated development can be achieved.

Not just this, in fact any kind of national conflict (inter or intra) may also be avoided and resolved following the above structure.

Inference from the Models of Communication

It can therefore be concluded that ICT uses the right portions of every model and theories to suit best in the position of weapon for social change. It can also be speculated that ICT has a role at micro as well as macro levels of the society. One of the primary things that should be kept in mind is the know-how to use it in the way to usher development. Inference can be summarized as:

1. Proper message (policies and schemes) should be designed in order to get the desired result.
2. ICT success depends on the way it is used. Proper use of ICT can bring peace and harmony and lessening misunderstandings and minimizing conflict. Improper use of ICT for rural development may serve the other way by making the target audience lose interest and trust in it thus leading to maximization of agitation and conflict.
3. ICT through proper planning can be strategically placed to gain higher degree of penetration at the grassroots level, i.e. through opinion leaders; thereby ICT can minimize the gaps between those privileged and underprivileged.
4. ICT, as in the technological part should be updated and upgraded for smooth flow of information in order to reduce miscommunication or technical noise that may hinder the flow of information. For example, slow internet connection may cause serious problems in the e- health sector.
5. ICT has effective role both at the micro as well as macro level, which means, its scope is not just limited to rural development programs.
6. ICT requires systematic functioning of the planned programs. The State is responsible for proper training and guidance as infrastructure building won't help alone.

ICT: A Look into the Future Journey

Till now the journey of ICT in India has been discussed in this chapter, but it is also very important to know what is happening outside India and thereby an overview of the outside world is also very important. Predicting the future is one of the important areas in research and thereby a statistical data is very important. As the progress of ICT is highly measurable by its daily usage, therefore a mathematical view of the same will give the clear picture. Statistically proved and stated that, by the end of 2014, there will be almost 3 billion internet users of which two-third of them coming from the developing countries. Also speculated that the number of mobile-broadband subscription will reach 2.3 billion globally by the end of 2014 and Fifty-five per cent of these subscriptions are expected to be in the developing world (Sanou, 2014).

The facts and figures also throw light on that there is 44% growth in all fixed-broadband subscriptions in Asia-Pacific, compared with only 0.5% in Africa.

The above stated statistics greatly predict a bright future of ICT in the developing countries and India being a microcosm of it also shows great hopes in the coming future as universally experts and specialists are looking into the investment from an optimistic point of view. ICT apart from rural development also fosters macro level communication, which also guarantees its longer stay.

Future Research Directions

Since the success of ICT is a proven fact, therefore future research directions may include the ways to improve it more in terms of application and maintenance. Maintenance is a markable factor in ICT implementation as contradictions are there (Upadhyaya, 2010) and several academic authors have criticized about it. Crores of money is being spent in ICT rural developmental projects and technologies are installed, but lack of maintenance pulls all the effort backward. So, improving maintenance and developing policies for that is the first initiative that should be concerning the future research.

Again, ICT implementation for rural development, although gained success in a short span, however it is felt that still, in the remote village; for instance take Meghalaya where a lady sitting in the government office affirmed that she did not know how to use it (Dutta, 2012). Therefore it can be inferred that building infrastructure won't work alone. So, focus should also be given on exhaustive training programs over 'just' building infrastructure and very importantly, there should be no compromise made in the way with these training programs.

ICT rural development plans still need to be developed in the North- East India. Proper plans and programs require to be implemented in the underprivileged area. E-literacy needs to be promoted more. Social Inclusion and proper citizen participation is of high requirement here in the North- Eastern part of India in order to foster development, peace and prosperity in this region of India. Therefore, one-step-ahead of state level plans like SWAN and national level plans like NeGP is required as the ethnographic culture and population demands that.

Like the concept of development is limitless and always expanding, thereby, ICT development plans must also look for the other sides in order to find ideas to develop it more giving a better result. Afterall it's the age of technological innovation and every individual is targeting to form an information society. So, the future research area may include in finding and inventing ways to develop it more for voluntary participation and integrated development.

CONCLUSION

Crossing the boundaries of digital divide, social exclusion and technology driven development concept; developing countries worldwide are steadily moving towards the acceptance of ICT's role in fostering integrated development. With lots of e-Governance projects launching more recently each year, government too takes active role in it by building infrastructure supporting the cause. Not just this, the public- private venture is also adding a lot of positivity in the scenario.

In a developing country like India, where the population is counted to be one of the largest in the world, development is hard to penetrate the grassroots due to social taboos, less understanding, poor education and mental rigidity. Rural sector in India is highly pluralistic in nature as one can witness a large variety of culture, systems and norms prevailing even till today. The challenge therefore is to meet the minds of this heterogeneous audience and bring development at individual level primarily. Development in such a heterogeneous society demands regular interaction with the modern world through e-Governance, assisted by specialized and trained volunteers, NGO workers and formation of SHGs.

E-Governance lets every individual to participate in the program and exchange vital resources necessary for smooth flow of information and thereby participate in the horizontal communication process. In order to initiate this communication and make it highly successful it is also very necessary to reach the audience in their own language and today's computer technology highly supports it. Kudos to Software options for language and translation! Receiving information from the new media technology in 'my own language' creates a 'my space' which is not just motivating but highly emotional. The rural vulnerable mass, which often alienate themselves from the outer world 'Our World, Their World' concept is instantly broken down and they could actually open up their emotion and cognition to necessary information and perceive things to get persuaded. Actually, the acceptance level both in sensory terms as well as psychological terms are attained which readily initiates active participation through motivation. This is also the aim of e-Governance. e- Governance therefore fosters social inclusion and breaks the digital divide. ICT is the right medium to do the needful and the overall responsibility goes in the hands of the State. Keeping an eye over the penetration factor of ICT, The State should initiate some more programs relating to rural development. ICT strategies not just handovers the power of technology in the hands of the poor but also empowers them with e-Learning facility. Distance Learning, DTP classes and basic hardware and software trainings help find employment in the modern world.

The summary of all the factors on basis of observations and inferences with respect to this chapter can compiled as under:

1. ICT is a technology driven endeavour to foster 'sustainable development' in rural India.
2. ICT uses schemes and programmes that directly relates to the rural audience and their problems.
3. ICT supports Development Support Communication (DSC) and therefore involves greater audience participation.
4. ICT imbibes two-step-flow theory in order to gain greater acceptance among the rural mass.
5. ICT brings transparency through smooth flow of information, thus the rural mass gets close to the administration and its policies. Therefore, the public- government conflict is minimized.
6. ICT enhances horizontal knowledge sharing process which is followed by group debates and discussions forming opinions.
7. ICT takes aid in building an information society, whereby every individual will be an equal participant irrespective of their financial background.
8. ICT serves to provide an integrated sustainable development to its target group that includes better quality of living, sanitation, health, employment and less climatic an economic vulnerabilities.

In a nutshell, ICT serves towards bringing positive and radical change in a developing society, blessing it with harmony, peace and prosperity. The State playing a crucial role; it is predicted that, with proper planning and better schemes, ICT will prove to bring about more positive changes in the near future.

REFERENCES

Accra, J. (2012). [Web log comment]. Retrieved from http://collegeassignments.wordpress.com/2012/10/01/provide-five-definitions-of-ictit-indicate-the-author-and-year-what-are-the-similarities-and-differences-in-these-definitions-provide-your-own-definition-of-ictit/

Andal, N. (2011). Communication Theories and Models. India: Himalaya Publishing House. ISBN Number: 978-93-524-588-0

Archmann, S., & Guiffart, A. (2014). ICT: Obstacle or Enabler for Social Inclusion? The Impacts of New Technologies on Governance. In S. Baum & A. Mahizhnan (Eds.), *E-Governance and Social Inclusion: Concepts and Cases* (pp. 45–61). Hershey, PA: Information Science Reference. doi:10.4018/978-1-4666-6106-6.ch004

Brants, K., & Frissen, V. (2003). Inclusion and exclusion in the Information Society. Retrieved from http://www.lse.ac.uk/media@lse/research/EMTEL/reports/brants_2003_emtel.pdf

Bhalla, A., & Lapeyre, F. (1997). Social Exclusion: Towards an Analytical and Operational Framework. *Development and Change*, *28*(3), 413–433. doi:10.1111/1467-7660.00049

Bhatnagar, S. (2000). Information Technology and Development: Foundation and Key Issues (pp. 1-13). In S. Bhatnagar, & R. Schware (Eds), *Information and Communication Technology in Rural Development: Case Studies from India*. World Bank Institute (WBI) Working Papers, WBI Publications.

Bhatnagar, S. (2014). Strategies for Digital Inclusion: Experience from India. In S. Baum & A. Mahizhnan (Eds.), *E-Governance and Social Inclusion: Concepts and Cases* (pp. 243–255). Hershey, PA: Information Science Reference. doi:10.4018/978-1-4666-6106-6.ch015

Bhatnagar, S., & Singh, N. (2010). Assessing the Impact of EGovernment: A study of E-Government Projects in India. *Information Technologies and International Development*, *6*(2), 109–127.

Castro Sardi, X., & Mlikota, K. (2002). *Overview on E-governance: Working Paper prepared in the framework of the ICT cross –cutting project ICTs as Tools for Improving Local Governance.* Paris, France: UNESCO.

Chhavi, M. (2008). ICT as a Tool For Poverty Reduction. Proceedings of the 2nd National Conference; INDIACom-2008, Computing for National Development. New Delhi: INDIACom.

Daly, A., Gong, C. H., Dugdale, A., & Abello, A. (2014). Social Inclusion of Australian Children in the Digital Age. In S. Baum & A. Mahizhnan (Eds.), *E-Governance and Social Inclusion: Concepts and Cases* (pp. 164–181). Hershey, PA: Information Science Reference; doi:10.4018/978-1-4666-6106-6.ch010

Das, R. (2010). Scope of E-governance in Rural India. *Media Watch*, 1(2). Print ISSN: 0976-0911

Dutta, S. (2012). ICT for the Development in North East India. Retrieved from http://enajori.com/ict-for-the-development-in-north-east-indi-asatyakam-dutta/

Emma, L. G., Gary, B., & Joanie, W. (2013). The role of local perceptions in the marketing of rural areas. Journal of Destination Marketing & Management, 2(1), 4-13.

eGov Reach: A Nasscom initiation. (n. d.). Core Infrastucture projects. Retrieved from http://egovreach.in/social/node/488

Govt. of Kerala (n. d.). *Project Akshaya.* Retrieved from http://www.akshaya.kerala.gov.in/index.php/e-literacy

Huang, I., Guo, R., & Xie, H. WU, Z. (2012). *The Convergence of Information and Communication Technologies Gains Momentum.* The Global Information Technology Report.

Portal, I. T. C. Retrieved from http://www.itcportal.com/sustainability/philosophy.aspx

Kataria, S. (2005). Dewang Mehta award for innovation in IT for NIIT Chief Scientist Sugata Mitra. Retrieved from http://www.niit.com/niit/ContentAdmin/NWS/NWSPR/NWSPR2/pr-010405-sugata-dewang.htm/

Katz, E., & Lazarsfeld, P. (1955). Personal Influence. New York: The Free Press.

Kokil, P. (n. d.). SAP-LAP Analysis. Retrieved from http://www.csi-sigegov.org/3/29_290_3.pdf

Lazarsfeld, P. F., Berelson, B., & Gaudet, H. (1944). *The people's choice: How the voter makes up his mind in a presidential campaign*. New York: Columbia University Press.

Macintosh, A. (2004). Characterizing e-participation in policy-making. *Proceedings of the 37th Annual Hawaii International Conference on System Sciences* (pp. 10). doi:10.1109/HICSS.2004.1265300

Magno, F. A. (2014). E-Governance and Social Inclusion: Community E-Centers in the Philippines. In S. Baum & A. Mahizhnan (Eds.), *E-Governance and Social Inclusion: Concepts and Cases* (pp. 256–270). Hershey, PA: Information Science Reference; doi:10.4018/978-1-4666-6106-6.ch016

Mahizhnan, A. (2014). E-Government and Social Inclusion: Concepts. In S. Baum & A. Mahizhnan (Eds.), *E-Governance and Social Inclusion: Concepts and Cases* (pp. 1–9). Hershey, PA: Information Science Reference. doi:10.4018/978-1-4666-6106-6.ch001

McNamara, K. S. (2003). Information and Communication Technologies, Poverty and Development: Learning from Experience. In *A background paper for the info Dev Annual Symposium.* Geneva: The World Bank.

Melkote, S. R., & Steeves, H. L. (2001). *Communication for Development in the Third World- Theory and Practice for Empowerment* (2nd ed.). New Delhi, India: SAGE. doi:10.4135/9788132113751

Molinari, F., McPherson, M., & Singh, G. (2014). Democratising E-Democracy: A Roadmap for Impact. In S. Baum & A. Mahizhnan (Eds.), *E-Governance and Social Inclusion: Concepts and Cases* (pp. 25–44). Hershey, PA: Information Science Reference; doi:10.4018/978-1-4666-6106-6.ch003

Jamaluddin, N. (2013). Adoption of E-commerce Practices among the Indian Farmers, a Survey of Trichy District in the State of Tamilnadu, India. *Procedia Economics and Finance*, *7*, 140–149.

Niall, H. and Chris, W. (2012). Context and the processes of ICT for development. *Inf. Organ.*, *22*(1), 23-36. DOI=10.1016/j.infoandorg.2011.10.001

Oakley, K. (2002, June 10-11). '*What is e-governance?*' *e*-Governance Workshop. Strasbourg. Retrieved from http://www.coe.int/t/dgap/democracy/activities/ggis/e-governance/work_of_egovernance_committee/kate_oakley_egovernance_EN.asp

Pradip, T., & Bhoomi, G.G. (2009). e-governance and the right to information: ICTs and development in India. *Telemat. Inf.,* 26(1), 20-31. DOI=10.1016/j.tele.2007.12.004

Rahman, H. (2008). Information Dynamics in Developing Countries. In C. Van Slyke (Ed.), *Information Communication Technologies: Concepts, Methodologies, Tools, and Applications* (pp. 104–114). Hershey, PA: Information Science Reference; doi:10.4018/978-1-59904-949-6.ch008

Sanyal, M. K., Das, S., & Bhadra, S. K. (2014). E-District Portal for District Administration in West Bengal, India: A Survey to Identify Important Factors towards Citizen's Satisfaction, Procedia Economics and Finance, Volume 11, Pages 510-521, ISSN 2212-5671,10.1016/S2212-5671(14)00217-2

Sarrocco, C. (n. d.). Elements and Principles of the Information Society. Retrieved August 10, 2014, from http://www.itu.int/osg/spu/wsis-themes/access/backgroundpaper/IS%20Principles.pdf

ICTs and the fight against HIV/AIDS in India. (2013). SAATHII.

Shah, N. & Panchal, A. (2004). ICT revolution in Rural Gujarat. *An e- Governance Bulletin*.

Shortall, S. (2008). Social inclusion, civic engagement, participation, and social capital: Exploring the differences. *Journal of Rural Studies*, 24(4), 450–457. doi:urstud.2008.01.001.10.1016/j.jr

Singh, R., & Raja, S. (2010). *Convergence in Information and Communication Technology*. The World Bank; doi:10.1596/978-0-8213-8169-4

Siriginidi, S. R. (2009). Achieving millennium development goals: Role of ICTS innovations in India. *Telematics and Informatics*, *26*(2), 127–143. doi:10.1016/j.tele.2008.02.001

The World in 2014: ICT FACTS AND FIGURES, Retrieved http://www.itu.int/en/ITU-D/Statistics/Documents/facts/ICTFactsFigures2014-e.pdf

Creating an Inclusive Society: Practical Strategies to Promote Social Integration. (2009). United Nations Department of Economic and Social Affairs. Retrieved from http://www.un.org/esa/socdev/egms/docs/2009/Ghana/inclusive-society.pdf

Upadhyaya, H. (2010, May 1-15). e-Waste. Kerala's e-Gov getting nowhere. *Governance Now*. Retrieved from http://indiaenvironmentportal.org.in/files/%20Akshaya.pdf

West Bengal. (2014, August 10). *Vikaspedia*. Retrieved from http://vikaspedia.in/e-governance/states/west-bengal#section-1

Warschauer, M. (2003). *Technological and Social Inclusion: Rethinking the Digital Divide*. Cambridge, MA: MIT Press.

Yoneji Masuda. (1980). Computopia: Rebirth of Theological Synergism. In Masuda, Y. (Ed.), The Information Society as Post-Industrial Society (pp. 146-154). Tokyo: Institute for the Information Society and 1981 by World Future Society.

KEY TERMS AND DEFINITIONS

Communication Model: Models of communication refer to the conceptual diagrammatic representation used to explain the human communication process which primarily consists of a transmitter, a channel, a receiver and a destination. Models are used for the sake of simplification and presentation of the complex communication structure and often help to identify the type or pattern of communication. Models also help to predict the nature of communication and the type of its outcome.

Convergence: Convergence is the coming together of telecommunications, computing and broadcasting into a single digital bit-stream. The rise of digital communication in the late 20th century has made it possible for media organizations (or individuals) to deliver text, audio, and video material over the same wired, wireless, or fibre-optic connections. This digital convergence of news media, in particular, was called "Mediamorphosis" by researcher Roger Fidler, in his 1997 book by that name. An example of device supporting convergence is smart phone that can involve n parallel work of a phone, pc, music system, compass, library, newspaper and so on.

Digital Divide: Digital divide is used to describe the discrepancy between people who have access to and the resources to use new information and communication tools and people who do not have the resources and access to such technology. The term also describes the discrepancy between those who have the skills, knowledge and abilities to use the technologies and those who do not. The digital divide can exist between those living in rural areas and those living in urban areas, between the educated and uneducated, between economic classes, and on a global scale between more and less industrially developed nations.

Digitalization: Digitalization is the integration of digital technologies into everyday life by the digitization of everything that can be digitized. The literal meaning of digitalization gives an apparent idea of development and technology dependent world. In this chapter, digitalization means computerization of systems and jobs for better ease and accessibility.

Development Communication: Development communication refers to the use of communication to facilitate social development. Development communication techniques include information dissemination and education, behaviour change, social marketing, social mobilization, media advocacy, communication for social change and community participation. Erskine Childers defined it as development support communications which is a discipline in development planning and implementation in which more adequate account is taken of human behavioural factors in the design of development projects and their objectives.

E-Governance: e-Governance is the public sector's use of the most innovative information and communication technologies, like the Internet, in order to deliver citizens with improved services, reliable information and greater knowledge in order to facilitate access to the governing process and encourage deeper participation (UNESCO). It is a generic term that refers to any government functions or processes that are carried out in digital form over the Internet. Local, state and federal governments essentially set up central websites from which the public (both private citizens and businesses) can find public information, download government forms and contact government representatives.

ICT: The term ICT (Information and Communication Technology) is used to refer to the convergence of audio-visual and telephone networks with computer networks through a single cabling or link system. There are large economic incentives (huge cost savings due to elimination of the telephone network) to merge the telephone network with the computer network system using a single unified system of cabling, signal distribution and management.

Information Society: Information Society is a term for a society in which the creation, distribution, use, integration and manipulation of information is a significant economic, political, and cultural activity. The aim of the information society is to gain competitive advantage internationally, through using information technology (IT) in a creative and productive way. The knowledge economy is its economic counterpart, whereby wealth is created through the economic exploitation of understanding. People who have the means to partake in this form of society are sometimes called digital citizens. This is one of many dozen labels that have been identified to suggest that humans are entering a new phase of society.

Public Participation: Public participation is a political principle or practice, and may also be recognized as a right (right to public participation). Public participation may be regarded as a way of empowerment and as vital part of the democratic governance. Public participation is marked by debates and discussion along with social inclusion. Generally public participation seeks and facilitates the involvement of those potentially affected by or interested in a decision. The principle of public participation holds that those who are affected by a decision have a right to be involved in the decision-making process. It initiates and enhances the knowledge sharing process within a community.

Social Inclusion: Social inclusion is a process by which efforts are made to ensure equal opportunities for all. The multi-dimensional process aimed at creating conditions which enable full and active participation of every member of the society in all aspects of life, including civic, social, economic, and political activities, as well as participation in decision making processes. Social inclusion may also be interpreted as the process by which societies combat poverty and social exclusion. Social inclusion aims to empower poor and marginalized people to take advantage of burgeoning global opportunities. It ensures that people have a voice in decisions which affect their lives and that they enjoy equal access to markets, services and political, social and physical spaces.

Social Exclusion: Social exclusion (or marginalization) is social disadvantage and relegation to the fringe of society. Social exclusion is the process in which individuals or entire communities of people are systematically blocked from (or denied full access to) various rights, opportunities and resources that are normally available to members of a society, and which are fundamental to social integration within that particular society.

Sustainable Development: Sustainable development or integrated development deals with an overall development which includes improved quality of living, health, education, employment along with economic development. Sustainable development can greatly be related to developing countries like India, where economy is not just the problem, but lack of proper sanitation and clean drinking water also.

ENDNOTE

1 The development of mass media technology in the developed nations imparted news about themselves, amplifying and glorifying their own society, events and people as the primary content of news; while portraying the third world or the developing nations to be a poor place to live in by mostly referring to the crimes and issues of distress. This was recognized as the one way flow of information or biased information from developed nations to the developing ones.

Chapter 22
Contingency Factors Impacting the Rural Information and Communication Technology Hubs

P Govindaraju
Manonmaniam Sundaranar University, India

M Maani Mabel
VELS University, India

ABSTRACT

A thorough glance of the ICT and development researches reveal that the qualitative studies reasonably depend on the grounded theory as it is obtained from the phenomenon unlike the study begins with the theory and proves it. Most of the researches concentrated on the adoption of technology, receptiveness of the target audience, organizational structure of the project agencies and of course, the impact of intervention. Fewer researches have been done to gauge the factors affecting the positive or negative impact of the technology. None of the above stated theories were relevant except meta-theoretical perspectives of ICT and society. The authors propose a chapter discusses the contingency factors which affect the positive or negative impact of the rural Information and Communication Technology hubs in India by analyzing the researches which were published after the year 2000. It shall be specifically dealing with the researches which are based on primary data. Thus it could reflect the challenges the Indian rural ICT initiatives face.

INTRODUCTION

Being evident from the history, any technology would not be deployed unless it is within the community, controlled and used by the community. The Information Kiosk emerged as new revolutionary change and reaches the rural locations in developing environments to use ICTs and to bring new access to content and services to rural consumers. Such installations have generally been termed as Telecenters, Knowledge Centers, Community Information Centers, Information Centers

DOI: 10.4018/978-1-4666-8598-7.ch022

and Information Kiosks. Information Kiosks/ Knowledge Centers are becoming the window of the world of knowledge for villages and to reap the benefits of e-governance, tele-education, telemedicine, e-commerce and e-judiciary initiatives need to be strengthened on a war footing.

The interventions have a measurable impact on commerce, marketing, public services, governance and education. Information and Communication Technologies enable the technological, social, cultural and economical change through participation, opportunity and accountability. Remote villages are witnesses of change effected by the new technology.

There are a number of success stories like how agriculturists interacted with professionals to save their crops from seasonal diseases, school drop outs and women have completed school education through e-educational services, fishermen who lost were considered at sea have found their way back using the services of Geo Positioning Satellites, poor farmers and fishermen have eliminated middlemen in their buying and selling of products, children have become familiar with teaching of computer applications, narrowing down of gender and caste discriminations, the list goes on.

Before a decade, there was Pro-ICT wave with the Indian budget assuring huge amount to enable the ICT to diffuse among the rural masses. Within a short span of time then, the first ICT for development initiative in Tamilnadu envisaged and run by the eminent IIT-Madras has agreed its failure and came off the screen. On the other hand the Government of India has announced Rs. 23000/- crores towards National e-Governance Plan (NeGP). These two instances contradicted and placed some serious questions and the researcher has stepped out to study the other initiatives in Tamilnadu.

Though various studies have identified the issues of sustainability, misconception of the role of ICTs, lack of awareness among rural folks on the usefulness of ICT, lack of community ownership and participation, the rural masses considerably have shown signs of interest towards these initiatives being geared up to break up the conservative bounding and acknowledged the need of technology for future development of the individual and the community as a whole. At various occurrences, it is abruptly known that the issues are around the improper planning and approach. Hence the researcher has focused to find the issues pertaining the effect of rural ICT initiatives.

ICT (Information and Communication Technologies) and development researches have widely adopted and done on almost theories of all social science disciplines focusing more on Technological Acceptance Model, Diffusion of Innovation and Social Learning Theory. It is also noted that various researchers have inculcated the concepts and built their research framework instead of evolving from theories in ICT research as against other researches. The following paragraphs attempt to give a synopsis of theories predominantly and significantly used in ICT and development research. This would later exemplify why the researchers have endeavored to look on the contingency factors.

A thorough glance on the ICT and development researches reveal that the qualitative studies reasonably depend on the grounded theory as it is obtained from the phenomenon unlike the study begins with the theory and proves it. Strauss and Corbin point out, "it is discovered, developed, and provisionally verified through systematic data collection and analysis of data pertaining to that phenomenon. Therefore, data collection, analysis and theory stand in reciprocal relationship with each other" (Strauss & Corbin, 1990).

Evusa has adopted the social construction of technology theory while studying the Huruma Community Telecentre of Kenya. Social construction of technology theory has evolved as the criticism to diffusion of innovation and more specifically technological determinism. This theory helped to outline the perception of diffusion of innovation and technological determinism and their relation between ICT and socioeconomic development altering the traditional approach of looking at the relation between communication and development either in mainstream (dominant) or alternative (critical) perspectives (Evusa, 2005).

Lee has integrated technology acceptance model, theory of planned behavior and diffusion of innovation to study the mobile technology adoption and whether imitation and innovation influences in ICT adoption. The integration contributed to explore the imitation and innovation influences in ICT adoption; the imitation influence construct; which and by how much these innovation influences affect ICT adoption; and finally, how much and which imitation factors influence ICT adoption (Lee, 2003).

Most of the researches concentrated on the adoption of technology, receptiveness of the target audience, organizational structure of the project agencies and of course, the impact of intervention. Fewer researches have been done to gauge the factors affecting the positive or negative impact of the technology. As stated in the research objectives, this present study focuses primarily to assess the factors affecting the effectiveness of the selected initiatives. To address this issue, none of the above stated theories were relevant except meta-theoretical perspectives of ICT and society.

Tracing back the history, it is evident that the researches on influence/ impact of any innovation on the society have been frequently done unlike its impact on industry, government and education. In the past the social impact of technology on the society has been studied under various contexts of satellite television (Contractor, Singhal, & Rogers, 1988), telephone (Pool, 1977) and computing (Kling, 1980) using four meta-theoretical perspectives.

META-THEORETICAL PERSPECTIVES OF ICT AND SOCIETY

The meta-theoretical perspectives focus on evaluating the technology in four views - the utopian view, the dystopian view, the neutral view and the contingency view. As part of the Harvard Programme on *The Role of Technology in Society,* Emmanuel G. Mesthene (1969) has made remarkable contributions to the domain. The following few paragraphs explain the excerpts from his views on technology and society.

The utopian view denotes "the technology is an unalloyed blessing for man and society". The technology as "the motor of all progress", is believed to possess solution for all the social issues, source of "permanent prosperity" and freed the human kind "from the clutches of a complex and highly organized society". This utopian thinking has its modern origins in the 19th century philosophers like Saint-Simon, Karl Marx and Auguste. The dystopian view stresses that "technology is an unmitigated curse". Any technological innovation is considered as autonomous and uncontrollable and it is believed that it fosters 'materialistic values', destroy 'religion' and brings 'technocratic society and bureaucratic state'. Dystopian views have been embossed by "artists, literary commentators, popular social critics and existentialist philosophers" who believed that technology would 'poison nature and blow up the world'.

The neutral view argues that "technology as such is not worthy of special notice". Industrial revolution changed the belief then that "technology has done little to accelerate the rate of economic productivity since the 1880s". The primary reason was that there was no significant difference in the time period between technological invention and widespread adoption of new technology. There are a number of empirical evidences to support this notion but it ignores a number of social, cultural, psychological and political effects of technological change.

Each of the views is distinct within itself and reflects the relationship between technology and society in its own way. Mesthene finds oversimplifications which lacks understanding. There are empirical foundations to support each of the notions 'without gaining much knowledge about the actual mechanism by which technology leads to social change or significant insight into its implications for the future'. All are too uncritical or too partial to guide inquiry. Researches reveal differentiated conclusions and more subtle relationships.

The contingency view recognizes the desirable and undesirable impacts of a technology that are differentially determined by the context in which the technology is introduced at a particular time (Contractor, Singhal, & Rogers, 1988). Mesthene argued that the utopian, dystopian and neutral view points are by themselves "unhelpful" to policymakers and he proposed a "dual effects hypothesis". According to him, the technology has "both positive and negative effects and it usually has the two at the same time and in virtue of each other". New technologies play a bi-lateral function by creating new opportunities as well as new problems. They bring about structural changes along with dislocations of business and people.

Mesthene states of few factors to explain how the technological development bring out both positive and negative effects. Technological innovations offer individuals and societies new options to choose from than ever before fulfilling what has been impossible before. Technological advances are always aimed at achieving some predetermined goals which highly demands changes in the existing social system to attain changes using the new opportunities. He explains further that, "the functions of existing social structures will be interfered with the result that other goals which were served by the older structures are now only inadequately achieved".

Mesthene cites the impact of transportation technology and private automobiles as an example explain his phenomenon. Mesthene cited the study on adoption and effect of transportation technology on the Americans. John R. Meyer and John F. Kain in their study on *transportation technology and urbanform* found that the improved transportation and private ownership of automobiles resulted in mobility and articulating many high level of economic activities. But the problem is felt when the mobility is denied to the largely populated poor and black citizens in the core cities for economic reasons and restrictions on choice of residence. It resulted in the economic divide and increase in unemployment among the "Negroes" which hampered the "traditional functions of providing employment opportunities for all segments and an integrated social environment that can temper ethnic and racial differences". The new opportunities could neither upgrade nor integrate their core populations into new system.

One of the reasons of negative effect lies in the fact that either the technology is not used at all or the technology is not used to its full capacity. The existing traditional system is not capable of or inadequate to respond to the issues and realizing the possibilities for resolving them, which is resulted by new opportunities or technological change. There is a need from the Government side to be equipped foreseeing the possibilities created by the technological change. The new opportunities or the technology is not independent by itself but is highly dependent on the institutional structures and cultural attitudes.

Thus, any technology possesses new possibilities and problems of social and psychological displacement. These issues are neither new nor unconnected and it occupies a prominent place in research. The social scientists have to spot the contingencies/ factors that establish the positive and negative effects of a technology. Society can then attempt social, technological and political reform to gauge the positive effects while minimizing the negative effects. Thus the contingency approach analyzes the desirable and undesirable impacts of the technology in the context. The contingency approach endorses that the technology is both "a problem-solver and problem-generator".

Various researches have given a glimpse of the potential of new Information and Communication Technologies in bringing development and the issue of widening the socio-economic and digital divide. Hence this chapter is intended to optimize the contingency factors which affect the potentially desirable (development/ positive change in our understanding) and undesirable (no development / negative change) effects of the ICT in the rural society by analyzing various cases, which were aimed at measuring the success and challenge factors of ICT among the rural community.

CONTINGENCY FACTORS

Community Participation and Ownership

Participation emphasizes the decision making role of the community. Participatory model allows the community members to choose the project. It encourages the participation "regardless of caste or gender to participate and have their say and to gain confidence in their ability to work together and influence agencies". In a Canadian participatory initiative in Nepal, the community members overcame "physical, bureaucratic and interpersonal difficulties". She also quotes that the participation brings out "a strong sense of community identity, an open decision-making structure, many people with recognized leadership skills.... Increased sensitivity toward gender and social equality, heightened self confidence in dealing with local issues, better two-way awareness of/ interaction with resource agencies". Participatory framework makes it possible for the community "to make healthier choices for themselves and their communities" and "increase in socially responsible efficacies". (Morris, 2003).

Participatory models result in "empowerment, community building and social equity". They concentrate on dual focus "to achieve some specific development end" and "to empower communities via participation" (Morris, 2003). Community can have a better perception of reality and improve conversation among "the poor people, external and local agents" (Altafin, 1991).

Scholars differentiate the participation as weak participation and strong participation. Weak participation is where "intended beneficiaries [are] consulted during the project design so as to take into account their felt needs, aspirations and capabilities" (IFAD, cited in World Bank, 1992). Chambers define strong participation as "an educational and empowering process in which people, in partnership with each other and those able to assist them, identify problems and needs, mobilize resources, and assume responsibility themselves to plan, manage, control and assess the individual and collective actions that they themselves decide upon" Chambers(1983, 94, 97).

In a democracy, lagging in participation would result in ineffective functioning of any structure. Possibility of success becomes viable only when participation is made primary. Participation is considered as the involvement in decision making process which is preceded by "analysis of the context, problem sensing, formulation and framing" and it needs responsibility. Participation is something associated with democracy and horizontal approach of development. It is also closely linked to the questions of empowerment (Pastrana, 2005). The secret lies in "who participates? What do they participate in? How do they participate? And for what reasons do they participate?" (Bailur, 2008)

At times the participatory models do have "unrealistic expectations" and "over-ambitious goals". All the participatory models do not claim success (Morris, 2003). A weak participatory approach "may be ritualistic and unproductive" and the strong approach "may be unrealistic, too expensive and politically different for development agencies to conduct, and most of all, too demanding of beneficiaries" (Brett, 2003). He also raises a question as it is quoted, "I am highly educated, and can access immense amounts of information, but I rely on professionals to service almost all of my needs. Why should poor people with fewer skills and less information be expected to organize their own services?" (Brett, 2003).

There are many researches which question the realism of participation as the representatives might not be the "real" representatives of the community and its needs. They might reflect the needs or they might be selected for their affiliation to education, articulation and politics. When looking at the development projects, only few people become key users and it would never address or can be addressed as "community". If it is seen critically the notion of participation itself is a top-down approach as an outsider designs the project and the community is expected to take the charge. As the project proceeds, the development agents push it towards an angle to reach the goals and not proceed in the way the community expects. (Bailur, 2008)

David Sill raises the doubt that the "uninformed" participants might be of no use and they might manipulate the interests and hinder the development. Robert Dahl(1966) comments, "a high level of participation could lead to controversy, fragmentation and instability" and is "not possible & desirable". The participants are not conceived as active subjects but as passive receivers and the project experts as the protagonists (Pastrana, 2005).

The notion of participation becomes incomplete without ownership (Bailur, 2008). Collective ownership "perform the function of keeping the village folk engaged, keeping stakeholders engaged, continually sounding out different individuals so as to regenerate the idea and continually seek affirmation amongst the participants" (Kanungo, 2003) which also has the risk when the individual's needs contradict with those of which with others.

The available literatures on telecentre stress on the community participation and community ownership. It has been proved in many studies that "user participation will create better relationships between designers and users" (Kawalek and Wood-Harper, 2002). Roman and Colle urge the voice for consideration to participation as "it conveys a sense of community ownership; it provides indigenous wisdom; it helps reflect community values and needs; it provides important resources, such as volunteers or technical expertise, at a favourable cost" (Roman & Colle, 2002).

Community Mobilization

Pedagogy of the Oppressed argues that "community involvement" and "dialogue" trigger the "individual or community empowerment". Cleaver (2001) posited "excel[s] in perpetuating the myth that communities are capable of anything, that all that is required sufficient mobilization and the latent capacities of the community will be unleashed in the interests of development". Development projects in spite of the goals need to considerable space to "participatory campaigns" which mostly comprises of "interpersonal channels", "group meetings, workshops and sometimes localized small media such as community theatre or interactive posters" (Morris, 2003).

UNDP-MOST project in China has set the development of "community awareness (promotion) strategies and materials" as one of the major activities in a list of deliverables (Jinqiu, 2007). Jinqiu documents the efforts of UNDP and Ministry of Science & Technology of China in hosting an advertising campaign to promote the project in local newspapers, radio, television, wall posters, bus banners and sign boards to target the rural residents (Jinqiu, 2007) and it resulted in the rise of awareness level of residents towards the new technology which was essential at the inception level.

The researcher who investigated the sustainability of ICT in Uganda documents the facilitation of policy which made sure the process of awareness creation by local institutional agents through effective and accurate media information. He further adds the project incorporated action research and it resulted in the "awareness of ICTs among the local target groups, especially among local policy makers and several researchers". Moreover they had also initiated strategies in business and the public sector to create awareness of the usefulness of ICTs for social and economic development. The researcher concludes that awareness creation have "a greater impact on the national ICT policy formulation process and potential impact on women" (Ofir Z. M., 2003).

Ofir (2003) cites the instances at Mozambique, Senegal, South Africa and Uganda that the community responded when the awareness has increased on the role of ICTs in development. "Influential ICT champions" have set an agenda to create awareness among decision-makers and the public to enhance its functionality. The results of action results were deployed to the target beneficiaries through awareness campaigns to create understanding between the policy makers and users which stimulated debate. Policy makers have also often utilized advocacy, awareness campaigns and lobbying as "policy influence instruments". In Mozambique and Senegal, the awareness campaign process is structured in such a way that people and institutions could provide "inputs into policy formulation processes". It is proved that awareness creation in turn influence others, strengthen negotiating power and argument bases at different levels through informal and formal gatherings (Ofir Z. M., 2003).

Reports have acknowledged the urgence of increase of awareness. The researcher identified that any strategic advocacy should be combined with capacity building and awareness raising. Lack of awareness did not end up in functional stability and gender considerations. Ela posits that the UK government has set "raise awareness of benefits" as one of the strategies to achieve the goal of Information Society as it believed encouragement to use or access the services would increase overall access and there were consistent efforts to fulfill the same.

Stephen M. Mutula explains the awareness created helped the target group to access the Multipurpose Community Telecentres (MCTs) of Tanzania in full pledge. He also further states that the diversity and the socio-economic scenario of sub-saharan Africa demands "extra-ordinary measures" like "outdoor advertising, use of roadshows, billboards, and promotion posters, advertisements around strategic places such as shops, churches, schools, stadium, airports, clubs and public transport" to create awareness "about the increasing digital opportunities that can be accessed by the populace" and he also warns of inculcating the rural and the needy people in this circle. Community video programmes and theatre were seemed to be effective in a rural area to create awareness.

A report on a health programme stresses on the need lies with the funding agencies to create awareness about the project explaining its processes using "formal and informal" strategies. Interpersonal communication and advertisements in media helped to establish the Pawtucket Heart Health Programme and the project has set "awareness" about the initiative as one of the goals and strategies, which would allow the users to avail the benefits. Community awareness always remains as a challenge for appropriate use of any innovation since its inception. The accessibility of services depends on the awareness of functions and it will be one of the main components in any M&E (Monitoring & Evaluation) research. The formal and informal communication media enhance awareness creation. The report concludes that the initiative could not achieve its goals as there was "limited awareness initially".

Queensland based Community based ICT – Women Empowerment Project did create awareness about a range of issues, topics and activities of interest to women and how the Information and Communication Technology could be a solution, which in turn produced "mental stimulation and broadened participants' thinking" to access or adopt the innovation. "New knowledge, awareness and understanding" created about new ICTs ended in potential benefits and impact among women. The funding agency realized that awareness is needed "when women of diverse backgrounds and levels of skills and knowledge are brought together".

Nature of Approach

In development, the urgence for design and implementation of bottom-top interventions arose when Top-down development projects faced a death blow by the 1980s (Brett, 2003). Development projects focused to start from bottom-up criteria and focus on the poorer communities while the economic sustainability may be an overall goal. "Bottom-up" approach influenced need based and relevant policy formulation coming to other countries where top-down approach was in function.

Altafin states in *Participatory Communication in Social Development Evaluation* that "people are called not only to answer surveys and to provide information; they are directly involved in programme planning and production, with access to professional help, technical facilities and resources" and "not be a mere echo of the outsiders' voice", but contradictorily development agents hold the control. Optimistic argue that "bottom-up approach will lead to more relevant and effective projects" (Altafin, 1991).

UNDP-MOST programme which aimed to alleviate poverty and narrow the digital divide in China failed as the model strictly followed a four-tier top-to-down approach. The communicators' "target goals" were prioritized than the "recipients' need for the Internet". The partnership agencies also did not share a common goal, whereas the government and UNDP fostered on poverty reduction and the local government concentrated on infrastructure development (Jinqiu, 2007).

Delman also reflects the same about the UNDP-MOST programmes. The project in a perfect top-to-down approach cross through all the levels of "bureaucratic system" and the policies of every department made it inflexible to make necessary adjustment to suit local conditions. It also led the bureaucrats to make the project benefit for themselves rather than the community (Delman, 1993).

Literature survey projects that bottom-up projects have proved successful while addressing "digital exclusion". "Local authorities, the third sector and community groups" need to be given an important role in leading and supporting initiatives. Sustainability of projects demand sustained interest and participation of the community members from the beginning.

The participatory and "grounded" bottom-up approach demand the community to "describe their perceived needs and to articulate their viewpoints in relation to social and business-related factors". Top-down approach may be appropriate for private businesses but if something is focused on behavioural change or community development, bottom-up approach cannot be replaced (Duncombe, Heeks, Morgan, & Arun, 2005).

In a course of period, there were evidences that the focus on bottom-up approach was shifted to conceptualize an integrated model of joining both the bottom-up and top-down approaches. The adoption of combined top-down approaches with bottom-up approaches was a mandate put forth by science and technology panel of the UN Convention to Combat Desertification and Drought (UNCCD).

Most of the Telecentre projects have followed the same as quoted by Roman and Colle that "a telecenters is the product of an eclectic strategy for social change that mixes a prescriptive top-down technology transfer with a bottom-up community leadership to make the technology work for self-determined development goals". ICT for development projects depend highly on the technology and the community based centers are entrusted for technology transfer "to provide information and communication opportunities to the rural poor". It clearly focuses on the very nature of top-down approach. But the increasing criticism and evident scope of bottom-up approach leaves the funding agencies to mix up "top-down and bottom-up approaches" in which the community defines the communication and information needs and the project agencies with the help of telecenter staff play an active role in "identification, retrieval, processing and diffusion of content" (Roman & Colle, 2002).

Most of the participatory theories stress on the people-centered bottom-up approach. But there are strong evidences of tension exists between "top-down bureaucratic imperatives and the bottom-up requirements of local communities". Visions and the reality often collide with each other and if untreated in an appropriate time would concede in failure of the process. The commencing vision should be "sufficiently sustained and not lost".

Partnership and Networking

Affiliations and alliances with groups of multiple-stakeholders are critical to the success of community based technological interventions (Aranda & Fontaine, 2001). Funding agencies collaborate with local farmers' organizations, educational institutions and NGOs to create locally relevant content (Oestmann & Dymond, 2001). Finance of matching contributions is often co-ordianted in partnership with various stakeholders. The cases which have neglected the notion of partnerships could not stand in the long run (Ernberg, 1998). The following paragraphs give a document on how partnerships help to make the telecenters sustainable and viable. It focuses on the cases s documented by various researchers rather than looking at what other researchers or authors have to discuss on these key issues.

Large-scale projects with joint partnerships between private and government have left success in the case of Karnataka and Andhra Pradesh in India (Jinqiu, 2007). The Gaseleka Telecentre of South Africa initiated and owned by a local Non Governmental Organization had a committee of 15 reputed members from the village. They were the influential persons within the community and local government. This alliance has helped them to secure support from the local government and also these members influenced the community to access the services and that was "crucial to the success of the centre" (Benjamin, 2001).

After an interim evaluation at the Western Australia Telecentre Network, it was recommended to reconstitute the Advisory committee with representations from public and private sectors to encompass a full range of government and non-government services (Short, 2001). The consulting agency strongly suggested The Australian Open Learning Network in Australia to develop alliances and partnerships with local government, industries, business firms, community organizations, universities, government departments and commercial organizations to achieve its goal (Gooley, 2001).

The telecenters at Canada has allied with the "federal and provincial health departments to develop and test new approaches to primary healthcare delivery in rural communities". This alliance has brought new user groups (Sheppard, 2001). In some cases, the partnerships and alliances with local government, schools, non-governmental organizations or libraries help to get access for physical space and technical space (Murray, 2001).

A telecottage / telecenter under a network with focus on development of rural economies maintain a "network of networks" to provide and link intranets and extranets among the various stakeholders "to maximize access to information and resources, encourage knowledge sharing, promote online partnerships and help communities build a better future (Evans, 2001). The AMIC@ telecenters at Paraguay had strategic partners like Internet Service Providers for connectivity, Higher Educational Institutions for students to serve as volunteers and professors to train and facilitate the employees, radio and television stations for advertisements and US Peace Corps for facilitation with managerial and operational tasks (Aranda & Fontaine, 2001).

Uganda's Multipurpose Community Telecenter forged partnerships with "institutions and individuals who had the required resources or who could provide access to potential users". They initiated partnerships at three levels – international, national and local which yielded technical resources and support at free of cost and thus ends up in "programming and content creation" (Mayanja, 2001). In Mozambique, the partnerships with educational institutions, professional groups, local government and community organizations helped to build the user network and the government departments did come forward to offer services to make the telecenters more viable. But the private sector did not show much interest as the telecenters were of less profit and secluded targeting the rural households (Gaster, 2001).

Ghana's Community Learning Centers have had partnerships with two major stakeholders of the region – a teachers' (primary and secondary) association and the regional development commission. They have taken different roles to ascertain development (Akakpo & Fontaine, 2001). Learning Centre at Lesotho had partnerships with international agencies for financial support and the Universities for content delivery apart from communication services. The Universities provided information and the centre acted as a hub for "gathering and disseminating information for education, training, development and business, and for providing office and communications services" (Howard, 2001).

Need Assessment and Evaluation

International communities have accepted the notion of locally relevant content. But in most cases, it is apparent that "there is limited content on the Internet relevant to the needs of rural users" and telecenters are often seen as "supply-driven rather than demand driven" (Oestmann & Dymond, 2001). In china, the deployment of ICT was questioned and proved to be failure as the content was not relevant to the users in anyway, though the system has followed Public-Private Partnership patterns. In Tongnan of China, the residents did not find any of the services relevant to them and it failed to address its capability to reduce poverty level (Jinqiu, 2007). Absence of content in local language was one of the major reasons for the failure of telecenters in South Africa (Khumalo, 1998).

Telecentres in the African nations have proved that "if technology is adapted to address real needs of people, they will use it". Initial phase of the ICT based interventions focus on information needs assessment and determine the economic viability of rural areas to support the communication services and assess the resources needed and costs involved to meet the requirements of rural areas. At the end identified communication and information needs would be inculcated in policy. It involves the men and women of the community to define their needs and develop content. The ICT policies did not focus on the attitudes and needs of the users but assumed the policies would bring benefits to all, which is THE wrong assumption in any ICT based intervention. More importantly it helps the community to understand their own information needs and it would reciprocate in accessing the ICT services (Ofir Z. M., 2003).

Nabanna ICT initiative which is functioning in West Bengal of India conducted an initial research to find their views of ICTs, expectations, usage and internal & external resources using in-depth interviews with different groups in the network, participant observation, field notes and mapping exercises. After the initiation of centres, the information agents maintained dairies to document their "thoughts, ideas and observations" which served as a window of everyday's lives and practices. Those notes helped to identify information needs and to generate content

The Gaseleka Telecentre in South Africa had monthly review meetings to identify problems and suggestions and to "measure impact and determine what else the telecenter can do to people" among from different stakeholders including the users but there had been no formal evaluation. They shared the findings with the community for further change or revision in the process (Benjamin, 2001). The

Western Australia Telecentre Network had two formal evaluations and also subjected itself to external reviews which helped them to focus on the goals, retain and generate resources (Short, The Western Australia Telecentre Network, 2001).

The Queensland Open Learning Network has gone through evaluations at various phases to "examine levels of access to, and levels of literacy in, information and communication technologies for students" and thus made amendments accordingly (Gooley, 2001). Canada's Newfoundland and Labrador telecenters have carried out a series of baseline focus groups, interviews and interim evaluations developing contextualized tools and techniques to retain the ongoing support for the services (Sheppard, 2001).

Among the network of telecottages (telecenters) in Hungary, the Hungarian Telecottage Movement initiated a "Telecottage Fact-finding, Monitoring and Evaluation" and the results were "of great value as a source of advice and guidance to new and existing telecottages and as input to the plans for the national telecottage managers training programme" (Murray, 2001). Evans documents the evaluations held at the WREN Telecottage at Warwickshire to review the which it turn would "make Internet access affordable for a larger proportion of the population and allowing telecottages to maintain an acceptable level of technology at a reasonable cost" (Evans, 2001).

Though the KITIMAT Community Skills Centre in Canada lacked formal evaluation due to lack of funding, the centre held client response as the effective informal evaluation tool and the negative feedbacks were dealt "instantly through self-evaluative staff workshops and follow-up with the client" (Hartig, 2001). USAID and the municipality of Asuncion's AMIC@ Project in Paraguay after its mid-term evaluation has made changes "to the operations to make the centres even more user-friendly and to offer and automate more of the Municipality's services" by employing new arrangements between the public, private and voluntary sectors differing from the original strategy and functioning (Aranda & Fontaine, 2001).

Financial Sustainability

Scholars, who have studied the financial viability, always questioned its existence after the demonstration/ pilot phase after three or four years of its inception. The key success factors of ICT initiatives are directly related to the financial outcomes of the centre (Duncombe, Heeks, Morgan, & Arun, 2005). There is a clear evidence of misconception between the "full costs involved in running information centers as well as the social and economic benefits that accrue from improved access to information via the internet" (Oestmann & Dymond, 2001).

UNDP-MOST Internet project in China failed after the demonstration phase and some farmers attribute the collapse of the Internet project to the termination of the funding (Jinqiu, 2007). A review of the project suggested along with the designing and execution of need based content, the project could have linked e-commerce activities as a means for providing financial sustainability to telecenters (Quibria & Tschang, 2001). In Venezuela, Internet access was given in all the public libraries to enable the mass of all social classes to access the information in nominal charges. But later after three years of its initiation, President has declared the usage of Internet and computer in the *Infocentros* at free of cost and the additional services may be charged which questioned the financial sustainability of the project and became a threat which resulted in the urgence of a business model for survival (NCIT, 2000).

Information Kiosks at Melur in Tamil Nadu, the first rural ICT initiative in TamilNadu had to shut the centers as they were not financially sustainable. Most of the centers were installed on personal loans by the entrepreneurs and some were run by the women Self Help Groups. Either one of them could take up revenue to run the centers. It could not render financial support to the infrastructure facilities, electricity and connectivity services (Govindaraju & Mabel, 2010). The biggest and major challenge for Melur Kiosks was financial sustainability and it led to the closure of the project (Narender & Nirmala, 2003).

Women based ICT enterprises are often subjected to financial vulnerabilities caused by "non-payment of monies owned, corruption, market competition, dependence on a single source of income, downturn in demand, illness and low traces of income-generating activities". They are required to earn income to cover costs and attain profit and re-invest them in the business to make it financially viable. Local networking and partnerships promise financial sustainability to some extent (Duncombe, Heeks, Morgan, & Arun, 2005).

There is always a demand from the project agencies and other stakeholders that the telecenters' "pricing strategies and guidelines are often lacking, and the prices do not reflect the cost of providing the services" (Oestmann & Dymond, 2001). "The service-fee-charging model proves to be an effective way of keeping the rural Internet services financially viable, sustainable or even profitable" (Quibria & Tschang, 2001).

In the developed countries, the telecenters are funded by the government but in the case of developing countries the external agencies fund the projects for a period of time and sustainability becomes an issue when the funding period ends in the latter cases with the lack of long-term financial support (Oestmann & Dymond, 2001). The Australian telecenters receive grants every year for its maintenance and functioning (Short, The Western Australia Telecentre Network, 2001) & (Gooley, 2001). Most of the projects incorporate the investigation of possible financial sustainability strategies in the need assessment phase itself for the longer term (Banks, 2004).

The early stages of telecenters require subsidies towards services "to offset the high start-up costs and piloting of new ideas" and they could not charge at full cost. With or without external financial assistance they have to move towards financial sustainability which is possible in the developed countries. In the due course of introduction of ICT based interventions, the developing countries' initiatives are not expected to function after three or four years of operation. Some scholars suggest of national ICT policies which would give benefits to the telecenters. But it remains a problem as the ownership pattern differs in every telecenter ranging from commercial to public focus.

Amidst the cloud of subsidies and financial support, the rural users face "higher costs and poorer levels of service", unreliable and high communication costs (Gooley, 2001). Few of the African countries which have taken ICT as one of the strategies towards development offer telephone subsidies and tax exemptions to maintain the centers functional (Gaster, 2001). When the financial sustainability has become an issue among the developing agencies and ICT researches, there have been a flow of suggestions regarding a commercial model.

But Gaster (2001) rightly states that though the commercial model through public-private partnership assures of sustainability by high economic benefits, the real target audience that is the rural users would be excluded from the process by "the more prosperous farmers, small entrepreneurs and community members" in "content gathering, production and dissemination". Any commercial entity would not sacrifice the most needed "time, effort and money" to achieve development for the underdeveloped.

Social and Demographic Variables

A study of the sustainability issues of UNDP-MOST Internet project revealed those individual characteristics and the pre-existing disparities in "age, gender, income, education and social positions resulted in an unbalanced access and usage of the Internet services". The Internet project did not acquire as "a natural stage of its socioeconomic development" but was forced by the change agents which failed in China. Mobilization of social, financial and human resources can ensure the implementation and sustainability of the Internet Project (Jinqiu, 2007). Khumalo also indicates "lack of culture" for the under usage of personal computers and Internet in the telecenters (Khumalo, 1998). There is a causal alarm that the digital revolution will result in disbanding of "communities and local cultures" (Gooley, 2001).

In the developing countries, level of literacy always remains as a constraint in deploying ICT for development (Brown, 2001; Chowdhury, 2000; Heeks, 1999). Literacy blocks the pavement even if access becomes possible. Technological innovation needs skills from its user to be benefitted. It becomes ineffective when the users of low demographics profile lack them (Jinqiu, 2007). "Farmers' command of basic IT skills and the complimentary role of the Internet to traditional means of communication" influence the adoption of technology for development (Quibria & Tschang, 2001).

Universal Service Agency (USA) conducted a survey of telecenters in South Africa and found that "illiteracy in general and computer illiteracy in particular" was the major cause of underutilization of Internet in the rural hubs (Khumalo, 1998). In Peru, with the low rate of literacy, primarily they had to focus on improving the educational level and the implementation of modernization in agriculture on the secondary basis. Mayan population, the indigenous population with no knowledge either in English or Spanish did not find the Internet interesting as 90 percent of the web content is in English (Dagron, 2001).

Though the Internet provides tremendous opportunities, the cost is very huge which is not affordable for a commoner (Dagron, 2001). High costs to access internet opt the "farmers" to stay away from technology (Jinqiu, 2007). High cost of Internet connection did affect the usage of telecenters in South Africa (Khumalo, 1998). The study, *Assessing the Need and Potential of Community Networking for Development in Rural India* recommended "low-cost services may be more equalizing than strategies aimed at wide coverage" and suggested of "a need for low-cost, affordable technologies in order to avoid economic barriers to access as much as possible" (Blattman, 2003).

The pioneering ICT initiative of South India at Melur of Tamil Nadu had to call off as it could not be financially sustainable. The technical support agency did provide subsidies to the farmers initially for about 6 months who access the centers. Those farmers who were low in economic profile did make use of the chance and earned money for merely asking questions in the kiosks over webcam. The project initiators had believed the farmers would adopt the new trend. But the kiosks being run by the rural entrepreneurs, they could not give subsidies after the stipulated time and that became the major reason with the failure of Melur kiosks (Govindaraju & Mabel, 2010).

Alfonso opposes the notion of technology is the solution and he posits that, "technology alone may not be the answer if culture and identity are not at the heart of the discussion". The biggest challenge in the diffusion of any technology/ innovation is "to change the attitude of the society" (Dagron, 2001). A study among the fishermen revealed that they were reluctant to learn new technology from the kiosk operator, who happened to be a woman. Immersed in the patriarchal society, the fishermen oppose the view of being dependant on women for anything (Govindaraju & Mabel, 2010).

Rural communities expect the ICT hubs to be within their community and they really do mind travelling far distances (Cohen, 2008). Social disparities hinder the development process and thus the effective deployment of technology among the community. In the case of Government of India's project of Common Service Centers, rural entrepreneurs were selected to initiate the centers in their rural helmet. They run the centers in their own buildings or rent buildings. But if the entrepreneurs belonged to the lower social status, they were either denied buildings for rent or given for higher rents. In other cases, people of lower social status were not allowed to access the Internet hubs which is situated in the higher class area. Socio-economic divide leads to the digital divide in most of the cases and "therefore the disparities would continue to widen with the uneven diffusion and adoption of the Internet" (Camacho, 2001).

Development practitioners consider technology alone is transferred to a community and often lacks to concentrate on "a set of assumptions and practices that emerged from another context and other needs" (Dagron, 2001). The researcher finds underdeveloped economy, handicapped access to the centre, lack of adequate telecommunication infrastructure and the lack of personal skills as the vital reasons for the failure of UNDP project in China. Farmers at the bottom of the structure would not opt for Internet unless and until they witness any economic benefits. The planners often do not understand that "the will of bringing about changes, no matter how good natured it was, could not substitute for individuals' motivation for change" (Jinqiu, 2007).

Physical and Technical Support

Prevalence of lack of customer skills among the managers and staff of telecenters has a profound effect on the existence of telecenters (Oestmann & Dymond, 2001). At some places they have been called as facilitators, as 'they facilitate the process of integration between people and the technologies and services". They will be recruited and or in some cases they may be the owners of the telecenters (Aranda & Fontaine, 2001).

Most of the ICT interventions function among the diverged communities which lay the need for a committed personality who overlooks the functioning of the project and shortage of staff results in adverse effect of the intervention after the sponsoring agency or any Non-Governmental Organization sketches the strategies (Dagron, 2001). He/ she helps to "overcome the challenge of working in a large area" and is willing to work without time, space and social limitations (Cohen, 2008).

Many telecenters have had a policy and provision for employing volunteers to make it free from financial sustainability. Telecenters rely on part time employees with specific skill sets and have a flexible timing of working with the users combining commitment to the family and work for both the parties. Part time workers and users can fix up the own timing conveniently. Some telecenters in Australia have highly relied upon the volunteers rather than full-time or part-time employees (Short, The Western Australia Telecentre Network, 2001). But on the later phases they had learnt that the volunteers lacked essential skill sets to run the centre and changed to employ full time efficient workers to 'keep up with user demand' and in the content creation, community mobilization and to offer technical support to the users (Sheppard, 2001).

As budgets allow, the full-time employees recruit instructors, programme assistants, tutors and mentors as consultants on short term basis for the arising needs. But they maintain the rhythm of the centers through bi-weekly staff meetings and newsletter to ensure even the consultants could go along with the determined objectives and strategies (Hartig, 2001). Hungarian telecenters recruited full- time workers and volunteers. The volunteers are the community members and they serve as assistants to the staff which helped the centres to have the assistance of capable and efficient main staff and at the same time the volunteers worked round the clock in accordance with the need of the community even though the chief has to come from the far off place (Murray, 2001). The presence of both the full-time and part-time workers in the centers assure success in 'creating local employment and making extensive use, as necessary of teleworkers, freelance project staff and student placements' (Evans, 2001).

South African telecenters recruited more than one staff with more skill sets which seem to be practical for the viability of the centre. But salary remains as a big threat in the telecenters if they employ more than one staff. The author cites of an example of a South African telecenter where both the husband and wife with different skills are recruited, in which salary is not a big deal comparing to other cases where employees are not related to one another (Benjamin, 2001).

An interim evaluation of Newfoundland and Labrador telecenters revealed that, "while volunteers can play a major role in building and sustaining a telecenter, there is a need for one individual whose only focus is building use of the telecenter by the community" (Sheppard, 2001). Case studies reveal that the operators in the telecenters, either full-time employees or volunteers are responsible for the functioning of the centres. It is essential that they belong to the community as it has direct effect on the need assessment, content creation and community mobilization rather. Rural users easily adopt themselves with someone from their community comparing to a stranger from other places (Aranda & Fontaine, 2001).

Though the telecenter projects choose highly committed person as staff in the centers, they need to be given adequate training through print materials, conferences, workshops and tranings. Neglecting this would result in the lacking of 'new strategic directions, the introduction of new technologies, programmes and services, and means of improving client service and learner support' and thus in the disfunctioning of centres (Gooley, 2001). Apart from training the employees, the project agencies train the interested people from the villages along with them, so that others who attain technical and functioning knowledge of the centre volunteer themselves to consistently run the centre (Evans, 2001).

Many ICT and development researches have stressed the significance of operational support and the delivery of adequate materials whenever necessary from the external support agencies to sustain the functioning (Cohen, 2008). "Technical know-how is at a premium" and the partner agencies do not give adequate training for the people of the community to handle the issue then and there it arises (Dagron, 2001). But they need to wait till someone arrives from the headquarters which creates intolerance among the villagers and force them not to be totally dependent on the technology (Govindaraju & Mabel, 2010). Lack of ICT skills threatens the long existence of ICT based interventions (Ofir Z. M., 2003).

CONCLUSION

The above factors have clearly emphasized its importance in the impact of any rural initiative inspite of its geographical, cultural and political significances. When looking at the development projects, only few people become key users and it would never address or can be addressed as "community".

The notion of participation becomes incomplete without ownership (Bailur, 2008). Collective ownership "perform the function of keeping the village folk engaged, keeping stakeholders engaged, continually sounding out different individuals so as to regenerate the idea and continually seek affirmation amongst the participants" (Kanungo, 2003) which also has the risk when the individual's needs contradict with those of which with others.

The researchers identified that any strategic advocacy should be combined with capacity building and awareness raising. Ela posits that the UK government has set "raise awareness of benefits" as one of the strategies to achieve the goal of Information Society as it believed encouragement to use or access the services would increase overall access and there were consistent efforts to fulfill the same (Klecun, 2008).

Most of the participatory theories stress on the people-centered bottom-up approach. The participatory and "grounded" bottom-up approach demand the community to "describe their perceived needs and to articulate their viewpoints in relation to social and business-related factors". Top-down approach may be appropriate for private businesses but if something is focused on behavioural change or community development, bottom-up approach cannot be replaced (Duncombe, Heeks, Morgan, & Arun, 2005). Visions and the reality often collide with each other and if untreated in an appropriate time would concede in failure of the process. The commencing vision should be "sufficiently sustained and not lost" (Rheingold, 2003).

The cases which have neglected the notion of partnerships could not stand in the long run (Ernberg, 1998). Affiliations and alliances with groups of multiple-stakeholders are critical to the success of community based technological interventions (Aranda & Fontaine, 2001). The telecenters at Canada has allied with the "federal and provincial health departments to develop and test new approaches to primary healthcare delivery in rural communities". This alliance has brought new user groups (Sheppard, 2001). In some cases, the partnerships and alliances with local government, schools, non-governmental organizations or libraries help to get access for physical space and technical space (Murray, 2001).

The ICT policies did not focus on the attitudes and needs of the users but assumed the policies would bring benefits to all, which is THE wrong assumption in any ICT based intervention. International communities have accepted the notion of locally relevant content. But in most cases, it is apparent that "there is limited content on the Internet relevant to the needs of rural users" and telecenters are often seen as "supply-driven rather than demand driven" (Oestmann & Dymond, 2001).

The key success factors of ICT initiatives are directly related to the financial outcomes of the centre. ICT enterprises are often subjected to financial vulnerabilities caused by "non-payment of monies owned, corruption, market competition, dependence on a single source of income, downturn in demand, illness and low traces of income-generating activities". They are required to earn income to cover costs and attain profit and re-invest them in the business to make it financially viable. Local networking and partnerships promise financial sustainability to some extent (Duncombe, Heeks, Morgan, & Arun, 2005). Any commercial entity would not sacrifice the most needed "time, effort and money" to achieve development for the underdeveloped.

In the developing countries, level of literacy always remains as a constraint in deploying ICT for development (Heeks, 1999). Literacy blocks the pavement even if access becomes possible. Technological innovation needs skills from its user to be benefitted. "Illiteracy in general and computer illiteracy in particular" was the major cause of underutilization of Internet in the rural hubs. The biggest challenge in the diffusion of any technology/ innovation is "to change the attitude of the society" (Dagron, 2001).

Most of the ICT interventions function among the diverged communities which lay the need for a committed personality who overlooks the functioning of the project and shortage of staff results in adverse effect of the intervention after the sponsoring agency or any Non-Governmental Organization sketches the strategies (Dagron, 2001). Though the telecenter projects choose highly committed person as staff in the centers, they need to be given adequate training through print materials, conferences, workshops and tranings. Neglecting this would result in the lacking of 'new strategic directions, the introduction of new technologies, programmes and services, and means of improving client service and learner support' and thus in the disfunctioning of centers (Gooley, 2001).

The above discussion has clearly identified and proved that the predicted contingency factors play a big role in determining the positive or negative impact of any Information and Communication Technology project. Of all the factors, community participation, community ownership and need based content decide the direction of the project. It is also revealed that if something is essential, the rural communities can pay for it. It lies between who decides on what is needed. The model should evolve from the community and no agency can stand among the rural communities with their business models. In those villages where the ICT has been deployed very well, it is obviously seen that they have taken ICT as a complimentary tool to other development strategies and not supplementary tool. It is appreciative that ICT hubs have enabled the rural students to attain computer education and training which paves a way for them to advance in knowledge search using Internet.

REFERENCES

Akakpo, J., & Fontaine, M. (2001). Ghana's Community Learning Centers. In C. Latchem, & D. Walker (Eds.), Telecentres: Case Studies and Key Issues. Vancouver: The Commonwealth of Learning.

Altafin, L. (1991). Participatory Communication in Social Development Evaluation. *Community Development Journal: An International Forum, 26*(4), 312–314. doi:10.1093/cdj/26.4.312

Aranda, S., & Fontaine, M. (2001). The AMIC@ in the Municipality of Asuncion, Paraguay. In C. Latchem & D. Walker (Eds.), Telecentres: Case Studies and Key Issues. Vancouver: The Commonwealth of Learning.

Bailur, S. (2007). The Complexities of Community Participation in ICT for Development Projects: the Case of "Our Voices." *Proceedings of the 9th International Conference on Social Implications of Computers in Developing Countries Brazil*. Brazil.

Bailur, S. (2008). *Deconstructing Community Participation in Telecentre Projects*. Development Informatics.

Banks, K. (2004). *Lessons Learned: Building Strong Internet-based Women's Networks*. Canada: IDRC.

Benjamin, P. (2001). The Gaseleka Telecentre, Northern Province, South Africa. In C. Latchem, & D. Walker (Eds.), Telecentres: Case Studies and Key Issues (pp. 75 - 84). Vancouver: The Commonwealth of Learning.

Bhatnagar,, B., , & Williams,, A., (Eds.). (1992). *Participatory Development and the World Bank, World Bank Discussion Papers*. Washington, DC: World Bank.

Blattman. (2003). Assessing the Need and Potential of Community Networking for Development in Rural India. *The Information Society, 19* (5), 349 - 364.

Brett, E. (2003). Participation and Accountability in Development Management. *The Journal of Development Studies, 40*(2), 1–29. doi:10.1080/00220380412331293747

Brown, M. M. (2001). *Can ICTs address the needs of the poor?* Retrieved.

Camacho, K. (2001). *Evaluating the impact of the Internet in civil society organizations of Central America: A summary of a research framework*. Retrieved.

Chambers, R. (1983). *Rural Development: Putting the Last First*. London: Longman.

Chambers, R. (1994). Participatory Rural Appraisal (PRA): Challenges, Potentials and Paradigm. *World Development, 22*(10), 1437–1454. doi:10.1016/0305-750X(94)90030-2

Chambers, R. (1997). *Whose Reality Counts? Putting the First Last*. London: Intermediate Technology. doi:10.3362/9781780440453

Chowdhury, N. (2000). *Information and communications technologies and IFPRI's Mandate: A conceptual framework*. Retrieved from http://www.ifpri.org/divs/cd/dp/ictdp01.pdf

Cleaver, F. (2001). Institutions, Agency and the Limitations of Participatory Approaches to Development. In B. Cooke & U. Kothari (Eds.), *Participation, the New Tyranny?* (pp. 36–55). London: Zed.

Cohen, E. R. (2008). *Community Engagement in Global Health Research: Case Studies from the Developing World - The Zomba District, Malawi Case Study* [PhD dissertation]. Canada: Simon Fraser University.

Contractor, N. S., Singhal, A., & Rogers, E. M. (1988). Metatheoretical Perspectives on Satellite Television and Development in India. *Journal of Broadcasting & Electronic Media*, *32*(2), 129–148. doi:10.1080/08838158809386690

Dagron, A. G. (2001). *Making Waves: Stories of Participatory Comunication for Social Change*. New York: The Rockefeller Foundation.

Delman, J. (1993). *Agricultural extension in Renshou County, China: A case-study of bureaucratic intervention for agricultural innovation and change*. Hamburg: Institut fur Asienkunde.

Duncombe, R., Heeks, R., Morgan, S., & Arun, S. (2005). *Supporting Women's ICT-Based Enterprises - A Handbook for Agencies in Development*. Manchester: Institute for Development Policy and Management.

Ernberg, J. (1998). *Towards a Framework for Evaluation of Multipurpose Community Telecentre. Partnerships and Participation in Telecommunications for Rural Development*. Ontario: University of Guelph.

Evans, D. (2001). The WREN Telecottage. In C. Latchem, & D. Walker (Eds.), Telecentres: Case Studies and Key Issues. Vancouver: The Commonwealth of Learning.

Evusa, J. E. (2005). *Information Communication Technologies as Tools for Socio-Economic and Political Development: The National Council of Churches of Kenya (NCCK) Huruma Community Telecentre as a Case Study*. MI: ProQuest Information and Learning Company.

Gaster, P. (2001). A Pilot Telecentres Project in Mozambique. In C. Latchem, & D. Walker (Eds.), Telecentres: Case Studies and Key Issues. Vancouver: The Commonwealth of Learning.

Gooley, A. (2001). THe Queensland Open Learning Network, Australia. In C. Latchem, & D. Walker, Telecentres: Case Studies and Key Issues. Vancouver: The Commonwealth of Learning.

Govindaraju, P., & Mabel, M. M. (2010). The Demise of a Digital Solution: A Study of Melur Kiosks in Tamilnadu, India. *Journal of Communication*.

Hartig, N. (2001). The KITIMAT Community Skills Center in British Columbia, Canada. In C. Letchem, & D. Walker (Eds.), Telecentres: Case Studies and Key Issues (p.). Vancouver: The Commonwealth of Learning.

Heeks, R. (1999, March). *The tyranny of participation in information systems: Learning from development projects*. Retrieved from http://idpm.man.ac.uk/publications/wp/di/di_wp04.pdf

Heeks, R. (2002). Information systems and developing countries: Failure, success, and local improvisations. *The Information Society*, *18*(2), 101–112. doi:10.1080/01972240290075039

Howard, L. (2001). The DaimlerChrysler Distance Learning Support Centre in Maseru, Lesotho. In C. Latchem, & D. Walker (Eds.), Telecentres: Case Studies and Key Issues. Vancouver: The Commonwealth of Learning.

Jinqiu, Z. (2007). The Sustainability of Public Internet Access Centers: Lessons from ICT Projects in Rural China. Empowering Rural Communities through ICT Policy and Research. Chennai.

Kanungo, S. (2003). Information Village: Bridging the Digital Divide in Rural India. In S. Madon & S. Krishna (Eds.), *The Digital Challenge: Information Technology in the Development Context* (pp. 103–123). Aldershot: Ashgate.

Kawalek, P., & Wood-Harper, T. (2002). The Finding of Thorns: User Participation in Enterprise Systems Implementation. *The Data Base for Advances in Information Systems*, *33*(1), 13–22. doi:10.1145/504350.504355

Khumalo, F. (1998). *Preliminary Evaluation of Telecenter Pilot Projects*. South Africa: Universal Service Agency.

Kling, R. (1980). Social Analyses of Computing: Theoretical Perspectives in Recent Empirical Research. *Computing Surveys*, 61-110.

Lee, S.-G. (2003). *An Integrative Study of Mobile Technology Adoption Based on the Technology Acceptance Model, Theory of Planned Behavior and Diffusion of Innovation Theory*. MI: ProQuest Information and Learning Company.

Mayanja, M. (2001). The Nakaseke Multipurpose Community Telecentre in Uganda. In C. Latchem, & D. Walker (Eds.), Telecentres: Case Studies and Key Issues. Vancouver: The Commonwealth of Learning.

Morris, N. (2003). A Comparative Analysis of the Diffusion annd Participatory Models in Development Communication. *Communication Theory*, *13*(2), 225–248. doi:10.1111/j.1468-2885.2003.tb00290.x

Murray, B. (2001). The Hungarian Telecottage Movement. In C. Latchem, & D. Walker, Telecentres: Case Studies and Key Issues. Vancouver: The Commonwealth of Learning.

Narender, K., & Nirmala. (2003). Information Communication Technology for Women. *Women and Information and Communication Technologies in India and China.* Adelaide: The Hawke Institute.

November 19, 2005, from http://www.acceso.or.cr/publica/telecom/frmwkENG.shtml

November 23, 2006, from http://www.undp.org/dpa/choices/2001/june/j4e.pdf

Oestmann, S., & Dymond, A. C. (2001). Telecentres - Experiences, Lessons and Trends. In C. Latchem, & D. Walker (Eds.), Telecentres: Case Studies and Key Issues (pp. 1 - 31). Vancouver: The Commonwealth of Learning.

Ofir, Z. M. (2003). *Information & Communication Technologies for Development (ACACIA): The Case of Uganda*. South Africa: The IDRC Evaluation Unit.

Ofir, Z. M. (2003). *Synthesis Report of Case Studies: ICTs for Development in Mozambique, Senegal, South Africa and Uganda*. South Africa: The IDRC Evaluation Unit.

Pastrana, S. (2005). The contributions of participation toward efficacy of community economic development projects in Morelos, Mexico. [Master of Arts Dissertation]. Simon Fraser University.

Pool, I. (1977). *The Social Impact of the Telephone*. Cambridge, MA: MIT Press.

Quibria, M. G., & Tschang, T. (2001, January). Information and communication technology and poverty: An Asian perspective. Retrieved from http://www.globalknowledge.org/gkps_portal/aprm2002/workshop/ADBI.pdf

Regional Human Development Report. Promoting ICT for Human Development in Asia: Realizing the Millennium Development Goals. (2007). New Delhi: Elsevier.

Rogers, E. M. (2003). The Generation of Innovations. Diffusion of Innovations (5th ed.). New York: Free Press..

Roman, R., & Colle, R. (2002). Themes and Issues in Telecentre Sustainability. *University of Manchester Development Informatices Working Paper Series*.

Roman, R., & Colle, R. (2002). *Creating a Participatory Telecenter Enterprise*. Barcelona: International Association for Media and Communication Research.

Sheppard, K. (2001). The Remote Community Service Telecentres of Newfoundland and Labrador, Canada. In C. Latchem, & D. Walker (Eds.), Telecentres: Case Studies and Key Issues. Vancouver: The Commonwealth of Learning.

Short, G. (2001). The Western Australia Telecentre Network. In C. Latchem, & D. Walker (Eds.), Telecentres: Case Studies and Key Issues. Vancouver: The Commonwealth of Learning.

Strauss, A., & Corbin, J. (1990). *Basics of Qualitative Research: Grounded Theory Procedures and Techniques*. Newbury Park: Sage Publications.

The Impact of ICT on Europe's Fishing Industry: a Case Study Approach. (2003).European Foundation for the Improvement of Living and Working Conditions. Retrieved from www.eurofound.eu.int

ADDITIONAL READING

Report of the Conference of FAO. (2001). Retrieved from http://www.fao.org/docrep/MEETING/004/Y2650e/Y2650e00.HTM

Sarewitz, D., & Pielke, R. Jr. (2001). Extreme Events: A Research and Policy Framework for Disasters in Context. *International Geology Review*, *43*(5),406–418.doi:10.1080/00206810109465022

Subramanian, S., Nair, S., & Sharma, S. (n. d.). Local Content Creation and ICT for Development: Some Experiences. Retrieved from http://www.unescobkk.org/fileadmin/user_upload/ict/e-books/ICT_for_NFE/Local_Content_Creation_-_Savithri_Subramanian_et_al.pdf

KEY TERMS AND DEFINITIONS

Access: Approach or entrance to a place.

Community Mobilization: A capacity building process, through which individuals, groups and families as well as organizations plan, carryout and evaluate activities on a participatory and sustained basis to achieve an agreed goal.

Development: A process which enables human beings to realize their potential, build self-confidence, and lead lives of dignity and fulfillment. It is a process which frees people from fear of want and exploitation. It is a movement away from political, social or economic oppression. Through development, political independence acquires true significance. A change towards betterment.

Financial Sustainability: The assessment that a project will have sufficient funds to meet all its resource and financial obligations, whether the fund continues or not.

Information: One or more statements or facts that are received by a human and that have some form of worth to the recipient.

Ownership: Ownership is perceived at three levels as a process by which voices are heard and considered legitimate or valid – who has influence over the outcome through decision making – how the effects of a decision are distributed, accepted and "owned" both spatially and temporally (Lachapelle, 2008).

Participation: A social process whereby specific groups with shared needs living in a defined geographic area actively pursue identification of their needs, take decisions and establish mechanisms to meet these needs (Chamala, 1995).

Compilation of References

25% Nigerian mobile phone subscribers use smartphones. (2013, January 8). *Punch.* Retrieved from http://www.punchng.com/business/technology/25-of-nigerian-mobile-subscribers-use-smartphones-tns

3. *news.* (2013, June 21). Police reap benefits of social media. Retrieved from http://www.3news.co.nz/Police-reap-benefits-of-social-media/tabid/423/articleID/302718/Default.aspx

A new goldmine. (2013, May 18). *The Economist.* Retrieved from http://www.economist.com/news/business/21578084-making-official-data-public-could-spur-lots-innovation-new-goldmine

Aamodt, A. (1993). A Case-Based answer to Some Problems of Knowledge-Based Systems. In E. Sandewall & C.G Jansson (Eds.) *Proceedings of the Scandinavian Conference on Artificial Intelligence (pp 168-182). IOS Press.* Retrieved from http://www.idi.ntnu.no/~agnar/publications/scai-93.pdf

ABC7News. (2014, June 25). Oakland Police Department turns to social media to find new recruits. Retrieved from http://abc7news.com/technology/oakland-police-uses-social-media-to-recruit/140708/

Abdoli, M.A., (1993). Municipal solid waste management system and its control methods. *Metropolitan recycling organization publication*, 142-154.

Accenture. (2012, January 11). Tap the Power of Social Media to Drive Better Policing Outcomes. Retrieved from http://www.accenture.com/us-en/Pages/insight-tap-power-social-media-drive-better-policing-outcomes.aspx

Accenture. (2013, June). Preparing Police Services for the future. Retrieved from http://www.accenture.com/us-en/landing-pages/Documents/13-1583/download/preparing-police-services-for-the-future.pdf

Accra, J. (2012). [Web log comment]. Retrieved from http://collegeassignments.wordpress.com/2012/10/01/provide-five-definitions-of-ictit-indicate-the-author-and-year-what-are-the-similarities-and-differences-in-these-definitions-provide-your-own-definition-of-ictit/

Ackoff, R. L. (1989). From data to wisdom. *Journal of Applied Systems Analysis, 16*, 5.

Adams, F. (2003). The informational turn in philosophy. *Minds and Machines, 13*(4), 471–501 Retrieved from http://www.uio.no/studier/emner/matnat/ifi/INF5020/h04/undervisningsmateriale/F-ADAMS-informational-turn-in-philosophy.pdf. doi:10.1023/A:1026244616112

Adams, M., & Oleksak, M. (2010). *Intangible Capital: Putting knowledge to work in the 21st century organization.* Santa Barbara: ABC-CLIO.

Adeoti, O.O., Osotimehin, K.O., & Olajide, O.T. (2012). Consumer Payment Pattern and Motivational Factors using Debit Card in Nigeria. *International Business Management*, 6(3), 352-355

Adler, P., & Kwon, S. (2002). Social capital: Prospects for a new concept. *Academy of Management Review, 27*(1), 17–40.

Afzali, A., Samani, J. M. V., & Rashid, M. (2011). Municipal landfill site selection for Isfahan City by use of fuzzy logic and analytic hierarchy process. *Iranian Journal of Environmental Health Sciences & Engineering, 8*(3), 273–284.

Agri Price Information Index. (2014). Mobitel Pvt Ltd. Retrieved from http://www.mobitel.lk

Ahituv, N., & Neumann, S. (1982). *Principles of Information Systems for Management*. Dubuque, IA: Wm. C. Brown Publishers.

Ahmad, H. A., Zainura, Z. N., Rafiu, O. Y., Fadhil, M. M. D. D., & Ariffin, M. A. H. (2013). Assessing environmental impacts of municipal solid waste of Johor by analytical hierarchy process. *Resources, Conservation and Recycling*, *73*, 188–196. doi:10.1016/j.resconrec.2013.01.003

Aigner, S. M., Flora, C. B., Tirmizi, S. N., & Wilcox, C. (1999). Dynamics to Sustain Community Development in Persistently Poor Rural Areas. *Community Development Journal: An International Forum*, *34*(1), 13–27. doi:10.1093/cdj/34.1.13

AIRO. (2012). The Atlas of the Island of Ireland - Mapping Social and Economic Change, All Ireland Research Observatory. Retrieved from http://www.airo.ie

Ajayi, O., Salawu, R. I., & Raji, T. I. (n. d.). A century of telecommunications development in Nigeria –what next? Retrieved from http://www.vii.org/papers/nigeria.htm

Ajzen, I. (1991). The Theory of Planned Behavior. *Organizational Behavior and Human Decision Processes*, *50*(2), 179–211. doi:10.1016/0749-5978(91)90020-T

Akakpo, J., & Fontaine, M. (2001). Ghana's Community Learning Centers. In C. Latchem, & D. Walker (Eds.), Telecentres: Case Studies and Key Issues. Vancouver: The Commonwealth of Learning.

Akbari, V., Rajabi, M. A., Chavoshi, S. H., & Shams, R. (2008). Landfill site selection by combining GIS and fuzzy multi-criteria decision analysis, case study: Bandar Abbas, Iran. *World Applied Sciences*, *3*(1), 39–47.

Akbiyik, C. (2010). Can affective computing lead to more effective use of ICT in Education? *Revista de Educacion*, *352*, 179–202.

Akçomak, S., Akdeve, E., & Fındık, D. (2013). *How do ICT firms in Turkey manage innovation? Diversity in expertise versus diversity in markets (No. 1301)*. STPS-Science and Technology Policy Studies Center, Middle East Technical University. Retrieved from http://stps.metu.edu.tr/sites/stps.metu.edu.tr/files/1301.pdf

Akoojee, S., & Nkomo, M. (2007). Access and quality in South African higher education: The twin challenges of transformation. *South African Journal of Higher Education*, *21*(3), 385–399.

Alabi, G. A. (1996). Telecommunications in Nigeria. University of Pennsylvania, African Studies Centre. Retrieved from www.africa.upenn.edu/ECA/aisi_inftl

Alderson, J. (1979). *Policing freedom*. Macdonald and Evans Plymouth.

Alexander, B. (2006). Web 2.0: A new wave of innovation for teaching and learning? *EDUCAUSE Review*, *41*(2), 32–44. Retrieved from https://net.educause.edu/ir/library/pdf/erm0621.pdf

Alexander, J. E., & Tate, M. A. (1999). *Web wisdom: How to evaluate and create Information Quality on the Web*. Mahwah, NJ: Lawrence Erlbaum Associates.

Al-Hanbali, A., Alsaaideh, B., & Kondoh, A. (2011). Using GIS-Based weighted linear combination analysis and remote sensing techniques to select optimum solid waste disposal sites within Mafraq City, Jordan. *Journal of Geographic Information System*, 3, 267-278. Retrieved from http://www.SciRP.org/journal/jgis doi:10.4236/jgis.2011.34023

Alhudaithy, A.I. and Kitchen, P.J., (2009). Rethinking models of technology adoption for Internet banking: The role of website features. *Journal of Financial Services Marketing*, 14(1), 56–69.

Ali, S., & Shahwar, D. (2011). Men, women and TV ads: The representation of men and women in the advertisements of pakistani electronic media. *Journal of Media and Communication Studies*, *3*(4), 151–159.

Allen, L. (2014). URL badman (Audio CD ed.). London, GB: Parlophone UK.

Altafin, L. (1991). Participatory Communication in Social Development Evaluation. *Community Development Journal: An International Forum*, *26*(4), 312–314. doi:10.1093/cdj/26.4.312

Alvarez, R., & Crespi, G. (2003). Determinants of technical efficiency in small firms. *Small Business Economics*, *20*(3), 233–244. doi:10.1023/A:1022804419183

Amsler, S. (2013). The politics of privatisation: insights from the Central Asian university. In Educators, Professionalism and Politics: Global Transitions, National Spaces and Professional Projects. NY and London: Routledge, 2012.

Andal, N. (2011). Communication Theories and Models. India: Himalaya Publishing House. ISBN Number: 978-93-524-588-0

Anderka, M., Stein, B., & Lipka, N. (2012). *Predicting Quality Flaws in User-generated Content: The Case of Wikipedia*. Retrieved from http://www.uni-weimar.de/medien/webis/publications/papers/stein_2012i.pdf

Anik, A.A. & Pathan, A.K. (2002). A framework for managing cost effective and easy electronic payment system in the developing countries.

Anthony, D., Smith, S. W., & Williamson, T. (2005). *Explaining Quality in Internet Collective Goods: Zealots and Good Samaritans in the Case of Wikipedia*. Retrieved from http://web.mit.edu/iandeseminar/Papers/Fall2005/anthony.pdf

Anthony, D., Smith, S. W., & Williamson, T. (2007). *The quality of Open Source Production: Zealots and good Samaritans in the case of Wikipedia [Technical Report* TR2007-606]. Dartmouth College, Computer Science. Retrieved from http://www.cs.dartmouth.edu/reports/TR2007-606.pdf

Aoki, M. (1989). *Information, incentives and bargaining in the Japanese economy: A microtheory of the Japanese Economy*. New York: Cambridge University Press.

Aponte, V. (2014, January 31). Police use social media to inform public about crime hot spots. *ValleyCentral.com*. Retrieved from http://www.valleycentral.com/news/story.aspx?id=1001273

Aranda, S., & Fontaine, M. (2001). The AMIC@ in the Municipality of Asuncion, Paraguay. In C. Latchem & D. Walker (Eds.), Telecentres: Case Studies and Key Issues. Vancouver: The Commonwealth of Learning.

Archmann, S., & Guiffart, A. (2014). ICT: Obstacle or Enabler for Social Inclusion? The Impacts of New Technologies on Governance. In S. Baum & A. Mahizhnan (Eds.), *E-Governance and Social Inclusion: Concepts and Cases* (pp. 45–61). Hershey, PA: Information Science Reference. doi:10.4018/978-1-4666-6106-6.ch004

Arkalgud, S. (2000). Electronic Payment Systems [Unpublished student report]. San Jose State University.

Armenakis, A. A. (1999). Organizational Change: A Review of Theory and Research in the 1990s. *Journal of Management*, *25*(3), 293–315. doi:10.1177/014920639902500303

Arya, U. (2010). Public relations facet of information and communication technologies: A cross sectional analysis of public grievances variables. *Governance & Public Policy*, *5*(4), 7–30.

Asaolu, O. T., Ayoola, J. T., & Yemi, E., (May 2011). Electronic payment system in Nigeria: implementation, constraints and solutions. *Journal of Management and Society*. 1(2).16-21

Astleitner, H. (2000). Designing emotionally sound instruction: The FEASP-approach. *Instructional Science*, *28*(3), 169–198. doi:10.1023/A:1003893915778

Atiyas, I. (2011). Regulation and competition in the Turkish telecommunications industry. In *The Political Economy of Regulation in Turkey*. New York: Springer. doi:10.1007/978-1-4419-7750-2_8

Atrostic, B. K., Motohashi, K., & Nguyen, S. V. (2008). Computer Network Use and Firms' Productivity Performance: The United States vs. Japan (US Census Bureau Center for Economic Studies Paper No. CES-WP-08-30). Retrieved from http://papers.ssrn.com/sol3/papers.cfm?abstract_id=1269425

Atrostic, B. K., & Nguyen, S. V. (2005). IT and productivity in US manufacturing: Do computer networks matter? *Economic Inquiry*, *43*(3), 493–506. doi:10.1093/ei/cbi033

Auer, S. R., Bizer, C., Kobilarov, G., Lehmann, J., Cyganiak, R., & Ives, Z. (2007). Lecture Notes in Computer Science: Vol. 4825. *DBpedia: A Nucleus for a Web of Open Data* (p. 722). The Semantic Web; doi:10.1007/978-3-540-76298-0_52

Aufderheide, P., & Firestone, C. M. (1993). *Media Literacy: A Report of the National Leadership Conference on Media Literacy.* Washington, DC: Aspen Institute.

Australian Institute of Police Management. (2012, June). *Preparing police services for the future: Six steps toward transformation. Australian Institute of Police Management.* Retrieved from http://www.aipm.gov.au/know-it-now/police/preparing-police-services-for-the-future-six-steps-toward-transformation/

Average Indian household pays 42 bills online a year: study. (2006, April 14). *Business Line*, 135, 9.

Averdijk, M., & Elffers, H. (2012). The discrepancy between survey-based victim accounts and police reports revisited. *International Review of Victimology*, *18*(2), 91–107. doi:10.1177/0269758011432955

Aw, B. Y., & Batra, G. (1998). Technology, exports and firm efficiency in Taiwanese manufacturing. *Economics of Innovation and New Technology*, *7*(2), 93–113. doi:10.1080/10438599800000030

Axelrod, L., & Hone, K. S. (2006). Affectemes and all affects: A novel approach to coding user emotional expression during interactive experiences. *Behaviour & Information Technology*, *25*(2), 159–173. doi:10.1080/01449290500331164

Ayo, C. K., Adewoye, J. O., & Oni, A. A. (2010). The State of e-banking Implementation in Nigeria: A Post-Consolidation Review. *Journal of Emerging Trends in Economics and Management Science*, *1*(1), 37–45.

Baban, S. J., & Flannagan, J. (1998). Developing and implementing GIS-assisted constraints criteria for planning landfill sites in the UK. *Planning Practice and Research*, *13*(2), 139–151. doi:10.1080/02697459816157

Babbie, E. (2005). *The basics of social research.* Australia: Wadsworth.

Backus, M. (2001). *E-Governance and developing countries-Introduction and examples* [IICD Research Report No. 3]. Retrieved from http://www.ftpiicd.org/files/research/reports/report3.doc

Bagozzi, R. P. (1980). *Causal Models in Marketing.* New York, NY: Wiley.

Baig, A. (2013). Data protection designed for the cloud era. *GigaOM research.*

Bailur, S. (2007). The Complexities of Community Participation in ICT for Development Projects: the Case of "Our Voices." *Proceedings of the 9th International Conference on Social Implications of Computers in Developing Countries Brazil.* Brazil.

Bailur, S. (2008). *Deconstructing Community Participation in Telecentre Projects.* Development Informatics.

Balassa, B. (1978). Exports and economic growth: Further evidence. *Journal of Development Economics*, *5*(2), 181–189. doi:10.1016/0304-3878(78)90006-8

Balit, S. (1998). Listening to farmers: communication for participation and change in Latin America. In Training for agriculture and rural development: 1997-98, 29-40. Rome Italy: FAO.

Bandura, A. (1997). *Self-efficacy: The exercise of control.* New York: W. H. Freeman.

Banks, J. (2009). Co-creative expertise: Auran Games and Fury –A case study. *Media International Australia, 130*, 77-89. Retrieved from http://eprints.qut.edu.au/26176/1/26176.pdf

Banks, J. A., & Deuze, M. (2009). Co-creative labour. *International Journal of Cultural Studies*, *12*(5), 4194–4431 Retrieved from http://eprints.qut.edu.au/31340/2/c31340.pdf doi:10.1177/1367877909337862

Banks, K. (2004). *Lessons Learned: Building Strong Internet-based Women's Networks.* Canada: IDRC.

Barber, M. J., Paier, M., & Scherngell, T. (2009). *Analyzing and modeling European R&D collaborations: Challenges and opportunities from a large social network. Analysis of Complex Networks: From Biology to Linguistics.* Chicago: Willey-Blackwell

Bargent, J. (2013, April). Mexico Crime Tracking Social Media Page Disappears. *InSight Crime | Organized Crime in the Americas.* Retrieved from http://www.insightcrime.org/news-briefs/mexican-crime-tracking-social-media-pages-disappear

Bargh, J., & McKenna, K. (2004). The Internet and social life. *Annual Review of Psychology, 55*(1), 573–590. doi:10.1146/annurev.psych.55.090902.141922 PMID:14744227

Bar-Hillel, Y., & Carnap, R. (1952). *An outline of a theory of Semantic information* [Technical report No. 247]. Cambridge, Massachusetts. Retrieved from http://dspace.mit.edu/bitstream/handle/1721.1/4821/RLE-TR-247-03150899.pdf?sequence=1

Barker, B. (2013, March).Social Media and Criminal Organizations. *Security Management*. Retrieved from http://www.securitymanagement.com/article/social-media-and-criminal-organizations-0010271

Barnard, H., Cowan, R., & Müller, M. (2012). Global excellence at the expense of local diffusion, or a bridge between two worlds? Research in science and technology in the developing world. *Research Policy, 41*(4), 756–769. doi:10.1016/j.respol.2011.12.002

Barney, J. (1991). Firm resources and sustained competitive advantage. *Journal of Management, 17*(1), 99–120. doi:10.1177/014920639101700108

Bartlett, A., & Henderson, M. (2013). *Things that liberate: An australian feminist wunderkammer*. Newcastle, GB: Cambridge Scholars Publishing.

Basden, A. (2010). On using spheres of meaning to define and dignify the IS discipline. *International Journal of Information Management, 30*(1), 13–20. doi:10.1016/j.ijinfomgt.2009.11.006

Basu, S., & Fernald, J. (2007). Information and communications technology as a general-purpose technology: Evidence from US industry data. *German Economic Review, 8*(2), 146–173. doi:10.1111/j.1468-0475.2007.00402.x

Bateson, G. (1972). *Steps to an ecology of mind* (p.459). New York: Ballantine Books. Retrieved from http://www.edtechpost.ca/readings/Gregory%20Bateson%20-%20Ecology%20of%20Mind.pdf

Bathelt, H. (2007). BuzzandPipeline Dynamics: Towards a Knowledge Based Multiplier Model of Clusters. *Geography Compass, 1*(6), 1282–1298. doi:10.1111/j.1749-8198.2007.00070.x

Bathelt, H., Malmberg, A., & Maskell, P. (2004). Clusters and knowledge: Local buzz, global pipelines and the process of knowledge creation. *Progress in Human Geography, 28*(1), 31–56. doi:10.1191/0309132504ph469oa

Battese, G. E., & Coelli, T. J. (1992). *Frontier production functions, technical efficiency and panel data: with application to paddy farmers in India*. Netherlands: Springer.

Baxter, N. (1996). Constitutionally, can police officers be replaced by soldiers in times of crisis. *The Police Journal, 69*, 119.

BBC News. (2011, November 18). Thousands in force "tweet-a-thon." Retrieved from http://www.bbc.co.uk/news/uk-england-birmingham-15790457

BBC News. (2012, December 7). Social media "benefits police." Retrieved from http://www.bbc.co.uk/news/technology-20641190

BBC News. (2014, July 2). Plea for no new social-media laws. Retrieved from http://www.bbc.com/news/uk-politics-28104937

Beale, R., & Creed, C. (2009). Affective interaction: How emotional agents affect users. *International Journal of Human-Computer Studies, 67*(9), 755–776. doi:10.1016/j.ijhcs.2009.05.001

Beccheti, L., Londono Bedoya, D. A., & Paganetto, L. (2003). ICT Investment, Productivity and Efficiency: Evidence at Firm Level using a Stochastic Frontier Approach. *Journal of Productivity Analysis, 20*(2), 143–167. doi:10.1023/A:1025128121853

Beer, D., & Burrows, R. (2007). Sociology and, of and in Web 2.0: Some initial considerations. *Sociological Research Online, 12*(5), 17. Retrieved from http://www.socresonline.org.uk/12/5/17.html doi:10.5153/sro.1560

Beer, M., & Eisenstat, R. A. (2011). How to have an honest conversation about your business strategy. *Harvard Business Review, 82*(2), 82–89. PMID:14971272

Belkin, N. J. (1978). Information concepts for Information Science. *The Journal of Documentation, 34*(10), 55–85. doi:10.1108/eb026653

Bell, D. (1976). In Webster (1997), Theories of the Information Society. London: Routledge.

Bell, D. (1976). The Coming of Post-Industrial Society: a Venture in Social Forecasting. In (2013, November), What Is An Information Society Media Essay. *UK Essays*. Retrieved from http://www.ukessays.com/essays/media/what-is-an-information-society-media-essay.php?cref=1

Bell, D. (1980). *Sociological Journeys 1960-1980*. London: Heinemann.

Bell, D. (1989). *The Third Technological Revolution and its Possible Socio-Economic Consequences*. Dissent. Spring.

Bell, M. (1998). The Dialogue of Solidarities, or Why the Lion Spared Androcles. *Sociological Focus*, *31*(2), 181–199. doi:10.1080/00380237.1998.10571100

Benjamin, P. (2001). The Gaseleka Telecentre, Northern Province, South Africa. In C. Latchem, & D. Walker (Eds.), Telecentres: Case Studies and Key Issues (pp. 75 - 84). Vancouver: The Commonwealth of Learning.

Benkler, Y. (2006). *The Wealth of Networks: How Social Production Transforms Markets and Freedom*. New Haven, CT: Yale University Press. Retrieved from http://yalepress.yale.edu/yupbooks/excerpts/benkler_wealth.pdf

Bennett, J. (2012, December 11). Study Shows That Social Media Benefits Police. *Social Media Today*. Retrieved from http://www.socialmediatoday.com/content/study-shows-social-media-benefits-police

Bennett, R. J. (1986). The impact of Non-Domestic rates on profitability and investment. *Fiscal Studies*, *7*(1), 34–50. doi:10.1111/j.1475-5890.1986.tb00412.x

Benneworth, P., & Dassen, A. (2010). *Strengthening Global-Local Connectivity in Regional Innovation Strategies–A Theoretical and Policy Reflection.* CHEPS. Twente, Netherlands.

Berghall, E. (2014). Has Finland advanced from an investment to an innovation-driven stage*? LTA*, *1*(14), 11–32.

Bergh, D. D., & Lim, E. N. (2008). Learning how to restructure: Absorptive capacity and improvisational views of restructuring actions and performance. *Strategic Management Journal*, *29*(6), 593–616. doi:10.1002/smj.676

Berner, S. (n. d). *Information overload or Information deficiency?* Retrieved from http://www.samberner.com/documents/KM/infoglut.pdf

Berners Lee, T. (1999). *Weaving the Web: The Original Design and Ultimate Destiny of the World Wide Web, Orion Business Books* (1st ed.). Collins.

Bertot, J. C., & Jaeger, P. T. (2006). User-centered e-government: Challenges and benefits for government web sites. *Government Information Quarterly*, *23*(2), 163–168. doi:10.1016/j.giq.2006.02.001

Bertschek, I., Fryges, H., & Kaiser, U. (2006). B2B or Not to Be: Does B2B e-commerce increase labour productivity? *International Journal of the Economics of Business*, *13*(3), 387–405. doi:10.1080/13571510600961395

Bessen, J., & Hunt, R. M. (2007). An empirical look at software patents. *Journal of Economics & Management Strategy*, *16*(1), 157–189. doi:10.1111/j.1530-9134.2007.00136.x

Best Practice Sharing. (2015, May 16). University Economic Development Association. Retrived from http://universityeda.org/value-to-members/best-practice-sharing/

Bhalla, A., & Lapeyre, F. (1997). Social Exclusion: Towards an Analytical and Operational Framework. *Development and Change*, *28*(3), 413–433. doi:10.1111/1467-7660.00049

Bharadwaj, S. N. (2014, February 4). Open Data Apps are All the Rage in India-Enterprise Efficiency. Retrieved from http://www.enterpriseefficiency.com/author.asp?section_id=2405&doc_id=272552

Bharadwaj, A. S. (2000). A Resource-Based Perspective on Information Technology Capability and Firm Performance: An Empirical Investigation. *Management Information Systems Quarterly*, *24*(1), 169–196. doi:10.2307/3250983

Bhaskar News. (2004, September 22). Man dies on the municipal committee counter in Delhi. *Dainik Bhaskar*.

Bhatnagar, S. (1990). E governance and social exclusion: Experiences from the fields.

Bhatnagar, S. (2000). Information Technology and Development: Foundation and Key Issues (pp. 1-13). In S. Bhatnagar, & R. Schware (Eds), *Information and Communication Technology in Rural Development: Case Studies from India*. World Bank Institute (WBI) Working Papers, WBI Publications.

Bhatnagar, S. (2000). Land/Property registration in Andhra Pradesh. *WorldBank*. Retrieved from www1.worldbank.org/publicsector/egov/cardcs.htm

Bhatnagar,, B., , & Williams,, A., (Eds.). (1992). *Participatory Development and the World Bank, World Bank Discussion Papers*. Washington, DC: World Bank.

Bhatnagar, S. (2014). Strategies for Digital Inclusion: Experience from India. In S. Baum & A. Mahizhnan (Eds.), *E-Governance and Social Inclusion: Concepts and Cases* (pp. 243–255). Hershey, PA: Information Science Reference. doi:10.4018/978-1-4666-6106-6.ch015

Bhatnagar, S., & Singh, N. (2010). Assessing the Impact of EGovernment: A study of E-Government Projects in India. *Information Technologies and International Development*, *6*(2), 109–127.

Bhushan, N., & Rai, K. (2004). *Strategic Decision Making: Applying the Analytic Hierarchy Process* (p. 172). New York: Springer-Verlag.

Bianchi-Berthouze, N., & Kleinsmith, A. (2003). A categorical approach to affective gesture recognition. *Connection Science*, *15*(4), 259–269. doi:10.1080/09540090310001658793

Biedenbach, T., & Söderholm, A. (2008). The challenge of organizing change in hypercompetitive industries: A literature review. *Journal of Change Management*, *8*(2), 123–145. doi:10.1080/14697010801953967

Birdshall, N., & Nellis, J. (2003). Winners and losers: Assessing the distributional impact of privatization. *World Development*, *31*(10), 1617–1633. doi:10.1016/S0305-750X(03)00141-4

Bishop, J. (2012). Tackling internet abuse in great britain: Towards a framework for classifying severities of 'flame trolling'. *The 11th International Conference on Security and Management (SAM'12)*. Las Vegas, NV.

Bishop, J. (2014a). 'U r bias love:' Using 'bleasure' and 'motif' as forensic linguistic means to annotate twitter and newsblog comments for the purpose of multimedia forensics. *Proceedings of the 11th International Conference on Web Based Communities and Social Media*. Lisbon, PT.

Bishop, J. (2014d). Using the legal concepts of 'forensic linguistics,' 'bleasure' and 'motif' to enhance multimedia forensics. *Proceedings of the 13th International Conference on Security and Management (SAM'14)*. Las Vegas, NV.

Bishop, J. (2013a). The art of trolling law enforcement: A review and model for implementing 'flame trolling' legislation enacted in great britain (1981–2012). *International Review of Law Computers & Technology*, *27*(3), 301–318. doi:10.1080/13600869.2013.796706

Bishop, J. (2013b). The effect of deindividuation of the internet troller on criminal procedure implementation: An interview with a hater. *International Journal of Cyber Criminology*, *7*(1), 28–48.

Bishop, J. (2013c). Increasing capital revenue in social networking communities: Building social and economic relationships through avatars and characters. In J. Bishop (Ed.), *Examining the concepts, issues, and implications of internet trolling* (pp. 44–61). Hershey, PA: IGI Global. doi:10.4018/978-1-4666-2803-8.ch005

Bishop, J. (2013d). The psychology of trolling and lurking: The role of defriending and gamification for increasing participation in online communities using seductive narratives. In J. Bishop (Ed.), *Examining the concepts, issues and implications of internet trolling* (pp. 106–123). Hershey, PA: IGI Global. doi:10.4018/978-1-4666-2803-8.ch009

Bishop, J. (2014b). 'YouTube if you want to, the lady's not for blogging': Using 'bleasures' and 'motifs' to support multimedia forensic analyses of harassment by social media. *Oxford Cyber Harassment Research Symposium*. Oxford, GB.

Bishop, J. (2014c). Representations of 'trolls' in mass media communication: A review of media-texts and moral panics relating to 'internet trolling'. *International Journal of Web Based Communities*, *10*(1), 7–24. doi:10.1504/IJWBC.2014.058384

Bjoko, A. (2006). Using eye tracking to compare web page designs: A case study. *Journal of Usability Studies*, *3*(1), 112–120. Retrieved from http://uxpajournal.org/using-eye-tracking-to-compare-web-page-designs-a-case-study/

Black, J. (1999). Losing Ground Bit by Bit. *London BBC News Online*. Retrieved from http://news.bbc.co.uk/1/hi/special_report/1999/10/99information_rich_information_poor/472621.stm

Blattman. (2003). Assessing the Need and Potential of Community Networking for Development in Rural India. *The Information Society, 19* (5), 349 - 364.

Bock, R. D. (1960). Components of Variance Analysis as a Structural and Discriminal Analysis for Psychological Tests. *British Journal of Statistical Psychology, 13*(2), 151–163. doi:10.1111/j.2044-8317.1960.tb00052.x

Bock, R. D., & Bargmann, R. E. (1966). Analysis of Covariance Structures. *Psychometrika, 31*(4), 507–533. doi:10.1007/BF02289521 PMID:5232439

Bodman, P. M. (1996). On export-led growth in Australia and Canada: Cointegration, causality, and structural stability. *Australian Economic Papers, 35*(67), 282–299. doi:10.1111/j.1467-8454.1996.tb00051.x

Bőgel, G. (2009). *Az informatikai felhők gazdaságtana, (The Economics of IT clouds)* (pp. 673–688). Közgazdasági Szemle.

Boland, R. J., Jr. (1987). In Z.J. Gackowski (Ed.), Informing for Operations: Framework, Models and the First principles (pp. 47). USA: Informing Science Press.

Boland, R. J. Jr. (1987). The in-formation of information Systems. In R. J. Boland & R. A. Hirscheim (Eds.), *Critical issues in Information Systems Research* (pp. 363–379). New York: John Wiley & Sons.

Bollenn, K. A. (1989). *Structural Equations with latent Variables*. New York, NY: Wiley. doi:10.1002/9781118619179

Bolter, J. D., & Grusin, R. (2000). *Remediation: Understanding new media*. Massachusetts: MIT Press.

Bonneau, J., Muniz, J., Anderson, R., & Stajano, F. (2009). Eight Friends are Enough: Social Graph Approximation via Public Listings.*Proceedings of the Second ACM Workshop on Social Network Systems*. doi:10.1145/1578002.1578005

Bontcheva, K., Gorrell, G., & Wessels, B. (2013). *Social Media and Information Overload: Survey Results*. arXiv.

Borgo, M. D., Goodridge, P., Haskel, J., & Pesole, A. (2013). Productivity and growth in UK Industries: An intangible investment approach. *Oxford Bulletin of Economics and Statistics, 75*(6), 806–834. doi:10.1111/j.1468-0084.2012.00718.x

Bortolotti, B., D'Souza, J., Fantini, M., & Megginson, W. L. (2002). Privatization and the sources of performance improvement in the global telecommunications industry. *Telecommunications Policy, 26*(5), 243–268. doi:10.1016/S0308-5961(02)00013-7

Bosworth, B. P., & Triplett, J. E. (2000). *What's new about the new economy? IT, economic growth and productivity*. Washington, DC: Brookings Institution, Mimeo.

Bourdieu, P., & Wacquant, L. (1992). *An Invitation to Reflexive Sociology*. Chicago: University of Chicago Press.

Bowman, N. A. (2010). College Diversity Experiences and Cognitive Development: A Meta-Analysis. *Review of Educational Research, 80*(1), 4–33. doi:10.3102/0034654309352495

Boyd, D. (2007). Why youth (heart) social network sites: The role of networked publics in teenage social life. In D. Buckingham (Ed.), *MacArthur Foundation Series on Digital Learning –Youth, Identity, and Digital Media Volume*. Cambridge, MA: MIT Press. Retrieved from http://www.danah.org/papers/WhyYouthHeart.pdf

Boyd, D. (2008). *Taken Out of Context: American Teen Sociality in Networked Publics* [Doctoral Dissertation]. University of California, Berkeley. Retrieved from http://www.danah.org/papers/TakenOutOfContext.pdf

Boyd, D. M., & Hargittai, E. (2010). Facebook Privacy Settings: Who cares? First Monday peer reviewed journal of the web, *13*(6). Retrieved from http://firstmonday.org/article/view/3086/2589

Boyd, D. (2006). Friends, Friendsters, and MySpace Top 8: Writing community into being on social network sites. *First Monday, 11*(12). Retrieved from http://firstmonday.org/article/view/1418/1336 doi:10.5210/fm.v11i12.1418

Boyd, D. M., & Ellison, N. B. (2007). Social network sites: Definition, history, and scholarship. *Journal of Computer-Mediated Communication, 13*(1), 210–230. doi:10.1111/j.1083-6101.2007.00393.x

Boyd, N. M., & Bright, D. S. (2007). Appreciative Inquiry as a Mode Action Research for Community Psychology. *Journal of Community Psychology*, *35*(8), 1019–1036. doi:10.1002/jcop.20208

Brandt, D. S. (1996). Evaluating information on the Internet. *Computers in Libraries*, *16*(5), 44–46.

Brants, K., & Frissen, V. (2003). Inclusion and exclusion in the Information Society. Retrieved from http://www.lse.ac.uk/media@lse/research/EMTEL/reports/brants_2003_emtel.pdf

Brasini, S., & Freo, M. (2012). The impact of information and communication technologies: An insight at micro-level on one Italian region. *Economics of Innovation and New Technology*, *21*(2), 107–123. doi:10.1080/10438599.2011.558175

Brendle, A. (2002, November 20). Police Use GIS in D.C. Area Sniper Case and More. *National Geographic*. Retrieved from http://news.nationalgeographic.com/news/2002/11/1120_021120_GIScrime.html

Breschi, S., & Cusmano, L. (2004). Unveiling the texture of a European Research Area: Emergence of oligarchic networks under EU Framework Programmes. *International Journal of Technology Management*, *27*(8), 747–772. doi:10.1504/IJTM.2004.004992

Brett, E. (2003). Participation and Accountability in Development Management. *The Journal of Development Studies*, *40*(2), 1–29. doi:10.1080/00220380412331293747

Brezzi, M., Piacentini, M., Rosina, K., & Sanchez-Serra, D. (2012). Redefining urban areas in OECD countries. In *Redefining "Urban": A New Way to Measure Metropolitan Areas*. OECD. doi.10.1787/9789264174108-en

Brier, S. (2004). Cybersemiotics and the problems of the information-processing paradigm as a candidate for a unified science of information behind library information science. *Library Trends*, *52*(3), 629.

Brillouin, L. (1962). *Science and Information Theory*. New York: Academic Press.

British Columbia - CBC News. (2011, June 15). Riots erupt in Vancouver after Canucks loss. Retrieved from http://www.cbc.ca/news/canada/british-columbia/riots-erupt-in-vancouver-after-canucks-loss-1.993707

Broadbent, M. (1984). Information management and educational pluralism. *Education for Information*, *2*(3), 209–227.

Broekens, J., & Brinkman, P. (2009). Affect button: A method for reliable and valid affective self report. *International Journal of Human-Computer Studies*, *71*(6), 641–667. doi:10.1016/j.ijhcs.2013.02.003

Brogan, C. (2010). *Social media 101* (1st ed.). Hoboken, N.J.: Wiley. doi:10.1002/9781118256138

Brown, J. (2000). *Realising the Potential, Market place of ideas, Utilizing the First Amendment to Advance Universal Service and Access to the Internet.* Paper presented at 83rd Annual AEJMC Convention, Communication Technology & Policy Division. Phoenix Arizona.

Brown, J. S. (2000). Growing up digital: how the web changes work, education, and the ways people learn. *Change*, *32*(2), 10–20. Retrieved from http://www.johnseelybrown.com/Growing_up_digital.pdf doi:10.1080/00091380009601719

Brown, J., & Alder, R. (2008). Minds on fire: Open education, the long tail and learning 2.0. *EDUCAUSE Review*, *43*(1), 16–32.

Brown, M. M. (2001). *Can ICTs address the needs of the poor?* Retrieved.

Brown, M. M. (2001). *Democracy and the Information Revolution*. United Nations Development Programme.

Bruns, A. (2008). The Future Is User-Led: The Path towards Widespread Produsage. *Fibreculture Journal*, *11*. Retrieved from http://eprints.qut.edu.au/12902/1/12902.pdf

Buckel, E. E., Trapnell, P. D., & Paulhus, D. L. (2014). *Trolls just want to have fun. Personality and Individual Differences, Butler, A. J. P. (1992). Police management*. Aldershot, GB: Dartmouth Publishing Company Limited.

Buest, R., & Miller, P., (2013). *The state of Europe's homegrown cloud market*, GigaOM research

Bull, M., & Brown, T. (2012). Alternative workplace strategies Change communication : The impact on satisfaction with alternative workplace strategies. *Facilities*, *30*(3), 135–151. doi:10.1108/02632771211202842

Bundeskriminalamt (2012). *BKA Electronic Search and Information Systems.* Retrieved from http://www.bka.de/nn_194550/EN/SubjectsAZ/ElectronicSystems/electronicSearchAndInformationSystems__node.html?__nnn=true

Burki, A. A., & Terrell, D. (1998). Measuring production efficiency of small firms in Pakistan. *World Development, 26*(1), 155–169. doi:10.1016/S0305-750X(97)00122-8

Burns, A., & Eltham, B. (2009). Twitter free Iran: An evaluation of Twitter's role in public diplomacy and information operations in Iran's 2009 election crisis.

Burns, D., & Perron, Z. (2014). Considerations for Social Media Management and Strategy. *The Police Chief,* (81): 31–32.

Burson, J. K. (2010). *Measuring media literacy among collegiate journalism students* [Thesis]. Oklahoma State University.

Buttler, M. (2013, July 7). Criminals use social media to track police. *Herald Sun.* Retrieved from http://www.heraldsun.com.au/news/law-order/criminalss-use-social-media-to-track-police/story-fni0fee2-1226675624831

Byrne, E., & Sahay, S. (2007). Participatory Design for Social Development: A South African Case Study on Community-Based Health Information Systems. *Information Technology for Development, 13*(1), 71–94. doi:10.1002/itdj.20052

Byrne, J., & Marx, G. (2011). Technological Innovations in Crime Prevention and Policing. A Review of the Research on Implementation and Impact. *Journal of Police Studies, 3*(20), 17–40.

Cabo, P. G. (1999). Industrial participation and knowledge transfer in joint R&D projects. *International Journal of Technology Management, 18*(3), 188–206. doi:10.1504/IJTM.1999.002766

Cairncross, F. (1977). *The Death of Distance: How the Communications Revolution will Change Our Lives.* London: Orion Business Books.

Caldeira, M. M., & Ward, J. M. (2002). Understanding the successful adoption and use of IS/IT in SMEs: An explanation from Portuguese manufacturing industries. *Information Systems Journal, 12*(2), 121–152. doi:10.1046/j.1365-2575.2002.00119.x

Callaos, N., & Callaos, B. (2002). Toward a systemic notion of information: Practical consequences. *In-forming Science: the International Journal of an Emerging Transdiscipline, 5*(1), 1–11. Retrieved from http://www.inform.nu/Articles/Vol5/v5n1p001-011.pdf

Callon, M. (1986). Some elements of a sociology of translation: domestication of the scallops and the fishermen. In J. Law (Ed.), *A sociology of monsters: Essays on power, technology and domination* (pp. 196–229). London: Routledge.

Callon, M. (1991). Techno-economic networks and irreversibility. In J. Law (Ed.), *A sociology of monsters: Essays on power, technology and domination* (pp. 132–165). London: Routledge.

Camacho, K. (2001). *Evaluating the impact of the Internet in civil society organizations of Central America: A summary of a research framework.* Retrieved.

Cameron, K. S., & Caza, A. (2004). Contributions to the Discipline of Positive Organizational Scholarship. *The American Behavioral Scientist, 47*(6), 731–739. doi:10.1177/0002764203260207

Campus for Research Excellence and Technological Enterprise (CREATE). (2015, May 16). National Research Foundation. Retrieved from http://www.nrf.gov.sg/about-nrf/programmes/create

Capgemini Consulting. (n.d.). Page 7 - The Open Data Economy, Unlocking Economic Value By Opening Government & Public Data. Retrieved from http://ebooks.capgemini-consulting.com/The-Open-Data-Economy/files/assets/basic-html/page7.html

Carlsoon, B. (2004). The Digital Economy: What is New and What is Not? *Structural Change and Economic Dynamics, 15*(3), 245–264. doi:10.1016/j.strueco.2004.02.001

Caroli, E., & van Reenen, J. (2001). Skill-biased organizational change? Evidence from a panel of British and French establishments. *The Quarterly Journal of Economics, 116*(4), 1449–1492. doi:10.1162/003355301753265624

Carr, N. (2010). *The Shallows: What the Internet Is Doing to Our Brains.* New York: W.W. Norton & Company.

Carroll, A., Barnes, S. J., Scornavacca, E., & Fletcher, K. (2007). Consumer perceptions and attitudes towards SMS advertising: Recent evidence from New Zealand. *International Journal of Advertising*, *26*(1), 79–98.

Cash-less Nigeria. (n. d.). Central Bank of Nigeria. Retrieved November 22, 2014 from http://www.cenbank.org/cashless/

Cassell, C., & Symon, G. (2004). *Essential guide to qualitative methods in organizational research.* New Delhi: Sage Publications. Retrieved from http://preview.tinyurl.com/4s84c84

Castellani, D., Zanfei, A., & Muendler, M. A. (2006). *Multinational firms, innovation and productivity*. Cheltenham: Edward Elgar. doi:10.4337/9781847201591

Castells, M. (1989). *The Informational City: InformationTechnology, Economic Restructuring and the Urban-Regional Process*. Oxford: Blackwell.

Castells, M. (1994). European Cities, the Informational Society, and the Global Economy. *New Left Review*, *204*(March-April), 18–32.

Castells, M. (1996). *The rise of the network society: The information age, economy, society and culture*. Oxford, MA: Blackwell Publishers.

Castells, M. (2001). *The internet galaxy: Reflections on the internet, business and society*. Toronto: Oxford University Press. doi:10.1007/978-3-322-89613-1

Castiglione, C. (2012). Technical efficiency and ICT investment in Italian manufacturing firms. *Applied Economics*, *44*(14), 1749–1763. doi:10.1080/00036846.2011.554374

Castiglione, C., & Infante, D. (2014). ICTs and time-span in technical efficiency gains. A stochastic frontier approach over a panel of Italian manufacturing firms. *Economic Modelling*, *41*, 55–65. doi:10.1016/j.econmod.2014.04.021

Castro Sardi, X., & Mlikota, K. (2002). *Overview on E-governance: Working Paper prepared in the framework of the ICT cross–cutting project ICTs as Tools for Improving Local Governance*. Paris, France: UNESCO.

Central Bank of Sri Lanka. (2013a). *Annual Report 2013*. Colombo: Si Lanka. Central Bank of Sri Lanka.

Central Bank of Sri Lanka. (2013b). *Sri Lanka Socio-Economic Data 2013* (Vol. XXXVI). Colombo, Sri Lanka: Central Bank of Sri Lanka.

Chambers, R. (1983). *Rural Development: Putting the Last First*. London: Longman.

Chambers, R. (1994). Participatory Rural Appraisal (PRA): Challenges, Potentials and Paradigm. *World Development*, *22*(10), 1437–1454. doi:10.1016/0305-750X(94)90030-2

Chambers, R. (1997). *Whose Reality Counts? Putting the First Last*. London: Intermediate Technology. doi:10.3362/9781780440453

Chandler, D. (2001). *Technological or Media Determinism*. Retrieved from http://www.aber.ac.uk/media/Documents/tecdet/tdet01.html

Chang, K. T. (2010). *Introduction to Geographic Information System* (5th ed.). Mc Graw-Hill.

Chang, N. B., Parvathinathan, G., & Breeden, J. B. (2008). Combining GIS with fuzzy multicriteria decision-making for landfill siting in a fast-growing urban region. *Journal of Environmental Management*, *87*(1), 139–153. doi:10.1016/j.jenvman.2007.01.011 PMID:17363133

Charnpratheep, K., Zhou, Q., & Garner, B. (1997). Preliminary landfill site screening using fuzzy geographical information systems. *Waste Management & Research*, *15*(2), 197–215. doi:10.1177/0734242X9701500207

Chau, P. Y. K. (1997). Reexamining a Model for Evaluating Information Center Success: Using a Structural Equation Modeling Approach. *Decision Sciences*, *28*(2), 309–334. doi:10.1111/j.1540-5915.1997.tb01313.x

Checkland, P., & Scholes, J. (1990). *Soft systems methodology in action* (p. 303). Chichester: John Wiley and Sons.

Chen, H.-T. (n. d). *Understanding Content Consumers and Content Creators in the Web 2.0 Era: A Case Study of YouTube Users*. Retrieved from http://citation.allacademic.com/meta/p_mla_apa_research_citation/2/3/3/7/0/pages233709/p233709-1.php

Cheng, J. M. S., Blankson, C., Wang, E. S. T., & Chen, L. S. L. (2009). Consumer attitudes and interactive digital advertising. *International Journal of Advertising*, *28*(3), 501–525. doi:10.2501/S0265048709200710

Chen, J. (2012). The synergistic effects of IT-enabled resources on organizational capabilities and firm performance. *Information & Management*, *49*(3-4), 142–150. doi:10.1016/j.im.2012.01.005

Chen, Y.-C., & Dimitrova, D. V. (2006). Electronic government and online engagement: Citizen Interaction with government via web portals. *International Journal of Electronic Government Research*, *2*(1), 54–76. doi:10.4018/jegr.2006010104

Chermack, T. J., van der Merwe, L., & Lynham, S. A. (2007). Exploring the relationship between scenario planning and perceptions of strategic conversation quality. *Technological Forecasting and Social Change*, *74*(3), 379–390. doi:10.1016/j.techfore.2006.03.004

Chesbrough, H. W. (2003). *Open innovation: The new imperative for creating and profiting from technology*. Boston, MA: Harvard Business School Press.

Chesbrough, H. W. (2006b). *Open business model: How to thrive in the new innovation landscape*. Boston, MA: Harvard Business School Press.

Chhavi, M. (2008). ICT as a Tool For Poverty Reduction. Proceedings of the 2nd National Conference; INDIACom-2008, Computing for National Development. New Delhi: INDIACom.

Chittaro, L., & Sioni, R. (2014). Affective computing vs. affective placebo: Study of a biofeedback controlled game for relaxation training. *International Journal of Human-Computer Studies*, *72*(8-9), 663–673. doi:10.1016/j.ijhcs.2014.01.007

Chowdhury, N. (2000). *Information and communications technologies and IFPRI's Mandate: A conceptual framework*. Retrieved from http://www.ifpri.org/divs/cd/dp/ictdp01.pdf

Christopherson, S., Garretsen, H., & Martin, R. (2008). The world is not flat: Putting globalization in its place. *Cambridge Journal of Regions. Economy and Society*, *1*(3), 343–349.

Chung, O., & Rodriguez, L. (2012). *Information Source Use and dependencies for Investment Decision-Making*. Communication Technology and Policy 2000 Abstracts.

Cid, F., Moreno, J., Bustos, P., & Nunez, P. (2014). Muecas: A multi-sensor robotic head for affective human robot interaction and imitation. *Sensors (Basel, Switzerland)*, *14*(5), 7711–7737. doi:10.3390/s140507711 PMID:24787636

Cisneros, T. (2009, April 1) Santa Ana launches online crime-reporting tool. http://www.ocregister.com/news/reports-168503-police-online.html

Cleaver, F. (2001). Institutions, Agency and the Limitations of Participatory Approaches to Development. In B. Cooke & U. Kothari (Eds.), *Participation, the New Tyranny?* (pp. 36–55). London: Zed.

CNN. (2012). Official: Los Angeles arson suspect under investigation in Germany. Retrieved from http://articles.cnn.com/2012-01-04/us/us_california-arson_1_los-angeles-arson-fireshollywood-apartment?_s=PM:US

Code For Honor - Awards 2014 (2014). *Open Government Data (OGD) Platform India*. Retrieved from https://data.gov.in/event/code-honor-awards-2014

Coe, D. T., Helpman, E., & Hoffmaister, A. W. (1995). North-South R&D spillovers. *The Economic Journal*, *107*(440), 134–149. doi:10.1111/1468-0297.00146

Cohen, E. R. (2008). *Community Engagement in Global Health Research: Case Studies from the Developing World - The Zomba District, Malawi Case Study* [PhD dissertation]. Canada: Simon Fraser University.

Cohen, G. A. (2000). In Dogra, (2001). *ICTs for development: A paradox of hope & hype*. Paper presented at International Conference on Community for Development in the Digital Era. University of Madras, Chennai.

Cohen, W. M., & Levin, R. C. (1989). Empirical studies of innovation and market structure. Handbook of Industrial Organization, 2, 1059-1107.

Cohen, W. M., & Levinthal, D. A. (1990). Absorptive capacity: A new perspective on learning and innovation. *Administrative Science Quarterly*, *35*(1), 128–152. doi:10.2307/2393553

Coleman, J. S. (1988). Social capital in the creation of human capital. *American Journal of Sociology*, *94*(s1Supplement), S95–S120. doi:10.1086/228943

Columbus, L. (2013). *Gartner Predicts Infrastructure Services Will Accelerate Cloud Computing Growth*. Retrieved from http://www.forbes.com/sites/louiscolumbus/2013/02/19/gartner-predicts-infrastructure-services-will-accelerate-cloud-computing-growth/

Commissioner for Law Enforcement Data Security. (2012). *Social Media and Law Enforcement*. Retrieved from http://www.cleds.vic.gov.au/content.asp?a=CLEDSBridgingPage&Media_ID=98370

Commissionerate Of Municipal Administration (CMA) And ThoughtWorks Conduct Hackathon Dedicated To Improving Governance In The City. (2013, December 20). *E. F. Y.Times*. Retrieved from http://efytimes.com/e1/124753/Commissionerate-Of-Municipal-Administration-CMA-And-ThoughtWorks-Conduct-Hackathon-Dedicated-To-Improving-Governance-In-The-City

Comninos, A. (2013). The Role of Social Media and User-generated Content in Post-Conflict Peacebuilding. Retrieved from http://www.tdrp.net/PDFs/TDRP_%20SocialMediaInPostConflictPeaceBuilding.pdf

Composite Project. (2012, December 7). *COMPOSITE deliverable - Best Practice in Police Social Media Adaptation*. Retrieved from http://www.composite-project.eu/tl_files/fM_k0005/download/COMPOSITE-social-media-best-practice.pdf

Comreg -. (2014). *Quarterly Key Data Report - Data as of Q4 2013 Document No: 14/19*. Dublin: The Irish Communications Regulator.

Contractor, N. S., Singhal, A., & Rogers, E. M. (1988). Metatheoretical Perspectives on Satellite Television and Development in India. *Journal of Broadcasting & Electronic Media*, *32*(2), 129–148. doi:10.1080/08838158809386690

Cooke, P., Gomez Uranga, M., & Etxebarria, G. (1997). Regional innovation systems: Institutional and organisational dimensions. *Research Policy*, *26*(4), 475–491. doi:10.1016/S0048-7333(97)00025-5

Copitch, G., & Fox, C. (2010). Using social media as a means of improving public confidence. *Safer Communities*, *9*(2), 42–48. doi:10.5042/sc.2010.0226

Cordner, G. W. (2014). *Police administration* (S. Decker-Lucke, E. S. Boyne, & J. Haynes, Eds.). 8th ed.). Waltham, MA: Anderson Publishing.

Cormode, G., & Krishnamurthy, B. (2008). Key differences between Web 1.0 and Web 2.0. First Monday peer reviewed journal of the web, *13*(6). Retrieved from http://firstmonday.org/article/view/2125/1972

Cormode, G., & Krishnamurthy, B. (2008). Key differences between Web 1.0 and Web 2.0. *First Monday*, *13*(6), 2. Retrieved from http://firstmonday.org/article/view/2125/1972 doi:10.5210/fm.v13i6.2125

Corrado, C., Haskel, J., Jona-Lasinio, C., & Iommi, M. (2013). Innovation and intangible investment in Europe, Japan, and the United States. *Oxford Review of Economic Policy*, *29*(2), 261–286. doi:10.1093/oxrep/grt017

Corrado, C., Hulten, C., & Sichel, D. (2009). Intangible capital and US economic growth. *Review of Income and Wealth*, *55*(3), 661–685. doi:10.1111/j.1475-4991.2009.00343.x

Cover, R. (2006). Audience inter/active: Interactive media, narrative control and reconceiving audience history. *New Media & Society*, *8*(1), 139–158. Retrieved from http://www.academia.edu/655898/Audience_Inter_Active_Interactive_Media_Narrative_Control_and_Reconceiving_Audience_History doi:10.1177/1461444806059922

Cragg, P. B., & Zinatelli, N. (1995). The evolution of information systems in small firms. *Information & Management*, *29*(1), 1–8. doi:10.1016/0378-7206(95)00012-L

Crawford, A., & Lister, S. (2006). Additional security patrols in residential areas: Notes from the marketplace. *Policing and Society*, *16*(02), 164–188. doi:10.1080/10439460600662189

Crawford, R., & Disney, R. (2012). *Reform of ill-health retirement benefits for police in england and wales: The roles of national policy and local finance. (No. w18479)*. Cambridge, MA: National Bureau of Economic Research. doi:10.3386/w18479

Creating an Inclusive Society: Practical Strategies to Promote Social Integration. (2009). United Nations Department of Economic and Social Affairs. Retrieved from http://www.un.org/esa/socdev/egms/docs/2009/Ghana/inclusive-society.pdf

Crede, A. (1998) Electronic payment System, Electronic money and the Internet: The United Kingdom Experience to Date. University of Sussex. Retrieved from www.susx.ac.uk/spru

Criscuolo, C., & Waldron, K. (2003). E-commerce and productivity. *Economic Trends*, *60*, 52–57.

Cronin, B. (1985). Towards information based economics. *Journal of Information Science*, *12*(3), 129–137. doi:10.1177/016555158601200305

Crump, J. (2011). What Are the Police Doing on Twitter? Social Media, the Police and the Public. *Policy & Internet*, *3*(4), 1–27. doi:10.2202/1944-2866.1130

CSO. (2011). Census of Population 2011, Preliminary Results *(PDF download)* Central Statistics Office. Retrieved from www.cso.ie

Csobán, J. (2014). *A felhőalapú számítástechnika elterjedésének empirikus vizsgálata a magyar vállalatok körében, (The empirical study of the spread of cloud-based computer technology among the Hungarian enterprises)*. Szakdolgozat, Miskolci Egyetem.

Cullen, S. M. (1993). Political violence: The case of the british union of fascists. *Journal of Contemporary History*, *28*(2), 245–267. doi:10.1177/002200949302800203

Cummins, J. G. (2005). A new approach to the valuation of intangible capital. In C. Corrado, J. Haltiwanger, & D. Sichel (Eds.), *Measuring capital in the new economy* (pp. 47–72). USA: University of Chicago Press. doi:10.7208/chicago/9780226116174.003.0003

Curran, J., & Blackburn, R. (1994). *Small firms and local economic networks: the death of the local economy?* London, UK: Paul Chapman.

Czerniewicz, L., Ravjee, N., & Mlitwa, N. (2005). Information and communication technologies (ICTs) and South African higher education: Mapping the landscape.

Dagron, A. G. (2001). *Making Waves: Stories of Participatory Comunication for Social Change*. New York: The Rockefeller Foundation.

Daly, A., Gong, C. H., Dugdale, A., & Abello, A. (2014). Social Inclusion of Australian Children in the Digital Age. In S. Baum & A. Mahizhnan (Eds.), *E-Governance and Social Inclusion: Concepts and Cases* (pp. 164–181). Hershey, PA: Information Science Reference; doi:10.4018/978-1-4666-6106-6.ch010

Damaskopoulos, P., & Evgeniou, T. (2003). Adoption of new economy practices by SMEs in Eastern Europe. *European Management Journal*, *21*(2), 133–145. doi:10.1016/S0263-2373(03)00009-4

Daneshvar, R., (2004). Customizing Arcmap Interface to Generate a User- Friendly Landfill Site Selection GIS Tool. Department of Civil Engineering. University of Ottawa Canada, 7-13.

Daneshvar, R., Fernandes, L., Warith, M., & Daneshfar, B. (2005). Customizing arcmap interface to generate a user- friendly landfill site selection GIS tool. *Journal of Solid Waste Technology Management*, *31*(1), 1–12.

D'Arcy, P. (2011). *7 trends driving the evolving workforce - are you ready for change?* Retrieved from http://en.community.dell.com/dell-blogs/direct2dell/b/direct2dell/archive/2011/10/18/7-trends-driving-the-evolving-workforce-are-you-ready-for-change.aspx

Das, R. (2010). Scope of E-governance in Rural India. *Media Watch*, 1(2). Print ISSN: 0976-0911

Das, L. K. (2005). Culture as the Designer. *Design Issues*, *21*(4), 41–53. doi:10.1162/074793605774597523

DavideChicco. (2012, May 29) Which soft skills for research career? [Web log comment]. Retrieved from http://academia.stackexchange.com/questions/1799/which-soft-skills-for-research-career (2015, May 16).

Davis, F. D. (1989). Perceived Usefulness, Perceived Ease of Use and User Acceptance of Technology. *Management Information Systems Quarterly*, *13*(3), 319–340. doi:10.2307/249008

de Lange, P., Suwardy, T., & Mavondo, F. (2003). Integrating a virtual learning environment into an introductory accounting course: Determinants of student motivation. *Accounting Education*, *12*(1), 1–14. doi:10.1080/0963928032000064567

De Silva, H. (2008). *Using ICTs to create efficient agricultural markets: A future vision for Sri Lanka* [PDF document]. Retrieved from http://www.lirneasia.net/wp-content/uploads/2008/03/de-silva_transaction-costs-in-sri-lanka-the-future.pdf

De Silva, H., & Ratnadiwakara, D. (2008). Using ICT to reduce transaction costs in agriculture through better communication : A case-study from Sri Lanka. Retrieved from http://www.lirneasia.net

De Silva, L. N. C., Goonetillake, J. S., & Wikramanayake, G. N. (2012). A holistic mobile based information system to enhance farming activities in Sri Lanka. In *Engineering and Applied Science (EAS 2012), IASTED Conferences, Vol 785* (pp. 91–99). ACTA Press. doi:10.2316/P.2012.785-092

de Soyza, M. (2014). Dialog Tradenet. *Digital Knowledge Center*. Retrieved from http://digitalknowledgecentre.in

De Vries, G. J., & Koetter, M. (2011). ICT Adoption and heterogeneity in production technologies: Evidence for Chilean retailers. *Oxford Bulletin of Economics and Statistics*, *73*(4), 539–555. doi:10.1111/j.1468-0084.2010.00622.x

Deb, S. (2001, June 25). Hits, Misses and Missing Pride. *Outlook*. Hathway: New Delhi.

Defining Open in Open Data, Open Content and Open Knowledge. (n. d.). *Open Definition*. Retrieved from http://opendefinition.org/od/index.html

Delgado, M. A., Farinas, J. C., & Ruano, S. (2002). Firm productivity and export markets: A non-parametric approach. *Journal of International Economics*, *57*(2), 397–422. doi:10.1016/S0022-1996(01)00154-4

Delman, J. (1993). *Agricultural extension in Renshou County, China: A case-study of bureaucratic intervention for agricultural innovation and change*. Hamburg: Institut fur Asienkunde.

Delone, W. (1988). Determinants of success for computer usage in small business. *Management Information Systems Quarterly*, *12*(1), 51–61. doi:10.2307/248803

Demeure, V., Niewiadomski, R., & Pelachaud, C. (2011). How is believability of a virtual agent related to warmth, competence, personification, and embodiment? *Presence (Cambridge, Mass.)*, *20*(5), 431–448. doi:10.1162/PRES_a_00065

Denef, S., Bayerl, P. S., & Kaptein, N. A. (2013). Social Media and the Police: Tweeting Practices of British Police Forces During the August 2011 Riots. In *Proceedings of the SIGCHI Conference on Human Factors in Computing Systems* (pp. 3471–3480). New York, NY, USA: ACM. doi:10.1145/2470654.2466477

Denning, P., Horning, J., Parnas, D., & Weinstein, L. (2005). Wikipedia risks. *Communications of the ACM*, *48*(12), 152. doi:10.1145/1101779.1101804

Denning, S. (2010). *The leader's guide to radical management: Re-inventing the workplace for the 21st century*. San Francisco: Jossey-Bass.

Department of Communications. Energy and Natural Resources (DCENR) (2012). Delivering a Connected Society, A National Broadband Plan for Ireland. Retrieved from http://www.dcenr.gov.ie/Communications/Communications+Development/Next+Generation+Broadband/

Department of Economic and Social Affairs. Division for Public Administration & Development Management, United Nations, (2013). Guidelines on Open Government Data for Citizen Engagement. Retrieved from http://workspace.unpan.org/sites/Internet/Documents/Guidenlines%20on%20OGDCE%20May17%202013.pdf

Dervin, B. (1983) quoted in Zbigniew J. Gackowski (Ed.) Informing for Operations: Framework, Models and the First principles (2011, p.47). USA: Informing Science Press.

Deschatres, S. (2014, July 8). Social Engineering: Attacking the Weakest Link in the Security Chain. Retrieved from http://www.symantec.com/connect/blogs/social-engineering-attacking-weakest-link-security-chain

Determining Total Cost of Ownership for Data Center and Network Room Infrastructure, White Paper #6. (2003). *American Power Conversion*. Retrieved from http://www.linuxlabs.com/PDF/Data%20Center%20Cost%20of%20Ownership.pdf

Deuze, M. (2009). Convergence Culture and Media Work. In J. Holt & A. Perren (Eds.), *Media Industries: History, Theory, and Method* (pp. 144–156). Malden, MA: Wiley-Blackwell.

Devaraj, R. (2000). *South Asia: Digital Divide Sharpens Rich-Poor Gap*. Retrieved from http://www.ipsnews.net/2000/07/south-asia-digital-divide-sharpens-rich-poor-gap/

Devlin, K. (1991). *Logic and Information*. Cambridge: Cambridge University Press.

Dhaliwal, R. K., & Joshi, V. (2010). Mobile Phones - Boon to Rural Social System.[LICEJ]. *Literacy Information and Computer Education Journal*, *1*(4), 261–265.

Dharmaratne, T. A. (2013). Agricultural market information system in Sri Lanka: Costs, transmission, reliability, volatility and adequacy to the policy needs. Proceedings of the International Conference on Agricultural Statistics VI. Rio de Janeiro, Brazil. Retrieved from http://www.fao.org

Dialog Axiata, P. L. C. (2009). Dialog Tradenet and GGS partnership set to revolutionise agri market access. Retrieved from http://www.dialog.lk

Diekman, A. B., & Murnen, S. K. (2004). Learning to be little women and little men: The inequitable gender equality of nonsexist children's literature. *Sex Roles*, *50*(5), 373–385. doi:10.1023/B:SERS.0000018892.26527.ea

Dilling-Hansen, M., Madsen, E. S., & Smith, V. (2003). Efficiency, R&D and ownership–some empirical evidence. *International Journal of Production Economics*, *83*(1), 85–94. doi:10.1016/S0925-5273(02)00302-X

Dimelis, S. P., & Papaioannou, S. K. (2010). Technical efficiency and the role of information technology: a stochastic production frontier study across OECD countries. In S. Allegrezza & A. Dubrocard (Eds.), *Internet Econometrics* (pp. 43–62). UK: Palgrave McMillan.

Dimelis, S. P., & Papaioannou, S. K. (2014). Human capital effects on technical inefficiency: A stochastic frontier analysis across industries of the Greek economy. *International Review of Applied Economics*, *28*(6), 797–812. doi:10.1080/02692171.2014.907246

Dissanayake, D. M. L. B., Wijekoon, R. R. A., Madana, P., & Wickramasinghe, Y. W. (2009). Awareness and effectiveness of the toll free agricultural advisory service of the department of agriculture. *Abstract of Final Year Research Symposium 2009, Volume 03*. Faculty of Agriculture Rajarata University of Sri lanka. Retrieved from http://repository.rjt.ac.lk/7013/1685

Dissanayeke, U. I., Wickramasuriya, H. V. A., & Wijekoon, R. (2009). Evaluation of Computer Based Learning Materials in Agricultural Information Dissemination in Sri Lanka. *Tropical Agricultural Research*, *21*(1), 73–79.

Dissanayeke, U., & Wanigasundera, W. A. D. P. (2014). Mobile based information communication interactions among major agriculture stakeholders: Sri Lankan Experience. *Electronic Journal of Information Systems in Developing Countries*, *60*, 1–12.

Dittrich, K., & Duysters, D. (2007). Networking as a means to strategy change: The case of open innovation in mobile telephony. *Journal of Product Innovation Management*, *24*(6), 510–521. doi:10.1111/j.1540-5885.2007.00268.x

Dixon, J., Durrheim, K., Tredoux, C., Tropp, L., Clack, B., & Eaton, L. (2010). A paradox of integration? Interracial contact, prejudice reduction, and perceptions of racial discrimination. *The Journal of Social Issues*, *66*(2), 401–416. doi:10.1111/j.1540-4560.2010.01652.x

Dodgson, M., Gann, D., & Salter, A. (2006). The role of technology in the shift towards open innovation: The case of Procter & Gamble. *R & D Management*, *36*(3), 333–346. doi:10.1111/j.1467-9310.2006.00429.x

Dogra, V. (2002). *ICTs for Developments Paradox of Hope and Hype*. Paper presented at International Conference on Community for Development in the Digital Era. University of Madras, Chennai.

Donath, J., & Boyd, D. (2004). Public displays of connection. *BT Technology Journal*, *22*(4), 71–82. doi:10.1023/B:BTTJ.0000047585.06264.cc

Donlon-Cotton, C. (2012, January). Implementing Social Networking into Law Enforcement Ops: Community Relations. *Hendon Publishing*. Retrieved from http://www.hendonpub.com/resources/article_archive/results/details?id=1185

Donnermeyer, J., & Hollifield, C. (2003). Digital Divide Evidence in Four Rural Towns. *IT & Society*, *1*(4), 107–117.

Donovan, K. (2011). Anywhere, anytime - mobile devices and their impact on agriculture and rural development. Proceedings of the ICT in Agriculture: Connecting Smallholders to Knowledge, Networks, and Institutions (pp. 49–70). Washington. Retrieved from http://www.ictinagriculture.org

Donthu, N., & Yoo, B. (1998). Cultural Influences on Service Quality Expectations. *Journal of Service Research*, *1*(2), 178–186. doi:10.1177/109467059800100207

Dooley, P. L. (2010). Wikipedia and the two-faced professoriate. In *Proceedings of the 6th International Symposium on Wikis and Open Collaboration*. New York: ACM. doi:10.1145/1832772.1832803

Doukidis, G. I., Lybereas, P., & Galliers, R. D. (1996). Information systems planning in small business: A stages of growth analysis. *Journal of Systems and Software*, *33*(2), 189–201. doi:10.1016/0164-1212(95)00183-2

drandreagalli. (2011, November 27). Organized Crime in Central Europe. *Economic crime intelligence*. Retrieved from http://economiccrimeintelligence.wordpress.com/2011/11/27/organized-crime-in-central-europe/

Driffield, N., & Munday, M. (2001). Foreign manufacturing, regional agglomeration and technical efficiency in UK industries: A stochastic production frontier approach. *Regional Studies*, *35*(5), 391–399. doi:10.1080/713693833

Druck, G., Miklau, G., & McCallum, A. (n. d.). *Learning to Predict the Quality of Contributions to Wikipedia*. Retrieved from https://people.cs.umass.edu/~mccallum/papers/druck08wikiai.pdf

Drucker, P. (2001). *The Next Information Revolution*. Retrieved from http://www.s-jtech.com/Peter%20Drucker%20-%20the%20Next%20Information%20Revolution.pdf

Dubois, A., Copus, A., & Hedström, M. (2012). Local embeddedness and global links in rural areas: Euclidean and Relational Space in Business Networks (pp. 103-121). In C. Hedberg & R.M. do Carmo (Eds.), Translocal Ruralism. Springer Netherlands. doi:10.1007/978-94-007-2315-3_7

Duggan, M., & Brenner, J. (2012). *The Demographics of Social Media Users — 2012*. Retrieved.

Duncombe, R., Heeks, R., Morgan, S., & Arun, S. (2005). *Supporting Women's ICT-Based Enterprises - A Handbook for Agencies in Development*. Manchester: Institute for Development Policy and Management.

Durrheim, K., & Dixon, J. (2010). Racial contact and change in South Africa. *The Journal of Social Issues*, *66*(2), 273–288. doi:10.1111/j.1540-4560.2010.01645.x

Dutta, S. (2012). ICT for the Development in North East India. Retrieved from http://enajori.com/ict-for-the-development-in-north-east-indiasatyakam-dutta/

Dutton, W. H., Sweet, P. L., & Rogers, E. M. (1989). Socioeconomic status and the early diffusion of personal computing in the United States. *Social Science Computer Review*, *7*(3), 259–271. doi:10.1177/089443938900700301

Eastin, M. S. (2001). Credibility assessments of online health information: The effects of source expertise and knowledge of content. *Journal of Computer-Mediated Communication*, *6*(4). Retrieved from http://www.ascusc.org/jcmc/vol6/issue4/eastin.html

Ebersole, S. (2000). Uses and gratifications of the web among students. Journal of Computer Mediated Communication. University of Southern Colorado, 6(1).

Edwards, J., & Chapman, C. (2000). Women's political representation in wales: Waving or drowning? *Contemporary Politics*, *6*(4), 367–381. doi:10.1080/713658377

eGov Reach: A Nasscom initiation. (n. d.). Core Infrastucture projects. Retrieved from http://egovreach.in/social/node/488

Eijkman, H. (2008). Web2.0 as a non-foundational network-centric learning space Campus-Wide. *Information Systems*, *25*(2), 93–104.

Ein-Dor, P., Segev, E., & Orgad, M. (1993). The Effect of National Culture on IS: Implications for International Information Systems. *Journal of Global Information Management*, *1*(1), 33–44. doi:10.4018/jgim.1993010103

Eisenhardt, K. M. (1989). Building theories from case study research. *Academy of Management Review*, *14*(4), 532–550.

Ekman, P. (1972). *Universal and cultural differences in facial expressions of emotion*. Lincoln: University of Nebraska Press.

Ellison, N. B., Steinfield, C., & Lampe, C. (2007). The benefits of Facebook "friends:" social capital and college students' use of online social network sites. *Journal of Computer-Mediated Communication*, *12*(4), 1143–1168. doi:10.1111/j.1083-6101.2007.00367.x

Ellison, N., Heino, R., & Gibbs, J. (2006). Managing impressions online: Self-presentation processes in the online dating environment. *Journal of Computer-Mediated Communication*, *11*(2), 415–441. doi:10.1111/j.1083-6101.2006.00020.x

eMarketer. (2013). Social Networking Reaches Nearly One in Four around the World. Retrieved from http://www.emarketer.com/Article/Social-Networking-Reaches-Nearly-One-Four-Around-World/1009976

Emma, L. G., Gary, B., & Joanie, W. (2013). The role of local perceptions in the marketing of rural areas. Journal of Destination Marketing & Management, 2(1), 4-13.

Employer Demand for Researchers in Australia, Report to the Department of Innovation, Industry, Science and Research. (2010). *Allen Consulting Group*. Retrieved from http://www.industry.gov.au/research/ResearchWorkforceIssues/Documents/EmployerDemandforResearchersinAustraliareport.pdf

Engel, R. S. (2001). Supervisory styles of patrol sergeants and lieutenants. *Journal of Criminal Justice*, *29*(4), 341–355. doi:10.1016/S0047-2352(01)00091-5

Eriksson, S. (2006). Cluster creation and innovation within an emerging Taiwanese high-tech sector. *International journal of technology transfer and commercialisation, 5(3),* 208-236.

Ernberg, J. (1998). *Towards a Framework for Evaluation of Multipurpose Community Telecentre. Partnerships and Participation in Telecommunications for Rural Development*. Ontario: University of Guelph.

Ernst & Young's. (2010). *Cloud computing issues and impacts*, Global Technology Industry Discussion Series. Retrieved from http://www.ey.com/Publication/vwLUAssets/Cloud-computing_issues_and_impacts/$FILE/Cloud_computing_issues_and_impacts.pdf

Espinoza, M. M. (1999). Assessing the cross-cultural applicability of a service quality measure A comparative study between Quebec and Peru. *International Journal of Service Industry Management*, *10*(5), 449–468. doi:10.1108/09564239910288987

European Commission - MEMO. 12/713 (2012). *A számítási felhőben rejlő potenciál felszabadítása Európában - mi is jelent ez pontosan és milyen módon érint bennünket? (Unleashing the Potential of Cloud Computing in Europe - What is it and what does it mean for us?)*, Retrieved from http://europa.eu/rapid/press-release_MEMO-12-713_hu.htm

European Commission. (n. d.). ECRIS (European Criminal Records Information System) - Justice. Retrieved from http://ec.europa.eu/justice/criminal/european-e-justice/ecris/index_en.htm

European Crime Prevention Network. (2009, December 30). Good practice documents - Virtual Community Policing. Retrieved from http://www.eucpn.org/goodpractice/showdoc.asp?docid=247

Europol. (n. d.). About Europol. Retrieved from https://www.europol.europa.eu/content/page/about-europol-17

Evans, D. (2001). The WREN Telecottage. In C. Latchem, & D. Walker (Eds.), Telecentres: Case Studies and Key Issues. Vancouver: The Commonwealth of Learning.

Evusa, J. E. (2005). *Information Communication Technologies as Tools for Socio-Economic and Political Development: The National Council of Churches of Kenya (NCCK) Huruma Community Telecentre as a Case Study*. MI: ProQuest Information and Learning Company.

Eyben, F., Weninger, F., Lehment, N., Schuller, B., & Rigoll, G. (2013). Affective video retrieval: violence detection in Hollywood movies by large-scale segmental feature extraction. *PLoS ONE*, *8*(12), 1–9. doi:10.1371/journal.pone.0078506 PMID:24391704

Facebook Penetration Growth. (2013). Miniwatts Marketing Group. Retrieved from http://www.internetworldstats.com/facebook.htm

Facebook statistics. (2014, June 30). Facebook. Retrieved from http://www.xmarks.com/site/www.facebook.com/press/info.php%3Fstatistics

Fafchamps, M., & Minten, B. (2012). Impact of SMS-based agricultural information on Indian farmers. *The World Bank Economic Review*, *26*(3), 383–414. doi:10.1093/wber/lhr056

Fairclough, S. H. (2009). Fundamentals of physiological computing. *Interacting with Computers*, *21*(1-2), 133–145. doi:10.1016/j.intcom.2008.10.011

Fajszi, B., Cser, L., & Fehér, T. (2010). *Üzleti haszon az adatok mélyén, Az adatbányászat mindennapjai, (Business gains in the depth of data, The daily routine of data mining)*. Alinea Kiadó- IQSYS.

Fallis, D. (n. d.). *A Conceptual Analysis of Disinformation*. Retrieved from http://ischools.org/images/iConferences/fallis_disinfo1.pdf

Farradane, J. (1979). The nature of Information. *Journal of Information Science*, *1*(1), 13–17. doi:10.1177/016555157900100103

Farrell, M. J. (1957). The measurement of productive efficiency. *Journal of the Royal Statistical Society. Series A (General)*, *120*(3), 253–290. doi:10.2307/2343100

Faye, I., & Hopgood, T. (2012). Thank you hater (MP3 ed.). London, GB: mar.

Feagin, J. R. (2014). *Racist america: Roots, current realities, and future reparations*. London, GB: Routledge.

Feather, N. T., & McKee, I. R. (2012). Values, Right-Wing authoritarianism, social dominance orientation, and ambivalent attitudes toward women. *Journal of Applied Social Psychology*, *42*(10), 2479–2504. doi:10.1111/j.1559-1816.2012.00950.x

Feder, G. (1983). On exports and economic growth. *Journal of Development Economics*, *12*(1), 59–73. doi:10.1016/0304-3878(83)90031-7

Feenberg, A. (2005). Critical theory of technology: An overview. *Tailoring Biotechnologies, 1* (1), 47-64. Retrieved from https://www.sfu.ca/~andrewf/books/critbio.pdf

Fernandez, S., & Rainey, H. G. (2006). Managing successful organizational change in the public sector. *Public Administration Review*, *66*(2), 168–176. doi:10.1111/j.1540-6210.2006.00570.x

Flanagin, A. J., & Metzger, M. J. (2008). (Eds.), Digital media, youth, and credibility (pp. 5-28). Cambridge, MA: The MIT Press. doi:10.1162/dmal.9780262562324.005

Flanagin, A. J., & Metzger, M. J. (2000). Perceptions of Internet information credibility. *Journalism & Mass Communication Quarterly*, *77*(3), 515–540. Retrieved from http://www.jasonmorrison.net/iakm/4006074.pdf doi:10.1177/107769900007700304

Flanagin, A. J., & Metzger, M. J. (2007). The role of site features, user attributes, and information verification behaviors on the perceived credibility of Web-based information. *New Media & Society*, *9*(2), 319–342. doi:10.1177/1461444807075015

Flanagin, A. J., & Metzger, M. J. (2011). From Encyclopædia Britannica to Wikipedia Generational differences in the perceived credibility of online encyclopedia information. *Information Communication and Society*, *14*(3), 355–374. doi:10.1080/1369118X.2010.542823

Floridi, L. (2001). What is the philosophy of information? *Metaphilosophy*, *33*(1/2), 123–145. Retrieved from http://www.philosophyofinformation.net/publications/books/blackwell/chapters/introduction.pdf

Floridi, L. (2003). Two approaches to the philosophy of information. *Minds and Machines*, *13*(4), 459–469. Retrieved from http://www.philosophyofinformation.net/publications/pdf/tattpi.pdf doi:10.1023/A:1026241332041

Floridi, L. (2005). Is Semantic Information Meaningful Data? *Philosophy and Phenomenological Research*, *70*(2), 351–370. Retrieved from http://www.philosophyofinformation.net/publications/pdf/iimd.pdf doi:10.1111/j.1933-1592.2005.tb00531.x

Floridi, L. (2010). *Information: A Very Short Introduction*. Oxford: Oxford University Press. doi:10.1093/actrade/9780199551378.001.0001

Food and Agriculture Organization of the United Nations (FAO). (2014). *Agriculture Management Information System. Department of Agriculture, Government of Sri Lanka (DOASL)*. Retrieved from http://www.agmis.lk/

Foster, P., Borgatti, S. P., & Jones, C. (2011). Gatekeeper search and selection strategies: Relational and network governance in a cultural market. *Poetics*, *39*(4), 247–265. doi:10.1016/j.poetic.2011.05.004

Foucault, M. (1988). Technologies of the self: A seminar with Michel Foucault. In L. H. Martin, H. Gutman, & P. H. Hutton (Eds.), *Technologies of the self* (pp. 16–49). Amherst: University of Massachusetts Press.

Four Steps to Setting the Right Budget for Downtime Prevention. (2012, April). *Aberdeen Group*. Retrieved from http://www.stratus.com/~/media/Stratus/Files/Library/AnalystReports/Aberdeen-4-Steps-Budget-Downtime.pdf

Fox, E. (2008). *Emotion Science: An integration of cognitive and neuroscientific approaches*. Palgrave: MacMillan.

Freeman, C. (1995). The 'National System of Innovation in historical perspective. *Cambridge Journal of Economics*, *19*(1), 5–24.

Friedmann, R. R. (1992). Community policing: Comparative perspectives and prospects.

Fritch, J. W., & Cromwell, R. L. (2001). Evaluating Internet resources: Identity, affiliation and cognitive authority in a networked world. *Journal of the American Society for Information Science and Technology*, *52*(6), 499–507. Retrieved from https://courses.washington.edu/info320/wi10/readings/fritch.pdf doi:10.1002/asi.1081

from http://www.pewinternet.org/2013/02/14/the-demographics-of-social-media-users-2012/

Funding Higher Education: A View across Europe. (2010). *European Platform Higher Education Modernisation*. Retrieved from http://www.utwente.nl/bms/cheps/publications/Publications%202010/MODERN_Funding_Report.pdf

Gabel, D., & Pollard, W. (1995). *Privatization, deregulation, and competition: learning from the cases of telecommunications in New Zealand and the United Kingdom*. Retrieved from http://citeseerx.ist.psu.edu/viewdoc/download?doi=10.1.1.230.4447&rep=rep1&type=pdf

Gallup (2010). Mobile phone access varies widely in sub-Saharan Africa: Average phone owner is more likely to be male, educated, and urban. Retrieved from http://www.gallup.com/poll/149519/mobile-phone-access-varies-widely-sub-saharan-africa.aspx

Gartner (2013). Predicts 2014: *Government CIOs Are Key to Moving the Digital Enterprise Forward*. Retrieved from http://www.gartner.com/document/2625824

Gasser, U. Cortesi, G., Malik, M., & Lee, A. (2012). Youth and Digital Media: From Credibility to Information Quality. Retrieved from http://dmlcentral.net/sites/dmlcentral/files/resource_files/youthanddigitalmedia-credibilityreport2.16.12.pdf

Gassmann, O., & von Zedtwitz, M. (2003). Trends and determinants of managing virtual R&D team. *R & D Management*, *33*(3), 243–262. doi:10.1111/1467-9310.00296

Gaster, P. (2001). A Pilot Telecentres Project in Mozambique. In C. Latchem, & D. Walker (Eds.), Telecentres: Case Studies and Key Issues. Vancouver: The Commonwealth of Learning.

Gates, B. (1995). *The Road Ahead*. London: Viking.

Gatlin, L. (1972). *Information Theory and the Living System*. New York: Columbia University Press.

Gazaway, C. (2011) KSP turning to social media for recruits. http://www.wave3.com/story/15176887/kspturning-to-social-media-for-recruits

Gazette of India. (2012). National Data Sharing & Accessibility Policy (NDSAP). Retrieved from http://data.gov.in/sites/default/files/NDSAP.pdf

Gbanie, S. P., Tengbe, P. B., Momoh, J. S., Medo, J., & Tamba Simbay, K. V. (2013). Modelling landfill location using geographic information systems (gis) and multi-criteria decision analysis (MCDA): Case study Bo, Southern Sierra Leone. *Applied Geography (Sevenoaks, England)*, *36*, 3–12. doi:10.1016/j.apgeog.2012.06.013

Geetha, K., & Malarvizhi, V. (2012). Assessment of a Modified Technology Acceptance Model among E-Banking Customers in Coimbatore City. *International Journal of Innovation, Management and Technology.*, *3*(2).

Gemitzi, A., Tsihrintzis, V. A., Voudrias, E., Petalas, C., & Stravodimos, G. (2007). Combining geographic information system, multicriteria evaluation techniques and fuzzy logic in siting MSW landfills. *Environ Geol*, *51*(5), 797–811. doi:10.1007/s00254-006-0359-1

Gertler, M. S., & Levitte, Y. M. (2005). Local nodes in global networks: The geography of knowledge flows in biotechnology innovation. *Industry and Innovation*, *12*(4), 487–507. doi:10.1080/13662710500361981

Gianelle, C., & Tattara, G. (2009). Manufacturing abroad while making profits at home: a study on Veneto footwear and clothing global value chains. In M. Morroni (Ed.), *Corporate Governance, Organization and Design and Inter-Firm Relations: Theoretical advances and Empirical Evidence* (pp. 206–213). UK: Edward Elgar. doi:10.4337/9781848446120.00019

Giddens, A. (1990). *The consequences of modernity*. Cambridge: Polity.

Gilbert, E., Karahalios, K., & Sandvig, C. (2008). *The Network in the Garden: An Empirical Analysis of Social Media in Rural Life*. University of Illinois at Urbana-Champaign.

Giles, J. (2005). Internet encyclopaedias go head to head. *Nature*, *438*(7070), 900–901. doi:10.1038/438900a PMID:16355180

Girard, J.P. (n. d.). *Combating Information Anxiety: A Management Responsibility*. Retrieved from http://www.johngirard.net/john/documents/Vadyba%2035-Girard.pdf

Glaser, B. G., & Strauss, A. L. (2009). *The discovery of grounded theory: Strategies for qualitative research*. New Jersey: Transaction Books.

Glynn, I., Kelly, T., & MacÉinrí, P. (2013). *Irish Emigration in an Age of Austerity. Project funded by The Irish Research Council Hosting Institutions: Department of Geography and the Institute for the Social Sciences in the 21st Century*. University College Cork.

Goddard, J. B. (1992, February22). *New Technology and the Geography of the UK Information Economy*. London Times. *Times Higher Education Supplement*.

Golden, B. (2009). *Capex vs. Opex: Most People Miss the PointAbout Cloud Economics*, Retrieved from http://www.cio.com/article/484429/Capex_vs._Opex_Most_People_Miss_the_Point_About_Cloud_Economics

Golder, S., Wilkinson, D., & Huberman, B. A. (2007). Rhythms of social interaction: messaging within a massive online network. In C. Steinfeld, B. T. Pentland, M. Ackerman, & N. Contractor (Eds.), *Communities and Technologies 2007: Proceedings of the Third Communities and Technologies Conference* (pp. 41–66). London: Springer-Verlag Limited. Retrieved from http://www.redlog.net/papers/facebook.pdf

Goldman, S. L., Preiss, K., & Nagel, R. N. (1995). *Agile Competitors and Virtual Organizations: Strategies for Enriching the Customer*. New York, NY: Van Nostrand Reinhold.

Gomez-Rodriguez, M., Gummadi, K. P., & Scholkopf, B. (n. d.). Quantifying Information Overload in Social Media and its Impact on Social Contagions. Retrieved from https://www.mpi-sws.org/~gummadi/papers/icwsm2014-overload.pdf

González, X., Jaumandreu, J., & Pazó, C. (2005). Barriers to innovation and subsidy effectiveness. *The Rand Journal of Economics*, *36*(4), 930–950.

Goodchild, J. (2012, December 20). Social Engineering: The Basics. *CSO Online*. Retrieved from http://www.csoonline.com/article/2124681/security-awareness/social-engineering-the-basics.html

Goodhue, D. L. (1988). IS attitudes: Towards theoretical and definition clarity. *Database*, *41*, 6–15.

Goodman, S. E., & Green, J. D. (1992). Computing in the middle east. *Communications of the ACM*, *35*(8), 21–25. doi:10.1145/135226.135236

Goodwin, J., & Rhoades, E. (2009). Agricultural Legislation: The Presence of California Proposition 2 [YouTube video]. Proceedings of the *Annual National Agricultural Education Research Conference*. Louisville, Ky.

Gooley, A. (2001). THe Queensland Open Learning Network, Australia. In C. Latchem, & D. Walker, Telecentres: Case Studies and Key Issues. Vancouver: The Commonwealth of Learning.

Gordhamer, S. (2010). 5 Levels of Effective Communication in the Social Media Age. *Mashable*. Retrieved from http://mashable.com/2010/02/08/communication-social-media/

Görzig, B., & Andreas, S. (2002). Outsourcing and firm level performance (DIW Berlin (Discussion Paper No. 309). Retrieved from http://www.econstor.eu/bitstream/10419/18045/1/dp309.pdf

Gould, R. V., & Fernandez, R. M. (1989). Structures of mediation: A formal approach to brokerage in transaction networks. *Sociological Methodology*, *19*, 89–126. doi:10.2307/270949

Goulev, P., Stead, L., Mamdani, E., & Evans, C. (2004). Computer aided emotional fashion. *Computers & Graphics*, *28*(5), 657–666. doi:10.1016/j.cag.2004.06.005

Govindaraju, P., & Mabel, M. M. (2010). The Demise of a Digital Solution: A Study of Melur Kiosks in Tamilnadu, India. *Journal of Communication*.

Govt. of Kerala (n. d.). *Project Akshaya*. Retrieved from http://www.akshaya.kerala.gov.in/index.php/e-literacy

Grabher, G., & Ibert, O. (2013). Distance as asset? *Journal of Economic Geography*, lbt014.

Graf, H. (2011). Gatekeepers in regional networks of innovators. *Cambridge Journal of Economics*, *35*(1), 173–198. doi:10.1093/cje/beq001

Graf, H., & Krüger, J. J. (2011). The performance of gatekeepers in innovator networks. *Industry and Innovation*, *18*(1), 69–88. doi:10.1080/13662716.2010.528932

Grant, G., & Chau, D. (2006). *Developing a Generic Framework for e-Government. Advanced Topics in Global Information Management. Idea Group Inc.* IGI.

Green, D. (2011, August 8). London riots: why did the police lose control? *Telegraph*. Retrieved from http://www.telegraph.co.uk/news/uknews/crime/8689004/London-riots-why-did-the-police-lose-control.html

Greenhow, C., & Robelia, B. (2009). Old communication, new literacies: Social network sites as social learning resources. *Journal of Computer-Mediated Communication*, *14*(4), 1130–1161. doi:10.1111/j.1083-6101.2009.01484.x

Grether, J. M. (1999). Determinants of technological diffusion in mexican manufacturing: A plant-level analysis. *World Development*, *27*(7), 1287–1298. doi:10.1016/S0305-750X(99)00054-6

Gretton, P., Gali, J., & Parham, D. (2004). The effects of ICTs and complementary innovation on Australian productivity growth. In OECD (Ed.), *The economic impact of ICT: Measurement, evidence and implications* (pp. 105–130). Paris, FR: OECD Publishing.

Griliches, Z. (1998). Issues in assessing the contribution of research and development to productivity growth. In Z. Griliches (Ed.), *R&D and Productivity: The Econometric Evidence* (pp. 17–45). USA: University of Chicago Press. doi:10.7208/chicago/9780226308906.001.0001

Grinstead, J. (2013, August 22). The Soft Skills of International Project Management. Retrieved from http://www.nasa.gov/offices/oce/appel/ask/issues/49/49s_soft_skills_ipm.html

Guidelines for Managing and Reporting on Intangibles. (2002). *MERITUM Project*. Retrieved from www.pnbukh.com/files/pdf_filer/pdf_filer/MERITUM_Guidelines.pdf

Gumbau-Albert, M., & Maudos, J. (2002). The determinants of efficiency: The case of the Spanish industry. *Applied Economics*, *34*(15), 1941–1948. doi:10.1080/00036840210127213

Gupta, M. P. (Ed.), *Promise of E-Governance: Operational Challenges*. New Delhi: Tata McGraw-Hill Publishing Company Limited.

Gürses, S., Troncoso, C., & Diaz, C. (2011). Engineering privacy by design. *Computers, Privacy & Data Protection, 14*

Hackathon, C. M. A. (2013). Code of Urban Governance. India: Government of Tamil Nadu; Retrieved from cma.tn.gov.in/cma/en-in/Pages/Hackathon.aspx

Haghighat, E. (2013). Social status and change: The question of access to resources and women's empowerment in the middle east and north africa. *Journal of International Women's Studies*, *14*(1), 273–299.

Hala, A. E., & Mohamed, N. H. (2012). Mapping potential landfill sites for North Sinai cities using spatial multicriteria evaluation. *The Egyptian Journal of Remote Sensing and Space Sciences*, *15*, 125–133. doi:10.1016/j.ejrs.2012.09.002

Halfaker, A., Geiger, R. S., Morgan, J., & Riedl, J. (n. d.). The Rise and Decline of an Open Collaboration System: How Wikipedia's reaction to popularity is causing its decline. Retrieved from http://www-users.cs.umn.edu/~halfak/publications/The_Rise_and_Decline/halfaker13rise-preprint.pdf

Halfaker, A., Kittur, A., & Riedl, J. (2011). Don't bite the newbies: How reverts affect the quantity and quality of Wikipedia work. In *Proceedings of the 7th International Symposium on Wikis and Open Collaboration, WikiSym '11* (pp. 163–172). New York: ACM Press. Retrieved from http://files.grouplens.org/papers/halfaker11bite.personal.pdf

Halfaker, A., Kittur, A., Kraut, R., & Riedl, J. (2009). A jury of your peers: Quality experience and Ownership in Wikipedia. In *Proceedings of the 5th International Symposium on Wikis and Open Collaboration WikiSym '09* (Article No. 15). *New York: ACM Press.* Retrieved from http://kraut.hciresearch.org/sites/kraut.hciresearch.org/files/open/halfaker09-JuryOfYourPeers.pdf

Hall, J. (1952). Police and law in a democratic society. *Indiana Law Journal (Indianapolis, Ind.), 28*(2), 133.

Hamidinava, F., & Madhoushi, M. (2010, December). Evaluating the features of electronic payment systems in Iranian bank users' view. *International Review of Business Research Papers,* 6(6), 78–94

Hammer, M., & Qahtani, F. A. (2009). Enhancing the case for electronic government in developing nations: A people-centric study focused in Saudi Arabia. *Government Information Quarterly, 26*(1), 137–143. doi:10.1016/j.giq.2007.08.008

Hampton, K., & Wellman, B. (2003). Neighboring in Netville: How the Internet supports community and social capital in a wired suburb. *City & Community, 2*(4), 277–311. doi:10.1046/j.1535-6841.2003.00057.x

Hanna, R., Rohm, A., & Crittenden, V. L. (2011). We're all connected: The power of the social media ecosystem. Northeastern University, Boston, MA.

Hardaker, C. (2013). Uh.... not to be nitpicky, but... the past tense of drag is dragged, not drug.": An overview of trolling strategies. *Journal of Language Aggression and Conflict, 1*(1), 57–85. doi:10.1075/jlac.1.1.04har

Harmon-Jones, E., Gable, P. A., & Price, T. F. (2013). Does negative affect always narrow and positive affect always broaden the mind? Considering the influence of motivational intensity on cognitive scope. *Current Directions in Psychological Science, 22*(4), 301–307. doi:10.1177/0963721413481353

Harper, A., Olivier, N., Thobakgale, S., & Tshwete, Z. (2002). *Institutional Forums.* Sunnyside, South Africa: Centre for Higher Education Transformation.

Harris, T. (2013). *Cloud Computing - An Overview, School of Software,* Sun Yat-sen University Retrieved from http://south.cattelecom.com/rtso/Technologies/CloudComputing/Cloud-Computing-Overview.pdf

Harrison, L., & Ollis, D. (2015). Stepping out of our comfort zones: Pre-service teachers' responses to a critical analysis of gender/power relations in sexuality education. *Sex Education, 15*(3), 318–331. doi:10.1080/14681811.2015.1023284

Hartig, N. (2001). The KITIMAT Community Skills Center in British Columbia, Canada. In C. Letchem, & D. Walker (Eds.), Telecentres: Case Studies and Key Issues (p.). Vancouver: The Commonwealth of Learning.

Hartley, R. V. L. (1928). Transmission of Information. *The Bell System Technical Journal, 7*(3), 535–563. Retrieved from http://www.uni-leipzig.de/~biophy09/Biophysik-Vorlesung_2009-2010_DATA/QUELLEN/LIT/A/B/3/Hartley_1928_transmission_of_information.pdf doi:10.1002/j.1538-7305.1928.tb01236.x

Harvey, J. M. (1989). *Space in the embedding society.* Retrieved from http://www.geocities.com/jp marshall.geo/cybermind/cybertopls.rtf

Haskel, J., Jona-Lasinio, C., & Iommi, M. (2012). Intangible capital and growth in advanced economies: Measurement methods and comparative results (IZA Discussion Paper No.6733). Retrieved from ftp://ftp.mpls.frb.fed.us/pub/research/mcgrattan/sr472/data/MacroData/Intangibles/Corrado12.pdf

Hayek, F. A. (1945). The Use of Knowledge in Society. *The American Economic Review, 35*(4), 519–530. http://www.kysq.org/docs/Hayek_45.pdf Retrieved December 29, 2013

Haythornthwaite, C. (2005). Social networks and Internet connectivity effects. *Information Communication and Society, 8*(2), 125–147. doi:10.1080/13691180500146185

He, D. H., & Lu, Y. B., (2007). *Consumers Perceptions and Acceptances towards Mobile Advertising: An Empirical Study in China.* IEEE.

Heatherly, R., Kantarcioglu, M., & Thuraisingham, B. (2013). Preventing private information inference attacks on social networks. *Knowledge and Data Engineering. IEEE Transactions on*, *25*(8), 1849–1862.

Hector Kobbekaduwa Agrarian Research and Training Institute (HARTI). (2014). Mobitel agri price information index. Retrieved from http://www.harti.gov.lk

Heeks, R. (1999). Information and communication technologies, poverty and development. Retrieved from http://www.man.ac.uk/idpm/diwpf5.htm

Heeks, R. (1999, March). *The tyranny of participation in information systems: Learning from development projects.* Retrieved from http://idpm.man.ac.uk/publications/wp/di/di_wp04.pdf

Heeks, R. (2002). Information systems and developing countries: Failure, success, and local improvisations. *The Information Society*, *18*(2), 101–112. doi:10.1080/01972240290075039

Heidegger, M. (1962). *Being and time* (J. Macquarrie & E. Robinson, Trans). Blackwell: Oxford UK, and Cambridge USA. Retrieved from http://www.naturalthinker.net/trl/texts/Heidegger,Martin/Heidegger,%20Martin%20-%20Being%20and%20Time/Being%20and%20Time.pdf

Heider, D., & Harp, D. (2000). *New hope or old power: New communication, pornography and the internet.* Retrieved from http://www.AEJMC.orq/convention/abstracts/2000%20/ctp.html

Heiskanen, T., & Hearn, J. (2004). *Information society and the workplace: spaces, boundary and agency* (pp. 1–25). London: Routledge.

Helliwell, J. F., & Putnam, R. D. (2004). The social context of well-being. *Philosophical Transactions of the Royal Society*, *359*(1449), 1435–1446. doi:10.1098/rstb.2004.1522 PMID:15347534

Helmbrecht, U. (2014). *ENISA Annual Report 2013, European Union Agency for Network and Information Security.* Luxembourg: Publications Office of the European Union.

Hempel, P. S., & Martinsons, M. G. (2009). Developing international organizational change theory using cases from China. *Human Relations*, *62*(4), 459–499. doi:10.1177/0018726708101980

Heshmati, A. (2003). Productivity growth, efficiency and outsourcing in manufacturing and service industries. *Journal of Economic Surveys*, *17*(1), 79–112. doi:10.1111/1467-6419.00189

Heylighen, F. (1999). Change and information overload: Negative effects. In F. Heylighen, C. Joslyn and V. Turchin (Eds.), *Principia Cybernetica Web.* Brussels: Principia Cybernetica. Retrieved January 29, 2014 from http://pespmc1.vub.ac.be/chinneg.html

Hey, V., & Morley, L. (2011). Imagining the university of the future: Eyes wide open? Expanding the imaginary through critical and feminist ruminations in and on the university, Contemporary Social Science. *Journal of the Academy of Social Sciences*, *6*(2), 165–174.

Hiltz, S. R., & Turoff, M. (1985). Structuring computer mediated communications to avoid information overload. *Communications of the ACM*, *28*(7), 680–689http://www.researchgate.net/profile/Starr_Hiltz/publication/220420820_Structuring_Computer-Mediated_Communication_Systems_to_Avoid_Information_Overload/links/0deec51fd15b970b51000000.pdf. RetrievedJanuary272014. doi:10.1145/3894.3895

Hindman, D. B. (2000). Infrastructure issues in computer-mediated communication. Retrieved from http://www.AEJMC.org/convention/abstracts/2000/20/ctp.html

Ho, K. K. W., Yu, C. C., & Lai, M. C. L. (2014). Engaging and Developing the Community Through Social Media: A Pragmatic Analysis in Policing Context in Hong Kong. In L. G. Anthopoulos & C. G. Reddick (Eds.), Government e-Strategic Planning and Management (pp. 263–285). Springer New York; Retrieved from http://link.springer.com/chapter/10.1007/978-1-4614-8462-2_14 doi:10.1007/978-1-4614-8462-2_14

Hoffmann, D. L., Novak, T. P., & Peralta, M. A. (1999). Information privacy in market space: Implications for the commercial uses of anonymity on the web. *The Information Society*, *15*(2).

Hofkirchner, W. (2010). Twenty questions about a unified theory of information: A short exploration into information from a complex systems view. Litchfield Park AZ: Emergent Publications (p.62). Retrieved from http://emergent-publications.com/documents/9780984216475_contents.pdf?AspxAutoDetectCookieSupport=1

Hofstede, G. (2001). *Culture's Consequences* (2nd ed.). Thousand Oaks: Sage.

Hollenstein, H. (2004). Determinants of the Adoption of Information and Communication Technologies. *Structural Change and Economic Dynamics*, *15*(3), 315–342. doi:10.1016/j.strueco.2004.01.003

Holt, D., & Challis, D. (2007). From policy to practice: One university's experience of implementing strategic change through wholly online teaching and learning. *Australasian Journal of Educational Technology*, *23*(1), 110–131.

Hone, K. (2006). Empathic agents to reduce user frustration: The effects of varying agent characteristics. *Interacting with Computers*, *18*(2), 227–245. doi:10.1016/j.intcom.2005.05.003

Hopkins, R. (1995). Countering information overload: The role of the Librarian. *The Reference Librarian*, *23*(49), 305–333. doi:10.1300/J120v23n49_21

Horrigan, J. (2006). Home Broadband Adoption 2006. *Pew Internet & American Life Project*. Retrieved from http://www.pewinternet.org/files/old-media/Files/Reports/2006/PIP_Broadband_trends2006.pdf.pdf

Hossain, M., & Dias Karunaratne, N. (2004). Exports and economic growth in Bangladesh: Has manufacturing exports become a new engine of export-led growth? *The International Trade Journal*, *18*(4), 303–334. doi:10.1080/08853900490518190

Hovland, C. I., Irving, J. L., & Harold, K. H. (1953). *Communication and Persuasion. Psychological Studies of Opinion Change*. New Haven, CO: Yale University Press.

Howard, L. (2001). The DaimlerChrysler Distance Learning Support Centre in Maseru, Lesotho. In C. Latchem, & D. Walker (Eds.), Telecentres: Case Studies and Key Issues. Vancouver: The Commonwealth of Learning.

Howard, P. N., & Hussain, M. M. (2011). The role of digital media. *Journal of Democracy*, *22*(3), 35–48. doi:10.1353/jod.2011.0041

Hsieh, C., & Lin, B. (1998). Internet commerce for small businesses. *Industrial Management & Data Systems*, *98*(3), 113–190. doi:10.1108/02635579810213116

Huang, I., Guo, R., & Xie, H. WU, Z. (2012). *The Convergence of Information and Communication Technologies Gains Momentum*. The Global Information Technology Report.

Huang, C. J., & Liu, J. T. (1994). Estimation of a non-neutral stochastic frontier production function. *Journal of Productivity Analysis*, *5*(2), 171–180. doi:10.1007/BF01073853

Hudson, H. E., & Parker, E. B. (1990). Information Gaps in Rural America: Telecommunications policies for rural development. *Telecommunications Policy*, *14*(3), 193–205. doi:10.1016/0308-5961(90)90040-X

Hulten, C. R., & Hao, X. (2008). What is a Company Really Worth? Intangible Capital and the" Market to Book Value" Puzzle (NBER Working Paper No. w14548). Retrieved May 14, 2015 from http://infolab.stanford.edu/pub/gio/CS99I/nber_w14548.pdf

Hydén, L., & Bülow, P. (2003). Who's talking: Drawing conclusions from focus groups – some methodological considerations. *International Journal of Social Research Methodology*, *6*(4), 305–321. doi:10.1080/13645570210124865

ICT Technology Audit Study for Turkey. (2011). *Middle East Technical University*. Retrieved from http://stps.metu.edu.tr/sites/stps.metu.edu.tr/files/task9.pdf

ICTs and the fight against HIV/AIDS in India. (2013). SAATHII.

IDC (2012). *Quantitative Estimates of the demand for cloud Computing in Europe and the likely barriers to take-up*

Idota, H., Bunno, T., & Tsuji, M. (2014). An Empirical Analysis of Innovation Success Factors Due to ICT Use in Japanese Firms. In T., Tsiakis, T., Kargidis, & P. Katsaros (Eds.), Approaches and Processes for Managing the Economics of Information Systems, (pp. 324-347). Hershey, PA: IGI. doi:10.4018/978-1-4666-4983-5.ch020

Idota, H., Ogawa, M., Bunno, T., & Tsuji, M. (2012c). An empirical analysis of organizational innovation generated by ICT in Japanese SMEs. In S., Allegrezza, & A., Dubrocard (Eds.), Internet econometrics (pp. 259-287). Hampshire, UK: Macmillan. doi:10.1057/9780230364226.0020

Idota, H., Akematsu, Y., Ueki, Y., & Tsuji, M. (2013a). Empirical Analysis on Innovative Capability and ICT Use in Firms of Four ASEAN Economies.*Proceedings of 2013 AAA ITS Regional Conference* (pp. 1-30). Perth, Australia.

Idota, H., Bunno, T., & Tsuji, M. (2010). Open innovation success factors by ICT use in Japanese firms.*Proceedings of the 21th European regional ITS Conference* (pp. 1-23). Copenhagen, Denmark.

Idota, H., Bunno, T., & Tsuji, M. (2011). Empirical Analysis of Internal Social Media and Product Innovation: Focusing on SNS and Social Capital.*Proceedings of the 22nd European regional ITS Conference* (pp. 1-20). Budapest Hungary.

Idota, H., Bunno, T., & Tsuji, M. (2012a). Open innovation strategy of Japanese SMEs: From viewpoint of ICT use and innovative technology.*Proceedings of the 23th European regional ITS Conference* (pp. 1-14). Vienna, Austria.

Idota, H., Bunno, T., & Tsuji, M. (2012b). Empirical Study on ICT Use and Business Strategy for Innovation among Japanese SMEs.*Proceedings of the 19th ITS Biennial Conference* (pp. 1-17). Bangkok, Thailand.

Idota, H., Bunno, T., & Tsuji, M. (2013b). Covariance Structure Analysis of Innovation and ICT Use among Japanese innovative SMEs.*Proceedings of the 24th European Regional ITS Conference* (pp. 1-22). Florence, Italy.

Igbaria, M., Zinatelli, N., & Cavaye, A. L. M. (1998). Analysis of information technology success in small firms in New Zealand. *International Journal of Information Management*, *18*(2), 103–119. doi:10.1016/S0268-4012(97)00053-4

Ige, O. (n. d.). Evolution of the telecommunications industry. Retrieved from http://www.ncc.gov.ng/archive/Archive%20of%20Speeches/telecomevolution-olawale_ige170402.pdfSlide presentation 49pp

Information and Communication Technology Agency of Sri Lanka (ICTA). (2013). List of Interactive Information Services. Retrieved from http://www.icta.lk

Information Anxiety - Towards Understanding (2012). *Landscape Urbanism Journal 02: Buzz or Noise?* Retrieved from http://scenariojournal.com/lu-information-anxiety/

Information Infrastructures: their impact and regulatory requirements. (1997). OECD. Retrieved from http://www.oecd.org/sti/broadband/2095181.pdf

Information Needs Assessment for Rural Communities: An Indian Case Study (2003). Retrieved from http://ruralinformatics.nic.in/files/4_12_0_229.pdf

Information Overload [Ascent White Paper]. Retrieved *from*http://atos.net/content/dam/global/ascent-whitepapers/ascent-whitepaper-information-overload.pdf

Intaganok, P., Waterworth, P., Andsavachulamanee, T., Grasaresom, G., & Homkome, U. (2008). Attitudes of staff to information and communication technologies. *The Electronic Journal on Information Systems in Developing Countries*, *33*(3), 1–14.

International Association of Chiefs of Police. (2013). *92% of U.S. law enforcement agencies use social media*. Retrieved from http://www.iacpsocialmedia.org/Portals/1/documents/2013SurveyResults.pdf

International Association of Chiefs of Police. (n. d.). Houston, Texas, Police Department – Blogging for recruitment and beyond. Retrieved from http://www.iacpsocialmedia.org/Resources/CaseStudy.aspx?termid=9&cmsid=4734

International ICT Policies and Strategies. (2011, September 2). International ICT Policies and Strategies: CCTNS Project of India to Be Launched Shortly. Retrieved from http://ictps.blogspot.com/2011/09/cctns-project-of-india-to-be-launched.html

Ipsos, M. R. B. I. (2014). Social Networking Quarterly. Retrieved from http://www.ipsosmrbi.com/social-networking-may-2014.html

Irani, Z., Love, P. E. D., & Montazemi, A. (2007). e-Government: Past, present and future. *European Journal of Information Systems*, *16*(2), 103–105. doi:10.1057/palgrave.ejis.3000678

Ireland Facebook Statistics. (2014). Social Bakers. Retrieved from http://www.socialbakers.com/facebook-statistics/ireland

Irving, L. (1999) *Losing Ground Bit by Bit*. London BBC News Online. Retrieved from http://news.bbc.co.uk/1/hi/special_report/1999/10/99information_rich_information_poor/472621.stm

Isaías, P., Miranda, P., & Pífano, S. (2009). *Critical Success Factors for Web 2.0 –A Reference Framework.* Heidelberg: Springer-Verlag Berlin. doi:10.1007/978-3-642-02774-1_39

Isen, A. M., & Reeve, J. (2005). The influence of positive affect on intrinsic and extrinsic motivation: Facilitating enjoyment of play, responsible work behavior, and self-control. *Motivation and Emotion*, *29*(4), 297–325. doi:10.1007/s11031-006-9019-8

ISIC REV.3 Technology intensity definition, classification of manufacturing industries into categories based on R&D intensities. (2011). OECD. Retrieved from http://www.oecd.org/sti/ind/48350231.pdf

Isiguzo, K. (2010). Foreword. In *The impact of mobile services in Nigeria: How mobile technologies are transforming economic and social activities*. Pyramid Research.

ITU, & UNPD. (2014). *Internet Live Stats*. Retrieved from http://www.internetlivestats.com/internet-users/

Jackson, L. (2006). *Women police: Gender, welfare and surveillance in the twentieth century*. Manchester, GB: Manchester University Press.

Jackson, M. (2009). *Distracted: The Erosion of Attention in the Coming Dark Age*. Amherst: Prometheus books.

Jaeger, Paul T., & Bertot, J. (2010). Designing, implementing, and evaluating user-centered and citizen-centered e-government. In C. G. Reddick (Ed.), *Citizens and e-government: Evaluating policy and management* (pp. 1-19).

Jafri, A., Dongre, A., Tripathi, V.N., Aggrawal, A., Shrivastava, S. (2002, April). Information and communication technologies and governance: The Gyandoot experiment in Dhar district of Madhya Pradesh, India. *Overseas Development Institute*.

Jalava, J., & Pohjola, M. (2008). The roles of electricity and ICT in economic growth: Case Finland. *Explorations in Economic History*, *45*(3), 270–287. doi:10.1016/j.eeh.2007.11.001

Jamaluddin, N. (2013). Adoption of E-commerce Practices among the Indian Farmers, a Survey of Trichy District in the State of Tamilnadu, India. *Procedia Economics and Finance*, *7*, 140–149.

Jamieson, K. (2012, October 15-17). *SMS Advertising: A Cross-national Study on Acceptance and Response. Proceeding of the 13th West Lake International Conference on Small and Medium Business, (WLICSMB 2011)*. Hangzhou, China.

Janes, J. W., & Rosenfeld, L. B. (1996). Networked information retrieval and organization: Issues and questions. *Journal of the American Society for Information Science*, *47*(9), 711–715. doi:10.1002/(SICI)1097-4571(199609)47:9<711::AID-ASI7>3.0.CO;2-V

Jayathilake, H. A. C. K., Jayaweera, B. P. A., & Waidyasekera, E. C. S. (2010). ICT adoption and its' implications for agriculture in Sri Lanka. *Journal of Food & Agriculture*, *1*(2), 54–63. doi:10.4038/jfa.v1i2.1799

Jenkins, H. (2006). Convergence culture: Where old and new media collide. New York: New York University Press. Retrieved from http://faculty.georgetown.edu/irvinem/theory/Jenkins-ConvergenceCulture-Intro.pdf

Jenkins, H. (2006). *Fans, bloggers and gamers: Exploring participatory culture*. New York: New York University Press.

Jha, R., & Majumdar, S. K. (1999). A matter of connections: OECD telecommunications sector productivity and the role of cellular technology diffusion. *Information Economics and Policy*, *11*(3), 243–269. doi:10.1016/S0167-6245(99)00017-7

Jinqiu, Z. (2007). The Sustainability of Public Internet Access Centers: Lessons from ICT Projects in Rural China. Empowering Rural Communities through ICT Policy and Research. Chennai.

Johar, M.G.M., & Awalluddin, J.A.A.(2011). The role of technology acceptance model in explaining effect on e-commerce application system. *International Journal of Managing Information Technology*, *3*(3).

Johnson, K. (2010, December 11). Police recruits screened for digital dirt on Facebook, etc. *USA TODAY*. Retrieved from http://usatoday30.usatoday.com/tech/news/2010-11-12-1Afacebookcops12_ST_N.htm

Johnson, L. (2007). The maverick: Dispatches from an unrepentant capitalist. Hampshire, UK: Harriman House Limited. Retrieved from http://tinyurl.com/amara-law

Johnson, T. J., & Kaye, B. K. (1998). Cruising is believing? Comparing media and traditional sources on media credibility measures. *Journalism & Mass Communication Quarterly*, *75*(2), 325–340. Retrieved from http://www.aejmc.org/home/wp-content/uploads/2012/09/Journalism-Mass-Communication-Quarterly-1998-JohnsonKay-325-340.pdf doi:10.1177/107769909807500208

Johnston, K. A., Kawalsky, D., Lalla, N., & Tanner, M. (2013). Social Capital: The Benefits of Facebook "Friends". *Behaviour & Information Technology*, *32*(1), 24–36. doi:10.1080/0144929X.2010.550063

Johnston, P., Pestel, R., Mladenic, D., Grobelnik, M., & Stefan, J. (2003). *European Research Co-Operation as a Self-Organising Complex Network: Implications for Creation of a European Research Area*. Brussels: DG Information Society.

Jonathan-Zamir, T., & Harpaz, A. (2014). Police understanding of the foundations of their legitimacy in the eyes of the public the case of commanding officers in the israel national police. *The British Journal of Criminology*, *54*(3), 469–489. doi:10.1093/bjc/azu001

Jonscher, C. (1999). *In Webster (2007), Theories of the Information Society*. London: Routledge.

Jungwirth, B. (2002). *Information overload: Threat or Opportunity?* Retrieved from http://people.lis.illinois.edu/~chip/pubs/03LIA/13-003.pdf

Kagami, M., Giovannetti, E., & Tsuji, M. (Eds.). (2007). *Industrial Agglomeration: Facts and Lessons for Developing Countries*. Cheltenham, U.K.: Edward Elgar.

Kahn, J. G., Yang, J. S., & Kahn, J. S. (2010). 'Mobile' Health Needs and Opportunities in Developing Countries. *Health Affairs*, *29*(2), 252–258. doi:10.1377/hlthaff.2009.0965 PMID:20348069

Kajtazi, M., & Haftor, D. M. (2011). Exploring the Notion of Information: A Proposal for a Multifaced Understanding. Retrieved from http://www.triple-c.at/index.php/tripleC/article/viewFile/280/270

Kalam, A. P. J. (2005, May 16). Technologies for societal transformation. *The Hindu*.

Kaliouby, R., Picard, R. W., & Cohen, S. B. (2006). Affective computing and autism (1093, 228–248). New York: Annals New York Academy of Sciences.

Kamberelis, G., & Dimitriadis, G. (2008). Focus groups: Strategic articulations of pedagogy, politics, and inquiry. In N. K. Denzin & Y. S. Lincoln (Eds.), *Collecting and interpreting qualitative materials* (p. 396). New Delhi: Sage.

Kamensky, J. M. (2013, November 5). Fighting Crime in a New Era of Predictive Policing.*Governing| The State and Localities*. Retrieved from http://www.governing.com/blogs/bfc/col-crime-fighting-predictive-policing-data-tools.html

Kang, H., Bae, K., Zhang, S., & Sundar, S. S. (2011). Source cues in online news: Is the proximate source more powerful than distal sources? *Journalism & Mass Communication Quarterly*, *88*, 719–736. Retrieved from http://www.researchgate.net/profile/Shaoke_Zhang/publication/230608544_Source_Cues_in_Online_News_Is_Proximate_Source_more_Powerful_than_Distal_Sources/links/09e41502130a5a870a000000.pdf

Kankanhalli, A., Tan, B. C. Y., & Wei, K. K. (2005). Contributing Knowledge to Electronic Knowledge Repositories: An Empirical Investigation. *Management Information Systems Quarterly*, *29*(1), 113–143.

Kanungo, S. (2003). Information Village: Bridging the Digital Divide in Rural India. In S. Madon & S. Krishna (Eds.), *The Digital Challenge: Information Technology in the Development Context* (pp. 103–123). Aldershot: Ashgate.

Kao, J. J., & Lin, H. Y. (1996). Multifactor spatial analysis for landfill siting. *Journal of Environmental Engineering*, *122*(10), 902–908. doi:10.1061/(ASCE)0733-9372(1996)122:10(902)

Kao, J. J., Lin, H., & Chen, W. (1997). Network geographic information system for landfill siting. *Waste Management & Research*, *15*(3), 239–253. doi:10.1177/0734242X9701500303

Kaplan, A. M., & Haenlein, M. (2010). Users of the world, unite! The challenges and opportunities of Social Media. *Business Horizons*, *53*(1), 59–68. doi:10.1016/j.bushor.2009.09.003

Kapoun, J. (1998, July/August). Teaching undergrads WEB evaluation: A guide for library instruction. *C&RL News*, 522-523.

Karahanna, E., Agarwal, R., & Angst, C. M. (2006). Re-conceptualizing compatibility beliefs in technology acceptance research. *Management Information Systems Quarterly*, *30*(4), 781–804.

Kaspersky Lab. (2013, September 17). Taking a malware hit – more than one in three attacks costs users money. Retrieved from http://www.kaspersky.com/about/news/press/2013/Taking_a_malware_hit_more_than_one_in_three_attacks_costs_users_money

Kataria, S. (2005). Dewang Mehta award for innovation in IT for NIIT Chief Scientist Sugata Mitra. Retrieved from http://www.niit.com/niit/ContentAdmin/NWS/NWSPR/NWSPR2/pr-010405-sugata-dewang.htm/

Katz, E., & Lazarsfeld, P. (1955). Personal Influence. New York: The Free Press.

Kauremaa, J., Kärkkäinen, M., & Ala-Risku, T. (2009). Customer initiated interorganizational information systems: The operational impacts and obstacles for small and medium sized suppliers. *International Journal of Production Economics*, *119*(2), 228–239. doi:10.1016/j.ijpe.2009.02.007

Kavanaugh, A. L., Fox, E. A., Sheetz, S. D., Yang, S., Li, L. T., Shoemaker, D. J., & Xie, L. et al. (2012). Social media use by government: From the routine to the critical. *Government Information Quarterly*, *29*(4), 480–491. doi:10.1016/j.giq.2012.06.002

Kawalek, P., & Wood-Harper, T. (2002). The Finding of Thorns: User Participation in Enterprise Systems Implementation. *The Data Base for Advances in Information Systems*, *33*(1), 13–22. doi:10.1145/504350.504355

Kealhofer, L. A. (2011). *Cinematic voices of maghrebi migrant women in France*.

Keller, J. M. (1987). Development and use of the ARCS model of instructional design. *Journal of Instructional Development*, *10*(3), 2–10. doi:10.1007/BF02905780

Kellner, D. (1998). Multiple literacies and critical pedagogy in a multicultural society. *Educational Theory*, *48*(1), 103–122. doi:10.1111/j.1741-5446.1998.00103.x

Kelly, H. (2012, August 30). Police embrace social media as crime-fighting tool. *CNN*. Retrieved from http://www.cnn.com/2012/08/30/tech/social-media/fighting-crime-social-media/index.html

Kelly, H. (2014, May 26). Police embracing tech that predicts crimes. *CNN*. Retrieved from http://www.cnn.com/2012/07/09/tech/innovation/police-tech/index.html

Kelly, K. (1988). *New rules for the new economy: Ten ways the networking economy is changing everything*. London: Fourth Estate.

Kennedy, G., Krause, K.-L., Judd, T., Churchward, A., & Gray, K. (2008). First Year Students' Experiences with Technology: Are they really Digital Natives. *Australasian Journal of Educational Technology*, *24*(1), 108–122.

Kepes, B. (2012). *Cloudonomics, The Economics of Cloud Computing*, Retrieved from http://www.cloudstratagem.com.au/Cloudonomics-The_Economics_of_Cloud_Computing.pdf

Kerber, K. W., & Buono, A. F. (2007). Enhancing Change Capacity. Client-Consultant Collaboration. *SYMPHONYA Emerging Issues in Management, n*(1), 81-96.

Kettinger, W. J., Lee, C. C., & Lee, S. (1995). Global measures of information service quality: A cross-national study. *Decision Sciences*, *26*(5), 569–588. doi:10.1111/j.1540-5915.1995.tb01441.x

Khalili Amozad, H., Ebrahimi Babak, S., & Nalchigar, S. (2012, May). Evaluation of e-payment systems in Iran using analytic hierarchy process. *African Journal of Business Management*, 6(19), 5950-5956. http://www.academicjournals.org/AJBM

Khondker, H. H. (2011). Role of the New Media in the Arab Spring Role of the New Media in the Arab Spring. *Globalizations*, *8*(5), 37–41. doi:10.1080/14747731.2011.621287

Khorasani, N., & Nejadkorki, F. (2000). Site selection for urban waste in arid lands by the application of GIS: A case study for the city of Kerman, Central Iran.[in Persian]. *BIABAN*, *5*(1), 59–66.

Khumalo, F. (1998). *Preliminary Evaluation of Telecenter Pilot Projects*. South Africa: Universal Service Agency.

Kim, Y., & Baylor, A. L. (2006). A social-cognitive framework for pedagogical agents as learning companions. *ETR & D*, *54*(6), 569–596. doi:10.1007/s11423-006-0637-3

Kirkpatrick, D. (2010). *The Facebook Effect: The Inside Story of the Company That Is Connecting the World.* Simon & Schuster.

Klapp, O. E. (1982). Meaning Lag in the Information Society. *Journal of Communication, 32*(2), 56–66. doi:10.1111/j.1460-2466.1982.tb00495.x

Klapp, O. E. (1986). *Overload and Boredom: Essays on the quality of life in the information society.* New York: Greenwood Press.

Klapp, O. E. (1991). *Inflation of Symbols: Loss of Values in American Culture.* New Brunswick, New Jersey: Transaction publishers.

Klein, S. M. (1996). A management communication strategy for change. *Journal of Organizational Change Management, 9*(2), 32–46. doi:10.1108/09534819610113720

Kline, R. B. (2005). *Principles and Practice of Structural Equation Modeling.* NY: The Guilford Press.

Kling, R. (1980). Social Analyses of Computing: Theoretical Perspectives in Recent Empirical Research. *Computing Surveys*, 61-110.

Kmieciak, R., Michna, A., & Meczynska, A. (2012). Innovativeness, empowerment and IT capability: Evidence from SMEs. *Industrial Management & Data Systems, 112*(5), 707–728. doi:10.1108/02635571211232280

Knell, N. (2013, January 3). Pinterest Helps Police Catch Criminals. *Governing The State and Localities.* Retrieved from http://www.governing.com/news/local/gt-pinterest-helps-police-catch-criminals.html

Koda, T., & Maes, P. (1996). *Agents with faces: The effect of personification.* Paper presented at the 5th IEEE International Workshop on Robot and Human Communication. Tsukuba, Japan. doi:10.1109/ROMAN.1996.568812

Kogut, B., & Metiu, A. (2001). Open-source software development and distributed innovation. *Oxford Review of Economic Policy, 17*(2), 248–264. Retrieved from https://www0.gsb.columbia.edu/faculty/bkogut/files/OpensourceSoftware_withMetiu_OREP_2001.pdf doi:10.1093/oxrep/17.2.248

Kokil, P. (n. d.). SAP-LAP Analysis. Retrieved from http://www.csi-sigegov.org/3/29_290_3.pdf

Kollock, P. (1999). The Production of trust in online markets. In E. J. Lawler, M. Macy, S. Thyne, & H. A. Walker (Eds.), Advances in Group Processes, 16, 99-123. Greenwich, CT: JAI Press.

Konieczny, P. (2009). Governance, Organization, and Democracy on the Internet: The Iron Law and the Evolution of Wikipedia. *Sociological Forum, 24*(1), 162–192. doi:10.1111/j.1573-7861.2008.01090.x

Kontos, T. D., Komilis, D. P., & Halvadakis, C. P. (2005). Sitting MSW landfills with a spatial multiple criteria analysis methodology. *Waste Management (New York, N.Y.), 25*(8), 818–832. doi:10.1016/j.wasman.2005.04.002 PMID:15946837

Koopmans, T. C. (1951). Analysis of production as an efficient combination of activities. *Activity Analysis of Production and Allocation, 13*, 33–37.

Korsgaard, T. R., & Jensen, C. D. (2009). Reengineering the Wikipedia for Reputation.*Proceedings of the 4th International Workshop on Security and Trust Management (STM 08)*, 71-84.

Kort, B., Reilly, R., & Picard, R. (2001). *An affective model of interplay between emotions and learning: reengineering educational pedagogy—building a learning companion.Proceedings of the IEEE International Conference on Advanced Learning Technology: Issues, Achievements and Challenges.* Madison, USA. doi:10.1109/ICALT.2001.943850

Korte, R. F., & Chermack, T. J. (2007). Changing organizational culture with scenario planning. *Futures, 39*(6), 645–656. doi:10.1016/j.futures.2006.11.001

Krueger, R. A. (1994). *Focus groups: A practical guide for applied research.* Thousand Oaks, California: Sage.

Kubiszewski, I., Noordewier, T., & Costanza, R. (2011). Perceived Credibility of Internet Encyclopedias. *Computers & Education, 56*(3), 659–667https://www.uvm.edu/giee/pubpdfs/Kubiszewski_2011_Computers_and_Education.pdf. RetrievedJanuary222014. doi:10.1016/j.compedu.2010.10.008

Kujath, C. L. (2011). Facebook and Myspace: Complement or substitute for face-to-face Interaction? *Cyberpsychology, Behavior, and Social Networking, 14*(1-2), 75–78. doi:10.1089/cyber.2009.0311 PMID:21329446

Kukreja, S., & Grover, M. (2004). Quoted In M.P. Gupta (Ed.), Promise of E-Governance: Operational Challenges. New Delhi: Tata McGraw-Hill Publishing Company Limited.

Kumbhakar, S. C., & Lovell, K. (2000). *Stochastic frontier analysis*. UK: Cambridge University Press. doi:10.1017/CBO9781139174411

Kumbhakar, S. C., Ortega-Argilés, R., Potters, L., Vivarelli, M., & Voigt, P. (2012). Corporate R&D and firm efficiency: Evidence from Europe's top R&D investors. *Journal of Productivity Analysis*, *37*(2), 125–140. doi:10.1007/s11123-011-0223-5

Kuo, E. C. Y., & Low, L. (2001). Information economy and changing occupational structure in Singapore. *The Information Society*, *17*(4).

Kwon, H. J., & Hong, K. S. (2013). A method to predict human emotion using sentimental similarity. *International Journal of Bio-Science and Bio-Technology*, *5*(3), 93–101.

Kykyri, V., Puutio, R., & Wahlstrom, J. (2010). Inviting Participation in Organisational Change through Ownership Talk. *The Journal of Applied Behavioral Science*, *46*(1), 92–118. doi:10.1177/0021886309357441

Lacity, M. C., & Willcocks, L. P. (1998). An empirical investigation of information technology sourcing practices: Lessons from experience. *Management Information Systems Quarterly*, *22*(3), 363–408. doi:10.2307/249670

Lakoff, G., & Johnson, M. (1980). Metaphors We Live By. Chicago: University of Chicago Press. Retrieved from http://shu.bg/tadmin/upload/storage/161.pdf

Lall, S. (2001). *Competitiveness, Technology and Skills. Williston*. Edward Elgar Publishing. doi:10.4337/9781781950555

Lamb, R., & Davidson, E. (2002, March 7-10). Social scientists: Managing identity in socio-technical networks. Paper presented at the Hawai'i International Conference on System Sciences. Big Island, Hawaii. doi:10.1109/HICSS.2002.994034

Lamb, R. (1996). Informational Imperatives and Socially Mediated Relationships. *The Information Society*, *12*(1), 17–38. doi:10.1080/019722496129684

Lam, P. L., & Shiu, A. (2010). Economic growth, telecommunications development and productivity growth of the telecommunications sector: Evidence around the world. *Telecommunications Policy*, *34*(4), 185–199. doi:10.1016/j.telpol.2009.12.001

Lampe, C., Ellison, N., & Steinfield, C. (2006). A Face(book) in the crowd: Social searching vs. social browsing.[New York: ACM Press.]. *Proceedings of CSCW-2006*, 167–170.

Lampe, C., Ellison, N., & Steinfield, C. (2007). A familiar Face(book): Profile elements as signals in an online social network.*Proceedings of the SIGCHI Conference on Human Factors in Computing Systems* (435–444). New York: ACM Press. doi:10.1145/1240624.1240695

Lanata, A., Valenza, G., & Scilingo, E. P. (2012). A novel EDA glove based on textile-integrated electrodes for affective computing. *Medical & Biological Engineering & Computing*, *50*(11), 1163–1172. doi:10.1007/s11517-012-0921-9 PMID:22711069

Landauer, R. (1996). The Physical nature of Information. *Physics Letters. [Part A]*, *217*(4-5), 188–193http://cqi.inf.usi.ch/qic/64_Landauer_The_physical_nature_of_information.pdf. RetrievedJanuary252014. doi:10.1016/0375-9601(96)00453-7

Langefors, B. (1993). Essays on Infology: Summing up and planning for the Future. In B. Dahlbom (Ed.) Gothenburg studies in Information Systems Report 5 (pp.111). Gothenburg: University of Gothenburg Press.

Laszlo, K. (2007). *Information society- what is it exactly?*. Budapest: European Commission. Retrieved from http://www.ittk.hu/netis/doc/ ISCB_eng/02_ZKL_final.pdf

Latour, B. (1987). *How to follow scientists and engineers through society*. Milton Keynes: Open University Press.

Latour, B. (1992). The sociology of a few mundane artefacts. In W. Bijker & J. Law (Eds.), *Shaping technology/building society studies in sociotechnical change*. Cambridge, MA: MIT Press.

Latour, B. (1999). *Pandora's hope: Essays on the reality of science studies*. Cambridge: Harvard University Press.

Latour, B. (2005). *Reassembling the social. An introduction to actor network theory*. New York: Oxford University Press.

Lawal-Adebowale, O. A. (2008). Fixed Wireless telephony system: A help line for bridging rural digital divide and transformation of rural communities in southwest Nigeria. Proceedings of the 16th Annual Conferee of the Nigerian Rural Sociological Association (pp. 241 – 245).

Lawal-Adebowale, O. A. (2010). Telecom sector policy deregulation and mobile phone diffusion in Nigeria – an assessment of impact on adoption and usage. *Proceedings of the 3rd Annual Conference of African Society for Information and Communication Technology* (pp. 177 – 185).

Lawal-Adebowale, O. A., & Adebayo, K. (2006). *Information and Communication Technologies: Pathways for Effecting Feedback in Mass Method of Extension Message Delivery. In proceedings of Agricultural Extension Society of Nigeria* (pp. 183–189). AESON.

Law, J., & Mol, A. (2001). Situating technoscience: An inquiry into spatialities. *Environment and Planning. D, Society & Space*, *19*(5), 609–621. doi:10.1068/d243t

Lawlor, A., Sandel, V., & Peterson, C. (2001). What works: Tarahaat's portal for rural India. Retrieved from www.digitaldividend.org/pdf/tarahaat.pdf

Lawson, B., & Samson, D. (2001). Developing innovation capability in organisations: A dynamic capabilities approach. *International Journal of Innovation Management*, *5*(3), 377–400. doi:10.1142/S1363919601000427

Lazarsfeld, P. F., Berelson, B., & Gaudet, H. (1944). *The people's choice: How the voter makes up his mind in a presidential campaign*. New York: Columbia University Press.

Lazonick, W. (1990). *Competitive advantage on the shop floor*. USA: Harvard University Press.

Leadbeater, C. (2008). *We-Think. Mass Innovation, Not Mass Production*. London: Profile Books.

Leao, S., Bishop, I., & Evans, D. (2001). Assessing the demand of solid waste disposal in urban region by urban dynamics modeling in a GIS environment. *Resources, Conservation and Recycling*, *33*(4), 289–313. doi:10.1016/S0921-3449(01)00090-8

Lee, C. (2103, August 27). New Media Knowledge - Social media's role in recruitment unveiled. *New Media Knowledge*. Retrieved from http://www.nmk.co.uk/article/2013/8/27/social-media%E2%80%99s-role-in-recruitment-unveiled

Lee, B., & Barua, A. (1999). An integrated assessment of productivity and efficiency impacts of information technology investments: Old data, new analysis and evidence. *Journal of Productivity Analysis*, *12*(1), 21–43. doi:10.1023/A:1007898906629

Lee, G., & Xia, W. (2006). Organizational size and IT innovation adoption: A meta-analysis. *Information & Management*, *43*(8), 979–985. doi:10.1016/j.im.2006.09.003

Lee, H. H., Fiore, A. M., & Kim, J. (2006). The role of the technology acceptance model in explaining effects of image interactivity technology on consumer responses. *International Journal of Retail & Distribution Management*, *34*(8), 621–644. doi:10.1108/09590550610675949

Lee, J. W. Y., Kim, B., Lee, T. L., & Kim, M. S. (2012). Uncovering the Use of Facebook During the Exchange Program. *China Media Research*, *8*(4), 62–76.

Lee, K. J. (2001). Globalization and infocom industries in Asia: Opportunities and threats. *Media Asia*, 28–29.

Lee, S.-G. (2003). *An Integrative Study of Mobile Technology Adoption Based on the Technology Acceptance Model, Theory of Planned Behavior and Diffusion of Innovation Theory*. MI: ProQuest Information and Learning Company.

Leimbach, T. (2014). *Potential and impacts of cloud computing services and social network websites*. Brussels: European Union.

Leishman, F., Loveday, B., & Savage, S. P. (2000). *Core issues in policing*. Pearson Education.

Lenhart, A., & Madden, M. (2007). Teens, Privacy and Online Social Networks: How teens manage their online identities and personal information in the age of Myspace. *Pew Internet and American Life Project Report*. Retrieved from http://www.pewinternet.org/files/old-media/Files/Reports/2007/PIP_Teens_Privacy_SNS_Report_Final.pdf.pdf

Lepenye, T. (2010). *Felhős ég az IT felett - Bevezetés a számítási felhők világába, (A cloudy sky over information technology – An introduction into the world of cloud computing)* Retrieved from http://lepenyet.wordpress.com/2010/04/23/felhos-eg-az-it-felett-%E2%80%93-bevezetes-a-szamitasi-felhok-vilagaba/

Lessig, L. (2004). *Free Culture: How big media uses technology and the law to lock down culture and control creativity.* London: Penguin Books. Retrieved from http://www.free-culture.cc/freeculture.pdf

Lessig, L. (2006). Code: Version 2.0. New York: Basic Books. Retrieved from http://codev2.cc/download+remix/Lessig-Codev2.pdf

Lessig, L. (2008). *Remix: Making Art and Commerce Thrive in the Hybrid Economy.* London: Bloomsbury. doi:10.5040/9781849662505

Lev, B. (2000). *Intangibles: management, measurement, and reporting*. Washington, DC: Brookings Institution Press.

LeVeque, T. (2011) Introducing social media to an emergency operations center. Retrieved from http://lawscommunications.com/category/tom-le-veque

Levin, J., & Fox, J. A. (2000). *Elementary statistics in social research* (8th ed.). Needham Heights, MA: Allyn & Bacon.

Levy, M., & Powell, P. (2000). Information systems strategy for small and medium sized enterprises: An organizational perspective. *The Journal of Strategic Information Systems*, *9*(1), 63–84. doi:10.1016/S0963-8687(00)00028-7

Lewins, K. (2010). The Trauma of Transformation: A Closer Look at the Soudien Report. *South African Review of Sociology*, *41*(1), 127–136. doi:10.1080/21528581003676077

Li, H. Y., & Huang, J. (2009). Applying Theory of Perceived Risk and Technology Acceptance Model in the Online Shopping Channel. *International Journal of Bank Marketing*, *2*(2).

Lim, S., & Kwon, N. (2010). Gender differences in information behaviour concerning Wikipedia, an unorthodox information source? *Library & Information Science Research*, *32*(3), 212–220. doi:10.1016/j.lisr.2010.01.003

Lin, C. A. (2000). *Predicting on-line news activity via motives, innovative traits and news media use.* html

Lin, H., & Kao, J. (1998). Enhanced spatial model for landfill siting analysis. *Journal of Environmental Engineering*, *125*(9), 845–851. doi:10.1061/(ASCE)0733-9372(1999)125:9(845)

Lister, S., Hadfield, P., Hobbs, D., & Winlow, S. (2001). Accounting for bouncers: Occupational licensing as a mechanism for regulation. *Criminology & Criminal Justice*, *1*(4), 363–384. doi:10.1177/1466802501001004001

Lobo, A., & Balakrishnan, S. (2002). Report card on service of Bhoomi kiosks: An assessment of benefits by users of the computerized land records system in Karnataka. Retrieved from http://www.nisg.org/egovgateway/kb_docs/casestudy/Bhoomi%20evaluation%20Nov%202002.pdf

Lohr, S. (2009). *Sampling: design and analysis*. Boston: Cengage Learning.

Lon, C. (2010, March).6 Ways Law Enforcement Uses Social Media to Fight Crime. *Mashable*. Retrieved from http://mashable.com/2010/03/17/law-enforcement-social-media/

Longe, O. M., & Longe, O. D. (n. d.). An overview of the development in the telecommunication industry of Nigeria. Retrieved from http://www.ircabfoundation.org/ journals/st/an%20overview%20of%20the%20development%20in%20the%20telecommunication%20industr%20of%20nigeria.pdf

Losee, R. M. (1998). A discipline independent definition of information. *Journal of the American Society for Information Science*, *48*(3), 254–269. Retrieved from http://www.ils.unc.edu/~losee/book5.pdf doi:10.1002/(SICI)1097-4571(199703)48:3<254::AID-ASI6>3.0.CO;2-W

Loten Angus. (2014, January 8). Open Data a Boon for Entrepreneurs - WSJ. Retrieved from http://online.wsj.com/news/articles/SB10001424052702304887104579307000606208592

Lough, J., & Ryan, M. (2010). Research note: Psychological profiling of australian police officers: A three-year examination of post-selection performance. *International Journal of Police Science & Management*, *12*(3), 480–486. doi:10.1350/ijps.2010.12.3.188

Louime, C., Jones, J. V., & Jones, T.-A. (2015). Developing Research-Based Partnerships: Florida A&M University's US-Brazil Cross-Cultural Initiative. In S. B. Sutton & D. Obst (Eds.), Developing Strategic International Partnerships: Models for Initiating and Sustaining Innovative Institutional Linkages. New York: Institute of International Education and the AIFS Foundation; Retrieved from http://www.tec.govt.nz/Funding/Fund-finder/Performance-Based-Research-Fund-PBRF-/

Louwerse, M. M., Graesser, A. C., Lu, S., & Mitchel, H. M. (2005). Social cues in animated conversational agents. *Applied Cognitive Psychology*, *19*(6), 693–704. doi:10.1002/acp.1117

Lovink, G. (1997). *Information inequality: An interview with Herbert Schiller.* Retrieved from http://www.ljudmila.org/nettime/zkp4/20.htm

Low, L. (2000). The Social Impact of New Communication "Technologies. *Media Asia*, *27*(2), 84.

Lozanov, G. (1978). *Suggestology and Suggestopedia: Theory and practice*. Paris: UNESCO. Retrieved online at: http://unesdoc.unesco.org/images/0003/000300/030087eb.pdf

Lucassen, T. (2013). Trust in Online Information. Retrieved from http://teunlucassen.nl/wp-content/uploads/2013/02/Teun-Lucassen-Trust-in-Online-Information.pdf

Lucassen, T., & Schraagen, J. M. (n. d.). Trust in Wikipedia: How Users Trust Information from an Unknown Source. Retrieved from http://wwwconference.org/proceedings/www2010/wicow/p19.pdf

Luftman, J., Zadeh, H. S., Derksen, B., Santana, M., Rigoni, E. H., & Huang, Z. D. (2013). Key information technology and management issues 2012–2013: An international study. *Journal of Information Technology*, *28*(4), 354–366. doi:10.1057/jit.2013.22

Luhmann, N. (1990). Meaning as sociology's basic concept. In N. Luhmann (Ed.), *Essays in Self Reference* (pp. 21–79). New York: Columbia University press.

Luis, E. M., Vicente, T., Andrea, B., José, A., Reyna, O. P., & Hernández-Espriú, A. et al. (2012). Identifying suitable sanitary landfill locations in the state of Morelos, México, using a Geographic Information System. *Physics and Chemistry of the Earth*, *2*(9), 37–39.

Luke, A. (1998) quoted in Sreekumar, T.T. (2004). E governance and social exclusion: Experiences from the fields. Retrieved from www.11iacc.org/download/add/WS11.2/TTS%20Paper.pdf

Luntz Research Company. (1997). *The Wired/Merril Lynch Forum Digital Citizen Survey.* Retrieved from http:// hotwired.lycos.com/special/citizen/

Mabillot, D. (2007). User generated content: Web 2.0 taking the video sector by storm. *Communications & Stratégies*, *65*, 39–49. Retrieved from http://mpra.ub.uni-muenchen.de/4579/1/

Machlup, F. (1962). *The production and distribution of knowledge in the United States* (Vol. 278). USA: Princeton University Press.

Machlup, F. (1984). *Knowledge, its creation, distribution, & economic significance: The economics of information and human capital.* New Jersey: Princeton University Press. doi:10.1515/9781400856022

Macintosh, A. (2004). Characterizing e-participation in policy-making.*Proceedings of the 37th Annual Hawaii International Conference on System Sciences* (pp. 10). doi:10.1109/HICSS.2004.1265300

MacKay, D. M. (1969). *Information, mechanism and meaning*. Cambridge, MA: MIT Press.

Madden, M., & Fox, S. (2006). Riding the Waves of "Web 2.0": More than a Buzzword, But Still Not Easily Defined. Pew Internet Project. Retrieved from http://www.pewinternet.org/2006/10/05/riding-the-waves-of-web-2-0/

Magno, F. A. (2014). E-Governance and Social Inclusion: Community E-Centers in the Philippines. In S. Baum & A. Mahizhnan (Eds.), *E-Governance and Social Inclusion: Concepts and Cases* (pp. 256–270). Hershey, PA: Information Science Reference; doi:10.4018/978-1-4666-6106-6.ch016

Mahini, S. A., & Gholamalifard, M. (2006). SitingMSWlandfills with a weighted linear combination (WLC) methodology in a GIS environment. *International Journal of Environmental Science and Technology*, *3*(4), 435–445. doi:10.1007/BF03325953

Mahizhnan, A. (2014). E-Government and Social Inclusion: Concepts. In S. Baum & A. Mahizhnan (Eds.), *E-Governance and Social Inclusion: Concepts and Cases* (pp. 1–9). Hershey, PA: Information Science Reference. doi:10.4018/978-1-4666-6106-6.ch001

Mahmood, O., & Selvadurai, S. (2006). Modeling "Web of Trust" with Web 2.0. In the *Proceedings of World Academy of Science, Engineering and Technology, 18.*

Malerba, F., Vonortas, N., Breschi, S., & Cassi, L. (2006). *Evaluation of progress towards a European Research Area for information society technologies. Report to European Commission.* Brusells: DG Information Society and Media.

Malhotra, C. Chariar, V. M & Das, L. K. (2011). *Citizen-centricity for e-Governance initiatives in Rural Areas.* Retrieved from http://indiagovernance.gov.in/files/initiatives_in_Rural_Areas.pdf

Malhotra, C. Chariar, V. M & Das, L. K. (2013). Citizen-Centric Approach for Converging Indigenous Knowledge Systems using ICT. In U.M. Munshi & V. Sharma (Eds.), Strategizing Knowledge Management and Environmental Paradigm. New Delhi: Jain Publishing House.

Malhotra, C., Chariar, V. M & Das, L. K. (2009 April). User Centered Design Model (G2C2G) for Rural e-Governance Projects. *International Journal of e-Governance,* 1742-7509.

Malhotra, C; Chariar, V.M.& Das, L.K. (2014). A Validated Citizen-Centric Approach using Delphi Technique for Converging Indigenous Knowledge Systems using ICT. *International Journal of e-Government Research (IJEGR), 4.* USA: IGI publications.

Malhotra, Charru & Chatterjee, T. (2014, August). *ICT4D: Innovating Governance to be more Citizen-Centric using ICT.* Department of Administrative Reforms and Public Grievances, Government of India.

Malmberg, A., & Maskell, P. (2006). Localized learning revisited. *Growth and Change, 37*(1), 1–18. doi:10.1111/j.1468-2257.2006.00302.x

Manoharan, B. (2007). Indian e-Payment System and Its Performance. *Professional Banker, 7*(3), 61–69.

Mantel, B. (2000). Why Don't Customers Use e-Banking Products: Towards a Theory of Obstacles, Incentives and Opportunities [FRB Chicago Working Paper No. EPS-2000-1].

Margetts, H. (1996). Public management change and sex equality within the state. *Parliamentary Affairs, 49*(1), 130–142. doi:10.1093/oxfordjournals.pa.a028663

Mariano, N., & Pilar, Q. (2005). Absorptive capacity, technological opportunity, knowledge spillovers, and innovative effort. *Technovation, 25*(10), 1141–1157. doi:10.1016/j.technovation.2004.05.001

Marin, A., & Bell, M. (2006). Technology spillovers from Foreign Direct Investment (FDI): The active role of MNC subsidiaries in Argentina in the 1990s. *The Journal of Development Studies, 42*(4), 678–697. doi:10.1080/00220380600682298

Martin, C. J. (1989). Information management in the smaller business: The role of the top manager. *International Journal of Information Management, 9*(3), 187–197. doi:10.1016/0268-4012(89)90006-6

Martin, J. P., & John, M. Jr. (1983). The impact of subsidies on X-Efficiency in LDC industry: Theory and an empirical test. *The Review of Economics and Statistics, 65*(4), 608–617. doi:10.2307/1935929

Maskell, P., Bathelt, H., & Malmberg, A. (2006). Building global knowledge pipelines: The role of temporary clusters. *European Planning Studies, 14*(8), 997–1013. doi:10.1080/09654310600852332

Mason, R., & Rennie, F. (2007). Using Web 2.0 for learning in the community. *The Internet and Higher Education, 10*(3), 196–203. doi:10.1016/j.iheduc.2007.06.003

Masuda, Y. (1990). *Managing in the information society: Releasing synergy Japanese style.* Oxford: Basil Blackwell.

Maturana, H. R., & Varella, F. J. (1980). R.S. Cohen & M.W. Wartofsky (Eds.), *Autopoiesis and cognition.* Dordrecht Holland: D. Reidel publishing company. Retrieved from http://topologicalmedialab.net/xinwei/classes/readings/Maturana/autopoesis_and_cognition.pdf

Mawoli, M. A. (2009). Liberalisation of the Nigerian telecommunication sector: A critical review. *Journal of Research in National Development, 7* (2), not paged. Retrieved from http://www.transcampus.org/JORIND-V7Dec2009/journalV7NO2Dec2009.html

Mayanja, M. (2001). The Nakaseke Multipurpose Community Telecentre in Uganda. In C. Latchem, & D. Walker (Eds.), Telecentres: Case Studies and Key Issues. Vancouver: The Commonwealth of Learning.

Maynard, M. (2013, October 31). Public agencies still don't do social media very well. *Governing- The State and Localities*. Retrieved from http://www.governing.com/news/headlines/Public-Agencies-Still-Dont-Do-Social-Media-Very-Well.html

Mazerolle, L., Rogan, D., Frank, J., Famega, C., & Eck, J. E. (2003). *Managing citizen calls to the police: an assessment of non-emergency call systems*. Washington, DC: United States Department of Justice.

Mcdonagh-Philp, D., & Lebbon, C. (2000). The emotional domain in product design. *The Design Journal, 3*(1), 31–43. doi:10.2752/146069200789393562

McDonald, J., & Dahlberg, J. (2010, March 8-10). US Consumer Attitudes Toward And Acceptance Of SMS Mobile Text Advertising, *Proceeding of the 4th International Technology, Education and Development Conference (INTED).* Valencia, Spain.

McEneaney, J. E. (2013). Agency effects in human–computer interaction. *International Journal of Human-Computer Interaction, 29*(12), 798–813. doi:10.1080/10447318.2013.777826

McNamara, K. S. (2003). Information and Communication Technologies, Poverty and Development: Learning from Experience. In *A background paper for the info Dev Annual Symposium.* Geneva: The World Bank.

McQuail, D. (2000). *McQuail's Mass Communication Theory.* New York. *Sage (Atlanta, Ga.).*

Measuring the Information Society CH 1211. (2012). (p. 213). International Telecommunication Union. Geneva, Switzerland. Retrieved from http://www.itu.int

Melkote, S. R., & Steeves, H. L. (2001). *Communication for Development in the Third World- Theory and Practice for Empowerment* (2nd ed.). New Delhi, India: SAGE. doi:10.4135/9788132113751

Mell, P., & Grance, T. (2011). *The NIST Definition of Cloud Computing*. Retrieved from http://csrc.nist.gov/publications/nistpubs/800-145/SP800-145.pdf

Menguc, B., & Auh, S. (2010). Development and Return on Execution of Product Innovation Capabilities: The Role of Organizational Structure. *Industrial Marketing Management, 39*(5), 820–831. doi:10.1016/j.indmarman.2009.08.004

Meola, M. (2004). Chucking the checklist: A contextual approach to teaching undergraduates Web evaluation. *Portal: Libraries and the Academy, 4*(3), 331–344. doi:10.1353/pla.2004.0055

Mesch, G. S., & Talmud, I. (2011). Ethnic differences in internet access: The role of occupation and exposure. *Information Communication and Society, 14*(4), 445–471. doi:10.1080/1369118X.2011.562218

Metzger, M. J., & Pure, R. *Flanagin,A.J., Markov, A., Medders,R. & Hartsell, E.* (2013). The Special Case of Youth and Digital Information Credibility. In M. Folk and S. Apostel (Eds.) *Online Credibility and Digital Ethos: Evaluating Computer-Mediated Communication* (pp. 148-163). *Hershey PA: IGI Global.* Retrieved from http://www.comm.ucsb.edu/faculty/flanagin/CV/Metzgeretal2013%28CredEthos%29.pdf

Metzger, M. J. (2007). Making sense of credibility on the Web: Models for evaluating online information and recommendations for future research. *Journal of the American Society for Information Science and Technology, 58*(13), 2078–2091. doi:10.1002/asi.20672

Metzger, M. J., & Flanagin, A. J. (Eds.). (2008). *Digital Media, Youth, and Credibility.* Cambridge, MA: MIT Press.

Metzger, M. J., Flanagin, A. J., & Medders, R. (2010). Social and heuristic approaches to credibility evaluation online. *Journal of Communication, 60*(3), 413–439. Retrieved from http://www.pensierocritico.eu/files/Metzger---Social-and-Heuristic-Approaches-to-Credibility-Evaluation-Online.pdf doi:10.1111/j.1460-2466.2010.01488.x

Meyers, M. (1996). *News coverage of violence against women: Engendering blame*. London, GB: Sage Publications Ltd.

Miettinen, R. (1997, July). The concept of activity in the analysis of heterogeneous networks in innovation processes. Proceedings of the CSTT Workshop, Actor Network and After. University of Helsinki. Retrieved from http://communication.ucsd.edu/MCA/Paper/Reijo/Reijo.html

Milana, C., & Zeli, A. (2002). The contribution of ICT to production efficiency in Italy: firm-level evidence using data envelopment analysis and econometric estimations (No. 2002/13). Paris: OECD Publishing. Retrieved from http://www.oecd-ilibrary.org/docserver/download/5lgsjhvj7m5d.pdf?expires=1431686341&id=id&accname=guest&checksum=235816053C0ABA10933BC3CB14BE1F82

Millennium Development Goals, 149. (2004). Millennium Development Goals. Retrieved from http://www.un.org/millenniumgoals/

Mills, M. B. (1999). Thai women in the global labor force: Consuing desires, contested selves. *The Journal of Asian Studies*, *59*(01), 217–219.

Milner, E. M. (2002). *Delivering the vision: Where are we going? Delivering the vision: Public services for the information and knowledge economy* (pp. 172–174). London: Routledge.

Mingers, J. (2001). Combining IS research methods: Towards a pluralist methodology. *Information Systems Research*, *12*(3), 240–259. Retrieved from http://gkmc.utah.edu/7910F/papers/ISR%20combining%20IS%20research%20methods.pdf doi:10.1287/isre.12.3.240.9709

Mingers, J. C. (1995). Information and meaning: Foundations for an intersubjective account. *Information Systems Journal*, *5*(4), 295. doi:10.1111/j.1365-2575.1995.tb00100.x

Ministry of Housing & Local Government Malaysia (MHLG), (2009). *National strategic plan for solid waste management*.

Ministry of Law & Justice, Government of India. (2005). Right to Information Act. Retrieved from http://rti.gov.in/rti-act.pdf

Miranda, R. (2000). The Building Blocks of a Digital Government Strategy. *Government Finance Officers Association*, *16*(5), 9.

Misra, D. P. (2013, May 25). The Launch of in Pursuit of an Idea - Creative Collaboration on Open Government Data for Innovation-Informatics. Retrieved from http://informatics.nic.in/news/newsdetail/newsID/450

Mitra, A. (1999). Agglomeration economies as manifested in technical efficiency at the firm level. *Journal of Urban Economics*, *45*(3), 490–500. doi:10.1006/juec.1998.2100

Mlitwa, N. (2005). Higher education and ICT in the information society: A case of UWC. 2nd Annual Conference of the Community Informatics Research Network (CIRN). 24-26 August, 2005, Cape Peninsula University of Technology (CPUT), South Africa.

Mlitwa, N. (2007). Technology for teaching and learning in higher education contexts: Activity theory and actor network theory analytical perspectives. *International Journal of Education and Development using Information and Communication Technology, 3*(4), 54-70.

Mobility Nigeria. (2013). Nigerian smartphone market figures for 2012. Retrieved from http://mobility.ng/nigerian-smartphone-market-figures-for-2012/

Mobility Nigeria. (2014a). Mobipedia Nigeria: Facts and figures. Retrieved from http://mobility.ng/quick-facts/

Mobility Nigeria. (2014b). 2014 Stats: Is Nigeria becoming a smartphone market? Retrieved from http://mobility.ng/2014-is-nigeria-becoming-a-smartphone-market/

Mokhtar, A. M. D., & Wan, Z. W. J. Rev. M.M. O., & Wan M.A.W.H., (2008). How Gis Can Be A Useful Tool To Deal With Landfill Site Selection. *Proceedings International Symposium on Geoinformatics for Spatial Infrastructure Development in Earth and Allied Sciences, Hanoi, Vietnam, 4-6 December 2008, ISBN 978- 4-901668-37-8, pp 377-382.*

Molinari, F., McPherson, M., & Singh, G. (2014). Democratising E-Democracy: A Roadmap for Impact. In S. Baum & A. Mahizhnan (Eds.), *E-Governance and Social Inclusion: Concepts and Cases* (pp. 25–44). Hershey, PA: Information Science Reference; doi:10.4018/978-1-4666-6106-6.ch003

Molnár, B., Szabó, Gy., Benczúr, A., & Tarcsi, Á. (2012). *Felhő számítástechnika a közigazgatásban, (Cloud computing in public administration)*. Információs Rendszerek Tanszék

Montserrat, Z., & Emilio, M. (2008). Evaluation of a municipal landfill site in Southern Spain with GIS-aided methodology. *Journal of Hazardous Materials*, *160*(2-3), 473–481. doi:10.1016/j.jhazmat.2008.03.023 PMID:18423853

Moodysson, J. (2008). Principles and practices of knowledge creation: On the organization of "buzz" and "pipelines" in life science communities. *Economic Geography*, *84*(4), 449–469. doi:10.1111/j.1944-8287.2008.00004.x

Moore, G., & Benbasat, I. (1991). Development of an Instrument to Measure the Perceptions of Adopting an Information Technology Innovation. *Information Systems Research*, *2*(3), 173–191. doi:10.1287/isre.2.3.192

Morgan, D. L. (1988). *Focus groups as qualitative research*. Newbury Park, CA: Sage.

Moridis, C. N., & Economides, A. A. (2008). Toward computer-aided affective learning systems: A literature review. *Journal of Educational Computing Research*, *39*(4), 313–337. doi:10.2190/EC.39.4.a

Moridis, C. N., & Economides, A. A. (2012). Affective learning: Empathetic agents with emotional facial and tone of voice expressions. *IEEE Transactions on Affective Computing*, *3*(3), 260–272. doi:10.1109/T-AFFC.2012.6

Morris, S. (2011, October 28). Joanna Yeates murder: the full truth may never be known. *The Guardian*. Retrieved from http://www.theguardian.com/uk/2011/oct/28/joanna-yeates-case-vincent-tabak

Morris, N. (2003). A Comparative Analysis of the Diffusion annd Participatory Models in Development Communication. *Communication Theory*, *13*(2), 225–248. doi:10.1111/j.1468-2885.2003.tb00290.x

Mory, E. H. (1992). The use of informational feedback in instruction: Implications for future research. *Educational Technology Research and Development*, *4*(3), 5–20. doi:10.1007/BF02296839

Moskvitch, K. (2012, October 29). Can you predict crime with tech? *BBC News*. Retrieved from http://www.bbc.co.uk/news/technology-20068722

Mossberger, K., Tolbert, C., & McNeal, R. (2008). *Digital Citizenship: The Internet, Society, and Participation*. Cambridge, MA: The MIT Press.

Motohashi, K. (2007). Firm-level analysis of information network use and productivity in Japan. *Journal of the Japanese and International Economies*, *21*(1), 121–137. doi:10.1016/j.jjie.2005.08.001

Mouelhi, R. B. A. (2009). Impact of the adoption of information and communication technologies on firm efficiency in the Tunisian manufacturing sector. *Economic Modelling*, *26*(5), 961–967. doi:10.1016/j.econmod.2009.03.001

Mowlana, H. (1996). *Global communication in transition: The end of diversity?* New Delhi. *Sage (Atlanta, Ga.)*.

Mowlana, H. (1997). *Communication and development--the emerging orders: Global information and world communication*. New Delhi: Sage. doi:10.4135/9781446280034.n10

Moynihan, B., Kabadayi, S., & Kaiser, M. (2010). Consumer acceptance of SMS advertising: A study of American and Turkish consumers. *International Journal of Mobile Communications*, *8*(4), 392–410. doi:10.1504/IJMC.2010.033833

Mozsik, T. (2010): *5 tipp a számítási felhők felhasználásához, (5 tips of using cloud computing)* Retrieved from http://bitport.hu/vezinfo/5-tipp-a-szamitasi-felho-vallalati-felhasznalasahoz

Mubarak, C. (2009). e-Sri Lanka: What is in it for agriculture. Proceedings of *Joint National Conference on Information Technology in Agriculture* (pp. 7–10). Colombo, Si Lanka. University of Moratuwa, Sri Lanka and University of Ruhuna, Sri Lanka.

Mueller, B. (2014). Participatory culture on YouTube: A case study of the multichannel network Machinima. Retrieved from http://www.lse.ac.uk/media@lse/research/mediaWorkingPapers/MScDissertationSeries/2013/msc/104-Mueller.pdf

Muianga, X. (2004). Blended online and face-to-face learning – a pilot project in the faculty of education at the Eduardo Mondlane University, Mozambique. Emerge2004 Online Conference. South Africa: University of Cape Town; Retrieved from http://emerge2004.net/connect/site/UploadWSC/emerge2004/file19/emerge2004paperfinal. pdf

Muk, A. (2007). Consumers' intentions to opt in to SMS advertising - A cross-national study of young Americans and Koreans. *International Journal of Advertising*, *26*(2), 177–198.

Muniz, A. M. Jr, & Schau, H. J. (2011). How to inspire value-laden collaborative consumer-generated content. *Business Horizons*, *54*(3), 209–217. doi:10.1016/j.bushor.2011.01.002

Murray, B. (2001). The Hungarian Telecottage Movement. In C. Latchem, & D. Walker, Telecentres: Case Studies and Key Issues. Vancouver: The Commonwealth of Learning.

Mustian, J., & Wallace, B. (2014, July 2). Police using social media to track down criminals. *The New Orleans Advocate*. Retrieved from http://www.theneworleansadvocate.com/news/9576282-171/gotcha-police-using-social-media

Muttiah, R. S., Engel, B. A., & Jones, D. D. (1996). Waste disposal site selection using GIS-based simulated annealing. *Computers & Geosciences*, *22*(9), 1013–1017. doi:10.1016/S0098-3004(96)00039-8

Nanterme, P., & Cole, M. (2013). *Accenture Technology Vision 2013*, Every Business Is a Digital Business, Retrieved from http://www.accenture.com/SiteCollectionDocuments/PDF/Accenture-Technology-Vision-2013.pdf

Narender, K., & Nirmala. (2003). Information Communication Technology for Women. *Women and Information and Communication Technologies in India and China*. Adelaide: The Hawke Institute.

Nargundkar, R. (2002). *Marketing Research*. New Delhi: Tata McGraw-Hill.

Narula, R., & Dunning, J. H. (2000). Industrial development, globalization and multinational enterprises: New realities for developing countries. *Oxford Development Studies*, *28*(2), 141–167. doi:10.1080/713688313

Nas, B., Cay, T., Iscan, F., & Berktay, A. (2008a). Selection of MSW landfill site for Konya, Turkey using GIS and multi-criteria evaluation. *Environmental Monitoring and Assessment*, *160*(1–4), 491–500. PMID:19169836

National Agricultural and Forestry Extension Service (NAFES). (2005). Consolidating Extension in the Lao PDR (p. 77). Retrieved from http://www.laolink.org

National Communication Commission - NPT. (2000). National Policy on Communication. Ministry of Communication. Retrieved from http://www.ncc.gov.ng

National Communication Commission. (2014). Subscriber data base. Retrieved from http://www.ncc.gov.ng/index.php?Option=com_content&view=article&id=1390:vanguard-23rd-april-2014-telecom-activities-may-keep-nigerias-rebased-gdp-green&catid=86:cat-Mediapr-headlines

Nayar, M. (2004, October 22). Aiming to get a true picture of corruption. *The Hindu*.

NCHE. (1997). Education White Paper 3 - A Programme for Higher Education Transformation. Retrieved from http://www.info.gov.za/view/DownloadFileAction?id=70435

Ndukwe, E. C. A. (2003a). Telecommunication in national development. A Slide Presentation, 45pp. Retrieved from http://ncc.gov.ng/archive/speeches_presentations/EVC's%20Presentation/The%20Role%20of%20Telecommunications%20in%20National%20Devep.pdf

Ndukwe, E. C. A. (2003b). An overview of evolution of the telecommunication industry in Nigeria and challenges ahead (1999-2003). Retrieved from http://www.ncc.gov.nig/ speeches-presentation/EVC's%20Presentation/overview%20of %20Telecom%20.

Ndukwe, E. C. A. (2003c). The role of telecommunications in national development. Proceedings of the 19th Omolayole Annual Management Lecture, held at the Chartered Institute of Bankers' Auditorium Victoria Island, Lagos. Retrieved from http://ncc.gov.ng/archive/speeches_presentations/EVC's%20Presentation/The%20Role%20of%20Telecommunications%20in%20National%20Devep.pdf

Ndukwe, E. C. A. (2003d). Telecommunication regulation: Nigerian challenges & direction. Proceedings of Telecommunications workshop NICON. Hilton, Abuja.

Ndukwe, E. C. A. (2004). Communications technology in the 21st century. Proceedings of annual general meeting of the Nigerian Society of Engineers, Enugu Branch, Enugu.

Ndukwe, E. C. A. (2004). The imperative of accelerating the deployment of Information and communications technologies (ICTs) for social and economic development. Proceedings of the 11th Herbert Macaulay Memorial Lecture. Retrieved from http://www.ncc.gov.ng/archive/speeches_presentations/EVC's%20Presentation/11th%20Herbert%20Maculay%20Memorial%20-%20220704.pdf

Ndukwe, E. C. A. (2005). Telecom liberalization in Nigeria: Opening up the market and sector reform. Proceedings of SATCOM. Retrieved from http://ncc.gov.ng/archive/speeches_presentations/EVC's%20Presentation/Telecoms%20Liberalisation%20in%20Nigeria.pdf

Ndukwe, E. C. A. (2006). Country experience in telecom market reforms [Slideshow]. Retrieved from http://ncc.gov.ng/archive/EVCSpeches/2009_NITDEL_Lecture.pdf

Ndukwe, E. C. A. (n. d.). Telecommunications as a vehicle for socio-economic development. Slide presentation. 12pp. Retrieved from http://www.ncc.gov.ng/archive/speeches_presentations/EVC's%20Presentation/2009/socio.pdf

Ndukwe, E. C. A. (2009). Telecom in the service of the modern society.

Negroponte (1995). In Preston (2001), Reshaping communications: Technology information and social change. New Delhi: Sage.

Ngulube, P. (2007). The nature and accessibility of e-government in Sub Saharan Africa. *International Review for Information Ethics*. Retrieved from http://www.i-r-i-e.net/about_irie.htm#Publication%20Agreement

Nhan, J. (2014). Police culture. In G. Bruinsma & D. Weisburd (Eds.), *The encyclopedia of criminology and criminal justice*. London, GB: Blackwell Publishing Ltd.

Niall, H. and Chris, W. (2012). Context and the processes of ICT for development. *Inf. Organ., 22*(1), 23-36. DOI=10.1016/j.infoandorg.2011.10.001

Nie, N. H. (2001). Sociability, interpersonal relations, and the Internet: Reconciling conflicting findings. *The American Behavioral Scientist, 45*(3), 420–435. doi:10.1177/00027640121957277

Nigeria mobile market: Insight statistics and forecast. (2014). *BudeComm*. Retrieved from [REMOVED HYPERLINK FIELD]http://www.budde.com.au/Research/Nigeria-Mobile-Market-Insights-Statistics-and-Forecasts.html

Nigeriafirst (2003), *Telecommunication in Nigeria*. Retrieved from http://www.nigeriafirst.org/Tcom

Norris, P. (2002). The Bridging and Bonding Role of Online Communities. *The Harvard International Journal of Press/Politics, 7*(3), 3–13. doi:10.1177/1081180X0200700301

November 19, 2005, from http://www.acceso.or.cr/publica/telecom/frmwkENG.shtml

November 23, 2006, from http://www.undp.org/dpa/choices/2001/june/j4e.pdf

Nua Internet Surveys (n. d.). In Lee (2001), *Globalization and infocom industries in Asia: Opportunities and threats*. Retrieved from [REMOVED HYPERLINK FIELD]http://www.AEJMC.org/convention/abstracts/2Q01conabs/Olmcs.html

Nunnally, J. C., & Bernstein, I. H. (1994). Psychometric Theory. New York: McGraw-Hill.

O'Flinn, J. (2014, January 14). Twitter trolls: the existing legal framework. *The Lawyer*. Retrieved from http://www.thelawyer.com/analysis/opinion/twitter-trolls-the-existing-legal-framework/3014808.article

O'Leary, A. (2013, April 18). One on One: Tim Jones of Buzzient, Hunting Chatter on Explosives. *Bits Blog*. Retrieved from http://bits.blogs.nytimes.com/2013/04/18/buzzient-boston-marathon-investigation/

O'Mahony, S. (2003). Guarding the commons: How community managed software projects protect their work. *Research Policy, 32*(7), 1179–1198. Retrieved from http://flosshub.org/sites/flosshub.org/files/rp-omahony.pdf doi:10.1016/S0048-7333(03)00048-9

O'Reilly, N. (2014, July 2). Halton police get homicide tip in tweet-a-thon. *The Spec*. Retrieved from http://www.thespec.com/news-story/4610107-halton-police-get-homicide-tip-in-tweet-o-thon/

Oakley, K. (2002, June 10-11). *'What is e-governance?'* *e*-Governance Workshop. Strasbourg. Retrieved from http://www.coe.int/t/dgap/democracy/activities/ggis/e-governance/work_of_egovernance_committee/kate_oakley_egovernance_EN.asp

Observer, J. (2012, May 11). Showing the human side of the police. *Jamaica Observer*. Retrieved from http://www.jamaicaobserver.com/letters/Showing-the-human-side-of-the-police_11430692

OECD, & Eurostat (2005). *Oslo Manual: Guidelines for collecting and interpreting innovation data* (3rd ed.). Paris, FR: OECD Publishing.

OECD. (2010). *Ministerial report on the OECD Innovation Strategy*. Retrieved from http://www.oecd.org/sti/45326349.pdf (2015, May 16).

Oestmann, S., & Dymond, A. C. (2001). Telecentres - Experiences, Lessons and Trends. In C. Latchem, & D. Walker (Eds.), Telecentres: Case Studies and Key Issues (pp. 1 - 31). Vancouver: The Commonwealth of Learning.

Ofir, Z. M. (2003). *Information & Communication Technologies for Development (ACACIA): The Case of Uganda.* South Africa: The IDRC Evaluation Unit.

Ofir, Z. M. (2003). *Synthesis Report of Case Studies: ICTs for Development in Mozambique, Senegal, South Africa and Uganda*. South Africa: The IDRC Evaluation Unit.

Ojo, J. (2011). Appraisal of a decade of GSM revolution in Nigeria. Public Affairs Analyst. Retrieved from http://jideojong.blogspot.com/

Oliner, S. D., Sichel, D. E., & Stiroh, K. J. (2008). Explaining a productive decade. *Journal of Policy Modeling*, *30*(4), 633–673. doi:10.1016/j.jpolmod.2008.04.007

Open Data 500 Open Government Partnership. Companies. (n. d.). Retrieved from http://www.opendata500.com/list/

Open data and economic growth: which link, if any? (2012, July 21). Retrieved from http://www.opengovpartnership.org/blog/blog-editor/2012/07/20/open-data-and-economic-growth-which-link-if-any

Open Data Driving growth, ingenuity and innovation. (2012). *Deloitte Analytics Paper*. Retrieved from https://www.deloitte.com/assets/Dcom-UnitedKingdom/Local%20Assets/Documents/Market%20insights/Deloitte%20Analytics/uk-insights-deloitte-analytics-open-data-june-2012.pdf

Open Knowledge Foundation. (2012, November 14). Open Data Handbook Documentation. Retrieved from http://opendatahandbook.org/pdf/OpenDataHandbook.pdf

OpenDataApps Challenge. (n. d.). *Open Government Data (OGD) Platform India*. Retrieved from https://data.gov.in/event/opendataapps-challenge

Ornebring, H. (2008). The consumer as producer of what?. *Journalism Studies*, *9*(5), 771-785. doi: 10.1080/14616700802207789

Ortega, J. L., & Aguillo, I. F. (2010). Shaping the European research collaboration in the 6th Framework Programme health thematic area through network analysis. *Scientometrics*, *85*(1), 377–386. doi:10.1007/s11192-010-0218-4

Osman, K. (2013). The role of conflict in determining consensus on quality in Wikipedia article. Retrieved from http://opensym.org/wsos2013/proceedings/p0206-osman.pdf

Padovitz, A., Loke, S. W., & Zaslavsky, A. (2004). *Towards a Theory of Context Spaces. Proceedings ofWorkshop on Context Modeling and Reasoning (CoMoRea), at* 2nd IEEE International Conference on Pervasive Computing and Communication *(PerCom'04)*. Orlando, Florida. doi:10.1109/PERCOMW.2004.1276902

Palfrey, J., & Gasser, U. (2008). Born Digital: Understanding the first generation of digital natives (Review of the Book). *International Journal of Communication*, *4*(2010), 1051–1055. Retrieved from http://ijoc.org/index.php/ijoc/article/viewFile/950/474

Paniyil, M. M. (2001). Media/Information Technology. *Asia Times Online*. Retrieved from http://www.atimes.cpm

Paoline, E. A. III. (2004). Shedding light on police culture: An examination of officers' occupational attitudes. *Police Quarterly*, *7*(2), 205–236. doi:10.1177/1098611103257074

Papadopoulos, I., Tilki, M., & Lees, S. (2004). Promoting cultural competence in healthcare through a research-based intervention in the UK. *Diversity in Health & Social Care*, *1*(2), 107–116.

Park, W. G., & Ginarte, J. C. (1997). Intellectual property rights and economic growth. *Contemporary Economic Policy*, *15*(3), 51–61. doi:10.1111/j.1465-7287.1997.tb00477.x

Park, Y., Fujimoto, T., & Hong, P. (2012). Product architecture, organizational capabilities and IT integration for competitive advantage. *International Journal of Information Management*, *32*(5), 479–488. doi:10.1016/j.ijinfomgt.2011.12.002

Pastrana, S. (2005). The contributions of participation toward efficacy of community economic development projects in Morelos, Mexico. [Master of Arts Dissertation]. Simon Fraser University.

Patterson, R., & Wilson, E. (2000). New IT and social equality in Africa: Resetting the research and policy agenda. *The Information Society*, *16*(1).

Pavlou, P. A., & Chai, L. (2002). What Drives Electronic Commerce across Cultures? A Cross-Cultural Empirical Investigation of the Theory of Planned Behavior. *Journal of Electronic Commerce Research*, *3*(4), 240–253.

Paxton, P. (1999). Is social capital declining in the United States? A multiple indicator assessment. *American Journal of Sociology*, *105*(1), 88–127. doi:10.1086/210268

Pedrotti, M., Mirzaei, M. A., Tedesco, A., Chardonnet, J.-R., Mérienne, F., Benedetto, S., & Baccino, T. (2014). Automatic stress classification with pupil diameter analysis. *International Journal of Human-Computer Interaction*, *30*(3), 220–236. doi:10.1080/10447318.2013.848320

Pekrun, R., Goetz, T., Titz, W., & Perry, R. P. (2002). Academic emotions in students' self-regulated learning and achievement: A program of qualitative and quantitative research. *Educational Psychologist*, *37*(2), 91–105. doi:10.1207/S15326985EP3702_4

Pelgrin, W. (2013, June 5). 3 reasons why criminals exploit social networks (and tips to avoid getting scammed). *CSO Online*. Retrieved from http://www.csoonline.com/article/2133563/social-engineering/3-reasons-why-criminals-exploit-social-networks--and-tips-to-avoid-getting-scamme.html

People's Daily Online. (2014, July 4). Chengdu police use social media to boost recruitment. Retrieved from http://english.peopledaily.com.cn/n/2014/0704/c98649-8750616.html

Perdomo-Ortiza, J., González-Benito, J., & Galende, J. (2009). The intervening effect of business innovation capability on the relationship between Total Quality Management and technological innovation. *International Journal of Production Research*, *47*(18), 5087–5107. doi:10.1080/00207540802070934

Perelman, S. (1995). R&D, technological progress and efficiency change in industrial activities. *Review of Income and Wealth*, *41*(3), 349–366. doi:10.1111/j.1475-4991.1995.tb00124.x

Perkin, H. (1990). *The rise of professional society: Britain since 1880*. London: Routledge.

Peter, B. (2001). Telecentres and universal capability: A study of the telecentre programme of the Universal Service Agency in South Africa, 1996 - 2000 [Unpublished doctoral dissertation]. Aalborg University, Denmark.

Pew Research Center's Internet & American Life Project. (2013, December 30). Social Media Update 2013. Retrieved from http://www.pewinternet.org/2013/12/30/social-media-update-2013/

Phillips, W. (2011). LOLing at tragedy: Facebook trolls, memorial pages and resistance to grief online. *First Monday*, *16*(12). doi:10.5210/fm.v16i12.3168

Picard, R. W. (2003). Affective computing: Challenges. *International Journal of Human-Computer Studies*, *59*(1-2), 55–64. doi:10.1016/S1071-5819(03)00052-1

Picard, R. W. (2010). Affective computing: From laughter to IEEE. *IEEE Transactions on Affective Computing*, *1*(1), 11–17. doi:10.1109/T-AFFC.2010.10

Pichandy, C. (1994). *Communication and Social Influence: A study of uses and effects of Home Video (VCR Technology) on the urban and rural audiences* [Unpublished doctoral dissertation]. PSG College of Arts & Science, Coimbatore.

Piesse, J., & Thirtle, C. (2000). A stochastic frontier approach to firm level efficiency, technological change, and productivity during the early transition in Hungary. *Journal of Comparative Economics*, *28*(3), 473–501. doi:10.1006/jcec.2000.1672

Pikkarainen, K., Pikkarainen, T., &Karjaluoto, H., & Pahnila, S. (2006). The measurement of end-user computing satisfaction of online banking services: empirical evidence from Finland. *International Journal of Bank Marketing*, 24(3), 158-172. Retrieved from www.emeraldinsight.com

Piller, F. T., & Walcher, D. (2006). Toolkits for idea competitions: A novel method to integrate users in new product development. *R & D Management*, *36*(3), 307–318. doi:10.1111/j.1467-9310.2006.00432.x

Planning Commission, Government of India. (2013). 12th Five Year Plan Hackathon. Retrieved from http://planningcommission.gov.in/hackathon/

Plant, E. A., Goplen, J., & Kunstman, J. W. (2011). Selective responses to threat the roles of race and gender in decisions to shoot. *Personality and Social Psychology Bulletin*, *37*(9), 1274–1281. doi:10.1177/0146167211408617 PMID:21566078

Polanyi, M., & Sen, A. (1967). *The tacit dimension*. New York: Doubleday.

Pool, I. (1977). *The Social Impact of the Telephone*. Cambridge, MA: MIT Press.

Poon W.-C. (2008). User's adoption of e-banking services: The Malaysian perspective. *Journal of Business and Industrial Marketing*, *23*(1), 59–69.

Porat, M. U. (1977). *The information economy: Definition and measurement*. Washington, DC: US Department of Commerce.

Portal, I. T. C. Retrieved from http://www.itcportal.com/sustainability/philosophy.aspx

Porter, L. E., & Prenzler, T. (2012). Police oversight in the united kingdom: The balance of independence and collaboration. *International Journal of Law, Crime and Justice*, *40*(3), 152–171. doi:10.1016/j.ijlcj.2012.03.001

Porter, M. E. (2000). Location, competition, and economic development: Local clusters in a global economy. *Economic Development Quarterly*, *14*(1), 15–34. doi:10.1177/089124240001400105

Posey, C., Lowry, P. B., Roberts, T. L., & Ellis, T. S. (2010). Proposing the online community self-disclosure model: The case of working professionals in France and the U.K. who use online communities. *European Journal of Information Systems*, *19*(2), 181–195. doi:10.1057/ejis.2010.15

Postgraduate Taught Experience Survey (PTES). (2015, May 16). *Higher Education Academy*. Retrieved from https://www.heacademy.ac.uk/consultancy-services/surveys/ptes

Postman, N. (1985). *Amusing Ourselves to Death: Public Discourse in the Age of Show Business*. USA: Penguin Books. Retrieved from https://zaklynsky.files.wordpress.com/2013/09/postman-neil-amusing-ourselves-to-death-public-discourse-in-the-age-of-show-business.pdf

Postman, N. (1993). *Technopoly: The surrender of culture to technology*. New York: Vintage Books. Retrieved from https://mafhom.files.wordpress.com/2013/06/technopoly-neil-postman.pdf

Postman, N. (1998). *Five things we need to know about Technological change*. A Talk delivered in Denver Colorado on March 28. Retrieved from http://web.cs.ucdavis.edu/~rogaway/classes/188/materials/postman.pdf

Potter, W. J. (2004). *Theory of media literacy: A cognitive approach*. Thousand Oaks, California: SAGE Publications, Inc. doi:10.4135/9781483328881

Potts, J., Cunningham, S., Hartley, J., & Ormerod, P. (2008). Social network markets: A new definition of the creative industries. *Journal of Cultural Economics*, *32*(3), 167–185. doi:10.1007/s10824-008-9066-y

Pradip, T., & Bhoomi, G.G. (2009). e-governance and the right to information: ICTs and development in India. *Telemat. Inf.*, 26(1), 20-31. DOI=10.1016/j.tele.2007.12.004

Prahalad, C. K., & Ramaswamy, V. (2004). Co-Creation Experiences: The Next Practice in Value Creation. *Journal of Interactive Marketing*, *18*(3), 5–14. Retrieved from http://deepblue.lib.umich.edu/bitstream/handle/2027.42/35225/20015_ftp.pdf doi:10.1002/dir.20015

Presidential Committee on Information Literacy: Final report. (1989). *American Library Association*. Retrieved from http://www.ala.org/acrl/publications/whitepapers/presidential

Presser, S., Couper, M. P., Lessler, J. T., Martin, E., Rothgeb, J. M., Bureau, U. S. C., & Singer, E. (2004). Methods for Testing and Evaluating Survey Questions. *Public Opinion Quarterly*, *68*(1), 109–130. doi:10.1093/poq/nfh008

Preston, P. (2001). *Reshaping communication: Technology, information & social change*. New Delhi: Sage.

Preston, P., Cawley, A., & Metykova, M. (2007). Broadband and Rural Areas in the EU: Recent Research and Implications. *Telecommunications Policy*, *31*(6-7), 389–400. doi:10.1016/j.telpol.2007.04.003

Procter, R., Crump, J., Karstedt, S., Voss, A., & Cantijoch, M. (2013). Reading the riots: What were the police doing on Twitter? *Policing and Society*, *23*(4), 413–436. doi:10.1080/10439463.2013.780223

Prokos, A., & Padavic, I. (2002). 'There oughtta be a law against bitches': Masculinity lessons in police academy training. *Gender, Work and Organization*, *9*(4), 439–459. doi:10.1111/1468-0432.00168

PTI. (2013). *2.97 million professionals employed in IT-ITeS sector in FY13: Government*. Retrieved from http://articles.economictimes.indiatimes.com/2013-05-03/

Public Intelligence. (2013, October 13). Social Media and Tactical Considerations for Law Enforcement. Retrieved from http://publicintelligence.net/cops-social-media/

Pujar, S.M., Kamat, R.K., Bansode, S.Y., Kamat, R.R., & Katigennavar, S.H. (2008). Identifying and exploiting human needs for a people centric evolving knowledge society: A case study of Indian ICT Emergence. *The International Information & Library Review*, 40, 165-170.

Pulutchik, R. (2011). The nature of emotions. *American Scientist*, *89*(4), 344–350. doi:10.1511/2001.4.344

Purvis, C. (2011, June 17). A Look at Mexican Drug Cartel Membership Trends. *Security Management*. Retrieved from http://www.securitymanagement.com/news/a-look-mexican-drug-cartel-membership-trends-008644

Purvis, C. (2012, January 20). Researcher Reports a Surge in Social Media Use By Subversive Groups. *Security Management*. Retrieved from http://www.securitymanagement.com/news/researcher-reports-a-surge-social-media-use-subversive-groups-009428

Quibria, M. G., & Tschang, T. (2001, January). Information and communication technology and poverty: An Asian perspective. Retrieved from http://www.globalknowledge.org/gkps_portal/aprm2002/workshop/ADBI.pdf

Quinn, R. (2014). An analysis of Facebook as a Communication Tool in Community Development [Student Research Paper]. University College Dublin.

Quon, A. (2001). Information rich vs information poor: Turning the digital divide into digital dividends. *Media Asia*, *28*(3).

Quotes of Heraclitus of Ephesus. (540-480BC). Heraclitus of Ephesus. Ancient Greece.

Qureshi, I. M., Batool, I., & Shamim, A. (2012). Consumer Perception In Response To E-Marketing Stimuli: The Impact of Brand Salience, *Actual. Problems of Economics*, *2*(4), 137–143.

Rabaiah. A, & Vandijck. (2009). *A Strategic Framework of e-Government: Generic and Best Practice*. Electronic journal of e-Government, 7(3), 242.

Racskó, P. (2014). A felhőalapú számítástechnika az elektronikus közigazgatásban, (Cloud computing in the field of electronic public administration) (pp. 191-209). Budapest: E-közszolgálatfejlesztés, Nemzeti Közszolgálati Egyetem.

Racskó, P. (2012). *A számítási felhő az Európai Unió egén, (Computerized clouds in the sky over the European Union)* (pp. 1–16). Vezetéstudomány.

Radovan, M. (2001). Information technology and the character of contemporary life. *Information Communication and Society*, *4*(2), 230–246. doi:10.1080/13691180110044498

Rahman, H. (2008). Information Dynamics in Developing Countries. In C. Van Slyke (Ed.), *Information Communication Technologies: Concepts, Methodologies, Tools, and Applications* (pp. 104–114). Hershey, PA: Information Science Reference; doi:10.4018/978-1-59904-949-6.ch008

Rahman, M. M., Sultana, K. R., & Hoque, M. A. (2008). Suitable sites for urban solid waste disposal using GIS approach in Khulna city, Bangladesh. *Proceedings of Pakistan Academy of Sciences*, *45*(1), 11–22.

Rainie, L., & Tancer, B. (2007). Wikipedia Users. Pew Internet & American Life Project. Washington, DC. Retrieved from http://www.pewinternet.org/2007/04/24/wikipedia-users/

Rajagopalan, M. S., Khanna, V., Stott, M., Leiter, Y., Showalter, T. N., Dicker, A., & Lawrence, Y. R. (2010). Accuracy of cancer information on the Internet: A comparison of a Wiki with a professionally maintained database. *Journal of Clinical Oncology*, *28*(15), 6058. Retrieved from http://jdc.jefferson.edu/cgi/viewcontent.cgi?article=1008&context=bodinejournal

Rajkumar, S. (2005). *Activity theory*. Retrieved from www.slis.indiana.edu/faculty/yrogers/act_theory

Ramalingam, A. (2006, January 22). Now, no long queues to pay your bills. *The Times of India*.

Ramana, R.N.R.V. (2002, December). A study on value network theoretical model to examine the e-banking services. *Indian Journal of Research*, 1(12).

Ramani, D. (2007). The E-Payment System. *E-Business*, *7*(5), 35–41.

Ramdass, K. (2009). The challenges facing education in South Africa. Proceedings of *Educational and Development Conference* (pp. 111 – 130). Thailand. Tomorrow People Organisation.

Ramli, N. S., Hassan, S., Samah, B. A., Sham, M., & Ali, S. (2013). Comparison of crop, fisheries and livestock information displayed on agriculture websites. *Journal of Basic and Applied Scientific Research*, *3*(6), 760–765.

Ram, R. (1985). Exports and economic growth: Some additional evidence. *Economic Development and Cultural Change*, *33*(2), 415–425. doi:10.1086/451468

Ravi, V., Mahil, C., & Sagar, N.V. (2007). Profiling of internet banking users in India using intelligent techniques. *Journal of Service Research*, *6*(2).

Raymond, J. (2013). Sexist attitudes: Most of us are biased. *Nature*, *495*(7439), 33–34. doi:10.1038/495033a PMID:23467152

Reddy, P., & Ankaiah, R. (2005). A framework of information technology-based agriculture information dissemination system to improve crop productivity. *Current Science*, *88*, 1905–1913.

Regional Human Development Report. Promoting ICT for Human Development in Asia: Realizing the Millennium Development Goals. (2007). New Delhi: Elsevier.

Rennie, F., & Mason, R. (2005). Bits or Baubles: The opportunities for broadband to add value to education and learning. *Scottish Affairs*, *53*(1), 31–47. doi:10.3366/scot.2005.0055

Repkine, A. (2009). Telecommunications Capital Intensity and Aggregate Production Efficiency: a Meta-Frontier Analysis (MPRA Working Paper No. 13059). Retrieved from http://mpra.ub.uni-muenchen.de/13059/1/MPRA_paper_13059.pdf

Repkine, A. (2008). ICT Penetration and Aggregate Production Efficiency: Empirical Evidence for a Cross-Section of Fifty Countries. *Journal of Applied Economic Sciences*, *3*(2), 137–144.

Resnick, P. (2001). Beyond bowling together: Sociotechnical capital. In J. Carroll (Ed.), HCI in the New Millennium (247–272). Boston, MA: Addison-Wesley.

Reynolds, C., & Picard, R. W. (2005). *Evaluation of affective computing systems from a dimensional metaethical position*. Paper presented at the First Augmented Cognition Conference, Las Vegas, Nevada.

Rhoades, E., & Aue, K. (2010). Social agriculture: Adoption of social media by agricultural editors and broadcasters. Proceedings of *107th Annu. Mtg. Of Southern Association of Agricultural Scientists* (pp. 1–20). Orlando, Florida.

Rich, M., Woods, E. R., Goodman, E., Emans, S. J., & DuRant, R. H. (1998). Aggressors or victims: Gender and race in music video violence. *Pediatrics*, *101*(4), 669–674. doi:10.1542/peds.101.4.669 PMID:9521954

Rincon, A., Robinson, C., & Vecchi, M. (2005). The productivity impact of e-commerce in the UK: 2001 evidence from microdata (NIESR Working Paper No. 257). Retrieved from http://www.researchgate.net/profile/Michela_Vecchi/publication/5200599_The_Productivity_impact_of_E-Commerce_in_the_UK_2001_Evidence_from_microdata/links/09e4150a4a6e814ae1000000.pdf

Ritzer, G., & Jurgenson, N. (2010). Production, Consumption, Prosumption: The Nature of Capitalism in the Age of the Digital 'Prosumer'. *Journal of Consumer Culture*, *10*(1), 13–36. Retrieved from https://sociologiaconsumului.files.wordpress.com/2011/10/overview-production-consumption-prosumption.pdf doi:10.1177/1469540509354673

Rivera, L. A. (2010). Status distinctions in interaction: Social selection and exclusion at an elite nightclub. *Qualitative Sociology*, *33*(3), 229–255. doi:10.1007/s11133-010-9152-2

Rizzo, T. (2013, October 15). Most Gang Members Use Social Media, Study Finds. *Government Technology Solutions for State and Local Government*. Retrieved from http://www.govtech.com/public-safety/Most-Gang-Members-Use-Social-Media-Study-Finds.html

Roberts, K. (2005). *Lovemarks: The Future Beyond Brands*. New York: Powerhouse.

Roediger-Schluga, T., & Dachs, B. (2006). *Does technology affect network structure?-A quantitative analysis of collaborative research projects in two specific EU programmes (No. 041)*. United Nations University.

Roediger-Schluga, T., & Barber, M. J. (2006). *The structure of R&D collaboration networks in the European Framework Programmes* (p. 36). UNU-MERIT.

Roger, E., & Shukla, P. (2001). The role of telecenters in development communication and the digital divide. *The Journal of Development Communication*, *12*, 26–30. Retrieved from http://wsispapers.choike.org/role_telecenters-development.pdf

Rogers, E. M. (2003). The Generation of Innovations. Diffusion of Innovations (5th ed.). New York: Free Press..

Rogers, E. M. (1962). *Diffusion of Innovation* (1st ed.). New York: Free Press.

Rogers, E. M. (1986). *Communication technology: The new media in society?* New York: The Free Press.

Roling, N. (1988). *Extension Science: Information Systems in Agricultural Development* (p. 233). UK: Cambridge University Press.

Roman, R., & Colle, R. (2002). Themes and Issues in Telecentre Sustainability. *University of Manchester Development Informatices Working Paper Series.*

Roman, R., & Colle, R. (2002). *Creating a Participatory Telecenter Enterprise*. Barcelona: International Association for Media and Communication Research.

Romero, Q. C., & Rodríguez, R. D. (2010). E-commerce and efficiency at the firm level. *International Journal of Production Economics*, *126*(2), 299–305. doi:10.1016/j.ijpe.2010.04.004

Romijn, H., & Albaladejo, M. (2002). Determinants of innovation capability in small electronics and software firms in southeast England. *Research Policy*, *31*(7), 1053–1067. doi:10.1016/S0048-7333(01)00176-7

Rose, M. A. (1991). The post-modern and the post industrial. Cambridge: Cambridge University Press.

Rose, A., Timm, H., Pogson, C., Gonzalez, J., Appel, E., & Kolb, N. (2010). *Developing a cybervetting strategy for law enforcement*. Alexandria: International Association of Chiefs of Police.

Rosegrant, M. W., & Cline, S. A. (2003). Global food security: Challenges and policies. *Science*, *302*(5652), 1917–1919. doi:10.1126/science.1092958 PMID:14671289

Ross, J. W., Beath, C. M., & Goodhue, D. L. (1996). Develop long-term competitiveness through IT assets. *Sloan Management Review*, *38*(1), 31–42.

Ruddell, R., & Jones, N. (2013). Social media and policing: Matching the message to the audience. *Safer Communities*, *12*(2), 64–70. doi:10.1108/17578041311315030

Ruet, J. (2002). *IT and development: Clusters as economic policy tools for India*. Retrieved from http://www.joef.ruet@esh-Deihi.com

Ruiz-Mercader, J., Meroño-Cerdan, A. L., & Sabater-Sánchez, R. (2006). Information technology and learning: Their relationship and impact on organizational performance in small businesses. *International Journal of Information Management*, *26*(1), 16–29. doi:10.1016/j.ijinfomgt.2005.10.003

Rural telephony: Huge investments, low impact. (2011). *TheNigerianDaily.com*. Retrieved from http://www.thenigeriandaily.com/

Russell, J. (1980). A Circumplex model of affect. *Journal of Personality and Social Psychology*, *39*(6), 1161–1178. doi:10.1037/h0077714

Rutter, T. (2014, January 27). How police can join the digital revolution – roundup. *The Guardian*. Retrieved from http://www.theguardian.com/public-leaders-network/2014/jan/27/police-digital-revolution-roundup

Ryan, V., Kerry, D., Agnitsch, A., Zhao, L., & Mullick, R. (2005). Making Sense of Voluntary Participation: A Theoretical Synthesis. *Rural Sociology*, *70*(3), 287–313. doi:10.1526/0036011054831198

Saaty, T. L., & Kearns, K. P. (1985). Analytical planning: the organization of systems. A. Wheaton & Co. Ltd. GB ISBN 0-08-032599-8.

Saaty, T. (1980). *The Analytic Hierarchy Process*. New York, USA: McGraw-Hill.

Saaty, T. L. (1977). A scaling method for priorities in hierarchical structures. *Journal of Mathematical Psychology*, *15*(3), 234–281. doi:10.1016/0022-2496(77)90033-5

Saaty, T. L. (1996). *Decision making with dependence and feedback: The analytic network process*. Pittsburgh: RWS Publications.

Safranka, M. (2013). *A felhő definíciója, System Center Mindenkinek, (The definition of cloud computing – System Centre for everyone)* Retrieved from http://blogs.technet.com/b/scm/archive/2013/02/08/a-felh-defin-237-ci-243-ja.aspx

Sahadath, K. C. (2011). Leading Change One Conversation at a Time.*ACMP Global Conference* (pp. 1 – 10). Orlando, Florida.

Samoilenko, A., & Yasseri, T. (2014). The distorted mirror of Wikipedia: A quantitative analysis of Wikipedia coverage of academics. *EPJ Data Science*, *3*(1). Retrieved from http://www.epjdatascience.com/content/pdf/epjds20.pdf

Samuelson, P., & Nordhaus, W. (1987). Közgazdaságtan I-II. (Economics Vol. 1-2.) (pp. 667). Budapest: Közgazdasági és Jogi Könyvkiadó,.

Sandhya, S. (2013, April 9). Planning Commission's hackathon gets over 1,000 participants. *The Times of India*. Retrieved from http://timesofindia.indiatimes.com/tech/tech-news/internet/Planning-Commissions-hackathon-gets-over-1000-participants/articleshow/19460398.cms?referral=PM]

Sanyal, M. K., Das, S., & Bhadra, S. K. (2014). E-District Portal for District Administration in West Bengal, India: A Survey to Identify Important Factors towards Citizen's Satisfaction, Procedia Economics and Finance, Volume 11, Pages 510-521, ISSN 2212-5671,10.1016/S2212-5671(14)00217-2

Sanzogni, L., Sandhu, K., & Ghaith, A. W. (2010). Factors influencing the adoption and usage of online services in Saudi Arabia. Retrieved from http://www.ejisdc.org

Sarah, W., & Susan, J. E. (2000). Environmental risk perception and well being: Effects of the landfill siting process in two Southern Ontario Communities. *Social Science & Medicine*, *50*(7–8), 1139–1154. PMID:10714933

Sarantakos, S. (2005). *Social research* (3rd ed.). Basingstoke: Palgrave Macmillan.

Sarrocco, C. (n. d.). Elements and Principles of the Information Society. Retrieved August 10, 2014, from http://www.itu.int/osg/spu/wsis-themes/access/backgroundpaper/IS%20Principles.pdf

Sassen, S. (1991). *The Global City: NewYork, London, Tokyo*. Princeton, New Jersey: Princeton University Press.

Sasvari, P. (2012). Adaptable Techniques for Making IT-Related Investment Decisions. *International Journal of Advanced Research in Computer Science and Software Engineering*, *2*, 2.

Savage, S. P. (1984). Political control or community liaison? *The Political Quarterly*, *55*(1), 48–59. doi:10.1111/j.1467-923X.1984.tb02562.x

Savard, I., Bourdeau, J., & Paquette, G. (2008). Cultural variables in the building of pedagogical scenarios. In E. Blanchard & D. Allard (Eds.), *Culturally aware tutoring systems* (pp. 83–94). Montreal, Canada: University of Montreal.

Schacter, D. L. (2011). *Psychology*. New York: Worth Publishers.

Schinasi, K., & Schultz, I. (2012). Paying Attention to Society and Culture. In B. V. Ark (Ed.), The Linked World: Executive Editor Bart van Ark (pp. 118 – 134).

Schmidt, P., & Sickles, R. C. (1984). Production frontiers and panel data. *Journal of Business & Economic Statistics*, *2*(4), 367–374.

Scholes-Fogg, T. (2013, December 12). Police and Social Media, a report for the Independent Police Commission of England and Wales. *ConnectedCOPS.net*. Retrieved from http://connectedcops.net/2012/12/13/police-social-media-report-independent-police-commission-england-wales/

Scholz-Crane, A. (1998). Evaluating the future: A preliminary study of the process of how undergraduate students evaluate Web sources. *RSR. Reference Services Review*, *26*(3/4), 53–60. doi:10.1108/00907329810307759

Schumpeter, J. A. (1934). *The theory of economic development*. Oxford, UK: Oxford University Press.

Segars, A., & Grover, V. (1993). Re-examining Perceived Ease of Use and Usefulness: A Confirmatory Factor Analysis. *Management Information Systems Quarterly*, *17*(4), 517–527. doi:10.2307/249590

Sekaran, U., & Bougie, R. (2010). Theoretical framework In theoretical framework and hypothesis development. In *Research Methods for Business: A Skill Building Approach* (p. 80). United Kingdom: Wiley.

Sellers, M. D. (2014). Discrimination and the transgender population: Analysis of the functionality of local government policies that protect gender identity. *Administration & Society*, *46*(1), 70–86. doi:10.1177/0095399712451894

Sen, M. (2006). *Effects of English lessons, based on multiple intelligences theory, on students' motivation, self efficacy, self-esteem and multiple intelligences.* [Masters Dissertation]. Ankara University Institute of Social Sciences, Ankara Turkey. Retrieved from www.yok.gov.tr(191346)

Şener, Ş., Şener, E., Nas, B., & Karagüzel, R. (2010). Combining AHP with GIS for landfill site selection: A case study in the Lake Beyşehir catchment area (Konya, Turkey). *Waste Management (New York, N.Y.)*, *30*(11), 2037–2046. doi:10.1016/j.wasman.2010.05.024 PMID:20594819

Shafeea Leman M., Komoo I., Roslan Mohamed K., Aziz Ali C., Unjah T., Othman K. & Yasin M. H.M., (2008). Geology and geoheritage conservation within langkawi geopark, Malaysia. *Articles and Publications*.

Shafeea Leman, M., Abdul Ghani, K., Komoo, I., & Ahmad, N. (Eds.). (2007). *Langkawi Geopark*. Bangi: Lestari, Ukm and Lada publication.

Shah, N. & Panchal, A. (2004). ICT revolution in Rural Gujarat. *An e- Governance Bulletin*.

Shahid, S., Krahmer, E., Neerincx, M., & Swerts, M. (2013). Positive affective interactions: The role of repeated exposure and copresence. *IEEE Transactions on Affective Computing*, *4*(2), 226–237. doi:10.1109/T-AFFC.2012.39

Shamshiry, E., Nadi, B., Mokhtar, B. M., Komoo, I., & Saadiah, H. H. (2011). Urban solid waste management based on geoinformatics technology. *Journal of Public Health and Epidemiology*, *3*(2), 54–60.

Shannon, C. E. (1948). A Mathematical Theory of Communication. *The Bell System Technical Journal*, *27*(3), 379–423, 623–656. Retrieved from http://worrydream.com/refs/Shannon%20-%20A%20Mathematical%20Theory%20of%20Communication.pdf doi:10.1002/j.1538-7305.1948.tb01338.x

Shao, B. B., & Lin, W. T. (2001). Measuring the value of information technology in technical efficiency with stochastic production frontiers. *Information and Software Technology*, *43*(7), 447–456. doi:10.1016/S0950-5849(01)00150-1

Shapiro, C., & Varian, H. R. (2013). *Information rules: a strategic guide to the network economy*. USA: Harvard Business Press.

Shareef, M. A., Kumar, U., Kumar, V., & Dwivedi, Y. K. (2011). E-government Adoption Model (GAM): Differing Service Maturity Levels. *Government Information Quarterly*, *28*(1), 17–35. doi:10.1016/j.giq.2010.05.006

Shareef, M. A., Kumar, V., Dwivedi, Y. K., & Kumar, U. (2014). Global Service Quality of Electronic-Commerce. [IJICBM]. *International Journal of Indian Culture and Business Management*, *8*(1), 1–34. doi:10.1504/IJICBM.2014.057947

Sharma, N. K. (2014, June 30). Criminal tracking system in a limbo. *Times of India*. Retrieved from http://timesofindia.indiatimes.com/city/jaipur/Criminal-tracking-system-in-a-limbo/articleshow/37484919.cms

Sharma. S., & Gupta, J. (2003). Building Blocks of an E-Government—A Framework. *Journal of Electronic Commerce in Organizations*, 1, 1-15.

Shastri, P. (2001, June 25). *Time Travel and Time Warps*. Outlook: New Delhi: Hathway.

Shaw, N. (2011). *The Cloud Broker Business Paradigm*, Retrieved from http://blogs.perficient.com/businessintelligence/2011/08/15/the-cloud-broker-business-paradigm/

Shekhar, R. (2014, July 16). Delhi cops teach how to fight cyber crime. *Times of India*. Retrieved from http://timesofindia.indiatimes.com/india/Delhi-cops-teach-how-to-fight-cyber-crime/articleshow/37875118.cms

Shen, L., Wang, M., & Shen, R. (2009). Affective e-learning: Using "emotional" data to improve learning in pervasive learning environment. *Journal of Educational Technology & Society*, *12*(2), 176–189.

Shen, Y. W. (2012). The narrative express of the concept of structure-pagoda in the fantian temple of shen kuo as example. *Applied Mechanics and Materials*, *209*, 122–125. doi:10.4028/www.scientific.net/AMM.209-211.122

Sheppard, K. (2001). The Remote Community Service Telecentres of Newfoundland and Labrador, Canada. In C. Latchem, & D. Walker (Eds.), Telecentres: Case Studies and Key Issues. Vancouver: The Commonwealth of Learning.

Sherman, A. (2011, August 31). How Law Enforcement Agencies Are Using Social Media to Better Serve the Public. *Mashable*. Retrieved from http://mashable.com/2011/08/31/law-enforcement-social-media-use/

Short, G. (2001). The Western Australia Telecentre Network. In C. Latchem, & D. Walker (Eds.), Telecentres: Case Studies and Key Issues. Vancouver: The Commonwealth of Learning.

Shortall, S. (2008). Social inclusion, civic engagement, participation, and social capital: Exploring the differences. *Journal of Rural Studies*, 24(4), 450–457. doi:urstud.2008.01.001.10.1016/j.jr

Shri Kapil Sibal inaugurates Conference on 'Open Data Apps for Innovation in Governance. (2013, August 8). *Press Information Bureau (PIB), Government of India*. Retrieved from http://www.pib.nic.in/newsite/erelease.aspx?relid=97925

Siddiqui, M. Z., Everett, J. W., & Vieux, B. E. (1996). Landfill siting using geographic information system: A demonstration. *Journal of Environmental Engineering*, *122*(6), 515–523. doi:10.1061/(ASCE)0733-9372(1996)122:6(515)

Singh, J.P. (2001). *Satellite broadcasting and distributing technology: Retrospect and prospect*. Manthan: DECU-ISRO Publication.

Singh, M., & Kaushal, R. (2012). Factor Analysis Approach to Customers' Assessment of Electronic Payment and Clearing System in Indian Banking Sector. *The IUP Journal of Information Technology, 11(3), 64-75.*

Singhal, A., & Roger, E. (1990). *India's information and communication revolution*. New Delhi: Sage Publications.

Singh, R., & Raja, S. (2010). *Convergence in Information and Communication Technology*. The World Bank; doi:10.1596/978-0-8213-8169-4

Siriginidi, S. R. (2009). Achieving millennium development goals: Role of ICTS innovations in India. *Telematics and Informatics*, *26*(2), 127–143. doi:10.1016/j.tele.2008.02.001

Siti Zubaidah, A., Mohd Sanusi, S. A., & Mohd Suffian, Y. (2013). Spatial comparison of new landfill sites using criteria derived from different guidelines. *International Surveying Research Journal*, *3*(2), 29–40.

Sklansky, D. A. (2007). Seeing blue: Police reform, occupational culture, and cognitive burn-in. *Sociology of Crime Law and Deviance*, *8*, 19–45.

Small and Medium Enterprises in Japan-Finding Vitality through Innovation and Human Resources [White Paper]. (2009). The Small and Medium Enterprise Agency. Tokyo, JPN: Ministry of Economy, Trade and Industry (METI). Retrieved from http://www.chusho.meti.go.jp/pamflet/hakusyo/h21/h21_1/2009hakusho_eng.pdf

Smith, A. (2011). *Why Americans use social media*. Washington, DC: Pew Research Center.

Smith, A. G. (1997). Testing the Surf: Criteria for Evaluating Internet Information Resources. *The Public-Access Computer Systems Review*, *8*(3), 5–23. Retrieved from https://journals.tdl.org/pacsr/index.php/pacsr/article/download/.../5645

Smith, B., & Sparkes, A. C. (2012). Narrative analysis in sport and physical culture. *Research in the Sociology of Sport*, *6*, 79–99.

Smith, S. P. (1976). Government wage differentials by sex. *The Journal of Human Resources*, *11*(2), 185–199. doi:10.2307/145452

Solis, B. (2010). Facebook Connects 500 Million People: Defines a New Era of Digital Society. Retrieved from http://www.briansolis.com/2010/07/facebook-connects-500-million-people-defining-a-new-era-of-digital-society/

SØrensen. E. (2009). The materiality of learning. Cambridge, MA: Cambridge University Press.

Soudien, C. W., Michaels, S., Mthembi-Mahanyele, M., Nkomo, G., Nyanda, N., Nyoka, S., et al. (2008). *Report of the ministerial committee on transformation and social cohesion and the elimination of discrimination in public higher education institutions*. Department of Education, Republic of South Africa. Retrieved from http://www.vut.ac.za/new/index.php/docman/doc_view/90-ministerialreportontransformationandsocialcohesion?tmpl=component&format=raw

So, W. C. M., Wong, T. N. D., & Sculli, D. (2005). Factors affecting intentions to purchase via the internet. *Journal of Industrial Management & Data Systems*, *105*(9), 1225–1244. doi:10.1108/02635570510633275

Sparrow, M. K. (1993). *Information Systems and the Development of Policing*. US Department of Justice, Office of Justice Programs, National Institute of Justice.

Spiezia, V. (2011). Are ICT users more innovation? An analysis of ICT-enabled innovation in OECD firms. *OECD Journal: Economic Studies*, *2011*, 99–119. doi:10.1787/19952856

Sproull, L., & Kiesler, S. (2005). Public Volunteer Work on the Internet. In W. Dutton, B. Kahin, R. O'Callaghan, & A. Wyckoff (Eds.), *Transforming Enterprise*. Cambridge, MA: The MIT Press.

Srinivas, N. (2006, August 17). Not so simple life, farming can take a toll on health. *The Hindu*.

Srisawatsakul, C., & Papasratorn, B. (2013). Factors Affecting Consumer Acceptance Mobile Broadband Services with Add-on Advertising: Thailand Case Study. *Wireless Personal Communications*, *69*(3), 1055–1065. doi:10.1007/s11277-013-1065-4

Stacey, R. (2003). Learning as an activity of interdependent people. *The Learning Organization*, *10*(6), 325–331. doi:10.1108/09696470310497159

Stadd, A. (2013, June 24). How Burglars Are Using Social Media [INFOGRAPHIC] - AllTwitter. *Mediabistro*. Retrieved from http://www.mediabistro.com/alltwitter/burglars-social-media_b45302

Stark, D. (2009). *The sense of dissonance: Accounts of worth in economic life*. Princeton, New Jersey: Princeton University Press.

Starmer, K. (2013). *Guidelines on prosecuting cases involving communications sent via social media*. London, GB: Crown Prosecution Service.

Statistical market overview: Sri Lanka. (2014). International Telecommunication Union (ITU). Retrieved from http://www.itu.int

Stein, E. W., & Zwass, V. (1995). Actualizing Organizational Memory with Information Systems. *Information Systems Research*, *6*(2), 85–117. doi:10.1287/isre.6.2.85

Stenson, K. (2013). Community safety in middle england: The local politics of crime control. In G. Hughes & A. Edwards (Eds.), *Crime control and community: The new politics of public safety* (pp. 109–140). Collumpton: Willan Publishing.

Stern, M. J., Adams, A. E., & Boase, J. (2011). Rural Community Participation, Social Networks, and Broadband Use: Examples from Localized and National Survey Data. *Agricultural and Resource Economics Review*, *40*(2), 158–171.

Stern, M., & Dillman, D. (2006). Community Participation, Social Ties, and Use of the Internet. *City & Community*, *5*(4), 409–424. doi:10.1111/j.1540-6040.2006.00191.x

Steuer, J. S. (1991). *Audio-visual space: On the influence of auditory spatial perception in mediated experience* [Unpublished manuscript]. Stanford University, Institute for Communication Research, Stanford, CA.

Steve, A. (2013, July). Cambridge Police Launch Map Database Showing Crime Stats.*Boston Magazine*. Retrieved from

Stevens, L. (2010). Social media in policing: nine steps for success. *Police Chief Magazine, 77*.

Stevens, T. (2009). Regulating the 'Dark web': How a two-fold approach can tackle peer-to-peer radicalisation. *The RUSI Journal*, *154*(2), 28–33. doi:10.1080/03071840902965687

Stewart, D. (2005). Social status in an open-source community. *American Sociological Review*, *70*(5), 823–842. doi:10.1177/000312240507000505

Stewart, D. W., & Pavlou, P. A. (2002). From Consumer Response to Active Consumer: Measuring the Effectiveness of Interactive Media. *Journal of the Academy of Marketing Science*, *30*(4), 376–396. Retrieved from http://www.uk.sagepub.com/chaston/Chaston%20Web%20readings%20chapters%201-12/Chapter%209%20-%2036%20Stewart%20and%20Pavlou.pdf doi:10.1177/009207002236912

Steyaert, J. (2000). Local governments online and the role of the resident: Government shop versus electronic community. *Social Science Computer Review*, *18*(1), 3–16. doi:10.1177/089443930001800101

Stilgherrianon. (2011, August 25). Has Facebook killed the undercover cop? *CSO Online*. Retrieved from http://www.cso.com.au/article/398581/has_facebook_killed_undercover_cop_/

Stonier, T. (1996). Information as a basic property of the universe. *Bio Systems*, *38*(2-3), 135–140. doi:10.1016/0303-2647(96)88368-7 PMID:8734520

Straub, D. W. (1994). The Effect of Culture on IT Diffusion: E-Mail and FAX in Japan and the U.S. *Information Systems Research*, *5*(I), 23–47. doi:10.1287/isre.5.1.23

Strauss, A., & Corbin, J. (1990). *Basics of Qualitative Research: Grounded Theory Procedures and Techniques*. Newbury Park: Sage Publications.

Stuart, R. D. (2013, February). Social Media: Establishing Criteria for Law Enforcement Use. *Federal Bureau of Investigation*. Retrieved from http://www.fbi.gov/stats-services/publications/law-enforcement-bulletin/2013/february/social-media-establishing-criteria-for-law-enforcement-use

Stvilia, B., Twidale, M. B., Smith, L. C., & Gasser, L. (2005). Assessing information quality of a community-based encyclopedia. In F. Naumann, M. Gertz, & S. Mednick (Eds.), *Proceedings of the International Conference on Information Quality–ICIQ 2005* (pp. 442–454). Cambridge, MA: MITIQ. Retrieved from http://mitiq.mit.edu/ICIQ/Documents/IQ%20Conference%202005/Papers/AssessingIQofaCommunity-basedEncy.pdf

Stvilia, B., Twidale, M. B., Smith, L. C., & Gasser, L. (2008). Information quality work organization in Wikipedia. *Journal of the American Society for Information Science and Technology, 59*(6), 983-1001. Retrieved from http://www.researchgate.net/profile/Michael_Twidale2/publication/200772424_Information_quality_work_organization_in_wikipedia/links/00b7d517a7ed9703be000000.pdf

Su, C. (2012). One earthquake, two tales: Narrative analysis of the tenth anniversary coverage of the 921 earthquake in taiwan. *Media Culture & Society*, *34*(3), 280–295. doi:10.1177/0163443711433664

Sudhagar, S. (2012). A Study on Perception and Awareness on Credit Cards among Bank Customers in Krishnagiri District. *Journal of Business and Management,* 2(3), 14-23. (IOSRJBM) ISSN: 2278-487X

Sumathi, V. R., Natesan, U., & Sarkar, C. (2008). GIS-based approach for optimized sitting of municipal solid waste landfill. *Waste Management Journal*, *28*(11), 2146–2160. doi:10.1016/j.wasman.2007.09.032 PMID:18060759

Sumiani, Y., Onn, C. C., Mohd Din, M. A., & Wan Jaafar, W. Z. (2009). Environmental planning strategies for optimum solid waste landfill siting. *Sains Malaysiana*, *38*(4), 457–462.

Sundar, S. S., & Nass, C. (2001). Conceptualizing sources in online news. *Journal of Communication*, *51*(1), 52–72. Retrieved from http://www.researchgate.net/profile/Clifford_Nass/publication/2403100_Conceptualizing_Sources_in_Online_News/links/09e4151086146158ba000000.pdf doi:10.1111/j.1460-2466.2001.tb02872.x

Sun, H., Hone, P., & Doucouliago, H. (1999). Economic openness and technical efficiency: A case study of Chinese manufacturing industries. *Economics of Transition*, *7*(3), 615–636. doi:10.1111/1468-0351.00028

Survey, G. V. U. (2001). *GVU's 5th WWW User Survey.* Retrieved from http://www.cc.gatech.edu/gvu/user_surveys/survey-04-1996/

Sutton, S. B., Obst, D., Louime, C., Jones, J. V., & Jones, T. A. (2011).*Developing strategic international partnerships: Models for initiating and sustaining innovative institutional linkages.*

Sutton, J., Palen, L., & Shklovski, I. (2008). Backchannels on the front lines: Emergent uses of social media in the 2007 southern California wildfires.*Proceedings of the 5th International ISCRAM Conference* (pp. 624–632). Washington, DC.

Svoen, B. (2007). Consumers, participants, and creators: Young people's diverse use of television and new media. *ACM Computers in Entertainment*, *5*(2), 1–16. doi:10.1145/1279540.1279545

Szucsne, M. K. (2012). A Comprehensive Review of Scientific Literature on Methods for Determining Discount Rates in Corporate Practices. *Theory Methodology Practice: Club of Economics in Miskolc*, *8*(02), 81–87.

Tadmor, C. T., Hong, Y. Y., Chao, M. M., Wiruchnipawan, F., & Wang, W. (2012). Multicultural experiences reduce intergroup bias through epistemic unfreezing. *Journal of Personality and Social Psychology*, *103*(5), 750–772. doi:10.1037/a0029719 PMID:22905769

Tajfel, H. (1972). La Categorisation Sociale (Social categorization). In S. Moscovici (Ed.), *Introduction a La Psychologie Sociale, 1* (pp. 272–302). Paris: Larousse.

Talwar, S. P. (1999). IT and Banking Sector. *RBI Bulletin*, *53*(8), 985–992.

Tapscott, D., & Williams, A. D. (2006). Wikinomics: How Mass Collaboration Changes Everything. New York: Penguin Group. Retrieved from http://labeee.ufsc.br/~luis/egcec/livros/globaliz/Wikinomics.pdf

Tapscott, D., & Williams, A. D. (2008). *Wikinomics: How Mass Collaboration Changes Everything*. London: Atlantic Books.

Tassey, G. (1997). *The economics of R&D policy*. USA: Greenwood Publishing Group.

Taymaz, E., Voyvoda, E., & Yılmaz, K. (2008). Türkiye Đmalat Sanayiinde Yapısal Dönüşüm, Üretkenlik ve Teknolojik Değişme Dinamikleri (ERC Working Paper No. 08/04) (Structural Transformation of Turkey Manufacturing Industry, Productivity and Technological Change Dynamics). Retrieved from http://www.erc.metu.edu.tr/menu/series08/0804.pdf

Taymaz, E., & Saatci, G. (1997). Technical change and efficiency in Turkish manufacturing industries. *Journal of Productivity Analysis*, *8*(4), 461–475. doi:10.1023/A:1007796311574

Technology: Blessing or curse. (2009, November). *Awake!* New York: Watch Tower and Tract Society. (pp. 1 – 9).

Telecom Development Lecture (n. d.). NITDEL. Retrieved from http://ncc.gov.ng/archive/EVCSpeches/2009_NITDEL_Lecture.pdf

Telecommunications Regulatory Commission of Sri Lanka (TRCSL). (2013). *Statistical Report -2013*. Retrieved from http://www.trc.gov.lk

Temin, T. (1992). *Telecommuting: Many Would, Few Actually Can, NewYork*. McGraw-Hill.

Ten Principles for Opening up Government Information. (2010, August 11). Sunlight Foundation. Retrieved from http://sunlightfoundation.com/policy/documents/ten-open-data-principles/

The definition of educational technology. (1977AECT. Washington, D.C.: Association for Educational Communications and Technology.

The eCommerce B2B Report. (2001, February). *Emarketer.* Retrieved from http://www.emarketer.com

The Guardian. (2012, April 1). Government plans increased email and social network surveillance. Retrieved from http://www.theguardian.com/world/2012/apr/01/government-email-social-network-surveillance

The Impact of ICT on Europe's Fishing Industry: a Case Study Approach. (2003).European Foundation for the Improvement of Living and Working Conditions. Retrieved from www.eurofound.eu.int

The impact of mobile services in Nigeria: How mobile technologies are transforming economic and social activities . (2010). Pyramid Research. Retrieved from www.pyramidresearch.com

The Launch of in Pursuit of an Idea - Creative Collaboration on Open Government Data for Innovation. (n. d.). Retrieved from http://informatics.nic.in/news/newsdetail/newsID/450

The notions of information/noise, communication/meaning, author/literature as a self-regulating machine in Italo Calvino's Cybernetics and Ghosts (1967) and Thomas Pynchon The Crying of Lot 49 (1966). (n. d.). Retrieved from http://www.jfki.fu-berlin.de/academics/SummerSchool/Dateien2011/Presentation_Handouts/Handout_-_Iuli_-_September_19_-_Belloni.pdf

The Olusegun Obasanjo reforms: Telecommunication sector. (n. d.). Federal Ministry of Information and National Orientation – FMNIO.

The Police Chief Magazine. (2003). Connecting the Dots: Data Mining and Predictive Analytics in Law Enforcement and Intelligence Analysis, *70*(10). Retrieved from http://www.policechiefmagazine.org/magazine/index.cfm?fuseaction=display_arch&article_id=121&issue_id=102003

The Times of India Crime tracking system to connect south Goa police stations. (2014a, July 18).. Retrieved from http://timesofindia.indiatimes.com/city/goa/Crime-tracking-system-to-connect-south-Goa-police-stations/articleshow/38575478.cms

The Times of India. (2014b, July 19). Crime and Criminal Tracking Network System project in Allahabad district likely to be completed by December. Retrieved from http://timesofindia.indiatimes.com/city/allahabad/Crime-and-Criminal-Tracking-Network-System-project-in-Allahabad-district-likely-to-be-completed-by-December/articleshow/38667452.cms

The Times of India. (2014c, July 4). Police station to go online. Retrieved from http://timesofindia.indiatimes.com/city/kanpur/Police-station-to-go-online/articleshow/37766775.cms

The White House, Memorandum on Transparency and Open Government. (2009). Retrieved from www.whitehouse.gov/the_press_office/Transparency_and_Open_Government/

The World in 2014: ICT FACTS AND FIGURES, Retrieved http://www.itu.int/en/ITU-D/Statistics/Documents/facts/ICTFactsFigures2014-e.pdf

Themba, G., & Tumedi, B. C. (2012). Credit Card Ownership and Usage Behaviour in Botswana. *International Journal of Business Administration*, *3*(6). doi:10.5430/ijba.v3n6p60

Thibault, E. A., & Lynch, L. M. (1985). *Proactive police management*. Englewood Cliffs, NJ: Prentice Hall.

Thomas, K. T. (2005). Beware! cops may soon go mobile. *Business Line*, *105*, 1.

Thomas, P. E. (2001). Information society: A thematic percept of concepts and limits. *Journal of Educational Research and Extension*, *38*(3).

Thong, J. Y. L., & Yap, C. S. (1995). CEO characteristics, organizational characteristics and information technology adoption in small businesses. *Omega*, *23*(4), 429–442. doi:10.1016/0305-0483(95)00017-I

Tidd, J., Bessant, J., & Pavitt, K. (2001). *Managing Innovation - Integrating Technological, Market and organizational Change* (2nd ed.). Chichester, U.K.: Wiley.

Tim Berners-Lee. (n. d.). 5 star Open Data. Retrieved from http://5stardata.info/

Tinio, V. L. (2002). ICTs in Education. In e-Primers for the Information Economy, Society and Polity. Retrieved from http://www.eprimers.org/ict/index.asp

Tınmaz, E., & Demir, I. (2006). Research on solid waste management system: To improve existing situation in Corlu Town of Turkey. *Waste Management (New York, N.Y.)*, *26*(3), 307–314. doi:10.1016/j.wasman.2005.06.005 PMID:16112565

Todtling, F., & Trippl, M. (2007). Knowledge links in high-technology industries: Markets, Networks or Milieu? The case of the Vienna biotechnology cluster. *International Journal of Entrepreneurship and Innovation Management*, *7*(2), 345–365. doi:10.1504/IJEIM.2007.012888

Toffler, A. (1980). In P. Preston (2001). Reshaping Communication: Technology, Information & Social Change. New Delhi: Sage.

Toffler, A. (1980). *The Third Wave*. London: Collins.

Tonkin, E., Pfeiffer, H. D., & Tourte, G. (2012). Twitter, information sharing and the London riots? *Bulletin of the American Society for Information Science and Technology*, *38*(2), 49–57. doi:10.1002/bult.2012.1720380212

Torii, A., & Caves, R. E. (1992). Technical efficiency in Japanese and US manufacturing industries. In R. Caves (Ed.), *Industrial Efficiency in Six Nations* (pp. 423–457). Cambridge: MIT Press.

Toronto Police. (2012a). Toronto Police Service: To Serve and Protect. Retrieved from http://www.torontopolice.on.ca/yipi/

Toronto Police. (2012b). Toronto Police Service Social Engagement Guidelines. Retrieved from www.torontopolice.on.ca/publications/files/social_media_guidelines.pdf

Toumi, I. (2001). Internet, innovation, and open source: Actors in the network. *First Monday*, *6*(1). Retrieved from http://firstmonday.org/issues/issue6_1/tuomi/index.html

Townsend, A. (2001). The Internet and the Rise of the New Network Cities, 1969–1999. *Environment and Planning. B, Planning & Design*, *28*(1), 39–58. doi:10.1068/b2688

Trappey, R. J., & Woodside, A. G. (2005). Consumer responses to interactive advertising campaigns coupling short-message-service direct marketing and TV commercials. *Journal of Advertising Research*, *45*(4), 382–401.

Trippl, M., Tödtling, F., & Lengauer, L. (2009). Knowledge sourcing beyond buzz and pipelines: Evidence from the Vienna software sector. *Economic Geography*, *85*(4), 443–462. doi:10.1111/j.1944-8287.2009.01047.x

Trivedi, B., & Thaker, K. (2001). Social dimensions of media convergence in India. *Media Asia*, *28*(3).

Trottier, D., & Schneider, C. (2012). The 2011 Vancouver riot and the role of Facebook in crowd-sourced policing. *BC Studies*, *175*, 57–72.

Tsuji, M. (2005). Information technology use in Japan. In M., Kuwayama, Y., Ueki, & M., Tsuji (Eds.). Information technology for development of Small and Medium-sized Exporters in Latin America and East Asia (pp. 345-373). Santiago de Chili, Chili: ECLAC/United Nations.

Tsuji, M., & Miyahara, S. (2010). A Comparative Analysis of Organizational Innovation in Japanese SMEs Generated by Information Communication Technology. In A., Kuchiki, & M. Tsuji (Eds.). From Agglomeration to Innovation: Upgrading Industrial Clusters in Emerging Economies (pp. 231-269). Basingstoke: Palgrave Macmillan.

Tsuji, M., & Miyahara, S. (2011). Agglomeration and Local Innovation Networks in Japanese SMEs: Analysis of the Information Linkage. In A., Kuchiki & M., Tsuji, (Eds.). Industrial Clusters, Upgrading and Innovation in East Asia (pp. 253-294). Cheltenham, U.K.: Edward Elgar.

Tummons, J. (2009). Higher education in further education in England: An actor-network ethnography. *International Journal of Actor-Network Theory and Technological Innovation*, *1*(3), 55–69. doi:10.4018/jantti.2009070104

Turel, O., Serenko, A., & Bontis, N. (2007). User acceptance of wireless short messaging

Turel, O., Serenko, A., & Bontis, N.services. (2007, January). Deconstructing perceived value. *Information & Management*, *44*(1), 63–73. doi:10.1016/j.im.2006.10.005

Tybout, J., De Melo, J., & Corbo, V. (1991). The effects of trade reforms on scale and technical efficiency: New evidence from Chile. *Journal of International Economics, 31*(3), 231–250. doi:10.1016/0022-1996(91)90037-7

Tylor, J. (2012). *An examination of how student journalists seek information and evaluate online sources during the newsgathering process* [Published Undergraduate Honors Thesis]. Arizona State University. Retrieved from http://barrettdowntown.asu.edu/wp-content/uploads/2012/05/tylor_An-examination-of-how-student-journalists-seek-information-and-evaluate-online-sources.pdf

Upadhyaya, H. (2010, May 1-15). e-Waste. Kerala's e-Gov getting nowhere. *Governance Now*. Retrieved from http://indiaenvironmentportal.org.in/files/%20Akshaya.pdf

Urban population Data. (2014). World Bank. Retrieved from http://data.worldbank.org

Usoro, P. (2007). Telecommunications Law and Practice in Nigeria [Slideshow]. Proceedings of the Nigerian Bar Association Bar Week.

Uzzi, B. (1996). The sources and consequences of embeddedness for the economic performance of organizations: The network effect. *American Sociological Review, 61*(4), 674–698. doi:10.2307/2096399

Vainikka, E., & Herkman, J. (2013). *Generation of content-producers? The reading and media production practices of young adults*. Retrieved from http://www.participations.org/Volume%2010/Issue%202/7.pdf

Van Ark, B., Hao, J. X., Corrado, C., & Hulten, C. (2009). Measuring intangible capital and its contribution to economic growth in Europe. *EIB papers, 14*(1), 62-93.

Van Ark, B., & Piatkowski, M. (2004). Productivity, innovation and ICT in Old and New Europe. *International Economics and Economic Policy, 1*(2-3), 215–246. doi:10.1007/s10368-004-0012-y

Van Mieghem, J. A. (1999). Coordinating investment, production, and subcontracting. *Management Science, 45*(7), 954–971. doi:10.1287/mnsc.45.7.954

Vanguard (2010). Rural Telephony: MTN covers 350 uncovered villages with smart technology. Retrieved from http://www.thevanguardnr.com

Varano, S. P., & Sarasin, R. (2014). Use of Social Media in Policing. In G. Bruinsma & D. Weisburd (Eds.), Encyclopedia of Criminology and Criminal Justice (pp. 5410–5423). Springer New York; Retrieved from http://link.springer.com/referenceworkentry/10.1007/978-1-4614-5690-2_387 doi:10.1007/978-1-4614-5690-2_387

Venkatesh, V., Morris, M. G., Davis, G. B., & Davis, F. D. (2003). User Acceptance of Information Technology: Toward a Unified View. *Management Information Systems Quarterly, 27*(3), 425–578.

Victor, P. T., & Dalzell, T. (Eds.). (2014). *The concise new partridge dictionary of slang and unconventional english*. London, GB: Routledge.

Vijayaditya, N. (2002). *A wired village: The warana experiment* (S. Bhatnagar & R. Schware, Eds.). New Delhi: Sage Publications.

Villani, D., & Riva, G. (2012). Does interactive media enhance the management of stress? suggestions from a controlled study. *Cyberpsychology, Behavior, and Social Networking, 15*(1), 24–30. doi:10.1089/cyber.2011.0141 PMID:22032797

Virvou, M., Tsihrintzis, G. A., Alepis, E., Stathopoulou, O., & Kabassi, K. (2012). Emotion recognition: Empirical studies towards the combination of audio-lingual and visual-facial modalities through multi-attribute decision making. *International Journal of Artificial Intelligence Tools, 21*(2), 1–28. doi:10.1142/S0218213012400015

Vis, F. (2013). Twitter as a Reporting Tool for Breaking News. *Digital Journalism, 1*(1), 27–47. doi:10.1080/21670811.2012.741316

Visher, C. A. (1983). Gender, police arrest decisions, and notions of chivalry. *Criminology, 21*(1), 5–28. doi:10.1111/j.1745-9125.1983.tb00248.x

Vosselman, W. (1998). Initial guidelines for the collection and comparison of data on intangible investment. OECD. Retrieved from http://www1.oecd.org/dsti/sti/industry/indcomp/prod/intang.htm

Vygotsky, L. S., Cole, M., John-Steiner, V., Scribner, S., & Souberman, E. (1978). *Mind in society*. Cambridge: Harvard University Press.

Wagner, K. (2014, March 17). Police Turn to Social Media to Fight Crime, Dispel Rumors. *Mashable*. Retrieved from http://mashable.com/2014/03/16/police-departments-social-media/

Wagner, C. S. (2005). Six case studies of international collaboration in science. *Scientometrics*, *62*(1), 3–26. doi:10.1007/s11192-005-0001-0

Wagner, C. S., Cave, J., Leydesdorff, L., Allee, V., Graafland, I., Perez, R., & Botterman, M. (2004). *ERAnets Evaluation of Networks of Collaboration Between Participants in IST Research and Their Evolution to Collaborations in The European Research Area (ERA). Inception Report*. Brussels: DG Information Society and Media.

Walsh, K. (2010, October 21). *New Ideas, New Directions*. Proceedings of the Pobal All-Island Conference. Boyne Valley Hotel, Drogheda. KW Research & Associates Ltd.

Walter, J. A. (1989). *Overload and Boredom: When the Humanities Turn to Noise*. Paper presented at the Community College Humanities Association Conference (pp. 6). Dayton, Ohio.

Walter, T. (2014). New mourners, old mourners: Online memorial culture as a chapter in the history of mourning. *New Review of Hypermedia and Multimedia,* (ahead-of-print), 1-15.

Walters, J. (2014, July). Governments Struggling to Get Social Media Right. Retrieved from http://www.governing.com/topics/mgmt/gov-government-social-media.html

Walter, T., Hourizi, R., Moncur, W., & Pitsillides, S. (2011). Does the internet change how we die and mourn? an overview and analysis. *Omega*, *64*(4), 275–302. doi:10.2190/OM.64.4.a PMID:22530294

Wan Hussin, W. M. A., Shahid, K., Mohd Din, M. A., & Wan Jaafar, W. Z. (2010). Modeling landfill suitability based on multi-criteria decision making method. *Interdisciplinary Themes Journal*, *2*(1), 20–30.

Wang, X., Tang, L., Gao, H., & Liu, H. (2010). Discovering Overlapping Groups in Social Media. In *2010 IEEE 10th International Conference on Data Mining (ICDM)* (pp. 569–578). doi:10.1109/ICDM.2010.48

Wang, E. C. (2007). R&D efficiency and economic performance: A cross-country analysis using the stochastic frontier approach. *Journal of Policy Modeling*, *29*(2), 345–360. doi:10.1016/j.jpolmod.2006.12.005

Warren, M. (2007). The digital vicious cycle: Links between social disadvantage and digital exclusion in rural areas. *Telecommunications Policy*, *31*(6–7), 374–388. doi:10.1016/j.telpol.2007.04.001

Warschauer, M. (2003). *Technological and Social Inclusion: Rethinking the Digital Divide*. Cambridge, MA: MIT Press.

Wasserman, T. (2011, August 10). NYPD Creates Unit To Track Criminals Via Social Media. *Mashable*. Retrieved from http://mashable.com/2011/08/10/nypd-unit-social-media/

Waters, N. L. (2007). Why you can't cite Wikipedia in my class. *Communications of the ACM*, *50*(9), 15–17. doi:10.1145/1284621.1284635

Weaver, D., & Nair. (2008). Academic and student use of a learning management system: Implications for quality. *Australasian Journal of Educational Technology*, *24*(1), 30–41.

Webster, R. (2013, February 11). Social media for community policing. Retrieved from http://www.russellwebster.com/social-media-for-community-policing/

Webster, E. (1999). *The economics of intangible investment*. UK: Edward Elgar Publishing Limited.

Webster, F. (1997). *Theories of the Information society*. London: Routledge.

Weick, K. E., & Quinn, R. E. (1999). Organizational Change and Development. *Annual Review of Psychology*, *50*(1), 361–386. doi:10.1146/annurev.psych.50.1.361 PMID:15012461

Weissma, S., Ayhan, S., Bradley, J., & Lin, J. (n. d.). *Identifying Duplicate and Contradictory Information in Wikipedia*. Retrieved from http://arxiv.org/pdf/1406.1143.pdf

Wellenius, B., & Stern, P. A. (1994). *Implementing reforms in the telecommunications sector: Lessons from experience*. Washington, D.C.: World Bank Publications. doi:10.1596/0-8213-2606-6

Wellman, B., Haase, A. Q., Witte, J., & Hampton, K. (2001). Does the Internet increase, decrease, or supplement social capital? Social networks, participation, and community commitment. *The American Behavioral Scientist*, *45*(3), 436–456. doi:10.1177/00027640121957286

Wenninger, J. (2000). Emerging Role of Banks in e-Commerce. Current Issues in Economics and Finance. 6(3)

West Bengal. (2014, August 10). *Vikaspedia*. Retrieved from http://vikaspedia.in/e-governance/states/west-bengal#section-1

Western Australia Police. (2013). Check my crime now available. Retrieved from http://www.police.wa.gov.au/Aboutus/News/Checkmycrimenowavailable/tabid/2013/Default.aspx

Whetten D.A. (2000). *Developing "Good" Theory through Articulation and Examination*. Brigham Young University.

Why South Africa is Africa's top destination for smartphone debuts. (2014). *Technology Marketing Corporation*. Retrieved from http://www.tmcnet.com/usubmit/-why-south-africa-africas-top-destination-smartphone-debuts-/2014/10/19/8074353.htm

Whyte, A. (1999). *Understanding the role of community telecenters in development - A proposed approach to evaluation in telecenter evaluation – A global perspective*. Ottawa: Retrieved from https://rgomez.ischool.uw.edu/sites/rgomez.ischool.uw.edu/files/documents/99%20TC%20evaluation,%20global%20perspective.pdf

Wiener, N. (1948). Cybernetics or communication and control in the animal and the machine (pp.132). Cambridge: MIT Press. Retrieved from http://www.allen-riley.com/utopia/cybernetics.pdf

Wijekoon, R., Emitiyagoda, S., Rizwan, M. F. M., Rathnayaka, R. M. M. S., & Rajapaksha, H. G. A. (2014). Cyber extension : An information and communication technology initiative for agriculture and rural development in Sri Lanka. *Food and Agriculture Organization. Document for Technical Consultant*. Retrieved from http://www.fao.org

Wijerathna, S. (2011). Mobile telephony for agricultural development of Sri Lanka (p. 45). Retrieved from http://papers.ssrn.com/sol3/papers.cfm?abstract_id=1976180

Wijeratne, M., & Silva, N. D. (2013). Mobile phone intervention for Sri Lankan mushroom producers. Proceedings of *27th Annual Conference of Asian Association of Open Universities*. Pakistan: Allama Iqbal Open University, Pakistan.

Wikigoviya. (2014). Retrieved from http://www.goviya.lk/index.php/en

Wilkinson, K. (1991). *The Community in Rural America*. New York: Greenwood Press.

Williams, M. (2012, August 9). New York City Unveils Crime-Tracking Data Software. *Governing| The State and Localities*. Retrieved from http://www.governing.com/topics/technology/gt-nyc-unveils-crime-tracking-data-software.html

Williamson, O. E. (1973). Markets and hierarchies: Some elementary considerations. *The American Economic Review*, *63*(2), 316–325.

Wilson, M. (2000). *Understanding the International ICT and Development Discourse: Assumptions and Implications* [Unpublished doctoral dissertation]. Development Studies at Oxford University. United Kingdom.

Wilson, R. E., Gosling, S. D., & Graham, L. G. T. (2012). A Review of Facebook Research in the Social Sciences.

Wilson, J. (2000). Volunteering. *Annual Review of Sociology*, *26*(1), 215–240. doi:10.1146/annurev.soc.26.1.215

Wilson, J. M., & Castaneda, L. W. (2011). Most wanted: Law enforcement agencies pursue elusive, qualified recruits. *RAND Rev*, *35*(1), 25–29.

Wilson, J., & Musick, M. (1997). Who Cares? Toward an Integrated Theory of Volunteer Work. *American Sociological Review*, *62*(5), 694–713. doi:10.2307/2657355

Wimmer, M. (2002). *Towards Knowledge Enhanced E-Government: Integration as Pivotal Challenge*. Johannes Kepler University. Retrieved from http://www.iwv.jku.at/aboutus/wimmer/habilschrift.pdf

Windrum, P., Reinstaller, A., & Bull, C. (2009). The outsourcing productivity paradox: Total outsourcing, organisational innovation, and long run productivity growth. *Journal of Evolutionary Economics*, *19*(2), 197–229. doi:10.1007/s00191-008-0122-8

Winsted, K. F. (1997). The service experience in two cultures: A behavioral perspective. *Journal of Retailing*, *73*(3), 337–360. doi:10.1016/S0022-4359(97)90022-1

Wong, L. (2010). The e-learning experience - Its impact on student engagement and learning outcomes. Proceedings of *Business & Economics Society International Conference*. Bahamas.

Wong, L., & Tatnall, A. (2010). Factors determining the balance between online and face-to-face teaching: An analysis using actor-network theory. *Interdisciplinary Journal of Information, Knowledge, and Management*, *5*(1), 167-176. Retrieved from http://www.ijikm.org/Volume5/IJIKMv5p167-176Wong450.pdf

Wong, L., & Tatnall, A. (2009). The need to balance the blend: Online versus face-to-face teaching in an introductory accounting subject.[IISIT]. *Journal of Issues in Informing Science and Information Technology*, *6*(1), 309–322. Retrieved from http://iisit.org/Vol6/IISITv6p309-322Wong611.pdf

Wresch, W. (1996). *Disconnected: Haves and have-nots in the information age*. New Brunswick: Rutgers University.

Wryght, I. (2006). *How to date today's modern woman*. Bloomington, IN: AuthorHouse UK Ltd.

Wu, J.-H., Wanga, S.-C., & Lin, L.-M. (2007). Mobile computing acceptance factors in the healthcare industry: A structural equation model. *International Journal of Medical Informatics*, *76*(1), 66–77. doi:10.1016/j.ijmedinf.2006.06.006 PMID:16901749

Wunsch-Vincent, S., & Vickery, G. (2007). *Participative Web: User-created content*. A Report prepared for the OECD Committee for Information, Computer and Communications Policy.

Wurman (1989) cited by Girard, J. and Allison, M. (2008). Information Anxiety: Fact, Fable or Fallacy. *The Electronic Journal of Knowledge Management*, *6*(2), 111-124. Retrieved from www.ejkm.com/issue/download.html?idArticle=147

Yam, R. C. M., Lo, W., Tang, E. P. Y., & Lau, A. K. W. (2011). Analysis of sources of innovation, technological innovation capabilities, and performance: An empirical study of Hong Kong manufacturing industries. *Research Policy*, *40*(3), 391–402. doi:10.1016/j.respol.2010.10.013

Yang, S., & Li, J. (2012). The Use of ICT Products and "White- Collarization" of White-Collar Workers: An Everyday-Life Perspective. In P. Law (Ed.), *New Connectivities in China* (pp. 159–169). Springer Netherlands. doi:10.1007/978-94-007-3910-9_13

Yap, C. S., Soh, C., & Raman, K. (1992). Information systems success factors in small business. *Omega*, *20*(5-6), 597–609. doi:10.1016/0305-0483(92)90005-R

Yildiz, M. (2007). E-government research: Reviewing the literature, limitations, and ways forward. *Government Information Quarterly*, *24*(3), 646–665. doi:10.1016/j.giq.2007.01.002

Yin, R. K. (1994) Case study research Design and Methods (2nd ed.). Thousand Oaks: Sage publication.

Yoneji Masuda. (1980). Computopia: Rebirth of Theological Synergism. In Masuda, Y. (Ed.), The Information Society as Post-Industrial Society (pp. 146-154). Tokyo: Institute for the Information Society and 1981 by World Future Society.

Yong-Yeol, A., Han, S., Kwak, H., Moon, S., & Jeong, H. (2007). Analysis of topological characteristics of huge online social networking services.*Proceedings of the 16th international conference on World Wide Web* (pp. 835-844). New York, NY, USA

Young, A. (1998). Towards an interim statistical framework: selecting the core components of intangible investment. *OECD*. Retrieved from http://www1.oecd.org/dsti/sti/industry/indcomp/prod/intang.htm

Young, K. S. (1996). *Pathological Internet Use: The Emergence of a New Clinical Disorder*. Paper presented at University of Pittsburgh, Bradford.

Yu, P., Wu, M. X., Yu, H., & Xiao, G. C. (2006, June 21-23). The Challenges for the Adoption of M-Health. *IEEE International Conference on Service Operations and Logistics and Informatics (SOLI 2006)* (pp. 181-186).Shanghai, China. doi:10.1109/SOLI.2006.329059

Zahra, H., & George, G. (2002). Absorptive Capacity: A Review, Reconceptualization, and Extension. *Academy of Management Review*, *27*(2), 185–203. doi:10.5465/AMR.2002.6587995

Zaikman, Y., & Marks, M. J. (2014). Ambivalent sexism and the sexual double standard. *Sex Roles*, *71*(9-10), 333–344. doi:10.1007/s11199-014-0417-1

Zeng, D., Chen, H., Lusch, R., & Li, S.-H. (2010). Social media analytics and intelligence. *IEEE Intelligent Systems*, *25*(6), 13–16. doi:10.1109/MIS.2010.151

Zhang, J., & Mao, E. (2008). Understanding the acceptance of mobile SMS advertising among young Chinese consumers. *Psychology and Marketing*, *25*(8), 787–805. doi:10.1002/mar.20239

Zhang, R. J., & Li, X. Y. (2012). Research on Consumers' Attitudes and Acceptance Intentions toward Mobile Marketing. In L. Hua (Ed.), *2012 International Conference on Management Science & Engineering* (pp. 727-732). doi:10.1109/ICMSE.2012.6414259

Zhao, D., & Rosson, M. B. (2009, May). How and why people Twitter: the role that micro-blogging plays in informal communication at work. In *Proceedings of the ACM 2009 international conference on supporting group work* (pp. 243 - 252). ACM. doi:10.1145/1531674.1531710

Zics, B. (2011). Engineering experiences in biofeedback interfaces: Interaction as a cognitive feedback loop. *Journal of Visual Art Practice*, *10*(1), 71–82. doi:10.1386/jvap.10.1.71_1

Zimmermann, P., & Finger, M. (2005). Information- and Communication Technology (ICT) and Local Power Relationships : An Impact Assessment. *The Electronic. Journal of E-Government*, *3*(4), 231–240.

Zwick, D., Bonsu, S. K., & Darmody, A. (2008). Putting Consumers to Work: Co-creation and new marketing governmentality. *Journal of Consumer Culture*, *8*(2), 163–196. Retrieved from http://www.sagepub.com/ellis/SJO%20Readings/Chapter%203%20-%20Zwick,%20Bonsu%20&%20Darmody.pdf doi:10.1177/1469540508090089

About the Contributors

P.E. Thomas is the Associate Professor and Head of the Department of Communication & Media Studies, Bharathiar University, Coimbatore, India. His academic stint is over two decades and half with specialisation in the realm of Information Society and New Media. He teaches New Media, Journalism, Communication Theories and Advertising at the post graduate level. Besides, twelve research scholars are currently working under his supervision. Prior to embarking upon academics, he has had stretches in the media industry in the fields of reporting, media marketing, copy writing, printing and publishing. He has published over twenty articles in international and national level research journals. Besides, he has contributions of six book chapters in various publications. He is the member of boards of studies in various universities—Madras, Manonmaniam Sundaranar at Tirunelveli, Periyar at Salem, Kerala, and Pondicherry. He is the vice president of the Association of Communication Teachers (ACT), Tamilnadu and Pondicherry.

M. Srihari is Assistant Professor in the Department of Communication and Media Studies, Bharathiar University, Coimbatore, Tamil Nadu, India. He holds a doctoral degree in Journalism and Mass Communication from the Bharathiar University. He has teaching experience at the postgraduate level and handles subjects such as Print production and technologies as well as design elements. He extends his guidance to both M.Phil and Ph.D researchers in the Department. He is actively involved in the making of documentaries and short films on social issues and has undertaken several extension activities in the same. He has several national and international research publications to his credit till date. His specialization is in the area of New Media, Information and Communication Technology and Rural Development.

Sandeep Kaur is the Assistant Professor of the Department of Communication & Media Studies, Bharathiar University, Coimbatore, India. She has completed her Masters in Philosophy in Journalism and Mass Communication from PSG College of Arts and Science, Coimbatore, Tamil Nadu, India. Her specialization is in the realm of E-Governance and Media Convergence. She teaches Journalism, Advertising and Research Methods at the post graduate level. She has several national and international research publications to her credit till date.

* * *

Abdul-Mumin Abdulai holds a Bachelor's degree in Geography and Resource Development with Sociology from the University of Ghana, Master's degree in Sociology and Anthropology from the International Islamic University Malaysia and Doctorate degree in Environment and Development from the National University of Malaysia. He specialized in Environmental/Natural resource governance, socio-economic and poverty issues. He taught courses on socio-economic development and environmental governance at the International Islamic University Malaysia for almost 3 years and has conducted research in the same areas at the National University of Malaysia. He is a Visiting Researcher at the Institute for Environment & Development, National University of Malaysia from April 2014 to October 2014, and from February 2015 to July 2015.

Jashim Uddin Ahmed is an Associate Professor and former Chairman at the Department of Management, School of Business, North South University, Bangladesh. He also served as an Associate Director of BBA Program during 2007-2008 and Director during 2012-2013 at North South University. He also associated with InterResearch, Dhaka, Bangladesh. He received his Ph.D. in Management Sciences from The University of Manchester Institute of Science and Technology, UK. He has two Master degrees from the University of Northumbria at Newcastle, UK. He has published more than 60 research articles in reputed journals.

Cenk Akbiyik has formerly worked as an IT instructor and is currently working at Erciyes University, Faculty of Education as an assistant professor. He has a PhD degree in educational technology. Dr. Cenk Akbiyik has published many scientific articles in various journals and has attended many scientific organizations. His main research interests are use of information and communication technologies for educational purposes; instruction of information technologies, learning theories; thinking skills instruction; and research methods in educational sciences.

Umesh Arya is an Associate Professor in the Faculty of Media Studies, Guru Jambheshwar University of Science & Technology Hisar, Haryana - India. He is a Google certified power searcher and firm believer in the technology enabled learning. He has created 40 online courses on various aspects of media education and research. Dr. Arya has written one book, Newspaper Vocabulary, and contributed to various national and international journals. He has developed 24 indices to measure the coverage of states and union territories' news in media.

Kinkini Bhadra has completed her Bachelor's Degree in Mass Communication and Journalism from the University of Calcutta and then Master Degree in Mass Communication and Journalism from the University of Burdwan. Currently she is doing her M.Phil in Cognitive Science at the School of Cognitive Science, Jadavpur University, India.

Jonathan Bishop is an information technology executive, researcher and writer. He founded the Centre for Research into Online Communities and E-Learning Systems in 2005, which is now part of the Crocels Community Media Group. Jonathan's research and development work generally falls in the area of human-computer interaction. He has over 70 publications in this area, including on Internet trolling, cyber-stalking, gamification, cyberlaw, multimedia forensics, Classroom 2.0 and Digital Teens. In addition to his BSc(Hons) in Multimedia Studies and various postgraduate degrees, including in law, economics and computing, Jonathan has served in local government as a counselor and school governor, and has contested numerous elections. He is also a fellow of numerous learned bodies, including BCS - The Chartered Institute for IT; the Royal Anthropological Institute; the Royal Society of Arts, and the Royal Statistical Society. Jonathan has won prizes for his literary skills and been a finalist in national and local competitions for his environmental, community and equality work, which often form part of action research studies. In his spare time Jonathan enjoys listening to music, swimming and chess.

Teruyuki Bunno is a Professor of Business Management, Faculty of Business Administration, Kinki University, Osaka, Japan. He has completed his doctorate and currently serves as a board member of the Japan Academy of Small Business Studies and the Kansai Association for Venture and Entrepreneur Studies. His current research focuses on the roles of human resources in the process of firm growth. Major areas of specialty include Innovation Theory, Lifecycle of Firms and New Business Creation. Current research focuses on the roles of human resources in the process of firm growth.

Uvasara Dissanayeke is a Senior Lecturer in the Department of Agricultural Extension, University of Peradeniya, Sri Lanka. She received her M.Phil. from the Peradeniya University in 2010. She is presently reading for her Ph.D. at the University of Colombo, School of Computing. Her main areas of research interest are ICTs in agricultural education, computer based learning and mobile learning.

Erkan Erdil studied Political Science and Public Administration at Middle East Technical University (METU) in Ankara. He received a Bachelor of Science degree in 1990. In 1990, he started studying Economics at the same university. He received Master of Science degree in 1994. He further received Ph.D. in 2001 from University of Maastricht. He was appointed as instructor in 1997 and as the vice-chairman of the Department of Economics at METU. He was then appointed as an associate professor in 2005 and a professor in 2011. He is also been the director of the Science and Technology Policy Research Center (METU-TEKPOL) since 2002. He has served as a National Delegate for the 7th Framework Programme, Research Potential and Regions of Knowledge between 2007 and 2013. He teaches introductory economics, microeconomics, statistics, econometrics, and technology and work organization courses. His main areas of interest are labor economics, economics of technology, applied econometrics, economics of information and uncertainty. He worked in research projects of national and international organizations. He has been author/co-author, and referee of articles in American Economic Review, Applied Economics, Applied Economics Letters, Agricultural Economics, METU Studies in Development and presented papers to various international conferences.

Derya Fındık is a researcher affiliated with the Department of Management Information Systems at Yıldırım Beyazıt University, Turkey. She holds a BA degree in public finance, MA degree and Ph.D. in science and technology policy studies from the Middle East Technical University, Turkey. She has worked on issues relating to the adoption and diffusion of information technologies in Turkey. Her main research interests are innovation management, technological entrepreneurship, and the role of intangible assets in the economy. She has published articles in journals and working papers.

P. Govindaraju is the Professor and Head of the Department of Communication, Manonmaniam Sundaranar University, Tirunelveli, and Tamilnadu, India. He has academic experience of 30 years of teaching, research and administration under different academic designations. He was the visiting research scholar at the centre for mass communication research, Leicester, England and served in Malaysia for three years. He was one of the lead researchers in conducting nation-wide experimental studies in gauging the effects of the Country-wide Classroom program. His research area includes development communication and he is the coordinator of UGC-SAP phase I and II projects. Produced several Ph.D candidates and also guiding scholars on areas relating to development communication. He is a member of several academic associations like International Association for Media and Communication Research (IAMCR) and Association of Communication Teachers – Tamilnadu and Pondicherry.

Huseyin Guler is mainly focused on the development of policy tools for an innovation-oriented entrepreneurial ecosystem including triggering innovation and entrepreneurship in universities and boosting R&D intensive start-ups. Currently, he acts as Director for Strategy and Business Development at Kastamonu Integrated Wood Industry and part-time lecturer at Bahçeşehir University. As Head of STI Policy Department at TÜBİTAK, Dr. Güler coordinated several studies to identify priority research topics in strategic sectors like automotive, ICT, energy and food between 2009- 2013. He developed a model to monitor and assess the progress of different actors of the innovation ecosystem including public funded research centers. He also led the preparatory phase of the National Science Technology and Innovation Strategy from 2011 to 2016. He served as the National Coordinator of Turkey for EU Framework Programmes (2006-2009) at TUBITAK; coordinated the mapping studies of Turkish research potential in ICT, production technologies, nanotechnology and material sciences; and developed strategies to link Turkish research diaspora and the national landscape. He graduated from Marmara University, in the Department of Industrial Engineering and holds MBA degree from Uludağ University. In September 2013, he completed his PhD degree at Middle East Technical University with dissertation on international R&D collaboration dynamics in ICT specifically on local buzz/global pipeline dichotomy.

Shuaib Mohamed Haneef is an Assistant Professor in the Department of Electronic Media and Mass Communication at Pondicherry University, India. His PhD on intertextual and interactive experiences in hypertext analyses how readers/users construct narratives through multimodal texts. His research interests include digital media studies; interactivity and agency; game studies; and affect and interfaces in digital technologies. He was the recipient of the Asia Culture Fellow during September to December 2006 in Chonnam National University, Republic of Korea.

Hiroki Idota is a Professor of Management Information System, Faculty of Economics, Kinki University, Osaka, Japan. He has completed his Ph.D., CISA (Certificated Information System Auditor). Additionally, he serves as a Board Members for the Japan Society for Information and Management; and the Nippon Urban Management and Local Government Research Association. He received his B.A. in Economics from Kwansei Gakuin University; his M.A. in Informatics from Kansai University; and his Ph.D. in Economics from Osaka University. His major areas of specialty include Management Information Systems and Management of Technology. His current research focuses on innovation using ICT. He is also the recipient of the Telecom Social Science Encouragement Award from the Telecommunications Advancement Foundation in March 2005 for his remarkable research contribution.

Kevin Allan Johnston is an Associate Professor and current Head of the Department of Information Systems at the University of Cape Town. He has worked for 24 years for companies such as De Beers, Liberty Life, Legal & General and BoE. Kevin's main areas of research are ICT Strategic Management, IS educational issues, IS-related social issues and Open Source Software.

Salah Kabanda is a senior Lecturer in the Department of Information Systems at the University of Cape Town.

Ibrahim Komoo is Vice Chancellor of Universiti Malaysia Terengganu (UMT). Professor Dato' Dr. Ibrahim Komoo was the Director of Southeast Asia Disaster Prevention Research Institute (SEADPRI). Prior to his appointment, he was the Deputy Vice Chancellor (Research and Innovation) at Universiti Kebangsaan Malaysia. His research specialisations include Engineering Geology, Earth Heritage Conservation and Sustainability Science and Governance. He currently sits on the National Heritage Council, MARDI Science Council, Advisory Council of the Langkawi Geopark, Chair of the National Geological Heritage Registration Committee, Chair of both the Sustainable Development and Biodiversity Task Force and Natural Hazards Committee at the Academy of Sciences Malaysia. Through his work on the conservation of geological resources, he serves as the Chairman of the Geological Heritage of Malaysia and sits as an expert in the Expert Group of the Global Network of National Geoparks and Geoparks Bureau, part of the International Advisory Group of Experts on UNESCO Geoparks.

Uma Kumar is a Full Professor of Management Science and Technology Management and is the Director of the Research Centre for Technology Management at Carleton University. She has published over 140 papers in journals and refereed proceedings. Ten papers have won best paper awards at prestigious conferences. She has also won the Carleton's prestigious Research Achievement Award, and twice, the Scholarly Achievement Award. Recently, she won the teaching excellence award at the Carleton University. She has been the Director of Sprott School's Graduate Programs. She has consulted DND, CIDA, the Federal partners of technology transfer, and the Canadian association of business incubators. Uma has taught in executive MBA programs in Hong Kong and in Sprott MBA in Ottawa, Iran, and China. Over last twenty years, she has supervised more than 70 MBA, MMS and EMBA student's projects. She has also given invited lectures to academics and professionals in Brazil, China, Cuba and India.

Vinod Kumar is a Professor of Technology and Operations Management of the Sprott School of Business (Director of School, 1995–2005), Carleton University. He received his graduate education from the University of California, Berkeley and the University of Manitoba. Vinod is a well known expert sought in the field of technology and operations management and has published over 150 papers in refereed journals and proceedings. He has won several Best Paper Awards in prestigious conferences, such as the Scholarly Achievement Award of Carleton University for the academic years 1985–1986 and 1987–1988, and Research Achievement Award for the year 1993 and 2001. Vinod has given invited lectures to professional and academic organizations Australia, Brazil, China, Iran, and India among others.

Okanlade Adesokan Lawal-Adebowale lectures in the Department of Agricultural Extension and Rural Development, Federal University of Agriculture, Abeokuta, Ogun State, Nigeria. He holds a PhD degree in Agricultural Communication with bias for Information and Communication Technology (ICT) usage in Agriculture and Innovation communication. Arising from his research activities, the author has about 40 publications to his credit, in both local and international journals, as well as the proceedings of Learned Societies/Associations and chapters in books. He is a member of various Learned Associations such as: the Agricultural Extension Society of Nigeria (AESON); the Agricultural Society of Nigeria (ASN); the Farm Management Association of Nigeria (FAMAN); the Nigerian Rural Sociological Association (NRSA) and the African Society for Information and Communication Technologies (ASICT).

M. Maani Mabel is an Assistant Professor in the Department of Electronic Media, at the St. Thomas College of Arts & Science, Chennai. She was chosen as a project fellow under the UGC special assistance programme. She has conducted field studies among the rural ICT initiatives in Tamil Nadu during her doctoral tenure. She has published articles on ICT and Community Development. She had also anchored numerous events during her tenure as a research scholar exhibiting her quality as an effective team player. She has been taking responsibilities in positions for coordinating and organising seminars and department programmes, research and mass contact programmes in villages.

Orance Mahaldar is a doctoral candidate at Research Centre S:PAM – Studies in Performing Arts & Media, Ghent University, Belgium. He has completed Bachelor Degree in Philosophy (Honours) and then a Master Degree in Film Studies from Jadavpur University. He is interested in Communication and Media Studies, Cultural Studies and ICT.

Charru Malhotra is presently Associate Professor (e-Governance and ICT) at Indian Institute of Public Administration (IIPA), New Delhi, India. She completed her Ph.D. from IIT-Delhi in the field of 'e-Governance for Rural Development'. [Thesis Title: Design of Citizen-Centric e-Governance Approach: A Study of Select ICT based Rural Initiatives]. She is also a National e-Governance and Short term MIS/GIS consultant to several UN bodies (The World Bank, Winrock International, Asian Development Bank-ADB), as well as an accredited 'Trainer of Trainers' (Thames Valley University, U.K.) and a Recognised Trainer for the Government of India (GoI). With more than 20 research publications, (including Best Paper Award as Innovative Approaches for e-Governance in International Conference on E-Governance, Award committee ICEG-2012, Deakin University, Australia for her study titled 'A Validated Citizen-Centric Approach using Delphi Technique for Converging Indigenous Knowledge Systems using ICT') and almost 25 years of experience in teaching, training, software development and research in the field of Information Technology (IT), her current areas of interest include Design, Development, Monitoring, Evaluation and Capacity building for e-Governance Initiatives for Smart-Cities and sustainable rural development; ICT4D and Citizen-centricity; Study of Internet Technologies and its impact on the Society (e.g. Social Media-Transparency in Governance/ Gender-crimes, Cyber Security) and Development Research.

Amir Manzoor holds a bachelor's degree in Engineering from NED University, Karachi, an MBA from Lahore University of Management Sciences (LUMS), and an MBA from Bangor University, United Kingdom. He has many years of diverse professional and teaching experience working at many renowned national and internal organizations and higher education institutions. His research interests include electronic commerce and technology applications in business. He is a member of Chartered Banker Institute of UK and Project Management Institute, USA.

Alka Misra is presently working as Senior Technical Director at National Informatics Centre, Government of India. Her major areas of responsibility include the WWW Services at the National Level, Head of National Portal of India, Indian Open Data Initiative and MyGov (Citizen Engagement Platform). She has over 25 years of experience in the field of Information Technology. She has worked on various assignments during her career from Software Development, Software Engineering to Web Portal and Internet Technologies. She has also authored a number of articles in National and International Journals. She has also reviewed the Guidelines for Indian Government Websites, which has been adopted by the Govt. of India.

D.P. Misra is working as Principal Systems Analyst at National Informatics Centre, Government of India. In his present assignment, he is working as the Project Leader of the MyGov Platform, an Initiative of Hon'ble Prime Minister of India, the Open Government Data Platform of Govt. of India as well as a Few Apex Office Web Platforms. He has over 25 years of experience in the field of Information and Communication Technologies. He has worked on various assignments during his career right from Software Design, Development, Training, Implementation and management of large scale projects as well as Content Management Frameworks. His areas of interest are Social Inclusion, e-Participation and e-Governance domains.

Mazlin Bin Mohktar is a Professor of Environmental Chemistry at Universiti Kebangsaan Malaysia (UKM) where he has been with the UKM since 1985 as a Tutor. Prior to that he was at the UKM Sabah Campus as a lecturer since 1988 and was later promoted to Associate Professor in 1995 at the Faculty of Science and Natural Resources. He is currently a Principal Fellow (since 1999) as well as Director of the Institute for Environment and Development (LESTARI), UKM, since August 2005. Professor Mazlin received his BSc in Chemistry from the University of Tasmania, Australia, in 1984 and his PhD (Analytical and Environmental Chemistry) from The University of Queensland, Australia, in 1988. He is also a Member of the UKM Senate; Fellow of The Malaysian Institute of Chemistry (FMIC); Life Member & Former Secretary (1995-2005) of the Malaysian Society of Analytical Sciences (ANALIS); Life Member, & former Executive Committee (2005-2009) of the Malaysian Water Partnership (MyWP) that is linked to the Global Water Partnership (GWP), Sweden; Former Country Manager (2005-2008) of MyCapNet (Malaysian Capacity Building for Integrated Water Resources Management, IWRM) that is linked to International Cap Net headquartered in Pretoria-South Africa (prior in IHE Delft, Holland); and Chairman of the Langat River Basin Research Group affiliated with UNESCO-HELP network, based in Paris involving more than 90 river basins from more than 65 countries.

Zoltan Nagymate is currently teaching as a faculty member of Economics, at the University of Miskolc in Hungary. He is also a PhD student at the Enterprise Theory and Practice, Doctoral School at the same university. He received his MSc degree in Logistics Management with an excellent qualification at the University of Miskolc in 2013. As part of the Erasmus programme, he spent two semesters at Poznan University of Economics in Poland and Pushkin State Russian Language Institute in Moscow, Russia. His main field of research is the effects of using cloud computing applications on the economy. Exploring his subject, he has conducted research both in Russia and in Kazakhstan while he was working there as a process engineer in 2014.

Bane Nogemane, completed his post graduate degree in the Department of Information Systems at the University of Cape Town in 2013.Bane is currently a Calypso Technical Analyst at the Standard Bank Group in Johannesburg.

Sanghita Roy is a BCA, MBA and M.Phil in Information and Technology Management. She has also held the position of Assistant Professor in Institute of Business Management & Research and Head of the Department of IT. She is completing her research work on the risk and security aspect of Information Technology. Using her abilities she provides research guidance, counseling and teaching to MBA students. As visiting faculty, she has to her credit a rich experience of teaching and research guidance for students of postgraduate management courses in several management Institute affiliated with West Bengal University of Technology. Her research based articles, case studies, book review etc. are published in journals of high repute. She is the author of two books on Management Information System. She has practice of organizing seminars and workshops in advanced technology management for various colleges of West Bengal.

Peter Sasvari is an Associate Professor (2009) of the Institute of Business Science, Faculty of Economics, at the University of Miskolc, Hungary. He defended his doctoral thesis with the best receivable mark, 'summa cum-laude' for his dissertation titled 'The Development of Information and Communication Technology: An Empirical Study'. He is currently supervising 3 Ph.D. students' theses and has supervised more than 150 Bachelor's and Master's theses. He is a member of the public body at the Hungarian Academy of Sciences. He is the author of more than 30 international publications and serves as the Associate Editor for 3 international journals. Recently, the analysis of business information systems has been the focus of his research. With the co-operation of some local universities, he has conducted primary research among small and medium-sized enterprises in Austria, Bosnia-Herzegovina, the Czech Republic, Croatia, Poland, Portugal, Hungary, Germany, Italy, Spain and Slovakia.

Elmira Shamshiry has graduated with a Bachelor's degree in Natural Resource Engineering - Environment from the Shahid Chamran University, Iran. She obtained a Master of Environmental Science degree from Universiti Putra, Malaysia (UPM) in 2009, and a PhD in Environment & Development in 2013 from Universiti Kebangsaan, Malaysia (UKM). She has completed her post-doctoral research at Universiti Kebangsaan, Malaysia (UKM) in 2014, and is presently engaged at the Research Management Center of Universiti Terengganu, Malaysia (UMT) as a research fellow.

Mahmud Akhter Shareef is an Associate Professor of school of business, North South University, Bangladesh. He was a visiting faculty in DeGroote School of Business, McMaster University, Canada during his post doctorate research. He has done his PhD in Business Administration from Sprott School of Business, Carleton University, Canada. He received his graduate degree from both the Institute of Business Administration, University of Dhaka, Bangladesh in Business Administration and Carleton University, Ottawa, Canada in Civil Engineering. His research interest is focused on online consumer behavior and virtual organizational reformation. He has published more than 60 papers addressing consumers' adoption behavior and quality issues of e-commerce and e-government in different refereed conference proceedings and international journals. He was the recipient of more than 10 academic awards including 3 Best Research Paper Awards in the UK and Canada.

Aysit Tansel is a professor of Economics at the Middle East Technical University, Ankara. She received her BS from Middle East Technical University with high honors, her MA from University of Minnesota and her Ph.D. from State University of New York. She was a Fulbright Fellow at the Cornell University during 2011-2012.She was a research fellow at the Yale University during 1990-1993. She is also a research fellow of the Economic Research Forum (ERF) in Cairo. Her main area of interest is labor economics with a focus on economics of education, empirical models of economic growth with emphasis on health and education and educational inequalities and gender gap in education and economic growth, returns to education, private tutoring, economics of gender, labor force participation and unemployment.

Masatsugu Tsuji is a Professor of Economics, Graduate School of Applied Informatics, University of Hyogo, and Professor Emeritus of Osaka University. He has received a B.A. from Kyoto University in 1965; an M.A. from Osaka University in 1967; and a Ph.D. in Economics from Stanford University in 1976. His serves include visiting professors of Carnegie Mellon University, US and National Cheng Kung University, Taiwan; Board of Director, International Telecommunications Society and CPRsouth; Editorial Board, Journal of International Society of Telemedicine and eHealth, and Smart Homecare Technology and TeleHealth; Coordinator of e-Health Economics, International Society for Telemedicine and e-Health. Current research focuses on identifying factors promoting innovation in Japan and ASEAN economies, in particular the role of ICT in the innovation process.

H.V.A. Wickramasuriya, B.Sc. (Agric.), M.Ed. (Penn State), Ph.D. (Penn State), is the Head of the Department of Agricultural Extension, Faculty of Agriculture, University of Peradeniya, and the past Chairman, Board of Study in Agricultural Extension, Postgraduate Institute of Agriculture, University of Peradeniya. He teaches Management Information Systems to MBA and Organizational Management students, and has also developed a number of computer based learning material and information systems.

Pádraig Wims is Senior Lecturer in Rural Development at University College Dublin, Ireland. His main academic interest is rural development and agricultural extension and his main research interests include researching the contribution of ICT to rural development and agricultural education and the application of ICT to rural communities. Prior to joining University College Dublin, Dr Wims worked in the Information Section of the Irish public agricultural extension service, on the development of a videotex service for Irish farmers.

Index

V

W

X

Y

Printed in the United States
By Bookmasters

Printed in the United States
By Bookmasters